# GREECE 2001

**Nora Brennan Morrison** editor
**Jen Taylor** associate editor

researcher-writers
**Erzulie Coquillon**
**Ben Davis**
**Eric Green**
**Deirdre Aoife O'Dwyer**
**Kristi Schaeffer**
**Rianna Stefanakis**

**Theodora Sakata** map editor

**Macmillan**

## HELPING LET'S GO

If you want to share your discoveries, suggestions, or corrections, please drop us a line. We read every piece of correspondence, whether a postcard, a 10-page email, or a coconut. Please note that mail received after May 2001 may be too late for the 2002 book, but will be kept for future editions. **Address mail to:**

**Let's Go: Greece**
**67 Mount Auburn Street**
**Cambridge, MA 02138**
**USA**

Visit Let's Go at **http://www.letsgo.com,** or send email to:

**feedback@letsgo.com**
**Subject: "Let's Go: Greece"**

In addition to the invaluable travel advice our readers share with us, many are kind enough to offer their services as researchers or editors. Unfortunately, our charter enables us to employ only currently enrolled Harvard students.

Published in Great Britain 2001 by Macmillan, an imprint of Macmillan Publishers Ltd, 25 Eccleston Place, London, SW1W 9NF, Basingstoke and Oxford.
Associated companies throughout the world
www.macmillan.com



Published in the United States of America by St. Martin's Press.



ISBN: 0-333-90128-2
First edition
10 9 8 7 6 5 4 3 2 1

**Let's Go: Greece** is written by Let's Go Publications, 67 Mount Auburn Street, Cambridge, MA 02138, USA.


Printed in the USA on recycled paper with biodegradable soy ink.

# CONTENTS

# MAPS

# RESEARCHER-WRITERS

**Erzulie Coquillon** *Sterea Ellada, Saronic Gulf, Sporades, Evia, and Northeast Aegean Islands*

She hacked her hair and was off. Erzulie's wildly eclectic route took her all over Greece's reaches, and she always responded with attitude and honesty. With an eye for improvement and an acquired Sour Patch Kids addiction, Erzulie left nothing undone, cheering her editors with prompt copy and calls. As the summer wound down, she returned to clean up our spelling errors and bring us treats.

**Ben Davis** *Thessaly, Epirus, Macedonia, Thrace, and Northeast Aegean Islands*

Even bears, wolves, and desperate refugees couldn't stop Ben—and they tried. Ben's wits and guts pulled him through, and his fantastic observations about monasteries, Mt. Olympus, and rural villages convinced us that Northern Greece is a hiker's paradise; his late-night conversations with conspiracy theorists over burning *tsipouro* entertained us all summer, as did his recollections of being beaten like bread dough in an İstanbul hamam.

**Eric Green** *Athens and Cyclades*

Emerging from the chaos of Athens with a love for speed and a will to see it all, Eric charged ahead into the Cyclades. Hobnobbing with fellow travel guide writers, he cooled his heels only when wild winds blocked ferry routes. Eric communed with the Big Blue, reporting that his job was the best possible—and though we almost lost him to Amorgos, he never conked out.

**Deirdre Aoife O'Dwyer** *Crete, Cyclades, and Northeast Aegean Islands*

Earning her *Let's Go* stripes in Belfast, Deirdre knows the budget travel thing like the back of her hand; lucky for us, she inherited the family obsession with Greece. Her fantastic work gratified us endlessly, as her art historian's eye took apart ruins and routine streetcorners with verve. Befriending a self-possessed person of a pelican, Deirdre later returned to us to tell the tale; while she was at it, she polished up the post-research book with editorial skills honed while masterminding *Let's Go: Ireland 2000.*

**Kristi Schaeffer** *Peloponnese and Ionian Islands*

Undeterred by illness, undaunted by bizarre ferry schedules, uncorrupted by the Pink Palace, Kristi hunted down the best beaches in Greece and sent back tight prose about it all. Ever self-possessed, Kristi floated through the Peloponnese while taking careful note of everything. Super-independent, she churned out solid, attentive prose that brought Greek myth and culture alive.

**Rianna Stefanakis** *Cyprus and Dodecanese*

A native of Kea, Rianna braved wildfires and saucy Cypriot monks with an unflagging enthusiasm. Turned away at the Green Line, she instead learned to walk like an Egyptian, made a philosophical new friend, and dodged countless marriage proposals before attacking the Dodecanese. Her ever-entertaining tales spiced up her writing, letting us experience the life of a fabulously tan Grecian girl.

# ACKNOWLEDGMENTS

**We hellenophiles** love Greece. We also love everything that let us find out about Greece, our researchers in particular. You good kids, your hard work made it easy to put this book together. Thanks to our neighboring Turkish crew, Beth and Siobhan, who proved that in mixing a g&t, two wrongs *do* make a right. Thanks to Naz and Amélie; Ankur and the LG brass; and the Europeans (Kate, sniff), who'll make us a *star.* Thea, you and your various maritime monsters make our maps sing. if thanks, Let's Go, for being a good thing.

**Nora** takes a deep breath. Thanks to Dr. Heisler, who addicted me to the *Odyssey* and planted all those silver-footed Homeric epithets in my brain. Record Hospital and number 67 on the BAD took me out of the bubble. The Café de la Cité caffeinated me, and the city kids (John, Lucy, Brady, Melissa, Terry, Valerie, and the usurped Olivia) and Mapland welcomed me to my office away from office—rock over London, rock on Chicago! Office everybody, it's idyllic like camp. Ever-so-responsible Internetrix Jen, both I and this book owe you many. Morrisons, you're great. Eamon and fellow Johnson Dave introduced me to Slurpee madness; you are good. Dan, I hope this serves you well. And all the readers.

**Jen** sleeps. When she wakes, she will thank the whole office for making it fun to be at work at 2am and for helping out. Thanks to Nora, for giving me the job that I love so much and getting me addicted to all things Greek. Thanks to the girls and mcnabb for visiting and bringing provisions, Matthew and Chris for being online and talking me down, Laura and Sarah for putting up with my lack of e-communication, and Nick for making me go home sometimes. I would also like to thank the Berg for free eats, theonion.com, and Channel 66. Thank you Hot Pockets and diet Coke. Remember: everything is funnier in a Scottish accent. Hi Mom, Dad, and Mike!

**Editor**
Nora Brennan Morrison
**Associate Editor**
Jen Taylor
**Managing Editor**
Ankur Ghosh
**Map Editor**
Theodora Sakata

# HOW TO USE THIS BOOK

When you set foot in Greece, you've arrived in the land of philosophers, poets, conquerors, archaeologists, kings, apostles, generals, saints, goddesses, and mythic beasts. We at *Let's Go* are here to rescue you from the Gorgons and vengeful Furies along the way, letting you pass unscathed to the nymphs' grottoes and sacred sites that survive in present-day Greece. Welcome, and Παμε—Let's Go!

## THE ORGANIZATION OF THIS BOOK

**INTRODUCTORY MATERIAL.** The first chapter of this book, **Discover Greece,** provides you with an overview of travel throughout mainland Greece, the Peloponnese, and the hundreds of islands within the nation. **Suggested Itineraries** outline our absolute favorites: what you shouldn't miss, and how long it takes to see it. The **History & Culture** chapter provides you with a general introduction to the art, architecture, politics, and present-day culture of Greece. The **Essentials** section outlines the practical information you will need to prepare and execute your trip. **Cyprus** gets its own introduction at the beginning of the island's coverage.

**THE MEAT.** The book begins with Athens, the central city and major transportation hub; from there, the coverage radiates outward throughout the Peloponnese, the mainland, and then the islands hugging the coast. The **black tabs** in the margins will help you navigate between chapters quickly and easily.

**APPENDIX.** The appendix at the end of the book contains useful **conversions,** a **phrasebook** of handy phrases in Greek, and a **glossary** of useful Greek words that will help you navigate menus and museum exhibits. Find it all starting on p. 555.

## A FEW NOTES ABOUT LET'S GO FORMAT

**RANKING ESTABLISHMENTS.** In each section (accommodations, food, sights, nightlife, etc.), we list establishments in order from best to worst. Our absolute favorites win the highest honor Let's Go gives, the **thumbs up.**

**PHONE CODES AND TELEPHONE NUMBERS.** The **phone code** for each city or town appears opposite the name of that city or town, and is denoted by the ☎ icon. **Phone numbers** in text are also preceded by the ☎ icon.

**GRAYBOXES AND WHITEBOXES. Grayboxes** let us indulge our chatty side, with all the mythology, crude humor, and seemingly inexplicable Greek habits we could muster. **Whiteboxes** give important practical information, like warnings (eek!), helpful hints and further resources (), and border crossing information ().

**BEACHES, DAYTRIPS, AND THE OUTDOORS:** In addition to gentle-on-the-wallet coverage of Greece's archaeological and historical sites, in this year's edition of *Let's Go: Greece*, you'll find new emphasis on out-of-the-way beaches and superior strips of sand. You can follow your inner trekker by hiking our road-tested routes through olive groves and scrubby foothills. We also expand our listings of daytrips, describing strolls to seaside towns, trips to frescoed monasteries, and a new section of daytrips to the Turkish Aegean coast, just across from the Dodecanese and Northeast Aegean Islands.

**A NOTE TO OUR READERS** The information for this book was gathered by *Let's Go* researchers from May through August of 2000. Each listing is based on one researcher's opinion, formed during his or her visit at a particular time. Those traveling at other times may have different experiences since prices, dates, hours, and conditions are always subject to change. You are urged to check the facts presented in this book beforehand to avoid inconvenience and surprises.

# DISCOVER GREECE



Four thousand years after Greeks started engraving frescoes, scrawling Linear A letters, and passing on epic stories, every schoolkid still dreams of Hercules and the Medusa. When those kids grow up, they hanker after Greece's island beaches, free-flowing booze, and the heroes' landscape they've always loved. Generous Greek hospitality extends a welcoming hand to relic hounds muttering Keats' "Ode on a Grecian Urn," to hikers in search of the gods' abode on Mt. Olympus, to film-lovers on a pilgrimage to the Thessaloniki festival, and to slick partiers beginning the night with a drink at a starlit *kafeneion.*

Modern Greece envelops travelers in its all-encompassing lifestyle. Trains, buses, and ferries run at unpredictable hours and at breakneck speeds, while death-defying kids on mopeds buzz through plateias at all hours. Three-hour lunch breaks (complete with nap) are standard issue; dancing on tables till daybreak is a summer rite. The mix of high speed and sun-soaked relaxation can make Greece both frustrating and delicious. If you look at delays as chances to munch baklava or watch the sun set over the Acropolis, you can enter a Greek mindset that looks back patiently to ancient beliefs and traditional customs even as it charges forward into a new Europe and a new millennium.

**FACTS AND FIGURES**

**CAPITAL** Athens.

**POPULATION** 10,707,000.

**LENGTH OF COASTLINE PER GREEK CITIZEN** 1.3m.

**DRINK OF CHOICE** Ouzo.

**NUMBER OF ISLANDS** about 1400.

**PERCENTAGE OF ISLANDS THAT ARE UNINHABITED** 88%.

**RATIO OF FOREIGNERS TO LOCALS** 9 tourists for every 10 Greeks.

## WHEN TO GO

June through August is **high tourist season** in Greece and Cyprus. Disco-flanked beaches set the scene for Dionysian indulgence, as the hundred-degree sun warms ancient cities and modern-day sun-worshipers alike. Hotels, domatia, nightclubs, and sights are in full swing. If crowds or the frantic pace of summer travel grate on you, consider visiting during May, early June, or September, when the same gorgeous weather smiles on thinner crowds. In ski areas, winter brings another high season: you can hit the slopes at Mt. Parnassos (p. 166), Mt. Pelion (p. 186), or Metsovo (p. 211). The **low season,** from mid-September through May, generally has cheaper airfares, lodging, and food prices, but many sights and accommodations have shorter hours or close altogether. In winter, Greece hibernates, freed from summertime farming, fishing, and tourism; ferries, buses, and trains run considerably less frequently, and life is quieter. For a temperature chart, see **Climate,** p. 555. For a list of Greek festivals, see **Festivals,** p. 35.

# THINGS TO DO

Mountain chains, a multitude of islands, omnipresent olive groves, and a population of mythological monsters contribute to the Greek landscape. The varied land, full of isolated villages and islands, satisfies even the pickiest visitor with its infinite diversions. *Ouzo*-aided loafing on the beach accompanies countryside hikes from quiet villages and past ancient ruins. Don't be afraid to plot out your own route: that famous Greek hospitality will make you feel welcome wherever you go.

For more on specific regional bests, check out the **Highlights of the Region** boxes that begin each chapter.

## THE ROAD TO RUIN(S)

Antiquity junkies will get the best fix of their lives in Greece. The mother of all ruins, the **Acropolis** (p. 97), still rules modern Athens. The perfectly proportioned, gigantic columns of the **Parthenon,** combined with the sun's beating rays and the brilliant gleam of white marble, conjures up the same awe felt by millennia of worshipers and pilgrims. A trek around the **Peloponnese** will transport you back to the era of nymphs, satyrs, and gods in disguise. Wander through Phidias' workshop on the way to the original Olympic fields at **Ancient Olympia** (p. 137), peer into Agamemnon's tomb at **Mycenae** (p. 119), or experience catharsis after an ancient tragedy in the decidedly *not* ruined theater at **Epidavros** (p. 127). On the mainland, get to "know thyself" at the ancient **Oracle of Delphi** (p. 170). Chase after the floating island of **Delos,** birthplace of Apollo and Artemis, for a peek at the Temple of Apollo and an island-wide archaeological site (p. 366). More archaeological sites include: Heinrich Schliemman's reconstruction of the Minoan palace at **Knossos** (p. 472); Crete's *other* archaeological site, **Phaistos** (p. 478); Santorini's **Akrotiri,** a city frozen in time by a volcanic eruption (p. 407); onetime cult capital **Paleopolis** in Samothraki (p. 349); and the dual ruins of **Pella** and **Vergina** in Northern Greece, once hangouts for Philip II and sonny boy Alexander the Great (p. 231). From Rhodes, you can reach the remnants of three of the seven wonders of the ancient world by daytrip. The **Colossus of Rhodes** leaves no trace today, though you can contemplate what its giant leg span must have been (p. 426). Across the water on the Turkish coast, you can venture to the city of **Halicarnassus** in modern-day Bodrum (p. 549), and Ephesus' **Temple of Artemis** (p. 553).

## YOUR PLACE IN THE SUN

Greece's oceanside summertime schedule could pass for an instruction manual on **sloth:** roll out of bed and onto the beach around noon; head for an open-air, harborside dinner at 11pm; toss back after-dinner drinks, catch a movie, or hit the clubs till 5am, all under the stars; watch the sun rise over the ocean; and hit the hay before another sun-drenched day. It's virtually impossible to resist the allure of Greek sun and water. The islands have long been a sun-worshiper's paradise (though people today are more likely to love the sun instead of Apollo). As soon as you step outside Athens to the **Saronic Gulf Islands** (p. 285), the roasting Greek sun will brown your (entire) body and release your inhibitions. In the Aegean Sea, **Santorini**'s black-sand beaches cast back the sun's rays and stay warm long after the stunning sunsets over the Sea of Crete (p. 397). Swim below sea caves once frequented by pirates, on the coast of **Skyros** (p. 313), or bask on the Lesvian shore, where the beaches stretch for miles outside of **Skala Eressou** (p. 341). Rip off all those constraining clothes at **Myknonos**'s wild, nude Super Paradise Beach, or seek solace from all those bare butts at out-of-the way strips of sand (p. 360). The much-beloved haunt of boozed backpackers, **Corfu,** is ringed by fabulous beaches on all sides, in addition to hosting that legendary party haven, the Pink Palace (p. 259). Try snorkeling, waterskiing, or just loafing in the sun on **Ios** (p. 379) or **Naxos** (p. 390); perfect your tan around **Paleohora** in Crete (p. 494), at castle-crowned Haraki Beach in **Rhodes** (p. 426), or on the holy isle of **Patmos** (p. 458).

## HIKIN' AND MOTORBIKIN'

Leave behind hectic Athens and the nonstop beach party to wander over the mountains and hills that inspired centuries of pastoral poetry. Hiking or motorbiking—or a combination of both—lets you cruise from little village to little village without depending on bus routes. On foot, you'll cross through foothills covered with olive groves, passing mountain goats and wildflowers on the way. With a moped, the favorite means of transit for young Greeks, you'll jump-start your trip. Sleepy **Dimitsana** and cobblestoned **Stemnitsa** (p. 144) stand apart from the tourist bustle of the rest of the Peloponnese; in the Ionian Sea, Odysseus' kingdom of **Ithaka** is an undiscovered hiker's paradise, where the Cave of the Nymphs—the hiding place for Odysseus' treasure and the endpoint of a delightful hike—will seduce you (p. 280). Northerly **Thasos** (p. 349) is full of secluded ruins, superior hikes, and village-to-village strolls. Rural **Alonnisos,** a largely uninhabited island in the Sporades, is crisscrossed by trails and moped-friendly roads, and is hugged by beaches (p. 310); outlying islands are protected as part of the National Marine Park, and make a delicious daytrip. The untouched traditional Greek villages of the **Zagorohoria** (p. 212) and its surrounding wilderness make walking a pleasure. The neighboring **Vikos Gorge** (p. 214), the world's steepest canyon, challenges hikers with a six-hour-long trek. You can explore more gorgeous gorges in Crete: the **Samaria Gorge** (p. 492), Europe's longest gorge, and the quieter **Valley of Death** (p. 508) plunge you below eagles' eyries and trees clinging to the steep canyon sides.

Eighty percent of the Greek landscape is mountainous, to the delight of climbers. Clamber to the abode of the gods at **Mt. Olympus** (p. 233), ascending over 2900 steep, stunning meters to one of its eight peaks; most trekkers start far below at little Litohoro. During the summer, Dionysus's hangout **Mt. Parnassos** makes a great hikin' and mountain-bikin' trip (p. 166); in winter, skiers take over the 2400m slopes. The trails around **Zaros** in Crete wind up to mountainside sanctuaries and to Zeus' childhood hiding place, **Kamares Cave** (p. 475).

### LET'S GO PICKS

**BEST BEASTIES:** Grimace and cower before the predatory **raptors** (birds, not dinos) of Dadia National Reserve (p. 258). Pad quietly through the **Valley of the Butterflies** on either Paros (p. 382) or on Rhodes (p. 426), and don't disturb the mating bugs. Be prepared to be amazed at the wild animal antics at the **Pink Palace,** Corfu (p. 259). **Petros the Pelican** lives on in Mykonos (p. 360).

**BEST BEACHES:** Go for a swim **Moni Myrtidon** and **Myriotissa** on Corfu (p. 259), extolled by Lawrence Durrell as the best in the world. The famous **black** and **red** sand beaches of Santorini (p. 399) will satisfy those bored with golden pebbles. Get nekkid on **Paradise** (and for the truly daring, **Super Paradise**) beach on Mykonos (p. 360).

**BEST CASTLES:** Check out the famous Phaistos disc and sit in the throne room of the **Palace of Phaistos** on Crete (p. 478). Get medieval with the **Knights of St. John** in their old castle on Kos (p. 443). Wander through the restored **Old Fortress** and have a picnic with a view in the **New Fortress** on Corfu (p. 259).

**BEST GUT-WRENCHING RIDES:** Hold on tight if you make the ride from tiny Diakofto to tinier **Kalavrita** (p. 130) on the rattling and rolling rack-railway. Imagine the fear in the eyes of those who were hauled up via rope as you take the easy way up (climbing the stairs) to the monasteries of **Meteora** (p. 196).

**BEST STATUES:** See the **Colossus of Rhodes,** one of the seven wonders of the ancient world, in your mind's eye, as he stands guard over the City of Rhodes (p. 426). Mourn the absence of the **Venus de Milo** while sunning on Milos (p. 408), then console yourself by heading to Athens's National Archaeological Museum (p. 104) to check out the abs on the **Kritias Boy.**

**WILDEST PARTIES:** Visit **Pierro's,** the first gay bar in Greece, on wild Mykonos (p. 360). Win yourself a free t-shirt for downing 7 shots at **Blue Note** on Ios (p. 394). Catch a ferry to the **"Bedroom of the Mediterranean,"** a.k.a. Bodrum, Turkey (p. 549), for a night you won't remember.

# SUGGESTED ITINERARIES

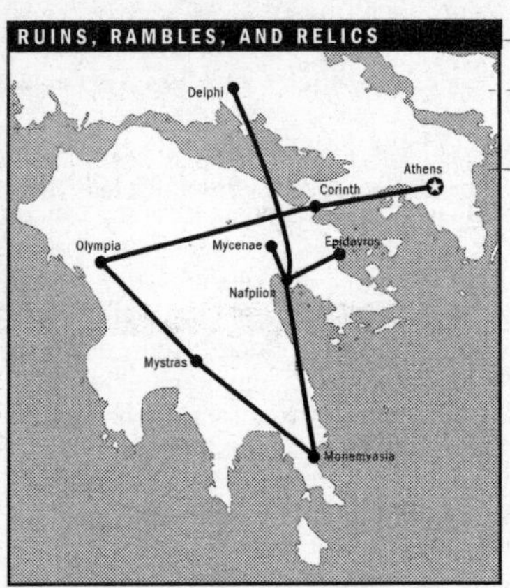


**RUINS, RAMBLES, AND RELICS (1 WEEK)** Put down that well-worn copy of the *Odyssey:* it's time to visit Classics-nerd Disneyland. Arrive in **Athens** (p. 79) and charge straight to the gleaming **Acropolis,** which still rules over the city (p. 97). After the hot sun (or brilliant floodlights) of the Acropolis blind you, head to the rooms and rooms of ancient treasure and statuary at the **National Archaeological Museum** (p. 104). Then head out from the capital to **Ancient Corinth,** with its fountain that once quenched Pegasus's thirst (p. 116). Take a lap around the stadium at **Ancient Olympia,** and feel your knees shake when you gaze at the Hermes of Praxiteles (p. 137). Clamber all over the Byzantine wonderland of **Mystras,** a semi-ruin and semi-city (p. 154), and to the otherworldly pedestrian and donkey-only city of **Monemvasia** (p. 159). Watch the setting sun color Venetian **Nafplion** (p. 123), then take a waterfront stroll in the evening. On the way back to Athens, visit the archaeological treasure trove of **Mycenae,** and walk beneath the Lion's Gate (p. 119); then exult in the perfect acoustics of the theater at **Epidavros** (p. 127). End your journey with a pilgrimage to **Delphi,** the ancient oracle that retains its mystic aura today (p. 168).

---

**POST-EURAIL PARTY (1 WEEK)** Finish up a Eurail trip by taking the ferry from Brindisi, Italy to **Corfu** (p. 259), home to gorgeous beaches and the infamous Pink Palace. Continue on via Patras to **Athens,** where you can catch an eyeful of the Acropolis before heading out to the islands (p. 79). As soon as you get off the ferry to **Mykonos,** start shedding those inhibitions: nude beaches abound, and nightlife sizzles (p. 360). When you've warmed up for a day, move on to **Ios,** an isle of pure bacchic hedonism (p. 394). Recuperate from the damage on the black sand beaches of **Santorini** (p. 399), then test out the tawny sand outside **Iraklion,** on Crete (p. 465).

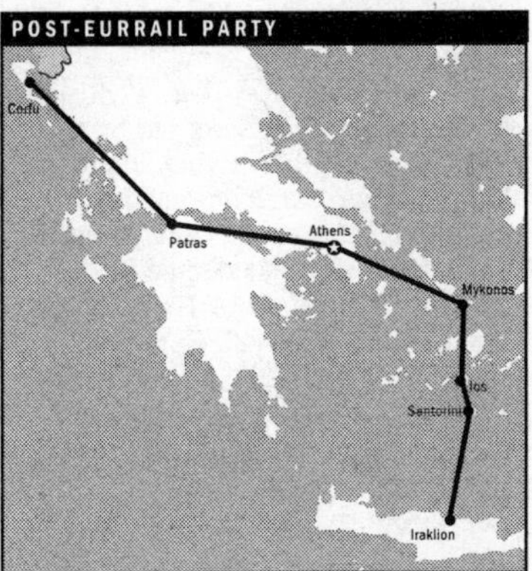


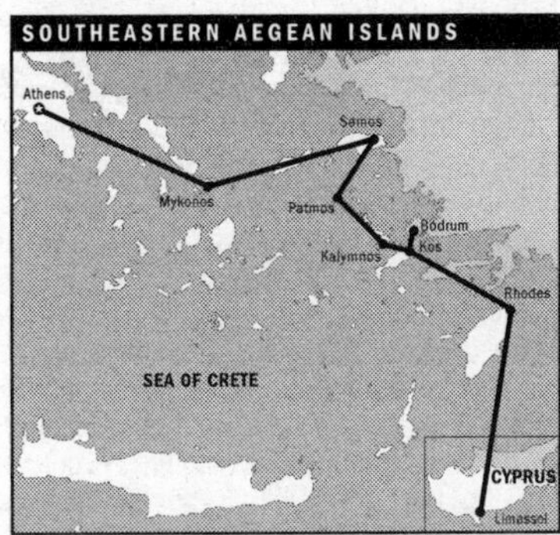


**SOUTHEAST AEGEAN ISLANDS (10 DAYS)** Start your trip from **Limassol,** Cyprus, where you can wander a castle occupied by crusading Knights Templar and visit the archaic ruins of Kourion; don't neglect the nearby beaches (p. 525). Sail on to **Rhodes,** imagining the giant Colossus that once towered over the harbor as you enter the City of Rhodes (p. 426). Drink a *frappé* as you sit between an Ottoman mosque and an Italian mansion on **Kos** (p. 443), then ferry across to the Turkish city of **Bodrum** to party until the morning ferry back (p. 549). Chill out along the deserted beaches that border the striking cliffs of

**Kalymnos** (p. 452). Find revelations on **Patmos,** where St. John wrote the last book of the Bible (p. 458), then move on to **Samos** and its superb collection of statues (p. 328). Break loose on wild **Mykonos** (p. 360), and return to **Athens** (p. 79) for a sight of the capital that governs them all.

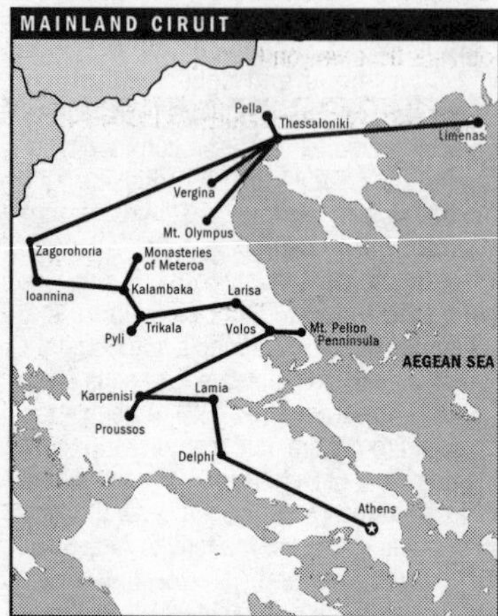


**MAINLAND CIRCUIT (2 WEEKS)** Set off from **Athens** (p. 79) to begin a trek through undertouristed mainland Greece, home of cliffside Byzantine monasteries, cobblestoned traditional villages, and the press of Thessaloniki. You'll probably need rented wheels of some kind. Set off for the oracle at **Delphi,** where perhaps you'll receive dream-advice about your upcoming travels (p. 168). Continue on to **Lamia,** where you can climb the built-and-rebuilt ruins of the town Castro (p. 179). **Karpenisi,** the capital of the mountainous Evritania region, is the next stop (p. 175). From here, hike out among the tiny villages of the neighborhood; **Proussos,** with its spectacular cliffside monastery, is a highlight (p. 178). Pass through Karpenisi again on the way to Volos and the **Mt. Pelion Peninsula,** the onetime haunt of centaurs and present-day hideaway of traditional village life (p. 186). Roll out through Larisa and Trikala, as you head for the frescoed church of Porta Pangia in tiny **Pyli,** where you can dine beside a Roman footbridge (p. 192). Past Kalambaka, avoid the traditional means of ascent to the **Monasteries of Meteora**—a terrifying, free-swinging rope—and save your prayers to give thanks for the fabulous view (p. 196). Pass through Ioannina on the way to the **Zagorohoria** villages, eminently hikeable and extremely friendly (p. 212). Stay in **Thessaloniki** (p. 216) as you daytrip to the ancient sites of gold-showered **Vergina** (p. 230) and nearby **Pella** (p. 231); Alexander the Great grew up in the neighborhood. For the greatest hike of them all—straight up to the gods' home on **Mt. Olympus** (p. 233). After the grueling, exulting climb, relax for a day in **Limenas** on offshore **Thasos** before you head out (p. 350).

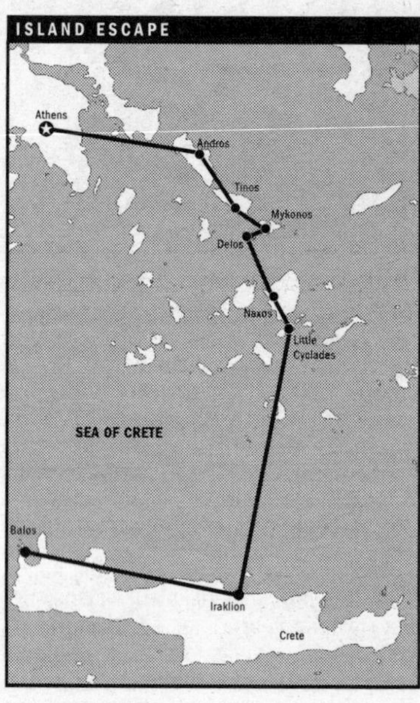


**ISLAND ESCAPE (2 WEEKS)** For a slower, more relaxing island tour, leave from Athens for **Andros,** a beach-lovers' paradise surrounded by neoclassical small towns (p. 352). Don't miss the sunsets; you certainly won't miss the crowds on other beach islands. Rip yourself away to **Tinos,** and throw yourself in the sand beside a ruined 4th century BC temple (p. 355). Stay with a local family at night for a truly local experience. Shake off your sloth at one of the crazed clubs of **Mykonos** (p. 360), and do penance during a daytrip to the sacred isle of **Delos,** the birthplace of Apollo and Artemis (p. 366). The next stop is **Naxos,** where you can snorkel among caves, sea urchins, and crystalline sand (p. 372). If the ferry schedule complies, slip away to one of the **Little Cyclades,** Koufonisia, Donousa, Iraklia, and Schinousa (p. 379). The total peace will saturate your being; ease back into reality with a stopover in western Crete, around **Balos** and **Rethymno** (p. 482).

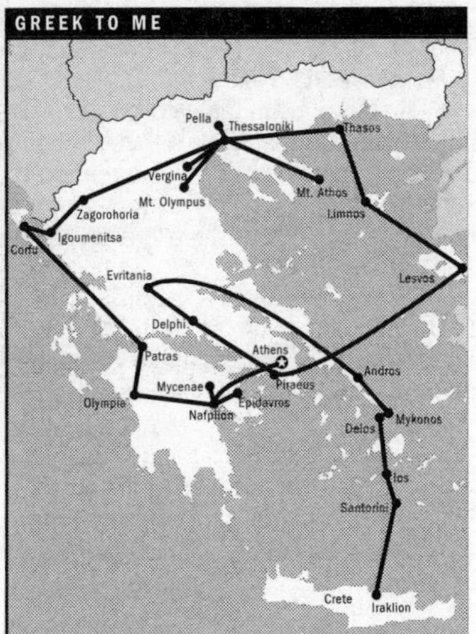


**GREEK TO ME (3 WEEKS)** To wander a large portion of Greece in a few weeks, you'll want to start in **Athens** (p. 79), the capital for millennia; the National Archaeological Museum, the Acropolis, and the many smaller museums will saturate you with Greek culture. Move on to **Nafplion** (p. 123), a gorgeous Venetian city and a perfect base to explore the neighboring sights of the theater of **Epidavros** (p. 127), the huge-scale dig at **Mycenae** (p. 119), and the original Olympic field at sacred **Olympia** (p. 136). Head to Patras to catch the ferry to **Corfu** (p. 259), island of mixed debaucherous overdevelopment and untouched wilderness. Cross back to the mainland at Igoumenitsa on your way to the **Zagorohoria** (p. 212), the district of petite towns that stick with traditional folkways. The Byzantine sights of **Thessaloniki** beckon (p. 216), with fabulous mosaics and the breathtaking archaeological sites of **Vergina** (p. 230) and **Pella** (p. 231) are a quick jaunt away. The industrious will set out for **Mt. Olympus** (p. 233), grappling with the gods' abode. Men who plan ahead and collect the proper approvals and forms may visit **Mt. Athos,** the ultratraditional monastic community jutting out of Halkidiki (p. 244). Recline for a few days on the shores of **Thasos** just offshore (p. 350), then circle down to **Limnos** (p. 343) off the Turkish coast. A ferry ride carries you to the widely varied landscapes of **Lesvos** (p. 336), Sappho's home and the birthplace of Nobel laureate Odysseus Elytis. Sail back to **Piraeus** (p. 109), Athens' modern port. From there, make a quick trip to the sacred oracle of **Delphi** (p. 168), then move on to **Evritania** (p. 174), a hilly rural district on the mainland. Hop the ferry to **Andros** (p. 352), a relaxing rural paradise that invites long hikes. Freak with hipsters on **Mykonos** (p. 360); pay for the sins incurred with a daytrip to the sacred isle of **Delos,** birthplace of Apollo and Artemis (p. 366). Party naked on **Ios** (p. 394), then snooze on the black sand beaches of **Santorini** (p. 399); the picturesque white cliffside buildings are postcard-perfect. Finish your excursion on **Crete,** exploring the ruins of Knossos and Phaistos just outside of **Iraklion** (p. 465).

# HISTORY AND CULTURE

For centuries, Greece has carved out its dominion of intellectual, governmental, literary, artistic, and religious majesty at the crossroads of Europe and Asia; the entire world has shared its wisdom. The relics of Crete's Minoan civilization betray Egyptian and Babylonian influence; in the bushy beards and long black robes of Orthodox priests, the mores of the Eastern Roman Empire survived through the Byzantine Era to the present time. Four hundred years under the Ottoman Turks left a spice in Greek food, an Eastern twang in its *bouzouki* music, and a skyline of minarets. Greece emerged independent in 1821, and now struggles to maintain the glory of Classical Athens, the splendor of Imperial Byzantium, and the religious purity of Ottoman folkways in an industrial world governed by a reborn democracy.

## HISTORY AND POLITICS

### ANCIENT GREECE (THROUGH AD 324)

Ancient Greece has long fed **fantasies**—Augustus Caesar, Shakespeare, and Napoleon have grasped at its glory, and today TV viewers hunker down for *Hercules: The Legendary Journeys*. The sculpture, architecture, literature, government, language, and philosophy of ancient Greece still influence much of our lives. Greek culture grew from agricultural or fishing communities: the coastal Aegean fostered prosperity, with its access to the ocean and its nearby olive trees, grapes, forests, and fertile land. Walled towns, constructed around a central high point, or **acropolis,** protected seaside settlements. Immigrants and traders from Anatolia, the Levant, and Egypt added a dash of global chic to the ancient Greek world.

### THROUGH THE TROJAN WAR (1250 BC)

**THE BRONZE AGE.** Though contemporary Greeks considered the **Bronze Age** (3000-1000 BC) a third-place finish after the earlier Golden and Silver Ages, the Bronze Age discovery of metalworking kicked off a high point in Greek culture.

**MY BRAIN HURTS** Philosophy—"the love of wisdom"—originated in 585 BC when **Thales of Miletus** asked, "What is everything made out of?" Thales answered "water" (wrongly), and fell into a well as a lesson. **Anaximander,** Thales' pupil, guessed more safely that everything springs from the "Indefinite" and exists "according to necessity." Soon others were jostling to assert their opinions: **Heraclitus** of Ephesus, called the "Dark One" for his sour attitude, claimed that reality is usually hidden, and that "war is the father and king of all, and some he shows as gods, others as men; some he makes slaves, others free." In reply, **Parmenides** answered that appearance and reality are separate: what is *must* be, and can't *not* be, so we shouldn't even bother thinking about what doesn't exist, because we can't grasp it. His pupil **Zeno** attacked the ideas of motion and plurality as naïve—silly people, there's no motion! Predicting a 70s rock band by several thousand years, **Empedocles** described the universe as composed of four elements—earth, air (wind), fire, and water; they constantly recombined to form everything in the world. Mr. Theorem, a.k.a. **Pythagoras,** played guru to a cult of vegetarians who were trying to get in touch with their past lives; once he heard the soul of a dead friend crying out to him in a puppy's yip. In his spare time, he figured out the properties of right triangles (remember $a^2+b^2=c^2$?).

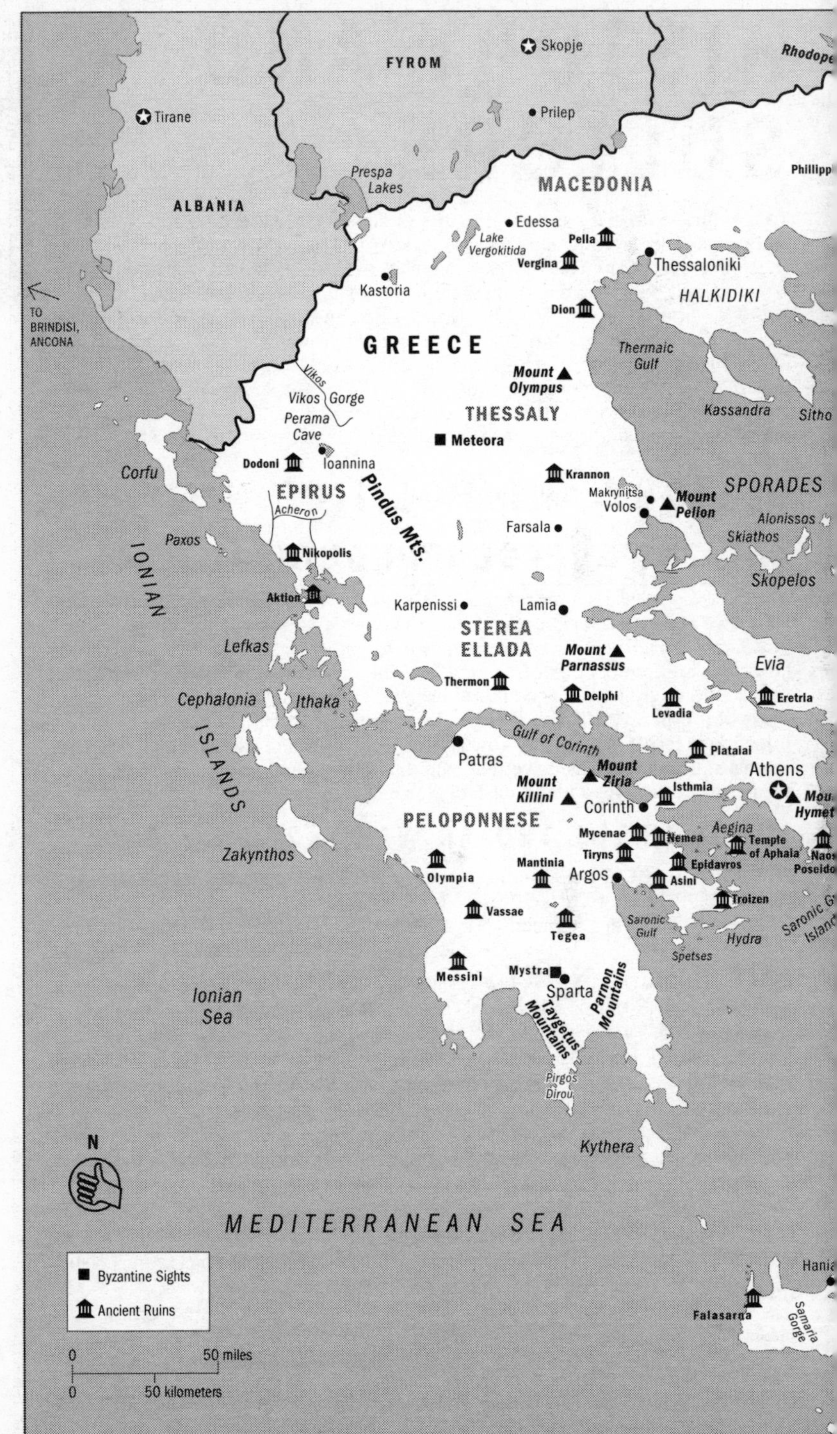
FYROM
Skopje
Tirane
Prilep
Rhodope
Prespa Lakes
ALBANIA
MACEDONIA
Phillippi
Edessa
Lake Vergokitida
Pella
Vergina
Thessaloniki
Kastoria
HALKIDIKI
Dion
TO BRINDISI, ANCONA
GREECE
Thermaic Gulf
Mount Olympus
Vikos
Vikos Gorge
Perama Cave
THESSALY
Kassandra
Meteora
Dodoni
Ioannina
Corfu
Krannon
SPORADES
EPIRUS
Pindus Mts.
Makrynitsa
Mount Pelion
Volos
Acheron
Alonissos
Farsala
Skiathos
Paxos
IONIAN
Nikopolis
Skopelos
Aktion
Karpenissi
Lamia
STEREA ELLADA
Lefkas
Mount Parnassus
Evia
Thermon
Delphi
Levadia
Eretria
Cephalonia
Ithaka
ISLANDS
Gulf of Corinth
Plataiai
Patras
Mount Ziria
Athens
Mount Killini
Isthmia
Corinth
PELOPONNESE
Aegina
Mycenae
Nemea
Temple of Aphaia
Zakynthos
Tiryns
Epidavros
Olympia
Mantinia
Argos
Asini
Troizen
Vassae
Saronic Gulf
Tegea
Hydra
Spetses
Messini
Mystra
Sparta
Parnon Mountains
Ionian Sea
Taygetus Mountains
Pirgos Dirou
Kythera
N
MEDITERRANEAN SEA
Byzantine Sights
Ancient Ruins
Hania
Falasarna
Samaria Gorge
0
50 miles
0
50 kilometers

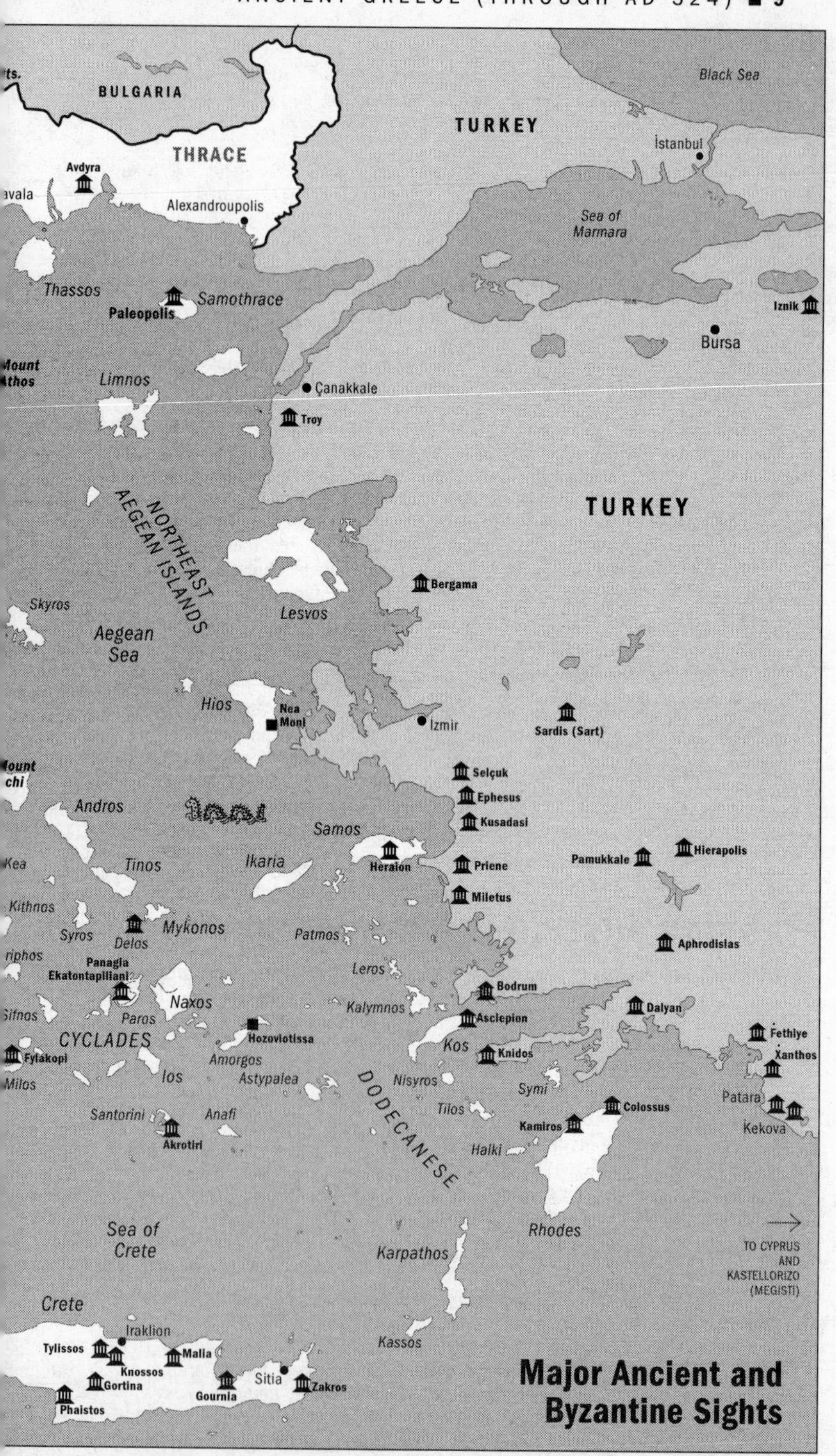
Major Ancient and Byzantine Sights
BULGARIA
THRACE
TURKEY
Black Sea
İstanbul
Sea of Marmara
Iznik
Bursa
Avdyra
Alexandroupolis
Thassos
Samothrace
Paleopolis
Limnos
Çanakkale
Troy
TURKEY
NORTHEAST AEGEAN ISLANDS
Bergama
Skyros
Aegean Sea
Lesvos
Hios
Nea Moni
İzmir
Sardis (Sart)
Selçuk
Ephesus
Kusadasi
Andros
Samos
Heraion
Priene
Miletus
Pamukkale
Hierapolis
Tinos
Ikaria
Kithnos
Syros
Delos
Mykonos
Patmos
Aphrodisias
Panagia Ekatontapiliani
Leros
Bodrum
Naxos
Paros
Kalymnos
Asclepion
Dalyan
CYCLADES
Hozoviotissa
Kos
Knidos
Fethiye
Xanthos
Fylakopi
Amorgos
Ios
Astypalea
DODECANESE
Nisyros
Symi
Milos
Tilos
Colossus
Patara
Santorini
Anafi
Kamiros
Kekova
Akrotiri
Halki
Sea of Crete
Rhodes
TO CYPRUS AND KASTELLORIZO (MEGISTI)
Karpathos
Crete
Iraklion
Kassos
Tylissos
Malia
Knossos
Gortina
Sitia
Zakros
Gournia
Phaistos

| BEGINNING OF TIME: WORLD EMERGES FROM CHAOS | The Start of the World as We Know It, and I Feel Fine. The universe's undefined mass separates into water, air, and the earth. Zeus ousts his pop Cronus to rule it; Pandora peeks into a box of evils, letting them loose on humans. |
|---|---|

Looking over the shoulders of their eastern neighbors, Greeks learned bronze toolmaking and weaponry. Three Aegean cultures built their reputations on bronze: the mainland Mycenaeans, Crete's Minoans, and the islands' Cycladic. Island civilization flourished early on. The wall frescoes and marble figurines of the **Cycladic** culture showed Middle Eastern influence and a strong geometric element. By about 2000 BC, the **Minoans** (named for the step-dad of the Minotaur) busily constructed palaces at Knossos (p. 472), Malia (p. 481), and Phaistos (p. 478) as centers of government, religion, and trade; a strong fleet made Minoans the mack daddies of the Aegean. Around 1500 BC, a **Mysterious Cataclysm**—tidal waves, volcanoes, and/or alien invasions—wiped the Minoans out of existence.

**TEAM HELEN.** The mainland **Mycenaeans** (a.k.a. Achaeans or Hellenes—named both for a tribe in Thessaly and for Helen of Troy), descended from invading warriors from Eastern Europe, took over the Aegean after the Minoans faded. Based in Mycenae and Tyrins, they built citadels surrounded by "Cyclopean" walls—so called because later Greeks thought only a muscle-bound **Cyclops** could lift such enormous stones. Mycenaean rule extended throughout the southern mainland, Crete, and the Cyclades and Dodecanese as far as Cyprus; archaeologists have uncovered remnants of Mycenaean culture throughout these areas. The Mycenaeans' language, **Linear A,** has long held to be a mystery as great as the cause of the Minoans' demise. **Linear B,** developed from the Minoan Linear A, has puzzled generations of linguists (cunning though they may have been); lately, it's been proven to be a pre-Greek tongue.

| 1250 BC: TROJAN WAR | Worst Marital Spat of All Time Causes Ten Years of War. Helen, source of the trouble and owner of the face that launched 1000 ships, laughs, "I got Menelaus good." |
|---|---|

The Mycenaeans attacked Troy in Asia Minor around 1250 BC, igniting the most mythologized, obsessed-over, and written-about war in history. Perhaps the greatest histories of the **Trojan War,** Homer's **Iliad** and **Odyssey,** compiled the oral lore of the war into two epic poems around 850 BC (during the following Dorian Era).

## DORIAN BUST-UP (1100–500 BC)

**THE DORIAN INVASION.** Bronze-age Aegean civilizations met an abrupt end in the 12th century BC, when invading **Dorians** burst in from the Balkan highlands just north of Greece. The invasion scattered the Mycenaeans in a **diaspora** that relocated Greeks to Asia Minor (where Homer may have lived) and to the Black Sea. A **Dark Age** of rule by decidedly un-dainty Dorians followed. It wasn't all bad under Dorian rule: the Greek language and alphabet settled into a single, national language, accompanied by a national identity. Tribal divisions still prevented a centralized government like the Mycenaeans'. Industry, agriculture, and trade passed into the hands of hundreds of small, independent villages peopled by self-sufficient farmers. The political independence of these villages and the Dorian destruction of "high" civilization in Greece paved the path to the city-state and to Classical splendor.

**THE RISE OF THE CITY-STATE.** From 800-500 BC, in the aftermath of the Dorian invasion, the *polis* or **city-state** rose as the major Greek political structure. A typical *polis* consisted of a city and the surrounding countryside which provided food and wood. Within the town, an **acropolis** (a fortified citadel and a religious center bedecked with **temples** to the people's patron deities) and an **agora** (the marketplace and the center of commercial and social life) were major landmarks. Within the agora, thinkers waxed philosophical and traders hawked their wares amidst the **stoas,** open-air paths lined with columns. Outside the city center, amphitheaters, stadia, and gymnasia hosted political and religious gatherings and athletic games.

**HALLUCINOGENIC HONEY** In the 5th century BC, King Cyrus of Persia recruited a ragtag troop of jack-booted Greek thugs to pillage various villages in Asia Minor. Among the 10,000 Greeks was **Xenophon,** who recorded their misadventures in the *Anabasis.* According to Xenophon, after making a hasty retreat laden with booty, the soldiers wandered among fields of beehives brimming with honey. The tired horde sampled the combs with disastrous results: some of the soldiers ended up unconscious or plagued with violent diarrhea and vomiting. Those who consumed the nectar in moderation reported **fantastical visions** (who knows what the bees were seeing!). The morning after, the entire legion woke up with a wicked hangover and some cool but embarrassing flashbacks. After enduring a few days of detox from too many psychotropic substances, the iron-hearted Hellenes marched west to Trabzon, on the eastern end of Turkey's Black Sea coast. Travelers near the Black Sea have reported similar mind-altering effects; scientists have concluded that the bees procure their heady honey from the *Azalea pontica*, a flower that grows in the area.

By the 9th century BC, many city-states began to expand and colonize overseas, spreading their military influence and culture throughout the Mediterranean. Colonization brought in the big bucks, as city-states became increasingly prosperous. The isolated city-states began forming economic, religious, and military ties amongst themselves, further uniting Greece. Religion and sports united in the **Olympic Games** (p. 137), where the athletic fields of Olympia hosted politically-charged competitions between states. Through similar transnational events, the residents of city-states began to feel more Greek, and less Athenian or Spartan. By 700 BC, the inhabitants of Greece called themselves **Hellenes,** or Greeks. This new identity made a contrast between Greeks and foreigners, whom the Hellenes called **barbarians** (**barbaroi,** after the sound of foreigners' language, which Greeks thought sounded like a savage "bar bar bar").

Starting in 495 BC, the Greeks were threatened by "barbarian" invasions from the eastern **Persians** under Xerxes, and from the empire of **Carthage** to the southwest. During the **Persian Wars** (490-477 BC), Athens and Sparta took the lead in defending Greece from invasion. The Greeks defeated five million Persians (according to Herodotus [p. 25]—a more realistic estimate suggests 25,000-35,000) in battles at Marathon, Salamis, and Platea. In Sicily and southern Italy (called **Magna Graecia**—wider Greece—by its Italian occupants), the western Mediterranean city-states fended off Carthaginian assaults from North Africa and saved western Greece from foreign rule. The Hellenic victories ushered in a period of unprecedented prosperity and artistic, commercial, and political success.

| 480 BC: BATTLE OF THERMOPYLAE | Leonidas, 300 Spartan Troops Block Persian Army. New words "bottleneck," "spartan," and "self-sacrifice" were defined by the battle, which killed every Spartan soldier. |
|---|---|

## CLASSICAL GREECE (500–400 BC)

**ATHENS IN THE LEAD.** At the end of the Persian Wars, **Athens** rose to prominence as the largest, most wealthy, and most influential *polis.* Equipped with a strong navy (built in preparation for the Persian Wars), Athens established itself as a power in the Mediterranean, and headed the **Delian League,** an organization of Greek city-states to defend against Persia (and which made Athens the de facto capital of Greece). Athens grew prosperous, and between 500 and 300 BC, Athens fostered the art, literature, philosophy, and government (including early democracy, a government for the ages) which still dominate Western culture. **Solon** freed debt-prisoners and ended aristocratic privilege during his rule, and **Pericles** opened his democratic government to all male citizens, who were randomly chosen to participate in the rule of Athens. Athens was no democratic paradise, however: almost 20% of the populace were slaves.

**BITE MY ASS** Early philosophical works, surviving on fragments of papyrus and in the reports of later writers, paved the road for **Socrates,** first of the **big three** (Plato, Socrates' student, and Aristotle, Plato's student, are the others). Socrates was a poor, ugly convict who described himself as a gadfly nipping at the ass of the horse that was Classical Athens. He brought philosophy down from the stars and into the muddy stalls of the *agora,* where he spent his days picking over the morals and beliefs of anyone who would stop for a chat. His impersonal style of asking questions is still called the Socratic method. All the while he insisted that he was more wise than anyone else only because he was aware of his own total ignorance. His radical lifestyle and constant questioning eventually angered influential Athenians, and he was sentenced to death for corrupting the youth. Socrates died by drinking hemlock in 399 BC.

**SPARTA STRIKES BACK.** Athens faced a rival city in controlling Greece: **Sparta,** the head of the **Peloponnesian League,** a collection of mainland city-states. The two powers could hardly be more different: Athens was commercial, democratic, and prided itself on its cultural achievements; Sparta was agricultural, oligarchical, and valued stoic military training above all else. Spartan men's lives from age seven to 60 were spent in military training, conquest, or defense; women trained to become fit mothers and models for their military sons. These opposing lifestyles resulted in the **Peloponnesian War** (431-404 BC), sparked in part by Athenian expansion in the Peloponnese and Sicily. The war ended in a nominal defeat for Athens after a hopeless attack on Syracuse. During this period, the structure of the Greek city-state began to rot from within; the Athenian historian **Thucydides,** our best source on the Peloponnesian Wars, identified the problem as a *stasis*—the Greeks lost their internal unity, while subject city-states chafed under Athenian rule.

## MACEDONIAN RULE (400–200 BC)

**PHILIP OF MACEDON.** Until the Peloponnesian Wars, Athens had been the single city-state powerful enough to lead a unified Greece against common foes. After the war, Sparta and later Thebes tried to hold together a Greek alliance, but succumbed to Persian political influence. A new political force in "barbarian" **Macedonia** soon took advantage of the weakness of the rest of Greece, and grabbed control. **King Philip II** and his Macedonian troops conquered the Greek city-states; in 338 BC, Philip snuffed other Greek powers at the battle of Chaeronea, where he crushed an Athenian resistance led by orator and statesman **Demosthenes.** He then bound the city-states into a union subject to his monarchy.

**RISE AND FALL OF EMPIRE.** After Philip's assassination in 336 BC, his 20-year-old son Alexander (soon to be called **Alexander the Great**) took the throne. Once a student of **Aristotle,** Alexander ruled Greece with an iron fist—in 335 BC, he mercilessly razed Thebes, and seized control of his father's empire. In military control of Greece, Alexander then turned his ambitions east. Within eleven years, by the time of his sudden death at 33 years of age, he ruled Egypt and the entire Persian Empire; he had spread the Greek culture and language throughout the eastern Mediterranean. During the **Hellenistic Era** that followed, Athenian literary and artistic forms diffused throughout the former empire and combined with Near Eastern influences to form a distinct hybrid culture.

| 323 BC: ALEXANDER DIES | Things Fall Apart. Upon Alexander the Great's death, the united Greek and barbarian empire shatters. |
|---|---|

The Macedonian empire quickly crumbled after Alexander's death, leaving three powers in its wake: the **Antigonids** in Macedonia, the **Seleucids** in Asia Minor, Syria, and Persia, and the Ptolemies in Egypt. The **Ptolemies** (of whom Cleopatra was the

**PLATO, PHILOSOPHER-KING** Most of what we know of Socrates comes from his disciple Plato, one of the youths he was executed for corrupting. In his dialogues, Plato paid tribute to Socrates' questioning technique, and later referred to Socrates as the originator of Plato's own moral and metaphysical doctrines. Plato's **Theory of Forms** described the sensory world as an illusion that was only an echo of the *real* truth of the distant, pure world of immutable **forms,** or ideas. People could understand the forms only through intense questioning of the world and concentrated Deep Thoughts. Plato embraced reason, and used Greek mythology to support his moral arguments. His rationalism convinced him that his country's famous democracy was for stooges. His *Republic* describes the ideal society, which was divided into ironclad classes by ability and birth and ruled by an enlightened **philosopher-king,** who would guide society out of the cave of ignorance into the light of wisdom.

last) remained particularly tied to Greek culture. The Ptolemy capital at **Alexandria** became a legendary center of culture. Again, the collapse of an empire restored a measure of independence to the Greek city-states. Three Greek powers ruled the 3rd century BC: the Peloponnesian **Achaean Confederacy,** the Delphi-based **Aetolian Confederacy,** and the city-state of Sparta.

## MAGNA GRAECIA TO MAGNA ROMA (200 BC–AD 324)

Greek self-rule was short-lived. In the 3rd century BC, Rome made alliances with Greek cities and began expanding its **empire** into Greek territory: rule of Greece was particularly satisfying for Romans, who had once been ruled by Greek colonial powers, and who admired and wished to adopt Greek culture. Roman influence filled the power vacuum left by Alexander, as the Romans defeated the Seleucids of Asia Minor and conquered Macedonia in the **First and Second Macedonian Wars.** At the end of the second war in 197 BC, Greeks gained a nominal "independence;" but as the Greeks soon realized, Rome treated Greece as its subject, not as a free state. Greek cities began to support their former enemies against Rome, and the Achaean Confederacy openly rebelled in 146 BC. In response, Rome destroyed Corinth and loaded Greece with oppressive restrictions. When the cities were organized by Augustus into the Roman province of **Achaea** in 27 BC, Greece finally fell under direct Roman rule. Rome had no consistent policy toward its Greek province; while the Roman Emperor Hadrian ran public works programs and a fair government, Emperor Sulla destroyed the economy and even massacred people. Even as Roman legions took hold of Greek lands, Hellenic culture took hold of Roman society: Greek slaves often tutored Roman children, Greek sculpture was brought to Roman homes, and Roman architects imitated Greek styles. Adopting what they admired of Greek culture, the Romans created a **Greco-Roman culture** that spread Greek influence to the farthest reaches of the Roman empire.

# BYZANTINE ERA (AD 324–1453)

Unlike other countries ruined by the decline and fall of the Roman Empire (Italy among them), Greece emerged from Roman rule into a **Byzantine** cultural rebirth, prosperity, and power that stretched from the Balkans through Greece to the Levant and Egypt. The Byzantines saw themselves as heirs of the classical Roman Empire; still, they were heirs to a culture more Greek than Roman, and they were Christian. Despite geographical and cultural differences between the Greeks, Syriacs, Egyptian Copts, Armenians, and Slavs in the empire, they forged a unified political state under one emperor, church, language (Greek), and tax system (even then, death and taxes were the only sure things in life). Internal pressure from religious spats and external attacks by raiders weakened the empire.

## ROMAN EMPIRE: EAST SIDE (324–500)

**SAILING TO BYZANTIUM.** At its height, the Roman Empire became too huge to control under a single government from Rome. Thus, the eastern half of the empire split into two regions controlled by a system of four rulers. The unusual political arrangement ended in a scramble for power, finally won by **Constantine** in AD 312. Before his decisive victory, Constantine saw a vision of a cross of light in the sun, bearing the fiery inscription, "In this sign, you will conquer." The newly installed eastern emperor interpreted this as a sign from the Christian God who was winning converts throughout the former Roman Empire. Later, Constantine legalized Christianity within his empire. Founding his own *polis*, **Constantinople** (modern Istanbul), in 324, he gave the Roman Empire a new capital over the ancient city of Byzantium. Known as **New Rome** or simply the **Polis** (City), Constantinople controlled the eastern and western portions of the empire from its strategic location between the Black Sea and the Aegean. Constantinople's new strength led to the eventual administrative division between the Greek-speaking east and the Latin-speaking west after the death of Emperor Theodosius in 395.

| **AD 324: CONSTANTINOPLE FOUNDED** | Brand-spanking-new Byzantium. Constantine grumbled, "I went through all this trouble to change the street signs to say Constantinople. This had better last *forever.*" |
|---|---|

**SLOUCHING TOWARD BETHLEHEM.** Constantine died in 338 after a deathbed Christian baptism; his empire didn't convert so easily. **Julian the Apostate,** a classically-educated nephew of Constantine's, challenged the upstart religion in 361-363, and tried to return to worshipping the traditional pantheon of gods. While Constantine had given state legitimacy to Christianity, many shunned the new faith: numerous pagan monuments still dotted the ostensibly Christian city of Constantinople. Yet the state grew increasingly supportive of Christian culture. Evangelical missions, Christian art, hymns, saints' biographies, theological tracts, spiritual poetry, church architecture, religious icons, and mosaics all spread the word. The church developed its doctrine through the **Seven Ecumenical Councils.** The **Council of Nicaea** in 325 (which produced the Nicene Creed still recited by Catholics daily) and the **Council of Constantinople** in 381 shaped the Orthodox Church into five **patriarchates,** or dioceses: Rome, Constantinople, Alexandria, Antioch, and Jerusalem. A patriarch or pope presided over each, as a religious and governmental official.

## SNIPPY NEIGHBORS (500–1453)

**VANDALS-1, GREEKS-0.** During the 6th century, **Emperor Justinian**'s battles against the Sassanians of Persia and the western Vandals (who had sacked Rome) overstretched the empire's strength. Justinian attempted to simplify the empire's aging Roman laws, and he undertook massive building projects, such as the **Agia Sophia,** a church that still stands in Istanbul. These expensive reforms, along with military campaigns and political corruption, left the empire vulnerable to raids by Slavs, Mongols, and Avars who attacked Greece as far as the Peloponnese around 500. In many areas of the mainland and Peloponnese, Greek culture and language were wiped out entirely, and the Greek language and script only returned after later missions from Constantinople.

**SMASHING, BABY!** Ensuing Arab conquests and the challenge of Islam consolidated and unified the empire, accompanied by the religious movement of **iconoclasm**—icon-smashing. Greek Christians came to believe that iconography (paintings of Christ and saints on boards or city walls for protection in battle, or any visual representation of God) violated the **second commandment** which demanded that the faithful make no graven image of God. They interpreted their defeats in battle as punishment for this violation. By the early 700s, Church doctrine demanded that all images be demolished—a policy whose enforcement

depended on the Greeks' performance in war. Eventually, iconoclasm itself was smashed in 843, to the benefit of latter-day art historians.

Non-Christian conquerors created the **Byzantine Commonwealth,** which further divided Constantinople from Rome and the west. The crowning of **Charlemagne** as Holy Roman Emperor in 800 finalized the split of west and east. The bitter **Great Schism** of 1054 caused a mutual excommunication between the Greek Orthodox and Roman Catholic Churches—each church declared the other a false church.

| 1054: GREAT SCHISM | "You're Out!" "No, *You're* Out!" Refusing to comment, pope and patriarch stick out their tongues. |
|---|---|

**THE CURSE OF CRUSADERS.** After the separation from Rome, Greeks attempted to extend Christianity as they protected themselves from invaders. **Missionaries** reached out from the empire's contracted borders into the Slavic kingdoms and Russia, sowing the seeds for Orthodox Christianity throughout Eastern Europe. In 1071, the Byzantines lost control of eastern Anatolia to the **Selçuk Turks;** Greek monasteries in the Aegean and Black Sea areas converted themselves to armed fortresses to ward off Turkish pirates. From 1200 to 1400, the Byzantine Empire was plagued by Norman and Venetian **Crusaders,** who conquered and looted Constantinople in 1204 and imposed western Catholic culture upon the city. Despite its strong emperors, Byzantium needed to ally with Latin, Slavic, and even Turkish rulers by marriage in order to survive. At last, the once-huge Byzantine Empire was reduced to only Constantinople and its environs, and in 1453 the **Ottoman Turks** overran the much-reduced city.

# UNDER THE OTTOMAN THUMB (1453–1829)

## ISTANBUL, NOT CONSTANTINOPLE

**GREECE UNDER TURKEY.** Old Byzantium suffered another undignified name change under the Ottoman Turks, this time renamed **Istanbul**—a Turkish adaptation of the Greek *steen Poli* (to the City)—in 1453. The city again became the seat of empire. For centuries the Ottoman Empire prospered, though eventually its diverse regions grew apart and caused its weakening. The Muslim Turkish rulers treated their Greek subjects as a **millet**—a separate community ruled by its own religious leaders. Greeks paid the *cizye*, a head tax dictated by Islamic law, but were otherwise free to worship as they chose. The Orthodox Greek church became the moderator of culture and tradition, and the foundation of Greek autonomy. Peacefully incorporated into Ottoman society, many Greeks fared better under Muslim rule than under the Christian crusaders. Greeks formed a new merchant class in towns, and served as soldiers, bureaucrats, and translators for the Turkish sultanate. Though rebellions were repressed ruthlessly, Ottoman rule brought relative peace and prosperity to Greece.

The sultans ensured army loyalty by doling out **tımars** (temporary, uninheritable land grants) as payment for military service. But as Ottoman expansion slowed (and land grants dwindled), *tımar* holders grew restless. In the 14th century, Sultan Murad I developed the **devşirme** draft system, in which male Christian children could be conscripted to serve the sultan in Istanbul, converted to Islam, and highly educated as civil servants. The position of **Janissary** (from *yeni çeri*, "new army") let Greeks rise in the military or the Ottoman bureaucracy, as *kulls* (slaves).

**GRRR.** Though Greeks could choose to integrate into Ottoman society, **anti-Turk nationalist sentiments** began to build, encouraged by Western Europe and Russia. Russia viewed Moscow as a Christian force and as a third Rome; Istanbul, a Muslim city that ruled Christians, the former seat of empire, naturally interested Russia immensely. Russia wanted a Greek Orthodox state at the Bosporus to control the entrance to the Black Sea, while Greeks chafed under the weakening Turkish rule. By the 19th century, Greeks were pushing for independence from the empire.

# THE GREAT IDEA (1821–1900)

## GREEK NATIONALIST REVOLT

**WAR FOR INDEPENDENCE.** On March 25, 1821, after 400 years of Ottoman rule, Bishop Germanos of Patras raised a Greek flag at the monastery of Agia Lavra and sparked an empire-wide **rebellion.** Middle-class rebels hoped that the Orthodox Russian czar and Greek peasants would join the revolt; when they didn't, the rebels met a crushing defeat. Disorganized but impassioned guerrillas in the Peloponnese and Aegean islands waged sporadic war on the Turkish government for 10 years. The day of the revolt, **25 Martiou,** and the names Botsaris, Koundouritis, Miaoulis, Mavrokordatos, and Ypsilanti (famous rebels) now appear as street names throughout the country (and the rest of the world—Ypsilanti, Michigan, for example). The liberation movement was carefully planned for nine months before Christmas Day (see "Conceived in Liberty...?," p. 292).

In an era of European revolutions, the Greek cause attracted the attention of hundreds of **philhellenes,** Europeans seeking to restore Greece to the Classical glory they idolized. These philhellenes came to fight (and often die) for Greece's independence, drawing international attention especially after British Romantic poet George Gordon, **Lord Byron,** died there of pneumonia in 1824. The persistent Greeks and their allies finally won the nervous support of the anti-revolutionary European Great Powers, and in 1827, Russia, Britain, and France pressured the Turkish sultan to ease up on Greece. After the Turkish fleet was wrecked at the **battle of Navarino** (now called Pylos, p. 148) the hesitant Russian czar declared war. The **Treaty of Adrianople** in 1829 finally freed Greece.

| 1829: GREECE LIBERATED | I'm a Big Kid Now. For the first time in 2000 years, Greece controls its own destiny, a grown-up country again. |
|---|---|

**A ROOM OF THEIR OWN.** Russia, Britain, and France wanted a free Greece, but also wanted to restrict its power. The borders of the new Greece were narrow, including only a fraction of the six million Greeks living under Ottoman rule. For the next century, Greek politics centered around regaining the Byzantine boundaries of Greece, and unifying the Greek population scattered around the Mediterranean. The vision of unification, called the **Megali Idhea**—the Great Idea—eventually ended in considerable expansion, including Crete, in 1913. However, Greece never gained its great goal—making Constantinople its capital.

Post-liberation nationalism also encouraged the creation of the **Church of Greece** in 1833, although it was not recognized by the patriarch until 1850. One of a number of independent Eastern Orthodox churches, the Church of Greece became the official state church.

## POST-REVOLUTION POLITICS

**OUT OF THE FRYING PAN, INTO THE FIRE.** After the War of Independence, joy soon dissolved into disappointment. Puny and poor, the new Greek state was divided by the **agrarian problem** that would plague it for the rest of the century: landowners clung to their traditional privileges, while peasants demanded the redistribution of lands that had motivated them to fight for independence.

The first president, **Ioannis Capodistrias,** was elected in 1827, and made an earnest (if autocratic) attempt to create a strong government. His assassination in 1831 thwarted the democratic government, and prompted European intervention in Greek politics.

The European powers then declared Greece a **monarchy,** handing the crown to the young German **Prince Otho** (dubbed "Otto") in 1833. Often called an "insensitive" ruler, Otto was a rich, powerful teenager who angered Greeks by handing out

high-ranking positions to his German buddies. Otto moved the capital to **Athens,** and in 1843 created a parliamentary system. Though he embraced the *Megali Idhea* (and made friends in his new country that way), his bumbling government earned him exile in 1862 for ignoring the constitution. The British stepped in and installed a Danish prince, **George I,** as king. George's rule brought stability and a new constitution (in 1864), but the land distribution problem remained unsolved.

# TWENTIETH CENTURY

**EXPAND AND CONTRACT.** The 1864 constitution downplayed the king, and emphasized the elected prime minister. In 1920, Cretan Prime Minister **Eleftherios Venizelos** wrangled new Greek territory in the aftermath of the Balkan Wars and the First World War. Savvy Balkan alliances nearly doubled Greece's territory. Defying King Constantine's request for neutrality, Venizelos set up an Allied revolutionary government in Thessaloniki. After the First World War, Venizelos realized Greece wouldn't get land in Asia Minor, and so in 1919 he invaded Smyrna in Turkey. A young Atatürk rebuffed the attack, and Venizelos was soon voted out of office. The **Treaty of Lausanne,** signed in 1923, enacted a massive population exchange that sent a million Greeks who lived in Asia Minor to live in Greece, and sent 400,000 Turkish Muslims from Greece to Turkey. This **population exchange** ended the *Megali Idhea* but began a series of economic problems for Greece.

**THE SECOND WORLD WAR.** Political turmoil rocked the 1930s, as Greeks lived through brief intervals of democracy amidst a succession of monarchies and military rule. King George II was overthrown by a series of coups that instated a democracy; Venizelos, the former Prime Minister, headed the new government for five years, though royalists eventually forced his exile. The extreme nationalist **General Metaxas** succeeded him as Prime Minister in a fixed election, as George II again took the throne in 1936. Metaxas inaugurated an oppressive military state. Most notably, Metaxas rejected Mussolini's request that Italy occupy Greece during the Second World War with a resounding "No!" (**"Οχι!"**). Greece fell to Germany in 1941 and endured four years of Axis occupation, which destroyed ancient sites, caused widespread starvation and large-scale executions, and allowed the Nazi extermination of much of Greece's Jewish community. The communist-led resistance received broad popular support, though many right-wing resistance fighters were helped by the Western powers to prevent a communist Greece.

# FORMING THE MODERN GREEK STATE

**CIVIL WAR AND RECONSTRUCTION.** A civil war broke out in 1944, in an early Cold War stand-off that the left-wing, Soviet-backed Democratic Army (DA) eventually lost to the US-supplied anti-communist coalition government. Through a rather disgraceful American intervention, Greece instituted the Certificate of Political Reliability, which guaranteed that the bearer had politically acceptable views. Keeping a visible hand in Greek politics, the red-scared US helped place General Papagos, **Constantinos Karamalis,** and the right-wing Greek Rally Party in power. When Karamanlis resigned after the assassination of a communist official in 1963, left-wing **George Papandreou** came to power.

The right-wing respite was short-lived; the army staged a **coup** on April 21, 1967, which resulted in rule by a **military junta** for seven years. Making extensive use of torture, censorship, and arbitrary arrest to maintain power, the junta enjoyed official US support and investment at the height of the Cold War. It ultimately fell in 1973 after the government killed 20 protesting students and provoked a **Turkish invasion of Cyprus** by attempting to unite Cyprus and Greece (p. 512).

Former president Karamanlis returned to take power, instituting parliamentary elections and organizing a referendum on the form of government. Monarchy was defeated by a two-thirds vote, and a new constitution was drawn up in 1975, calling for parliamentary government with a ceremonial president appointed by the legislature—the system still in use today.

**1975: DEMOCRACY RETURNS** | Greece Goes Retro: Democracy Back in Style. The Prime Minister commented, "We *invented* democracy. We were into it *before* it was cool. Not like you poseurs."

## RECENT EVENTS

**TOWARD EUROPE.** Under Prime Minister and founder **Andreas Papandreou,** the leftist Panhellenic Socialist Movement (PASOK) won landslide electoral victories in 1981 and 1985. Appealing to voters with the simple campaign slogan **Allaghi** ("Change"), Papandreou promised a radical break with the past. In office, he steered Greece into the European Economic Community (EEC) and pioneered the passage of women's rights legislation, though many of his policies were anti-Western: he spoke against NATO and maintained friendships with Qaddhafi and Palestinian Liberation Organization leader Yasser Arafat. When a scandal involving the chair of the Bank of Crete implicated government officials in 1989, Papandreou lost control of Parliament. After three general elections in the space of 10 months, **Constantine Mitsotakis** of the New Democracy party (Nea Demokratia, or ND) became Prime Minister by a slim parliamentary majority.

**REFORM AND AUSTERITY.** Attempting to solve Greece's economic and diplomatic problems and align the country with mainstream European politics, Mitsotakis imposed an **austerity program** that limited wage increases and authorized the sale of state enterprises. This policy became tremendously unpopular when it threatened thousands of public sector jobs, and in 1993, Mitsotakis was defeated by a resurgent Papandreou in an emergency election. Just two years later, poor health forced Papandreou to leave his position.

Fellow socialist **Constantine Simitis** took control of the party and has since pursued aggressive economic reforms, privatizing banks and companies despite the opposition of perpetually striking labor unions. The ruling PASOK party has also made strides in international relations by being more NATO-friendly and opening talks with Turkey. The administration has also slashed Greece's budget deficit, brought inflation down, and cut the national debt in an attempt to meet the qualifying standards for entry into the **European Monetary Union** (EMU). Simitis, who was barely re-elected in the 2000 election, has supported Greece in its successful bid to enter the EMU in January 2001, so that visitors to the **2004 Olympics in Athens** (eagerly anticipated and in elaborate preparation) will be shelling out euros instead of drachmas.

**GREECE AND TURKEY: BREAKING THE ICE.** One of Simitis's continuing projects is normalizing relations with nearby Turkey. The two nations have been on less-than-friendly terms in the past (see p. 16), but in January **Financial Minister George Papandreou** traveled to Turkey, the first such visit in 37 years. While there, he signed four cooperation agreements concerning tourism, the environment, the protection of investments, and terrorism. Furthermore, talks have begun concerning the touchy issue of Cyprus, which remains divided into Turkish and Greek Cypriot states. Although neither country wants to relinquish hold of the island, both sides appear to be open and optimistic.

# ART & ARCHITECTURE

> Such is the bloom of perpetual newness upon these works which makes them ever to look like untouched by time, as though the unfaltering breath of an ageless spirit had been infused in them.
>
> —Plutarch

Order, proportion, and symmetry have shaped the tradition of Greek art from its earliest stages. Works by masters like Praxiteles and Lysippus still make us gasp, and we still scurry to see them in museums. Greek art is typically divided into three eras: Ancient, Byzantine, and Modern. Three highly influential periods of the Ancient Era still stand out: the **Archaic** (700-480 BC; see p. 10), the **Classical** (480-323 BC; see p. 11), and the **Hellenistic** (323-46 BC; see p. 12).

# PERFECTION WITH A PURPOSE: ANCIENT GREECE (THROUGH AD 324)

The ancient Greeks prized beauty above all else, as their technically perfect and carefully crafted works affirm. But Greeks didn't produce art just to admire its beauty. Ancient works of art served religious or practical functions: decorative pottery was a hot export item, used for storing (and chugging) wine, while sculptures represented gods in temples, or served as offerings and monuments to the dead. Architecture developed through the construction of temples, commercial buildings, and stadia for performance of religious plays and for governmental gatherings. The mythological scenes painted on vases and in frescoes expressed religious values, political propaganda, or even made penis jokes.

Greek art grew around the belief that "man is the measure of all things." The living human form became artists' favorite subject, after years of experimentation with abstract and stylized geometrical shapes. Meanwhile, Greek temples incorporated light and space as integral parts of the place of worship. It is impossible to overestimate how much Western culture owes to the architectural and artistic achievements of the ancient Greeks—Augustus Caesar, Michelangelo, Jacques-Louis David, Thomas Jefferson, Constantine Brancusi, and even Salvador Dalí found inspiration in Greek works. Present-day artists still learn their art from 2500-year-old Greek masterpieces, though many exist only as fragments.

## ROOTS

**CYCLADIC AND MINOAN PERIOD (3000-1100 BC).** The Bronze Age Cycladic civilizations produced a minimalist style of sculpture, mostly small marble statuettes. These miniature pieces gracefully simplified the human form; a nude goddess, arms folded straight across her body, is a typical figure. Many of these enigmatic idols dazzle visitors to the **Goulandris Museum of Cycladic and Ancient Greek Art** in Athens (p. 105).

The Minoans of Crete also created scores of miniature votive statuettes, like the two earthenware **snake goddesses,** decorated with opaque colored glazes which reside in Iraklion's **Archaeological Museum** (p. 469). It was Minoan **architecture,** however, that brought the Minoans glory, as Cycladic cultures took their cue from Minoan palaces like **Knossos** (p. 389). The palaces were cities unto themselves, and their labyrinthine complexity echoed the complicated administrative and religious roles of Minoan priest-kings. The palaces' massive pillars, ceremonial stairways, and decorative stucco show Near Eastern aesthetic and structural influence, which arrived via commercial contact with Egypt and Mesopotamia.

Minoan artists delighted in plaster, sculpting bull-leaping ceremonies (p. 478), magical gardens, and leaping dolphins in vividly painted and lifelike frescoes. Several Minoan **frescoes** were preserved in the ash of a volcanic eruption that destroyed much of Thira (present-day Santorini) near 1500 BC, and can be seen at the **National Archaeological Museum** in Athens (p. 104). Similar fresco paintings, restored by Sir Arthur Evans, can be seen at Knossos or in Iraklion's **Archaeological Museum** (p. 469). The Minoans were also renowned throughout the Aegean for their multicolored **Kamares-style pottery,** which consisted of red and white ornamentation on a dark background. Kamares-style designs included curving, abstract patterns and stylized ocean and plant motifs.

**MYCENAEAN PERIOD (1600-1100 BC).** The architecture of the mainland Mycenaean culture developed in response to the Cretan Minoans. The Mycenaeans' palaces at **Mycenae** (p. 131), **Tiryns,** and **Pylos** (p. 160) followed a more symmetrical design than earlier architecture, and centered around the **megaron,** a Near East-inspired reception room. Decorative frescoes remade the fanciful Minoan model according to Mycenaean warrior taste.

The Mycenaeans were the first Europeans to produce sculpted monuments, as in the **royal tombs** and triangular **Lion's Gate** sculpture at Mycenae (p. 130). Dated to the 13th century BC, the Lion's Gate is the earliest monumental sculpture known.

By 1500 BC, Mycenaean royal graves had evolved into **tholos,** beehive-shaped stone structures covered in packed earth. The relief work on these tombs shows Minoan influence; the large-scale masonry is distinctly Mycenaean.

**GEOMETRIC PERIOD (1100-700 BC).** A new ceramics-based art evolved out of the collapse of Mycenaean civilization and the Dark Age that followed. Athens stood at the center of the movement; Athenian pottery of the **Proto-Geometric Period** (1100-900 BC) was decorated with Mycenaean-inspired spirals, arcs, wavy lines, and concentric circles. These patterns became more intricate in the **Geometric Period,** when artists covered pottery and clay figurines with geometric motifs that resembled woven baskets. Identically posed stick-figure humans and grazing animals began to appear among the continuous, patterned bands and tight rows of thick black lines. Near Eastern contact with Greece showed up again in Syrian and Phoenician floral and animal designs, earning the period the title of the **Orientalizing** phase. At this time, Corinth joined Athens as a major ceramic center.

Architects of the Geometric Period focused on the development of one-room temples with columned porches. These temples were essentially regarded as the houses of the gods or goddesses they honored, and each **oikos** (house) came complete with a sculpture of its inhabitant.

## ARCHAIC PERIOD (700-480 BC)

During the **Archaic Period,** Greek art and architecture morphed from the stylization of the Geometric Period to the curving, human realism of the Classical Period. Sculptors and vase painters produced abstracted images of the human form, and architects perfected temple-building and proportion in construction. The city-states basked in a prosperity that allowed new, expensive, and artfully conceived architecture. During this period, the acropolis, agora, amphitheater, and gymnasium were all perfected. The city-states' public buildings imitated the temples which architects had pored over for hundreds of years.

**COLUMNS, ON THE STRAIGHT AND NARROW.** During the Archaic Period, the Doric and Ionic architectural orders—whose columns have lined many an art history student's nightmares—departed along their own paths. The **Doric order** gave a stone face-lift to the makeshift wood and mud-brick Geometric temple in the 7th century BC. The former design of a one-room *cella,* or inner sanctum, and its surrounding peristyle were spiced up with new columns and classy marble. Around the 6th century BC, Greece's colonies along the coast of Asia Minor branched off into the more exotic **Ionic order.** The curlicued Ionic columns differed from the more austere Doric order in gracing the tops of each column (the capitals) with twin **volutes,** or scrolled spiral uppers, and in the slender, fluted bodies of each column. Ionic temples, ornate and fussy, boasted forests of columns: the **Temple of Hera** at Samos (p. 328) sported 134.

**BUCK NAKED AND GRINNING.** Early Archaic sculptors began to craft large-scale figures called **kouroi.** Each *kouros* was a naked, idealized young man, symmetrically posed, with one leg forward and his hands clenched at his sides, smiling goofily under stylized curls. The *kouroi* stood in temples as offerings to deities or as memorials to fallen warriors. An early example dedicated to Poseidon at Sounion (c. 590 BC) now stands in the **National Archaeological Museum** of Athens (p. 104). In the 6th century BC, technical advances and an increasing concern with the natural human form led to more life-like *kouroi,* such as the stunning **Anavissos kouros,** also in the National Archaeological Museum. The female equivalent of the *kouros,* the **kore,** posed in the latest fashions instead of in her birthday suit; Archaic sculptors focused on the drape of the *kore*'s clothing, suggesting the female form through straight and bunched folds and zig-zag hemlines.

In the beginning of the 5th century BC, sculpture turned toward realistic depiction, which would reach its height soon afterward in the Classical Period. The relaxed posture of the free-standing **Kritios Boy** (490 BC), now in the **Acropolis Museum** in Athens (p. 100), broke the stiff, symmetrical mold of the archaic *kouroi* with an individualized personality: the Kritios Boy's weight is shifted onto one leg, and his hips and torso tilt naturally.

**ARISTOTLE, SCIENTIST** Although a student of Plato's, Aristotle reacted critically against his teacher's methods and teachings. Aristotle took up biology and grounded himself in concrete examples and specimens; he appreciated the palpable world and rejected abstract ideas. His empirical approach virtually founded Western science, and his work remained at the forefront of scientific thought throughout the Middle Ages. But Aristotle was also a political philosopher: he disagreed with Plato and Socrates' belief (a belief shared by many even in the present) that a politically active man can't live a moral life. He saw a moral life in civic responsibility to the Greek *polis*. Indeed, his later life was spent in political service: when Athens came under pressure from **Philip of Macedon** (p. 12), Aristotle returned to his native Macedonia, where he took on a none-too-shabby job as tutor to **Alexander the Great** (p. 12).

**AT TEMPLE-TOP.** During the Archaic Period, architectural sculpture integrated the human form into building decoration. Sculptors quit trying to fill the awkward triangular pediments above temples with mythological narratives, and looked to battle scenes to fill them. The new style placed a standing god at the central high point of the pediment, and lined falling bodies on each side. For an example, see the **Temple of Aphaia** at Aegina (p. 288). Showing the intertwined, warring figures challenged sculptors to model the human form, presaging the Classical Period's interest in the body both in architecture and in free-standing sculpture.

**WALK LIKE AN EGYPTIAN.** As for two-dimensional art, Athenian **vase painters** depicted humans using Corinth's **black figure technique,** drawing black silhouettes with carved features. Human figures appeared in the half-profile of ancient Egyptian art: moving figures' chests faced forward, and each person stared straight out with both eyes. The figures conveyed emotion with gestures rather than facial expression, and many figures pulled their hair in grief or flailed their limbs in joy.

## CLASSICAL PERIOD (480-323 BC)

The arts flourished during the Classical Period, as Athens reached the peak of its political and economic power under Pericles and his successors (p. 11). Perfecting Doric architecture and dabbling in the Ionic style, Classical temples were more spacious and fluid than the stocky temples of the Archaic Period. The peerless Athenian **Acropolis** (p. 97), built during this period, embodied "classic" for the entire Classical world; its star attraction, the **Parthenon,** shows the fullness of the Greek obsession with perfect proportions. *Everything* on the Parthenon—from its floor space to the friezes above the columns—is in a four-to-nine ratio.

**WHAT A BOD!** Sculptors mastered the natural representation of the human form during the Classical Period. The milestone sculptures of the **Temple of Zeus** at Olympia (p. 139) exhibit a newfound mastery of anatomical detail. Although the figures bear Archaic-style stylized hair, their unique bodies and faces expressed emotion for the first time in Greek sculpture. Indeed, the personal and mood-evoking Classical style fully broke from formulaic Archaic sculpture. Notable sculptures from the Classical Period include the bronze statues of the **Charioteer** (470 BC) at Delphi (p. 171) and the **Poseidon** from the Artemisium wreck (465 BC), now in Athens's **National Archaeological Museum** (p. 104). The charioteer's grace and Poseidon's heroism show the twin ideals toward which Classical sculpture—and Classical society—strove.

By the middle of the 5th century BC, Classical sculptors had scrapped the stylized stiffness of the early Archaic Period, favoring a detailed realism that still lacked much emotion or realism in facial features. Sculptors pursued a universal perfection of the human form, suppressing particular imperfections that make people unique. The impersonal, idealized **Severe style** embodied the idealization of Plato's forms (see "Plato, Philosopher-King," p. 13) and the athletic heroism that Pindar praised in his Olympic odes (p. 25). It remained in vogue through the start

of the 4th century BC. By this time, sculptors like the genius **Praxiteles** had created free-standing sculptures that virtually breathe. This new generation of sculptors turned their talent away from the monumental and impersonal Severe Style toward vivid representations of individual people.

**OLD-SCHOOL POT.** Classical potters swooned over the **red figure technique** that had been gaining steam since 540 BC; the older black figure style was *so* passé. Red figure vase painting featured a black painted background, allowing the naturally reddish clay to show through as the drawn figures. Vase-makers then painted on details with a fine brush. Inspired by the new-found realism in sculpture, anonymous early Classical masters known as the **Berlin Painter** and the **Kleophrades Painter** lent their subjects an unparalleled level of psychological depth.

Although they still showed only a limited profile of the head, vase-painters experimented with foreshortening and three-quarter views of the body, suggesting a variety of new poses, gestures, and emotions. With this newfound expressive freedom, Classical red-figure artists tackled more ordinary subjects, like boozing at parties, women lounging at home, and athletic contests. By the mid-5th century BC, vase painting fell by the wayside of the art world because of growing interest in sculpture. But vase-painters left their mark: their vigorous, sinuous lines and careful anatomical detail inspired many later European painters.

## HELLENISTIC PERIOD (323-46 BC)

**ALAS, POOR DORIC...** After the death of Alexander the Great, a new Hellenistic Period rose out of the ashes of Classical Greece. Eastern Greeks made architecture a flamboyant affair. Scuttling the simpler Doric and Ionic styles, they whipped up ornate, flower-topped **Corinthian-style columns.** Hellenistic architects worked on a monumental scale, building complexes of temples, *stoas* (colonnaded walkways), and palaces. Astoundingly precise **acoustics** graced the enormous amphitheaters at **Argos** (p. 121) and **Epidavros** (p. 127); a coin dropped onstage is audible in the farthest seat of the theaters, even 2200 years after their construction.

Hellenistic sculpture exuded passion, displaying all the technical mastery and twice the emotion of Classical works. Artists tested the aesthetic value of ugliness, sculpting the grotesque figure of **Laocoön** as snakes writhe around him, dragging him to death; only a Roman copy of the Hellenistic original survives. The final frontier of Greek sculpture was **portraiture,** which began with the appointment of **Lysippus** as court sculptor to Alexander the Great.

**DO AS THE ROMANS DO.** With the arrival of the **Roman empire** in Greece, the Hellenistic style shifted to suit Roman tastes. Greek artists painted, sculpted marble, and assembled mosaics for Romans in Italy and for the old Hellenistic kingdoms of the east. Architects built mostly Christian churches; even the Parthenon was temporarily converted to a church, though it was (fortunately) left unaltered in its structure. Under the Romans, Greek art and architecture spread throughout the empire, but its innovative glory had passed.

# BYZANTINE & OTTOMAN (AD 324-1829)

Ensconced in a throne and surrounded by elaborate mechanical animals and golden birds, the **Byzantine emperor** administered his holy city in the image of God ruling the cosmos. The art and architecture in Greece under Byzantine and Ottoman rule belonged more to these imperial cultures that had overtaken Greece than to native Greek culture. The Byzantine empire unified religion and government, a combination that shaped the art and architecture of the empire. Byzantine artistry developed within a set of religious conventions that limited creative experimentation, but still created magnificent mosaics, iconography, and church architecture.

In 529, Emperor **Justinian** restricted art to Christian subjects; afterward, Byzantine art and architecture evolved in a unified, religiously themed vein even after the fall of Constantinople in 1453.

## ARCHITECTURE

**GOING TO THE CHAPEL.** Early Byzantine churches show their roots in Roman Christianity: based on the Roman **basilica** layout, the Byzantine versions were long buildings with a semicircular **apse** at one end, and with windows lining a wooden ceiling (forming a **clerestory**). A column-lined outer courtyard stood on a church's western side; on the eastern side, people entered the **vestibule** through two doors, often bronze or inlaid with silver. These doors opened onto the **naos,** the church proper. Inside, a central **nave** reached from the church's inner door to the choir rows, and was separated from two side aisles by arched colonnades.

Constantinople's **Agia Sofia,** built during Justinian's rule over the remains of a church from Constantine's time, stands as the prime example of Byzantine architecture. The Byzantines used two revolutionary architectural techniques: incorporating the **squinch,** an arch tucked into the corners of the square base, and the **pendentive,** a triangular section of vaulting with concave sides that transferred the dome's weight to the ground. By the reign of **Basil I** (867-886), domed basilicas like the Agia Sofia evolved into a **cross-in-square** plan, with four equal-vaulted arms holding up a central dome (see **Osios Loukas,** p. 165). On occasion, the vaulted roofs above the four arms of the cross-shaped church were replaced by four small domes, producing a five-domed church called a **quincunx.**

**RETRO-CHIC ICONS.** The floor and lower parts of the walls were usually covered in **marble,** while the upper parts were reserved for **mosaics** and occasionally **frescoes.** After the end of **iconoclasm** (p. 14) in the 9th century, **icon** layout in Byzantine churches was standardized along a hierarchical scheme determined by Byzantine theology. The inside of the central dome usually portrayed the **Pantocrator** (Creator of All Things); in iconoclast churches, a large cross replaced the image of Christ (smashed by Church order); the image in the central dome formed the physical and spiritual center of the rest of the church's images. Angels and evangelists lined the dome's base, and rows of saints covered the walls. The **Virgin Mary** appeared in the half-dome above the apse. The **Festival Cycle,** twelve scenes from the life of Christ that corresponded to the 12 major feast days of the Byzantine calendar, further adorned the church. The faithful assembled below these images, making the church a complete, earthly microcosm of the Christian universe.

## ENLIGHTENMENT IN TWO DIMENSIONS

Byzantine artists transformed almost any flat surface they encountered into art: they illuminated manuscripts, carved ivory panels, embossed bronze doors, and covered *cloisonée* enamels with jewels. The dazzling **mosaics** and **icons** of Byzantine churches showed the greatest of Byzantine talent: artists underwent years of spiritual and technical training before gaining permission to portray sacred subjects. Byzantine icons aimed for religious authenticity, intended to transmit—not just represent—the spiritual power of the subject. Based on evocative swathes of color rather than exacting form, the Byzantine pictorial style showed flat figures with idealized facial features, wearing stylized clothes. Each figure stared out with a **soul-searing gaze,** adding to the power of the images; a determined frontal pose against a gold background created the illusion of the figure floating between the wall and the viewer in the church's dim light.

Byzantines used enamel, ivory, gold, wood, and mosaic to make icons. Mosaics were composed of **tesserae,** small cubes of stone or ceramic covered in glass or metallic foil. A unique shimmering effect was produced by contrasting gold and silver tesserae at sharp angles to reflect light. Sparkling examples of Byzantine mosaics can be seen in the churches of **Thessaloniki** (p. 216), at the **Monastery of Osios Loukas** (p. 166), on **Mt. Athos** (p. 244), and at **Meteora** (p. 196).

One Greek artist did separate himself from the dominant Ottoman tradition of flat, stylized, religious paintings. Domenikos Theotokopoulos (1541-1614)—**El Greco** to the world, and "god-touching" in literal Greek—was influenced by the Venetian tradition in his native Crete. El Greco moved to Spain at age 35, and there forged an international reputation (see "It's El Greco to Me," p. 470).

## MODERN ART (1829-PRESENT)

Nationalist sentiment after Greek independence led the government to subsidize Greek art. King Otto (p. 16) encouraged young artists to study their craft in Munich, and the **Polytechneion,** Greece's first modern art school, was established in 1838. The first wave of post-independence Greek painters—**Nicephoros Lytras** (1832-1904) and **Nicholas Gyzes** (1842-1901) among them—showed strong evidence of their German training. Sculptors, on the other hand, looked to Classical Greek works as their inspiration. **Giannoules Halepas** (1854-1938) produced graceful works which are still unparalleled among modern Greek sculpture.

**FOR EUROPE.** Twentieth century Greek painters have contended with European trends: painter **Konstantinos Parthenes** (1879-1965) brought Impressionism to Greece, while Expressionist **George Bouzianis** (1885-1959) used thick, vivid brush strokes to convey emotion. **Nikos Engonopoulos** (1910-85) adopted Surrealism.

**FOR GREECE.** Other painters rejected foreign influence, among them the much-adored Theophilos Chatzimichael (1873-1934), known simply as **Theophilos.** Though undistinguished in his own lifetime, this eccentric folk artist has been called the Greek Van Gogh. His oddly primitive paintings of natural and historical scenes are now admired for their harmonious composition.

In the twentieth century, painter **Photis Kontoglou** (1896-1965) returned to a different set of roots, leading a movement for the revival of Byzantine art. Kontoglou also took a cue from Greek folk art, as did **Spyros Vassiliou** (1902-85)—who portrayed Greek customs and daily life in urban landscapes—and **Yiannis Tsarouhis** (1910-89), who painted his native country with emotion and sympathy. Tsarouhis, along with Yiannis Moralis (b. 1916) and Giorgos Sikeliotis (1917-84), focused his work on the relationship between artist and art.

In the present day, the paintings of **Yiannis Psychopedis** (b. 1945) combine social and aesthetic criticism. Painter **Opy Zouni** (b. 1941) has won international renown for her almost metaphysical geometric art.

# LANGUAGE & LITERATURE

Wherever literature consoles sorrow or assuages pain; wherever it brings gladness to eyes which fail with wakefulness and tears, and ache for the dark house and the long sleep, there is exhibited in its noblest form the immortal influence of Greece.
—Thomas Babington Macaulay

## ANCIENT GREECE

Greek writing goes way back. Tablets scrawled with pre-Greek writing were found among Minoan palace ruins, preserved, ironically, by baking in the fires that destroyed the palaces themselves. Somewhat uninspiring in content (how many bushels of grain were received, how many cows), these palace treasury records were inscribed on tablets in two-syllable scripts called **Linear A** and **Linear B** near the end of the Bronze Age (roughly 1100 BC; see p. 7). During the Dark Age under the Dorians (see p. 10), Linear B disappeared from archaeological sight. Greeks were generally illiterate, though their language eased into a more solid form.

### EARLY MASTERS

**SING IN ME, OH MUSE.** The first written Greek did not appear until the middle of the 8th century BC, but the Greek literary tradition may have begun as much as 150 years earlier, with the epic-crooning mystery-man **Homer.** The original bard may have recorded or dictated the **Iliad** and **Odyssey** in his own lifetime (if he was indeed one guy); most scholars believe that Homer simply began an oral tradition that would lead to a written epic literature in the next century. Regardless of whether or not Homer wrote the poetry, his mythic history of the **Trojan War** (see p. 10 and p. 28) still drives readers to **ecstasy.**

**I LAUGHED, I CRIED...** Born out of the 5th century BC from a tradition of **goat songs** *(tragodoi)* dedicated to the god Dionysus, the plebeian roots of Greek drama are worlds away from our view of theater as high art. Greek drama began as a religious rite in which all attendants were both performers in the chorus and audience members. Individual acting began when, at a public competition of masked choruses in Dionysus' honor, young **Thespis** stepped out of the crowd to become Athens's first actor—hence, "thespian." By adding a second actor and other characters, **Aeschylus** (525-456 BC) composed the plays *Prometheus Bound* and the *Oresteia,* a trilogy about Agamemnon's ruinous return home from the Trojan War. **Sophocles** (496-406 BC) followed, creating the creepy, cathartic *Oedipus* trilogy, which details the ruinous tale of Oedipus, a man who becomes king by killing his father and marrying his mother. **Euripides** (485-406 BC), Sophocles' contemporary, added *Medea* and the *Bacchae* to the tradition. **Aristophanes** (450-385 BC) tossed aside the tragic medium, and wrote *The Clouds, Lysistrata,* and *The Frogs* in bawdy, slapstick "Old Comedy" form; Aristophanes' swipes at Socrates helped cause the philosopher's execution. **Menander,** creator of "New Comedy," wrote more sunny and well-mannered works; his star-crossed lovers paved the way for endless happy endings throughout Western literature.

**POEMS POETS POETRY.** Homer's contemporary **Hesiod** composed the **Works and Days,** a farmer's-eye view of life that lamented the oppression of the aristocracy; he also composed the **Theogony,** the first Greek account of the creation of the world and the gods' wacky exploits. During the 7th century BC, anti-everything **Archilochus** of Paros inscribed the first known written poetry—anti-heroic, anti-Homeric elegies. In one particularly sour fragment, Archilochus expresses no shame at tossing his shield aside in battle to run for his life.

On the island of Lesvos, during the 6th century, lyric poet **Sappho,** the lone female poet of the ancient world, sang of love, lovin', and nature's beauty. Sappho's poems survive only in fragments, as the medieval monks who preserved much of Greek literature considered her verses filthy and evil, largely because she was a woman. **Alcaeus,** a contemporary of Sappho's, was embroiled in Lesvos's political feuds; his angry stance colors his very personal lyric poems. **Pindar** of Thebes (518-438 BC), acclaimed by the ancients as the greatest of lyric poets, wrote Olympic odes commissioned by sports-nut nobles to commemorate athletic victories. **Theocritus,** a pastoral poet, portrayed scenes from the subdued lives of shepherds and goatherds.

Roman poet **Horace** later revived the Greek poetic model, taking its images and meters (the *sapphic* and *alcaic*), and looking to latter-day Greek poet **Callimachus** as his master. Callimachus (305-240), living in Alexandria, wrote elegies in Hellenistic Greek about the origins of rites and customs—only fragments of his work remain. Callimachus's influence shaped the Alexandrian revival in Rome, where poet **Catullus** took up his slogan **mega biblion, mega kakon**—big book, big bore.

**STORY BECOMES HISTORY. Herodotus,** geographer, anthropologist, and the so-called "Father of History," wrote up the monumental battles and personalities of the **Persian Wars** in his most monumental (and rather sensationalist) **Histories.** His incredibly detailed account of the wars came from interviews with elderly men with sharp memories, as the Persian Wars took place during Herodotus's childhood. **Thucydides** immortalized the **Peloponnesian Wars,** chronicling Athens's conflict with Sparta; he took the opportunity to examine the effects of war on nations and people while he was at it. **Xenophon** too wrote histories: see **Hallucinogenic Honey** for a sticky example (p. 11).

**BLINDED BY SCIENCE.** The philosophic-scientific writings of the ancient Greeks awed even the practical-minded Romans. Other civilizations sought religious answers to ultimate questions, but the scattered Greek pantheon gave no easy answers, and philosophical reasoning took over instead. The first philosopher, according to Hellenic tradition, was the 6th century BC thinker

**Thales of Miletus** (see p. 7); as none of his writings survive, we'll have to take their word for it. Thales believed that the universe had an ordered structure, and that everything moved toward a predetermined end. This **teleology,** or end-oriented worldview, contributed to every major Greek philosophy. **Pythagoras,** a math whiz, came up with theorems that still make math homework unsavory (see **My Brain Hurts,** p. 7).

**Plato** (428-348; see p. 13) and **Aristotle** (384-322 BC; see p. 21) mused about the cosmos—to them, heavenly bodies were literally divine, as their circular shapes were the most perfect in existence. The ancient Greek **universe** centered around the earth; spherical planets traveled in circular orbits. Aristotle observed spontaneous events: his science had no need for pesky experimental proof, since experiments were unnatural, fake constructions, not spontaneous and real. In the same century, **Euclid** wrote the *Elements*, the source of geometry even to the present. Euclid's geometry is one of the most widely translated works ever. **Archimedes** stole the show by creating complex mathematical formulas with circles and cylinders, and by inventing the **Archimedes screw,** a device to move water.

Greeks sliced into **medicine** as well. Oath-man **Hippocrates** suggested in the 5th century BC that disease might not be the result of divine punishment, but of natural causes. Combined speculation and observation yielded the idea of **four humors** flowing through the body (yellow bile, black bile, phlegm, and blood); an imbalance caused illness. Research at the museum of **Alexandria,** Egypt, in the 3rd century BC pushed medical knowledge further. Work on animal brains, hearts, and organs inspired **Galen of Pergamum** to try dissection. A pioneer in the queasy art of human dissection, Galen's work expanded knowledge about the human anatomy.

Under Roman rule, Greek natural science wilted. The Romans were impressed by the vast body of knowledge the Greeks had acquired, but confused by the concept of "knowledge for knowledge's sake." Science should be a means to a useful and practical end, thought the hard-nosed Latins. During the Middle Ages, the advancements in European medical knowledge evaporated entirely. Luckily, Greek scientists had about written their findings, and we can still read them today.

# BYZANTINE LITERATURE

The pseudo-historical romance took Greece by storm in the first century AD, along with personal love poems like *Erotopaegnia (Love Games)* and erotic novels. The era of the romance novel also produced the most-read work of literature ever, the Greek-language **New Testament** of the Bible. After Emperor Constantine converted to Christianity in 338 (see p. 14), most literature was written by monastery-bound theologians or court historians.

**TELL-ALL CELEBRITY BIO. Plutarch,** writing around AD 100, constructed biographies of famous Greeks and Romans in *Parallel Lives*. In the 6th century, **Procopius,** one of emperor Justinian's generals, reported on all aspects of his boss's reign. He wrote two conventional tracts for publication, *On the Wars* and *On the Buildings*, and left behind a **Secret History**—an insider's account of the **deviant debauchery** common in the court of Justinian and his wife Theodora. **Photios** (820-893), twice appointed Patriarch of Constantinople, admired the "pagan" works of Homer and encouraged their study. This avid reader was a writer as well; his massive *Biblioteca* chronicled Greek works in over 270 articles.

**A LATTER-DAY HERO.** Around the 10th century, folk singers began recounting a Byzantine epic about the hero **Digenis Akritas.** This epic was written down several times between the 12th and 17th centuries in both popular (Koine) and literary Greek. Akritas probably really lived, serving as an 8th-century border guard who helped defend the empire from Arabic and Turkish marauders. In the 16th century, Greek marauders composed folk ballads between raids on Ottoman posts. These bandits, called **kleftes,** would be among the first to fight for Greek independence.

# MODERN LITERATURE

the language I speak has no alphabet
since even the sun and the waves are a syllabic script which you decode
only in times of grief and exile
—Odysseas Elytis

As with its ancient predecessor, modern Greek literature crosses genre and subject matter, defying categories. Like Greece's modern artists, its contemporary authors feel torn between ancient heritage and new accomplishment. Some turn to mythology, epics, the Orthodox religious legacy, and the oral tradition of folk ballads and fairy tales for inspiration; others struggle to step outside the past's long shadow. This process has forged a new national literary identity for Greece.

**REVOLUTIONARY POETS.** Greek independence in 1821 (see p. 16) gave rise to the **Ionian School** of modern literature, which dealt with the political and personal issues of the Greek revolution. **Andreas Kalvos**'s (1796-1869) lyrical poetry pays tribute to freedom. **Dionysios Solomos** (1798-1857)—whose *Hymn to Liberty* became the Greek national anthem—is often called the "national poet of Greece." Solomos used the demotic, or spoken, Greek language, not the official *katharevousa*, a "purified" Greek that borrows obsolete words from ancient Greek; this choice proclaimed a new, modern literature for a new, free Greece.

**TAKING ON HISTORY: YOUNG POETS.** A flock of 20th century poets challenged the ancient writers, and together remade Greek poetry. **Angelos Sikelianos** (1884-1951) took up the literary use of demotic Greek pioneered by Dionysios Solomos, writing lyric poetry for a modern age. **Constantine Cavafy** (1863-1933) treated Greece's ancient past with ironic nostalgia. **George Seferis** (1900-63), a 1963 Nobel Laureate, was the first Greek Modernist, and wrote with an obsessive memory of Greek history and spoke of the suffering of exile on personal, national, and mythic levels. **Kostas Palamas** (1859-1943) also reached out to ancient Greek myths and history, and combined them with the Byzantine Christian tradition and modern Greek folklore. **Yiannis Ritsos** (1909-90), a socialist, was arrested and exiled by the military dictatorship in 1967, and his writings were banned until the junta's fall. Winner of a 1979 Nobel Prize, **Odysseas Elytis** (1911-96) looked at politics in a different light, and incorporated French Surrealism in hope of personal and national redemption. This national rebirth would combine humanity, nature, and religion.

**PROSE REVIVAL.** Short-story writer **Alexandros Papadiamantis** (1851-1911)—whose last name means "father of love"—set his works on his home island of Skiathos, and used the official high-register Greek, *katharevousa*. Papadiamantis's stories describe the failings of humanity and society, but hold faith in an ultimate spiritual redemption. **George Vizyenos** (1849-96) borrowed liberally from the oral folk tradition; though he wrote in *katharevousa*, Vizyenos's work touches the mysterious and the supernatural in the realm of everyday life. **Nikos Kazantzakis** (1883-1957) may be the best known modern Greek author. His many novels

**THEATRICAL TERROR** Classical Greek theater survives as an influence on modern theater, as a body of work read and studied, and as a living, performed art. In Greece, the **Athens Festival,** held from June to September, features Classical drama at the ancient **Theater of Herod Atticus** (p. 101), as well as concerts, opera, choruses, ballet, and modern dance. At the **Epidavros Festival** (p. 127), from July to September, even a language barrier won't detract from the ominous chorus that, in Aeschylus's time, made "boys die of fright and women have miscarriages." Tickets and programs for the festivals are available two weeks in advance at the **Athens Festival Box Office,** Stadiou 4, inside the arcade (see p. 85); this office also sells tickets to many smaller theaters and festivals, including those at Philippi, Thassos, and Dodoni.

include *Odyssey*, a modern sequel to the Homeric epic, *Report to Greco*, **Zorba the Greek** (1946), and **The Last Temptation of Christ** (1951); the last two have been made into successful films. *Freedom or Death*, his homage to Greek revolts against Ottoman rule on his home island of Crete, analyzes the Greek-Turkish conflict, and looks into the Greek concept of masculinity.

**PLACES TO GO, PEOPLE TO SEE.** The landscape and culture of Greece has also inspired inventive travel writing by English-speaking authors, such as **Edward Lear**'s lively *Journals of a Landscape Painter in Greece and Albania*, the **Henry Miller** classic *The Colossus of Maroussi*, and the work of brothers **Lawrence and Gerald Durrell,** whose house on Corfu attracts visiting fans (see p. 270). **Patricia Storace** continues the travel-writing tradition with her 1996 collection of short essays, *Dinner With Persephone*, which inspects contemporary Greek life with an eye for paradox and ear for poetry.

# RELIGION

## ANCIENT GODS

Greek myths bubble with spicy, titillating **scandal** as they tell us how the world got to be the way it is. The colorful adventures of the often childish gods and their long-suffering mortal counterparts have inspired visual artists, writers, and even psychoanalysts.

| GREEK GOD(DESS) | ROMAN FAKE ID | JOB DESCRIPTION |
|---|---|---|
| Zeus | Jupiter | King of gods; sexual gymnast; law-maker; kept order with handy thunderbolt. |
| Hera | Juno | Queen of Olympus; goddess of women and marriage; Zeus's sister and wife (eek!). |
| Ares | Mars | God of war and the spirit of battle; represented the gruesome aspects of fighting. |
| Hephæstus | Vulcan | Fire god; divine smith and patron of all craftsman; Aphrodite's ugly hubby. |
| Demeter | Ceres | Goddess of the Earth and fertility. |
| Aphrodite | Venus | Love goddess; patron of prostitutes; Cupid's mom and boss; noted philanderer. |
| Hestia | Vesta | Goddess of the family and city hearth; forever virgin (like Athena and Artemis). |
| Athena | Minerva | Goddess of war, handicraft, reason; Athens's protectress; born from Zeus's head. |
| Hades | Pluto | Menacing god of the Underworld; Zeus's brother; always looking for new residents. |
| Poseidon | Neptune | God of the sea and of water; brother of Zeus; rode around in a wavetop car. |
| Apollo | Apollo | Sun god; patron of music, song, and poetry; python-slayer; Artemis's twin. |
| Artemis | Diana | Goddess of the hunt, the moon, wild animals, vegetation, chastity, and childbirth. |
| Hermes | Mercury | Messenger god; presided over animals, commerce, shrewdness, and persuasion; patron god of travelers. |

## FROM HISTORY TO MYTH

Greek mythology explained natural phenomena and connected human events with a divine order, tying history to the gods. Greek literature and mythology are inextricably intertwined: from epic poems we learn of the Greek gods and their habits, and the characters of early literature become a part of mythology themselves.

**Homer**'s semi-divine heroes project mythic shadows of Mycenaean kings and military leaders (see p. 24). **Achilles,** the hero of the *Iliad* who spends much of the epic sulking in his tent, later rejoins battle to slay **Hector,** the Trojan royal prince. Though the Trojan War was long believed to be fictional, the discovery of Troy's ruins by amateur archaeologist **Heinrich Schliemann** in the 1880s proved the city really had existed, and that perhaps the Trojan War had, too. (For more on Schliemann, see p. 119.) The constant conflict between kingdoms of Greece and those on the Aegean coast of Anatolia makes a Trojan War even more likely, though in Homer's version, the gods play favorites and fight alongside the mortals.

The story of **Odysseus,** tricky hero of the *Odyssey,* reveals more than the overt guidelines of the story. As his story passed through generations of storytellers and across regional lines, it evolved to reflect Greek political and religious concerns. Homer's version reflects this development, as do other mythic histories that tell conflicting stories.

## GODS AND MONSTERS

Greek religion evolved alongside this mythic history. Worship in the Greek pantheon centered around praying and leaving offerings to gods whose all-too-human exploits Greeks chronicled. Religious sects lacked any overarching unity or mutual exclusivity. Worship revolved around specific locations, temples, and rites. People were free to worship whomever they chose (and to develop patron gods—and enemy gods). Greek religion was thus a changeable and multifaceted creature. Though individual rites and ceremonies were preset, overall religious practices could change drastically through the centuries.

**GOD, NOT THE DEVIL, MADE ME DO IT.** Rituals of communion with the gods were often as scandalous as the myths that inspired them: extreme chemical **intoxication** and large-scale **orgies** were legitimate routes to a state of religious ecstasy. The Greek gods behaved very much like humans who could never die—they lacked strong morals, and got into lots of silly arguments without fear of any real retribution. Appeasing the gods by rituals pleasing to humans (drunken debauchery) made sense.

But the Greeks by no means thought their gods were lightweights to be trifled with: indeed, mythology is full of ugly examples of what happens to those who challenge gods. Humans were often unwilling participants in religious myths. The talented weaver **Arachne**—because she dared to compete with Athena—was turned into a spider (hence the word "arachnid"). **Tantalus** was condemned to stand in a pool in Hades, forever tormented by hunger and thirst with oh-so-tantalizing food and water just beyond his grasp. **King Minos,** poor fool, didn't make a sacrifice on time, so Poseidon gave Minos's wife **Pasiphaë** an insatiable lust for a bull. Pasiphaë then bore a baby, a cannibal bull-boy, the **Minotaur.**

**THEY MOVE IN MYSTERIOUS WAYS.** The twelve deities of the Greek **pantheon** were roommates on **Mt. Olympus** (Hades, down below, makes thirteen). Zeus, the team captain, liberated the higher gods from the gut of their cannibal dad, the titan Cronos, who had eaten each as he or she was born. Zeus had escaped, concealed from his father at birth. Indebted to Zeus, the rest of the gods were subject to his will. Many gods were Zeus's children, begotten from his thundering sexual exploits with Hera, various mortals, animals, and other gods. **Athena,**

**SLEAZY DEITY** Although **Zeus** threw a mighty lightning bolt, **Ovid**'s lurid account in the Latin *Metamorphoses* report that his real prowess lay in the world of romance. A bona fide nymphomaniac, Zeus would do it with almost anyone or anything, as long as his baleful and long-suffering wife **Hera** wasn't looking. Even when mortal women were unwilling or inaccessible, he always managed to get the girl: he impregnated **Danae,** safely locked away in a tower by her father, by visiting her as a golden shower of light. Oftentimes he assumed the shape of an animal in his conquests: a cuckoo when he seduced **Hera,** a swan with **Leda,** or a bull when he carried off **Europa.** His wife, powerless to injure her husband directly, lavished vengeance on the unfortunate objects of his lust. Io was turned into a cow chased by an enormous, stinging gadfly. **Leto,** pregnant with **Artemis** (goddess of the hunt) and **Apollo** (god of light and music), was forbidden to rest on solid ground; the itinerant island of Delos lent its shore to her to give birth. **Semele,** one of Zeus's *voluntary* cohorts, dissolved into ash. **Callisto** got off relatively easy in comparison–she was changed into a bear. What's the moral of Zeus's mythic sexcapades? *Mortals never win.*

patron goddess of Athens, burst fully-formed from Zeus's head, a unique birth if ever there was one. Despite fantastic powers and immortality, gods' lives could be irritating. **Hera** endured her husband's endless philandering, **Persephone** sat bored in Hades six months of the year, fire god **Hephaestus** limped around with a lame leg, and demigod **Atlas** quite literally had the world on his shoulders (see also chart p. 28).

Many humans and minor deities figured prominently in Greek mythology, too. The three **Fates**—Atropos, Clotho, and Lachesis—spun, measured, and snipped the threads of human lives. The **Furies,** or *Eumenides* ("Kindly Ones") punished evil-doers; their kindness was extremely one-sided. The nine **Muses** aided poets, artists, and musicians; Homer begins both the *Iliad* and the *Odyssey* with a plea for Muse-given inspiration. **Dryads** and **naiads** inhabited trees and streams; **nymphs** cavorted in the fields; **satyrs,** or goat-men with long beards and tails, frolicked with **maenads** in the holy groves.

## ORTHODOX CHRISTIANITY OUSTS ZEUS

Greece, famed for its fabulous paganism, nevertheless served as a gateway for Christianity in Europe. In AD 49, **St. Paul** arrived in Philippi, Macedonia and began five years of successful preaching throughout the Greek mainland. By the 3rd century AD, the books of the **New Testament** had been written down—in Greek. In the following century, **Constantine** (see p. 14) followed the flaming cross in the sky, and plastered crosses across the shields of his troops. He then legalized Christianity in the empire, and even converted moments before his death. Thus began the modern church, called the **Orthodox Catholic Church** in its own canonical texts, but commonly known as the "Eastern" or "Greek Orthodox" Church. Orthodoxy is defined by its adherence to the teachings of the first **seven ecumenical councils**—held in Ephesus in AD 431—and by a belief that spiritual truth is preserved not only in the Bible, but in the living **traditions** of the church. Orthodox Christianity is an **Apostolic** religion: its members believe their church upholds the true faith as delivered to the saints by the Holy Spirit. Orthodox believers look to the lives of the saints as models for their own lives.

Orthodox practice is based on seven sacraments. Life in the church begins with **baptism,** a ritual immersion in holy water. This process of initiation is later completed by **confirmation,** an official, conscious affirmation of faith marking mature entrance into the church. The **eucharist,** or communion, recreates the Last Supper, wherein bread and wine represent the body and blood of Jesus, cleansing the faithful of sins and offering a taste of eternal life. In **confession,** supplicants ask to be forgiven for their transgressions. **Ordination** is considered the completion of apostolic succession, as the new priest is joined in spiritual lineage to St. Peter, to whom Jesus originally entrusted the church. **Marriage** is the process by which a man and a woman are united in the eyes of the church; Orthodox priests (unlike Roman Catholics) are permitted to marry before ordination. The last sacrament, **holy unction,** is the healing anointment of the sick with sanctified oil.

## RELIGION TODAY

**Greek Orthodoxy** is the religion of 98% of the Greek population. Fortunately for the minority 2% (primarily Muslims), the constitution guarantees freedom of religion, and the Greek Orthodox Church remains separate from the Greek state.

**THE CHURCH.** The **Orthodox Church** is rigidly hierarchical in structure, with one archbishop of Athens, 85 bishops in 77 dioceses, and 7500 parishes. The **bishops** take responsibility for keeping the church faithful to its doctrines, and for ensuring apostolic succession by ordaining new priests. Bishops don't have a lot of contact with their congregations on an everyday basis. **Priests,** easily recognizable by their long black robes, beards, and cylindrical hats, interact more closely with the people, but still remain fairly removed from secular life. Orthodox clergy spend

**OPA!** Greeks have made music since the Bronze Age: early musical instruments from this period have been found on Crete. Although they had no system of musical notation before the 5th century BC, they devised a theory of harmonics. It was necessary for early poets to remember musical formulas, since poems were sung or chanted (partially to help poets remember endless epics). The musical choruses of religious rites naturally became part of evolving drama, and music remained essential to Classical theater. Folk music and dances flourished in the Byzantine Era. Dances from southern Greece were often tragic or mourning; northern dances celebrated war and the harvest. Cretans danced in religious and burial rites. Today, these regional distinctions have blurred. In many areas, it's common to see a wide circle of locals and tourists, hands joined, dancing to clarinets and lyres. The group leader flashes fancy footwork, twirling in circles while winding around a white handkerchief. Some dancers throw backwards somersaults. The dance steps for the followers are comfortably repetitive. Don't hesitate to join in—stamp your feet, yell *Opa!* and enjoy yourself.

most of their time praying, reflecting, and preparing the sacraments, rather than pursuing missions in the secular world at large. Greece's many isolated **monastic communities** (such as Mt. Athos, p. 244) have had considerable trouble adapting to the modern world and face dwindling numbers of recruits.

**THE FAITHFUL.** For the **laity**—the community of believers—faith and deed are intertwined; Orthodoxy is less an institution than a worldview. The sacraments are the backbone of Orthodox doctrine, though they occur only a few times in an Orthodox Christian's life. The church plays a role in any decision made by an Orthodox Christian. Many Greeks wear crosses around their necks and hang icons in their homes. Most celebrate their **name days** (Greek children are always named after a saint) set aside for their patron saint, rather than their birthdays.

# PEOPLE

**THE MANY...** A Greek census will take place in 2001, but current estimates put the population at about **10.7 million** people. The population is 98% ethnically Greek, and 98% Greek Orthodox in religion (see p. 31), although historical and recently emerging minorities inhabit Greece, too. The extremely homogeneous ethnic and religious population may be hidden by the large number of foreign visitors who travel in Greece.

**...AND THE FEW.** Both the Greek government (which does not recognize official ethnic divisions) and the Greek people generally deny any overt racism. However, there is a growing concern about and widespread prejudice toward a rapidly expanding refugee and migrant population. (For more information, see p. 47.)

Roughly 350,000 ethnic **Albanians** in northern Greece make up the country's largest minority population; recently, reports of violence perpetrated by the Greek border patrol against illegal Albanian immigrants have cropped up.

The **Gypsies,** or **Roma,** make up another significant minority group; they have remained on the fringes of Greek society for centuries, and are now concentrated in Athens and Thessaloniki. Plagued by poor health, low literacy rates, and extensive poverty, the Gypsy population is typically viewed by Greeks as one of the country's largest social problems.

The most populous religious minority group is made up of over 130,000 Slavic and Turkish **Muslims** in Thrace who remain separated from the Greeks in both language and culture. The sizable Turkish population in Western Thrace is a result of 1923 **Population Exchange** (see p. 17). **Jewish** communities have lived in Greece since the first century AD, but the majority of the Jewish population was deported to concentration camps during the Nazi occupation during the Second World War. Only about 5,000 Jews live in Greece at the present moment.

Other officially recognized minorities include the **Vlachs** and the **Sarakatsans,** both nomadic shepherds descended from Latin-speakers who settled in Greece. The Greek region of Macedonia is inhabited by some 60,000 **Slavic** peoples still unrecognized by the Greek government as an ethnic or cultural minority.

# GOVERNMENT AND ECONOMY

**ADMINISTRATION.** The present Greek constitution was created on June 11, 1975, establishing a **presidential republic** and a **parliamentary democracy.** True to the oldest model of democracy, power is divided between three branches: executive, legislative, and judicial. Legislative power is vested in a single-chamber **Vouli** (parliament) composed of 300 members, who are popularly elected by secret ballot—voting is the compulsory privilege of all Greeks age 18 and older. Each member of parliament serves a 4-year term. The **President** is elected by parliament and serves a five-year term. A constitutional amendment in 1985 significantly decreased the presidential powers, reducing the position to little more than a figurehead. The executive branch consists of the powerful **Prime Minister** (the leader of whichever party wins the national election) and the **Cabinet,** selected from the elected representatives by the Prime Minister. The full and independent judiciary has three types of courts: administrative, civil, and criminal.

**PARTIES.** In the Greek party system, the **New Democracy** (ND) and **Panhellenic Socialist Movement** (PASOK) dominate the political landscape, with the **Communist Party of Greece** (KKE) gaining a few third-party votes (see **The KKE,** p. 32). The two major parties ran with similar platforms in the most recent elections, touting economic reforms aimed at gaining admission to the European Monetary Union (EMU) and the need for improved foreign relations—these reforms have succeeded, and Greece will join the EMU in 2001. The KKE, endorsing a Soviet-style communism, vocally opposes Greece's joining the EMU.

**Constantine Karamalis,** leader of the ND, has accused **Constantine Simitis,** current Prime Minister and leader of PASOK, of neglecting rural Greek society and the workers. Simitis responded by promising to improve social welfare and reduce governmental bureaucracy during his latest term. In an April 2000 election (held five months early to avoid disruption of EMU negotiations), Simitis and his party were edged out by the surprisingly strong conservative New Democracy party, winning 158 seats to ND's 125, with the KKE coming in at 11 seats; the remaining few went to fringe parties. In a meeting with current **President Constantine Stephanopoulous,** Simitis vowed to bring Greece up to the level of its European neighbors, economically, socially, and politically.

**ECONOMY.** With its limited natural resources and partial industrialization, the Greek economy is one of the least advanced in the European Union, with the second-to-lowest average income of all EU countries. A large **public sector** controls over 60% of the country's assets (including many banks) and is often blamed for slow economic growth. The Simitis government's austerity policies have reduced the massive budget deficit and lowered the rate of inflation by privatizing much of

**THE KKE** The Greek Communist Party, or KKE, is the third-strongest political party in Greece, after the conservatives and socialists. Looking askance at NATO, the West, and US influence, KKE members cringe at American cultural dominance. Leave those Union Jack backpacks and Old Glory bathing suits at home, that famous Greek hospitality notwithstanding. Many KKE supporters have strong anti-Western sentiments, particularly the youthful, extremist set. Be prepared for a lot of angry graffiti, equating Bill Clinton with Hitler and Americans with Nazis. Noisy Western patriots will probably meet with no more than angry glances or verbal harassment, but it's a good idea to lie a bit low, out of respect and common sense. (For more info, see p. 47.)

the former public sector, though these reforms have led to rising unemployment and unrest among strong labor unions.

**Agriculture** has benefited from EU subsidies, and the huge **shipping** industry remains strong. Greece **exports** fruit, olives, some natural resources (including chromium, marble, and petroleum), and has a growing industrial sector focusing on textiles, plastics, and chemical production.

Many fear that the economy is perilously dependent on the **tourist industry,** which caters to a yearly number of tourists greater than the country's total population. This booming business creates a need for seasonal employment, puts tremendous pressures on Greek infrastructure, and causes environmental damage.

# MEDIA

Several years ago, much of Greek media was state-owned and prone to propagandist portrayals of government policy. More recently, private companies have bought several outlets. Many Greek-language **newspapers** are still sensationalistic (and hence exciting to read, though not overly factual). The more reputable papers include the weekly newspaper *Bima* (published Sundays), and partisan political dailies like the center-left leaning *Eleftherotipia* and *Ta Nea*, and the conservative *Kathimerini* and *Eleftheros Typos*.

Page through some glossy **magazines** like the bubble-gummy *Clique* or the more sophisticated *Taxydromos*, whose glamorous American and British cousins (*Vogue*, *Cosmopolitan*, and the like) also circulate in Greek. More academic types should try the scholarly journals *Diabazo* and *Anti*. The most noticeable recent change in Greek media has been in the **television** industry. Whereas ERT1 and 2 were the original stations, both state-owned and private channels like Mega Channel and ANT-1 have brought hi-tech production and, of course, those inescapable, wacky American sitcoms to the Greek viewing public. Greek **radio** plays a range of international, genre-crossing music in large cities, but in more remote locales, you'll have to learn to love Greek pop.

# CINEMA

Although most of the films shown in Greece are American or European imports with Greek subtitles, the theaters themselves have an atmosphere all their own. You'll find small movie houses filled with relaxed viewers chatting, munching food, and drinking throughout the film. Blockbuster movies pass through Greece quickly, about six months to a year after being released in other parts of the world. Some theaters show sequences of film classics, but these are similarly fleeting: if you're lucky enough to catch a good series, don't expect it to be around for long.

Summertime **outdoor movies** are an essential part of the Greek experience. At twilight, cinemas set up screens in vacant lots or on high-rise rooftops, or daytime theaters may have slide-away roofs that reveal the stars. Earlier shows can be difficult to *see*, and later shows are often difficult to *hear*, as the volume is lowered to accommodate neighbors. Bring bug spray to ward off vicious mosquitoes.

**REPRESSION.** Greek **art house films** are a different story. During the reign of the junta, government censorship forced Greek artists to move west to comment on the political situation at home. Set in a Francophone Thessaloniki and the product of French and Greek collaboration, **Z,** directed by Costas Gavras with Yves Montand in 1969, is a thrilling, humorous, and tragic account of the regime's assassination of a rising opposition candidate and the ensuing sloppy cover-up (for a more detailed account of the political situation that inspired *Z*, see p. 17).

**AND FLOWERING.** After suffering under the colonels' junta, the Greek film industry rebuilt itself throughout the 1980s and has recently emerged as a distinguished and prolific presence in the international arena. This revitalization

## BOUZOUKI PUNK ROCK

I'll become a little old monk and wear a monkish habit
And I'll carry a string of beads, sweetheart, just to please you.
Your lips tell me one thing... and your friends tell me another.
I'd rather be stabbed twice... than hear the words you're saying.
I fixed myself up as a monk, stayed in a monastery.
Then I fell into your hands, nagging bitch,
And got myself defrocked.
—*Rembetika* lyrics

Many Greek lyric songs are romantic and poetic. But a new musical style emerged from Turkey's western coast in the late 19th century, and unsettled these classical notions. Gritty, urban **rembetika** used traditional Greek instruments to sing about the ugly side of modern life, focusing on **drugs, prison, and alienation.** Convicts sang *rembetika* laments about smoking hashish and life on the run. During the population exchange with Turkey in the 1920s (see p. 17), it emerged as the cry of the underclass, as newly transplanted refugees living in urban shantytowns embraced its sorrowful expressiveness. *Rembetika* is still played on the *bouzouki* and *baglama,* although today players are few and far between. Read lyrics and find out more in Gail Holst-Warhaft's book *Road to Rembetika.*

has been significantly helped along by the 1982 reestablishment of the **Greek Film Center,** a state-supported institute involved in the production of many of the most highly regarded modern Greek films. The Greek Film Center has assisted in making works by **Nikos Perakis** *(Loafing and Camouflage, Arpa-Colla),* **Pantelis Vougaris** *(The Engagement of Anna, Elefterios Venizelos),* **Nikos Panayotopoulos** *(Varieties, O Ergenis),* and **Theo Angelopoulos** *(Voyage to Kythera, The Beekeeper, Ulysses' Gaze,* and *Eternity and a Day).* Greece's most acclaimed filmmaker, Angelopoulos, won the 1998 Cannes Palme d'Or for *Eternity and a Day.* The most important event in the Greek film world (and an important event in the world film scene) is the **Thessaloniki Film Festival,** held every November (see p. 229).

# SPORTS

Everything from handball to water polo has fans in Greece, but **football** (soccer) and **basketball** are national favorites. Most major Greek cities have their own municipal football teams. In addition to their home team, Greeks also favor an A-League Athenian team. Three top Athenian teams stand out in the hearts and apparel of Greek sports fans: red-jerseyed **Olympiakos** from Athens, green **Panathinaikos** from Piraeus, and the number-three team, yellow **AEK.** Almost everyone wears their favorite team's colors. **Basketball** is the country's newfound passion. The primary teams are the same as in football, but—unlike football—the Greek basketball association is among the premier European leagues. It has featured such NBA stars as Roy Tarpley, Byron Scott, Dino Radja, and Dominique Wilkins.

Hydrophilic visitors will dream of Greek **watersports** for years afterward: windsurfing, waterskiing, sailing, and (of course) swimming are welcomed at most beaches. **Scuba diving** is generally forbidden, but it's allowed under supervised conditions in Mykonos, Santorini, Corfu, Kephalonia, and Zakynthos. **Tennis** has also gained great popularity in Greece, especially with the success of Greek-American Pete Sampras; there are now public tennis clubs throughout the country. **Snow skiing** has become popular among Greeks, and ski resorts can be found throughout the country's mountainous regions. Figuring prominently on the horizon of Greek sporting events are the **2004 Olympic Games,** to be held in Athens. The 28th Olympiad is scheduled for August 13-19, and is expected to attract enormous crowds. Check out the official Athens 2004 Olympics website at http://www.athens2004.gr.

# FOOD & DRINK

Greek food is simple and nutritious. Greek drink is simple and nefarious. Sample several varieties of both to get an idea of the regional varieties within Greece.

**AT THE SOUVLAKI STAND.** Medical studies highlight the Greek diet as super-**healthy;** its unsaturated olive oil and vegetables prevent heart disease in spite of the fairly sedentary lifestyle of the populace. Penny-pinching carnivores will thank Zeus for lamb, chicken, or beef **souvlaki** and hot-off-the-spit **gyros** stuffed into a pita. Vegetarians can eat their fill of feta-piled **horiatiki** (a.k.a. Greek salad), savory pastries like **spanakopita** (cheese pie, a pastry full of feta) and **tiropita** (spinach pie), and the fresh fruits and vegetables found at markets and vendor stands in most cities. Big bottles of **spring water** go for dirt cheap, so there's no excuse not to keep hydrated. When you need to cool off and beat the heat, there are **ice cream bars** for sale on almost every corner. Greek-style liquid relaxation typically involves a few basic options: the old standbys are **ouzo** (a Greek spirit that will earn your respect) and the hard core grainy sludge that is **Greek coffee** (drip coffee is for wimps). In the summer, people chill out with frothy, iced coffee ***frappés.***

**DINNER BELL. Breakfast,** served only in the early morning, is a simple affair: a piece of toast with *marmelada* or a pastry suffices. **Lunch,** a hearty and leisurely meal, can begin as early as noon, but is more likely eaten sometime between 2 and 5pm. After a few hours' nap, it's time to eat again. **Dinner** is a drawn-out, relaxed affair served late; don't expect a restaurant to be ready to feed you at 7:30pm, since you are *very* unfashionably early for dinner. Eat with the Greeks sometime between 10pm and midnight—then party all night or head home for another nap.

**THE PROTOCOL.** A Greek restaurant is known as a **taverna** or **estiatorio;** a grill is a **psistaria.** Don't be suspicious of restaurants without menus; this is common. Waiters will ask you if you want salad, appetizers, or the works, so be careful not to wind up with mountains of food—Greek portions tend to be large. Restaurants often put bread and water on the table as a matter of course, adding an extra charge for the bread, often listed on the menu as the **couvert.** You may never see ice in the glasses or butter on the table; many restaurants don't have them. Service is included in the check, but it's customary to leave a few drachmas as an extra tip.

# HOLIDAYS AND FESTIVALS: 2001

Greece celebrates a host of religious and political holidays throughout the year. Banks, shops, and most museums and sights close on holidays.

**Jan. 1: Feast of St. Basil/New Year's Day.** Carrying on a Byzantine tradition, Greeks cut a New Year's sweet bread called *Vassilopita,* baked with a coin inside. The person who gets the coin-hiding slice will be lucky all year.

**Jan. 6: Epiphany.** Orthodox Epiphany celebrates Jesus' baptism by St. John. *Kallikantzaroi* (goblins) prowl between Christmas and Epiphany; village bonfires attempt to scare them away. At Epiphany, Greeks bless the waters and throw crosses into harbors. The evil spirits leave the earth, and young men are blessed for retrieving the crosses.

**Feb. 25: Carnival.** Three weeks of feasting and dancing at Carnival precede Lenten fasting. Patras (p. 131) and Kephalonia (p. 274) host particularly fun celebrations.

**March 18: First Sunday in Lent.** A season of four weeks of fasting anticipates Easter.

**March 25: Greek Independence Day.** Commemorates the 1821 struggle against the Ottoman Empire. Not coincidentally, also the **Feast of the Annunciation,** celebrating when the angel Gabriel told Mary that she would bear God a son in nine months.

**April 13: Good Friday.** Remembers Jesus' crucifixion. Greek Orthodox believers carry candles in a procession through town and around the church on a most holy day.

**April 15: Easter.** The single holiest day in the Greek calendar celebrates Jesus' resurrection from the dead. After a midnight mass and a meal, Easter celebrations commence with dancing and feasting on spit-roasted lamb and dyed red hard-boiled Easter eggs.

**April 23: St. George's Day.** Honors the dragon-slaying knight. Festivities at Limnos (p. 343) and Hania (p. 487) include horse races, wrestling matches, and dances.

**May 1: Labor Day.** A celebration of workers and a communist demonstration. Also called the **Feast of the Flowers,** because flower wreaths deck doors.

**May 25: Ascension.** Commemorates Jesus' ascension into heaven. Celebrated 40 days after Easter, with different rituals in each region.

**June 4: Pentecost.** The Day of the Holy Spirit, remembering the appearance of tongues of flame (and the Holy Spirit) over Jesus' disciples. Celebrated 50 days after Easter.

**Aug. 15: Feast of the Assumption of the Virgin Mary.** A celebration throughout Greece, particularly on Tinos (p. 408), that honors Mary's ascent to Heaven.

**Sept. 8: The Virgin Mary's Birthday.** To celebrate Mary's birthday, some villages hold auctions for the honor of carrying the Virgin's icon. The money pays for a village feast.

**Oct. 26: Feast of St. Demetrius.** Celebrated with particular enthusiasm in Thessaloniki (p. 216). The feast coincides with the opening of a new stock of wine.

**Oct. 28: National Anniversary of Greek Independence.** Called **Ohi Day** in honor of Metaxas's cry of *"Οχι!"* (No!) to Mussolini's demand to occupy Greece (see p. 17.)

**Nov. 17:** Commemoration of an **uprising of Greek university students** against the 1974 junta. Speeches are presented at the University of Athens.

**Dec. 25: Christmas.** Greeks celebrate both Christmas Eve and Christmas Day. As part of the festivities, children make the rounds singing *kalanda* (Christmas carols).

# ESSENTIALS



## DOCUMENTS AND FORMALITIES

**ENTRANCE REQUIREMENTS**

**Passport** (p. 38). Required for citizens of Australia, Canada, Ireland, New Zealand, the UK, and the US.

**Visa** (p. 39). Required for citizens of South Africa.

**Work Permit** (p. 39). Required for all foreigners planning to work in Greece.

**Driving Permit** (p. 69). Required for all those planning to drive.

## GREEK CONSULAR SERVICES ABROAD

**Australia Embassy:** 9 Turrana St., Yarralumla, **Canberra,** ACT 26000 (☎(02) 6273 3011; fax 6273 2620). **Consulate:** 366 King William St., 1st Fl., **Adelaide,** SA 5000 (☎(08) 8211 8066; fax 8211 8820); Stanhill House, 34 Queens Road, **Melbourne,** VIC 3004 (☎(03) 866 4524; fax 866 4933); 15 Castlereagh St., Level 20, **Sydney,** NSW 2000 (☎(02) 9221 2388; fax 9221 1423); 16 St. George's Terrace, **Perth,** WA 6000 (☎(08) 9325 6608; fax 9325 2940).

**Canada Embassy:** 76-80 MacLaren St., **Ottawa,** ON K2P 0K6 (☎(613) 238-6271; fax 238-5676). **Consulate:** 1170 Place du Frère André, 3ème Etage, **Montréal,** QC H3B 3C6 (☎(514) 875-2119; fax 875-8781; email congrem@citenet.net); 365 Bloor St. E, Suite 1800, **Toronto,** ON M4W 3L4 (☎(416) 515-0133; fax 515-0209; email grconsulate@weblink.com); 688 West Hastings, Suite 500, **Vancouver,** BC V6B 1P1 (☎(604) 681-1381; fax 681-6656).

**Ireland Embassy:** 1 Upper Pembroke St., Dublin 2 (☎(01) 6767 2545; fax 661 88 92).

**New Zealand Consulate:** 57 Willeston St., 10th Fl., Box 24066, Wellington (☎(04) 473 7775 or 473 7776; fax 473 7441).

**South Africa Embassy:** 995 Pretorius St., Arcadia, 0083, **Pretoria** (☎(012) 437 35 13; fax 43 43 13). **South African Consulate,** 11 Wellington Rd., Parktown, 2193, **Johannesburg** (☎(011) 484 17 69; fax 484 17 94).

**UK Embassy:** 1a Holland Park, London W113TP (☎(0171) 229 38 50; fax 229 72 21). **Consulate:** 1a Holland Park, London W113TP (☎(0171) 221 64 67; fax 243 32 02).

**US Embassy:** 2221 Massachusetts Ave., N.W., **Washington, D.C.** 20008 (☎(202) 939-5800; fax 939-5824; email greece@greekembassy.org). **Consulate:** 2211 Massachusetts Ave. NW, **Washington, D.C.** 20008 (☎(202) 939-5818; fax 234-2803); 69 East 79th St., **New York,** NY 10021 (☎(212) 988-5500; fax 734-8492; email nycons@greekembassy.org); 650 North St. Clair St., **Chicago,** IL 60611 (☎(312) 335-3915/6; fax 335-3958); 2441 Gough St., **San Francisco,** CA 94123 (☎(415) 775-2102/3; fax 776-6815); 12424 Wilshire Building, Suite 800, **Los Angeles,** CA 90025 (☎(310) 826-5555; fax 826-8670; email grecon@earthlink.net); 86 Beacon St., **Boston,** MA 02108-3304 (☎(617) 523-0100 or 523-1083; fax 523-0511); Tower Place, 3340 Peachtree Rd. NE, Suite 1670, **Atlanta,** GA 30326 (☎(404) 261-3313, or 261-3391; fax 262-2798); 1360 Post Oak Blvd., Suite 2480, **Houston,** TX 77056 (☎(713) 840-7522; fax 840-0614); World Trade Center, 2 Canal St., Suite 2318, **New Orleans,** LA 70131 (☎(504) 523-1167; fax 524-5610).

## CONSULAR SERVICES

A full listing of embassies is available at the Athens tourist office (p. 82). Embassies generally open only in the morning. All embassies, unless noted, are in **Athens.**

**Albania:** Karahristrou 1, 115 21 (☎723 4412; fax 723 1972). Open M-F 8:30am-noon.

**Australia:** D. Soutsou 37, 115 21 (☎644 7303 or 645 0404; fax 644 3633). Open M-F 8:30am-12:30pm.

**Brazil:** Filikis Eterias 14 (☎721 3039). Open M-F 9am-3pm.

**Canada:** Ioannou Genadiou 4, 115 21 (☎725 4011 or 727 3400; fax 725 3994 or 727 3460). Open M-F 8:30am-12:30pm.

**Czech Republic:** Seferi 6 (☎671 3755). Open M-F 9am-noon.

**European Community:** Vasilissis Sofias 2 (☎725 1000). Open M-F 8:30am-1pm.

**Germany:** Karaoli Dimitriou 3, 106 75 (☎728 5111; fax 725 1205). Open M-F 9am-noon.

**Hungary:** Kalvou 16 (☎672 5337 or 672 3753). Open M-F 8:30am-12:30pm.

**Ireland:** Vas. Konstandinou 7, 106 74 (☎723 2771; fax 724 0217). Open M-F 9am-3pm.

**Romania:** Em. Benaki 7 (☎672 8875). Open M-F 8am-1pm.

**South Africa:** Kifissias 60, 151 25 Maroussi (☎680 6645; fax 680 6640). Open M-F 8am-1pm.

**Turkey:** Vas. Georgiou B. 8, 106 74 (☎724 5915; fax 722 9597). Open M-F 8:30am-12:30pm.

**UK:** Ploutarchou 1, 106 75, Athens (☎727 2600; fax 727 2722). Open M-F 8:30am-1pm.

**US:** American Embassy, Vas. Sophias 91, 101 60 Athens (☎721 2951; fax 645 6282; www.usisathens.gr). Open M-F 8:30am-5pm, for visas 8-11am. Consulate General, Tsimiski 43, 7/F, 546 23 **Thessaloniki** (☎(031) 242 905; fax: 242 924; email cons@compulink.gr). You can also contact US Information Services at USIS, Makedonon 8, 115 21 Athens (☎(01) 643 4710 or 643 2977).

**Yugoslavia:** Vas. Sofias 106 (☎777 4355). Open M-F 8:30-1pm.

# PASSPORTS

**REQUIREMENTS.** Citizens of Australia, Canada, Ireland, New Zealand, South Africa, the UK, and the US need valid passports to enter Greece and to re-enter their own country.

**PHOTOCOPIES.** Be sure to photocopy the page of your passport with your photo, passport number, and other identifying information, as well as any visas, travel insurance policies, airplane tickets, or traveler's check serial numbers. Carry one set of copies in a safe place, apart from the originals, and leave another set at home. Carry an expired passport or an official copy of your birth certificate in a part of your bag separate from other documents.

**LOST PASSPORTS.** If you lose your passport, immediately notify the local police and the nearest embassy or consulate of your home government. To expedite its replacement, you will need to know all information previously recorded and show identification and proof of citizenship. In some cases, a replacement may take weeks to process, and it may be valid only for a limited time. Visas stamped in your old passport will be irretrievably lost. In an emergency, ask for immediate temporary traveling papers that will permit you to re-enter your home country. Your passport is a public document belonging to your nation's government. You may have to surrender it to a foreign government official, but if you don't get it back in a reasonable amount of time, inform the nearest mission of your home country.

**NEW PASSPORTS.** All applications for new passports or renewals should be filed several weeks or months in advance of your planned departure date. Get a passport from your local post office, passport office (available in most major cities), or travel agency. Most passport offices offer emergency passport services for a steep fee. Citizens residing abroad who need a passport or renewal should contact the nearest consular service of their home country.

**ONE EUROPE.** The idea of European unity has come a long way since 1958, when the European Economic Community (EEC) was created to promote solidarity and cooperation between its six founding states. Since then, the EEC has become the **European Union (EU),** with political, legal, and economic institutions spanning 15 member states: Austria, Belgium, Denmark, Finland, France, Germany, Greece, Ireland, Italy, Luxembourg, the Netherlands, Portugal, Spain, Sweden, and the UK.

What does this have to do with the average non-EU tourist? Well, 1999 established **freedom of movement** across 14 European countries—the entire EU minus Denmark, Ireland, and the UK, but plus Iceland and Norway. This means that border controls between participating countries have been abolished, and visa policies harmonized. While you're still required to carry a passport (or government-issued ID card for EU citizens) when crossing an internal border, once you've been admitted into one country, you're free to travel to all participating countries. For more important consequences of the EU for travelers, see **The Euro** (see p. 42) and **Customs** (see p. 40).



# VISAS AND WORK PERMITS

**VISAS.** EU members, as well as citizens of the US, Canada, Australia, and New Zealand are all automatically granted leave for a three-month stay in Greece, though they are not eligible for employment during that time. South Africans need a visa. Apply to stay longer at least 20 days prior to the three-month expiration date at the **Aliens Bureau,** Alexandras 175, Athens 11522 (☎(01) 642 3094), or check with a Greek embassy or consulate.

**WORK PERMITS.** For long-term employment in Greece, you must first get a **work permit** from a pre-arranged employer. Permits are available at the **Ministry of Labor,** Pireos 40, Athens 10437 (☎(01) 523 3110). Make all arrangements and negotiations before you leave. (For more information, see p. 76.)

# IDENTIFICATION

When you travel, always carry two or more forms of identification on your person, including at least one photo ID. A passport combined with a driver's license or birth certificate is usually adequate. Many establishments, especially banks, require several IDs to cash traveler's checks. Never carry all of your forms of ID together; split them up in case of theft or loss. Bring extra passport-size photos to affix to the various IDs or passes you may acquire on the way.

**STUDENT AND TEACHER IDENTIFICATION.** The **International Student Identity Card (ISIC),** the most widely accepted form of student ID, provides discounts on sights, accommodations, food, and transport. In Greece, the card will procure you discounts at many sights and museums, a few hostels, and on the occasional ferry and Olympic Airways flight. If discounts are not listed, make sure to present the card and ask. The ISIC is preferable to an institution-specific card (such as a university ID) because it is more likely to be recognized (and honored) abroad. All cardholders have access to a 24-hour emergency helpline for medical, legal, and financial emergencies (in North America, ☎(877) 370-ISIC, elsewhere call US collect +1 (715) 345-0505), and US cardholders are also eligible for insurance benefits (see **Insurance,** p. 52). Many student travel agencies issue ISICs, including STA Travel in Australia and New Zealand; Travel CUTS in Canada; usit in the Republic of Ireland and Northern Ireland; SASTS in South Africa; Campus Travel and STA Travel in the UK; Council Travel (www.counciltravel.com/idcards/default.asp) and STA Travel in the US (see p. 61). The card is valid from September of one year to December of the following year and costs AUS$15, CDN$15, or US$22. Applicants must be

degree-seeking students of a secondary or post-secondary school and must be of at least 12 years of age. Because of the proliferation of fake ISICs, some services (particularly airlines) require additional proof of student identity, such as a school ID or a letter attesting to your student status, signed by your registrar and stamped with your school seal.

The **International Teacher Identity Card (ITIC)** offers the same insurance coverage as well as similar but limited discounts. The fee is AUS$13, UK£5, or US$22. For more info, contact the **International Student Travel Confederation (ISTC),** Herengracht 479, 1017 BS Amsterdam, Netherlands (☎+31 (20) 421 28 00; fax 421 28 10; email istcinfo@istc.org; www.istc.org).

**YOUTH IDENTIFICATION.** The International Student Travel Confederation issues a discount card to travelers who are 26 years old or younger but not students. Known as the **International Youth Travel Card** (**IYTC;** formerly the **GO 25** Card) this one-year card offers similar benefits to the ISIC, and is sold by most of the same organizations. To apply, you'll need a passport, driver's license, or copy of a birth certificate, and a passport-sized photo. The fee is AUS$15, CDN$15, or US$22.

# TOURIST BOARDS

**Tourist info** in Greece is available in English 24 hours a day by dialing 171.

Start early when trying to make contact with tourist offices—like most things Greek, they run on their own relaxed schedule. Polite persistence and genuine excitement about visiting works wonders. Two national organizations oversee tourism: the **Greek National Tourist Organization (GNTO)** and the tourist police *(touristiki astinomia)*. The GNTO can supply general information about sights and accommodations throughout the country. (For additional info and offices abroad, see www.gnto.gr.) The main office is in Athens at Amerikis 2 (☎(01) 327 13 00). Note that the GNTO is known as the **EOT** in Greece. The tourist police deal with more local issues: where to find a room, what the bus schedule is, or what to do when you've lost your passport. The offices are open long hours and the staff is often quite willing to help, although their English may be limited. On many islands and in smaller towns, travel agencies will be more helpful (and more likely to exist) than tourist offices; feel free to stop in and ask for advice. **Nikis** and **Filellinon** in Athens are lined with agencies and organizations geared toward budget and student travelers. *Let's Go* lists similar establishments in different cities in the **Practical Information** section for most cities.

**Australia:** 3rd Fl., 51-57 Pitt St., Sydney, NSW 2000 (☎(02) 9241 1663; fax 9235 2174; email hto@tpg.com.au).

**Canada:** 1300 Bay St., **Toronto,** ON M5R 3K8 (☎(416) 968-2220; fax 968-6533; email grnto.tor@sympatico.ca; www.aei.ca/gntomtl); 1170 Place du Frére André, Suite 300, **Montréal,** PQ, H3B 3C6 (☎(514) 871-1535; fax 871-1498; email gntomtl@aei.ca).

**UK:** 4 Conduit St., London W1R DOJ (☎(4207) 734 5997; fax 287 1369; email EOTgreektouristoffice@btinternet.com; www.tourist-offices.org.uk).

**US:** Head Office, Olympic Tower, 645 Fifth Ave., 5th Floor, New York, NY 10022 (☎(212) 421-5777; fax 826-6940; email gnto@greektourism.com).

# CUSTOMS

Upon entering Greece, you must declare if you've brought currency above US$1000 or if you've brought certain items from abroad. You must pay a duty on the value of those articles if it exceeds the allowance established by Greek customs. Importing biological hazards (agricultural products, raw meat, etc.) is prohibited. Selling anything while abroad is illegal; authorities expect you to return with everything except your money.

Upon returning home, you must declare all articles acquired abroad and pay a duty on the value of articles in excess of your home country's allowance. To ease your return home, make a list of any valuables brought from home and register them with customs before traveling. Keep receipts for all goods required abroad.

**DUTY-FREE ITEMS.** You should also be aware that duty-free was abolished on June 30, 1999 for travel between EU member states; however, travelers between the EU and the rest of the world still get a duty-free allowance when passing through customs. Goods and gifts purchased at duty-free shops abroad are not exempt from duty or sales tax at your point of return and thus must be declared as well; "duty-free" merely means that you need not pay a tax in the country of purchase. Keeping receipts for purchases made in Greece will help establish values when you return. If you will be carrying valuables, you should make a list of their serial numbers and register it with customs. An official customs stamp will ensure that you avoid import duty charges and simplify your return. Be especially careful to document items manufactured abroad.

ESSENTIALS

**EUROPEAN CUSTOMS** As well as freedom of movement of people within the EU (see **P. 39**), travelers can also take advantage of the freedom of movement of goods. This means that there are no customs controls at internal EU borders (i.e., you can take the blue customs channel at the airport), and travelers are free to transport whatever legal substances they like as long as it is for their own personal (non-commercial) use–up to 800 cigarettes, 10L of spirits, 90L of wine (60L of sparkling wine), and 110L of beer.

**VALUE ADDED TAX.** The European Union imposes a value added tax (VAT) on goods and services purchased within the EU, which is included in the marked price. Non-EU citizens may obtain a **refund** for taxes paid on retail goods (but not services). In Greece, you must spend over 40,000dr to receive a refund. The percentage of your refund will vary from 11.5% to 15.3%. To file for a refund, first obtain a Tax-Free Shopping Cheque, available from shops sporting the blue, white, and silver Europe Tax-Free Shopping logo, and then save the receipts from all of the purchases for which you want to be partially refunded. Upon leaving Greece, you can present your goods, invoices, and Tax-Free Shopping Cheque to customs, which will then validate the Cheque. An immediate cash refund may be available at an ETS cash refund office, or you may have to file for a refund at home. Refunds are available for purchases made by credit card and check. Allow two hours to apply for customs endorsement at your point of departure.

There are some **restrictions** on VAT refunds. Goods must be taken out of the country within three months after the end of the month of purchase, and they must be unused. For more information, visit www.globalrefund.com.

# MONEY

## CURRENCY AND EXCHANGE

Greek **drachmas** (abbreviated "dr") are issued in both paper notes (100, 200, 500, 1000, 5000, and 10,000dr) and coins (5, 10, 20, 50, and 100dr). If you're carrying more than US$1000 in cash when you enter Greece, you must declare it upon entry. This rule does not apply to traveler's checks. You can bring up to US$445 worth of drachmas into Greece. No more than 20,000dr can be taken out of the country when you leave. The currency chart below is based on August 2000 exchange rates. Check a large newspaper or the web (e.g. finance.yahoo.com, www.bloomberg.com, or www.letsgo.com/thumb) for the latest exchange rates.

It's generally cheaper to convert money in Greece and Cyprus than at home. Banks in Greece charge a commission of 2% with a minimum of 50dr and a

GREEK DRACHMAS

| | |
|---|---|
| US$1 = 369DR | 100DR = US$0.27 |
| CDN$1 = 239DR | 100DR = CDN$0.42 |
| UK£1 = 529DR | 100DR = UK£0.19 |
| IR£1 = 427DR | 100DR = IR£0.23 |
| AUS$1 = 209DR | 100DR = AUS$0.48 |
| NZ$1 = 166DR | 100DR = NZ$0.60 |
| SAR1 = 50DR | 100DR = SAR2.01 |
| EUR€ = 336DR | 100DR = EUR€0.30 |
| TRL1000 =0.6DR | 100DR = TRL173,185 |
| CYP£1 = 590DR | 100DR = CYP£.17 |

maximum of 4500dr on cashing traveler's checks. However, you should bring enough foreign currency to last for the first 24 to 72 hours of a trip to avoid being penniless should you arrive after banking hours or on a holiday. Travelers from the US can get foreign currency from the comfort of home: **International Currency Express** (☎ (888) 278-6628) deliver foreign currency or traveler's checks overnight (US$15) or second-day (US$12) at competitive exchange rates.

When changing money abroad, try to go only to banks or exchange bureaus with at most a 5% margin between their buy and sell prices. Since you lose money with every transaction, **convert large sums** (unless the currency is depreciating rapidly), **but no more than you'll need.**

An **ATM card** or a **credit card** (see p. 43) will often get you the best possible conversion rates. Most towns and islands in Greece now have ATMs that are linked into major international networks.

If you use traveler's checks or bills, carry some in small denominations (the equivalent of US$50 or less) for times when you are forced to exchange money at disadvantageous rates. Bring a range of denominations, since charges may be levied per check cashed. Store your money in a variety of forms. Ideally, you will at any given time be carrying some cash, some traveler's checks, and an ATM and/or credit card. Travelers should consider carrying about US$50 or 95 German marks, which local tellers may prefer; however, avoid using non-Greek money when possible, since it marks you as a foreigner and invites price hikes and robbery.

**THE EURO** On January 1, 1999, 11 countries of the European Union, including Italy, officially adopted the Euro as their common currency. Euro notes and coins will not be issued until January, 1, 2002, and until that time the Euro will exist only in electronic transactions and traveler's checks. *Let's Go* lists all prices in drachmas, as they will continue to be used throughout 2001. Travelers who will be passing through more than one nation in the Euro-zone should note that exchange rates between the national currencies have been irrevocably fixed. Henceforth, Euro-zone currencies will be exchanged at the official rate with **no commission,** though there may still a nominal service fee. Euro-denominated traveler's checks may also be used throughout the Euro-zone, and can be exchanged commission-free in any of the 11 Euro nations. At the time of press, the permanent exchange rate for the drachma wasn't yet available. For more info, see www.europa.eu.int.

## TRAVELER'S CHECKS

Traveler's checks are one of the safest and least troublesome means of carrying funds, and are accepted in Greece (generally only at large hotels and chains; but they can be exchanged at almost any bank or exchange kiosk in urban and rural areas alike). **American Express** and **Visa** are the most recognized. Several agencies and banks sell them for a small commission. All agencies provide refunds if your

checks are lost or stolen, and many provide additional services, like toll-free refund hotlines abroad, emergency message services, and stolen credit card assistance.

While traveling, keep check receipts and a record of which checks you've cashed separate from the checks themselves. Also leave a list of check numbers with someone at home. Never countersign checks until you're ready to cash them, and always bring your passport with you to cash them. If your checks are lost or stolen, immediately contact a refund center of the company that issued your checks; they may require a police report verifying the loss or theft in order to reimburse you. Less-touristed countries may not have refund centers at all, in which case you might have to wait for a refund. Ask about toll-free refund hotlines and the location of refund centers when purchasing checks, and always carry emergency cash.



**American Express:** Call (800) 251 902 in Australia; in New Zealand (0800) 441 068; in the UK (0800) 521 313; in the US and Canada (800) 221-7282. Elsewhere call US collect +1 (801) 964-6665; www.aexp.com. If your checks are lost, call the regional refund number, 00 800 441 27 569. Traveler's checks are available in Australian, British, Canadian, Dutch, French, German, Saudi Arabian, and US currencies at 1-4% commission at AmEx offices and banks, commission-free at AAA office. *Cheques for Two* can be signed by either of 2 people traveling together.

**Citicorp:** In the US and Canada, call (800) 645-6556; in Europe, the Middle East, or Africa, call the UK +44 (020) 7508 7007; elsewhere call US collect +1 (813) 623-1709. Traveler's checks available in 7 currencies at 1-2% commission. Call 24hr.

**Thomas Cook MasterCard:** In the US and Canada, call (800) 223-7373; in the UK, call (0800) 62 21 01; elsewhere call UK collect +44 (1733) 31 89 50. Checks available in 13 currencies at 2% commission. Thomas Cook offices cash checks commission-free. Call toll-free in Greece at 800 441 28 455.

**Visa:** In the US call (800) 227-6811; in the UK call (0800) 89 50 78; elsewhere call UK collect +44 (1733) 31 89 49. Call for the location of their nearest office.

# CREDIT CARDS

Credit cards are accepted in the more touristed areas of Greece; if you're traveling off the beaten path, be prepared to use other forms of payment. Where they are accepted, credit cards often offer superior exchange rates—up to 5% better than the retail rate used by banks and other currency exchange establishments. Credit cards may also offer services such as insurance or emergency help, and are sometimes required to reserve hotel rooms or rental cars. **MasterCard** (a.k.a. EuroCard or Access in Europe) and **Visa** (a.k.a. Carte Bleue or Barclaycard) are most welcomed, with Visa being the most popular by far; **American Express** cards work at some ATMs and at AmEx offices and major airports. Credit cards often offer an array of other services, from insurance to emergency assistance. Check with your company to find out what is covered.

Credit cards are also useful for **cash advances,** which allow you to withdraw drachmas from associated banks and ATMs throughout Greece instantly. Transaction fees for credit card advances (up to US$10 per advance, plus 2-3% extra on foreign transactions after conversion) make them a costly way to withdraw cash, (more expensive than traveler's checks or cash cards), but they are very useful in emergencies. To be eligible for an advance, you'll need a **Personal Identification Number (PIN)** from your credit card company. Call in advance to arrange a PIN (see **Cash Cards (ATM Cards),** below). In certain circumstances, companies have started to charge a foreign transaction fee. It's also never a bad idea to warn your credit card company that you will be traveling and will thus have an unusual spending pattern; companies have been known to freeze their customers accounts because they thought the card had been stolen and was being used illegally.

**CREDIT CARD COMPANIES.** **Visa** (US ☎(800) 336-8472) and **MasterCard** (US ☎(800) 307-7309) are issued in cooperation with banks and other organizations. **American Express** (US ☎(800) 843-2273) has an annual fee of up to US$55. AmEx

cardholders may cash personal checks at AmEx offices abroad, access an emergency medical and legal assistance hotline (24hr.; in North America call (800) 554-2639, elsewhere call US collect +1 (202) 554-2639), and enjoy American Express Travel Service benefits (including plane, hotel, and car rental reservation changes; baggage loss and flight insurance; mailgram and international cable services; and held mail). The **Discover Card** (in US call (800) 347-2683, elsewhere call US +1 (801) 902-3100) offers small cashback bonuses on most purchases, but is useful only for advance arrangements: it isn't accepted in Greece.

## CASH CARDS (ATM CARDS)

Cash cards—popularly called ATM (Automated Teller Machine) cards—are widespread in larger towns, cities, and ports in Greece; only the smallest towns and remotest areas are without. You can most likely access your home checking account from abroad—savings accounts are harder to access. ATMs get the same wholesale exchange rate as credit cards, but there is often a limit on the amount of money you can withdraw per day (around US$500), and unfortunately computer networks sometimes fail. They typically charge an extra US$5 per withdrawal. Memorize your PIN code in numeric form, and if your PIN is longer than four digits, ask your bank for a new number.

The two major international money networks are **Cirrus** (US ☎(800) 424-7787) and **PLUS** (US ☎(800) 843-7587). To locate ATMs around the world, call the above numbers, or consult www.visa.com/pd/atm or www.mastercard.com/atm. All ATMs are linked to at least one of these major networks.

**Visa TravelMoney** (for customer assistance in Greece, call 800 114 810 304) allows you to access money from any Visa ATM. After depositing money before you travel (plus an administration fee), you can withdraw up to that sum. These cards give you the same favorable exchange rate as a regular Visa, and are especially useful if you plan to travel through many countries. Check with your local bank to see if it issues TravelMoney cards. **Road Cash** (US ☎(877) 762-3227; www.roadcash.com) issues cards in the US with a minimum US$300 deposit.

**ATM ALERT** To use a cash or credit card to withdraw money from a cash machine (ATM) in Europe, you must have a four-digit **Personal Identification Number (PIN).** If your PIN is longer than four digits, ask your bank whether can just use the first four, or whether you'll need a new one. **Credit cards** in North America don't usually come with PINs, so if you intend to hit up ATMs in Europe with a credit card to get cash advances, call your credit card company before leaving to request one. People with alphabetic, rather than numerical, PINs may also be thrown off by the lack of letters on European cash machines. The following handy chart gives the corresponding numbers to use: 1=QZ; 2=ABC; 3=DEF; 4=GHI; 5=JKL; 6=MNO; 7=PRS; 8=TUV; and 9= WXY. If you mistakenly punch the wrong code into the machine three times, it will swallow your card for good.

## GETTING MONEY FROM HOME

**AMERICAN EXPRESS.** Cardholders can withdraw cash from their checking accounts at any of AmEx's major offices and many representative offices (up to US$1000 every 21 days; no service charge, no interest). AmEx "Express Cash" withdrawals from any AmEx ATM in Greece are automatically debited from the cardholder's checking account or line of credit. Green card holders may withdraw up to US$1000 in any seven-day period (2% transaction fee; minimum US$2.50, maximum US$20). To enroll in Express Cash, cardmembers may call (800) 227-4669 in the US; elsewhere call the US collect +1 (336) 668-5041. The toll free AmEx national number in Greece is 00 800 12 3211.

**WESTERN UNION.** Travelers from the US, Canada, and the UK can wire money abroad through Western Union's international money transfer services. In the US, call (800) 325-6000; in Canada, (800) 235-0000; in the UK, (0800) 833 833; through-

out Greece, call (01) 927 1010. The rates for sending cash are generally US$10-11 cheaper than with a credit card, and the money is usually available at the place you're sending it to within an hour. To locate the nearest Western Union location, consult www.westernunion.com or call the national access number listed above.

**US STATE DEPARTMENT (US CITIZENS ONLY).** In dire emergencies, the US State Department will forward money within hours to the nearest consular office, which will then disburse it (according to instructions) for a US$15 fee. Contact the Overseas Citizens Service, American Citizens Services, Consular Affairs, Room 4811, US Department of State, Washington, D.C. 20520 (☎(202) 647-5225; nights, Sundays, and holidays ☎(202) 647-4000; http://travel.state.gov).

## COSTS

The cost of a trip to Greece will vary considerably, depending on where you go, how you travel, and where you stay. The single biggest cost of your trip will probably be your round-trip **airfare** (see p. 61). If you choose to buy a **Eurail pass** for travel throughout Europe, it will be valid in Greece, but will cost a substantial sum (see p. 66). Before you go, spend some time calculating a reasonable per-day **budget** that will meet your needs. To give you a general idea, a bare-bones day in Greece, staying at hostels, campgrounds, or domatia (rooms to let), and buying food at supermarkets or at outdoor food stands, costs about US$35. Note that camping can save a substantial sum of money: about US$10-15 per day. A day with more creature comforts, with accommodations in a more expensive domatia or budget hotel, eating one meal a day in a restaurant, and going out at night, runs US$50. For a luxurious day, the sky's the limit. Also, don't forget to factor in emergency reserve funds (at least US$200) when planning how much money you'll need.

Saving US$5 per day for a week will fund an entire additional day of travel, so learning to pinch pennies pays off. Take advantage of freebies: hit the **beach,** go **hiking,** tour churches, wander winding streets, and hunt down free open-air **concerts,** traditional **dances,** and outdoor **festivals** (especially in the summer). Do your **laundry** in the sink (where it is allowed). Split **accommodations** costs (in hotels, hostels, and domatia) with trustworthy fellow travelers, since multi-bed rooms are cheaper per person than singles. Buy food in **supermarkets** instead of eating out, split **restaurant** meals, or eat cheap, divine souvlaki from outdoor **food stands.** But don't go overboard with money management. Though US$1 may seem like peanuts at home, many travelers obsess over money while abroad. Staying within budget is important, but don't sacrifice your sanity or your health to save a buck.

## BARGAINING AND TIPPING

**BARGAINING.** Bargaining skills are essential in Greece, but you must know when to bargain. Paying the asked price for street wares will have the seller marveling at your naïveté, while bargaining at the shop of a master craftsman whose crafts are worth the stated tag will be seen as rude and disrespectful. The more informal the venue, the more flexible the price. If in doubt, hang back and watch someone else buy. Keep the cooperative spirit of bargaining in mind: everyone involved is looking for a fair, agreed-upon price. Merchants with any pride in their wares will refuse to sell to someone who has offended them in the negotiations.

**Domatia** (rooms to let, see p. 55) have varying price flexibility according to season: prices rise in summer and fall in the winter. Bargain before you get into a **taxi** (be it a boat, car, truck, or guided tour), if your trip won't be metered or ticketed. **Clothing** in general is negotiable. Obvious conveniences like pharmaceutical goods and grocery items are priced as marked, as are street food, taverna fare, and books. **Jewelry** stores usually mark up 10-50%, so shop around to get an idea of what an item is really worth. Then go back to your favorite shop and ask for a lower price. (At a good store, expect 10 to 20% off, more in cheaper stores; you should also be able to get deals on multiple purchases.)

**TIPPING.** As with bargaining, when tipping, you should offer enough to show respect, for the goods, but not so much to seem like a show-off. At all but the ritziest restaurants, service is included in the bill. A few hundred drachmas for a several thousand drachma meal is usually sufficient. There is no tipping for any other services (including taxis).



# SAFETY AND SECURITY

**EXPLORING.** Solo travelers may feel quite conspicuous among Greeks, who don't usually travel alone. Westerners in particular may feel nervous around pro-KKE, anti-American, and anti-Western graffiti (see **The KKE,** p. 32). Don't worry about it; if you are heckled by anti-Westerners, just walk away.

To stay safe, familiarize yourself with your surroundings before setting out, and carry yourself with confidence. If you must check a map, duck into a shop to do it. If you are traveling alone, be sure someone at home knows your itinerary. **Never admit that you're traveling alone.** When walking at night, stick to busy, well-lit streets and avoid dark alleyways. Do not attempt to cross through parks, parking lots, or other large, deserted areas. Look for children playing, women walking in the open, and other signs of an active community. Find out about unsafe areas from tourist offices, or from the manager of your hotel or hostel. You may want to carry a whistle to scare off attackers or attract attention. If you feel uncomfortable, leave as quickly and directly as you can, but don't allow fear of the unknown to turn you into a hermit. Careful, persistent exploration will build confidence and make your stay even more rewarding.

**SELF DEFENSE.** There is no sure-fire way to be completely prepared for every threatening situation you might encounter, but a good self-defense course will give you concrete ways to react to unwanted advances. Impact, Prepare, and Model Mugging can refer you to local self-defense courses in the US (☎(800) 345-5425) and Vancouver (☎(604) 878-3838). Workshops (2-3hr.) start at US$50; full courses run US$350-500.

**TRAVEL ADVISORIES** The following government offices provide travel information and advisories by telephone, by fax, or via the web:

**Australian Department of Foreign Affairs and Trade:** ☎(2) 6261 1111; www.dfat.gov.au.

**Canadian Department of Foreign Affairs and International Trade (DFAIT):** In Canada call (800) 267-6788 in Canada, elsewhere call +1 (613) 944-6788; www.dfait-maeci.gc.ca. Call for their free booklet, *Bon Voyage...But.*

**New Zealand Ministry of Foreign Affairs:** ☎(04) 494 8500; fax 494 8511; www.mft.govt.nz/trav.html.

**United Kingdom Foreign and Commonwealth Office:** ☎(020) 7238 4503; fax 7238 4545; www.fco.gov.uk.

**US Department of State:** ☎(202) 647-5225, auto faxback (202) 647-3000; http://travel.state.gov. For *A Safe Trip Abroad,* call (202) 512-1800.

**GETTING AROUND.** Driving in Greece requires a fearless temperament and all your attention: the thousands of roadside shrines on every winding road commemorate those killed in car and moped accidents. Roads, especially on the islands and in rural areas, are narrow and poor, some lack shoulders, barriers, and gas stations; others are plagued by roaming goats. These roads wind around Greece's mountainous terrain. Native Greek drivers careen around the roads with astonishingly reckless confidence, but visiting drivers should take the shrines as a warning and drive slowly.

Learn local driving signals and wear a seatbelt in **cars.** Children under 40 lbs. should ride only in a specially designed carseat, available for a small fee from most car rental agencies. Always wear a helmet on a **moped** (required by law). Driving

any vehicle at night on winding roads is incredibly dangerous and even foolish; plan to take a cab instead if at all possible. Be forewarned that driving a moped is harder than it looks, and countless tourists injure themselves on the bikes.

Study route maps before you hit the road, and plan ahead. You may want to bring spare parts. If your car breaks down, wait for police assistance, or locals may help you. **Sleeping in your car** is dangerous and illegal—don't do it. For info on the perils of **hitchhiking,** see p. 71.

**TERRORISM.** Though certainly not rampant, Greece does have some issues with terrorism, particularly with the high-profile, anti-Western, anti-NATO, anti-US **November 17** group. Claiming responsibility for the deaths of 23 people in the last 25 years, the group is responsible for the assassination of the British diplomat Stephen Saunders in the spring of 2000. Although the government has pledged to begin combatting terrorism more effectively, it remains on the US list of countries that have not arrested anyone for a terrorist act in over 25 years. Tourists are never targeted by these terrorist groups but should be aware of their existence.

**PROTECTING YOUR VALUABLES.** In Greece, you are much more likely to be **ripped off** by a cab driver, restaurant owner, or hotel owner than you are to be outright **mugged** in the street. However, **pickpocketing** is somewhat common, especially at major tourist sites and in Athens: be especially careful in these locations. To avoid being swindled, do your homework. Ask around for prices for hotel rooms, food, and cab rides to find out what a fair price is: don't take a first offer. Always, always, always negotiate cab fare or accommodation price ahead of time; pay only what you agreed upon, even if they try to change the price on you later. If you think someone is trying to rip you off, contact the tourist police (listed in the **Practical Information** section for each town).

Minimize financial risks by leaving expensive watches, jewelry, cameras, and electronics (like your Discman) at home; chances are you'd break them, lose them, or get sick of lugging them around anyway. Second, carry as little cash as possible; instead carry traveler's checks, an ATM card, or credit cards (along with your passport and ID cards) in a **money belt**—not a "fanny pack." Third, keep a small cash reserve separate from your primary stash. Keep the equivalent of US$50 sewn into or stored in the depths of your pack, along with your traveler's check numbers and photocopies of your passport, plane ticket, Eurail pass, and any other valuable documents you're carrying. Leave a set of photocopies at home.

Don't put a wallet with money in your back pocket. Label every piece of luggage both inside and out. Never count your money in public, and carry only as much as you'll need for the day. If you carry a purse, wear it across your body, away from the street, with the clasp against you. Always have emergency cash stashed away, in case you are robbed.

**CON ARTISTS.** In larger cities and touristy towns (especially Athens), you may run into **con artists.** They often work in groups. In a classic Athenian scam, you might be invited to a club by a new friend; there you'll meet several of his friends, and everyone will have several drinks. When you get up to go, you'll be stuck with the bill for several dozen *very* expensive drinks. Be wary of such invitations, since they can cost you everything you have.

Beware of certain classic cons: sob stories that require money, rolls of bills "found" on the street, mustard spilled (or saliva spit) onto your shoulder distracting you for enough time to snatch your bag. In a suspicious situation, don't respond or make eye contact, and walk away quickly. Don't ever hand over your passport to someone whose authority you question (ask to accompany them to a police station if they insist), and **don't ever let your passport out of your sight.** Similarly, don't let your bag out of sight; never trust a "station-porter" who insists on carrying your bag or stowing it in the baggage compartment or a "new friend" who offers to guard your bag while you buy a train ticket or use the rest room. Beware of **pickpockets** in city crowds, especially on public transportation. Also, be alert in public telephone booths. If you must say your calling card number, do so very quietly; if you punch it in, make sure no one can look over your shoulder.

**ACCOMMODATIONS AND TRANSPORTATION.** Never leave your belongings unattended; crime occurs in even the most demure-looking hostel or hotel. Bring your own **padlock** for lockers: don't trust the original locks, and don't store valuables in lockers. If you feel unsafe, look for places with a curfew or night attendant.

Be particularly careful on **buses** and **trains;** some determined thieves wait for travelers to fall asleep. Carry your backpack in front of you where you can see it. When traveling with others, sleep in alternate shifts. When alone, use good judgement in selecting a train compartment: never stay in an empty one, and lock your pack to the luggage rack. In hostels, sleep on top bunks with your luggage above you or in bed with you. Keep important documents and valuables on your person. Don't leave valuables in a **car** while you are away from it; hide tape decks, radios, and baggage in the trunk, or take them with you.



**DRUGS AND ALCOHOL.** You're subject to the laws of the country in which you travel when you're abroad, so familiarize yourself with those laws before leaving. If you carry **prescription drugs,** it is vital to have both a copy of the prescriptions themselves and a note from a doctor, especially at border crossings. Never try to bring any illegal substances into Greece. Authorities are especially vigilant at the Turkish and Albanian borders (major drug trafficking routes cross these borders) and might carefully search your bag for anything you shouldn't have.

# HEALTH

Common sense is the simplest prescription for good health while you travel. Travelers complain most often about their feet and their gut, so take precautionary measures: drink lots of fluids to prevent dehydration and constipation; wear sturdy, broken-in shoes and clean socks, and use talcum powder to keep your feet dry. Bring moleskin to cover blisters.

## BEFORE YOU GO

In your **passport,** write the names of people you wish to be contacted in case of a medical emergency, and add a list of your **allergies** or medical conditions. Carry up-to-date, legible prescriptions or a statement from your doctor stating the trade name, manufacturer, chemical name, and dosage of any medicine you're carrying. Matching a prescription to a foreign equivalent is not always easy, safe, or possible. While traveling, keep all medication with you in your carry-on luggage. You should also put together a first-aid kit (see p. 53).

**IMMUNIZATIONS.** Travelers over two years old should have the following up-to-date immunizations: MMR (for measles, mumps, and rubella); DTaP or Td (for diptheria, tetanus, and pertussis); OPV (for polio); HbCV (for haemophilus influenza B); and HBV (for hepatitis B). Hepatitis A vaccine and/or immune globulin (IG) are recommended. For recommendations on immunizations and prophylaxis, consult the CDC (see below) in the US or the equivalent in your home country, and be sure to check with a doctor for guidance.

**MEDICAL CONDITIONS.** Those with diabetes, allergies to antibiotics, epilepsy, heart conditions, or other conditions can obtain a stainless steel **Medic Alert** identification tag (US$35 the first year, $15 annually thereafter), which identifies the condition and gives a 24-hour collect-call information number. Contact the Medic Alert Foundation, 2323 Colorado Ave., Turlock, CA 95382 (☎(800) 825-3785; www.medicalert.org). Diabetics can contact the **American Diabetes Association,** 1660 Duke St., Alexandria, VA 22314 (☎(800) 232-3472), for the article "Travel and Diabetes" and a diabetic ID card, which carries messages in 18 languages explaining the carrier's diabetic status.

**USEFUL ORGANIZATIONS AND PUBLICATIONS.** The **US Centers for Disease Control and Prevention (CDC;** ☎(877) FYI-TRIP; international hotline ☎(404) 332 4559;

www.cdc.gov/travel), an excellent source of information for travelers, maintains an international fax information service. The **US State Department** (http://travel.state.gov) compiles Consular Information Sheets on health, entry requirements, and other issues for various countries. For information on health and other travel warnings, call the **Overseas Citizens' Services** (☎(202) 647-5225; after-hours 647-4000), contact a US passport agency or a US embassy or consulate abroad, or send a self-addressed, stamped envelope to the Overseas Citizens' Services, Bureau of Consular Affairs, #4811, US Department of State, Washington, D.C. 20520. The **British Foreign and Commonwealth Office** also gives health warnings for individual countries (www.fco.gov.uk).

For detailed information on travel health, including a country-by-country overview of diseases, try the **International Travel Health Guide,** Stuart Rose, MD (Travel Medicine, US$20; www.travmed.com). For general health info, contact the **American Red Cross** (☎(800) 564-1234).

# ONCE THERE

**MEDICAL ASSISTANCE.** In Greece, all EU travelers receive free health care with the presentation of an **E111 form.** There is a doctor on every island and in every town, and emergency treatment is available to all nationalities in public hospitals. Medical training in Greece is of high quality, but the health care system is vastly underfunded. Public hospitals are overcrowded, and hygiene may not be the best. Private hospitals generally have better care for more money; to use them, you will need good **health insurance.** If your regular policy does not cover travel abroad, you may wish to purchase additional coverage (see p. 52).

**Pharmacies** *(farmakia)*, labeled by green or red crosses, are on every street corner. In most towns and cities, at least one pharmacy (known as *efimerevon*) is open 24 hours every day—all pharmacies post listings of 24-hour pharmacies in their windows. Greek pharmacists often prescribe medicines, so consult one if you encounter minor problems, before going to a hospital.

If you are concerned about being able to access medical support while traveling, there are special support services you may employ. The **International Association for Medical Assistance to Travelers (IAMAT;** US ☎(716) 754-4883, Canada ☎(416) 652-0137, New Zealand ☎(03) 352 2053; www.sentex.net/~iamat) has free membership, lists English-speaking doctors worldwide, and offers detailed info on immunization requirements and sanitation. The *MedPass* from **Global Emergency Medical Services (GEMS),** 2001 Westside Dr. #120, Alpharetta, GA 30004, USA (☎(800) 860-1111; fax (770) 475-0058; www.globalems.com), provides 24-hour international medical assistance, support, and medical evacuation resources coordinated through registered nurses who have online access to your medical information, your primary physician, and a worldwide network of screened, credentialed English-speaking doctors and hospitals. Subscribers also receive a personal medical record that contains vital information in case of emergencies. GEMS will pay for medical evacuation if necessary. Prices run from US$35 for a 30-day trip to about US$100 for annual services. If your regular **insurance** policy does not cover travel abroad, you may wish to purchase additional coverage (see p. 52).

**ENVIRONMENTAL HAZARDS.** The **hot sun** beats down on all of Greece all summer long: this may be why you're going to Greece. It's easy to overheat, get sunburned, and forget to drink enough water. Especially on beaches, at outdoor sights, and hiking in the sun, beware of dehydration, sunburn, and heat exhaustion. These conditions can be avoided by drinking enough water, wearing a hat and sunglasses, using sunscreen, and taking a nap during the heat of the day like Greeks do.

In the **winter** or on **high-altitude** hikes, travelers should look out for hypothermia and exposure. Always dress warmly; on hikes, bring plenty of water, take it slowly to adjust to thin air, and go with a partner.

**Heat exhaustion and dehydration:** Heat exhaustion, characterized by dehydration and salt deficiency, can lead to fatigue, headaches, and wooziness. Avoid it by drinking plenty of clear fluids, eating salty foods (like crackers), and avoiding dehydrating beverages (e.g. alcohol, coffee, tea, and caffeinated soda). Continuous heat stress can lead to heatstroke, characterized by a rising temperature, severe headache, and cessation of sweating. Victims should be cooled off with wet towels and taken to a doctor.

**Sunburn:** Even if you're not prone to sunburn, bring sunscreen with you—though you can buy it in Greece, it's better to have sunscreen on hand as soon as you arrive in this sometimes fiercely hot country. Apply it liberally and often to avoid burns and risk of skin cancer. Even if you don't think you'll be in the sun much, you probably will be, and the sun is merciless, even through clouds. If you get sunburned, drink more fluids than usual and apply an aloe-based lotion.

**High altitude:** While skiing or hiking in the mountains, allow your body a couple of days to adjust to the reduced oxygen content before doing demanding work. At high elevations alcohol is more potent and UV rays are stronger.



**FOOD- AND WATER-BORNE DISEASE.** Prevention is the best cure: be sure that everything you eat is cooked properly and that the water is clean. In Greece, the tap water is fairly safe. However, as bottled water is dirt cheap and widely available, drink it whenever possible. Always wash your hands before eating, or bring a quick-drying purifying liquid hand cleaner. Your bowels will thank you.

**Traveler's diarrhea** results from drinking untreated water or eating uncooked foods. If the nasties hit you, have quick-energy, non-sugary foods with protein and carbohydrates to keep your strength up. Over-the-counter remedies (such as Pepto-Bismol or Immodium) may counteract the problems, but they can complicate serious infections. The most dangerous side effect of diarrhea is dehydration; drink 8 oz. of water with a half teaspoon of sugar or honey and a pinch of salt, try soft drinks without caffeine, or munch on salted crackers. If you develop a fever or your symptoms don't go away after four or five days, consult a doctor. Consult a doctor for treatment of diarrhea in children.

Microbes, tapeworms, and other **parasites** hide in unsafe water and food. **Giardia,** for example, is acquired by drinking untreated water from streams or lakes. Symptoms include swollen glands or lymph nodes, fever, rashes or itchiness, digestive problems, eye problems, and anemia. Boil water, wear shoes, avoid bugs, and eat only cooked food.

**OTHER INFECTIOUS DISEASES.** There are several other diseases you should be aware of before you head out on your trip to sunny Greece.

**Rabies:** Transmitted through infected animals' saliva; fatal if untreated. When symptoms appear (thirst and muscle spasms), it has reached its terminal stage. Wash animal bites, seek immediate medical care, and seek the animal. A vaccine (3 shots given over a 21-day period) is available but is only semi-effective.

**Hepatitis B:** A viral infection of the liver transmitted via bodily fluids or needle-sharing. Symptoms may not surface until years after infection. Vaccinations are recommended for health-care workers, sexually-active travelers, and anyone planning to seek medical treatment abroad. The 3-shot vaccination series must begin 6 mo. before traveling.

**Hepatitis C:** Like Hep B, but the mode of transmission differs. IV drug users, those with occupational exposure to blood, hemodialysis patients, and recipients of blood transfusions are at the highest risk, but the disease can also be spread through sexual contact or sharing items like razors and toothbrushes that may have traces of blood on them.

**AIDS, HIV, AND STDS.** The World Health Organization estimates that 30 million people have been infected with the **HIV** virus, the virus that causes **AIDS.** The easiest mode of HIV transmission is through direct blood-to-blood contact with an HIV-positive person, usually through shared needles; the most common way to transmit HIV is through sexual intercourse. **Latex condoms** can help prevent transmission; since they can be scarce in Greece, take a supply with you before you depart for your trip.

For detailed information on **AIDS** in Greece, call the **US Centers for Disease Control**'s 24-hour hotline at (800) 342-2437, or contact the **Joint United Nations Programme on HIV/AIDS (UNAIDS),** Appia 20, CH-1211 Geneva 27, Switzerland (☎+41 (22) 791 36 66; fax 791 41 87). Council Travel's brochure, *Travel Safe: AIDS and International Travel*, is available at their offices and on their website (www.ciee.org/Isp/safety/travelsafe.htm). Greece does not require HIV tests for tourists or those with visas.

**Sexually transmitted diseases** (STDs) such as gonorrhea, chlamydia, genital warts, syphilis, and herpes are easier to catch than HIV and can be just as deadly. **Hepatitis B** and **C** are also serious STDs (see **Other Infectious Diseases,** above). Condoms may protect you from some STDs, but oral or tactile contact transmits them, too. Warning signs include swelling, sores, bumps, or blisters on sex organs, the rectum, or the mouth; burning and pain during urination and bowel movements; itching around sex organs; swelling or redness of the throat; and flu-like symptoms. If these symptoms develop, see a doctor immediately.

**WOMEN'S HEALTH.** Women traveling in unsanitary conditions are vulnerable to **urinary tract** and **bladder infections,** which cause a burning sensation as well as painful and frequent urination. To try to avoid these infections, drink plenty of vitamin-C-rich juice and clean water, and urinate frequently, especially right after intercourse. Untreated, these infections can lead to kidney problems, sterility, and even death. If symptoms persist, see a doctor.

**Vaginal yeast infections** may flare up in hot, humid areas of Greece. Wearing loosely fitting trousers or a skirt and cotton underwear will help, as will over-the-counter remedies like Monostat or Gynelotrimin. Bring supplies from home if you are prone to infection, as they may be difficult to find on the road. In a pinch, some travelers use a natural alternative such as a plain yogurt and lemon juice douche.

**Tampons** and **pads** are readily available at pharmacies in cities and large towns; when heading for a remote village, bring your own supply. Although some pharmacies may be able to fill a birth control pill prescription, it is best to bring enough from home to avoid problems. Other methods of contraception, like condoms, may also be unavailable.

Women considering an **abortion** should contact the **International Planned Parenthood Federation (IPPF),** Regent's College, Inner Circle, Regent's Park, London NW1 4NS (☎(020) 7487 7900; fax 7487 7950; www.ippf.org) for more information.

For additional women's health information, check out the *Handbook for Women Travellers* by Maggie and Gemma Moss (Piatkus Books, US$15).

# INSURANCE

Travel insurance generally covers four basic areas: medical/health problems, property loss, trip cancellation/interruption, and emergency evacuation. Although your regular insurance policies may extend to travel-related accidents, consider purchasing travel insurance if the cost of potential trip cancellation or interruption is greater than you can absorb. Separately purchased travel insurance generally costs about US$50 per week for full coverage, and trip cancellation or interruption insurance may be purchased separately for about US$5.50 per US$100 of coverage.

**Medical insurance** (especially university policies) often covers costs incurred abroad; check with your provider. **US Medicare** does not cover foreign travel. **Canadians** are protected by their home province's health insurance plan for up to 90 days after leaving the country; check with the provincial Ministry of Health or Health Plan Headquarters for details. **Homeowners' insurance** (or your family's coverage) often covers theft during travel and loss of travel documents (passport, plane ticket, railpass, etc.) up to US$500.

**ISIC** and **ITIC** (see p. 39) provide basic insurance benefits, including US$100 per day of in-hospital sickness for up to 60 days, US$3000 of accident-related medical reimbursement, and US$25,000 for emergency medical transport. Cardholders have access to a toll-free 24-hour helpline for medical, legal, and financial emer-

gencies overseas (US and Canada ☎(877) 370-4742, elsewhere call US collect +1 (713) 342-4104). **American Express** (US ☎(800) 528-4800) grants most cardholders automatic car rental insurance (collision and theft, but not liability) and ground travel accident coverage of US$100,000 on flight purchases made with the card.

For information on getting car insurance, see **Car Insurance,** p. 69.

**INSURANCE PROVIDERS.** **Council** and **STA** (see p. 61) offer a range of plans that can supplement your basic coverage. Contact your local travel agency about extended insurance coverage.



# PACKING

**Pack light:** lay out only what you absolutely need, then take half the clothes and twice the money. The less you have, the less you have to carry—or lose. For information on hiking, see **Camping and the Outdoors** (p. 56).

**LUGGAGE.** If you plan to cover most of your itinerary by foot, a sturdy **frame backpack** is unbeatable. (For the basics on buying a pack, see p. 57.) Make sure your luggage is compact and easy to transport: a **suitcase** is a very bad idea if you're going to be moving around a lot. In addition to your main piece of luggage, a **daypack** (a small backpack or courier bag) is a must.

**CLOTHES.** If you are in Greece at the height of summer, you'll need very little other than **comfortable shoes,** a few changes of **light clothes,** and a **fleece** or sweater. **Flip-flops** are crucial for grubby hostel showers. To visit monasteries or churches, men will need a lightweight pair of pants and women will need a long skirt; both will need covered shoulders. If you plan on taking ferries or hiking, you'll want a warm wool sweater and a windproof jacket.

**CONVERTERS AND ADAPTERS.** Greek electricity is 220 volts AC, enough to fry any 110V North American appliance. **Americans** and **Canadians** should buy an **adapter** (which changes the shape of the plug) and a **converter** (which changes the voltage; US$20). Don't make the mistake of using only an adapter, unless appliance instructions explicitly state otherwise. **New Zealanders** and **South Africans** (who both use 220V at home) and **Australians** (who use 240/250V) won't need a converter, but will need a set of adapters to use anything electrical.

**TOILETRIES.** Toothbrushes, towels, soap, talcum powder (to keep feet dry), razors, deodorant, tampons, and the all-important sunscreen and aloe vera are readily available at Greek pharmacies. However, contact lenses can be expensive and difficult to obtain; bring enough extra pairs and solution for your entire trip. Also bring your **glasses** and a copy of your prescription in case you need emergency replacements. If you use heat-disinfection, you might switch temporarily to a chemical disinfection system if it's safe with your brand of lenses.

**FIRST-AID KIT.** For a basic first-aid kit, pack bandages, aspirin or other painkiller, antibiotic cream, a thermometer, a Swiss army knife, tweezers, sunscreen and aloe, moleskin for foot woes, decongestant, motion sickness remedy, diarrhea and upset-stomach medication, an antihistamine, insect repellent, and burn ointment.

**FILM.** Film and film developing in Greece can be expensive (about US$10 for a roll of 24 color exposures, though it is more reasonable in some places); try to bring enough film for your entire trip and definitely develop it at home. **Disposable cameras** may be a better option than expensive permanent ones. Airport security **X-rays** *can* fog film, so ask security to hand inspect it; pack film in your carry-on luggage, since higher-intensity X-rays are used on checked luggage.

**OTHER USEFUL ITEMS.** For safety purposes, you should bring a **money belt** and a small **padlock.** Basic **outdoors equipment** (plastic water bottle, compass, waterproof matches, pocketknife, sunglasses, hat) may also prove useful. Quick repairs can be done on the road with a **needle and thread** or with **electrical tape** patches. Doing

your **laundry** by hand (where it is allowed) is both cheaper and more convenient than doing it at a laundromat—bring detergent, a small rubber ball to stop up the sink, and string for a makeshift clothes line. **Other things** you're liable to forget: an umbrella; sealable **plastic bags** (for damp clothes, soap, food, shampoo, and other spillables); an **alarm clock;** safety pins; rubber bands; a flashlight; earplugs; garbage bags; and a small **calculator.**

**IMPORTANT DOCUMENTS.** Don't forget your passport, traveler's checks and receipts, ATM and/or credit cards, and adequate ID (see p. 39). If you need them, make sure you have a driver's license, your railpass, and travel insurance forms.



# ACCOMMODATIONS

Relative to the US and elsewhere in Europe, accommodations in Greece and Cyprus remain a bargain. Budget accommodations in Greece are usually found in domatia (rooms to let), hostels, campgrounds, and budget hotels. **Prices** given in this guide are for the high season. Off-season prices (Oct.-May) are 20 to 40% cheaper than in high season. Prices may rise on weekends and are usually reduced for extended stays; when renting a room in a *domatia*, prices are completely negotiable, especially during the week and off-season. This guide was researched during summer 2000, and prices may rise 10-20% in 2001. During high season (especially July and August), consider making **reservations**—you may not be able to find a room if you wait until you arrive on an island.

**DOMATIA (ROOMS TO LET).** Private homes all over Greece put up signs offering domatia (rooms to let). Domatia are perhaps the ideal budget accommodation: they are cheap and as safe as hotels, and allow you to stay in a Greek home and absorb some local culture. At more popular destinations, proprietors with rooms to let will greet your boat or bus, a practice which is theoretically illegal, but common. Always negotiate with domatia owners before settling a price. Before you accept an offer at portside, have a set destination in mind and look for people whose domatia are in the area you want. Many rooms offered at the port or bus stop are inexpensive; since the proprietors are in direct competition with the other domatia owners, good deals abound. Make owners pinpoint the location of their houses to make sure that "ten minutes away" means ten minutes on foot. Don't pay until you've seen the room.

While domatia may be run like small hotels in tourist towns, domatia in out of the way places promise warm offers of coffee at night and friendly conversation. Prices are quite variable, but you can expect to pay about 4000-5000dr for a single (8000dr for a double) in the more remote areas of northern and central Greece, and 6000-8000dr for a single (8000-12,000dr for a double) on heavily traveled islands. Never pay more for domatia than you would for a hotel in town, and remember domatia owners can often be bargained down, *especially* when the house is not full. If in doubt, ask the tourist police: they'll usually set you up with a room and conduct the negotiations themselves. Most private rooms operate only in high season and are the best option for those arriving without reservations.

**HOSTELS.** Hostels—typically dorm-style accommodations, sometimes in single-sex large rooms with bunk beds—are not as prevalent in Greece as they are throughout the rest of Europe. Those that exist (usually in the most popular tourist destinations) are almost never affiliated with an international hosteling organization. Thus, a hosteling membership won't do you much good. In Greece, a bed in a hostel will average around 2000dr. You can expect showers, sheets (free or a few hundred drachma), and towels; since hostels are not regulated, don't be surprised if you find some that are less than clean or don't offer sheets and towels.

Some Greek hostels offer private rooms for families and couples. They sometimes have kitchens and utensils for your use, bike or moped rentals, storage areas, and laundry facilities. Some hostels have a maximum stay of five days. Greek **youth hostels** generally have fewer restrictions than those farther north in

Europe. Many are open year-round and a few have midnight or 1am curfews (strictly enforced—you may be left in the streets if you come back too late). In summer, they usually stay open from 6-10am and 1pm-midnight (shorter hours in winter). It's advisable to book in advance in the summer at some of the more popular hostels in Athens, Santorini, Crete, or Nafplion.

**HOTELS.** The government oversees the construction and (seemingly random) classification of most hotels. Proprietors are permitted to charge 10% extra for stays of less than three nights, and 20% extra overall in from July until September 15. Most D- and E-class hotels start at 5000dr for singles and 6000dr for doubles. A hotel with no singles may still put you in a room by yourself. More information is available from the **Hellenic Chamber of Hotels,** Stadiou 24, Athens 10564 (☎(01) 331 0022; fax 322 5449; grhotels@otenet.gr). If a hotel owner solicits you, offering to drive you, make sure you establish the location on a map: it may be miles away.

Late at night, in the off season, or in a large town, it's a buyer's market and bargaining is appropriate. As a security deposit, hotels often ask for your passport and return it when you leave. Don't give it to them—suggest that they take down your passport number or offer to pay up front. You can often leave your luggage in the reception area during the afternoon, though check-out is at 11am or noon.

To charge you more, hotel owners may offer you only their most expensive rooms, compel you to buy breakfast, squeeze three people into a hostel-size triple and charge each for a single, or quote a price for a room that includes breakfast and private shower and then charge extra for both. Don't pay until you've seen the room. If a room seems unreasonably expensive, stress that you don't want luxuries and they may give you a cheaper option. The **tourist police** are on your side. If a hotel flagrantly violates the prices shown by law at the front desk or behind each room's front door, or if you think you've been exploited, threaten to report the hotel to the tourist police. The threat alone often resolves "misunderstandings."

**TRADITIONAL SETTLEMENTS.** Several traditional villages and buildings that have been preserved and restored by the government in an effort to maintain Greece's architectural heritage. The restoration of these Greek villages offers visitors a taste of small town Greek life and improves the regional economy. More than ten settlements host guests: **Makrynitsa** on Mt. Pelion (p. 186), **Fiscardo** on Kephalonia (p. 279), and **Papingo-Zagorohoria** in Epirus (p. 212). There are 12 reconstructed towers in **Vathia, Mani** (p. 155), and an expensive hotel in the Castro in **Monemvasia** (p. 159). Doubles range from 5000 to 10,000dr; tourist offices can make reservations and provide information.

# CAMPING AND THE OUTDOORS

Camping in Greece releases you from monotonous hotel rooms and hostel regulations, and saves you a large amount of money. The Greek National Tourist Organization (GNTO, see p. 40) is primarily responsible for campgrounds; most official GNTO campgrounds have drinking water, lavatories, and electricity. Many campgrounds rent tents for a low fee (a few hundred drachma). The Hellenic Touring Club also runs a number of campgrounds, especially in northern Greece (ask at local tourist offices for more information). In addition, Greece has many private campgrounds, which may include pools, discos, mini-markets, and tavernas. **Prices** depend on the facilities; you'll usually pay roughly 1200dr per person, plus 1000dr per tent. GNTO campgrounds tend to be ritzier and more expensive (up to 1700dr).

On many islands, some campers choose to bivouac on the beaches. While this is commonplace during July and August, when hotels are booked solid, it is **illegal.** Some police have ben known to ignore sleeping bags in the sand, while others charge penalties from stern chastisement to stiff fines. Those who camp on beaches should always clean up after themselves. *Let's Go: Greece* doesn't recommend camping illegally. For more information on camping and the outdoors, check out **Other Resources** (p. 77)

**ENVIRONMENTALLY RESPONSIBLE TOURISM** Leave no trace: keep your campsite at least 150 ft. (50m) from water; bury your feces at least six inches (10cm) deep, above the high-water line, and 150 feet or more from water supplies; carry out your toilet paper with you; and keep your trash together and carry it with you until you reach the next trash can. For more information, contact one of the organizations listed below.

**Earthwatch,** 680 Mt. Auburn St., Box 403, Watertown, MA 02272, (☎(617) 776-0188; fax 926-8532; email info@earthwatch.org; www.earthwatch.org).

**Ecotourism Society,** P.O. Box 755, North Bennington, VT 05257 (☎(802) 447-2121; email ecomail@ecotourism.org; www.ecotourism.org/tesinfo.html).

**EcoTravel Center:** www.ecotour.com.

**Tourism Concern,** Stapleton House, 277-281 Holloway Rd., London N7 8HN, England (☎(0170) 753 3330; www.gn.apc.org/tourismconcern.



# CAMPING AND HIKING EQUIPMENT

**WHAT TO BUY.** Good camping equipment is both sturdy and light. It's also more expensive in Australia, New Zealand, and the UK than in North America.

**Sleeping Bag:** Good sleeping bags are rated by season ("summer" means 30-40°F at night; "four-season" or "winter" often means below 0°F. Sleeping bags are made of **down** (warmer and lighter, but more expensive and miserable when wet) or **synthetic** (heavier, more durable, and warmer when wet). Although Greece is quite dry, a synthetic bag is a safer bet. Prices range from US$80-210 for a summer synthetic to US$250-300 for a down winter bag. Bring a **stuff sack** to keep your bag dry.

**Tent:** The best tents are free-standing (with their own frames and suspension systems), set up quickly, and only require staking in high winds. Low-slung dome tents are good for all-season camping, but are a bit heavy and hot in summer; good two-person tents start at US$90, four-person tents at US$300. Seal the seams of your tent with waterproofer and make sure it has a rain fly. For summer camping, **bivy-sacks,** one-man shelters that slide over a sleeping bag, allow sleeping under the Greek stars (US$120-200). A **battery-operated lantern**, a **plastic groundcloth**, and a **nylon tarp** might be useful.

**Backpack: Internal-frame packs** mold better to your back, keep a lower center of gravity, and flex adequately to allow you to hike difficult trails. **External-frame packs** are more comfortable for long hikes over even terrain, as they keep weight higher and distribute it more evenly. Make sure your pack has a strong, padded hip-belt to transfer weight to your legs. Any serious backpacking requires a pack of at least 4000 in$^3$ (16,000cc), plus 500 in$^3$ for sleeping bags in internal-frame packs. Sturdy backpacks cost anywhere from US$125-420—this is one area in which it doesn't pay to economize. Fill up any pack with something heavy and walk around the store with it to get a sense of how it distributes weight before buying it. Don't forget a **waterproof backpack cover.**

**Boots:** Be sure to wear hiking boots with good **ankle support.** They should fit snugly and comfortably over 1-2 pairs of wool socks and thin liner socks. Break in boots over several weeks first to spare yourself from painful and debilitating blisters.

**Other Necessities:** Synthetic layered clothes, like polypropylene, and a pile jacket will keep you warm when wet. A **"space blanket"** helps retain body heat and doubles as a groundcloth (US$5-15). Plastic **water bottles** are virtually shatter- and leak-proof. Bring **water-purification tablets** for when you can't boil water. Don't forget a **first-aid kit** (p. 49), **pocketknife, insect repellent, Calamine lotion, waterproof matches** or **lighter.**

**WHERE TO BUY IT.** Mail-order/online companies offer lower prices than many retail stores, but keep in mind that a visit to a local camping or outdoors store will give you a better sense of the look and weight of items.

## WILDERNESS SAFETY

**Stay warm, stay dry, and stay hydrated.** Most life-threatening wilderness situations result from a breach of this rule. On any hike, however brief, pack enough equipment to keep you alive should disaster befall. This includes **raingear, hat** and **mittens,** a **first-aid kit,** a **reflector,** a **whistle, high energy food,** and extra **water.** Don't rely on **cotton** for warmth; it is useless when wet.

Check **weather forecasts** and pay attention to the skies when hiking. Weather patterns can change suddenly. Whenever possible, let someone—a friend, hostel-owner, park ranger, hiking organization—know when and where you are going hiking. Do not attempt a hike beyond your ability—you may be endangering your life.



# KEEPING IN TOUCH

## BY MAIL

Let's Go lists **post offices** in the **Practical Information** section for each city and most towns. Post offices in Greece are generally open Monday to Friday 7:30am to 2pm, although certain branches may extend their hours into the afternoon and evening, as well as into the weekend.

### SENDING MAIL TO GREECE

Envelopes should be marked "air mail" or "par avion." Most countries offer both an airmail and express mail option for sending mail to Greece. For exact prices per weight, see the websites for each post office.

**Australia:** Allow 5-7 days for regular **airmail** to Greece. Postcards and letters up to 50g cost AUS$1.50; packages up to 0.5kg AUS$13, up to 2kg AUS$46. **EMS** can get a letter to Greece in 2-3 days for AUS$32. www.auspost.com.au/pac.

**Canada:** Allow 7-10 days for regular **airmail** to Greece. Postcards and letters up to 20g cost CDN$0.95; packages up to 0.5kg CDN$8.50, up to 2kg CDN$28.30.www.canadapost.ca/CPC2/common/rates/ratesgen.html#international.

**Ireland:** Allow 3-4 days for regular **airmail** to Greece. Postcards and letters up to 25g cost IR£0.32. Add IR£2.30 for **Swiftpost International**. www.anpost.ie.

**New Zealand:** Allow 6-10 days for regular **airmail** to Greece. Postcards NZ$1.10. Letters up to 20g cost NZ$1.80; small parcels up to 0.5kg NZ$15, up to 2kg NZ$39. www.nzpost.co.nz/nzpost/inrates.

**UK:** Allow 3 days for **airmail** to Greece. Letters up to 20g cost UK£0.36; packages up to 0.5kg UK£2.67, up to 2kg UK£9.42. **UK Swiftair** delivers letters a day faster for UK£2.85 more. www.royalmail.co.uk/calculator.

**US:** Allow 4-10 days for regular **airmail** to Greece. Postcards/aerogrammes cost US$0.55/0.60; letters under 1 oz. US$1. Packages under 1 lb. cost US$7.20; larger packages cost a variable amount (around US$15). **US Express Mail** takes 2-3 days and costs US$19 for 0.5 lb., US$24.50 for 1 lb. http://ircalc.usps.gov.

**Federal Express:** FedEx can get a letter from New York to Athens in two days for a whopping US$28.50; rates from non-US locations are prohibitively expensive. Australia ☎ 13 26 10; US and Canada ☎ (800) 247-4747; New Zealand ☎ (0800) 73 33 39; UK ☎ (0800) 12 38 00; Greece ☎ (01) 901 6752. www.fedex.com.

**Surface mail:** This is by far the cheapest and **slowest** way to send mail. It takes one to three months to cross the Atlantic and two to four to cross the Pacific–appropriate for sending large quantities of items you won't need to see for a while. When ordering books and materials from abroad, always include one or two **International Reply Coupons (IRCs)** as a way of providing the postage to cover delivery. IRCs (US$1.05) should be available from your local post office and those abroad.

## RECEIVING MAIL IN GREECE

There are several ways to arrange pick-up of letters sent to you by friends and relatives while you are abroad. Mail can be sent to Greece through **Poste Restante** (the international phrase for General Delivery) to almost any city or town with a post office. Address Poste Restante letters to:

Tom WAITS
Poste Restante
Paphos, Greece 8900

The mail will go to a special desk in the central post office, unless you specify differently. As a rule, it is best to use the largest post office in the area, because mail may be sent there regardless of what is written on the envelope. When possible, it is usually safer and quicker (though much pricier) to send mail express or registered. When picking up your mail, bring a form of **photo ID,** preferably a passport. There is no surcharge for picking up Poste Restante mail in Greece. The **Practical Information** of each city and town contains information for post office listings.

**American Express**'s travel offices throughout the world will act as a mail service for cardholders if you contact them in advance. Under this free **Client Letter Service,** they will hold mail for up to 30 days and forward upon request. Address the letter in the same way shown above. Some offices will offer these services to non-cardholders (especially those who have purchased AmEx travelers checks), but you must call ahead. *Let's Go* lists AmEx office locations in **Practical Information** when available. A complete list is available free from AmEx (US ☎(800) 528-4800).

## SENDING MAIL HOME FROM GREECE

**Aerogrammes,** printed sheets that fold into envelopes and travel via airmail, are available at post offices. You should mark letter both "par avion" and "air mail." Most post offices will charge exorbitant fees or simply refuse to send aerogrammes with enclosures. Airmail from Greece can take anywhere from one to two weeks, although times are much more unpredictable from smaller towns.

Sending a postcard via airmail to an international destination costs 170dr within Europe and 200dr to the US. Domestically, postcards require 120dr. To send a letter (up to 50g) via airmail to another European country costs 200dr and to anywhere else in the world, 240dr (up to 150g).

For **express** mail service, ask for *katepeegon;* to **register** a letter, *systemeno;* for **air mail,** *aeroporikos*, and write "air mail" on the envelope.

# BY TELEPHONES

## CALLING HOME FROM GREECE

A calling card is your cheapest bet. Calls are billed either collect or to your account. MCI WorldPhone also provides access to MCI's Traveler's Assist, which gives legal and medical advice, exchange rate information, and translation services. Other phone companies provide similar services to travelers. To obtain a calling card from your national telecommunications service before you leave home, contact: Telstra Australia Direct (☎13 22 00); Bell Canada Canada Direct (☎(800) 565-4708); Telecom Éireann Ireland Direct (☎(800) 25 02 50); Telecom New Zealand (☎(0800) 00 00 00); Telkom South Africa (☎09 03); British Telecom BT Direct (☎(800) 34 51 44); AT&T (☎(888) 288-4685); Sprint (☎(800) 877-4646); or MCI (☎(800) 444-4141).

Wherever possible, use a calling card for international phone calls, as the long-distance rates for national phone services are often exorbitant (a 20- or 30-minute call to the US from Greece costs US$50). All pay phones in Greece are card-operated, and you will need to purchase a card to operate the phone, even if you are going to use your own calling card to place the call (see **Calling Within Greece,** below). Although incredibly convenient, in-room hotel calls invariably include an arbitrary and sky-high surcharge (as much as US$10). For instructions on dialing direct, see **Placing International Calls.**

**TO USE A CALLING CARD** To call home from Greece using a calling card, simply contact your service provider's Greek operator:
**AT&T:** ☎00 800 13 11.
**Sprint:** ☎00 900 14 11.
**MCI WorldPhone Direct:** ☎00 800 12 11.
**Canada Direct:** ☎00 800 16 11.
**BT Direct:** ☎00 800 44 11.
**Ireland Direct:** ☎155 11 74.

The expensive alternative to using a calling card is using an international operator to place a **collect call.** An English-speaking operator from your home nation can be reached by dialing the appropriate service provider listed above, and they will typically place a collect call even if you don't possess one of their phone cards.

**PLACING INTERNATIONAL CALLS** To call Greece from home or to place an international call from Greece, dial:

1. The **international dialing prefix.** To dial out of **Greece,** the **Republic of Ireland, New Zealand,** or the **UK,** 00; **Australia,** dial 0011; **Canada** or the **US,** 011; **South Africa,** 09.
2. The **country code** of the country you want to call. To call **Greece,** 30; **Australia,** dial 61; **Canada** or the **US,** 1; the **Republic of Ireland,** 353; **New Zealand,** 64; **South Africa,** 27; the **UK,** 44.
3. The **city or area code.** Let's Go lists the phone codes for cities and towns in Greece across from the city or town name, alongside the following icon: ☎. If the first digit is a zero (e.g., 031 for Thessaloniki), omit it when calling from abroad (e.g., dial 011 30 31 from Canada to reach Thessaloniki).
4. The **local number.**

## CALLING WITHIN GREECE

The only way to use the phone in Greece is with a **prepaid phone card.** You can buy the cards at street side kiosks and *peripteros* in denominations of 1000, 3000, and 5000dr. The time is measured in minutes or talk units; a 1000dr card will buy you 100 units, roughly equal to 30 minutes of local calling within Greece and 5-10 minutes long-distance within Greece or internationally.

A few warnings about using card phones: Type the number slowly; Greece's quirky phones get confused if you type fast. Don't remove the card until the phone tells you to do so or you will lose your remaining credit. Finally, do not make long calls from card phones, or a long line of irate people is likely to form behind you.

# TIME DIFFERENCES

**TIME ZONES**

| Seattle<br>San Francisco<br>Los Angeles | Toronto<br>New York<br>Ottawa | London<br>(GMT) | **Athens**<br>Istanbul<br>Nicosia | Hong Kong<br>Manila<br>Singapore | Sydney<br>Canberra<br>Melbourne |
|---|---|---|---|---|---|
| 4am | 7am | noon | 2pm | 8pm | 10pm |

# BY EMAIL AND INTERNET

The availability of the Internet in Greece is rapidly expanding. In all big cities, in most small cities and large towns, and on many islands, you will able to find Internet access. Expect to pay between 1000-2000dr per hour. **Cybercafe Guide** (www.cyberiacafe.net/cyberia/guide/ccafe.htm) can help you find cybercafes in Greece. Travelers with laptops can call an internet service provider via a **modem.** Long-distance phone cards specifically intended for such calls can defray nor-

mally high phone charges; check with your long-distance phone provider to see if it offers this option. **Internet cafes** and the occasional free internet terminal at a public library or university are listed in the **Orientation and Practical Information** sections of major cities. Free, web-based email accounts have become popular because of their easy accessibility; try Yahoo Mail (www.yahoo.com), Operamail (www.operamail.com), or OneBox (www.onebox.com). Many free email providers are funded by advertising and some may require subscribers to fill out a questionnaire. Almost every search engine has an affiliated free email service.



# GETTING THERE

## BY PLANE

When it comes to airfare, a little effort can save you a bundle. If your plans are flexible enough to deal with the restrictions, courier fares are the cheapest. Tickets bought from consolidators and standby seating are also good deals, but last-minute specials, airfare wars, and charter flights often beat these fares. The key is to hunt around, to be flexible, and to persistently ask about discounts. Students, seniors, and those under 26 should never pay full price for a ticket. See **Other Resources** (p. 77) for further information.

Airfares to Greece peak between **June** and **September;** holidays are also expensive. Midweek (M-Th morning) round-trip flights run US$40-50 cheaper than weekend flights, but are generally more crowded and less likely to permit frequent-flier upgrades. Flights between capitals or regional hubs (particularly Athens and Thessaloniki) will offer the cheapest fares. Traveling with an **"open return" ticket** (arriving in and departing from different cities, e.g. London-Athens and Thessaloniki-London) can be pricier than fixing a return date when buying the ticket. tickets tend to be pricier. If Greece is only 1 stop on a more extensive globe-hop, consider a **RTW** ticket. Tickets usually include at least 5 stops and are valid for about a year; prices range US$1200-5000. Try **Northwest Airlines/KLM** (US ☎(800) 447-4747; www.nwa.com) or **Star Alliance,** a consortium of 13 airlines including United Airlines (US ☎(800) 241-6522; www.star-alliance.com).

In the high season, flights to **Athens** range from under US$300 (from London) to nearly US$2000 (from Sydney). Flights from New York cost at least US$550 in the high season. In the low season, fares drop by at least US$100.

## BUDGET AND STUDENT TRAVEL AGENCIES

A knowledgeable agent specializing in flights to Greece can make your life easy and help you save, too, but agents may not spend the time to find you the lowest possible fare—they get paid on commission. Students and under-26ers holding **ISIC and IYTC cards** (see **Identification,** p. 39), respectively, qualify for big discounts from student travel agencies. Most flights from budget agencies are on major airlines, but in peak season some may sell seats on less reliable chartered aircraft.

**usit World** (www.usitworld.com). Over 50 usit campus branches in the UK (www.usitcampus.co.uk), including 52 Grosvenor Gardens, **London** SW1W 0AG (☎(0870) 240 1010); **Manchester** (☎(0161) 273 1721); and **Edinburgh** (☎(0131) 668 3303). Nearly 20 **usit Now** offices in Ireland, including 19-21 Aston Quay, O'Connell Bridge, **Dublin** 2 (☎(01) 602 1600; www.usitnow.ie), and **Belfast** (☎(02890) 327 111; www.usitnow.com). There is an office in **Athens** Ethinikis Antistaseos 31, 18531 Pireaus (☎+30 1 41 32 950; fax 30 1 41 32 901; email etospir@usitetos.gr; www.usitetos.gr). Offices also in Auckland, Brussels, Frankfurt, Johannesburg, Lisbon, Luxembourg, Madrid, Paris, Sofia, and Warsaw.

**Council Travel** (www.counciltravel.com). US offices include: 273 Newbury St., **Boston,** MA 02116 (☎(617) 266-1926); 1160 N. State St., **Chicago,** IL 60610 (☎(312) 951-0585); 931 Westwood Blvd., Westwood, **Los Angeles,** CA 90024 (☎(310) 208-3551);

254 Greene St., **New York,** NY 10003 (☎(212) 254-2525); 530 Bush St., **San Francisco,** CA 94108 (☎(415) 566-6222); 3301 M St. NW, **Washington, D.C.** 20007 (☎(202) 337-6464). **For US cities not listed,** call (800) 2-COUNCIL (226-8624). In the **UK,** 28A Poland St. (Oxford Circus), **London,** W1V 3DB (☎(020) 7437 7767).

**CTS Travel,** 44 Goodge St., **London** W1 (☎(020) 7636 0031; fax 7637 5328; email ctsinfo@ctstravel.com.uk).

**STA Travel,** 6560 Scottsdale Rd. #F100, Scottsdale, AZ 85253 (☎(800) 777-0112; fax (602) 922-0793; www.sta-travel.com). A student and youth travel company with over 150 offices worldwide. Ticket booking, travel insurance, railpasses, and more. Call for the nearest office. In the UK, STA is at 11 Goodge St., **London** WIP 1FE (☎(020) 7436 7779 for North American travel). In New Zealand, 10 High St., **Auckland** (☎(09) 309 0458). In Australia, 366 Lygon St., **Melbourne** VIC 3053 (☎(03) 9349 4344).

**Travel CUTS (Canadian Universities Travel Services Limited),** 187 College St., **Toronto,** ON M5T 1P7 (☎(416) 979-2406; fax 979-8167; www.travelcuts.com). Also in the UK, 295-A Regent St., **London** W1R 7YA (☎(020) 7255 1944).

ESSENTIALS

## COMMERCIAL AIRLINES

**FLIGHT PLANNING ON THE INTERNET** The web is a great place to look for travel bargain. Many airline sites offer special last-minute deals on the web. Check out **www.greeceflights.com; www.easyjet.com** lists cheap London-Athens flights; see **www.studentuniverse.com** should you happen to be a student traveler. Other sites do the legwork and compile the deals for you–www.bestfares.com, www.onetravel.com, www.lowestfare.com, and www.travelzoo.com. **STA Travel** (www.sta-travel.com) and **Council Travel** (www.counciltravel.com) provide quotes on student tickets, while **Expedia** (www.expedia.com) and **Travelocity** (www.travelocity.com) offer full travel services. **Priceline** (www.priceline.com) lets you specify a price, and obligates you to buy any ticket that meets or beats it; expect antisocial hours and odd routes. **Skyauction** (www.skyauction.com) lets you to bid on both last-minute and advance-purchase tickets. One last note–to protect yourself, make sure that the site uses a secure server before handing over any credit card details.

The commercial airlines' lowest regular offer is the **APEX** (Advance Purchase Excursion) fare, which provides confirmed reservations and allows "open-jaw" tickets. Generally, reservations must be made seven to 21 days ahead of departure, with seven- to 14-day minimum-stay and up to 90-day maximum-stay restrictions. These fares carry hefty cancellation and change penalties (fees rise in summer). Book peak-season APEX fares early; by May you will have a hard time getting your desired departure date.

Major airlines like American Airlines in the US, Virgin Atlantic Airways in the UK, and Qantas in Australia will have frequent flights and many departure points for Greece. Smaller "budget" airlines may have cheaper fares, but they will have limited departure points and times. Rather than going through a particular airline, it may be easier to go through a budget agency or online service (see above) to get the best deal on airfare. APEX fares from the commercial airlines will not be the cheapest ones to Greece, but they will give you an idea of the fares out there.

**Olympic Airways** (in Greece Sygrou 96, Athens 11747, ☎+30 01 926 7221, fax 926 7858, www.olympic-airways.gr; in US 645 Fifth Ave., New York, NY 10022, ☎(800) 223-1226, www.omogenia.com/olympicairways) the national Greek airline, flies to and within Greece. Domestic flights in particular can be very inexpensive, saving time and money for those traveling long distances within Greece.

## OTHER CHEAP ALTERNATIVES

**TICKET CONSOLIDATORS. Ticket consolidators,** or **"bucket shops,"** buy unsold tickets in bulk from commercial airlines and sell them at discounted rates. Look in the Sunday travel section of any major newspaper (such as the *New York Times* or

SLOVENIJA
15-06-1999
MARIBOR

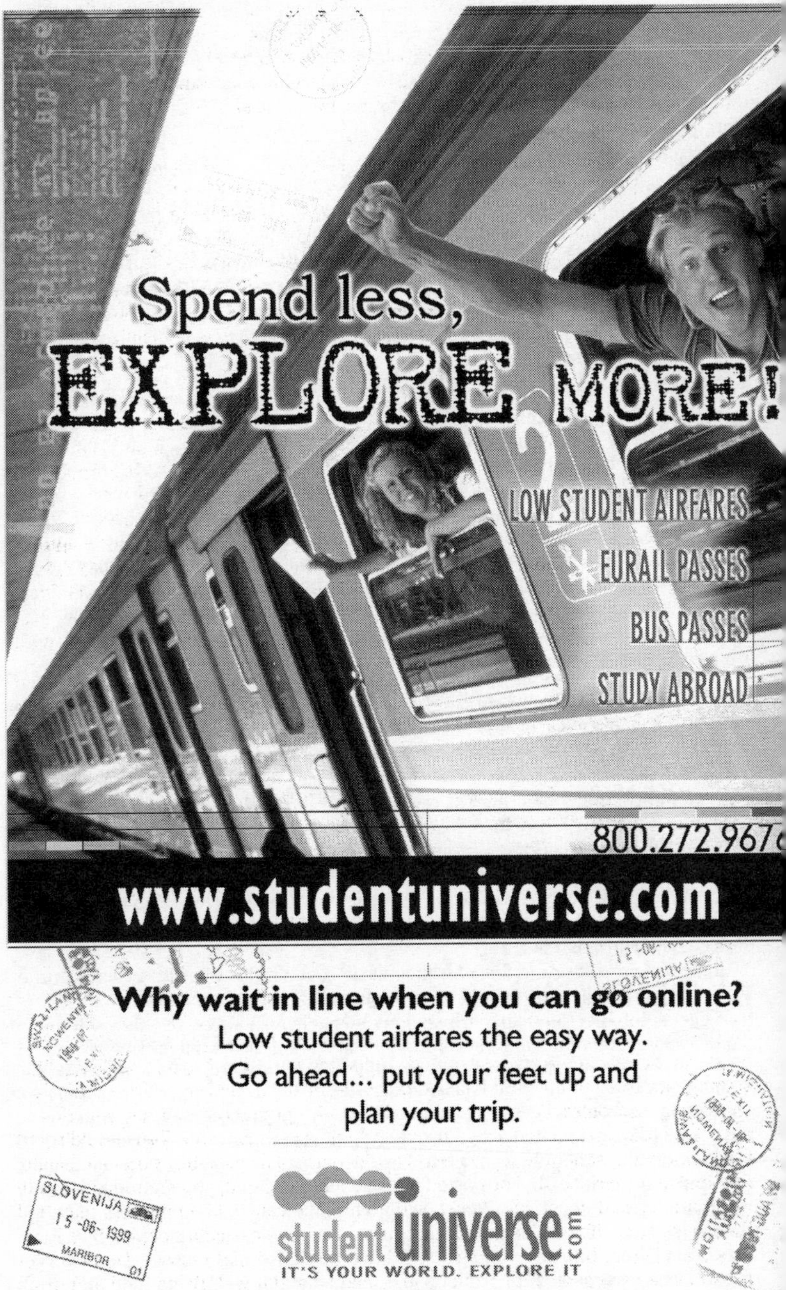

student universe.com
IT'S YOUR WORLD. EXPLORE IT

the *Sydney Morning Herald*) for tiny ads from many bucket shops. Call quickly, as availability is typically extremely limited. Not all bucket shops are reliable, so insist on a receipt that gives full details of restrictions, refunds, and tickets, and pay by credit card (in spite of the 2-5% fee) so you can stop payment if you never receive your tickets. For more info, see www.travel-library.com/air-travel/consolidators.html or pick up Kelly Monaghan's *Air Travel's Bargain Basement* (Intrepid Traveler, US$8).

**CHARTER FLIGHTS.** Charters are flights a tour operator contracts with an airline to fly extra loads of passengers during peak season. Charter flights fly less frequently than major airlines, make refunds particularly difficult, and are almost always fully booked. Schedules and itineraries may also change or be canceled at the last moment (as late as 48 hours before the trip, and without a full refund), and check-in, boarding, and baggage claim are often much slower. **Travelers Advantage,** Stamford, CT (☎(800) 548-1116; www.travelersadvantage.com; US$60 annual fee includes discounts, newsletters, and cheap flight directories) specializes in European travel and tour packages.

**AIR COURIER FLIGHTS.** Couriers help transport cargo on international flights by guaranteeing delivery of the baggage claim slips from the company to a representative overseas. Generally, couriers must travel light (carry-ons only) and deal with complex restrictions on their flight. Most flights are round-trip only with short fixed-length stays (usually one week) and a limit of a single ticket per issue. Most of these flights also operate only out of the biggest cities, like New York. Generally, you must be over 21 (in some cases 18), have a valid passport, and procure your own visa, if necessary. Groups such as the **Air Courier Association** (☎(800) 282-1202; www.aircourier.org) and the **International Association of Air Travel Couriers,** 220 South Dixie Hwy. #3, P.O. Box 1349, Lake Worth, FL 33460 (☎(561) 582-8320); email iaatc@courier.org; www.courier.org) provide their members with lists of opportunities and courier brokers worldwide for an annual fee.

**STANDBY FLIGHTS.** Companies that specialize in standby flights don't sell tickets but the promise that you will get to your destination (or near your destination) within a certain window of time (anywhere from one to five days). One established standby company in the US is **Airhitch,** 2641 Broadway, 3rd fl., New York, NY 10025 (☎(800) 326-2009; fax 864-5489; www.airhitch.org) and Los Angeles, CA (☎(888) 247-4482), which offers one-way flights to Europe from the Northeast (US$159), West Coast and Northwest (US$239), Midwest (US$209), and Southeast (US$189). Intracontinental connecting flights within the US or Europe cost US$79-139. Airhitch's has European offices in Paris (☎+33 (01) 47 00 16 30); or Amsterdam (☎+31 (20) 626 32 20). Carefully read agreements with any company offering standby flights, as tricky fine print can leave you in the lurch.

# BY FERRY

Ferry travel is a popular way to get to and travel within Greece and Cyprus; their ports can be reached from a seemingly unlimited number of points, and finding a boat agency to facilitate your trip should not be difficult. Be warned that **ferries run on irregular schedules.** A few websites, like www.gptnet.com and www.ferries.fr, have tried to keep updated schedules online and are worth a try. You should try to take a look at a schedule as close to your departure as possible; you can usually find one at a tourist office or posted at the dock. That said, you should also make reservations, and check in at *least* two hours in advance; late boarders may find their seats gone. If you sleep on deck, bring warm clothes and a sleeping bag. Bicycles travel free, but motorcycles will have an additional charge. Don't forget motion sickness medication, toilet paper, and a hand towel. Bring food and drink to avoid high prices on board.

The major ports of departure from **Italy** to Greece are Ancona and Brindisi, on the southeast coast of Italy. Bari, Otranto, and Venice also have a few connections.

For schedules from Greece to Italy, see Patras (p. 131), Kephalonia (p. 274), Corfu (p. 259), or Igoumenitsa (p. 199). The **Brindisi-Patras** route (17hr.) is heavily traveled; a Eurail pass is accepted at **HML** ferry lines (**Patras,** on Iroon Polytechniou; ☎452 521. **Brindisi,** C. Garibaldi 8; ☎08 31 52 85 31). **Adriatica,** C. Garibaldi 85/87, in Brindisi, also accepts Eurail passes. (☎08 31 52 38 25.) Deck passage to Brindisi is 6000-8000dr, plus 2200dr port tax. The Eurail pass does not cover port tax.

Ferries also run from Greece to various points on the Turkish coast. Trips from Greek islands that nearly touch the mainland are brief and fairly inexpensive. For prices, schedules, and more information, see **Turkish Daytrips** (p. 549).



## BY BUS AND TRAIN

**BY BUS.** Although trains and railpasses are extremely popular in most of Europe, buses are a sometimes cheaper alternative. Unfortunately, there are almost no buses running directly from any European city to Greece. **Busabout,** 258 Vauxhall Bridge Rd., London SW1V 1BS, is one of the very few European bus lines that also runs to Greece (☎0171 950 1661; fax (0) 171 950 1662; email info@busabout.co.uk; www.busabout.com). Only truly useful if you plan to travel elsewhere in Europe, there are five interconnecting bus circuits covering 60 cities and town, with **"Add-ons"** that extend to Greece (via Italy) and environs. Standard/student passes are valid for times ranging from 15 days (US$259, UK£155) up to unlimited (US$1109, UK£659). "Add-ons" to **Patras** go through **Venice** (US$49, UK£29) and **Brindisi** (US$29, UK£17). Faster and more efficient than most trains to Greece, the inconvenience of finding a bus to Greece may outweigh the benefits. The **Hellenic Railways Organization (OSE)** runs buses to **Athens** from **Sofia** (13 hr.; 1 per day 8:30am; one-way 14,000dr, round-trip 25,500dr), and **Tirana** (17hr.; 1 per day 8am; one-way 12,000dr, round-trip 21,500dr). These buses are expensive and slow.

**BY TRAIN.** Greece is served by a number of international train routes that connect Athens, Thessaloniki, and Larisa to most European cities. **Eurail** passes are valid in Greece, and may be a useful purchase if you plan to visit the 17 other European countries in which they are valid. Fifteen-day youth passes (ages 25 and under) are US$388, adults are US$554. Eurail passes are available through travel agents, student travel agencies like STA and Council (see p. 61), and **Rail Europe,** 500 Mamaroneck Ave., Harrison, NY 10528 (US ☎(888) 382-7245, fax (800) 432-1329; Canada ☎(800) 361-7245, fax (905) 602-4198; UK ☎(0990) 84 88 48; www.raileurope.com). Unfortunately, the Greek rail system is one of Europe's most antiquated and least efficient—for example, a trip from Vienna to Athens will take at least three days. For information on specific routes and fare see the **OSE** website at www.osenet.gr.

# GETTING AROUND

## BY FERRY AND HYDROFOIL

Widespread but unpredictable, cheap but slow, ferries will form the backbone of your travel-adventure tales. Be prepared to arrive at the dock one to two hours before departure for a decent seat (though a five-minutes-early and a three-hours-late departure are both real possibilities) and bring a good book, a bottle of water, food to last you the trip (snack-bars are pricey), and a **windbreaker** (you'll want to wander the deck at sea). For short distances, indoor seats fill up fast; bring a hat to shield you from the sun on upper decks. For longer distances, bring **sleeping bags** or upgrade to a **cabin;** though the latter are usually expensive and disappointing, the former can be paired with insulated mats for starry sea nights on the deck.

**MAKING SENSE OF FERRIES.** The key to making good use of ferries is understanding ferry routes and planning your trip accordingly. Most ferries, rather than shuffling back and forth between two destinations, trace a four- or five-port route.

Most ferry companies will allow you to buy your round-trip ticket **"split,"** meaning that you can ride the Piraeus-Syros-Tinos-Mykonos ferry from Piraeus to Syros, get off, get back on when the same ferry passes Syros several days later, proceed to Tinos, and so on. Besides convenience, traveling along ferry routes gives you a Greek (rather than guidebook) grouping of islands, based on commuters, local traffic, trade, and historical connections. Remember that geographic proximity is **no guarantee** that you'll be able to get to one island from another later on. For example, there is no ferry service from Skyros to the rest of the Sporades, nor is there service from Skyros to the northeast Aegean, or from any of the Cyclades to any of the Dodecanese.

Understanding ferry routes will also help you make sense of discrepancies in ticket prices (going to Hydra from Athens via Poros and Aegina is more expensive than simply going via Poros) and travel times. **Ferry schedules,** generally available for the region from the ferry companies or posted at the port police *(limenarcheio),* are published weekly and give the departure times, routes, and names of each departing ferry. As particular ferries, even within companies, vary hugely in quality, local travelers pay close attention to the names. Ask around or check on the web (www.ferries.gr) for tips, ferry schedules, and prices.



**DOLPHIN RIDES.** Twice the price and twice the speed, **Flying Dolphins** provide extensive, standardized, and sanitized human transport (no cars) between islands; offices and services are listed in the **Getting There** sections of all towns. However, traveling by Dolphin is like traveling by seaborne airplane: passengers are assigned seats and required to stay in the climate-controlled cabin for the duration of the trip, which may be less than ideal for the easily seasick. If you have the money to spare and want to minimize travel time, Dolphins are convenient enough and they run like clockwork; otherwise, why sail the Aegean in a craft that won't let you get salt on your fingers and wind in your hair?

# BY BUS

Spending time in Greece means traveling by bus. Service is extensive and fares are cheap. On major highways, buses tend to be more modern and efficient than in the mountainous areas of the Peloponnese or northern Greece. The **OSE** (see **By Train,** p. 66) offers limited bus service from a few cities. Unless you're sticking close to train routes, **KTEL** bus service should be sufficient.

Always check with an official source about scheduled departures; posted schedules are often outdated, and all services are curtailed significantly on Saturday and Sunday; major holidays run on Sunday schedules. The English-language weekly newspaper *Athens News* prints Athens bus schedules, and like almost everything else, they are available online (www.ktel.org). Try to arrive at least 10 minutes ahead of time, as Greek buses have a habit of leaving early. In major cities, KTEL bus lines may have different stations for different destinations, and schedules generally refer to **endpoints** ("the bus leaves Kalloni at three and arrives in Mytilini at four") with no mention of the numerous stops in between. In villages, a cafe or *zaccharoplasteio* (sweet-shop) often serves as the bus station, and you must ask the proprietor for a schedule.

**ALL ABOARD!** Ask the **conductor** before entering the bus whether it's going to your destination (the signs on the front are often misleading or wrong), and ask to be warned when you get there. If stowing bags underneath the bus, make sure they're in the compartment for your destination (conductors take great pride in packing the bus for easy unloading, and may refuse to open the "final destination" compartment at the "halfway" stop). If the bus passes your stop, stand up and yell **"Stasi!"** (STASH). On the road, stand near a Stasi sign to pick up an intercity bus. KTEL buses are generally **green** or occasionally **orange,** while intercity buses are usually **blue.** For long-distance rides, you should buy your ticket beforehand in the office (if you don't, you may have to stand throughout the journey). Prices vary by the duration of the trip; short hops cost only a few hundred drachma, while longer

rides cost thousands. For shorter trips, pay the conductor after you have boarded; reasonably close change is expected. Some lines discount round-trip fares by 20%.

## BY PLANE OR TRAIN



**BY PLANE.** In Greece, **Olympic Airways** can be found in **Athens,** Syngrou 96-100, 11741 Athens (☎(01) 926 91 11), in **Thessaloniki,** Koundouritou 3, Thessaloniki 54101(☎(031) 26 01 21), and in many large cities and islands. In the US, contact 645 Fifth Ave., New York, NY 10022 (☎(212) 735-0200; fax (212) 735-0212). In England, contact 11 Conduit St., **London** W1R OLP (☎(870) 606 04 60; fax (207) 629 98 91). The Olympic Airways website (www.olympic-airways.com) lists information for every office around the globe. For further flight information within Greece, check regional **Practical Information** listings of airports, destinations, and prices, or get an Olympic Airways brochure at any Olympic office.

In recent years, Olympic's domestic *(esoteriko)* service has increased appreciably; from Athens, an hour's flight ($60-90) can get you to almost any island in Greece. Even in low season, more remote destinations (Limnos, Hios) are serviced several times weekly, while more developed areas (Thessaloniki, Crete) can have several flights per day. Though somewhat frivolous for short distances, fairly cheap flights seem like more of a deal if they exempt you from overnight ferry rides and potential cost of food and beds on-board (e.g., the 22-hour ferry ride from Limnos to Piraeus). Make sure to reserve your tickets one week in advance.

**BY TRAIN.** Although trains can be cheaper than buses, they run less frequently and take longer: as a rule, Greece has one of Europe's slowest train services. If you're lucky, you may come across a new, air-conditioned, intercity train, which is a different entity altogether: although they are slightly more expensive and rare, they are worth the price. **Eurail** passes are valid on Greek trains. **OSE** (www.osenet.gr) connects Athens to major Greek cities (like Volos and Thessaloniki). For schedules and prices in Greece, dial 145 or 147. Lines do not go to the west coast, and they are rarely useful for remote areas or archaeological sites. Bring food and a water bottle, because the on-board cafe can be pricey, and the water undrinkable. Lock your compartment and keep valuables on your person.

## BY MOPED

**BE CAREFUL.** A word of caution about travel by moped: **most tourist-related accidents each year occur on mopeds.** Regardless of your experience driving a moped, winding, often poorly maintained mountain roads and reckless drivers make driving a moped hazardous. Always wear a helmet, and never ride with a backpack.

Motorbiking is a popular way of touring Greece's winding roads. Although renting wheels is the best and most cost efficient way to assert your independence from unreliable or inconvenient public transportation systems, you should be aware that they can be uncomfortable for long distances, dangerous in the rain, and unpredictable on rough roads. On many islands, navigable roads suddenly turn into tiny trails that can only be walked. Furthermore, moped rental shop owners often loosen the front brakes on the bikes to discourage riders from using them (relying on the front brakes makes accidents more likely), so use the back brakes. If you've never driven a moped before, a cliffside road is not the place to learn.

**RENTING.** Shops renting mopeds are everywhere, and most require only some sort of drivers' license (a Greek licence or International Driving Permit is not necessary). Bike quality, speed of service in case of breakdown, and prices for longer periods vary drastically, but you should expect to pay at least 4000dr per day for a 50cc scooter, the cheapest bike with the power to tackle steep mountain roads.

More powerful bikes cost 20 to 30% more and usually require a Greek motorcycle license. Many agencies will request your passport as a deposit, but it's wiser just to settle up in advance; if they have your passport and you have an accident or mechanical failure, they may refuse to return it until you pay for repairs. Ask before renting if the price quote includes tax, insurance, and a full tank of gas, or you may pay several hundred unexpected drachmas. Information on local moped rentals is in the **Practical Information** section for individual cities and towns.



# BY CAR

Cars are a luxury in Greece, a country where public transportation is nonexistent after 7pm. Ferries will take you island-hopping if you pay a transport fee for the car. Drivers must be comfortable with a standard transmission, winding mountain roads, reckless drivers (especially in Athens), and the Greek alphabet—signs in Greek appear roughly 100m before the transliterated versions. Driving can be a cheaper alternative to trains and buses for groups of travelers, and is especially useful for exploring remote villages in northern Greece, though having a car might detract from the traveling experience.

Agencies may quote low daily rates that exclude the 20% tax and **Collision Damage Waiver (CDW)** insurance (2500dr per day). Without CDW, the driver is responsible for the first 15,000dr worth of damage if theft or accident is not the driver's fault, and the full amount otherwise. Expect to pay 16,000-18,000dr per day for a rental. Some places quote lower rates but hit you with hidden charges, such as exorbitant refueling bills if you come back with less than a full tank, 1.5 to 2.5dr per kilometer drop-off or special charge, or 100km per day minimum mileage. Most companies won't let you drive the car outside Greece.

The cheaper and larger rental agencies are **Just, InterRent,** and **Retca,** with offices in Athens and other mainland cities (see the **Practical Information** sections for towns and cities), as well as on Crete and several islands. At **Avis, Hertz, Europcar,** and **Budget,** reliable service mitigates steep rates. Hertz and InterRent rent to 21-year-olds, but the others rent only to those over 23.

Foreign drivers are required to have an **International Driving Permit** and an **International Insurance Certificate** to drive in Greece (see below). The **Automobile and Touring Club of Greece (ELPA),** Messogion 395, Athens 11527 (☎(01) 606 88 00), provides assistance and offers reciprocal membership to foreign auto club members. They also have 24-hour emergency road assistance (☎104) and an information line (☎174 in Athens, (01) 60 68 838 elsewhere in Greece; open M-F 7am-3pm). More information can be found at www.fia.com/tourisme/infoclub/grece.htm.

**INTERNATIONAL DRIVING PERMIT (IDP).** If you plan to drive a car while in Greece, you are legally required to have an International Driving Permit (IDP). Although Greek proprietors may ignore the law, get one if you know you plan on driving. Your IDP, valid for one year, must be issued in your own country before you depart; AAA affiliates cannot issue IDPs valid in their own country. You must be 18 years old to receive the IDP. A valid driver's license from your home country must always accompany the IDP.

**CAR INSURANCE.** Most credit cards cover standard insurance. If you rent, lease, or borrow a car, you will need a **green card,** or **International Insurance Certificate,** to certify that you have liability insurance and that it applies abroad. Green cards can be obtained at car rental agencies, car dealers (for those leasing cars), some travel agents, and some border crossings. Rental agencies may require you to purchase theft insurance in areas that they consider to have a high risk of auto theft. Contact the automobile association in your country for information on obtaining an international driving permit and car insurance.

## BY FOOT

*Let's Go: Greece* describes hikes and trails in town and city listings; local residents and fellow travelers can suggest even more. Always make sure you have comfortable shoes and a map. There's rarely any reason to trek during the hottest part of the day (1-5pm). Besides the sweltering heat and the threat of dehydration, many destinations (hilltop monasteries, campgrounds) close for the afternoon and reopen only in the evening. Good sunscreen, a hat, and water are essential.

Most islands in Greece have untamed areas through which to hike; the mainland offers an abundance of mountainous trails to trek. Some of the more famous, popular, and time-consuming hikes include **Mount Olympus** (p. 233), **Vikos Gorge** (p. 214), the villages of **Zagorohoria** (p. 212), and the monasteries of the **Meteora** (p. 196). Some hikes take more than one day to complete; be sure that you are well-informed about places to stop and sleep along your hike.



## BY THUMB

*Let's Go* strongly urges you to consider the risks before you choose to hitch. We do not recommend hitching as a safe means of transportation, and none of the information presented here is intended to do so.

Think before you hitch: those who hitchhike entrust their life to whoever stops beside them on the road, risking theft, assault, sexual harassment, and unsafe driving. Safety-minded hitchers avoid getting in the back of a two-door car and never let go of their backpacks. If they feel threatened, they **insist on being let off,** regardless of where they are. They may also act as if they are going to open the car door or vomit on the upholstery to get a driver to stop. Experienced hitchers pick a spot outside of built-up areas, where drivers can stop, return to the road without causing an accident, and have time to inspect potential passengers as they approach; at night, experienced hitchers stand in well-lit places and expect drivers to be leery of nocturnal thumbers. Women should avoid hitching in Greece.

Greeks are not eager to pick up foreigners, and foreign cars are often filled with other travelers. Sparsely populated areas have little or no traffic—those who hitchhike risk being **stuck** on the road for hours. Hitchhikers write their destination on a sign in both **Greek and English** letters. Successful hitchers travel light and stack their belongings in a visible, compact cluster.

# SPECIFIC CONCERNS

## TRAVELING ALONE

There are many benefits to traveling alone, among them greater independence and challenge. Travelling alone in Greece can be a fantastic way to interact with locals and to see less-touristed areas than you might visit with a group of sightseeing friends. Talk to people, ask them to show you around, make a few friends, and go out. You could even write a great travelogue in the tradition of Mark Twain, Lord Byron, or Homer's *Odyssey*. On the other hand, solo travelers are more vulnerable to harassment and street theft. Lone travelers need to be well organized and look confident at all times. Follow **local customs and dress,** and be inconspicuous. **Never admit that you are traveling alone.** Maintain regular contact with someone at home who knows your itinerary.

There are basic **common sense rules** to follow when traveling alone. Remember that no one knows where you are at all times, so be careful of going anywhere with a newfound friend. Be equally wary when hitting the nightlife, as your defenses may drop as your ouzo consumption increases. Stay alert and pay attention to

your surroundings. If you feel nervous about an area or place, leave. To avoid standing out as a tourist in villages, make a *stavros* (a cross: up, down, right, left) in front of all churches as a sign of **respect** for the country's culture and customs; locals are much more likely to accept you once they realize that you respect them in return. In most Greek villages, xenophobia is directed only at rude outsiders; as soon as you show familiarity with Greek customs, people are much more friendly.



## WOMEN TRAVELERS

Women exploring on their own face additional safety concerns (and **Health Concerns,** p. 49), but you can be **adventurous** without taking undue risks. If you are uneasy about traveling alone, stay in hostels with single rooms that lock from the inside or offer rooms for women only. Check the safety of communal showers in hostels before settling in. Stick to centrally located accommodations and avoid solitary nighttime treks. When traveling, carry extra money for a phone call, bus, or taxi. **Hitching** is never safe for lone women in Greece, or even for two women traveling together. Look as if you know where you're going, even when you don't.

When Greek women travel together, it tends to be to the beach, so Greeks might be curious if they see a woman or group of women traveling in what is not resort territory. The subtext of most blunt questions is: "I can't imagine anyone I know doing what you're doing. Do you really enjoy it?" Explain that you do, and insist gently on respect. **Older Greek women** in villages, towns, and cities can help you if you get in a bind; they're sharp, wise, fearless, and your best allies if you need information, advice, or a respite from persistent amorous attempts by local men.

In **cities,** you may be harassed no matter how you act or what you look like. Your best answer to verbal harassment is no answer at all: ignore catcalls and questioning by sitting motionless, and staring straight ahead, or walking away. Wearing a conspicuous **wedding band,** mentioning a "husband" back at the hotel, or carrying pictures of a "husband" or "children" may help ward off unwanted overtures. If you do feel threatened, call attention to what is going on: yell **"vo-EE-thee-ah"** (help) and **"as-te-no-MEE-ah"** (police). Alternatively, you might carry a **whistle** on your keychain to blow in an emergency. *Let's Go: Greece* lists emergency numbers (including rape crisis lines) in the **Practical Information** listings of most cities. Memorize the emergency numbers in the places you visit. An **IMPACT Model Mugging** self-defense course prepares people for potential attacks, and raises confidence and awareness about your surroundings (see **Self Defense,** p. 47).

## BISEXUAL, GAY, & LESBIAN TRAVELERS

Though legal in Greece since 1951, homosexuality is still socially frowned upon, especially in more conservative villages. Athens and Thessaloniki offer a slew of gay bars, clubs, and hotels. The islands of **Hydra, Lesvos, Rhodes,** and **Mykonos** (arguably the most gay-friendly destination in Europe) offer gay and lesbian resorts, hotels, bars, and clubs. Gays are not legally protected from discrimination. Consult these organizations, and for more information see **Other Resources,** p. 77.

**Gay Greek Guide**, TΘ 4228, Athens 10210 (☎(01) 381 5249; English speaker M-F 7-9m). Call this hotline while in Greece for information on nightlife options.

**Go Greece Gay and Lesbian Links** at gogreece.about.com/travel/gogreece/msub47.htm connects you to internet resources about gay and lesbian travel.

**International Gay and Lesbian Travel Association,** 4331 N. Federal Hwy., Suite 304, Fort Lauderdale, FL 33308 (☎(954) 776-2626 or (800) 448-8550; fax 776-3303; email IGLTA@aol.com; www.iglta.com). Organization of over 1350 companies serving gay and lesbian travelers worldwide. Call for lists of travel agents, accommodations, and events.

**GayGreece** at http://travel.to/gayGREECE describes various towns and cities in Greece, listing bars and clubs in Athens, and offers a virtual tour of Mykonos.

**Pridenet** (www.pridenet.com/greece.html) links to other Greece-specific gay sites, and offers listings and information organized by area and island groupings.

# OLDER TRAVELERS

People in Greece have great respect for their elders, so don't expect any problems while traveling. Be aware that many sites are only reachable by strenuous hikes and the hot sun can be dangerous. Senior citizens are eligible for a wide range of discounts on transportation, museums, movies, theaters, concerts, restaurants, and accommodations. If you don't see a senior citizen price listed, ask, and you may be delightfully surprised. See **Other Resources** (p. 77) for information about organized trips in Greece with other older travelers, or consult:

**Elderhostel,** 75 Federal St., Boston, MA 02110, USA (☎(617) 426-7788 or (877) 426-2166; email registration@elderhostel.org; www.elderhostel.org). Organizes 1- to 4-week "educational adventures" in Greece on varied subjects for those 55+.

**Walking the World,** P.O. Box 1186, Fort Collins, CO 80522, USA (☎(970) 498-0500; fax 498-9100; email walktworld@aol.com; www.walkingtheworld.com), organizes hiking trips in Greece for travelers over 50.



# TRAVELERS WITH DISABILITIES

Greece and Cyprus are only slowly beginning to respond to the needs of travelers with disabilities; those with severe physical disabilities won't have it easy. Even the most renowned sights—even the Acropolis—are not wheelchair accessible. Some hotels, train stations, and airports have installed facilities for the disabled, as have some cruise ships that sail to Greek islands. Special air transportation is available aboard Olympic Airways to many of the larger islands.

Those with disabilities should inform airlines and hotels of their disabilities when making arrangements for travel; some time may be needed to prepare special accommodations. Call ahead to restaurants, hotels, parks, and other facilities to find out about ramps, door widths, elevator sizes, and such. **Guide dog owners** should inquire as to the specific quarantine policies ahead of time, and should carry proof of immunization against rabies. Greece's **rail** systems have very limited resources for wheelchair accessibility, but they are probably the best bet for disabled travelers. There are no handicapped-accessible **buses.** Some major **car rental** agencies (Hertz, Avis, and National) offer hand-controlled vehicles. The following organizations offer more information for disabled travelers (see **Other Resources,** p. 77, for useful publications):

**Mobility International USA (MIUSA),** P.O. Box 10767, Eugene, OR 97440 (☎(541) 343-1284 voice and TDD; fax 343-6812; email info@miusa.org; www.miusa.org). Sells *A World of Options: A Guide to International Educational Exchange, Community Service, and Travel for Persons with Disabilities* (US$35).

**Moss Rehab Hospital Travel Information Service** (☎(215) 456-9600 or (800) CALL-MOSS; email netstaff@mossresourcenet.org; www.mossresourcenet.org). An information resource center on travel-related concerns for those with disabilities.

# MINORITY TRAVELERS (NON-GREEKS)

Greeks stare, point, whisper, and gossip with a passion that makes pre-teens look like Miss Manners. The first thing to notice is that they're not just staring at *you*. Even the larger cities Greece retain a small-village, island worldview, where everyone and everything is gossip material. While the Greeks culture tends to hold stereotypes about every group of people imaginable, they place a great value on **individualism;** you may be asked (out of curiosity, not maliciousness) all manner of questions or referred to continually as "the (insert your nationality here)," "the (insert religion here)," or simply "the foreigner" *(xenos)*. If you deal with individual Greeks for any period of time, they'll treat you as you seem to be (honest, trustworthy, friendly). Still, Greek stereotypes remain global enough to be almost laughable. Black travelers should expect to field questions about basketball (or

sports, or whether they know Michael Jordan); Asian travelers will probably be called "Chinese" (regardless of their ethnicity or the language they speak).

Greece presents two strong and entirely different views about foreigners, and travelers should expect to encounter both. One one hand, the Greek tradition of hospitality **(philoxenia)** is unmatched in the Mediterranean. Greeks consider it almost a sacred duty to help travelers, loading them with homemade food and advice. On the other hand, it's important to remember Greece's historical position as the crossroads of empire: most European nations have at one time or another invaded, burned, betrayed, or colonized part of Greece, forging an intense "us-versus-them" Greek nationalism. If you're not obviously Greek, everyone will want to know who you are. **Minority travelers** will have more trouble blending in, and will have to deal with more stares, questions, and comments. While such curiosity may seem in-your-face and invasive by Western standards, think of its roots: 3000 years of experience have taught the Greeks to beware foreigners (who could be spies, fugitives, or gods, or at the very least good for an interesting break) even when they bear gifts. Once their curiosity is satisfied, people will realize that you are a trustworthy person after all; they'll be happy to have you in the village, and take great pleasure in showing you around.

# TRAVELERS WITH CHILDREN

Greeks and Cypriots adore children. Expect a stream of compliments, advice, candy, and substantial discounts on transportation throughout Greece or Cyprus. Many museums and archeological sites allow children under 18 in for free. Children under two generally fly for 10% of the adult airfare on international flights (this does not necessarily include a seat). International fares are usually discounted 25% for children from two to 11.

Family vacations often require that you slow your pace, and always require that you plan ahead. When deciding where to stay, call ahead to make sure the hotels and pensions allow children; plenty of hotels and domatia have large rooms for families and roll-away beds for children. If you rent a car, make sure the rental company provides a car seat for younger children. Be sure that your child carries some sort of ID in case of an emergency or in case he or she gets lost.

# DIETARY CONCERNS

Greek meals are traditionally organized as follows: bread and olive oil, followed by a lot of largely vegetable or seafood appetizers (fresh vegetables, vegetable pies, fried octopus), followed by a meat or fish dish, followed by fresh fruit. **Vegetarians** (but not vegans, as it is virtually impossible to avoid all animal products in Greek food) will have plenty of options if they don't mind occasionally making a meal of appetizers—green beans in oil *(fasolia)*, the omnipresent Greek salad *(horiatiko)*, cooked vegetables *(laderakia)*, spinach-phyllo-feta pastry *(spanakopita)*, greens *(horta)*, flat-beans *(yigandes)*, fresh bread, and wine. In smaller towns, many seemingly vegetarian entrees (like *moussaka*, lasagna with eggplant instead of noodles; or *yemista*, stuffed vegetables) can contain meat, especially in agricultural areas; **ask before you order.** There are almost no Greek vegetarians, though, so if questioned your best bet is to argue weather ("It's so hot I only want vegetables") or allergies ("I'm allergic to pork and beef and I'll get a headache and a terrible stomachache if I eat it"), as opposed to some kind of ideology: "I don't want to eat meat" will be taken with as much seriousness as "I don't want to eat my vegetables" by well-meaning local grandmothers. As far as actual **allergies** are concerned, the same rule applies: ask before you order, especially at local tavernas that simply serve you whatever is cooking in the kitchen.

Travelers who keep **kosher** should contact synagogues in larger cities for information on kosher restaurants; your own synagogue or college Hillel should have access to lists of Jewish institutions across the nation. If you are strict in your observance, you may have to prepare your own food on the road. **The Jewish Travel**

**Guide,** which lists synagogues, kosher restaurants, and Jewish institutions in over 100 countries, is available in Europe from Vallentine Mitchell Publishers, Newbury House 890-900, Eastern Ave., Newbury Park, Ilford, Essex IG2 7HH, (☎(020) 8599 8866; fax 8599 0984) and in the US ($16.95 + $4 S&H) from ISBS, 5804 NE Hassallo St., Portland, OR 97213 (☎(800) 944-6190).



# ALTERNATIVES TO TOURISM

## STUDYING ABROAD

Studying abroad is Greece is fun and easy. Several different types of programs are available: studying directly at a Greek university, studying through an international program, or going to a language school. Most of these programs are located in Greece's most highly traveled areas, especially in Athens, on Crete, and throughout the Cyclades. In addition, aspiring archeologists have a fairly unique opportunity to work on current digs while studying abroad in Greece.

Citizens of countries that can travel in Greece only on a passport need do nothing (see p. 38). For semester- or year-long study programs, you must first obtain admission into an academic or language program in Greece. Then, as long as you can prove financial support, you need to apply to your embassy for a student visa for however long you want to study (US$20).

Programs vary tremendously in expense, academic quality, living conditions, degree of contact with local students, and exposure to local culture and languages. Peterson's also publishes a popular book on studying abroad (US$30).

**The Athens Centre,** Archimidous 48, Athens 11636 (☎(01) 701 2268; fax 701 8603; email athenscr@compulink.gr; www.athenscentre.com). Offers a Modern Greek Language program. Semester and quarter programs on Greek civilization in affiliation with US universities. Offers 4- to 6-week summer Classics programs, a yearly summer theater program, and Modern Greek Language programs in summer on the island of Spetses.

**College Year in Athens,** P.O. Box 390890, Cambridge, MA 02139 (☎(01) 756 0749 from Greece, ☎(617) 868-8200 from the US; fax (617) 868-8207; email cyathens@aol.com; www.cyathens.org). Runs a semester-long or full-year program for undergraduates (usually juniors), which includes travel as well as classroom instruction (in English). The program has two tracks, one in Ancient Greek civilization and one in Mediterranean area studies. Scholarships available. Students are housed in apartments in Athens' Kolonaki district. College Year in Athens also offers summer programs, including a 3-week intensive course in modern Greek on Paros, a 6-week study-travel program, and two 3-week modules that cover different subjects every year.

**Beaver College Center for Education Abroad,** 450 S. Easton Rd., Glenside, PA 19038 (☎(888) 232-8379; www.beaver.edu/cea). Summer, semester, and year-long programs in Greece. Costs range from $1900 (summer) to $20,000 (full-year).

**School for International Training, College Semester Abroad,** Admissions, Kipling Rd., P.O. Box 676, Brattleboro, VT 05302 (☎(800) 336-1616 or (802) 258-3267; www.sit.edu). Semester- and year-long programs in Greece run US$9500-12,900.

**International Association for the Exchange of Students for Technical Experience (IAESTE),** 10400 Little Patuxent Pkwy. #250, Columbia, MD 21044, USA (☎(410) 997-3068; www.aipt.org). Operates 8- to 12-week programs in Greece for college students who have completed 2 years of technical study. US$50 application fee.

**www.studyabroad.com,** 1450 Edgemont Ave., Chester, PA 19013 (☎(610) 499-9200; fax (610) 499-9205; email webmaster@studyabroad.com). Information and links to every type of study abroad program imaginable in Greece.

**Languages Abroad,** Box 502, 99 Avenue Road, Toronto, ON M5R 2G5 (☎(800) 219-9924; www.languagesabroad.com). Runs programs from 1 to 36 weeks long in Athens. Cost varies with length, but 3 week programs start at US$1800.

**Language Immersion Institute,** 75 South Manheim Blvd., The College at New Paltz, New Paltz, NY 12561 (☎(914) 257-3500; www.newpaltz.edu/lii). Two-week summer language courses in New Paltz or New York City and some overseas courses in Greek. Program fees are about US$295 for a weekend or US$750 per 2 weeks.

# WORKING AND VOLUNTEERING



**WORKING.** For citizens of Greece and of **EU** countries, getting a job in Greece is relatively simple. For all others, finding work in Greece can be difficult. Job opportunities are scarce and the government tries to restrict employment to citizens and visitors from the EU. If your parents were born in an EU country, you may be able to claim dual citizenship or at least the right to a work permit. Those who can teach English find a host of job openings in Greece, and in some sectors (like agricultural work) permitless workers are rarely bothered by authorities. Students can check with their universities' foreign language departments, which may have connections to job openings abroad. Friends in Greece can expedite work permits or arrange work-for-accommodations swaps. (For info on work permits, see p. 39.)

Arrive in the spring and early summer to search for **hotel jobs** (bartending, cleaning, etc.). Most night spots offer meager pay but don't require much paperwork. Check the bulletin boards of hostels in Athens and the classified ads in the *Athens News*. Check out **Other Resources** (p. 77) for more information.

**International Schools Services,** Educational Staffing Program, P.O. Box 5910, Princeton, NJ 08543 (☎(609) 452-0990; fax 452-2690; email edustaffing@iss.edu; www.iss.edu). Recruits teachers and administrators for American and English schools in Greece. All instruction in English. Applicants must have a bachelor's degree and two years of relevant experience. Nonrefundable US$150 application fee.

**Office of Overseas Schools,** US Department of State, Room H328, SA-1, Washington, D.C. 20522 (☎(202) 261-8200; fax 261-8224; email OverseasSchools@state.gov; www.state.gov/www/about_state/schools/). Keeps a comprehensive list of schools abroad and agencies that arrange placement for Americans to teach abroad.

**American Farm School** runs a summer work and recreation program for high schoolers (grades 10 and up; US$500 donation). Write to: 1133 Broadway, New York, NY 10010 (☎(212) 463-8434; fax 463-8208; email nyoffice@amerfarm.org; www.afs.edu.gr); or P.O. Box 23, GR-55102, Thessaloniki, Greece (☎(31) 49 27 00; fax 49 27 10).

**ARCHAEOLOGICAL DIGS. Archaeological Institute of America,** 656 Beacon St., Boston, MA 02215-2006 (☎(617) 353-9361; fax 353-6550; email aia@bu.edu; www.archaeological.org), puts out the *Archaeological Fieldwork Opportunities Bulletin* (US$16 for non-members), which lists field sites in Greece. This can be purchased from Kendall/Hunt Publishing, 4050 Westmark Dr., Dubuque, Iowa 52002 (☎(800) 228-0810). **The American School of Classical Studies at Athens,** 54 Souidias, Athens 10676 (☎(01) 72 36 313; fax 72 50 584; email info@ascsa.edu.gr; www.ascsa.org), is a highly competitive school offering a variety of archaeological and classical studies programs for undergraduates, graduate students, and Ph.D. candidates. Visit the website to find a list of publications and links to other archaeological programs.

**VOLUNTEER.** Volunteer jobs are readily available almost everywhere. You may receive room and board in exchange for your labor. You can sometimes avoid high application fees charged by organizations that arrange placement by contacting the individual workcamps directly; check with the organizations (see **Other Resources,** p. 77).

**Service Civil International Voluntary Service (SCI-IVS),** 814 NE 40th St., Seattle, WA 98105 (☎/fax (206) 545-6585; www.sci-ivs.org). Arranges placement in workcamps in Greece for those 18+. Registration fee US$65-150.

**Volunteers for Peace,** 1034 Tiffany Rd., Belmont, VT 05730 (☎(802) 259-2759; www.vfp.org). A nonprofit organization that arranges speedy placement in 2-3 week workcamps in Greece comprising 10-15 people. Most complete and up-to-date listings provided in the annual *International Workcamp Directory* (US$20). Registration fee US$200. Free newsletter.

# OTHER RESOURCES

*Let's Go* tries to cover all aspects of budget travel, but we can't put *everything* in our guides. Listed below are books and websites that can serve as jumping off points for your own research.

# USEFUL PUBLICATIONS

### FINDING CHEAP AIRFARE

*The Worldwide Guide to Cheap Airfare,* by Michael McColl. (Insider Publications, US$15).

*Discount Airfares: The Insider's Guide, by* George Hobart. (Priceless Publications, US$14).

*The Official Airline Guide,* an expensive tome available at many libraries, has flight schedules, fares, and reservation numbers.

### CAMPING AND THE OUTDOORS

*How to Stay Alive in the Woods,* by Bradford Angier (Macmillan, US$8).

*Soft Paths,* by Bruce Hampton and David Cole (Stackpole Books, US$15).

*Camping Your Way through Europe,* by Carol Mickelsen (Affordable Press, US$15).

*Exploring Europe by RV,* by Dennis and Tina Jaffe (Globe Pequot, US$15).

### BISEXUAL, GAY, AND LESBIAN TRAVELERS

*Spartacus International Gay Guide,* by Bruno Gmunder Verlag (US$33).

*Damron's Accommodations,* and *The Women's Traveller* (Damron Travel Guides, US$14-19).

*Ferrari Guides' Gay Travel A to Z, Ferrari Guides' Men's Travel in Your Pocket, and Ferrari Guides' Women's Travel in Your Pocket* (Ferrari Guides, US$14-16).

### OLDER TRAVELERS

*No Problem! Worldwise Tips for Mature Adventurers,* by Janice Kenyon (Orca Book Pub., US$16).

*A Senior's Guide to Healthy Travel,* by Donald L. Sullivan (Career Press, US$15).

*Unbelievably Good Deals and Great Adventures That You Absolutely Can't Get Unless You're Over 50,* by Joan Rattner Heilman (Contemporary Books, US$13).

### WORKING AND VOLUNTEERING

*International Jobs: Where they Are, How to Get Them,* by Eric Kocher and Nina Segal (Perseus Books, US$17).

*Directory of Jobs and Careers Abroad* (Peterson's, US$17-18 each).

*International Directory of Voluntary Work,* by Louise Whetter (Vacation Work Publications, US$16).

# THE WORLD WIDE WEB

Almost every aspect of budget travel is accessible via the **web.** Even if you don't have internet access at home, seeking it out at a public library or at work would be well worth it; within 10 minutes at the keyboard, you can make a reservation at a hostel in Greece, get advice on travel hotspots or experiences from other travelers who have just returned from the Cyclades, or find out exactly how much a ferry from Kephalonia to Corfu costs.

## GENERAL TRAVEL SITES

**Let's Go:** www.letsgo.com. Our newly revamped website features photos and streaming video, info about our books, a travel forum buzzing with stories and tips, and links that will help you find everything you could ever want to know about Greece.

**How to See the World:** www.artoftravel.com. A compendium of great travel tips, from cheap flights to self defense to interacting with local culture.

**Air Traveler's Handbook:** www.cs.cmu.edu/afs/cs/user/mkant/Public/Travel/airfare.html. Help finding cheap airfare.

ESSENTIALS

**Rec. Travel Library:** www.travel-library.com. A fantastic set of links for general information and personal travelogues.

**Shoestring Travel:** www.stratpub.com. An e-zine focusing on budget travel.

**Foreign Language for Travelers:** www.travlang.com will help you brush up on your Greek.

**Great Outdoor Recreation Pages:** www.gorp.com can provide hiking information.

**Internet Guide to Hostelling:** www.hostels.com provides a directory of hostels around the world and oodles of information about hosteling and backpacking worldwide.

**Eurotrip:** www.eurotrip.com. This site has information and reviews on budget hostels, as well as info on traveling alone.



## GREECE-SPECIFIC SITES

**The Internet Guide to Greece:** www.gogreece.com features maps, references, discussions, and extensive listings of Greek businesses, schools, news sources, and sports.

**Phantis:** www.phantis.com. A Greek-specific search engine that accommodates region-specific queries, and contains links to Greek city sites.

**Hellenic Federation of Mountaineering and Climbing:** www.climbing.org.gr. Learn about great hikes in Greece.

**The Perseus Project:** www.perseus.tufts.edu. "An evolving digital library," provides a library of classical Greek texts, translations, and an online dictionary.

**United Hellas:** www.united-hellas.com. A would-be database of all things Greek, from small businesses and folk art sources to places to buy a boat.

**The Greek Orthodox Archdiocese of New York:** www.goarch.org lists information about the religion of most Greeks.

**Greek Travel:** www.greektravel.com. Talky, marbled pages based on one man's enjoyable and rather earnest scoping of the country.

**Greek Ferries:** www.ferries.gr and www.greekislands.gr claim to maintain a complete and updated list of ferry schedules over all the Greek islands.

**The Ministry of Culture:** www.culture.gr. Events, history, "cultural maps of Greece," and other fun stuff.

**The Greek Government online:** www.government.gr. In Greek with sections in English.

**Cyprus homepage:** kypros.org/Government. Links to most Cypriot government agencies and to the Cyprus virtual tour guide.

**Greek poetry:** www.webexpert.net/vasilios/gpoetry.htm. An extensive compilation of links to Greek poetry resources, modern and ancient.

**The CIA World Factbook:** www.odci.gov/cia/publications/factbook/index.html has tons of statistics on Greece, including an overview of Greek economy and an explanation of its system of government.

**G.S.T. (GREEK STANDARD TIME)** Greeks are known the world over for their slow-paced and contemplative enjoyment of life. "Be flexible! Relax! Have fun!" This *philosophia,* unfortunately, doesn't make it particularly easy for travelers accustomed to reliable timetables. Restaurant menus and hours rotate, depending on whim. Train, bus, and ferry schedules are notoriously fickle, and owners of establishments may close up shop at any given moment to pay their respects to the sun god Helios—at the beach. Summer dance clubs return to their city locations in the winter, but will often swap beach locations from year to year. Prices for everything from food to accommodations to that garish head scarf you'll buy for Aunt Barbara are subject to change, depending on various circumstances (season, availability, whether or not you said *"yassou"* [see p. 556]). When a proprietor tells you your food will be here "in a minute," be warned that something might get lost in translation.

# ATHENS ΑΘΗΝΑ

Athens, the eye of Greece, mother of arts
And eloquence.
—John Milton

One minute of dodging the packs of mopeds in Pl. Syndagma convinces you that Athens refuses to become a museum. Athens's historical skeletons aren't bottled in the closet, though: they jut up through the modern city in glowing white marble. The Acropolis looms larger than life over the city at its feet, a perpetual reminder of ancient glory. Byzantine churches recall an era of foreign invaders, when Athens was ruled from Macedonia, Rome, and Byzantium. The reborn democracy of the past two centuries has revived the city in a wave of madcap construction: the conflicted, oddly adolescent metropolis gutted its crumbling medieval mansions to become a dense concrete jungle.

Countless vantage points from Athens's seven hills look out over this sprawling work of centuries: Lycavittos, the Acropolis, Pnyx, Strefi, Phillippapou, Hymettus, and the Hill of the Nymphs. Crowded, noisy, polluted, and totally alive, Athens will get you stuck in traffic at 2am on a Tuesday. A new subway system is in the works to connect the city in the next century; it should be completed for the 2004 Olympic Summer Games. Still, civil engineers refuse to "destroy everything in the name of the underground," picking their way among subterranean antiquities, cisterns, and the springs of lost, ancient rivers that sleep beneath the city.



**HIGHLIGHTS OF ATHENS**

**STROLL PAST CHIC OUTDOOR CAFES** in Kolonaki (p. 85) and ascend Mt. Lycavittos (p. 103) to watch the sun set over the Acropolis, with all Athens stretched out below.

**SURVEY ANCIENT RELICS** at the National Archaeological Museum (p. 104), then chill with a *frappé* among the Exharia's internationals (p. 96).

**THREAD THROUGH THE MEDIEVAL ALLEYWAYS** of Plaka (p. 85).

**MAKE A PILGRIMAGE** to Athena's Parthenon on the Acropolis (p. 100).

**HAGGLE** with wily merchants at Monastiraki's flea market (p. 85), then dine in style at an open-air table in the charming streets of Psiri.

**SALUTE** skirted, tasseled *evzones* who guard the Parliament in Pl. Syndagma (p. 84).

**STARE OUT INTO THE BLUE** of the Aegean from Cape Sounion, where the marble Temple of Poseidon still worships the sea below it (p. 108).

## HISTORY

Athens's recorded history began when the Olympian gods got in a tug-of-war over who would be the Attic city's patron and namesake. They decided that whoever gave it the best gift would earn the city. Poseidon struck the Acropolis with his trident, and a sea gushed forth from a well. But **Athena**'s wiser gift, an olive tree, won her the right to rule. Rising to political power as early as the 16th century BC, Athens was united as a *polis*, or city-state, by the hero **Theseus** (onetime slayer of the Minotaur). By the 8th century, it became the artistic center of Greece; an initial fame for geometric pottery foreshadowed a shining future. Two centuries later, law-giver and poet **Solon** ended the enslavement of native citizens, restoring rights to some slaves. After dramatic victories over the Persians at Marathon and Salamis in the 5th century BC, Athens experienced a 70-year **Golden Age** under the democracy of Pericles, the era that produced the Parthenon; masterpiece tragedies of Aeschylus, Sophocles, and Euripides; and Aristophanes' ribald comedies.

Pericles' Athens fell apart during the bloody, drawn-out **Peloponnesian War** (431-404 BC) against Sparta. Political power shifted north under Philip of Macedon and his son **Alexander the Great;** Athens remained a cultural center throughout the 5th and 4th centuries BC. In this period, Athens produced three of the most influential philosophers in western history—**Socrates** (p. 12), **Plato** (p. 13), and **Aristotle** (p. 21)—as well as the orator Demosthenes. By the 2nd century AD, the Roman Empire gobbled up the city, and in AD 324, Constantine passed over Athens and moved the capital of the Roman Empire to Byzantium, leaving the former city-state as an overtaxed backwater. It remained the center of Greek education, but its status (and buildings) lapsed into ruin when the emperor Justinian banned the teaching of philosophy in 529.

Around 1000, Byzantine emperor **Basil II** visited Athens. After praying to the Virgin Mary in the Parthenon, Basil ordered craftsmen to restore Athens to its former glory. The city was reborn again and again under successive conquering crusaders—the Franks in 1205, the Catalans in 1311, the Accajioli merchant family in 1387, and the **Ottomans,** whose 400-year rule began in 1456. In 1821, Greek independence (see p. 16) brought further waves of renovation and restoration and a new spirit of nationalism. Modern Athens's plateias, wide boulevards, and National Garden follow the plan of architects hired by the new German-born monarch King Otho.



In the 20th century, Athens's population and industry have skyrocketed. A 1923 **population exchange** with Turkey (see p. 17) brought an influx of ethnic Greeks from Turkish land, swelling the city; since then, rural workers have flocked to industrial jobs here. In the past 100 years, the city's population has exploded from an official count of 169 families to almost half of Greece's residents. The approaching 2004 Olympic Games have sparked another urban renewal, as the transit authority fights the sinister *nephos* (smog cloud) overhead by banning cars from historic Plaka, limiting driver access downtown to alternate days, and building a new mass-transit subway.

## GETTING THERE AND AWAY

**Flights:** To get from the airport to Athens, look to your left after exiting customs for the blue and yellow express **bus #091** (250dr before 11pm, 500dr after). A **taxi** costs 2500-3000dr (3500-4000dr after midnight), with an extra 50dr charge for each piece of luggage over 10kg, and a 300dr surcharge from the airport. Watch drivers very carefully; some have been known to rig the meters. Drivers may be unwilling to pick up travelers laden with luggage and might also make you share a taxi. Express buses and taxis are the most reliable travel option. To get to the airport, take the express **bus #091** from either Pl. Syndagma or Pl. Stadiou near Pl. Omonia (40min., every 20min. 7:10am-9:00pm, 12 per night 9:50pm-6:45am). **East Air Terminal** is for international and charter flights by international carriers; **West Air Terminal** is only for domestic and international Olympic Airways flights (☎936 3363; dial 144 for a timetable recording). The **New Charter Terminal** is only for charter flights. There's a branch of the national **tourist office** (☎961 2722; fax 964 1627) also in the East Terminal, on the left after exiting baggage claim. Open M-F 9am-9pm, Sa-Su 10am-9pm.

**Buses:** Unlike much else in Greece, **KTEL** (ΚΤΕΛ) buses are punctual, so be on time. For longer trips, take the orange or green long-distance buses. The OSE runs international buses to: **Sofia, Bulgaria; Tirana, Albania;** and **Istanbul, Turkey** (see **Trains** above for info).

**Terminal A:** Kifissou 100 (☎512 4910). Take blue **bus #051** there; catch it at the corner of Zinonos and Menandrou near Pl. Omonia (every 15min. 5am-11:30pm, 120dr). The "information" booth at Terminal A is a privately run agency; don't buy their useless "vouchers." Buses depart for: **Corinth** (1½hr., 1 per hr. 6am-10:30pm, 1750dr); **Thessaloniki** (7½hr., 6 per day 8am-6pm, 8700dr) via **Larissa; Corfu** (10hr., 4 per day 7:30am-8:30pm, 8150dr); **Igoumenitsa** (8½hr., 4 per day 6:30am-9pm, 8850dr); and **Patras** (3hr., 20 per day 6am-9:45pm, 3650dr).

**Terminal B:** Liossion 260 (☎831 7153, except Sa-Su). Take blue **bus #024** there; catch it on Amalias street outside the National Gardens on Panepistimiou, and allow 45min. for the trip (every 20min. 5am-11pm, 120dr). Watch the numbers labeled on street signs–Liossion 260 is near

several car mechanic shops. Buses depart for: **Katerini** (6hr., 3 per day 9:45am-10pm, 7250dr); **Delphi** (3hr., 6 per day 7:30am-8pm, 2900dr); and **Halkida** on **Evia** (1¼hr.; every 30min. 5:30am-9pm, with extra buses Su; 1350dr).

**Mavromateon 29:** in Exarhia, between the National Archaeological Museum and Areos Park in Exarhia; take **trolley #18, 11, 5, 2,** or **9.** Buses to: **Sounion** (2hr., every hr. 6:30am-6:30pm, 1300dr; or 2¼hr., every hr. 6am-6pm, 1200dr); **Marathon** (1½hr., every hr. 5:30am-10:30pm, 700dr); and **Rafina** (1hr., every 30min. 5:40am-10:30pm, 460dr).

**Pl. Eleftherias:** from Pl. Syndagma, go west on Ermou, turn right on Athinas, and turn left on Evripidou. Buses to **Eleusis** and **Daphni.**

**Ferries:** Check schedules at the tourist office, in the *Athens News,* with the Port Authority of Piraeus (☎422 6000), or at any travel agency. Ferry schedules change daily; check as close to your departure as possible, and be flexible. Most ferries dock at **Piraeus** (p. 109); some arrive at nearby **Rafina** (p. 109). Those headed for the Sporades leave from **Ag. Konstantinos** (p. 182) or **Volos** (p. 183). Those headed for the Ionian Islands leave from **Patras** (p. 131).

**Piraeus:** Take the subway south to its end, or take green **bus #40** from Filellinon and Mitropoleos (every 10min.). To: **Iraklion,** Crete (10hr.; 7:30am, 8pm; 6400dr); **Hania,** Crete (10hr., 8:30pm, 5400dr); and **Rethymno,** Crete (10hr., 7:30pm, 6500dr). Also to: **Aegina, Poros, Spetses,** and **Hydra** (1-4hr., 2 per day, 1900-3100dr); **Chios** and **Lesvos** (9-11hr., 1 per day, 5400dr); **Ios** (7½hr., 5090dr); **Mykonos** (6hr., 2 per day, 4800dr); **Naxos** and **Paros** (6hr., 3 per day, 4800dr); **Rhodes** (16hr.; 2pm, 4pm; 8600dr); **Santorini** (9hr., 5630dr); and **Sifnos, Kythnos, Serifos,** and **Milos** (3-5½hr., 1 per day, 3900-4800dr). International ferries run to **Limassol, Cyprus;** and **Haifa, Israel.**

**Rafina:** Take the subway south to the last stop, or take green **bus #40** from Filellinon and Mitropoleos (every 10min.). **Karystos** in Evia (1¾hr., 2 per day, 1770dr); **Marmari** in Evia (1¼hr., 4-6 per day, 1240dr); **Andros** (2hr., 4 per day 7:20am-7pm, 2500dr); **Tinos** (4hr., 3 per day 7:20am-5:30pm, 3600dr); **Mykonos** (4¾hr., 3 per day 7:20am-5:30pm, 4000dr); **Paros** (5hr., 1 on Th, 4100dr); and **Naxos** (6hr., 2 per day, 4200dr). **Hydrofoils** sail to: **Andros** (1hr., 2 per week, 4700dr); **Tinos** (1½hr., 2 per day, 7200dr); **Amorgos** (10hr., 2 per week, 9500dr); and **Mykonos** (2½hr., 2 per day, 8200dr). **Nel Lines** goes to **Ag. Efstratios, Limnos,** and **Kavala** (3 per week), and **Lesvos** (1 per week).

**Lavrio:** take a taxi from Syndagma, or the orange bus (950dr) that leaves from Mavromateon near Areos Park. Ferries to: **Kea** or **Kithnos** (1650-2300dr).

**Flying Dolphins:** Hydrofoils serve the mainland and Saronic Gulf Islands, the Sporades, and the Cyclades; try **Minoan Flying Dolphins** (☎428 0001). Open M-Sa 8am-6:30pm, Su and holidays 8am-1pm. The hydrofoils, roughly twice as expensive and twice as fast as ferries, leave from **Zea Port** near Piraeus; Ag. Konstantinos; and Volos.

**Trains:** Call 145 or 147 for timetables; schedules are subject to change. Contact the railway offices to confirm schedules before your trip.

**Larissis Train Station** (☎529 8837) serves northern Greece and Europe. Open 24hr. Take **trolley #1** from Panepistimiou in Syndagma (every 10min. 5am-midnight, 120dr). Trains depart for: **Thessaloniki** (7¼hr., 10 per day, 4100-5850dr); **Sofia, Bulgaria** (16,000dr); **Istanbul, Turkey** (15hr., 20,000dr, must change trains at border); **Bratislava, Slovakia** (30,000dr); **Prague, Czech Republic** (35,000dr); **Bucharest, Romania** and **Budapest, Hungary** (40,000dr). To get to Sofia, Istanbul, Bratislava, Prague, Bucharest, and Budapest, take the train from Larissis Station to **Salonica** and change there; an 8300dr surcharge is included in prices listed above.

**Peloponnese Train Station** (☎513 1601) is in a Victorian building with a silver roof. Open 24hr. From Larissis, exit to your right and go over the footbridge; from Panepistimiou in Syndagma, take blue **bus #057** (every 15min. 5:30am-11:30pm, 120dr). Serves **Patras** (1580dr) and major towns in the Peloponnese. For more info and a booklet, try the office of **Hellenic Railways (OSE),** Sina 6 (☎362 4402 or 362 4406; www.ose.gr).

**Luggage Storage:** At the **East Terminal** of the airport, exit the baggage claim and customs and look for the yellow "LOCKERS" sign, 150m outside on your right. At the **West Terminal,** exit the baggage claim building and look for the "LOCKERS" sign on the right by a pharmacy. Keep your ticket stub to reclaim; pay when you collect. 1000dr per piece per day (until midnight); 1500dr for bicycles, surfboards, or extra-large boxes. Open 24hr. Also several offices on Nikis and Filellinon, including **Pacific Ltd.,** Nikis 26 (☎324 1007). 500dr per day, 1500dr per week, 3000dr per month. Open M-Sa 8am-8pm, Su 8am-2pm. Many **hotels** and **hostels** have free or inexpensive luggage storage.

# GETTING AROUND

**Buses:** KTEL (ΚΤΕΛ) buses are punctual, so be on time. Buses around Athens and its suburbs are blue and designated by 3-digit numbers. These buses are good for travel throughout the city, and ideal for daytrips to Daphni and Kesariani. Buy blue bus/trolley **tickets** (good for both) at any street **kiosk** and stamp it yourself at the orange machine on board (120dr). Kiosks only sell tickets for Athens and its suburbs; buy several tickets at once if you plan to use buses and trolleys frequently while in Athens. **Hold on to your ticket:** if you drop or don't stamp your bus, trolley, or subway ticket–even when it seems like nobody is there to make you pay–you can be fined (eek!) 1500dr by police. The map of Athens from the tourist office has the most frequented **routes** labeled on it.

**Trolleys:** Yellow, crowded, and sporting 1- or 2-digit numbers, trolleys are distinguished from buses by their electrical antennae. Trolleys don't accept money; buy a trolley/bus **ticket** ahead of time at a **kiosk** (120dr). Service is frequent and convenient for short hops within town. See the detailed tourist office map for trolley **routes** and stops.



**Subway:** The Athens **Metro** is under construction, creating branches from the current single line from Piraeus to Kifissia in northern Athens. There are 20 stops on this line, including Omonia and Monastiraki. Trains depart from either end of the line every 5min. 5am-midnight. Buy **tickets** (120dr) at booths or at automatic machines in the station (which give no change), and remember to **hold on to your ticket.**

**TAXI SMART** Beware! Some drivers tinker with their meters, while others may not turn on the meter at all, taking you somewhere and then charging an exorbitant fee. Ask the cost of the fare in advance, and if you don't see the meter running, yell "Meter! Meter!" In addition, if you ask for a hotel, the taxi driver may have another one in mind for you–a hotel that has paid him off. Be firm about where you're going; don't trust a driver who says your hotel is closed or there are no hostels in town.

**Taxis:** Meter **rates** start at 250dr, with an additional 66dr per km within city limits, 130dr per km in the suburbs, 33dr per stationary min. Rates double between midnight and 5am. There's a 300dr surcharge for trips from the airport and a 150dr surcharge for trips from ports and bus and railway terminals; plus 50dr extra for each piece of luggage. Pay what the meter shows rounded up to the next 50dr as a **tip.** Hail your taxi by shouting your destination–not the street address, but the area (e.g. "Kolonaki"). The driver will pick you up if he feels like heading that way. Get in the cab and tell the driver the exact address or site. Most drivers don't speak English, so write your destination down, in Greek if possible; include the area of the city, since streets in different parts of the city can share the same name. Empty taxis are rare; it's common to ride with other passengers going in the same direction. For an extra 400dr, call a radio taxi: **Ikaros** (☎515 2800); **Ermis** (☎411 5200); **Kosmos** (☎801 1300). You can get a full list of radio taxis in the *Athens News* or at the tourist office.

**Car Rental:** Try the many places on **Singrou.** All charge 10,000-15,000dr for a small car with 100km mileage included (prices include tax and insurance). Some have student discounts up to 50%. Prices rise in summer. International Driver's License not needed.

# PRACTICAL INFORMATION

## TOURIST AND FINANCIAL SERVICES

**Tourist Office:** The **central office** and **information booth** are at Amerikis 2 (☎331 0561 or 331 0562; fax 325 2815; www.areianet.gr/infoxenios/GNTO), off Stadiou near Pl. Syndagma. Offers: bus, train, and ferry schedules and prices; lists of museums, embassies, and banks; brochures on travel throughout Greece; and an indispensable **map** of Athens. There's also an office in the airport **East Terminal** (☎961 2722; fax 964 1627), on the left after exiting baggage claim. Open M-F 9am-9pm, Sa-Su 10am-9pm.

**Tourist Agencies:** You can buy ISIC (2800dr) and FIYTO (3000dr) ID cards (see p. 39) at **USIT Youth Student Travel,** Filellinon 3 (☎324 1884; fax 323 8447). Open M-F 9am-5pm, Sa 10am-2pm. **International Student and Youth Travel Service Limited,** Nikis 11 (☎322 1267; fax 322 1531), sells ID cards and has student rates on ferries, trains, and planes to the rest of Europe. Open M-F 9am-5pm, Sa 9am-1pm. **Consolas Travel,** Aiolou 100 (☎325 4931; fax 321 0907), is next to the post office, with a second office at Filellinon 18 (☎323 2812). Budget travel agencies are along Nikis.

**Banks: National Bank of Greece,** Karageorgi Servias 2 (☎334 0015), in Pl. Syndagma. Open M-Th 8am-2pm, F 8am-1:30pm; open for currency exchange only M-Th 3:30-6:30pm, F 3-6:30pm, Sa 9am-3pm, Su 9am-1pm. American Express, the post office, some hotels, and other banks (list available at tourist office) offer **currency exchange.** Expect commissions of about 5%. Currency exchange available 24hr. at the airport, but exchange rates and commissions may be exorbitantly high.

**American Express:** Ermou 2, P.O. Box 3325 (☎324 4975 or 324 4979), above McDonald's in Pl. Syndagma. This A/C-endowed office cashes traveler's checks commission-free, holds mail for a month, and provides travel services for cardholders. Open M-F 8:30am-4pm, Sa 8:30am-1:30pm (only travel and mail services Sa).



## LOCAL SERVICES

**International Bookstores: Eleftheroudakis Book Store,** Panepistimiou 17 (☎331 4180) and Nikis 4 (☎322 9388). A browser's delight, with Greek, English, French, and German books, classical and recent literature. Open M, W 9am-4pm; Tu, Th-F 9am-8:30pm; Sa 9am-3pm. **Pantelides Books,** Amerikis 11 (☎362 3673), overflows with variety, mostly in English, including a wide philosophy/critical theory selection. Open M and Sa 9am-4pm, Tu-F 9am-8:30pm. **Compendium Bookshop,** Nikis 28 (☎322 1248), has popular new and used books and large fiction and poetry sections, with monthly poetry readings and a **children's book room**—part store, part library. Open M-F 8:30am-4:30pm, Tu and Th-F 4:30pm-8:30pm, Sa 9am-3pm.

**Libraries:** The **American Library,** Massalias 22 (☎363 8114), on the 4th floor of the Hellenic American Union behind the university. Open M and Th 3-7pm, Tu-W and F 11am-3pm. The 7th floor of the Union has a **Greek Library,** with English books on Greece. Open M-Th 9am-8pm, F 9am-5pm. The **British Council Library,** Pl. Filikis Eterias (☎363 3215) is open M-F 9:30am-1:30pm; closed in Aug.

**Laundromats:** Most *plinitirios* have signs reading "Laundry." A kind Greek grandmother will wash, dry, and fold your laundry for 2000dr at **Angelou Geront 10** in Plaka. Open M-Sa 8am-8pm, Su 9am-2pm. Launder one load for 2700dr near the train stations, at **Psaron 9** (☎522 2856; open M-F 8am-9pm, Sa 8am-5pm, Su 8am-2pm) or get the same for 2300dr at **Kolokinthous 41 and Leonidou** (☎522 6233). Open M-F 9am-9pm, Su 9am-3pm. Giorgos at **Xenokratous 48,** in Kolonaki, charges 2500dr per load.

## EMERGENCY AND COMMUNICATIONS

**Emergencies: Police** (☎100). **Doctors** (☎105) from Athens, 101 elsewhere; line open 2pm-7am. **Ambulance** (☎166). **Poison control** (☎779 3777). **AIDS Help Line** (☎722 2222). *Athens News* lists emergency hospitals. Free emergency health care for tourists.

**Tourist Police:** Dimitrakopoulou 77 (☎171). Great for information, assistance, and emergencies. English spoken. Open 24hr.

**Pharmacies:** Identified by a **red** or **green cross** hanging over the street. They're absolutely everywhere. One is always open 24hr.; check *Athens News* "Useful Information," which lists the day's emergency pharmacies, or look at the chart in pharmacy windows.

**Hospitals: Geniko Kratiko Nosokomio** (Public State Hospital), Mesogion 154 (☎777 8901). **Hegia,** Erithrou Stavrou 4 (☎682 7904), is a private hospital in Maroussi. **Aeginitio** state hospital, Vas. Sofias 72 (☎722 0811 or 722 0812) and Vas. Sofias 80 (☎777 0501), is closer to Athens's center. Near Kolonaki is a **public hospital,** Evangelismou 45-47 (☎722 0101). "Hospital" is *nosokomio* in Greek; call an operator at 131.

**Post Offices:** In **Omonia,** Aiolou 100 (☎321 6023); **postal code:** 10200. In **Syndagma** (☎322 6253), on the corner of Mitropoleos; **postal code:** 10300. In **Exarhia,** at the

corner of Zaimi and K. Deligiani; **postal code:** 10691. Open M-F 7:30am-8pm, Sa 7:30am-2pm, Su 9am-1pm. An **Acropolis** branch sells stamps and exchanges currency; **postal code:** 11702. Open M-F 8am-5:30pm, Sa 7:30am-2pm, Su 9am-2pm.

**Shipping:** To send packages abroad, try parcel post, **Koumoundourou 29** (☎524 9359; open M-F 7:30am-8pm) and **Stadiou 4** (☎322 8940; open M-F 7:30am-2pm). **D. Alatzoglou Parcel Post and Gift Shop,** on the first floor of the American Express Building, provides shipping and packing services; 19,500dr to the US (up to 7lb.).

**Internet Access:** Internet cafes are listed individually with bars and cafes.

**Telephones: OTE,** Patission 85 (☎821 4449 or 823 7040) or Athinas 50 (☎321 6699). Offers overseas collect calls, recent phonebooks for most European and Anglophone countries, and currency exchange (until 3pm). Open M-F 7am-9pm, Sa 8am-3pm, Su 9am-2pm. For information on **overseas calls** dial 161; for **directory assistance** in and outside Athens, dial 132. Most phone booths in the city operate by **telephone cards** (1000dr, 7000dr, or 11,500dr at OTE offices, kiosks, and tourist shops). Push the "i" button on the phones for English instructions. For rate and general info call 134; for complaints, call 135; for a domestic operator speaking English, call 151.

**PHONE CODES** The phone code for all of Athens is **01.**

# ORIENTATION

Athenian geography mystifies newcomers and natives alike. When you're trying to figure out the city, don't neglect the detailed **free maps** from the tourist office (p. 82): city map includes bus, trolley, and subway routes, and the *Greece-Athens-Attica* magazine has a more exacting street plan. If you lose your bearings, ask for directions back to well-lit **Syndagma** or look for a cab; if you get lost, the **Acropolis** provides a reference point, as does **Mt. Lycavittos.** Athenian streets often have **multiple spellings or names,** so check the map again before you panic about being lost.

Several English-language **publications** can help you navigate Athens. The free tourist office publication *This Week in Athens* gives addresses, hours, and phone numbers for weekly happenings. Listings, news, and ferry information appears in the daily **Athens News** (300dr). *Athenorama* lists entertainment information.

Covering southwest Attica, near the coast, Athens and its suburbs occupy seven hills. **Syndagma,** the central plateia containing the Parliament building, is encircled by the other major neighborhoods. Clockwise, they are **Plaka, Monastiraki, Omonia, Exarhia, Kolonaki,** and **Pangrati.** To get around, you can walk or take a trolley or the expanding subway line (subway maps are available at the tourist office). A ½hr. car, bus, or taxi ride south takes you to the seaside suburb of **Glyfada,** where Bacchantes head to party.

**SYNDAGMA.** Pl. Syndagma (Συνταγμα; Constitution Square) stands at the center of Athens. The **Greek Parliament** occupies a pale yellow Neoclassical building on the edge of the **National Gardens,** once the royal gardens of Kings Otho and Amalia. The **Greek** National Tourist Office (EOT), post office, American Express office, transportation terminals, and a number of travel agencies and banks ring the plateia; airport buses also stop here. Within Pl. Syndagma itself, overpriced outdoor cafes, luxury hotels, and car and moped traffic mingle perilously with spaced-out pedestrians. Budget-friendly travel offices, restaurants, and hotels line **Filellinon** and **Nikis,** parallel thoroughfares that head out from Syndagma toward Plaka; **Ermou** and **Metropoleos,** which head toward Monastiraki, are similarly cheapskate-friendly. These streets are just removed enough to provide some nocturnal quiet and safety. The plateia itself buzzes around the clock: people-watchers can spy on lounging kids and mangy dogs, tourists and executives hailing cabs, blank-eyed drug addicts and street musicians sitting on sidewalks, and brightly clad panhandlers begging for coins.

**PLAKA.** Southwest of Syndagma, Plaka (Πλακα) is the center of the old city, and the temporary home of most visitors to Athens. Busy and relatively safe at night, Plaka undergoes a daily transformation; a vendor-vacuum by morning, it becomes the perfect place to linger over a coffee while observing the warm hum of Athenian life by night. Bounded by the city's two largest ancient monuments—the **Temple of Olympian Zeus** (p. 102) and the **Acropolis** (p. 97)—the neighborhood also contains the only medieval buildings to survive the double-edged shovel of archaeologists and the frantic building of the past few decades. Many of the city's cheap hotels and tourist eateries are here, as are legions of *kamakia* ("octopus spearers," or sleazy pick-up artists) who catcall at passing women. Just keep walking; harassment is usually only verbal.

**MONASTIRAKI.** In daylight, Monastiraki's (Μοναστηρακη) frenetic **flea market** is home to vendors who sell rugs, furniture, leather, *bouzoukis*, and all varieties of souvenirs. Test your bargaining mettle on a stubborn merchant—haggling is the only way not to get ripped off. Because it borders the central food and flea markets, the neighborhood's three-alarm noise never pipes down. The Acropolis and the subway are nearby, it's practically on top of the Agora, and the old buildings of **Psiri**—north of Ermou, bounded by Evripidou on the north and Athinas on the east—now house hot nightspots and restaurants. Go for an evening stroll—or a late night (and morning) bender—along Monastiraki's streets.

**OMONIA.** Northwest of Syndagma, Pl. Omonia (Ομονια) is the site of the city's **central subway station.** Trains run to Kifissia (40min.), Monastiraki (3min.), and Piraeus (20min.), among other destinations. The HQ of the **Greek Communist Party** (KKE)—a Red House of sorts—towers overhead. After indulging in literal opiates, junkies roam the plateia at night. Cheap lodgings, food, clothing, and jewelry abound in Omonia, but lately the area has become increasingly unsafe. Beware of pickpockets, mind your own business, and don't travel alone at night.

Two parallel avenues, **Panepistimiou** and **Stadiou,** connect Syndagma to Omonia. The **University** and **library** are on Panepistimiou between the two plateias. Larissis Station, serving northern Greece, and Peloponnese Station, serving the south, are on **Konstantinoupoleos,** northeast of **Pl. Karaiskaki,** accessible from Deligiani.

**EXARHIA.** Pl. Omonia's neighbor to the east, progressive Exarhia (Εξαρχια) was once the spiritual home of Greek anarchists. In the past 10 years, international models have imported the values of capitalism, and a new population of students have arrived to match. Thanks to the crazy kids at the **University** on Panepistimiou, Exarhia sports some of Athens's most bumpin' nightlife. Cafes overflow throughout the night, as the outdoor tables open a window onto the revelry of students.

**KOLONAKI.** If you've got money to burn, you've found the place. Models move and shake in Exarhia, but Kolonaki's (Κολονακη) got the glitz. On this posh foothill of Mt. Lycavittos, swanky Greeks drop drachmas in designer boutiques, sip *frappés*, and jockey for spots for their BMWs and for high-profile seats in the cafes, bars, and restaurants on Plutarchou and Loukianou. Kolonaki houses the **British Academy,** the **American School of Classical Studies,** and an enclave of expat students. With the sights of Plaka just down the hill and an exceptional view of the Acropolis below, Kolonaki shelters Athens's trendiest nightspots. The dethroned Greek royal family once called it home.

**PANGRATI.** Athenian youth chat over Fanta or coffee, jabber into mobile phones, and play backgammon in Pangrati (Πανγρατι), southeast of Kolonaki. Though close to the city center, Pangrati is remarkably intimate. Not much *happens* in this peaceful area, but the safe streets allow quiet strolls and exploration. Several Byzantine churches, a park, the **Olympic Stadium,** and the **National Cemetery** mark the area's major monuments. Take trolley #2, 4, or 11 from Syndagma to get here.

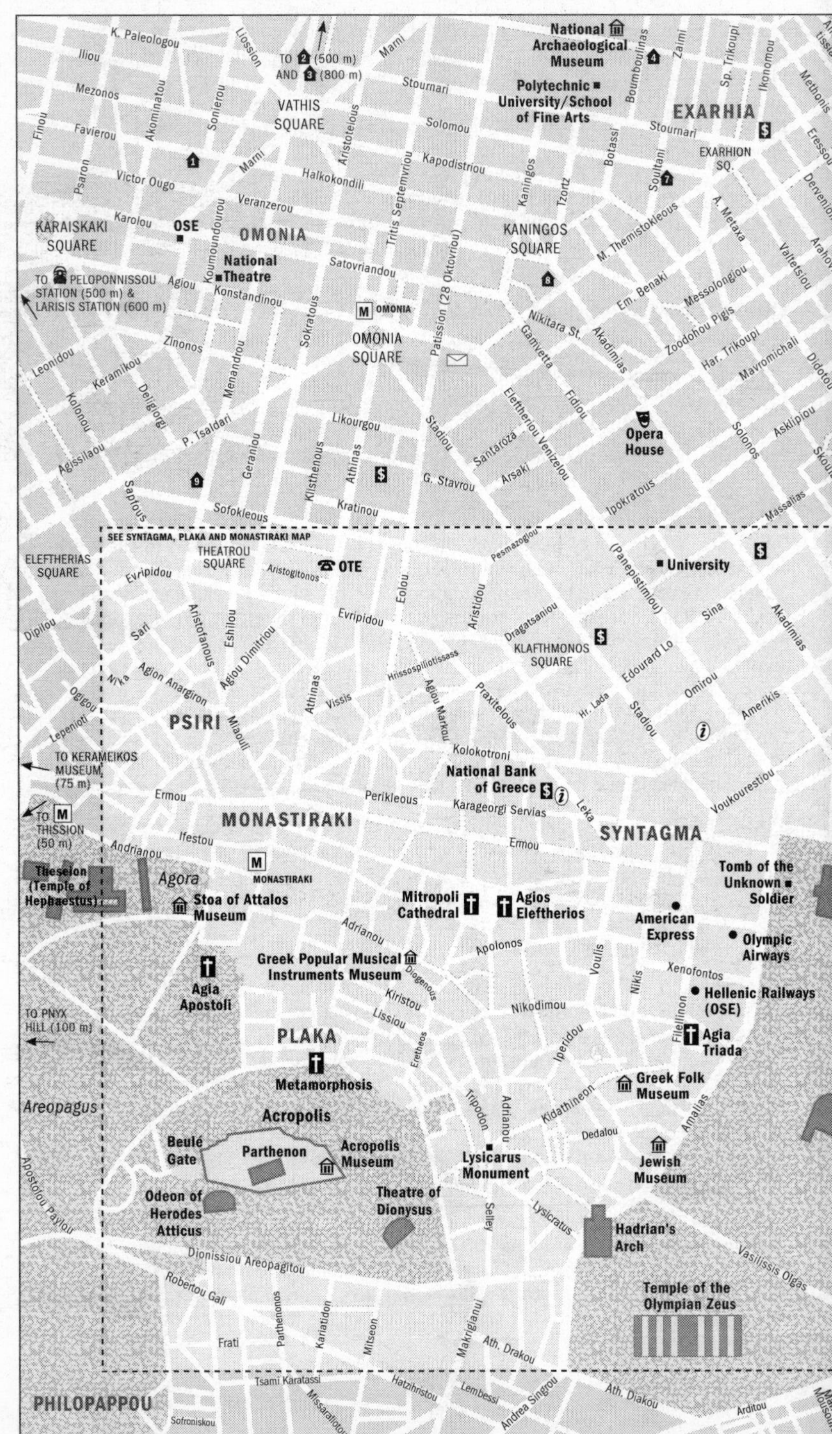
K. Paleologou
Iliou
Mezonos
Finou
Favierou
Psaron
Victor Ougo
Karolou
KARAISKAKI SQUARE
TO PELOPONNISSOU STATION (500 m) & LARISIS STATION (600 m)
Agiou Konstandinou
Akominatou
Sonierou
Liossion
TO 2 (500 m) AND 3 (800 m)
VATHIS SQUARE
Marni
Aristoteleous
Halkokondili
Veranzerou
Koumoundourou
OSE
OMONIA
National Theatre
Satovriandou
Tritis Septemvriou
Patission (28 Oktovriou)
OMONIA
OMONIA SQUARE
Sokratous
Zinonos
Menandrou
Leonidou
Keramikou
Kolonou
Deligiorgi
P. Tsaldari
Agissilaou
Geraniou
Likourgou
Klisthenous
Athinas
Kratinou
Sofokleous
Saplous
G. Stavrou
Stadiou
Stournari
Solomou
Kapodistriou
National Archaeological Museum
Polytechnic University/School of Fine Arts
Kaningos
Tzortz
KANINGOS SQUARE
Boumboulinas
Botassi
Zaimi
Sp. Trikoupi
Ikonomou
EXARHIA
Stournari
EXARHION SQ.
Soultani
A. Metaxa
M. Themistokleous
Valtetsiou
Methonis
Eressou
Derveniou
Arahovis
Em. Benaki
Messolongiou
Zoodohou Pigis
Har. Trikoupi
Mavromichali
Didotou
Nikitara St.
Gamvetta
Akadimias
Fidiou
Eleftheriou Venizelou
Santaroza
Arsaki
Opera House
Solonos
Asklipiou
Skoufa
Ipokratous
Massalias
SEE SYNTAGMA, PLAKA AND MONASTIRAKI MAP
THEATROU SQUARE
Aristogitonos
OTE
Evripidou
Eolou
Pesmazoglou
Aristidou
(Panepistimiou)
University
Sina
Akadimias
ELEFTHERIAS SQUARE
Dipilou
Sari
Aristofanous
Eshilou
Agiou Dimitriou
Dragatsaniou
KLAFTHMONOS SQUARE
Edourard Lo
Omirou
Amerikis
Nika
Agion Anargiron
Athinas
Vissis
Hrissospiliotissass
Agiou Markou
Praxitelous
Hr. Lada
Stadiou
Ogigou
Lepeniotí
PSIRI
Miaouli
TO KERAMEIKOS MUSEUM (75 m)
Kolokotroni
National Bank of Greece
Voukourestiou
Ermou
Perikleous
Karageorgi Servias
Leka
TO THISSION (50 m)
MONASTIRAKI
Ifestou
Andrianou
Ermou
SYNTAGMA
Theseion (Temple of Hephaestus)
Agora
MONASTIRAKI
Stoa of Attalos Museum
Mitropoli Cathedral
Agios Eleftherios
Tomb of the Unknown Soldier
American Express
Olympic Airways
Adrianou
Apolonos
Greek Popular Musical Instruments Museum
Diogenous
Voulis
Nikis
Xenofontos
Agia Apostoli
Kiristou
Lissiou
Nikodimou
Hellenic Railways (OSE)
TO PNYX HILL (100 m)
PLAKA
Eretheos
Iperidou
Filellinon
Agia Triada
Metamorphosis
Greek Folk Museum
Areopagus
Tripodon
Adrianou
Kidathineon
Amalias
Acropolis
Dedalou
Beulé Gate
Parthenon
Acropolis Museum
Lysicarus Monument
Jewish Museum
Odeon of Herodes Atticus
Theatre of Dionysus
Selley
Lysicratus
Hadrian's Arch
Apostolou Pavlou
Dionissiou Areopagitou
Vasilissis Olgas
Robertou Gali
Temple of the Olympian Zeus
Parthenonos
Kariatidon
Mitseon
Makrigianni
Frati
Ath. Drakou
Tsami Karatassi
Hatzihristou
Lembessi
Andrea Singrou
Ath. Diakou
Missaraliotou
PHILOPAPPOU
Sofroniskou
Arditou

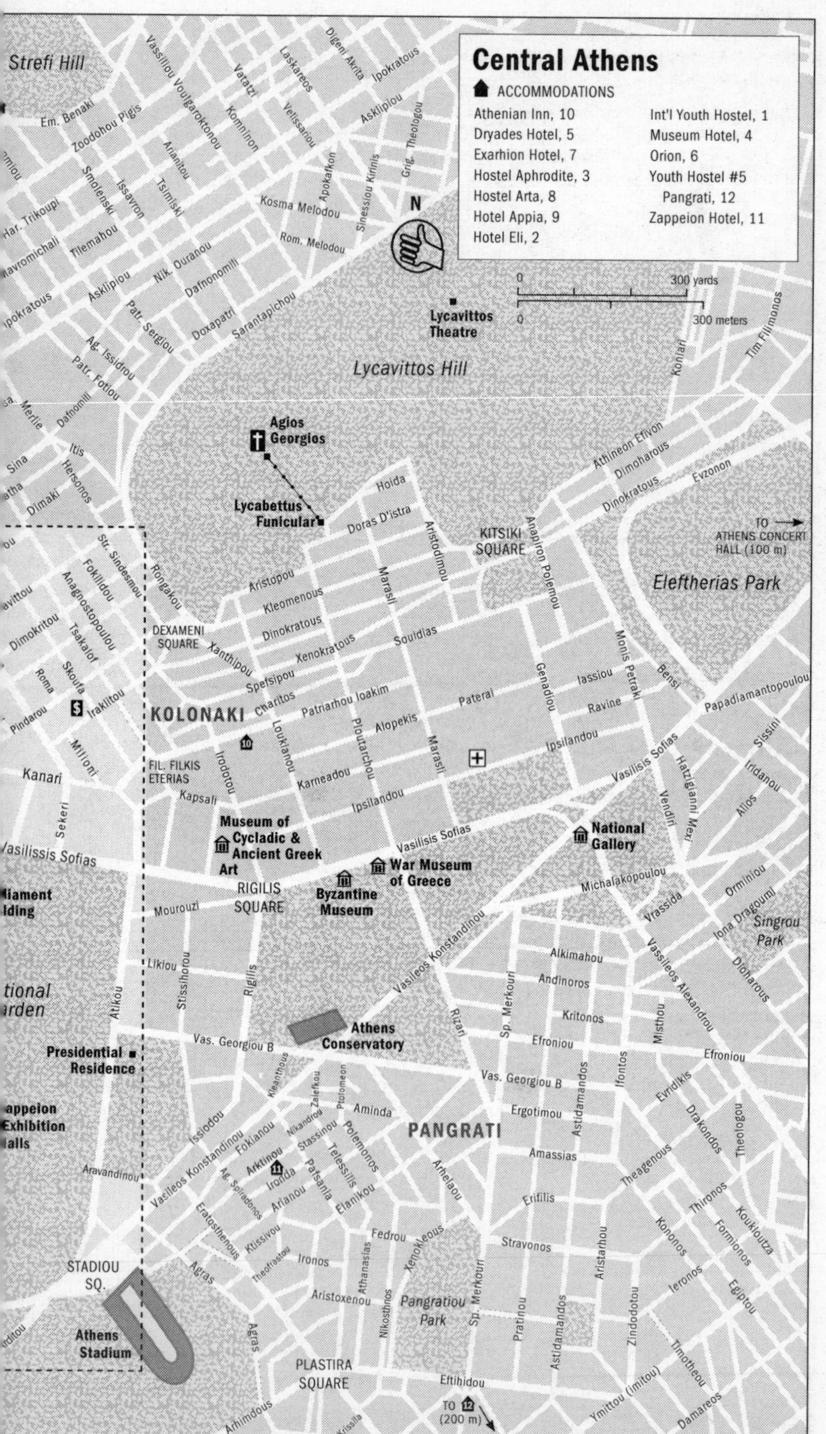
Central Athens
ACCOMMODATIONS
Athenian Inn, 10
Dryades Hotel, 5
Exarhion Hotel, 7
Hostel Aphrodite, 3
Hostel Arta, 8
Hotel Appia, 9
Hotel Eli, 2
Int'l Youth Hostel, 1
Museum Hotel, 4
Orion, 6
Youth Hostel #5
Pangrati, 12
Zappeion Hotel, 11
N
0
300 yards
0
300 meters
Strefi Hill
Lycavittos Theatre
Lycavittos Hill
Agios Georgios
Lycabettus Funicular
KITSIKI SQUARE
TO ATHENS CONCERT HALL (100 m)
Eleftherias Park
DEXAMENI SQUARE
KOLONAKI
FIL. FILKIS ETERIAS
Museum of Cycladic & Ancient Greek Art
War Museum of Greece
National Gallery
RIGILIS SQUARE
Byzantine Museum
Singrou Park
Athens Conservatory
Presidential Residence
PANGRATI
STADIOU SQ.
Athens Stadium
Pangratiou Park
PLASTIRA SQUARE
TO 12 (200 m)
Vassiliou Voulgaroktonou
Laskareos
Digeni Akrita
Ipokratous
Asklipiou
Vatatzi
Komninon
Velissariou
Em. Benaki
Zoodohou Pigis
Arianitou
Apokafkon
Sinessiou Kirinis
Grig. Theologou
Kosma Melodou
Rom. Melodou
Smolenski
Issavron
Tsimiski
Har. Trikoupi
Tilemahou
Nik. Ouranou
Dafnonomili
Asklipiou
Patr. Sergiou
Doxapatri
Sarantapichou
Ipokratous
Ag. Issidrou
Patr. Fotiou
Dafnomili
Merlie
Itis
Sina
Hersonos
Dimaki
Kontari
Tim Filimonos
Athineon Efivon
Dimoharous
Dinokratous
Evzonon
Hoida
Doras D'istra
Aristodimou
Anapiron Polemou
Str. Sindesmou
Fokilidou
Anagnostopoulou
Rongakou
Aristopou
Kleomenous
Dinokratous
Marasli
Dimokritou
Tsakalof
Xanthipou
Xenokratous
Souidias
Spefsipou
Charitos
Patriarhou Ioakim
Paterai
Genadiou
Monis Petraki
Iassiou
Ravine
Bensi
Papadiamantopoulou
Roma
Skoufa
Iraklitou
Pindarou
Milioni
Kanari
Loukianou
Ploutarchou
Alopekis
Marasli
Ipsilandou
Sissini
Irodotou
Karneadou
Vasilisis Sofias
Hatzigianni Mexi
Iridanou
Kapsali
Ipsilandou
Vendiri
Alkou
Sekeri
Vasilissis Sofias
Vasilisis Sofias
Michalakopoulou
Orminiou
Iona Dragoumi
Vrassida
Mourouzi
Vassileos Konstandinou
Alkimahou
Andinoros
Vassileos Alexandrou
Dioharous
Likiou
Stissihorou
Rigilis
Atikou
Sp. Merkouri
Kritonos
Misthou
Rizari
Vas. Georgiou B
Efroniou
Efroniou
Vas. Georgiou B
Kleanthous
Zalefkou
Ptolemeon
Aminda
Astidamandos
Ifontos
Evridikis
Drakondos
Theologou
Ergotimou
Issiodou
Vasileos Konstandinou
Fokianou
Nikandrou
Stassinou
Polemonos
Telessilis
Amassias
Theagenous
Arktinou
Ironda
Pafsania
Archelaou
Aravandinou
Ag. Spiridonos
Arianou
Erifilis
Thironos
Koukloutza
Kononos
Formionos
Eratosthenous
Etanikou
Kissivou
Fedrou
Xenokleous
Stravonos
Aristarhou
Agras
Theofrastou
Ironos
Ieronos
Eglptou
Aristoxenou
Athanasias
Nikosthnos
Sp. Merkouri
Pratinou
Astidamandos
Zindodotou
Timotheou
Agras
Eftihidou
Ymittou (Imitou)
Damareos
Arhimdous
Krissila

PSIRI
MONASTIRAKI
PLAKA
ANCIENT AGORA
ROMAN FORUM
AREOPAGUS
ACROPOLIS
KLAFTHMONOS SQ.
IROON SQ.
MONASTIRAKI SQ.
MITROPOLI SQ.
FLEA MARKET
OTE
Agii Theodori
Athens City Museum
Agios Georgios
Agios Irini
Kapnikarea
Hadrian's Library
Stoa of Attalus Museum
Athens Cathedral (Metropolis)
Agios Eleftherios
Greek Popular Musical Instruments Museum
Andronicus Kyrrhestes Clock
Ag. Apostoli
Center of Folk Art & Tradition
Metamorfossis
Agios Nikolaus
Agios Ioannis Thelogos
Propylaea
Erechtheion
Beulé Gate
Parthenon
Acropolis Museum
Temple of Athena Nike
Odeon of Herodes Atticus
Theater of Dionysos
Lysikrates Monument
Sofokleous
Armodiou
Aristogitonos
Evripidou
Athinas
Eolou
Ermou
Adrianou
Pandrossou
Mitropoleos
Dionysiou Areopagitou
Rovertou Gkalli
Kolokotroni
Perikleous
Athinaidos
Thrassilou
Makrigiani
Vironos
Kidathineon
Apolonos
Kekrops
Hatzimihali
Tripodon
Erehtheos
Mnissikleous
Kiristou
Lissiou
Erotokritou
Pritaniou
Theorias
Tholou
Polignotou
Pelopida
Diogenous
Dioscouron
Panos
Vrissakiou
Kladou
Pikilis
Dexipou
Areos
Nissou
Kinetou
Normanou
Ifestou
Astingos
Filipou
Miaouli
Eshilou
Aristofanous
Menandrou
Sokratous
Filopimenous
Aristeidou
Pesmazoglou
Stadiou
Dragatsaniou
P.P. Germanou
Praxitelous
Paparigopoulou
Parnassou
Leoharous
Havriou
Agiou Markou
Evangelistrias
Romus
Thisseos
Fokionos
Petraki
Ipatias
Thoukididou
Nikodimou
Adrianou
Flessa
Schollou
Rangava
Selei
Thespidous
Epimenidi
Herefodus
Afroditis
Lissikra
Frinhou
Hrissospiliotissas
Miltiadou
Nikiou
Libona
Skouze
Klitou
Agathonos
Voreou
Avramiotou
Kari
Vlahava
Poliklitou
Kalamida
Melanthiou
Ag. Dimitriou
Palados
Protogenous
Eleoussis
Kakourgodikiou
Themidos
Papanikoli
Kevitos
Artemidos
Pitaki
Karatskaki
Essopou
Mikonos
Taki
Hristokopidou
Aviton
Arionos
N. Apostoli
Lepenioti
Agatharhou
Ag. Anargiron
Nika
Sari
Palamidou
Sahtouri
Epikourou
Korinis
Spafous
Ag. Andrea
Benizelou
Andokidou
M. Avriliou
Ekate

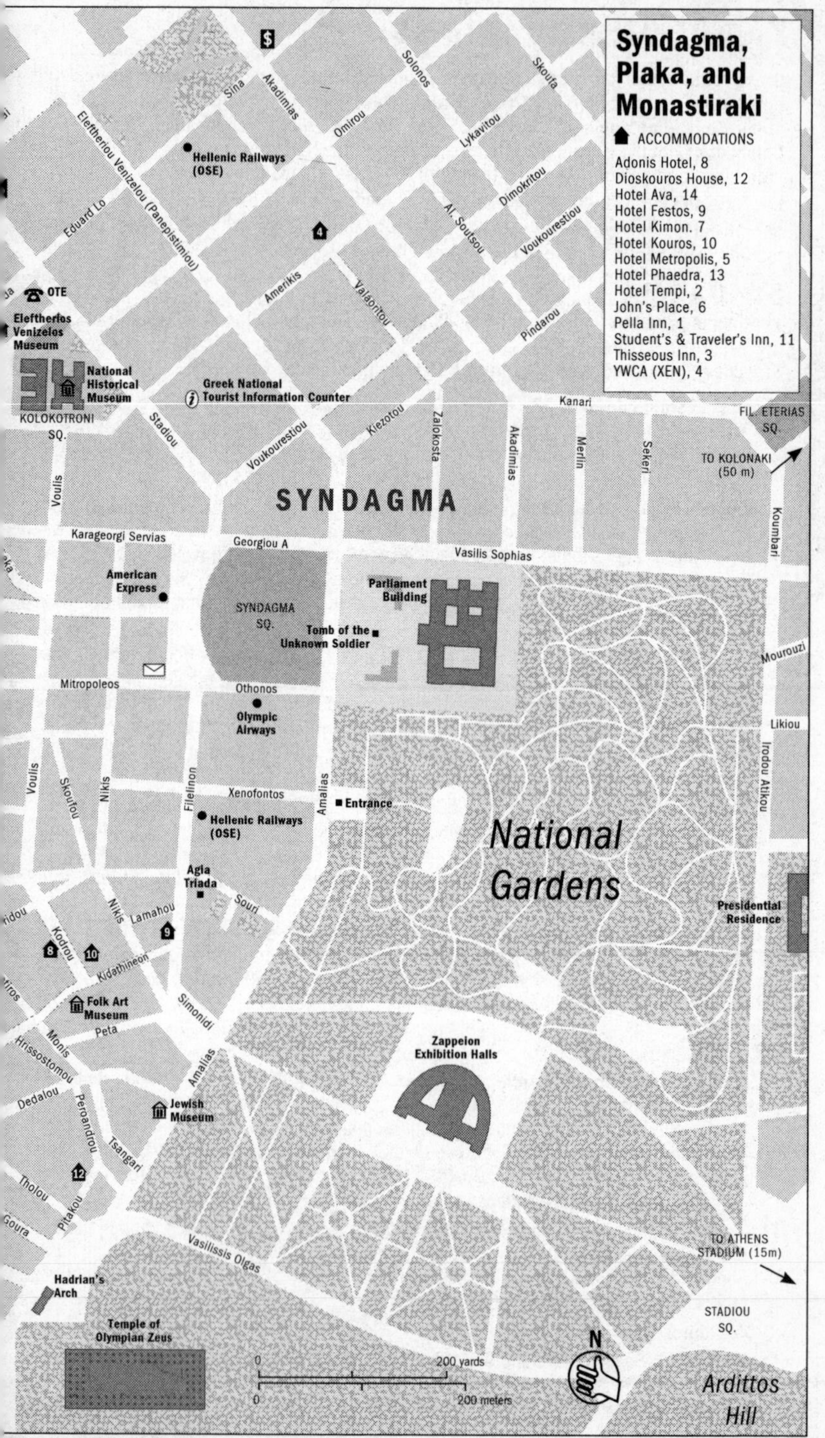

Syndagma, Plaka, and Monastiraki
ACCOMMODATIONS
Adonis Hotel, 8
Dioskouros House, 12
Hotel Ava, 14
Hotel Festos, 9
Hotel Kimon. 7
Hotel Kouros, 10
Hotel Metropolis, 5
Hotel Phaedra, 13
Hotel Tempi, 2
John's Place, 6
Pella Inn, 1
Student's & Traveler's Inn, 11
Thisseous Inn, 3
YWCA (XEN), 4
Solonos
Skoufa
Sina
Akadimias
Omirou
Lykavitou
Hellenic Railways (OSE)
Eleftheriou Venizelou (Panepistimiou)
Dimokritou
Eduard Lo
Al. Soutsou
Voukourestiou
Amerikis
Valaoritou
OTE
Pindarou
Eleftherios Venizelos Museum
National Historical Museum
Greek National Tourist Information Counter
Kanari
KOLOKOTRONI SQ.
Stadiou
Kiezotou
Zalokosta
Akadimias
Merlin
Sekeri
FIL. ETERIAS SQ.
TO KOLONAKI (50 m)
Voukourestiou
Voulis
SYNDAGMA
Koumbari
Karageorgi Servias
Georgiou A
Vasilis Sophias
American Express
SYNDAGMA SQ.
Parliament Building
Tomb of the Unknown Soldier
Mourouzi
Mitropoleos
Othonos
Olympic Airways
Likiou
Voulis
Skoufou
Nikis
Filelinon
Xenofontos
Amalias
Entrance
Irodou Atikou
Hellenic Railways (OSE)
National Gardens
Agia Triada
Souri
Presidential Residence
Nikis
Lamahou
Kodrou
Kidathineon
Folk Art Museum
Simonidi
Peta
Monis
Hrissostomou
Amalias
Zappeion Exhibition Halls
Dedalou
Peroandrou
Jewish Museum
Tsangari
Tholou
Pitakou
Goura
Vasilissis Olgas
TO ATHENS STADIUM (15m)
Hadrian's Arch
STADIOU SQ.
Temple of Olympian Zeus
0
200 yards
0
200 meters
N
Ardittos Hill

# ACCOMMODATIONS

**Greek Youth Hostel Association,** Dragatsaniou 4, 7th floor, lists hostels in Greece. Go up Stadiou and then left on Dragatsaniou, then take the elevators on the right as you enter the arcade. (☎323 4107; fax 323 7590. Open M-F 9am-3pm.) The **Hellenic Chamber of Hotels,** Karageorgi Servias 2, inside the National Bank of Greece, provides info and reservations for hotels of all classes throughout Greece. Reservations require a cash deposit, length of stay, and number of people; you must call, fax, or email one month in advance. (☎323 7193; fax 322 5449; www.users.otenet.gr/~grhotels/index.htm. Open M-F 8:30am-2pm, Sa 9am-12:30pm.)

## SYNDAGMA



Syndagma is at the heart of Athens. Tourist services and cheap accommodations are plentiful. Though it can be a noisy area, it's a good bet for those looking for dirt-cheap hostel rates and proximity to transportation.

**Hotel Festos,** Filellinon 18 (☎323 2455; email consolas@hol.gr). This backpacker-friendly hostel charges rock-bottom prices. Breakfast 500dr, dinner 1000dr. A/C. Dorms 2000–3500dr; singles 5000-7000dr; doubles 6000-8000dr; triples 12,000dr; quads 14,000dr. Monthly rates for students: single 80,000dr; double 100,000dr.

**George's International Students Inn**, Nikis 46 (☎322 6474). Cross 2 streets with your back to the Parlaiment building and turn left onto Nikis. Nikos and his wife Maria welcome you to their simple, no-frills hostel geared toward student travelers. Most rooms have huge windows and open-air balconies. Curfew 1:30am (though you can try ringing the bell after hours). Dorms 3000dr; singles 5000dr; doubles 7000dr; triples 9000dr. Usually closed Jan.-Feb.

**YWCA (XEN),** Amerikis 11 (☎362 4291), up the street from the tourist office. For women only. Spacious building has hand-wash laundry facilities, refrigerators on each floor, and a mini-cafeteria open M-F 10am-2pm. 600dr membership fee or valid YWCA membership required. Central and safe location compensates for strict regulations and an occasionally grumpy staff. Renovated in summer 2000, to reopen in fall 2000. Singles 6000dr, with bath 7500dr; doubles 9000dr/9500dr; triples 12,000dr.

**Thisseos Inn,** Thisseos 10 (☎324 5960). Take Karageorgi Servias, which becomes Perikleous, and Thisseos is on the right. This home-turned-hostel is close to Syndagma's sights but far from its noise. Friendly staff speaks English. TV in reception area, full kitchen. Towels upon request. Dorms 3500dr; singles 5000dr; doubles 7000dr; covered roof available in July for 2000dr (bring your own sleeping bag).

**John's Place,** Patroou 5 (☎322 9719); near Metropoleos. Well located yet off the major streets, John's has basic amenities and thankful quiet. Dim hallways and quiet nights enhance this simple guest house's gothic feel. Singles 7000-8000dr; doubles 9000-10,000dr; triples 12,000-14,000dr.

## PLAKA

**Student's and Traveler's Inn,** Kidathineon 16 (☎324 4808 or 324 8802; fax 321 0065; email Students-inn@ath.forthnet.gr). The location couldn't be better. This hotel courts young backpackers with its inviting rooms, large courtyard, travel services, and Internet access at the Cyber Cafe (see below). Breakfast 6-11am (1000-1500dr). Singles 8000-9000dr; doubles 10,000-11,000dr; triples 12,000-13,500dr; quads 14,000-16,000dr. 10% discount with student ID, youth card, or hostel card.

**Hotel Metropolis,** Mitropoleos 46 (☎321 7871 or 321 7469), opposite Mitropoli Cathedral. Newly renovated, this hotel is a roomy step up at a good price. Its welcoming husband-and-wife owners cater to privacy-oriented travelers. Private baths in 15 of the 21 rooms. Singles 8000dr; doubles 12,000dr.

**Dioskouros House,** Pitakou 6 (☎324 8165), on the southwest corner of the National Gardens by the Temple of Olympian Zeus. The simple wood-floored rooms are sheltered from the city center; a secluded outdoor bar serves breakfast (500dr) and drinks until 11pm. Singles 7000-9000dr; doubles 8000-10,000dr; triples 12,000-15,000dr.

**Adonis Hotel,** Kodrou 3 (☎324 9737 or 324 9741; fax 323 1602). From Filellinon on the way from Syndagma, turn right on Nikodimou and left on Kodrou, which meets Voulis. A perfect family hotel, with bath, A/C, and phone in each plush room, and a delightful rooftop lounge with a view of the Acropolis. Singles 11,500dr; doubles 16,000dr, with A/C 19,400dr; triples 22,300dr. Discounts for stays of more than 2 days.

**Hotel Kimon,** Apollonos 27 (☎/fax 331 4658), one block from the Mitropoli Cathedral. Friendly, safe, and close to the sights; there's a relaxing, quiet roof garden. A/C 2000dr extra. Doubles 10,000dr, with bath 13,000dr; triples 11,000dr/13,000dr.

## MONASTIRAKI

Like Plaka and Syndagma, Monastiraki lies at the center of things. You'll be close to the flea market and nightlife of Psiri. It's noisy fun.

**Pella Inn,** Karaiskaki 1 (☎325 0598; fax 325 0598). Walk 10min. down Ermou from Pl. Syndagma; it's 2 blocks from the Monastiraki subway station. Near the hip hangouts of Monastiraki, Pella features a large terrace with impressive views of the Acropolis to complement the comfy rooms. Breakfast 800dr, free luggage storage. Dorms 3000dr; singles 6000-8000dr; doubles 6000-9000dr, with bath 8,000-11,000dr, with A/C 13,000dr; triples 9000dr; quads 10,000. 20% discount for *Let's Go* users.

**Hotel Tempi,** Eolou 29 (☎321 3175 or 324 2940; fax 325 4179; www.travelling.gr/tempihotel). Wedged between an assortment of street vendors, Tempi rents simple rooms with a self-service breakfast. Rooms facing the rear are much dimmer—ask for a front-facing room. Laundry 1000dr. Free luggage storage. Single 6800dr, with bath 8500dr; double 9500dr/11,000dr; triple 13,000dr. 20% less in off season.



## OMONIA

If you're leaving Athens on an early morning bus or train (or arriving on a late-night one), you'll be able to roll out of bed to your ride from Omonia. Don't travel alone at night, as it's deserted.

**Athens International Hostel (HI),** Victor Hugo 16 (☎523 4170; fax 523 4015). Walk down Tritis Septembriou from Pl. Omnia, and take a left on Veranzerou, which becomes Victor Hugo after crossing Marni. A continental crowd packs this HI-affiliated youth hostel, the only one in Greece. You'll need to be an HI member or buy a membership (4200dr) to stay here. Full kitchen facilities. Hot water 6-10am and 6-10pm. Bar with internet access (1200dr per hr.) across the street. Dorms 1720dr, including sheets.

**Hostel Aphrodite,** Einardou 12 (☎881 0589 or 883 9249; fax 881 6574; email hostelaphrodite@ath.forthnet.gr). From the Victoria subway, follow Heiden two blocks, then Paioniou two more. Turn right on Michail Voda and left on Einardou. From the train station, take Filadelfias to Michail Voda. A staircase with an erotic mural leads to a swingin' 24hr. basement bar. Small, comfy rooms. Breakfast 500-1500dr. Dorms 3000dr; doubles 10,000dr; triples 13,500dr; quads 16,000dr.

**Hotel Appia,** Menandrou 21 (☎524 5155 or 524 4561; fax 524 3552). From Pl. Omnia, follow Tsaldari to Menandrou, in a shady area. Reception staff speaks English. Phones, ceiling fans, and radios in all rooms; 24hr. bar. Breakfast 1000dr. Singles with bath 6700dr; doubles 6500dr/9500dr; triples 9000dr; quads 9500dr.

**Hotel Arta,** Nikitara 12 (☎382 7753 or 382 2881). Take Stadiou to Benaki from Omnia, turn left, and take the third left onto Nikitara. It's in a nice part of Omonia, and very clean. Rooms vary widely so ask to see another if you don't like what you see. All rooms have bath and A/C. Breakfast 1500dr. Singles 8000dr; doubles 12,000dr.

## EXARHIA

Home to Athens's student population, Exarhia has some of Athens's hippest digs. Convenient to the National Archaeological Museum, the neighborhood is within walking distance of major public transportation, but is quieter and safer than nearby Pl. Omonia. This area is a good choice for young budget travelers.

**Hotel Dryades,** Dryadon 4 (☎382 7116 or 330 2387). Elegant Dryades offers some of Athens's nicest accommodations, with large rooms and private baths. Full kitchen and TV lounge. Breakfast 1500dr. Singles 10,000dr; doubles 14,000dr; triples 17,000dr.

**Hotel Orion,** Em. Benaki 105 (☎382 7362 or 382 0191; fax 380 51 93). From Pl. Omonia, walk up Em. Benaki or take bus #230 from Pl. Syndagma. Filled with hip travelers intent on seeing more than Athens's tourist magnets, Orion rents small rooms with shared baths. Sunbathers relax on the rooftop with music, the TV, and board games. Breakfast 1500dr. Singles 7000dr; doubles 9000dr; triples 11,000dr.

**Museum Hotel,** Bouboulinas 16 (☎380 5611 or 380 5612; fax 380 0507). An ideal family hotel–safe, convenient, and near the National Museum. Singles 7500dr; doubles 11,500dr; triples 13,800dr. Discount for student groups.

**The Exarcheion,** Themistokleous 55 (☎380 0731 or 380 1256; fax 380 3296). Enjoy the stairway's stylish mural as you walk up to one of 50 rooms, each with phone and TV, and a view of Exarhia. Some A/C, breakfast 1000dr, private bathrooms, credit cards accepted. Singles 9000dr; doubles 13,000dr; triples 14,000dr. Make reservations.



## KOLONAKI AND PANGRATI

High prices and the sizeable distance from the major sights makes **Kolonaki** better to visit than to stay in. Accommodations generally break the bank, since they're as high-class as the storefront shops. Though a bit far from Athens's main attractions, Pangrati offers much cheaper accommodations. Just be ready to trek a while to get around the rest of Athens.

**Youth Hostel #5 Pangrati,** Damareos 75 (☎751 9530; fax 751 0616). From Pl. Syndagma take trolley #2 or 11 to Filolaou, or walk through the National Garden, down Eratosthenous Efthidiou, then 3 blocks to Frinis, and down Frinis until Damareos on the right. There's no sign for this cheery hostel–just the number 75 and a green door. Bulletin boards spread hosteler wit and wisdom, and the owner speaks English. TV lounge, full kitchen facilities. Hot showers 50dr for 20min.; sheets and pillowcases 100dr each; laundry 800dr. Quiet hours 2-5pm and 11pm-7am. Dorms 2000dr. Roof beds 1500dr; bring a sleeping bag. Discounts for stays over a week.

# FOOD

## SYNDAGMA

Cheap fast food saturates Syndagma like a grease stain on paper. Chains like Goody's, Wendy's, and McDonald's dispense cheeseburgers, french fries, and sodas for 1100dr, or traditional *tost* (a grilled sandwich) with feta and lettuce for 360dr. **Everest** and **Delikiosk** make cheap sandwiches like ham and cheese croissants for 590dr. For quickie eats, try the family-owned joints on Nikis: **Makrigianni,** #54, **Mirabelle,** #34, or **To Apollonion,** #10.

**Kentrikon,** Kolokotroni 3 (☎323 2482 or 323 5623), near Stadiou, next to the National Historical Museum. Traditional (and lovely) Greek lunches cost around 2500dr, or branch out with pasta *bolognaise* (2100dr) or veal with spinach ragout (1400dr). Vegetarian options too. Open M-F noon-6pm.

**Sandwichland,** Korai 2 (☎331 0556). A thoroughly American operation with bright lighting and speedy service. Various vegetarian (and flesh) sandwiches go for around 600dr.

**Restaurant Palea Athina,** Nikis 48 (☎324 5777). Inexpensive elegance washes over you here; owner Thimios makes delicious, creamy *tzatziki* (700dr). Grilled feta 800dr, vegetable risotto 1200dr, and mussels with bacon 1900dr. Open noon-12:30am.

**Nikis Cafe,** Nikis 3 (☎323 4971), near Ermou. Nikis stands out from the other Syndagma cafes with its bright modern art and equally bright cocktails: strawberry, banana, and kiwi frozen margaritas go for 2000dr. The menu melds Greek and French: fresh baguette sandwiches 900-1000dr, seasonable fresh fruit salad 1200dr, and sangria 1000dr per glass. Open Su-Th 8am-1am, F-Sa 8am-3am.

## PLAKA

For do-it-yourself meals, **minimarkets** on Nikis sell basic groceries. Most of the tavernas along Kidathineon, Plaka's main drag, are roughly equivalent; explore quieter streets like **Tripodon** and **Lysiou** for the gems. The restaurants are pretty traditional. New, more innovative places are in Kolonaki and Monastiraki.

**Eden Vegetarian Restaurant,** Lissiou 12 (☎324 8858). Take Kidathineon to Tripidon, then left on to Lysiou; it's on the first corner. Greece's first vegetarian restaurant isn't just for herbivores. It *is* a mini totalitarian organic state—vegetables, beer, wine, cheese, the whole shebang. Enormous dishes like eggplant salad (900dr), hummus (each 900dr), *moussaka* with organic soy (1800dr), a spinach special (2200dr), and flavorful mushrooms *stifado* with onions and peppers. Open noon-midnight; closed Tu.

**O Platanos,** Diogenous 4 (☎322 0666), on a street parallel to Adrianou. This restaurant takes its name from the *platanos* tree towering over the table-filled courtyard. Specialty veal with potatoes, rice, or *fricasse* 1800dr. Open M-Sa noon-4:30pm, 8pm-midnight.

**Kouklis Ouzeri,** a.k.a. **To Gerani,** Tripodon 14 (☎324 7605), on a wide sidestreet of Kidatheneon. Kouklis occupies a quiet niche with a delightful balcony. Waiters bring a selection of 11 or 12 mouth-watering dishes to your table for inexpensive instant gratification (800-1400dr each), while street musicians serenade you from below.

**T. Stamatopoulos,** Lissiou 26 (☎322 8722 or 321 8549). Family-owned since 1882, the restaurant has an outdoor terrace and—the star attraction—Greek dancing to live music nightly (9:30-11pm). Veal special in wine sauce 2150dr. Open 7pm-2:30am.

ATHENS

## MONASTIRAKI

Give up fresh breath in exchange for cheap food by eating some *tzatziki*-smothered gyros at the flea market; if your image is too cool to stink of garlic and onions, sate yourself on grilled bananas. You can explore the chic options that stretch the boundaries of regulation Greek cooking. **Market Sophos,** Mitropoleos 78 (☎322 6677), near Aiolou, lets you stock up on groceries to cook at your hostel's kitchen.

**Oineas,** Aisopou 9 (☎321 5614), off Karaisaki by the Pella Inn. The best food in Monastiraki. Nostalgic Greek posters, bottles, and old Singer sewing machine ads adorn the walls, and the menu is just as quirky: pink beet *tzatziki* (800dr), sausage in orange sauce (1400dr), veal filet in wine sauce (5000dr), pastas (2000dr), and salads (200-2500dr). Open Tu-Su 11am-2am.

**Savas,** Mitropoleos 86 (☎324 5048), tucked in a corner off Ermou. For takeout, this grill is a budget eater's dream, with heavenly, el cheapo gyros (350dr). Don't sit down—prices skyrocket 1500dr extra. Open 8am-3am.

**Revekka,** Miaouli 22 (☎321 1174). At this menu-less authentic eatery outside the touristy square, you'll get a plate of Greek delicacies the owner prepared that day (2000dr).

**Dia Tafta,** Adrianou 37 (☎321 2347), near the Agora. A huge bar snakes through Dia Tafta, but it's the streetside tables that make it popular. Fresh, delectable Greek salad 1700dr, variety platters to serve four people 3500-6500dr. Open 9:30am-1:30am.

**Attalos Restaurant,** Adrianou 9 (☎321 9520), near the Thisseon area. Frequented by VIPs from the US Embassy, this traditional Greek taverna serves skewered souvlaki (2400dr), as well as wild mushroom *saganaki* with bacon (1400dr). The food is tasty, but you're paying for the view of the Agora. Open 9am-2am.

## OMONIA

As in Syndagma, the immediate area around Pl. Omnia is filled with fast food joints—busy thoroughfares **30 Septembriou** and **28 Octouvriou** (Pastission) are alive at all hours. For those with kitchen access, pick up ingredients at **Galaxias Discount Market,** Tritis Semptembriou 26. To quiet late-night stomach rumblings, stop by the meat market (no, not another club) on **Athinas** between Monastiraki and Omonia, where night-owl restaurants open from 3-7am.

**Healthy Food Vegetarian Restaurant,** Panepistimiou 57 (☎321 0966; fax 321 2043). Wholesomeness to make a souvlaki stand blush. Everything's made fresh. Try the potato carrot pie (400dr), breakfast *mueslix* (950dr), and the scrumptious carrot apple juice (500-600dr). Open M-F 8am-9:30pm, Sa 8am-8:30pm, Su 10am-3:30pm.

**Dafni Taverna,** Ionlianou 65 (☎821 3914). From Pl. Victoria, walk down Aristotelous and turn right on Iolianou. The second you enter the grapevine-shaded courtyard walled by barrels of *retsina,* you'll know it's a classic. Traditional Greek entrees 1500dr or less; wash it down with a slug of the homemade *retsina*. Open noon-1am.

**Souvlaki Pitta Pan,** Patission 8. Bite this, Captain Hook! This Greek version of the neighboring fast food behemoths serves it with fairy dust. Try the souvlaki (chicken 390dr) and special meals with fries, pita, tomato, and *tzatziki* (1400dr). Open 11am-11pm.



## EXARHIA

Starving twentysomethings demand inexpensive food around Exarhia; you'll be sure to find some, too. Many of the options are bare-bones, but savory: think souvlaki, Greek classics, and a jug of wine.

**O Barba Giannis,** Em. Benaki 94 (☎330 0185). From Syndagma, walk up Stadiou and make a right on Em. Benaki. Athenian students, execs, and artists all agree that "Uncle John's" is the place for cheap, delicious food and outstanding servic... Lots of fish (from 950dr), meatballs (1500dr), vegetarian dishes (950dr), and cheap wine (700dr); ask about today's choices. Open M-Su 9am-1am; closed Su in summer.

**Souvlaki Kavouras,** Themistokleous 64 (☎383 7981). Although its name promises souvlaki crabs, there's no seafood here, just super-cheap souvlaki (260dr) and beer (300dr) in the rear courtyard. Open 10am-6am.

**The Oasis,** Baltetsion 44 (☎330 1369). Surrounded by fountains and trees, Oasis is a green respite from the hot street; try the reasonably priced fresh fish (1500dr) and beer (500dr). Open 1pm-1am.

## KOLONAKI

The surest bargain is the Friday morning **street market** on Xenokratous, where you can grab a week's supply of peanuts, potatoes, and fresh clementines. Otherwise, this is the place to splurge with a super-swanky meal.

**Pluto,** Plutarchou 38 (☎724 4713). Owner and chef extraordinaire Constantine has created a one-of-a-kind restaurant with warm ambience and a staggeringly good international menu. Waves of Greek and international customers keep this place hopping every night. Entrees range from seafood paella (3400dr) to fabulously simple salads. Don't miss the chef's specialties: the seafood risotto is divine. Open 1-5pm, 9pm-2:30am.

**Jackson Hall,** Millioni 4 (☎361 6098), dominates the small footpath 2 blocks down the hill from Kolonaki. The spot for homesick Americans and Yankophiles, and a place to be seen. This noisy restaurant, bar, cafe, and nightclub serves food (and kitsch) to please any red-blooded American. Chicken fillet 2900dr, BBQ chicken risotto 3700dr, and pasta *Taste* 2800dr. A DJ spins 70s, 80s, and 90s pop. Open 10am-2:30am.

**Apokentro Pizzeria and Creperie,** Deinokratous 2 (☎725 1982 or 721 6898). From Vas. Sofias, walk up Karaoli-Dimitrioun (which becomes Loukianou) to Xenokratous and make a right. Petros and Artemis have been known to take on expat students like family. Try one of their unreal crepes with chocolate, banana, and Bailey's (1500dr). Over 20 pizzas include margarita, garlic, vegetarian, and Hawaiian (1200-1500dr). Free delivery to Vas. Konstandinou. Open M-Sa noon-12:30am, Su 6pm-12:30am.

**Under the Olive Tree,** Ploutarchou 32 (☎721 6578). Brimming with students at lunch and dinner, this is an outpost of cheap Greek food in Kolonaki. Open noon-midnight.

## PANGRATI

You can pick up fresh food Thursday mornings at the **street market** off Pl. Plastira.

**Evdokia,** Pl. Plastira 2 (☎756 4879). Try the cheap, yummy veggie pizza (400dr) or *spanakopita* (350dr) in this cafe at the heart of Plastira.

**Kallimarmarou,** Eforiouos 13 (☎701 9727 or 701 7234). Rabbit with mustard sauce (3100dr) and shrimp baked in salted biscuits (3700dr) will wow you–try splurging.

**Dragon Palace,** Andinoros 1 (☎724 2795 or 723 5783). From Syndagma, take Vas. Sofias, turn right onto Rizari at the War Museum, cross the lights and take a left onto Andinoros. Both the restaurant and the Peking duck (6700dr) are large and elegant; Szechuan chicken (2100dr) packs a spicy jolt. Take-out and delivery. Open noon-1am.

## CAFE-BARS AND NIGHTLIFE

That uniquely Greek hybrid, the cafe-bar, flourishes throughout Athens. You can start your night early with a coffee and proceed to a boozy binge at the same place.

Come summertime, the very Greek Athens club scene moves from Amerikis street to the seaside clubs of **Glyfada,** past the airport. The most popular clubs are on **Poseidonos** along the beach, where serene ocean views counteract a frenzied scene. Primarily male **gay clubs** are around Lembessi and the northern end of Singrou. Look for Camel Club on **Pergamon** street; +Soda, King Size, Bedside, Privilege, and Karting on **Poseidonos;** and Prime and Bo on **Alkynonidon.** In general, American or British tunes blare until 2 or 3am, at which point Greek music (live or recorded) takes over. Look suave—many clubs will not permit shorts—and bring lots of cash (covers 3000-5000dr; beers 1500-2000dr, cocktails 2000-3000dr). Head out before midnight to catch bus A3 (240dr) from Pl. Syndagma to Glyfada (the last stop). Then take a taxi down the beach away from the bars, cafes, and shopping on Vouliagmenis to your club, and later back to the city (2500-3000dr). Traffic back to Athens is heavy after 3am; the trip takes around 40 min.

ATHENS

### SYNDAGMA

**Sofokleous.com Internet Cafe,** Stadiou 5 (☎ 324 8105; email sofos1@ath.forthnet.gr), just up Stadiou from Pl. Syndagma. Owner Giorgos Kolios is helpful, friendly, and PC-proficient. Open 10am-10pm. 1500dr per hr., minimum 15min. for 500dr.

**Skynet Internet Centers** (☎322 7551; fax 331 0853; www.skynet.gr), at the corner of Apollonos 10 and Voulis 30. Computer use 1500dr per hr., minimum 15min. (500dr). Open M-F 9am-8:30pm, Sa 9am-5pm.

**Lava Bore,** Filellinon 25 (☎324 5335), on the corner of Simonidi by Amalias. This dance club is cheaper, less crowded, and more convenient than its hopping Glyfada counterparts. 1000dr cover includes a drink. Open Su-Th 10pm-4am, F-Sa 10pm-5am.

### PLAKA

Nearby in **Dora Stratou Theatre,** on Philopappou Hill, Greek dancers kick and holler to live music on an open-air stage, celebrating traditions from all regions of the country. (☎324 4395, 9am-1:30pm; 921 4650 after 7:30pm. Shows May-Sept., nightly at 10:15pm, W and Su 8:15pm. 3000dr, students 1800dr.)

To get a spellbindingly 360° view of Athens at night, go up to **Pnyx Hill** just opposite the Acropolis. Formerly the meeting place of the ancient Athenian assembly, the hill now brings Athenians and tourists together to listen to guitar-strumming by the city lights. Take care in ascending the smooth, slippery stairs.

**Cine Paris,** Kidatheneon 22 (☎322 2071 or 324 8057). Enjoy your own *cinema paradiso* in the Athenian night breeze. Check *Athens News* for showtimes of the twice-nightly second run English-language films. Tickets 2000dr.

**Bretto's,** Kidatheneon 41 (☎323 2110). The walls are lit up with colorful bottles of ouzo, brandy, and other liqueurs, all made by friendly Dimitris in his family's 100-year-old distilleries. Buy a bottle to go (5ml-1L), or get an immediate fix sitting at the bar. Open 10am-midnight.

**Cyber Cafe**, Kidathineon 16 (☎324 8808/02; email: ccave1@otenet.gr), located inside the Student and Traveler's Inn. Open 10am-noon, 5-11pm.

## MONASTIRAKI

The **Psiri** district is the new place to see and be seen in Athens, and Monastiraki's nightlife has revved to up to rival Glyfada.

**Bee,** at the corner of Miaoli and Themidos, off Ermou; a few blocks from the heart of Psiri. DJs spin upstairs in this 3-floor, patio-equipped Athenian artistic hub. The basement sunflower room glows orange and lights up sculpted-utensil chandeliers. The friendly staff keeps the booze flowing. Drinks 1000-2500dr. Open 8pm to 3 or 4am.

**Aristophanes Music Club,** Taki 2 (☎321 8408). Iron Maiden lives! A rowdy crowd bounces to 80s hard rock under Doors and Led Zeppelin t-shirts elevated on high.

**Asfron Bar,** Taki 3. Stops traffic, literally: mopeds can't squeeze past the gyrating partiers spilling into the narrow alleyway. Wiggle your way inside to eye the photos.

## OMONIA

**Moc@fe Internet Cafe,** Marnis 49 and Venanzerou (☎522 7717). This hip cafe jacks you in to a fast connection and cheap drinks. Coffees 500dr, beers 700-1000dr. 500dr for the first 20min., 1500dr per hour. Open 9am-midnight, depending on business.

**Internet Cafe,** Stournari 49 (☎383 8808). Athenian students crowd this hidden seventh-floor joint. Gaze at the city below while checking email (1000dr per hr.).

**Web Cafe,** Tzortz 10 (☎330 3063). Video games downstairs, Internet access upstairs. 1300dr per hr., minimum 800dr per 30min. Open 9am-2am.

**Merlin Cafe,** Kanigos 2. An overwhelming blue decor colors your hours spent sipping espresso (700dr) or Irish coffee (1100dr). Come early in the day. Open 8am-10:30pm.

## EXARHIA

Exarhia exudes its funkiness in its many bars, which showcase everything from backgammon to death metal. Check *Athens News* for showtimes of second-run movies at **Cinema Rivera,** Baltetsiou 46 (tickets 1800dr).

**Deligrece Internet Cafe,** Akademias 87 (☎330 2929). This Internet cafe is cool enough to stand on its own, with big-screen MTV broadcasts and cheap espresso (650dr). Internet connection 1000dr per hr.; minimum 15min. Open 7:30am-midnight.

**Metal Cafe,** Em. Benaki 69. Like the Flintstones meeting the Jetsons, superficial conflict gives way to ultimate fun here. Open 9am-1:30am.

**Underground,** Motaxa 1821 (☎382 2019). For a British flavor, try this cafe/bar.

**Cafe Floral,** (☎330 0938), in Pl. Exarhia. Floral offers *fredo* cappuccinos (900dr) and beer (1000dr). Play pool and watch TV, or groove outside to the nighttime DJ.

**Museum Internet Cafe,** Patission 46 (☎883 3418). After visiting the Archaeological Museum, luxuriate in oh-so-modern email. 500dr per 20min. Cappuccino 700dr, drinks 1100-1500dr, beers 600-1100dr.

**Astor Cafe,** Kapodistriou 27 (☎523 8546). Email 1500dr per hr. Often packed, but not for the computers: sandwiches and pizza 500-800dr. Open 9am-1am.

## KOLONAKI

Kolonaki is brimming with cafes/bars. Try Millioni street by **Jackson Hall**—home to **La Tasse Cafe** (Millioni 8), **Caffé Millioni,** and **Al Buon Caffé**—or Haritos street by Pluto, where you'll find **Azul, Baila,** and **Mousa** (Μουσα). Don't stand outside these bars too long; when it gets noisy, residents periodically toss buckets of water or Coke out the windows on those below.

Summertime performances are staged in Lycavittos Theater as part of the **Athens Festival** (p. 27), which has included acts from the Greek Orchestra to Pavarotti to the Talking Heads. The **Festival Office,** Stadiou 4, sells student tickets. An English-language schedule of events is available in mid-June. (☎322 1459 or 322 7944. Open M-F 9:30am-4pm, Sa-Su 9:30am-2pm. Tickets 3000-5000dr.) *Athens News* has showtimes for year-old Hollywood flicks at **Cine Athenaia,** Haritos 50. (☎721 5717. Tickets 1800dr.)

**Jazz in Jazz,** Dinokratous 4. From behind the well-worn wooden bar, Kostas can be persuaded to muse about jazz and teach swing lessons. Endless old jazz records on the box draw Athens's faithfuls. 1500dr cover includes a drink. Open noon-3am.

**The Daily,** Xenokratous 47 (☎722 3430). A cafe/bar hybrid, the Daily is where Kolonaki's chic foreign student populations converge to imbibe, take in Latin music and reggae, and watch soccer and basketball on TV. Fabulous, shaded outdoor seating and open-air bar. Pints of Heineken 1000dr. Open 9am-2am.

**Cafe 48,** Karneadou 48 (☎725 2434), 2 blocks up the hill from Vas. Sofias. Pictures of boozed patrons pepper the walls of this student bar, showing you what you'll look like when you leave. Expat classicists hang here, as do student travelers. With your student ID, beer costs 800dr and punch 1000dr. Open M-Sa 9am-2am, Su 4pm-2am.

## PANGRATI

The cafes along Imittou let you people-watch in style.

**Babylon Cafe,** Imittou 103 (☎751 4024). Throw dice on this streetside cafe's backgammon boards; gambling debts are up to you. Try the *frappés* (900dr). Open 9am-3am.

**Sideradiko Cafe,** Imittou 128 (☎701 8700). This cafe shines, with fresh pear, orange, peach, apple, or banana juices (1300dr). Tea 800dr; beer 700dr. Open 9am-3am.

**Pan Tsan,** Krisila 26 (☎701 0369). Rambunctious Athenian kids play video games, pool, and chess. Billiards 1000dr per hr. Beer 500dr. Open 10am-midnight.

**Frangelico Cafe,** Eratosthenous 12 (☎701 9914). This undiscovered, small cafe near the Olympic Stadium serves an even smaller menu of drinks (500-1200dr). Open 11:30am-3pm, 7:30pm-midnight.

**Carousel-Cybercafe,** Eftixidou (Eftychidou) 32 (☎756 4305), by Pl. Plastira. Order a wood-oven-baked pizza (1150dr) after you empty your inbox (1500dr per hr; 400dr per 30min.); space out to satellite TV. Open 11am-midnight.

**Planet Net,** Kristila 5 (☎756 0949), near McDonald's. Upbeat music adds to the joy of getting new mail. 1500dr per hr., minimum 600dr per 20min. Open 11am-midnight.



# SIGHTS

## ACROPOLIS

*Reach the entrance on the west side of the Acropolis either from Areopagitou to the south, by following the signs from Plaka, or by exiting the Agora to the south, following the path uphill, and turning right. Not wheelchair accessible. The marble can be slippery, so wear shoes with good traction. ☎321 0219.* ***Open*** *8am-6:30pm; in winter 8am-2pm.* ***Admission*** *to site and Acropolis Museum 2000dr, students and EU seniors 1000dr, under 18 free.*

Perched on a rocky plateau above the city, the Acropolis has crowned Athens since the 5th century BC. The brilliant Parthenon at its center towers over the Aegean and the plains of Attica, the greatest achievement of Athens's Classical glory and the era's most enduring architectural contribution. Although each Greek *polis* had an *acropolis* ("height of the city"), Athens's magnificent example has effectively monopolized the name. It stands timelessly, awe-inspiringly upright—though steel scaffolding and restoration work often embrace it—amidst otherwise rubble-strewn grounds. Make sure you visit as early in the day as possible to avoid massive crowds and the broiling, humbling midday sun.

### HISTORY

**BEGINNINGS.** With its view toward both land and sea, the Acropolis began as a strategically located military fortress. It was initially controlled by one ruler, who lived in a palace that doubled as a temple to a nature goddess, later to Athena. Around the 12th century BC, the original aristocrats, wealthy landowners calling themselves the **Aristoi** ("excellent ones"), ousted the monarch. They shifted government away from the Acropolis to the city's northern foothills, in an area that later became the Agora (see p. 101). The Acropolis became a purely religious center for worshiping Athena, whose wooden shrine celebrated both Athena Polias,

**GAUDY GREEKS** The blinding white of the Parthenon seems like an essential part of its beauty and wonder. Likewise, the simplicity of Ancient Greek marble and bronze artifacts impresses us. In comparison to their purity, tourists' Hawaiian shirts and fluorescent hats seem unbearably garish. But before you go postal over your fellow tourists' screaming duds, take a deep breath and count to ten. Bad news: the ancients didn't see their statues in monochrome; many statues were brightly painted (you can see traces on paintings in the National Museum, p. 104, and the Acropolis Museum, p. 100), and wore semi-precious stones in their eyes. Even by our day-glo standards, these decorations seem hideous. While you can applaud the effects of time for good taste and subtlety, remember that the Greeks were just as gaudy as we are.



goddess of crops and fertility, and Pallas Athena, loving virgin and protectress of the city (she added the name Pallas in honor of a mortal friend who found immortality in name only, becoming part of the goddess's name itself). Money was entrusted to Athens's protector, Athena, so the Acropolis also housed the city treasury.

**PERICLEAN PROJECT.** The Acropolis's world-famous form took shape in 507 BC, when the *Aristoi* were overthown and Athens began its experiment with democracy. In 490 BC, Athenians began constructing a new temple on the Acropolis, this time in marble. Ten years later, under attack from the Persians, Aegean rulers formed the Delian League, and **Pericles** started piling up a slush fund from the taxes paid by the league to beautify Athens. He continued this practice long after the Persian threat evaporated, blowing the money on projects like the temples of the Acropolis, the **Hephaesteion** in the Agora, and the **Temple of Poseidon** at Sounion. As is the fate with all public works, Pericles' program was mocked as lavish and unscrupulous; Plutarch reports that Pericles was "gilding and bedizening" the city like a "wanton woman adding precious stones to her wardrobe." Nevertheless, after delays caused by the Peloponnesian War (431-404 BC), the Periclean project was completed. Four of the buildings erected thus still stand today: the **Parthenon,** the **Propylaea,** the **Temple of Athena Nike,** and the **Erechtheion.**

**CAPTURE AND RESTORATION.** Almost as soon as the Acropolis was completed, it fell to Sparta; ever since, its function has changed whenever it changed hands. **Byzantine Christians** added the symbolic power of the Parthenon to their faith arsenal; they turned the temple into the Church of Ag. Sophia ("Sophia," like "Athena," means wisdom). In 1205, **Frankish Crusaders** turned back the clock and again made the Acropolis into a fortress/palace/headquarters, this time for the Dukes de la Roche. Eventually, the Parthenon served as a Catholic church, Notre Dame d'Athènes. In the 15th century, **Ottomans** used the Parthenon as a mosque and the Erechtheion as the Ottoman commander's harem. In a 1687 **Venetian** siege, Ottoman gunpowder stored in the Parthenon blew its roof off; squalor ensued as Ottoman guards and their families settled on the Acropolis. In 1833, the newly independent Greeks reclaimed the hill, dismantling remnants of the Turkish occupation and resurrecting the Temple of Nike.

The subsequent preservation and restoration of the Acropolis has kicked up a swirl of impassioned controversy. The first wave of large-scale restoration began in 1898 and lasted almost forty years, transforming the site by demolishing and reconstructing the Temple of Nike. Many of the Parthenon's most important pieces have survived, having been spirited away to the British Museum in London, nicked by English ambassador Lord Elgin. In the last 20 years, acid rain has forced works formerly displayed outside to take cover in the on-site museum.

## RUINS

When you enter the Acropolis, the reconstructed Temple of Athena Nike lies before you. Though the Classical-era ramp that led to the Acropolis no longer exists; today's visitors still make an awe-inspiring climb. The path leads through

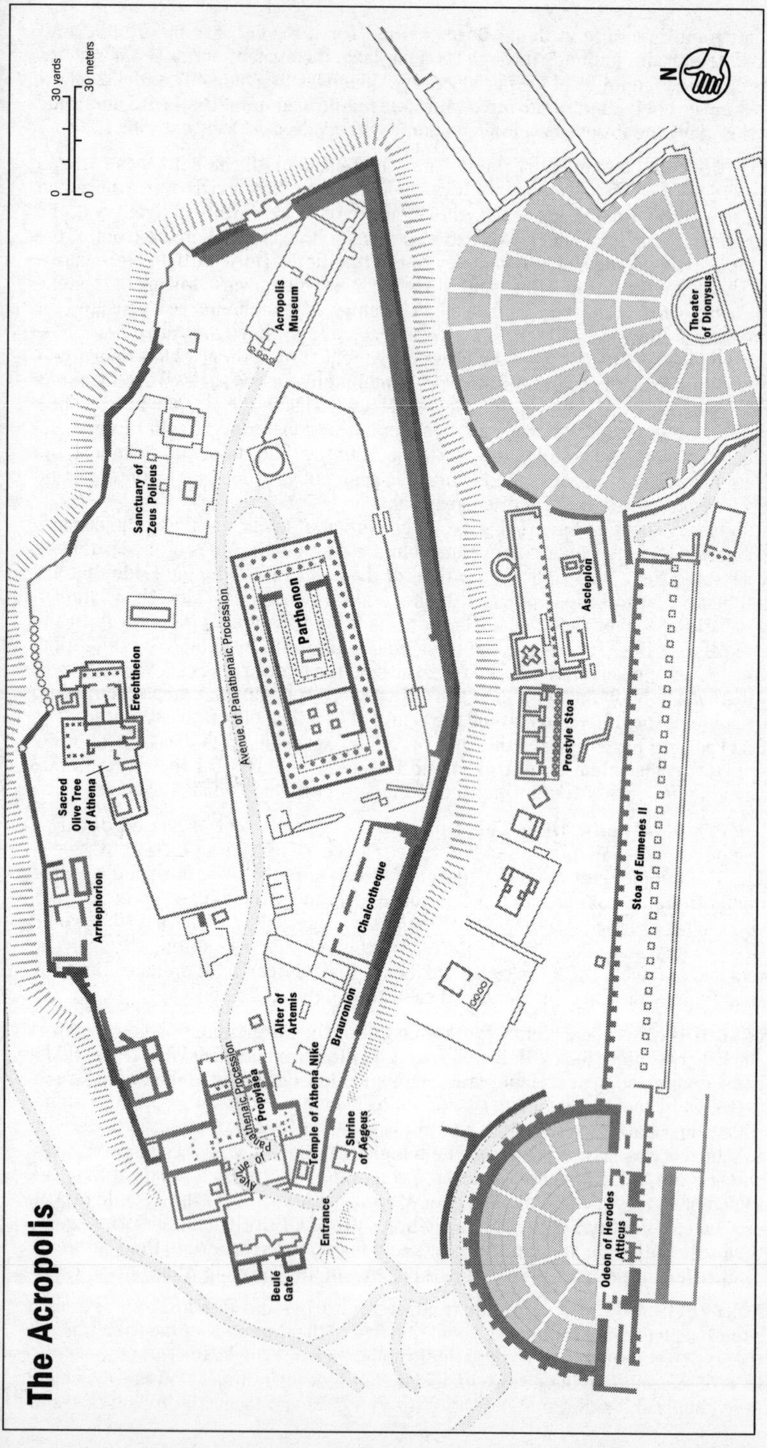

# The Acropolis

0 30 yards
0 30 meters
N

Acropolis Museum
Sanctuary of Zeus Polleus
Theater of Dionysus
Erechtheion
Sacred Olive Tree of Athena
Avenue of Panathenaic Procession
Parthenon
Asclepion
Arrhephorion
Prostyle Stoa
Chalcotheque
Stoa of Eumenes II
Alter of Artemis
Brauronion
Propylaea
Avenue of Panathenaic Procession
Temple of Athena Nike
Shrine of Aegeus
Entrance
Beulé Gate
Odeon of Herodes Atticus

the crumbling Roman **Beulé Gate,** named for a French archaeologist who unearthed it. It continues through the **Propylaea,** the ancient entrance famous for its ambitious multi-level design begun by Mnesikles between 437 and 432 BC; it was never completed. Innovative Mnesikles improved upon the Doric and Ionic styles, tying the Propylaea's Ionic columns with a massive Doric exterior.



**PARTHENON.** Looming over the hillside, the **Temple of Athena Parthenos** (Athena the virgin), known more commonly as the Parthenon, keeps vigil over Athens and the modern world. Iktinos designed the Parthenon to be the crowning glory of the Periclean project; he added two extra columns to the usual six in the front of the temple, thus adding a stately majesty to the traditional Doric design. More subtle refinements transformed the usual Doric boxiness: the upward bowing of the temple's *stylobate* (pedestal) and the slight swelling of its columns compensated for the optical illusion in which, from a distance, straight lines appear to bend. The Parthenon's elegance shows the Classical Athenian obsession with proportion—everything from the layout to the carved entablature shared the same four-to-nine ratio in size (a variation on the "Golden Mean"). Inside the temple, in front of a pool of water, stood Phidias's greatest sculptural masterpiece, a 40 ft. chryselephantine (ivory and gold) statue of Athena. Although the statue has been lost, the National Museum houses a 2nd-century Roman copy, which is fearsomely grand even at one-twelfth the size of the original.

Ancient Athenians saw their city as the capital of civilization, and the **metopes** (scenes in the open spaces above the columns) around the sides of the Parthenon celebrate Athens's rise. On the far right of the south side—the only side that has not been defaced—the Lapiths battle the Centaurs; on the east side, the Olympian gods triumph over the giants. The north side faintly depicts the victory of the Greeks over the Trojans, and the west side revels in their triumph over the Amazons. A well-preserved, bas relief frieze around the interior walls shows a group of Athenians hobnobbing with the gods. The **pediments** (triangular areas propped up by columns) at either end marked the zenith of Classical decorative sculpture. The **East Pediment** once depicted the birth of Athena, springing from Zeus's head, while the **West Pediment** showed Athena and Poseidon's contest for the city's eternal devotion; fragments are now housed in the Acropolis and British Museums.

**TEMPLE OF ATHENA NIKE.** This tiny cliff's-edge temple was raised during a respite from the Peloponnesian War called the Peace of Nikias (421-415 BC; see p. 11). The temple, known as the "jewel of Greek architecture," is ringed by eight miniature Ionic columns and once housed a statue of the winged goddess Nike. One day, in a paranoid frenzy, the Athenians were seized by a fear that Nike would flee the city and take peace with her, so they clipped the statue's wings. The remains of the 5m-thick **Cyclopean wall** lies below the temple. It predates the Classical Period, and once surrounded the entirety of the Acropolis.

**ERECHTHEION.** The Erechtheion, to the left of the Parthenon, was completed in 406 BC, just before Sparta defeated Athens in the Peloponnesian War. The building housed many gods in its time, grabbing its name from snake-bodied hero Erechtheus. Old Erechtheus couldn't stand up to Poseidon, who speared him with his trident in a battle over the city's patronage. When Poseidon struck a truce with Athena, he was allowed to share the temple with her—the east is devoted to the goddess of wisdom and the west to the god of the sea. The east porch, with its six Ionic columns, sheltered an olive wood statue of Athena; like the Temple of Athena Nike, it contrasts with the Parthenon's dignified Doric columns. The Erechtheion's south side is supported by six women frozen in stone, the Caryatids. They're actually copies—the originals are safe in the Acropolis Museum (p. 100).

**ACROPOLIS MUSEUM.** This museum neighboring the Parthenon shelters a superb collection of sculptures, including five of the Caryatids of the Erechtheion; the sixth has been whisked off to the British Museum. The statues seem to be replicas of one another, but a close look at the folds of their drapery reveals delicately individualized detail. Compare the stylized, entranced faces and frozen poses of

the Archaic Period *Moschophoros* (calf-bearer) sculpture to the more idealized, more human Classical Period **Kritias** boy for a trip through developing Greek sculpture. Only a few pieces from the Parthenon are here, since British Lord Elgin helped himself to the rest. *(Open M noon-6:30pm, Tu-Su 8am-6:30pm; in winter M 11am-2pm, Tu-Su 8am-2pm. Cameras without flash allowed; no posing next to the objects. Labels in Greek and English.)*

**ELSEWHERE ON THE ACROPOLIS.** The southwest corner of the Acropolis looks down over the reconstructed **Odeon of Herodes Atticus,** a functional theater dating from the Roman Period (AD 160). See the *Athens News* for a schedule of concerts and plays there. You'll also see nearby ruins of the Classical **Theater of Dionysus,** the **Asclepion,** and the **Stoa of Eumenes II.** *(Entrance on Dionissiou Areopagitou street. ☎322 4625. Open Tu-Su 8:30am-2:30pm. 500dr, students 250dr, children under 18 free.)*



## AGORA

*Enter the Agora in one of three ways: off Pl. Thission, off Adrianou, or as you descend from the Acropolis. ☎321 0185. Open Tu-Su 8:30am-3pm. 1200dr, students and EU seniors 600dr, EU students and under 18 free.*

The Agora is Athens's heart, just below its soul, the Acropolis above: it has served as the city's marketplace, administrative center, and center of daily life from the 6th century BC through AD 500. The debates of Athenian democracy were argued in the Agora; Socrates, Aristotle, Demosthenes, Xenophon, and St. Paul all preached it here. After the 6th century AD, the Agora, like the Acropolis, passed through the hands of innumerable conquerors. The ancient Agora emerged again in the 19th century, when a residential area built above it was razed for excavations. Inhabited since 3000 BC, the Agora still stands at the center of Athens. Today, visitors have free reign over the 30-acre archaeological site it has become.

**HEPHAESTEION.** The Hephaesteion, on a hill in the northwest corner of the Agora, is the best-preserved classical temple in Greece. The 415 BC temple still flaunts cool **friezes,** which depict Hercules labors and Theseus's adventures. The closer you look, the more impressed you'll be. Unlike most sites, the temple can be viewed up close.

**ODEON OF AGRIPPA.** The Odeon of Agrippa, a concert hall built for Roman Emperor Augustus's son-in-law and right-hand man, now stands in ruins on the left of the Agora as you walk from the museum to the Hephaesteion. When the roof collapsed in AD 150, the Odeon was rebuilt at half its former size. From then on, it served as a lecture hall. The actors' dressing room was turned into a porch supported by colossal statues, three of which still guard the site.

**STOA OF ATTALOS.** The elongated Stoa of Attalos was a multi-purpose building filled with shops and home to informal philosophers' gatherings. Attalos II, King of Pergamon, built the Stoa in the 2nd century BC as a 3-D thank-you note to Athens for the education he had gotten there. Reconstructed between 1953 and 1956, it now houses the **Agora Museum,** which contains relics from the site. Stars of the collection are the excellent black figure paintings by Exekias, and a calyx-krater depicting Trojans and Greeks quarreling over Patroclus's body.

**STOA BAILEIOS.** Plato reports that Socrates' first trial was held at the recently excavated Stoa Basileios, the Royal Promenade of the Agora. As you cross the subway tracks at the Adrianou exit, it's on the left.

## OTHER ANCIENT SITES

**KERAMEIKOS.** The Kerameikos's rigidly geometric design becomes clearly visible from above, before you enter the grounds; the site includes a large-scale cemetery and a 40m-wide boulevard that ran from through the Agora and the Diplyon Gate and ended at the sanctuary of Akademos (where Plato founded his academy in the 4th century BC). **Public tombs** for state leaders, famous authors, and battle victims

lined this sacred road, and worshipers began the annual Panathenaean procession along its path. The Sacred Gate arched over the Sacred Way to Eleusis, traversed in annual processions. The **Oberlaender Museum** displays finds from the burial sites; its excellent collection of highly detailed pottery and sculpture is a highlight. *(Ermou 48, northwest of the Agora. From Syndagma, walk toward Monastiraki on Ermou for 25min. ☎346 3552. Open Tu-Su 8am-2:30pm. 500dr, students and EU seniors 300dr, EU students and under 18 free.)*

**TEMPLE OF OLYMPIAN ZEUS AND HADRIAN'S ARCH.** In the middle of downtown Athens, you'll spot the final trace of the largest temple ever built in Greece. The 15 majestic Corinthian columns of the Temple of Olympian Zeus mark where the temple once stood. Started in the 6th century BC, it was completed 600 years later by Roman emperor Hadrian. None too shy, Hadrian attached his name to the centuries-long effort by adding his arch, which marked the boundary between the ancient city of Theseus and Hadrian's own new city. A Roman bath (tiles and all) borders the site. (*Vas. Olgas at Amalias. Next to the National Garden. ☎922 6330. Open Tu-Su 8:30am-3pm. Temple admission 500dr, students and EU seniors 300dr, EU students and under 18 free. Arch free.*)



## BYZANTINE ATHENS

*Viewing hours depend on each church's priest; mornings are best. Dress appropriately: long skirts for women, long pants for men, no bare shoulders.*

Like their Classical counterparts, Byzantine sanctuaries have become a part of Athens's landscape. Religious Greeks often pause before churches to pay their respects before going about their business. Many of these churches are in the busiest areas of Athens; they grant refuge to pedestrians looking for spiritual relief from the busy sidewalk and hot sun. Ducking into a few churches lets you get a glimpse of Greece's modern-day culture and faith.

Shoppers and pedestrians on Ermou will run right into **Kapnikaria Church,** which is stranded in the middle of the street one block beyond Aiolou. A bas relief decorates its west wall; it escaped destruction in 1834 only by the clemency of Louis I of Bavaria. Walking down Mitropoleos from Syndagma, you may notice a tiny red church on the corner of Pentelis—it's engulfed in a modern building; you'll also pass **Agios Eleftherios** and the **Mitropoli Cathedral. Agia Apostoli,** a well-preserved Byzantine church, stands at the east edge of the Agora in the heart of Athens. White-walled **Metamorphosis,** in Plaka near Pritaniou, was built in the 11th century and restored in 1956; look up to its dome, painted with Christ's face. Eleventh-century Russian Orthodox **Agia Triada,** a few blocks from Pl. Syndagma at Filellinon 21, is filled with silver angel icons.

## MODERN ATHENS

**OLYMPIC STADIUM.** The Panathenaic Olympic Stadium is wedged between National Gardens and Pangrati, carved into a hill. The site of the first modern Olympic Games in 1896, the stadium lay under a cloud of disappointment in 1996, when the centennial games were held in Atlanta. Still, in 1997, the stadium held the opening ceremonies of the World Track and Field Championships. The city is ecstatic about hosting the **2004 Summer Olympics** at the new Irini Stadium.

The Byzantines destroyed the Classical-era stadium, but in 1895 it was restored in Panteli marble. Before the stands were built, spectators peered down from the two hills hugging the stadium. Today, 70,000 people can pack in the stands of this preserve for athletes and sun bathing students; military parades and gymnastic displays are held here, and it's the finish line of *the* marathon. Marble *steles* near the front honor Greece's Olympic gold and silver medalists. Stand in the middle of the field and get an idea of what Olympians feel—imagine your legion of cheering fans. *(On Vas. Konstandinou. From Syndagma, walk up Amalias for 15min. to Vas Olgas, and follow it to the left. Or take trolley #2, 4, or 11 from Syndagma. Open 8am-8:30pm. Free.)*

**NO STRINGS ATTACHED** According to one story, Greek folk **shadow puppet theater** traces its origins to the 14th-century Ottoman Empire. Two men working on Sultan Orhan's new mosque, a stonemason named Karagöz and his foreman, Hacivat, were constantly distracting the rest of the crew with their fabulously witty, ribald conversations. In a rash fury, Orhan had the two jokesters executed, but soon after he found himself missing their humor. An inventive dervish attempted to entertain the bored, melancholic sultan with figures of the late twosome made from transparent camel skin, which he manipulated behind a screen lit with candles or oil lamps. Passed on from one anonymous puppet-master to the next over the following centuries, these **Karagöz** shadow shows evolved into bewitching spectacles of color, music, bawdy comedy, clever word play, slapstick, and political satire, migrating west in the early 19th century to usher in the distinctly Greek **Karaghiozis** shadow theater. Expert shadow puppet players, often an illiterate, itinerant bunch, traveled the countryside, sailed around the islands, and performed before cafe crowds sipping ouzo or coffee under the night sky. After the show, owner and puppet master split the proceeds from the food and drink. Today you can occasionally see shadow puppets on children's TV programs, or live at the one remaining permanent theater in the Athenian suburb of **Nea Smirni.** Ask at the Pl. Syndagma tourist information window for details.



**AROUND SYNDAGMA.** Don't miss the **changing of the guard** in front of the **Parliament** building. Every hour on the hour, two sets of *evzones* (guards) wind up like toy soldiers, kick their tassled heels in unison, and fall backward into symmetrical little guardhouses on either side of the **Tomb of the Unknown Warrior.** Unlike the stoic British beefeaters, *evzones* are known to give a wink and a smile. Their jovial manner matches their attire—pom-pommed clogs, *foustanelas* (short pleated skirts), and tasseled hats. Sunday at 10:45am, there's a ceremony with a band and the full guard troop.

Athens's endangered species, greenery and shade, are preserved in the **National Gardens,** their natural environment. The tranquil paths welcome siesta-seekers. There's a duck pond and a sad little zoo. Grab a drink (600-800dr) or pastry (800dr) from the *kafeneion* at the Irodou Atikou entrance (open 8am-8pm) to accompany you. Women shouldn't stroll here alone.

**OUTDOOR MARKETS.** Athens's two major markets attract bargain-hunters and browsers alike. The **Athens Flea Market,** adjacent to Pl. Monastiraki, has a festive bazaar atmosphere, with its potpourri of second-hand junk and high-rent antiques. Though tourists flock, you'll still be able to find treasures. *(Open daily 8am-3pm; Tu, Th, F till 8pm.)* If you're hankering for a **bouzouki,** seek out the master, Bill Aevorkian at Ifestou 6 (☎321 0024). On Sunday, a sprawling **food market** takes over Athinas between Evripidou and Sofokleous. Not for the faint of heart, the **meat market** overwhelms with sights and smells of livers, kidneys, and skinned rabbits. Early risers can jostle with Athenian cooks (restauranteurs and moms alike) for choice meat, fish, fruits, vegetables, breads, and cheeses. *(Open M-Sa 8am-2pm.)*

**MT. LYCAVITTOS.** Of Athens's seven hills, Lycavittos is the largest and most central. Try ascending at sunset, when you can catch a last glimpse of Athens's densely packed continuous rooftops in daylight, and watch the city light up for the night. Take the **funicular** to the top (2 min.; every 10-15min.; round-trip 1000dr, children 500dr)—the station is a healthy walk from the end of Ploutarchou. Or hike up: it's a nice 15- to 20-minute walk from any approach as long as you bring water, watch out for slippery rocks, and don't climb alone (especially at night, when crimes, accidents, and misnavigation are most frequent). At the top you'll see the **Chapel of St. George,** where you might spy a couple tying the knot (open 8:45am-12:15am, Th 10:30am-12:15am); you can light a candle (30dr) under the ornately painted ceilings. A leisurely stroll around the church will delight you with views of Athens's endless panoramic expanse. Using the Acropolis as a point of reference,

the neighborhoods of Monastiraki, Omonia, and Exarhia are on your right. Continuing clockwise, you will see Areos Park behind a small circular patch of green—that green is Strefi, another hill. The flashy lights and music of the Lycavittos Theatre are 180° from the Acropolis. The eastern view looks out on more parks, Mt. Hymettus, and—back near the Acropolis—a glimpse of the Panathenaic Olympic Stadium, the National Garden, and the Temple of Olympian Zeus. On a clear day, you'll see the Aegean blue to the south. The smog hasn't inhibited (and may have enhanced) the Athenian sunset's hazy blues and reds.

**NATIONAL CEMETERY.** The National Cemetery houses deceased politicians, actors, poets, and foreigners who died in Athens. There are currently two kinds of graves—family graves and rented graves that give up their bones to boxes after three years. Soon, space limits will allow only three-year graves. Even VIPs will spend three years in the ground before moving to the Mausoleum Commons.



As you enter the main gate, the Greek-speaking information bureau is on your left. The first graves are larger and more elaborate than most, as the rich and famous try to take it with them. On the left side of the first courtyard, archaeologist **Heinrich Schliemann,** excavator of Troy and Mycenae, lies in a pseudo-temple. To the left of the large statue of an angel is the tomb of **Melina Mercury,** a national film icon, who starred in *Never on Sunday* before becoming the Minister of Culture. On the main path, there is a small church where ceremonies are held for the dead. *(In Pangrati. From Pl. Syndagma walk down Amalias, turn left on Athenisiou Diakou, and then walk down Anapavseos. ☎922 1621. Open 8:30am-5:30pm. Free. For guided tours call the Cultural Center, Akademias 50. ☎361 2705 or 363 9671.)*

# MUSEUMS

## NATIONAL ARCHAEOLOGICAL MUSEUM

*Patission 44. A 20min. walk from Pl. Syndagma down Stadiou until Aiolou and right onto Patission. Take trolley #2, 4, 5, 9, 11, 15, or 18 from the uphill side of Syndagma, or trolley #3 or 13 from the north side of Vas. Sofias. Or take the metro to Victoria, leave the station and walk straight to the first street, 28 Octovriou. Make a right and walk 5 blocks; the museum is on your left. ☎821 7717. Open Apr.-Oct. M 12:30-7pm, Tu-Su 8am-5pm; Nov.-Mar. 8am-5pm. 2000dr, seniors 1500dr, students and EU seniors 1000dr; free Su and holidays. No flash photography; no posing in front of the exhibits.*

The jaw-dropping collection in the National Archaeological Museum deserves a spot on even the most rushed itinerary. Even a few pieces from this, the world's most extensive array of Greek artifacts, would steal the show in any other museum. First, check your bags (free) and grab a free **map** of the museum. Hold on to your ticket, since the museum's arrangement redirects you to the entry several times, and you'll have to pay again if you lose it.

The museum begins with prehistoric pieces (room 4), including Heinrich Schliemann's **Mycenae** excavations (p. 119). At first glance you may think the German archaeologist discovered the Midas touch: it is a world of gold, including the **Mask of Agamemnon** (the death mask of a king who lived at least 3 centuries earlier than Agamemnon himself). You'll also see samples of Bronze Age jewelry and pottery and, in the side rooms, magnificent examples of Cycladic art.

The next exhibition, made up of 29 rooms, surveys Greek **sculpture** from the 8th century BC through the 5th century AD. Buck-naked **kouroi,** or standing young men, allow the viewer to trace every last inch of Greek sculpture's development from early Archaic to late Roman; you'll see examples in the round, low relief, high relief, marble, and bronze. In room 11, don't miss the detailed, rippling abs of statue 13, a lifelike 540 BC work found at Megara. In room 12, a red backdrop brings out the ruddiness and vitality of the **Anavyssos Kouros** (item 3851). Compare the massive 530 BC Kouros of Sounion (item 2720), in room 8, to the 520 BC kouros named Kroisos (item 3851), in room 13; you'll notice how smoothness and fluidity seeped into sculpture over a decade. The 460 BC **bronze of Poseidon** poised

to throw his trident (item 15161) seems to move—it was an inspiration to Renaissance artists in Western Europe. In room 21, the perfect bronze **Jockey of Atemision,** recovered from the sea and restored this century, is full of dynamic life.

Move on to the fabulously sexy sculptures in room 32. The luscious neck, lips, and expression of the bust of **Antinous** (item 417), a favorite of the emperor Hadrian, will move you, while the suggestive pose of the sleeping maenad (item 261) may remind you of similar art from the pages of *Penthouse.* After the jolt of this sleazy stuff, check out the finds in room 48 on the second floor. Exquisite wall paintings and other finds here come from **Anotiri Thira,** a 16th century BC civilization buried by volcanic eruption. Resembling both Egyptian and Minoan art, these images of dolphins, reeds, and a boy holding a fish, highlight early fresco work.

Finally, rooms 49-56 hold an extraordinary (and overwhelming) collection of **pottery** from the 11th to 4th centuries BC, featuring pieces of every shape and style.



## OTHER MUSEUMS

**GOULANDRIS MUSEUM OF CYCLADIC & ANCIENT GREEK ART.** This 15-year-old museum is an unusually graceful teenager, displaying a stunning collection. The high-density exhibition space shows off its famous Cycladic figurines, sleek, abstract marble works, some with painted details that may represent tattoos. Many pieces were either looted from archaeological sites about 100 years ago or found in graves in the Cyclades. The figurines may represent goddesses, guides to the Underworld called *psychopompoi*, or concubines. Bronze jewelry from Skyros, a collection of vases, and Hannibal Lecter-lookalike Corinthian helmets share the space. Visit the extension of the Cycladic collection on the corner of Vas. Sofias and Herodotou. *(Neophytou Douka 4. A 20min. walk toward Kolonaki from Syndagma on Vas. Sofias; turn left on Neophytou Douna. It's ½ block up, on the right. Accessible by trolleys #3 and 13 (120dr). ☎722 8321. Open M, W-F 10am-4pm, Sa 10am-3pm. 1000dr, students 200dr.)*

**BYZANTINE MUSEUM.** In an elegant Neoclassical building, the Byzantine Museum's excellent collection of Christian art spans the 4th through 19th centuries. Early Byzantine sculptures, icons from the entire Byzantine period, and three reconstructed early **Christian basilicas** squeeze into the space. Room 4, in the back left corner of the ground floor, has a ceiling cut in the shape of the cross and mosaic-studded floor; it centers around an *omphalos* (belly button) representing an eagle and a snake. Also on the ground floor, you'll find an ornately reconstructed 17th-century Kephalonian church, with the 1863 throne of the Patriarch of Constantinople. A chandelier from Halkidiki presents scenes from Christ's life. Not all the exhibits are well marked; you might want to buy a guidebook beforehand. A new wing is scheduled to open in 2001; the construction work doesn't interfere with a visit. *(Vas. Sofias 22. Open Tu-Su 8:30am-2:30pm. ☎723 1570. 500dr; students 300dr; EU students, under 18, and classicists free. Guidebooks 2500dr.)*

**NATIONAL GALLERY.** The National Gallery (a.k.a. Alexander Soutzos Museum) exhibits the work of Greek artists, with periodic international displays. The permanent collection includes outstanding work by El Greco, as well as drawings, photographs, and sculpture gardens. Call the museum about current exhibits. *(Vas. Konstandinou 50. Set back from Vas. Sofias, next to the Hilton. ☎721 1010 or 721 7643. Open M and W-Sa 9am-3pm, Su 10am-2pm.1500dr, students and seniors 500dr, under 12 free.)*

**WAR MUSEUM.** Canons and fighter jets mark the museum, which traces Greek armaments from Neolithic times to now. It's cool if you're into submachine guns, 5th century BC Persian invasions, Alexander the Great, or the modern Greek arsenal. Model tanks, submarines, bombs, and booby traps delight your inner psycho. *(Rizari 2. Next to the Byzantine Museum, off Vas. Sofias. ☎723 9560. Open Tu-F 9am-2pm, Sa-Su 9:30am-2pm. Free.)*

**FOLK ART MUSEUM.** Exhibiting *laiki techni* (popular art) from all over Greece, the museum has embroidered textiles, costumes, puppets, ornamental church sil-

verwork, and household pottery. Don't miss the temporary exhibits or **Theophilos**'s (p. 24) paintings. *(Kedatheneon 17, in Plaka. ☎322 9031 or 323 9813. Open Tu-Su 10am-2pm. 500dr, students and seniors 300dr, EU students and children free. No flash photography.)*

**POPULAR MUSICAL INSTRUMENTS MUSEUM.** This interactive museum displays 18th-, 19th-, and 20th- century instruments. Grab the headphones at each exhibit to hear frenetic *kementzes* (bottle-shaped lyres) or *tsamboura* (goatskin bagpipe) music from the islands; tapping metal coins jingle as dancers cavort. *(Diogenous 1-2, in Plaka. ☎325 4119. Open Tu and Th-Su 10am-2pm, W noon-6pm. Free.)*

**ILIAS LALOUNIS JEWELRY MUSEUM.** Ilias Lalounis's jewel-studded art is displayed here, in his former home. Over 3000 designs from a 50-year period gleam in cases; you'll also find displays tracing Greek jewelry from ancient to modern times. There's also a workshop where visitors can watch the magic happen. You can begin with "Goldsmithery," a free short film on the first floor. The second floor houses the "Silver Frolics" collection, designed by children and produced by the museum goldsmiths. *(Kallisperi 12, south of the Acropolis. ☎922 1044. Open M and Th-Su 9am-4pm, W 9am-9pm. 800dr, students and seniors 500dr; free W after 3pm.)*



**JEWISH MUSEUM.** Occupying a brand new, seven-story building, this museum charts the Jewish experience in Greece from the Hellenistic Period. The collection includes textiles, religious artifacts, and a thorough library. A reconstructed Synagogue of Patras and an exhibit on the Holocaust are also there. *(Nikis 39, in Plaka. ☎322 5582. Open M-F 9am-2:30pm, Su 10am-2pm. Library Tu, Th 11am-1pm. 500dr.)*

**CHILDREN'S MUSEUM.** This museum offers a colorful, friendly, hands-on experience in the heart of Plaka, faithfully subscribing to the motto "I hear and I forget; I see and I remember; I do and I understand." Learn about the in-progress subway system or play dress-up in a bedroom from times past. In summer 2000, the museum was being renovated, and is expected to reopen soon; call ahead. *(Kidathineon 14, in Plaka. ☎331 2995 or 331 2996. Open M, Th, F 9:30am-1:30pm; W 9:30am-6:30pm; Sa-Su 10am-2pm. Free.)*

**THEATER MUSEUM.** Thespians and other interested parties should look into the **Theater Museum,** which displays costumes, models, photo equipment, and dressing rooms. *(Akademias 50. ☎362 9430. Open M-F 9am-2:30pm, W 5-8pm. Free.)*

# DAYTRIPS FROM ATHENS

The whites and grays of Athens's marble and smog quickly give way to the greens, browns, and blues of Greece's coast. Monasteries, ancient religious centers, and battlegrounds skirt Athens, while the ports of Piraeus and Rafina are gateways to the mixed frenzied and peaceful pace and pleasures of the islands.

## MONASTERY OF KESARIANI Μονη Καισσαριανης ☎01

*Take **blue bus #224** from the Athens KTEL stop two blocks up Vas. Sofias from Pl. Syndagma (20min., every 15min., 120dr). Get off at the last stop, follow the asphalt road uphill for 10min., and bear right under the overpass; stay to the right through two forks. The road splits again; stay to the right, which ascends the mountain. After 5min., you'll see another fork. Take a stone path up to the monastery. Bring water. ☎723 6619. **Open** Tu-Su 8:30am-2:30pm. **Admission** 800dr, seniors and students 400dr, EU students free.*

For serenity, or perhaps salvation, the Monastery of Kesariani is a total escape from nearby Athens. Near the peak of **Mt. Hymettus,** and with a bird's-eye view of Athens, the site was originally a temple to Demeter, goddess of agriculture and nature. In the Roman Period (AD 100-300), a new temple took its place; the old temple's stones served as building blocks. Well-preserved 17th-century frescoes by Ioannis Ypatios adorn the tiny, cave-like chapels. The 30-40min. walk rewards you with a fabulous, peaceful view of Athens. If you run out of water along the way, a 15min. walk up the main road leads to a small store with a drinkable fountain and spinach and cheese pies for sale (400dr). The staircases near the monastery lead up to three levels of wooded picnic area. Short trails meander away from the road and throughout the area; take a picnic and explore.

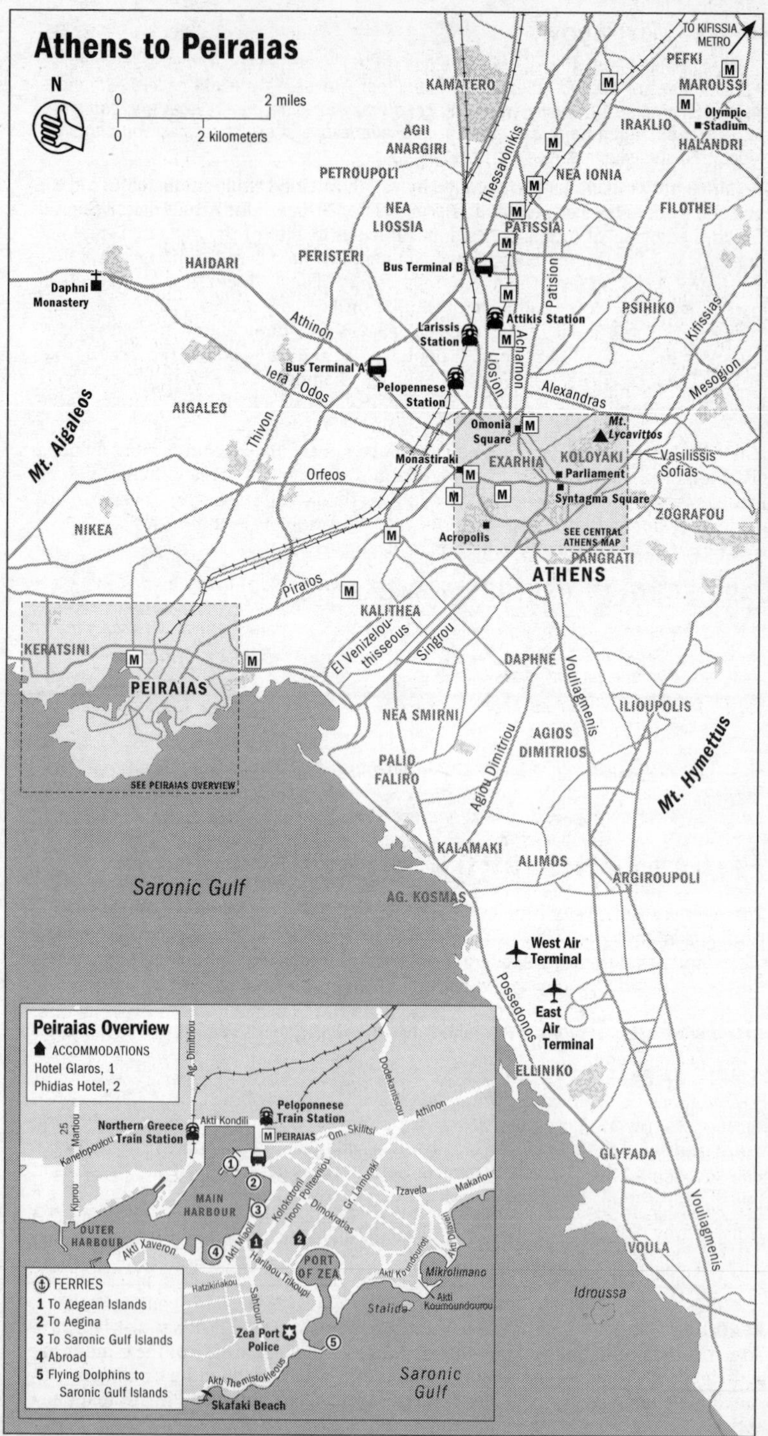
Athens to Peiraias
N
0 2 miles
0 2 kilometers
TO KIFISSIA METRO
PEFKI
MAROUSSI
KAMATERO
Olympic Stadium
IRAKLIO
HALANDRI
AGII ANARGIRI
Thessalonikis
PETROUPOLI
NEA IONIA
NEA LIOSSIA
FILOTHEI
PATISSIA
PERISTERI
HAIDARI
Bus Terminal B
Daphni Monastery
Patision
Attikis Station
PSIHIKO
Kifissias
Athinon
Larissis Station
Acharnon
Bus Terminal A
Liosion
Iera Odos
Pelopennese Station
Alexandras
Mesogion
Mt. Aigaleos
AIGALEO
Thivon
Omonia Square
Mt. Lycavittos
EXARHIA
KOLOYAKI
Vasilissis Sofias
Monastiraki
Parliament
Orfeos
Syntagma Square
ZOGRAFOU
NIKEA
Acropolis
SEE CENTRAL ATHENS MAP
PANGRATI
ATHENS
Piraios
KALITHEA
KERATSINI
El Venizelou-thisseous
Singrou
DAPHNE
PEIRAIAS
Vouliagmenis
ILIOUPOLIS
NEA SMIRNI
AGIOS DIMITRIOS
PALIO FALIRO
Agiou Dimitriou
SEE PEIRAIAS OVERVIEW
Mt. Hymettus
KALAMAKI
ALIMOS
ARGIROUPOLI
Saronic Gulf
AG. KOSMAS
West Air Terminal
East Air Terminal
Possedonos
ELLINIKO
GLYFADA
VOULA
Vouliagmenis
Idroussa
Peiraias Overview
ACCOMMODATIONS
Hotel Glaros, 1
Phidias Hotel, 2
Ag. Dimitriou
Dodekanissou
Peloponnese Train Station
Northern Greece Train Station
Akti Kondili
Athinon
PEIRAIAS
Om. Skilitsi
25 Martiou
Kanelopoulou
Kiprou
MAIN HARBOUR
Kolokotroni
Iroon Politexniou
Gr. Lambraki
Tzavela
Makariou
Dimokratias
OUTER HARBOUR
Akti Xaveron
Akti Miaoli
PORT OF ZEA
Akti Dilaveri
Hariliaou Trikoupi
Akti Koumoundourou
Mikrolimano
FERRIES
1 To Aegean Islands
2 To Aegina
3 To Saronic Gulf Islands
4 Abroad
5 Flying Dolphins to Saronic Gulf Islands
Hatzikiriakou
Sahtouri
Stalida
Akti Koumoundourou
Zea Port Police
Saronic Gulf
Akti Themistokleous
Skafaki Beach

## DAPHNI Μονη Δαφνι ☎01

*To reach Daphni from Athens, take* **blue bus #A16** *(20min., every 30 min., 120dr) from Pl. Eleftherias or from Pl. Koumoundourou. From Piraeus, take* **#804** *or* **845** *(35min., every 15min. 6am-11:30pm). When you get off the bus, cross the highway and go right. ☎581 1558.* **Open** *daily 8:30am-2:30pm.* **Admission** *800dr, students and seniors 400dr, EU students free. No flash photography.*

The Monastery of Daphni, surrounded by a high fortified wall, is a peaceful retreat caressed by cool breezes. It stands 10km west of Athens, along the Ancient Sacred Way at the corner of Iera and Athinon. Built on the site of the ancient Temple of Daphnios Apollo, the monastery owes its name to the sacred *daphnai* (Apollo's own laurels) that graced the ancient sanctuary. The 11th-century structure has flower-shaped windows and a smattering of birds' nests outside, while the inside holds a dozen cats and celestial mosaics of Jesus' life. Immediately to your right as you enter the octagonal room is a depiction of the *anastasis* (resurrection of Christ). The four corners of the ceiling portray (counterclockwise from near right) the angel's announcement of Mary's pregnancy, Christ's birth, His baptism in the Jordan River, and His *apotheosis* (or transfiguration). Mosaics in the narthex depict Judas's betrayal, the Last Supper, Mary's birth, and Her blessing as a young girl. Christ scowls down upon visitors from the masterful mosaic dome; His displeasure with man's misdeeds was a common theme in 11th-century Christian art. This expression perhaps prophesied the later violation of the monastary's sanctity: it was used as an army camp and then an insane asylum.

## CAPE SOUNION PENINSULA Ακρωτηριο Σουνιο ☎01

Place me on Sunium's marbled steep,
Where nothing, save the waves and I,
May hear our mutual murmurs sweep;
There, swan-like, let me sing and die.
—Lord Byron, *Don Juan*

*Two* **orange-striped KTEL buses** *travel to Cape Sounion from* **Athens:** *one leaves from the Mavromateon 14 bus stop near Areos Park and stops at all points on the Apollo Coast (2hr., every hr. 6:30am-6:30pm, 1300dr); the other follows a less scenic inland route (2¼hr., 1 per hr. 6am-6pm, 1200dr). Get off the bus at the last stop and head up to the right (facing the water), past the cafeteria to a ticket booth. Accommodations are at the* **Aegaeon Hotel,** *(☎(0292) 39 200; fax 39 234) a large yellow building five minutes from the main bus stop, visible from the temples. Singles 15,000dr; doubles 18,000dr.*

The majesty of the Aegean as seen from the cliffs of Sounion so captivated Lord Byron that he included Cape Sounion in his praise of Greek independence in the "Isles of Greece." Even his lyricism can't fully prepare you for the sight of the shimmering Aegean in every direction below the 60m rocky promontory. The rich, unique color of the Sounion-view ocean could only be described as Aegean blue.

**TEMPLE OF POSEIDON.** Gracing the highest point on the Cape, the Temple of Poseidon has been a dazzling white landmark for sailors at sea for millennia. Gazing past its towering columns at the sea below, you may feel transported to the world of Homer, with a glimpse of Odysseus sailing in the distance. Originally constructed around 600 BC, the fortress of Sounion was destroyed by the Persians in 480 BC and rebuilt by Pericles in 440 BC. The 16 remaining Doric columns rise above the coast. Look closely at the graffiti on the columns for the name of Lord Byron (on the square column as you face away from the cafeteria). Scattered bits of the **Temple of Athena Sounias,** the patron goddess of Athens, litter the lower hill. *(☎39 363. Open daily 10am-sunset. 800dr, students 400dr, EU students free.)*

**BEACHES.** After an hour at the temple, many people head down to the beaches. To reach the ocean, follow one of the paths from the inland side of the temple; the agile and adventurous can negotiate the cliff on the ocean side. Swarmed with vacationing families, the beaches along the **Apollo Coast** between Piraeus and Cape

Sounion have a carnival atmosphere on summer weekends. Some are owned by hotels, which charge admission (150dr). Towns usually have free public beaches, and some seaside stretches along the bus route remain almost empty. Drivers will let you off almost anywhere if you ask.

## MARATHON Μαραθωνας ☎0294

*The bus from the Mavromateon 29 station in Athens heads to Marathon (1½hr., every hr. 5:30am-10:30pm, 700dr); sit in the front and keep reminding the driver of your destination, and flag the bus down on the way back.*

Gasping out two words—*Νικη ημιν*, "Victory to us"—Phidippides announced the Athenian victory over the Persians in the bloody 490 BC battle of Marathon; he collapsed and died immediately after. His 42km sprint to Athens remains legendary, and today runners trace his Marathon route twice annually, beginning at a commemorative plaque.

With a car, you can explore nearby sights and beaches. At **Ramnous,** 15km to the northeast, lie the ruins of the **Temple of Nemesis**—goddess of divine and just retribution—and **Thetis,** goddess of law and justice (and Achilles' mom). Coastal **Schinias** to the north and **Timvos Marathonas** to the south are popular **beaches.** Some choose to camp illegally beneath Schinias's trees, but bloodthirsty mosquitoes act as a cruel modern Nemesis—a potential hefty fine completes the punishment.

To reach the **Archaeological Museum of Marathonas,** ask the bus driver to drop you at the "Mouseion and Marathonas" sign, after Marathon Town and the beach. Follow the signs through 2km of farms, bearing right at the fork, to the end of the paved Plateion road at #114. The small museum's five packed rooms focus on **death rituals:** you'll find Neolithic grave pieces (4000-2500 BC), Geometric sepulchres (2500 BC), Cycladic funeral offerings, Athenian and Plateion tombs and remains from the battle of Marathon, and—the coup de grace—a first century BC baby skeleton surrounded by two beehives. An **Athenian trophy** commemorates the battle with the Persians. Marble heads of Marathon's arts patron Herodes Atticus and his star pupil Polydenkion are on display, as are some Egyptian statues probably from a temple of Isis, and one of Atticus's poems. An arched gate in the museum courtyard, dedicated to Atticus's wife Regilla, displays marble replicas of the couple's heads. *(☎55 155. Open Tu-Su 8:30am-3pm. 1000dr, students 500dr, EU students, children under 18, student classicists and archaeologists free.)*

# PIRAEUS Πειραιας ☎01

The natural harbor of Piraeus (also Pireas, Peiraias—literally, "port") has been Athens's port since 493 BC, when Themistocles concocted an ambitious plan to create a naval base for the growing Athenian fleet. A hilly peninsula gridded with big white apartment buildings, Piraeus has all the dirt and grime of a commercial hub, including a waterfront lined with junk shops, shipping offices, travel agencies, and banks bordered by run-down neighborhoods. Still, the port stands on former glory: its quietude in Kazantzakis's *Zorba the Greek* shows a recent beauty, and Plato set his *Republic* in Piraeus during the height of Athenian power. An alluring cosmopolitan center, it bustled with rich *metoikoi* (resident aliens) and exotic cults. The destruction of the Long Walls by the victorious Spartans in 405 BC ended Athenian dominance. Centuries later, Piraeus is mainly a useful point of departure for the Greek isles, though an active nightlife attracts some Athenian party-goers.

**GETTING THERE AND GETTING AROUND.** To get to Piraeus, take the subway west from Athens to the last stop. (125dr, 20 min.) The subway deposits you at the top of Akti Poseidonos; head toward the water past Akti Zelepi.

An enormous number of ferries run from Piraeus. Unfortunately, the ferry schedule changes on a daily basis, and these listings are only approximate. **Be flexible** with your plans, since ferries are notoriously changeable. Check the *Athens*

*News* for schedules before you go. **Ferries** sail to nearly all Greek islands (except the Sporades and Ionian Islands). Among them are: **Iraklion,** Crete (10hr.; 7:30am, 8pm; 6400dr); **Hania,** Crete (10hr., 8:30pm, 5400dr); and **Rethymno,** Crete (10hr., 7:30pm, 6500dr). Also to: **Aegina, Poros, Spetses,** and **Hydra** (1-4hr., 2 per day, 1900-3100dr); **Chios** and **Lesvos** (9-11hr., 1 per day, 5400dr); **Ios** (7½hr., 5090dr); **Mykonos** (6hr., 2 per day, 4800dr); **Naxos** and **Paros** (6hr., 3 per day, 4800dr); **Rhodes** (16hr.; 2pm, 4pm; 8600dr); **Santorini** (9hr., 5630dr); and **Sifnos, Kythnos, Serifos,** and **Milos** (3-5½hr., 1 per day, 3900-4800dr). International ferries run to **Limassol, Cyprus** and **Haifa, Israel.** Long-distance **trains** for **Patras** and the **Peloponnese** leave daily from the train station on **Akti Kalimassioti.** Long-distance trains for northern Greece (Larissis) leave daily from the station on **Ag. Dimitriou** across the harbor.



**ORIENTATION AND PRACTICAL INFORMATION.** **Akti Poseidonos** merges with Akti Miaouli street at **Pl. Themistokleous,** where ferries depart for the Saronic Gulf Islands and hydrofoils leave for Aegina. The larger ferries dock at **Akti Miaouli,** international ferries are at the end toward the **Customs House,** and small ferries depart from **Akti Poseidonos.** On the opposite side of the peninsula is the port of **Zea,** a 10min. walk away from the water on any of the roads off Akti Miaouli. Private boats dock in the harbor on the left; hydrofoils depart from the right to the Saronic Islands. Boat and ticket agencies are on Akti Poseidonos and **Akti Miaouli.**

The subway station **tourist office** doles out advice on ferries and sells tickets. (☎412 1181 or 412 1172. Open 6am-8pm.) A second office is above the Zea post office. (☎452 2586 or 452 2591. Open M-F 8am-2:30pm.) Most **banks** along the waterfront **exchange currency. Citibank,** Akti Miaouli 47-49, has **ATMs.** (☎417 2153. Open M-Th 8am-2pm, F 8am-1:30pm.) There is an **American Express** office (☎429 5120) right next door. The Piraeus **port police** (☎422 6000) are at Akti Zelopi; the Zea **port police** (☎459 3144) are along the water and under the sidewalk. For the **tourist police,** dial 171. Stop in at **Telstar Booksellers,** just down the street, to grab last-minute summer reading. (Open M-F 7am-8pm, Sa 8am-4pm.) The **OTE,** Karaoli Dimitriou 19, is open M-F 7am-2:40pm. Surf the internet at **Dios Internet and...,** Sotiros Dios and Androutsou 170 (☎412 4220), behind McDonald's, or at **Surf In Internet Cafe,** Polytexneiou 42-44 and Platonos (☎422 7478). The main **post office** is on Tsamadou, one block inland from Pl. Themistokleous. (☎412 4202. Open M-F 7:30am-2pm.) Zea's **post office** is near the port police. (☎418 3380. Open M-F 7:30am-2pm.) **Postal code:** 18502 (Piraeus), 18504 (Zea).

**ACCOMMODATIONS AND FOOD.** Don't stay in Piraeus unless you must: inexpensive, quality accommodations are much easier to find in Athens. An adequate option is **Hotel Glaros,** Char. Trikoupi 4, off Akti Miaouli. (☎451 5421; fax 453 7889. Singles 7500dr; doubles 10,000dr; triples 13,000dr). Or try **Hotel Phidias,** Koundouriotou 189, near Zea off Bouboulinas (off Akti Miaouli), for private baths and TVs, A/C, and bar with a TV. (☎429 6160. Breakfast 1700dr. Singles 12,000dr; doubles 16,000dr.) Dockside fast food joints hawk average food for cheap. You can stock up on staples at **Peiraikon Supermarket,** one block up Antistasseos (open M-F 8am-9pm, Sa 8am-4pm). The extensive menu at **Drosopigi,** Akti Moustopoulou 24, doesn't distract most from the rolled souvlaki (400dr). Mouth-watering *baklava* (300dr) is made fresh at **Europa Bakery,** Koundouriotou 166-168 (☎412 2577). If you've got time to kill, chill in a Kolokatroni cafe, near Tsamadou: **Belle Epoque** and **Demotikon Ouzeri** both brew coffee (450dr) and *frappés* (1200dr).

**SIGHTS.** The prize possession of the **Piraeus Archaeological Museum,** Char. Trikoupi 31, is the ancient **Piraeus Apollo,** a hulking hollow bronze with outstretched arms. Three other bronze statues of Athena and Artemis were found near the port in 1959; they had been shelved in a storeroom for safekeeping when Piraeus was besieged by Sulla in 86 BC. (☎452 1598. Open Tu-Su 8:30am-3pm. 500dr, students 300dr.) Farther south at Zea, a stroll down the ramp to the dock at Akti Themistokleous and Botassi leads to the **Hellenic Maritime Museum,** which traces the Greek navy's history using detailed ship models. Of particular note in

Room 3 is a model of the Athenian trireme "Olympias," used in the Persian Wars (490-480 BC). The courtyard holds torpedo tubes, naval weapons, and the top part of the Second World War submarine *Papanikolis*. (☎451 6822. Open Tu-Sa 9am-2pm. 500dr; Sa free.)

## RAFINA Ραφηνα ☎0294

Rafina feels like a smaller, quieter version of Piraeus. There's less to do, but its easier on the eyes, ears, and lungs than its bigger, badder counterpart.

**ORIENTATION AND PRACTICAL INFORMATION.** The ramp up from the waterfront leads to **Pl. Plastira. Ferries** sail to: **Karystos** in Evia (1¾hr., 2 per day, 1770dr); **Marmari** in Evia (1¼hr., 4-6 per day, 1240dr); **Andros** (2hr., 4 per day 7:20am-7pm, 2500dr); **Tinos** (4hr., 3 per day 7:20am-5:30pm, 3600dr); **Mykonos** (4¾hr., 3 per day 7:20am-5:30pm, 4000dr); **Paros** (5hr., 1 on Th, 4100dr); and **Naxos** (6hr., 2 per day, 4200dr). **Hydrofoils** sail to: **Andros** (1hr., 2 per week, 4700dr); **Tinos** (1½hr., 2 per day, 7200dr); **Amorgos** (10hr., 2 per week, 9500dr); and **Mykonos** (2½hr., 2 per day, 8200dr). **Nel Lines** goes to **Agios Efstratios, Limnos, and Kavala** (3 per week) and **Lesvos** (1 per week). The **port authority** (☎22 300 or 22 487) has more info. Along the waterfront, English-speaking **Strintzis Lines, Goutos Lines, Agoudimos Lines,** and **Ventouris Ferries** operate various ferries, while **Ilios Lines** and **Hermes Lines** run **hydrofoils.** Rafina is accessible by frequent **buses** from Athens's station at Mavromateon 29, two blocks up along Areos Park (1hr., every 30min. 5:40am-10:30pm, 460dr). Return buses leave Rafina from the ramp on the waterfront.

Both **Commercial Bank,** two blocks inland from the plateia (☎25 182; open M-Th 8am-2pm, F 8am-1:30pm), and **Ionian Bank,** on the far left corner of the plateia (☎24 152; open M-Th 8am-2pm, F 8am-1:30pm), **exchange currency** and have 24hr. **ATMs. Taxis** line up in front of the plateia; call one at 23 101. Facing inland at the dock, the **post office** is two streets to the right on El. Venizelou. (☎23 777. Open M-F 7:30am-2pm.) The **OTE** is across from the post office on the plateia. (☎25 182. Open M-F 7:30am-3pm.) **Postal code:** 19009.

**ACCOMMODATIONS AND FOOD.** Don't stay in Rafina unless you get stuck here; if you do, be prepared to pay. **Hotel Korali,** Pl. Plastira 11, rents cramped rooms with shared baths. (☎22 477. Singles 6000dr; doubles 9500dr; triples 14,000dr.) Other tiny inlets let you **swim** or **sunbathe** if you've got a spare hour. Go right at the top of the ramp, then right again at the end of the blue fence, then follow the coast and pick your spot. Cafes, pizzerias, and tavernas line the plateia and waterfront. Early ferry-catchers can try **Arktopolia,** an inexpensive bakery; it's on the left side of the plateia when you're facing away from the water. (Fresh bread 150dr, filled croissants from 200dr, yogurt 250dr. Open 6:30am-11pm.) A **minimarket** sells fruits, vegetables, and toiletries off Pl. Plastira, two buildings from Arktopolia. (Open 8am-1:30pm, 5-9pm.)

# PELOPONNESE ΠΕΛΟΠΟΝΝΗΣΟΣ

We let the features gather, the low skies and mists, the hilltops edged with miles of old walls, fallen battlements, that particular brooding woe of the Peloponnese.

—Don DeLillo

A hand-shaped peninsula stretching its fingers into the Mediterranean, the Peloponnese is steeped in history and folklore that contribute to its magical, otherworldly atmosphere. The remnants of ancient civilizations and achievements mark the present-day peninsula, and its timeless natural beauty remains unchanged. The majority of Greece's best archaeological sites are here, including Olympia, Mycenae, Messene, Corinth, Mystras, and Epidavros. Uncommon landscapes, from the barren crags of the Mani to the forested peaks and flower-blanketed pastures of Arcadia, grace Pelops' former home. A world apart from the islands, the serenely beautiful and sparsely populated Peloponnese remembers 5000 years of continuous habitation, from the ancients to traditions of village life.



**HIGHLIGHTS OF THE PELOPONNESE**

**WALK BENEATH THE LION'S GATE,** past Cyclopean walls, and into *tholos* tomb at the home of the dysfunctional Atreus clan, Mycenae (p. 119).

**THE BYZANTINE GHOST TOWN** Mystras, once the capital of the Greek part of the empire, invites you into the living architectural museum it has become (p. 154).

**TAKE A BREAK FROM ANTIQUITY** in the exquisite Arcadian mountain villages of mountainside Dimitsana (p. 143) and medieval Stemnitsa (p. 144).

**TOAST THE GODDESS OF LOVE** on the gorgeous beaches and rocky mountains of nearly uninhabited Kythera (p. 160).

**ENVISION GREASED-UP ATHLETIC GRAPPLING** at ancient Olympia, where Mediterranean Greek city-states squared off in the original Olympic Games (p. 137).

**STRIKE A MATCH** on the stage center of the acoustically marvelous theater of Epidavros, and a friend can hear it in the last row (p. 127).

## CORINTHIA ΚΟΡΙΝΘΙΑ AND ARGOLIS ΑΡΓΟΛΙΔΑ

Back in the day, Argos, a monster endowed with 100 unblinking eyes, stalked the north Peloponnese, subduing unruly satyrs and burly, bad-boy bulls. Today's Corinthia and Argolis still hold a lion's share of impressive archaeological sites, but, alas, the population of roving mythological beasts has declined sharply. Consider making Nafplion (p. 123) your base for exploring the region, as it allows access to Mycenae, Corinth, Tiryns, and Epidavros, and the smaller sites of Nemea, Isthmia, and Argos's Heraion.

### NEW CORINTH Κορινθος ☎0741

New Corinth rests on the Gulf of Corinth just west of the canal that separates the Peloponnese from the Greek mainland. Like its ancient predecessor (7km southwest of the city), New Corinth has been victimized by several earthquakes, most

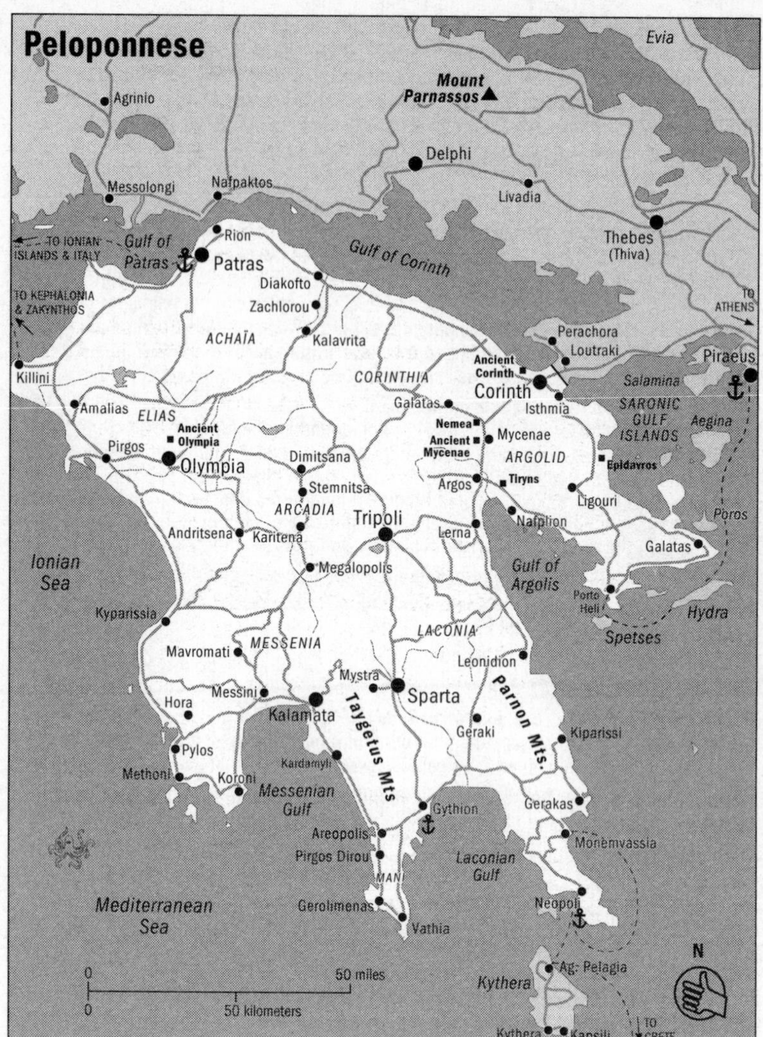


recently in 1981; people wisely rebuilt their city low, secure, and shake-proof, giving it a very sturdy but none too aesthetically pleasing appearance. Since most travelers merely pass through en route to nearby ancient sites, the city is relatively tourist-free. Despite an attractive harbor, Corinth remains fairly dirty, busy, and hot; consider bypassing this experience by staying at the campgrounds outside the city, near the ruins, or one easy bus ride away in Loutraki (p. 117).

## ORIENTATION AND PRACTICAL INFORMATION

New Corinth spreads out in a neat grid, which makes it fairly simple to navigate. The main drag, **Eth. Antistasis,** runs perpendicular to the waterfront. Both **Ermou** (to the east) and **Kolokotroni** (to the west) are parallel to Eth. Antistasis. All three intersect **Damaskinou,** which borders the harbor. Two blocks inland from the shore, between Eth. Antistasis and Ermou, is the city's central park. This area is the heart

of town, where most of the shops and restaurants are located. Buses deposit their passengers and taxis line up at the city's central park, between Eth. Antistasis and Ermou. The train station is a few blocks southeast. To find the waterfront from the station, turn left out of the building onto Demokratias, then take the first right onto Damaskinou.

**Buses: Ermou** and **Koliatsou Station** (☎24 481), corner of Ermou and Koliatsou. To **Athens** (1½ hr., 32 per day 5:30am-9:30pm, 1750dr) and **Loutraki** (20min., 2 per hr. 5:30am-10pm, 320dr). The **Argolis Station** (☎24 403) is located at the intersection of Eth. Antistasis and Aratou, just past the park. Buses to: **Isthmia** (10min., 4 per day, 250dr) and **Nemea** (1hr., 7 per day, 750dr). Buses to: **Mycenae** (40min., 750dr) via **Fihtia** (1.5km from the site); **Argos** (1hr., 900dr); and **Nafplion** (1½hr., 1200dr) leave at 7am and then every hr. 8:30am-9:30pm. To get to **Sparta** or other points south, take the Loutraki bus to the Corinth Canal and pick up the Athens bus to Sparta, Kalamata, Koroni, or Tripoli. You can also depart for these destinations from a new bus station south of town, but you'll have to take a taxi (1000dr).

**Trains:** The **station** (☎22 523) is on Demokratias. To **Athens** (2hr., 14 per day, 900dr) via **Isthmia.** Two major train lines serve the Peloponnese: one travels the northern coast from Corinth to Pirgos and south to Kyparissia; the other goes south from Corinth to Tripoli and Kalamata. To: **Argos** (1hr., 6 per day, 700dr); **Diakofto** (1½ hr., 8 per day, 800 dr); **Kalamata** (5hr., 4 per day, 1700dr); **Kyparissia** (5hr., 6 per day, 2050dr); **Patras** (2½hr., 8 per day 8am-midnight, 1150dr); **Pirgos** (4½hr., 7 per day, 1600dr); and **Tripoli** (2hr., 4 per day, 900dr). Express trains 400-1000dr extra.

PELOPONNESE

**Taxis:** (☎24 844), along the park side of Eth. Antistasis.

**Moped Rental: Libropoulos,** Eth. Antistasis (☎72 937). 5500dr per day for 50ccs of road dominance. Open 8am-1:30pm and 5-8:30pm.

**Tourist Police:** Ermou 51 (☎23 282), upstairs. Maps, brochures, and assistance. English spoken. Open M-Sa 8am-2pm and 5-8pm.

**Banks: National Bank,** Eth. Antistasis 7, one block up from the water, has **currency exchange** and a 24hr. **ATM.** A number of other banks with these services are also on Eth. Antistatis. Banking hours are mostly 8am-2pm.

**Public Toilets:** Across from the park on Eth. Antistasis. Open 24hr.

**Police:** Ermou 51 (☎100 or 22 143), facing the park. Open 24hr.

**Pharmacy:** Lots along Eth. Anastasis and Koliatsou, most open 8am-2pm and 5-8pm.

**Hospital** (☎25 711), on Athinaion; cross the train tracks and turn left. It's quite a walk, so use a cab or call the hospital for an **ambulance** in an emergency. Open 24hr.

**Telephones: OTE,** Kolokotroni 32 (☎22 111). Open M-F 7am-10pm.

**Internet Access: Stretto** (☎71 143), on Theotoki. Sip coffee (600dr) and check your email (1000dr per hr., 500dr minimum charge). Open M-Sa 8am-2pm and 5-11pm.

**Post Office:** Adimantou 35 (☎22 015). Adimantou borders the park on the end farthest from the water. Open M-F 7:30am-2pm. **Postal code:** 20100.

## ACCOMMODATIONS

Most travelers on their way to the nearby sites don't spend much time in New Corinth, so domatia, hostels, and budget hotels are rare. New Corinth's few hotels tend to be pricey, and are mostly on Eth. Antistasis and Damaskinou.

**Hotel Akti,** Eth. Antistasis 3 (☎23 337), is your best bet for an inexpensive stay in New Corinth. Simple, utilitarian bedrooms have private sink (toilet and showers shared), and some have balconies with great views of the water at no extra charge. A really low rate for its prime location. Singles 4000dr; doubles 8000dr.

**Hotel Apollon,** Pirinis 18 (☎22 587). Turn left onto Damaskinou after exiting the train station, Apollon is at the first intersection, to your right. At press time, the hotel was open, but undergoing renovations. Wood-paneled rooms with linoleum floors and private baths. Singles 5000dr; doubles 8000dr; TV and A/C 2000dr extra.

**Ephira Hotel,** Eth. Antistasis 52 (☎24 021; fax 24 514), two blocks inland from the park. Posh 45-room hotel has well-furnished rooms with private bath, A/C, TV, and balcony. Continental breakfast 1500dr. Singles 9500dr, 9000dr in winter; doubles 15,000dr, 13,000dr in winter; triples 18,000dr, 16,000dr winter.

New Corinth's two beachfront **campgrounds** present inexpensive alternatives. Catch a bus (every 30min., 210dr) on Kollatsou near Kolokotroni, and get off at the signs for the campground. **Camping Korinth Beach** is 3km out of town. (☎27 920. 1400dr per person, 850dr per tent.) **Blue Dolphin** is 1.5km farther, with campsites on Lecheon beach. (☎25 766. 1200dr per person; 600dr per small tent; 1000dr per large tent; 700dr per car; electricity 800dr; tents rented for 2000dr.) The campgrounds are near the archaeological site, and you can catch the Ancient Corinth-New Corinth bus back to town if the driver notices you waiting by the campground stop: make yourself visible if you want to snag the bus.

## FOOD

After 9pm, downtown New Corinth springs to life, as residents flock to the waterfront to dine outdoors in the balmy evening air. As in the daytime, speed seems to be a virtue in New Corinth; fast food is *de rigeur* and waiters deftly dodge the traffic on Damaskinou to shuttle between restaurants and their outdoor seating areas across the street on the waterfront plateia.

**Axinos** (Αχινος), Damaskinou 41 (☎28 889), on the waterfront plateia. The blue wooden chairs and bright tablecloths add a cheerful touch to summer evening dining al fresco. *Pastitsio* (1400dr) and Greek salad (1200dr) are among the many Greek specialty dishes. Open for breakfast (omelette 1000dr).

**24 Oro,** Ag. Nicholou 19, on the waterfront, a few blocks east of the museum. This taverna serves classic staples prepared with fresh ingredients, less grease, and more attention to detail. Cucumber and tomato salad 700dr, *pastitsio* 1500dr, *orzo* in clay bowl 1700dr.

**Neon Cafeteria**, at the corner of Damaskinou and Eth. Antistasis, is a glowing display of lights, mirrors, and brass with a wide selection of foods. Hearty entrees (1450-1750dr), a salad bar (950dr), and mouth-watering desserts (550dr) lure you in. Open late.

## NIGHTLIFE

New Corinth feels serious by day, but it tosses down its hair at night when motorcycle-mounted teens head west of the city to **Kalami Beach.** To reach Kalami without a motorcycle, walk four blocks past the park along Eth. Anistasis, turn right, and walk 10 blocks. As the neighborhood is disconcertingly dark and empty at night, women may prefer taking a taxi from the park (500dr); tell the driver "Kalami" or "*Thalisa*" (the sea). Ask a restaurant owner to call a taxi for you.

Kalami's strip has something for everyone. Behind the street, looking out at the sparkling lights of Loutraki, an assembly of cafes and clubs strut their stuff, each with thumping bass and expansive umbrellas. At places like **Pregio** and **La Plaza,** you'll find Corinth's hip young things sipping beer (700dr) or mixed drinks (1500dr), motorcycle-watching, and listening to American dance tunes. On the beach side of the main drag, humbler cafes draw family crowds. Rambunctious children play while adults gaze at the ocean and sip coffee (300dr) and beer (500dr). **Pizza Ami,** out of earshot of the raucous bars, serves pasta dishes (1100-1500dr) and a lengthy list of pizzas (small 1800-2100dr, large 2700-3250dr).

If you'd rather hang downtown, try car-free **Theotoki** street as an alternative to the beach. Walking away from the harbor on Eth. Antistasis, turn right halfway down the second block. Past the intersection with Koloktroni, the street fills with outdoor tables of cafes, pubs, and small restaurants. The typical and trendy **Blue Note Club** gathers a perpetual crowd of people under its umbrellas.

## DAYTRIPS FROM CORINTH

### ANCIENT CORINTH Αρχαια Κορινθος

*7km southwest of New Corinth. Buses from Corinth city leave from a stop along the central park, on Koliatsou (20min.; to Ancient Corinth every hour 8am-9pm, return 8:30am-9:30pm; 300dr). ☎31 207. Open 8am-7pm, in winter 8am-5pm. Guidebook 2200dr. Museum and site 1200dr, students 600dr.*

Strategically located on the isthmus between the Corinthian and Saronic Gulfs, Ancient Corinth was once a powerful commercial center and one of the most influential cities in ancient Greece. At its height in the 5th century BC, Corinth joined forces with southern neighbor Sparta against the naval muscle of Athens—a power struggle that led to the Peloponnesian Wars (p. 12). While the war won dominance for Sparta, it weakened Corinth considerably. After Romans sacked the city in 146 BC, destroying buildings and pocketing precious objects, Corinth remained deserted until Julius Caesar rebuilt it in 44 BC. You'll want to spend several hours at the site to hike around and poke at the ruins.

PELOPONNESE

**ANCIENT SITE.** The remains of the ancient city stand at the base of the **Acrocorinth.** Past the exit of the museum, the archaeological site is down the stairs to your left. Its reconstructed columns from the 6th-century BC Temple of Apollo contrast strikingly with the vivid blue sky. Columns, engraved friezes, and pediments lie around the courtyard in delicious chaos. As you pick your way through the rubble, an unparalleled view of New Corinth and the Gulf stretches out below you. Facing the entrance of the museum, the Corinthian columns on your left make up the facade of a Roman shrine. Behind the museum is the **Fountain of Glauke,** named after Jason's second wife, who was consumed by flames from an enchanted robe given to her by Jason's jilted first wife, Medea. Standing at the Temple of Apollo and facing the mountainous Acrocorinth, the remains of the forum—the center of Roman civil life—lie in front of you. Walk down the middle of the row of central shops and you'll see the **Julian Basilica.**

To the left, near the exit at the edge of the site farthest from the museum, a broad stone stairway descends into the **Peirene Fountain,** perhaps the most impressive structure on the site. Although smoothed and patinated by the water that still flows today, the columns and fresco-covered tunnels inside the fountain have survived the centuries unharmed. The ancients believed that winged Pegasus was drinking here when he was captured by Bellerophon. Just past the fountain is the **Perivolos of Apollo,** an open-air court surrounded by yet more columns. On the uphill edge of the site on the side farthest from the museum, somewhat shabby sheds cover the mosaic floors of a Roman villa. Unfortunately, you'll have to peer through a rusted chain link fence, as entry is not permitted.

**ARCHAEOLOGICAL MUSEUM.** The Archaeological Museum houses an impressive collection of statues, well-preserved mosaics, tiny clay figurines, and pottery, tracing Corinth's history through Greek, Roman, and Byzantine rule. The Roman frescoes and mosaics date from the same period as Pompeii, and changes in pottery technique follow Greece's evolution from Neolithic to Byzantine times. The museum's collections of sarcophagi (one with a skeleton under glass) and its headless statues in the open-air courtyard are morbidly appealing. While the exhibits are noteworthy, there isn't much explanation of their history or relationship to the site, so it's worthwhile to purchase a guidebook (2200dr).

**FORTRESS AND ACROCORINTH.** Getting to the fortress at the top of Acrocorinth is a strenuous 90min. walk, and only for the truly dedicated. At the summit, the Temple to Aphrodite, once served by "sacred courtesans" who initiated diligent disciples into the "mysteries of love," remains largely intact. The relatively empty fortress contains acres of towers, mosques, gates, and walls. *(To get there from the archaeological site, call a taxi (1500dr), which will wait for you for an hour. ☎31 464. From Corinth, 1500dr; hr. wait 4000dr.)*

## ISTHMIA Ισθμια

*Take the bus (20min., every 30min. 8am-7pm, 300dr) from Corinth to Isthmia, getting off at the green museum to the right of the bus stop. Open Tu-Sa 8:45am-7pm, Su and off-season 9:30am-2:30pm. 500dr, students 300dr, EU students free.*

Like Olympia, Isthmia was the site of prestigious athletic contests every four years. An excellent museum compliments the remains of the ancient complex, displaying carefully diagrammed exhibits of finds from the Temple of Poseidon and the sites of the Isthmian games. Of particular interest are the glass *opus sectile* (mosaic panels), which survived the earthquake of AD 375 to be discovered at nearby Kenchreai. The entrance to the ruins lies to the right of the museum. All that remains of the **Temple of Poseidon** is its foundation. The **theater** is below and to the right of the temple. Caves where people enjoyed dinner and entertainment during the Archaic Period lie above the theater.

## NEMEA Νεμυα

*4km from modern Nemea; coming by bus from Corinth (1hr., 7 per day, 750dr), ask to be let off at the ancient site. ☎22 739. Site and museum open Tu-Su 8am-2:30pm. 500dr, students 300dr, EU students free.*

The temple of **Nemean Zeus** has dwindled to three columns, but it's still worth a look. The walkway takes you past a wall built around a glass-encased grave, skeleton included. The site also includes a stadium (500m down the road to Corinth), well-preserved baths, and a museum with excellent explanatory notes in English, some artifacts, and reconstructions of the site.

PELOPONNESE

# LOUTRAKI Λουτρακι ☎0744

The pebbled beach of Loutraki, just over the isthmus of Corinth on the mainland, has attracted sun-seeking vacationers since ancient times. Visitors still come to soak in the natural springs for their reputed healing powers. This potent stuff is also the water bottled and hawked all over Greece. Though clearly a tourist haven whose downtown is marred by nigh-tacky hotels, Loutraki's relaxed vacation pace and hospitality toward travelers allows for a tranquil overnight stay on the way to visit neighboring sites.

**ORIENTATION AND PRACTICAL INFORMATION.** To get to Loutraki from Isthmia, cross the canal bridge and find the bus stop next to a railroad station sign. Stay on the bus until the last stop, a triangular road island where **El. Venizelou,** the main street, meets Periandou and Eth. Antistasis. Running parallel to the water, El. Venizelou curves at the port and becomes Georgiou Lekka. **Buses** (☎22 262) from Loutraki go to: **Athens** (1½hr., 1 per hr. 6:05am-9pm, 750dr); **Corinth** (20min., 2 per hr. 5:30am-10:30pm, 320dr); and **Perahora** (20min., 9 per day 6am-8pm, 250dr). Boat excursions are available at the dock past the park. **Albona Cruises** sail to **Lake Vouliagmeni** (Tu-Th, 3000dr). Cruises down the **Corinth Canal** leave Sundays at 10am and Thursdays at 5pm (4500dr). For a **taxi,** call 22 555, or stop by their stand next to the Tourist Info center on El. Venizelou. For **moped rentals,** visit **Moto-Rent,** on the left of Damaskinou, two blocks before the ocean. (☎67 277. 50cc bike 6000dr.)

A **tourist information center** kiosk is located about one block down from the bus station. To get to the **National Bank,** Pl. 25 Martiou, bear left where the road forks. (☎/fax 21 937. Open M-Th 8am-2pm, F 8am-1:30pm. 24hr. **ATM** available.) Periandrou, the first side street on the right across from the bus station's road island, is home to **Laundry Self-Service,** which provides wash and dry (3000dr) and ironing. (☎63 854. Open M-W and Sa 8:30am-2pm, F 8:30am-2pm and 5:30-9pm.) The **police,** El. Venizelou 7 (☎63 000 or 22 258), are in the same building as the **tourist police.** (☎65 258. Open M-F 8am-2pm.) The **health center** is roughly 5km from the center of town: walk five blocks up from El. Venizelou, turn right, and continue straight. (☎63 444. Open 24hr.) There is a **pharmacy** (☎21 787) at El. Venizelou 21. **Internet access** is available at **NetCafe@Loutraki,** on the waterfront off El. Venizelou. The **OTE** is at El. Venizelou 10. (Open M-F 7:30am-3:10pm.) From the bus station, walk down El. Venizelou with the water to your left; the **post office,** 28 Octovriou 4, is a block down on your right. (Open M-F 7:30am-2pm.) **Postal code:** 20300.

**BIG DIG** For years, the pesky **isthmus of Corinth** forced ships sailing between the Aegean and Adriatic seas to circumnavigate the entire Peloponnese, adding an extra 185 nautical miles to an already lengthy journey. Late 7th or early 6th century BC Greeks came up with a solution, building the limestone-paved road called the *Diolkos*, which connected the Corinthian and Saronic Gulfs. *Olkos*, huge wheeled vehicles, carried ships overland along the *Diolkos*. The possibility of building a canal was proposed time and time again by the powers that were, including Periander of Corinth, Julius Caesar, and Caligula, but none of them ever followed through. It looked like the work might get done when **Nero** removed the first bucket of earth himself at the Isthmian Games of 67 (AD, that is). With that fiery flair for the dramatic, Nero thrust a golden pick into the ground to start the project. But Nero had bigger fish (like Rome) to fry, and the project never got underway. Not until 1893 did Greek and French engineers complete their 11-year project, creating a canal 6343m long and 24.6m wide.



**ACCOMMODATIONS.** Loutraki draws a near-constant stream of monied vacationers; the result is a lack of budget hotels. To reach **Le Petit France,** Marcou Botsari 3, from the bus station, take El. Venizelou in the direction you face upon exiting the station building; Botsari is your third right. Friendly owners keep free bottled water for the guests of the blue-shuttered hotel; rooms come with balconies, ceiling fans, and bath. (☎22 401. Singles 6000dr; doubles 8000dr.) To find **Hotel Marko,** go left from the bus station (facing the water) and take your second right onto L. Kalsoni. Though it may appear a few decades outdated, the locale (practically on the beach) and cleanliness make it livable. All rooms have balcony and bath. (☎63 542. Singles 9000dr; doubles 10,000dr; A/C extra. Breakfast included.) For domatia, call 22 456 or stop by the corner of El. Venizelou and G. Lekka. (Open 9am-1:30pm and 5-10pm.) **Camping** is available 16km away at stunning Lake Vouliagmeni, but you'll have to arrange transportation.

**FOOD AND NIGHTLIFE.** If the best food is whatever is most abundant, then Loutraki's best is fish. **Theonoros** (Θεονορος), on El. Venizelou next to the National Bank, has peaceful outdoor seating overlooking the waterfront. It serves generous portions of delicious fare. Seafood variety plates (2000-4000dr) and veal with spaghetti (1500dr) are two of the best options. **Taverna Astoria,** on El. Venizelou near the OTE, offers scrumptious and inexpensive dinners both à la carte (chicken *yiouvetsi* 1400dr, *tzatziki* 600dr) and prix-fixe (3-course meal 1900dr). **Horiatiki Taverna,** El. Venizelou 70, has been serving fruits and stellar fish dishes for over 30 years, drawing crowds with its elegant garden seating area to the freshest seafood around (fish entrees 6500-13,000dr per kg). If seafood doesn't suit you, tiny **Il Guosto Pizza,** one block behind the bus station on El. Venizelou, has an impressive variety of pizzas (1700-2300dr) and Italian dishes like four-cheese tortellini for 1850dr. (☎69 200. Delivery available. Open until 1am.)

Nightlife consists of a ritual vacillation between eating and dancing. Waterfront restaurants swell in summer, staying full until midnight and beyond, when taxis transport the footloose to discos on the fringe of the city. The flagship disco in Loutraki is undoubtedly **Baby-O,** precariously placed between a vast, lonely looking bottling company and a shrub-covered wasteland. Baby-O caters to a weekend crowd of 1000 to 1500 people, and is the only disco open year-round in the Corinth-Loutraki area. **Biblos** and **Club Bazaar** are both in town and near the waterfront.

**WATER FUN.** Those seeking solace in Loutraki's healing waters can indulge in sauna treatments, whirlpool baths, and hydromassage at the **Hydrotherapy Thermal Spa,** G. Lekka 26. Four-, five-, six-, and 10-day programs are offered; call for prices and group discounts. The spa will cure "rheumoatoarthritic, spondycarthritic" and "chronic gynecological diseases," or so the bilingual sign printed on the door promises. (☎22 215. Open M-Sa 8am-1pm.) At the theme parky **waterfalls** on the edge of town away from Corinth, you can hike to the top and watch the water funnel out from fountains at the base of the cliff. (Open 10am-3am.)

## AT&T Direct® Service

The easy way to call home from anywhere.

### AT&T Access Numbers

| | |
|---|---|
| Austria ● ......0800-200-288 | France........0800-99-00-11 |
| Belarus ✖ ........8◆800-101 | Gambia ● ..............00111 |
| Belgium ● ....0-800-100-10 | Germany ....0800-2255-288 |
| Bosnia ▲ ......00-800-0010 | Ghana ......................0191 |
| Bulgaria ▲ ......00-800-0010 | Gibraltar ....................8800 |
| Cyprus ● ........080-900-10 | Greece ● ......00-800-1311 |
| Czech Rep. ▲00-42-000-101 | Hungary ● ....06-800-01111 |
| Denmark ........ 8001-0010 | Iceland ● ..........800-9001 |
| Egypt ● (Cairo)‡....510-0200 | Ireland ✓......1-800-550-000 |
| Finland ● ......0800-110-015 | Israel ......1-800-94-94-949 |

| | | | |
|---|---|---|---|
| **Italy●** | **172-1011** | **Russia (Moscow)◗▲●** | **755-5042** |
| **Luxembourg✚** | **800-2-0111** | **(St. Petersbg.)◗▲●** | **325-5042** |
| **Macedonia●** | **99-800-4288** | **Slovakia▲** | **00-42-100-101** |
| Malta | 0800-890-110 | **South Africa** | **0800-99-0123** |
| **Monaco●** | **800-90-288** | **Spain** | **900-99-00-11** |
| Morocco | 002-11-0011 | **Sweden** | **020-799-111** |
| **Netherlands●** | **0800-022-9111** | **Switzerland●** | **0800-89-0011** |
| **Norway** | **800-190-11** | **Turkey●** | **00-800-12277** |
| **Poland▲●** | **00-800-111-1111** | **Ukraine▲** | **8◆100-11** |
| **Portugal▲** | **800-800-128** | U.A. Emirates● | 800-121 |
| **Romania●** | **01-800-4288** | **U.K.** | **0800-89-0011** |

FOR EASY CALLING WORLDWIDE

*1.* Just dial the AT&T Access Number for the country you are calling from. *2.* Dial the phone number you're calling. *3.* Dial your card number.

For access numbers not listed ask any operator for **AT&T Direct®** Service.
In the U.S. call 1-800-331-1140 for a wallet guide listing all worldwide AT&T Access Numbers.
Visit our Web site at: **www.att.com/traveler**
Bold-faced countries permit country-to-country calling outside the U.S.

- ● Public phones require coin or card deposit to place call.
- ▲ May not be available from every phone/payphone.
- ✚ Public phones and select hotels.
- ◆ Await second dial tone.
- ◗ Additional charges apply when calling from outside the city.
- † Outside of Cairo, dial "02" first.
- ✖ Not available from public phones or all areas.
- ✔ Use U.K. access number in N. Ireland.

When placing an international call ***from*** the U.S., dial 1 800 CALL ATT.

EMEA © 8/00 AT&T

# MYCENAE Μυκηνες ☎0751

Excavations of ancient Mycenae have continued for 126 years, since Heinrich Schliemann first turned a spade here. Now one of the most visited sites in Greece, mobs stampede to the famed Lion's Gate and Tomb of Agamemnon. Most make Mycenae a daytrip from Athens, Argos, or Nafplion, but you may find the tourist-friendly modern village a pleasant place to spend the night.

**ORIENTATION AND PRACTICAL INFORMATION.** The only direct **buses** to **Mycenae** are from **Nafplion** (30min., 4 per day, 600dr) via **Argos** (15min., 300dr). A bus from **Athens** (2½hr., 15 per day, 1800dr) stops at **Fihtia,** 1.5km away. The site is on the Corinth-Argos road; from Fihtia, follow the sign to Mycenae. Four buses make the return trip to **Argos** and **Nafplion,** stopping in the town of **Mycenae** (in front of the Hotel Belle Helene) and at the **site** (a 20min. walk from the town). **Trains** (5 per day) run from **Athens** to Fihtia via Corinth. Although Mycenae has no banks, the **post office** offers **currency exchange.** (Open Apr.-Oct. M-F 9am-3:15pm.) **Postal code:** 21200.

**ACCOMMODATIONS AND FOOD.** Mycenae is short on cheap accommodations—if campgrounds aren't your thing, browse the signs off the main road for a good-priced domatia. The quiet **Hotel Belle Helene** opened its doors in 1862; Heinrich Schliemann and crew promptly moved in for two years in the 1870s. In the lobby you can read framed photocopies of the hotel guest book, with signatures from Virginia Woolf, Claude Debussy, William Faulkner, Agatha Christie, Hans Himmler, Goebbels, and Allen Ginsberg. Grab room #3, where Schliemann stayed; it's got an iron bed and period furniture. Other rooms are modern and carpeted. (☎76 225; fax 76 179. Singles 7000dr; doubles 10,000dr; triples 12,000dr.) More luxurious (albeit less historic) lodgings are available down the main road toward the archaeological site at **Dassis Rent Rooms.** This gorgeous, Class "A" domatia boasts spacious rooms with balconies, baths, and even some bathtubs. (☎76 385 or (094) 688 576. Singles and doubles from 6000dr.) **Camping Mykines,** shaded by pine trees in the middle of town, offers laundry facilities, free hot showers, and a nicely-priced taverna (☎76 121. 1000dr per person; 500dr per car; 500dr per small tent; 800dr per large tent.)

A few good restaurants hide among the overpriced multitude of tour-bus troughs bearing the name of gods or unfortunate members of Atreus family. With a vast dining area that seats 500, **Achilleus Restaurant** (☎76 027) doesn't sacrifice quality for quantity as they serve up delicious traditional Greek fare to crowds of hungry sight-seers. Across the street, inexpensive **Spiros Restaurant and Taverna** is another source of tasty food at reasonable cost. (Omelettes 500-700dr, grilled meats 1400-2500dr, *tosts* 400-600dr, *dolmades* 1300dr.) The J and M of **J & M Cocktail Bar** are John and trilingual, ex-Canadian Mireille; their nighttime-only bar mixes great drinks (cocktails 1000dr, ouzo 400dr), palm trees, and lots of locals.

# ANCIENT MYCENAE

*The bus drops off at the end of the asphalt road; the ruins are on your right. Open Apr.-Sept. 8am-7pm, Oct.-Mar. 8am-5pm. 1500dr, students 800dr, EU students free. Keep your ticket after the main site for Agamemnon's Tomb or you'll pay twice. Bring a flashlight.*

Excavated ancient Mycenae rests on a rocky knoll between Mt. Ag. Elias to the north and Mt. Zara to the south. Gargantuan **Cyclopean walls,** 13m high and 10m thick, surround the site; they get their name from ancients who believed that Perseus and his descendants—the city's founders—could only have lifted such stones with the help of a superhuman Cyclops. Outside the central fortified city, several *tholoi*—most notably the so-called **treasury of Atreus**—stand guard outside the walls. The bulk of the ruins left standing today date from 1280 BC, when the city was the center of a far-flung Mycenaean empire. Many of the unearthed relics number among the most celebrated archaeological discoveries in modern history,

and are treasured at the National Museum in Athens (see p. 104). A large on-site museum is underway at the moment. A good guidebook can add to the experience of the site: try the one by S. E. Iakovidis, covering both Mycenae and Epidavros, which includes a map and is well worth the 2500dr. Another by George E. Mylonas, director of the excavation, takes a more scholarly approach (1700dr). If you want info on other ruins, buy *The Peloponnese*, by E. Karpodini-Dimitriadi (3000dr).

## HISTORY

Mycenae's origins, interactions with other Near Eastern civilizations, and decline have long puzzled historians. Settled as early as 2700 BC by a colonizing tribe from the Cyclades, Mycenae (along with other nearby cities like Pylos) remained under the control of the Minoan capital Knossos for centuries. It wasn't until the cataclysmic collapse of Minoan civilization in the mid-15th century BC that Mycenae surged to the head of the Greek world, lending its name to an entire period of Greek history (p. 10). Mycenaean culture flourished for the next centuries, until the warrior Dorians attacked from the north, burning and looting anything in their path. The Dorians conquered Greece, and Mycenae lost its hold on the Greek culture it had helped to create. Mycenae was inhabited through the Roman period, but Byzantine times saw it swallowed up by earth and forgotten.

In 1874, the German businessman, classicist, amateur archaeologist, and human dynamo that was **Heinrich Schliemann,** burst into Mycenae. Fresh from his successful dig at Troy and eager to further establish that Homeric epics were factual, he went looking for Agamemnon's city. To his delight, he found massive walls and elaborate tombs laden with dazzling artifacts, fitting Homer's description of a "well-built citadel... rich in gold." Schliemann began his dig just inside the citadel walls at the spot where several ancient authors described royal graves. Discovering 15 skeletons "literally covered with gold and jewels," Schliemann decked his new 17-year-old Greek bride with the baubles and had her pose for photographs. Believing he had unearthed the skeletons of Agamemnon and his followers, he sent a telegram to the Greek king that read, "Have gazed on face of Agamemnon." Moments after he removed its mask, the "face" underneath disintegrated. Shedding a tear at the initial reckless excavation, modern archaeologists now date the tombs to four centuries before the Trojan War.



## RUINS

**LION'S GATE AND GRAVE CIRCLE A.** Uphill from the entrance booth, you'll spot the imposing **Lion's Gate,** the portal into the ancient city, with two lions carved in relief above the lintel. They symbolized the house of Atreus, and their heads—now missing—bore eyes of precious gems. The sculpture is one of the earliest known

**BLOODBATH, TRAGIC STYLE** Think you have a dysfunctional family? Thank the gods that your problems pale in comparison to the epic, bloody background of Mycenae. Atreus, Mycenae's first chosen ruler, gleefully cooked his nieces and nephews for dinner to serve them to his hated brother (and the children's father), Thyestes—vengeance against Thyestes, who seduced Atreus's wife. The cannibal feast upset the gods, who pitied Thyestes and put a curse on the House of Atreus; Thyestes' son Aegisthus axed Atreus. Atreus's two kiddies, Agamemnon and Menelaus's, fared little better. They stirred up the Trojan War when smooth Paris ran off with Menelaus' gorgeous wife Helen. On the ship to the war, Agamemnon disemboweled his daughter Iphigeneia for a good-luck sacrifice. Ten years later, Agamemnon returned to Mycenae as a war hero; his wife Clytemnestra just wanted her daughter back, and she and her lover Aegisthus (remember? Her father-in-law's nephew and killer?) stabbed him in the bath. Agamemnon's other kids, Orestes and Electra, avenged the murder of their father by murdering their mother. The Furies then tormented Orestes until Athena finally pardoned him. Phew!

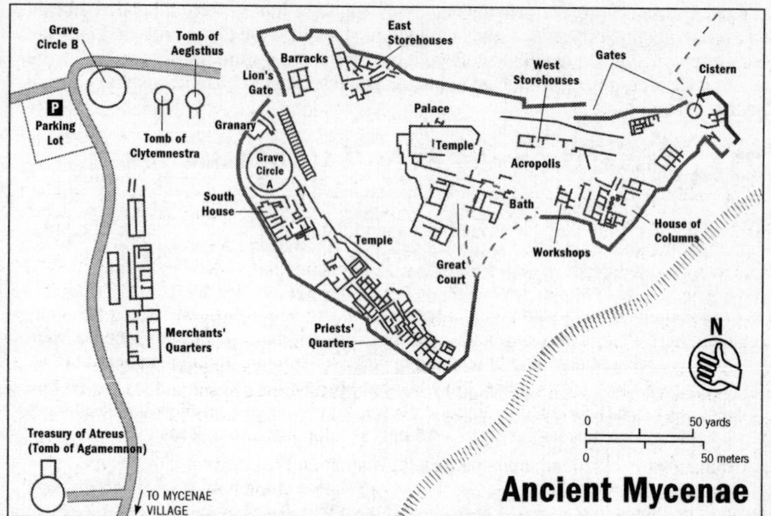

Ancient Mycenae

examples of sculpture being incorporated into a structure's support system. Schliemann found most of his artifacts in **Grave Circle A,** a large hollow area to the right, just outside the original city walls, which contains six 16th-century BC shaft graves. The barracks are up the stairs to your left just after the gate. The gate and the Cyclopean Walls of the upper citadel date from the 13th century BC.

**BUILDINGS.** The ruins on the hillside are the remnants of various homes, businesses, and shrines. The **palace** and the **royal apartments** are at the highest part of the citadel on the right. The open spaces here include guard rooms, private areas, and public rooms; look for the **megaron,** or royal chamber, with its round hearth framed by the bases of four pillars. To the left of the citadel sit the remaining stones of a Hellenistic **Temple of Athena.** At the far end of the city, between the palace and the **postern gate,** is the underground **cistern,** silently offering solitude and complete darkness. A flashlight is essential to explore its depths; be careful if you make the descent: the steps are worn and slippery, and suddenly drop off.

**ROYAL TOMBS.** Follow the asphalt road 150m back toward the town of Mycenae to the **Tomb of Agamemnon** (a.k.a. the Treasury of Athens), the largest and most impressive *tholos*, named by Schliemann for the king he desperately wanted to discover here. On your way, stop at two often-overlooked *tholoi*, the **tomb of Aegistheus** and the more interesting **tomb of Clytemnestra;** take the paths on your left and hang on to your flashlight. Once you get to the main event, head down a 40m passage cut into the hillside that leads to Agamemnon's resting place, looking up at the 120 ton lintel stones above you. The dim, quiet interior of the *tholos* conveys a ghostly majesty befitting the grave of such a famous and tragic figure; but the tomb was found empty, having lost its valuables to grave robbers.

## ARGOS Αργος ☎0751

According to Homer, Argos was the kingdom of the hero Diomedes, and claimed allegiance from Mycenae's powerful king, Agamemnon. Later, Dorians invaded and captured the city in the 12th century BC, using it as their base for control of the Argolid Peninsula. Argos remained the most powerful state in the Peloponnese through the 7th century BC, defeating even Kleomenes and the Spartans, who, in the famous 494 BC battle, were unable to penetrate the city walls. Like many other ancient cities in Greece, each period of Argos's history has obliterated or buried the remains of the era preceding it. The modern city is no exception: it is built

almost entirely on top of previous layers of inhabitation; despite a healthy ribbon of archaeological red tape, it has managed to grow into the dirty, crowded, breezeless city you see today. Nonetheless, the excellent museum and the ruins of the ancient theater, *agora*, and Roman baths on the southeast edge of town are worth seeing if you're in the area.

## ORIENTATION AND PRACTICAL INFORMATION

Argos has few landmarks and can be tough to navigate, so pick up a copy of the archaeological museum's free laminated **map.** Most amenities, hotels, and restaurants are in or around the plateia, marked by the **Church of St. Peter.** Behind the church, a small shady park extends toward the train station.

**Buses:** There are two stations. The **Argolida** station (☎66 300), on Kapodistriou very near the plateia, sends buses to: **Athens** (2½hr., 14 per day, 2300dr) and **Nafplion** (20min., every 30min. from 6:30am-9pm, 250dr). From the **Arcadia-Laconia Station,** Feidonos 24 (☎67 157), buses go to **Mycenae** (30min., 4 per day, 300dr) and **Nemea** (1hr., 2 per day, 600dr). To find the station from the plateia, follow Vas. Olgas two blocks past the museum, turn left, and walk past the Agricultural Bank.

**Trains:** (☎67 212), 1km from the plateia. Walk down Nikitara past the OTE and follow the signs to Nafplion from the five-point intersection. At the next big intersection head toward Athens; the station is at the end of the street. Trains go to: **Athens** (3hr., 5 per day, 1100dr) via **Fihtia** (10min., 120dr), **Nemea** (20min., 250dr), and **Corinth** (1hr., 510dr); and **Kalamata** (4hr., 4 per day, 1300dr) via **Tripoli** (1hr., 600dr).

**Bank: National Bank** (☎29 911), on Nikitara, off the plateia behind the church, has **currency exchange** and an **ATM.** Open M-Th 8am-2pm, F 8am-1:30pm.

**Hospital:** (☎24 455), north on Corinth, opposite St. Nicholas Church. Open 24hr.

**Police:** (☎67 222), on the corner of Inaxou and Papaoikonomou; head out from Vas. Sofias. English spoken. Open 24hr.

**Telephones: OTE,** Nikitara 8 (☎67 599). Facing the park from the main plateia, take the street along the park's left side past the National Bank and around the bend to the right–it's on the right. Open 7am-2pm.

**Post Office:** (☎68 066). Follow the signs from Hotel Telesilla. Open M-F 7:30am-2pm. **Postal code:** 21200.

PELOPONNESE

## ACCOMMODATIONS AND FOOD

Since the sights can be seen in half a day and Argos has few accommodations, it's a good idea to make Argos and Mycenae a daytrip from Nafplion. If you stay overnight, try the **Hotel Apollon,** Papaflessa 13; take Nikitara from the plateia, then follow the road by Mickey's. It's on the left; follow the signs to its spacious rooms with large shared baths, TVs, and ceiling fans. (☎68 065; fax 61 182. Singles 6000dr, with bath and A/C 7000dr; doubles 7000dr/8000dr.) The **Hotel Palladion,** Vas. Sophias 5, opposite the museum on the plateia, is convenient, and has private baths and TV. (Singles 5000dr; doubles 7000dr; triples 10,000dr, extra 1000dr for A/C.)

Argos has the Peloponnese's largest **open-air market** in the empty plateia across from the museum; vendors sell everything from olives to used clothing (W and Sa). Food, however, is discouragingly bad in Argos, and tavernas are scarce. The well-stocked **Dia Discount Supermarket,** to the left of the National Bank in the central plateia, may be a lifesaver. (Open M-F 9am-2pm and 5:30-8:30pm, Sa 8:30am-6pm.) Next to the Hotel Mycenae, the **Retro Pub and Restaurant** is discordantly decorated with chrome inside and wicker outside. (Greek salads 1000dr, ice cream 1000-1400dr, thick or thin pizzas 1500-2500dr, extra-large pizzas 2800-3500dr.) **Restaurant Aigli,** in the corner of the plateia facing the church next to the Hotel Mycenae, has the most taverna-like menu of any establishment in the area. (Calamari 1000dr, *pastitsio* 1300dr, *moussaka* 1300dr.) For a post-Mycenae snack, head to **Cafe Croissant,** past the museum. (☎63 013. Ice cream 300-1100dr, pastries 250-450dr.)

## SIGHTS

**ARCHAEOLOGICAL MUSEUM.** Argos's superb archeological museum has a large Mycenaean collection, including pottery, jewelry, and weaponry, as well as a garden courtyard with notable Roman sculptures and mosaics. In the most striking of the mosaics, twelve figures personify the months of the year in their dress, expression, and accoutrements. On the ground floor of the museum, a detailed shard of *krater* from the 7th century BC depicts Odysseus putting out the eye of Polyphemus. In the same room, the well-preserved helmet and cuirass from the Geometric period also deserves a careful look. *(Off the plateia on Vas. Olgas. ☎68 819. Open Tu-Su 8:30am-3pm; in Aug. 8:30am-7pm. 500dr, students 300dr, EU students free.)*

**ANCIENT ARGOS.** Archaeologists hope to uncover a large part of the ancient city of Argos, but at this point, most of it remains buried beneath the modern version. Major excavations have taken place on the city's western fringe at the site of the ancient *agora.* With a seating capacity of 20,000, the 4th-century BC **theater** was the largest of its time in the Greek world, although now it's not as well preserved as its famous counterpart in Epidavros. Across from the theater are the remains of the extensive **Roman bath complex,** whose remaining walls convey the magnitude of the structure. Many of the original wall-to-wall floor mosaics are intricate, colorful, and intact. The **Roman Odeum,** 30m from the baths, survives mostly as an outline, as the rows dissolve into the hillside. Across the street from the theater, baths, and odeon are the scattered remains of the *agora*, built in the 5th century BC and destroyed by Alaric's Visigoths in AD 395. *(Walk past the post office, turn right, and walk to the end of Theatron.)*

**THE FORTRESS OF LARISA.** In medieval times, Franks, Venetians, and Ottomans in turn captured and ruled Argos. As a result, the fortress is an architectural hodgepodge, combining these disparate medieval elements with Classical and Byzantine foundations. The ruins, which lie among overgrown weeds, are mainly of interest to scholars. *(Walk along Vas. Konstantinou for roughly 1hr., or climb the foot path from the ruins of the ancient theater.)*

**OTHER SIGHTS.** The **Argive Heraion,** north of Argos, dedicated to Hera, goddess of the Argives, was built in the 5th century BC. It prospered well into the 2nd century AD, hosting the celebrations that followed the official ending of the Heraia Games (archery contests held at Argos in the second year after each Olympiad, see p. 137) and other annual festivals. **Prosimni,** several kilometers northeast of Argos and past the Heraion, is home to a series of prehistoric graves. A few kilometers east of Agias Trias are the remains of the city of **Dendra,** where tombs yielded the preserved suit of bronze armor now in the Nafplion museum (p. 127).

# NAFPLION Ναυπλιο

☎0752

Beautiful old Nafplion glories in its Venetian architecture, fortresses, pebble beach, and hillside stairways. Though it's the perfect base for exploring the ruins of the Argolid, it may entice you to spend a few days away from the ruins. The convenient layout connects the rich past that lingers in the stone walkways of the Old Town to the modern bustle of the newer district. A delightful central park links the two sides over shady flower-lined paths and a large children's playground. Before the Venetians built Nafplion—named for Poseidon's son Nafplius—on a swamp in the 15th century, the city consisted entirely of the two hilltop fortresses. Passing from the Venetians to the Ottomans and back again, in 1821 it served as headquarters for the Greek revolutionary government and later as Greece's first capital (1829-1834). John Kapodistrias, former president of Greece, was assassinated here in Ag. Spyridon Church; the bullet hole is still visible in the church walls—the assassins hid behind the fountain across the street. Palamidi, the Venetian fortress where the Ottomans imprisoned Kolokotronis before the Revolutionary War of 1821, and the Bourtzi, a small island fortress that once housed retired executioners, still stand as testaments to Nafplion's politically checkered past.

## ORIENTATION AND PRACTICAL INFORMATION

**Bouboulinas** is the waterfront promenade. Three principal streets run off **Singrou** in the Old Town. Moving inland, the first is **Amalias,** the shopping street. The second, **Vasileos Konstandinou,** ends in **Pl. Syndagma,** full of tavernas, a bookstore, bank, museum, and at night, scores of aspiring soccer stars. The third is **Plapouta,** which becomes **Staikopoulou** in the vicinity of Pl. Syndagma; it is home to Nafplion's best restaurants. Across Singrou, Plapouta becomes **25 Martiou,** Nafplion's largest avenue. This side of Singrou—behind the statue of Kapodistrias—is the new part of town. Radiating outward from the five-way intersection split by the road to Argos and the road to Tolo is the New Town, home to the city's inexpensive hotels. The bus terminal is on **Singrou,** near the base of the Palamidi fortress. To reach **Bouboulinas,** the waterfront promenade, from the bus station, go left as you exit it and follow Singrou to the harbor—the **Old Town** is on your left. If you come by ferry, Bouboulinas is in front of you across the parking lot, parallel to the dock.

**Buses:** (☎28 555), on Singrou, off Pl. Kapodistrias. To: **Athens** (3hr., every hr. 5am-8pm, 2650dr) via **Corinth** (2hr., 1100dr); **Argos** (30min., 2 per hr. 5am-10:30pm, 260dr); **Mycenae** (45min., 4 per day, 600dr); **Tripoli** (2½hr., 4 per day, 1100dr); **Epidavros** (1hr., 4 per day, 600dr); and **Tolo** (20min., every hr. 7am-9:30am, 260dr).

**Boat Excursions: Staikos Travel,** Bouboulinas 50 (☎27 950), runs **island cruises** on to **Hydra**, **Spetses**, and **Poros** (M-W, F 8:30am-8pm; 10,000dr per person, buy tickets 2 days in advance). Open 9am-2pm, and 6-9pm.

**Taxis:** (☎24 120 or 24 720). Congregate on Singrou across from the bus station. Pay less by finding drivers who are returning to your destination.

**Moped Rental: Motortraffic Rent-A-Moto,** Sidiras 15 (☎22 702), parallel to 25 Martiou on the other side of the park. 50cc mopeds 4500dr, 100cc 8000dr per day. Open 8am-11pm.

**Tourist Office:** (☎24 444), on 25 Martiou, across from the OTE. Free pamphlets and brochures on Nafplion and surroundings. Open 9am-1pm and 4-8pm.

**Banks: National Bank** (☎23 497), in Pl. Syndagma, has an **ATM.** Other banks in Pl. Syndagma and on Amalias charge 500-700dr commission for **currency exchange.** Open M-Th 8am-2pm, F 8am-1pm.

**Bookstore: Odyssey** (☎23 430), in Pl. Syndagma. Bestseller romance novels, sci-fi, and Greek plays, all in English. Open 8am-11pm.

**Laundromat: Self-Service Laundry Astraftero,** Papanikolaou 22 (☎24 256). From the bus station, go right on Singrou, walk two blocks, and turn right. It'll be on your left.

**Tourist Police:** (☎28 131). From the Old Town, walk along 25 Martiou, 6 blocks past the turn-off for the road to Tolo and Epidavros. English-speaking. Open 7am-10pm.

**Police:** (☎27 776) on Praitelous, a 15min. hike along 25 Martiou from the bus station. Follow the signs. Open 24hr.

**Hospital: Nafplion Hospital** (☎27 309) is a 15min. walk; go down 25 Martiou and turn left onto Kolokotroni, which becomes Asklipiou. You can also call the tourist police.

**Telephones:** (☎22 139), on the left side of 25 Martiou as you walk toward the New Town. Open 7am-10pm.

**Internet Access: Filion** (☎27 651), past the post office on Sidhiras Merarchias. 1500dr per hr. Cocktails 1000dr.

**Post Office:** (☎24 230), in a large yellow building on the corner of Sidhiras Merarchias and Singrou. Open M-F 7:30am-2pm. **Postal code:** 21100.

## ACCOMMODATIONS

Rooms in the Old Town are charming and beautifully situated, but those in the New Town are cheaper and have more amenities.

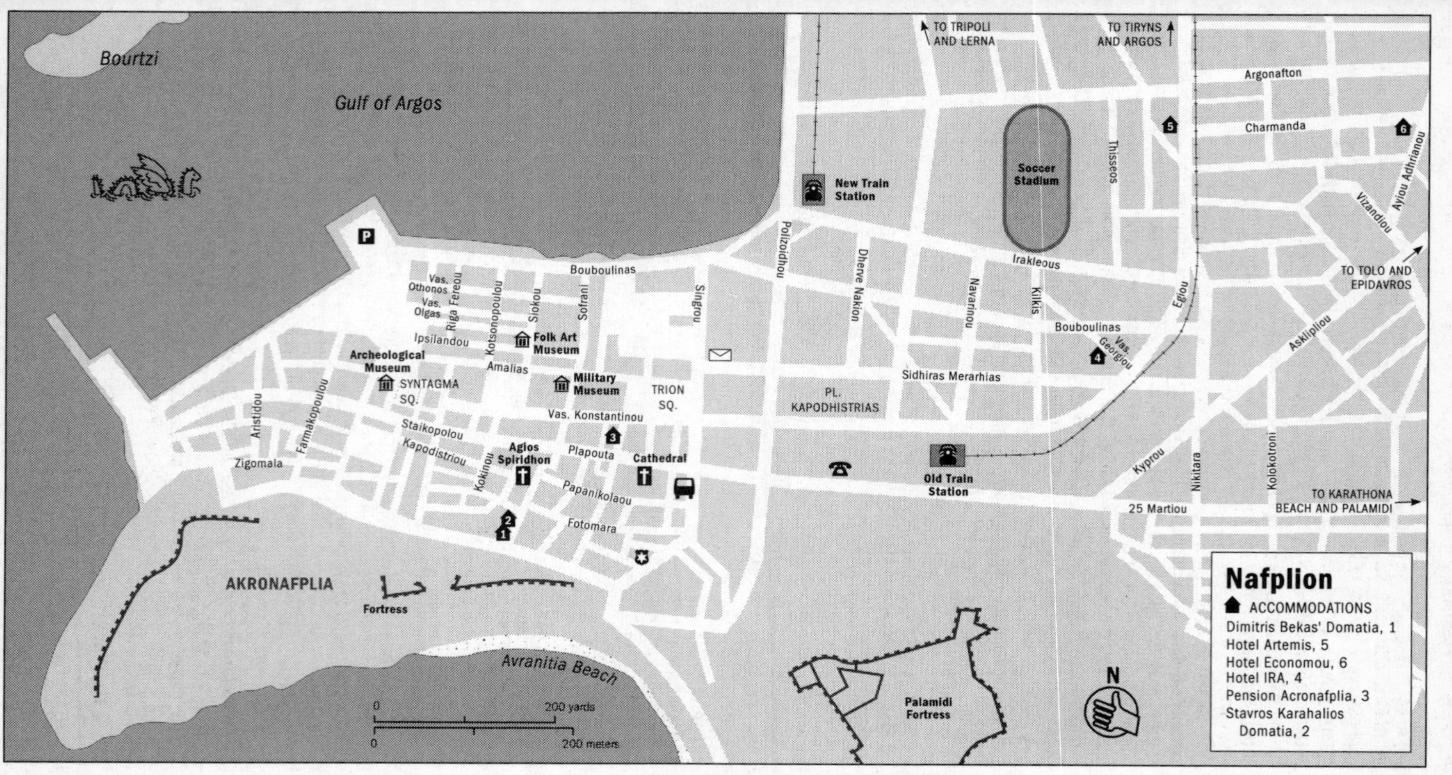
Nafplion
ACCOMMODATIONS
Dimitris Bekas' Domatia, 1
Hotel Artemis, 5
Hotel Economou, 6
Hotel IRA, 4
Pension Acronafplia, 3
Stavros Karahalios Domatia, 2
Bourtzi
Gulf of Argos
TO TRIPOLI AND LERNA
TO TIRYNS AND ARGOS
Argonafton
Charmanda
Soccer Stadium
Thisseos
New Train Station
Ayiou Adhrianou
Vizandiou
TO TOLO AND EPIDAVROS
Irakleous
Polizoidhou
Dherve Nakion
Navarinou
Kilkis
Egiou
Asklipiou
Bouboulinas
Vas. Georgiou
Sidhiras Merarhias
PL. KAPODHISTRIAS
Singrou
Sofrani
Siokou
Kotsonopoulou
Riga Fereou
Vas. Othonos
Vas. Olgas
Ipsilandou
Folk Art Museum
Archeological Museum
Amalias
Military Museum
SYNTAGMA SQ.
TRION SQ.
Vas. Konstantinou
Aristidou
Farmakopoulou
Staikopolou
Kapodistriou
Kokinou
Agios Spiridhon
Plapouta
Cathedral
Zigomala
Papanikolaou
Fotomara
Old Train Station
Kyprou
Nikitara
Kolokotroni
25 Martiou
TO KARATHONA BEACH AND PALAMIDI
AKRONAFPLIA
Fortress
Avranitia Beach
0
200 yards
200 meters
Palamidi Fortress
N

### NEW TOWN

**Hotel Artemis** (☎27 862), on Argos. Large rooms with balconies and baths. Closed curtains keep the room cool. Singles 6000dr; doubles 8000dr.

**Hotel IRA,** Vas. Georgiou B9 (☎28 184), off Bouboulinas. Bare lobby but airy rooms, terrorist-free. Singles 5000dr, with A/C, TV, bath 6000dr; doubles 8000dr/12,000dr.

**Hotel Economou** (☎23 955), on Argonafton, off the road to Argos; a 15min. walk from the bus station. Hostel-like (up to 4 beds in one room) Dorms 2500dr.

### OLD TOWN

**Dimitris Bekas' Domatia** (☎24 594). Turn up the stairs onto Kokinou, following the sign for rooms off Staikopoulou. Climb to the top, turn left, then go up another 50 steps. An evening on the roof, with its wonderful view of ocean and Palamidi, is well worth the climb. Small rooms with shared baths and fridges. Singles 5000dr; doubles 7000dr.

**Pension Acronafplia,** Vasileos Konstandinou 23 (☎24 481). If it's full, owner Dimitris can show you one of his 3 other charming hotels, all conveniently located. Singles with shared baths 6000dr, with private baths and A/C 9000dr; doubles 8000dr/17000dr.

**Stavros Karahalios Domatia** (☎27 696), just down the stairs from Dimitris Bekas. Clean, spacious rooms with fridges; it's worth a splurge. Singles 8000dr; doubles 11,500dr; A/C 1500dr extra.

PELOPONNESE

## FOOD AND NIGHTLIFE

The food in Nafplion is excellent, but often not cheap. The beautiful alleys of the Old Town hold an endless number of romantic tavernas, lit by soft flood lights and strewn with plants, balconies, and people. The waterfront is lined with fish restaurants that charge as much as 7000dr per entree. The best dining options are on Staikopoulou, the street above Pl. Syndagma, behind the National Bank. **Marinopoulos,** an excellent modern supermarket, is behind the post office.

**Taverna O Vasiles,** a street above the plateia on Staikopoulou. Fresh fish (8000-12,000dr per kg), and a divine rabbit in onions and red sauce (1650dr) that would seduce the most devoted Beatrix Potter fan. Salads 600-1000dr; *pastitsio* 1200dr.

**Ellas,** in Pl. Syndagma. The cheapest place around, with lots of seating facing the action of the plateia. Salads 500-1100dr, veal stew 1700dr, fish entrees 1000-1800dr.

**To Fanaria,** just to the left of O Vasiles on Staikopoulou. Another intimate taverna with tantalizing entrees. Soups 1000dr, spaghetti bolognese 1200dr, *dolmades* 1100dr, and salads 500-1100dr.

**The Agora Music Cafe,** Vas. Konstandinou 17. It's the best place for an evening cocktail or ice cream. Decorated with traditional household and farm implements. R&B and Greek pop plays inside. Drinks 800-1400dr, beer 700dr, ice cream 800-1200dr.

Although similar trendy cafes are strung along the waterfront, the search for nightlife may land you in a taxi (1500dr) for the 15min. ride to **Tolo.** At the far end of the waterfront is **Luna Park,** a carnival under neon lights. You can also take a **minicruise** of the harbor (until 7pm), and get a close-up view of the Bourtzi. Small *caïques* leave from the end of the dock (600dr round-trip).

## SIGHTS AND BEACHES

The Old Town's architectural diversity is a historical sight in itself. Pl. Syndagma alone boasts a Venetian mansion, a Turkish mosque, and a Byzantine Church.

**PALAMIDI FORTRESS.** The grueling 999 steps that once provided the only access to the 18th-century fort have since been supplemented by a 3km road (taxis 1000dr). If you opt for the steps, they begin on Arvanitias, across the park from the bus station; bring water and climb in the morning. At the top, you'll be rewarded with spectacular views of the town, gulf, and much of the Argolid. Note the Vene-

tian lion *steles* that adorn some of the lower citadel's walls. Years ago there were eight working cisterns at the site; today you can tour the cool interiors of the two remaining underground reservoirs. *(☎28 036. Open M-F 8am-6pm, Sa-Su and off season 8:30am-3pm. 800dr, students 400dr, EU students free.)*

**ACRONAFPLIA.** The fortress walls of the Acronafplia were fortified by three successive generations of conquerors—Byzantines, Franks, and Venetians. To reach the fort, take the tunnel, which runs into the hill, from Zigomala to the Xenia Hotel elevator. The views of the Palimidi, the Gulf, and the Old Town are fantastic. Ludwig I, King of Bavaria, had the huge Bavarian Lion carved out of a monstrous rock as a memorial to the men who died in an epidemic in 1833-34. Today the lion oversees a small park. *(Make a left onto Mikh. Iatrou and walk 200m.)*

**MUSEUMS.** Nafplion's **Folk Art Museum,** winner of the 1981 European Museum of the Year Award is open again after years of renovation. Ask the tourist office for more information. The **Military Museum,** toward the New Town from Syndagma, displays artifacts and high-quality black-and-white photos from the burning of Smyrna (İzmir), the population exchanges of the 1920s, and the Second World War. *(Open Su 9:30am-2pm. Free.)* The **Archaeological Museum,** in the Venetian mansion on Pl. Syndagma, has a small but esteemed collection of pottery and idols from nearby Mycenaean sites, plus a Mycenaean suit of bronze armor. Don't miss the great geometric period vases on the second floor. *(☎27 502. Open Tu-Su 8:30am-3pm. 500dr, students 300dr, EU students free.)*

**BEACHES. Arvanitia,** Nafplion's small, pebbly beach, is along the road that curves around the left-hand side of Palamidi. On hot days the shore is packed, and pop music blares over the noise of the sun-drenched crowd. For a nicer (cleaner) alternative, try the footpath that runs along the water from the parking lot, between Palamidi and the end of Polizoidou. The scenic 45min. walk will reveal three quiet, rocky **coves.** If you're desperate for a long, sandy beach, head to **Tolo.** You can rent jetskis (5000dr per 15min.), umbrellas (2000dr per day), and paddle boats (1500dr per hr.), or go windsurfing (2000dr per hr.). Buses leave from Nafplion every hour (260dr), and on summer days, scads of pre-teens head for the water.



## DAYTRIPS FROM NAFPLION: TIRYNS Τιρυνθα

*Take the Argos bus from Nafplion (10min., 2 per hr. 5am-10:30pm, 260dr). ☎22 657. Open 8am-7pm. 500dr, students 300dr, EU students free.*

About 4km northwest of Nafplion on the road to Argos lie the Mycenaean ruins of Tiryns, or **Tiryntha,** birthplace of Hercules. Heinrich Schliemann's excavation of the site began in 1875 and has been continued by the German Archaeological Institute ever since. The site is now one of the finer prehistoric sites outside Mycenae. Perched atop a 25m high hill, Tiryns was nearly impregnable during ancient times, until its capture and destruction by the Argives in the 5th century BC. Parts of the stronghold date as far back as 2600 BC, but most of what remains was built 1000 years later, in the Mycenaean era. Standing 8m high, the massive walls surrounding the site are evidence of the immensity of the original fortifications; on the eastern and southern slopes of the ancient acropolis, they reach a width of 20m. Inside these structures lurk vaulted galleries. While gems like the palace's frescoes have been taken to the National Archaeological Museum in Athens (p. 104), one huge limestone block remains to form the bathroom floor. Follow the signs left from the site to a remarkably well-preserved Mycenaean-era *tholos* tomb in a hillside.

# EPIDAVROS Επιδαυρος

*Buses travel to and from Nafplion (1hr., 4 per day, 600dr). Bring lunch; there is no town near the site. Museum ☎22 009. Open daily 7:30am-7pm. Ticket office open M-Sa 9am-5pm, F-Sa 5-9pm during festival season. 1500dr, students 800dr, EU students free.*

Like Olympia and Delphi, Epidavros was once both a town and a sanctuary—first to an ancient deity Maleatas, then to Apollo, who assumed the god's name and aspects of his identity, and finally to Apollo's son by Koronis, the healer Asclepius. Under the patronage of Asclepius, Epidavros became famous across the ancient world as a center of medicine, reaching its height in the early fourth century BC, when the sick would travel hundreds of kilometers for cures that mixed medical and mystical. Recent finds indicate that both surgeries and direct deity intervention took place in the sanctuary—diagnoses were made by the god in dream visitations. Over the centuries, the complex became increasingly grand with the benefactions of former patients, growing to include temples to Themis, Aphrodite, and Artemis. Operating until AD 426, the sanctuary complex was closed along with all other non-Christian sanctuaries by Byzantine emperor Theodosius II.

The theater, built in the early 2nd century BC, is the grandest structure at the site. Initially constructed to accommodate 6000 people, its capacity was expanded to 14,000 later in the same century. Despite severe earthquakes in AD 522 and 551, the theater has survived the centuries almost perfectly intact. Today, Greece's most famous ancient theater has come alive again after centuries of silence: in July and August it hosts the **Epidavros Theater Festival.**



**THEATER.** Built into a lovely hillside, the 55 tiers of Theater of Epidavros face half-forested, half-flaxen mountains so pretty they almost distract from the tragedies played out on the stage. The theater's acoustics are unbelievably good, as yelling, singing, coin-dropping, whispering, and even match-lighting tourists from all nations demonstrate eagerly. Every sound can be heard from even in the last row.

**FESTIVAL.** The modern sets left on stage by drama troupes may annoy those visiting the theater for its history alone, but the sets redeems themselves at the Friday and Saturday night shows. The festival, from late June to mid-August, trots out the National Theater of Greece and visiting companies to perform classical Greek plays translated into modern Greek. Performances begin at 9pm, and tickets can be purchased at the site. (4000-6000dr, students 2000dr; children under six prohibited.) You can also buy tickets in advance in Athens at the Athens Festival Box Office (☎(01) 322 1459; see p. 96) or Nafplion's bus station. On performance nights, KTEL buses make the round-trip circuit from Nafplion (7:30pm, 1500dr).

**MUSEUM.** The museum is on the way from the theater to the ruins. Most of the museum's finest pieces, most notably the exquisite architectural carvings of the site's maze (called the **tholos**) have been under restoration and hidden from visitors for years. Fortunately, the three open rooms contain great pieces. The intricately carved **entablature** from the temple of Asclepius and the *tholos* compose the first room, along with a marble pillar inscribed with a hymn to Apollo, and an array of ancient medical implements. The second room is filled with elaborately decorated architectural reconstructions and randomly placed statuary. In the third room, most of the *tholos*'s beautiful decorative elements have been removed and replaced temporarily with plaster copies. Authentic and impressive, however, is the perfectly preserved Corinthian capital. It is thought to be the architect's prototype for all of the capitals of the temple of Asclepius. Archaeologists found it buried in the ground away from the site, apparently unconnected with any ruin.

**SANCTUARY OF ASCLEPIUS AND THOLOS.** The extensive ruins of the sanctuary can be confusing. Walking from the museum, you will pass the **Xenon** or hostel, a maze of foundations. The gymnasium containing the remains of a Roman Odeon is the first structure of the more concentrated complex of ruins. To the left is a stadium, of which only a few tiers of seats and the athletes' starting blocks survive. Two of the most important structures of the ancient sanctuary, the **Temple of Asclepius** and the famous *tholos*, are in front and to the left. The **tholos,** thought to have been built by Polycleitos the Younger in the mid-4th century BC, is an architectural masterpiece, richly decorated with carvings. Although certainly a place of worship, its exact function is unknown. Beside the *tholos* are the remains of the **abaton,** where the sick would rest, hoping to have the correct therapy revealed in their dreams by the god. Farther from the *tholos*, along the path on the eastern edge of the site, lie the ruins of 2nd-century AD Roman baths.

# ELIAS ΗΛΕΙΑΣ AND ACHAIA ΑΧΑΙΑ

In rural Elias and Achaia, tomatoes and beachgoers alike redden beneath the blazing sun. Corn fields, golden beaches, and occasional ruins stud the road between their capitals, Pyrgos and Patras (Greece's most popular western port of entry). First settled by Achaians from the Argolid, Romans ruled the region; Franks, Ottomans, and Venetians all violently disputed this land and left their legacy behind.

## DIAKOFTO Διακοφτο ☎0691

Halfway between Corinth and Patras, at the base of precipitous mountains, Diakofto is famous for its rack-railway trains that chug past waterfalls and over steep cliffs through the mountains to Kalavrita. With its fruit-tree-lined streets and turquoise waters, Diakofto is a town with tourist potential. Houses are planted between orange and lemon trees, with magenta bougainvillea providing shade. Accommodations are better in Kalavrita (p. 130), but if you plan to catch an early train toward Athens or Patras, Diakofto is an agreeable place to spend the night.

**ORIENTATION AND PRACTICAL INFORMATION.** The **train station** (☎43 206) intersects Diakofto's main road about 200m from the beach. Flanked by cafes and restaurants, it is the town's social center. Tiny rack-railway trains to **Kalavrita** make for an exhilarating ride (1hr., 4 per day, 1000dr). Trains going to **Patras** (40min., 6 per day, 1200dr) and **Corinth** (1hr., 8 per day, 1500dr) leave from the opposite side of the tracks.

Walk down the main road toward the sea to pass through a picturesque residential area and end up at the harbor and public beach. If you walk inland on the winding main road toward the mountains, you will see the **National Bank** offering **currency exchange** and 24hr. **ATM** (open M-Th 8:45am-12:45pm, F 8:45am-12:15pm) as well as the **post office** on the left side of the road. (☎41 343. Open M-F 7:30am-2pm.) **Postal code:** 25003.

**ACCOMMODATIONS.** **Hotel Lemonies,** halfway between the train station and the beach on the main road, offers spacious rooms with bath, balcony and A/C. Downstairs is a mellow taverna, and the surrounding residential neighborhood is lovely and quiet. (☎41 820. Singles 7000dr; doubles 10000dr; triples 12000dr; prices may be higher in peak summer.) **Hotel Helmos** provides small, simple chambers on the main road on the inland side of the tracks. Rooms have a distinctly aged feel; the back door locks at 11pm, so make sure you get a key from the owner if you plan to be out late. (☎41 236. Singles 5500dr; doubles 7500dr; triples 9,000dr; extra for A/C and private bath.) If you prefer to be closer to nature, a half-hour hike to the left on the beach will bring you to **Camping Eleon Beach,** where you can enjoy a small playground, washing machines, a nice kitchen and dining area, a restaurant, beach bar, mini-market, and a nearby discotheque. (☎41 539. 1200dr per person; 600dr per small tent. Electricity 700dr.)

**FOOD AND ENTERTAINMENT.** Several cafes and bars line the train station and the main street inland from the station. **Festaria Taverna** (☎43 228) has quick service, pleasant outdoor seating, delicious tzatziki (500dr), grilled meats (1100-1450dr), and quick salads (500-1100dr). On the beach, **Taverna Kohuli** (Κοχυλι) sits beside a docking area for small boats and serves, among other offerings, fresh cucumber and tomato salad (600dr), savory grilled chicken (1200dr), and lamb (1800). Next door, **El Fuego Cafe Bar** is the place for an evening drink under stars and large straw umbrellas. Its fashionable counterpart on the main drag is **Mess Cafe Bar,** right across from the National Bank, with framed old-fashioned travel posters adorning its walls, and ouzo and *mezedes* (ouzo and snacks) for 500dr.

## GREAT CANYON MONASTERY Μονη Μεγαλου Σπηλαιου

Located 9km inland from Diakofto, the famous monastery is accessible only by a combination of 19th-century rack-railway and hiking. Getting there is half the fun:

PELOPONNESE

the 30-minute railway ride winds into smoke-blackened tunnels, through spectacular canyons and gorges created by the Vouraikos River, and over old bridges, offering the same excitement as a rollercoaster (1000dr round-trip). For the monastery, get off at the **Zahlorou,** the first stop on the line. Don't forget a water bottle, long-sleeved shirt, and sturdy shoes.

The small mountain village conjures up stock images of mining or timber towns in the old American West. A few well-shaded rustic buildings cluster around the tracks where they pass over the river. The path that leads to the monastery is marked in English. Take frequent water breaks, if only to admire the panoramic views. After about 45 minutes of walking, you should reach a paved road: turn left and follow the road to the sign for Mega Spilaeou on your right. Stairs in front of the monastery lead to the main entrance. A monk will lead you to the upstairs museum with its gold-encased relics and beautiful icons (some say one was painted by St. Luke). Photographs show the destruction of the centuries-old monastery by an explosion of stored gunpowder in 1934. The new monastery is built up against the cliff wall, and one of the cliff's caves is accessible from the second floor of the building—peer into the darkness in search of the cave's miraculous icon.



## KALAVRITA Καλαβρυτα ☎0692

In a small valley at the end of the rack-railway line, Kalavrita is a close-knit mountain village that caters more to winter skiers than to summer visitors. However, the green mountain vistas and shaded, quiet streets make the warmer months a pleasant time to visit. Although it has only one sight, those who wish to make the rack-railway a two-day event may find Kalavrita an enjoyable place to stay.

### PRACTICAL INFORMATION

Kalavrita is accesible by a tiny and fun-to-ride rack-railway line from **Diakofto** (1hr., 4 per day, 1000dr). The two roads perpendicular to the train station that lead to the plateia are **Konstantinou** (later called **Ag. Alexiou**) to the left and **Syngrou** (later called **25 Martiou**) to the right. The **National Bank of Greece,** 25 Martiou 4, offers **currency exchange** and a 24hr. **ATM.** (☎22 212. Open M-Th 8am-2pm, F 8am-1:30pm.) The **police,** Fotina 7, are 3 blocks beyond the OTE, to the right off Ag. Alexiou. (☎23 333. Open 24hr.) The **OTE** is at Ag. Alexiou 10 (open weekdays 8am-4:30pm). The **post office,** on 25 Martiou, is to the right of the town hall at the lower right corner of the plateia coming up from the train station. (☎22 225. Open M-F 7:30am-2pm.) **Postal code:** 25001.

### ACCOMMODATIONS AND FOOD

Hotels in Kalavrita are pleasant but expensive, especially during ski season. Fortunately, affordable, well-appointed domatia abound; numerous signs nearby the train station will lead you to them.

**Achrysa** (☎22 443) is easy to find; just cross the tracks behind the train station and go straight down the road running perpendicular to the tracks. It's a block down on the right. Comfortable ground-floor singles with bath open up onto a fragrant garden (5000dr in summer and 8000dr in winter); there are more luxurious rooms on the third floor (8000dr in summer and 10000dr in winter, higher on weekends).

**Mitsopoulos Rooms** (☎22 481). With your back to the rail station, turn right and walk three blocks. Turn right immediately after the hospital and then continue two blocks; the rooms are on the right. Spacious rooms with baths and lovely mountain views. Singles 6000dr, 9000dr in winter; doubles 9000dr/12,000dr.

**Hotel Megas Alexandros** (☎22 221), on Ag. Alexiou two blocks before the plateia, has spacious rooms with wood floors and tiny showers in private baths. Singles 8000dr; doubles 10,000dr; triples 12,000dr.

**Hotel Maria,** (☎22 296). Across the street, two blocks before the plateia on Ag. Alexiou, this luxurious hotel has TVs, telephones, and lavender furniture. Singles 8000dr; doubles 12,050dr; in winter only doubles are available 17,000dr.

A collection of similar tavernas line Ag. Alexiou and 25 Martiou. Centrally located **Taverna Stani** has entrances on both streets and offers standard fare served by a friendly staff (Greek salad 1000dr, veal with potatoes 1800dr, coffee 100dr, menu in Greek). **Taverna Aistralos,** part of the Anesis Hotel, just off Ag. Alexiou facing the plateia, serves tasty dishes like spicy sausage (1500dr), and lamb with vegetables (1900dr) in a light and spacious dining room.

### SIGHTS AND ENTERTAINMENT

The town's only sight is a morbid memorial to the Kalavritan men who were killed on December 13, 1943. In retaliation for the murder of one of their troopers, the occupying Nazis gathered all of the town's men and boys over age 15 on a hill outside of town under the pretext of giving a stern reprimand about the murder. Instead, at 2:34pm from the trees above the hill, lurking troopers opened fire on command and then burned the town itself. Today the clock of the town's church is set permanently to 2:34, and an extensive memorial stands alongside a hanging oil lamp shrine, symbolizing the awaited resurrection of the murdered Kalavritans.

Aside from walking around the town enjoying the mountain air, there is nothing in the way of entertainment come summer. In the winter months, travel to the nearby **Mt. Helmos** for fantastic skiing. The **Ski Centre** on 25 Martiou provides information and rentals. (☎(0692) 22 175. Open December-April 8:30am-3:30pm.)



## PATRAS Πατρα ☎061

Patras, Greece's third-largest city, sprawls noisily and dustily along its harbor. Location, location, location—on the northwestern tip of the Peloponnese—makes Patras a busy transportation hub. Much of Patras is under construction; rumbling semi-trailers menace hapless pedestrians amidst the general chaos. Island-bound tourists often see Patras as flyover, never looking beyond the tourist agencies and cafes. Patras's noisy exuberance makes for a lively social life; with the second-largest number of bars of any European city, Patras's cafe-lined plateias and pedestrian-only streets overflow every night. From mid-January to Ash Wednesday, Patras breaks out with pre-Lenten Carnival madness—music, food, and an all-night festival. The port transforms into one vast dance floor; for once, the people stand a chance against massive speeding vehicles. When you're here, buy your ferry ticket, store your luggage, and head for the hills. The peaceful upper city invites afternoon strolls among the elegant garden-terraced homes perched above the mad lower city, turning toward the turquoise gulf below.

### GETTING THERE AND GETTING AROUND

If you're coming from Athens by car, choose between the **New National Road,** which runs inland along the Gulf of Corinth, and the slower, scenic **Old National Road,** which hugs the coast. Those coming from the north can take a ferry from **Antirio** across to **Rion** on the Peloponnese (30min.; every 15min. 7am-11pm; 300dr per person, 1800dr per car), then hop on bus #6 (30min., 270dr) from Rion to the stop at **Kanakari** and **Aratou** streets, four blocks uphill from the main station.

**Ferries:** From Patras, boats reach **Kephalonia, Ithaka,** and **Corfu** in Greece, and **Brindisi, Trieste, Bari, Ancona,** and **Venice** in **Italy.** Most ferries to Italy leave at night. Daily ferries go to **Vathy** on Ithaka (3¾hr., 3500dr) via **Sami** on Kephalonia (3hr., 3200dr), and to **Corfu** (6-8hr., 5800dr). Deck passage to **Brindisi** is 6000-8000dr, plus 2200dr port tax. Several ferry lines make the trip, so check the travel offices along Iroon Polytechniou and Othonas Amplias; discounts are available for those under 25. If you have a **railpass,** make sure to go to **HML** (☎452 521), on Iroon Polytechniou, near the customs complex–*don't let other agencies tell you your pass no longer works; they're trying to scam you.* The folks at **Strintzis Tours,** Othonas Amalias 14 (☎622 602), the main office of Strintzis Lines, are helpful. Open 9am-11pm.

**Buses: KTEL** (☎623 886, 887, or 888), on Othonos Amalias between Aratou and Zaïmi. Buses go to: **Athens** (3hr., 28 per day, 3800dr); **Egion** (17 per day, 750dr); **Ioannina** (4hr., 4 per day, 4550dr); **Kalamata** (4hr., 2 per day, 4350dr); **Kalavrita** (2hr., 4 per day, 1600dr); **Pyrgos** (2hr., 10 per day, 1900dr); **Thessaloniki** (9½hr., 3 per day, 8800dr); **Tripoli** (4hr., 2 per day, 3250dr), and **Volos** (4hr., 2 per day, 5300).

**Trains:** (☎639 109), on Othonos Amalias. To: **Athens** (8 per day; slow 5hr., 1600dr; express 3½hr., 3000dr); **Egio** (slow 320dr, express 800dr); **Kalamata** (4½hr., 2 per day, 1500dr); and **Pyrgos,** where you can transfer to **Olympia** (2hr.; 8 per day until 10pm; slow 820dr, express 1220dr). The trains to Athens are packed, so reserve seats, even if you have a railpass. **Ticket booth** open 6:30am-2:30am.

**Car Rental:** many along Ag. Andreas. **National Car Rental/Alamo,** Ag. Andreas 1 (☎273 667), has reasonable rates. Open M-F 9am-9pm, Sa and Su 9am-2pm.

## ORIENTATION AND PRACTICAL INFORMATION

Patras is on a grid; most hotels, restaurants, and shops are condensed in the heart of the lower city. **Iroon Polytechniou** runs parallel to the water, toward downtown. Just before the train station, the road curves and shakes off its name, becoming **Othonos Amalias.** Just beyond the train station, it runs past the palm trees, cafes, and kiosks of **Pl. Trion Simahon.** Car-free **Ag. Nikolaou,** full of hotels and cafes, runs inland from the plateia and intersects the major east-west streets of the city. From the corner of Ag. Nikolaou and **Mezanos,** walk three blocks from the water and turn right to find open **Pl. Georgiou** and its sculpted fountain near the waterfront. The heart of New Patras lies between Pl. Georgiou and shaded **Pl. Olgas,** three blocks to the west. To skip the grime of the lower city's plateias, climb the daunting steps on Ag. Nikolaou to the upper-crust upper part of town.



**Tourist Office:** (☎430 195), on the water at the customs entrance. Multilingual staff hands out bus and boat timetables, lodging advice, and maps. Open M-F 7am-9pm.

**Banks: National Bank** (☎221 643), in Pl. Trion Simahon on the waterfront, has a 24hr. **ATM,** as do other banks on the plateia. Open M-Th 8am-2pm, F 8am-1:30pm.

**Luggage Storage:** In the pink building near the customs complex. 500dr per day. Also at train station: 500dr per day with ticket, 1000dr otherwise. Open 7am-10pm.

**International Bookstore: Lexis Bookshop,** Patreos 90 (☎274 831). Useful selection for travelers: language dictionaries and various books about Greek history and culture.

**Laundromat:** Zaïmi 49 (☎620 119), near Korinthou. Wash and dry 2300dr. Open M-F 9am-3pm; 5-8:30pm; Sa 9am-6pm.

**Tourist Police:** (☎451 833 or 451 893), inside the customs complex. Offers the same services, but is more helpful than the tourist office. Open 7am-11pm.

**Hospital: Red Cross Emergency Station** (☎227 386), on the corner of 28 Oktovriou and Ag. Dionysiou, dispenses first aid. Open 8am-8pm. **Rio Hospital of Patras University** (☎999 111) is 5km away, accessible by taxi or bus #6.

**Telephones: OTE** (☎421 998) is at the customs complex, across from the tourist office. Open 7:30am-2:30pm and 3-9pm. To make international collect calls, go to the OTE at Pl. Trion Simahon. Open M-F 7am-2:30pm, Sa-Su 7:20am-1pm.

**Internet Access:** Hilltop **Rocky Raccoon Online Cafe,** Gerokostopoulou 56 (☎223 398), near the upper city steps. 1500dr per hr., 750dr minimum. Open 9am-3am.

**Post Office:** (☎223 864), on Mezonos at the corner of Zaïmi. Open M-F 7:30am-8pm, Sa 7:30am-2pm. **Postal code:** 26001.

## ACCOMMODATIONS

The tangle of buildings on **Ag. Andreas,** parallel to and one block up from the waterfront, houses hotels galore. Many of Patras's cheap hotels—some part-time bordellos—have closed, leaving vacant buildings with bright plastic signs. The hotels you'll see are often budget in appearance, not in price.

**Patras**

ACCOMMODATIONS
Hotel El Greco, 5
Hotel Hellas, 3
Pension Nicos, 4
Rio Camping, 2
Youth Hostel, 1

0 300 yards
0 300 meters

Gulf of Patras

TO 1 (1 km), 2 (8 km)
Customs House
Iroon Polytechniou
Gianitson
Ipirou
PL. NIKIS
Ag. Sofias
Ioaninon
Kilkis
TO CORINTH (134 km) & ATHENS
Athinon
Faverou
Mourouzi
Makedonias
Konstantinoupoleos
Norman
Astigos
28 Oktovriou
Korinthou
Kanakari
Maniakiou
Gotsi
Train Station
PL. TRION SIMAHON
Mihalakopoulou
Satovriandou
Zaimi
PL. OLGAS
Aratou
Othonos Amalias
Ermou
Mezonos
Korinthou
Kanakari
Kolokotroni
Ypsilandou
Ag. Nikolaou
PL. GEORGIOU
Frouriou
Artemidos
Athinas
Acropolis
Papadiamantopoulou
Patreos
Pantanasis
Votsi
Filopimenos
Gerokostopoulou
Boumboulinas
Ag. Andreou
Riga Fereou
D. Gounari
Kanari
Miaouli
Tsamadou
Sahtouri
Karaiskaki
Pantokratoros
ANCIENT ODEON
Trion Navarhon
Agios Andreas
Korai
Genadiou
Kalamogdart
Germanou
Ag. Dimitriou
N
TO PYRGOS (100 km) & AG. ANDREAS
Papaflessa
Diakou
PL. IPSILON ALONION
D. Gounari
TO KALAVRITA (77 km) & TRIPOLI (170 km)

**Youth Hostel,** Iroon Polytechniou 68 (☎427 278). From the docks, walk away from town with the water on your left for about 1.5km. The slightly remote hostel occupies a creaky turn-of-the-century mansion that sat empty for 40 years after being used by occupying Germans. You can leave valuables at the reception desk. Dorms 2000dr per person.

**Pension Nicos,** Patreos 3 (☎221 643), two blocks off the waterfront. The best bet in Patras, conveniently located and cheery. Wood-paneled rooms have large, modern shared baths with tubs. Bar and roof terrace. Singles 4000dr; doubles 6500dr.

**Hotel El Greco,** Ag. Andreas 145 (☎272 931 or 272 932), two blocks up from the waterfront, four blocks past Pl. Trion Simahon. Clean, cute rooms have shared hall bathrooms. Singles 6000dr; doubles 8000dr; 2000dr extra for private bath and TV.

**Hotel Hellas,** Ag. Nikolaou 14 (☎273 352), two blocks inland from the waterfront, on the right. Aged and slightly musty, the bare rooms have balconies and communal bathrooms with huge bathtubs. Singles 4000dr; doubles 6000dr.

**Rio Camping** (☎991 585), 8km east in Rion, a beach-and-club suburb of Patras. Catch bus #6 at the corner of Aratou and Kamakari, get off at Rion, and follow signs. 1200dr per person, 600dr per child; 1100dr per tent; 700dr per (small) car. Electricity 800dr.

## FOOD

Patras's bazillion pubs and cafes are generally indistinguishable and overpriced, and tavernas are scarce. If wholesome is your bag, you can self-cater from **Dia Discount Supermarket,** on Ag. Andreas near Kolokotroni. (Open Tu-Sa 9am-5pm.)

**Taverna O Nikolas,** on Ag. Andreas just past Ag. Nikolaou as you approach from the train station. The finest restaurant in Patras, and cheap, too. Chatty Nikolas will patiently explain the menu to you in English. Greek salad 900dr, extra garlicky *tzatziki* 600dr, baby calamari 2000dr. All entrees 800-2000dr; classy bottle of vino 1000dr per liter.

**Europa Center** (☎437 006), on Oth. Amalias a few blocks after the customs exit. This friendly cafeteria-style eatery is run by Greek-Americans ready to assist weary backpackers stumbling off ferries. In addition to tasty, low-priced dishes (entrees 900-1700dr), they provide services like free luggage storage, maps, and information.

**Taverna Nikolaras,** Ag. Nikolaou 50 (☎624 595), three blocks inland. This old-school taverna isn't flashy, but the food is delicious—the owner's family has perfected the recipes over 90 years. A changing menu of hot dishes including *fasolia* (giant beans, 950dr) and stuffed eggplant (1300dr). Beer 500dr.

**Signore** (☎222 212), on Ag. Andreas near Ag. Nikolaou. A casual, quasi-Italian place serves everything from calzones (700dr) and pizza (650dr per slice) to sweet and savory crepes (700-1050dr). Delivery available.

## NIGHTLIFE



At night, the wall of cafes and pubs swells with patrons of all tastes: younger, hardcore beer-swillers rub elbows with dainty spiked-*frappé* sippers. All gesticulate with cigarettes and jabber into cell phones. The two main plateias, Radinou (a pedestrian-only alley one block east of Pl. Olgas), and the upper part of Gerokostopolou (extending uphill from Pl. Georgiou), are especially dense with cafe umbrellas. **Club Mondo** is on Aratou with seating on Pl. Olgas. A boisterous crowd divides its time between the indoor video games and table-hopping on the plateia. **Blue Monday,** along Radinou, is a veritable shrine to 1950s America, chock full of rock memorabilia and playing the best oldies-but-goodies. (Open until 3 am.)

Though Patras itself has a lot to offer in the way of bars and cafes, the wildest party-goers head out of town. **Rion,** a beach satellite 8km to the northeast, accommodates Patras's club junkies with a summertime stretch of bars, clubs, restaurants, and discos. Decor is a big deal at the beach bars—the most exciting resemble theme parks. To get to Rion, take bus #6 from Kamakari and Araton (30min., 230dr) all the way to the port. From the port, walk along the beachside road with the water on your right. The start of the strip is within 100m. Buses to Rion only run until 11pm, so count on taking a cab home if you're having any fun at all (1000dr). At **Mioiouia 105,** a bright yellow plane from the Second World War hangs above the dance floor, and plastic soldiers engage in desert combat under plexiglass at the bar (beer 600dr, *frappés* 500dr). **Soka Bay** goes for the jungle motif: green lighting illuminates rope-wrapped trees and fake ruins, and you can play on the giant tree swing as you sip your beer (500dr).

## SIGHTS

**ACHAIA CLAUSS WINERY.** A narrow road meanders uphill through grapevines and shaded countryside to the internationally renowned Achaia Clauss winery, 8km southeast of Patras. Founded in 1861 by German-born Baron von Clauss, its weathered stone buildings have aged well, as has the wine. Try a complementary sample of their famous Mavrodaphne, a superb dessert wine named for the black eyes of Clauss's ill-fated fiancée Daphne. Though a bit out of the way, a visit is highly recommended, if only for the invigorating breath of country air. *(Take bus #7 (30min., 260dr) from the intersection of Kolokotroni and Kanakari; it stops at the main gate to the winery at the bottom of the hill. Free English tours every hr.)*

**VENETIAN CASTLE.** Built atop ruins of an ancient acropolis and temple to Panachaian Athena, Patras's 13th-century castle looks down on the teeming beehive of Patras. At the castle's center is a verdant courtyard with chirping birds, bright flowers, and olive and orange trees that lend the site a cheerfully medieval feel. *(If the entrance near the steps from the lower city is closed, walk around to the main entrance at the opposite corner of the castle. Open 8am-7pm. Free.)*

**ANCIENT ODEUM.** West of the castle in the upper city, this ancient Roman theater was built sometime before AD 160 and used until the 3rd century. Ancient travel writer Pausanias described it as the second most impressive in Greece, after Athens's Theater of Herodus Atticus (p. 101). Excavated in 1889, the theater was restored with brick and marble after the Second World War. *(Open Tu-Su 8:30am-3pm. Free.)* In the summer, the theater hosts the **Patras International Festival,** where Greek and international music groups play nightly. *(June 15-Oct. 15 9pm. 1500dr.)*

**AGIOS ANDREAS.** The largest Orthodox cathedral in Greece, Ag. Andreas is dedicated to St. Andrew, a Patras native martyred here on the X-shaped crucifix he requested, feeling unworthy to die on a cross like Jesus'. A decade ago, the Catholic Church presented the Bishop of Patras with the über-relic, St. Andrew's holy head. The crown of the head is visible through its reliquary, an ornate silver replica of the cathedral around it. The cathedral's frescoes, gold mosaics, and delicately latticed windows enhance its otherworldly beauty. To the right of the cathedral is the equally beautiful **Church of St. Andrew,** with a small well allegedly built by the saint himself. Spy the well through a doorway to the right of the church. Legend says that whoever drinks from it will return to Patras again. *(Follow Ag. Andreou with the water to your right, roughly 1.5km from the port (20min.). Open 9am-dusk. Dress modestly.)*

**ARCHAEOLOGICAL MUSEUM.** This small museum's collection will captivate history buffs. Its most striking pieces are Roman, with statuary, mosaics, glassware, oil lamps, and surprisingly intact delicate gold jewelry. *(☎220 829. Mezonos 42, next to Pl. Olgas at the corner of Mezonos and Aratou. Open Tu-Su 8:30am-3pm. Free.)*

**CARNIVAL SEASON.** From mid-January to Ash Wednesday, *karnavali* sweeps the entire town up in an indescribable energy. A 12-hour parade takes to the streets the last Sunday of Carnival. The final night climaxes in a ritual burning of King Carnival's effigy and a boozy all-night harborside party. Every hotel room within a 100km radius fills up, so reserve ahead.



## KYLLINI Κυλληνη ☎0623

For a port town that handles almost all the tourist traffic to Zakynthos, Kyllini is surprisingly underdeveloped; the town has almost no bus service, few accommodations, and very little to occupy the passing traveler. If find yourself stuck here overnight, make the best of it by spending the afternoon at the wide sandy beach right in the center of town, and later indulging in delicious home-cooked food found at its many tiny tavernas. To bypass Kyllini entirely, take a direct bus from Zakynthos Town to any of the stops on the Patras-Athens route (p. 131).

**PRACTICAL INFORMATION.** To leave Kyllini, take the **bus** from the kiosk near the port gate to **Pirgos** (30min., 3 per day until 4:30pm, 500dr). Once safely in Pirgos, catch a bus to **Olympia** (40min., 16 per day, 450dr) or a train to **Athens, Patras, Kalamata,** or **Tripoli.** For all other bus connections you will have to spend 3000dr on a **taxi** (☎71 764) to **Lehena,** the nearest town on the main Patras-Pirgos highway. **Ferries** sail from Kyllini to: **Argostoli** (2hr., 11:30am, 2800dr); **Poros** on Kephalonia (1½hr., 6:30 and 10:30pm, 2000dr); and **Zakynthos** (1hr., 1-2 per day, 1400dr). Buy tickets from one of the two kiosks on the dock; facing inland, the kiosk on the right, near the gate, sells tickets to Zakynthos, and the one on the left sells tickets to Kephalonia. The **port police** are on the dock (☎92 211; open 24hr.), while the path to town will take you to the **police** (☎92 202; no English spoken). The **post office** is a few blocks farther down, on a side street leading inland (open 7:30am-2pm). **Postal code:** 27068.

**ACCOMMODATIONS AND FOOD.** **Sea Garden Domatia,** above the Sea Garden Restaurant two blocks inland from the port, is nothing fancy but has pleasant rooms with ceiling fans, TVs, balconies and private baths. (☎92 165. Singles 8000dr, doubles 10,000dr.) **Hotel Ionion,** across the tracks and down the beach, rents large rooms decorated in vivid shades of gray. (☎92 318. Singles

8000dr; doubles 12,000dr; triples 14,000dr; private baths available.) **Stivas** (☎92 045), down the street from the port gate, facing the entrance to the Sea Garden domatia, serves up divine dishes cooked in a tiny, family-run kitchen to be savored under a vine-laden trellis on the side patio. Dishes change daily, but a full meal with wine will cost about 2500-3000dr per person.

**DAYTRIPS FROM KYLLINI.** Nearby **Karitena** is the village pictured on the 5000dr bill. The birthplace of **Kolokotronis** (a Greek nationalist revolutionary), Karitena has ruins of a Frankish castle and a 13th-century church dedicated to Ag. Nikolaos. If its beauty entices you to stay, **Stamata Kondopoulos** has rooms near the post office. (☎31 206. Singles 5000dr; doubles 7000dr.)

# OLYMPIA Ολυμπια ☎0264

Set among meadows and shaded by cypress and olive trees, modern Olympia is a friendly and attractive town reduced to a sleeping-and-eating stopover for visitors to that gold mine tourist attraction, the ancient Olympic arena. Intense tourism has inspired vigorous recruiting tactics amongst the locals who hock their wares.

PELOPONNESE

## ORIENTATION AND PRACTICAL INFORMATION

Olympia consists primarily of a 1km main street called **Kondili;** buses stop in front of the tourist office on this street. Head out of town on the main road for a 5min. walk to the Olympia ruins and archaeological museum. The road curves left just outside town; follow the signs to the site. The side road running downhill opposite the youth hostel has the train station, convenience store, and pricey tavernas.

**Buses:** Across from the tourist info shack's posted schedule. To: **Pirgos** (40min., 16 per day 6:30am-10pm, 450dr); **Tripoli** (4hr., 3 per day, 2500dr); **Dimitsana** (M and F 8:45am, 1550dr); and **Lala** (30min., 1:20pm, 350dr). Service reduced Sa-Su.

**Trains:** At the end of the road that begins opposite the youth hostel, perpendicular to the road to Pyrgos. Trains run to **Pirgos** (5 per day, 210dr), which connects to more cities.

**Tourist Office:** (☎23 100), on Kondili, toward the ruins. Helpful staff, photocopier, stamps, and free **maps.** Open M-F 8am-9pm, Sa 10am-5pm, closed Su.

**Bank: National Bank,** on Kondili, has an **ATM** and **exchanges currency.** Open M-Th 8am-2pm, F 8am-1:30pm.

**Police:** Em. Kountsa 1 (☎22 100), one block up from Kondili. Open 9am-9pm, but someone is there 24hr. **Tourist police** usually around in the morning (hours vary).

**Health Center:** (☎22 222; Pirgos hospital (0621) 22 222). Olympia uses Pirgos's hospital, but has its own **health center.** Walk from the ruins down Kondili and turn left before the church on your left. Continue straight as the road winds right and then left, then take a left. Open M-F 8am-2pm.

**Telephones:** On Kondili by the post office. Open M-F 7:30am-2pm.

**Post Office:** (☎22 578), on a nameless uphill side street just past the tourist office. Open M-F 7:30am-2:30pm. **Postal code:** 27065.

## ACCOMMODATIONS

Most of Olympia's dozens of hotels offer private baths and balconies. Prices hover around 8000dr per double.

**Youth Hostel,** Kondili 18 (☎25 580). Convenient location, clean. Lockout 10:30am-noon. Breakfast 600dr. Check-out 10:30am. Dorms 1700dr, free hot showers.

**Pension Poseidon** (☎22 567), 2 blocks uphill from the National Bank, on the right. Run by a nice Francophone family. Clean, shared hallway baths. Singles 6000dr; doubles 7500dr; triples 9000dr.

**Rooms for Rent.** Ask at the **Anesi Cafe-Tavern,** 13 Avgerinou and Spiliopoulou (☎22 644), on a road uphill just off Kondili (toward Pirgos). Private baths. Singles 4000dr; doubles 6500dr; triples 8000dr.

**Pension Achilleus** (☎22 562), across the street and one block down from Pension Poseidon. Private bathrooms. Singles 5000dr; doubles 7000; triples 9000dr.

**Camping Diana** (☎22 314), uphill from the Sports Museum. With a clean pool, hot water, mini-market, helpful info (schedules and maps), and breakfast (1000dr). 1600dr per person; 1000dr per car; 1200dr per small tent, 1600dr per large tent; adult with sleeping bag 1800dr. Electricity 1000dr. 10-20% student discounts.

**Camping Olympia** (☎22 745), 1km toward Pirgos. Has a pool. 1300dr per person; 900dr per car; 1050dr per small tent; 1300dr per large tent. Electricity 850dr.

## FOOD

Numerous **minimarkets** along Kondili sell picnic fixings. Most eateries on Kondili are cramped and overpriced, but a walk toward the railroad station or up the hill reveals charming and inexpensive tavernas. Most restaurants are open 8am-1am.

**Ambrosia** (☎23 414), in the woods beside the train station. Exceptionally delicious food in an elegant setting overlooking a quiet, cypress-lined meadow. *Mezedes* plate 2600dr, veal with red sauce and pasta 2000dr, lamb chops 1950dr.

**Pension Poseidon** (☎22 567), beside the pension. The smiling owner George serves *retsina* made from the grapes that hang on the lattices overhead (800dr per L), and generous, succulent portions of food made by his wife and mother. Entrees change daily, *moussaka* 1500dr, grilled chicken 1500dr, omelettes 800dr.

**Taverna Olympia,** on the road to the train station. Away from the crowds, and low-key. Greek entrees 900-1550dr, Italian pastas 650-1100dr.

## SIGHTS

At the top of the hill, on the side of town toward Pirgos, the **Museum of the Olympic Games,** a.k.a. the **Sports Museum,** on Angerinou, two blocks uphill from Kondili, explains the recent history of the Olympics and has interesting paraphernalia from each of the modern games, including medals, posters, and photographs of athletes. (☎22 544. Open M-Sa 8am-3:30pm, Su 9am-4pm. 500dr.)

PELOPONNESE

# ANCIENT OLYMPIA

***Site:*** *☎22 517. Open 8am-7pm.* ***Museum:*** *Through the parking lot opposite the ancient site. ☎22 742. Open M noon-7pm, Tu-Su 8am-7pm. Cameras with flash prohibited.* ***Admission*** *to museum and site 2000dr; museum only 1200dr, students 600dr, EU students and children under 18 free. A guidebook and map are vital, as the ruins are practically unmarked. Several thorough guides are available at the site–try the red* Olympia *(2000dr) and* Olympia: Complete Guide *(1500dr) both by Spiros Photinos, or* The Blue Guide to the Museum and Sanctuary *by A. and N. Yalouris (2500dr).*

A green and tranquil tract between the rivers Kladeo and Alphios, Olympia was one of the most important cultural centers of the Greek world for a millennium. Here, participants from Sicily, Asia Minor, North Africa, Macedonia, and all of Greece convened to worship, compete, and get some cultcha among poets, musicians, and masterpieces of art and architecture. Every four years, warring city-states would call truces and travel reverently to Olympia for the most splendid pan-Hellenic assembly of the ancient world.

Olympia was settled by the 3rd millennium BC, when it was dedicated to **Gaia,** the Earth Mother, who had an oracle at the site. Kronos disposed of Gaia and his father, who were in turn kicked out by Kronos's son Zeus and his Olympian thugz in the Battle of the Gods and the Titans. Olympia's allegiance was quick to follow this succession, and the first athletic games commenced in Zeus's honor, only to

**NO GIRLS ALLOWED** In ancient Olympia, although female athletic abilities were showcased in the prestigious Heraion footrace held every four years, most women were not allowed to attend the Olympic Games. Only young girls (more specifically, virgins) and the priestess of Demeter were allowed to watch the events. This rule was strictly enforced; as the rules specified, any women caught at the games would be thrown to her death off the summit of Mt. Typaion. While there is no record of anyone ever suffering this gruesome fate, one notable woman was caught breaking the rules. **Kallipateira,** mother of the Olympic athlete Peisirodos, entered the stadium disguised as a male trainer; her husband had died, and she wanted to watch her son compete as he could not. Peisirodos won the games, and as his victory was announced she leapt up to embrace him, disrobing herself in the process and revealing her definitely-not-manhood. Out of respect for her son, brother, and deceased husband, all of whom were Olympic champions, officials did not order her death. They *did* preventively decree that from then on, all trainers had to wear their birthday suits.

be forgotten again until 884 BC. The first Olympic revival took place on the Oracle of Delphi's orders to Iphtos, King of Elias; prophecy had it that the games would save Greece from civil war and plague. The first recorded Olympiad was in 776 BC, with **Koroibos of Elias** emerging victorious. Every four years thereafter, another champion added his name to the illustrious list, which became the first accurate chronology of Greek history. Initially, a foot-race of 192m (the stadium's length) was the only event, but longer races, wrestling, boxing, the pentathlon (long jump, discus, javelin, running, wrestling), the hoplite race (in full bronze regalia), and equestrian events eventually joined the roster. The games were celebrated through the 4th century AD, when Theodosius the Great (and No Fun) abolished them.



## SIGHTS AND RUINS

The central sanctuary of the Olympic complex, which was eventually walled and dedicated to Zeus, was called the **Altis.** Over the centuries, it held temples, treasuries, and a number of monuments to the gods. It was surrounded by various facilities for participants and administrators, including the stadium on the far east side. Pausanias, a traveler who wrote in the 2nd century AD, mentions a whopping 69 separate monuments built by victors thanking the gods.

Although the ruins are not especially well preserved, the site's colossal dimensions remain impressive. Few sections are corded off; you can climb up the steps of the Temple of Zeus and wander through Phidias's workshop as you please.

**TRAINING GROUNDS.** As you enter the site, you face south, and the 2nd-century BC **Gymnasium**'s thigh-high remains lie to your right. The Gymnasium was an open-air quadrangle surrounded by Doric columns used by runners and Pentathlon athletes for training. If you wander through the Gymnasium toward the south, you will come to the re-erected columns of the **Palaestra,** or wrestling school, built in the 3rd century BC. Always more than just an athletic facility, the Palaestra had an educational function as philosophical as it was athletic. Young men trained their minds and bodies, wrestling one moment and studying Homer the next.

**PHIDIAS'S WORKSHOP.** The next group of buildings to the south includes the workshop of **Phidias,** the marvelous sculptor who came to Olympia after his banishment from Athens in a cloud of scandal (it had to do with the statue of Athena he had created for the Parthenon; use your imagination). Commissioned to sculpt for the Temple of Zeus, he produced an ivory-and-gold statue of the god so magnificent that it was later called one of the **seven wonders of the ancient world.** Seven times larger than life, it stood about 12.4m high, and portrayed the god seated on his throne, his face a revelation of benevolence and glory. After viewing the sculpture, poet Philip of Salonica wrote, "Either God came down from Heaven to show you his image, Phidias, or you went to see God." When the games were abolished

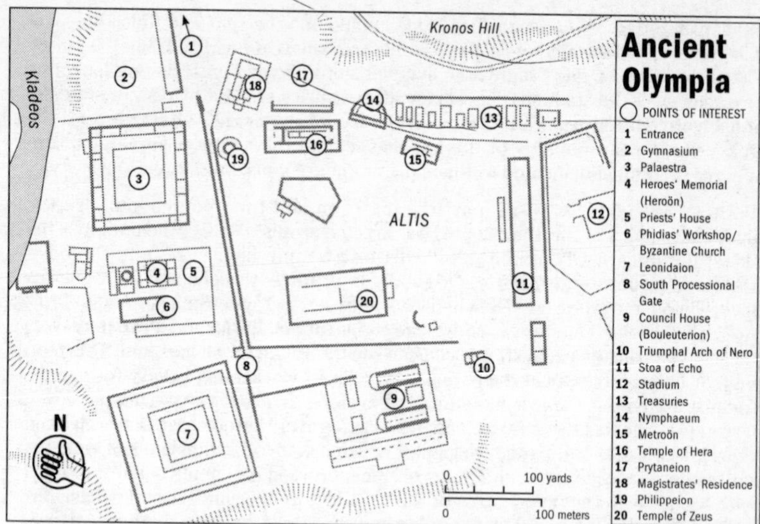




in the 4th century AD, the statue was moved to Constantinople; it burned in a fire there in AD 475. Adding insult to injury, the Byzantines built a church on top of the sculptor's workshop in the 5th century AD, constructing new walls but leaving the foundation intact. For years, the identity of the site was debated. Recent excavations of the building, however, have affirmed the traditional sources, yielding moulds, sculpting tools and, most amazing of all, shards of a plain wine jug that, when they were cleaned and mended, bore the inscription ΦΕΙΔΙΟ ΕΙΜΙ—"I belong to Phidias." These finds are in the museum (see below). Just beyond the workshop to the south is the huge **Leonidaion,** built by a wealthy man from Naxos named Leonidas and dedicated to Zeus sometime after 350 BC, and used to house game officials and other VIPs.

**BOULETERION.** Across from the northeast corner of the Leonidaion and Palaestra lies the remains of the South Processional Gate to the **Altis.** Here the procession of athletes and trainers entered the sacred area on their way to the Bouleuterion (to the right of the Gate), where the Olympic council met and the official documents were kept. Each athlete was required to make a sacrifice to Zeus and take the sacred oath, swearing their eligibility and intent to abide by the rules of the Games.

**TEMPLE OF ZEUS.** To the north of the Bouleterion are the ruins of the once-gigantic Temple of Zeus, the centerpiece of the Altis after its construction in 457 BC. Home to Phidias's awe-inspiring statue of Zeus (see above), the 27m long temple was the largest completed on the Greek mainland before the Parthenon. The temple's elegant facade, slim columns, and accurately modeled pedimental sculpture exemplified the Classical design that evolved before the Persians invaded Greece. Toppled in segments, the tremendous columns lie as they fell in a 6th-century AD earthquake. Parts of the original mosaic floor remain on the temple base.

**STADIUM.** Continuing east past the temple, you will reach the remains of the **Stoa of Echo,** which was used for the competitions between trumpeters and heralds, whose musical prowess was no doubt enhanced by the seven-fold echo the Stoa is said to have had. At the northern edge of the Stoa is the **Krypte,** the official entrance to the stadium used by athletes and judges. This domed passageway (of which only one arch survives) and the stadium as seen today are the work of the Hellenistic period, built over the remains of the earlier, similarly positioned stadium. Despite the efforts of powerful earthquakes, the stadium appears today

much as it did 2300 years ago. The judges' stand and the start and finish lines are still in place, and the stadium's grassy banks can still seat nearly 40,000 spectators. Take a lap around, and bond with Olympians of millennia past. As you leave the passageway to the stadium, the remains of treasuries erected by distant states to house votive offerings are in a row on the bank to your right. East, beyond the treasuries, lie the remains of the **nymphaeum** and the **metroön,** an elegant 4th-century BC temple dedicated to Rhea, the mother of gods, built in the Doric style.

**HERA'S TEMPLE.** Westward, past the metroön and the nymphaeum, are the dignified remains of the Temple of Hera. Erected around 600 BC, the temple is the oldest building at Olympia, the oldest Doric temple in Greece, and the best-preserved structure at the site. Originally built for both Zeus and Hera, it was devoted solely to the goddess when Zeus moved to grander quarters in 457 BC. The *cella* of the Temple is where the magnificent **Hermes of Praxiteles** was unearthed during its excavations; you can see the statue in the museum. This temple figured prominently in the **Heraia,** a women's foot-race held every four years. Today, the Olympic flame is lit at the Altar of Hera, to the east of the temple. From here, it is borne to Athens by runners who each travel 1km, then pass it from hand to hand to the site of the modern games, which can involve thousands of runners, or draw upon more modern methods of transportation like boats, planes, or even laser beam (as in the unique case of the 1976 Montreal Games). The **Prytaneion** is northwest of the Temple of Hera and contains a sacred hearth, the **Altar of Hestia.** The spirit of the Games reached its culmination here with the celebratory feasts on behalf of the victors and official guests that expressed a collective appreciation for the virtues of discipline and honor that they embodied.



## MUSEUM

Many find the gleaming new **Archaeological Museum** a greater attraction than the ancient site itself. A team of French archaeologists began unearthing the site from 1400 years of silt in 1829; the systematic excavations that continue today commenced in 1875. Most of what has been extracted in these 124 years, from the mundane to the wildly spectacular, resides in the museum. Since military victors from across the Greek world sent spoils and pieces of their own equipment to Olympia as offerings to the gods, the new museum doubles as a museum of Greek military history, with entire rooms filled with helmets, cuirasses, greaves, swords, spear points, and other military paraphernalia. The most spectacular military offering is a common **Corinthian helmet,** partially destroyed by oxidation. While richer, better preserved headgear can be found elsewhere in the museum, the helmet's lodestone is the faint inscription on the chin guard, which reads ΜΙΛΤΙΔΕΣ ΑΝΕΘΕΚΕΝ ΤΟΙ ΔΙΙ—"Miltiades dedicated this to Zeus." The victor of one of the most famous battles in all antiquity, **Miltiades** led the outnumbered Greeks to victory over the Persians at Marathon in 479 BC; he may have worn the helmet in the battle. Beside it is another headpiece whose inscription reveals it to be from the Persians in the same battle. The museum's awesome array of sculpture includes some of the greatest extant pieces in the world. Gape at the graceful perfection of the **Hermes of Praxiteles** and the **Rape of Ganymede,** and see how the **Nike of Paionios** seems to float. The pedimental sculptures and the metopes depicting the twelve labors of Hercules come from the Temple of Zeus. Even the lesser-known objects astound—every case holds objects that would be highlights of a lesser collection.

# ARCADIA ΑΡΚΑΔΙΑ

Beyond the noisy bustle of Tripoli, mountainous Arcadia is heavily forested and lightly speckled with red-roofed villages and lonely monasteries. The region's lush mountain landscapes and undisturbed serenity ushered it into mythology and literature as the pastoral archetype, home to Pan, Dionysus, and the nymphs, satyrs,

and the lucky mortals who cavorted with them. While few foreign tourists make it to Arcadia's pristine outer reaches, those who do are amply rewarded by the sight of stone-paved villages atop precipitous slopes and solitary walks accompanied by the tin bells of grazing mountain goats.

## TRIPOLI Τριπολη ☎071

The transportation hub of Arcadia, Tripoli is crowded and fast-paced, a place where tourists are merely an annoyance to its otherwise-occupied residents. The narrow streets are crammed with clothing and furniture stores, and cafes and tavernas are relegated to the area bordering the park, an oasis of space amidst the suffocating city. If the infrequent buses into the mountains force you to spend the night, amuse yourself by sipping a *frappé* in the park while watching the children wreak havoc in their bumper cars, or try to join the somewhat adolescent nightlife of the techno-blaring bars along Deligianni.

### ORIENTATION AND PRACTICAL INFORMATION



Think of Tripoli as a cross. At the center joint is **Pl. Ag. Vasiliou,** marked by the Church of Ag. Vasiliou. Four other plateias form the ends of the cross, at the ends of the four roads that radiate out from Ag. Vasiliou. Most buses arrive at Arcadia station in **Pl. Kolokotronis,** to the east of the center. From the station, **Georgiou** street will take you to Pl. Ag. Vasiliou, from behind the Church. Facing the Church of Ag. Vasiliou, turn a left and head north on **Eth. Antistasis** to reach **Pl. Petrinou,** recognizable by the large, neoclassical Maliaropouli Theater. Along with Pl. Kolokotronis, Pl. Petrinou sees most of the city's activity. Continue along Eth. Antistasis, the main shopping boulevard, and the park will be on your right, occupying eight city blocks. At the center of the park is **Pl. Areus,** with its 5m high statue of War of Independence hero Kolokotronis. The blocks around the park house boutiques, cafes, and clubs, and provide an excellent spot for people-watching.

**Buses: Arcadias Station** (☎222 560), in Pl. Kolokotronis, runs buses to: **Athens** (3hr., 14 per day, 3200dr); **Andritsena** (2½hr., 2 per day, 1600dr); **Dimitsana** (1hr.; M-F 1:30pm and 6:30pm, 8:30am only on M and F, Sa-Su only 1:30pm; 1000dr); **Megalopolis** (45min., 9 per day, 700dr); **Nafplion** and **Argos** (4 per day, 1100dr); and **Pirgos** (3½hr.; 8:30am and 6:30pm, Sa-Su only 11am; 2850dr). The **KTEL Messinia and Laconia** depot (☎242 086) is across from the train station; from Arcadias Station, exit by the taxi line, and turn right onto Lagorati, following it for about 300m until it ends at the train station, where you'll see the depot on your left. Buses go to: **Kalamata** (2hr., 12 per day, 1550dr); **Patras** (3hr., 2 per day, 3100dr); **Pylos** (3hr., 5 per day, 2400dr); and **Sparta** (1hr., 10 per day, 1000dr). **Blue buses** leave from Pl. Areus for **Tegea** and **Mantinea** (15min., every hr., 200dr).

**Trains:** (☎241 213), across from the Messinia and Laconia depot; go down Lagorati from Arcadias bus station. Four trains per day go to **Athens** (4hr., 1500dr); **Argos** (1½hr., 590dr); **Corinth** (2½hr., 900dr); and **Kalamata** (2½hr., 840dr).

**Tourist Information:** There's no real tourist office, just Vzettou Vanna a woman in city hall who might be able to give you some information. She's on the third floor of the new city hall, a glass-fronted building that's not very well marked (☎231 844). Follow Eth. Antistasis, past Pl. Petrinou, taking the second left onto N. Dimitrakopoulou after you pass the old city hall on your left–it has a Greek flag in front. The new building is about 2 blocks down the street on your left. Open M-F 7am-2:30pm.

**Bank: National Bank** (☎225 489), on Eth. Antistasis, one block from Pl. Agios Vasiliou. **Exchanges currency** and has a 24hr. **ATM.** Open M-Th 8am-2pm, F 8am-1:30pm.

**Police:** (☎222 411), on Eth. Antistasis, in Pl. Petrinou. Open 24hr.

**Hospital:** (☎238 542), on Panargadon road (on the far western ring of the city). Walk due west from Pl. Agios Vasiliou; the road becomes E. Stavrou, which intersects with Panargadon after 500m. At the intersection, turn left. After 300m, look right.

**Telephones: OTE,** 28 Octovriou 29 (☎226 399). From Pl. Agios Vasiliou, take Eth. Antistasis and bear left on 28 Octovriou. Open M-F 7am-10pm.

**Internet Access: Forth Net** is on Deligianni, a cafe-lined pedestrian road just off Eth. Antistasis near the park. 2000dr per hr.

**Post Office:** (☎222 565). With your back to the church in Pl. Ag. Vasiliou, cross the plateia and pass the Galaxy Hotel on your left, taking the alley that leads past a few cafes for about 20m, until you see the post office in front of you on the corner across Nikitara. Open M-F 7:30am-2pm. **Postal Code:** 22100.

## ACCOMMODATIONS

Tripoli presents numerous bloated, mid-range hotels with spotty lighting, better suited to business conventions than to budget travelers.

**Hotel Alex,** Vas. Georgios 26 (☎223 465; fax 242 442), between Pl. Kolokotronis and Pl. Ag. Vasiliou. Acceptable rooms in varying shades of puce are improved by TVs and private baths. Back rooms are quieter. Singles 7000dr with bath; doubles 10,000dr, with bath 13,500dr.

**Galaxy Hotel** (☎225 195; fax 225 197), opposite the church of Agios Visiliou. The decor and amenities of the rooms are nearly identical to Alex, although pricier. Singles 10,000dr; doubles 14,000dr.

PELOPONNESE

## FOOD AND ENTERTAINMENT

The best restaurants in Tripoli border the park; elsewhere in the city, trendy cafes and fast food dominate. Sandwich shops on Eth. Antistasis and Georgiou pile tasty baguettes with meat and cheese (300-500dr). **Atlantik Supermarket,** on Lagorati, is well stocked. (Open M-F 8am-9pm, Sa 8am-6pm.)

**Kipos Sosoli Restaurant,** in a garden-like backyard on Pavlou, one block off Eth. Antistasis. Traditional entrees under 1700dr. Menu is in Greek, but the staff will translate.

**H Gonia Taverna,** in Pl. Agios Vasiliou. No fancy decor, but cheap and filling. *Tzatziki* 600dr, Greek salad 1000dr, grilled chicken 1100dr, pork steak 1600dr.

**'Gaea,** in Pl. Areus, facing the park. More of a cafe atmosphere, but serves tasty fare like their rigatoni special (1600dr) and feta cheese (600dr).

At night you can rub shoulders with Tripoli's high school students at the bars along Eth. Antistasis past Pl. Petrinou. Especially popular is the **Cinema Classic Billiards Club,** on Deligianni, the pedestrian street off Eth. Antistasis, just before the park. With a big screen TV and A/C, this place fills up every night. (Beer 400-600dr; 1hr. of pool 1600dr.) Numerous cafes crowd this narrow area, like **Azur,** at the corner of Deligianni and Eth. Antistasis; **The American Music Bar,** 20m down the street, is among the entrants in the loudest music competition.

In the summer, posters advertise dance groups, choirs, and plays performed in the city's main plateias and nearby villages. Traveling companies and local performance groups stage Greek-language shows in the attractive **Maliaropoulio Theater;** make queries at the tourist office (tickets 1000-2000dr). The **Lera Panigyris** is a 10-day cultural **festival** that starts August 15. During Easter, the town's bishop roasts a lamb for all to eat in one of the plateias.

## SIGHTS

The **Archaeological Museum** is on Evangelistrias, in a yellow flower-bedecked building. From Pl. Kolokotronis to Pl. Ag. Vasiliou, take the first left and then turn left again. The museum has an especially large prehistoric collection, with room after room of pottery, jewelry, and weaponry from the Neolithic to the Mycenaean periods. Among the later pieces is a Hellenistic relief showing a figure with a scroll in hand: it's one of the few surviving artistic depictions of modern books' predecessor. (☎242 148. Open Tu-Su 8:30am-2:45pm; 500dr.) The large **Church of Ag. Vasiliou** is in the plateia of the same name; the shop underneath has great religious art.

# DIMITSANA Δημητσανα ☎0795

About 60km west of Tripoli lies the quintessential Arcadian village of Dimitsana, clinging to a steep, rocky mountainside covered with pines. Built on the ruins of ancient Teuthis with a view of the plain of Megalopolis and the Lousios River, Dimitsana has been a center of Greek learning and revolutionary activity since the 16th century, producing several notable church fathers during the War of Independence. Today, the town is almost untouched by modern life or tourist intrusions. Wander the streets and you'll see elderly men whiling away the afternoons in cafes, and catch the scent of fresh-baked bread (a local specialty) wafting from the open windows of immaculately kept stone homes.

**ORIENTATION AND PRACTICAL INFORMATION.** Transportation can be tricky in the mountains, and locals are roughly indifferent to the passage of time. When planning connections, keep in mind that the two taxis in some towns might siesta all afternoon. **Buses** run to Dimitsana from **Tripoli** (1½hr.; M and F 3 per day, Tu-Th 2 per day, Sa-Su 1 per day; 1200dr) and **Olympia** (1hr., M and F 8:45am, 1500dr). From Dimitsana, buses go to Tripoli (M-F 7:30am and 7pm, Sa-Su 7:30am; 1200dr). Buses to **Tripoli, Pirgos,** and **Olympia** make frequent stops in **Karkalou,** a 20min. taxi ride (1000dr); you can also catch a daily bus to Tripoli from Karkalou (3pm, 1200dr) across from the cafe that sells tickets. Take a taxi from Dimitsana or ask directions to get to the stop.

In Dimitsana, the bus deposits you in **Pl. Pesonton,** the heart of town, or 30m down **Labardopoulou** (the main street), across from the cafe that doubles as a taxi stand. Walking uptown, you will first pass the **OTE** on your right, just before the plateia. (Open M-F 7am-2:30pm.) Continue through the plateia and around the second bend; the **National Bank,** with an **ATM,** will be on your left. (☎31 503. Open M-Th 8am-2pm, F 8am-1:30pm.) The **post office** is past the bank. (☎22 007. Open M-F 7:30am-2:30pm.)

**ACCOMMODATIONS AND FOOD.** Widespread **domatia** are really the only option, but fortunately, most establishments are beautifully furnished and more like bed-and-breakfasts than the boxlike rooms to let often found elsewhere. Rooms to let are also available above the grocery store in the main plateia and elsewhere around town; look for prominent signs. The home of **Basilis Tsiapa** is set back from the road with a fragrant garden, sweeping mountain views, and extremely gracious owners. Walking through the plateia, take the last right before the road bends to the left (you'll see the Rooms to Let signs). Gorgeous rooms have double beds, polished hardwood floors, TVs, and kitchenettes. (☎31 583. Singles 9000; doubles 10,000.) Equally luxurious, **Domatia Kousteni** has big, brand-new rooms with baths, TVs, kitchenettes, and access to a beautiful lounge and full kitchen. The lovely proprietor, Anna, makes cakes and cookies for breakfast, which is included in the room price. Ask at the Teythis Cafe, beside the OTE. (☎31 550 or 31 571. Rooms for one, two, or three 12,000dr.)

The ouzo flows freely in the cafes lining Labardopolou, but tavernas serving full meals are less common. **Barougadiko** (☎31 629; ΜΠΑΡΟΥΓΑΔΙΚΟ), just past the plateia downhill from the OTE, is a good choice. They serve skillfully prepared traditional Greek dishes like grilled pork with potatoes (1900dr). The friendly staff speak some English, and will help with menu-translation difficulties.

**SIGHTS.** Two small museums commemorate the town's ecclesiastic, scholarly, and revolutionary heritage. The **Historical Museum** within the library, halfway up the main road, displays an eclectic collection including vintage War of Independence pistols, two 15th-century illuminated psalters, and a handful of Italian edition Greek-Latin **incunabula** of various church fathers and ancient authors. To find the museum and library, climb the steps at the bus stop or at the main plateia. Look for a church across from an elementary school in a small gravel courtyard; the entrance is at the far end of the elementary school, facing the plain of Megalopolis in the distance. (☎31 219. Open M-F 9am-1:30pm, Su 8am-noon.) Walking away from the bus station, the **Icon Museum** is off the main plateia up the second alley on the right. (☎31 465. Open Sa-Tu and Th 10am-1:30pm and 5-7pm.)

### STEMNITSA Στεμνιτσα ☎0795

From Dimitsana, walk an easy, beautiful 11km (about 2½hr.) along the winding road, or pay 1000dr for a taxi, to Stemnitsa, where narrow, irregular cobbled streets betray medieval roots. With its unspoiled mountain scenery and an abundance of flowers, greenery, and stucco-roofed homes, it is easy to see why this town has been called one of the most beautiful in Greece. The **post office** is behind the church in the plateia. (☎81 280. Open M-F 7am-2pm.) **Postal code:** 22024.

Fortunately, the only Hotel in town offers outstanding quality at a reasonable price. The splendid **Hotel Triokolonion** is on the left side of the main road as you go away from Dimitsana, with an inviting terrace that offers a relaxing place to unwind after a day hiking the mountain paths. Its spacious rooms have hardwood floors, private baths, and amazing views. (☎0795 81 297; fax 81 483. Singles 7800dr; doubles 10,600dr; buffet breakfast included. Call ahead to ensure availability.) Although there are few signs advertising domatia, locals claim there are rooms to be had if you ask around at the tavernas and cafes in the plateia. From among these several restaurants, consider the tiny **Taverna Klinitsa,** just out of the plateia on the way to Dimitsana, for an inexpensive treat. They specialize in creative vegetarian fare (*fasolacia* 600dr, *briam* 500dr) and Mama's special fried bread.

Off the road from Dimitsana to Stemnitsa are several monasteries, some built right into the mountain face. At the **Monastery of Ag. Ioannis Prodromos,** 12km from Dimitsana and still inhabited by 12 monks, you can see icons painted on the bare stone walls and gravity-defying monastic cells that seem to hang off the mountain. Follow the road as it goes from asphalt to dirt, and finally becomes a footpath. (☎31 279. Open dawn-dusk. Modest dress required. Free.)



# MESSENIA ΜΕΣΣΗΝΙΑ

Messenia is an oasis in the arid Peloponnese. World-renowned olives, figs, and grapes spring from the rich soil on the region's rocky coastline, which remains largely tourist-free. Most Messenians live at the head of the gulf around sprawling Kalamata, though visitors may prefer to stay in the sleepy coastal towns of Pylos, Methoni, Koroni, or Kardamyli, which luxuriate in clean, nearly empty beaches and quiet streets perfumed with the scent of fragrant blossoms.

## KALAMATA Καλαματα ☎0721

Kalamata, the second largest Peloponnesian city, flourishes as a port and beach resort. The town played a key role in igniting the War of Independence, when, on March 23, 1821 (two days before a Greek revolt was planned to begin), a group of impatient Kalamatans massacred local Ottomans in their sleep. A yearly reenactment of the grisly Greek victory is followed by parades and dancing. Today, fast-growing Kalamata has all the down sides of a large Greek city (excessive noise, confusing transportation networks, and horrid traffic), which detract from its vacation appeal; its clean, if crowded, 4km-long beach redeems it somewhat.

### ORIENTATION AND PRACTICAL INFORMATION

Kalamata sprawls inland from its long beachfront, with a frustratingly spread-out plan that means you'll need to walk or take a taxi for long stretches to traverse the city. The city is divided into three sections. Closest to the water is a **residential section,** distinguished by the municipal park; most of the hotels and restaurants are here, clustered by the water. Next is **Pl. Georgiou,** with the train station and most amenities, like stores, banks, and the post office. The **Old Town,** with its castle, market, and bus station, is 3km from the beach. Navigating from one end to the other can be confusing; get a **map** from the tourist office. **Aremidos** is the street where the bus station and post office are. Turn right, and follow this street to **Aristomenous,** Kalamata's main street. A left takes you to the plateia and the Old Town. A right takes you to the waterfront. **Navarinou** runs parallel to the water.

**Buses:** Unfortunately for the motor-less traveler, the city's bus system is overpriced (200dr per ride) and limited in scope. To get to the waterfront from the bus station, take a taxi (500-700dr), a good idea if you have heavy baggage, or trudge down **Aremidos,** the bus station's street, until you come to Iatropoulou on your right just before the post office (☎28 581 or 22 851 info line, open 7am-10pm). Buses go to: **Athens** (4hr., 11 per day, 4400dr) via **Megalopolis** (1hr., 1150dr); **Corinth** (3hr., 3000dr); **Finikoundas** (2½hr., 4 per day, 1500dr); **Koroni** (1½hr., 8 per day, 950dr); **Mavromati** and **Ancient Messene** (1hr., 2 per day, 500dr); **Methoni** (1¾hr.; 6 per day, 1150dr); **Patras** (4hr., 2 per day, 4150dr) via **Pirgos** (2hr., 2350dr); **Pylos** (1½hr., 9 per day, 950dr); **Sparta** (2hr., 2 per day, 1150dr) via **Artemisia** (30min., 450dr); and **Tripoli** (2hr., 1550dr). To get to **Areopolis** (15min., 220dr) and **Gythion** (1½hr., 400dr), go to **Itilo** (2hr., 4 per day, 1500dr) and change buses. The bus passes **Kardamyli** (650dr) and **Stoura** (700dr) before it reaches Itilo.

**Flights:** Two flights per week (Su, M 9:15pm) to **Athens** (30min.; 15,000dr, under 24, 13,400dr). **Olympic Airways,** Sideromikou Stathmou 17 (☎22 376), just before the train station. Open 8am-2pm. Taxis to the airport, which is 6km from town near **Messini,** cost 1500dr, or you can bus to Messini from the KTEL station.

**Trains:** (☎95 056), on Sideromikou Stathmou. Turn right on Frantzi at the end of Pl. Georgiou and walk a few blocks. To: **Athens** (7hr., 4 per day, 2160dr) via **Tripoli** (2½hr., 840dr); **Argos** (4hr., 1280dr); **Corinth** (5¼hr., 1640dr); to **Patras** (5½hr., 4 per day, 1500dr) via **Kyparissia** (2hr., 590dr); **Olympia** (3hr., 900dr); and **Pirgos** (3¼hr., 860dr).

**City Bus:** Depart near Pl. 25 Martiou. **Bus #1** goes down Pl. Aristomenous and then runs along the water (200dr). Runs 8am-10pm.

**Taxi Service:** (☎22 522, 28 181, or 27 366).

**Moped Rental:** At **Alpha Rental** (☎93 423), on Vironos near the waterfront, mopeds go for 5000dr per day. Open 8:30am-8pm. They're the same price at **Bastakos,** Faron 192 (☎23 392), just off the waterfront.

**Bank: National Bank** (☎28 047), on Aristomenous off the north end of Pl. Georgiou, and smaller branches in the plateia and on Akrita at the waterfront. All have 24hr. **ATMs** and **currency exchange.** Open M-Th 8am-2pm, F 8am-1:30pm.

**Medical Emergency:** ☎ 25 555.

**Tourist Police:** (☎95 555), on Maouli in the port, on the second floor of a yellow building to the right of the post office. **Free maps.** Open 8am-2pm. More extensive tourist info and free **maps** are available in town at **D.E.T.A.K.,** Poliviou 6, just off Aristomenous near the Old Town. Open M-F 7am-2:30pm.

**Port police:** (☎22 218), on the harbor near the tourist police in a blue building.

**Police:** (☎22 622), in Pl. Georgiou on Aristomenous. Open 24hr.

**Hospital:** (☎85 203), on Athinou.

**Telephones:** The **OTE** is in Pl. Georgiou, opposite National Bank. Open M-Th 7am-1:15pm, F 7am-1pm.

**Internet Access: Diktyo Internet Cafe,** Nedontos 75 (☎97 282), just off Aristomenous and close to the OTE. 1000dr per hr. Open 10am-1am.

**Post Office:** Iatropolou 4 (☎22 810). Follow this street from the south end of Pl. Georgiou. There's another branch on the waterfront next to the tourist police. Open M-F 7:30am-2pm. **Postal code:** 24100.

## ACCOMMODATIONS

Most of Kalamata's hotels are expensive, loaded with amenities, and on the waterfront. Rooms to let and budget accommodations are uncommon here.

**Hotel Nevada,** Santa Rosa 9 (☎82 429), off Faron one block up from the water (heading inland on Faron, take the first left, or take bus #1 from town and get off as soon as it turns left along the water. Large, comfortable rooms wildly decorated with an assortment of kitschy posters, figurines, and artificial flowers. Shared bath and kitchen. Singles 5000dr; doubles 7000dr; triples 8000dr.

**Pension Avra,** Santa Rosa 10 (☎82 759). Sunny rooms with hard-wood floors and interesting decorations; shared baths and kitchen. Singles 6000dr; doubles 7000dr.

**Hotel George** (☎27 225), right near the train station. Very convenient and charming, with TVs, balconies, and private baths. Singles 7000dr; doubles 8000dr.

**Camping Maria's Sea and Sun** (☎41 060). Take bus #1 east past the other campsites. Hot showers. 1500dr per person; 1000dr per small tent; 1200dr per large tent; 1000dr per car. Electricity 1000dr.

## FOOD AND NIGHTLIFE

Before leaving town, sample the famous Kalamata olives and figs. The immense **New Market,** just across the bridge from the bus station, is a collection of meat, cheese, and fruit shops, as well as a daily farmer's market. Great sit-down meals can be found along the waterfront (all of the listed restaurants are there).

**Taverna Tzamaika** (☎24 940), 2km down the road from the port, with the water on your right. With its own outdoor oven, a large collection of Agricultural Revolution-era farm implements, and even a horse, it stands out among the waterfront tavernas. It's also the farthest from town. Grilled lamb (1500dr) and stuffed tomatoes (1000dr) get raves.

**To Petrino.** Mellow waterfront dining under a thatched straw roof, accompanied by American R&B tunes. Eggplant stuffed with meat 1300dr, tomato and cucumber salad 700dr, those famous Kalamata olives 500dr.

**Tampaki Restaurant.** On the waterfront next to To Petrino. Lunch and dinner at reasonable prices. Country sausage 1300dr, pork in wine sauce 1450dr. Entrees 800-2200dr.

**Exociko Kentro.** Rather drab and fast-food-like from the exterior, this place shines when in comes to food, with a mean lamb and potatoes (1400dr) or veal (1500dr).

PELOPONNESE

Nightlife in Kalamata revolves around the beach. The strip (1km east of the port) lacks some of the over-the-top fun you'll overdose on in other towns: expect lots of umbrellas and subdued techno music. **Palladium,** Kalamata's newest disco, draws the crowds, but it's a bit expensive (cover and one drink 1200dr). Kalamata also supports two professional **theaters** and **cinemas;** ask the tourist police for info on events in the **Pantazopoulion Cultural Center** on Aristomenon.

## SIGHTS

**CASTLE OF VILLEHARDOUINS.** The survivor of a violent history, the Castle of the Villehardouins crowns a hill above the old city. Built by the Franks in 1208, it was blown up by the Ottomans in 1685, restored by the Venetians a decade later, and is still recovering from the damage it suffered in a 1986 earthquake. The castle encircles an open-air theater, which hosts "Cultural Summer of Kalamata" in July and August, featuring jazz, rock, classical Greek drama, and more. *(To get to the gates from Pl. 25 Martiou, walk up Ipapandis past the church on the right and take your first left. Ticket prices average 2000dr.)*

**CHURCHES.** At the foot of the castle you'll find the **Convent of Ag. Konstantinos and Ag. Elena,** where nuns sell bargain linen and lacework. At the far end of the site is the 14th-century **Church of the Ag. Apostoli** (Holy Apostles), site of the first Greek revolt against the Turks on March 23, 1821. A doe-eyed icon of the Virgin Mary was found here; today, the city name echoes the miraculous icon's appearance (good eyes). At the far end of the old city, there are the remains of a **Byzantine church;** scramble up it for a sublime view. *(All open 8am-dusk.)*

**ARTS.** The Old City's **Benakeion Museum** presents its small collection more artfully and professionally than most Greek museums. Highlighted by an exceptionally well-preserved mosaic floor from a ruined Roman villa nearby, the collection is enlivened by lengthy, informative placards in English. *(Open Tu-Sa 8am-2:30pm, Su 8:30am-3pm.)* Just off the waterfront, Kalamata's **School of Fine Arts** exhibits work by Greek artists. *(Faron 221. Open 9am-1pm and 6-10pm.)*

**OUTDOORS.** Shady trees arch over lovely **Train Park**'s cafes, performance space, duck pond, restaurant, and ice cream parlor, which occupies a converted old train station. Antique trains repose on the tracks. It's at the end of Aristomenous toward Pl. Georgiou. Kalamata's gravelly **beaches** empty as you go eastward, but Pylos, Methoni, and other southern beach towns are a much better bet.

## DAYTRIP FROM KALAMATA: ANCIENT MESSENE

*Take the bus to Mavromati (1hr.; leaves M-Sa 5:40am and 2pm, returns 2:30pm; 500dr). Taxis 4000-5000dr. If you rent a* ***moped,*** *you'll need 50ccs to handle the steep hills. Open 8:30am-3pm. 500dr, students 300dr, EU students free.*

Excavations on **Mt. Ithomi** over the last 15 years have yielded one of the most impressive ancient archaeological sites in Greece. The site dates back 2300 years. When the battle of Leuctra in 371 BC ended Spartan domination of the Peloponnese, Theban general and statesman **Epaminodas** built Messene, naming the town for the region's first queen. While the remains of a theater, stadium, gymnasium, public baths, and nine different temples have been uncovered, it is the city's **defensive walls** that usually receive the most attention. The 3m thick walls circle 9km, and represent the massive heft of 3rd- and 4th-century BC military architecture. Originally, huge gates reinforced with two-story towers and battlements interrupted the circuit, taking their names from the roads that they barricaded. Of the four surviving, the Arcadian gate is the best preserved, and the stone-slab road that proceeds from it still bears the traces of chariot wheels. A **museum** at the site houses statues and other objects. Also outside Mavromati, the 17th-century **Monastery of the Vourkan** was a starting point for rebels in the War of Independence. Its library protects several priceless manuscripts.

PELOPONNESE

# KARDAMYLI

☎0721

The sleepy, one-road town of Kardamyli is the first major bus stop south of Kalamata near Taygetus. The seaside town possesses just a few stone houses and restaurants, but its gorgeous white-pebble beaches and views of the surrounding mountains captivate an increasing number of foreign visitors.

**ORIENTATION AND PRACTICAL INFORMATION.** Four buses run from Kalamata every day, dropping off near the *periptera* off the main plateia. **Buses** go to **Kalamata** (1hr., 5 per day, 700dr) and **Itilo** (30 min., 3 per day, 650dr), where you can switch to the **Areopolis** bus (20min., 500dr). Through the main plateia, on the road to Itilo, are the **post office** (open M-F 7:30am-2pm) and the **police station** (☎73 209). A **pharmacy** (☎73 512) sits across from the post office. Walking toward Itilo, turn right after the police station for **Cafe Internet Kourearos.** (☎73 148. Open until 1am. 1000dr per 30min., minimum 700dr.)

**ACCOMMODATIONS AND FOOD.** Domatia are everywhere, but start with the excellent, cheap rooms let by **Olympia Domatia.** To get there, turn right off the main road at M Travel and follow the side street. Rooms are spacious, with clean shared baths and kitchen. (☎73 623. Singles 6000dr; doubles 8000dr; triples 10000dr for two rooms.) If you want beachfront (rental) property, walk toward Kalamata and turn left at the signs for **Camping Melitsana,** which is 1.5km down the main beach. (☎73 461. 1300dr per person; 1100dr per small tent; 1300dr per large tent; 1000dr per car. Electricity 800dr.)

When you get hungry, walk back toward Kalamata to find two large **supermarkets.** For delicious traditional food with a waterfront view, try the daily special menu at family-run **Taverna Kiki,** downhill from O Kypos Rooms near the main plateia. (Entrees 1000-1400dr.) **Taygetos,** on Kardamyli's main beach, 1km north toward Kalamata, serves appetizers and snacks from feta cheese (500dr) to fried calamari (1400dr), plus standard entrees (950-1700dr). A creative pizzeria just outside town toward Kalamata, **Paulos** serves eight different pizzas; each feeds two (2000-2500dr). Their macaroni with bleu cheese is a crowd pleaser (1200dr). Fast food greases down the area near the post office (souvlaki 200dr, gyros pita 300dr).

**REALLY BIG SKYLIGHTS** Throughout Greece, private homes and commercial buildings with completely finished, furnished, inhabited first floors are often topped by two or three stories of structural skeleton. Both in Greece and in Turkey, most people simply build the essentials of a house as high as they can imagine ever finishing, then fill in such niceties as walls and ceilings when they can afford them. That way, commercial ventures need not invest a load of capital before their businesses are an assured success, and families can expand their homes as they grow. Greek law specified that a house could not be taxed until it was completed—and it wasn't completed until it had a roof. Thrifty Greeks gleefully left their top floors roofless for years of freedom from at least half of supposedly inescapable death and taxes. A few years ago, the government revamped the tax laws and closed the loophole.

**SIGHTS AND BEACHES.** Beaches are Kardamyli's main attraction, but there are a few other things to see. A short stroll up the road to Itilo will bring you to the small but interesting ruins of the **Old Town.** Nearby, the frescoed **Monastery of Dekoulo** and the 17th-century Ottoman **fortress** are poised on a hill.

Three kilometers along the bus route from Kalamata, you'll spot the magnificent **Neo Itilo beach.** On an enormous natural bay encircled by barren mountains, the white-pebble shore is ideal for swimming. From Neo Itilo, the winding uphill road looks out over **Limani,** the old harbor of Areopolis and home to the Mavromichaeli **Castle of Potrombei.** From here, buses continue down the bad roads blessed by beautiful vistas all the way to Areopolis.



**DAYTRIP FROM KARDAMYLI: MT. TAYGETUS.** The bus ride there is bumpy and the roads are twisting, but the views at Mt. Taygetus are absolutely breathtaking. Southeast of Kalamata, this limestone mountain divides Messenia and Laconia, running from Megalopolis down through the Taenarian promontory. Sacred to Apollo and Artemis, the mountain was named after **Taygete,** daughter of Atlas, mother of Lacedaemon, and lover of Zeus. Long glorified for its size, Mt. Taygetus has been dubbed "Perimiketon," or the "long one," by Homer, while Aristophanes mentions in *Lysistrata* that "I would climb as high as the peak of Taygetus, if thus I could find peace." With its highest peak, Profitis Ilia, reaching 2407m, the mountain is home to unusual amphibians, 23 species of endemic plants, the rare *testudo marninata* turtle, and a slew of adventurous hikers, mountain bikers, climbers, and paragliders. For serious hiking, carry lots of water and stick to the **Laconian side** (the eastern half) of the mountain: its slopes get more rain and thus bubble up beautiful springs and sprout fir and black pine forests. It's best to hike in the spring, as summer heat and aridity make the strenuous terrain rather exhausting to navigate for more than an hour or two. **Brochures** with suggested routes are available in the tourist office in Kalamata and Sparta; you can also find detailed **hiking maps** in tourist shops and bookstores. One popular 1½hr. **trail** is marked in black and yellow, and begins from Kardamyli, heading to Old Kardamyli, Agia Sophia, then to Petrovouni.

## PYLOS Πυλος ☎0723

With its delightful beaches, Ottoman fortress, museum, and splendid views of Navarino, the Peloponnese's largest natural bay, the town of Pylos is wonderfully and mystifyingly untouristed. Flower-decked buildings line the track of narrow streets and steep stairways from the waterfront plateia up to the residential town. Pylos' harbor cuts a silhouette marked by the vertical cliffs of Sfakteria Island.

**ORIENTATION AND PRACTICAL INFORMATION.** Most of the town's businesses line the plateia/bus stop and the road leading up to Methoni. The tiny **beaches,** one sand and one pebble, lie to the right of the waterfront as you face inland, as does the 16th-century Ottoman **Neocastro** fortress on a forested hill.

**Buses** (☎22 230) go to: **Kalamata** (1½hr., 9 per day, 1000dr); **Athens** (6½hr., 2 per day, 2300dr); and **Finikoundas** (1hr., 4 per day, 450dr) via **Methoni** (15min., 6 per day, 250dr). No buses travel directly to **Koroni,** but you can go through Finikoundas and take a bus to **Horokorio,** the stop nearest Koroni. Buses leave for **Kyparissia** (1½hr., 5 per day, 1200dr), stopping at **Nestor's Palace** (30min., 400dr) and **Hora** (45min., 500dr); service is reduced on weekends. **Rent-A-Bike,** 100m off the plateia on the road running by the police station, has a moped monopoly. (☎22 707. 6000dr per day. Open 9am-2pm and 5-9pm.) The **police** are on the second floor of a building on the left side of the waterfront on a road going uphill. (☎22 316. English spoken. Open 24hr.) The **tourist police** are in the same building. (☎23 733. Open 8am-2pm.) Continue around the curve of the waterfront road to reach the **port police** (☎22 225). A **National Bank** with an **ATM** is in the plateia. (Open M-Th 8am-2pm, F 8am-1:30pm.) To get to the **hospital,** take the road right of the plateia. (☎22 315. Open 24hr.) To get to the **OTE,** pass the post office and take your first left; then take your second right. (☎22 399. Open M-F 7:30am-3:10pm.) The **post office** is on Nileos (the road toward Hora and Kiparissia), uphill to the left (facing the water) from the bus station. (☎22 247. Open M-F 7:30am-2pm.) **Postal code:** 24001.

**ACCOMMODATIONS AND FOOD.** There are several **Rooms to Let** signs as the bus descends into town from Kalamata. In general, expect to pay 4000-6000dr for singles, 6000-10,000dr for doubles, and 8000-12,000dr for triples. Perhaps the cheapest accommodation in town is the **Pension,** just before the OTE, with its basic high-ceilinged rooms with private baths and A/C. (☎22 748. Singles 5000dr; doubles 7000dr; triples 9000dr.) **Hotel Nilefs,** Rene Pyot 4, has big rooms with baths and sea-view balconies. It's on the road running uphill from the waterfront on the right side of the plateia, facing inland, by Hotel Miramare. (☎22 518. Singles 9000dr; doubles 10,000-12,000dr; triples 13,000dr.) **Navarino Beach Camping** is 6km north at **Yialova Beach** (☎22 761. 1400dr per person; 1000dr per small tent; 1300dr per large tent. Electricity 800dr.)

Many waterfront restaurants cook up taverna staples served alongside sunset views over the waterfront. The best of four eating establishments with the same name, the **Navarino** on the right side of the waterfront has good, cheap meals (Greek salad 1000dr, entrees 1000-1700dr.) Delicious **Tessera Epohes** (Τεσσερα Εποχεζ), the last taverna on the water to the right of town, is unpretentious but masterful: everything is large, cheap, and well-prepared. (*Tzatziki* 350dr, *tarama* 600dr, *moussaka* 1000dr, lamb chops 1500dr.) Uphill from the plateia, opposite the police station, **La Piazza** prepares wonderful pasta and pizza. (Entrees 800-1500dr. Open 6:30pm-1am.) The expensive-leaning **1930 Restaurant,** on the road into town from Kalamata, is accented by wood paneling, antique fishing paraphernalia, and a seafood menu with grilled octopus (2500dr) and fish soup (1000dr).

**SIGHTS AND BEACHES.** Fortresses guard both sides of Navarino Bay. **Neocastro,** to the south, is easily accessible from the town; walk up the road to Methoni and turn right at the sign reading Καστρο. The well-preserved walls enclose a fast-decaying church (originally a mosque), along with a citadel and a collection of Greece-hugger engravings. The restored hexagonal courtyard, up the hill to your right after entering the castle, shows a room of photographs detailing its restoration. (☎22 448. Open Tu-Su 8:30am-3pm. 800dr, seniors and students 400dr, EU students free.) The slight **Archaeological Museum,** just before the castle on the road to Methoni, shows the contents of Mycenaean and Hellenistic tombs. A Mycenaean battle helmet made of boar's tusks catches the eye, while three richly colored glass vessels highlight the Hellenistic period. (☎22 448. Open Tu-Su 8:30am-3pm. 500dr, seniors and students 300dr, EU students free.) The tourist police claim that the badly preserved ruins of the **Paleocastro** north of Pylos aren't worth the dangerous trip there. If you disagree, you'll need your own transportation and their directions.

To see the island of **Sfakteria** up close, you can take a **boat tour** from the port; they stop at various monuments to the allied sailors of the Battle of Navarino and show a sunken Ottoman ship. Inquire at the small booth on the waterfront or at the

coffee bar under the police station, where the captains often toss back a few. (1½hr. 10,000dr for 4 people. July-Aug. only.) A few small **beaches** surround the town. Although the sand is devoured by the ocean when the tide is in, the clear, choppy water makes splashing around fun. The beautiful, long, and much wider **Yialova Beach** is 6km north of town; ask the bus driver to let you off there.

**DAYTRIP FROM PYLOS: NESTOR'S PALACE.** In the Mycenaean world, Pylos was second only to Mycenae in wealth and artistic development. The centerpiece of the archeological site is the **palace** where Nestor met Telemachus, Odysseus's son, in Homer's *Odyssey*. The palace is thought to have been built in the 13th century BC by Nestor's father Neleus, the founder of the Neleid dynasty. It was destroyed by fire around 1200 BC. Still under excavation, the thigh-high remains of the site make up three buildings. The main building, possibly the king's residence, originally had a second floor with official and residential quarters and storerooms. Archaeologists think an older, smaller palace stood to the southeast. To the northeast lie the ruins of a complex of isolated workshops and storerooms. Archaeologists have turned up pottery, jewelry, various bronze and ivory objects, and a cache of **Linear B tablets** explaining some of the palace's administrative operations. Most finds are displayed at the National Archaeological Museum in Athens; some pottery and surviving fragments of wall paintings are at the Hora village museum, 5km away. For 1500dr you can supplement your tour with the *University of Cincinnati's Guide to Nestor's Palace.* Buses from Pylos run through Kyparissia (1½hr., 5 per day, 1200dr), and stop at Nestor's Palace (30min., 400dr) on the way to Hora (45min., 500dr); service is reduced weekends. The last bus returns at 5:30pm. ☎31 437 or 31 358. Open Tu-Su 8:30am-3pm. 500dr, non-EU students 300dr, EU students free.

PELOPONNESE

## METHONI Μεθωνη ☎0723

With hibiscus-lined streets and a relaxed atmosphere, Methoni is a restorative reprieve from the bustle of Kalamata and Tripoli. Known as the "Camelot of Greece," Methoni was once used as bait by Agamemnon to lure the sulking Achilles back to war. The town's spectacular 15th-century castle shoots its narrow stone walkways out onto rocky outcroppings in the bay. Inspired by it, Miguel de Cervantes churned out romances here while imprisoned under Ottoman guard.

**ORIENTATION AND PRACTICAL INFORMATION.** The town's two main streets form a Y where the Pylos-Finikoundas buses stop. There's no **bus** station, but the schedule hangs on the door of a market across from where the buses stop and depart. Buses go to **Pylos** (15min., 7 per day, 250dr) and **Finikoundas** (30min., 4 per day, 300dr), with a reduced schedule Saturday and Sunday. The main town **beach** is a few blocks to the left of the end of the lower street, beside a little beachfront plateia. To get to the **castle,** follow the upper street to its end. The campgrounds and several beach bars are on the road bordering the lengthy beach; there's also a stone walkway perfect for evening strolls by the water. The **police** are near the bus station on the upper street, just past the bank. (☎31 203. Open 24hr.) The **National Bank** with a 24hr. **ATM** is 40m down the right fork. (☎31 570. Open M-Th 8am-2pm, F 8am-1:30pm.) The **OTE** is in a cream-colored building with blue shutters that's not very well marked; go down the lower fork and turn left, toward the beachside plateia. (Open M-F 7:30am-3:10pm.) The **post office** is two blocks down the lower street on the left side. (☎31 266. Open M-F 7:30am-2pm.) **Postal code:** 24006.

**ACCOMMODATIONS.** Since Methoni receives a fair amount of August tourism, rooms can be a bit expensive. Dozens of **Rooms to Let** signs hang along both forks of the road; although the rooms usually lack hotel amenities, their prices are slightly cheaper. Near the end of the lower road, make a left (heading toward the plateia) to find the unassuming **Hotel Galini,** which has rooms similar in quality to its flashier counterparts, but at cheaper prices. (☎31 467. Singles 7000dr, doubles 10,000dr.) On the upper street, over a taekwondo center about 4 blocks away from the bus stop, **Ioannis Psiharis** lets spacious rooms with double beds, private baths,

and balconies (☎31 406. Singles 7000dr; doubles 9000dr.) **Hotel Alex** (☎31 219; fax 31 212) and **Hotel Giota** (☎31 290 or 31 291), run by the same family and located opposite one another in the beachfront plateia, have modern rooms with A/C, balconies, and private baths. (Singles 9000dr; doubles 12,000dr.) At Alex, the rooms also have refrigerators, and triples and quads are available. (14,000dr and 17,000dr.) **Seaside Camping Methoni** is a 5min. walk down the beach to the right of the plateia. (☎31 228. 1100dr per person; 610dr per car; 700dr per small tent; 810dr per large tent; prices lower May-June and Sept.-Oct.)

**FOOD.** Several excellent tavernas and restaurants pepper Methoni. In the waterfront plateia, the dignified, multilingual proprietor of **Meltemi** serves excellent traditional entrees. (Feta with olive oil 700dr, *moussaka* 1400dr.) **Restaurant Venetiko,** two blocks down the lower street on the left, serves Italian food under leafy banana trees. (Entrees 700-2000dr. Salads 600-1400dr.) Humble **Oraia Methoni** makes up for its lack of a swanky atmosphere with its quality and low price. Turn left one block down the lower road and walk 30m; the restaurant will be on your right. (Tomato and cucumber salad 400dr, *moussaka* 900dr, souvlaki 200dr.) **Kali Kardia,** four blocks down the upper street, has higher prices than Oraia, but the atmosphere and reputation are second to none.

**SIGHTS.** No visitor to the southwest Peloponnese should miss Methoni's **Venetian fortress,** a 13th-century mini-city. Venture behind the fortified gate to wander paths over overgrown fields strewn with wildflowers and crumbling walls. Frankish foundations, Venetian battlements, and Turkish steam baths testify to the castle's varied history. At the tip of the peninsula, a narrow bridge connects an islet and its fortified tower to the main structure with a whimsical touch of medieval defensive architecture. Early morning is the best time to visit, when the tide crashes against the steadfast stone walls and the cool earth is just warming. *(Open M-Sa 8am-8pm, Su 9am-8pm. Free.)*

PELOPONNESE

# LACONIA ΛΑΚΩΝΙΑ

In the 12th century BC, the Indo-European Dorians invaded Greece from the north, driving out the Mycenaean inhabitants and ushering in the so-called Dark Age. Laconia, the territory of the ancient Spartans, has long prided itself on its minimalist aesthetic, coining its own adjective, "laconic"—terse and concise. The starkly dramatic Taygetus Mountains match the stern personality of the people. Although Laconia boasts one of the Peloponnese's most popular sites—Byzantine Mystras—the region as a whole offers a peaceful break from the more touristed urban hurry in other Peloponnesian towns.

## SPARTA Σπαρτη ☎0731

Citizens of today's quiet Sparta make olive oil, not war. Built directly on top of the ancient warrior city, modern Sparta leaves meager ruins to occupy its tourists. Its clean, pleasant public gardens and its broad, palm-lined boulevards make it hospitable and by far the best base for exploring the ruins of Byzantine Mystras, 6km away. Today's lovely Sparta barely hints at its belligerent past. The capital of Laconia, aggressive Sparta dominated the Peloponnese with its legendary sense of discipline and its invincible armies. Spartans traced their austere daily regimens back to 8th-century law-giver **Lycurgus,** who demanded plain dress, simple food, and strict training for all citizens from a young age. Men and women were educated differently, but with equal severity. The Spartans produced little memorable literature, art, or architecture—but in arms, they took the cake. Finally capturing Athens in 404 BC to end the 28-year Peloponnesian War (see p. 12), Sparta won its greatest victory and effectively ruled Greece. Although their domination of Athens was brief, even temporary hold over *the* Classical power is testimony to Sparta's unparalleled military prowess. In the end, the earthquake-shaken empire collapsed under the combined stress of slave revolts and a depleted male population.

## ORIENTATION AND PRACTICAL INFORMATION

Sparta lies on a grid. The main streets, **Paleologou** and **Lykourgou** (named for law-giver Lycurgus), hold the necessary amenities, and intersect in the center of town. The town plateia is one block up from this intersection. To reach the center of town from the bus station, walk ten blocks west on Lykourgou. The **bus station** is crowded and not tourist friendly; ticket takers and drivers don't usually answer questions. The trick is to find a Greek traveler heading to your destination and follow her to ensure you end up at the right bus. There are often confusing and unmentioned transfers on the bus routes, but if you stick with your travel stalkee, you'll be sure to get where you're going.

**Buses:** (☎26 441). Walk downhill on Lykourgou away from the plateia and continue past the fire station until the road peters out The station will be on your right, 1500m from the center of town. Buses go to: **Athens** (3½hr., 9 per day, 3800dr) via **Corinth** (2hr., 2400dr) and **Tripoli** (1hr., 1100dr); **Gerolimenas** (3hr., 3 per day, 1850dr); **Gythion** (1hr., 5 per day, 800dr); **Kalamata** (2hr., 2 per day, 1150dr); **Monemvasia** (2hr., 3 per day, 1800dr); **Neapoli** (2½hr., 2 per day, 2600dr); and **Pirgos Dirou** (1½hr., 1 per day, 1400dr) via **Areopolis** (1½hr., 4 per day, 1300dr). Buses to **Mystras** (20min., 9 per day, 250dr) also stop at the corner of Lykourgou and Leonidou on the left, two blocks past the town plateia away from the main bus station.

**Tourist Office:** (☎24 852), to the left of the town hall in the plateia. English spoken. Bus schedules, hotels, and information are available on specific request. They will direct you to a nearby photo store to purchase their map (700dr). Open 8am-2pm.

**Banks: National Bank** (☎26 200), on Paleologou, 3 blocks north of Lykourgou, has a 24hr. **ATM** and **currency exchange.** Open M-Th 8am-2pm, F 8am-1:30pm.

**Police:** Hilonos 8 (☎26 229), on a side street off Lykourgou, a block past the museum. Open 24hr. Earnestly helpful, English-speaking **tourist police** (☎20 492) are housed in the same building. Open 8am-3pm and 7-9pm.

**Hospital:** (☎28 671/5), on Nosokomeio, 1km to the north of Sparta. Open 24hr.

**Telephone: OTE,** Kleombrotou 11 (☎23 799), off Lykourgou across from the museum. Open M-F 7:45am-1pm.

**Internet: Hellas Internet Cafe,** Paleologou 34 (☎21 500), 1100dr per hr.

**Post Office:** (☎26 565), on Arhidamou off Lykourgou. Open M-F 7:30am-2pm. **Postal code:** 23100.

## ACCOMMODATIONS

Among the numerous mid-range hotels on Paleologou, a bargain is hard to find, but TVs and private baths are a drachma a dozen.

**A HARD-KNOCK LIFE** A young Spartan's training for a life of war began early—before conception. Lycurgus believed two fit parents produced stronger offspring, so he ordered all Spartan women to undergo the same rigorous training endured by men. Furthermore, newlyweds were permitted only an occasional tryst on the theory that the heightened (desperate?) desire of the parents would produce more robust children. If they weren't winnowed out as weak or deformed, seven-year-old boys began a severe regimen of training under an adult, away from their parents. They were forced to walk barefoot to toughen their feet, and wore only a simple, single garment both summer and winter to expose them to drastic weather changes. The Spartan creed dictated that young men be guarded against temptations of any kind, so strict laws forbade everything from drinking to pederasty. Moreover, young Spartans were given the plainest and simplest foods for fear that rich delicacies would stunt their growth. One visitor to Sparta, upon sampling the fare, allegedly quipped, "Now I know why they do not fear death."

**Hotel Laconia** (☎28 952), on Paleologou. Offers slightly dim rooms with TV, dark-wood furniture, carpeting, and even shower curtains. Singles 8000dr; doubles 12000dr; student discounts available.

**Hotel Cecil** (☎24 980), five blocks north of Lykourgou on the corner of Paleologou and Thermopilion. Lemon yellow inside and out, you'll spot this bright hotel from down the block. TV, A/C, and phones. Singles 8000dr; doubles 10000dr.

**Hotel Apollon,** 84 Thermopylon (☎22 491). Walking up Lykourgou, bear right after you pass Hotel Cecil; Apollon is about a block further on your right. The flashy, red, mirrored lobby and bar don't represent the rooms, which are more sedately decorated. TVs, private baths, phones, and A/C. Singles 8000dr; doubles 11,000dr; breakfast 1500dr.

**Camping Castle View** (☎83 303), near Mystras. Take the Mystras bus and get off at the signs. Pool, modern showers and toilets, and a mini-market. 1500dr per person; 900dr per car; 900dr per small tent; 1200dr per large tent. Electricity 800dr.

## FOOD AND NIGHTLIFE

Sparta's restaurants provide uniform, standard menus at pretty reasonable prices.

**Elyssé Restaurant** (☎29 896), on Paleologou, 200m north of the main intersection. Superior service and a large selection spice up this pink-tabled place, which specializes in local dishes like chicken *bardouniotiko* (1500dr) and lamb *horiatiko* (1600dr).

**Diethnes** (☎28 636), on Paleologou, a few meters south of Elyssé. Tasty Greek food in a garden behind the restaurant. *Moussaka* 1300dr, *taromasalata* 500dr.

**Menelaion Hotel Restaurant** (☎22 161), in the Menelaion Hotel on Paleologou. Excellent meals served in an elegant and quiet poolside setting, with surprisingly low prices. Meatballs and potatoes 1300dr, shrimp 1800dr, cucumber and tomato salad 600dr.

At night, the side of the plateia near the town hall fills with young people chilling at outdoor cafes; head indoors for some clubbing. **The Imago,** a hip, artsy bar, is in the alley behind the town hall (open 10pm-3am). **Caprice,** another popular club with an outside bar, faces the town hall (cover 500dr).



## SIGHTS

**ANCIENT SPARTA.** What little remains of ancient Sparta lies in an olive grove 1km north of the town plateia down Paleologou. At the north end of Paleologou stands an enormous statue of **Leonidas,** the famous warrior king who fell at the Battle of Thermopylae in 480 BC. The Spartans built a large, vacant tomb for their leader, hopefully awaiting his remains, but his body was never found. The tomb is in a public park, on the left of the road heading up to the ruins. The ruins consist of the outline and lower rows of one of the larger theaters of antiquity, along with a few fragments of the acropolis. *(To find the tomb and the ruins, walk down Paleologou to the right from the bus station, to the statue of Leonidas. Turn left and then right at the signs for the ruins about 50m from the statue. From the sign, the ruins are about 400m up the road.)*

**MUSEUMS.** Sparta's **Archaeological Museum** hedges a beautiful, well-kept park with a fountain and assorted ancient statuary. The varied collection is worth an hour; it includes spooky votive masks used in ritual dances at the sanctuary of Artemis Orthia, a large marble statue of a warrior thought to be Leonidas, and various representations of the Dioskouri, the brothers Castor and Pollux, locally revered as symbols of brotherly love and honor. A room is devoted to prehistoric pottery, weaponry, and jewelry. Especially impressive are the "unpublished" mosaics from the Roman period. *(On Lykourgou. Head from Paleologou toward the bus station. ☎28 575. Open Tu-Sa 8:30am-3pm, Su 9:30am-2:30pm. 500dr, students 300dr, EU students free.)* The **National Art Gallery** has a small, strong collection of 19th-century French and Dutch paintings, mostly still-lifes and portraits, including one attributed to Gustave Courbet. Upstairs is a more contemporary exhibit by modern Greek artists, with a number of watercolor landscapes. *(Paleologou 123. ☎81 557. Open Tu-Sa 9am-3pm, Su 10am-2pm. Free.)*

**OTHER RUINS.** Finding the various surrounding ruins may be a challenge, but is worth it for history buffs. Before you set out, ask the tourist police for a hand-drawn map. Three remaining platforms of the **Shrine to Menelaus and Helen** (history's most sought-after beauty and her ditched hubby) are 5km away. The remains of a **Shrine to Apollo** are on the road to Gythion. A short walk east on the banks of the Eurotas River leads to the **Sanctuary of Artemis Orthia,** where Spartan youths proved their courage by enduring public floggings.

**EXCURSIONS.** For an evening away from Sparta, share an expensive cab to the village of **Paroli,** 2km from Mystras. There you can sip a cool *frappé* while watching the nearby waterfalls. Two kilometers farther, the village of **Tripi** has larger waterfalls, some of which run right under the excellent restaurant **Exochiko Kentro.**

## MYSTRAS Μυστρας

***Buses** that leave from **Sparta**'s main station (see above) drop off at the Castro entrance, near the top of the city; buses from the corner of Lykourgou and Kythonigou drop off 50m down the road from the main gate (20min., 9 per day, 250dr). It's hot out there, so come early and bring water. You'll want good hiking shoes, 3hr. to see the sights, and perhaps the great* Guidebook Mystras *by Manolis Chatzidakis (2000dr). Dress modestly. No bathrooms. ☎83 377. **Open** 8am-7pm; in winter 8:30am-3pm. **Admission** 1200dr, students 600dr, EU students free.*



Mystras was once the religious center of all Byzantium, and the locus of Constantinople's rule over the Peloponnese. Its extraordinary ruins make up a city of Byzantine churches, chapels, and monasteries. Mystras was founded by French crusader **Guillume de Villehardouin** in 1249 with the building of a central castle. After the final attempt to establish Frankish sovereignty over the Peloponnese failed, Mystras was ceded to the Greeks in 1262, giving them an important military base and cultural center. In the centuries following, it grew from a village to a city, draining Sparta of its inhabitants as they sought protection in the city's fortress. By the early 15th century, Mystras was an intellectual center with a thriving silk industry. Unhappy under the thumb of repressive feudal lords and clergy, restless countryfolk surged into town, set up schools, and became an early bourgeoisie. When Turks invaded in 1460, Mystras's glory days were over. By the early 19th century, the city had crumbled to ruin. When King Otto founded modern Sparta in 1831, Mystras's fate was sealed with a table-turning exodus to its revived neighbor.

Crowned by the original castle, an intricate network of paths traces through three tiers of ruins, descending from royalty to nobility to commoners. Although less well preserved than many of the religious edifices that encircle it—they're almost completely intact, if a bit faded at the frescoes—the dramatic castle delivers a breathtaking view of the site and the surrounding countryside. It's easiest to take the bus to the upper entrance, climb to the castle, then work your way down through the rest of the site; otherwise, you'll have to make the grueling, steep climb up from the main gate (at the bottom of the hill) to the castle.

In the two centuries after Mystras's founding, churches, monasteries, a palace, and many luxurious homes sprang up behind its projectile walls. Don't miss the beautiful **Metropolis of Ag. Demetrios** on the lower tier, with its detailed frescoes, flowery courtyard, and museum of architectural fragments. Wander toward the two churches of the monastery of **Vrontochion. Aphentiko** glows with magnificent two-story frescoes, and **Ag. Theodoros** is its neighbor. On the same tier is the **Pantanassa,** a convent with an elaborately ornamented facade, frescoes, and a miracle-working icon of Mary. Finally, at the extreme left of the lower tier, every centimeter of the awe-inspiring **Church of Peribleptos** is bathed in exquisitely detailed religious paintings. Though many were vandalized by invading Ottomans, digging the eyes out of saints and saviors alike, they remain Mystras's most stunning relic.

# MANI ΜΑΝΗ

The name of the province of Mani comes from the Greek word *manis*—wrath or fury. History has affirmed this etymology time and again. Sparsely settled and encircling unforgiving Mt. Taygetus (p. 148), the region juts out into the surrounding sea unprotected. In Roman times, Mani founded the league of Laconians and broke free of Spartan domination. Ever since, Maniots have ferociously resisted foreign rule, boasting even today that nary an Ottoman set foot on their soil. But this rage has also been directed inward; savage, long-lasting family feuds flare up in Mani from seemingly trivial offenses. While Maniots revel in their historical ferocity, they are also warm hosts to the visitors who stay in their traditional greystone tower houses, seeking beautiful beaches and views.

## GYTHION Γυθειο ☎0733

Gythion, "Gateway to the Mani," has a much livelier, more Mediterranean feel than the bleak landscapes to the south. Bright fishing boats bustle in and out of the port, where dockside restaurants hang strings of octopi out to dry. A short causeway connects Gythion to the tiny island of **Marathonisi,** where Paris and Helen consummated their ill-fated love, and beautiful sand and stone beaches are a short ride (but long walk) away. For those who'd like to explore the Mani on their own, Gythion is the only city in the area that rents motorbikes (p. 155).

PELOPONNESE

### ORIENTATION AND PRACTICAL INFORMATION

Heading north into town along the main harbor road, the causeway to Marathonisi branches off to the right before you reach Gythion's center. As you continue along the main road, the waterfront becomes lined with outdoor tavernas tables, and the road leads directly to the quay, where ferries depart. To the left of the quay, the waterfront curves inland and forms a crescent, where most of the hotels and amenities can be found. The bus stop is on the north side of the waterfront (facing inland, to the right of the crescent). Small **Pl. Mavromichali,** consisting mostly of cafe seating, is on the southern side of the crescent near the quay.

**Buses:** The user-friendly **station** (☎22 228) is on the north end of the waterfront, opposite a large triangle of palms. Service to: **Athens** (4hr., 6 per day, 4700dr) via **Sparta** (1hr., 850dr); **Tripoli** (2hr., 1850dr); **Corinth** (3hr., 3350dr); **Kalamata** (2 per day, 2050dr) via **Itilo** (1hr., 750dr); **Gerolimenas** (2hr., 3 per day, 1150dr); **Areopolis** (1hr., 4 per day, 500dr), via the campgrounds south of town (250dr); and **Pirgos Dirou** (1¼hr., 10:15am, 700dr).

**Ferries:** To **Diakofti** on Kythera (2hr.; Su-Tu 5pm, Th 9pm; 2300dr) and on to **Kasteli** on Crete (7hr., 4900dr).

**Taxis:** (☎23 423, 23 492, or 22 755). Available 24hr.

**Moped Rental: Moto Makis Rent-A-Moped** (☎25 111), on the waterfront near the causeway. 5000dr per day including 80km, tax, and insurance. Open 8:30am-8:30pm.

**Travel Agency: Theodore V. Rozakis** (☎22 650) sells ferry tickets during late July and Aug. Other months, check at the booth at the end of the pier where the ferry departs.

**Banks: National Bank** (☎22 313), just beyond the bus stop toward the water, has **currency exchange** and a 24hr. **ATM.** Open M-Th 8am-2pm, F 8am-1:30pm.

**Police:** (☎22 100), on the waterfront, halfway between the bus station and Pl. Mavromichali. English spoken. Open 24hr.

**Port Police:** (☎22 262), before the causeway, past the plateia.

**Health clinic:** (☎22 001, 002, 003), on the water near the causeway.

**Telephones: OTE** (☎22 799), corner of Herakles and Kapsali. Open M-F 7:30am-3:10pm.

**Internet: Escape Cafe** (☎25 177), on Kapsali, one block behind the National Bank, at the corner. 1500dr per hr. Open 10am-1am.

**Post Office:** (☎22 285), on Ermou. Open M-F 7:30am-2:30pm. Turn right onto Herakles from the bus station and then left onto Ermou. **Postal code:** 23200.

## ACCOMMODATIONS

While seaside accommodations are prohibitively expensive, you can find a few cheap, charming options inland. Gythion's campgrounds are a pleasant (and more interesting) alternative to city lodging—all are about 4km south of town toward Areopolis, and can be reached by city bus (4 per day there and back); a taxi costs about 900dr. If you stay in Gythion, get some wheels for easy beach access.

**Xenia Karlaftis Rooms** (☎22 719), on the water 20m from the causeway. Voula and her mother, Xenia, have been letting cheap, spacious rooms for over 20 years, and their experience and gracious hospitality show. Kitchen with free coffee, fridges on every floor, and laundry. Clean, standard rooms with private baths. Singles 5000dr; doubles 6000dr; triples 7000dr.

**Koutsouris Rooms** (☎22 321). From Pl. Mavromichali, go up Tzanaki Gregoraki, turn right at the clock tower, and look for a sign and the gate just past the bakery on your left. Quiet, elegant home with huge upstairs suites; private baths, balconies, fridge, and coffee makers at surprisingly low prices. Only a few rooms are available, so call ahead. Singles and doubles 5000-7000dr; quads 8000dr.

**Meltemi Camping** (☎22 833), 4km south on the road toward Areopolis. Washing machine, mini-market, restaurant, and pool. 1500dr per person, 950dr per child; 850dr per car; 1300dr per tent. Electricity 1100dr.

**Gythion Bay Campgrounds** (☎22 522), 4.5km south on the road toward Areopolis. Washing machine, mini-market, restaurant, playground, and pool. 1600dr per adult, 1000dr per child; 1100dr per car; 1100dr per tent. Electricity 900dr.

**Mani Beach** (☎23 450), 5km south on the road toward Areopolis. Washing machine, mini-market, and restaurant. 1350dr per person, 700dr per child; 700dr per car; 800dr per small tent; 1100dr per large tent. Electricity 800dr.



## FOOD

Virtually identical waterfront tavernas serve up fresh seafood and views at moderate prices. A **fruit store** and **bakery** are across the street from Masouleri Kokkalis.

**Taverna To Nisi,** on Marathonisi, across from the church. This charming outdoor taverna is a favorite with locals and has a great view of Gythion's unique architecture. *Tzatziki* 400dr, grilled chicken 1200dr, heaping seafood variety plate 3000dr. Other entrees 1000-1400dr.

**Saga** (☎23 220), on the water between the causeway and the plateia. Delicious food served on tables pulled right up to the water. Crispy grilled and seasoned bread, cheap vegetarian salads. Meat entrees 1200-1700dr; fish 8000-10,000dr per kg. For a real treat, try the shrimp *saganaki* (4000dr).

**Gonia Corner,** from the bus station, it's past the plateia on the corner as the road straightens. *Moussaka* 1400dr, minnows 1400dr, and octopus 1500dr.

**Masouleri Kokkalis** (☎22 832), at the center of the plateia behind all the cafe chairs. Where locals head for fast food. Gyros 300dr, souvlaki 200dr, Greek salad 700dr, roasted chicken plate 750dr.

## SIGHTS AND BEACHES

**ANCIENT THEATER.** The compact, masterfully built, 240° theater of Gythion has endured the centuries remarkably well. Even its class distinctions remain: note the differences between the seats for dignitaries in front and the simpler seats farther back. Arrive early in the evening and you can join the soldiers getting their nightly pep talk; any other time of day, it will most likely be deserted. Next to the theater and scattered up the grassy hill are crumbling Roman walls. *(Walk down Herakles from the bus station, go to Ermou, and then right onto Archaiou Theatrou.)*

**PALIATZOURES ANTIQUE SHOP.** The last of its kind in the Peloponnese, this antique shop has furnished a number of museums in its day, as owner Costas will gladly tell you. The majority of the collection consists of 19th-century household items, artwork, furniture, coins, and assorted trinkets, but he claims to have a few medieval and even ancient items interspersed throughout. By Greek law, only items made after the fall of Constantinople in 1453 are exportable by foreigners, but unless you plan on spending a *lot* of money, this probably won't be a concern. *(#25 on the waterfront. ☎22 944. Open 11am-2pm and 6-9pm.)*

**ON THE ROAD TO AEROPOLIS.** When traveling from Gythion to Areopolis, look for the Frankish **Castle of Pasava** on the right (roughly 10km down the road; tours available). Farther along, the **Castle of Kelefa** looks out to sea.

**BEACHES.** There is a disappointing **public beach** just north of the bus station, but better beaches lie out of town. Four kilometers south, near the campgrounds, is the wide, pebbly beach of **Mavrovouni,** with a high surf and a number of bars (mixed drinks 900-1000dr, beer 500dr). Three kilometers north is rocky **Selinitsa,** a beach honored by the EU for its clean water. *(Neither beach is accessible by bus–ride a moped, take a taxi (700dr), or walk.)*

PELOPONNESE

## AREOPOLIS Αρεοπολη ☎0733

Though Areopolis neighbors the sea, its buildings dominate the scenery: stone tower houses and cobbled streets just wide enough for donkey carts are framed by the dramatic purple peaks of the Taygetus. Tourists flocking to nearby coastal towns often pass right through Areopolis, leaving plenty of inexpensive, romantic accommodations in the traditional tower houses that once defended the insular, suspicious clans of the Mani. The town musters little entertainment besides its striking scenery; closeby, you'll find the caves at Pirgos Dirou, the beautiful beach at Limenas (which doubles as Areopolis's port), and lively Gythion, the harbor town on the opposite side of the peninsula.

**ORIENTATION AND PRACTICAL INFORMATION.** All local services can be found off Kapetan Matapan or in the plateia. The bus stops in front of **Nicola's Corner** in the main plateia, pointing toward the main street of the Old Town, **Kapetan Matapan.** The **bus "station"** (☎51 229) is in the Europa Grill on the eastern edge of the plateia, opposite the Hotel Kouris. Buses from Areopolis go to: **Gythion** (30min., 4 per day, 500dr), and then on to **Sparta** (1½hr., 1300dr) and **Athens** (6hr., 5000dr); and **Kalamata** (2½hr., 2 per day, 1400dr) via **Itilo** (30min., 230dr). A bus running into the Mani takes you to the **Vlihada Lake Caves** (leaves 11am, returns 12:45pm; 250dr) and **Vatheia** (1hr., 1:45pm, 750dr) via **Gerolimenas** (30min., 500dr). The **police** are in the plateia at the end of a little street that starts behind the statue. (☎51 209. Open 24hr.) The **post office** is just off the plateia on Kapetan Matapan. (Open M-F 7:20am-2pm.) To find the **National Bank** and its 24hr. **ATM,** walk down Kapetan Matapan, turn right at the first small church, and continue up the street. (Open M-F 9am-noon.) The bus station and the post office **exchange currency** and **traveler's checks** for a hefty fee. The **OTE** (☎51 399) is 50m down a street that starts in the main plateia; the statue's right hand points down the street with its sword. Opposite the OTE is a 24hr. **health center** (☎51 242). A **pharmacy** is on Kapetan Matapan. **Postal code:** 23062.

**ACCOMMODATIONS AND FOOD.** Staying at either **Tsimova's Rooms** or the **Pension** opposite may amount to taking sides in what appears to be long-standing feud. Both proprietors spend their days staring menacingly at one another's doors, but are delightful individually; choose at your own risk. To find them, turn left at the end of Kapetan Matapan. **Tsimova** rents narrow rooms with tiny doors and windows typical of tower houses; Kolokotronis supposedly slept here, and the living room displays rifles, swords, and uniforms passed down through the owner's family from the War for Independence. Shared baths may require a trip outside.

(☎51 301. Singles 6000dr; doubles 8000dr; triples 12,000dr; quads 14,000dr; continental breakfast 750dr.) Tsimova's neighbor and rival, friendly **Pierros Bozagregos Pension,** lets doubles with private baths. (☎51 354. Singles 6000dr; doubles 10,000dr.) Spacious and new, **Hotel Mani** has huge rooms with private baths, balconies, and TVs. Walk 50m from the bus station on Kapetan Matapan, turn right at the first small church, and walk another 200m. (☎51 190; fax 51 269. Singles 8000-9000dr; doubles 12,000-14,000dr; A/C 2000dr extra.)

The simple sign reading "Taverna" in front of the yellow building on the left of Kapetan Matapan marks the splendid **Oinomageireio** (☎51 205), with intimate garden seating and first-class cooking by its internationally recognized chef and owner. Try "flower of the zucchini with mixed vegetables" (1200dr) or traditional chicken with spaghetti (2000dr). In the plateia, **Nicola's Place** (☎51 366), serves rotating specials, including stuffed omelets (1000dr), and their specialty, souvlaki *ikilo* (1800dr), accompanied by grilled, seasoned bread (200dr).

## PYRGOS DIROU CAVES Σπηλαιο Πυργος Διρουυ

*4km from **Areopolis,** accessible by daily bus (leaves Areopolis 11am, returns 12:45pm; 250dr). Some tour guides speak only Greek, so you may want to purchase the guidebook* Caverns of Mani *for 1500dr at the cave entrance ticket booth. Open June-Sept. 8am-5pm; Oct.-May 8am-5:30pm. 3500dr includes tour.*

Part of a subterranean river, the unusual **Vlihada Cave** (Spilia Dirou or Pyrgos Dirou) is cool, quiet, and strung with tiny crystalline stalactites. Vermilion stalagmites slice the 30m deep water's surface. Discovered at the end of the 19th century, it was opened to the public in 1971; it has yet to be fully explored. Experts speculate that the cave is 70km long and may extend all the way to Sparta. The 1200m boat ride through the cave lasts about 30min.; the tiny boats rock their way through the narrow channels of the cave, forcing passengers to duck at times to avoid low-hanging stalactites. The close quarters and the cavernous echo of dripping water create an eerie calm. Lights floating in styrofoam rings illuminate the tour, but unlit recesses of the cave branch off to the left and right. Don't miss **Poseidon's Foot,** a striking hanging formation resembling (lo and behold!) a giant foot. You'll rejoice in sunlight again when you emerge.

PELOPONNESE

# GEFYRA Γεφυρα ☎0732

Byzantine nuts on the way to their paradise, Monemvasia, may be puzzled when the bus drops them off in the unabashedly modern—albeit pleasant—coastal town of Gefyra. Just beyond the breaking waves off Gefyra's shore lies an impressive island, dominated by spectacular vertical cliffs. "The rock," as it is known, looks uninhabited from the mainland; only after crossing the causeway and walking along the main road for 15min. does Monemvasia appear. Before you cross, however, it's wise to take care of your needs in cheaper Gefyra.

**ORIENTATION AND PRACTICAL INFORMATION.** During late July and August, an **orange bus** runs between the causeway and Monemvasia gate all day long (every 10min. 8am-midnight, 100dr). In Gefyra, **23 Iouliou,** the principal thoroughfare, runs along the waterfront to the causeway leading to the island. The **bus station** (☎61 432) is on 23 Iouliou, opposite the post office in the helpful **Malvasia Travel Agency,** which provides pretty much any service you would need, including **moped rental** (5000dr per day) and **currency exchange.** (☎61 752; fax 61 432. Open M-Sa 8:15am-2:15pm and 5-9pm, Su 10:15am-3:15pm.) All **buses,** except for the direct express to **Athens** (6hr., 4:10am, 4300dr), connect or stop in **Molai.** Three buses per day leave to: **Athens** (6hr., 5800dr) via **Molai** (20min., 500dr); **Corinth** (5hr., 4450dr); **Sparta** (2½hr., 1900dr); and **Tripoli** (4hr., 2950dr). Twice a day, **Flying Dolphins** go to **Spestes, Hydra, and Portoheli** (8900dr). **Ferries** leave for **Piraeus** and **Crete** (F 1 or 2am, 4000dr). Check out the boat schedules at the **ticket office** (☎61 219), next to the Mobil station on the island.

Across from the bus station, the **National Bank** has a 24hr. **ATM.** (☎61 201. Open M and W 9am-1:30pm, F 9am-1pm.) The **post office** is next door. (☎61 231. Open M-F 7:30am-2pm.) The **police** (☎61 210) and **tourist police** are in the same building, past Malvasia Travel, toward the causeway. (☎61 941. Open 24hr.) Bear left from the bus station to reach the **OTE,** 200m uphill, on the left in a second-floor balcony. (☎61 399. Open M-F 7:30am-3pm.) **Postal code:** 23070.

**ACCOMMODATIONS AND FOOD.** As Gefyra's hotels tend to be expensive, the waterfront **domatia** are your best bet (doubles 5000-8000dr). **Hotel Sophos** has recently renovated rooms for decent prices. (☎61 360. Singles 8000dr; doubles 10,000dr.) **Camping Paradise,** 3.5km along the water on the mainland, is more affordable. (☎61 123. 1400dr per person; 950dr per car; 900dr per small tent; 1200dr per large tent; 20% discount for longer stays.) The helpful information center on the main road leading uphill from the gate can help you find a place to sleep.

Restaurants on the island are much more expensive and have less space for outdoor seating, so the many harborfront tavernas of Gefyra are probably a better option. **To Limanaki,** offering lots of waterside seating on the mainland beside the harbor, serves exceptional Greek food, including the best *pastitsio* (1300dr) and stuffed tomatoes (1100dr) you could ever ask for. **Pipinellis Taverna,** 2km from Monemvasia on the road to Camping Paradise, has featured home-grown produce for the past 25 years. (☎61 004. Entrees 1300-1900dr.) In the island's old city, pricier **Matoula** boasts fig trees and a plant-decorated stone terrace with a spectacular view to the sea. (☎61 660. Entrees 1300-2000dr, veal with spaghetti 1800dr.)

**DAYTRIPS FROM GEFYRA: MONEMVASIA.** Monemvasia (Μονεμβασια) deserves the constant attention it gets; an undeniable otherworldliness pervades the old city. Passing through the single gateway (hence the town's name, which means "one way") into old Monemvasia, you may feel as if you've entered a city frozen in time. No cars or bikes are allowed through the gate, so packhorses bearing groceries and cases of beer are led back and forth to restaurants. The winding cobbled street that passes the town's tourist shops and restaurants appears immediately upon entering the gate; it continues past the strip of tourist shops to reach the central plateia. Facing the ocean, the church of **Christos Elkomenos** (Christ in Chains) is on the left. To get to the oft-photographed 12th-century **Agia Sofia,** balanced on the edge of the rock cliffs, work your way through the maze of narrow streets—with hidden stairways, child-sized doorways, flowered courtyards, and the occasional cactus—to the edge of town farthest from the sea at the base of the mountain. There, a path climbs the cliffside to the tip of the rock; you'll find the church on the far side of the rock. Modeled after the monastery at Daphni (p. 108), the structure of the church is still beautiful, although the faded frescoes were badly vandalized by invading Turks who held the castle for a time. The top of the rock, scattered with crumbling castle ruins, offers splendid views of the town and sea below. Back in town, a very small but excellently labeled **Archaeological Museum** holds an air-conditioned single room full of masonry, pottery, and ecclesiastical sculpture attesting to Monemvasia's 13th-century prominence. Open Tu-Su 8am-7pm, M noon-7pm. Free.

## NEAPOLI Νεαπολις ☎0734

A necessary but uneventful stop on the path between Kythera and the southeastern Peloponnese, Neapoli is a little coastal town with lots of waterfront restaurants, a few luxury hotels, and an increasing number of Greek tourists. The pebble beaches are an uncrowded and refreshing break from the towel-to-towel sunbathers of more popular vacation spots. Unfortunately, there's not much besides Neapoli's waterfront to keep visitors occupied, so you'll probably want to stay only long enough to catch a boat or a bus to a more exciting destination.

The **port police** are on the waterfront near the sole pier. To the left of the pier, a blue and white hut on the water's edge provides **info** and posts ferry schedules.

**Ferries** go to **Kythera** (1hr.; W-Su 4 per day, M-Tu 3 per day; 1600dr) and **Elefonnisos** (every hr., 400dr). **Flying Dolphins** depart 5 times per week (except Tu and W) to **Kythera** and **Monemvasia** (9000dr). The **bus station** (☎23 222), on the same street, sends buses to: **Molai** (40min., 3 per day, 1200dr); **Athens** (1 per day, 4200dr); **Sparta** (3 per day, 2600dr); and **Ag. Nikolaos** (20min., 3 per day, 250dr). The **National Bank** is one block from the port police, on the other side of the street (open M-Th 8am-2pm, F 8am-1:30pm). The town's main street along the water is home to many services. The **post office** is one block inland on Leoforos Democratias on the left (open M-F 7:30am-2pm). If you get stuck in Neapoli overnight, scour the streets for domatia, or try **Hotel Arsenakos,** run by a friendly ex-New Yorker, which is a five-minute walk to the left of town on the water. Rooms have A/C, TV, private baths, balconies, and refrigerators. (☎22 991. Singles 8000dr; doubles 11,000dr.)

# KYTHERA ΚΥΘΗΡΑ



According to ancient myth, the island of Kythera rose from the waters where Zeus cast his father Kronos's severed godhead into the sea after castrating him. Springing from Kronos's foamy misfortune, Aphrodite washed up onto Kythera's shores and made it her homeland. In antiquity, the island supported a large temple to the goddess, where she was worshiped as Aphrodite Urania, goddess of chaste love. Though one might not associate the island's barren, mountainous landscape with the fertility for which Aphrodite is known and worshiped, its flowering shrubs, sandy beaches, and secluded villages do hold a potent beauty. Like the other Ionian Islands, Kythera passed through the hands of the Venetians and the French before ending up as a British possession. However, it is distinct from the other islands in its extremely rugged scenery—desert-like in places—and its nearly untouristed feel. Only about 3000 people live on Kythera, fewer during the winter, but improved ferry schedules (see below) have made it a more convenient destination for budget travelers; the two main island ports are northerly **Agia Pelagia** and the newer, less accessible east-coast port of **Diakofti.** While bus service is nearly nonexistent, mopeds are cheap, and having some sort of vehicle at your disposal is virtually essential to taking full advantage of all the island has to offer. Kythera's major sites can be seen in a day or two if you've got wheels, but if you enjoy clean sand beaches and the unhurried island life, you'll probably want to stay longer.

## AGIA PELAGIA Αγια Πελαγια ☎0735

If you plan a short stay on the island, and especially if you're catching a ferry, Agia Pelagia is a good place to set up camp to avoid paying for an overpriced cab to the docks. The town is smaller and less picturesque than southerly Hora or Kapsali, but accommodations and moped rentals are considerably cheaper, and its long, convenient stretch of beach offers up both sand and pebbles to choose from.

**ORIENTATION AND PRACTICAL INFORMATION.** The island's main road runs between Agia Pelagia and **Kapsali** in the south, with small villages connected by subsidiary roads. This road also passes through **Potamos** (the island's largest town), **Livadi,** and **Kythera (Hora). Ferries** leave Agia Pelagia daily for **Neapoli** (1hr., 1500dr) and from **Diakofti** to **Gythion** (2½hr., 1550dr) and **Kastili** on Crete (5hr., at least 1 per day, 3850dr). **Flying Dolphins** leave Diakofti to **Spestes** (2hr., 6700dr) and for **Piraeus** (4hr.; M,W, and F-Su at 5pm; 10,400dr) via **Monemvasia** (1hr., 5000dr). In Agia Pelagia, a cottage to the left of the quay is a **Volunteer Tourist Office,** where friendly staffers provide information about accommodations and sights. (☎33 815. Open July-Sept. 10am-noon and 5:30-8pm.) A daily **bus** runs between Agia Pelagia and Kapsali in late July and August (leaves 8am, returns noon; 300dr). **Easy Rider,** to the right of Agia Pelagia, rents mopeds (3000dr per day for 50cc, 5000dr for 125cc). Ferry tickets and schedules are also a available at the two tiny shacks at the end of the pier and from the **port police** (☎33 280).

**ACCOMMODATIONS AND FOOD.** The tourist office has a list of the few domatia owners in town and will put you in contact with them. Otherwise, **Hotel Kythereia,** right beside the ferry pier in blue and white, has rooms with private baths, A/C, and lovely views (of either mountains or sea) for good prices. It's run by an extremely hospitable Greek-Australian family. (Singles 8000dr; doubles 10000dr; breakfast included.) The other hotels in town are more luxurious (and expensive), like the **Vernados Hotel,** with a score of amenities such as A/C, TVs, free laundry, and a beautiful buffet breakfast. The hotel is just 50m down the road to Potamos, on your right and up a small hill. (☎34 205 or 34 206. Singles 13,000-20,000dr; doubles 22,000-24,000dr.)

**Taverna Faros,** the first taverna to the right of the pier, has lots of waterfront seating and scrumptious *pastitsio* (1200dr). (Appetizers 300-600dr, salads 600-1000dr, entrees 700-2000dr. Fish 9000-11,000dr per kilo, and worth every last drachma.) Agia Pelagia has a well-stocked **supermarket** opposite the beach, beside the fruit market.

# AROUND KYTHERA

The pint-size island has a lion's share of sights, enough to keep any visitor occupied. The peaceful beach town of **Kapsili,** east of Hora, has clear waters and a long shore. At Paleohora, in the east, are the ruins of the former fortified capital of the island, **Agios Dimitrios,** built during Byzantine rule. The town was destroyed by pirates led by the notorious Barbarossa in 1537. Even more compelling are the island's natural wonders, like the **Cave of Agia Sofia,** near the village of Milopotamos on the western side of the island, which is the most impressive of the island's several caves. Inquire at the cafe in the plateia of Milopotamos about boat tour information. Kythera's **beaches** are gorgeous, with the ocean's variety of blues contrasting with the rocky brown landscape. The best beaches are a bit difficult to reach, accessible only by bumpy dirt roads, perilous for moped-riders; a car is safer. On the eastern coast, a steep staircase leads down to the spectacular **Kaladi** beach, with sparkling coves and striking rock formations. **Halkos,** near the village of Kalamos on the southern coast, is another out-of-the-way beach, but its quiet beauty makes it well worth the trip.



## POTAMOS Ποταμας ☎0735

Pretty, residential Potamos, with narrow hilly streets bedecked with flowers and an abundance of fresh fruit markets, is on a hill 9km south of Agia Pelagia on the main road, and is the largest town on the island. Accommodations are scarce here, and most visitors to the island choose to stay in places closer to the sea. However, it's worth a visit to stroll through the streets and admire the traditional Kytherean architecture, and to take advantage of the services in the small central plateia, where most of the island's amenities can be found. There you'll see an **Olympic Airlines** office, although the airport is a taxi ride away on the eastern half of Kythera. (☎33 362. Open M-F 8am-4pm.) Olympic runs **flights** to and from Athens (1 per day, 15,400dr). The **National Bank** with a 24hr. **ATM** is also in the plateia. (☎33 350. Open M-Th 8am-2pm, F 8am-1pm.) The **post office** is uphill from the plateia (☎33 225. Open M-F 7:30am-2pm.) The **police station** is behind the National Bank, tucked in a lemon-tree lined corner. (☎33 222. No English spoken.) The **hospital** is on the road to Hora. (☎33 325. English spoken.) **Taxis** (☎33 676) park in the plateia. **Selana Cafe,** in the plateia, has **Internet access** for 2000dr per hour, and rich Greek coffee (250dr). **Postal code:** 80200.

## HORA Χωρα ☎0735

The whitewashed plaster houses of the island's southerly capital, Hora (also called **Kythera Town**), gleam in the bright sun, especially along the main street running downhill from the plateia to the castle. Hora hosts many of the island's visitors. This plateia holds Hora's **post office** (☎31 274; open 7:30am-2pm) and a **National**

**Bank** branch with a 24hr. **ATM.** Facing the water, Hora's main street starts from the plateia's lower left-hand corner; along it you'll find the **police** (☎31 206) and **tourist police** (open mornings only), 50m down toward the water. **Kithira Travel** has **Flying Dolphin** schedules, **currency exchange,** and is the island's main **Olympic Airways** office. (☎31 390. Open 9am-2pm and 7-10pm.) The **OTE** is up the stairs to the left of Kithira Travel. (☎31 299. Open 7:30am-2pm.) If you're catching a ferry in Diafkoto, a **taxi** (☎31 320) from Hora will cost about 5000dr.

Expensive domatia fill Hora's sparkling buildings. To reach **Pension Pises,** head downhill and turn left off the main road on Ag. Elesis. It's the place for great views, shared baths, and creative decor. (☎31 070. Doubles 6000dr.) At the end of the main road, wildflowers have sprouted around the remains of the town's **castle,** where the wind-swept plateau offers intoxicating views of nearby Kapsali's double harbor. The small, under-funded **Archaeological Museum,** on Kythera's highway just before the turn-off for Hora, has pottery, sculpture, and coins from the Classical to the Byzantine periods. It also has gravestones, which are all that remain of the island's 19th-century English military base. (Open Tu-Sa 8:45am-3pm, Su 9:30am-2:30pm. Free.)

# CENTRAL GREECE

Under 19th-century Ottoman rule, Thessaly and Sterea Ellada acquired a Byzantine flavor. Follow them along forgotten mountain-goat paths that lead to these Byzantine treasures. Along the way, you'll encounter glorious mountain-top vistas that look out over silvery olive groves, fruit-laden trees, and patchwork farmland.

## HIGHLIGHTS OF CENTRAL GREECE

**ASCEND TO THE CLOUD-SWEPT** Meteora monasteries like Byzantine saints (p. 196).

**WANDER THE DREAMY** traditional holdout of Makrynitsa (p. 186).

**GLUT YOUR EYES** on the frescoes and gold mosaics at the Monastery of Osios Loukas (p. 165), an oasis of Byzantine decorative art.

**DITCH THE PSYCHIC HOTLINE** for the real deal—Apollo's oracle at Delphi (p. 170).

**SUNBATHE** on the pristine, deserted stone beaches of Galaxidi (p. 171).

**SKI AND SWIM** in a single afternoon: the slopes of Mt. Parnassos, Greece's premier ski town, and the shores near Arahova await (p. 166).

# STEREA ELLADA ΣΤΕΡΕΑ ΕΛΛΑΔΑ

Small mountainside villages, monumental ruins, the country's finest honey, and superb ski slopes make up Sterea Ellada (the "Greek Continent," the only section of the mainland to join the new Greek state after the War of Independence; see p. 16). For thousands of years, pilgrimages from all over the Mediterranean and Asia Minor led to the Delphic Oracle; ponderous questions met cryptic replies. The 10th century Monastery of Osios Loukas, a modern religious center not far from Delphi, displays the Byzantines' architectural mastery. Be kind to strangers you meet on the road below the monastery: at the crossroads, an unknowing Oedipus met and murdered his father on the way to Thebes, where he married his mother.

## THEBES (THIVA) Θηβα ☎0262

Buried beneath the sleepy streets and tavernas of modern Thebes lies its claim to fame—its illustrious (and notorious) past. Some ruins are visible at the archaeological museum and in the slightly overgrown excavation pits haphazardly scattered around town. Theban history provides many street names: take a walk down the avenues of **Cadmus** (the city's legendary first king), **Oedipus** (exiled king and originator of the complex), **Antigone** (Oedipus' rebellious daughter and sister and heroine of Sophocles' play), and **Pindar** (the 5th-century BC lyric poet). Rising to prominence in the heyday of the Greek polis, from the 6th to the 4th centuries BC, Thebes capitalized on its fertile plains and strategic location between northern Greece and the Peloponnese. Alexander the Great's army cut this prosperity short around 335 BC, when its invasion from Macedonia reduced the city to rubble and spared only temples and Pindar's ancestral home. It seems that Thebes is still attempting to recover from that blow; it now warrants a brief daytrip.



**ORIENTATION AND PRACTICAL INFORMATION.** Thebes is built on a high hill with two parallel main streets, **Epaminonda** and **Pindarou,** running from the top of the hill into the valley below. These two streets provide everything a visitor needs. Cafes line the side streets between them.

From Terminal B, platform 4 at Liossion 260 in **Athens,** take the **bus** to Thebes (1½hr., every hr. 6am-8pm, 1650dr). Buy tickets inside the station from the desk labeled ΘΗΒΑ (Thebes). The main **bus station** is in the valley below Thebes, on Estias (☎27 512). If you ask nicely upon your arrival, the bus driver might let you off in the center of town. Otherwise, to get to town from the station, cross the parking lot, with your back to the station, and turn right, following the first road uphill. You will see Eteokleous; follow it up the hill to a plateia where the two main roads begin. Pindarou is your immediate right, and Epaminonda is perpendicular to Eteokleous. Turn right onto Epaminonda to find hotels, tavernas, and other comforts. From Thebes, buses depart from the station for **Athens** (1½hr., every hr. 6am-8pm, 1650dr). To travel to **Halkida,** take the Athens bus to the Skimatari stop (30min., 600dr); across the street from the Skimatari stop, catch the Athens-Halkida (10min., every 30min., 350dr). Regular buses run to **Livadia** (45min., every hr. 6am-8pm, 950dr) from a stop about 4km out of town: walk all the way down Pindarou, past the Archaeological Museum, and go down the steps. Follow this road as it curves around the hill and crosses the perpendicular road at the base of the hill. Going straight along the same road, follow the blue signs to Λει βαδεια (Livadia) until the small metal bus shelter just before the Shell gas station, on your right. Buy your ticket on board; the conductor will come and collect your money. For **taxis** call 27 077. Pindarou St. is lined with **banks** and **pharmacies.** The **National Bank,** Pindarou 94, has a 24hr. **ATM.** (☎23 331 or 25 144. Bank open M-Th 8am-2pm, F 8am-1:30pm.) The **hospital,** Pindarou 105 (☎24 444) is between the church and the archaeological museum—look for Greek and Red Cross flags. The brand-new **OTE,** 14 Vourdouba, is off of Epaminonda (open M-F 7:45am-1pm). The **post office,** Drakou 17, lies on a side street between Pindarou and Epaminonda. (☎27 810. Open M-F 7:30am-2:30pm.) **Postal code:** 32200.

**ACCOMMODATIONS AND FOOD.** If you decide to spend the night in Thebes, **Hotel Niobi,** Epaminonda 63, offers rooms with TVs, beautifully tiled private baths, and an English-speaking staff at the best rates in town. (☎29 888. Singles 8000dr; doubles 10,000dr; triples 12,000dr; breakfast 1000dr.) The **Hotel Meletiou,** Epaminonda 58, across the street, has comparable rooms (TVs, private baths) at slightly higher prices. (☎22 111. Singles 9000dr; doubles 13,000-15,000dr.) By evening, young people, families, and retirees fill the pedestrian-only sections of Epaminonda, as tavernas and cafes move tables into the street. A multitude of tavernas tumble across Epaminonda, and its side streets to Pindarou offer similar fare at similar prices (500-1500dr); bakeries, fruit stands, and small gyro and souvlaki restaurants scattered among the tavernas provide cheaper eats (300-900dr).

**SIGHTS AND ENTERTAINMENT.** Thebes' antiquities are its main attraction. The **Archaeological Museum** at the end of Pindarou has an extensive collection of Mycenaean artifacts, including jewelry and pottery from the era of the *Iliad* and *Odyssey*, pinch-faced idols and intricate funerary boxes lamenting those trapped inside. The museum also displays Boeotian statuary from the 5th and 4th centuries BC, and pottery galore. Especially notable are the Geometric style vases *(larnakes)*, dating from 900 to 700 BC, before black-figure vase painting became commonplace (p. 21). Mosaics and funerary *steles* accent the courtyard, where more than half the museum's collection is simply lying about. (☎27 913. Open Tu-Su 8:30am-3pm. 500dr, seniors 400dr, students 300dr, children and EU students free.)

Peer into the open **excavation pits**—the source of the museum's collection—sprinkled between buildings throughout the central city. Tantalizing segments of a Mycenaean palace and acropolis (dated to 1400BC) are partially visible. The largest of these, the **House of Cadmus,** shows its ancient palace walls; it is along the way to the museum on Pindarou, just between the church and the hospital.

In mid-August, the town hosts **Pindaria,** a festival of arts named in honor of hometown poet Pindar. Activities vary from year to year, but typically feature drama and traditional music. The festival can last up to a whole month. For their daily dose of fun, locals chat, chill, and sip coffee at cafes off Epaminonda.

**DAYTIP FROM THEBES: LIVADIA (Λειβαδεια).** Livadia's treasures cluster around the sacred river **Herkina** that flows below the **Oracle of Trophonius**. Herkina bubbles up from the dual **springs of Kyra,** called *Lethe* (forgetfulness) and *Mnemosyne* (memory). Pilgrims bathed in these waters to empty their minds of everything but the oracle's instruction just before visiting the oracle. Across from the oracle, a now-graffitied 14th-century **Frankish castle** towers overhead. Though the castle permits no visitors, a smooth stone path through the hills beyond the castle is open to all. Two tiny, whitewashed chapels are perched high in the cliffs to the left and right of the trail. The hike up the path and the stairs carved into the hill takes about an hour and provides a splendid view of the countryside. *(Accesible by bus via Thebes (2hr., every hr. 6am-8pm, 2550dr) or from Terminal B in Athens (see* p. 80*). From the bus stop, cross the street to Boufidou, which becomes Georganta, and ends in a plateia full of cafes. Turn left and follow the road straight into another busy plateia. The oracle and streams are on your left, and the castle is on your right.)*

## OSIOS LOUKAS Οσιος Λουκας ☎0267

***Bus** travel between Livadia and Osios Loukas is sporadic at best; as a result, the monastery is difficult to reach. Without a car, you'll need to hire a **taxi** (☎22 322; 5000-6000dr each way) or **walk** along the hilly, narrow road from the town of Distomo, 9km west. ☎22 797. Open May 3-Sept. 15 8am-2pm and 4-7pm; Sept. 16-May 2 8am-5pm. Dress modestly (long skirts for women, long pants for men, no bare shoulders). 800dr, seniors 600dr, under 18 and students with ID free.*

Osios Loukas delights the eye with its mountain vistas and stunning Byzantine architecture. The exquisite monastery, built in the 10th and 11th centuries and still in use today, overlooks Boeotia and Phokis from the green slopes of Mt. Elikon

more than 1700m above sea level. Gold-laden mosaics, vibrant frescoes, and intricate brick- and stonework adorn Osios Loukas, the most famous and perhaps the most gorgeous monastery in Greece.

**HISTORY.** Ironically, Christian saint Osios Loukas was born in AD 896 in Delphi (p. 168), the former religious center of the Olympian gods (see p. 28). Inclined to an ascetic life from early on, he became a monk at the age of 14. In 946, Osios Loukas settled at the lush and enchanting site of the monastery that now bears his name, building a cell, a small church, and a garden. Rumors that his relic worked miracles brought believers to his church, which led to an expansion of the grounds and the beginning of a monastery. With aid from fellow hermits and money from admirers, Osios Loukas began construction of two churches. The first, the **Church of the Panagia** (Church of the Virgin Mary), was finished soon after the saint's death in 953. The larger **Katholikon of Osios Loukas,** built in 1011, became the site of his reliquary. Osios Loukas was famed as a miracle worker during his lifetime; since his death, thousands have found cures at his tomb. Unfortunately, the monastery still bears damage from a 13th-century Frankish occupation.

**MONASTERY.** Today, the monastery consists of the two churches, the crypt, a bell-tower, and monks' cells. Also on the grounds are an archaeology museum and several tourist shops. The handful of black-robed, bearded monks who live in the monastery and tend its gardens cheerfully accommodate tourists.

The archaeology museum, on the right after the arched stone gate, sells tickets for entrance into the monastery. The museum holds a few relics from the monastery's architectural past (chunks of molding and such) and merits little more than a quick look.

The **Katholikon,** on the right after the museum, is the most impressive piece of the monastery. Built on the classic "Greek cross" basilica plan (see p. 23), the church is resplendent with brilliant frescoes and mosaics. The mosaics, crafted from minute pieces of stone, enamel, and gold, depict scenes of Christian lore: the birth, baptism, and crucifixion of Christ, and **Christ Pantokrator** (Christ in heaven, reigning in glory as savior and ruler).

A small passageway in the Katholikon's northwest corner links it to the smaller **Church of Panagia.** In this passageway is the monastery's most prized relic: the desiccated body of the saint himself, lying in state in a transparent glass coffin. Orthodox pilgrims come here to pray at Osios Loukas's velvet-slippered feet. Some have been even bolder: Loukas's left hand, which protrudes from his habit to hold a rosary, has lost a few fingers to relic-seekers. The Church of Panagia down the passage features extremely fine exterior brickwork and an inlaid mosaic floor.

Between the museum and the churches and accessible by an entrance in the southern exterior of the Katholikon is the **crypt;** its stunning frescoes should not be missed. Protected from the elements, the frescoes retain their original brilliance, giving us an idea of what the churches looked like originally.



## PARNASSOS Παρνασσος AND ARAHOVA Αραχωβα ☎0267

Winter is peak season on Mt. Parnassos (2455m), as Apollo and the muses share their abode with ski buffs and ski bunnies flocking to the best slopes in Greece. Summer trekkers can hike the slopes undisturbed. Outdoor enthusiasts will adore Parnassos regardless of the season. From December to May, the little village of Arahova (24km away from Parnassos) becomes Greece's largest ski resort, thanks to its prime location. Arahova is the most common point of departure for excursions to the mountain. Drowsy and picturesque in the summer months, Arahova offers local delights like delicious unresinated red wine, Boeotian honey, that peculiar grape-seed brandy called *tsipouro* (see **Moonshine,** p. 174), and an overwhelming view of the valley 4800m below. A three-day **festival** in mid-April commemorates Arahova's role as the site of a pivotal victory over the Turks during the

Ottoman War in 1821. In honor of St. George, the renowned dragon-slayer and the town's patron saint, the festival consists of athletic competitions, dances, and general merrymaking; during the festivities, residents don their best costumes.

**ORIENTATION AND PRACTICAL INFORMATION.** From **Terminal B** in Athens (see p. 80), take the Delphi bus to **Arahova** (3½ hr, 6 per day, 2850dr). A brown and yellow "Celena" sign identifies the **bus station** (☎28 226), which doubles as a restaurant. Find the bus station in the center of town on the left side of Delphon (the main road), approaching from Delphi. From here, an additional seven **buses** make the run from Arahova to **Delphi** (20min., 6:15am-7:50pm, 250dr). From Arahova, the trip to Parnassos is easy: either drive in a **car,** or those without cars can hire a **taxi.** (☎31 566. Round-trip 10,000-12,000dr.) Arahova centers around a single road, **Delphon,** which points downhill toward Delphi and has all a tourist could want. Most townspeople live on lovely, mainly pedestrian paths parallel to Delphon, both above and below the town on the mountain. Three main plateias lie in town; directions assume you are heading into town from Delphi.

The **police** (☎31 133) are reachable by phone. Several **pharmacies** offer balm for bruises and blisters; there's one in the second plateia, beside the big taverna, and another just past it down an alley to the right. A little past the post office, on the left, lies the **National Bank,** with a 24hr. **ATM.** (Open M-Th 8am-2pm, F 8am-1:30pm.) **Alpha Bank,** in the second plateia of cafes on the right, **exchanges money.** (Open M-Th 8am-2pm, F 8am-1:30pm.) Farthest downhill in the first of the town's three plateias you'll find the **post office.** (Open M-F 7:30am-2pm.) **Postal code:** 32004.

**ACCOMMODATIONS AND FOOD.** Several hotels, pensions, and domatia cluster near the first plateia. The low-end prices listed refer to summer prices; high-end prices refer to ski season rates. In the first small alley to the right after the first main plateia on Delphon, little hotel **Petrino** (Πετρινο) offers gorgeous rooms with private baths, fridges, balconies, and high wooden ceilings at decent rates. Ask about discounts on weekdays during ski season. (☎31 384; fax 32 663. Singles 5000-12,600dr; doubles 8000-18,000dr; triples 11,000-22,000dr.) Farther down the road past the center of town, **Hotel Apollon,** Delphi 20, has comfortable rooms with shared hall bathrooms; some rooms have balconies blessed with an uninterrupted view of the mountainside. (☎31 057. Singles 5000-10,000dr; doubles 6000-12,000.) The same friendly, English-speaking owner runs the **Apollon Inn,** Delphi 106, just off Delphon to the left across from the main plateia. Private baths, TVs, phones, and occasional balconies off sparkling rooms make it a great deal. (☎31 540 or 31 427. Singles 6000dr; doubles 8000dr. Breakfast 1000dr. AmEx.)

Small, inexpensive souvlaki stands set up shop near the first plateia at the end of town, toward Delphi. The bakeries along the road to Delphi sell fresh bread and savory pastries (300-500dr). Tavernas are plentiful but indistinct and can be found along the main road. The usually moderate prices, like everything else, go up in winter. **O Terouiovrahos** (Ο Τερουιοβραχος), just past the second main plateia on the left, is one of the better of the lot. They serve a savory *moussaka* (1800dr) and other moderately priced dishes (900-2200dr).

**SKIING, HIKING, AND THE OUTDOORS.** The **Parnassos Ski Center** whisks you up the mountain with its multitude of lifts. (☎22 493/689/694. Lifts 7000dr per day on weekends and as little as 4500dr on weekdays. Ski rental 5000dr per day).

Though more goats than tourists frequent Parnassos in the summer months, it's a peaceful spot for hiking and rock climbing, with literally breathtaking views: the air becomes noticeably thinner higher up. Ski centers on the mountain provide free parking and an easy starting destination for most trips. Consult the **Greek Alpine Club** in Athens (☎(01) 321 2429) about routes and refuges for climbers. In most cases, the hike will take no more than three hours. Summer hikers should note that trails are unmarked and usually deserted (goats aside). Be sure to take water and sunscreen along, and be aware of the thin air and rocky paths: Parnassos provides a challenge to those looking for a tough hike.

# DELPHI Δελφοι ☎0265

The god whose oracle is at Delphi neither utters nor hides his meaning but shows it by a sign.

—Heraclitus

As any Delphinian will proudly attest, this town of 2500 marks the belly button *(omphalos)* of the earth. According to the ancients, Zeus discovered this fact by simultaneously releasing two eagles, one toward the east and one toward the west. They collided, impaling each other with their beaks, directly over Delphi. A sacred stone (the belly button itself) marks the spot. Nearby stood the most important oracle of the ancient Mediterranean. The oracle was initially devoted to Gaia (Mother Earth). Gaia was overthrown by the Olympian gods around 800 BC, when Apollo defeated the Python, Gaia's snaky, underworldly son and ruler of the site. The Apollonian oracle drew pilgrims from far and wide, who sought guidance from Pythia, priestess of the oracle.

The temples and treasury building of the ancient oracle have mostly crumbled to rubble, but Delphi remains a place of pilgrimage. Jewelry stores, overpriced restaurants, "Greek Art" trinket shops, and hotels litter the present-day town. Beyond the touristy glitter, the tiny town's mountainside perch and its incredibly beautiful ruins make ancient Delphi a must-see daytrip.

## ORIENTATION AND PRACTICAL INFORMATION



Delphi consists of two streets, **Apollonas** and **Friderikis** (which becomes **Pavlou**), that run parallel through the center of town and connect at each end. The **bus station** is at the western end of town, on Pavlou. The oracle and museum are on Pavlou at the opposite end of town, toward Athens.

**Buses:** From **Terminal B** in Athens (see p. 80), take a bus to **Delphi** (3½hr., 6 per day, 3100dr). Buy your ticket at the booth labeled Δελφοι (Delphi). From Delphi, buses leave for: **Thessaloniki** (5½hr.; M-Sa 10:15am, Su 3:15pm; 6950dr) via **Volos, Larisa,** and **Katerini; Patras** (3hr., 1 per day, 2500dr); **Lamia** (2hr., 3 per day, 1800dr); **Nafpaktos** (2½hr., 4 per day, 2150dr); **Amphissa** (30min., 7 per day 6:30am-8pm, 450dr); **Itea** (30min., 7 per day 6:30am-10pm, 380dr); and **Galaxidi** (50min., 4 per day with a switch in Amphissa, 600dr).

**Taxi Stand** (☎82 000), at the eastern end of Pavlou.

**Tourist Office:** Friderikis 12 (☎82 900), housed in the town hall. Signs marked "Information" in a stucco courtyard on your left (walking toward Athens with the mountain on your right) identify the office; go up the stairs to the first door, where incredibly helpful, quadrilingual **Mrs. Efi** will assist you with bus schedules and accommodations. Open M-F 7:30am-2:30pm. If the office is closed, the bus station (☎82 317) can provide directions and bus information. Open 7:30am-10:30pm.

**Police** (☎82 222), directly behind the church at the peak of Apollonas.

**National Bank:** Pavlou 32 (☎82 622), has a 24hr. **ATM.** Open M-Th 8am-2pm, F 8am-1:30pm.

**Public Toilets:** at the eastern end of Pavlou across from the taxi stand.

**OTE:** In the town hall, next to the tourist office.

**Post Office:** (☎82 376) at Pavlou 25. Open M-F 7:30am-2pm. **Postal code:** 33054.

## ACCOMMODATIONS

Delphi is full of hotels; most are expensive. Almost all of the many hotels can be found on Apollonas or Pavlou. Prices tend to rise during the ski season. Camping is available on the road heading west from Delphi.

**Hotel Sibylla,** Pavlou 9 (☎82 335), provides wonderful views (often balconies) and private baths at the best prices in town. Singles 4000dr; doubles 6000dr; triples 8000dr.

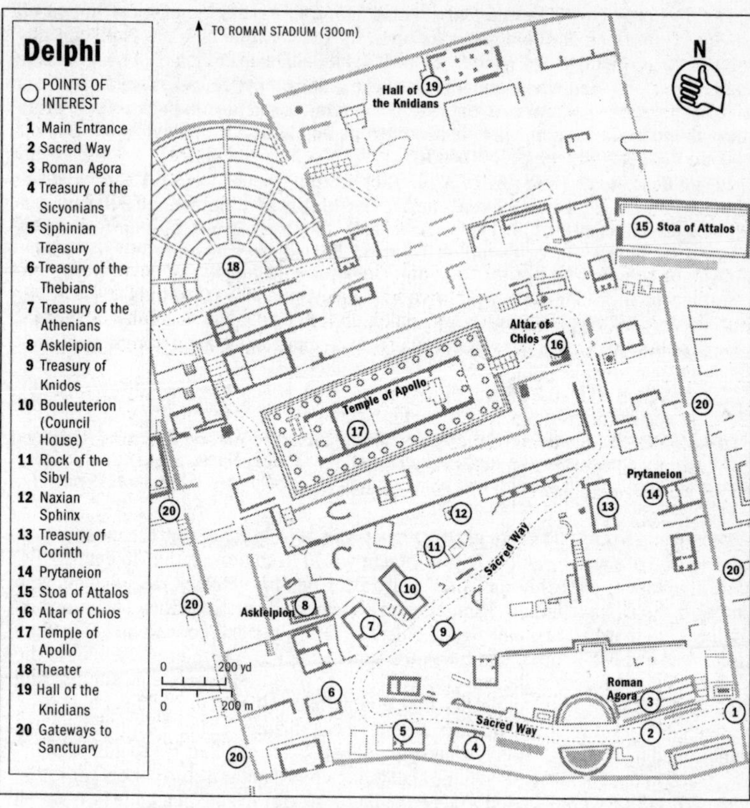




**Hotel Stadion,** Apollonas 21 (☎82 251; fax 82 775). Private balconies accent tiled rooms with TVs, phones, and private baths. Show the jolly, English-speaking owner your *Let's Go* guide and he may give you a discount. Singles 6000dr; doubles 11,000dr.

**Sunview Pension,** Apollonas 84 (☎82 815/349). From the bus station, facing the sea, take a left up the street behind the gas station. The road meets Apollonas at the supermarket; take a left at the top of the hill. Sparkling rooms with private baths and balconies overlook the Gulf. Singles 7000dr; doubles 10,000dr; breakfast included.

**Camping:** The bus can drop you at **Delphi Camping** (☎82 745), 4km from the bus station (1300dr per person; 900dr per tent; 750dr per car); or **Chrissa Camping** (☎82 050), 10km out of town (1400dr per person; prices vary by season). Both sites have swimming pools.

## FOOD AND ENTERTAINMENT

Several **mini-supermarkets** and a **bakery** along Pavlou and Apollonas provide for self-caterers. Delphi's tavernas are fairly indistinguishable and a bit pricey. They do, however, have English menus. Not one, not two, but four pizza places beckon from the western end of Pavlou. Many restaurant terraces overlook the mountains and the Gulf of Corinth. **Taverna Elatos,** Pavlou 65, serves inexpensive starters (*tzatziki* 700dr, *saganaki* 1000dr), with a view. Added bonus: watch your meal a-cooking. (☎82 830. Entrees 1500-2300dr.) The "Belly-Button Taverna", **Taverna Omphalos,** at Apollonas 30, has a lovely vine-covered terrace that overlooks the mountains and serves tasty, relatively inexpensive entrees (1000-2400dr).

Delphi's only two nightclubs are within stumbling distance of most hotels on Pavlou. Both open at 10pm and stay open till the customers leave (substantially later in the more crowded winter season). **Katoi Cub,** near Pavlou 65, boasts a large dance floor, wooden walls, and a view of the gulf. Happy Hour sloshes along from 10 to 11pm with free shots. (Cover 2000dr, includes one drink; beer 1000dr.) Rub elbows with tourists and the local youth at **Delphi at Night,** Pavlou 33. (Cover 1000dr; beer 1000dr; cocktails 1500dr.)

**Delphi Consultants** (☎82 151 or 82 086) organizes traditional **Greek dances** at the Symposium Center. Call for events and dates. In July and August, the **European Cultural Center of Delphi** (☎82 731) puts on a **Festival of Greek Drama** with performances in the ancient stadium of Delphi in July and August; they also present temporary international art exhibitions. (For more on Greek drama, see p. 27.) To find the Center, follow the Amphissa/Itea road down the hill out of town to the blue signs, turn right and head up the hill. (Open 9am to 2pm.) Delphi is home to several other summer **festivals,** so ask around and keep a sharp eye out for posters.

## ORACLE OF DELPHI

*Head out of town toward Athens, following the highway until you see the paved path on the left, which leads to the ruins and museum. ☎82 312. Museum and site 2000dr, museum only 1200dr, students and seniors 600dr, EU students free. Site only 1200dr, students and seniors, 600dr, EU students free.*

A sacred site from 1500 BC or earlier, the Oracle of Delphi became the most important source of sacred wisdom in the ancient world from around the 7th century BC until the advent of Orthodox Christianity after the 4th century AD. Pilgrims ventured to the Delphic Oracle from all over Greece and the Near East (where Alexander the Great had brought Greek culture); later, visitors from Rome's far-flung provinces came in droves, and today the oracle still attracts pilgrims. After all, the Delphic oracle foretold **Cadmus**' founding of Thebes and prophesied the horrific fate of **Oedipus**—to kill his father and marry his mother. The oracle's authority extended beyond religious matters and personal fortune-telling; Delphic approval sanctioned many political decisions, including the reforms that led to pure democracy in Athens. The oracle's pronouncements altered nations and set off (or extinguished) military conflicts. Hoping to make powerful friends, city-states from all over the Greek world erected treasuries and donated immense sums, showing their respect to the oracle with old-fashioned attempts at bribery.

CENTRAL GREECE

The oracle's operation is a bit unclear. The **Pythia,** an older Delphic priestess, would sit over a chasm and inhale the vapors wafting from below. These vapors—the breath of the Python—possessed her, and she became delirious, muttering gibberish. Several priests would then interpret the mutterings, translating them into advice. The chasm, referred to in many ancient texts and whose existence no one

**KNOW THYSELF (OR ELSE)** The Delphic Oracle was known for giving obscure, deceptive, metaphorical answers to pilgrims' questions. Many a suppliant went home more confused than he or she had come, having failed to draw meaning from the answer, or—worse still—having drawn the *wrong* meaning. **Croesus of Sardis,** ruler of a vast territory encompassing most of Asia Minor and the richest man in the ancient world, came to the oracle in the 6th century BC to ask about the Persian threat to his kingdom. The oracle's answer: "A great empire will be destroyed." The king returned to Sardis thinking that he would administer a slamdown to the Persians, whose empire was as large as his own. Croesus found out the hard way that the oracle had meant his own great empire would crash, as he watched his home fall to Persian invaders. Athenian leader **Themistocles** fared better when he asked the oracle how to prepare for another war with ever-pesky Persia. He was told to "build wooden walls." Most interpreted this as an order to enclose Athens in wooden walls, but Themistocles set to work building a fleet of ships. Only after Athens' decisive victory in the First Persian War at the naval battle of Salamis did the Athenians realize their leader's smarts.

in the ancient world doubted, was supposedly accessible from the Temple of Apollo. However, there is no evidence today of one ever existing. The geological instability of the area, however, makes it possible that the original story is true.

**ARCHAEOLOGICAL SITE.** The inscription "Know thyself" (Γνοθι σεαυτον) has long crumbled from the portal of the ancient temple, but still governs the meditative atmosphere of peaceful, windswept ancient Delphi. Cut into the steep mountainside, the ancient oracle reigns over the brush-dotted valley below, and overlooks eagles that fly below the lofty temple. Now, as then, the thrice-destroyed **Temple of Apollo** is the centerpiece of the oracle site. A largely wooden incarnation of the temple was burned in 548 BC; it was again shattered, this time by an earthquake, in 373 BC; it still lies in ruin today. Ancient proclamations are still visible etched along the stone base. To reach the Temple of Apollo, visitors follow the **Sacred Way,** which winds up the site in the footsteps of ancient pilgrims. To the left, you will pass the reconstructed **Treasury of the Athenians,** excavated in the early 20th century. Past the Temple of Apollo, the **theater,** with its geometric perfection and amazing acoustics, is no less impressive. For a taste of the oracle's life as a Roman site, slip your way up the slick steps to the **stadium** at the very top of the hill. Through the archway at the entrance, you'll see the golden brown and green dappled mountains framed before you. If you're exhausted by the thin air and the hundreds of steps, sit among Roman ghosts in the stadium's seats. Before you go, take a few laps around the stadium and imagine the turning posts and cheering crowds. *(Open 7:30am-7:30pm.)*

**ARCHAEOLOGY MUSEUM.** The museum contains many precious artifacts mined from the site: the frieze and two *kouroi* (see p. 20) from the Siphian Treasury, the haunting bronze **Charioteer of Delphi,** the altar from the temple of Athena Pronaia, enormous 7th-century bronze shields, and many ornaments and figurines in gold, silver, and ivory offered to the oracle. Nearly all of the collection was unearthed in 1939 by the **Ecole Française d'Athens.** Most labels are written in French and English as well as Greek, but a guidebook (1000-4000dr) is still helpful. *(Open M noon-6:15pm, Tu-Su 7:30am-2:45pm.)*

**OTHER SITES.** Before calling upon the oracle, pilgrims cleansed themselves both physically and spiritually in the **Castalian Spring,** 300m past the main ruins along the road to Athens. The remains were covered by rocks until the beginning of this century, when a clever archaeologist cleared them out of the lush ravine. You can still see the niches carved into the rock for votive offerings. Drinking from the spring is said to confer the gift of eloquence. Just past the spring, the **Temple of Athena Pronaia** served as a lounge for pilgrims before they entered the sanctuary. The three remaining Doric columns of the **Tholos,** a round building used for an unknown purpose, are the sole evidence of its architectural mastery.



## GALAXIDI Γαλαξιδι ☎0265

The town shares its name with a bittersweet drink made of *gala* (milk) and *xithi* (vinegar), which may be an allusion to the difficult existence of a seaman's wife—Galaxidi used to be a prominent naval base. In its charmed modern incarnation, seafaring has evolved into pleasure boating, as locals lead tours for vacationing Swedes, Danes, and Germans. Quiet throughout most of the year, Galaxidi delights visitors with its peaceful waterfront, sedate gulf-side residences, pebble beaches, and gorgeous view of the surrounding mountains.

**PRACTICAL INFORMATION.** Galaxidi's main street, **Nik. Mama,** leads down from the sole town plateia (and the **bus station**) to the cheapest hotel in town, Hotel Poseidon. **Naucharchou Aggeli** (Ναυαρχου Αγγελη) leads down to the plateia, the harbor, and the waterfront. **Buses** run from Galaxidi to Nafpaktos (1hr., 5 per day 6:15am-9:20pm, 1500dr) and to Itea, where you can transfer to Delphi (1 hr., 3 per day 7:15am-12:30pm, 380dr). Find the **police** (☎41 620) in the main

## SO HE'LL GO NO MORE A-ROVING

Seek out—less often sought than found—
A soldier's grave, for thee the best;
Then look around, and choose thy ground,
And take thy rest.
—George Gordon, Lord Byron, "On This Day I Complete My Thirty-Sixth Year"

Though **Messolongi,** a stop on the Athens-Delphi-Astakos bus route, may not walk in beauty like the night, it does hold **Lord Byron**'s heart—literally. The city has the sad distinction of being the place Lord Byron caught fever and met his end in 1824, while leading the local troops in the War of Independence (see p. 16). A small **War of Independence Museum** in the old town hall at the center of the plateia includes an unexceptional collection of Byron memorabilia. A Byron pilgrim's trail points to the large statue of the poet dressed in Greek garb, in front of the Hotel Liberty, just before the entrance to the Garden of Heroes. The park consists mainly of crumbling busts and other poorly maintained monuments to national war heroes; **Byron's heart** is buried beneath his statue. The noise and dirt of modern Messolongi may be tragically unromantic, but Byron would be content that the city is indeed free.

plateia across from the bus station. The **pharmacy** is one block to the right of the bus station up Nik. Mama. (☎41 122. Open M-Sa 8:30am-1pm and 6-9pm.) The **National Bank** is several blocks further down Nik. Mama, past the Hotel Poseidon on the left. (With 24hr. **ATM.** Open M-Th 8:30am-2pm, F 8:30am-1:30pm). **Public toilets and showers** are in the harbor before the forest on the right. Galaxidi's **post office** is next to the bank on Nik. Mama. (Open 7:30am-1:30pm.) **Postal code:** 33052.



**ACCOMMODATIONS AND FOOD.** From the bus stop, turn right and head down Nik. Mama to find **Hotel Poseidon,** a breezy old home-turned-hotel blessed with an ultra-friendly manager, **Costas,** who just may break open a bottle of *ouzo* on the evening of your arrival. Choose rooms with old-world charm or modern convenience (A/C, TV, and private bath). (☎41 426. Singles 7000-10,000dr; doubles 11,000-14,000dr.) On a summer weekend, expect prices to be 20% higher. There are also a few **domatia:** keep your eyes peeled for signs or ask at the bus station.

**To Perasma,** across from the National Bank, sells old standbys for typical prices (gyros 400dr, souvlaki 250dr). On Kon. Satha to the left of Nik. Mama before the Hotel Poseidon, **Taverna Albatross** is a cheap, sit-down alternative (starters 500-900dr, entrees 1000dr and up). If you're splurging, head to one of the tavernas along the harbor for a great view and tasty seafood. For the best deal, head to the bakeries on Nik. Mama.

**SIGHTS AND ENTERTAINMENT.** The **Nautical Museum,** off Kon. Satha to the left from Nik. Mama, houses a plethora of artifacts covering most of the town's long history, from 4th century BC black and red pots to navigational equipment from the 19th century AD. (Open M-F 8:30am-1:30pm, 500dr.) Farther down Kon. Satha, the **Church of Agios Nicholas** houses many fine mosaics. The 13th-century **Monastery of Transfiguration,** with sublime centuries-old wood carvings and a great view of town, is 6km from Galaxidi on the uphill road outside of town. Though the unshaded, uphill trip takes an hour by foot, on a cool day the views make it a perfect hike; follow K. Papapetrou out of town past the school and into the terraced orange orchards. Otherwise, consider hiring a taxi in front of the bus station. In the early spring, Galaxidi shakes off its sleepiness with the leftover Bacchanalian frenzy that is **Pre-Lenten Carnival.** Ouzo bottles are emptied by the hundreds as fantastically costumed people come from miles around for extraordinary once-a-year carousing. Revelers gyrate in traditional dances around a fire and throw brightly colored pigments at each other. If you want to keep your costume clean, stick to the dances by the town's children; they'll be in traditional garb.

**BEACHES.** Rocky shoreline stretches out past the docks on the forest side of the harbor; small, wonderful, pebbly beaches are scattered throughout. Walk Nik. Mama to the waterfront, then follow the harbor toward the forest to your left until you find a resting place that suits you. Several tiny islands are within easy swimming distance, ideal for solitary tanning, snoozing, or snuggling.

## NAFPAKTOS Ναυπακτος ☎0634

From the towering battlements of the Venetian castle on the hill above the city, you can look down over all of Nafpaktos, a bustling port city and a hot beach spot. Relatively untouristed by foreigners, summer brings weekending urbanites and Greek families from Patras and Athens. Nafpaktos derives its name from its ancient role as a ship-building naval colony—its name literally means "manufacturing ships." Although less peaceful and idyllic than some Sterea Ellada port towns, Nafpaktos's nightlife hops in summer; its beaches are pretty and it provides key ferry service to the Peloponnese via nearby Antirrio.

**ORIENTATION AND PRACTICAL INFORMATION.** For help navigating the city, consult Chris Zographos in his kiosk, the first on the plateia next to the bus stop. He happily offers advice in an Iowa-educated American accent. Buses from points east drop off at **Athinon** at the base of the main town plateia. The **bus station** itself is across from the church just down the street that intersects Athinon at the bus stop. Take a **bus** to Antirrio (15min., 2 per hr. 6am-10pm, 280dr) to catch the **ferry** that serves the Peloponnese. Buses leave for Athens (3½hr., 1 per hr. 5am-11pm, 3800dr) and Thessaloniki (4hr., 1:30 and 3pm, 7750dr). **Taxis** (☎27 792 or 27 878) are in the plateia, as are phones for calling them. In case of emergency, call the **police** (☎27 258). The **Second Alpha** (Τραπεζα Πιστεως) and the **National Bank** both have 24hr. **ATMs** and identical hours. (Open M-Th 8am-2pm, F 8am-1:30pm.) There are **pharmacies** around the plateia, all with varying hours; if one's closed, there should be a sign telling you which others are open. Follow Athinon as it curves slightly downhill and then to the right past the Old Port to find an **Internet cafe.** (Open 10am-2pm and 5-11pm, 1500dr per hr.) You can also get connected at the **Golden Beach Hotel** on Psani beach. (☎21 444. 1500dr per hr., 30min. minimum.) The **post office** is several blocks down Athinon from the banks, on the right side of the street. (☎27 232. Open M-F 7:30am-2pm.) **Postal code:** 30300.



**ACCOMMODATIONS AND FOOD.** **Hotel Diethnes** on Odos Messologgiou, across from the Internet cafe, has hardwood floors and blindingly white private baths. Look for the purple shutters on the right. (☎27 342. Singles 6000dr; doubles 7000dr.) **Pension Aphrodite,** on the waterfront to the left of the Old Port, has it all: private baths, TVs, phones, and a view, at a great price. (☎27 370. Singles 6000; doubles 8000. Be sure to specify pension and not hotel.) **Hotel Niki** is a convenient place to plunk down your pack. Follow Athinon two blocks to the right from the main plateia for spare rooms with phones and private baths on a busy, noisy street. (☎28 901. Singles 6000dr; doubles 12,000dr.)

Bakeries, souvlaki stands, and fast food restaurants jumble together near the central plateia and Old Port. Head to the waterfront for tavernas; veer left for the best prices. The first of the bunch, **O Stavros,** offers starters for around 500dr (entrees 800-1600dr). Dozens of trendy cafes surround the small port protected by the castle walls; these more expensive places become lively only after 10pm.

**SIGHTS AND ENTERTAINMENT.** The 15th-century **Venetian castle** dominates the picturesque town, with five zones of fortification from port to crest. Footpaths wind around the walls, past fountains, and through century-old gates; one begins off Athinon just past the post office, on the right. A leisurely walk to the main fortifications on the hill takes about 25min. For a more circuitous route, stop at the fountains and detour through the original castle buildings.

Most leisure time around Nafpaktos is spent on the town's beaches; many villagers take a break every afternoon to relax on the beach and swim. The best beaches are to the right of the Old Port, as you face the water. Families dominate **Psani Beach;** small amenities, like playgrounds and a few **public showers,** add to the experience. Calm waters and flat, pebbly shores invite swimmers to explore both sides of the Old Port. Cafes and *ouzeris* along the waterfront to the left and in the port are filled with customers from 8:30 until 11:30pm, when families hit the road and everyone else hits the clubs. **Club Cinema** is conveniently located one block up from the waterfront, on Messinion. (☎26 02[illegible] Cover 1000dr, drinks 900dr. Open F and Sa 11:30pm until late.) **The Blue Lake** claims to be open "all day, everyday" and features traditional Greek music on Friday, Saturday, and Sunday nights. (☎51 900. Cover 1000dr, drinks 2000dr.) You'll need a taxi ride to get there. Nafpaktos's week-long **Pre-Lenten carnival celebration** is nothing to sniff at (although some townsfolk migrate to **Patras**'s larger scale festivities), with music everywhere, dancing, free wine, and free souvlaki in the Old Port.

# EVRITANIA EYPITANIA

Often called the "Switzerland of Greece," this mountainous land was once a refuge for Greeks escaping Ottoman rule. Now it's a paradise for nature enthusiasts and hikers, with its clean air, green forests of fir and walnut, trails that wander past tiny mountain villages to the highest peaks of the Louchi Mountains, and opportunities to raft, canoe, and kayak the Achelos and Tavropos Rivers. Evritania's winding trails lure visitors through pristine forests and meadows, past mountain lakes, to tiny hamlets of stone farmhouses beside rolling fields. Old churches and shrines dot the mountains and overlook steep gorges formed by the rushing Karpenisiotis, Krikelopotamos, and Tavropos Rivers.



The best way to explore Evritania is either by car or by foot (or by switching back and forth between hiking and driving), and with plenty of time to explore the mountains' hidden treasures. There's no place to rent a car or moped in Karpenisi; the nearest rental office is **Hillco Rent-a-Car** (☎(0231) 37 086) in Lamia (p. 179), where cars cost 4200-6400dr per day (prices higher from July to September). They deliver cars for an extra charge of 120dr per km.

Backpackers should contact the **Hellenic Alpine Club (EOS),** which runs several mountain refuge huts throughout Evritania. (Karpenisi Office: ☎(0237) 23 051; Lamia Office: ☎(0231) 26 786). The more adventurous can be outfitted at **Trekking Hellas,** past the Karpenisi plateia down Zinopoulou on the right (☎(0237) 25 940), which offers kayak, rafting, 4x4 driving, and ski services and supplies. The best map of the region is on sale at the *periptero* in the plateia in Karpenisi, and is well worth the 2000dr for hiking routes, a topographical key, and an invaluable guide to the area's history.

**MOONSHINE** Ask almost any taverna owner in Evritania for a taste of *tsipouro* and he'll give you a knowing wink, disappear into the back, and reappear with a chilled bottle of clear Greek moonshine. Regular old legal wine is distilled all over Evritania, using local grapes. When they're done with the grapes, however, the farmers don't throw them away. Instead, they boil down the leftovers for a couple of days before distilling the residue in clear river water. The result is a fiery transparent alcohol that will burn your throat and clear your sinuses with a vengeance. Though illegal, *tsipouro* can be found at virtually every taverna in Evritania. Beware, though: it packs a powerful punch, and tastes a bit like wine-flavored tequila mixed with lighter fluid.

## KARPENISI Καρπενησι ☎0237

Karpenisi (pop. 10,000), at the tip of a long stretch of hairpinned roadway, is Evritania's relaxed capital and the perfect base for outdoor explorations in the surrounding countryside and villages. Founded when five agrarian settlements in the foothills of Mt. Timfristos merged early in the era of Ottoman rule, Karpenisi has acquired a healthy tourist industry, catering mainly to Greek outdoor enthusiasts.

Unlike some of its neighboring cities, Karpenisi's post-Civil War and post-Second World War rebuilding was executed with some eye toward aesthetic appeal. In the broad main plateia, where old men still occasionally strum a guitar and join in a melancholy sing-along, a floor mosaic of whorled designs spells out the names of the region's old towns. South of Karpenisi, the streets give way to rolling pastures populated only by stone farmhouses and herds of curious goats. Karpenisi's friendly atmosphere, natural beauty, and stunning views make it the perfect getaway from the noise of other, more touristed areas.

**ORIENTATION.** Karpenisi sits at the foot of Mt. Velouchi, which rises up about 70km west of Lamia in central Sterea Ellada. Everything of importance is within a 5min. walk from the **bus station.** From the station, Tsamboula leads downhill to the spacious plateia, where it changes its name to **Zinopoulou.** After passing the plateia, the road splits in a V, with **Karpenisioti** heading down to the right and Zinopoulou continuing on the left. Most of the town's shops are on these two streets. The other main road, **Eth. Antistaseos,** forks off to the right from Zinopoulou at the top end of the plateia. As Eth. Antistaseos passes the plateia, **Grigoriou Tsitsara** branches off to the left, running roughly parallel to Zinopoulou and Karpenisioti. The largest **church** and the **town hall** are on the north end of the plateia, near a **monument** to Greek soldiers who died in 20th century wars. Above the bus station, the town climbs up the hillside in a tangle of steep, winding streets and narrow stairways, where you can catch a view of the gorgeous valley below.

**PRACTICAL INFORMATION. Buses** run to **Agrinio** (3½hr., 9am and 3:15pm, 2150dr); **Athens** (5hr., 3 per day 9am-3:30pm, 5000dr); **Koryshades** (10min., 6am and 1pm, 250dr); **Lamia** (1¾ hr., 3 per day 6:30am-12:30pm, 1450dr); **Proussos** (M, W, F 1pm; 650dr); and **Mikro Horio** and **Megalo Horio** (20min., 7am and 1pm, 350dr). Ask at the bus station about bus service to smaller villages. In winter, buses to the **Velouchi Ski Center** (12km away) can be arranged for larger groups (1500-2000dr). **Taxis** (☎22 666 or 22 100) line up at the stand just downhill from the bus station.

The **tourist office** is on the left as you walk down from the bus. The basement office is behind an inconspicuous door beneath a green handpainted sign. The friendly English-speaking staff offers regional maps, brochures, and ideas for excursions into the Evritanian countryside, including hiking, rafting, camping, canyoning, and parachuting. (☎/fax 21 016. Open M-Sa 10am-2pm and 5-9pm, Su 10am-2pm.) Brochures with maps of Karpenisi and the surrounding villages, including extensive hiking trails, can be purchased at the *periptero* across the street. There are a number of 24hr. **ATMs,** including one at the **National Bank** in the plateia. (Open M-Th 8am-2pm, F 8:30am-1:30pm.) The **police station** (☎25 100. Open 24hr.) and the **OTE** (Open 7am-10pm.) are on Eth. Antistaseos. The **hospital** (☎80 680) is a 10min. walk past the police station. The **post office** is just off to the left of the bottom of Karpenisioti. (Open M-F 7:30am-2pm.) **Postal code:** 36100.

**ACCOMMODATIONS.** The best option is to stay in one of many **domatia:** Karpenisi brims with cheap rooms to let. The tourist office lists available rooms and prices. Friendly former Boston resident **Konstantinos Kousigos** offers rooms at his house down the hill from the bus station at the top of a tall flight of stone steps; a view, private bath, and comfy beds make it homey. (☎21 400. Double rooms 8000-10,000dr depending on season.) **Taverna Megampelia** (☎23 171), in the countryside on the road to Mikro Horio, has small but clean and quiet rooms for 9000dr.

Rates at Karpenisi's hotels increase during ski season and summer, often by as much as 100%. In both high seasons, hotel prices also jump on weekends. **Hotel Galini,** Riga Feriou 3, is set back on a quiet side street; to reach it, walk down G. Tsitsara and make your second right. True to its name ("peace"), it offers simple, comfortable rooms with balconies, TVs, phones, and private baths at very cheap rates. (☎22 914; fax 25 623. Singles 6000dr; doubles 8000dr.) **Hotel Elvetia,** Zinopoulou 7, has pleasant but noisy rooms with TVs, radios, phones, balconies, private baths, and a cozy lounge area. Also offers group rates in season. (☎80 111; fax 80 112. Singles 6500-13,000dr; doubles 9000-16,000dr; family suite 16,000-32,000dr. Breakfast 800-1200dr.)

**FOOD.** To scrounge up your own meal, visit the **bakery** and large **supermarket** on Karpenisioti. **I Klimataria,** Kosmai Etolou 25 (☎22 230), downhill and around the corner from Hotel Galini, is decorated with antique local handicrafts like a handwoven tapestry and an old-school butter churn; a 1953 Rock-Ola American jukebox brings the restaurant into the 20th century. The gregarious owner, whose family has owned the restaurant for over a century, will translate the menu for you. Excellent local dishes run from 1600-1900dr. On the road toward Mikro Horio about 2km south of town, dine outdoors on local specialties like rustic salad and fresh trout from the neighboring river at the brookside **Taverna Megampelia.** Stay the night upstairs in their domatia if the walk back to Karpenisi seems too far. (☎23 171. Entrees 500-1500dr. Open for dinner.) The three-inch thick crumbly slab of baklava at **Kitsios**, Zinopoulou 13 (☎25 504), is full of enough honey, nuts, and flaky pastry to merit a trip to Karpenisi by itself (300dr).

**NIGHTLIFE AND ENTERTAINMENT.** If there's still life in your legs after dinner, you might want to hit one of the many bars near the plateia. Karpenisi's most popular club, **Nemesis,** is about 1.5km south of town on the road to Koryshades. Tourists and Karpenisians groove to house and trance until 2:30am, and then it's strictly Greek music until dawn. (Drinks 1000-2300dr. Cover 1500dr. Open F and Sa, midnight-6am.) Young people crowd into **Pieros** on Zinopoulou, and sip beers and *frappés* at tables on the street. (☎22 382. Drinks 1000-1500dr. Open 7am-1am.) Later, head down the street to **Byzantio,** the bar of choice for most young Karpenisian late nights; it doesn't start rocking until well after midnight. (☎35 606. Open 12am-6am.) **De Facto,** just past the police station on Eth. Antistaseos, has an all-Greek jukebox and outdoor seating. (☎24 455. Drinks 1000-2000dr. Open 6am-3am.) Down the road from Nemesis, a replica stagecoach announces the American-themed **Saloon,** where the stereo blares country music, patrons slug Jack Daniel's, and dancing begins on the floor and ends up on the tables. (☎24 606. Drinks 1000-1500dr. Open 10am-6am.) For traditional Greek music, head to **Musikes Epafes,** Kosma Aitovou 17, a door down from Klimataria restaurant. (☎25 555. Open F-Sa.) Throughout summer, saints' days are celebrated with religious services in the mornings and food, music, and dancing at night. In mid-July, the town hosts a 15-day *Yiortes Dhassous* ("Celebration of the Forest") replete with exhibitions and, of course, more food and music.



## NEAR KARPENISI

Outside Karpenisi, small villages and traditional settlements beckon visitors to gorgeous rural views and hikes. The forested, mountainous terrain encourages rambles. Old-fashioned stone houses abut lakes, and omnipresent herds of goats snooze on hillsides. Hotels can be expensive in the area: domatia offer much better deals. Some people choose to camp off trails, but this is illegal.

The side-by-side villages of **Gorgianades** and **Koryshades** (4km southwest of Karpenisi) are traditional settlements with beautifully preserved stone mansions, terraced farmland, and elaborate wooden balconies characteristic of the area. To get there, follow the main highway downhill out of town, take the right at the fork in the road, and follow the signs for Gorgianades. The National Council convened

in 1944 in the schoolhouse in Koryshades; the site has been turned into a small **museum.** West of Karpenisi lies the village of **Klafsion** (8km away), a village whose name—derived from the Greek verb "to cry"—is a tribute to the hardships endured by the townspeople when they survived a 279 BC disaster caused by Galates. The church dates to the 5th century and features an ancient mosaic floor. Beyond lie **East** and **West Frangista** (40km from Karpenisi), home of a fresco-covered church well worth visiting. Find fresh local trout, traditional sausages, *katiki* cheese, and wonderful, fresh country bread at the village tavernas. The **Monastery of Tatarnas,** west of Frangista and 70km from Karpenisi, was built in 1555 and served as a refuge for rebels against the Turks. The extensive Byzantine art collection includes an icon of "The Lord of Glory," painted in 1350. Backpackers can take the **Trans-European Footpath E4** where it passes through Evritania on a two-day hike from Karpenisi, through the village of **Krikelo,** all the way to **Mount Oxia** in the southwestern extreme of Evritania.

## MIKRO HORIO Μικρο Οριο

Fifteen kilometers down the road from Karpenisi and accessible by bus (15min., 280dr) are the forested new and old "little villages," Neo and Paleo Mikro Horio. **Paleo Mikro Horio** was largely destroyed by a landslide in 1962; a 19th century church and the village square, consisting of five old water fountains, survived. The cool, shaded plateia overlooks terraced farmland rising from the gorge below. After the disaster, the population relocated down the hill to **Neo Mikro Horio** (pop. 250), on the slopes of **Mt. Xelidona.** WWII bombs scarred the new village, and occupying Nazis executed the town's 13 leading dignitaries in 1944. The route to the top of the mountain (about 3hr.) starts near the bus stop; from the summit, a view of the river valleys and Kremaston Lake rewards you. Mikro Horio has just begun to direct its attention to tourism. Lodgings range from simple, cheap domatia to expensive ski lodge-style hotels. **Taverna Nyonia** has rooms to let above a restaurant. (☎41 393. Doubles 8000dr.)

## MEGALO HORIO Μεγαλο Οριο

A visit to Megalo Horio ("Big Village," with a whopping population of 300) seems like a time warp back to 1900, complete with flagstone streets, dilapidated churches, and low stone houses. Old shepherds argue with each other in the plateia and bang their crooks on the ground for emphasis. The *kafeneio* tables on the plateia overlook the breathtaking gorge of the Karpenisiotis River. A gnarled plane tree shades the plateia and a large lime tree tints the summer air with the delicate scent of its blossoms; village women gather these flowers to make tea, which you can sample by asking for *tsa* at a village cafe. The red sign by Megalo Horio's post office, visible from the plateia, marks the trailhead for the path up **Mount Kaliakouda,** a 3hr. climb posted with red blazes. The **Lacomata,** a monument to the Battle of Kaliakouda in 1821, borders the village of Aniada. A charmingly crusty old man leads tours at the **Folk Art Museum,** easily found by following the signs from the plateia. The collection houses traditional farming equipment, a shepherd's goat-wool *kapa* (coat), a 19th century Turkish grain sieve made of goat hide, a Revolution-era rifle, and a still for brewing *tsipouro*—Greek moonshine. (☎41 502. Open 10am-2am and 6-8pm; Nov.-May Th, Sa-Su only. Free.)

Reach Megalo Horio by the bus from Karpenisi that runs through Mikro Horio. Like the rest of Evritania, Megalo Horio abounds with homes offering domatia. Cheap rooms can be hard to find during high season, however, so look around before settling into one. The rooms at **Petrino** have TVs and fireplaces, and can be economical if shared with someone else. (☎41 187. Doubles 15,000-25,000dr.) Local tavernas dot the nearby countryside. Ask for **Maria Mahalioti** at the store (☎41 263) in the plateia, and she'll display her selection of homemade sweets, jams, honey, and teas. Enjoy the sunshine, clear blue skies, the shade of a twisted old tree, and the view of a river gorge at **Antigone** (☎41 395) in the plateia. They serve sandwiches, omelettes, and Greek coffee all day in the open air.

## PROUSSOS Προυσσος ☎0237

Though small and easy to skip over accidentally, Proussos is an absolutely gorgeous little town, with stunning views over the neighboring gorge and mountainside. The views from Proussos are some of the highlights of the Evritania region.

**ORIENTATION AND PRACTICAL INFORMATION.** Getting to **Proussos,** 15km past Megalo Horio, is an adventure in itself; enjoy the roadside scenery and admire the KTEL driver's uncanny ability to maintain control of his vehicle as it swerves alongside steep ravines past intermittent, flimsy guardrails and shrines to drivers killed on the road. From Megalo or Mikro Horio, you'll need to walk back down to the main road, or to the tiny hamlet of **Gavros,** to catch the Proussos-bound bus from Karpenisi (M, W, F 1pm, 650dr). The village climbs upward from a central plateia, which overlooks the gasp-inducing gorge below.

**ACCOMMODATIONS AND FOOD.** Proussos has no hotels, but like most of the villages in Evritania, many homes offer domatia for fairly inexpensive prices; most are on the road through the main village. The plateia in Proussos sports many local tavernas, most of which overlook the gorge and the river below. **I Proussiotissa** (☎80 768) has the best location of them all, with balcony tables hanging over the valley and looking out on the monastery and clock tower. The owner cooks up local specialties such as roast goat with tomato sauce (1600dr); ask him and he'll serve you a bit of his homebrewed bathtub *tsipouro* (see **Moonshine,** p. 174), which may well knock you flat.



**SIGHTS.** Just before reaching the village, a road leads down from the statue of Karaiskakis, to the serene **Monastery of the Virgin of Proussiotissa** that clings spectacularly to the cliffside. Founded in the 12th century, the monastery's innermost sanctuary is blasted out of the stone itself, and contains a miracle-working icon of the Madonna said to have been painted by St. Luke the Evangelist (see below). Dress modestly (long skirt or pants, shoulders covered) to visit the monastery, where a monk will hospitably offer you a piece of "special delight," the Greek version of the Turkish. In the evenings, monks' chants mingle with the sound of rushing water from the Karpenisiotis River echoing through the ravine. Above, Proussos' clock tower belts out the hour from its precarious hilltop perch. The **Castle Of Karaiskakis** is a small stone fortress near the monastery; though it's more of a crumbling tower than a castle, it adds a mood of mystery. The eerie **Black Cave,** allegedly an ancient oracle and a hideout for Greek women and children during the War of Independence, can be found along a trail that begins on the far side of Proussos, near a bridge. Bring a flashlight if you want to explore more.

**HAVE ICON, WILL TRAVEL** Local legend has it that the Virgin Mary herself visited Proussos in the 8th century, during the Iconoclast period (see p. 14). The Church had recently declared that traditional paintings and relief-icons of Christ and the Virgin, popular all over the Byzantine empire, violated the Second Commandment against worshiping idols; all icons were ordered destroyed. The Virgin Mary didn't cotton to this anti-icon business, and personally delivered an icon to Proussos all the way from the Turkish city of Prousa. On the way, she left her footprints in the rocks near Gavros and passed through Mt. Kaliakouda, leaving a hole in her wake. Another tradition holds that two monks brought the icon when they founded the Monastery of the Virgin of Proussiotissa in the 12th century. In either case, the icon remains greatly revered throughout the area.

# LAMIA Λαμια

☎0231

Bustling, rarely touristed Lamia conceals a multifaceted charm beneath a drab appearance: the repetitive, concrete exterior hides a town that considers itself a nightlife capital of Greece. Lamia's four central plateias and tiny, criss-crossing pedestrian streets brim with non-stop energy. Lazy, shaded squares where old men argue for hours give way to streets crammed with slickly dressed teenagers on motorcycles. A key strategic town during the War of Independence (see p. 16), Lamia became the border gateway for the newly independent Greece before the annexation of Thessaly in 1884. A snappy archaeological museum high up within the *kastro* walls, a nighttime scene that never seems to go to bed, and the beautifully tended gardens of Agios Loukas are all worthwhile reasons to stop in Lamia.

## GETTING THERE AND GETTING AROUND

Lamia apportions one individual KTEL bus station and *kafeneion* for nearly every major city in Greece, making it one of the most inconvenient transportation hubs. To reach the city center from the local **train station** or the **bus stations** serving Athens, Thessaloniki, Karpenisi, and most local destinations, walk uphill on **Satovriandou,** which ends in Pl. Parkou. If arriving at the Delphi or Trikala/Larisa/Patras **bus stops,** walk up **Thermopylon** across the railroad tracks and make a left on Kapodistrion for Pl. Parkou. From the Volos bus stop, take Rozaki Angeli away from the intersection to **Kolokotroni,** turn right, and follow it to Pl. Laou.

**Buses:** From the largest station (☎51 345 or 51 346), south of the town center at Papakiriazi 27, buses run to **Athens** (3hr.; 5am-4pm every hr., 5:30pm, 6:20pm; 4000dr) and **Thessaloniki** (4hr.; Su-Th 9:15am F and Su also 7pm; 5500dr). The station for **Karpenisi** (2hr., 5 per day 7am-9pm, 1450dr) and the Evritania region, at Botsari 3 (☎28 955), is to the left, one block down from Satovriandou. Between these two, the road leads downhill to the local station (☎51 347 or 51 348) at Konstantinopoulos 2, which runs buses to **Thermopylae** (15min., 5 per day 5:40am-4:35pm, 450dr), among other small locales. To the east, across the railway track on the right, is the station for **Delphi** (2hr., 3 per day 10:40am-7pm, 2200dr) at Thermopylon 58 (☎35 494). The Thessaly station (☎22 802) is a little farther south at Thermopylon and Nikopoleos 1. To: **Larisa** (2hr., 3 per day 11:15am-6:15pm, 2750dr); **Patras** (4hr., 3 per day 12:30pm-12:45am, 3700dr); and **Trikala** (1¾hr., 7 per day 9:45am-7:45pm, 1950dr). The Volos station, Rosaki Angeli 69 (☎22 627), in the northeast runs buses to: **Volos** (2hr.; Su-F 9am, 3pm, Sa 9am; 2550dr); the beaches of **Agia Marina** (20min.; every 30min. 8am-1pm, every hour 1pm-9pm; 280dr); and **Raches** (5min., 5 per day 5:45am-8pm, 650dr).

**Local buses:** Buses marked "Stauros" (Σταυρος) also make stops at Lionokladi, departing frequently at the corner of Drosopolou and Hatzopolou streets at Pl. Parkou.

**Trains:** Trains to **Athens** run from the orange trees of the town station, Konstantinopoulos 1 (☎22 990), across from the local buses. **Lionokladi Station** (☎06 161) runs trains to **Thessaloniki** (3¾hr., 8 per day 9:28am-3am, 3000dr) and **Athens** (3½hr., 5 per day 9:00am-2:50am, 2600dr). Take the local bus (10min., 13 per day 8:25am-10:30pm, 400dr) from the OSE office, Averof 28. Walk down E. Venizelou from the southwest corner of Pl. Parkou, and make the third right onto Averof.

## ORIENTATION AND PRACTICAL INFORMATION

Just inland off the Maliakos Gulf and 160km north of Athens, Lamia's tangle of streets climbs gently into a northwesterly ridge, crowned by the **Kastro** in the north. The city sprawls outward from the roughly rectangular arrangement of its four central plateias, all with umbrella-filled outdoor cafes. Southeastern **Pl. Parkou** is broad, crowded, and swarming with motorcycles; it's also the busy departure point for the local buses. From here, **Kolokotroni** leads north to leafy and mellow **Pl. Laou,** shaded by plane trees and filled with *kafeneia* and the Greek men

who idle there. West from Pl. Parkou up **Karagiannopolou** is sleepy, spacious **Pl. Diakou.** From here, Diakou runs northeast to pulsing **Pl. Eleftherias,** home to Lamia's trendiest nightlife. Pl. Eleftherias connects back to Pl. Parkou along **Rigou Ferias;** several small stairways lead to nearby Pl. Laou. On the north side of Pl. Eleftherias, Lamia's largest **church** and **town hall** face each other on the corner of **Ipsilandon.** A network of small, pedestrian streets like **Rozaki Angeli** and **Karaiskaki** interlace the four squares and burst with small cafes, shops, and bakeries.

**Tourist office,** Pl. Laou 3 (☎30 065), next to the Hotel Neon Astron. A friendly, English-speaking staff can inform you about Lamia and Central Greece. Open M-F 7am-2:30pm.

**Banks:** There are several banks with 24hr. **ATMs** on Pl. Parkou, including one on the west side that offers currency exchange. Open M-Th 8-2pm, F 8-1pm.

**Police** (☎22 331), on Patroklou, one street below Pl. Parkou, but they speak very little English. Open 24hr.

**Hospital** (☎30 126/121), on Karaiskaki, 5min. north of the town center. Open 24hr.

**OTE:** On the west side of Pl. Eleftherias. Open 24hr.

**Internet Access: Internet Cafe,** Ipsilandon 6 (☎22 133); just off of Pl. Eleftherias. Provides Internet access and coffee. 1000dr per hr., minimum 5dr. Open 9am-midnight.

**Post office** (☎47 718; fax 33 727), on Pl. Diakou and offers Post Restante. Open M-F 7am-8pm. **Postal Code:** 35100.

## ACCOMMODATIONS



Few tourists or budget travelers see Lamia, so hotels are scarce and expensive.

**Hotel Neon Astron** (☎22 246), on Pl. Laou. Though noisy from street traffic, offers an excellent location, airy rooms with ceiling fans, private baths, and balconies at good rates. Singles 6000dr, with TV 7000dr; doubles 8000dr.

**Thermopylae Hotel,** Rozaki Angeli 36 (☎26 393 or 21 366), two blocks east of Pl. Laou. Has 15 rooms that are small and drab but clean and comfortable, and include TVs, phones, A/C, and private baths. Singles 8000dr; doubles 10,000dr.

**Hotel Athena,** Rozaki Angeli 41 (☎20 700 or 27 700), has pricey, small, dark, bare rooms. Singles 8500dr, with breakfast 10,000dr; doubles with breakfast 15,000dr.

## FOOD

Lamia is a diner's paradise: virtually every street and side alley is crammed with pizza joints, stands hawking souvlaki and gyros, *ouzeris*, tavernas, pastry shops, and coffee bars. For fresh fruits and veggies, head to the **markets** along Rozaki Angeli and Othonos, both off Pl. Laou. Strolling south from Pl. Laou along the pedestrian street Karaiskaki, carnivores will drool at the windows of countless souvlaki joints featuring whole lambs warming on spits.

**Taverna O Togos** (☎23 501), right off Pl. Laou on Aristoteli, is a romantic outdoor eatery that serves tasty specialties like *tsoukalaki* (beef in wine sauce; 1600dr) and lamb *exohiko* (lamb, cheese, and potatoes baked in paper; 1700dr).

**Allo Schedio** (☎42 711) serves an array of foods, including fresh fish. Walk along the east end of Pl. Eleftherias past the three sidewalk bars, and descend the stairs. There's no menu—just follow the waiter into the kitchen and select your fish.

**Aman Aman,** a few meters north of Pl. Laou and to the left, offers tasty *mezedes* (500-1000dr). "Aman," which means mercy in Turkish, is the opening wail to many of the *rembetika* (see **Bouzouki Punk Rock,** p. 34) that the local intellectual crowd gathers to hear. Open 9am-12:30am.

## NIGHTLIFE AND ENTERTAINMENT

Young people from the Lamia area congregate around Pl. Eleftherias every night, zooming in on motor bikes and crowding around the bars and cheap gyro stands. For

those looking to dance, there are plenty of clubs; for a more sedentary night out, check out the three similar bars in northeast Pl. Eleftherias: **Camelot** (☎34 490), **Contratta** (☎39 595), and **Diva** (☎34 840) offer plentiful outdoor seating in the plateia (beer 800dr).

On summer nights, most intrepid party-goers head to the seashore at **Raches** or **Agia Marina** in the countryside. These clubs are best reached by private vehicle—a taxi to the most popular clubs, **Bojo** or **Active** at Raches, or **Yazz Club** will cost 4000 to 5000dr until midnight, when the rates double. The **Municipal Theatre** (☎33 325) on Ipsilandon, a few blocks past Internet Cafe, offers a year-long program of plays, music, and movies. Visit their offices in the **movie theater** across the street.

**Fuego** (☎23 180), behind the Municipal Theater on Ipsilandon, is like a small, happening cave, staffed by folks who speak good-natured, sarcastic English. Beer 1000dr, drinks 1500-2000dr. Open 6pm-3:30am.

**Splendid** (☎52 726), on Ipsilandon, off Pl. Eleftherias. This ultra-trendy night spot serves drinks and beer to the hip and hot until 3am.

**Venezia** (☎36 808), on the left between Pl. Diakou and Pl. Eleftherias, is a pretentious place to see and be seen among Lamia's would-be cosmopolitan youth. Put on your tightest garb and make your way through the clutter of motorbikes on the curb. Beer 1000dr, drinks 1300dr. Open 8am-4am.

## SIGHTS

**KASTRO.** The imposing remains of the Kastro fortifications loom eerily over the city in nighttime illumination. Built in the Classical period, it has been subsequently added to by virtually everyone who has invaded Greece since, including the Romans, Franks, Catalans, and Ottomans. Before Greece's 1884 annexation of Thessaly and Domokos, Lamia's Kastro served as the core of the country's border defenses. Now in ruins, the castle still offers a stunning view of Lamia, the plains, and the mountains beyond. The barracks building, built by King Otto in 1880, was used until the Second World War, but now serves as a spacious and well-organized **Archaeological Museum.** It displays finds from the Neolithic to Roman periods found in burial tombs outside Lamia. Aside from the standard ceramic figurines and amphoras, highlights include the earliest preserved vase depicting a naval battle, a large engraving showing a pregnant mother's sacrifice to Artemis, and a fearsome collection of rusty spears and axe-heads. *(To reach the Kastro and museum walk for 20min. north of Pl. Laou and up one of the stairways to the main road, which leads up to the museum gate. ☎29 992. Open Tu-Su 8:30am-3pm. 500dr., students with ID and under 18 free.)*

**GARDENS OF AGIOS LOUKAS.** The way to the Gardens of Agios Loukas (atop Agios Loukas hill) begins at the top of Pl. Diakou behind a gloriously posed **Statue of Athanasios Diakos,** his sword broken in battle. A War of Independence hero, he was burned to death in Lamia by the Turks in 1821. Continue up the steps behind Athanasios and you'll arrive in the beautiful shady gardens. It's a steep climb, but lovely panoramic views of the surrounding countryside, cool mountain breezes, and stone paths lined with rosebushes, mulberry trees, and benches make the trek rewarding as a hot afternoon respite or a romantic evening rendezvous. On occasional summer evenings, live music fills the gardens.

## DAYTRIPS FROM LAMIA

### THERMOPYLAE Θερμοπυλες

*Take the bus from Lamia's local station (15min, 5 per day 6am-5pm, 450dr) and ask to be let off at the baths (BAN-yo), not the village of Thermopylae. To return, walk 1.5km to the village and catch the bus there.*

More a highway roadstop than a destination in itself, Thermopylae (18km south of Lamia) is richer in history than anything else. As the gateway to southern Greece, Thermopylae's strategic location has made it a prime target for invading armies for

thousands of years. **Leonidas** and his army of 300 Spartans fought to their heroic deaths here in 480 BC, holding back Xerxes' vast Persian army—estimated by Herodotus to be five million strong—from invading Thessaly. More recently, both the Ottomans and the Nazis launched fierce attacks at the straits. Sulfurous **hot springs** originate in the mountains above, and attract visitors not for their rotten egg stench, but because legend says that the healing power of their 41°C waters once helped Hercules regain his strength.

From the hot springs parking lot, walk down the dirt path lined with eucalyptus and oleanders, and swarming with pale yellow butterflies in summer. Continue through a highway underpass and follow the path, with the mountains on your right, to a highway rest stop consisting of the **Monument to the Thespians** and the **Statue of Leonidas.** The defiant inscription on the statue reads "Molon Labe" ("Come and get it"). Across the highway from the statue is the **Archaeological Site,** where you can scramble around a network of trails, see the ruins of a Classical-era wall, and catch the view from craggy outlook points. Continue walking alongside the highway until the path reaches the miniscule Thermopylae village, consisting of a deserted square with a bone-dry fountain and some crumbling benches. You can flag down one of the frequent buses to **Lamia** (450dr) here at the rusty **bus stop.**

## AGIOS KONSTANTINOS
## Αγιος Κωνσταντινος ☎0235

Although tourists flood the streets of Agios Konstantinos, few visitors are lured by the town itself. Most come because it is the closest port to Athens with ferries to the sun-soaked Sporades. The rare visitor who resists the Sporades' siren song (or misses the ferry) and spends a night in Agios Konstantinos has little to regret. The town's charms are surprisingly accessible, from its late-night gyros-filled plateia to the beauty of the Church of Agios Konstantinos, capped by a red-tile roof and a clock tower that displays a time all its own.



**PRACTICAL INFORMATION.** If you're facing inland, the **bus station** (☎32 223) is about 150m to your left along the waterfront. Buses go to: **Athens** (2½hr., every hr. 9:45am-9:30pm, 3250dr); **Lamia** (1hr., every hr. 6am-8pm, 950dr); and **Thessaloniki** (5hr.; 7:15am, 2:15, 5pm; 6500dr). The pier, immediately seaward of the plateia, serves both **ferries** and **Flying Dolphins** (☎31 874). Buy your tickets at the right-hand side of the park (facing inland). One to three ferries (depending on the season) leave daily for: **Alonnisos** (5½hr., 4400dr); **Skiathos** (3½hr., 3300dr); and **Skopelos** (4½hr., 4100dr). One to five hydrofoils go daily to: **Alonnisos** (2¾hr., 8800dr); **Skiathos** (1½hr., 6600dr); and **Skopelos** (2½hr., 8200dr). Departure times are usually posted outside of the ticket offices.

Besides a few bakeries and a barbershop on side streets, the action is in the main plateia. The **port police** (☎31 920), along the harbor, can help with ferry schedules. Facing seaward from the park, a right-hand turn toward the bus station takes you past the National Bank with a 24hr. **ATM.** (Open M-Th 8am-2pm, F 8am-1:30pm). A turn to the left takes you past the **OTE** (Open M-F 8am-3:10pm) and a sign for the **post office,** which lies 20m inland on a street just parallel to the park (Open M-F 7:30am-2pm). **Postal code:** 35006.

**ACCOMMODATIONS AND FOOD.** Accommodations are somewhat limited. The first in the strip of hotels, **Hotel Olga** is both classy and reasonably priced. Rooms have A/C, telephones, and TVs. (☎32 266. Singles 5000-5500dr; doubles 7500-8500dr; triples 9000-10,000dr.) Take a right from the ferries and continue along the waterfront away from the park. In the center of town, **Hotel Poulia,** 20 ft. down the alley between souvlaki shops at the right side of the park facing inland, may be a bit older, but its central location makes it attractive. (☎31 663. Singles 5000-6000dr; doubles 6000-8000dr.)

Sit down and eat just past the main plateia. You can devour toothsome souvlaki (300-600dr), play backgammon, and do some quality people-watching. In the morning, warm bread and pastries from **Artopolia,** next door to Hotel Poulia, make painful early-morning ferries less heinous (100-400dr).

# THESSALY ΘΕΣΣΑΛΙΑ

Thessaly oscillates between the mundane and the ethereal. The region is the earthly anchor to the transcendent Meteora monasteries; at the same time, it harbors some of Greece's more drab cities. **Medea** dropped her witch's potions in Thessaly after returning here with Jason from Colchis; the legend won the region a reputation for sorcery and magical plants in ancient times. Thessaly's plains were once home to farmers who tended sheep and goats in summer before returning home to fish from the waters of the Pinios River. Though traditional farming has given way to modern methods, you can still buy a field guide and gather herbs off the mountain slopes or buy them in the villages. These small towns bear witness to the culture and character of a Greece that few tourists ever see. In these out-of-the-way places to the north of Karpenisi and in the green Pelion Peninsula, you'll find little English, much genuine hospitality, generations-old folk songs, and reverence for all things *hiropitios* (hand-made; literally, "poetry of the hands").

## VOLOS Βολος ☎0421

Volos looms large in two of ancient Greece's best-loved myths. Jason and the Argonauts set sail from Volos on their quest for the Golden Fleece, a fact which the city won't let you forget. Two important streets and half a dozen hotels name themselves after the Argonauts' voyage. Volos was also the site of the marriage of the sea-nymph Thetis to King Peleus, a wedding that would have cataclysmic repercussions (see **Who is the fairest of them all?** p. 187). A century ago, Volos was a small, sleepy town on the Pagasitic Gulf. But after the 1922 population exchange (see p. 17), ethnic Greek refugees from Turkey enlivened the port town with their love for carousing: Volos quickly became famous for the *ouzeria* that popped up all over town. Now a fast-growing industrial center and transportation hub connecting mainland Greece with the Sporades, Volos seems to have a split personality. By day, the port is filled with cranes and ugly oil tankers, the long avenues host an endless succession of cars, trucks, and motorbikes, and an oppressive haze pervades the air above the city. Come nightfall, the harborside fills with strolling couples, fruit vendors hawk their sweet produce, and dozens of cafes and seafood restaurants spread tables up to the water. On lazy afternoons, residents head for the beach east of town, where the splashing waves and seaside cafes will almost make you forget the tankers in the distance.



### ORIENTATION AND PRACTICAL INFORMATION

Volos, about 220km south of Thessaloniki, sprawls on the shores of the Pagasitic Gulf, due west of the Sporades. The city's bus station lies at the end of **Lambraki,** an easy 15min. walk from town and the waterfront. This main road, leading from the bus station to town, runs past the train station, **Riga Feriou Park,** and the tourist office. Lambraki splits at a fountain to become **Dimitriados** on the left and **Iasonos** on the right, which both run parallel to **Argonafton** on the waterfront. The intersecting roads leading away from the harbor are lined with various hotels and other services like banks, pharmacies, and the post office. A walk along the waterfront for about 10min. from the ferry docks past a long park brings you to the large **Church of Agios Konstantinos,** which juts out into the harbor. Here, Argonafton and Dimitriados join to become **Nik. Plastira,** which leads to the hospital, the archaeological museum, and various restaurants before ending at the **beach. Ermou,** the next street inland after Dimitriados and running parallel, is a pedestrian street lined with shops selling women's clothes, shoes, and the occasional icon. Ermou leads to an open plateia containing the **Church of Agios Nikolaos.**

**Ferries:** Service to: **Skiathos** (3hr., 3 per day 8:30am-5:30pm, 2700dr); **Skopelos** (4½hr.; 2-3 per day M-F 1pm and 5:30pm, also W and F 8:30am; 3400dr); **Alonnisos** (5hr.; 1-2 per day M 5:30pm, Tu and F 1 and 5pm, W 1pm; 3700dr); and **Glossa** (3hr.; 2 per day M-Tu, Th-F 8:30am and 5:30pm, also Tu, W, F 1pm; 3100dr). On Tuesdays at 1am, boats depart for **Tinos, Paros, Santorini,** and **Iraklion** (more on Su, fewer in off-season). Several waterfront agencies sell tickets; **Falcon Tours** (☎21 626 or 25 688), which also sells Flying Dolphin tickets, is by the docks.

**Flying Dolphins:** Daily service to: **Skiathos** (1hr., 4-6 per day, 5500dr); **Skopelos** (2½hr., 5-6 per day, 6800dr); **Alonnisos** (2¾hr., 4-7 per day, 7500dr); and **Glossa** (1¾hr., 4 per day, 6200dr). Tickets available at Falcon Tours (see above).

**Buses:** The **bus station** (☎33 254 or 25 527), is in the Old Town, all the way at the end of Lambraki. Buses to: **Athens** (4½hr., 10 per day 6am-10pm, 5500dr); **Larisa** (1hr., 12 per day 6am-9pm, 1150dr); **Kalambaka** (3hr., 5 per day 6:15am-8:30pm, 3200dr); and **Thessaloniki** (3hr., 6 per day 6:15am-10:30pm, 3700dr). For service to **Trikala,** take the 1pm bus to Kalambaka. Buses to Mt. Pelion Peninsula run to: **Makrynitsa** and **Portaria** (45min.; M-F 9 per day 6:15am-8:45pm, Sa-Su 7 per day, 8am-8pm; 300dr); **Milies** (1hr., 6 per day 5:15am-6pm, 450dr); **Tsagarada** (2hr., 3 per day 5:15am-2pm, 1050dr); and other locales. Inquire at the bus station or tourist office; most villages have daily service and can be reached in less than 3hr. Service is reduced on weekends and in winter.

**Trains:** The **station** (☎24 056 or 28 555) is 1 block west of the tourist office. From town, turn right at the kiosk past the tourist office. Walk 2-3min. down the parking lot parallel to the track. Service to: **Athens** (5hr., 1 per day 7am, 5850dr); **Thessaloniki** (3hr., 8 per day 8:55am-9:10pm, 3500dr); and **Larisa** (1hr., 13 per day 5:45am-9:10pm, 600dr).

**Car Rental: Avis,** Argonafton 41 (☎20 849; fax 22 849). **European Car Rental,** Iasonos 83 (☎36 238; fax 24 192). High-season rentals from 16,000dr per day.

**Tourist Office** (☎23 500 or 37 417), on Lambraki next to the town hall in Pl. Riga Feriou. Ask for information about Volos and the Pelion Peninsula. Maps of the villages available. Open M-F 7am-2:30pm.

**Banks:** All major banks, including **National Bank** (☎23 382), **Agricultural Bank** (☎23 411 or 54 030), and **Bank of Greece** (☎23 442) on Iasonos. Most offer **currency exchange** (M-Th 8am-2pm, F 8am-1:30pm) and **ATMs.** There's also a **Citibank** on the corner of Argonafton and El. Venizelou with a 24hr. **ATM.**

CENTRAL GREECE

**Police** (☎72 412). Open 24hr.

**Tourist Police,** 28 Octovriou 179 (☎72 421). Locals still call the street by its former name, "Alexandras". Open 7am-11pm.

**Hospital** (☎30 126), next to the museum on the eastern waterfront. Open 24hr.

**Telephone: OTE,** on the corner of El. Venizelou and Sokratous, across from the fruit market. Open 24hr.

**Internet Access: Diavlos Info Cafe,** Topali 14 (☎25 363), off Dimitriados, offers free access for an hour at a time. Crowded, it has 6 terminals and free backgammon. Open 10am-2pm, 6-10pm. **Magic Cafe,** Argonafton 56 (☎20 992), in a loud arcade, has 9 terminals and 2 printers operated by 100dr coins. 100dr per 5min., 1000dr per hr.

**Post Office:** P. Melo 63, off 28 Octovriou away from the water. Open M-F 7am-8pm. Poste Restante available. **Postal code:** 38001.

## ACCOMMODATIONS

Volos doesn't make its money from tourism—it's shipping and manufacturing that pay the bills around here. Volos's hotels vary tremendously in size, location, appeal, and amenities, but almost all are quite expensive for the financially constrained traveler. Most of the cheaper options are clustered on the small streets leading away from the noisy harbor. Wave a student ID in the air and ask for a simple room *(aplo domatio)* for a small discount.

**Hotel Jason,** P. Melo 1 (☎26 075; fax 26 975), on the waterfront across from the harbor. Most of the gleaming, scrubbed-white rooms are filled with light and have balconies looking over the waterfront. All have phones, baths, and TVs. Singles 6000dr; doubles 10,000dr; triples 13,000dr.

**Hotel Roussa,** Iatrou Tzanou 1 (☎21 732; fax 22 987), on the corner of Plastira and Iatrou Tzanou, a 40min. walk on the waterfront from the bus station. Quiet white rooms with neat blue trim, tiny baths, phone, and TV. Singles 6500dr; doubles 8500dr.

**Hotel Santi,** Topali 13, off Argonafton. These rooms, near the ferry docks, are clean and bright, if sparsely furnished. Pleasant bathrooms, phones, and lots of noise from the harbor. Singles 8000dr; doubles 10,000dr.

**Hotel Phillipos,** Solonas 9 (☎37 607 or 37 608; fax 39 550), just off Dimitriados. Polished wood floors and comforters for the beds make Phillipos one of Volos's most attractive hotel options; if you're up for a splurge, try it. Each spacious room has A/C, phone, TV, and a balcony. Singles 12,000dr; doubles 17,000dr.

## FOOD

A **supermarket** on Papadiamanti, across from the train station, and a **farmer's market** every day along Lambraki on the way to the bus station can provision you for a seaside picnic. The plentiful *ouzeria* and *tsipouradika* along Volos's waterfront are the town's saving grace. They specialize in fresh seafood and *spetsofai* (spicy sausages), washed down with stinging *tsipouro* (see **Moonshine,** p. 174); nearly all provide outdoor seating. Find fast food vendors near the docks.

**Rotonda,** Plastira 15 (☎34 973), past the Church of Agios Konstantinos on the eastern edge of town near Hotel Roussas. Specializing in fresh fish, served whole, Rotonda offers delicious calamari *psito* and swordfish souvlaki. Walk into the kitchen to pick your critter, which they'll grill up fresh. Simple, amazing food. Entrees 2000-3000dr.

**Klasico** (☎32 891), on Argonafton by the ferry docks, specializes in seafood but serves everything from fried octopus to goat soup, including a squid stuffed with cheese. Pricey but worth it. Entrees 1000-8000dr, all delicious.

**Enidrio** (☎27 765), on Plastira across from the beach. One of the most consistently popular restaurants in the city, with tables right next to the water, Enidrio specializes in fish and other seafood; the name means "Aquarium." Experimenting with the menu is worth it. It's also a perfect spot for a romantic dinner. Open until 1am. Entrees 1500-2200dr.



## NIGHTLIFE AND ENTERTAINMENT

The waterfront turns into a hive of activity at night, with cafes spilling revelers into the streets. Western-side cafes, on Argonafton before the church, push tables up to the water for romantic cocktail-sipping. By the museum and the beach, east side bars thump with pounding disco beats and more tight black pants than you can shake your booty at. **Ammos** and **Yiousouri,** side by side on the beachfront across from Rotonda, both alternate between pulsing house and disco's greatest misses. (Beers 800dr, drinks 1500-2500dr. Open until 6am.) Plenty of cafes await your *frappé*-sipping needs along Argonafton: **Cafe Memory** includes a British phone booth and a gramophone, while **Achillion** is *the* spot for the young and suave. These pleasant harborside cafes become packed bars by 11pm. Volos's **outdoor movie theater,** Dimitriados 263 (☎29 946), near the shore behind the park of Agios Konstantinos, is not to be missed. Films run for one week, showing nightly at 9pm, in English with Greek subtitles (2000dr). Some weekend nightspots in Volos, including **Psigeia,** are near the bus station. In late July and August, Volos hosts a **festival** in Riga Feriou Park with concerts, dances, and theater.

## SIGHTS

The **Archaeological Museum,** Athonassaki 1, a 40min. walk along the water from the ferry docks, houses tidbits from the later Paleolithic era through the Roman period in

a lovely Neoclassical mansion. Check out the painted grave *steles* from ancient Demetrias in Room 4 and the rather morbid reconstructed tombs in Room 6. The panoply of miniature Neolithic objects in Room 3 includes collections of figurines, seals, spindle wheels, bits of jewelry, carbonized seeds, and small tools of bone and stone. (☎25 285. Open Tu-Su 8:30am-3pm. 600dr, students 400dr.) Inquire here or at the tourist office for information on the nearby archaeological sites at **Dimini** and **Sesklo.** Sesklo is the oldest known settlement in Thessaly, with the oldest acropolis in Greece. Accessible by bus, the sites represent two of the oldest finds in the region: Dimini dates from 4000 BC, and Sesklo from 6500 BC. The **Art Center of Giorgio de Chirico,** Metamorphoseos 3, around the corner from Hotel Ialkos, showcases representative Greek landscape painting, accompanied by out-of-tune violins from the music school next door. The center features a collection of monotypes, lithographs, and copper prints reaching back to the Ottomans. The works of adopted Italian native and surrealist Giorgio de Chirico are upstairs, in a special collection only accessible in the morning. (☎31 701. Open Tu-Su 10am-1pm. Free.) The **Kitsos Makris Museum,** in Kitsos's own home at Afendoli 50 (a.k.a. Kitsos Makris 50), includes works by *laiki* (folk) painters **Theophilos** (see p. 24) and **Christopoulos,** as well as Byzantine icons, pottery, and wood carvings. (☎37 119. Open M-F 8:30am-2pm, Su 10am-2pm. Free.)

## MOUNT PELION PENINSULA Ορος Πηλιο

Way back when, rowdy centaurs—half-men, half-horses with enormous sex drives—called the rugged Pelion Peninsula (named for King Peleus) home. There they had their way with any hot young nymph they could find. Chiron, a renowned healer and tutor to Achilles, settled in Pelion despite its frat-house atmosphere; its abundant supply of over 1700 medicinal herbs lured him to the region. This plant variety stems from the peninsula's cool, moist climate, much appreciated today by tourists weary of the scorching sun. Over the years, the mountains of Pelion have protected the area from invasion. While the rest of Greece groaned under Ottoman rule, the peninsula was a virtually autonomous center of Greek nationalism. Many of Pelion's villages look as they did centuries ago, hidden in lush groves of beech, chestnut, and oak. Coastal towns lie alongside excellent beaches.



### MAKRYNITSA Μακρυνιτσα ☎0428

In Makrynitsa, one of Pelion's most beautiful villages, narrow flagstoned paths creep through pomegranate and plane trees to stunning lookout points, well-preserved *archondika* (mansions), and crumbling churches. Thanks to its designation by the European Community as a protected traditional settlement, the town's roads are closed to cars; the only sounds you hear come from more than 50 splashing fountains and streams, the kids in the plateia, and the evening songs of the resident birds. Nicknamed "the balcony of Pelion," the town overlooks the Pagasitic Gulf like a box seat in a giant opera house. At nightfall, the valley fills with deep indigo, broken only by the shimmer of city lights, while lamps hanging from an immense hollow tree illuminate the central plateia like a stage filled with strolling residents and visitors.

**ORIENTATION AND PRACTICAL INFORMATION.** Makrynitsa clings to the side of the large hill behind Volos. Its plateia overlooks the city below, and the cobblestone streets wind up and down the hill from the center. From the parking lot on the outskirts of town, a low road (17 Martiou) and a high road lead to the plateia. The low road passes various shops purveying both tourist kitsch and local medicinal and kitchen herbs. The high road runs past the village **clock tower** and the **Kimisi Theotokou church.** Buses run to **Volos** from the turn-around point on the road outside the village (45min., 7 per day 7am-8:30pm, 280dr). From nearby **Portaria village** (a 10min. walk down the Volos road), buses to other Pelion destinations can be caught, including the beaches at **Agia Iannis** and **Milopotamos.** A **tourist information booth** (☎90 150), on the side of the road leading to the village just after the bus turn-around, offers helpful maps and advice on touring Makrynitsa and the entire peninsula. The **mailbox** is behind the fountain in the plateia; stamps can be bought with postcards. Portaria has a **post office** which also offers **currency exchange. Phones** are in the plateia and the main parking lot.

**WHO IS THE FAIREST OF THEM ALL?** Everyone has heard of the Trojan War, with its horses and subsequent odyssey. But not everyone knows that the whole 10 year conflict began on Mt. Pelion with a social no-no. When **King Peleus** married **Thetis,** the sea nymph and future mother of **Achilles,** he invited all the gods and goddesses to the wedding–except for **Eris,** goddess of strife. Eris was infuriated by the snub, and responded by crashing the party and rolling the **golden apple of discord** across the floor. The apple was labeled "For the Fairest." Hera, Athena, and Aphrodite soon scared off other competitors for the title. The three goddesses demanded that a Trojan prince ignorant of his birth, **Paris,** judge the contest. Each goddess tried to bribe him: white-armed Hera offered him rule of the whole world, bright-eyed Athena promised him all-surpassing wisdom, and governor of love Aphrodite offered him the love of the most beautiful woman in the world. (Inconveniently, this woman, **Helen,** was already married to the Spartan king Menelaus.) Like any red-blooded adolescent, Paris chose Aphrodite and Helen's love. The Trojan War followed, ending in Paris's death, the fall and burning of Troy, and Helen's return to Sparta. **Hormones in an uproar** have never caused a bigger disaster.

**ACCOMMODATIONS AND FOOD.** Since Makrynitsa has been designated a traditional settlement, staying here will cost an arm and a leg. Either stay in Volos and save by making Makrynitsa a daytrip, or splurge on one of the town's cozy pensions. There are loads of homes offering domatia on the road into town, but most of them cater to well-heeled European visitors. The cheapest rooms are in the house of **Katsani Litsa,** on top of the last tourist shops as you walk to the plateia, just below Kentavros Hotel. The comfortable rooms are large, offering private hall baths and (sometimes) views. There's also a nice communal kitchen. (☎99 287. Singles 7000dr; doubles 9000dr.) Uphill and behind the Galini Restaurant in the plateia, **Pension Archontiko Diomides** has a cozy communal living room and an outdoor terrace. (☎99 430. Singles 8000dr; doubles 10,000dr; triples 12,000dr.)

On the plateia, the restaurants **Pantheon** (☎99 143; open 9am-11pm) and **Galini** (☎99 256; open 9am-5pm) offer similar fare, but while Pantheon's tables for two provide an achingly romantic setting to sip a *frappé*, Galini inundates the ears with the pervasive sound of saccharine, sentimental Greek tunes. Galini specializes in rabbit stew and *spetsofai* (spicy sausage), while at Pantheon the *moshari* or *kokopoulo kokkonisto* (braised veal or chicken), *fasolada* (bean soup), and ice cream parfaits are all delicious.

**SIGHTS.** Makrynitsa's **Museum of Folk Art and the History of Pelion** lies down a path that leads past the public telephones. The curator gives free tours of the authentic clothes, scabbards, and folk art. Housed in a converted 1844 mansion with a gorgeous view, the museum highlights old *tsipouro* stills, a collection of 16th and 17th century Bibles, and paintings by **Christopoulos,** all of which depict ships, gorgons, and sundry sea-related subjects. (☎99 505. Open Tu-Su 10am-5pm. Free.) In the plateia, cafe **O Theophilos** contains a somewhat dim wall mural painted by folk artist Theophilos himself (see p. 24). Notable **churches** include the one-room **Church of Agios Yiannis the Baptist** in the main plateia, and the crumbling but pretty **Metamorphosi,** just downhill from the Folk Art Museum. The peaceful, still functional church of **Kimisi Theotokou** once housed the *krifto skolio*, a secret school that taught the forbidden Greek language during the Ottoman era. The town's churches remain open at the whim of their caretakers; early to mid-morning and evenings are your most likely opportunities for a visit. From the main parking lot, the narrow road leads steeply uphill to the **Monastery of Agios Gerasimou** (a 20min. walk). The view alone is worth the trip up. The last three churches require modest dress (long skirts for women, pants for men, no bare shoulders). If you can keep your eyes off Makrynitsa's steep stone walkways, look up to see the adornments of the town's old houses—stained glass lanterns, false painted windows, and symbols to ward off evil spirits festoon many outer walls.

# LARISA Λαρισα ☎041

Seemingly uninterested in tourists, Larisa is nonetheless a pleasant place to get stranded while traveling around Central Greece. The town invites you to stroll through the elegant, tree-lined central plateias and their pedestrian sidestreets to find suave cafes and bars. Window shop at fine bookstores and alarmingly chic boutiques, explore the partially excavated ancient theater, or dance the transit-hub blues away at one of the packed discos outside of town. A rash of graffiti covers Larisa's outdoor surfaces: be warned. Bearing the dubious distinction of being Greece's hottest city (temperature-wise), Larisa is a ghost town on steamy summer Sundays when folks head east to the beach; on these days you can hear backgammon pieces shuffle in the *kafeneia* as you walk down the empty sidewalks.

## ORIENTATION AND PRACTICAL INFORMATION

Surrounded by miles of fertile corn and wheat fields, Larisa is directly southeast of the **Pinios River,** smack dab in the middle of Eastern Thessaly. The bus station in the north and the train station in the south mark the boundaries of the city's main commercial downtown district. At the heart of it all is **Pl. Ethnarhou Makariou** (a.k.a. Pl. Tahydromiou, "post office plateia") where plenty of cafes and bars extend outward in all directions on shady pedestrian arcades. **Papakyriazi** runs east-west on the north side of the main plateia. Walking a few blocks to the north from Pl. Tahydromiou, you'll find the large, open **Pl. Mikhail Sapka** to the left, and the fountains of **Pl. Laou** to the right, with **Kyprou** running east-to-west between the two. Two main streets run north and south through town: **Panagouli** on the east of Pl. Tahydromiou, and **Papanastasiou** on the west. In the north of town, **Olympou** runs south from the bus station to Pl. Laou, where it meets Panagouli. At the southern end of town, **Iroön Polytechniou** runs east-west, meeting Panagouli in a massive five-way intersection close to the train station.

CENTRAL GREECE

**Buses:** (☎537 777). The main **station** is 150m north of Pl. Laou on Olympou. Buses to: **Athens** (4¼hr., 6 per day 7am-midnight, 6300dr); **Thessaloniki** (2hr.; 13 per day 6am-7:30pm, fewer Sa-Su; 3200dr); **Volos** (1hr.; 12 per day M-F 6am-9pm, Sa-Su 7am-9pm; 1200dr); **Kastoria** (4hr.; 3 per day noon-1:15am; 2800dr); and **Ioannina** (4hr., 2 per day 9:30am and 3pm, 3700dr). Buses for **Trikala** (1hr., 21 per day 5:45am-10:30pm, 1250dr) and **Karditsa** (4hr., 11 per day 6am-8:15pm, 1300dr) leave from a station on Iroön Polytechniou (☎537 777); to get there, head south on Panagouli, turn right at the 5-way intersection, and walk 600m to the gas station/bus stop on your left.

**Trains:** (☎236 250), at the end of Paleologou: head south on Panagouli and make a soft left (*not* sharp left) at the 5-way intersection. **Intercity** express trains run to: **Athens** (4hr., 5 per day 10:24am-2am, 6670dr); **Thessaloniki** (2hr., 7 per day 7:48am-7:53pm, 2920dr), and **Volos** (45min, 1 per day 3pm, 1690dr). Regular *(aplo)* service to: **Athens** (5hr., 13 per day 6:44am-2am, 2970dr); **Thessaloniki** (2½hr., 8 per day 11:06am-4:59am, 1370dr); and **Volos** (1hr., 12 per day 6:21am-10:17pm, 590dr).

**Tourist Office,** Koumoundourou 18 (☎250 919), off Papanastasiou, 2 blocks south of Papakyriazi and Pl. Tahydromiou. Friendly staff doles out city maps and advice in broken English. Open M-Sa 7am-2:30pm.

**Banks:** There is a 24hr. **Commercial Bank ATM** at the train station. Fully functioning banks with 24hr. **ATMs** can be found all along Pl. Tahydromiou and Iroön Polytechniou.

**Police** (☎683 137), on Papanastasiou, four blocks north of Iroön Polytechniou.

**Hospital** (☎230 049), on Georgiadou, east of the bus station. Open 24hr.

**Internet Access: Planet Cafe,** Skarlatou Soutsou 20 (☎252 300), founded in 1996, is Greece's first cyber cafe. To find it, walk along Papakyriazi to the west (right when facing Pl. Tahydromiou) about 5 blocks until you reach A. Gazi; the cafe is directly in front of you. Use one of its eight high-tech terminals in the cool, quiet cafe (1000dr per hr.). Open M-Sa 10am-2:30am, Su 6pm-2:30am. A slew of **arcade parlors** along pedestrian Roozvelt, running south off Pl. Tahydromiou, also offer Internet access.

**Telephones: OTE** (☎995 341 or 995 342), on Filellinion, which branches northward from Kyprou off of Pl. Sapka. Open M-F 7:30am-9pm.

**Post Office** (☎532 312), on the corner of Papanastasiou and Diakou, a block north of the tourist office. Open M-F 7:30am-8pm. Poste Restante service and currency exchange provided. **Postal code:** 41001.

## ACCOMMODATIONS

Though Larisa isn't a tourist town, it's full of inexpensive accommodations. The cheapest options are convenient to the train station and not too far from the Trikala bus, but they're a 1.5km hike south from the main bus station.

**Hotel Pantheon** (☎234 810 or 236 726), on Paleologou near the train station, on top of a small taverna. Cheap, serviceable rooms with TVs and phones. Ask for one with a balcony. Singles 3500dr, with bath 5550dr; doubles 9000dr.

**Hotel Diethnes** (☎234 210), next to Pantheon. Affable management and lots of small, comfy rooms with shared baths and hot water. Balconies or big leafy windows give a lovely, treehouse feel. Lounge and common space furnished in the style of a 60s throwback. Cheap, but beware bugs. Singles 5000dr; doubles 7000dr.

## FOOD AND CAFES

Most of Larisa's cafes, bars, and tavernas are centered around Pl. Tahydromiou and its adjacent pedestrian streets, where the different eating establishments blend into one never-ending series of chairs, tables, and blaring TVs. **Restaurant Philoxenia** (☎258 660, literally "foreigner-loving") and **To Sidrivani** (☎535 933 or 531 400), both on the south side of the plateia, offer old favorites like *pastitsio* and *moschari* for good prices (entrees 1000-1800dr). Vegetarians will enjoy the rice-stuffed tomatoes and green peppers at To Sidrivani, along with palate-pleasing string beans (1600dr). On the opposite side of the plateia, you can find an excellent *moussaka* and other Greek classics (and the occasional free glass of ouzo) at the quieter **Ta Dio Fengaria** ("The Two Moons"), on Asklepiou, which runs north-south from the center of Pl. Tahydromiou. Tempting scents will entice you toward the *psistaria* grills on Panos, north of Kyprou one block east of the OTE. The main roads of Larisa are teeming with very good *zaccharoplasteia*, where glass-encased confections and treats will dazzle the sweet-toothed traveler.

Dissatisfied *frappé* and Nescafe drinkers who yearn for the fresh-ground, hard-core stuff will find sweet fulfillment at various *kafekopteia* (coffee sellers), including one just north of Pl. Laou on the corner of Olympou, and a very good one on Skarlatou Soutsou, which runs northeast from Planet Cafe. Overpoweringly rich aromas from huge vats of stirred-up coffee beans pervade these old-fashioned stores, which also sell imported foodstuffs, candies, nuts, dried fruit, and herbs. If you prefer your groceries in neat straight aisles, head to the southern end of Panagouli, where you'll find a large **supermarket.**



## NIGHTLIFE

For after-dinner hijinks, the lively bars of Larisa will not disappoint; hip joints like **Cafe del Mar** (☎252 464) and **Ermes** (☎621 022), face to face on the corner of Roozvelt and Mandilara, are always packed until 3am. After drinks, check out some of Larisa's dynamic discos. **Club Hoya** (☎288 845), a 1000dr taxi ride from downtown, is an enormous open-air nightclub boasting a row of towering fountains, ten bars, and a mini club-within-a-club called **Planet Babe.** The crowd usually starts to arrive around 1am; dancing on the tables doesn't start until at least 4am. A 1500dr taxi ride in the other direction brings you to **Baby Boom,** Larisa's most popular club, on the outskirts of town. Packed crowds gyrate nightly to American and Greek favorites under the enormous Thessalian night sky. Nearby, about 500m toward town, is ultra-chic **Blaze,** open weekends only. All clubs have a 2000dr cover, which includes one drink.

## SIGHTS

Larisa's **ancient theater,** fenced off in the northwest corner of town at the end of Papanastasiou, is mostly covered up by the boutiques and asphalt roads of the neighborhood. From the excavations, though, you can get a sense of the theater's size, which would approach that of the theater of Epidavros (see p. 127) if fully unearthed. Just to the north are the unspectacular remains of the ancient **acropolis,** completely overgrown with weeds, the **Temple to Pallas Athena,** and the **frourio,** the city's former fortress. A slightly upscale restaurant of the same name now occupies the spot, circling the still-standing Ottoman **Bedesten** (covered marketplace), built in the 15th and 16th century by leader Türhanoğlu Omar Bey. Further northeast are the **Pinios River** (a mere trickle in summer) and shady **Alcazar Park.** Modern art museum **Pinakothiki,** at Roozvelt 59, has one of the better 20th century art collections in Greece. (☎621 205. Open W-Su 9am-1pm and 6-8pm. 100dr.) The **Museum of Folk Art,** Mandilara 74, features rotating temporary exhibits and a permanent collection of men's and women's traditional dress, a setup of the precursor to the farmhouse kitchen, and a selection of 19th century weapons. The temporary exhibits are organized around the themes of Thessalian farming life, such as threshing (featuring wooden farm implements and carts), fishing (with a large wooden canoe, nets, and traps for Pinios fishing trips), and bread (explaining the complex procedures of traditional Thessalian baking). The captions are in both Greek and English. (☎287 516 or 287 493. Open Su-F 10am-2pm. Free.) Larisa's **Archaeological Museum** was closed for repairs in summer 2000; it is scheduled to reopen by summer 2001. Found in the northeast corner of Pl. Laou, it exhibits local finds like Late Empire *steles,* parts of a Hellenistic sarcophagus, and Archaic sculpture, all in an old Ottoman building. (☎288 515. Open Tu-Su 8am-1pm. Free.)



# TRIKALA Τρικαλα ☎0431

Greeks may snicker to hear you've vacationed in Trikala; many consider it a provincial replica of Larisa. However, Trikala is much more pleasant than either Larisa or Volos, and is wonderful for walking. The lazy Letheos River, named for the ancient Underworld's river of forgetfulness, divides Trikala in half; banks of acacias, chestnuts, plane trees, and pedestrian-friendly footbridges lend the town charm. The striking remains of a mosque designed by Ottoman-era master architect Sinan, breezy views from the *frourio* (fortress), the labyrinthine old quarter, and the Katsikoyianni Museum will keep you from twiddling your thumbs at the bus station. At night, young people fill the streets, strolling the broad pedestrian arcades and dancing the night away in packed clubs outside town. Devotees of Asclepius, the god of healing who was born in Trikala (then known as Trikkis), can make a pilgrimage to his all-but-decimated sanctuary. According to ancient belief, a nap in the sanctuary (or maybe in a nearby hotel room?) brings a nocturnal dream-visit from Asclepius himself, who reveals the cure for whatever ails you.

## ORIENTATION AND PRACTICAL INFORMATION

Trikala lies 70km west of Larisa. The curvaceous Letheos River bisects the town roughly northwest to southeast: the two main plateias lie directly across the river from each other, **Pl. Riga Feriou** in the south and the larger **Pl. Iroön Polytechniou** in the north (complete with a statue of a boy perpetually relieving himself into a small pond). The bus station is on **Othonos,** on the south bank of the river, to the east of Pl. Riga Feriou. **Asklepiou,** Trikala's main road, runs south from Pl. Riga Feriou, where it begins as a broad pedestrian arcade designed for glamorous strutting and coy ogling. It turns into a regular car-laden street after hitting Kapodistriou, on its way to the train station south of town. On the north bank, **Sarafi** leads west out of Pl. Iroön Polytechniou to **Varousi,** the old Turkish quarter, and the remains of the fortress in the northwest.

**Buses:** On the river's south bank, the **bus station** (☎73 130) is at the corner of **Othonos** and **Garivaldi** streets, about 150m east of Pl. Riga Feriou. Buses depart for: **Athens** (4½hr., 8 per day 7am-8:30pm, 5650dr); **Ioannina** (3½hr., 2 per day 8:30am-3pm, 2900dr); **Kalambaka** (30min., 20 per day 5:45am-8:45pm, 450dr); **Larisa** (1¼hr., 22 per day 5:45am-8:30pm, 1250dr); **Pyli** (30min., 13 per day 5:45am-8:45pm, 360dr.); **Thessaloniki** (3¼hr., 6 per day 7:30am-8pm, 3750dr); and **Volos** (2½hr., 4 per day 7:30am-7pm, 2750dr).

**Trains:** The **train station** (☎27 214) is located at the far southern end of Asklepiou, about 700m south of Pl. Riga Feriou. In summer 2000, the train station was closed for construction of a new, larger branch of Kalambaka-bound track; construction will most likely continue throughout 2001.

**Police:** The **station** (☎27 303) is about 500m from town center on the corner of Iannitson and Farmaki.

**Banks:** A National Bank with **ATM** is located right on the north side of Pl. I. Polytechniou. Open M-Th 8am-2pm, F 8am-1:30pm. There's also a 24hr. ATM on Asklepiou just south of Pl. Riga Feriou.

**Internet Access:** On Vyronos between Garivaldi and Asklepiou, **Neos Kosmos** (☎72 591) has 9 terminals, a printer, and a full bar. 1000dr per hr. Open 9am-1am.

**Telephone: OTE** (☎95 328; manager 95 315), 25 Martiou. 25 Martiou runs parallel to Sarafi, two blocks away from the river; turn left after Pl. I. Polytechniou.

**Post Office:** The main **post office,** Sarafi 15 (☎27 615), provides exchange and Poste Restante. Open M-F 7am-2pm. Walk across the bridge from Pl. Riga Feriou and turn left on the street directly in front of you (Sarafi). A smaller post office, Asklepiou 44 (☎32 983), sells stamps and offers mail-related services only. Open M-F 7:30am-2pm. **Postal code:** 42100.

## ACCOMMODATIONS AND FOOD

The most affordable digs in town are at the **Hotel Palladion,** Vyronos 4, right along the riverbank, and one street behind Pl. Riga Feriou. Spacious, comfortable, light-filled rooms catering to business travelers have marbled floors, phones, balconies, sinks, and TVs that receive more than 20 channels. The shared baths are clean and in the hallway. (☎28 091 or 37 260. Singles 6000dr; doubles 8000dr.) **Hotel Lethion,** in the bus station, has rooms with phones and TVs, and is the next-cheapest place in town. (☎20 690. Singles 10000dr; doubles 15000.)

Ypsilandou, leading northwest from Pl. Iroön Polytechniou, has a taverna on every corner, each with outdoor seating and plenty of ouzo. **Archontissa,** Patriarchou 16, right off Ypsilandou, concocts lamb and veal specialties. (☎33 603. Entrees 800-2500dr.) **Taverna O Babis,** just off of Asklepiou on Karanasion, near Dinas Hotel, serves Greek specialties, including a particularly good *pastitsio* (baked macaroni), chicken in wine sauce, and a range of vegetarian options such as stuffed tomatoes and peppers. (☎34 900. Entrees 1000-2000dr. Open noon-4:30pm and 7pm-1am.) Pl. Riga Feriou is home to hordes of souvlaki and pizza places, including **Trikki,** Asklepiou 35, where the Special Pizza (800dr) is a Special Bargain. (Open 6pm-2:30am.) A good-sized **supermarket** on Vyronos, next door to Palladion Hotel, sells mini-icons of the *Panagia* (Virgin) shelved between shoe polish and thimbles, in addition to average foodstuffs.

## NIGHTLIFE AND CAFES

Pl. Riga Feriou and Asklepiou are packed with loud cafes blasting dance music and serving drinks, while the pedestrian area around Ypsilandou in the north is lined with streetside tavernas and corner bars serving drinks until 3am. Both are centers of Trikala's after-dinner existence. Just off Pl. Riga Feriou on Asklepiou are **Black Door Cafe** (not as ominous as it sounds) and **Lotus** right next door; both offer ear-splitting music, relatively affordable drinks, and a lively setting near Pl.

Riga Feriou. On the north side, **Mezedo Kamanata,** Ypsilandou 16-18 (☎76 741), and **Thea Artemis,** Ypsilandou 4 (☎77 533), both serve drinks and *mezedes* in a less frenetic setting more conducive to hours-long discussions over tiny cups of Greek coffee or ouzo. **Chain,** the biggest disco in the area, is about 5min. from town by taxi (12,000dr) on the Trikala-Kalambaka road. With its exuberant beach decor and blend of Greek and American music, Chain attracts a crowd of rowdy revelers (cover 1000dr). On your way there, keep an eye out for the ruined foundation of the once-majestic **Sanctuary of Asclepius** on your right. Just down the road is **Verykono,** which pounds out Greek music in a spacious open-air setting. The 2000dr cover includes one drink. Friday and Saturday nights, locals flock to **Xantres,** a dinner theater club specializing in syrupy live Greek pop (cover 2000dr). Partying begins around 12:30am on the weekends.

## SIGHTS

**VAROUSI.** Trikala's old quarter, **Varousi,** was home to the Christian community under the Ottomans. Cobblestone streets wind through the crumbling walls, each leading to beautiful old churches. Varousi is on the north side of town. Walk 150m across the bridge to Pl. Iroön Polytechniou, turn left on Sarafi, and walk until you see the signs; the neighborhood is on your right. One of Varousi's churches, **Agios Faneromeni,** is open to the public from 7-9am and 5:30-7:30pm.

**FORT TRIKKIS.** Looming above Varousi are the grand stone walls and bell tower of Fort Trikkis, first constructed in the 4th century BC and dedicated to Artemis; it's currently being excavated. As of summer 2000, the bell tower is closed to the public, but excavation might be finished by summer 2001. The lovely, fountain-decked park and cafe at the *frourio* is an ideal setting for a cool *frappé* with a view (700dr). At the base of the *frourio* is the **Katsikoyianni Museum,** which houses all the paintings and sculptures of local artist and ardent communist Legos Katsikoyiannis. His surrealist work—busts with hands and faces springing out of them— glorifies the Greek resistance against the Nazis and the simple pastoral life of the farmer. *(Open 9am-1:30pm, also M and Th 5:30-8:30pm, though hours vary. Free.)*



**FOLK ART MUSEUM.** Trikala's inevitable Folk Art Museum, Garivaldi 6, on the street which meets Othonos at the bus station, features an extremely enthusiastic curator and two floors of household objects including an Orthodox icon stamp for making bread, looms, and the local barber's grim medical supplies (bloodletting tools and tooth-yanking pliers). There are also several rooms full of Theodoros Markelos' paintings. *(☎76 613. Open M-Sa 11am-1pm. Free.)*

**KOURSOUN TZAMI.** The fascinating 400-year-old Koursoun Tzami mosque lacks the top half of its minaret. It's in the south side of town: from the bus station, head away from Pl. Riga Feriou, turning right onto Venizelou at the end of Othonos; walk about 5min. until you see the huge dome of the mosque rising up over the spires of the neighboring modern church. Suleiman the Magnificent's chief architect Sinan, who pioneered the multi-domed trademark look for Ottoman mosques, built the mosque in 1550. Used as a church in the 16th century, the mosque is now under renovation for use as a performance space.

# PYLI Πυλη ☎0434

The seemingly endless plains of Thessaly finally end in tiny Pyli, portal to the forested mountains rising in the west. Notable mostly for its 12th century Byzantine church, the Porta Panagia, Pyli is home to two spectacular monasteries and to trails that climb through the trees of **Mount Kosakas.** Visit Pyli for its churches and for the cool serenity of the mountains, since it has little else to offer: the town consists of one main road and a handful of stores and tavernas. Try a daytrip from Trikala to the church and monasteries, and perhaps relax with dinner by the river.

**ORIENTATION AND PRACTICAL INFORMATION.** Located at the foot of Mt. Kosakas, 20km southwest of Trikala, Pyli heralds the end of Thessaly's boundless flatness as it flows into mountainous terrain: *pyli* means "gateway." The highway from Trikala to Artis runs parallel to the river and directly through the center of town, where it becomes **Trikalon,** Pyli's main street and home to most of the shops and the bus station. The small, shady plateia is on the main road, right next to the footbridge over the river. The other major street, **Ermou,** breaks off from Trikalon just below the plateia, only to rejoin it after 200m near the **bus station.** The bus station runs buses to Trikala (30min, 20 per day 6:15am-9:20pm, 380dr) and some of the other villages in the area; inquire for service to Ellaki and Kotroni, among others. Between the two is a **National Bank of Greece** offering **currency exchange** and a 24hr. **ATM.** (Open M-Th 8am-2pm, F 8am-1:30pm.) The **post office** is on Trikalon, about 400m from the bus station in the direction of Trikala. (Open M-F 7:30am-2pm.) The **OTE** is one block further down. **Postal Code:** 42032.

**ACCOMMODATIONS.** The only budget place to stay in Pyli is the **Hotel Babanara,** right across the street from the bus station. Housed upstairs from a cafe, Babanara has spacious, comfortable rooms with TV, phone, and bath. The lobby doubles as a cafe, and fills up in the evening with regulars; it's the perfect place to argue politics over a glass or two of ouzo. (Singles 6500dr; doubles 9000dr.)

**FOOD AND ENTERTAINMENT.** Many *psiterias* and cheap fast food places can be found along Trikalon and Ermou. **Taverna O Theodoras,** on Ermou just below the plateia, serves good (if greasy) local specialties, including an excellent *moussaka.* (☎22 217. Entrees 700-1800dr.) Pyli is quiet at night; after dinner, the streets are by and large empty. The only noise comes from **La Porta,** on the plateia, where Pyli's hip, black-clad contingent shake their groove thangs till 4am. (☎22 696. Beers 700dr, drinks 1000-1500dr.) **Cafe Kittara** (☎22 672), right next door, serves beer and drinks to a crowd of regulars until 2am. Follow Trikalon out of town to the north for 500m and you'll find **Neromylos** on the banks of the river. The water wheels and leafy, romantic patio provide a perfect setting for a *frappé* by day or a cocktail by night, just across the river from the Porta Panagia. (☎22 085. Open 10am-1am. Drinks 500-2000dr.)

**CHURCH OF PORTA PANAGIA.** Most visitors come to Pyli to ogle the extraordinary **Church of Porta Panagia.** The church has rested on the banks of the Aheloös River since 1283, when it was built by Despot of Epirus **Ioannis Dukas** on the site of an ancient Greek temple. Despite a smallish, drab appearance from outside, the church's interior mosaics are jaw-dropping; light slants in from lofty windows to illuminate them. A domed *Pantokrator* ("Creator of All Things") graces the vestibule. The church's main area, the *naos*, is built in a *trikliti stavrepisteli* style: its intersecting three vertical parts and single horizontal part meet to form a cross. The church's treasures are in the *naos*: a pair of 700-year-old mosaic icons, one of the *Panagia* (Virgin) and one of Christ. The positioning of Porta Panagia's icons is a bit unusual in that the icon of the *Panagia* is located to the right of Christ, not to the standard left. Beautiful frescoes painted with flower-extract dyes adorn the walls of both the vestibule and the *naos*. Some frescoes, especially in the vestibule, have been damaged by fire, earthquakes, and Nazi bullets, but most remain unscathed. *(Start in Pyli's plateia and, ignoring the signs for a moment, cross the river on the narrow footbridge. Turn left on the other side and you'll find the church on your left very shortly. ☎22 420. Open 8am-noon and 4-6pm; winter 9am-noon and 3-5pm. 400dr.)*

## KALAMBAKA Καλαμπακα ☎0432

Kalambaka sits directly at the base of the Meteora rocks: its name is derived from the Turkish phrase for "the rock with the cowls of monks." The lone main road channels countless package-tour buses past the town, to the rocks' summit. Though Kalambaka itself doesn't offer much beyond access to the famed monasteries, it makes a quiet, pleasant, convenient base. If the lonely wilds of Thessaly have made you lonesome for backpacker banter, Kalambaka is the place to be.

## ORIENTATION AND PRACTICAL INFORMATION

Kalambaka is in the northwestern corner of Thessaly, 30km north of Trikala, near the border with Epirus. The town's central plateia is uphill from the bus station at the intersection of all the town's major thoroughfares. Most streets are unlabeled, but standing in this plateia with your back to the fountains and restaurant tables, **Vlachara** is straight behind you, and **Ioanninon** runs downhill to the right toward the police station. **Patriarchou Dimitriou** goes off to your right, while **Trikalon** leads left to **Pl. Riga Feriou,** home of various banks and restaurants.

**Buses: Main station** downhill from the local bus station on the left, past the taxi stand. To: **Athens** (5hr., 8 per day 7am-8:30pm, 5500dr); **Ioannina** (3hr., 8:45am and 3:20pm, 2550dr); **Lamia** (2hr., 8 per day 7am-8:30pm, 2500dr); **Metsovo** (2hr., 8:45am and 3:20pm, 1550dr); **Patras** (6hr., Tu and Th 9am, 5800dr); **Thessaloniki** (3hr., 6 per day 7:30am-8pm, 3700dr); **Trikala** (30min., 24 per day 6:15am-9:45pm, 500dr); and **Volos** (3hr., 4 per day 7am-6:30pm, 3150dr). Buses bound for **Meteora** (20min., 9am and 1:20pm, 250dr) and **Kastraki** (10min., 24 per day 6:30am-9pm, 150dr) pick up passengers in front of the **central plateia** at the sign reading "Bus stop to Kastraki/Meteora." The 9am bus to Meteora allows you time to hike around the monasteries. Most people walk back to Kalambaka (6km downhill), visiting monasteries along the way, but you can also take a bus back from **Grand Meteoron** at 2pm.

**Trains:** The station (☎22 451), on the corner of Pindou and Kondyli, is closed for at least another year to construct a larger branch of railroad running into town.

**Taxis:** (☎22 310 or 22 822) congregate at a small kiosk across from the central plateia. Taxi to Meteora 1500dr. Open 6:30am-midnight.

**Tourist Office:** (☎75 306), on Kondyli. From the central plateia, walk down Trikalon to the end of Pl. Riga Feriou, then turn right and go downhill—you'll see a sign for the office a few doors down on the right. Maps, bus schedules, lists of hotels and rooms to let, and information on the monasteries. After hours information available from xeroxes left in boxes by the door. Open M-F 8am-3:20pm. The **kiosk** by the taxi stand also provides maps of the town and of Meteora.

**Banks:** Both the National Bank in Pl. Riga Feriou and the Ionian Bank near the central plateia have 24hr. **ATMs.**

**Police and Tourist Police:** (☎76 100), on the road to Ioannina, about a 10min. walk from the center of town. Open 24hr. English sometimes spoken.

**Health Center:** (☎24 111), 1km from town, on the road to Ioannina. Open 24hr.

**Telephones: OTE** (☎22 121), down Ioanninon. Open M-F 7:30am-2pm.

**Internet Access: Cafe Hollywood,** Trikalon 67 (☎24 964), a few blocks past Pl. Riga Feriou. 500dr per 30min. for use of one of its five coin-operated, snail-mail paced terminals. Open 10am-1am.

**Post Office:** (☎22 467), between the two plateias on Trikalon. Poste Restante available. Open M-F 7:30am-2pm. **Postal code:** 42200.

## ACCOMMODATIONS AND CAMPGROUNDS

Think carefully before you accept domatia offers from the dock hawks; some of Kalambaka's room-peddlers are known to lure travelers with promises of good prices only to change their rates or add surcharges when it comes time to pay. Be skeptical if someone tells you that the place you're going has raised its rates or is closed, and make sure you agree on a rate before you agree to spend the night.

A number of **campsites** line the roads in all directions around Kalambaka and Kastraki; many also rent rooms at cheap prices. **Kalambaka** (☎22 309), about 1km down the road to Trikala, is the closest campground out of town. **Vrachos** is about as far away in the opposite direction, in nearby Kastraki. (☎22 293 or 23 134. 2000dr per car; 400dr per tent.) Other camping proprietors include **International** (☎22 239), **Philoxenia** (☎24 466), and **Theopetra** (☎81 406).

**Koka Roka** (☎24 554). A 15min. walk from the central plateia; follow Vlachara until it ends, then bear left following the signs to Kanari. On a quiet side street right at the base of footpath to the rocks, Koka Roka offers large, airy, comfortable rooms in a family setting, fantastic food in the taverna below, and awe-inspiring views of Meteora. Call from the bus station and they may give you a lift. 3500dr per person without bath; singles with bath 6000dr; doubles with bath 8000dr; triples with bath 10,000dr.

**G. Tostis** offers bare, bright rooms to let on quiet Kon. Masouta. To find the house, face Pl. Riga Feriou with Trikalon behind you, and take the street to your left. Signs will point the way to the small cafe that doubles as a reception desk. Shared baths and some balconies. Singles 3000dr; doubles 6000dr.

**Alsos Rooms** (☎24 097 or mobile 097 660 929), on Kanari before Koka Roka. Small multinational flags blow over the front gate. 14 presentable little rooms with shared baths and great views, over two small patios. Singles 5000d;, doubles 6000dr and up.

## FOOD AND NIGHTLIFE

Most of Kalambaka's restaurants and almost all of its bars are on **Trikalon,** past Pl. Riga Feriou. There's a **discount supermarket** just down Kondyli from the tourist office, and various **fruit stands** on Vlachara. On Fridays, Vlachara and intersecting Kondyli become a full-scale **marketplace** for produce and sundry household goods.

The nightlife mainly centers on **Trikalon,** south of Pl. Riga Feriou, where enough motorcycles, cheap fast food joints, and neon signs line the streets to recall your worst strip-mall nightmare. There are plenty of indistinguishable bars all along Trikalon, most offering beers for 500dr and drinks for 1000dr-1500dr. **Kivotos,** on Dimoula, has a laid-back atmosphere, outdoor tables, and fewer tourists than most. (☎77 577. Open until 2am.)

**Koka Roka Taverna** (☎24 554), inside its namesake hotel. Homey, roofed outdoor tables under whimsically hung dried gourds make the perfect spot for chatting, backgammon, guitar serenades, and Kyria Sakkas's specialties. Entrees around 1000dr.

**Restaurant Panellinio** (☎24 735). Panellinio pretty much *is* the central plateia, and very popular at night. Vegetarian eggplant *papoutsakia* (1400dr) and *briam* (1000dr), as well as a host of Greek lamb and veal specialties. Entrees 800-1700dr.

**Taverna Vaxchos** (☎24 678), up a hill at the end of Patriarchou Dimitriou, has a large, fun-filled patio right under the Meteora rocks. Entrees change nightly; you might find *moussaka*, lamb-and-vegetable dishes, and all kinds of country salads (800-2000dr). Open noon to midnight.

## SIGHTS

In the land of monasteries, it is no surprise that Kalambaka's foremost attraction is the Byzantine **Church of the Assumption of the Virgin,** once the seat of the bishop of Kalambaka and Trikala. Follow the signs in the central plateia; after several blocks you'll spy the graceful bell tower of the old church. Built in the 11th century on the ruins of a 5th-century basilica, the main structure was remodeled in 1573. Unfortunately, many of the interior frescoes, painted by the Cretan monk **Neophytos** and priest **Kiriazis** have been badly blackened by centuries of candles and incense. Of particular interest is the church's marble *amdo* (pulpit), located in the center of the nave. (Open 9am-2pm. Dress modestly. 400dr.) In late July, the town honors its patron saint with a **glendi** (celebration) of music, dance, and food. Nearby Kastraki holds a three-day **wine festival** with dancing and free samples in late August.

The Monasteries of Meteora are by far the biggest attraction near Kalambaka; a trip to the town would be incomplete without a visit to the monasteries far above.

# MONASTERIES OF METEORA Μετεωρα

*For information on getting to Meteora from Kalambaka by* **bus,** *see p. 194. Each monastery closes for one day of the week, and their opening hours vary slightly. All are open Apr. to end of Sept. Sa-Su and W 9am-12:30pm and 3:20-6pm.* **Admission**: *500dr per monastery. Dress modestly: long skirts for women, long pants for men, no bare shoulders, or you will not be admitted. Men with long hair may be asked to wrap it in a bun (as the monks do). Photography and filming inside most of the monasteries are forbidden. Though you can buy snacks from small carts at Varlaam, Grand Meteoron, and Ag. Stephanos, it is better to pack a picnic to eat during the mid-day closing hours.*

No one knows how the majestic, iron-gray pinnacles of the Meteora (meh-TEH-o-rah, "rocks of the air") formations were created, but they're probably the remains of large salt deposits from a primordial sea. Whatever their origin, the Meteora rear up from the plains of Thessaly and yield astonishing views of fields, forests, mountains, and monolithic stone; they'd be a must-see even without the 24 gravity-defying, frescoed Byzantine monasteries that cling to them. Six of these monasteries are still inhabited by religious orders and are open to the public. The largest monasteries, Grand Meteoron and Varlaam, have the most spectacular displays and cater to bus loads of tourists. The other monasteries are quieter and more intimate; you might even meet one of the reclusive monks. The Meteora require a full day's visit, and it's well worth the time and the walk.

## HISTORY

CENTRAL GREECE

The origins of the settlements perched atop the Meteora rocks are unknown: one theory holds that the first recluse was a monk named **Barnabas,** who founded the *skite* of the Holy Ghost in the mid-10th century. By the 11th century, hermits and ascetics followed his example, moving to the wind-beaten pinnacles and crevices of the Meteora, worshiping in a church dedicated to the **Theotokos** (Mother of God), which can still be seen below the Agios Nikolaos monastery. As religious persecution at the hands of Serbian marauders increased in the 12th century, devout Christians hid on the summits of these impregnable columns of rock.

In 1344, the region's first monastic community was founded when the monk **Athanasios,** his spiritual father **Gregorios,** and 14 fellow mountain-climbing monks began to build Grand Meteoron. Athanasios was a highly educated monk whose journeys brought him from his native Patras to Constantinople, Crete, and finally Mt. Athos, which he fled to avoid Turkish invasions. He preferred to occupy his time weaving baskets in a nearby cave, referring to women as "the sling" (that vaults the stones of sin into man's hearts) or as "the affliction" (addicting men to the sinful pleasures of the flesh). When the Ottomans ruled most of Greece, Meteora served as an outpost of Christianity along with Mount Athos (see p. 244), growing in the 16th century into a powerful, rich community of 24 monasteries, each embellished by the age's finest artists. As donations fell off and interest in the monastic life dwindled in the late 1700s, many treasured manuscripts and books were sold off to foreign visitors for a fraction of their actual worth. A small brotherhood still exists at **Grand Meteoron, Varlaam, Agia Triada,** and **Agios Nikolaos,** while **Agios Stephanos** and **Roussanou** are now convents.

## WALKING THE MONASTERIES

The first ascetics scaled the sheer cliffs of the Meteora by wedging timbers into the rock crevices to construct small platforms; traces of these platforms can still be seen along the Meteora walls. After the monasteries were completed, visitors usually arrived by means of extremely long rope ladders. When these were pulled up, the summit became virtually inaccessible. Visitors who were either too weak or too timid to climb the ladders were hoisted up in free-swinging rope nets. The 30min. ascent no doubt injected yet more of the fear of God into pilgrims to the site. Motorized winches have since replaced monk-powered rope-spool cranes,

and today only provisions, not pilgrims, are yanked up by rope. In 1922, steps were carved into the rocks and bridges built between the pillars, so even the vertigo-prone could feel secure.

It's best to begin your walking tour from **Grand Meteoron,** the uppermost monastery, and then to visit the others on your way down. From Grand Meteoron, a road leads down to Varlaam. After Varlaam, the road splits in two. The right fork leads to Roussanou, Agios Nikolaos, and, eventually, the village of Kastraki. The left fork, after about 1km, splits again. The road to the right (a dead end) leads to Agia Triada and Agios Stephanos; the road to the left ends up, in a long and roundabout way, at **Kalambaka.**

**GRAND METEORON.** The **Monastery of the Transfiguration,** known as Grand Meteoron (Μεγαλου Μετεορου), is the oldest, largest, most important, and most touristed monastery in the area. Built in the late 14th century on the most imposing of the inhabited stone columns, **Platys Lithos,** the Grand Meteoron complex looms 613m above Thessaly's plain. According to legend, Athanasios took the wings of the Holy Spirit and flew to the rocky peak to found the original church on this site, called the **Theometor.** The monastery rose to prominence when Ioannis Uresis Angelos Komninos Paleologos, many-named son of the Greco-Serbian King of Thessaly and Epirus, forsook the worldly vanities of royal power and retired to Meteora in 1388, taking on the monkish (and much more manageable) name of **Ioasaph.** Ioasaph spearheaded a period of great artistry at Grand Meteoron and is considered its second founder. Grand Meteoron reached its peak in the 16th century, when it was visited by the reigning patriarch and accorded the same privileges as the autonomous Mt. Athos. Around this time the **Church of the Transfiguration** *(Metamorphosis)* was built, to be capped by an exalted dome with a *Pantokrator* (a central image of Christ); prepare yourself for the narthex's gruesome frescoes of Christians being stoned, dismembered, skinned, hammered, beheaded, burned, boiled alive, and otherwise mangled by Romans. The monastery houses a **folk museum,** exhibiting domestic items, including a large former kitchen, holy books, traditional dress, and a mausoleum with neatly stacked skulls and bones. *(Open W-M 9am-1pm and 3:-6pm; winter Th-M 9am-1pm and 3-5pm.)*

**VARLAAM MONASTERY.** Some 800m downhill from Grand Meteoron stands Varlaam, the second-largest Meteora monastery. Varlaam was founded in the 14th century by a contemporary of Athanasios who, in a show of monkish humility, named the monastery after himself. Brothers Theophanis and Nektarios built the **Church of All Saints** in 1541. The *katholikon's* 16th-century frescoes, thought to be executed by the Theban artist Frangos Katelanos, depict desert hermits, martyrs, an apocalyptic sea serpent swallowing unfortunate sinners, and St. Sisoes chatting up Alexander the Great's skeleton (symbolic of the vanity of worldly achievements). Meteora's best scribes and calligraphers worked at Varlaam in the 16th and 17th centuries; the monastery's **library** contains 290 manuscripts, some of which are housed in the museum, including a miniature Bible from 960 that belonged to Emperor Constantine Porfitogenitou. Varlaam also has an extensive **net and pulley system,** now used for supplies, which shows how earlier visitors were hoisted up. *(Open Sa-Th 9am-1pm and 3:20-6pm; winter Sa-W 9am-1pm and 3-5pm.)*

**ROUSSANOU.** Bear right at the fork in the road to reach Roussanou. Visible from most of the valley, it is spectacularly situated and frequently photographed. More than the other monasteries, Roussanou feels less like a creation of man than a natural continuation of the boulders: its steep sides—three of which overlook the sheer drop to the valley below—were built almost flush to the rock face and seem to spring out of the formation, in an especially ornate flourish of stone. Founded in 1380 by the monks **Nikodemos** and **Benedict,** Roussanou was renovated and enlarged in the 16th century. Despite continuous renovation, the interior—which includes paintings of the criminal in paradise and a portrait of Constantine the

Great—can't match the heavenly exterior. Still, the *katholikon*, illuminated by stained glass, is quite beautiful. Roussanou celebrated its greatest moment when it housed Greek refugees fleeing the Turks in 1757 and 1897. *(Open 9am-6pm; in winter Th-Tu 9am-1pm and 3-5pm.)*

**AGIOS NIKALAOS.** Farther down the road lies the Monastery of Agios Nikolaos Anapafsas, only 2.5km from Kastraki. Built in 1527 by the Archbishop of Larisa and expanded in 1628, its highlight is the incomparable fresco work painted by the 16th century Cretan master **Theophanes Strelitzas-Bathas,** whose son, Neophytus, painted Kalambaka's Church of the Assumption of the Virgin (p. 195). Situated on a very narrow boulder, Agios Nikolaos was forced to grow vertically rather than horizontally; it is now the second tallest of the monasteries, next to Grand Meteoron. Excellent views open from the rooftop and the small balcony beneath it. Visitors are admitted only in small groups; wait at the top of the steps for the door to open. *(Open 9am-5:45pm; closed in winter.)*

**AGIA TRIADA.** Walking back toward Roussanou, a footpath across from the arched bridge into Roussanou leads to the road above, which is the left fork at the main intersection. Follow the road and keep bearing right to find Agia Triada ("Trinity"); movie buffs will recognize if from the James Bond flick *For Your Eyes Only*. Looming above Kalambaka, the peak of Agia Triada gives a soul-searing view of the Kalambaka and the distant, snow-capped Pindos Mountains. The monk Dometius built the monastery in 1438, but most of the **wall paintings** weren't added for another 200 years. Sadly, most of the monastery's prized manuscripts and heirlooms were lost in the Second World War. Triada is now one of the least-touristed and most intimate monasteries, well worth the hike from Grand Meteoron. To get to **Kalambaka** from Agia Triada, take the (unmarked) 3km footpath leading from the monastery's entrance. At the base of the cliff and with your back to the monastery, walk a few meters to your left, and then descend on the small left-hand fork in the path. The narrow, overgrown trail soon evolves into a cement-paved stone path ending up at Koka Roka hotel. *(Open F-W 9am-12:30pm and 3-5pm.)*

**AGIOS STEPHANOS.** At the end of the road, past Agia Triada, is Agios Stephanos, founded as a hermitage by the Archmandrite Antonius Katakouzinos and the priest-monk Philotheos. According to an 18th-century report, it was originally a convent; it became a monastery in the early 15th century. Today it is once again home to a large, active community of nuns. Of its two churches, only the more modern **Agios Charalambos,** built in 1798, is open to the public. The **museum** displays well-preserved icons, manuscripts, liturgical vestments, and crosses. Its wooden *iconostasis* is intricately carved into figures of birds, animals, and people. The peaceful garden in back offers spectacular views of the entire valley. *(Open Tu-Su 9am-1pm and 3:20-6pm; in winter Tu-Su 9am-1pm and 3-5pm.)*

# NORTHERN GREECE

Snide Athenians regarded the residents of Macedonia and Thrace as primitive barbarians in ancient times. Perhaps they didn't know that Orpheus, the mythical Pied Piper who tamed wild animals with his divinely inspired songs, first sang in Thrace, where cults of his devotees filled the northern hills. Having ventured to the underworld and back in a vain search for his beloved Eurydice, Orpheus recounted his tale of woe in poems resembling musical guidebooks to the underworld; commentary on one of these "Orphic" poems was found on a papyrus at Derveni outside Thessaloniki. A few rural festivals still preserve pre-Christian rites that probably stem from these ancient pagan practices. Parts of Northern Greece did hang on to the ancient ways for a good long time: Romans who came to pave the Via Egnatia across the Balkans encountered uncivilized, cityless Thracian tribes. Today, the northern reaches of Greece vary greatly in their connection with modern life; Thessaloniki is a step ahead of the Next Big Thing, while the Zagorohoria region's residents barely test the waters of the 19th century.

**HIGHLIGHTS OF NORTHERN GREECE**

**SIDESTEP SCORPIONS** while trekking through super-steep Vikos Gorge into the time-warped villages of the Zagorohoria (p. 212).

**ABSORB 2000 YEARS** of Byzantine and Ottoman monuments, then wake up to techno at Theatro, an amphitheater/disco outside brightly lit Thessaloniki (p. 216).

**DROOL** over the treasures unearthed from the tombs, palaces, and mosaics at Pella (p. 231) and Vergina (p. 230), and consider how Alexander the Great was human, too.

**WALK LIKE A GOD** to the top of Mt. Olympus; the vistas are divine (p. 233).

**SUBMIT** to 10th century monastic rituals among Mt. Athos' monasteries (p. 244).

**RELIVE THE MAYHEM, INTRIGUE, AND SODOMY** of Albanian "Lion of Epirus" Ali Pasha amid the fortresses and mosques of Ioannina (p. 205).

**DIVINE YOUR FORTUNE** from the rustling leaves of Dodoni's oracular oak (p. 209).



# EPIRUS ΗΠΕΙΡΟΣ

If you came in search of idyll and isolation, consider roaming Greece's northwest coast. The postcard-pretty towns and beaches of Parga see their share of visitors, but the mountains and timeless villages of Zagorohoria near the Vikos Gorge remain undisturbed. Epirus links itself to a living past—the old Latin dialect of Vlachi is still spoken in the mountain towns, and the almost perfectly preserved mosques of the dreaded Ali Pasha still grace the beautiful city of Ioannina. The region's mountains draw international hikers for some of Greece's most rewarding outdoor rambles, with paths that link to trails through Greece and beyond.

## IGOUMENITSA Ηγουμενιτσα ☎0665

For many, Igoumenitsa is the first (disappointing) glimpse of the Greek mainland. Greece's third largest port and consummate transportation hub, the city links Central and Northern Greece, the Ionian islands, and Italy. Tourist agencies line the

streets, harried backpackers scurry about in search of their ship, loitering old men by the docks keep an eye on all the comings and goings, and everyone seems in a desperate hurry. Though you may prefer to avoid staying the night in Igoumenitsa, the prevalence of early morning ferries makes this easier said than done. If you're stuck here, the waterfront is the most pleasant spot to pass your spare hours.

## GETTING THERE AND GETTING AROUND

**Ferries:** Tickets to **Corfu** (1½hr., 21 per day 7:30am-10pm, 1500dr) can be purchased at the Corfu Port, in one of several white kiosks. For tickets to **Italy,** shop around at the waterfront agencies. Budget carriers vary from year to year: some have student rates, and some accept Eurail and Inter-Rail passes; bargain before you buy. Destinations include: **Ancona** (24hr., 2 per day, 14,000-16,000dr); **Bari** (12hr., 1-2 per day, 10,500-12,000dr); **Brindisi** (8hr., 4-6 per day, 7500-8500dr); and **Venice** (25hr., 1-2 per day, 12,000-15,000dr). Prices do not include port dues. Most boats depart before noon or late in the evening. Note that the endlessly long **port** has three subdivisions. **Old Port,** on the waterfront's north edge (to the right facing the water), mostly sends boats to Italy. **Corfu Port** is in the middle of the three. **New Port,** beyond the Corfu Port, sends boats to both Italy and Corfu.

**Buses:** Kipou 17 (☎22 309). To: **Athens** (8hr., 4 per day 8:30am-8:15pm, 8850dr); **Ioannina** (2hr., 9 per day 6:30am-8pm, 1900dr); **Parga** (1hr., 4 per day 5:45am-5:15pm, 1200dr); **Preveza** (2hr., 11:45am and 3:30pm, 2200dr); and **Thessaloniki** (7hr., 11:45am, 8200dr). To reach the **bus station** from the ports, walk up Zalogo (past the Ionian Bank). When you reach the town plateia, turn left and walk two blocks to the **ticket office,** behind a cafe on the left marked with a blue KTEL sign.

## ORIENTATION AND PRACTICAL INFORMATION

Igoumenitsa is on the westernmost corner of mainland Greece, about 20km from the Albanian border. **Eth. Antistaseos,** which becomes **Ag. Apostolon,** runs along the waterfront, and teems with travel agencies. To the north, after it divides, the tree-lined inland side of the street is bordered by an array of cafes. Igoumenitsa's main shopping area is on the first pedestrian street parallel to the waterfront. To reach the uninspiring central plateia, walk four blocks inland on **Zalogo.**



**Tourist Office:** (☎22 227), in the old port. Helps with transportation and accommodations, plus a free map. Multilingual. Open 7am-2pm and 5-10pm. A second **tourist office** is in the New Port, Eth. Antistaseos 68 (☎23 564). Open 7am-10pm.

**Banks: National Bank** (☎22 415), across the road from the Old Port in a string of banks with 24hr. **ATM** and automatic **currency changer.**

**American Express:** Eth. Antistaseos 14 (☎22 406 or 24 333). Will **change money,** issue traveler's checks, cash all traveler's checks without commission, and give you cash from an AmEx card. Open M-F 7:30am-2pm and 4pm-11pm; Sa 4pm-11pm.

**Police:** Ag. Apostolon 5 (☎22 100), across from Corfu Port. Available 24hr.

**Port Police:** (☎25 833), in a Corfu Port booth, near customs and passport control.

**Medical Center:** (☎24 420). Basic health care. If necessary, they will help you get to the **hospital** (☎(0664) 22 203), 15min. away. Open 24hr.

**Telephones: OTE** (☎22 399), in the same building as the post office. Open 7am-3pm. The new port also has an **OTE** (☎27 757). Open 7am-10pm.

**Internet Access: Cafe Planet** (☎29 180), on the north end of the waterfront in the cafe strip. 6 fast terminals for 800dr per hour. Open 11:30am-12:30am.

**Post Office:** (☎22 599). Go left from the bus station, and turn left at the first corner; it's in the same building as the OTE. Open M-F 7am-2:45pm. A larger post office is at Tzaveninas 2 (☎46 100), 1km north along the waterfront on the corner of a large playground. Poste Restante. Open 7:30am-2pm. **Postal code:** 46100.

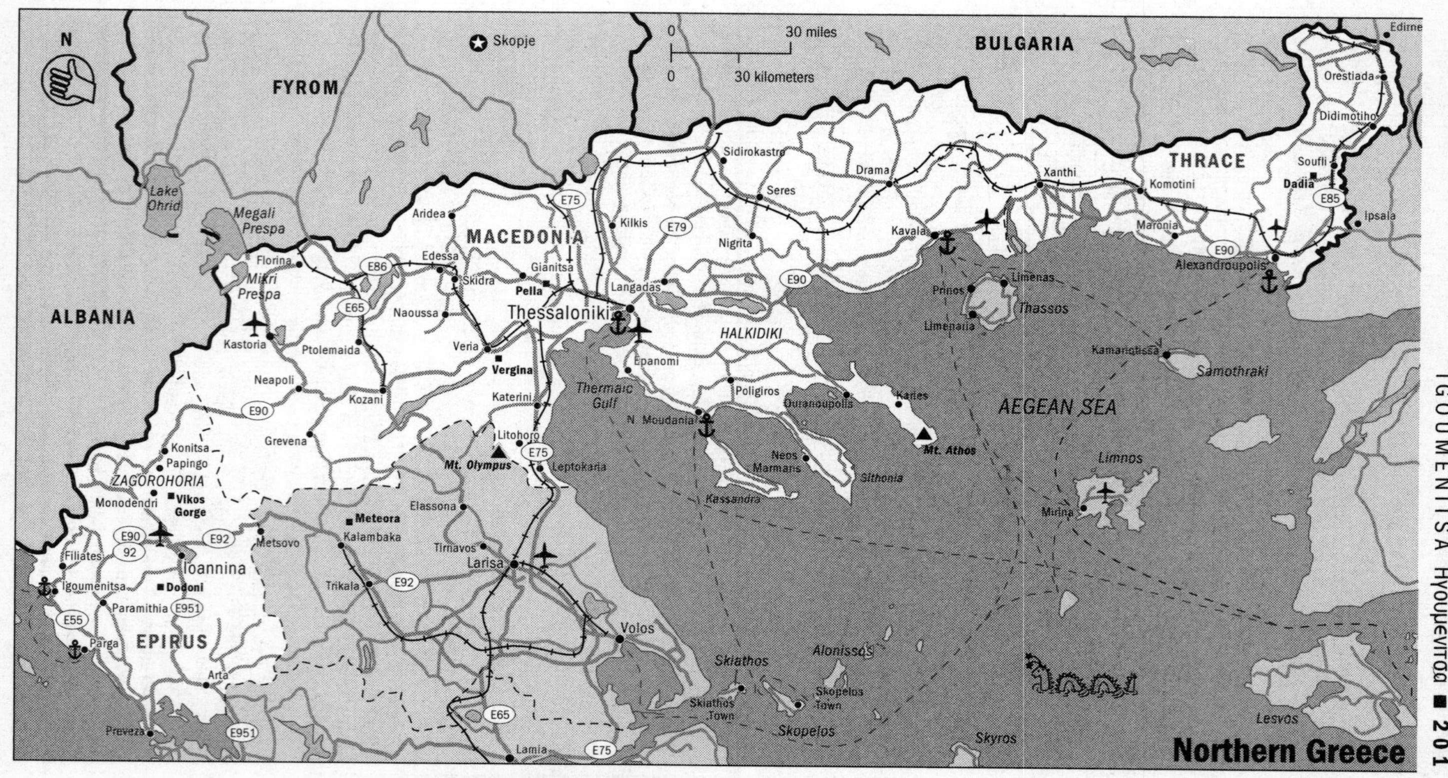


NORTHERN GREECE

## ACCOMMODATIONS

**Stavrodromi,** Souliou 16 (☎22 343). Walk uphill from the InterAmerican Hotel in the main plateia, and you'll see Stavrodromi on your right. Spacious, light-filled, airy rooms above a cafe, some with private baths (BYO toilet paper). Comfy beds. Singles 4000dr; doubles 6000dr; triples 9000dr.

**Hotel Acropolis** (☎22 349 and 28 346), on the waterfront in Old Port (look for the sign). Pretty, small rooms with wooden floors, shared baths, and thick-carpeted hallways; feels like a decaying mansion. Singles 6000dr; doubles 8000dr.

**Hotel Rex,** Grigariou 12 (☎22 255). From the port, walk up Zalogo and turn left at the first corner. Up the steep stairs in the white building with green shutters. Cramped, dark rooms with shared baths. Singles 3000dr; doubles 4000dr; triples 6000dr.

**Hotel Egnatia,** Eleftherias 2 (☎23 648). Sign at the central plateia's far right corner. Bare rooms with bath/shower, TVs, phones. Singles 7500dr; doubles 13,750dr.

## FOOD AND NIGHTLIFE

The best—and most locally popular—among the city's very average restaurants are on the north edge of the **waterfront,** past the ports and junk shops. Dozens of bakeries and small markets line the pedestrian street just inland from the harbor. Igoumenitsa's none-too-happening nightlife centers on a strip of bars just past the cafes along the waterfront. **Traffic** (☎23 505) and **Factory** (☎32 625), side by side along the water, both pump out American and Greek tunes all night on the weekends. There's also a **cinema,** right next to Taverna Aleko, that shows American movies at 9:30pm and 11:30pm. (1500dr per ticket.)

**Mykonos** (☎27 567), at the beginning of the waterfront strip, with a vine-hung patio full of earnestly arguing Greeks. Boasts a varied menu (entrees 1400-2300dr) consisting mainly of fish specialties. Try the feta-stuffed souvlaki for a break from the seafood.

**Paravda** (☎28 169). Follow the colorfully painted signs from the waterfront to the quiet side street behind the Ionian Bank. Imaginative takes on traditional fare and carafes of *retsina,* with live music at night under the grapevines. Entrees 500-1500dr.

**Alekos** (☎23 708), next door to Mykonos. Specializes in fish, big and small, from the pristine harbor waters. Entrees 1400-2000dr.



# PARGA Παργα ☎0684

Attached to the mainland by an arc of green mountains, Parga looks and feels like a Greek island town. With its luxurious beaches and bustling waterfront, Parga draws the fun- and sun-loving crowd, as well as overpriced jewelry shops, "effervescent nightlife," t-shirt vendors, and dozens of Scandinavian children wielding inflatable alligators. In high season, Parga bloats, attracting more than 15 times its winter population of 1700 in fuschia-nosed tourists. Parga's narrow, curling streets, its Neoclassical buildings, its house-high bougainvillea bushes, and the Venetian fortress that crowns it all create a pleasant and romantic mood that seems to have infected even the pastel pink supermarket.

Venice controlled Parga for close to four centuries, supporting it against raids by the Ottoman rulers of neighboring Epirus and marauding pirates. Rocky, reef-strewn cliffs and a high fortress made the town nearly impregnable by sea or land. For the Venetians, Parga was "the eye and ear of Corfu," an optimal spot to keep an eye on nearby Turkey. After Venice fell to Napoleon, Parga fell into British hands, and was in turn sold to Ali Pasha (see **Ali Pasha, Turkish Bogeyman,** p. 204) in exchange for the Ionian islands. Faced with the impending arrival of this notorious tyrant, many residents sought refuge in off-shore islands, taking the bones from their cemetery with them. After Ali Pasha's death, the townspeople gradually returned, only to labor under the Ottomans until Parga's 1913 liberation.

**ORIENTATION AND PRACTICAL INFORMATION.** Parga is organized around its waterfront. The main waterfront road, which brims with tavernas, bars, and tourist agencies, has three different names: from west to east, they are **Lambraki, Anexartissias,** and **Athanassiou.** At **Krioneriou Beach,** which runs alongside Athanassiou, the road forks: its uphill branch is **R. Feraiou.** Running inland from the waterfront is **Al. Baga,** which leads uphill to most of Parga's municipal buildings. Al. Baga meets **Sp. Livada** at the town's main intersection.

**Ferries** run to **Corfu Town** (1¾hr., Su and Th 8:30am, 5500dr). **Buses** run from Parga to: **Athens** (8½hr., 3 per day 7am-7:15pm, 8000dr); **Igoumenitsa** (1¼hr., 4 per day 7am-6:30pm, 1250dr); **Preveza** (1½hr., 5 per day 7am-9:45pm, 1500dr) and **Thessaloniki** (8hr., 7am, 9500dr). The bus station is a small booth next to the Chinese restaurant, at the top of Al. Baga.

The **municipal tourist office,** right across from the ferry dock, offers maps of the area and information about renting boats, cars, and mopeds. (☎32 107; fax 32 511. Open 8am-11pm.) **Tourist agencies** pack the streets around the waterfront, ready to help you find rooms, rent mopeds, and arrange daytrips; they're generally open M-Sa 9am-2pm and 5:30-10pm. **Axis Travel,** on Riga Fereou, just up from the Balthazar Restaurant, is a good bet, and provides **Internet access** on slow computers at 20dr per min. (☎31 766. Open 9am-10pm.)

With the **OTE** building (☎31 699; open M-F 7am-2:40pm) on your left and the shore behind you, straight ahead are the **bus stop, police station** (☎31 222; open 24hr), and **post office** (☎31 295; open M-F 7am-2pm). To the left is the **health center** and the **National Bank;** going right will bring you to a junction with the main road. **V.E. Vasila,** running parallel to the waterfront and having the highest density of tourist shops, leads up to the **Venetian castle** at the far southwest corner of town. From here, a stone path leads down the other side to **Valtos Beach.** For **emergencies** you can also call the **port police** (☎31 227). **Postal code:** 48060.

**ACCOMMODATIONS AND FOOD.** Parga's hotels are expensive, and prices spike in the summer months. For a cheaper bed, look around the south end of the town and the top of the hill for **rooms to let** (expect to pay 8000-10,000dr in high season). **Thomas House,** on Tzabela, has light rooms with shared bath and a large, full kitchen. From the bus station, walk downhill past the OTE and make a right at V.E. Vasila, then another right just before the Blue Bar: the rooms are upstairs from the shop directly ahead selling body-care products. (☎31 211. Doubles 5000-7000dr.) **Andreou Nausika**'s rooms, 10 steps below the castle on Gaki Zeri, are another good deal. Call ahead and someone will meet you in town. (☎31 306. Singles and doubles 5000dr, with bath 7000dr; triples 12,000dr.) Budget travelers can skip Parga's high-priced lodging altogether and camp on the nearby beaches. The closest is **Parga Beach Camping** (☎31 161), but **Valtos Camping,** by neighboring Valtos beach, is a bit cheaper. (☎31 287. 1200-1400dr per person.) **Elia Camping** (☎31 130) is 500m out on the Igoumenitsa road.

Although there are outright tourist traps among Parga's waterfront-centered restaurants, some offer memorable food at good prices. To find the best options, avoid establishments with extensive advertisements in English or German. Parganites and visitors enjoy O Psaras, one of the first restaurants along the dock, where Christos Giakis cooks up innovative renditions of the standard Greek repertoire: he makes his *pastitsio* (1200dr) with a mix of cheeses instead of pasta. (Entrees 1000-2200dr.) By the town beach, Restaurant Ionio (☎31 402) has a daily *prix fixe* three-course menu that's a steal at 1900dr, and Balthazar Restaurant (☎31 388) offers good atmosphere, a varied menu, and entrees from 1000 to 2000dr. If you're in the mood to splurge, swank Rudis serves creative Greek and Italian cuisine in a corner nook by the ferry dock. (Entrees 1500-3800dr.)

**NIGHTLIFE AND ENTERTAINMENT.** Scuttling waiters and rambunctious children run willy-nilly through crowds of happily inebriated northern Europeans at Parga's many waterfront bars and cafes. **Caravel,** near the ferry dock, is one of

the town's most popular bars, with an upstairs balcony. (☎31 359. Drinks 1800-2000dr.) The more removed **Blue Bar** (☎32 067), on the road leading to the castle, is the better bet, with stunning views of the sea and an attractive decor to go with the 96 cocktails cooked up by the bartenders. Try the Happy Company (6000dr)—served in a massive ceramic jug, it packs a punch to cold-cock you and three of your friends. Though the tourists here are of the family ilk, there are a couple of discos, which don't really start kickin' until around 2am. The biggest scenes are **Camares** (☎32 000) behind Caravel, and **Arena** (☎31 871), down behind the town beach. Camares packs more drunk Swedes into its cave-like interior than you'll find at a Stockholm beer festival, while Arena caters to the young, hip, beautiful set. **Factory,** whose neon signs point up side streets from near the ferry dock, and **Island** (☎32 446), along the waterfront between the ferry dock and the hill, are larger but slightly less packed. All clubs stay open until 4am on weekdays and at least 6am on weekends; they have a 1000dr cover, which includes one drink.

**SIGHTS AND BEACHES.** Poised above Parga, the massive **fortress,** or Kastro, was built by the Normans, but controlled by the Venetians from 1401 to 1797. A surprising number of walls still stand, and it's a perfect spot for a shady picnic, stroll, or dramatic re-enactment of a Venetian-Ottoman battle. It's five minutes from the water; follow the steps from the harbor up the hill. (Open 7am-10pm.)

**Krionerou Beach,** Parga's little waterfront, sees mostly the over-60 or under-8 set, but you can rent pedal-boats (2000dr per hr.) to paddle the 100m to the islet that holds the small **Church of the Panagia. Golfo Beach,** five minutes to the left of the town beach, is more secluded, but it has rocks the size of golfo (and tenniso) balls. Vastly nicer is long **Valtos Beach,** on the other side of the castle: a voluptuous crescent of sole-tickling pebbles turns to sand near the middle. Endless hordes of sun-worshipers sidle up to the rim of clear turquoise water. Here you can rent anything from a beach ball to a paragliding trip, or enjoy shots and revelry at the packed **pool club.** Boats travel to the smaller beaches, including the more secluded **Lignos Beach** (2km away), accessible by car or boat.

Tour companies along the waterfront and on the ferry dock book a variety of prepackaged excursions, most of which include cheery stops at the **River Acheron**—the River Styx, mythical gateway to the Underworld—and the **Necromonteion,** the Oracle of the Dead, excavated in 1958. It was here that Odysseus conversed with the Shades, who spoke to him only after drinking offerings of blood. (Open 8:30am-3pm. 500dr, students 300dr.) Both are about a 20min. drive from Parga, but trips by **boat** are significantly cheaper than by bus. **Axis Travel**'s daily boat tour visits both sites and several beaches. (Leaves at 9:30am, returns 4pm. 4000dr.)



**ALI PASHA, TURKISH BOGEYMAN** Ali Pasha's black shadow hangs over the Greek folk tradition, embodying ruthless Turkish evil and greed. Although nominally subject to the Sultan in Istanbul, Ali Pasha did pretty much whatever he wanted during his 34-year rule over Ioannina, purportedly handing out horrifying punishments to all transgressors and oppressing the locals. He is said to have drowned the **Lady Phrosyni** and 17 of her attendants in Pamvotis Lake, either because she was having an affair with his oldest son or because she had rejected his advances. Famed for his cunning and debauchery, Ali cavorted with his harem of hundreds of men and women, caroused with Lord Byron, and engaged in endless vindictive skirmishes. On the other hand, all was not misery under Ali. He was more tolerant of other religions than his predecessors, abolishing second-class-citizen status for Christians. His reign brought stability, economic progress, and an intellectual flowering to the region. His court was home to many up-and-coming Revolutionary War heroes, including Kar̈iskakis, Botsaris, and members of the secret revolutionary group *Filiki Eteria* ("Friendship Society"). These rebels strategically sided with Ali against the Sultan, encouraging his disregard of the sublime Porte in the hopes that the Ottoman regime's internal division would help the cause of Greek independence.

# IOANNINA Ιωαννινα ☎0651

On the shores of Lake Pamvotis, 96km miles east of Igoumenitsa, lies Epirus's capital, largest city, and transportation hub. Ioannina itself might not detain you for long, but the surrounding mountains and calm lake below deliver scenic views and an uplifting breeziness to Ioannina. Likewise, the city's post-Second World War architecture is redeemed by the small, older streets near the lake and the absolutely magnificent fortress, both remnants of its Ottoman past. No visitor to Ioannina can escape the foreboding, half-legend of Ali Pasha, "Lion of Ioannina" (see p. 204). The Albanian-born Pasha of Trikala seized Ioannina in 1788 and built himself a sumptuous, well-fortified palace there. Intending to make the city the capital of his Greek-Albanian Empire, Ali ruled with an iron fist, alternately fighting with and serving the Ottoman Sultan, who was theoretically his ruler. In his quest for power, Ali flirted with Napoleon, the British, and the Venetians, until finally the Sultan axed him for high treason in 1822. Ali left his imprint on the city: his immense fortress and private Xanadu are here, and he died on nearby Nisi Island.

## ORIENTATION AND PRACTICAL INFORMATION

Ioannina is at the center of Epirus, edging along the side of steely Lake Pamvotis, circled by Pindos peaks. Not far out into the lake is a small, hilly island simply called Nisi or Nissaki ("the island" or "the islet"). Ioannina's streets change names frequently, when they have names at all.

The **city center** is a major intersection near the **clock tower** in Litharitses park. **G. Averof** street has most necessities; it's a broad avenue that runs from the main gate of the old city to the city center. To reach the city center from the main **bus station,** walk uphill about 20m from the station to an intersection, where you'll see an **Agricultural Bank.** Facing the bank, walk uphill along the street on the left, which is **M. Botsari**—the enormous Hotel Egnatia sign makes a useful landmark. You'll pass the **post office,** which is on a corner across from the **OTE** and will emerge next to the **Ionian Bank** on Averof, facing the park. On your right, past the long building labelled "Nomarchion Ioanninou" ("Prefecture of Ioannina"), the road splits. The right side (*not* the sharp right) is **Napoleonda Zerva,** to the left is **Leoforos Dodoni.** At the set of lights before the Prefecture building, a road leads downhill on your left past the city bus stop and on to the smaller of the two intercity bus stations. To reach the **Frourio** (fortress) and the **waterfront,** follow the signs from the city center to Averof's opposite end, and veer left at the Frourio walls. You will now be on **Karamanli,** which passes the main gate of the Frourio to the dock and waterfront.

**Buses:** There are two terminals in town.

**Main terminal,** Zosimadon 4 (☎27 442). To: **Athens** (7hr., 9 per day 7:15am-midnight, 7500dr); **Igoumenitsa** (2hr., 10per day 5am-7:45pm, 1800dr); **Konitsa** (1hr., 6 per day 5am-6:45pm, 1250dr); **Larisa** (4hr., 6 per day 7am-9pm, 3750dr); **Metsovo** (1½hr., 2 per day 5am-2pm, 1200dr); **Parga** (2½hr., 8:30am, 2250dr); and **Thessaloniki** (7hr., 6 per day 7am-9pm, 6200dr).

**Smaller station:** Bizaniou 21 (☎25 014). To: **Agrinio** (3hr., 6 per day 5:30am-7:15pm, 3000dr); **Arta** (1hr., 10 per day 5:45am-7:15pm, 2050dr); **Dodoni** (30min., 2 per day, 450dr); **Patras** (4hr., 2 per day 8:30am-5pm, 4550dr); and **Preveza** (2hr., 10 per day 6am-7:15pm, 2050dr).

**Flights:** daily to **Athens** (50min.; 10:35am and 8:35pm, plus W-F 2:35pm; 19,000dr) and **Thessaloniki** (45min.; 4:30pm, plus Th and Su 3:55pm; 13,500dr). **Olympic Airways** (☎26 218; reservations 23 120), across from tourist office. Open M-F 9am-3pm.

**Taxis:** (☎46 777, 778, or 779) also in the city center and at the bus station.

**Tourist Office: EOT office** (☎46 662; fax 49 139), about 500m down Leoforos Dodoni on the left; it's a trek from the city center, so think twice before going. Has **maps** and a Ioannina prefecture propaganda, with a list of rooms to let in the province. Open M-F 7:30am-2:30pm and 5:30-8pm; in winter 9am-2:30pm, Sa 9:30am-1pm.

**Banks:** There are a number of banks with 24hr. **ATMs,** including **National Bank,** on Averof, just after the archaeological museum as you walk toward the waterfront.

**Police:** (☎26 326). Walk along Botsari to the post office–the police and the tourist police are just around the corner on 28 Octovriou. Open 8am-10pm, but available 24hr.

**Tourist Police:** (☎25 673), with the police. **Free maps** and other info available. Open 8am-10pm. Another kiosk is on the waterfront on Filosoffou.

**Hospital:** Two hospitals, each about 5km from the center of town. One handles emergencies on even dates (☎80 111); the other on odd dates (☎99 111).

**Telephones: OTE** (☎22 350 or 42 777), opposite police. Open 8am-2:30pm.

**Internet Access: Web@r,** Stoa Sarka 31-32 (☎83 215), is tucked away among shops off Nap. Zerva. Turn right after down the arcade after the Wendy's. You'll see the blue-edged windows through the passageway to the left of the Casbah Cafe. Nine fast terminals, 600dr per hr. Open 11am-4am.

**Post Office:** (☎25 498), at the intersection of 28 Octovriou and Botsari. Open M-F 7:30am-8pm. **Postal code:** 45221.

## ACCOMMODATIONS

**Hotel Paris,** Tsirigoti 6 (☎20 541). Walk uphill from the station to the Agricultural Bank and look left for the hotel's sign. Small, functional rooms, close to the main bus station. Free luggage storage. Singles 6000dr, with bath 8000dr; doubles 9000/10,000dr.

**Hotel Metropolis,** Kristali 2 (☎26 207), on the corner of Averof as you walk toward the waterfront. Comfortable, spacious rooms with wooden floors and furnishings that walk the fine line between quaint and too quaint. Singles 5000dr, with bath 6000dr; doubles 8000/10,000dr. Prices lower from Oct.-Apr.

**Hotel Ermes** (☎75 992), across from the main bus station. Bare, cell-block rooms with sinks, shared baths, lots of street noise. But cheap. Singles 4000dr; doubles 6000dr.

## FOOD AND NIGHTLIFE

Several souvlaki stands are at the end of Averof near the Frourio (and elsewhere). Seafood restaurants circling the north side of the **waterfront** serve critters straight from the lake.

**Nousias,** Karamanli 1. Take the street that passes the main gate of the Frourio toward the dock and the waterfront; it's a little sweetshop. Enough confections, pastries, chocolate things, gooey concoctions, honey, nuts, and crispy delights to drive you wild.

**Oasis** (☎75 400), in the city center park. An enormous, popular, open-air restaurant serving generous portions of good food at good prices, and nice lake views in back. Classic Greek entrees like *kokoretsi* (lamb liver) and awesome feta-stuffed beef are 700-3000dr. English menu posted at the gate on the sidewalk. Open 24hr.

**Filippas** (☎31 170), on the waterfront before Stin Ithaki. Delicious fish from the river and eel from the lake (a delicacy in classical Athens). Open 1:30pm-midnight.

**Stin Ithaki** (☎73 012), on the waterfront about midway down. This local favorite has blue tablecloths and straw roofs. Entrees 1000-1900dr.

**Propodes** (☎81 214), on the island along the path to the Ali Pasha Museum. Secluded tables by the lake shore. Your meal is either whisked out of the cage (quail) or the tank (trout, frogs, eels, crayfish). Entrees 800-1800dr.

Most of Ioannina's bars are at the far western end of the waterfront, about a 15min. walk from the castle. **Ev. Ioanninos** (☎21 669) takes up three sides of a small square off the road, serving drinks from its outdoor bar until 3:30am; get ready to see and be seen. **Skala** (☎37 676) is on the fourth side, churning loud music for piercing-heavy wannabe Sex Pistols. **Millenio** (☎78 087) is right around the corner, with a blue-lit dance floor and late-night dancing. **Monopolio** is Ioannina's biggest disco, where locals dance to Greek or Latin tunes every night. It's on the opposite end of town, past the seafood restaurants. (Drinks 500dr; cover 1000dr. ☎35 985.)

## SIGHTS

### FROURIO (OLD CITY)

The town's fortress, the Frourio (a.k.a. the **Kastro** or **Old City**) looms regally over the shore, a slender minaret at each end. Its massive, overgrown stone walls enclose a placid neighborhood of narrow streets and old Turkish-style homes. The Frourio contains two separate walled areas; the larger is the **Itş Kale** (Inner Citadel). Like any self-respecting fortress, the Frourio's main entrance on Karamanli has several sharp turns, making invasion tricky. Just outside this entrance is the shrine to **St. George the Neomartyr,** Ioannina's patron saint, whose Turkish overlords tortured and hanged him in 1838 for marrying a Christian. The Frourio's old **Synagogue,** Ioustinianon 16, is inside along the wall that faces Karamanli; go left from the main gate and follow the wall until you reach the white walls with a large brick-red double door. Ioannina's Jewish population shrank from 2000 to 150 after the Second World War, but the building still has services on Friday and Saturday.

**HISTORY.** Most of the castle was built in the 14th century by **Thomas Preljubovic,** the Serbian ruler of Ioannina who was also known as **Albanitoktonos:** "Albanian-killer." In order to secure the city's bloodless surrender in 1430, the Turks assured the Greeks that they could remain in their houses within the walls. After a failed 1611 Greek insurrection led by **Skilosofos,** fanatical Bishop of Trikala, however, the Turks cracked down. One Sunday, when all the Greeks were in church, the Turks

seized their houses and moved right in. Skilosofos, the rebellious Bishop, was flayed alive on the cliff near his namesake esplanade, which runs lakeside beneath the castle walls. When Ali Pasha came to power in 1795, he forced his Greek subjects to rebuild the pre-existing Byzantine walls on a grander scale to fortify the capital of his dreamed-of empire. The project connected the ends of a partially existing moat, insulating the walls with lake water.

**ITŞ KALE.** To reach the Itş Kale from the main entrance, walk generally forward, veering left, following the signs. The small ruined buildings to the left and right as you enter the walls were guard posts, and the cafe on the left was originally a kitchen. Over to the immediate right along the wall are the remnants of Ali Pasha's **hamam** (baths). Around what is now the Silverworks gallery, the *serai* once housed Ali, his harem, and his ornately decorated audience chambers. Ali Pasha held most of his notorious tortures and executions at the plane tree near the *serai*, running the gory gamut from skinning to impaling and suspending on hooks hung from the tree's branches. Independence War hero **Katsandonis** is said to have sung patriotic hymns while being brutally hammered to death here, a scene re-enacted frequently in Greek folk shadow puppet theater. The ruins on the right of the complex are partially preserved, and are well worth a scramble. *(Open 7am-10pm.)*

The **Byzantine Museum** in the Itş Kale displays intricately carved wooden sanctuary doors, stone carvings, calligraphied manuscripts, and post-Byzantine icons. Informative English wall plaques chronicle the history of Epirus and Ioannina. *(☎27 761 or 39 580. Open July-Oct. M 12:30-7pm, Tu-Su 8:30am-5pm; Nov.-June Tu-Su 8am-2:30pm. 500dr, students free.)* The **Fethiye Camii** (Victory Mosque) next to the museum is the third mosque in its location, a space once occupied by a 13th-century church: the first was built of wood in 1430 and the second in 1611. The current mosque was rebuilt in 1795 by Ali Pasha himself. In front of the mosque, weeds and rubble obscure the **Tomb of Ali Pasha,** a family sarcophagus that contains his headless body; from the neck up, he's buried in Istanbul. The tomb was originally decorated with a gilded cage that was looted by Nazis in 1943. For splendid lake views, walk behind the mosque. Ioaninna is the silversmithing capital of Greece, and at the **Silverworks Gallery,** you'll find snuffboxes, tea services, and belt buckles to prove it. An 1843 etching beside the ticket desk depicts the Frourio's former glory. *(☎25 989. Show your Byzantine Museum ticket for admission to the gallery.)*

**MUNICIPAL MUSEUM.** The smaller of the Frourio's walled inner areas is a little farther to the left of Itş Kale—follow signs through the crooked streets to the museum housed in the lovely **Aslan Pasha Camii.** Most of the ruins are clearly labeled. On the left as you enter is the long, rectangular *medrasa* (school for Koranic study). The tombstones engraved in Arabic are the remains of an **Ottoman cemetery,** and the small building behind the mosque is Aslan Pasha's mausoleum.



**GOING OUT WITH(OUT) A BANG** When Ali Pasha heard that the Sultan had finally tired of his rebellious, empire-dreaming antics, he decided not to go gently into that good night. Holing up on Nisi, he gave orders to Selim, his most trusted servant, to stand guard over the castle's immense casks of gunpowder with a lighted torch. If Selim heard gunshots from the island, he was to blow himself, the castle, and the city with all its inhabitants clear into Lake Pamvotis. If anyone arrived bearing Ali's rosary, all was well and he could put out the torch. The sultan's envoys, however, managed to convince Ali's Greek wife Vasilikis to betray Ali's instructions, telling her it was her duty as a Greek to save the town from destruction. Vasilikis stole Ali's rosary as he slept, and presented it to the Turks, who immediately used it to convince Selim to put out his torch. When the gun battle began on Nisi the next day, Ali waited in vain for the explosion from the mainland before discovering his rosary had vanished. Before he could order revenge against his wife, he was killed by shots fired through the floor. For her part, Vasilikis retired to the coast of Turkey, where she lived with the captain of the force sent to kill her husband.

In 1618, following Bishop Skilosofos's rebellion, the Turks destroyed the former church of St. John Prodromus and replaced it with this elegant mosque, painted with green and terra-cotta. Worshipers washed their hands and feet in the fountains outside and left their shoes in small grooves along the entranceway before going inside to pray. The Municipal Museum focuses on Ioannina's diverse ethnic past, featuring a sword that belonged to War of Independence hero Karaiskaki, a golden dress worn by Ali Pasha's wife, Lady Vasilikis, and embroidered clothing and temple decorations donated by the city's Jewish community. *(☎26 356. Open June-Sept. 8am-8pm; Oct.-May 8am-3pm. 700dr, students 300dr.)*

## OTHER SIGHTS

**ARCHAEOLOGICAL MUSEUM.** Aside from local finds, Paleolithic to Roman, the museum's highlights are the **lead tablets** used by puzzled ancients to inscribe their questions to that divine Dear Abby, the oracle to Zeus in nearby **Dodoni** (p. 209). Questions range from petty suspicions ("Has Pistos stolen the wool from the mattress?") to love advice ("Am I her children's father?"), and much angst seems to have surrounded the dilemma of which deity to honor for which cause. Check out the **copper statues** from the oracle, which would speak the words of Zeus through batons they held in their hands. The cafe and terrace behind the museum have very nice views. A trip to the museum really adds to a visit to Dodoni. *(The museum is on a small road off Averof near the city center, across from the yellow town hall building with its three white arches. ☎33 357 or 25 490. Open Tu-Su 8am-2pm. 500dr, students free.)*

**NISI (THE ISLAND).** Wandering chickens, cheap silver shops, a tiny whitewashed village, and five deteriorating monasteries cover Ioannina's peaceful island, a ten-minute ferry ride from the harbor. Ali Pasha met his death here after falling out of the sultan's favor in a big way. Discovered and trapped in the second story of the island's **St. Pantaleemon monastery,** he was killed by shots fired up through the floorboards—you can still see the bullet holes (see **Going Out With(out) a Bang,** p. 208). The victors hung Ali's severed head out for public viewing for several days before transporting it on horseback all the way to the sultan in Constantinople. The monastery now houses the **Ali Pasha Museum,** which displays Ali Pasha's enormous *nargileh,* from which he happily puffs in almost every portrait, other personal relics, and a large painting of the sultan ceremoniously receiving the head of his fearsome ex-governor. What goes around comes around. *(Open 8am-8pm. 150dr.)*

Signs point the way to St. Pantaleemon and the other four monasteries. Near the museum, the **frescoes of St. Nicholas Philanthropinos,** painted by Katelanou in 1542, depict saints, the life of Jesus, and seven ancient sages (including Plato, Aristotle and Plutarch) who were said to have proclaimed the coming of Jesus. At the nearby *krifto scholio* ("secret school"), the forbidden Greek language was kept alive during the Ottoman reign. The monastery of **St. John Prodromos** has a crypt leading to a secret exit and path to the lake. *(To reach the island, take one of the little ferries from Ioannina's waterfront (10min.; every hr. 6:30-11:30am and every 30min. 11:30am-11pm; in winter every hr. 7am-9pm; 150dr). ☎25 885.)*

**VRELLIS' WAX-WORKS MUSEUMS.** Brother **Antanasios**' unconvincing wax people pose for a handful of cheesy historical and mythological scenes: Socrates drinks the hemlock, Diogenes asks Alexander the Great to step out of his sunlight, and a mechanized eagle teeters over Prometheus for another go at his regenerating liver. Flashing colored lights make for a disco feeling. *(Karamanli 15. ☎22 414. Open M-Sa 9am-4pm, Su 10am-4pm.)*



## DAYTRIPS FROM IOANNINA

## DODONI Δωδωνη

*Your best bet is the **bus** to Melig (30 min; 2pm M, Th, F; 450dr) from **Ioannina**'s smaller station–ask to be let off at the theater. You can then catch the return bus at 5:15pm. The bus to Dodoni (30min.; 4:30pm M-W, F; 400dr) will leave you with barely 15min. to view the site. Otherwise, hire a **taxi** (at least 5000dr round-trip). ☎82 287. Open 8am-7pm; in winter 8am-5pm. 500dr, students free.*

In an unprecedented example of tuber lust, **Zeus** put down roots (literally) in Dodoni—while trying to get with a nearby cypress tree, he made a guest appearance as a giant oak's undercarriage. Years later, a dove perched on the tree and told Dodoni's inhabitants that there should be an oracle to Zeus on the spot. Countless visitors have since brought questions on the meaning of life and the intricacies of sex: Zeus was clearly an expert on both subjects.

Ancient Dodoni, the site of mainland Greece's oldest oracle, hugs up to the base of a mountain 22km southeast of Ioannina. The name Dodoni descends from the Linear B language, and may mean "great mother of civilization;" Dodoni was probably the deity worshipped there before being supplanted by Zeus. Excavations suggest that the oracle was used from the Bronze Age (2600-1100 BC) through Christianity's arrival in the late 4th century AD. Worship of Zeus at Dodoni was well established by Homer's time: Odysseus himself came to the oracle at "wintry Dodona" for advice on ridding his house of Penelope's suitors. At its height, Dodoni was one of the ancient world's greatest oracles and home of the **Naia festival,** a series of athletic and dramatic contests held every four years in Zeus' honor.

The large **amphitheater** near the entrance to the site was built in the third century AD; the original design seated 18,000, before the Romans expanded it and improved the drainage system to accommodate their bloodsports. The annual ancient **theater festival** may have been revived, but the theater is in sad need of restoration. Beyond the amphitheater are the ruins of the oracle itself, where Zeus would answer queries through a still-standing oak tree. A clan of priests called the **Hellopes, Helloi,** or **Selloi** interpreted the wind's effect on the oak tree leaves' rustling, the flight of doves in its branches, and the sound of wooden batons held by a bronze statue of a boy striking a row of copper cauldrons. Using their sonic data, the priests made prophecies; trying to absorb the god's messages through the soil, they walked barefoot. Wild priestesses prone to divine frenzy eventually replaced the male *Selloi*. Little remains today of the original building that housed the tree and its horde of pilgrims. Additional buildings, now almost totally vanished, once surrounded the oracle: a 5th-century BC temple and the 350 BC *bouleuterion* and *prytaneion*. Following the Aetolian sack in 219 BC, a larger Ionic temple to Zeus was built in 168-167 BC, and the great amphitheater in the early 3rd century AD.



## PERAMA CAVES

*Take local bus #4, 5, or 8 from the park behind the city center (15min., every 20min., 360dr round-trip). At Perama, follow the blue signs reading EPHLAIO ("cave"). ☎81 251 or 81 440. Open 8am-8pm; in winter 8am-5pm; tours run every 45min. 1500dr, students 700dr.*

A 163-step stairway leads through the spectrally lit, sickly-yellow Perama Caves, believed to be the largest in the Balkans. Excavations have turned up bears' teeth and bones in the almost two million-year-old stalagmites and stalactites, as well as **paintings** devoted to the ancient worship of Hades and Persephone. The path leads from narrow passageways to immense **caverns** hanging with eerie rock formations. The 45-minute Greek-only guided tour mainly introduces selected stalagmites which have been named after other stalagmite-shaped things they uncannily resemble: "Tower of Pisa," "Egyptian Sphinx," and so on.

## PINDOS MOUNTAINS

Those who prefer their air fresh and sunlit might consider using Ioannina as a base for outdoor activities in the Pindos Mountains. The **European E6** path runs nearby, as well as the **national 01** and **03 routes.** The 03 brings hikers through the Vikos Gorge and past an array of mountaintops and villages, and is known to offer some of the best hiking in Greece. Rock climbers can scale the faces of **Eamila, Tsouka Rossa,** and **Pirgos Astraka,** and avid spelunkers can attempt the **Provatihas Cave,** the second-deepest cave in the world, at 407m. Most of these expeditions are best undertaken with an experienced guide or after consulting an outdoors agency in Ioannina, since maps of the region tend to be unreliable. The **Hellenic Mountaineering Club** (EOS), Despotatou Ipirou 2, can be reached by following the signs for

the Folklore Museum down Mikhail Angelou; it's a few blocks past the museum at a multi-pronged intersection. The club supplies information and leads weekend trips throughout the region. (☎22 138. Open M-Sa 7:30-9pm.) **Robinson's Agency,** Merarchias 8, 2km from city center on the airport road, arranges walking and canyoning trips. (☎29 402. Open M-F 9am-3pm.) The **Paddler Kayaking and Rafting School** (☎(0655) 23 777 or (0655) 23 101) in Konitsa gives lessons and oversees outings to local rivers. For alpine flowers, April through June is the best hiking season; colored foliage flares brilliantly in the dry autumns.

## METSOVO Μετσοβο ☎0656

On a forested mountainside below the Pindos Mountains' 1690m-high Katara Pass, Metsovo is almost painfully quaint: think ski town meets teensy traditional village. Once upon a time, Marc Antony used to pack his wife off to Metsovo when he wanted to carry on more freely with Cleopatra. Now, daytripping tour buses of all nations frequent this officially designated "traditional" settlement. There's a booming trade in postcards and handmade wooden trinkets, most of which are made across the border in Albania. Despite its kitschiness, Metsovo makes an excellent base for hiking, exploring Metsovo Lake, and trekking down the European E-6 trail, which passes nearby. Metsovo was once an important outpost on the route from Rome to Constantinople, and its inhabitants today trace their roots to the Vlachi, a tribe of Latin-speaking Romans who served as guards; today, older villagers are among the few in the world who still speak their Latin-like tongue, and local surnames and place names still show vestiges of their Latin origins. Way back when, Metsovo's wealth came from its relative independence under Ottoman rule, which attracted rich refugees; Metsovo owes its current prosperity to Mihail Tositsas, a Metsovo-born Swiss baron, who gave most of his fortune to the town.

**ORIENTATION AND PRACTICAL INFORMATION.** Metsovo is about 100km inland in eastern Epirus, halfway between Kalambaka and Ioannina. On a stone wall in the main plateia, a large, nearly illegible English-language **town map** lists hotels, sights, monasteries, restaurants, discos, and a 24-hour "sanitary station" (☎41 111) for **medical emergencies.** From the main plateia, **buses** depart for Ioannina (1½hr.; M-F 4 per day 6:15am-4:30pm, Sa-Su 2 per day; 1100dr) and to Trikala via Kalambaka (2hr., 8:15am and 3:15pm, 1800dr). Buses to Thessaloniki stop at the main highway above town (about 5 times per day); ask the owner of the Hotel Athens for a more complete schedule. For **schedule info,** check any of the cafes near the bus stops. Some six or seven streets radiate out of the large, open plateia, none of which has a labeled name. Standing with your back to the big town map, the street on the left side of the souvenir shop you're facing leads slightly downhill to the municipal **police** (☎41 233; open 24hr.) and the **OTE** (☎42 199; open 8am-1pm). The main road is on your left, choked with souvenir stands and tavernas; it leads uphill to the path to the Tositsas Museum and the **post office.** (☎44 200. Open M-F 7:30am-2pm.) The **town hall,** the large building in the park where the main road meets the plateia, can provide you with a few glossy brochures of the area. (☎41 207. Open 7:30am-2pm; walk around to the building's back entrance.) On your immediate right, a road runs downhill to Hotel Athens and Agios Nikolaos monastery, while another wraps around the plateia past a **National Bank** with 24-hour **ATM** and the art museum. **Postal code:** 44200.

**ACCOMMODATIONS.** Room prices peak during the two high seasons: from mid-July to early September, and from December to March for the ski season. It's best to call ahead for the price *du jour.* The **Hotel Athens,** just below the main plateia, offers cozy rooms with private baths at the best rates in town; a taverna is below. (☎41 725. Singles 4000dr; doubles 8000dr.) Hikers and campers are welcome to store their gear here free of charge during visits to Pindos Mountain. The owners can also suggest hiking routes, and are in fact your best source of information in Metsovo. **Tsanaka** rents scrubbed, comfortably spacious rooms with TVs

and phones. To find it, follow the signs from the road leading to the OTE. (☎41 806. Prices fluctuate by season, with doubles ranging from 5000dr to 10,000dr.) **John Xaralabapoulos**'s rooms are large and comfortable, with TVs and phones, some with fridges and stoves. To get there from the plateia, take the left fork where the road splits before the OTE, and then turn left at the schoolyard. The house is in front of you, across from a fruit market. (☎42 086. Singles 6000dr, doubles 8000-9000dr, triples and suites 12000dr and up; prices may rise in high season.)

**FOOD AND ENTERTAINMENT.** The restaurant in **Hotel Athens** serves Greek specialties on their shady patio. The *fasolada* (bean soup, 750dr), stuffed vegetables (1000dr), and *Katogi* (local wine, 500dr), are cheaper (entrees 600-1700) and better than most restaurants in the plateia. If you'd like to eat in the plateia, try local favorite **Krifi Folia** for its grilled meats, like *kokoretsi* (1600dr) and *kontosoufli* (1400dr). Also on the plateia is **Kria Vrisi,** which specializes in *hilopittes fournou* (a pasta), and **Galaxias,** on the patio atop the grassy hill overlooking the plateia, which has Metsovo's largest selection of dishes. Metsovo has little to no nightlife, but if you need a drink or three after dinner, head to **Tositsas** street, leading uphill from the plateia. There's little difference between the bars; all charge 500dr for beer and 1500dr for cocktails, and quiet down by midnight.

**SIGHTS.** Thanks to the generosity of Baron Tositsas and Evangelos Averoff-Tositsas, Metsovo has far more sights than you'd expect of a 3500-person village with one main road. Off the main plateia, the spacious, well-lit **E. Averoff Gallery** exhibits 19th- and 20th-century Greek art labeled in English and Greek, including the private collection of Averoff-Tositsas. Some highlights of the museum's 200-plus paintings include impressionistic landscapes by Pantazis (1849-84), the *Burning of the Turkish Flagship* by Lytras (1832-1904), and the postmodern *Erotic* by Gravvalos (b. 1933). Green clay dinosaurs gaze amiably upon visitors in the colorful **children's art room** downstairs, where dried-bean collages and delightful tempera paintings are a welcome complement to their oily counterparts above. (☎41 210. Open W-M 10am-7pm. 500dr, students 300dr.)

The **Tositsas Museum,** the family abode of the town benefactors, is the stone and timber *arhontiko* (mansion) up from the main road on the left; look for the sign opposite the Shell station. In the museum's rooms you'll find the beds, sofas, rugs, jewelry, clothing, and kitchen utensils used by the Tositsas clan from 1661 until 1950, when the last descendant, Mihail, died. In addition, there's also a collection of local folk art and dress. The museum's upper floor served as Averoff-Tositsas' apartment until his death in 1990. (Open F-W 9:30am-1:30pm and 4-6pm. 500dr. Visitors are admitted only in small groups; wait at the museum's door for the guide, who appears every 30min.)

A 30-minute walk from the plateia, you'll find the **Agios Nikolaos Monastery;** signs point the way. Built in the 14th century and subsequently abandoned, the crumbling chapel was for years a refuge for itinerant shepherds. The smoke from their fires completely covered the luminous frescoes painted in 1702 by noted saint biographer Efsiat Chios, perfectly preserving their colors until they were rediscovered in 1950 by Averoff-Tositsas. A family now lives in the monastery, so knock to be admitted and wander around through the chickens and cats. For information about skiing, hiking, and rafting in Metsovo and in nearby **Valiakalda National Park,** contact the town hall (☎41 207) or the family that owns Hotel Athens (☎41 725).



## ZAGOROHORIA Ζαγοροχωρια

The Zagorohoria is a cluster of 46 villages north of Ioannina. According to the strictures of Zagori custom—and Greek preservation laws—buildings are crafted out of gray stone from the surrounding mountains. With nary a whitewashed concrete *polikatikia* apartment building in sight, the villages appear, from a distance, as oddly geometric rock formations poking humbly out of the green hills. Bridging streams between villages are the famous two- and three-arched stone bridges of

Epirus, best exemplified in the village of Kipi. While the natural beauty hasn't prevented native Zagorians from heading to the big city, some villages have reinvented themselves as quiet getaways for Greek and European tourists seeking clear air, simple food, and extraordinary hiking. Outside Monodendri, the Papingo villages, and Tsepelovo, however, no more than a handful of tourists visit each year, leaving the other villages as pristine as they were hundreds of years ago.

**OUTDOOR FUN.** Although the villages themselves are well worth a day or two, most tourists come to this rugged region for what lies in the hinterlands—untamed rivers, stark peaks, and the renowned **Vikos Gorge.** Outdoor enthusiasts of every skill level will find more than enough to satisfy them in the Zagorohoria and the surrounding **Vikos-Aoös National Park.** For more information, contact the **Hellenic Mountaineering Club (EOS)** in Ioannina (☎(0651) 22 138), Mario at **Pension Monodendri** (☎(0653) 71 300), or Nikos at **Koulis Restaurant** in Megalo Papingo (☎(0653) 41 138). Rafting and kayaking trips can be arranged in spring through **Konitsa's Paddler School** (☎(0655) 23 777 or 23 101). **Robinson Expeditions** runs guided tours, rock climbing expeditions, and rafting trips out of their office in Ioannina (☎(0651) 74 989; fax (0651) 25 071) and their activity center in Kipi (☎(0653) 71 041). The best times for hiking are late May, early June, and September. Make sure to get good maps (available through the EOS) and good directions through reliable sources before heading out. Maps of the region are surprisingly difficult to come by; it's said that because of the Zagorohoria's proximity to the Albanian border, the Greek army doesn't like maps to circulate widely. Check in hotels and with Robinson Expeditions in Kipi.

## MONODENDRI Μονοδενδρι ☎0653

Many an enchanted traveler have tripped dreamily through Monodendri's cobbled maze, illuminated only by celestial bodies and, in summer, multitudes of flirting fireflies. Despite a smattering of hikers, skiers, and city-escapees in summer and winter, the village remains as peaceful, unsullied, and perfect as a mountain stream. Its natural and architectural beauty makes it a pleasant base for hikers.

**ORIENTATION AND PRACTICAL INFORMATION.** The single paved road in Monodendri runs through the upper end of the village; the bus stop, all the hotels, and most of the restaurants cluster there. Buses go to **Ioannina** (45min., 2 per day 7am and 5pm, 750dr). The town plateia is accessible by a footpath descending to the right as you leave the bus stop; follow the path downhill and turn left when the road forks. There is **no bank,** but some hotels may be able to cash traveler's checks or change money in a pinch. There is a card **phone** on the paved road after Zarkada. There is a **post box** in the plateia, but you'll have to get up early and catch the postman if you want to buy any stamps.

**ACCOMMODATIONS.** Monodendri's plentiful accommodations are generally high in quality and low in price, making it one of the most affordable villages in the Zagorohoria. **Pension Monodendri,** just up the road from the bus stop, has light, extremely comfortable rooms in the traditional Zagori style, with low platform beds strewn with cushions; there's a garden in back and a great restaurant downstairs. It's a great place for hikers; the owner's English-speaking son Mario is full of info on trekking the area. His parents, Dimitris and Katerina Daskalopoulou, can also arrange to pick you up in the surrounding villages after your day-hike (from Vikos village 8000dr; from Megalo Papingo 10,000dr) and can provide a bagged lunch (950dr) to take on the trail. (☎71 300 or 71 410. Singles 5000dr; doubles 8000dr.) Down the road after the taverna, cozy **Zarkada** provides homey, spacious rooms with wide balconies and great views. (☎71 305 or 71 405. Singles 7000dr; doubles 10,000dr; breakfast 2000dr.) Closest to the bus station on the left is **Ladia,** a castle-like structure at the entrance to the village offering comfy, modern rooms with private

baths, TVs, rugs, and the occasional fireplace. (☎71 483. Singles 7000dr; doubles 12,000dr; breakfast 2000dr.) **Kaliterimi,** to the right off the main road just before Pension Monodendri, boasts spacious, comfortable rooms, some with great views. (☎71 510 or 71 484. Singles 6000dr; doubles 10,000dr, 12,000dr with breakfast; triples 12,000dr.)

**FOOD AND SIGHTS.** Interspersed among these pensions on the main road are a few tavernas. The best and always the most crowded is **Katerina's,** at the porch of Pension Monodendri, where Mrs. Daskalopoulou prepares a changing set menu for two (4500dr), including an array of delicious traditional Zagori pies. **Oxia,** between Ladia and Zarkada, is a favorite of tour buses laden with visiting Germans, and has fresh local trout (1300dr) and lots and lots of goat, cooked many different ways (1200-1600dr).

There isn't much to see or do in Monodendri beyond admiring the architecture, breathing the mountain air, and stocking up for a foray into Vikos Gorge. Those unwilling to tackle Vikos head-on, however, can enjoy breathtaking, unparalleled views of the entire gorge at a not-to-be-missed natural **"Balcony,"** about an hour's walk on the main road uphill from the village. The road gives way to a small footpath, leading to a vantage point for gazing down the length of the gorge's three main chasms; it's glowingly spectacular at sunset. The abandoned **Monastery of Agia Paraskevi,** about 600m from the plateia, also has impressive views. Signs from the plateia point the way to **Megali Spilia,** a nearby cave where Zagori people used to stock food and water, and hide from occasional Albanian marauders.

## VIKOS GORGE Χαραδρα Βικου

According to the *Guinness Book of World Records*, the Vikos Gorge, whose walls are 900m deep but only 1100m apart, is the steepest canyon on earth. This "Greek Grand Canyon" stretches from the village of Kipi in the south to Megalo Papingo at its northernmost tip, winding its way through the center of the Zagorohoria. In spring, the river that has taken millions of years to form its namesake gorge rushes along the 15km stretch of canyon floor; by summer this mighty force is reduced to a half-hearted trickle through huge, white boulders in the bone-dry riverbed. Rusted iron deposits in the gorge's sedimentary rock give the walls an orange-pink tint that suggests the last gleamings of sunset, even at high noon. Even more colorful are spring wildflowers, summer butterflies, autumn foliage, and views of the bright-green spring below Vikos village running under the crags. The long hike through the gorge is impressive: the nearly vertical canyon sides, to which throngs of trees cling stubbornly, tower hundreds of meters over your head.



**THE HIKE.** The well-marked and maintained Vikos trail is part of the **Greek National 03 route.** Before you go, make sure you get a **map.** If you get confused, just look for the red diamonds on white square backgrounds with "O3" stencilled on them, which consistently mark the path. Most enter the gorge from **Monodendri,** the highest of the villages, but it can also be accessed from **Kipi,** the **Papingo** villages, and from **Vikos village.** It takes 4½hr. to walk between Vikos village and Monodendri, and six hours between the Papingos and Monodendri.

To reach the gorge from Monodendri, take the marked path from the plateia. After about 40 minutes along the steep descending trail, you'll reach a fork in the path. Go left to enter the canyon's dry riverbed of smooth rocks; to the right, about an hour away, lies the village of Kipi with its trademark stone bridges. Follow the path as it climbs above the left side of the riverbed, leaving the canyon floor. Further along, the path forks on a small slide of scree without markers: go right and the trail will take you down to avoid the rocky cliffs. The way continues for some time, fairly level and pleasant, through a mossy, shady woodland along the riverbank. After about two hours, there will be a sign for a **water tap** where you can fill

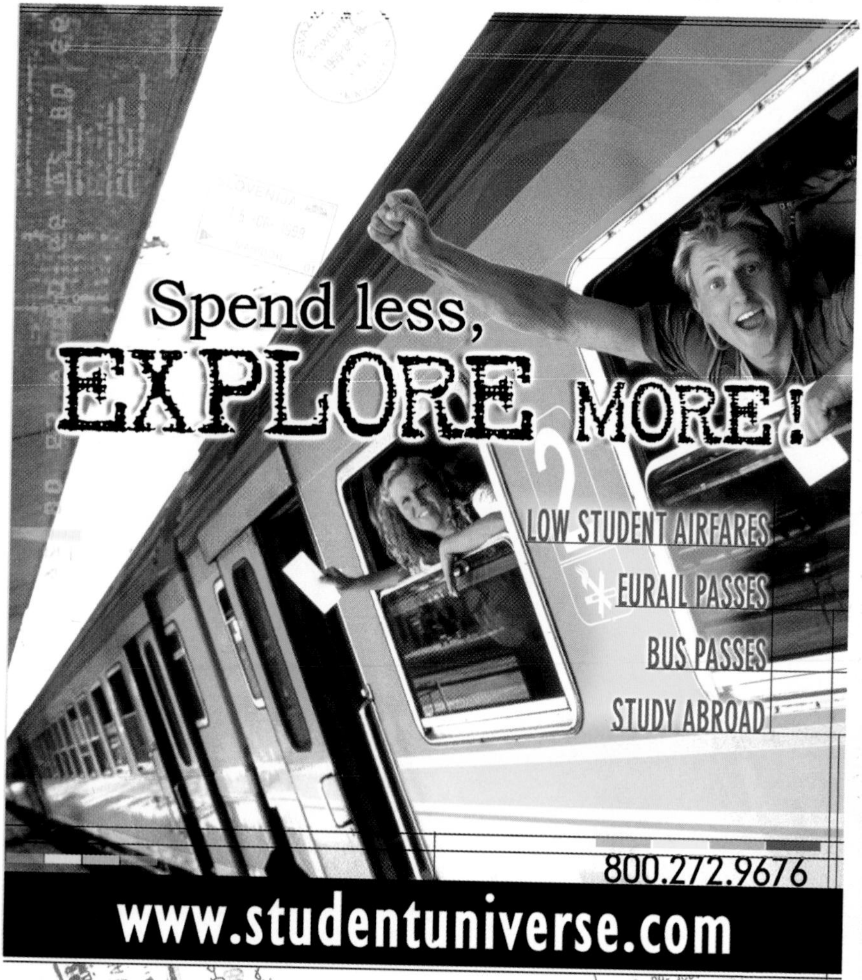
Spend less,
EXPLORE MORE!
LOW STUDENT AIRFARES
EURAIL PASSES
BUS PASSES
STUDY ABROAD
800.272.9676
www.studentuniverse.com

your water bottle—you've reached the halfway point. Continuing straight back on the trail after the water tap, you'll pass some open groves mowed clean by grazing horses; finally you'll emerge in very bare, exposed, sunny terrain. Around this area (about 5 hours from Monodendri), listen for the sound of gushing water from the previously bone-dry riverbed. These are the Voidhomatis Springs, bubbling at a poorly marked major crossroads.

Continue on the path uphill to reach **Vikos** village, about 45 minutes farther away. Vikos has only one accommodation: smallish 12,000dr rooms rented by **Sotiris Karpouzis** (☎(0653) 41 176). For the **Papingo** villages, make a right and go down the slope to the inviting springs, which lie beneath a large, flat area with a campfire circle, good for tenting. Cross over the riverbed (on the right where it's still dry) and head uphill. The green, shady springs are the perfect place for a swim, if you have the time; at least wade and refill your water bottle. From here, an arduous 90-minute ascent brings you to the twin villages of **Megalo Papingo** and **Mikro Papingo.** On the hike up, check out the eerie pillars of stone on the mountainside. You'll also find another small stream to drink from, and soon after, a sign in Greek pointing the way: Megalo Papingo to the left, Mikro Papingo to the right.

## MEGALO PAPINGO Μεγαλο Παπινγο ☎0653

The two Papingo villages are the most developed of the Zagorohoria. Their position at the end of the Vikos Gorge ensures their popularity with backpackers and independent travelers. In recent years, Megalo Papingo, the larger of the two, has also become a favorite spot for vacationing Greeks seeking a breath of fresh air from Thessaloniki and Ioannina. These villages boast seventeen separate lodging choices, while most of their 44 Zagori cohorts don't have seventeen full-time residents. Luckily, the influx of visitors hasn't diminished the village's peculiar stony beauty, which feels, at certain hours, something like an enchanted kingdom frozen into rock. The only indications of a larger tourist presence are somewhat classy hotels and slightly higher prices.

The large, austere stone **church** and its attendant bell tower stand at the entrance to the village, at the end of the road to the outside world and next to the **bus stop.** From here, one cobblestone main street snakes around the town, containing most of the pensions and restaurants. **Buses** go to **Ioannina** (1hr.; M, W, and F 7am, Su 10:30am; 1200dr). Megalo Papingo has a **phone** and a **mailbox,** both on its main street. For information on the village and on all outdoor activities, ask for Nikos at **Koulis Restaurant** (☎41 138); to reach it, walk uphill to the left when facing the clock tower from the main road.

**ACCOMMODATIONS AND FOOD.** Because of its popularity with rich Greeks, lodging in Papingo is extremely expensive. The low-ceilinged rooms at **Koulis Restaurant,** with fireplaces and baths, are the best deal. (☎41 138. Singles 9000dr; doubles 12,000dr; triples 15,000dr.) Behind its beautiful entranceway of hanging grape vines, the 120-year-old **Astraka,** on the other end of the main road, offers comfortable, pleasantly decorated rooms with baths, fireplaces, and TVs, plus a cozy living room. (☎41 693. Singles 9000dr; doubles 15,000dr; triples 17,000dr; quads 20,000dr.) The rest of the hotels in town have prices starting at 10,000dr a night, and the food isn't much cheaper. **O Nikos,** with outdoor tables just off the main road, has the standard menu for reasonable rates; look for the blue "Food" sign uphill from the bell tower. (Entrees 1500-1850dr.) **Restaurant Papingo** (☎41 121), to the right of the belltower in the Papingo Pension, is popular and serves delicious traditional Zagori pies.

About 3½ hours from Papingo is a **refuge** for tired hikers, 20 minutes from **Mt. Atraska.** (Open May 20-Oct. 30; 2500dr per person; hot meals available.) Call Nikos at Koulis Restaurant for information or to make a reservation (☎41 115). You can also hike from Megalo Papingo to **Dracolimni** ("dragon-lake"; 4½hr.), or to **Provatina Cave** (4hr.) and **Mt. Gamila** (6hr.). If you're running low on time or energy, pleasant **rock pools** await a mere 300m from Megalo Papingo.

### KIPI Κηποι ☎0653

Another option for hiking the gorge begins at its lowest point, in the tiny village of Kipi. One of the most beautiful and least touristed villages in the Zagorohoria, Kipi climbs up a hill above the one main road, its cobbled streets and stone walls rising in a gentle slope to the church and clock tower at the top. Kipi's biggest attractions, besides the peace and quiet, are its traditional **stone bridges,** built in the 17th and 18th centuries at the height of Zagori culture. The double- and triple-arched bridges are just outside the village; four lie within 1km from each side of the village. **Robinson Expeditions** runs an activity center in Kipi, right across the road from Hotel Artemis. The center sells hiking maps and has information on the area, as well as offering extensive guided tours of the gorge, rock climbing expeditions, rafting, and a weekly platter of events. Call ahead to find the schedule; trips are occasionally canceled if there's not enough interest. (☎71 041. Open M 2-6pm, Tu-Su 9am-3pm.) The best way to enter the gorge from Kipi is to head out on the road toward Ioannina, and look for paths to the gorge floor by the bridges. The hike to Monodendri is about 2 hours along the riverbed.

The **bus** to Ioannina (45min.; M, W, F 8am; 700dr) leaves from the road right at the bottom of the hill. To find the small plateia and the church, pick a street and follow it to the top—the town is so small the clock tower is hard to miss. There aren't many places to stay in Kipi; your best bet are the rooms offered at **Artemis,** which are big, comfortable, and decorated in the traditional Zagori style. Follow the sign up the hill off the main road.(☎71 644. Singles 9000dr with breakfast; doubles 9000dr without breakfast.) The best dining option is **Stou Mikalis,** on the road opposite the bus stop, which serves delicious Zagori pies (chicken, vegetable, and cheese) and gourmet omelettes. (Entrees 900-2500dr. ☎71 632.)

# MACEDONIA ΜΑΚΕΔΟΝΙΑ



Some of the finest Greek landscapes and sights belong to Macedonia, including the sublimely beautiful Olympian hiking trails, millions of sparkling mosaic *tesserae* from Thessaloniki's Byzantine churches, Karala's Ottoman *imaret*, the Royal Tombs from Vergina, the austere monasteries of Mt. Athos, and lots surf and sand on Halkidiki's two secular peninsulas. Greece's largest province tops the mainland like a gold-wrought ancient burial crown. You'll encounter the region's symbol, a 16-pointed star, on everything: the sidewalk at the OTE, the backs of 100-drachma coins, bumper stickers saying "Macedonia is Greece," and even Philip II's gold casket in Vergina. Although it receives few tourists, you won't feel like you've entered a backwater: hip, thriving Thessaloniki, Greece's second-largest city, keeps the whole region on its toes.

## THESSALONIKI Θεσσαλονικη ☎031

Thessaloniki fans out from its hilltop Byzantine-Turkish fortress to the Thermaic Gulf, a jumble of ancient, Byzantine, European, Turkish, Balkan, and contemporary Greek cultural and historical debris. At its peak, the fortress oversees the Old Town's placid streets and long, tree-lined, congested avenues. Among glitzy and lackluster concrete facades, well-heeled Thessalonikians strut their stuff, their hip-clipped cell phones swinging inches from the beggars and street children sitting below them on the sidewalk. Golden mosaics, frescoes, and floating domes still gleam in the industrial city's side-street Byzantine churches. Most travelers spend a couple of days in Thessaloniki clubbing and seeing the sights, and then head out for countryside hikes or more sight seeing, or ship out to islands.

Macedonia's capital and Greece's second city, Thessaloniki was founded in 316 BC. Needing a new city to name after his wife (Alexander the Great's sister), Cassander, the ruler of Macedon, picked the Thermaic Gulf shore and forcibly

transplanted the inhabitants of 26 pre-existing towns to his new Salonica. The new burg flourished under Macedonian and later Roman rule, as the only port on the Via Egnatia and a vital link between trade centers; cultural luminaries flocked there. In the first century AD, the apostle Paul put Thessaloniki on the map by writing First, and possibly Second, Thessalonians to churches he founded there. A thousand years later, missionary followers of the brothers Cyril and Methodius—inventors of the Cyrillic alphabet—arrived, and set up their influential headquarters.

Despite frequent and bloody raids by Goths, Avars, Slavs, Bulgars, and Latin Crusaders, Salonica rose to become the Byzantine Empire's second-most important city, after Constantinople. The Turks ended these glory days, conquering the city by siege in 1421. Throughout the centuries of Ottoman rule, Thessaloniki remained a cultural and intellectual center, dominated largely by its population of Sephardic Jews, who had fled the Spanish Inquisition and arrived in 1492. In 1881, Salonica saw the birth of Mustafa Kemal, who would rise to world fame as Atatürk, founder of the Turkish Republic. Ottomans ruled Thessaloniki until the First Balkan War in 1912, 90 years after most of Greece became independent. The Great Fire of 1917 destroyed a huge portion of the city's historical downtown area, damaging many of its churches. Although it began the 20th century with a population more European than Hellenic, the population exchange (see p. 17), the partitioning of the Ottoman Empire, and the death of virtually all of the city's 50,000 Jews during the Holocaust have left Thessaloniki almost homogeneously Greek.

## GETTING THERE AND AWAY

### BY BUS

| DESTINATION | TIME | FREQUENCY | PRICE | STATION |
|---|---|---|---|---|
| **Alexandropoulis** | 5hr. | 6 per day 8am-10:30pm | 5400dr | Koloniari 17 (☎51 411) |
| **Athens** | 6hr. | 20 per day | 9000dr | Monastiriou 69 (☎527 265) |
| **Corinth** | 7½hr. | 10:30am | 9200dr | Monastiriou 69 (☎527 265) |
| **Edessa** | 2¾hr. | 14 per day 6am-8pm | 1550dr | Anagenisseos 22 (☎525 100) |
| **Florina** | 3hr. | 6 per day 7:30am-7pm | 3150dr | Anagenisseos 42 (☎522 161) |
| **Halkidiki** | 2hr. | 8 per day 6am-7pm | 2500dr | Karakassi 68 (☎924 444/5) |
| **Igoumenitsa** | 8½hr. | 8pm | 7800dr | Monastiriou 51 |
| **Ioannina** | 7hr. | 5 per day 7:30am-9:30pm | 6050dr | Giannitsa 39 (☎512 444) |
| **Kastoria** | 3½hr. | 7 per day 7:30am-7:30pm | 3700dr | Anagenisseos 4 (☎522 162) |
| **Katerini** | 1hr. | every 30min. 6:30am-10:15pm | 1250dr | Sapfous 10 (☎519 109) |
| **Kavala** | 2½hr. | every hr. 6am-8pm; 10pm | 2850dr | Langadas 59 (☎525 530) |
| **Kozani** | 2½hr. | every hr. 6am-8pm | 2250dr | 26 Oktovriou 20 (☎522 488) |
| **Larisa** | 2hr. | 14 per day 7am-9:15pm | 3000dr | Enotikon 4 (☎544 133) |
| **Litohoro** | 1½hr. | 11 per day 6:30am-10:15pm | 1700dr | Sapfous 10 (☎519 109) |
| **Ouranopolis** | 3hr. | 8 per day 6am-8pm | 2500dr | Karakassi 68 (☎924 444/5) |
| **Parga** | 8¾hr. | 10am | 9400dr | Monastiriou 69 (☎527 265) |
| **Patras** | 8hr. | 8:15am and 3:15pm | 8250dr | Monastiriou 87 (☎525 253) |
| **Ancient Pella** | 40min. | every 15-20min. | 750dr | Anagenisseos 22 (☎525 100) |
| **Trikala** | 3hr. | 6 per day 8am-9pm | 3600dr | Monastiriou 75 (☎510 110) |
| **Veria** | 1½hr. | every hr. 8am-7pm | 1400dr | Monastiriou 75 (☎522 160) |
| **Volos** | 3½hr. | 6 per day 8am-10pm | 3550dr | Monastiriou 79 (☎512 122) |
| **Xanthi** | 6½hr. | 8 per day 8am-1:30am | 3550dr | Ag. Nestoriou 22 (☎526 526) |

**KTEL** buses run out of dozens of stations, each serving a region or large city. Most stations are in the no-man's-land between the port and the railway station, or just north of the railway. Some hand out printed timetables, while others post schedules on chalkboards and signs. The **EOT** has info (in Greek) on schedules, fares, duration, station locations, and telephone numbers, and will call to figure out anything they don't know.

**International buses** (☎599 100) leave from the **main train station** (☎517 517), on Monastiriou in the city's western part; take any bus down Egnatia to get there (100dr). Buses go to: **Istanbul, Turkey** (12hr., 2:30am, 24,300dr); **Koritsa, Albania** (6hr., 8am and midnight, 6600dr); and **Sofia, Bulgaria** (6hr., 4 per day 7am-10pm, 5600dr).

**Domestic buses** leave from different stations; check in advance.

## BY BOAT

**Ferries:** Buy tickets at **Karacharisis Travel and Shipping Agency,** Koundouriotou 8 (☎524 544; fax 532 289), on the corner. Open M-F 9am-9pm, Sa 9am-3pm. Ferries go to: **Chios** (21hr.; Tu, F, Sa midnight; 8300dr); **Ios** (23½hr., F 7:30pm, 9200dr); **Lesvos** (9hr., W and Su 1am, 8300dr); **Limnos** (7hr.; Tu 6pm and midnight, W, F, Sa midnight; 5300dr); **Kos** (18½hr., W 1pm, 12,300dr); **Iraklion** (24hr., 5 per week, 11,900dr); **Mykonos** (16hr.; M 2pm, Tu 3pm, and F 7:30pm; 9200dr); **Naxos** (21hr., F 7:30pm and Th 9:30pm, 8700dr); **Paros** (18hr., 4 per week, 9300dr); **Rhodes** (21½hr., W 4pm, 14,600dr); **Samos** (14hr., W 1pm, 9500dr); **Santorini** (26hr., 5 per week, 9900dr); **Syros** (13hr.; M 2pm, Th 9:30pm, and F 7pm; 8400dr); and **Tinos** (16hr.; Tu 3pm, F 7:30pm, and Sa midnight; 9100dr).

**Flying Dolphins:** Buy tickets at **Crete Air Travel,** Dragoumi 1 (☎547 407 or 534 376), across from the main port. Open M-F 8:30am-9pm, Sa 8:30am-3pm, Su 9am-3pm. June-Sept., every day at 8am and Th-M in the afternoon (usually 4:30pm) to: **Alonnisos** (5hr., 9300dr); **Skiathos** (3¾hr., 8500dr); and **Skopelos** (4½hr., 9300dr).

## BY TRAIN



To reach the **main terminal** (☎517 517), on Monastiriou in the western part of the city, take any bus down Egnatia (100dr).

**International trains** to: **Istanbul, Turkey** (13hr., 7:25am, 13,000dr); **Skopje, FYR Macedonia** (5hr., 6:15pm, 5000dr); and **Sofia, Bulgaria** (10½hr., 10pm, 7000dr). An **OSE** office (☎518 113), on the corner of Aristotelous and Ermou, sells **tickets** and has **schedules.** Open M-Sa 8am-2:30pm.

**Domestic trains** to: **Alexandroupolis** (7hr., 5 per day 7am-11:40pm, 3300dr); **Athens** (6 or 8hr., 10 per day 7am-11:40pm, 4250dr); **Edessa** (2½hr., 8 per day 6am-10pm, 950dr); **Florina** (4hr.; 7:30am, 9:15am, and 6pm; 1450dr); **Larisa** (2½hr., 12 per day 5:20am-11:40pm, 1500dr); **Volos** (4hr., 4 per day 8am-10:20pm, 2100dr); and **Xanthi** (4½hr., 5 per day 5:50am-11:00pm, 2270dr).

## BY PLANE

The **airport** (☎473 720), 16km east of town, can be reached by **bus #78** (120dr) from the train station or Pl. Aristotelous, or by **taxi** (2200dr). There's an **EOT** tourist office branch (☎985 215) at the airport.

**Olympic Airways:** office at Koundouriotou 3 (☎230 240 or 260 122; fax 229 725), is open M-Sa 7am-3:30pm. Call for reservations (☎281 880) M-Sa 7am-8pm. To: **Athens** (50min., 10 per day, 18,000dr); **Iraklion** (1¾hr.; M and W 10:40am, Sa 8:30am; 24,600dr); **Hania** (1¾hr.; Tu 8:30am, F 10:40am; 24,600dr); **Cyprus** (2hr., Tu and F 4pm, 50,000dr); **Ioannina** (35min.; M-W, and F-Sa 3pm, Th and Su 2:40pm; 10,400dr); **Lesvos** (50min., W-F and Su 6am, 17,400dr); **Limnos** (50min., 6am, 13,000dr); **Rhodes** (1¼hr., Tu and Th 11pm, 26,200dr); **Istanbul,** Turkey (2hr., Th and Su 5:30pm, 59,000dr). Also to: **Chios, Corfu, Larnaca, Mykonos, Samos,** and **Santorini** (2-3 per week).

## GETTING AROUND

Thessaloniki and its suburbs (up to one hour away) are connected by an extensive public transportation network. **Local buses** cost 100dr and run throughout the city. An **office** across from the train station provides limited schedules and the **EOT** has a route chart. Buses #8, #10, #11, and #31 run up and down Egnatia. Buy tickets at *periptera* or ticket booths at major stations.

## ORIENTATION

Thessaloniki stretches out along the waterfront of the Thermaic Gulf's north shore. Its rough grid layout—established after the Great Fire of 1917—and the orienting presence of the sea make it nearly impossible to get lost; still, street signs are haphazard, so a map can be quite helpful. **Egnatia** runs straight down the middle of town; the road was originally part of highway from Rome to Byzantium. The city's buses, sights, and cheapest hotels congregate there. From Egnatia, running parallel to the water, the main streets are **Ermou, Tsimiski, Mitropoleos,** and **Nikis,** which go along the waterfront. Inland from Egnatia is **Ag. Dimitriou** and the **Old Town** beyond. Intersecting all these streets and leading from the water into town are **I. Dragoumi, El. Venizelou, Aristotelous, Ag. Sophias,** and **Eth. Aminis.** Tsimiski, Mitropoleos, Ag. Sophias, and all the little streets between Aristotelous and Ipodromiou are the main shopping streets. The cheaper hotels are on Egnatia, banks on Tsimiski, and waterfront bars and cafes on Nikis. Nikis leads east, past various popular bars and cafes, to the **White Tower** (Λεφκος Πυργος), Thessaloniki's favorite monument, which presides over the harbor like an oversized chess piece. The roads north of Ag. Dimitriou grow increasingly tiny and steep, toward the **Old Town**'s ancient fortress walls, marvelous walks, panoramic views, and cheap tavernas. Between Tsimiski and the Arch of Galerius, **Pl. Navarino,** with its Roman ruins, is a meeting ground for Thessaloniki's young people. Facing inland, head left on Mitropoleos past **Pl. Elefterias** to reach **Ladadika,** a former red-light district now restored into a lovely pocket of turn-of-the-century cafes, bars, and tavernas.



## PRACTICAL INFORMATION

**Tourist Offices: EOT** (☎271 888, 222 935, or 265 507; fax 265 504), Pl. Aristotelous, 1 block from the water, has **free maps,** hotel listings, transportation schedules and prices, and festival information. Exceedingly helpful; English spoken. Open M-F 9am-9pm, Sa 10am-6pm, Su 10am-5pm; reduced in winter. Another EOT office (☎985 215) is at the **airport. UTS,** Mitropoleos 28 (☎286 756; fax 283 156), is near Pl. Aristotelous; ring the bell by the door labeled "28" on the right and go to the 7th floor. Ask for English-speaking Liza (make sure you're carrying *Let's Go* first.) Open M-F 9am-5pm.

**Permits for Mt. Athos:** Visit the **Holy Executive of the Holy Mt. Athos Pilgrims' Bureau,** Kou. Karamanli 14, 1st fl. (☎861 611; fax 861 811). Letter of recommendation not needed, but make sure you bring your passport. Karamanli is the eastern extension of Egnatia; take **bus #12** from Mitropoleos at Pl. Aristotelous and ask to be let off at Papafio. English spoken. Open M-Sa 9am-1pm, but call ahead.

**Consulates: Bulgaria:** N. Manou 12 (☎829 210). Open M-F 10am-noon. **Cyprus:** L. Nikis 37 (☎260 611). Open M-F 9am-1pm. **Turkey:** Ag. Dimitriou 151 (☎248 452). Open M-F 9am-noon. **United Kingdom:** Venizelou 8 (☎278 006). Open M-F 8am-1pm. **United States:** Tsimiski 43 (☎242 900). Open M, W and F 9am-noon.

**Banks:** Banks with currency exchange and 24hr. **ATMs** line Tsimiski, including **National Bank,** Tsimiski 11 (☎538 621). Open M-F 7:45am-2pm and 6-8pm.

**American Express: Memphis Travel,** Aristotelous 3, 1st floor (☎282 351). Cashes **traveler's checks** (no commission) and **exchanges currency** (500dr flat commission). Open for these services M-F 9:30am-3:30pm and Sa 9am-2pm.

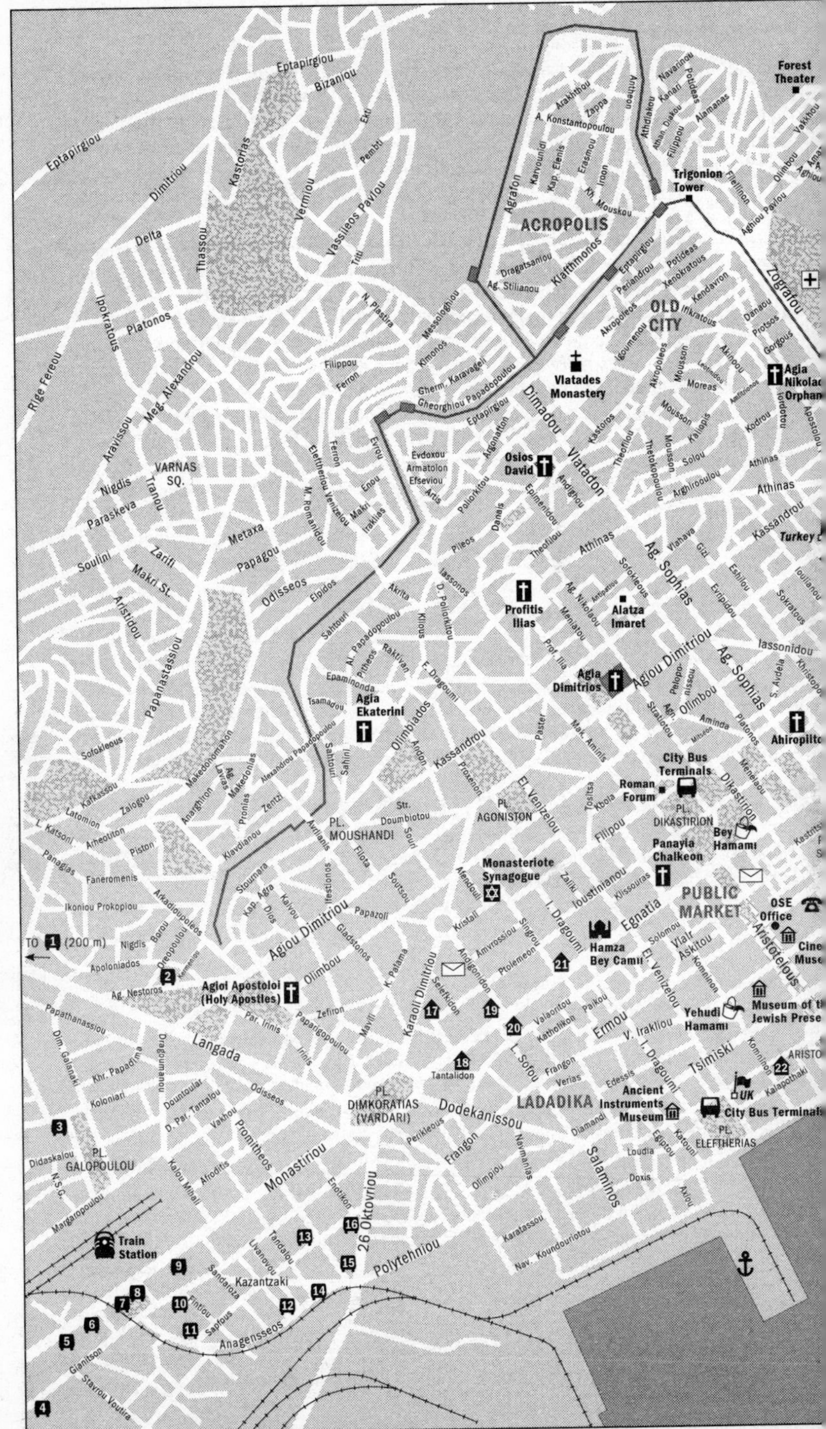
Forest Theater
Trigonion Tower
ACROPOLIS
OLD CITY
Vlatades Monastery
Osios David
Agia Nikolaos Orphanos
Profitis Ilias
Alatza Imaret
Agia Dimitrios
Agia Ekaterini
Ahiropiitos
City Bus Terminals
Roman Forum
PL. DIKASTIRION
Bey Hamami
Panayia Chalkeon
PUBLIC MARKET
OSE Office
Monasteriote Synagogue
Hamza Bey Camii
Yehudi Hamami
Museum of the Jewish Presence
Agioi Apostoloi (Holy Apostles)
LADADIKA
Ancient Instruments Museum
City Bus Terminals
PL. ELEFTHERIAS
PL. DIMKORATIAS (VARDARI)
PL. MOUSHANDI
PL. AGONISTON
VARNAS SQ.
PL. GALOPOULOU
Train Station
TO 1 (200 m)
UK
Turkey
Eptapirgiou
Bizaniou
Kastorias
Dimitriou
Delta
Thassou
Vermiou
Vassileos Pavlou
Platonos
Ipokratous
Rige Fereou
Meg. Alexandrou
Aravissou
Nigdis
Tranou
Paraskeva
Soulini
Zarifi
Makri St.
Metaxa
Papagou
Odisseos
Aristidou
Papanastassiou
Sofokleous
Makedonomahon
Anaghiron
Latomion
Arheotiton
Piston
Panagias
Faneromenis
Ikoniou Prokopiou
Nigdis
Apoloniados
Ag. Nestoros
Papathanassiou
Langada
Dim. Galanaki
Khr. Papadima
Koloniari
Dragoumanou
D. Par. Tantalou
Vakhou
Promitheos
Afroditis
Kalou Mihali
Didaskalou
Margaropoulou
Monastiriou
Enotikon
26 Oktovriou
Polytehniou
Kazantzaki
Sandaroza
Livanovou
Tandalou
Anagensseos
Gianitson
Stavrou Voutira
Agiou Dimitriou
Olimbou
Zefiron
Papazoli
Gladstonos
Karaoli Dimitriou
Selefkidon
Antigonidon
Kristali
Amvrossiou
Ptolemeon
Singrou
I. Dragoumi
Egnatia
El. Venizelou
Valaoritou
Katholikon
Paikou
Ermou
V. Irakliou
Tsimiski
Komninon
Kalapothaki
Dodekanissou
Frangon
Tantalidon
L. Sofou
Verias
Edessis
Diamandi
Katouni
Egiptou
Loudia
Doxis
Salaminos
Karatassou
Nav. Koundourioutou
Aristotelous
Solomou
Vlali
Askitou
Kissouras
Ioustinianou
Filipou
Tositsa
Kolba
El. Venizelou
Proxenou
Kassandrou
Olimbiados
Sahtouri
Sahini
Zentzi
Pronias
Klavdianou
Stournara
Kalvou
Ilestionos
Soutsou
Doumbiotou
Souri
Flota
Akrita
Kilous
D. Poliorkitou
Iassonos
Pileos
Danais
Theofilou
Athinas
Ag. Sophias
Sofokleous
Vlahava
Epimenidou
Andigonou
Poliorkitou
Argonafton
Eptapirgiou
Dimadou
Vlatadon
Evdoxou
Armatolon
Efseviou
Artis
Evrou
Enou
Makri
Iraklias
Eleftheriou Venizelou
M. Romanidou
Ferron
Filippou
Gherm. Karavangeli
Gheorghiou Papadopoulou
Kimonos
Messologhiou
N. Plastira
Exti
Pembti
Titi
Agrafon
Karvounidi
Kap. Elenis
Erasmou
Iroon
Kh. Mouskou
A. Konstantopoulou
Arakithou
Zappa
Antheon
Athidiakou
Navarinou
Kanari
Potideas
Alamanas
Filippou
Dragatsaniou
Klafthmonos
Ag. Stilianou
Periandrou
Xenokratous
Kendavrou
Ifkratous
Akropoleos
Igoumenou
Akropoleos
Moussion
Moreas
Kalopis
Solou
Athinas
Kassandrou
Theotokopoulou
Arghiroulou
Danaou
Protsos
Gorgous
Akinou
Kodrou
Iordotou
Zografou
Olimbou
Agiou Pavlou
Fiellinon
Eptapirgou
Eskilou
Evripidou
Sokratous
Ioulianou
Iassonidou
Ag. Sophias
Olimbou
Aminda
Platonos
Meneleou
Dikastirion
Pasteur
Mak. Aminis
Prof. Ilia
Menatou
Ag. Nikolaou
Al. Papadopoulou
Pitheos
Raktivan
E. Dragoumi
Epaminonda
Tsamadou
Alexandrou Papadopoulou
Avrilianis
Kap. Agra
Dios
Reneiou
Paparigopoulou
Par. Irinis
Irinis
Mavili
K. Palama
Zaliki
Odisseos
Dountoular
Oreopoulou
Borou
Arkadioupoleos
Karkassou
L. Katsoni
Zalogou
N.S.G.

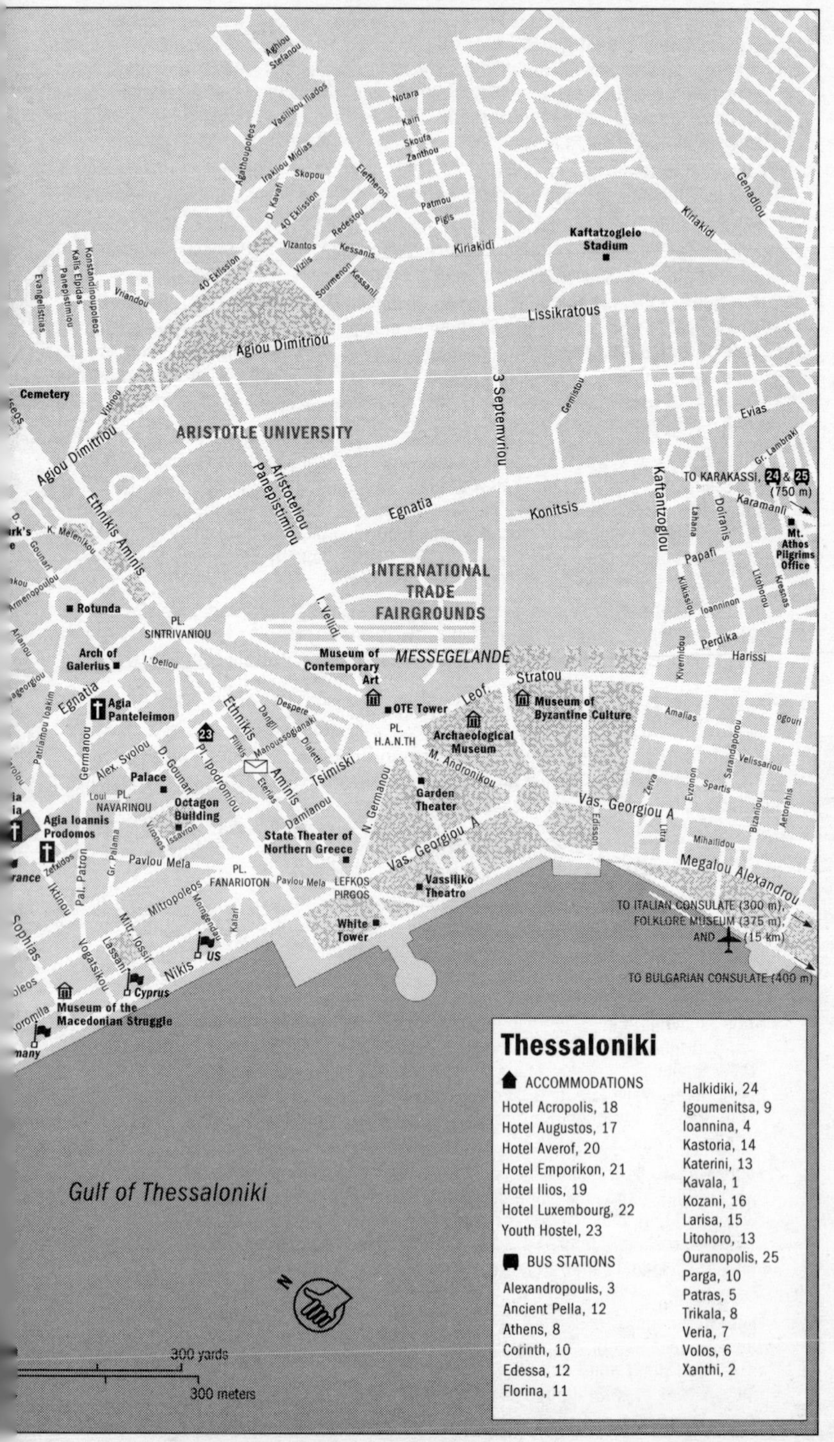
Thessaloniki
ACCOMMODATIONS
Hotel Acropolis, 18
Hotel Augustos, 17
Hotel Averof, 20
Hotel Emporikon, 21
Hotel Ilios, 19
Hotel Luxembourg, 22
Youth Hostel, 23
BUS STATIONS
Alexandropoulis, 3
Ancient Pella, 12
Athens, 8
Corinth, 10
Edessa, 12
Florina, 11
Halkidiki, 24
Igoumenitsa, 9
Ioannina, 4
Kastoria, 14
Katerini, 13
Kavala, 1
Kozani, 16
Larisa, 15
Litohoro, 13
Ouranopolis, 25
Parga, 10
Patras, 5
Trikala, 8
Veria, 7
Volos, 6
Xanthi, 2
Aghiou Stefanou
Vasilikou Iliados
Agathoupoleos
Irakliou Midias
Skopou
D. Kavafi
40 Eklission
Eleftherou
Redestou
Vizantos
Vizilis
Kessanis
Sourmenon
Kessanil
Notara
Kairi
Skoufa
Zanthou
Patmou
Pigis
Kiriakidi
Kaftatzogleio Stadium
Genadiou
Konstandinoupoleos
Kalis Elpidas
Panepistimiou
Evangelistias
Vriandou
Lissikratous
Agiou Dimitriou
Cemetery
Vizinou
ARISTOTLE UNIVERSITY
3 Septemvriou
Gemistou
Evias
Gr. Lambraki
TO KARAKASSI, 24 & 25 (750 m)
Karamanli
Mt. Athos Pilgrims Office
Aristoteliou Panepistimiou
Egnatia
Konitsis
Kaftantzoglou
Lahana
Doiranis
Papafi
Ethnikis Aminis
K. Melenikou
Gounari
Armenopoulou
INTERNATIONAL TRADE FAIRGROUNDS
I. Vellidi
Kilkissiou
Ioanninon
Litohorou
Kresnas
Rotunda
PL. SINTRIVANIOU
Perdika
Harissi
Arch of Galerius
I. Deliou
Museum of Contemporary Art
MESSEGELANDE
Kivernidou
Stratou
Agia Panteleimon
Patriarhou Ioakim
Despere
Dangli
Leof.
OTE Tower
Museum of Byzantine Culture
Amalias
Germanou
Alex. Svolou
D. Gounari
Pr. Ipodromiou
Filikis
Manoussogianaki
Dialetti
PL. H.A.N.TH
Archaeological Museum
Sarandaporou
Velissariou
Palace
PL. NAVARINOU
Octagon Building
Issavron
Eterias
Tsimiski
M. Andronikou
Garden Theater
Evzonon
Spartis
Zeva
Agia Ioannis Prodomos
Damianou
N. Germanou
Vas. Georgiou A
Edisson
Litra
Bizaniou
Aetorahis
Mihailidou
Gr. Palama
Pavlou Mela
State Theater of Northern Greece
Megalou Alexandrou
Zefxidos
Iktinou
Pal. Patron
PL. FANARIOTON
LEFKOS PIRGOS
Vassiliko Theatro
Mitropoleos
Morihendau
Kalari
TO ITALIAN CONSULATE (300 m), FOLKLORE MUSEUM (375 m), AND (15 km)
Sophias
Mitr. Iossif
Lassani
Vogatsikou
Nikis
US
White Tower
TO BULGARIAN CONSULATE (400 m)
Cyprus
Museum of the Macedonian Struggle
Gulf of Thessaloniki
N
300 yards
300 meters

**International Bookstore:** Many **kiosks** in Thessaloniki sell foreign newspapers and magazines. **Molchos Books,** Tsimiski 10 (☎275 271), across from the National Bank, has an excellent selection of English, Classical, religious, and art history books, plus international daily newspapers. Open M-Sa 8:30am-3pm. Two branches of **Prometheus International Bookstore,** Ermou 75 (☎263 786) and Vironos 4 (☎236 332), have a few shelves of novels. Open M-W and F-Sa 8am-3pm, Th 8am-2pm and 5:30-9pm.

**Laundromat: Bianca,** L. Antoniadou 3 (☎209 602), behind the church to your right as you face the Arch of Galerius. 1800dr for wash, dry, and soap. Open M-Sa 8am-3pm.

**Tourist Police:** Dodekanissou 4, 5th fl. (☎554 870/871). Free maps and brochures. English spoken. Open 24hr. For the **local police,** call 553 800 or 100. There are also police and tourist police booths at the train station.

**Hospital:** At **Ippokration Public Hospital,** A. Papanastasiou 49 (☎837 920), some doctors speak English. **Ahepa Hospital,** Kiriakidi 1 (☎993 111), is a private alternative. **Red Cross First Aid Hospital,** Koundouriotou 6 (☎530 530), offers free minor medical care at the entrance to the port. The **ETO** can help you find an English-speaking doctor.

**Telephones: OTE,** Karolou Diehl 27 (☎221 899), at the corner of Ermou, 1 block east of Aristotelous. Open M-F 7:15am-9:30pm.

**Internet Access: Pl@net**, 53 Alex. Svolou, across from the hostel, is the best in town. 14 fast terminals and jazzy tunes. 600dr per hour from 10am-6pm, 800dr per hour 6pm-3am. **The Web,** Gonata 4 (☎237 031), one block south of Svolou, near Pl. Navarino between Ipodromiou and Gounari, is often crowded but has fast terminals. 700dr per hr., 900dr per hr. after 5pm. Open 24hr. The **British Council,** Eth. Aminis 9 (☎235 236 or 235 237), has free access. Open M-F 9am-1pm.

**Post Office:** On Aristotelous, just before Egnatia. Open M-F 7:30am-8pm, Sa 7:30am-2pm, Su 9am-1:30pm. A **branch** office (☎227 640), on Eth. Aminis near the White Tower, is open M-F 7am-8pm. Both offer Poste Restante. **Postal code:** 54101.

## ACCOMMODATIONS



Welcome to the big city—don't expect to find comfort and cleanliness all at one low price, especially if you want your own bathroom (usually a tiny compartment partitioned from the bedroom). Most of Thessaloniki's less expensive hotels are clustered along the western end of **Egnatia,** between **Pl. Dimokratias** (500m east of the train station) and **Pl. Dikastiriou.** Most are a bit gritty, ranging from ramshackle sleaze to merely cheerless. Egnatia is loud at all hours, but rooms on the street have balconies (read: air circulation), while quieter back rooms have just a window. Women alone should be wary of the English-speaking "tourist information" people at the train station: they are often impersonators, and you shouldn't accept their offers of cheap rooms.

**Hotel Augustos,** Elenis Svoronou 4 (☎522 955; ☎/fax 522 500). Walking down Egnatia, turn north at the Argo Hotel; Augustos is straight ahead. The best budget deal in Thessaloniki. Cozy rooms with wooden floors, big wood closets, rugs, and painted ceilings. Rooms vary; ask for a balcony. Triples and doubles with bath have A/C and TVs; all rooms have phones. Singles 5000dr, with bath 8000dr; doubles 7000/11,000dr; triples with bath 13,000dr.

**Youth Hostel,** Alex. Svolou 44 (☎225 946; fax 262 208). Take bus#8, 10, 11, or 31 west down Egnatia and get off at the Arch of Galerius (Kamara stop); or walk toward the water and turn left 2 blocks later onto Svolou. The cheapest Thessaloniki option; fairly clean. Hot showers from 7am-11pm, in a basement somewhere between a cave and a prison. Lockout 11am-6:30pm, very loosely enforced curfew 1:30am. Reception open 9am-11am and 7-11pm. Open Mar. 1-Nov. 30. 2500dr per person.

**Hotel Acropolis,** Tantalidou 4 (☎536 170). Tantalidou is the second right off Egnatia after Dodekanissou, when coming from Pl. Dimokratias. A good bet if you like lots of quiet and don't mind shared baths. Light rooms with sinks and wood floors; family-owned. Singles 5500dr; doubles 6500dr; triples 7500dr.

**Hotel Averof,** L. Sofou 24 (☎538 840; fax 543 194), at Egnatia. Rooms are a bit bare and stuffy, but with new furniture, friendly staff, and a communal TV room with fridge. Singles 6000dr, with bath 9000dr; doubles 8000/12,000dr.

**Hotel Emporikon,** Singrou 14 (☎525 560 or 514 431), at Egnatia. Uncomplicated rooms with bright fluorescent lighting and balconies overlooking leafy, tranquil Singrou. Shared bathrooms and fridges, high ceilings. Quieter than most other hotels on Egnatia. Some doubles have a partitioned private shower, but all share toilets. Singles 5000dr; doubles 8000, with shower 10,000dr; triples 12,000dr.

**Hotel Luxembourg,** Komninon 6 (☎278 449 or 275 725), at the intersection with Tsimiski, with a turn-of-the-century facade. Small, overpriced rooms with TVs and shabby bathrooms. Close to the Ladadika district. Singles 7000dr, with bath 11,000dr; doubles 9000/12,000dr.

**Hotel Ilios,** Egnatia 27 (☎512 620/1). Comfortable, big-windowed, high-priced modern rooms with A/C, TVs, phones, and baths. Some doubles have armchairs. Ask for a room away from the noisy street. Singles 10,000dr; doubles 14,000dr; triples 16,000dr.

## FOOD

Pocketed on tiny sidestreets all over the city (and clustered along Aristotelous), Thessaloniki's *ouzeri* tables are mini altars of appetizer *mezedes*, upon which are placed offerings to the gods of good cheap food. Innovative places a block down from Egnatia between **Dragoumi** and **El. Venizelou** cater to a younger clientele and are open late. Probably the most pleasant setting is under the trees on **Komninon** between Tsimiski and the flower market, where Thessaloniki's busiest sidewalks melt into a languid calm. Tables teem around 3:30pm and again around 11pm.

The **open-air markets** of Vati Kioutou, just off Aristotelous to the east and west between Irakliou and Egnatia, are perfect for stocking up or walking around (see **Bedesten,** p. 227). The **Aretsou** area, along the bay about 4km toward the airport, has excellent seafood. The **Old Town** and **Ladadika** district brim with inexpensive, family tavernas; restaurants just below the **fortress**'s tower have sweeping views over the gulf. Thessaloniki contributes its local pig's feet soup, *boutsas*, to the Greek culinary universe. It's only for the bold and the cold.

**Ouzeri Melathron,** on an alleyway between El. Venizelou and Dragoumi. From Egnatia, walk past the Ottoman Bedesten on El. Venizelou and make a right into the passageway between storefronts. Witty, 4ft. long menus feature a spicy meat dish called "Lonely Nights" ("No nookie with this on your breath") and snails ("for friends of the hermaphrodite"). Entrees 1150-3600dr.

**THESSALONIKI'S JEWS** By the 16th century, Thessaloniki was nicknamed the "Mother of Israel" for its large, thriving Jewish population. The community began when Sephardic Jews escaped the Spanish Inquisition in 1492 and emigrated to Thessaloniki; Italian, French, and Sicilian Jews joined them. In the 17th century, the *Doenmah* ("converts") sectarian group followed the self-proclaimed prophet Shabbethai Zvi to join Islam, taking a bite out of the Jewish faithful. In 1917, the community suffered a second major setback when the Great Fire destroyed 31 synagogues and countless offices and libraries (along with the rest of Thessaloniki). In April 1941, the Axis powers occupied the city, and destroyed and looted Jewish homes, businesses, and synagogues, and ripped up the gravestones of a 500-year-old Jewish cemetery—the current site of Aristotle University—to pave roads and line swimming pools. Trains for Auschwitz and Birkenau left beginning in March 1943; 18 transports carried 46,000 people to their deaths. Around 4% of the Jewish populace either escaped—fleeing to the mountains or given secret refuge by Christian friends—or numbered among the 2000 survivors of the camps. Today, the **Museum of Jewish Presence** looks back on Thessaloniki's Jewish community throughout history (see p. 228).

**Ta Adelphi** (☎266 432), in laid-back Pl. Navarino. Carnivorous meals at good prices. Popular, delicious, and very busy. Try the special chicken: it's stuffed with cheese and wrapped in bacon. Entrees 980-2750dr. Open noon-midnight.

**Mesogeios,** Balanou 38 (☎288 460), east of Aristotelous, one block south of Egnatia. The largest *ouzeri* in the area—look for yellow and blue tablecloths. Delectable calamari, some English-speaking staff, and festive nighttime ambience. Entrees 1200-2200dr.

**Rogoti,** Venizelou 8 (☎227 766 or 227 794), on the corner. Since 1928. Try the secret recipe for *soutzoukakia* (meatballs, 1650dr) and enjoy all kinds of niceties—a black bowtie here, a tasty garnish there—at decent prices. Huge menu, but much of it is only available before 5:30pm. Entrees 1100-2250dr.

**O Loutros,** Komninon 15 (☎228 895), near the corner of Irakliou. A tasty, laid-back fish restaurant in and around a former Ottoman *hamam.* Entrees 1000-2800dr.

**Cafe Extrablatt,** Alex Svolou 46 (☎256 900), next to the hostel. Overpriced but delicious, European-influenced cuisine, and over 50 beer options. There's an entire menu for mushroom options, including a mushroom gyro and the special "mushrooms Extrablatt." Entrees 2000-3200dr.

# SIGHTS

**WHITE TOWER.** The White Tower is Thessaloniki's most easily recognized sight, and is a reference point for the harbor. All that remains of a 15th-century Venetian seawall, the tower was later the Ottoman Death Row where **Janissaries**—an elite corps of Ottoman soldiers recruited from the Greek populace—carried out gruesome executions. In those days it was known as the **Bloody Tower.** In 1890, a prisoner attempting to earn his release whitewashed the whole building and inaugurated the current name. The tower now houses exhibits on Thessaloniki's monuments in Greek and a bilingual **Museum of Early Christian Art.** Climb the spiral staircase and peruse a large collection of mainly 17th- and 18th-century iconography, including disheveled John the Baptist, coolly triumphant St. George rearing over pint-sized dragons, and Thessaloniki's patron Ag. Dimitrius slaying some hapless infidel from an enormous, flaming-red horse. Kodak moments are to be had atop the tower. *(At the far east end of Nikis. ☎267 832. Open Tu-Su 8am-3pm. Free.)*



## WALKING TOURS

Just below the surface of modern, bustling Thessaloniki lies a tangle of Roman, Byzantine, Ottoman, Sephardic, and Bulgarian legacies. Temples and baths became churches, churches were transformed into mosques, and minarets were toppled to make churches again, all in a many-layered pile. *Wandering Byzantine Thessaloniki*, a guide available at the White Tower for a pricey (but well-deserved) 6000dr, will glut history buffs with Byzantine gratification.

### ROMAN REMNANTS

**ROTUNDA.** Originally built as part of egotistical emperor Galerius' palace, the Rotunda later became a church and was renamed **Agios Georgios** by Theodosius the Great. The walls of the enormous, Pantheon-inspired, cylindrical Rotunda are plastered with some of the city's most lavish and gleaming **mosaics,** the earliest mural mosaics in the area. An estimated 36 million *tesserae* were assembled to represent gilded facades, birds, fruits, and saints, which are currently almost all covered up for restoration. You can still see the angels' heads and hands upholding a circle of stars, and pomegranates sheaved in a rainbow band. The Christ figure at the dome's key has been destroyed, but his sketch in charcoal can still be faintly seen. What mosaics can be seen are way up in the dome; bring a guidebook with pictures or a pair of binoculars. The scaffolded **minaret** outside dates from the building's use as a mosque in the 16th century. *(Open 7am-2:30pm.)*

**MORE OF GALERIUS' EGO TRIP.** A colonnaded processional led south from the Rotunda to the **Arch of Galerius** and the **Palace of Galerius,** once the three compo-

nents of an enormous complex. Galerius built the arch to commemorate his victory over the Persians in AD 305; it's covered with **relief sculptures** detailing his triumphs. Now supported by scaffolding to prevent further damage from pollution, the arch, at the intersection of Egnatia and Gounari, stands at the crossroads of two major thoroughfares of the ancient city. It was once paralleled by a similar structure to the east; together they formed a huge gateway commemorating the Persian defeat. The Palace of Galerius, south of the Arch on Dragoumi near Pl. Navarino, has been partially excavated. The centerpiece remains its well-preserved **octagonal hall,** best viewed from the southwest.

**ROMAN FORUM.** The not terribly spectacular Roman Forum, still under excavation, was the center of public life from the 2nd to 3rd centuries AD. It included a public records archive, mint, odeon, *boulaterion*, and library; today it offers a somewhat hyper-restored version of the **theater.** On the south side of the Agora's lower square was once the **colonnade** that held eight caryatid statues of mythological women. Known in Ladino, the language of the Sephardic Jews, as *las Incantadas* ("the enchanted women"), they were thought to have been magically turned to stone. When the portico was demolished in 1865, the statues were taken to their permanent home in the Louvre. *(On Egnatia, behind the Pl. Dikastiriou bus station.)*

## OLD CITY

North of Ag. Dimitriou you'll find the streets of the Old City. **Agios Nikolaos Orphanos,** off Apostelou Pavlou, has splendid 14th-century wall paintings, some of the most important in all of Macedonia and Serbia for their skillful illustration of biblical narratives. From the **White Tower,** follow the remains of the ancient wall north along Ipodromiou, past Ag. Dimitriou, to reach the 15th-century **Trigonion Tower,** a replacement of the Byzantine original. At the top of the hill are the **fortifications** originally erected by the Byzantines, and later refurbished by the Ottomans to strengthen and prepare them for the new technologies of artillery warfare. Rewarding views look out over the city and its gulf. Continue up through the crooked sprawl of the Old Town to reach the ruins of the **Eptapirgion Walls** ("Seven Gates"), erected during the reign of Theodosius the Great. *(To reach the Old City, take bus #22 from Pl. Eleftherias.)*

## BYZANTINE CHURCHES

Salonica was a Big Deal in the Byzantine Empire, which littered the town with enough churches to keep devout old women crossing themselves at a truly aerobic rate on a bus ride down Egnatia alone. Over the centuries, earthquakes, fire, and Muslim appropriations have severely damaged most of Salonica's 90 original churches, but many—especially Agios Dimitrios, Agios Sofia, and the Rotonda (Agios Giorgios)—still deserve a visit. Apart from Agios Dimitrios, most churches open early (6-7am), close sometime between noon and 2pm, and reopen for a few hours in the evening (usually around 5-8pm). Come in the morning to be sure of getting in, and dress modestly. Although there's no admission fee, donations are always a nice idea. To appreciate fully the dazzling mosaics on high, get your hands on some binoculars and/or a copy of *Wandering in Byzantine Thessaloniki*, available at the Byzantine Culture Museum, the White Tower, and many bookstores (paperback 6000dr).

**AGIOS DIMITRIOS.** The city's oldest and most famous church is named for the city's patron saint, a Christian Roman officer who was speared to death in the Roman bath complex that occupied this site during Galerius' reign. A small church was erected on the site of the martyr's grave in the 4th century AD. A 5th-century basilica soon supplanted it; pilgrims flocked to worship the saint and collect bottles of the myrrh said to flow from the wounds of his entombed corpse. Two fires, in 620 and 1917, decimated the church, and from 1493 to 1912 it served as the Ottoman's Kasimiye Camii. The surviving fragments of the **mosaics** that once covered the inner sides of the colonnades are absolutely stunning. The **crypt,** down a flight

of stairs on the east side, contains the shell of the original tiny church and the fountain where Dimitrios was killed. *(On Ag. Dimitriou, due north of Aristotelous. Open 8am-8pm. Crypt hours reduced Su-M. Holy Liturgy held in the crypt every F 9:30-11pm.)*

**PROFITIS ILIAS.** The domed, 14th century church of Profitis Ilias was once the *katholikon* (main church) of a monastery. Now it has lost most of its frescoes to the passage of time, and its uniqueness lies in its architectural layout: a cross-in-square with side choruses, a style invented in 1000 by the founder of Megistis Lavras on Mt. Athos. The remaining **frescoes** detail, faintly, Herod's slaughter of the innocents. *(On Ag. Dimitriou. Open 6am-noon and 6-9pm.)*

**OSSIOS DAVID.** Originally founded in the 5th century and funded by an anonymous female donor, the dim little church of Ossios David has one brilliant **mosaic** of the Epiphany in the apse. Jesus sits on a rainbow, the symbol of heaven, flanked by an angel, eagle, lion, and calf (the symbols of evangelists Matthew, John, Mark, and Luke), with the prophets Ezekiel and Habakkuk in the corners and fish swimming in the river Jordan below. According to legend, the anonymous donor was **Theodora,** daughter of Galerius (who was none too fond of Christianity); she commissioned the mosaic, which was miraculously completed overnight on top of the artist's sketch. The mosaic actually dates later, and was more likely covered as protection from the Iconoclasts of the 8th and 9th centuries than to avoid a father's wrath. *(On Ag. Dimitrios above Profitis Ilias. Open 8am-noon and 6-9pm.)*

**AGIA SOPHIA.** Named after the cathedral in Constantinople (the premier church of Orthodoxy), this magnificent, domed 7th-century Agia Sophia was erected on the site of an earlier 5th-century basilica. Starting in the 8th century, it served as Thessaloniki's cathedral until it was converted to mosquehood in 1523-24. The terra-cotta and blue-green interior has a forest-y feel, accentuated by column capitals of waving acanthus leaves. Gold *tesserae* gleam on the dome's 9th-century circular **mosaic** of the Ascension, where the awestruck Apostles, angels, and Virgin witness a somewhat truncated Christ ascending in a blue globe. *(On Ag. Sophia. Open 7am-1pm and 5-7pm.)*



**PANAGIA ACHIRPOEITOS.** If you're looking for easy-to-see **mosaics,** nearby Panagia Achirpoeitos, one of the first-known basilica-style churches, contains appetizing examples on the undersides of its arches. Visitors to the Museum of Byzantine Culture will recall the familiar motif of heavenly delights—glittery fruits, birds, vases of water, and fish. Throughout the Ottoman occupation, Panagia Achirpoeitos was the city's official mosque, and one of the columns in the north colonnade bears the inscription of the conquering Sultan Murad II. The church's name means "created without hands" and stems from a 12th-century legend of an icon's miraculous appearance in the church. Just around the corner, the **crypts of Agios Yiannis Prodromos** contain an underground church and winding paths with beautiful silver-plated icons. *(On Ag. Sofia. Open 7:30am-12:30pm and 6-9pm.)*

**DANGEROUS LIASONS** Now completely buried under Pl. Ipodromion, the **Hippodrome** once hosted one of the more horrendously scandalous Roman events. Back in 390 AD, troops were stationed along the old city walls to ward off intruding Goths and other barbarians threatening the refinement of Roman civilization. When one of the city's most popular circus charioteers fell in love with a young slave boy in the garrisons, the boy's general, **Botheriz,** ordered the lustful athlete to be jailed. An infuriated mass of chariot fans took their revenge, killing Botheriz and his officers and parading their maimed corpses through the city streets. Deciding to teach his unruly subjects a lesson, the sly **Emperor Theodosius** lured thousand of civilians to the Hippodrome, ostensibly to watch games. Once the fans had arrived, soldiers stationed around the circus attacked, slaughtering at least 7000 men, women, and children—some accounts claim as many as 15,000 casualties. Subsequently, the disapproving **Agios Ambrose** (St. Ambrose) recommended that Theodosius fill a public penance in Milan Cathedral to atone for his perhaps overzealous admonishment.

**CHURCH OF THE HOLY APOSTLES.** The early 14th-century church is noted for its naturalistic mosaics and wall paintings, which borrow from the Hellenistic tradition of illustrating scenes from the Bible and the life of Christ. It's difficult to see everything because the church is dimly lit—this would be the moment for those binoculars or a guidebook with photographs. Though associated with the Twelve Apostles due to the twelve domes of its roof, the church was most likely devoted to the Virgin. *(Open 5:30am-noon and 5:30-8pm.)*

## OTTOMAN HOLDOVERS

The Ottomans ruled Thessaloniki for almost 500 years, leaving an indelible imprint on the city's landscape. Many former mosques have reverted to Orthodox churches, but the vicinity south of the forum reveals the completely neglected but well-preserved remnants of the Ottoman legacy.

**BEY HAMAMI.** This 15th-century bathhouse featured a labyrinthine interior, with a cool antechamber leading to a "tepid" room and the immense, domed sauna beyond. The baths used to feature separate men's and women's quarters and a special apartment for the bathing bey himself. *(On Egnatia, between Platonos and Venizelou.)*

**HAZMA BEY CAMII.** Thessalonikians call this longtime mosque the **Alkazar,** for a movie theater that once screened flicks here; the Hazma Bey Camii is almost obscured by a confusing complex of storefronts. Built by a bey's daughter in 1467-68 as a *mesçid* (a hall of worship minus the minarets), the building gained a minaret and official mosque status in the late 16th century, and is today the largest mosque in Greece. *(On Egnatia, just past Venizelou.)*

**BEDESTEN.** A late 15th-century covered marketplace and craftsmen's workshop for luxurious merchandise, the Ottoman Bedesten was said to emit delicious perfumes of musk and amber. Inscriptions carved into the domes in French, Greek, Southern Slav, and Turkish show the variegated ethnicity of Thessaloniki in its cosmopolitan heyday. The **market** still bustles daily, with butchers, fish mongers, fruit sellers, and salesmen hawking every imaginable food and good, yelling prices amid the hubbub of families stocking up for dinner. Southeast of the market, on the corner of Komninon and Iraklion, the 16th-century **Yahudi Hamamı** once cleansed women and men. The name ("baths of the Jews") stems from its location in the old Jewish quarter. *(On Venizelou, one block south of Egnatia.)*

# MUSEUMS

**ARCHAEOLOGICAL MUSEUM.** The treasures from Vergina's royal Macedonian tombs, once the highlight of Thessaloniki's collection, returned to Vergina (p. 230) in 1998, but the museum still shelters many jewels. A permanent exhibit on **Macedonian gold** has replaced the Vergina pieces in room 9. Among the **sculptures** in room 2 are Roman copies of a famously erotic ancient Aphrodite and parts of the enormous statue of Athena that used to stand in the Roman library's central apse. Room 4 presents visual tableaux from Thessaloniki's history, from prehistoric burial figurines to the headless statue of three Muses from the Roman Forum's Odeon, accompanied by excruciatingly detailed wall texts on excavating the ruins. A grand **mosaic** from a wealthy home, depicting Dionysus with Ariadne, Apollo stalking Daphne, and Ganymede in Zeus's eagle talons, forms the centerpiece. There are also finds from an ancient Egyptian **temple of the Serapium,** including uncannily realistic votives of ears and feet. Surreal Room 6 is full of Roman heads, while mercifully air-conditioned room 8 displays extensive finds from 121 graves at Sindos, including gold death masks and jewelry, soldiers' swords and helmets, and figurines. The **Derveni Papyrus,** a version of an Orphic poem and the sole papyrus to have survived the Greek humidity, is being restored, but may have returned by 2001. *(Take bus #3 from the railway station to Pl. Hanth. ☎830 538 or 831 037. Open M 12:30-7pm, Tu-Su 8am-7pm; reduced in winter. 1500dr, students and seniors 800dr, EU students and under 18 free. Dual admission to the Archaeological and Byzantine museums 2000dr.)*

**MUSEUM OF BYZANTINE CULTURE.** The Byzantine Museum's massive brick building, informative wall texts, and displays tracing the evolution of early Christian art and life in some ways overshadow its neighbor, the Archaeological Museum. Room 1 showcases art salvaged from churches destroyed by the 1917 fire—check out the gold-spangled **mosaic fragments** from Ag. Dimitrios. Hit the next room for a flashback to everyday Byzantine life: fish-hooks, loom weights and embroidery, belt buckles, toiletries items, and dice. Well-preserved, frescoed **tombs** from the 3rd and 4th centuries fill the final room. Paintings of earthly abundance—vines, food, animals, and flowers—transform stone tombs into Elysian fields for the benefit of their occupants, who were awaiting their resurrection at the Second Coming. *(Behind the archaeological museum, across Septemvriou 3. ☎868 570 or 868 571. Open M 12:30-8pm, Tu-Su 8am-7pm; reduced in winter. 1000dr, students and seniors 500dr, EU students and under 18 free.)*

**MACEDONIAN MUSEUM OF CONTEMPORARY ART.** If enigmatic postmodern creations made of disco balls, papier maché, electric hot plates, and other such unconventional materials call to you, the Macedonian Museum is a must-see. Ponder **George Lazongas**' "Nike: the Idea of Nike as an Idea" and **Takis**' ambient "Musical." Temporary spaces feature exhibits such as the luminous "Fotometaphores: Perspectives on Transportation." Outside, the whimsical rain shower **water sculpture** by Giorgios Zogoulopoulo douses a flock of rising and falling mesh umbrellas. *(At the fairgrounds. Walk through the main gates past the info center and go left from the OTE tower. ☎240 002. Open Tu-Sa 10am-2pm and 6pm-9pm; Su 11am-3pm; Sept.-May Tu-Su 10am-2pm and 5-9pm. 500dr, students and artists free.)*

**MUSEUM OF JEWISH PRESENCE.** The petite museum's central exhibit chronicles Thessaloniki's Jewish community from 140 BC to the present, using a walk-through timeline of photographs and text. Artifacts include 19th century Jewish newspapers, like the Sephardic-language **El Lunar,** the first newspaper in Greece. The other half of the museum is an exhibit on the Holocaust as a whole. *(Irakliou 26, 1st floor. ☎273 767. Open M-F 10am-1:30pm. Free. Ring bell if door is closed. To visit the beautiful **Monasteriote Synagogue**, Singrou 35, you must make an appointment through the Jewish Community Office, Tsimiski 24. ☎272 840.)*

**MUSEUM OF THE MACEDONIAN STRUGGLE.** Through extensive artifacts and reconstructed scenes, this museum tells the tale of Macedonia's war of independence against both Turkey and Bulgaria, leading up to and including both **Balkan Wars.** The exhibits include personal artifacts of the rebel leader **Pavlou Melas** (including the bullet that killed him) as well as captured war loot: Turkish and Bulgarian arms and treasure. *(Koromila 23, one block in from the water, halfway between the White Tower and Pl. Aristotelous. ☎229 778. Open Tu-F 9am-2pm, Sa-Su 11am-2:30pm. Free.)*

**ATATÜRK'S HOUSE.** If you've just come from Turkey and miss the omnipresent statues, streets, and museums dedicated to the creator and leader of the modern Turkish state, here's a chance to get your fix. You'll also have a chance to walk back in time, through the pre-population exchange Ottoman household where Atatürk (aka Mustafa Kemal) lived until age seven. Pictures of the leader adorn all the walls, and various relics (including Atatürk's bathrobe) are on display upstairs. *(Apostolou Pavlou 17. Open 10am-5pm. Free. To visit, you must present your passport next door, at the Turkish consulate, Ag. Dimitriou 151.)*

**CINEMA MUSEUM.** Big old movie cameras and pictures of ground breaking Greek artists and directors like the Mannakis brothers and Takis Kanellopoulos fill this little museum. Check out the props and artifacts from early 20th century Greek films, as well as photos of *Never on Sunday* star and later political minister Dimitra Liani. *(Aristotelous 18. ☎257 051. Open M-F 7:30am-3pm. Free.)*

**MUSEUM OF ANCIENT, BYZANTINE, AND POST-BYZANTINE MUSICAL INSTRUMENTS.** The three floors of recreated ancient instruments music-makers have shapes and names—tambourades, zournades, citharas—as beautiful as the sounds they might have made. Ancient paintings lend context. The museum's concert hall hosts a series of **Byzantine music performances** from September to May.

*(Katouni 12-14. ☎555 263 or 555 264. Open Th-Su 9am-3pm and 5-10pm. Free.)* If you're inspired, head to **En Chordes** to try out lyres, lutes, and drums. Charidimos, the knowledgeable owner, plays just about everything and can help you choose from a great selection of Greek CDs. *(Ipodromiou 3. ☎282 248. Open M-Sa 9:30am-2:30pm.)*

**ETHNOLOGY AND POPULAR ART (FOLKLORE) MUSEUM.** Even if you're not into traditional Macedonian costumes, embroidery, and farm tools, you might like the display of photographs by Fred Boissonas. At press time, the museum was closed for renovation; call ahead or check at the EOT before making the trip. *(Vas. Olgas 68. Take bus #5, 33, or 39 from Pl. Eleftherias (10min.); ask to be let off at the "Laigrafiko Mouseio." ☎830 591. Open F-W 9:30am-2pm. 200dr.)*

## ENTERTAINMENT

Summer visitors looking for live *rembetika* music (see **Bouzouki Punk Rock,** p. 34) should spend a weekend night at **Iyoklima,** on tiny Axiou south of Nikis near the port, or **Palios Stathmos** (Old Station), Voutira 2 (☎521 892). **Alexandros,** at Eth. Aminis and Nikis by the White Tower, is an indoor movie theater, but when skies are clear, head outside to waterfront **Natali Cinema,** Vas. Olgas 3 (☎829 457), five minutes past the White Tower, or **Ellinis** (☎292 304), at Pl. Chanth across from the archaeological museum. You won't be able to miss the posters pasted up all over town for the big theater, dance, and music performances (more sporadic in summer) at venues like the **Dhasous Theater** ("Forest Theater;" ☎218 092), **Kiprou Theater** ("Garden Theater;" ☎275 806), **Damari Theater,** and **Kratiko and Vassiliko Theaters** (☎223 785 for both). The **International Fairgrounds,** across from the Archaeological and Byzantine Museums, holds festivals throughout the year, including the **Wine Festival** (August), **International Trade Fair and Song Festival** (September), the **Dimitria Festival** (October), the internationally respected **Thessaloniki Film Festival** (November), and the new **Documentary Festival** (March).

## NIGHTLIFE

There are three main hubs for late-night fun in Thessaloniki: the bars and cafes of the **Ladadika** district (once the city's red-light strip), the bustling **waterfront,** and the big, open-air discos that throb in the area around the **airport** exit (a 1000-2000dr taxi ride from the center). Although the clubs boom until dawn, summer nightlife in the city doesn't amount to much by Thessalonikian standards—everyone who can heads out of town to the beaches of Halkidiki (p. 243).

**Privilege,** 11 km east of the city along the main highway; further down the highway from Teatro, and across the street from Deka Dance. A huge, open-air dance spot with five bars, American and Greek tunes at ear-blasting volume, and dancing on every available surface. Packed on weekends. Cover 2000dr (includes one drink).

**Deka Dance** (☎471 768), across from Privilege. One of the most popular spots in town, Deka Dance is a booming US-style nightclub with deafening music. Cover 2500dr.

**Kouva,** Orvilou 7 (☎531 944), is a two story hotspot, with a split-level dance floor complete with catwalks and bumpin' Greek tunes. Cover 1000dr (includes one drink).

**Stala,** L. Nikis 3 (☎228 237), right at the western end of the waterfront, by the port. Cool, breezy tables outside, deafening rock music and a cave-like interior inside. Cocktails 2000dr.

**Mylos,** Andreou Georgiou 56 (☎525 968), in the far west of the city, accessible by bus #31 or by taxi. Once an old mill, now a massive entertainment center with art exhibits, a restaurant, and bars. Live shows include jazz and groups like Massive Attack and Patti Smith. The **EOT** has their free calendar and magazine.

**Teatro** (☎471 160), 11km east of the city along the main highway. For Greek music addicts only. The most sophisticated club in Thessaloniki has an equally sophisticated cover (3000dr includes one drink). Rub elbows with Thessaloniki's hip and monied in the club's amphitheatric bowl, or join the crowd on stage with the live Greek pop band.

# DAYTRIPS FROM THESSALONIKI

If you're coming from Thessaloniki and get an early start, it's possible to see both Vergina and Pella in one day. The town of **Skidra** (on the junction of the Edessa-Thessaloniki and Veria roadways) can serve as a transit point, from which there are frequent buses to both Veria and Thessaloniki via Pella.

## ANCIENT VERGINA Βεργινα ☎0331

***Buses** run from Thessaloniki (2hr., every 30min., 1300dr) and Edessa (1½hr., 6 per day 8am-4pm, 950dr) to Veria. From Veria, take the Alexandria bus and get off in Vergina (20min., 9 per day 6:30am-8pm, 300dr). Ask to be dropped off next to the complex housing the Royal Tombs ("tafi"). Buses run out of Vergina for **Veria** (20min., 8 per day 7:20am-8:20pm, 300dr). Open Tu-Su 8am-7pm, M noon-7pm; in winter Tu-Su 8:30am-3pm. 1200dr, students 600dr; EU students free.*

The discovery of the **ancient Vergina ruins,** 13km southeast of Veria, was an archaeological watershed, yielding fabulous burial finds, including Greek inscriptions that proved the ancient Macedonians were a Greek tribe. In 1861, French archaeologist L. Heusey discovered portions of the palace of ancient Aigai (now called Vergina); the ruins contained ancient Macedonian remains. The extent and significance of the ruins, however, weren't revealed until 1977, when Manolis Andronikos began excavating the remains of royal tombs and a large palace dating from 350 BC. The findings in the tombs display such superb artistry that scholars believe they could have belonged only to the royal Macedonian family of Philip II, father of Alexander the Great; it's likely, too, since the tombs date to 350-325 BC, during Philip's rule. Ancient sources report that one of Philip's legs was longer than the other, and the discovery of a tomb holding shin guards of different lengths made archaeologists jump up and down: the tomb is probably Philip's. Though the Macedonian capital moved from Aigai to Pella before Philip's time, the ruins are thought to be the former capital city, since Macedonian custom required kings to be buried in the original capital.



**MUSEUM.** At once eerily morbid and dazzlingly beautiful, Vergina's museum will without a doubt be the highlight of your visit. Housed until 1998 in Thessaloniki's Archaeological Museum (see p. 227), most of the finds from the Vergina tombs have come home to the subterranean museum. Visitors enter the **Great Tumulus,** itself a massive burial mound more than 12m high and 110m in diameter, the largest in Greece. The Tumulus was built before the mid-3rd century BC over the foundations of an earlier, smaller mound, and held the graves of many average joes in addition to the massive royal tombs. The atmospherically lit museum displays artifacts found in the Great Tumulus, including Attic vases, clay and ivory figurines, gold jewelry, and carved marble funerary *steles* of the commoners' graves.

Four of the majestic **royal tombs** lie in their original locations. The designs of all four are similar: each has an anterior Ionic or Doric colonnade, usually decorated with mythological scenes. The large room behind the colonnade contains the remains of the deceased and various items to accompany him or her into the afterlife. Tombs I and IV belong to unknown royal family members. Tomb IV, looted in antiquity, contained unusually beautiful and well-preserved **frescoes,** possibly by the master artist **Nikomachus.** The most intact depicts an anguished Persephone being abducted by a grim, stony Hades, while Demeter watches with cold sorrow.

The **Tomb of the Prince** probably belongs to Alexander IV, son of Alexander the Great; he was murdered along with his mother at age 13 by his relative, Cassander of Amphipolis. The silver hydra containing his bones and his spectacular leaf-mimicking gold myrtle wreath are on display, along with other artifacts. The grand **Tomb of Philip II** is accompanied by a magnificent gold chest and exquisite myrtle wreath, and by fragments of his chryselephantine couch, decorated with miniature figures made of gold, glass, and wood. A huge glass case displays the charred remains of the bountiful offerings thrown on Philip's funeral pyre; they include animal offerings, figurines, and all his treasured possessions. The flames of the

pyre acted as transformative agents, sending these items into the next world with the deceased. Philip's tomb also contained the remains of a woman, probably **Cleopatra,** one of his seven consorts. Her somewhat less grandiose gold couch remains, as do shreds of the gold-embroidered purple cloth that wrapped her bones.

**OTHER VERGINA RUINS.** Uphill and to the south of the museum are the open ruins of the 3rd-century BC **Palace of Palatitsa,** a 20-minute walk away. Although what remains of the palace is now little more than a large collection of toppled columns and ancient rubble, a lovely mosaic floor on the south side still depicts vegetal motifs and half-woman, half-flower creatures. *(Open Tu-Su 8am-7pm, M 12pm-7pm. 1000dr, students 500dr, EU students free.)*

On the walk up to Palatitsa, you'll encounter the **Rhomaios Tomb,** containing a stately marble throne, or a "Macedonian tomb;" its occupant remains a mystery. The tomb itself is locked, but you can peer through the gates at the still-intact inner chamber. Next to it (but still undergoing restoration) is the **tomb of Evridiki,** with a fresco of Persephone and Hades in the underworld rivaling that of Tomb IV. Farther up the road, a sign off to the left past a prickly meadow indicates the site of the **Ancient Theater.** It was here that Philip II was assassinated while celebrating the marriage of his daughter, Cleopatra. The theater is currently undergoing restoration and further excavation. Before it are the decimated remains of the **Sanctuary to Eucleia,** archaic goddess of marriage and childbirth.

## ANCIENT PELLA Πελλα ☎0331

*Along the main Edessa-Thessaloniki highway, 38km west of Thessaloniki.* ***Buses*** *(40min., every 15-20min., 650dr) to Pella depart from the station at Anagenniseos 22 (☎525 100); down Octovriou past the courthouse and turn right when you see it, near the train station—make sure you're let off at "Ancient Pella," not "Nea Pella." Buses to* ***Thessaloniki*** *(2-3 per hr.) pass the site; the bus stop is across from the small cafe by the archaeological site. ☎(0382) 31 160. Open Apr.-Oct. M noon-7pm, Tu-Su 8am-7pm; Nov.-Mar. Tu-Su 8:30am-2:30pm. Both site and museum 800dr, site or museum alone 500dr, students 300dr, EU students free.*

The name "Pella" derives from the ancient Macedonian word *pelli*, meaning "ashen-colored." According to legend, the city was founded by a gray ox. The ruins at Pella, discovered in 1957 by a farmer with an archaeological bent, date back to a time when the Aegean covered the surrounding fields, and Pella served as a Thermaic Gulf port and capital of the Macedonian Empire. As the remains of 26 Neolithic settlements indicate, the area around Pella was heavily inhabited in prehistoric times. According to legend, Pella's earliest Cretan inhabitants were rapidly replaced by Macedonians barreling in from the north. Around 400 BC, King Archelaus opted to move his capital here from Aigai (Vergina), taking advantage of his new position to simultaneously foster eastern trade and build stronger ties with southern Greece. Pella became the largest city in Macedonia, home of such cultural luminaries as Zeuxis, one of antiquity's greatest painters, and Euripides, who lived here in his old age. Later the birthplace of King Philip II, the capital prospered under his reign. As Philip united the Greek states, Pella became the first capital of a Greece ruled by Macedonian conquerors. The construction of a splendid new palace attracted great minds and talents from the entire Hellenic world to the court. Pella's halcyon days continued with the rule of Philip's son Alexander the Great and his Hellenistic successors. The gradual recession of the sea, however, made Pella a less-than-convenient port, and by the mid-4th century BC, one needed to sail upstream in a dugout boat to reach the city. A more abrupt end came when Pella was ransacked by the Roman general Aemilius Paulus in 168 BC after his victory over the Macedonians at the battle of Pydna.



**MUSEUM.** Pella only takes an hour to see, but the museum alone makes the trip worthwhile. It's treasures include gold-leaf jewelry, dozens of terra-cotta figurines, glazed and unglazed Macedonian pottery, and unusual molded pottery depicting some quite racy little episodes (think Debbie Does Mace-

donia). The collection's important objects are the exquisite **mosaics** of Dionysus riding a spotted panther, a lion hunt, and a gryphon devouring a deer, complete with grisly splashes of blood. The mosaics are composed of small sea pebbles and outlined with thin lead strips; the missing eyes were most likely semi-precious stones. They're the earliest-known mosaics to mimic a three-dimensional look. The extraordinary detail and colors of the mosaics, from Dionysus's graceful features to the lion's brilliant red mane, merit a trip to Pella by themselves.

**RUINS.** Directly across the highway from the museum is Pella's vast archaeological site, still under excavation by budding young diggers from the University of Thessaloniki. At the heart of the site are the remains of the **Agora,** the commercial center of the city in ancient times, and a few grand houses. The **House of Dionysos** and the **House of the Abduction of Helen** both have expansive, well-preserved mosaic floors. The beautifully executed scenes in the mosaics seem to breathe, with subtle muscle gradations and shadows in the stag-hunting scene, and the swirling skirts and rearing horses in Helen's abduction. The **House of Plaster** has no mosaics, but it does have a splendid rectangular Ionic colonnade. North of the houses and the Agora are the Acropolis and palace (off-limits to visitors). The palace, built in ten stages, is a makeshift blend of architectural styles. Expanded by Philip, it fell with the rest of Pella at the hands of Aemilius Paulus.

## LITOHORO Λιτοχωρο ☎0352

For most hikers, the gateway to **Mount Olympus** is the village of Litohoro, which caters to both fearless mountain-climbers and beach-loving hedonists (who come for the sands and bars of nearby Plaka). It's also possible to make the ascent from the western side of Olympus, beginning in Kokkinopilos village, but this route isn't as spectacular as the trails that originate in Litohoro.

NORTHERN GREECE

**ORIENTATION AND PRACTICAL INFORMATION.** Litohoro is 90km southwest of Thessaloniki, about 8km inland. **Ag. Nikolaou,** the main street in Litohoro, runs east to west, leading into the central plateia about 500m after the entrance to the town. Down Ag. Nikolaou from the bus station, you'll find the town **tourist office** in the park, providing free maps of the town and a 1000dr map of the mountain. (☎83 100. Open 8:15am-9pm.) **Buses** (☎81 271) from Litohoro's KTEL station, opposite the church in the main plateia, travel to: **Athens** (6hr., 3 per day 9:30am-midnight, 7400dr); **Larisa** (2hr., 8 per day 6am-7:45pm, 1600dr) via **Katerini**; Plaka (10min., 12 per day 9am-8pm, 250dr); and **Thessaloniki** (1½hr., 16 per day 6:15am-8:45pm, 1750dr) via **Katerini** (20min., 17 per day 6:15am-8:45pm, 470dr). **Trains** (☎22 522) stop at **Litohoro** on the **Thessaloniki-Volos** and **Thessaloniki-Athens** lines at the station 1km from the beach **bus stop** (by the BP station, left facing the water). **Trains** from Litohoro's station run to: Athens (7hr., 3 per day 9:15am-7:50pm, 3500dr); Larisa (1½hr., 6 per day 7:10am-8:40pm, 870dr); and Thessaloniki (1½hr., 5 per day 7:55am-8:20pm, 850dr). Call the Katerini station (☎0351 23 709) or the Litohoro tourist office for more information (☎83 100). A **taxi** from the train station should cost around 2000dr. You could also take the **train** to Katerini and catch a **bus** the 5km to **Litohoro** (20min., 13 per day, 250dr), though Katerini's train and bus stations are about 1km (a 15min. walk) apart. There's a **National Bank** (☎81 025) with a 24hr. **ATM** in the main plateia. The **police station** is just below the plateia, on the left as you walk downhill. (☎81 100 or 81 111. Open 24hr.) The **health center** (☎22 222) is about 5km outside of town, by the beach, and has 24hr. **emergency** facilities. From the plateia, cobblestoned **28 Octovriou** leads left, up to the **post office** (open M-F 7:30am-2pm). The **OTE** sits across from the tourist booth, farther down the main street. (Open 7:30am-3:10pm.) **Postal code:** 60200.

**ACCOMMODATIONS.** The most affordable hotel in town is the **Hotel Park,** Ag. Nikolaou 23, down Ag. Nikolaou from the plateia and past the tourist office; the small but cozy rooms have TVs, phones, and baths. (☎81 252. Singles 6500dr; doubles 8000dr; triples 9000dr.) The pleasant **Hotel Aphroditi,** next to the plateia, has the most attractive and comfortable rooms in town. There's a communal fridge and a cozy living room, and many of the rooms have stunning views of the mountain. (☎81 415; fax 22 123. Singles 7500dr; doubles 10,000dr; triples 12,000dr; breakfast 1000dr.) A friendly family owns **Hotel Enipeas,** across from Hotel Aphroditi on the plateia; the bright, very comfortable rooms have phones, TVs, and baths, and a lovely upstairs balcony cafe. (☎84 328; fax 81 328. Singles 7000dr, doubles 9000dr, breakfast 1000dr.) The **beach,** 5km from town, is full of **campgrounds,** of which **Olympus Zeus** (☎22 115, 116, 117) and **Olympus Beach** (☎22 112 or 22 113) are the largest and best situated. Don't freelance camp on the north side of the road between the town and the highway; it's a Greek army training ground.

**FOOD AND NIGHTLIFE.** If the munchies afflict you in Litohoro, you've got plenty of options. **To Vareladikon,** on Ag. Kinolaou past the line of bars, at the bottom of town, has a large, varied menu of local favorites and friendly, English-speaking staff. (Entrees 1200-1600dr.) Small **Taverna Pazari,** 15m from the Hotel Markesia, specializes in fish dishes like red snapper and octopus. (Entrees 900-1300dr.) On the street that forks to the right at the Commercial Bank and police station, popular **Zeus** roasts and grills meat dishes. (Entrees 1000-1400dr.)

If you want to party before (or instead of) hiking, the evening begins in the **bars** clustered around the bottom of Ag. Nikolaou, and moves over to Plaka by midnight. In Litohoro, **Bolero** and **Xaos** are popular for their selective American tunes. House and techno-booming **Status** and metal-loving **Garage**—alleged to be frequented by the prettiest girls in Greece—see a younger and hipper crowd. At **Plaka,** techno-blasting **Kavodimo** and **Michele Club,** right on the beautiful clear water, are popular, but the most kickin' spot of them all is **On the Rocks,** where the sleekest and hippest Litohorians get down with their black-clad selves all night long. A taxi to Plaka costs around 1200-1400dr.

NORTHERN GREECE

# MOUNT OLYMPUS Ολυμπος Ορος ☎0352

The charm of Olympus does not lie in its natural beauty; nor its physical magnitude; the beauty of Olympus is spiritual, it is divine.
—Boissonade

Erupting out of the Thermaic Gulf, the 3000m height and formidable slopes of Mt. Olympus once so awed the ancients that they named it the divine dwelling place of their immortal pantheon. The sharp peaks saw no successful mortal ascent until 1913, when Christos Kakalos, a Litohorian hunter, guided two Swiss adventurers up to Mytikas's zenith. Since then, Olympus has been harnessed by a network of well-maintained hiking trails that makes the summit accessible to just about anyone with sturdy legs and a taste for adventure; the climb is a fantastic must-do. Today some 20 mules make a daily trip up Olympus, carrying everything from cocoa to olive oil, walking the slopes that Iris, the ancient Olympian messenger, would leap over, going from sea level to the heavens on a dewy rainbow.

Mt. Olympus has eight peaks: **Kalogeros** (2701m), **Toumba** (2785m), **Profitis Ilias** (2803m), and **Antonius** (2817m) are dwarfed by the summits of **Skala** (2866m), **Skolio** (2911m), **Stefani** (also called "The Throne of Zeus," 2909m), and **Mytikas** (or "The Pantheon," 2917m). The entire region became Greece's first national park in 1938; 23 species of native wildflowers blanket its alpine heights.

## LOGISTICS OF THE CLIMB

You'll find the most reliable resources for all aspects of hiking, including updates on weather and trail conditions, advice on itineraries and routes, and reservations for any of the **Greek Alpine Club** (EOS) refuges, at the **EOS refuge Spilios Agapitos**, or "Refuge A." (☎81 800. See **Refuges** below for more info.) The staff have years of experience and are happy to give out information over the phone in fluent English. In Litohoro, follow the "Alpine Club" signs from near the plateia to reach the **EOS office,** where you'll get helpful information and a less helpful map. (☎84 544. Open M-F 9am-12:30pm and 6-8:30pm, Sa-Su 9am-noon.) The **SEO office** (Association of Greek Mountain Climbers; ☎83 262), behind Zeus Restaurant, acts more as a clubhouse than as an official resource, but if you happen to catch someone there they can answer questions. You can buy a colorful bilingual fold-out map with contour lines, all the major trails, and an aerial-photo map of Litohoro at the **tourist office** for 1000dr. (☎83 100. Open 8:15am-9pm.) The bilingual EOS/Acharnes fold-out contour map (2500dr), available at the "Olympos Maps" shop, has more trail coverage but is badly designed and hard to read.

**PLANNING.** Each winter, over 2m of snow buries Mt. Olympus, and even in late July there are snowfields in shady corners. Unless you're handy with an ice-axe and crampons, you'll want to make your ascent between May and October, when Persephone returns to Olympus from the Underworld and her mother, Demeter, warms the earth. Mytikas, the tallest peak, is still not accessible without special equipment until June. **Weather** conditions can change extremely rapidly near the summits; even in the peak of summer, be prepared for chilly damp clouds, rain, and unrelenting sun above the tree line. If you make the ascent between June and September, you'll need **equipment** but nothing too special: bring sturdy shoes, sunglasses, sunscreen, head covering, some snacks, at least two liters of water, a warm wool or synthetic fleece sweater or jacket, and, ideally, an extra shirt and waterproof windbreaker. Take a small day-pack and leave your luggage in Litohoro, as you'll come to resent every extra pound on your shoulders.

NORTHERN GREECE

## REFUGES AND FOOD

Though it's technically possible to get an early start from Prionia and climb to Mytikas and back in one day, to enjoy the mountain fully, you should try to take two or three days. This means an overnight stay in one of the friendly refuges or campsites on the mountain; the refuges provide blankets, beds, meals, and water, but you'll still want a full suit of warm clothes, a flashlight, and maybe earplugs. There are three refuges near the summits. The EOS-run **Spilos Agapitos refuge,** or "Refuge A," is at 2100m, about 800m below Skala and Mytikas peaks. It has 110 beds, making it the largest and cushiest, with a telephone and cold showers. The **kitchen** also serves meals until 9pm, with salads running around 750-1000dr and meat dishes around 1500dr. (☎81 800. Open mid-May to late Oct.; meals served 6am-9pm; doors close and lights out at 10pm. 2500dr per bed, 2000dr for members of any mountain club, 500dr to tent nearby and use their facilities.) The extremely friendly and knowledgeable management can also be reached via messages left at their Litohoro phone or fax (☎81 329; fax 83 655). On the other side, the other EOS refuge, **Kakalos,** "Refuge C" (Γ), at 2650m, has 14 beds, no phone, and charges the same prices as Agapitos. Make reservations through Agapitos. (Open July 1-Sept. 15. Meals served 7am-midnight. Doors open all night.) Fifteen minutes from Kakalos, beneath Stefani and Profitis Ilias, **G. Apostolidis** (better known as **SEO Refuge;** 2760m) sleeps 90 and can accommodate extras and latecomers in its glass-walled porch or living room. (Open July-Sept. Meals served 9am-9:30pm. Doors open all night. 2000dr per bed, 1500dr with any mountain club membership.) Make reservations through the **Thessaloniki SEO,** which runs the refuge. (☎021 244 710. Open M-F 8-10pm; leave messages for a reservation.) Although Kakalos is smaller and more expensive than the SEO refuge, it has the best view of the rosy-fingered Dawn as she rises above the clouds.

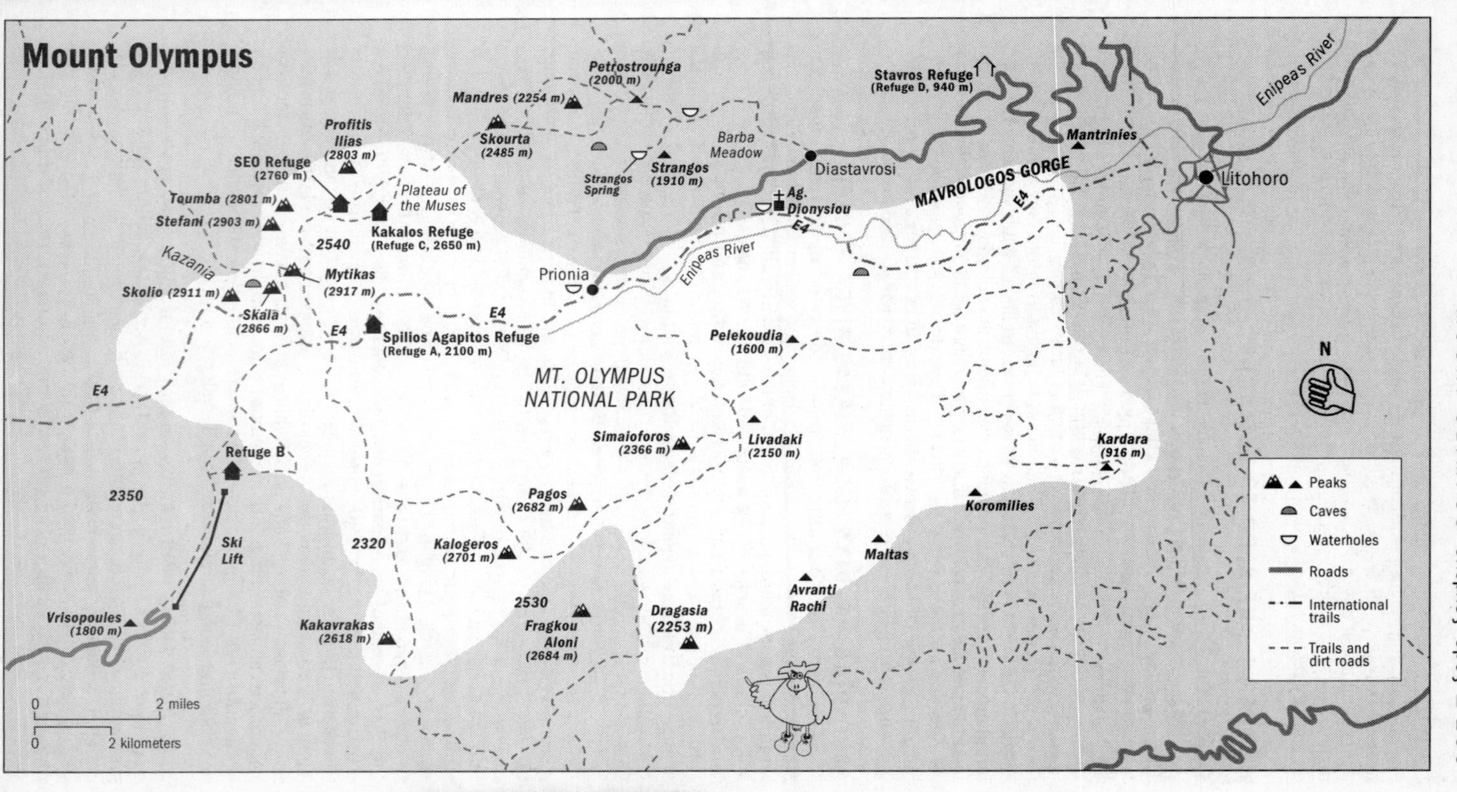
Mount Olympus
Petrostrounga (2000 m)
Mandres (2254 m)
Stavros Refuge (Refuge D, 940 m)
Enipeas River
Profitis Ilias (2803 m)
Skourta (2485 m)
Barba Meadow
Mantrinies
SEO Refuge (2760 m)
Strangos Spring
Strangos (1910 m)
Diastavrosi
MAVROLOGOS GORGE
Litohoro
Plateau of the Muses
Ag. Dionysiou
E4
Toumba (2801 m)
Stefani (2903 m)
Kakalos Refuge (Refuge C, 2650 m)
2540
Enipeas River
Kazania
Mytikas (2917 m)
Prionia
Skolio (2911 m)
Skala (2866 m)
E4
Spilios Agapitos Refuge (Refuge A, 2100 m)
Pelekoudia (1600 m)
MT. OLYMPUS NATIONAL PARK
N
Simaioforos (2366 m)
Livadaki (2150 m)
Kardara (916 m)
Refuge B
2350
Pagos (2682 m)
Koromilies
Ski Lift
2320
Kalogeros (2701 m)
Maltas
Avranti Rachi
2530
Vrisopoules (1800 m)
Kakavrakas (2618 m)
Fragkou Aloni (2684 m)
Dragasia (2253 m)
Peaks
Caves
Waterholes
Roads
International trails
Trails and dirt roads
0
2 miles
0
2 kilometers

All of the refuges, particularly the very popular Refuge A, tend to fill up on weekends in July and August—call at least a couple of weeks in advance for **reservations.** Otherwise, call one to two days ahead and you'll probably be fine. Meals tend to run about 800-900dr for soups and salads, 1400-1500dr for pasta and meat dishes, 1000dr for breakfast. The refuge managers are also prepared to handle emergency rescues if needed.

## TRAILS: THE SLOG TO THE GODS

There are three ways to take on Olympus: all three originate at **Litohoro** (elev. 280m), two involve heading straight to the trailheads, and one involves an alternate hike. The first trailhead is at **Prionia** (elev. 1100m), 18km from the village; the second trailhead is at **Diastavrosi** (also called **Gortsia;** elev. 1300m), 14km away. There is no bus to Prionia or Diastavrosi, so walk, drive, or take a cab (Prionia 6000dr, Diastavrosi 1500dr) along the asphalt road (eventually a dusty, unpaved path) that winds upward starting next to the police station in Litohoro, just below the plateia. The third route is more challenging, and involves hiking to Prionia via a trail along the **Enipeas River;** you'll eventually start at the Pronia trailhead. After spending the night at the Agapitos refuge, you'll wind to the summit the next day and head around to the SEO and Kakalos refuges. Hikers can stay another night there and walk down the next day to Diastavrosi (about 3-4 hr., depending on how you fare going downhill), or pass the refuges and arrive at Diastavrosi in late afternoon. The pretty hike to Refuge A from Litohoro takes 7-9 hours and really lets you see the mountain.

### ASCENDING MT. OLYMPUS (ENIPEAS RIVER ROUTE)

The fairly strenuous, beautiful trail from Litohoro to Prionia runs through the **Mavrologos Gorge** and along the Enipeas River, and is also an **E4 trail.** Wonderful stretches punctuate the 18km climb, but it's a difficult 4½ hours with many steep ups and downs. **Bring water.** To find the **trailhead,** walk uphill from Litohoro's main plateia past the Hotel Aphrodite, and follow signs to Mili (Μυλοι), past the town cemetery, to the Restaurant Mili. There is drinking water at the trailhead. Continue past the restaurant to the left, and when you reach the concrete walkway, make a right and walk along it a short distance. Then, at a fork in the trail, follow the yellow diamond markers emblazoned with "E4" up the left side of the Mavrologos Gorge. Keep following yellow diamonds, red blazes, spray-painted numbers, and orange-and-white plastic strips tied on trees. You'll need to cross the river several times. In springtime the water may be waist-high; crossing the river when full is inadvisable. By June the water is only knee-deep, and by July, barely calf-deep. Parts of the trail have views down into the gorge, and when the trail descends to the river, lovely clear green pools abound. After 3 hours you'll reach the tiny **chapel of Agios Spileo,** built at the source of a small spring inside a gaping cave. About 20 minutes farther, after a bridge crossing, follow the dirt road for 60m before turing left up the hill to see the charred shell of the **Monastery of Agios Dionysiou,** which gave refuge to Greek partisans during the Second World War until the Nazis burned it. A solitary monk lives there now, and there are a few beds he may let you use if you ask. You can leave a small donation here for the restoration of the large and beautifully situated monastery; you can also fill your water bottles. Follow the outside wall of the monastery to a fork in the road, and continue straight. You'll reach a second fork after 15min. or so—take the left for the **falls of Perivoli** and the right to reach **Prionia** in just under an hour's walk.



**ASCENDING FROM PRIONIA.** The most popular route toward the refuges begins at Prionia, where you'll find drinking **water, toilets,** and a small **restaurant.** From here, a three-hour walk uphill takes you to the Spilios Agapitos refuge ("Refuge A," elev. 2100m). The trail is unambiguous and well marked, and is part of the **European E4 path** from Spain to Greece. There's one last chance for water before the refuge, about 45min. up from Prionia. As you

approach the tree line, you'll be encouraged by the brilliantly colored masses of wildflowers. This hike can take just one day up and back, if you take the 6000dr **taxi** ride to Prionia from Litohoro.

**ASCENDING FROM DIASTAVROSI.** Another approach to the peaks begins at Diastavrosi, 14km from Litohoro. This longer but more picturesque route climaxes in a stunning **ridge walk** with dazzling views of Poseidon's Aegean, the Macedonian plain, and Thessaloniki's smog layer. It reaches the SEO and Kakalos refuges in about six hours. Begin at the parking lot by taking the uphill path on the left, and follow the red blazes, striped plastic strips on trees, and signs of the mule procession that uses this route. In about an hour you'll pass through the **Barba meadow,** and in about two hours you'll reach a cement **water tank** with an unhelpful painted map off to the left. Go straight here, not left, and the path leads up and up to **Petrostrounga** (1800m), about 2½ hours from the trailhead. Continue on; four hours from the trailhead you'll begin approaching the tree line, reaching Skourta Hill in another 30 minutes or so. The beautiful **Lemos** ridge (meaning "neck") leads you gently toward the peaks. About 5½ hours from the beginning of the hike you'll reach the **Plateau of the Muses** (Οροπεδιο Μουσον), a sweeping expanse of green under the Stefani, Toumba, and Profitis Ilias peaks. Take the clearly marked fork left for the **Kakalos shelter** (2650m) or right for the **SEO shelter** (2760m). There's also a trail up to the top of **Profitis Ilias,** where there's a tiny stone church. You can find **water** in two places along the Diastavrosi trail: at the turnoff between Barba and Spilla (1½hr. from the trailhead, marked on the trail), and at Strangos spring.

## SUMMITS

**ASCENDING MYTIKAS.** Up at the summit area, Mytikas (2917m) has the highest elevation of the Mt. Olympus summits; it's thus the most climbed peak. There are two possible routes of ascent. The nearly vertical, rockslide-prone **Louki** trail, on the east face of the peak, makes for a difficult climb straight up 300m. Dotted with small plaques to honor those who fell to Hades trying to make this ascent, Louki is the more dangerous route, especially due to the risk of loose rock falling on hikers below. The other trail runs along the south side of Mytikas by way of **Skala** peak (2860m), through a series of sinuous ups and downs that also involves rock-climbing by handhold and foothold. This way is generally thought safer, but both trails to Mytikas are moderately dangerous, and are prone to rock slides and avalanches. It's a bad idea to lug a large pack along the route or to attempt the climb in very wet weather, and acrophobes should take a good look at the trails to judge whether or not they can handle it. The Louki path in particular should only be tackled by the enthusiastic, fit, and **experienced** mountain hiker. Get an early start, because clouds often hover around the peaks by mid-afternoon.

To reach Mytikas from Refuge A, walk uphill; after about 45 minutes, you'll find a **map** at a fork in the road. The left takes you along the E4 trail to Skala and Skolio peaks; the right leads to the Louki ascent and the **Zonaria** trail that leads to the SEO and Kakalos refuges. If you're heading toward Louki, a 40-minute walk brings you to the base of the ascent; look for the short stone wall and red blazes going straight up. From there, it's about an hour of rock climbing to the summit. A slightly more dangerous trail goes up to **Stefani** peak a little farther along. Past this, 20 minutes along a stony trail brings you to the SEO refuge and Plateau of the Muses. The bowl-shaped slopes you traverse are known as the **Throne of Zeus.** The god of gods rested his enormous cranium on the Stefani (crown) peak above.

Back at the fork in the road, the way to **Skala** leads left; make a right at the unmarked fork (a left brings you to the top of Agios Antonios). An hour's walk brings you to Skala peak and the beginning of the **Kaki Skala** (Bad Ladder) trail to Mytikas, marked with paint blazes. The last 100m or so to the highest peak involves a fair amount of scrambling upward. The **Kazania** (Cauldron), named for the clouds of mist that usually steam up from it, drops 500m down sharply on your left. It's about a 3-hour hike from Refuge A to Mytikas' summit via the Skala route.

**ASCENDING SKOLIO.** If you decide not to tempt the gods by ascending Mytikas, take the 30-minute hike from Skala to Skolio, the second highest peak (2911m; 6m shorter than Mytikas). The best view of Olympus' sheer western face looks out from here. It takes about two hours to reach the Skolio summit from the Agapitos refuge. Approaching the peaks from the Plateau of the Muses, it's about 90 minutes up to Mytikas via Louki, or four hours to go around on the Skala route.

# EDESSA Εδεσσα ☎0381

Atop a steep butte in the foothills of Mt. Vermion, Edessa hangs on the brink of a cliff 90km west of Thessaloniki and 25km south of the border with FYR Macedonia. Here, numerous streams—channelled through stone waterways and under Edessa's arched bridges—form the country's only notable waterfalls, cascading 70m to the valley floor and causing one occupying Bulgarian army to name the town "the waters." Historic districts, including the former Christian Varousi district and the old mills, and beautiful views over the orchard-laden plains below, make lively Edessa a refreshing and worthwhile stopover.

## ORIENTATION AND PRACTICAL INFORMATION

Edessa's bus station is at the corner of **Filippou** and **Pavlou Mela,** near the center of town. With your back to the station, facing the kiosk across the street, Pavlou Mela leads straight ahead to meet **Dimokratias** (also called **Egnatia**). After three short blocks, it becomes one of the town's main thoroughfares, where most of Edessa's hotels hang their signs. A right turn on Dimokratias brings you past the cafe and playground of **Pl. Megalou Alexandrou** and leads to an intersection near the stadium, at a large, leafy park full of bars and cafes. The right fork, **25 Martiou,** leads to the waterfalls, while the left, **18 Octovriou,** leads to the train station. Filippou runs parallel to Dimokratias, then merges with it near the stadium at triangular **Pl. Timendon,** which consists of a cafe and playground.

**Buses** run from the main bus station (☎23 511) to: **Athens** (7hr., 3 per day 8am-8pm, 9300dr); **Thessaloniki** (2hr., 14 per day 6am-8pm, 1700dr); and **Veria** (1¼hr., 6 per day 8am-4pm, 950dr). Buses to **Florina** (1½hr., 6 per day 8:45am-8:15pm, 1650dr), **Kastoria** (2 hr, 4 per day 11:15am-6:15pm, 2200dr) and **Kozani** (2hr, 6 per day 10am-8:45pm, 2400dr) leave from a **stop** outside a small fast food joint next to the fruit market, on Filippou, a block past the main bus station; look for schedules posted in the window. From the **train station** (☎23 510), at the end of 18 Octovriou, trains run to: **Athens,** either directly (7hr., 3:06pm, 4310dr), or via **Plati** (1½hr., 8 per day 4:30am-9:09pm, 700dr); **Florina** (2hr., 4 per day 9:48am-8:06pm, 720dr); **Kozani** (2hr., 4 per day 7:59am-6:31pm, 820dr); and **Thessaloniki** (2hr., 8 per day 4:30am-9:09pm, 840dr) via Veria and Naoussa. **Taxis** (☎23 392 or 22 904) congregate on Dimokratias near the National Bank in Pl. Megalou Alexandrou.

The **Tourist Information Office,** to the right of the waterfalls, provides maps and brochures with information about sights, hotels, and transportation in English. (☎20 300. Open 9am-9pm; hours reduced in winter.) The **National Bank,** Dimokratias 1, surrounded by a fence on the corner of Arch. Penteleiminos 2, has an **ATM,** as do many other banks scattered throughout town. To find the **police station,** follow Dimokratias toward the waterfalls and turn left on Iroön Polytechniou; the station is at the intersection with Arhelaou. (☎23 333. Open 24hr.) Several cafes on Edessa provide **Internet access;** the cheapest are **Monitor Cafe,** Dimokratias 35, just before the intersection at the stadium (☎26 835; open 10:30am-2am) and **Net Cafe** just around the corner at Filellinon 17, on the street that flanks the stadium (☎29 629; open 9am-1am). Both charge 800dr per hr. The **OTE** is a blue and white building facing the Byzantine clock tower on Ag. Dimitriou (open 7am-2:40pm). Edessa also has two **post offices.** The larger (☎23 332) is at Dimokratias 26, and the smaller (☎26 030) is on Pavlou Mela a block up from the bus station; both are open 7:30am-2pm, and offer the usual services plus Poste Restante and **currency exchange. Postal code:** 58200.

## ACCOMMODATIONS

There are a few good deals among Edessa's handful of hotels. Centrally located **Hotel Alfa,** at the intersection with P. Mela, is convenient for bus riders, just a block up from the station. Alfa is a bit fancy, with an astounding *two* elevators. The wide, ample rooms come with TVs, phones, balconies, baths, and the reception has **free town maps.** (☎22 221 or 22 231; fax 24 777. Singles 7000dr; doubles 13,000dr; prices higher with A/C). Next door to Hotel Alfa, **Hotel Pella,** Egnatia 26, has generously spacious and light rooms with balconies, including phones, TVs, baths, and a communal eating area with a fridge. (☎23 541. Singles 6000dr; doubles 10,000dr.) **Olympia Rented Rooms,** Octovriou 51, is near the train station with the green neon sign. Gleaming white tiled rooms contain baths and TVs, and some have balconies. (☎23 544. Doubles 7000dr.) Across from the Pl. Timendon is the very modern **Hotel Elena,** D. Rizou 4, whose snazzy rooms come with phones, TVs, and tiled baths. (☎23 218; fax 23 951. Singles 8000dr; doubles 12,000dr; triples 13,000dr.)

## FOOD AND ENTERTAINMENT

Edessa has no shortage of those edible evil twins known as cheese pies and rotisserie chicken; it also has inexpensive restaurants scattered about town. The largest, most popular, and best situated restaurant in town is the **Public Waterfall Center Restaurant,** right at the top of the falls. It serves local and traditional specialties like *tseblek-kebab*, a combination of beef, eggplant, pepper, and cheese (1850dr), and *stamnato* (1750dr), a concoction with lamb, potatoes, vine leaves, and cheese. (☎26 810. Entrees 900-2500dr.) The fish taverna **Boulgouri,** under a striped awning near Octovriou 18 on the way to the train station, is a fairly pleasant place for a fish dinner (1200dr); tasty fresh trout and a mean *tzatziki* share the menu. (Entrees 800-1500dr.)

The most picturesque and popular of Edessa's cafes is the **Cafe High Rock** (Psilos Brahos), M. Alexandrou 2, in the southwest corner of town on—you guessed it—a high rock looking out over the cliff face. (500dr; cocktails 1200dr. ☎26 793.) You can find dinner, drinks and dancing at **Kanavourgeio,** at the bottom of the glass elevator by the old cannabis mill from which it derives its name. The restaurant has seafood, salads, and some grilled meats, and the disco blasts American and Greek music every Friday and Saturday night. (Entrees 1100-2400dr. ☎20 070 or 20 102. 1000dr cover goes toward one drink.) In the town center, the heart of nightlife is a shady park off Dimokratias right before the post office, where three similar cafe/bars draw masses of young people into tight clusters on the sidewalks. Bars popular with the youthful and fashionable are **Saloon** and **River,** both off Dimokratias.

## SIGHTS

**WATERFALLS AND ENVIRONS.** Edessa's best sights revolve around the waterfall, where the town's rivers runneth over into the valley below. To reach the impressive Katarrakton (waterfall), walk down Dimokratias past the stadium, where it becomes 25 Martiou, and watch for the large waterfall signs, which will tell you when to turn right. The roar of surging water and bustling souvenir stands will herald your arrival. The descending concrete terraces let you survey the falls and the agricultural plain below from varying angles, and to catch a little spray on your face. You'll spot a convent and the ruins of the ancient city, whose marble columns are visible in the distance. A none-too-impressive cave also beckons (50dr).

The area at the edge of the cliffs once supported a collection of water mills and textile factories. The entire area has been redesigned and reconstructed as Edessa's **Open-Air Water Museum,** featuring pre-industrial wheat and sesame mills and tanneries, built in the mid- to late-19th century, more modern textile factories, including the Tsitsis & Co. spinnery, the wool mill, and the cannabis factory **(Kanavourgio),** which produced rope for the ships. The tourist office has a great free

**HOT COALS, HOLY SOULS** Visitors to Northern Greece in the off season may witness some unique rural festivals. On May 21, the residents of **Langades,** north of Thessaloniki, celebrate the feast day of Saints Constantine and Helen with **fire-dancing,** which began back in the frenzied revelry of Dionysian worship. Orthodox Greeks imported the fire dance from Turkish Thrace during the population exchanges (p. 17), and it revolves around the **Anastenarides,** a religious brotherhood of men "possessed by the saint." On the feast day, a procession carries the sacred icons of Constantine and Helen through the village, accompanied by music and drumming. The Anastenarides begin to dance around a great bonfire—slowly at first, then faster as the music accelerates, gasping and sighing all the while (*anastenazo* means "to sigh"). They enter a sort of trance, leap into the flames, and dance barefoot, calling out: "Make your vows to the Saint!" and "Restore justice lest the Saint shall destroy you!" Those who dance without damaging the feet qualify to enter the brotherhood.

brochure showing the mill locations; get one before you go. To reach the Kannavourgio, you can follow the steps down along the waterfalls, but a more unique mode of transport is Edessa's **glass elevator.** Even those who haven't read Roald Dahl will enjoy the first of two glass-sided, A/C elevators sitting calmly and incongruously at the top of the cliff face like a mysterious magic portal. Though the elevators are short and marred with graffiti, the view descending over the plain is impressive. The path to the elevator begins to the right of the tourist office in the little park; follow signs for the Kannavourgiou disco-cafe complex.

**VAROUSI DISTRICT.** The old church-dotted town that remained a Christian enclave during Ottoman occupation, rests along the cliff's edge, beginning to the right of the waterfall park and continuing on behind the walls of the stadium. Examples of traditional architecture abound: upper stories protrude out miraculously on creaky old wooden beams over a stone base. The quarter's convenient location near the "safe escape" of the lowlands made it a popular spot not only for oppressed Christians but for Second World War resistance fighters—much of the area was burned by the Nazis in 1944. The narrow streets invite leisurely strolls. The new **Museum of Traditional and Folk Life** is housed in one of the old buildings on the side of the drop, a block down from the intersection of Arch. Panteleimonos and Megalou Alexandrou (ignore the big yellow "museum" sign and go left, away from Cafe High Rock). In addition to regional costumes and the expected array of bread-making, weaving, and farming tools, the museum showcases paraphernalia from Edessa's old silk mill, which thrived until the 60s nylon revolution supplanted silk. Old geography textbooks and a Koran, colorful woven rugs, and children's toys are set out on three floors. *(☎28 787. Open Tu-Su 10am-6pm. 500dr.)*



**SITES.** Below the town, about 3km to the southwest, the 4th-century BC ruins of the ancient city of **Loggos** are no longer terribly impressive, but a few columns along the main avenue still stand, one from a temple devoted to the goddess **Mas.** Loggos was once the lower town of the ancient city, which included present-day Edessa as the upper citadel. Try going in the evening, when the dying light makes the columns glow with unearthly beauty. The fastest way to the ruins begins at the landing between the two elevators. Walk to the right on the sandy path over the little mound to find a windy path. Follow it downhill (don't go through the gates on the left) and go straight; you'll reach the city in 15 minutes. The longer but prettier path begins at the restaurant and disco Kannavourgio: follow the road along the huge pipeline, and after the first bridge turn right to cross a second bridge. You'll pass the convent and then arrive at the ruins after a total of about 25 minutes.

The **Byzantine Clock Tower** occupies a block in the upstream direction from Dimokratias at Pl. Megalou Alexandriou. The very dilapidated, neglected remains of a 19th-century **Ottoman mosque** sink down on a side street: walk along Dimokratias a few blocks away from the city center, turn right after the Alpha Credit Bank, and veer left when the mosque's dome and de-crowned minaret come into view.

To see Edessa's rivers united, follow any of the tributaries upstream until you hit the **Byzantine Bridge.** The bridge arches over the main stream that eventually splits off to form the town's countless rivulets and narrow channels.

## KASTORIA Καστορια ☎0467

Although the unassuming town of Kastoria, rarely visited by tourists, has seen better days, it still manages enough charm and small-town bustle to make it worth a visit. Once upon a time, its proximity to a less-tumultuous Balkans brought border-town prosperity its way, and Kastoria became the fur capital of Greece. Many rich fur merchants built their permanent homes by the lake, and their decaying mansions still dot the Old Town. Hundreds of years later, 3000 local furriers continue to be the mainstay of the town's economy, despite the haggard appearance of their fading storefronts and mannequins. While Kastoria's natural setting on large, murky **Lake Orestiada** evokes a distant beauty that the rest of the city never quite lives up to, the city's broad waterfront streets and lovely crumbling churches make up for newer, more concrete touches.

Kastoria's prettiest neighborhood is the north waterfront, which has a small plateia and some cafes. Although the city doesn't merit a particularly long stay, the view of the lake at sunset will make the time you do spend pass pleasantly. Kastoria originally rested securely on an island in Lake Kastoria. Around the 10th century AD, the townspeople began dumping garbage into the lake to build a causeway to the shore. Today, the bulk of the city is squeezed onto this narrow isthmus, and the island proper is nearly deserted. Savor the beauty of the lake from a distance, but don't even think about taking a dip; the town only recently stopped dumping raw sewage into the water.

### ORIENTATION AND PRACTICAL INFORMATION

The town has two lakefronts, bounded by **Nikis** street on the north and **Megalou Alexandrou** street on the south, and two main plateias. To reach the roadway hub of **Pl. Davaki** and its many hotels from the bus station on the south waterfront's western edge, walk left (facing the lake), make your first left, walk one block, and you'll be on **Diakou.** Turn right, walk another two blocks, and veer right at the Commercial Bank to reach the plateia. From here, **Mitropoleos,** the main road, leads uphill to the right to the other main plateia, **Pl. Omonias** (700m southeast). On the left and uphill, **Ag. Athanasiou** leads toward the Byzantine Museum. On the left and downhill, **Ioustinianou** runs to the north waterfront, past the town hall. The **Old Town,** with its sagging mansions and churches, is past Pl. Omonias, at the foot of the hill on the easternmost edge of the city.

NORTHERN GREECE

**Buses: KTEL,** Diakou 14 (☎83 455). Buses run to: **Athens** (9hr., 3per day 7:30am-7:30pm, 10,200dr); **Edessa** (2hr., 3 per day 8am-6pm, 2200dr); **Kozani** (1hr., 3per day 7:30am-7:30pm, 1850dr); **Thessaloniki** (3½hr., 7 per day 6am-6pm, 3900dr); and **Veria** (2½hr., 4 per day 6am-4pm, 2750dr). With a little more ingenuity (i.e. connections, transfers), you can reach **Florina** (via Kozani or Edessa), **Ioannina** (via Neapoli), or **Kalambaka.**

**Flights: Olympic Airways,** Megalou Alexandrou 15 (☎24 648), on the southern waterfront, 5min. past the bus station, behind a big parking lot. Open M-F 8am-4pm. Four flights per week to **Athens** (1hr.; M, W, F, and Su 11am; 19,000dr, under 24 16,000dr). A taxi travels to the **airport,** 12km away in **Argos,** for 2000dr.

**Taxis:** (☎27 666 or 28 666), converging near the bus station. Available 24hr.

**Tourist services:** (☎22 777 or 23 068), under the town hall on Ioustinianou. Open M-F 8am-7pm, Sa-Su 10am-7pm. If the office is closed, try upstairs at the town hall.

**Banks:** Both **Ionian Bank,** on the south waterfront across from the taxi stand, and **Commercial Bank,** at the corner of Grammou and 11 Novembriou, have 24hr. **ATMs.**

**Police:** Gramou 25 (☎83 333), behind the bus station. No English spoken. Open 8am-3pm, but available 24hr.

**Hospital:** (☎28 341, 342, 343). On the southwestern edge of the waterfront, by the island and near the Mavrotissa Church. Open 24hr.

**Telephones: OTE,** Grammou 209 (☎22 599 or 22 135). Open 7am-10pm.

**Internet Access: Aer@s,** Ag. Anathasiou 48 (☎23 232). 1500dr per hr. for use of one of three speedy terminals in a jazzy, hip cafe with outdoor tables. Open 9am-12:30am.

**Post Office:** (☎22 991), on the southern lakefront road, Meg. Alexandrou, around the bend from the bus station. Poste Restante and currency exchange. Open 7:30am-2pm. **Postal code:** 52100.

## ACCOMMODATIONS

If you ask for an upper level room, you'll be able to look out on the lake.

**Hotel Keletron,** Artis 3 (☎22 525). Follow Grammou from behind the bus station, veer left onto 11 Novembriou, and make a left at the town hall. Large, carpeted rooms with phones, baths, TVs, above a shady, quiet plateia. Singles 7000dr; doubles 9000dr; triples 11,000dr.

**Hotel Anesis,** Gramou 10 (☎83 908; fax 83 768). A more expensive choice, but fancier. Spacious, comfortable rooms with baths and TVs; half of the rooms have balconies. Singles 10,000dr; doubles 12,600dr; triples 13,000dr.

**Lenonas,** Agio Theologou 6 (☎22 446), on the eastern part of the island, about 25 minutes from the bus station. Walk all the way down the harbor on the south side, make a left onto Agio Theologou, and look for the pretty yellow building on the left. A luxury splurge if you can afford it, with eight huge, comfortable rooms in a private home, with breakfast included. Singles 16,000dr; doubles 21,000dr.

## FOOD AND NIGHTLIFE

Good dining options are limited in Kastoria. Several locally favored restaurants line **Pl. Omonia,** serving classic Greek entrees for 500-2000dr. Mitropoleos is loaded with cafes, bars, fast food, and somewhat tacky arcade parlors.

**To Krontiri,** Oresteiados 13 (☎28 358), about a 15min. walk from the bus station on the eastern part of the southern waterfront. Meaty menu includes snails. Ask for anything in a crock. Open past 3am. Entrees 600-1500dr.

**Ta Kimata** (☎28 887), at Ioustinianou and Nikis, on the north waterfront with a swan statue at entrance. Lots of seafood in a bustling, open air place by the lake; not much variety but what's there is tasty (1000-1500dr). Dare to try the fish from the lake. Pleasant patio juts out over the water.

**Krasostamo** (☎22 218), on the southern waterfront, past Ta Klimata. Lots of fishy delights from the lake, as well as delicious salads and local recipes, with tables by the water. Entrees 800-2000dr.

## SIGHTS

Kastoria is renowned first for its voluminous fur garment industry (some 5000 garments produced per day) and second for its churches. There are 40 Byzantine and 36 post-Byzantine holy edifices scattered throughout the city, many with elaborate masonry and exquisite decoration, usually lurking in a state of near-collapse between apartment blocks. Most of the churches are in the Old City, where it's hard to go a block without seeing a green sign pointing the way to another church. The tiny Byzantine **Panagia Koumblelidhiki,** on Mitropoleos a block before Pl. Omonia, and the **Agia Anargiri,** on Vitsiou off Athanasiou at its near eastern end, house particularly spectacular frescoes. Sadly, some of the paintings—rare exterior fres-

coes—have recently been defaced by graffiti scratched into their surfaces. The walls of 11th-century **Mavrotissas Monastery,** about 3km from the southeast corner of town along the waterfront, are also laden with beautiful frescoes. The priest who lives in the church conducts tours in Greek or German. (Open 8am-8:30pm.) Also worth a look is the 10th century **Agios Stephanos,** on Eleussis off the end of Athanasiou, one of the oldest churches in Kastoria.

To be sure of gaining access to the churches, stop first at the **Byzantine Museum,** off Mitropoleos in Pl. Dexamenis, during their opening hours; a guide from the museum will open the churches for you. The museum's own collection illustrates the evolution of iconographic styles from its earliest icon (AD 1180) until the 17th century. (☎26 781. Open Tu-Su 8:30am-3pm. Free.) Kastoria's excellent **Folk Art Museum** resides in one of the town's many 17th century mansions, and houses a wine cellar, a gorgeous living room with a carved ceiling, and a reconstructed traditional fur-cleaning workshop. (Open 10am-12pm and 5pm-7pm.) One kilometer outside of town stands **Mt. Psalida,** where Alexander the Average decided to upgrade to Alexander the Great by conquering the world.

# HALKIDIKI ΧΑΛΚΙΔΙΚΗ

The fingers of the monument-free Halkidiki peninsula point south into the Aegean, like a shadow of Poseidon's three-pronged trident, yielding spectacular scenery and some of the finer beaches in Greece. Tourists with money and tanning lotion swarm to the middle and western prongs, **Sithonia** and **Kassandra,** where natural beauty tempers tourist gloss. On the eastern prong is **Mt. Athos,** a monastic community and living link to the traditions of the Byzantine Empire. Visits to Mt. Athos are strictly regulated; men must obtain permits, and women are entirely excluded. Reservations for serious pilgrims should be made up to six months in advance (see p. 219). In contrast, visitors to Kassandra and Sithonia have no hoops to jump through, excepting the Halkidiki public transportation system. Frequent buses run between the Karakassi 68 station in Thessaloniki (☎(031) 924 444) and the three peninsulas, but bus service does not accommodate those who want to hop from prong to prong; you'll just have to return to Thessaloniki and catch another bus. Moped rental allows for splendid cruises along Halkidiki's quiet, beautiful roads.



## SITHONIA PENINSULA Σιθονια ☎0375

A measure of tranquility persists on the more isolated beaches on the south and southwest coasts of Sithonia, though (like Kassandra), the peninsula has gradually sold its soul to BMWed visitors, plunging into the sordid world of tour buses and plastic souvenirs. There are two backroad routes through Sithonia: west via Neos Marmaras and east via Vourvourou. Not long ago, Neos Marmaras was a quiet fishing village, but with a push from the 900-room Porto Carras hotel complex just across the bay, the town has fallen from grace and into tourist hub hell. The beaches, however, remain gorgeous (if crowded), and sunset views from Neos Marmaras' north end of town will wow you.

**PRACTICAL INFORMATION.** You can get to Neos Marmaras by bus or boat. **Buses** run to Thessaloniki (2½hr., 7 per day, 6am-7:30pm, 2600dr) and nearby small towns, including Moudania (6 per day, 6am-7:30pm, 1000dr); timetables are posted outside of Dionysios' next door. There's an **Internet Cafe** (☎72 670) right across from the bus stop, offering 24hr. access at 800dr for 30min. **Taxis** (☎71 500) group by the beach. The nearest **ferry** service to the Sporades runs from the town of **Nea Moudania** in northernmost Kassandra. The English-speaking staff at **Marmaris Tours,** next to the bus stop, recommends rooms, **exchanges currency,** and books excursions. They also rent motorbikes and **mopeds** for 2000-4000dr per day. (☎72 232 or 72 010. Open 9am-2pm and 6-11:30pm.) The **National Bank,** with

24hr. **ATM,** is on the main street and offers **currency exchange** on Saturdays. (☎72 793. Open M-Th 8am-2pm, F 8am-1:30pm, Sa 9am-1pm.) The town **post office** is in the second plateia, to the left of Plaza Cafe. (☎71 334. Open M-F 8am-2pm.) **Postal code:** 61381.

**ACCOMMODATIONS.** Rooms are extremely expensive. Even with 76 proprietors in town, vacancies are few on midsummer weekends. A sign with a map by the beach lists every domatia; Marmaris Tours will also call around for availability. **Albatross Rooms To Let,** on Themistokli, has spacious, modern rooms with kitchenettes and large balconies; ask at Rigalo Jewelers, near the bus stop. They can also help you find another place if they're booked up. (☎/fax 71 738. Doubles with bath and kitchen 6000-8000dr; triples 10,000dr). **Hotel Glafos,** around the corner from the Internet cafe, has small, comfortable rooms with phones and private baths. Inquire at the *ouzeri* underneath. (☎71 205, fax 72 340. Singles 7000dr; doubles 9000dr). **Camping Marmaras** is clearly marked by road signs, and is 2km away on the beach. (☎71 901. Open May to early Oct.; 1600dr per person; 1750dr per tent.)

**FOOD AND NIGHTLIFE.** Popular pagoda impostor **Zoe's Little China** serves a variety of Chinese dishes. (Entrees 900-3500dr. Open 1pm-1:30am.) For Greek classics, head to a waterfront taverna like **Dionysos,** on the other side of the bus stop; it serves delicious seafood. (Entrees 1300-3000dr. ☎71 202.) Locals like smallish **Ta Kimata,** which serves higher-priced, savory fish dishes (entrees 1200-3300dr). Nightlife in Neos Marmaras centers on the strip of bars and a pair of discos on the beach. The most happening bar in town is the centrally located, waveside **Pluton,** where picky bouncers guard a split-level outdoor bar/club. No jeans or sneakers, bub. (2000dr cover includes one drink.) Next door at **Molos,** things are more laid back; Greeks and foreigners rub elbows, drink, and watch the surf. (1500dr cover includes one drink.) The big disco, **Vareladiko,** is about 4km away.

**RURAL SITHONIA.** Explore more of Sithonia by taking the **bus** around the peninsula to **Sarti** (1hr., 9 per day 9:15am-9pm, 700dr). The bus passes by the most deserted, desirable turf on the peninsula. If you climb the road 5km south of **Porto Carras,** you'll see a **beach** near **Agia Kiriaki,** with a small reef and an outlying island. It's a long, hard climb down, but you'll glory in the sand once you get there.



# MOUNT ATHOS Αγιον Ορος ☎0377

The monasteries on Mt. Athos (the "Holy Mountain"), the easternmost peninsula of Halkidiki, have been the standard bearers of Orthodox asceticism for more than a millennium. The community has existed since AD 883, when Basil I issued an imperial charter to Athos preventing local military officials from interfering with the monks. Today, the Holy Community of Mount Athos is an autonomous state comprised of 20 Orthodox monasteries and countless hamlets (skites), with some 1600 monks who live and work there full time. The absence of technological development has helped to preserve the peninsula's luxuriant foliage. Only the jagged marble peak of Mt. Athos itself, soaring 2033m above the encircling waves of the Aegean, is exposed, and wildlife ranging from eagles to foxes abounds all over the peninsula. Against the background of this lush turf, the monks of Mt. Athos isolate themselves from the outside world, attempting to transcend material pleasures and live a truly spiritual life. Emperor Constantine's edict of 1060 forbids women and even female domestic animals from setting foot on the peninsula.

## GETTING THERE VIA OURANOUPOLIS

Men who wish to see Mt. Athos must secure a permit in advance (see below). Those without a permit can view the monasteries by boat. A day cruise from **Thessaloniki** costs 10,500dr. From **Ouranoupolis,** tours (roughly 3½hr.) cost 4000dr. Contact **Doucas Travel,** Venizelou 8, Thessaloniki (☎(031) 269 984), or try **Avdimiotis**

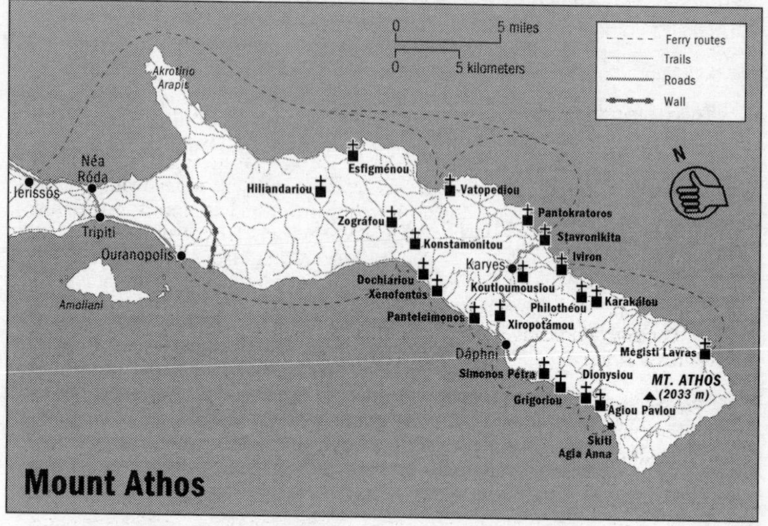


**Theophilos** in Ouranoupolis (☎(0377) 51 207 or (0377) 51 244). With permit in hand, arrive in Halkidiki the night before your entry date into Athos, or catch the 6am bus leaving Thessaloniki for **Ouranoupolis** the day of your visit. Ouranoupolis, the last settlement in secular Athos, functions dually as the gateway to monastic Athos and as a hedonistic beach resort popular among Germans.

Because Athos's hikes can be long and arduous, it's a good idea to pick up a copy of the brown **Mount Athos Tourist Map** or buy a **guidebook** with a map (1200-3000dr) in Ouranoupolis or Karies. Leave your pack in Ouranoupolis.

The standard approach to Athos is via Ouranoupolis, by boat to **Daphni,** then by bus to the capital city of **Karies. Buses** for Ouranoupolis leave from **Thessaloniki**'s Halkidiki station (☎924 444), at Karakassi 68 (3hr., 8 per day 6am-8pm, 2500dr). A bus for Thessaloniki will be waiting immediately after your return from Mt. Athos. There is one boat a day to **Daphni** from Ouranoupolis at 9:45am (3hr., 900dr); it returns to Ouranoupolis at noon. From Daphni you can take Athos' one **bus line** (1 per day, 600dr) to the capital, **Karies** (30min.), or to several of the monasteries. There is also limited (and expensive) monk-driven **taxi service** (☎23 266) between monasteries. **Boats** also travel throughout the peninsula. The main boat leaves Daphni for Agia Anna at 12:30pm; other more sporadic routes also exist. **Karies** has an **OTE** next to the Athonite Holy Council Building, a **post office** (Open M-F 8am-2pm), and two inexpensive hotels (1500dr per person). **Postal code:** 63086.



## PRACTICAL INFORMATION

A special entrance pass, issued only to males, is required to visit Mt. Athos. These passes are issued at **Ouranoupolis,** the main gateway to Athos, upon presentation of a special permit. To get the permit, you must call the **Mt. Athos Pilgrims' Bureau** in Thessaloniki (☎/fax (031) 861 611) six months in advance. If you can be flexible with your dates, you may call later and find a day that hasn't been fully booked up yet; only 10 non-Orthodox visitors are admitted to Mt. Athos per day. Then mail (not fax) a copy of your passport to the office at Kon. Karamanli 14, Thessaloniki, 54638; call two weeks ahead of your visit to confirm the reservation, and visit the office with your passport to pick up the permit. (Open 9am-1pm; call ahead.) In Ouranoupolis, bring your permit and passport to the Athos office, just uphill from the bus stop by the gas station, by 9am on the day your visit begins.

The regular permit is valid for a **four-day stay.** Passes cost 8000dr for foreigners and 4000dr for students with ISIC under age 27. You must strictly observe the **date of arrival** on your permit: if you arrive a day late, you will be turned away. Without your **passport,** you will not be admitted. To extend your stay, you must ask at the peninsula's capital, Karies. Unless you have an extremely compelling reason for extending your sojourn (i.e. to become a monk), your request will almost certainly be denied. Unofficial extensions are easier to come by; especially in low season, kind monks often allow considerate, genuinely interested visitors to stay longer.

## ACCOMMODATIONS AND FOOD

Those staying overnight have several reasonably affordable choices. Dozens of houses offer **domatia** throughout the town, and on your arrival you will probably be greeted at the bus by offers of cheap rooms. Most places will also store luggage while you're on Athos. **Hotel Athos,** above a supermarket one street back from the waterfront, offers elegant rooms with bath. (☎71 368. Singles 7000dr; doubles 10,000dr.) Those looking for a last non-fasting meal before their entrance into Mt. Athos—or a triumphal reward after experiencing the monks' spartan cuisine—should head to the row of similar-looking taverns on the waterfront. **Restaurant Pyrgos** (☎71 236) and **Restaurant Karydas** (☎71 280 or 71 180) are two of the more popular establishments in this strip.

## MOUNT ATHOS

Derived from the name of a Thracian giant buried by Poseidon beneath the mountain, the name "Athos" predates both Christianity and Hellenism. The Christian tradition began at Mt. Athos when the **Virgin Mary,** on a sea trip from Ephesus to visit Lazarus on Cyprus, was thrown off course and led by divine sign to the Athonite coast. The peninsula, known as **Akte,** had been a notorious center of paganism; the moment Mary's foot graced its soil, the false idols disintegrated in realization of their worthlessness. Even before Mary's time, many tried to tame the rowdy peninsula, from Alexander the Great to Xerxes.



Although legend claims that the first monastic settlements were founded by Constantine the Great and his mother, Helen, the first record of monkish habitation does not come until the 7th century. The first monastery, **Megistis Lavras,** was built in 963 by **St. Athanasios** with the support of the Byzantine emperor, Nikephoras Phokas. Over the centuries that followed, Athos alternately flourished—at one point containing 40 settlements and 40,000 monks—and declined, as it was buffeted by natural disasters, invasions by pirates, and internal squabbling. The edict banning women from the area was enacted in 1060, perhaps out of respect for the Virgin Mary, but likely because of scandalous frolicking between the monks and Vlach shepherdesses who had settled on the mountain. Unlike most of Greece, Mt. Athos retained its autonomy during the Turkish occupation by surrendering promptly to the Ottomans and accepting their rule.

During the centuries preceding the Greek liberation of 1821, Mt. Athos was supported and populated by Serbs, Bulgarians, Romanians, and Russians, who still have affiliations with particular monasteries. At the height of imperial Russia's expansionist policies, some 3000 Russian monks inhabited **Agios Panteleiomon,** supplied weekly by cargo-laden ships arriving straight from Odessa.

After World War I, the Treaty of Lausanne made Mt. Athos an official port of Greece while allowing it to retain an autonomous theocratic agreement (the so-called **Agia Epistasia**—a body of monks elected from the 20 monasteries which legislate and govern the peninsula). Due to gradual attrition and the diminishing influx of young novices, Mt. Athos' eminence slowly declined through the 1950s, when it became a prime target for greedy real estate developers. In recent decades, however, Athos has been rejuvenated by hundreds of young men inspired to take vows and don the black robes and cap of Orthodox monasticism.

## LIFE ON MOUNT ATHOS

Today more than 1600 predominantly Greek monks live in the 20 communal monasteries, the smaller skites, or alone in hermitages on the slopes of the mountain itself. Many of the monasteries were formerly idiorrhythmic communities, where each monk was allowed to keep some personal wealth to defray the immense taxes levied on the monasteries by the sultan. Today, all the monasteries are cenobitic, with totally communal money and duties. The last idiorrhythmic monastery, Pantokratoros, converted in 1992.

Athos retains an unsurpassed wealth of Paleologian and Late Byzantine art, manuscripts, treasure, and architecture. Each monastery houses *lipsana*, remains of dead saints that only Orthodox Christian men are allowed to see and venerate. Especially impressive are the **Hand of Mary Magdalene,** who bathed Jesus, that remains (skin intact) in **Simonos Petra** as warm as a living hand, and the **belt of the Theotokos** in **Vatopediou,** the only extant relic of the Virgin Mary. Several monasteries possess fragments of the **True Cross.** The **Gifts of the Magi**—gold, frankincense, and myrrh—presented to Christ at his birth, are housed in St. Paul's; 5 of the 28 pieces are displayed for veneration every night.

## BEING A PILGRIM

Life on Mt. Athos is dedicated to building faith and devotion to God—and, as such, is likely to induce complete culture shock. The monks operate on a schedule twice removed from our own: they use the **Julian calendar** (not Gregorian), which is 13 days behind our own, and mark the hours of the day according to the sunset as midnight. At most monasteries, the morning liturgy begins at 4am (our time) and stretches until 8am. Although only the most devout pilgrims attend the beginning of the service, the ringing of bells and tapping of wooden planks keep visitors turning in their beds until they too get up and go to church. Breakfast is served directly after service in fresco-covered *trapezaries* to the sound of a **chanter,** who reads the story of a different saint's life at every meal. Only the chanter talks during meals, and everyone ceases eating the moment the chanter stops. Non-Orthodox pilgrims must sit at a separate table from the monks and Orthodox visitors, and at some monasteries must eat after everyone else. Breakfast and dinner both generally consist of homegrown squash or zucchini, sour-ish bread, water, and fruit, with fish and other delicacies served on feast days.

Always reach the monastery where you plan to stay the night before sunset, when the gates close; earlier if you want anything besides leftovers to eat. When you arrive, look for the *arhodariki*, or guest house. There, a monk will welcome you with a glass of ice-cold water, *tsipouro*, and a piece of "special delight" as he explains the rules of the monastery. The evening *esperino* church service usually starts at 5pm and goes until 6:30pm or so, with dinner served immediately afterward. Relics are presented for veneration either before or after dinner, depending on the monastery. Both food and lodging are free at every monastery.

While at the monasteries, try to be as courteous and cooperative as possible: always address monks by their title, *Patera*, and instead of hello and good-bye, say *evlogite* (bless us, father). Avoid talking loudly, which disturbs monks' meditation, especially during siesta and after nightfall. Be aware of each monastery's rules: some allow non-Orthodox visitors into the church, others restrict them to the narthex, and still others forbid non-Orthodox from entering the church at all.

## MONASTERIES

Athos' 20 monasteries ring the peninsula's northern and southern coasts. Despite similar architecture (most consist of a large rectangular wall with lodging and churches within), each monastery has its own distinctive character. Since visitors can stay only one night in each monastery, it's a good idea to start hiking to your next destination right after breakfast. **Hikes** through Mt. Athos' winding mountain paths, speckled by fluorescent butterflies and chirping crickets, rival any in Greece. Take along a copy of the brown **Mount Athos Tourist Map** or guidebook from Ouranoupolis or Karies, and leave your pack behind in Ouranoupolis. **Paths**

**2001: AN ATHOS ODYSSEY** Mount Athos was once a land outside time. As the frenetic pace of the secular world accelerated beyond its borders, the monasteries of the Holy Mountain remained full of monks chanting the same hymns and pursuing the same austere lifestyles as their devout predecessors. But now, construction work takes place around the clock; newly paved roads are beginning to make hiking obsolete; and computers are sprouting throughout Athos. Lately, equality-minded Europeans are even attempting to force Mount Athos to let in female visitors for the first time in a millennium. Although most monks embrace the changes taking place, some remain reluctant. "The outside world is a living hell," thundered one monk at Karakallou Monastery. "Every little change we make—every little break with tradition—severs another one of our ties to God." A monk at Grigoriou had similar complaints: "When I look at the world beyond Mount Athos, I see people scurrying around blindly without any thought to where their final destination might be. Do we want the same kind of blindness to infect us too?"

are narrow, overgrown, and poorly marked; furthermore, the ones on the map might unexpectedly fork in four different directions or not exist at all. When possible, keep to the dirt roads for vehicles and to seaside routes, and travel in groups.

**MEGISTIS LAVRAS.** This monastery on the northwestern tip of the peninsula, is the oldest, largest, and richest of the monasteries—and the only one to escape destruction by fire at some point in its history. Its monks are known to be stern and conservative. The *katholikon* architecture is in the "Athonite" style, invented here in 963. The huge complex houses multiple churches, chapels, and cells for monks and visitors, and is one of the most visited of all the monasteries. It's also the most isolated: to get here, you will need to get a ride from Karies. *(☎23 745.)*

**IVIRON.** Iviron is beautifully situated by a meadow overlooking the northern coast, full of relics and icons such as the **Panagia Portaitissa,** the most renowned of Athos' miracle-working icons. According to legend, Athos will never fall as long as the Panagia Portaitissa remains within its borders. Founded by Georgian monks in 980, Iviron was the first non-Greek monastery on Mt. Athos, and rose throughout the years to a position second only to Megistis Lavras. Today, it is completely Greek (the last Georgian monk died in 1955) and one of the most popular monasteries—you will need to call ahead for a reservation. *(☎23 643.)*



**VATOPEDIOU.** Moated and turreted like a medieval castle, Vatopediou lies on the north coast in a beautiful, secluded bay. Built in 972 and ravaged by pirates for centuries, Vatopediou is now populated largely by Greek-Cypriot monks. It houses over 3000 priceless icons, and its treasures include the **belt of the Virgin Mary** and the largest known fragment of the **True Cross.** Vatopediou is the single most visited monastery on Mt. Athos; call at least two weeks ahead for a reservation. *(☎23 219.)*

**PANTOKRATOROS AND STAVRONIKITA.** Pantokratoros (☎23 253; The Almighty) and nearby Stavronikita (☎23 255), lie on the north coast, close to Karies and accessible by bus. Pantokratoros was founded by officials sent to the peninsula by the Byzantine emperor Ioannis V Paleologos, who built the present monastery on the ruins of a smaller, earlier church. The 14th century *katholikon* houses a wooden screen carved and painted by the great Cretan artist **Kimiss Theotokou.** Stavronikita is the smallest and "youngest" monastery, completed in 1536; it's also one of the friendliest and most peaceful, offering a more intimate atmosphere and more direct immersion in the lives of the monks than many of the larger communities.

**PHILOTHEOU.** Greek for "God-loving," one of Mount Athos's most stunningly located monasteries, is on a plateau near the top of a hill overlooking the north coast. The abbey is surrounded by orchards, gardens, and lush chestnut forests. Founded in 1015 by two ascetic monks from Megistis Lavras, Philotheou's greatest

treasure is the **arm of St. John Chrysostom,** which can be venerated every night by Orthodox visitors. Philotheou is also one of the stricter monasteries: non-Orthodox guests must eat after the faithful, and may not enter the church at all.

**SIMONOS PETRA.** Perched on the edge of a sheer cliff on the southern coast, is spectacularly beautiful. Dramatic, death-defying architecture and splendid **frescoes** might attract more visitors, but there's only room for ten. Travelers can relax in the roomy guest quarters, which extend out on a balcony overlooking the cliff out to the sea. Under constant renovation, Simonos Petra is frequently booked; you'll need to call at least two weeks in advance to get a bed. *(☎23 254.)*

**GRIGORIOU.** In a secluded bay just east of Simonos Petra is one of the more liberal monasteries, where the meals are a little tastier, the beds a little cushier, the monks a little friendlier, and the sunset views a little more poignant. Grape vines and flowers overhang the central courtyard, and guests are treated to their own private quarters just outside the monastery walls, with breeze-blown balconies overlooking the turquoise ocean. *(☎23 668.)*

**SLAVIC MONASTERIES.** In addition to these predominantly Greek monasteries, there exist several abbeys inhabited mostly by Slavs. At one time, there were nearly equal numbers of Greek and Slavic monks on the mountain. However, political turmoil (notably the 1917 Russian Revolution) cut off the supply of funds and novices at the source. Today, just three Slavic monasteries remain: onion-domed Russian **St. Panteleimon,** Bulgarian **Zagrafou,** and Serbian **Hilandariou.** The collapse of communism has reopened Russian wallets, and swelling church coffers now finance an ongoing restoration of Panteleimon. Though 5000 Russians seek to enter the monastery, its population is barred from exceeding that of its nearest Greek neighbor, and a community of 50 fills its walls.

**SKITES AND HERMITAGES.** Many of Athos's monks choose to live as ascetic hermits, eschewing the material comforts of the monasteries in favor of caves and huts on the harsh slopes of Mt. Athos itself. Dozens of huts, cells, and tiny churches dot the southernmost end of the island, between Megistis Lavras and Ag. Pavlou, all inhabited by monks who have given their lives to the lonely study of sacred texts and contemplation of God. Many hermits will allow you to stay with them, but you must bring your own food and sleeping bag and be careful not to disturb their constant meditations. The barren southeastern slope of Athos, called **Karoulia** after the pulleys the monks use to bring food to their caves, is home to some of the most extreme ascetics. The **hike** around the base of the mountain is a difficult one, but it traverses the most pristine areas of the peninsula.

More rough than the monastic life is the hike to the top of Mt. Athos itself. The approach is by path from the skitic community of **Agia Anna** (☎23 320), accessible by boat daily from Daphni. A five-hour climb will take you to the **Church of the Panagia,** with beds for an overnight stay, just one hour from the summit.



# KAVALA Καβαλα ☎051

Be warned: "Kavala" stems from the Greek verb meaning "to ride" (as in "cavalry"), a word connoting the same sexual innuendo as its English equivalent—that's why people may snicker when you say you're going to vacation "in Kavala." The tree-lined avenues of the bustling town stretch from the shores of the North Aegean to the slopes of Mt. Simvolo, 160km east of Thessaloniki. Modern Kavala rests upon the ruins of ancient Neapolis (later Christopolis), where the apostle Paul once preached; in the 18th century, Mehmet Ali, a future Pasha of Egypt, was born here. The makeup of Kavala changed dramatically during the population exchange of 1922 (see p. 17), when an influx of ethnic Greeks from Turkey arrived. After the Second World War, the former tobacco town and bastion of Communism became a commercial port. Most visitors use Kavala as a handy point of departure for the nearby Northeastern Aegean Islands; apart from the lovely, broad streets of the historic Panagia District, there isn't much reason to linger.

## ORIENTATION AND PRACTICAL INFORMATION

The city's main attraction, the **Panagia District,** is southeast of the port on its own peninsula, hemmed in by ancient walls under the turrets of the Byzantine fortress. The entrance is near **Pl. Eleftherias,** on Poulidou, a block in from the harbor. From here, Kavala's main streets, **El. Venizelou** and **Erithrou Stavrou** run west, parallel to the waterfront, and lead to **Pl. 28 Octovriou,** an open expanse of pigeons and little flags. **Eth. Andistassis** runs along the waterfront from the Thasos ferry dock. Most ferries leave from the eastern end of the port in front of the string of restaurants. Thasos boats all leave from the western dock.

**Buses:** (☎223 593), at the corner of Eterias and Kavalas, a block north from Vas. Pavlou and the waterfront, and a block south of the post office. To: **Athens** (9½hr., 3 per day 9:15am-7:15pm, 11,650dr); **Drama** (1hr., every 30min. 6am-9pm, 750dr); **Iraklitsa** (20min., every 20-30min. 6am-11pm, 280dr); **Philippi** (½hr., every 30min. 6am-9pm, 360dr); **Thessaloniki** (3hr., 20 per day 5:30am-8:30pm, 3000dr); and **Xanthi** (1hr., 16 per day 6am-8:30pm, 1100dr). Contact the **KTEL Office** (☎222 294) near the post office. Open 6am-8pm. To get to **Alexandroupolis** (2½hr., 6 per day 10:30am-1:30am, 3100dr), go to the **Dore Cafe,** Erithrou Stavrou 35 (☎227 601), beyond the Oceanis Hotel; there you'll find schedules, tickets, and the bus itself.

**Ferries: Nikos Milades** (☎220 067 or 223 421), in a back corner of the main harbor, has ferry info for islands other than Thasos. Open M-F 8:30am-1:30pm and 6-8pm, reduced hours Sa-Su. Ferries to: **Chios** (14hr., Su 8:30am, 7300dr); **Lesvos** (10hr., Th noon and Su 10am, 6300dr); **Limnos** (4½hr.; Th noon, Sa 5pm, and Su 10am; 3700dr); and **Piraeus** (25hr., Su 8:30am, 9700dr). **Arsinoi Travel,** K. Dimitriou 16 (☎835 671), a few doors down from Milates, sells tickets to **Samothraki** (4hr., 4-5 per week, 3000dr); schedules change monthly. Open M-F 8:30am-8:30pm, Su 8:30am-3pm. Buy tickets to **Thasos** (2hr., 8 per day 8am-10pm, 850dr) at the white port police kiosk on the Thasos ferry dock.

**Flying Dolphins:** Hydrofoils leave from near the Thasos ferry dock for **Thasos** (45min., 6 per day 7:15am-6:30pm, 2000dr) and **Samothraki;** buy your ticket on the boat.

**Flights: Olympic Airways** (☎223 622), a little west of the Thasos ferry dock on the corner of Eth. Andistassis and Kavalas. Open M-F 8am-2:30pm. Daily flights to **Athens** (1hr., daily except Tu 7:30am and 9pm, 18,300dr). **Public buses** to the airport leave before scheduled airplane departures (30min., 6am and 7:30pm, 850dr), and from the airport to Kavala center immediately following flight arrivals.

**Taxis:** (☎232 001 or 227 080), in Pl. 28 Octovriou. Available 24hr.

**Tourist Office:** (☎222 425, 228 762, or 231 653), on its own traffic island at the corner of El. Venizelou and Dragoumi, right on Pl. Eleftherias. Friendly; fluent English spoken; has city **maps** and a list of hotels. Open M-F 8am-8pm, winter M-F 8am-2pm.

**Police Station:** Omonias 111 (☎223 167), 4 blocks north of the port. **Port police** (☎224 472) at both ports. Open 24hr.

**Tourist Police:** (☎222 905), on the police station ground floor. Open 7:30am-10pm.

**Bank:** The **National Bank** (☎222 163), on the corner of Omonias and Pavlou Mela, one block north of the EOT, has a 24hr. **ATM** and **currency exchange.**

**Hospital:** Stavrou 113 (☎228 517). Open 24hr.

**Telephones: OTE** (☎222 699), on the east side of Pl. 28 Octovriou, near El. Venizelou. Open 7:30am-2:30pm.

**Post Office:** Main branch (☎833 330), at Kavalas and Stavrou, one block north of the bus station. **Exchanges currency.** Open M-F 7:30am-3:20pm. **Postal code:** 65110.



## ACCOMMODATIONS

The bad news: domatia are scarce, hotels aren't cheap, and many of Kavala's rooms overlook the port (the shipping industry doesn't shut down when you do).

**George Alvanos Rented Rooms,** Anthemiou 35 (☎221 781 or 228 412). Enter the Panagia District on Poulidou, bear left uphill on Mehmet Ali, and make a sharp left on Anathemiou. A centuries-old house in the heart of the scenic Panagia District has large rooms with fans for the lowest prices in town, far from the noise and fumes of the port. Many of the spacious, homey rooms look out over the sea; all have free use of a laundry machine and full kitchen. Singles 5000dr; doubles 6000dr.

**Hotel Aeropolis,** El. Venizelou 29 (☎223 543; fax 830 752). Bare, serviceable rooms have sinks and high ceilings; some have views of the bay—or fuming El. Venizelou. Singles 6000dr, with bath 7500dr; doubles 9000dr/14,000dr.

**Hotel Panorama** (☎224 205), on El. Venizelou across from Hotel Aeropolis. Pleasant rooms with phones, some TVs, and colorful drapes. Singles 6000dr, with bath 7500dr; doubles 7500dr/9500dr.

## FOOD AND NIGHTLIFE

Tavernas line the water and Poulidou in the Panagia District. Kavala's nightlife is surprisingly small. The young and hip tend to congregate at the few cafe-bars that line the waterfront past the ferry docks. **I Kriti** (☎223 097) is a popular choice, with outdoor tables and a constant rotation of Greek and American tunes. Otherwise, take a taxi to the nearby village of **Palio** (2000-3000dr) or the beach at **Iraklitsa.**

**Cafe-Restaurant Imaret,** Poulidou 32 (☎233 325 or 836 286). Kavala's most magnificent eating experience is here: upstairs, tables overlook the forest of chimneys and little domes that top this former Ottoman hostel for theology students. Come nightfall, it morphs into a breezy outdoor cafe/restaurant. The meat-heavy menu also has loads of fish options: try the octopus salad (1200dr). Entrees 1500-2200dr.

**O Vangelis** (☎838 885), on the east side of the harbor, by the ferry docks. A giant pink neon fish greets visitors. There are more fish options than you can identify and use in a sentence, including *lithrini, sargus, plaise,* and *mourmoura.* Entrees 1000-1800dr.

**Mikros Mylos Bakery** (☎228 132), on the corner of El. Venizelou and Dangli, a block south of the Municipal Museum. This first-rate bakery bakes it all, not just pastry made of *filo* and drenched in honey, although the *baklava* is fabulous. Try the *pasta flora* (marzipan and fruit tart) for 400dr.

**A TRIP DOWN MEMORY LANE** If you spend enough time in Northern Greece (or anywhere in Greece), you'll begin to notice that all the street and square names are the same.

**25 Martiou:** March 25, 1821 is *the* Greek national holiday, celebrating Greece's declaration of independence from the Ottoman Empire.

**3 Septemvriou:** On September 3, 1863, Greeks rioted against monarchical rule and demanded a constitution.

**11 Novemvriou:** Thessaloniki was liberated from the Ottomans on this day in 1912.

**28 Octovriou:** In 1940, President Metaxas answered Mussolini with his famous declaration of "Οχι!" (no!), refusing to submit to Italian occupation.

**Athanassiou Diakou:** A hero of the Greek Revolution who was roasted on a spit after being captured by the Turks.

**Pavlou Melas:** A guerrilla leader who freed Macedonian villages from Bulgarians.

**Iroön Polytechniou:** The heroes of the Polytechniou University—students who rioted against the military *junta* in 1974 and contributed to its downfall.

**Riga Fereou:** The great pre-Revolutionary Greek poet: "Better one day of freedom than 40 years of slavery and oppression."

**Averof:** The name of one of Greece's oldest, richest, and most philanthropic families. The primary recipient of their generosity is the village of Metsovo (p. 211).

## SIGHTS

**CASTRO.** Follow signs from the entrance to the Panagia. Originally built in the 5th century BC, the castle and its surrounding walls were later augmented by the Byzantines and the Ottomans. The well-preserved, turreted walls survey the wide panorama of the city and the island of Thasos to the south; after walking through the Panagia, you can see it again from above. The small **amphitheater** hosts occasional musical and cultural performances—ask the guard or the tourist office. In the **Eleftheria Festival** in late June, students celebrate Kavala's liberation from the Ottomans by performing dances at the castle. *(Open 9:30am-2:30pm and 5-8pm.)*

**OTTOMAN REMAINS.** While the **Imaret** is now a trendy cafe-bar and restaurant, it was once a charitable soup kitchen and hostel for theology students at the nearby *medrasa*, and is one of the largest Muslim-built edifices in Europe. Ask the restaurant's owners to show you around, or just admire the domes and courtyards over a *frappé.* On the corner of Pavlidou and Mehmet Ali stands the stone and timbered **House of Muhammad Ali.** Born here in 1769, Ali later seized rule of Egypt and was an important force in Ottoman politics in the 19th century. *(Open Tu-Su 10am-1pm and 5-7pm.)* The graceful, double-tiered 16th-century **Kamares Aqueduct,** at the north edge of the Old Town near Nikotsara, was built in 1556 by Süleyman the Magnificent to transport water from mountain springs above the city.

**ARCHAEOLOGICAL MUSEUM.** On the other side of town, overlooking the water, the Archaeological Museum on Stavrou holds polychrome busts of goddesses from Amphipolis and a Hellenistic mosaic of the rape of Europa from Abdera. Also check out the massive Ionian columns—all that remain of a Temple of Parthenos in Neapolis—and the ruins of a Macedonian tomb found near Kavala. *(☎222 335. Open Tu-F 8am-7pm, Sa-Su 8am-2:30pm. 500dr, students 300dr, EU students free.)*

**MUNICIPAL FOLK MUSEUM.** The ground floor of Kavala's small Municipal Museum houses works by famed Thassian sculptor Polygnotos Vagis (1894-1965). The marble, stone, and wooden pieces blend archaic Greek styles with modern influences like Chagall and Matisse, as in the roughly chiseled, mask-like faces of **The Moons.** Upstairs, a standard collection of traditional clothes, carpets, and farm tools stand alongside a bizarre taxidermy exhibit featuring some ragged stuffed vultures. *(Filippou 4, just behind Pl. 28 Octovriou. ☎222 706. Open 8am-2:30pm. Free.)*

**BEACHES.** Several sandy beaches west of Kavala are accessible by intercity bus—get off on impulse, or consult the tourist office first. The closest is just outside the city of **Kalamitsa.** There's a **GNTO campground** with a supermarket in **Batis,** 3km outside of Kavala. (☎243 051. 1200dr per person; 1500dr per large tent; 900dr per small tent; 750dr per child; 500dr to swim.) Blue bus #8 treks to Batis from Kavala every 30 minutes. The resort town of **Nea Iraklitsa,** 20km southwest of Kavala, luxuriates in long, golden beaches and some of the area's hottest nightlife.



## DAYTRIP FROM KAVALA: PHILIPPI

*Take the bus from Kavala (every 30min., 6am-9pm, 360dr). Make sure to tell the driver you want the archaeological site.*

Roughly 15km north of Kavala, the once-proud city of **Philippi** lies in splendid ruins. Philip of Macedon founded Philippi to protect Thassian goldminers from Thracian attacks, and named it all by himself. A 42 BC Roman Civil War battle made it famous: here, Octavian (later Augustus) and Antony defeated Cassius and Brutus, the assassins of Julius Caesar. In AD 50, missionaries St. Paul and St. Silas arrived from Anatolia to preach Christianity, in the process baptizing a woman named **Lydia** the first European Christian. The **Cell of Paul** is the apostle's own budget accommodation: shut the door and peek at the Roman **latrines,** where most of the 42 marble seats are intact. For shame! All the lids have been left up. *(☎516 470. Open 8am-8pm, winter 8am-2pm. 800dr.)*

# THRACE ΘΡΑΚΗ

Thrace is sliced into two halves by the Evros River—Greece holds the west, Turkey the east. The region remains a political and cultural frontier for both countries. Ruled by the Ottomans until 1913, the region fell under Allied control during the First World War, not joining the Greek state until 1919. Continued Western interference resulted in the 1923 Treaty of Lausanne, which handed over the eastern part of Thrace to Turkey. The scarring 1922 population exchange (see p. 17) relocated Greeks in Turkish territory to Greece, and Turks in Greek territory to Turkey. Although most Muslim Greeks were shipped off to Turkey, some stayed in Thrace. Seventy-five years later, they're still here. This tangle of cultures makes Thrace fascinatingly different from more homogenous Greek cities to the south. Today, the border between Greece and Turkey is one Europe's most tense. Forces on both sides are always on alert, and minor incidents of aggression occur daily.

## XANTHI Ξανθη ☎0541

Xanthi, Thrace's most charismatic city, is perhaps the most pleasant place to experience the somewhat edgy phenomenon of Greek multiculturalism. Strolling the sidewalks you'll see Muslims (about 10% of Xanthi's population), Christians, Gypsies, and occasional Pomaks, who descend from 16th-century Slavs forced to convert to Islam and speak a Bulgarian dialect. Getting lost in Xanthi's old town is highly recommended; exploring the narrow cobbled streets threads you through neighborhoods of Ottoman houses and elegant old mansions, the bounty of a tobacco industry that still keeps much of the town's economy humming. A winter student population from Xanthi's University of Thrace gives the modern city a smart, sophisticated feel all year-round; other perks include the restaurants, bars, and cafes that hungry, thirsty, sleepy scholars crave.

**ORIENTATION AND PRACTICAL INFORMATION.** Xanthi is Thrace's westernmost city, about 50km northeast of Kavala. Its most important plateia is **Pl. Kentriki,** also known as **Pl. Dimokratias,** easily recognizable by the clock tower in the center. Get here from the bus stop by making a left, passing the Kyklos Cafe onto Dimokritou (which becomes Karaoli) and following it straight about 800m, through the small traffic circle that is **Pl. Balsazi.** From the central plateia, streets run off like spokes of a wheel. Xanthi's main street, **28 Octovriou,** runs south to **Pl. Eleftherias,** and **Vas. Konstantinou** runs north into the heart of the old town.

From the **bus station,** Dimokritou 6 (☎22 684), buses go to: **Athens** (11hr., 9:30am and 7pm, 12,500dr); **Komotini** (45min., 18 per day 6:30am-8:15pm, 1100dr); and **Thessaloniki** (3½hr., 8 per day 5:45am-7pm, 2800dr) via **Kavala** (1hr., 800dr). Xanthi's **train station** (☎22 581) is about 2km southeast of the central plateia; to get there, head down Karaoli, go right at the rotary of Pl. Baltati, and then left onto Kapnergaton (a.k.a. Kondili). Walk straight until the road forks, and then take the cobblestone street going straight all the way to the station. You could also take a taxi from the central plateia for 500dr. **Trains** go to: **Athens** (14hr., 3 per day 8:45am-12:30am, 6260dr); **Komotini** (45min., 5 per day 4am-9:30pm, 420dr); and **Thessaloniki** (4hr., 5 per day, 2160dr). A few faster, cooler, pricier intercity trains run each day. Tickets are sold at the train station and the **OSE Office** in the Agora Nousi shopping area on Tsaldari, just east of the central plateia. (☎22 277 or 27 840. Open M-Sa 9am-1:30pm.) **Taxis** (☎25 900 or 22 702) wait in Pl. Dimokratias and Pl. Baltsazi. Xanthi has no tourist office, but the **town hall** (☎24 444), on the upper end of Vas. Konstantinou, provides a **city map.** The **National Bank,** which has a 24hr. **ATM,** is north of the main plateia on Konitsis, a pedestrian walkway. Two blocks southeast of Pl. Baltsazi is the **hospital** (☎72 131; open 24hr.). The **police** (☎23 333 or 28 888) are at Neston 2, north of Karaoli near the bus station. Surf the **Internet** at **Speedy Net,** Velissariou 11, north of Karaoli between the central plateia and Pl. Baltsazi,

for 1000dr per hr. (☎62 950. Open 10am-2pm and 5pm-2am.) The **post office** (☎22 511; open M-F 7:30am-2pm) and the **OTE** (☎22 499; open 7am-2:30pm) are just west of the central plateia. **Postal code:** 67100.

**ACCOMMODATIONS.** Neither tourists nor budget hotels have yet discovered Xanthi, and accommodations are scarce and expensive—they almost universally cost over 15,000dr. If you have good bargaining skills, this is the time to use them; if you don't, this is the time to learn them. Your best bet is the comfortable, modern **Hotel Orfeas,** Karaoli 40, which has carpeted rooms with A/C, TVs, phones, and private baths. (☎20 121 or 20 122; fax 20 998. Singles 10,000dr; doubles 13,000dr.) A more luxurious option is the gleaming black-glass **Hotel Vanthippion,** 28 Octovriou 212, below Pl. Eleftherias. Huge, well-furnished rooms come with TVs, phones, baths, A/C, and minibars. (☎77 061, 062, 063, 064, or 065; fax 77 076. Singles 13,000dr; doubles 16,000dr; triples 20,000dr.)

**FOOD AND NIGHTLIFE.** Many of Xanthi's culinary specialties, including its syrupy *kariokes* or the *soutzouk-lokum*, reflect the town's strong Turkish presence. Restaurants, cafes, and bars are clustered around the central plateia and on Vas. Konstantinou. A covered **market,** off 28 Octovriou just south of the main plateia, is the perfect place to stock up on fruit, vegetables, and baked goods, as well as fish and immense slabs of meat—whole goat, anyone? (Open daily until 3pm.) Just north of the plateia on a sidestreet is **Midos Taverna,** Stavrou 18, serving all kinds of Greek classics in a quiet, flagstoned courtyard. **I Klimataria,** packed with locals under the shadow of the clock tower in the main plateia, has a big, tasty, inexpensive menu, specializing in local pork and goat dishes. Grab a seat on their balcony to watch the passersby as you munch your stuffed tomatoes. (☎22 408. Entrees 900-1600dr.) **Gonia,** Konitsis 28, across from the National Bank, is a packed *ouzeri* that specializes in fish dishes. (Entrees 1050-3200dr.)

Nightlife in Xanthi is surprisingly quiet. Most of the action takes place in the central plateia, where young people gather for evenings of hanging out and people-watching. The best of the overpriced cafe-bars that line the plateia is **Retro,** where a DJ spins above-average American tunes, and the tables stretch to the middle of the square. **Kiverno,** on nearby Vas. Sofias, provides the perfect vantage point for watching the comings and goings of Xanthi's youth. Bust out your hair grease before you go. (Beer 800dr, cocktails 1500dr.)



**SIGHTS.** A ramble in Xanthi's **Old Town** will make you fall in love. On these quiet little streets you'll find stately mansions, churches, and old homes, many of them bristling with balcony satellite dishes to tune into the latest news from Turkey. Orthodox priests mingle with veiled Muslim women, and the corner stores sell a variety of Greek and Turkish newspapers. Xanthi's museums are in the Old Town, behind the Town Hall. The **Folklore Museum** houses a small, standard collection of folk clothing and farm equipment. *(Open Tu-Su 8am-2:30pm. Free.)* **Christos Pavlides Painting Gallery,** directly across the way, houses a collection of 20 brilliantly colored paintings by local luminary Christos Pavlides. *(☎76 363. Open Tu-Su 8am-2pm. Free.)* The hills northeast of town house a pair of lovely convents. **Panagia Archangeliotissa**'s vivid frescoes adorn its walls. Ask if an English-speaking nun can show you around. *(Open 7am-7pm.)* Farther down, **Panagia Kalamou** is more notable for its views of the town below than for its interior. *(Open 8am-1pm, 4-8pm.)*

## KOMOTINI Κομοτηνη ☎0531

Forty kilometers east of Xanthi, the broad Thracian plain begins to rise into the eastern Rodopi Mountains at rarely touristed Komotini. As in much of Thrace, Komotini's population is about 15% Turkish (or Greek Muslim, as the Greek authorities insist on calling them). Their influence is visible in the crooked streets of the Turkish Old Town and in the graceful minarets poking up from the forest of whitewashed apartments and church domes. Though Komotini has few sights, its relaxed charm and broad plateias make a stopover here painless.

**ORIENTATION AND PRACTICAL INFORMATION.** The **bus station,** G. Marmeli 1 (☎22 912 or 26 111), is about 800m from the city center on the corner of **Tsounta:** get there by walking west on Zoidi with your back to Pl. Vizinou. Buses go to: **Alexandroupolis** (1hr., 13 per day 6am-8pm, 1200dr); **Athens** (11hr., 8:30am and 6:30pm, 13,000dr); **Kavala** (2hr., 8 per day 5:30am-7pm, 1950dr); **Thessaloniki** (4hr., 8 per day 5:30am-7pm, 4650dr); and **Xanthi** (1hr., 10 per day 6:30am-8pm, 950dr). Komotini's **train station** (☎22 650) is at the far southwest corner of the city, a 20min. walk from the city center. Walk down Orfeos with your back to Pl. Eirinis. At the large five-way intersection, turn left onto Vironos and follow it as it turns first into Kiriakidi, then into Tsaldari (at the stadium), and finally hits the station. There is an **OSE (Hellenic Railways) office** in town on Zoidou. (☎26 804. Open M-F 8am-3pm.) **Trains** go to: **Athens** (12hr., 3 per day 8:20am-midnight, 6600dr); **Thessaloniki** (5hr., 5 per day 8:20am-11:45pm, 2500dr); **Xanthi** (30min., 7 per day 8:20am-midnight, 450dr); and **İstanbul, Turkey** (7hr., noon, 7500dr). Trains at 8:20am are intercity express, where a 30% higher fare gets you there 30% faster, in icy A/C.

**Pl. Eirinis** is in the very center of town. **Orfeos** runs east-west directly above it. To the north, in the Turkish part of town, is the smaller **Pl. Ifestou.** Following Orfeos east takes you to **Pl. Vizinou. Zoidi,** Komotini's other major thoroughfare, runs east-west through Pl. Vizinou, parallel to Orfeos. Komotini has no tourist office, but the **police** (☎34 444) on Zoidi, west of Pl. Eirinis, give out free **maps** and answer questions. The **post office** (☎23 195; open M-F 7:30am-2pm) and **OTE** (☎20 700; open M-F 7am-10pm, Sa-Su 7am-3pm) are neighbors on Parasiou, a side street south of Pl. Eirinis. The **National Bank,** Thisauis 1, just north of Pl. Eirinis at the east end of Orfeos, has an **ATM.** (Open M-Th 8am-2pm, F 8am-1:30pm.) The local **hospital** (☎22 222 or 24 601) is on Sismanoglou in the southeast part of town; follow Georgiou east out of Pl. Eirinis. **Postal code:** 69100.

**ACCOMMODATIONS.** Weary but choosy travelers take heed: Komotini's hotels are scattered, and it takes some ambling to find a decently priced room. Your best bet is the lovely **Adrianopolis Hotel,** Ifestou 25, in the shadow of a mosque just north of Orfeos—look for a yellow bell tower next to a dainty minaret. The rooms above the leafy courtyard are small but pleasant, with shared baths and a homey feel; listen for *muezzin* calls to prayer in the evening. (☎24 563. Singles 5000dr; doubles and triples 7000dr.) Another good deal is **Hotel Hellas,** Dimokritou 31, a tidy building bereft of balconies on a large intersection just north of the Archaeological Museum. Well-maintained, minimally furnished rooms with shared baths are off hallways adorned with the paintings and ceramics of the manager's artistic wife. (☎22 055. Singles 5000dr; doubles 7000dr; triples 8000dr.)

**FOOD AND NIGHTLIFE.** Komotini has the standard array of cafes and bars, but not too many restaurants. The center for both dining and nightlife is the area around **Pl. Eirinis. Taverna Aquarius,** just off Pl. Eirinis to the west, has a full menu of regional specialties, like ham and fried cheese in a pot, and chicken with mushrooms. (Entrees 700-1700dr. ☎73 226.) In Pl. Vizinou, popular, classy **Restaurant Dimokritos** serves shrimp dishes and classic *spetzofai* (spicy meatballs) in pink-walled splendor. (Entrees 1600-2500dr. Open noon-midnight.) For *frappés* (or headier brews), cafe-full Pl. Eirinis is the only place to be; beers cost 800-1000dr, cocktails 1500dr. **Cafe Nemesis,** Pl. Eirinis 69, is packed from morning until night. On the opposite side of the plateia is happening **Theatro** (☎30 691), where the small entryway leads to a cavernous interior packed with sharp-dressed teens. Right next door is the bigger, louder **Bo,** catering to a slightly older crowd.

**SIGHTS.** To reach Komotini's surprisingly excellent **Archaeological Museum,** follow Zoidi westward and bear right at the big five-way intersection onto Simeonidi; the museum will be on your right. Arranged in meticulous chronological order, the museum's artifacts are gleaned from archaeological sites from all over

Thrace, including nearby Dikaia, Mesemuria, Meronia, and the banks of the Lissos River. Meronia is the modern site of Homer's Ancient Ismaros, where **Odysseus** found the wine he later used to intoxicate the fearsome Cyclops, **Polyphemus.** Highlights include archaic funerary statues of lions and men, a painted terra-cotta sarcophagus, a golden bust of the Roman Emperor Septimius Severus, and the 2500-year-old soles of military sandals. (☎22 411. Open 9am-5pm. Free.) The converted mansion that houses the **Museum of Folk Life and History,** Ag. Georgiou 13, has household utensils, costumes, and manuscripts depicting Greek village life. Ag. Georgiou runs south from the east side of Pl. Eirinis. (☎27 344 or 25 975. Open M-Sa 10am-2pm. Free.) A 30min. taxi ride from Komotini, several lovely **beaches** spread along the coast, as does the sometimes tourist-ridden town of **Maronia,** whose little-known ruins are quite impressive.

# ALEXANDROUPOLIS Αλεξανδρουπολις ☎0551

Travelers often rush through Alexandroupolis on their way to Turkey, the Northeast Aegean Islands, and the hinterlands of northern Thrace. But in the hurry to get somewhere else, don't miss the considerable charms of Thrace's most bustling and sophisticated city. Rows of fashionable stores, cobblestone streets, and a lovely wooded waterfront make Alexandroupolis worthy of a night's pause.

## GETTING THERE AND GETTING AROUND

The **bus station** (☎26 479) is at the corner of El. Venizelou and 14 Maiou, 500m inland from the docks.

**Ferries:** The two main ferry lines are **Saos** and **Kikon Tours.** Saos (☎26 721 or 23 512) is on Kyprou, a few doors from the waterfront. Ferries to **Samothraki** (2½hr., 1-2 per day, 2300dr). Open 6am-4pm and 6-10pm. Kikon Tours, Venizelou 68 (☎25 455 or 32 378), sends one ferry per week (Tu 1pm) to: **Rhodes** (28hr., 11,500dr) via **Limnos** (5hr., 3300dr); **Lesvos** (11hr., 5000dr); **Chios** (16hr., 6700dr); **Samos** (21hr., 8300dr); and **Kos** (24hr., 10,800dr). Open M-F 9am-3pm and 6-10pm, Sa 9am-2pm.

**Flying Dolphins: Thraki** (☎81 700), on the corner of Koundouriotou and Emporion, two blocks east of Pl. Polytechniou. Hydrofoils to: **Limnos** (1½hr., M and W 3:30pm, 6600dr) and **Samothraki** (1hr., 2 per day, 4700dr). Tickets may be bought on board.

**Buses:** To: **Athens** (12hr., 6:15pm, 14,550dr); **Didimotiho** (2¾hr., 18 per day 4:30am-8:45pm, 1700dr) via **Soufli** (1½hr., 1200dr); **Kavala** (2½hr., 8 per day 7:30am-10pm, 3100dr); **Kipi** (30min., 6 per day 8:45am-7:30pm, 750dr); **Komotini** (1hr., 14 per day 6:10am-8pm, 1900dr); **Thessaloniki** (5hr., 8 per day 7:30am-10pm, 6000dr); and **Xanthi** (1½hr., 7 per day 8:30am-10pm, 2200dr). The bus to **İstanbul** leaves from the train station (7hr., 8:30am, 5000dr), where you can buy bus tickets.

**Trains:** The **station** (☎26 395 or 26 398) is about 400m away in front of Pl. Eleftherias. Open 6:30am-11:30pm. To: **Athens** (12½hr., 7:13am, 7000dr). A train runs 4 times per day to **Thessaloniki** (7½hr., 3000dr) via **Komotini** (1hr., 600dr) and **Xanthi** (1½hr., 800dr). There's also a faster intercity train with A/C to these three cities (leaves 7am), but it costs twice as much. Trains run daily to **İstanbul** (7hr., 1pm, 6500dr).

**Taxis:** (☎22 000 or 27 700). Available 24hr.

## ORIENTATION AND PRACTICAL INFORMATION

Though it's a large city, everything the traveler needs or wants is within a 10min. walk of the center and the ferry docks. Standing at these docks facing inland, the waterfront road, **Vas. Alexandron,** stretches left to the long row of cafes, and right toward the **train station. Kypron** leads straight from the lighthouse by the docks to small, leafy **Pl. Iroön Polytechniou.** The three main streets running parallel to Alexandrou (moving inland from the water)—**L. Dimokratias, El. Venizelou,** and **Paleologou**—lie about three blocks inland, linked by a row of narrow cobblestone streets.

**Tourist Office:** On the corner of L. Dimokratias and Mitropolitou Kaviri, toward the train station. Offers maps and info on transportation and lodging. Open M-F 8am-2pm.

**Banks:** L. Dimokratias is one long string of banks with 24hr. **ATMs.**

**Police:** Karaiskaki 6 (☎37 424), two blocks inland from the water, just before the lighthouse. Open 24hr. **Tourist Police:** (☎37 411), with the police. Open M-F 7:30am-2pm.

**Hospital:** Dimitras 19 (☎25 772). Open 24hr.

**Telephones: OTE,** on I. Kaviri, in the block between L. Dimokratias and El. Venizelou. Open M-Sa 7am-10pm, Su 7am-6pm.

**Internet Access: Arcade,** Dimokratias 363 (☎36 096), just past the intersection with Trikouri. 1000dr per hour. Open 9am-11:30pm.

**Post Office:** On the water, past Karaiskaki. Open M-F 7:30am-2pm. **Post code:** 68100.

## ACCOMMODATIONS

Hotels in Alexandroupolis are crowded and expensive. Lodging choices cluster near the bus and train stations. Call ahead, especially for weekends.

**Hotel Majestic,** Pl. Eleftherias 7 (☎26 444), a short building across the intersection from the train station. Pleasant, old-fashioned rooms with screened windows and shared baths. Singles 5000dr; doubles 7000dr; triples 10,000dr.

**Hotel Lido,** Paleologou 15 (☎28 808), behind the bus station. Functional if bare rooms come with well-kept shared baths. Singles 5000dr, with bath 6000dr; doubles 6000dr/7000dr; triples with bath 8000dr.

**Camping Alexandroupolis** (☎28 735), 2km west of town center on the water. 2000dr per person.

## FOOD AND NIGHTLIFE

Plenty of cheap fast food can be found on the waterfront and Dimokratias. Nightlife in Alexandroupolis centers almost exclusively around the waterfront, whose many cafes blend into one loud, lively, mile-long bar. Agreeably festive **Cafe Akrotiri** (☎45 308), under the grass roof on the far western edge, is an expansive, ideal spot to watch the sun set into the shimmering Aegean. A little farther east, the inviting and cozy **Cafe del Mar** (☎45 417) and mellow **Cafe Aeolus** (☎34 209) provide a quiet evening. If you'd rather watch a movie than sip ouzo, try the **Municipal Theater** (☎28 735) at the campground 2km west of the town center.

**Taverna Mulo** (☎35 519), on the left-hand side of the waterfront—look for the windmill. Delicious fresh seafood served at tables overlooking the dark North Aegean waters. Try the delectable octopus for 2000dr. Entrees 1000-3100dr. Open until midnight.

**Neraida** (☎22 827), diagonal from I. Klimataria on Pl. Polytechniou. Popular with locals. Listen for strains of the schmaltzy live music from next door as you bite into octopus pasta (1200dr). Entrees 500-2000dr.

**I. Klimataria,** on Pl. Polytechniou. A casual local hangout, with all the Greek standards. Entrees 860-3500dr.

## SIGHTS

Alexandroupolis's **Ecclesiastic Art Museum** is housed within the Cathedral of Ag. Nikolaos, two blocks inland from the National Bank. An 18th-century icon of Christ, portraying Jesus with his legs forming a heart, is the highlight of a collection of icons, decorative screens, and church frescoes. If you can, get an English-speaking priest to give you a tour. You'll pick up some Thracian history and the distinctions between icon styles. (☎37 205. Open M-Sa 8am-1pm. Donation 200dr.)

The other museum is the **Historical and Folklore Museum,** on the corner of Dimokratias and Kanari. Rotating exhibits focus on local art, Thracian history, and Greek tradition. (☎28 926. Open Tu-Sa 10:30am-1:30pm and 6:30-9:30pm.)

## DAYTRIPS FROM ALEXANDROUPOLIS: DADIA

*Take the **bus** from Alexandroupolis to Didimotiho; it stops in **Soufli** (1½hr., 18 per day 4:30am-8:45pm, 1200dr). From Soufli, catch the bus to Dadia (20min.; 7:30am, 11:30am, 1:30pm; 260dr). Get maps and information on the Reserve at the helpful **Ecotourist Center,** across the road from the bus stop; they also rent mountain bikes for 1000dr per hr. (☎0554 32 209. Open June-Aug. 8:30am-8:30pm; Sept.-May 9am-7pm.)*

The lush green expanse of the Dadia Forest Reserve lies 40km northeast of Alexandroupolis, covering 7300 hectares of thickly-wooded hills spread near the Turkish border. Created as a protected reserve in 1980, the forest serves as a home and breeding ground for hundreds of endangered **raptors**—no, this isn't Jurassic Park! They're rare birds of prey. Of the 38 European species of these huge hunters, 36 are found only in Dadia. A well-maintained network of clearly marked **hiking trails** runs throughout the oasis that is the reserve. Blazes show the way along rugged ridges that break up the golden Thracian plain. Its isolation ensures that it's one of Thrace's most beautiful and least-touristed natural attractions.

From the Ecotourist Center, a main trail leads up a hill to a **bird hide,** complete with free binoculars, where you can cringe as raptors, vultures, and other scary-looking birds feed in the valley opposite. Just follow the orange blazes uphill from the Center for about an hour along the clearly-marked hike. The center also runs a frequent **bus** to the bird hide (10min., every 20min., 500dr). From the hide, trails extend in all directions, most leading back to the center in a roundabout way. To head straight back down to the Center, take the trail marked with yellow blazes.

# IONIAN ISLANDS
# ΝΗΣΙΑ ΤΟΥ ΙΟΝΙΟΥ

Somewhere between Calabria and Corfu the blue really begins.
—Lawrence Durrell

Just to the west of mainland Greece, the Ionian Islands create a mystique from their rugged mountains, patchwork farmland, shimmering olive groves, and pristine beaches, all surrounded by an endless expanse of water reflecting varied blues. Even the most jaded travelers will gasp. Covetous invaders have conquered and re-conquered these lovely isles: Venetians, British, French, and Russians forces have all left cultural, commercial, and architectural fingerprints behind. Today the islands are a favorite among vacationing Brits, Italians, Germans, and ferry-hopping backpackers heading to Italy. Multicultural for millennia, the Ionian Islands are in no danger of losing their firm grip on their culture.

**HIGHLIGHTS OF THE IONIAN ISLANDS**

**PAD** through the British and Italian churches, fortresses, and palaces of the Old Town on Corfu (p. 259).

**LOUNGE** on the beach where Odysseus set foot again on Ithaka (p. 280).

**LEAVE A TRAIL OF CANDLES** to mark your path through the underground caves around a subterranean lake on Kephalonia (p. 274).

**GAZE** out over the brilliant blue sea from the western cliffs of Zakynthos (p. 282).

## CORFU ΚΕΡΚΥΡΑ

Homer first sang Corfu's praise, writing of its "honied fig," "unctuous olive," and "boisterous waves"; since then, Goethe, Wilde, the Durrell brothers, Sisley, and Lear have all thrown in their two cents about Corfu's perfection. Handed down from the Franks to the Venetians to the British to today's tourist hordes, Corfu (also called Kerkyra) has captivated them all. Sadly, Corfu's enchanting beauty has perhaps attracted too many, so some beaches have degraded. But as in most of Greece's beautiful places, those who stray from the beaten path are greatly rewarded by unspoiled, uncrowded beaches; you may need a pedal-boat to the next rocky inlet, or a rented moped for exploring. Try the less frenetic resorts at Pelekas, Kalami, or Ag. Stephanos, or make Corfu Town your daytripping base. Even party-central Corfu has hidden inland villages and beach towns remain distinctly Greek, with villagers still tending to their vineyards, olive trees, and sheep.



### CORFU TOWN Κερκυρα ☎0661

Corfu Town flutters with activity like the two rolled *r*'s of its Greek name, Kerkyra. Laundry lines stretch from balconies ornate with iron and greenery, and the perfect Venetian loveliness of yellow and rose buildings and green-shuttered alleyways persists today. A festive note pervades the secluded courtyards and thronged thoroughfares, and is amplified at dusk by swooping flocks of chirping sparrows inscribing circles in darkening sky. By night, romance settles on the city streets in a gentle cloud of expensive perfume, through which couples wander arm-in-arm.

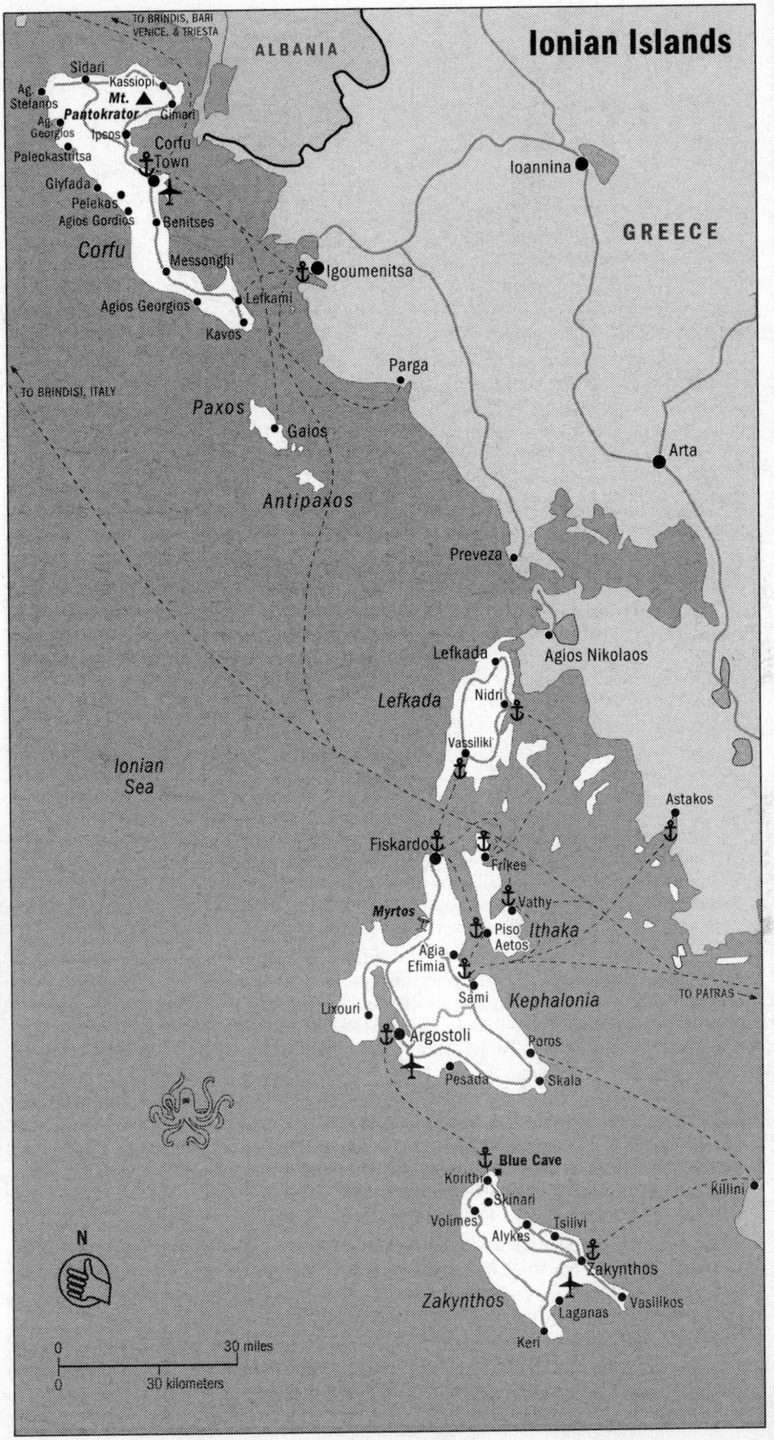

# Ionian Islands

TO BRINDIS, BARI VENICE, & TRIESTA
ALBANIA
GREECE
Sidari
Kassiopi
Ag. Stefanos
Mt. Pantokrator
Gimari
Ag. Georgios
Ipsos
Corfu Town
Paleokastritsa
Glyfada
Pelekas
Agios Gordios
Benitses
Corfu
Messonghi
Igoumenitsa
Ioannina
Agios Georgios
Lefkami
Kavos
Parga
TO BRINDISI, ITALY
Paxos
Gaios
Antipaxos
Arta
Preveza
Lefkada
Agios Nikolaos
Nidri
Lefkada
Vassiliki
Ionian Sea
Astakos
Fiskardo
Frikes
Vathy
Myrtos
Piso Aetos
Ithaka
Agia Efimia
Sami
Kephalonia
TO PATRAS
Lixouri
Argostoli
Poros
Pesada
Skala
Blue Cave
Korithi
Killini
Skinari
Volimes
Tsilivi
Alykes
Zakynthos
Zakynthos
Vasilikos
Laganas
Keri
N
0
30 miles
0
30 kilometers

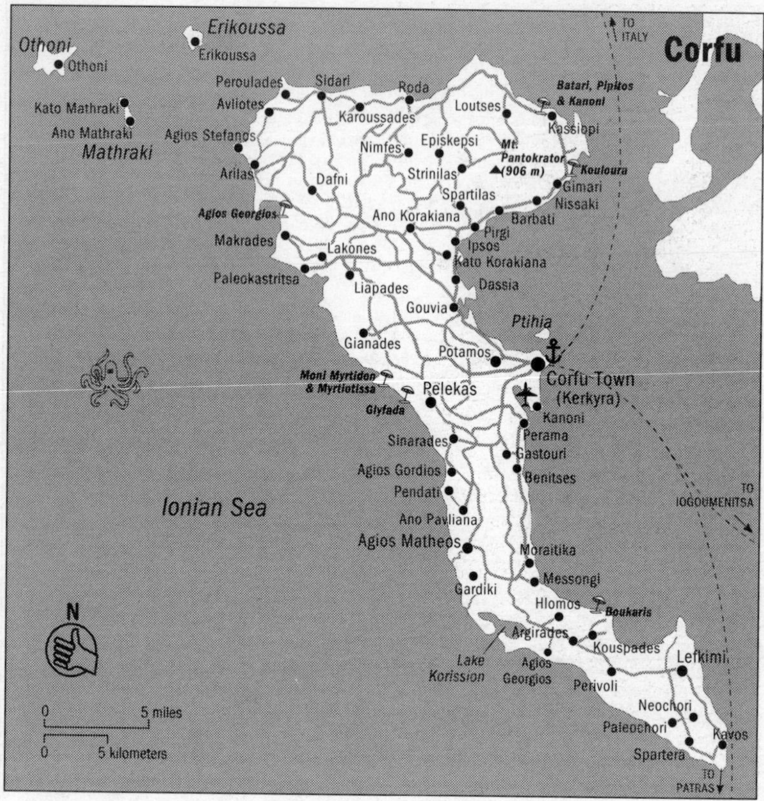


## GETTING THERE AND GETTING AROUND

**Ferries:** Get your tickets at least a day early in high season; when traveling to **Italy,** find out if the port tax (1500-2200dr) is included in the price of your ticket. Prices vary according to season, ferry line, and class. Try **Fragline** or **HML** for **Brindisi** and **Strindzi's Lines** for **Venice. Adriatica** and **HML** accept **Eurail** and **InterRail** passes. Shipping company agents line Xen. Stratigou, opposite the new port, so shop here for the lowest fares. The jovial staff of **Corfu Mare** (☎ 32 467), at the new port beneath the Ionian Hotel, sell tickets with a friendly *"kalo taxidi!"* (good journey). Ferries to: **Ancona** (21hr., 1 per day, 15,800-22,200dr); **Bari** (10hr., 1 every other day, 9000dr); **Brindisi** (8hr., 4 per day, 7500-19,500dr); **Kephalonia** (5hr., Sa 11am, 5200dr) in high season only; **Igoumenitsa** (1½hr., 21 per day 7:30am-10pm, 1300dr); **Patras** (9hr., 1-2 per day, 5800dr); **Trieste** (24hr., 2 per week, 14,500-19,400dr); and **Venice** (26hr., 1 per day, 15,800-22,200dr). High-speed **catamarans** go to **Brindisi** (3¼hr., 9am, 17,800-27,000dr; 5000-10,000dr discount for under 28). Schedules vary by season, and some routes run only in high season, so check before planning your trip.

**Flights: Olympic Airways,** Polila 11 (☎38 694; reservations ☎38 695, 38 696, or 38 187). From the post office, walk one block on Voulis toward the Old City and then turn right. It's behind the police station. Open M-F 7:30am-7:30pm. Flights to: **Athens** (50min., 4 per day, 23,300dr) and **Thessaloniki** (50min.; M, Th, Sa 1 per day; 20,800dr, 17,500dr if under 24). In summer, almost 50 charter flights per day fly through Corfu's airport; book 2-3 days ahead. A 5min. taxi ride (agree on 1500dr before getting in) is the only way to get to the **airport** (☎30 180).

**Buses:** Two main lines serve the island: **green KTEL buses** (☎30 627), just off I. Theotoki, and **blue municipal buses,** at Pl. Sanrocco. For a detailed green bus schedule, ask at the white info kiosk at the station, (open 6am-8pm); blue bus schedules are posted on the ticket kiosk window in Pl. Sanrocco (open 6:30am-10pm).

**Green buses** head to: **Agios Gordios** (45min., 6 per day 8:15am-8pm, 300dr); **Agios Stephanos** (1½hr., 6 per day 5:45am-7:30pm, 850dr); **Barbat** (45min., 3 per day, 400dr); **Glyfada** (45min., 8 per day 6:45am-8pm, 400dr); **Ipsos** and **Pirgi** (30min., 8 per day 7am-8pm, 300dr); **Kassiopi** (1hr., 7 per day 5:45am-6:30pm, 700dr); **Kavos** (1½hr., 11 per day 5am-7:30pm, 850dr); **Messonghi** (45min., 6 per day 9am-5:30pm, 450dr); **Paleokastritsa** (45min., 7 per day 8:30am-6pm, 500dr); and **Sidari** (1hr., 9 per day 5:45am-7:30pm, 650dr). Buy tickets on board; reduced schedules on weekends. **KTEL** also runs buses to: **Athens** (9hr., 3 per day, 8650dr) and **Thessaloniki** (9hr., 2 per day, 8350dr); prices include ferry. Buy these tickets at the green bus station.

**Blue buses: #10** to **Achilleon** (30min., 6 per day 7am-8pm, 230dr); **#6** to **Benitses** (25min., 13 per day 6:45am-1pm, 230dr); **#8** to **Ioannis** and **Aqualand** (30min., every hr., 230dr); **#2** to **Kanoni** (every 30min., 160dr) and **#11** to **Pelekas** (30min., about every 2 hours, 230dr).

**Taxis:** (☎33 811), at the old port, the Spianada, Pl. Sanrocco, and G. Theotoki.

**Car Rental:** A small car costs 14,000-18,000dr per day, but price varies by season. Ask if price includes 20% tax, third-party insurance, and mileage over 200km. **InterCorfu Rent a Car** (☎41 708), on the waterfront at the new port, offers reasonable rates.

**Moped Rental:** See those untouristed areas by renting from a place on Xen. Strategiou, near customs. Don't pay more than 8000dr per day. Make sure the brakes work and get a helmet. Rental fee should include third-party liability and property damage insurance.

## ORIENTATION AND PRACTICAL INFORMATION

Prepare to familiarize yourself with the Theotokos family, after whom four of Corfu Town's main streets are named: you may pass from N. to M. to G. to I. Theotoki without even realizing it. The city's peninsula juts northeast into the Ionian Sea. The endless **New Port** in the west and the smaller **Old Port** in the east span the north coast of town. From the customs house at the New Port, it's about 1km to Corfu Town's central **Pl. Sanrocco** (also called **Pl. G. Theotoki**). Cross the intersection and walk uphill on **Avramiou,** which becomes I. Theotoki. On the way, you'll pass the driveway for the **KTEL** (green bus) terminal on your left. East of Sanrocco, **G. Theotoki** leads into the Old Town, a beautiful, befuddling tangle of old alleyways. Continuing east, any reasonably straight walk will bring you to the **Spianada,** a large esplanade with a cricket pitch on its north side. The **Old Fortress** *(Paleo Frourio)* rises in the east. Arcaded buildings dotted with expensive cafes form the Parisian-row **Liston,** with narrow **Kapodistriou** running behind it. Kapodistriou runs uphill in the north and curves around along the waterfront, becoming **Arseniou** and **El. Venizelou** and leading back to the ports. South of town, **Dimokratias** makes a fine late-afternoon stroll along Garitsa Bay, leading to ancient Paleopolis and the Mon Repos estate. At the little obelisk, tree-lined **Alexandras** leads past the post office and back to Pl. Sanrocco.



**A BRIEF *ODYSSEY*** Besides enjoying notoriety for its revelry and beaches, Corfu claims the distinction of being widely regarded as the site of Homer's ancient Scheria, where Odysseus washed ashore and was taken in by the good-hearted Phaeacians. As the story goes, vengeful Poseidon, god of the sea, was looking to prevent Odysseus from returning home to his native Ithaka by attacking his ship, leaving Odysseus all washed up. Fortunately for our hero, Athena took pity on him and led Nausicaä, daughter of the King of the Phaeacians, to him as he lay on the shore. Her people nursed him back to health, and he recounted his 10-year adventure to them. Wishing to help Odysseus, the Phaeacians bestowed gifts of gold and silver on him, and offered him a ship to finish his journey. After depositing Odysseus in Ithaka, the ship returned to Scheria, where it was petrified by the furious Poseidon. Corfiot legend claims the ship can still be seen today, a large rock off the coast of Paleokastritsa—or maybe it's the small island of Pontikinossi, as a rival story claims.

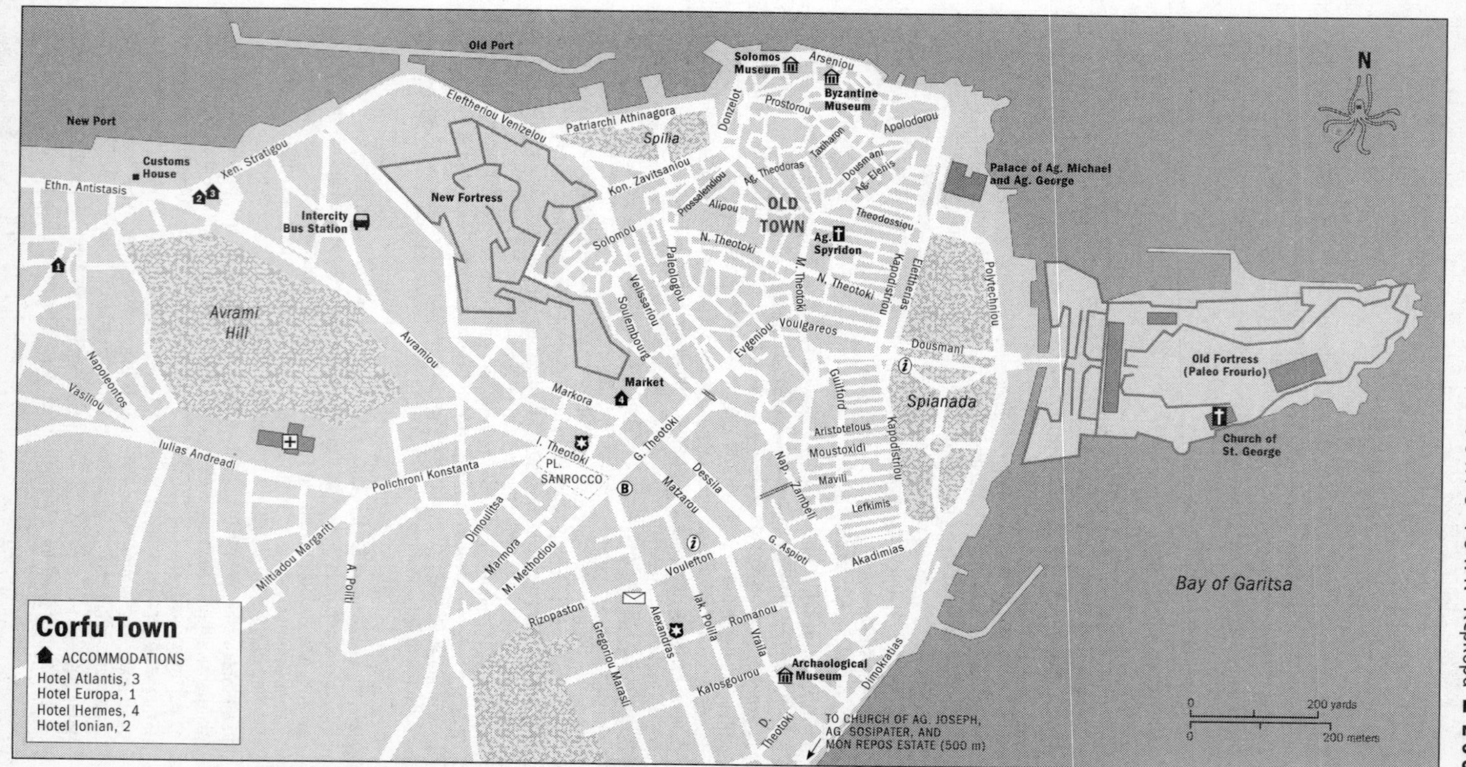


IONIAN ISLANDS

**Tourist Office: EOT** (☎37 520 or 37 638), at the corner of Rizospaston Voulefton and Iak. Polila. The building is marked, and a sign directs you up the first flight of stairs. Open M-F 8am-2pm, free maps and information. A **small tourist office** is in the customs building at the new port. Open 6am-2pm.

**Banks:** Banks with 24hr. **ATMs** line the larger streets and the waterfront by the ports, including **Ionian Bank** in Pl. Sanrocco and **Commercial Bank** on Voulgareous street.

**Luggage Storage:** In the customs building at the new port (1000dr per day).

**International Bookstores: Xenoglosso,** Markora 45 (☎23 923), near the public market, has classic novels, books on Greece, and language materials. Open M-Sa 8:30am-2pm; also Tu, Th-F 5-8:30pm.

**Laundromat: The Peristeri,** I. Theotoki 42 (☎35 304), just past Pl. Sanrocco. Wash and dry 2800dr per basket. Open M-Sa 8am-2pm, and Tu, Th, F 6-8pm. **New Port Laundry,** Eth. Antistaseos 12A (☎38 457), has dry cleaning and laundry: wash and dry 3200dr per load. Open M-Sa 8:30am-2:30pm and every day 5:30-7:30pm.

**Tourist Police:** (☎30 265). Walk along G. Theotoki in the direction of Pl. Sanrocco with the Old Town at your back. Turn right on I. Theotoki and take the first right; they're on the 4th floor of the big police building on your left. Maps available. Open 7am-10pm.

**Port Police:** Contact the port police (☎38 425), in the customs house at the new port, or the **port authority** (☎32 655 or 40 002) for updates on ferry schedules.

**Police:** (☎99 509), in the same building as the tourist police. Open 24hr.

**Hospital: Corfu General Hospital** (☎88 200; 24hr. emergency room 25 400), on Iulias Andreadi. The tourist office or the tourist police can help you find an English-speaking doctor. For an **ambulance,** call 166.

**Telephones: OTE,** Mantzarou 9, off G. Theotoki. Open M-F 8am-10pm. Card **phones** on the Spianada and in white mobile buildings at the old and new ports.

**Internet Access: Netoikos Cafe,** Kalochairetou 14 (☎47 481), near St. Spiridon church. 500dr per 20min. on speedy computers. Open M-Sa 9am-1am.

**Post Office:** (☎31 604), on the corner of Alexandras and Voulefton. Poste Restante and **currency exchange** available. Open M-F 7:30am-8pm. **Postal Code:** 49100.

## ACCOMMODATIONS

Corfu is expensive. Budget accommodations are few, and it may require extra footwork to find them. **The Association of Owners of Private Rooms and Apartments in Corfu,** Iak. Polila 24, has a complete list of rooms in Corfu and can give you the numbers of landlords to call for rooms within your price range. (☎26 133; fax 23 403. Open M-F 8:30am-2pm and 5:30-8pm.) Contact them several weeks prior to your trip to ensure availability. Consider staying outside the city in a base town with a nice beach and more domatia. Buses only run until 8 or 10pm, so you'll need to rent wheels to party-hop.



**Hotel Europa,** Giantsilio 10 (☎39 304). From the New Port customs house, cross the main street and make a right onto the street that leads back from the waterfront; Giantsilio is a tiny road on your left just after the road turns and becomes Napoleonta. Rooms are white and airy, at the best price in Corfu Town. Singles 4000dr, with bath 5000dr; doubles 6000dr/7000dr; triples 8000dr.

**Hotel Ionian,** Xen. Stratigou 46 (☎39 915 or 30 628), at the new port, offers relatively inexpensive rooms, with blessed fans and green turf-carpet suitable for mini-golf. Singles 7000-8000dr; doubles 9000-11,000dr; triples 12,000-16,000dr.

**Hotel Hermes,** Rue G. Markora 14 (☎39 268 or 39 321; fax 31 747), by the noisy public market. A charming lobby gives way to dimmer, high-ceilinged, bare rooms with baths and ceiling fans. Singles 8000dr; doubles 10,000dr; triples 12,000dr.

**Hotel Atlantis,** Xen. Stratigou 48 (☎35 560), at the new port. Big, carpeted rooms with A/C, baths, satellite TVs, and some ocean views. Singles 14,000dr; doubles 19,000dr.

## FOOD

The premier restaurant areas bookend N. Theotoki: near the Spianada and by the Old Port. While in Corfu, try the local meat specialties: *sofrito* (veal stewed in a wine sauce with pepper and garlic); *stifado* (beef stewed with onions), and *pastitsada* (lamb or beef with noodles, flavored with tomatoes, cinnamon, onion, and pepper). Traditional pork *nuombolo* resembles prosciutto, and is available at Corfu's famous butcher shops. Corfiot treats like *chadilia* (a dense cake of almonds, pistachios, rose water, and special citrus marmalade) are served at **bakeries** throughout town. The **kumquat** plant, introduced to Corfu by the British, fills bottles of "Koum Kouat" liqueur and jars of preserves. You can taste **homemade wines** all over the island: light white *kakotrygis* or richer white *moschato;* dry *petrokorintho* red and dark *skopelitiko.* Bottles of light yellow *tsitsibira* (ginger beer) are another imperial holdover. A daily open-air **public market** sells inexpensive produce on Dessila, off G. Theotoki below the new fortress (open 6am-2pm). There are **supermarkets** on I. Theotoki, one in Pl. Sanrocco and one further down the street, past the bus station (open M-F 8am-9pm, Sa 8am-6pm).

**Restaurant Antranik,** Arseniou 21 (☎38 858), looking out over the northern waterfront. Established in 1920 by Armenian refugees, Andronik specializes in Greek dishes and seafood and still draws large international crowds. Entrees 1300-3200dr.

**Restaurant Rex,** Kapodistriou 66 (☎39 649), one block back from the Spianada. A bit pricey, but long famed as one of Corfu's best restaurants. Try the savory *sofrito* or *stifado* (both 2800dr). Entrees 2200-3800dr.

**Best Top Restaurant**, Filellinon 33 (☎24 010), a small street perpendicular to the waterfront near Donzelot. Friendly staff serves Corfu specialties and other dishes under spacious umbrellas in a sunny plateia of its own. Entrees 1100-3250dr.

**Faliraki Restaurant** (☎30 392), on the water at the corner of Kapodistriou and Arseniou. A family crowd enjoys innovative entrees (1200-3500dr) and beautiful westward views over the Ionian Sea; the waves almost lap at your feet. Adjacent **En Plo Cafe** is one of the city's most picturesque spots for a drink.

**Art Cafe,** in the pretty garden behind the Palace of St. Michael and St. George. The preferred hangout of artsy local teens, it's a relaxing place to enjoy a late-afternoon ham and cheese sandwich (600dr), and a *frappé* (600dr).

## NIGHTLIFE

The undisputed focus of Corfu Town's nightlife is the so-called **Disco Strip,** on Eth. Antistaseos at the waterfront, 2km west of the New Port. The many bars and clubs on the strip bustle with a multicultural crowd of locals and tourists. Covers range from 500-2500dr; beers cost 1000-1500dr and cocktails 1500-2000dr. A **taxi** from Pl. Sanrocco costs about 500dr. The popular **Coca Club,** built into the hillside, begins the mayhem of the strip, which is exponentially intensified next door at **Sodoma,** which blasts mostly Greek music and flashes dizzying strobes inside with slower-paced drink-sipping on the outside patio. The decadent trio of **Mobile, Apocalypsis,** and giant **Hippodrome** requires you to wade through lines of parked cars. The elaborately stylized bastard child of an ancient temple and a construction site, Apocalypsis plays only techno in its pool-equipped expanse. The last of the strip, **Sax,** has a more sophisticated, toned-down feel inside an old stone building.

For a more mellow night, head to the Liston and the adjacent park under the big palm tree, where elegant little cafes stay lively until around 1am. By far the most popular among them is **Magnet,** at the top of Kapodistriou, where a babel of multilingual chatter and nearby croaking frogs echo in the shady little plateia. The **cinema** on G. Theotoki, a few blocks from Pl. Sanrocco, and another on the corner of Akadimias and G. Aspoti screen films in English—look for placards on G. Theotoki (tickets 1800dr). The **municipal theater** (☎33 598), between Dessila and Mantzarou one block from G. Theotoki, has occasional drama, dance, and music performances, publicized on bulletin boards all over town.

## SIGHTS AND MUSEUMS

After invading Vandals and Goths destroyed ancient Corfu (Paleopolis) in the 5th and 6th centuries AD, Corfiots built a more defensible city between the twin peaks (called *Koryfes*, a possible root for "Corfu") of the Old Fortress. Scared of Ottoman raids, the Venetians fortified this fortress, constructed the New Fortress, and built thick walls around the growing city. A series of **underground tunnels,** now closed, connected the Old and New Fortresses and all parts of Corfu Town. They later provided refuge for Corfiots after the first World War II air raids in 1940.

**OLD FORTRESS.** Finished in the late 14th century by the Venetians, the *Paleo Frourio* was considered impregnable—until the British blew it up in 1864 before leaving Corfu to the Greeks. Along with much of Corfu Town, the castle's imposing fortifications were restored to some semblance of their onetime glory for a 1994 EU summit. On the grounds are the **Church of St. George,** patron saint of infantry; a **Byzantine Gallery** houses mosaics and frescoes from an early Christian basilica, and a small neighboring **museum** is devoted to the role of Christianity in Byzantium, and a **bell tower** strikes the hour for all Corfu Town. *(Just east of the Spaniada. ☎48 311. Open 8am-7pm. 800dr, students 400dr, EU students free.)*

**NEW FORTRESS.** The younger, 350-year-old fort above the ferry docks opens out on panoramic views of Corfu Town ideal for sun-drenched picnics. The fort displays a small **gallery** of etchings, maps, and watercolors with nautical motifs, and an additional gallery with contemporary exhibits. Concerts and theatrical events are held here throughout the year. *(Look for signs as you walk along Velissariou from the Old Port. ☎27 477. Open 9am-9pm. 400dr.)*

**CHURCH OF AG. SPYRIDON.** This site of pilgrimage for Orthodox Christians was built in 1590, and contains the embalmed body of St. Spyridon, Corfu's patron saint. Spyridon, born in AD 270, lived and died on Cyprus. When invading Saracens threatened his body, his preserved corpse was brought to Corfu in a burlap sack slung on the back of a donkey. Each year, the faithful give him a new pair of embroidered slippers—he wears out the old pair wandering the island doing good deeds. If the priests open the gold cover of the saint's casket during your visit, you can see Spyridon's blackened face. Above him, dozens of silver lamps swing beside gold votive offerings (most of ships), offering thanks and prayer. Spyridon worked his latest major miracle in 1943: when the surrounding buildings were razed in an air raid, the church and the Corfiots sheltered within went unscathed. Corfiots parade the saint's remains four times a year: on Palm Sunday, the first Sunday in November (celebrating deliverance from 17th-century plagues); on Holy Saturday (for relief from a 1550 famine); and during the two-day **festival** beginning August 11 (for the end of a month-long 1716 Ottoman siege). His own festival runs December 11-13. *(Take Ag. Spyridon off the Spianada; it's on your left, with the rose-colored onion dome. Open 6am-9pm.)*



**BYZANTINE MUSEUM.** Housed in the 15th-century Church of the Most Holy Virgin Kyra Antivouniotissa, the museum's collection of **Cretan School** icons is worth seeing. After the fall of Rethymno in 1646, Corfu served as a pit-stop on the way to Venice for many artists from Venetian Crete; a wall chart in the museum details painters' movements and activities. Striking icons include St. George with a somewhat wussy dragon, a gaudy St. Cyril of Alexandria, and St. Pantalemon granting mercy to the suffering; they're housed in the uniquely Corfiot three-sided exonarthex. *(☎38 313. Look for signs for the museum on Arsenion as it curls downhill from the palace. Open Tu-Su 8am-2:30pm. 500dr, students and seniors 300dr, EU students free.)*

**ARCHAEOLOGICAL MUSEUM.** Relics of Corfu's Mycenaean and Classical past appear in this museum's large collection. The highlight is the fantastic **Gorgon Pediment** from the Temple of Artemis in ancient Corfu, which shows the ghoulish Medusa with her children—winged Pegasus and the **Chrysaor**—born at the moment Perseus cut her head off. Statuettes of Artemis, a fascinating collection of coins

depicting mythological figures from an ancient mint on Corfu, and funerary urns also deserve your attention. *(Vraila 1, on the waterfront south of Spianada. ☎30 680. Open Tu-Su 8:30am-3pm. 800dr, students and seniors 400dr, children and EU students free.)*

**PALACE OF SAINT MICHAEL AND SAINT GEORGE.** Presiding over the stately Spaniada is the even statelier palace, built by the Lord High Commissioner Sir Thomas Maitland to house himself, the Ionian Parliament and Senate, and various public services. It now holds the unique **Museum of Asian Art,** which displays a range of Oriental artifacts collected by diplomat Gregorios Manos. *(☎30 443. Open Tu-Su 8:30am-2:45pm. Free.)* The **Municipal Modern Art Gallery (Dimotiko Pinakothiki),** around the back of the Palace through the garden, has a small but growing collection of Corfiot paintings and rotating special exhibits. *(☎48 690. Open 10am-9pm, but hours may vary with special exhibits. 500dr, students 200dr.)*

**OTHER MUSEUMS.** The small **Solomos Museum** honors the national poet of Greece, Dionysios Solomos (see p. 27). Born in Zante in 1798, the poet spent much of his life on Corfu. After living in Italy, Solomos dropped out of law school and began to write poetry. He was the first to use popular (Demotic) Greek in poetry, and his "Hymn to Freedom" is the Greek National Anthem. The museum is housed in Solomos's house, reconstructed after a German bombing, and displays copies of original manuscripts, portraits, and memorabilia. *(Look for the sign on an alleyway on Arseniou just after the Byzantine Museum. ☎30 674. Open M-F 9:30am-2pm. 200dr.)* Fanatical capitalists will enjoy the **Museum of Paper Currency,** in the Ionian Bank Building down N. Theotoki from the Spianada, which holds the first bank note printed in Greece. *(☎41 552. Open M-F 9am-1pm. Free.)*

**MON REPOS ESTATE.** This former summer residence of the British Commissioner was given by the British government to the Greek royal family in 1864. Since the royals' exile in 1967, the lovely Neoclassical palace has fallen into disrepair, and the large gardens of rare trees are overgrown. The forested park and its many paths are far off the beaten track—you and the cicadas will probably have the place to yourselves. *(Open 8am-7pm. Free.)* The paths lead up to the Neoclassical palace, which looks out over the sea. Past this to the left is **Kardaki beach**—it's said that anyone who drinks from its spring will remain on the island forever. To the right, a path leads to two Doric temples, the decrepit **Temple to Hera** and the more impressive **Kardaki Temple,** perhaps dedicated to Poseidon, Apollo, or Asclepius.

**CHURCH OF AG. JASON AND SOSIPATER.** Within this 12th-century Byzantine church, dazzling silver and gold ornaments, medieval paintings, an impressive ceiling mural, and exquisite Byzantine icons are displayed. The church was once covered entirely by murals of saints, but the islanders painted over them to prevent their destruction by the Ottomans. *(Make a right onto Jason and Sosipater across from the Mon Repos beach. The church is currently open but under construction.)*

**ESCAPE FROM ENGLISH DEATH** Lawrence Durrell was born in India in 1912, the child of British colonialism. Sent to school in England, he recoiled from it, dubbing it the "Pudding Isle." He suggested his family ditch stuffy Britain for the sun and sand of Corfu, a former British colony. In 1935, at age 23, Durrell landed on Corfu with his wife, mother, sister, and two brothers. Durrell came of age on the island and called it a rebirth from the "English Death." He and his brother Gerald paid tribute to the island in books–Lawrence's poetic, Shakespeare-entwined *Prospero's Cell* and Gerald's jovial *My Family and Other Animals.* Among their friends were Greek Nobel Laureate George Seferis and Henry Miller, who abandoned his habitual obscenities to write the great travelogue *The Colossus of Maroussi.* Durrell left Greece when Hitler invaded Egypt, only to write his most renowned work, *The Alexandria Quartet.* After the war, Durrell returned and took on Rhodes in *Reflections on a Marine Venus,* and Cyprus, where he worked for the colonial government, in *Bitter Lemons.*

## FESTIVALS

If you come to Corfu at Easter, you can witness the procession of the embalmed body of **St. Spyridon** on Palm Sunday and Holy Saturday. It's a tradition for Corfiots to throw special pots full of water out their windows at 11am on Holy Saturday, a Venetian New Year's tradition that Orthodox Greeks have appropriated to celebrate the Resurrection. The evening religious ceremonies for Holy Saturday are held in the Spaniada, and followed by music, fireworks, and a special feast including red-dyed eggs and dove-shaped breads called *colombines*. Corfu's **Carnival** festivities see a mix of Greek and Venetian influence. The most striking traditions include the final Thursday's "The Gossip," a street theater performance in which women call out the latest gossip from windows across alleys in the center of the Old Town, and the last Sunday's burning of King Carnival, when the effigy "King" is tried and sentenced to death by fire for his hand in all the year's misfortunes.

## DAYTRIP FROM CORFU TOWN: ACHILLION PALACE

*In Gastouri. From Corfu Town, take bus #10 from 200m west of Pl. Sanrocco on Methodiou (30min., 6 per day 7am-8pm, 230dr). ☎56 210. Open 9am-4pm. 1000dr, students 500dr.*

The 1981 James Bond flick *For Your Eyes Only* was filmed in the gardens of the eccentric and ostentatious Achillion Palace, the secluded home of Empress Elizabeth of Austria from 1892 until her 1897 assassination by an Italian anarchist in Geneva. She named her home for Achilles, an obsession of hers; she, like Achilles's mother Thetis, lost two sons. Later, German Kaiser Wilhelm II summered here until the First World War diverted his attention. Achillion Palace became a hospital and barracks in both World Wars; it was again reborn as the first Greek casino in 1962. Now it's a museum, with the house as the subject: its grossly ornate interior, private chapel, and statue-ridden grounds overlooking the sea.

# EASTERN CORFU ☎0661

The east coast of Corfu is by far the most developed and least aesthetically pleasing part of the island. The first 20km north of Corfu Town are thoroughly Anglicized by throngs of rowdy expats, and the beaches are thin strips along a busy, clamorous coastal road. Despite its low points, Eastern Corfu *is* convenient and relatively inexpensive. Everything—beach, restaurants, hotels, nightlife—is consolidated in one strip, so you won't need to rent a moped, as in more remote parts of the island. It's cheaper than beautiful Corfu Town, but close enough to allow frequent trips. **Gouvia** and **Dassia,** the first two resorts north of town, thrive off package tours despite meager beaches. The visitors to notorious little **Ipsos,** a bit farther north, guzzle the day away at countless cheap bars and discos. Interchangeable souvenir stands, fast-food restaurants, and C-class hotels line the flat stretch of road across from the beach. **Pirgi,** a quieter extension of Ipsos, crawls up the base of the neighboring mountains. Hotels fill up quickly with package tour groups, so reserve ahead. There are also a few domatia and several beachside campsites in the area. Signs are posted prominently along the coastal highway for **Camping Corfu** (☎93 579), **Ipsos Ideal** (☎93 243), and **Paradise** (☎93 578). Ipsos and Pirgi are served by KTEL green **buses** (30min., 8 per day 7am-8pm, 300dr).



# WESTERN CORFU

Western Corfu is a beach lover's paradise, with wide expanses of golden sand, hidden crystal coves, and majestic cliffs and rock formations as a backdrop to the glimmering turquoise sea. While it sees its share of tour buses, it doesn't suffer from the same degree of overdevelopment that mars the beautiful east and sad south. Instead, its towering, untouched natural beauty makes it a continual delight to explore its towns and more remote beaches.

## GLYFADA Γλυφαδα ☎0661

Glyfada attracts more tourists than tiny Pelekas, 5km down the coast, but its seemingly endless shore accommodates them admirably. Scrubby cliffs bracket both of Glyfada's remarkably shallow **beaches,** where crashing waves make swimming extra fun. An eclectic crowd of internationals bask on the sun-speckled sand, including (gasp!) Greeks. Young sun-worshipers scope each other's tans and amuse themselves parasailing (7000dr) and water-skiing (9000dr for 15min). Green KTEL **buses** pull in here (8 per day 6:45am-8pm, 400dr), and a free bus connects Pelekas to Glyfada (10min., 6 per day 10am-9:40pm). Budget accommodations are scarce, but it's easy to make the trip from Pelekas or Corfu Town. The nearest camping is at **Vatos Camping** (☎94 505) in Vatos Village.

North of Glyfada, accessible via dirt path off the main Pelekas road, lie the isolated **beaches** of **Moni Myrtidon** and **Myrtiotissa,** extolled by Lawrence Durrell as the most beautiful beaches in the world. A section of sand at Myrtiotissa serves as an unofficial nude beach—unless local monks complain to the police, who reluctantly bring offending nudists to court.

## PELEKAS Πελεκας ☎0661

Removed from the mass tourism of the resorts, the village of Pelekas sits at the top of a hill, with great views and famously beautiful sunsets. The long, sandy **beach** is a pleasant 30min. walk from town along a very steep road. Rooms to let are plentiful and well priced in Pelekas, but call ahead in high season to secure a spot. Stay here only if you have a car or moped (or *love* walking), as it's off the beaten path. Take **bus** #11 from Pl. Sanrocco in Corfu Town (30min., 7 per day 7am-8:30pm, 230dr). Near the **Church of Agios Nikolaos, Takis Kontis**'s rooms are comfortable and airy, half with fantastic balcony views. (☎94 247. Singles 5000-6000dr; doubles 7000-8000dr; shared baths.) Next door, **Antonis** restaurant lets its upstairs rooms. (☎94 289. Doubles 5000dr; shared baths.) On the road to the beach, next to the fork for Glyfada, the rooms at the **Pension Paradise** are a good deal, and include kitchen use. (☎94 530 or 36 217. Doubles 5000-6000dr.) The well-situated **Pelekas Cafe** purees superb milkshakes (700dr) from a view over the island.

## PALEOKASTRITSA Παλαιοκαστριτσα ☎0663

Paleokastritsa beach rests among six small coves and sea caves that cast shadows over the blue. Although the beach is a bit narrow and can get crowded, it more than makes up for it to swim in the calm, dark-blue water protectively encircled by cliffs. Green KTEL **buses** leave Corfu Town (45min., 10 per day 8:30am-6pm, 650dr). You can hire a motorboat (2500dr per person; 30min. each way) or rent a pedal boat (3000dr per hr.) or canoe (2000dr per hr.) to reach the caves where Phaeacian princess Nausicaä found the shipwrecked Odysseus who had washed ashore (see **A Brief *Odyssey*,** p. 262). Jutting out on a hill over the sea, bright white **Panagia Theotokos Monastery** boasts a collection of Byzantine icons, nice views, and a **sea monster's skeleton.** Come as early as possible—by mid-morning it's a mess of tour buses—and take a little bread with you to feed the monastery's spectacular, tame peacocks (up the little road past the vegetable garden). The paved road up the hill leads to the monastery. The 12th-century fort of **Angelokastro** (Castle of the Holy Angels) sits above Paleokastritsa. A natural balcony, **Bella Vista,** rests halfway up—its magnificent view is a 1½hr. walk from Paleokastritsa: take the road from the bus stop back up to the Odysseos Hotel and turn left on the path going up through the olive groves. Continue on the trail, through a village, to the fortress. You can camp at **Paleokastritsa Camping** (☎41 105).

## AGIOS GORDIOS Αγιος Γορδιος ☎0661

Ten kilometers south of Pelekas, Agios Gordios is naturally beautified by impressive rock formations and a lovely **beach.** It's also the home of the infamous debauchery of the Pink Palace hotel/backpacker playground. Yet it remains surprisingly quiet. The main road runs uphill, perpendicular to the beach, with a short

stretch of restaurants, minimarts, and souvenir shops. The steep rock face on the southern end of the beach was once used as a lookout for pirates. Blue **buses** run to Agios Gordios from Pl. Sanrocco in Corfu Town (45min., 7 per day 8:15am-8pm, 300dr). The town's accommodation is the main attraction: the notorious **Pink Palace Hotel,** a favorite with American and Canadian backpackers in search of instant (and constant) gratification. Forget mingling with the locals—there's nary a word of Greek spoken at this reincarnation of MTV Spring Break. Some Greek traditions have been appropriated to heighten the fun: toga-wrapped partiers have been known to down countless shots of ouzo as they break plates on each other's heads, in a spirit of revelry that would make Dionysus proud. The Palace's impressive list of amenities makes it a self-contained party resort: there's laundry service (2500dr); Internet access (1000dr per 30min.); a jacuzzi; basketball, volleyball, and tennis courts; an on-site nightclub; clothing-optional cliff-diving (3000dr); boat daytrips; and various watersports. (☎53 103 or 53 104; fax 53 025. Quality-rated rooms: A-class—with A/C, telephone, private balcony, and private baths—9000dr; dorm-style, stuffier B-class 7000dr. Breakfast, dinner, and pick up/drop off at the Corfu Town ferry included.)

# NORTHERN CORFU

**TRAVEL ADVISORY: ALBANIA.** In June 2000, the US State Department issued a warning against unnecessary travel to Albania. Violent political turmoil affects southern Albania, where several great archaeological sites are. While improved relations between Greece and Albania have made Albania's Ionian coast accessible to tourists from Corfu, *Let's Go* discourages travel to Albania.

Past Pirgi, the road begins to wind below steep cliffs. **Mt. Pantokrator** towers 1000m above on your left, while dramatic vistas of Albania appear across the straits. Emperors Tiberius and Nero of Rome once vacationed here, though tourism has erased most traces of the ancient world on the north coast. The farther you get from overbuilt beach towns like Kassiopi and Sidari, the better off you'll be.

## AGIOS STEFANOS Αγιος Ετεφανος ☎0661

The most remote northern beach town is Agios Stefanos (not to be confused with the northeastern village of the same name). A mere 15-minute drive from bustling Sidari, Agios Stefanos is mercifully underdeveloped; the sandy, wide beach is set in a long curving gulf with high sandstone cliffs. The long waves roll in toward the few determined souls who have escaped Sidari and Kassiopi. The trip there is a treat in itself: the coastal road curves inland west of Sidari, past ferny hillsides of figs, olives, and cypresses, through a picturesque mountain village. **Buses** run from Corfu Town (1½hr., 6 per day 5:45am-7:30pm, 800dr) and Kassiopi, via Sidari (4 per day, 10:15am-4:45pm). The few who make it to town will find expensive hotels and plenty of domatia, some at reasonable prices (7000-9000dr); check the signs in front of some tavernas along the main road to track them down. Discuss price and location before going to see the room. Be warned: there is **no bank or ATM** in town, so bring enough cash to avoid having to make an extra trip to Sidari.



## BEACHES AND THE OUTDOORS ☎0661

Cradled by the sheer slopes of northeastern Corfu are several fine **beaches,** including **Barbati,** 10km north of Ipsos, nearby **Nissaki,** and the twin beaches **Kalami** and **Kouloura.** A green KTEL **bus** from Corfu Town runs to Kassiopi (1¼hr., 7 per day 5:45am-6:30pm, 700dr) and stops at every beach along the northeastern coast. Kouloura and Kalami beaches are a brief walk from the main road on the north side of Gimari village. Head down from where the bus stops on the main road; soon you'll see a rusted sign on the right marking the shortcut path to Kalami. If you're heading for Kouloura, continue down the road and turn left at the fork; the right fork leads you to Kalami by the long way.

**Kalami,** with its beautiful, relatively wide beach of flat stones, was home to author **Lawrence Durrell** and his family in the 1930s (see **Escape from English Death,** p. 267). His small white house is still "set like a dice on a rock" in the southern end of town; now it houses the pleasant **Taverna White Horse,** which serves typical Greek fare under wisteria vines with a sea view (entrees 1000-2500dr). Super-secluded **Kouloura,** a 10-minute walk along the road from Kalami, is a small, partially shaded beach composed of mixed sand, eucalyptus leaves, and stones, with nary an umbrella or paddleboat in sight. **Taverna Kouloura** has a nice view of the marina (entrees 1500-9000dr), and domatia are available in both towns.

To hike to the high plateau of **Mt. Pantokrator,** with its breathtaking views of all Corfu, start at Spartillas, a village 7km north and inland from Pirgi, along the bus route. From there, follow the same path used each summer by villagers on their way to the annual festival at Pantokrator Monastery.

# LEFKADA ΛΕΥΚΑΔΑ

Thucydides reports that Lefkada was part of the mainland until 427 BC, when inhabitants dug a canal and made their home an island. A modern bridge now connects Lefkada to the mainland, just 50m away; it's just recently replaced an archaic chain-operated ferry built by Emperor Augustus. Despite their ancestors' attempts to keep people away, modern Lefkadians are devoted to tourists. Souvenir shops and over-priced restaurants abound, especially in Nidri, which is mostly composed of tourist traps and a profusion of liquor stores. Still, miles of white-sand beaches and astonishing natural beauty remain; with a little effort, you can skirt the patches of tacky tourism and find the island's unspoiled secrets.

## LEFKADA TOWN ☎0645

Lefkada Town, across from the mainland, is a little too big and a little too crowded, but it's a break from heavy tourism. There are fewer gaudy signs, only a few leather and jewelry stores, and no unsightly fields of buses. If you stray from the waterfront and the pedestrian-only main thoroughfare, you'll find tiny alleyways full of pastel, flower-draped houses and roosters pecking in gardens—a sign that Lefkada Town retains a quiet charm beneath the busy surface.

**ORIENTATION AND PRACTICAL INFORMATION.** Archaeologist William Dörpfield claimed that Homer's Ithaka was really Lefkada; Lefkada Town thanked him by naming its main road, running down the middle of the peninsula that is the city's downtown, **Dörpfield.** It later becomes **Strategou Mela.** Dörpfield and all the little winding streets that branch off it are for pedestrians and bikes only, but cars can drive along the waterfront and inland from the peninsula.

From the **bus station** (☎22 364)—a yellow waterfront building with a gray and yellow striped awning—**buses** cross the canal to: **Athens** (5½hr., 5 per day, 6600dr) and **Aktion** (30min., 2 per day, 380dr). **Local buses** run to: **Nidri** (30min., 5 per day, 300dr); **Agios Nikitas** (20min., 6 per day, 260dr); **Poros** (45min., 2 per day, 500dr); and **Vasiliki** (1hr., 5 per day, 650dr). Pick up a bus schedule at the station for additional routes and return times; service is reduced on Sundays. **Ferries** leaving from **Nidri** and **Vasiliki** link Lefkada with **Ithaka** and **Kephalonia** to the south. From Nidri (☎92 427), ferries sail to **Frikes** on Ithaka (1½hr., 1 per day, 935dr), and then to **Fiskardo** (1220dr). From **Vasiliki,** a ferry leaves twice a day and goes to **Fiskardo** (950dr) and on to **Pisaeto,** Ithaka (1350dr). Check travel offices for current schedules. **Excursion boats** leave Nidri each morning at 9:45am and return at 6pm for cruises to **Kephalonia, Ithaka, Meganisi, Skorpios,** and **Madouri.** (7000dr. Call ☎92 577 for more information.) For other boat excursions, inquire at waterfront kiosks or travel offices, or read the hard-to-miss signs aboard the little boats.

There is no tourist office, but the **tourist police,** Iroön Politechniou 30, a few blocks to the right of Lefkada Town's bus station (facing the water), offers handy

brochures and helps locate rooms. (☎26 450. Open 8am-10pm.) The 24hr. **police station** (☎22 340) is in the same building. For detailed info about ferries, tours, or sights, try the numerous travel agencies around the bus station. There is a **National Bank** with a 24-hour **ATM** on Dörpfield (M-Th 8am-2pm, F 8am-1:30pm), and several **pharmacies.** Dörpfield also leads to the main plateia, with its cafes and occasional traveling music acts. For the **OTE,** turn right off St. Melas onto Pantaneromenis, head toward the waterfront, and look for the satellite tower. (Open 7am-10pm.) The **post office** is on Dörpfield. (Open M-F 7:30am-2pm.) **Postal code:** 31100.

**ACCOMMODATIONS AND FOOD.** There are few domatia in town; travel agencies suggest you check in **Lia,** a small village 4km outside town. In a hip, noisy neighborhood at the waterfront end of Dörpfield, **Hotel Byzantion** has friendly owners, a convenient location, and blue-trimmed hallways decorated with antiques. (☎22 629. Singles 4000dr-6000dr; doubles 7000dr, 9000dr in summer; shared bathrooms.) The cheapest hotel that the travel office vouches for is the rather deluxe A/C **Santa Maura,** off Dörpfield about three blocks from the water. (☎21 309. Singles 10000dr; doubles 12,000dr.)

**Taverna Regentos,** off the main plateia on Verrioti, has a whimsical decor and tasty food. Peek into the pots as your palate-pleasers are prepared. From the water, turn right at the old stone building on the plateia to get there. (Grilled chicken with beans and greens 1000dr, *retsina* 600dr per half-liter. Open 7:30pm-2am.) **Taverna Riviera,** near the bus station and just off the waterfront, has low-priced traditional dishes and is empty of tourists. (☎21 480. Entrees 1300-1700dr.)

**SIGHTS AND BEACHES.** The **Archaeological Museum,** in a modern building 1km down the waterfront road to Ag. Nikitas, has a collection of artifacts from ancient Leukas, a prominent island city from the 7th century BC. Panels thoroughly explain the objects in English, and give interesting information about Leukas's history and culture. (☎23 678. Open 9am-1:30pm. 500dr.) The **folklore museum** gives a taste of Lefkada's Italian legacy. It's off the main plateia; turn right and follow the signs. It may be temporarily closed for work on the building, so call ahead to check. (☎22 473. Open M-F 11am-1pm, 5-10pm. 500dr.) The unusual one-room **Phonograph Museum** not only houses old phonographs, but also antique trinkets from matchboxes to muskets. To find it, go to the left edge of the plateia (facing inland) and follow the alleyway for about two blocks, taking a left just after Metro Life. The museum is the yellow building facing you. (☎23 433. Open M-F 10am-2pm, 5-10pm. Free.) In the second half of August, Lefkada hosts the annual **Folklore Festival,** with music and dance performances in the outdoor theater just off the plateia. While Lefkada Town has no sandy beaches, the northwest coast has miles of white pebbles and clear water. To get there, rent a **moped** (3000dr per day for *Let's Go* users) at **Eurocar** (☎24 617) on the tip of the peninsula, or catch a bus to the best stretch of beaches, north of **Agios Nikitas** (3 per day, 260dr), to the sweeping view at the **Faneromenis Monastery.** (☎22 275. Open 7am-10pm. Free.)



## NIDRI Νιδρι AND ENVIRONS

The last stop on the delightful Fiskardo-Frikes-Nidri ferry, Nidri is a disappointing end of the line. The waterfront, crowded with pleasure boats, has a handsome view of the dappled coves of numerous offshore islands; the town itself is a strip of garish tourist shops and cafes. **Ferries** go to **Frikes** on Ithaka (1½hr., 1 per day, 935dr), and then to **Fiskardo** (1220dr). **Buses** from Nidri go to **Lefkada** (30min., 15 per day, 320dr) and **Vasiliki** (30min., 4 per day, 400dr). The **buses stop** at a small KTEL bus sign on the right end of the main street, between a florist and a supermarket. If you miss the last bus out of town, **taxis** make the trip for 2500dr. The crowds and glitz that make Nidri wholly unpleasant during the daytime transform it at night into a party zone, as strobe-lit clubs throw open their doors to tourists and locals alike: especially popular are **Byblos, Sail Inn,** and **Club Tropicana** (all conspicuously located on the main street).

To escape the glitz (but not the mosquitoes) of Nidri, climb the 3km to **Neochori** at dusk. The tiny village of **Vliho,** 3km south, has a striking church surrounded by wildflowers and cypress trees; you can take the **bus** there from Lefkada (13 per day, 300dr). Also near Nidri are the idyllic waterfalls at **Dimossari,** about 4km away; follow the signs from the main road.

## VASILIKI Βασιλικη ☎0645

Vasiliki's unique position between mountains creates distinct wind patterns that make it one of the world's premiere windsurfing towns. But don't be shy if you aren't one of the buff, outdoorsy tourists who keep to the windsurfing beach. The town keeps a neighborly, close-knit atmosphere—and its prettiness—despite the visitors. Smaller than Lefkada Town, and less touristy and tacky than Nidri, Vasiliki is the best Lefkada has to offer. With tiny pebbled coves, an attractive waterfront with excellent restaurants, and a ferry connection point for Kephalonia and Ithaka, Vasiliki is full of the quiet pleasures of a small beach town.

**ORIENTATION AND PRACTICAL INFORMATION.** Almost everything in Vasiliki lines the main road running inland. **Buses** run five times a day from **Lefkada** (30min., 650dr) and **Nidri** (30min., 380dr). From Vasiliki, **ferries** (☎31 555) sail to **Fiskardo** on Kephalonia (1hr., 12:30pm and 7pm, 950dr) and continue on to **Pisaeto,** Ithaka (2 hrs, 1350dr); inquire at the kiosk next to the pier. Up the street from the waterfront, **Star Travel** (☎31 833; fax 31 834) has info about ferries, buses, accommodations, boat excursions around the islands, and **Internet access** (Internet 500dr per 20min. Open 8am-11:30pm.) A little further down the street, **Samba Tours** offers the same services, including photocopying, safety deposit, and book swap. (☎31 555/520; fax 31 522. Open 8:30am-midnight.) Both offices offer weekly trips to Lefkada's best beach, the breathtaking **Porto Katsiki** (Port of the White Goat), at the base of towering white cliffs (40-50 min., 2500dr). Renting a **moped** is a good idea, especially to visit the pristine beaches on the southwest coast (1hr. to Porto Katsiki). **Christo's Alex's Rental** (☎31 580), on the main road at the corner of the intersection with the road to Lefkada Town, is the cheapest place (2500dr a day), and if you remark upon Alex's resemblance to Tom Cruise you may get a discount. For **emergencies,** contact the **health center** (☎31 065); on the main road, go straight through the intersection with the road to Lefkada Town and Nidri; it's about 100m on your right. The 24hr. **police station** (☎31 218) is a short distance inland along the main road. The **post office** is up from Star Travel, just after the crossroad. (Open M-F 7:30am-2pm.) **Postal code:** 31082.

**ACCOMMODATIONS.** Rooms are plentiful along the road leading uphill from the bus stop, on the waterfront, and along the main post road. The **fruit market,** around the corner at the back side of the ferry dock, lets spacious rooms with private bath, balcony, and fabulous views of the water. (☎31 221. Doubles 7000dr.) **Vasiliki Beach Camping,** popular among the windsurfing crowd, has superlative amenities and is only a hop, skip, and jump away from the beach; head for the beach to the left of town as you face inland, and make a right on the road running inland just before the **Windsurfing Club.** (☎31 308 or 31 457; fax 31 458. 1400-1800dr per person; 1100-1300dr per small tent; 900-1300dr per car.) **Hotel Lefkatas** on the main road, on the left as you walk out of town about 100m from the waterfront, is another option, with comfortable rooms equipped with private baths and ocean-view balconies. (☎31 801 or 31 803. Singles 10,000dr; doubles 13,000.)

**FOOD AND ENTERTAINMENT.** Nearly all the restaurants are a short stretch of the waterfront, where full meals can be inexpensive and well-prepared. **Alexandros Restaurant,** on the far left end of the waterfront, facing inland, has the largest number of tables—and they're usually filled with happy diners. Service may be slow because of the crowd, but the meal is worth the wait. (Pasta dishes 1000-1600dr; stuffed chicken fillet 1800dr; pizzas 1500-1700dr.) The extensive

menu at **Penguin Restaurant,** on the waterfront at the corner of the main road running inland, includes traditional Greek favorites (1600-2300dr), international appetizers (400-2200dr), great vegetarian dishes (800-1000dr), and salads (600-2600dr). **Dolphin Restaurant,** in the middle of the row of restaurants on the waterfront, has excellent service and tasty entrees to match. *Moussaka* 1300dr; *stifado* 1400dr. Local favorite **Miramare,** on the main road toward the water, specializes in pizza (2100dr) and seafood. After dark, try **Zeus' Bar,** which serves up orange juice with soda water (300dr) to soothe the salt- and sun-weary. It comes alive at night, when Happy Hour (7-9pm) cocktails are 1400dr. **Remezzo Beach Bar,** on the beach just before the Windsurfing Club, is also a local hotspot popular with the under-25 crowd, featuring good dance music and large indoor/outdoor bars.

**SIGHTS.** A **lighthouse** built on the site of the **Temple of Lefkas Apollo** sits at the southernmost tip of the island. Worshipers exorcised evil with an annual sacrifice at the temple, in which the victim, usually a criminal or a person thought to be possessed, was launched from the cliffs into the sea. For extra fun, live birds were tied to the victim's limbs. It was from these 70m cliffs that the ancient poet **Sappho,** rejected by her lady lover Phaon, leapt to her death. The best views of **Sappho's Leap** or *Kavos tis Kiras* (Cape of the Lady) are found on various **boat excursions.**

# KEPHALONIA ΚΕΦΑΛΟΝΙΑ

Massive mountains, subterranean lakes and rivers, caves, dense forests, and more than 250km of sand-and-pebble coastline make Kephalonia a nature lover's paradise. Its beauty has been fought over by the Byzantine, Frankish, Ottoman, Venetian, Napoleonic, and British Empires; during the Second World War, 9000 Italian soldiers occupying the island fought their alleged allies for seven days, when Germans invaded and killed all but 33 Italians. In 1953, a disastrous earthquake forced the island to rebuild, leaving only relatively undamaged Fiskardo with the Ionian pastel neoclassical look. Today, Kephalonia's beauty has emerged unscathed to draw a diverse crowd, from the upscale yachting set to budget-conscious backpackers. Inconvenient bus schedules and a plethora of things to see and do make Kephalonia a good spot for a longer stay.

## ARGOSTOLI Αργοστολι ☎0671



The capital and by far the largest town in Kephalonia and Ithaka, Argostoli is a busy, noisy, ugly city with palm tree-lined streets jammed with traffic. The countless postcards of the island will remind you that there are nearby places more worthy of your vacation time. There's no shortage of hotels, restaurants, or souvenir shops; still, Argostoli is unique among the Ionian islands in that it has a large population of locals who want nothing to do with the tourist industry (i.e. don't expect them to be nice to you). It's also Kephalonia's transportation hub, so when you tire of the fumes, just hop on the first outbound vehicle you see.

### GETTING THERE AND GETTING AROUND

**Ferries:** Kephalonia has multiple ports for different destinations. Buses connect **Argostoli** to other ports, including **Sami,** where ferries leave for **Patras** and **Italy** July-Aug. (see p. 131). Prices and times are seasonal; inquire at a travel agency. From Argostoli boats go to **Killini** on the Peloponnese (2 per day, 3200dr) and **Lixouri** in western Kephalonia (1 every 30min. until 11:30pm, 350dr). Ferries head to the tiny port of **Korithi** on the northern tip of Zakynthos from **Pesada,** a similarly small and inconvenient port on the southern coast of Kephalonia. Buses from Argostoli stop at the village of **Pesada** (30min. ride, 2 or 3 per day, 300dr), but from there you need to take an exorbitantly priced taxi to the port (4000dr).

**Buses:** The bus station (☎22 281) is on the south end of the waterfront. Open 7am-8pm. Buses head to: **Skala** (2 per day, 850dr); **Poros** (3 per day, 900dr); **Fiskardo** (1½hr., 2 per day, 1000dr); **Sami** (3 per day, 550dr); **Agios Gerasimos** (3 per day, 400dr); and **Kourkoumelata** (3 per day, 350dr). Buses meet the ferry and continue on to **Athens** (3 per day, 8000dr). Buses to Argostoli meet the ferry arriving in **Sami** (1 per day, 550dr). Service is reduced Sa, and no buses run Su.

**Flights: Olympic Airways,** R. Vergoti 7 (☎28 808, 28 881), has daily flights to Athens (15,000-20,000dr). Open M-F 8am-3:30pm.

**Taxis:** (☎24 305). Line up in the main plateia and respond to phone calls.

**Rentals: Myrtos Rent-a-Car** (☎24 230 or 25 023), on the waterfront. Must be over 23 to rent. 14,500dr per day (and up) includes the first 100km per day; 64dr per km thereafter. Open 9am-1:30pm, 6-9pm. **Sunbird** (☎23 723), near the port authority, rents cars (15,000dr), mopeds (4000dr), and bicycles (2000dr). Gas is not included, but it costs 1000dr at most. Open 8:30am-3pm and 5-10pm.



## ORIENTATION AND PRACTICAL INFORMATION

The town's main plateia is two blocks up from the water on **Calypsou Vergoti** (Καλυψους Βεργοτι); from the waterfront, follow the side street **21 Maiou** (from the bus station, face inland and look to the right) up two blocks. Left of the main plateia, **Lithostrotou** is a pedestrian-only shopping area with high-rent stores like Diesel and Benetton, and dozens of leather, postcard, and jewelry shops.

**Tourist Office:** (☎22 248 or 24 466), beside the port authority. Provides free maps and candid advice on accommodations, restaurants, and beaches. Has a list of rooms to let. Open M-Sa 8am-2:30pm, 5:30-9:30pm; in winter M-F 8am-2pm.

**Banks:** All over; try waterfront **National Bank** (**ATM** and 24hr. **exchange machine**).

**International Bookstore: Petratos Bookstore** (☎22 546), on Lithostrotou at the intersection of Ithakis, two blocks up from the water. English newspapers. Foreign newspapers and magazines. Open M-Sa 8am-10pm.

**Police:** (☎22 815 or 22 200), on I. Metaxa across from the tourist office.

**Tourist Police:** In the police station. Keeps irregular hours.

**Telephone:** At Rokou Vergoti and Georgiou Vergoti. Open M-Sa 7am-2:40pm.

**Post Office:** (☎23 173), two blocks up from the water on Lithostrotou, at the intersection of Kerkyras. Open M-F 7:30am-2pm. **Postal code:** 28100.

## A6CCOMMODATIONS

Private rooms are the cheapest option, though the waterfront hotels are much nicer. Signs advertising **domatia** are all over town; for guidance, go to a travel agency or the tourist office. Bargain hard, but in high season don't expect to find a room for much less than 8000dr. Unless you're stuck in Argostoli awaiting a ferry, it's more enjoyable (and less expensive) to stay in one of the omnipresent small town domatia, where you can at least be near the beach. If you have your own rented wheels, it's always fun to drive along the coast and take in the astonishing landscapes until you find a suitable locale for your stay.

**Hotel Tourist** (☎22 510 or 23 034), on the waterfront before the port authority. A surprisingly good deal for a hotel of considerable quality. Balconies and TVs help you forgive the name. Breakfast included. Singles 7000dr; doubles 14,000dr.

**Hotel Kephalonia Star** (☎23 180; fax 23 180), farther down the street on the waterfront, sign just says "Hotel C Star." More upscale, with extras like soundproof windows and A/C; great for families. Singles 13,000-14,500dr; doubles 13,000-18,000dr (depending on season).

**Hotel Allegro** (☎28 684), up from the waterfront on Andrea Choïda. A pleasant reception area, but rooms are rather bare and stuffy. Singles 7000dr, rooms with double beds and private baths 10,000dr.



## FOOD

Food is cheaper on the waterfront, but selection and quality are better in the plateia. A well-organized **farmers' market** takes over the waterfront near the bus station on Saturday mornings. Permanent fruit shops and bakeries line the water.

**Kalafatis Restaurant,** one of the first restaurants on the waterfront as you come from the bus station. Superior service, and their Kephalonian meat pie (1800dr) is said to be the best on the island. Salads 500-1000dr, many entrees under 1500dr.

**Portside Taverna,** on the waterfront, all the way across town from the bus station. Hosted by an expat New Yorker who serves frank island advice and a mean *moussaka* (1300dr). Salads 500-1000dr, souvlaki 500dr, *pastitsio* 1200dr, calamari 1600dr.

**Villa Diana,** on the waterfront next to Kalafatis. Well-prepared traditional dishes at budget-friendly prices. Kephalonian meat pie 1800dr, stuffed tomatoes 1200dr, chicken souvlaki 1950dr.

**Mister Grillo,** near the port authority, offers plenty of vegetarian options including black beans in oil (600dr) and stuffed peppers (800dr). Carnivores will appreciate the luscious Kephalonian meat pie (1200dr), octopus (2000dr), and *moussaka* (1300dr).

## SIGHTS

Argostoli's requisite **Archaeological Museum** is housed in the squat magenta building in the main plateia. (☎28 300. Open Tu-Su 8:30am-3pm. 400dr.) The **Historical and Folk Museum,** two blocks from Pl. R. Vergoti, is crammed with 19th-century

objects from household items to military medals. The French coffee cups, English top hats, and antique dolls illustrate Argostoli's history of colonialism. Particularly interesting are the photographs of Argostoli during the 20th century, including shots of the damage from the devastating 1953 earthquake and ensuing reconstruction. (☎28 835. Open M-Sa 9am-2pm. 500dr.)

## DAYTRIPS FROM ARGOSTOLI

Renting a moped gives you the freedom to roam between sights and beaches, like sandy **Lassi beach,** on the road between the town and the airport.

**CASTLE OF ST. GEORGE.** The Venetian-built castle is 9km southeast of Argostoli, overlooking the village of Travliata. From its battlements, you can admire a panorama that once inspired Lord Byron. *(By moped, head toward Skala and turn when the road splits. By bus, it's 10min. (2 per day, 200dr). Open M-Sa 8:00am-8pm, Su 8am-3pm. Free.)*

**LIXOURI.** In the center of the west peninsula, Lixouri, former home of satirical poet Andreas Laskaratos, offers miles of essentially tourist-free coastline. You can rent **mopeds** at several places in Lixouri, and **buses** run to smaller villages in the area. *(Get there from Argostoli by boat (30min., every 30min., 300dr).)*

**SOUTH COAST BEACHES.** A few beaches and interesting towns dot the area south of Argostoli. One of the best beaches is **Ormos Lourda,** in the middle of the south coast, but **Platis Gialos** is closer to Argostoli *(30min., 7 buses per day, 150dr).* Nearby **Metaza** (see **So He'll Go No More A-Roving,** p. 172) is one of the eminent Lord Byron's adopted towns; his house no longer exists. **Kourkoumelata** village was completely restored by a Greek tycoon after the 1953 earthquake. Check out the comfortable **Hotel Kourkoumi** if you decide to stay. *(☎41 645. Doubles with bath and breakfast 6000dr.)* Outside the city in the village of **Dargoti,** a multilayered **Mycenaean tholos tomb** is said to belong to Odysseus himself; locals can thus claim that Kephalonia is the site of Homer's ancient Ithaka. **Poros,** on the southeast coast, is a modern beach town; rooms to let are everywhere. *(Buses run from Argostoli to Poros (1½hr., 3 per day, 900dr).)*

**EAST OF ARGOSTOLI.** The **Monastery of Ag. Gerasimos** was founded by its namesake saint; his preserved body still rests here. On the night of August 15, nearby **Omala** hosts a festival and a vigil in the saint's church, and on the saint's name days (Oct. 20 and Aug. 16), the whole town goes wild; ask at the tourist office for info on all the fun. Omala has an excellent **Archaeological Museum** *(☎28 300. Open 8:30am-3:30pm. Buses run from Argostoli to Omala (3 per day, 400dr).)* **Skala** is yet another Kephalonian village with an exquisite beach; in this case, it's pebble-and-sand. The remains of a 2nd-century **Roman villa** are in town; almost all its structure is gone, but the mosaic floors are remarkably well preserved. *(Look for the signs. Open 9am-3pm. Free.)* Every day two buses come to Skala from Argostoli and three return; the last runs at 5pm (850dr each way). If you must stay, ask for rooms at **Skalini Tours** (they'll be expensive), and eat at the **Sun Rise Restaurant** (beef stew 1000dr).



# SAMI Σαμη ☎0674

As you stroll through Sami, stunning views in all directions make it difficult to decide which is more lovely: the tempestuous blue waves crashing on the long, white-sand beach, or the lush, green hills cradling the town. Despite high-season tourist traffic, Sami manages to maintain its village atmosphere. It's close to the natural wonders of Melissani Lake and Drograti cave; its own beauty makes it a good place to spend the afternoon and night—or even longer—before catching a ferry from its small but busy port. Sami was the set for the movie *Captain Corelli's Mandolin,* based on the best-selling novel.

**ORIENTATION AND PRACTICAL INFORMATION.** The street in front of the water is lined with restaurants and cafes, and intersects the main plateia. From Sami, **ferries** sail to: **Ithaka** (40min., 4 per day, 500dr); **Patras** (2½hr., 8:30am,

**SUBTERRANEAN MYSTERY** Melissani, a short walk from Sami, is one of Kephalonia's weirdest wonders. An underground lake and cave complex shaped like a B, it measures an astonishing 150m long, 25m wide, and 36m deep. Until 1963, the cave was accessible only to daring visitors willing to descend via a precarious rope and to swim through the lake's icy waters to reach the cave itself. Today, a tunnel eases the once-dangerous journey, and guided boat tours give the full view of the shimmering blue waters and 20,000-year-old **stalactites** (some of which twist into shapes like the "elephant's foot," "praying nun," and the ever-charming "lamb carcass"). Even more fascinating than Melissani's visual treat is its history as a place of worship of **Pan,** the musical goat-bodied god, and of the Nereids, or sea nymphs. From Mycenaean times on, worshipers descended into the cave by rope to make offerings within the eerie solemnity of an underground sanctuary. The name Melissani may be a tribute to a shepherdess who fell into the cave while looking for her lost sheep, or to the nymph Melissani, who took her life here, out of unrequited love for Pan; its root word means "Sweet" or "Honey," and remains a common English name—Melissa. Today, the cave stimulates the imagination, allowing you to discern deities hiding in the dark corners, and to mistake trickling water for a nymph's laughter.

3200dr); and **Astakos** (1½hr., 2 per day, 2000dr). In summer, international ferries go to **Brindisi** in Italy (2 per day beginning in early July, 10,000dr). **Buses** leave the station on the left end of the waterfront for **Argostoli** (4 per day, 500dr) and **Fiskardo** (2 per day, 700dr). **Taxis** (☎22 308) line up on the waterfront beside the plateia.

Exiting the ferry docks, turn right and follow the waterfront until you come to the plateia on your left. If you're coming from the bus station, facing the water, just turn left. You may be able to glimpse the top of the blue and white **Hotel Kyma,** which sits on the (unmarked) main road of Sami, at the end of the plateia away from the water. This main road leads to Argostoli, if you follow it with the water on your right. Heading in this direction, you'll come to the 24hr. **police station** (☎22 100), which is about three blocks from the plateia on the right. There is no official tourist office, but the police may be able to answer your questions. **Sami Travel,** near the port authority building off the right end of the waterfront on Akti Posidonos street offers rooms, tickets to Italy, excursion tickets, and general info. (☎23 050. Open 8am-9pm.) The **Marketou Travel/Strintzis Line Office** (☎22 055 or 23 021), on the waterfront just to the left of the ferry landing in Sami, is also helpful. There are several **banks; Emporiki Trapeza** on the waterfront, just to the right of the plateia, has an **ATM** (open M-Th 8am-2pm, F 8am-1pm). The **OTE** is one block further (open M-F 7am-2:40pm). The **post office** is on the road to Argostoli, two blocks out of the plateia (open M-F 7:30am-2pm). **Postal code:** 28080.



**ACCOMMODATIONS AND FOOD.** Because Sami is a convenient base for travel within Kephalonia, and because many people pass through to take ferries, there's a high demand for rooms, and they're relatively expensive. Try the **Hotel Kyma,** in the plateia, for spectacular views and cool breezes (☎22 064. Singles 6000dr; doubles 8000dr, 10,000dr with bath.) The **Riviera Restaurant** on the waterfront lets airy rooms with double beds, private baths, and balconies. However, prices can be rather steep in season. (☎22 777. Singles 10,000dr; doubles 12,000dr.) At similar rates, **Hotel Melissana,** two blocks back from the waterfront, has comfortable rooms with private bath, telephone, balcony, and minibar. Take the road running inland on the left side of the waterfront, near the ferry dock exit, and turn right at the top of the hill; it's a block down on your right. (☎22 467. Singles 10,000dr; doubles 15,000dr.) **Karavomilos Beach Camping,** a 15-minute walk down the beach from town with the water on your right, has a huge subdivided field with shade trees and blooming bushes. There are hot showers, electricity, laundry facilities, and a mini-market. (☎22 480. 1300dr per adult; 700dr per car; 800dr per small tent; 1200dr per large tent; prices higher July-Aug.) Good budget fare, like gyros (450dr), and warm service can be found at **Taka Taka Mam** on the

waterfront (open until 1am); more elegant meals can be found at its neighbor on the waterfront, the **Mermaid Restaurant** (*moussaka* 1400dr, *stifado* 1800dr).

**SIGHTS AND BEACHES.** Play the mole in the **underground caves** of Melissani and Drogarati. **Melissani** is part of huge, underground **Lake Karavomilos.** To get there, walk along the beach with the water to your right until you come to a small lake with a waterwheel on your right. Turn left after the restaurant by the lake, walk inland about 30m, and turn right at the first cross street. Down this street you'll see signs to the cave, which is only a few hundred meters away. The trip takes 15 minutes Lake guides will row you around the two large caverns flooded with sparkling water, studded with stalactites, and squirming with eels. Go when the sun is high. *(Open 9am-7pm. 1350dr, boatsman's tip 1000dr.)* **Drogarati** is a large cavern full of spectacular stalactites and stalagmites 4km from Sami. To get there, head inland on the road to Argostoli and follow the signs. *(Open until nightfall. 950dr.)*

**Agia Efimia,** a pretty harbor town 10km north of Sami, and lovely **Antisamos beach** deserve a visit. Take a taxi to **Antisamos** (500-1000dr per person), or take the hilly one-hour walk to the left from the plateia, on the road along the water.

**DAYTRIP FROM ARGOSTOLI: FISKARDO.** The road north ends at must-see Fiskardo, which escaped the 1953 earthquake to become the only remaining example of 18th- and 19th-century Kephalonian architecture. Fiskardo's crescent-shaped waterfront is tinged with the pastel hues of the modest buildings surrounding it. At night, a romantic aura pervades the town, as jazz notes drift over the harbor twinkling with the dim lights of boats resting in the water. A playground for wealthier visitors, Fiskardo remains free of the trappings that drag other tourist towns down. A splendid walk through the woods or swim from the rocks will take you to the forested tidbit of land across the harbor, where you'll find the lighthouse and ruins of a 15th-century Venetian fortress. For archaeology buffs, an open excavation of a 2nd-century Roman graveyard is right next door to the harbor, along the water. Fiskardo's unbeatable beach lies 500m out of town on the hilly road back to Argostoli, in a quiet cove that offers flat rocks for sunbathing.

Buses for **Argostoli** leave at 6:30am and 4:30pm from the parking lot next to the church, uphill from the town. One **bus** per day arrives from **Sami** (1hr., 700dr). Two buses per day arrive from **Argostoli** (1½hr., 1000dr). **Ferries** go to: **Pisaeto** on Ithaka (1 hr, 8:30pm, 480dr); **Vasiliki** (1hr.; 11am, 5:15pm; 950dr); and **Nidri** (3hr., 2pm, 1350dr) on Lefkada. For transportation and lodging questions or helpful info, stop by or call **Nautilus Travel Agency,** on the right end of the waterfront facing inland. (☎41 440. Open 9am-9pm.)

## NEAR ARGOSTOLI

Cliffs plunge into the sea along the coastal road north from Argostoli and Sami to Fiskardo. Just off this road lies one of the best beaches in Europe, **Myrtos,** which shouldn't be missed by any visitor to Kephalonia. The **buses** from Fiskardo to Sami and Argostoli stop at the turn-off to Myrtos, 4km from the gasp-inducing beauty of the beach—hop off there and hoof the rest of the way. Roughly 4km up the road from the Myrtos turn-off is the equally incredible Venetian castle of **Assos,** on a steep, wooded peninsula joined to the island by a narrow isthmus. Completed in the early part of the 17th century, much of the castle and its houses are well preserved. Much of the land inside the walls is privately owned and fenced; the owner's goats and chickens are penned in the crumbling shells of original castle buildings, adding or detracting from the medieval romance of the place, depending on your sensibilities. On August 15, the village of **Markopoulo** in the southeast celebrates the Assumption of the Virgin Mary with a strange, spooky festival involving an all-night church liturgy. According to local belief, hundreds of small snakes with black crosses on their heads slither over the icons during the service.

# ITHAKA ΙΘΑΚΗ

The least touristed and perhaps the most beautiful of the Ionian islands, Ithaka is often passed over for the tourist havens of Corfu and Kephalonia. Those who discover Ithaka find the island's pebbled, rocky hillsides and terraced olive groves quiet and welcoming. Ithaka was the kingdom that Odysseus left behind to fight the Trojan War (and to wander ten years on his way home). His wife Penelope faithfully waited 20 years for his return here: crowds of suitors pressed for her hand—and Odysseus's kingdom. She bought herself time by insisting she finish the bridal cloth she was weaving (and secretly unwinding each night). However fair Penelope may have been, it is easy to see why Odysseus's kingdom attracted so many would-be successors; Ithaka is an island fit for the gods themselves.

## VATHY Βαθυ ☎0674

Ithaka's lovely capital wraps around a circular bay, where colorful fishing and pleasure boats bob in the water. A precipitous green hillside nudges against the water. At dusk, the dying sun deepens the tint of the red-shingled roofs and pastel-painted houses. As you climb higher, Vathy becomes more striking; from the surrounding hills, the town's rich hues and small harbor gain an air of miniature, unworldly perfection.

**ORIENTATION AND PRACTICAL INFORMATION.** Facing inland, Vathy's **ferry docks** are to the right of the town plateia; depending on where you're coming from, you may need a taxi from **Piso Aetos** (10min., 2000dr) or **Frikes** (30min., 4000dr). **Ferries** connect Ithaka to Sterea Ellada (at **Astakos**), the Peloponnese (at **Patras**), and nearby **Lefkada** and **Kephalonia.** Schedules vary seasonally; check with the helpful staff at **Delas Tours** (☎32 104; fax 33 031; open 9am-2pm and 4-10pm), in the main plateia, or consult the daily departures schedule posted on the door of **Polyctor Tours** (☎33 120; fax 33 130; open 9am-1:30pm and 3:30-9pm) further left in the plateia. Ferries depart from **Frikes,** on the northern tip of Ithaka, to **Vasiliki** on Lefkada (2½hr., 9:45am, 1335dr) and **Fiskardo** on Kephalonia (30min., 9:45am, 450dr). Departures from **Piso Aetos** (near Vathy) go to: **Sami** on Kephalonia (45min., 4 per day, 500dr); **Fiskardo** on Kephalonia (45min., 5pm, 480dr); and **Vasiliki** on Lefkada (3hr., 5pm, 1335dr). Ferries go to mainland **Astakos** (4hr.; 10:15am, also 6:15pm on W, F, Su; 1700dr), and to **Patras** in the Peloponnese (6hr.; 7 am, 4:30pm; 3500dr). **Rent a Scooter,** just behind the plateia on the right side, has standard rates of 6000dr per day, plus gas. (☎32 840. Open 9am-2:30pm; 4:30-9:30pm in summer.) For car rental, try **AGS Rent a Car,** on the waterfront about two blocks to the right of the plateia. (About 14,000dr per day for a small car, including insurance. ☎32 702. Open daily 8:30am-1pm and 5-9pm.) **Taxis** (☎33 033) are expensive, but can be found at the waterfront, in front of the plateia.

To reach the **hospital** (☎32 222), turn left, facing inland, and walk out of the plateia 1km until you see a sign. Along the way, you will see the **police station** (☎32 205), where English is spoken (open 24hr.). There is a **pharmacy** on the right side of waterfront Delas Tours on the right side of the harbor. For **laundry** service, **Polifimos** is behind the plateia, on the right side, facing inland. (☎32 032. 900dr per kg, wash and dry.) The **National Bank** is in the left corner of the plateia, facing inland, and has a 24hr. **ATM.** (Open M-Th 8am-2:00pm, F 8am-1:30pm.) The **OTE** is on the water, left of the square, facing inland. (Open M-F 7:30am-1pm.) The **post office** is in the plateia, on the left side of the waterfront, facing inland. (☎32 386. Open M-F 7:30am-2:30pm.) **Postal code:** 28300.

**ACCOMMODATIONS AND FOOD.** Private **domatia** can cut you a very good deal, and hotels are expensive, so they're a good way to go. Be sure to discuss price and distance before leaving the town center. Many of the rooms on the island are rented through **Delas Tours** (see above), so you might want to contact them first to see what is available. **Hotel Mentor** lies on the water, next to the OTE. (☎32 433. Singles 11,000dr; doubles 16800dr; breakfast included.) **Dexa Beach** (☎32 855) allows free camping for one tent at a time, but unlimited sleeping bags are welcome. There are showers (350dr), a small cafe, paddleboat rentals, and wonderful swimming and sunning.

**Taverna To Trexantiri** dishes out huge portions and is the hands-down favorite among locals. (Salads 500-900dr, entrees under 1800dr. ☎33 066.) **Kantouni** (☎32 044) on the right side of the waterfront has delicious food like pork souvlaki (1600dr), superior service, and extra touches like complimentary honey yogurt. **O Nikos,** just down the street across from the National Bank, also serves traditional fare. (Entrees 1500-2500dr. ☎33 039.) On the waterfront, on the right end of town, **Lo Sputino** offers pizza, pasta, and other Italian dishes for similar prices.

**SIGHTS AND THE OUTDOORS.** By far the best entertainment in Vathy is to be had outdoors on the several lovely beaches, on the water, and relaxing and sipping *frappés* in the huge open air cafe. But museum-lovers aren't out of luck. The airy new **Folklore and Cultural Museum** houses fully assembled bedrooms, a kitchen, and a sitting room from Ithaka's colonial period, photographs of the 1953 earthquake devastation, and heirloom lace-trimmed clothing and linens. (☎33 398. Open M-Sa 9:30am-3:30pm; also 7-10pm July-Aug. 250dr.) The tiny **Vathy Archaeological Museum** displays finds from ongoing excavations at the **Apollo sanctuary** at Aetos, a site that may be Odysseus's palace. Follow the signs from the waterfront street to get to the museum. (Open Tu-Su 8:30am-3pm. Free.)

Homer fans and those with a poetic imagination can make the grueling 45-minute, 4km **hike** up to the **Cave of the Nymphs,** where Odysseus hid the treasure the Phaeacians gave him. The cave has been under archaeological excavation in recent years, and is sometimes closed to visitors. If it is closed, you can still walk around the site and view the two separate entrances (one for the gods and one for mere mortals), and perhaps chat with a few archaeologists. To get there, walk around the harbor with the water on your right and follow the signs along the road that winds up the mountain. The hike provides stunning views of Vathy; bring a flashlight for the cave. A two-hour **hike** southeast leads to the Homeric **Arethousa Fountain,** along a steep mountain path through orchards. In summer, the fountain is dry. To find the well-marked, rocky path to the fountain, follow Evmeou St. uphill until it becomes a dirt road. Keep an eye out for the signs.

**BEACHES.** Ithaka's beaches are beautiful, if a bit hard to reach. **Dexa** is the closest to Vathy, a 15-minute walk from town. According to legend, this is where Odysseus landed when he returned to Ithaka. To get there from Vathy, follow the main road out of town with the water on your right. On the other side of Vathy, you can visit gorgeous **Filiatro** and **Mniada** by following the waterfront with the water to your left; after Hotel Mentor, take the steep uphill road on your right—it's about a 20-minute walk. If you have your own transportation, **Ag. Yiannis** on the western side of the island is a favorite with locals. **Gidaki,** perhaps the island's best beach, is only accessible by boat. Little ferries around the island leave several times a day from the center square harbor in Vathy; schedules are posted near the water and on the boats' sides.



# NEAR VATHY

The small village of **Perahora** rests on the steep mountainside 5km above Vathy. It's a town devoted to the vine; it produces the island's best wine, and hosts a **wine festival** the last Sunday in July. If you make it up to Perahora, visit the ruins of **Paleohora,** the capital city of the island until it was abandoned in the early 16th century. Its stone walls crumble on the hillside next to Perahora. To get there, follow the signs in Perahora to the beginning of a footpath that leads through olive groves to the ruins. The town church ruins are the first you'll encounter; although the roof is gone and the walls have nearly fallen, frescoed icons still cling to the inner walls. The view of Vathy from here is unbeatable.

The secluded villages scattered along Ithaka's rocky coast are a must-see during a trip to Ithaka. Moped rental isn't cheap, but it's worth it for the mobility. The island's sole **bus** runs north from Vathy, passing through the villages of Lefki, Stavros, Platrithiai, Frikes, and Kioni. The bus doubles as a school bus, and schedules are erratic. Check in town, but in high season the bus usually runs three times

per day (1hr., 350dr to Frikes). Check the times of return buses before setting out, since **taxis** from Kioni to Vathy cost roughly 4500dr. The route covers both sides of the isthmus and opens superlative views of the strait and Kephalonia on the west and of the coastline on the east. **Frikes** and **Kioni,** both with small, crystal-blue harbors on the northern coast of the island, are exceptionally beautiful.

Little **Stavros** is high in the mountains on the way to Frikes and Kioni. Follow signs in town to a small museum full of excavated items from another contender for the site of Odysseus's palace. (Hours vary. Free, but a small tip is expected.) Homer described the palace site as a place from which three different waters could be seen; still visible from this point are the bays of Frikes, Aphales, and Polis, although several other sites of similar description on Ithaka and in Kephalonia compete for the same distinction. You can also visit the **Monastery of Panagia Katharon,** on the highest mountain in Ithaka. To get there, take a taxi or moped to Anoghi and follow the signs.

# ZAKYNTHOS ZAKYNΘΟΣ

Zakynthos's varied landscapes and seascapes compose an exceptionally subtle palette of colors—white cliffs rise from turquoise water, sun-bleached wheat waves in the shadow of evergreens, and magenta flowers frame the twisting streets. In Zakynthos Town or its neighboring beaches, all you'll see are the sweaty backs of other tourists. Set out for the countryside to appreciate Zakynthos's best natural sights, like its famous blue caves in the north; anyone who ventures there will understand why Lord Byron so loved this island, which the Venetians christened *Fior di Levante*—flower of the east.

## ZAKYNTHOS TOWN ☎0695

Bustling Zakynthos Town welcomes visitors with arcaded streets and whitewashed buildings. After an earthquake completely destroyed it in 1953, locals restored the city to its former state, recreating the Venetian architecture in areas like Pl. Solomou. Head north for remote beaches, and south for better nightlife.

### GETTING THERE AND GETTING AROUND

IONIAN ISLANDS

**Ferries:** Ferries from **Killini** (1½hr., 4-6 per day, 1400dr) arrive at Zakynthos Town port. Ferries from **Kephalonia** depart from Pessado for Korithi, north of Zakynthos Town (1½hr., 5:30pm, 950dr). Tickets are available at the **boat agencies** along the waterfront. For more information, call the **port police** (☎28 117).

**Buses:** Filita 42 (☎22 255), on the corner of Pl. Eleftheriou; from Pl. Solomou. Go six blocks along the water and one block inland. To **Patras** (3hr., 4 per day, 1550dr) and **Athens** (6hr., 1 per day, 5200dr); they meet the **ferry** to Killini (ferry ticket included in the price). Schedules for local service are posted outside the bus station; a complete list is at the info window. Buses run to: **Vasiliko, Porto Roma,** and **Ag. Nikolaos** (4 per day, 360dr); **Alykes** (4 per day, 340dr); **Argasi** (8 per day, 250dr); **Tsilivi** (11 per day, 250dr); **Laganas** (15 per day, 250dr); **Kalamaki** (8 per day, 250dr); and **Keri Lake** (2 per day, 380dr). There are also **excursions** around the island (W-Sa 10:15am, 2500dr). Schedules change often; ask for the schedule at the station.

**Flights:** The **airport** (☎28 322) is 6km south. Flights to **Athens** (45min., 2 per day, 17,500dr). **Olympic Airways,** Alex. Roma 16 (☎28 611), is open M-F 8am-3:30pm.

**Taxis:** (☎48 400) Lining the side streets off the waterfront. 24hr.

**Rentals: Hertz,** Lombardou 38 (☎45 706). Cars from 15,000dr per day including insurance, tax, and unlimited mileage. Must be over 21. Open 8am-2pm and 5:30-9:30pm. **Rent a Scooter,** toward the center of Lombardou, has the cheapest moped rates: 3500dr a day. **EuroSky Rentals** (☎26 278), one block inland on A. Makri, charges 4000dr per day for mopeds, and may not bug you with formalities. Open 9am-11pm.

## ORIENTATION AND PRACTICAL INFORMATION

The waterfront runs between **Pl. Solomou** at the right end (facing inland) and Agios Dionysios Church at the left end. Each end has a port at which boats from the mainland dock. **Lombardou** runs along the water between the two ports and is lined with restaurants, gift shops, and ferry agencies. The next street inland parallel to Lombardou is **Filita,** home to the bus station. Behind it are, in order, **Foskolou, Alexandrou Roma** (the main shopping street), and **Tertseti.** Three blocks inland from Pl. Solomou is **Pl. Agiou Markou,** a gathering spot with outdoor eateries. Ferries for the Peloponnese leave from the right end of the waterfront, facing inland.

**Banks: National Bank** (☎44 113), on Pl. Solomou, **exchanges currency** and has a 24hr. **ATM.** Open M-Th 8am-2pm, F 8am-1:30pm, Sa-Su 9am-1pm. Other **ATMs** on Alex. Roma and Lombardou.

**Police:** (☎22 200), Lombardou and Fra. Tzoulati, 5 blocks along the waterfront from Pl. Solomou. Open 24hr.

**Tourist police:** (☎27 367). English info, and help finding rooms. Open 7:30am-10pm.

**Hospital:** (☎42 514, 42 515), above the city center. Walk down Lombardou until Ag. Eleftheriou. Follow this road inland until Kokkini, where the road jogs right and becomes Ag. Spiridona. The hospital is at the end of this road, roughly 1km down. Open 24hr.

**OTE:** 2 Dimokratias, between the two plateias. Open 7am-2:30pm. **Currency exchange** available until 8pm.

**Internet Access: Top's Cafe,** Filita 34 (☎26 650), has a bar, billiards, video games, and web access (2000dr per hr.). Open 9:30am-2am.

**Post Office:** (☎42 418), on Tertseti, the 4th street inland parallel to the waterfront. **Exchanges currency.** Open M-F 7:30am-8pm. **Postal code:** 29100.

## ACCOMMODATIONS

Rooms in Zakynthos Town tend to be expensive and scarce in July and August. Look for the signs advertising domatia, and bargain.

**Rooms for Rent at 40 Alex Roma** (☎51 621), on the section of the street near the center of the shopping district—look for the prominent signs. Spacious rooms with private baths. Singles 6000dr; doubles 8000dr.

**Athina Marouda Rooms for Rent** (☎45 194), on Tzoulati and Koltoi, 2 blocks inland from the tourist police, on the left side of the street. The best prices, but rooms go fast. Singles 5000dr, doubles 10,000dr.

**Hotel Aegli,** on Lombardou, two blocks from Pl. Solomou. Large, cheap, rather dingy rooms. Singles 5000dr; doubles 7000dr.

## FOOD

Feeding yourself in Zakynthos is pleasure. Restaurants line the waterfront and Pl. Ag. Markou, and every other establishment on Alexandrou Roma is a cafe or candy shop. Zakynthian specialities include *melissaki* (a nougat-almond candy) and veal in tomato sauce. Fast food is everywhere; gyros cost 400dr. The **Coop Supermarket,** near the police station, caters to those who cater to themselves (open M-F 8am-9pm; Sat 8am-5pm).

**Molos Restaurant.** A popular waterfront joint with extremely affable owners and staff. Pizza 1650-2000dr, omelettes 700-1000dr, and English breakfast 1200dr.

**The Garden,** next to Ag. Dionysios, in a quiet, spacious plateia removed from the hectic waterfront. *Moussaka* 1600dr, beef stew 2400dr.

**The Village Inn,** on the waterfront. You're paying extra for the garden seating option, the live Greek music, and the huge servings. Mixed grill 2000-2800dr, salads 800-2200dr.

**House of Latas** (☎41 585), 2km above the city (follow the signs to Bohalis) near the Venetian castle. Spectacular views of Zakynthos, live local music, and inexpensive seafood (grilled swordfish 1900dr) every evening. Open 9am-midnight.

## SIGHTS AND HIKES

The **Church of Agios Dionysios** makes Zakynthos famous: it's named in honor of the island's patron saint and displays a silver chest that holds the saint's relics. *(Open 7am-1:30pm and 5-10pm. Dress modestly.)* In Pl. Solomou, the **Byzantine Museum** houses two floors of icons from the Ionian School, a distinctive local hybrid of Byzantine and Renaissance art styles, along with elaborately carved *iconostases*, chalices, and miscellaneous church items. Most were rescued by devout locals who risked their lives to pluck them from the steaming rubble of area churches after the 1953 earthquake; poignant photos document the effects of the disaster. (☎42 714. Open Tu-Su 8am-2:30pm. 800dr, students free.) If you enjoy a good **hike,** climb 2km above town to the **Venetian Castle,** where 19th-century poet Dionysios Solomos wrote the poem that became the Greek National Anthem. Take **Tertseti,** later called **N. Koluva,** to the edge of town, follow the signs uphill to Bohalis, turn left after 1km, and follow the signs to the Castro. You'll see panoramic views of the island. (Open Tu-Su 8am-2:30pm.)

## DAYTRIPS FROM ZAKYNTHOS

It's possible to see all of Zakynthos, including the otherwise-inaccessible **western cliffs,** by boat. Shop around for a cruise on Lombardou. Most tours leave in the morning, usually around 9am, return around 5:30 or 6pm, and prefer a reservation the night before. Don't buy from hawkers around gift shops—they'll charge a commission (2000-3000dr) on top of the agency's fee (usually 3000-6000dr, though price wars sometimes cut prices to 1500-2000dr). Cruises go to the **blue caves, turtle beach,** and the **"Smuggler's Wreck,"** a large boat skeleton you can swim through; inquire at the tourist police or agencies. **KTEL** also offers a **bus tour** of the island (W-Sa 10:15am, 2500dr). To explore independently (and with far less hassle), get a **moped**—there's a rental place at each beach (3000-4500dr per day). Because the island is developing rapidly, many new roads don't appear on maps; get a combination of road maps (400dr) and ask directions.

The closest beach to Zakynthos Town is **Tsilivi beach,** 6km up the waterfront road with the water on your right. Buses run there every day (30min., 10 per day, 250dr). Nearby **Planos** has plenty of domatia. **Zante Camping,** 3km past Planos, is Zakynthos's only beach campsite. It has a cafeteria and minimarket. (☎44 754. 1400dr per person; 810dr per car; 930dr per small tent; 1150dr per large tent.)

Unscathed beaches carpet the peninsula that stretches out 16km from Zakynthos Town to **Vasilikos,** especially near **Porto Roma** and **Porto Zoro.** Rooms to let signs dot the road to Vasilikos, especially near **Agios Nikolaos Beach.** On the other side of Vasilikos, facing Laganas Bay, lies **Gerakas beach.** The southern beaches near Vasilikos are pleasingly wide and sandy, with shallow, warm water full of splashing holiday-makers. Some are protected areas that must be vacated in the evenings to accommodate the sea turtles that come ashore to nest. **Buses** leave Zakynthos Town for **Vasiliko** (M-F 4 per day, Sa-Su 2 per day, 360dr). Romantic restaurants fill **Alykes,** 16m from Zakynthos Town. Fringed with soft, clean sand beaches, it's nicer and less crowded than its southern counterparts. Many signs along the main drag advertise domatia. **Buses** run here four times per day (340dr).



## KORITHI Κοριθη ☎0695

At the extreme northern tip of Zakynthos and a breathtaking drive away from Volimes is tiny **Korithi,** locally known as **Agios Nikolaos.** Ferries to Kephalonia depart from here. As with Volimes, bus service here is sporadic, so incoming ferry passengers often need to arrange their own transportation to Zakynthos Town. If you have to stay here, **La Grotta Restaurant/Snack Bar** has surprisingly nice rooms with waterfront balconies. (Singles 4000-6000dr, doubles 8000dr.) Just down the street, **La Storia Restaurant** serves divine fare with the water at your feet; try the seafood pasta (2000dr). Ex-Canadian owner Andreas may proudly show you the day's catch of massive lobsters awaiting their demise. During the day, you can buy tickets at the waterfront tourist office for a fishing boat tour of the weird **blue caves,** a main attraction of the island, accessible only by water (1hr., 100dr); you could also rent a canoe or small boat on the tiny, pebbled beach.

# SARONIC GULF ISLANDS ΤΑ ΝΗΣΙΑ ΤΟΥ ΣΑΡΩΝΙΚΟΥ

When 5 million Athenians flee the city each summer in search of beaches and *pareia* (Greek for something like "food, folks, and fun"), they don't flee far. Many head to the Saronic Gulf Islands. This means two things: first, you've chosen a destination approved by discriminating Greeks; second, you're not the only one. Keep in mind that, while good times are to be had *without* 50 of your closest package tourist friends, it may require a bit of creativity that shake them—as the best traveling always does. Beware: the islands' popularity makes them a bit of a stretch on a budget traveler's wallet. Despite their geographic proximity, each of the Gulf islands retains a distinct character. Just remember these cheat-sheet quick reference distinctions: Poros has the magnificent lemon grove, the Temple of Aphaia is on Aegina, Spetses' forests are pine-filled, and Hydra's streets are pollutant-free.

**HIGHLIGHTS OF THE SARONIC GULF ISLANDS**

**SCRAMBLE** up to the 5th-century BC Temple of Aphaia on Aegina (p. 291) and check out the 360-degree view of the coastline.

**FOLLOW THE SCENT OF LEMONS** as you walk past tens of thousands of trees on your way to a picnic in the Devil's Gorge, (p. 295) near Galatas on Poros.

**DON'T LOOK BOTH WAYS** while crossing the street on vehicle-free Hydra, (p. 296) but watch out for donkeys as you wander through the art fairs.

**MUNCH WATERMELON** as you gaze at the enrapturing blues of the Aegean from stunningly colorful Xylocheriza beach on the coast of Spetses (p. 300).

## AEGINA ΑΙΓΙΝΑ

Who does not know the renowned Aegina who went to bed with Zeus?
—Bacchylides

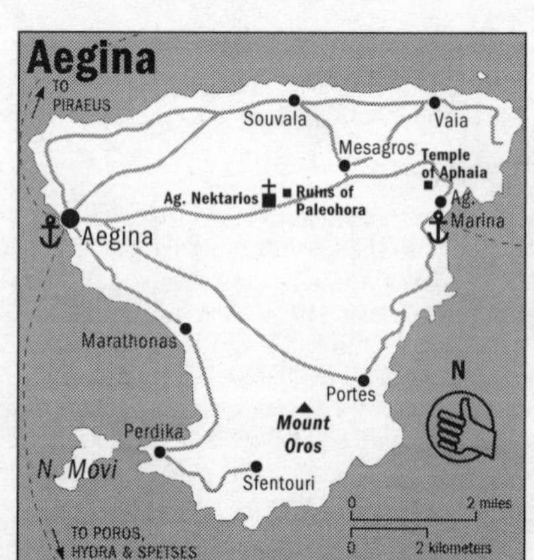


Bright, white-washed Aegina is an easy daytrip for city-weary Athenians, and summer weekends find the island saddled with the bustle of Greece's capital. Tour groups flood the beaches and swarm the resort town of Agia Marina; horns blast and exhaust clouds the air. But if you can elbow through the crowds, you'll find an island as lovely as it is convenient. The hamlet of Marathonas is

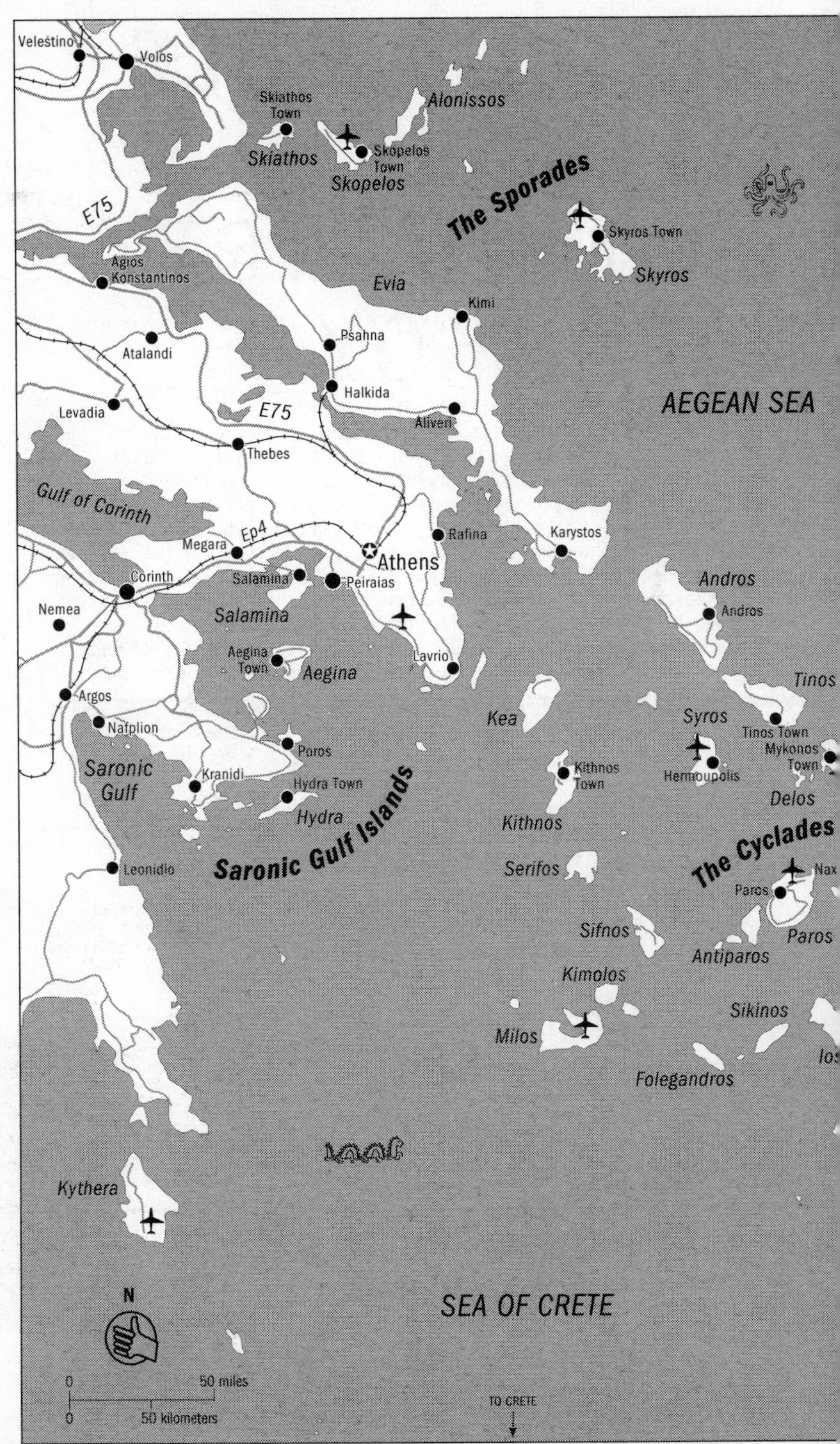
Velestino
Volos
Skiathos Town
Alonissos
Skiathos
Skopelos Town
Skopelos
The Sporades
E75
Skyros Town
Skyros
Agios Konstantinos
Evia
Kimi
Atalandi
Psahna
Halkida
Levadia
E75
Aliveri
AEGEAN SEA
Thebes
Gulf of Corinth
Megara
Ep4
Rafina
Karystos
Athens
Corinth
Salamina
Peiraias
Andros
Nemea
Salamina
Andros
Aegina Town
Aegina
Lavrio
Tinos
Argos
Kea
Syros
Nafplion
Poros
Tinos Town
Mykonos Town
Saronic Gulf
Kranidi
Hydra Town
Kithnos Town
Hermoupolis
Hydra
Saronic Gulf Islands
Delos
Kithnos
The Cyclades
Leonidio
Serifos
Paros
Sifnos
Paros
Antiparos
Kimolos
Sikinos
Milos
Folegandros
Kythera
N
SEA OF CRETE
0
50 miles
0
50 kilometers
TO CRETE

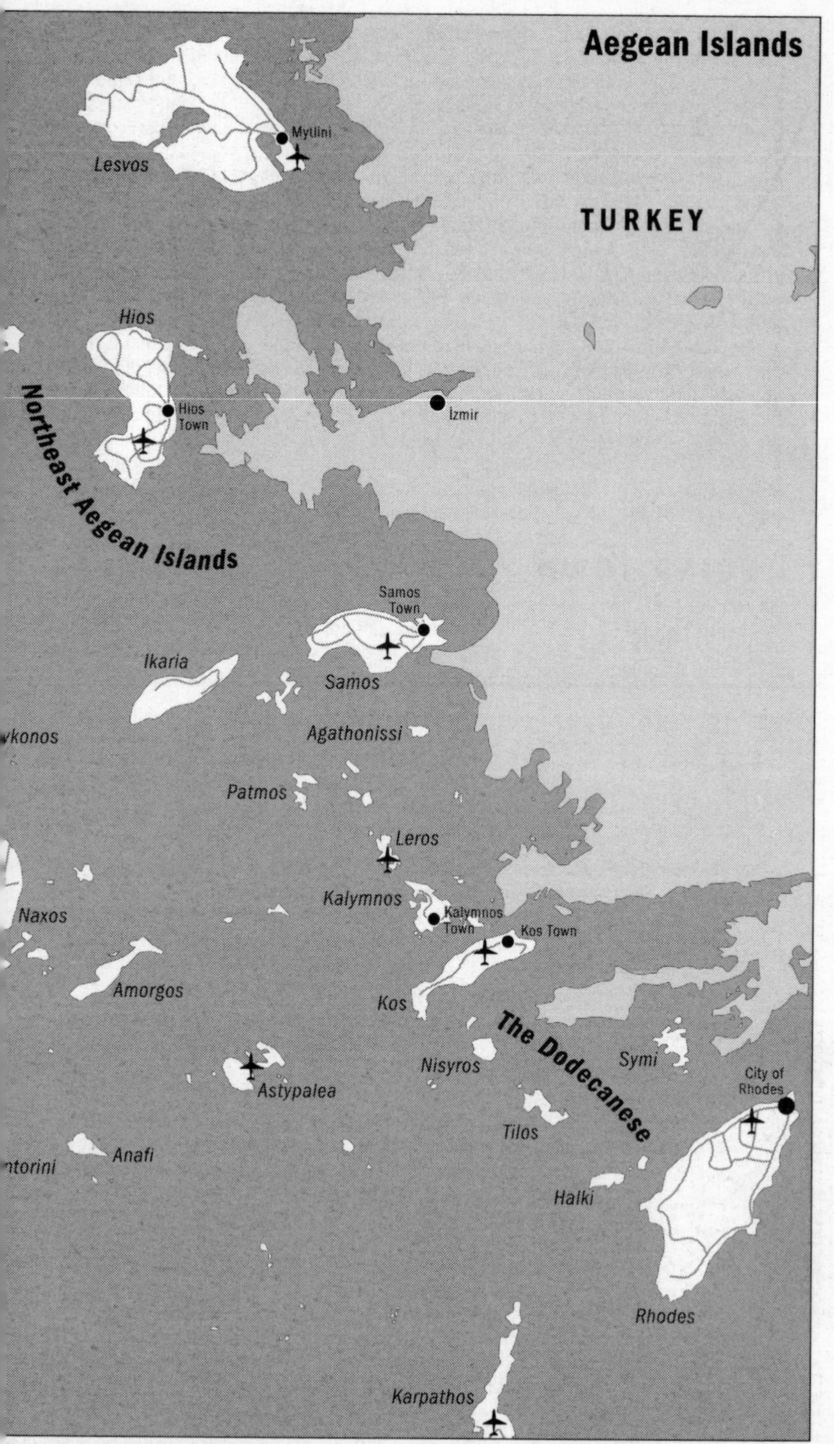
Aegean Islands
TURKEY
Mytlini
Lesvos
Hios
Hios Town
İzmir
Northeast Aegean Islands
Samos Town
Samos
Ikaria
Agathonissi
Patmos
Leros
Kalymnos
Kalymnos Town
Kos Town
Kos
Naxos
Amorgos
The Dodecanese
Symi
Nisyros
City of Rhodes
Astypalea
Tilos
Anafi
Halki
Rhodes
Karpathos

ideal for a swim on a beach *sans* rented chairs. Buses pass through olive-terraced mountains and the church of Agios Niktarios. The well-preserved remains of the Temple of Aphaia still stands, securing a view of the entire island and reminding visitors of the more noble past of the area.

Aegina's history is that of an island utterly different from the floating resort that exists now. Relations between Athens and the island were not particularly chummy in ancient times. The little island made up for its size with a self-determining spunk which irritated the mighty—and encroaching—Athens. The island produced the first Greek coins (silver "tortoises," which gained great financial leverage throughout the Greek world), and Aegina's sprinters, who practiced with jugs of water on their shoulders, zoomed past the competition at the pan-Hellenic games. With the onset of the Persian War in 491 BC, the citizens of Aegina sided at first with Xerxes' army, angering the besieged Athenians. In 480 BC they returned to the Greek side, winning the praise of the Delphic Oracle as the swiftest navy on the seas. In the peaceful inter-regnum that followed Persian defeat, island life flourished and Aegina's inhabitants built the magnificent Temple of Aphaia. With the eventual return of war, this time between Athens and Sparta, Aegina suffered the misfortune of siding with Sparta. Trounced by Athens in 459 BC, the islanders soon found themselves displaced by Athenian colonists. The island sank into geopolitical obscurity, only to emerge over two millennia later, in 1827, as the temporary capital of the partially liberated Greece.

## AEGINA TOWN ☎0297

As soon as your ferry docks in Aegina Town, you'll know that you've entered the Pistachio Capital of the World. Preserved, jellied, flavored, red, flaked, shelled, regular—there are at least as many ways to eat pistachios as there are package tour boats from the mainland. Fortunately, the tasty nuts are the greater influence.

### GETTING THERE AND GETTING AROUND

**Ferries:** Service to: **Piraeus** (1½hr., 22 per day, 1400dr); **Methana** and **Poros** (1hr., 3-4 per day, 950dr and 1200dr, respectively); **Hydra** (2hr., 2 per day, 1600dr); and **Spetses** (3hr., 1 per day, 2400dr). Each ticket stand at the edge of the quay represents only one ferry company. Schedules reduced on Su; check with port police.

**Flying Dolphins:** Ticket stand on the quay (☎27 462); an additional office is next to the port police. Sells hydrofoil tickets to: **Piraeus** (35min., 13 per day, 2100dr); **Methana-Poros** (25-40min., 3 per day, 2400dr); **Methana** (25min., 1 per day, 1900dr); **Hydra** (1hr., 2 per day, 2900dr); **Spetses** (2hr., 2 per day, 4300dr); and **Porto Heli** (2hr., 2 per day, 4500dr). **Catamarans** (☎26 974, at the kiosk on the quay) usually run to: **Piraeus** (5 per day, 1600dr), **Agistri** (7 per day, 600dr).

**Mopeds: Trust,** Leonardou Lada 1 (☎27 010), 1 block in from the waterfront. Mopeds go for 3000-5000dr pei day or less. Make sure you've got good brakes for steep island roads, and ask for a complimentary map.

**Taxis:** (☎22 635) Station immediately to the left of the quay along the waterfront; look for the line of grey, diesel-pumped Mercedes and Andis.

**Buses:** (☎22 787, station; 22 412, office), in Ethnegarcias Park, at the corner of the waterfront left of the ferry quay. Buses run to **Agia Marina** and the **Temple of Aphaia** (30min., every 45min. 6:30am-7:30pm, 450dr), and to **Perdika** via **Marathonas** (10min., 9 per day 7am-7:30pm, 250-500dr). For the temple, buy a round-trip ticket.

### ORIENTATION AND PRACTICAL INFORMATION

The central quay is expensive, but tavernas and hotels get cheaper toward either end of the waterfront. Running parallel to the waterfront, **Sp. Irioti** (1 block in) is lined with supermarkets, gritty restaurants, local markets, and the occasional moped rental, while **Sp. Aphaias** (2 blocks in) is home to more upscale shops, a historical museum, and an internet cafe.

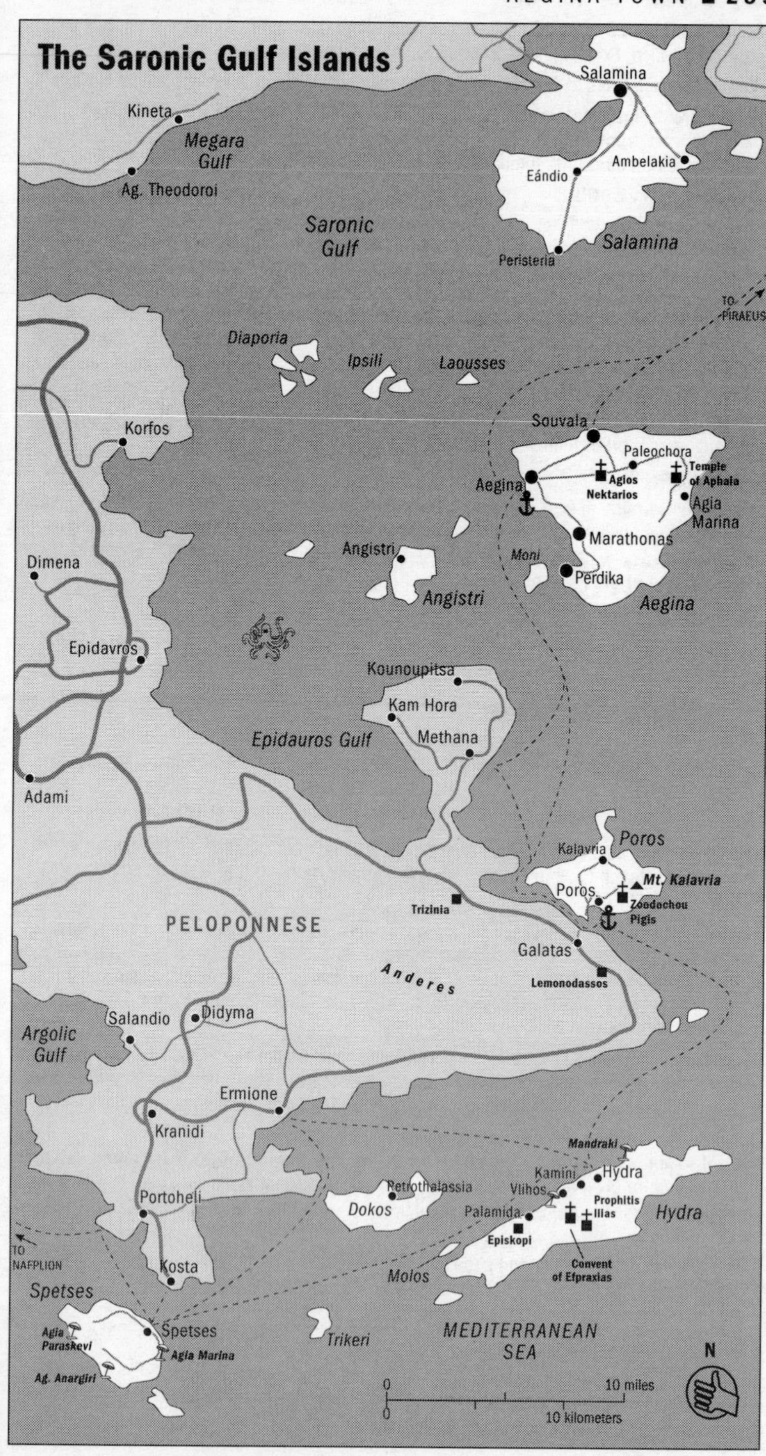
The Saronic Gulf Islands
Salamina
Kineta
Megara Gulf
Ag. Theodoroi
Ambelakia
Eándio
Saronic Gulf
Salamina
Peristeria
TO PIRAEUS
Diaporia
Ipsili
Laousses
Korfos
Souvala
Paleochora
Temple of Aphaia
Aegina
Agios Nektarios
Agia Marina
Marathonas
Angistri
Dimena
Moni
Perdika
Angistri
Aegina
Epidavros
Kounoupitsa
Kam Hora
Methana
Epidauros Gulf
Adami
Poros
Kalavria
Mt. Kalavria
Poros
Zoodochou Pigis
Trizinia
PELOPONNESE
Galatas
Anderes
Lemonodassos
Salandio
Didyma
Argolic Gulf
Ermione
Kranidi
Mandraki
Kamini
Hydra
Vlihos
Prophitis Ilias
Retrothalassia
Portoheli
Dokos
Palamida
Hydra
Episkopi
TO NAFPLION
Convent of Efpraxias
Kosta
Molos
Spetses
Agia Paraskevi
Spetses
Agia Marina
Trikeri
MEDITERRANEAN SEA
Ag. Anargiri
N
0
10 miles
0
10 kilometers

**Bank: National Bank** (☎25 697), to the right of the quay along the waterfront, just past the port police. Exchange and 24hr. **ATM**. Open M-Th 8am-2pm, F 8am-1:30pm.

**Exchange: Asco Tours** (☎25 697) on the corner of Irioti and Vas. Georgiou. Open 9am-10pm.

**Bookstore: Kalezis (International Press)** (☎23 874), one block to the right of the cafes on the waterfront. International books and magazines, phone cards, bus tickets, stamps. Credit cards 7% surcharge. Open 9am-10pm.

**Emergency**: ☎22 100.

**Tourist Police:** (☎27 777). Available mornings and afternoons only. Tourist and regular police in the same courtyard at Leonardou Lada 11.

**Police:** ☎23 333 or 22 100.

**Port Police:** (☎22 328), on the waterfront. Updated ferry schedules; English. Open 24hrs.

**Pharmacy:** Corner of Aiakou and Sp. Rodi (☎23 714). Open all day.

**Medical Center:** (☎22 222, 22 902, or 22 886), 2km along the waterfront to the left of the ferry quay. Call the tourist police (☎27 777; emergency ☎22 100) and they will arrange transport or refer you to doctors in town.

**Fire Brigade:** ☎22 912.

**OTE:** Paleas Choras 6 (☎22 399; dial 161 for assistance; costs 300dr); up Aiakou to the right. It's the building with the monstrous rooftop satellite dish. Open M-F 7:30am-3pm.

**Internet access: Nesant Internet Cafe,** Aphaias 13 (☎24 053). 1800dr per hour. **Prestige Internet Cafe** on Aiakou, 1500dr per hour. Both open late.

**Post Office:** Kanari 6 (☎22 398), Pl. Ethnegersias 1 behind the bus station. Express Mail Hellenic Post and **Poste Restante** available. Open M-F 7:30am-2pm. **Postal Code:** 18010.

## ACCOMMODATIONS

Rooms here are cheaper than on any of the other Saronic Gulf Islands. In the high season, doubles go for around 8000-12,000dr. *Domatia* owners often meet the ferries, but as always, bargain and discuss location before following anyone.

**Hotel Avra,** (☎22 303; fax 23 917) at the far left end of the waterfront. Checkered floors add a lively touch to simple rooms with phones and baths. Doubles 8000-10,000dr; triples 10-15,000dr.

**Hotel Plaza,** Kazatzaki 4 (☎25 600; fax 28 404), at the far left end of the waterfront. Friendly owner Michalis Kororos runs 3 roughly equivalent pensions—Plaza, Ulrikke and Christina—from the Plaza front desk. Rooms are modest and spotless, some have TVs and balconies. Doubles 8000-10,000dr, with A/C 12,000dr; triples 9000-12,000dr, with A/C 15,000dr.

**Hotel Areti** (☎23 593), at the left of the waterfront, before the Plaza and Avra hotels. Clean rooms have TVs, phones and private baths; seek your inner flower-child in the groovy lobby phone booth. Owners also run Hotel Togias and Hotel Aegina. Doubles 12-15,000dr; triples 17,000dr.

**Hotel Artemis** (☎25 195; fax 28466), set back to the left of the post office. White rooms with phones and the occasional balcony. Check-out noon, book exchange, A/C 1500dr. Singles 7500-9500dr, 8000-10,000dr with bath; doubles 13,000dr; triples 13-15,500dr.

**Hotel Marmarinos**, Leonardou Lada 24 (☎23 510, 22 474), up the road from the tourist police on the right. Neat but unremarkable; features refrigerators, private baths, and small balconies. Doubles 11-12,000dr; triples 13,000dr.

**Hotel Pavlou,** Aeginitou 21 (☎22 795), behind the church on the far right of the quay. Owned by the same man for 27 years. Come for the 70s decor (psychedelic curtains!) and comfortable rooms with balconies. Check-out noon. Breakfast 1500dr. Singles (no bath) 9100dr; doubles 11,100dr, with bath 13,000dr.

## FOOD AND ENTERTAINMENT

No-frills tavernas line P. Irioti street, which runs parallel to the waterfront one block inland along the right side of the harbor. For make-your-own meals, try the **supermarkets** on P. Irioti.

**To Patitiri** (☎51 520), in an alley to the left off of Aikaou. Serves marvelously fresh Greek meals in a quiet, bougainvillea-filled courtyard (salads 600-1000dr, entrees 1100-2400dr).

**O Babby's Restaurant and Snack Bar** (☎25 946), a 7min. walk along the waterfront to the right, serves cheap Greek specialties with a lovely view of the islands (salads 500-1000dr; family pizzas 1300-2000dr; entrees 1100-2100dr).

**Yacht Club,** on the waterfront. If you can't eat another *souvlaki,* walk upstairs to the Panagakis Cafe Bar/Crêperie. Fillings range from ice cream and strawberries to tunafish and mayo. (Crepes 1400-2400dr; cocktails 1400dr and up.)

**Zaccharo Plasteo Leo,** Afaes 48; just down from the internet cafe. Local desserts and chocolate ice cream, which goes for 200dr per scoop. Open 8am-11pm.

If you're tired of baking in the sun, visit Aegina's only **water park** (☎22 540), located 1km out of Aegina Town on the road to Marathonas (open 24hr.; 500dr, children under 11 free). During summer, watch American movies out-of-doors at **Anesis**, off of Aikou; to reach it, take the first hard left along the road to Marathonas (☎24 757. Shows at 9 and 11pm; 1800dr). In the winter, movies show at **Tinita** up the street.

Follow the searchlights or packs of mopeds to the dance club named, uh, **The Club,** a 10min. walk along the water to the right. Drink and dance under primary-colored lights. (☎24 570. Beer 1500dr, cocktails 2000dr. Cover 1500dr, includes first drink. Open 10:30pm-late.) The beach bar **Inn on the Beach** is just before The Club and packs a serious crowd on summer weekends. (☎26 440. Cover 1000dr, half off first drink.) Go tropical at **Aqua Loca** on Agios Basileos beach, a long walk along the waterfront to the right. (☎28 500. Beer 700-1200dr, cocktails 1500-2000dr. Open late morning-early morning.) Dream of enormous wealth while drinking your budget away at **Perdikiotika,** Afeas 38, a bank-turned-bar-and-restaurant. (Beer 1200-1400dr, cocktails 1200-2100dr. Open 9:30am-3pm, evening-4am.)

## SIGHTS

Aegina Town's archaeological fame teeters on the last half-column of the **Temple of Apollo.** The 8m-tall Doric column dates to 460 BC and stands on Kolona hill, a short walk out of town to the north. The **archaeological museum** at the site features artifacts from the Temple of Aphaia, a statue of Hercules from the Temple of Apollo, and some neolithic pots. (☎22 248. Open Tu-Su 8:30am-3pm. 500dr, students and seniors 300dr, EU students and children under 18 free.) The underground church of **Faneromeni,** a 15-minute walk inland just south of the town, houses a rare icon of the Virgin Mary. Locals say that the night before construction was to begin on a site above Faneromeni, the architect had a vision in which he was instructed to dig instead of build. Doing just that, he discovered the church and unearthed the icon. Contact a local travel agency to arrange a visit.

**NOTE TO SWIMMERS.** Colored flags on Aegina's beaches denote swimming regulations. A **white** flag means that swimming is allowed, a **yellow** flag means swim with caution, and a **red** flag means that swimming is forbidden.

## DAYTRIPS FROM AEGINA TOWN

**TEMPLE OF APHAIA.** The magnificent 5th-century BC remains of the **Temple of Aphaia** rest 2km from **Agia Marina.** Aphaia was one of Zeus' daughters, a hunting nymph worshipped on Aegina as protector of women. Her temple, built on the

foundation of a 6th-century BC temple, boasts a spectacular set of standing double-tiered columns. At night, peacocks roam the quiet hills by the temple. A small **museum** opens for 15 minutes at 9am, 11am, noon, and 1pm. *(The Agia Marina bus from Aegina Town stops right in front. Open M-F 8:15am-7pm and Sa, Su and holidays 8:30am-3pm. 800dr, students 400dr, children and EU students free.)*

**AGIOS NEKTARIOS.** The bronze and white church of Agios Nektarios is one of the largest places of worship in the Balkans. It's part of a complex that includes Nektarios' personal residence, bed, and books. The road behind Agios Nektarios leads to Paleohora (about 1½km), the "town of 300 churches," where locals used to take refuge from pirate invasions. It's worth exploring the 15 churches that remain to see their frescoes. *(For Agios Nektarios: Take the bus from Aegina Town (15min.), and dress appropriately: long pants for men, long skirts for women, no bare shoulders.)*

**AGIA MARINA.** If you find yourself inexplicably yearning to see hordes of sunburned tourists, overpriced beach toys and tacky towels, then by all means swing by Agia Marina. The summer resort town is at the end of a lovely 30-minute bus trip through the island's interior and offers some quality nightlife along with the exceedingly crowded beaches. The town is built around a main avenue parallel to the sea called **Aphaias.** A multitude of hotels surround the port, most are open only in the summer. **Hotel Myrmidon,** off Aphaias, sports a courtyard and a lovely footbridge. Rooms have private baths and fridges, and *Let's Go* users enjoy a 30% discount. (☎32 691; ☎/fax 32 558. Doubles 15,000dr; triples 18,000dr. Continental breakfast 1000dr in adjacent cafe.) If that's full, try **Hotel Neftarios** on a small road to the right off of Aphaias. The motherly owner provides large, sparkling rooms with private baths and common balconies. (☎32 438 or 71 564. Doubles 8000-9000dr; triples 10,000dr.) **Karras Travel,** next to the bus stop, offers **exchange** and sells **bus** tickets. (☎32 557. Open 9am-11pm).

Pick up a hamburger (500dr) and fries (400dr) at the **Fast Food Fresh** kiosk, on the road heading from the beach to the bus stop. A **supermarket** on Aphaias offers an alternative to eating out. You can rent paddle boats at the beach (2000dr per hr), but consider saving your money for discos like **Zorbas**; to find it take a right on Praxitelous two blocks past the bus stop, then follow the signs (opens 11pm). For authentic Greek music, head to **Disco Leos** (1½km out of town on the road to Aphaia; look for a sign and a road curving down to the right).

**MARATHONAS.** Turn seaward from the small newsstand at Marathonas for the best food and beaches on the island. Tiny and unassuming, the town—essentially a small taverna-lined detour along the beach—is a well-kept secret. **Cafe Ostria** (☎26 738) serves specialty *melizano* (eggplant) salads and calamari (entrees 800-2000dr, ice cream 500-1000dr). **Tassos** (☎24 040), family-owned for 40 years and renowned for its superb veal and fish, is the perfect place to finish off your perfect swim as you look out over a perfect Aegean sunset. Walk the 7km road from Aegina Town (it takes an hour) to see the island's most valuable coastline.



**CONCEIVED IN LIBERTY...?** On March 25, 1821, Greek forces began the rebellion against 400 years of Ottoman occupation. The date was no accident: any Orthodox Christian will recognize March 25 as exactly nine months before Christmas Day, and thus the day of the conception of Christ. Pragmatic enough to realize that rebuilding their land would take time, yet idealistic and spiritual enough to appreciate the endless significance of March 25, the Greeks chose the date in the hopes that the new republic would be ready for birth on December 25. In actuality it took years, but freedom was won and the modern state forged, and March 25 is still celebrated annually by Greeks as the anniversary of a doubly important conception.

# POROS ΠΟΡΟΣ

"Poros" is actually two islands, separated by a shallow channel. Little Sphaeria nuzzles the Peloponnesian mainland, mostly covered by the sprawl of touristy Poros Town. Its rugged big sister, Kalavria, still preserves large stretches of woods and dark-watered beaches. The name Poros means "passage," and refers to the 350m-wide channel separating it from the Peloponnese.

In the 6th century BC, a seven-city council called the Kalavrian League met in Poros to ward off hostile naval powers and ordered the building of the Temple of Poseidon. Three centuries later, the great orator Demosthenes, who improved his diction by speaking with marbles in his mouth, killed himself beside its columns. Poros was sparsely populated until Greeks arrived from Turkey in the 1920s.

## POROS TOWN ☎0298

Poros feels very much like a small town—even in thick crowds you'll be recognized as a tourist. Locals are curious and very helpful. Once you've got your bearings and a good meal, head out to Kalavria's pine woods and sandy beaches.

### GETTING THERE AND GETTING AROUND

**Ferries: Askeli Travel Agency** (☎24 900), across from the hydrofoil dock, sells ferry tickets and posts schedules. Six ferries per day run to **Piraeus** (2½hr., 2100dr) via **Methana** (30min., 800dr) and **Aegina** (1hr., 1200dr). Also service to **Hydra** (1hr., 2 per day, 1000dr) and **Spetses** (2½hr., 1 per day, 1600dr).

**Flying Dolphins:** (☎22 977 or 22 297). Hydrofoils dock at the main landing in the center of town. To: **Piraeus** (1¼hr., 9-11 per day, 4100dr); **Aegina** (30min., 1-3 per day, 2400dr); **Hydra** (30min., 6 per day M-Th, 2000dr); **Hermione** (1-2 per day, 2500dr); **Spetses** (1hr., 2-3 per day, 3300dr).

**Car Ferries: Poros-Galatas** (every 30min. 6:30am-10:30pm, 250-1000dr).

**Port Authority:** (☎22 274). Marked entrance one street in from the harbor by Seven Brothers Restaurant. Up a flight of stairs and down a long dreary hallway. Open 24hr.

**Moped Rental: Kosta's Bike Rental** (☎23 565), left of the waterfront past Ciné Diana. Mopeds start at 2500dr (4000dr for 80cc). Mountain bikes 1000dr. Open 9am-9pm.

**Buses:** Leave from the main plateia 7-8am until midnight. The green bus goes every 30min. to the **monastery** via **Askeli Beach** (200dr). The white bus goes every hr. to **Russian Bay** via **Neorion** (150dr). Buses leave **Galatas** to **Methana** (45min., 5 per day, 380dr); **Trizina** (20min., 3 per day, 250dr); **Nafplion** (1 per day); and **Epidavros** (2 per day), but not on Su; call 22 480 for schedules.

**Boat Taxis:** run 24hr. between Poros dock and **Galatas** (2min., 100dr). In high season, boats also run to Neorion, Askeli monastery, and Aliki (150-300dr; ask at port).

**Taxis:** (☎22 600 or 22 596) stop at the harbor just before the main plateia. Expect to pay more after midnight.

### ORIENTATION AND PRACTICAL INFORMATION

The hydrofoil quay is the center of transportation and tourist activity, while real life continues calmly on the waterfront (a block inland and a plateia to the right).

**Tourist Agencies: Saronic Gulf Travel** (☎24 555, 22 112; fax 24 802), is the most helpful of the waterfront travel agencies. Keep left from the ferry dock. Open 9am-9pm.

**Bank:** The **Alpha Trapeza Bank,** in the plateia to the right before the port police, has a **24hr. ATM.** Open M-Th 8am-2pm, F 8am-1:30pm.

**Bookstore: International Press** (☎25 205), 1 block left of Family Tours along the waterfront, has international newspapers. Open 8am-11pm. The quiet, unassuming **Skipper & Trout International Bookshop** (☎26 245), in the arcade behind Diana Cinema to

the left of the main landing, is a favorite haunt of the island's expats. Buys, sells, and exchanges new and used books in many languages. Also has telephone, fax, and translation services, greeting cards, stationery, and advice. Open M-Sa 9:45am-3:45pm.

**Showers:** 800dr at the **Yachting Supplies Mini Market** (☎22 992) to the left of the ferry dock along the waterfront, just after the road bends. Open 8am-midnight.

**Laundromats: Suzi's Launderette Service,** to the right of the OTE. Wash and dry 3000dr; ironing extra. Drop-off only. 2hr. service. Open M-Sa 9am-2pm and 7-9pm.

**Police:** (☎22 256). From the post office and pharmacy turn right and head up the stairs next to Igloo Ice Cream. At the top, turn right at the church and continue over and down past the Platanos Taverna. **Tourist Police** (☎22 462), in the same building.

**Clinic:** (☎22 600, 22 336), in Poros. Open 8am-2pm and, in high season, 6pm-8pm. **Galatas** has a 24hr. clinic (☎22 222), and emergencies including minor surgery can be handled at the **Naval School;** contact the tourist police.

**Telephone: OTE** (☎22 199 or 22 399), on the waterfront, left of the main landing. Telecards and telegrams. Open M-F 7:30am-3pm.

**Internet Access:** (☎25 404) Above Cafe Ermani across from the hydrofoil dock—look for signs up the stairs. 500dr per 15min. minimum; 1000dr per 30min. Fax and printing services available. Open 10am-2pm and 6-11pm.

**Post Office:** (☎22 275; fax 23 451), in the first plateia to the right along the water. Poste Restante; specify Poros Trinzinias. Open M-F 7:30am-2pm. **Postal code:** 18020.

## ACCOMMODATIONS

The best deals in Poros Town are the **domatia** advertised in almost every window; expect to pay 6000-9000dr. The tourist police and Saronic Gulf Travel offer fairly unbiased help. There's no pressing reason to stay in Poros Town, as **Galatas,** 2min. across the strait by boat (every 10-15min., 24hr., 100dr), has equivalent hotel rooms for less.

**Manos Pension** (☎22 000 or 23 456), in Galatas. Walk left when you disembark from the small boat from Poros Town. Family-run pension dedicated to your Greek experience. Manos and Beatrix can pick you up at the airport, tell you all about the area, rent you a motorbike (2500-4000dr), and invite you out to their farm for Greek dancing. Doubles 8300dr; triples 9600dr; apartments 12,000dr; discounts for longer stays.

**Hotel Seven Brothers** (☎23 412; fax 23 413), 40m inland in the center of the waterfront. One of the better deals for a decked-out portside hotel. Rooms with private bath, TV, A/C, and minibar. Singles 12,000dr; doubles 16,000dr; triples 19,000dr.

**Camping Kyragelo** (☎24 520), outside Galatas. Follow the waterfront road to the right and uphill to the left. Take the second right and continue for about 350m. 1000dr per person, 500dr per car or tent.



## FOOD AND NIGHTLIFE

Similar restaurants line the harbor, and "charming" waiters try to convince tourists to sit down; make your choice based on the view. **Nikolaos' Fruit Market and Grocery Store** (☎22 287) is to the right of the main plateia along the waterfront; several grocery stores are nearby. Poros isn't much of a party town, but there's plenty to do on weekends. Check billings by the bus station for **Diana open-air cinema,** to the left of Lela Tours, where you can see American movies (9 and 11pm; 1900dr, children 1300dr). The difference between bars and discos in Poros is that the former are required to shut off their music at 3am, while the latter keep up the beat for a few more hours. Most are about 1km to the right of the ferry landing on the waterfront; two more popular joints that meet your pulsating music needs are **Malibu** and **Cocomo** (drinks around 1500-2000dr). Cafes are open all day; more hardcore establishments start at 10:30pm. **The Posidonion** (☎22 361) is a hotel, bar, and disco 2km above the other clubs; take a cab.

# WORLDWIDE CALLING MADE EASY

**The MCI WorldCom Card, designed specifically to keep you in touch with the people that matter the most to you.**

MCI WORLDCOM WORLDPHONE

1·800·888·8000

J. L. SMITH

**www.wcom.com/worldphone**

Please tear off this card and keep it in your wallet as a reference guide for convenient U.S. and worldwide calling with the MCI WorldCom Card.

## HOW TO MAKE CALLS USING YOUR MCI WORLDCOM CARD

> **When calling from the U.S., Puerto Rico, the U.S. Virgin Islands or Canada** to virtually anywhere in the world:

1. Dial 1-800-888-8000
2. Enter your card number + PIN, listen for the dial tone
3. Dial the number you are calling :
   **Domestic Calls:** Area Code + Phone number
   **International Calls:**
   011+ Country Code + City Code + Phone Number

> **When calling from outside the U.S.**, use WorldPhone from over 125 countries and places worldwide:

1. Dial the WorldPhone toll-free access number of the country you are calling from.
2. Follow the voice instructions or hold for a WorldPhone operator to complete the call.

> **For calls from your hotel:**

1. Obtain an outside line.
2. Follow the instructions above on how to place a call.
   **Note:** If your hotel blocks the use of your MCI WorldCom Card, you may have to use an alternative location to place your call.

## RECEIVING INTERNATIONAL COLLECT CALLS*

Have family and friends call you collect at home using WorldPhone Service and pay the same low rate as if you called them.

1. Provide them with the WorldPhone access number for the country they are calling from (In the U.S., 1-800-888-8000; for international access numbers see reverse side).
2. Have them dial that access number, wait for an operator, and ask to call you collect at your home number.

** For U.S. based customers only.*

## START USING YOUR MCI WORLDCOM CARD TODAY. MCI WORLDCOM STEPSAVERS[SM]

Get the same low rate per country as on calls from home, when you:

1. **Receive international collect calls to your home** using WorldPhone access numbers
2. **Make international calls with your MCI WorldCom Card** from the U.S.*
3. **Call back to anywhere in the U.S. from Abroad** using your MCI WorldCom Card and WorldPhone access numbers.

** An additional charge applies to calls from U.S. pay phones.*

**WorldPhone Overseas Laptop Connection Tips** —
Visit our website, www.wcom.com/worldphone, to learn how to access the Internet and email via your laptop when traveling abroad using the MCI WorldCom Card and WorldPhone access numbers.

**Travelers Assist®** — When you are overseas, get emergency interpretation assistance and local medical, legal, and entertainment referrals. Simply dial the country's toll-free access number.

**Planning a Trip?**—Call the WorldPhone customer service hotline at 1-800-736-1828 for new and updated country access availability or visit our website:

**www.wcom.com/worldphone**

# MCI WorldCom Worldphone Access Numbers

*Easy Worldwide Calling*

MCI WORLDCOM[SM]

**Taverna Karavolos** (☎22 287), in an alley next to Lela Tours on the far left side of the waterfront. Hearty traditional treats are served with class at this small, unassuming taverna. If you're feeling wild, try to the house specialty and namesake–snails in tomato sauce (1200dr). Entrees 1400-1900dr.

**Taverna Poros** (☎25 267), one of the more relaxed waterfront restaurants, right across from sea taxi dock. Entrees 1500-3800dr.

**Igloo Ice Cream** (☎25 515), inland around the corner to the right of the post office. Serves breakfast, pastries, and ice cream (350dr per scoop).

## SIGHTS

**ARCHAEOLOGICAL MUSEUM.** In Poros Town itself, the archaeological museum in the middle of the waterfront has some interesting inscriptions and photographs of the ruins at Troizen in the Peloponnese; very little of the collection is actually from Poros. *(☎23 276. Open Tu-Su 8:30am-3pm. Free.)* For a pretty view of the harbor, climb the **clock tower** (the stairs are next to the library, 1 block inland).

**GALATAS.** If you look across a thin strait to the Peloponnesian mainland from Poros, you'll spy Galatas (Γαλατας), a working village with a different feel than tourist-frequented Poros. Surrounded by beautiful farmland and cut with flat, well-paved roads, Galatas is great for bike riding. When you arrive, turn left (facing inland) to find the pleasant sand beaches of **Plaka** and **Aliki.** Plaka is about 2km from Galatas, marked by a wall that reads "Poros Marine," while livelier Aliki is 1km further—only the water on the ocean side is safe for swimming. Bring your own food or eat at either of the Aliki Beach tavernas, where two can fill up for a costly 6000dr. A gravel path 1km past the turn-off for Aliki is on the right of the road and leads up through the enormous lemon grove of **Lemonodassos.** If you are riding a moped, leave it here before going up the dirt road. It is a pleasant, if dusty, 20min. walk up to **Kardasi Taverna** (☎23 100), to get a cool glass of fresh lemonade (350dr) and a view of windmills and 38,000 lemon trees. The beaches are quieter on the opposite side of the peninsula; try **Vlacheika.** *(Boats run between Galatas and Poros daily every 10min. (2min., 100dr).)*

**MONASTERY OF ZOODOCHOS PIGIS.** The 18th-century Monastery of Zoodochos Pigis (Virgin of the Life-Giving Spring) is secreted away in an overgrown glade 6km from Poros Town. Monks have been quaffing blessed, curative waters here since 200 BC. The monastery served as a meeting place for Greek naval leaders Miaoulis, Jobazis, and Apostolis, who strategized the uprising of 1821. Before hopping on the bus back, stop for delicious homemade spoon sweets at **Samali's,** opposite the monastic complex, and if you're curious, ask nicely about the tiny church next door. From the road below the monastery you can find the 6th-century BC **Temple of Poseidon.** The "ruins" may be best appreciated by true Greek history buffs, but the view will inspire all. *(Take the green bus from the stop next to the main port (20min., every 30min. 7am-11pm, 150dr). Open 8am-4pm. Modest dress required.)*



## BEACHES AND GORGES

The **white bus line** runs hourly along the shore to the beach at **Russian Bay**, where Russian ships first docked to aid the Greek rebellion. Along the way are classy **Neorion**—featuring a long sand beach, tavernas, a watersports center, and a waterski school (lesson 7500dr, rental 6000dr)—and the secluded blue-green waters and rocky sands of **Lover's Bay.** The tiny island just seaward from Lover's Bay was an undercover school during the Turkish occupation, when Greeks were forbidden an education. Ironically, it's now a popular sunning rock for kids playing hooky.

Fifteen kilometers from Galatas lies **Trizina,** mythical home to the hero **Theseus.** Take a bus (20min., 3 per day, 250dr) there form Poros. Meager ruins have been unearthed near the town, but of far more interest is the lovely **Devil's Gorge** that looms over both town and site. The shady, verdant area is not large, but is a per-

fect picnic spot, especially for those who miss trees. Head uphill from the bus stop in the center of town and go right, following the paved road past olive trees and fragrant lemon groves. At the fork in the road, head left and uphill (right and downhill will take you to the ruins). Keep right on the dirt road past the fork to reach the gorge.

# HYDRA ΥΔΡΑ

Steep and bright, proud Hydra (EE-drah) rises out of the sea in its own bubble of smog-free, screech-free air. Even bicycles are illegal here—the steep, scaled streets only accommodate pedestrians, donkeys, and three garbage trucks. Look inland to the huge mansions stacked against the rocks: Hydra was rich long before the influx of tourist cash, first coming to prosperity as the 15th-century refuge of wealthy Greek families escaping Turkish persecution. The island then struck a deal with the Ottomans, providing the Turkish navy with the service of 30 young Hydrian men every year in return for its freedom. Hydrian youth thus learned the art of naval battle, a perk when, in 1821, Admiral Miaoulis and the Hydrian elite dedicated their wealth and their fleet to the fledgling revolution. Everyone's still terribly proud of it, and Miaoulis is honored in the name of the main thoroughfare.

## HYDRA TOWN ☎0298

The sometimes baffling, cobbled streets of Hydra Town twist up the island's parched hills as they rise from the rich blues of the sea. Donkeys mingle with wheelbarrow-pulling fruit vendors in the quiet alleys that wend their way toward the famous mountaintop monasteries. Glowing a sleepy yellow-pink in the evenings, the port below bustles with art students and smiling tourists during the summer months. As gorgeous as summers in Hydra are, the pink-blossomed spring and salt-winded fall give the town an off season like no other. Outside of Hydra Town, the island's only real settlement, and hidden beaches (immortalized in a rash of 60s films) can be yours for the price of a sea taxi.

### ORIENTATION AND PRACTICAL INFORMATION

Hydra's waterfront is lined with cute, overpriced shops catering to Athenian day-trippers. The U-shaped harbor faces north toward the mainland; its east side is home to boat docks and museums, while the west has beaches, bars, and a disco.

**Ferries: Salanikos Ferries** ticket office (☎54 007), upstairs in the building with the gray door across from the ferry dock. Open 10am-6:30pm. Two ferries per day to: **Piraeus** (3¼hr., 2300dr) via **Poros** (1hr., 1000dr), **Methana** (1½hr., 1500dr), and **Aegina** (2¼hr., 1600dr). Also service to **Spetses** (1hr., 1 per day, 1200dr).

**Flying Dolphins:** The **ticket office** (☎53 813 or 53 814) is upstairs on the same floor as the ferry ticket office. Open 6:30am-9pm. To: **Hermione** (30min., 4 per day, 1700dr); **Piraeus** (1½hr., 9 per day, 4600dr); **Poros** (30min., 5 per day, 2000dr); **Portoheli** (45min., 8 per day, 2500dr); and **Spestes** (30min., 8 per day, 2300dr).

**Sea Taxis:** (☎53 690). Bright yellow motorboats park by the mule stand in the southwest corner of the harbor. Priced per boat (not per person), reflecting time of journey. Service to: **Kamina** (1800dr); **Miramare Beach** (2500dr); **Vlihos** (2500dr); **Palamidas** (3500dr); **Molos** (5500dr); **Metohi** (6000dr); **Agios Georgios** (10,000dr); **Agios Nikolaos** (13,000dr); **Hydra Beach** (13,000dr); and a daytrip around the island with beach stops for 28,000dr (bring food). Also to **Spetses** and **Piraeus** for mind-boggling rates (if you just can't wait for the ferry).

**Tourist Agency: Vassilis Tours** (☎54 190; fax 54 191), one block inland on Tombazi in the southwest corner of the harbor. Fax, photocopies, **currency exchange,** and English. Next door to the island's best bakery. Open 10am-10pm in summer; 2hr. daily in winter.

## HYDRA'S POET LAUREATE

Like a bird on a wire
Like a drunk in a midnight choir
I have tried in my way to be free.
—Leonard Cohen

In the late 60s, singer and songwriter Leonard Cohen spent several inspired years living on Hydra in a house he bought for $1500. Contemplating the invasion of telephone poles and other innovations on this technologically primitive island, he discussed the oppressive weight of such modernizing changes in his song "Bird on a Wire." For Cohen, Hydra was an oasis of pacific beauty, free from the materialism and overbearing religion he associated with his native Montreal. The Aegean fascinated him—its water, its colors, the light reflected from its surface—and he attributed the depth and meaning of his poetry to that shifting, magical body. As he said in 1963, "there's something in the light that's honest and philosophical." Cohen found Hydra inspiring beyond its natural beauty: "Thank god for hashish, cognac, and neurotic women who pay their debts with flesh," he wrote. He saw the mixed isolation and debauchery as a positive influence, writing, "I chose a lonely country / broke from love / scorned the fraternity of war / I polished my tongue against the pumice moon." Cohen found his muse on Hydra; in Greece, he says, he "just felt good, strong, ready for the task" of writing.

**Bank: National Bank** (☎53 233), on the waterfront. 24hr. **ATM.** Open M-Th 8am-2pm and F 8am-1:30pm.

**Laundry:** (☎53 380) in the small building behind the fruit market next to the post office. 3000dr per load. Open 9am-1:30pm and 5-8:30pm.

**Tourist Police:** (☎52 205). Follow the street to the right of the clock tower inland and go left at the fork. Look for the coat of arms on your right opposite the OTE. Open 24hr.

**Port Police:** (☎52 279), upstairs in the big gray building flying the Greek nautical flag, in the northwest corner of the harbor. Open 24hr.

**Pharmacy:** (☎52 059), inland from the tourist police and to the left. Open M-F 8:30am-1:30pm and 5-8:30pm.

**Hospital:** (☎53 150 or 53 151), inland on the street to the right of the clock tower, set back on the right just past the tourist police. Brown door with grates set in a stone wall. Open 9am-1pm and by appointment; in an **emergency,** call the 24hr. nurse (☎53 150) or the tourist police.

**Telephones: OTE** (☎52 199), facing the tourist police. Open M-F 8am-2pm.

**Internet Access: Flamingo Cafe** (☎53 485), on Tombazi across from Vassilis Tours. 2500dr per hr., 1300 per 30min. Open 11am-11pm.

**Post Office:** (☎52 262), one block inland in the alley to the left of the Bank of Greece. Open M-F 7:30am-2pm. **Postal code:** 18040.

SARONIC GULF

## ACCOMMODATIONS

Hydra has the most expensive accommodations in the Saronic Gulf. Singles are practically nonexistent and doubles generally coat at least 12000dr in the high season. Rooms in one of Hydra's famous old mansions are usually much more. Weekend accommodations are almost impossible to get due to the influx of vacationing Greeks; if you can, arrive on Thursday for the weekend or call ahead.

**Sophia Hotel** (☎52 313), right in the middle of the wharf; look for green, iron-railed balconies. In business for 66 years, it's run by the original Sophia's granddaughter's goddaughter. Five big, bright, balconied rooms (and common baths) in a lovely old house; reservations recommended. Doubles 8800dr; triples 11,500dr.

**Hotel Amarillis** (☎53 611, 52 249, 53 859; mobile (097) 411 065). Walk inland on Tombazi; hang right at the fork. Rooms at this welcoming, no-frills, family-run hotel have big windows, high ceilings, baths, and balconies. One single for 6000dr; doubles 12,000dr; triples 16,000dr.

**Hotel Delfini** (☎52 082), across from the ferry dock, before the cafes. Sunny white rooms with blue trim are clean and cheery. Private baths and phones. Check-out noon. Singles 13,000-15,000dr; doubles 15,000-17,000dr; triples 18,000-20,000dr.

**Hotel Argo** (☎52 452; fax 53 845), on the waterfront across from the water taxi stand above Osisalos Cafe. Nine nicely renovated rooms include the luxury of A/C, private baths, TVs, and phones. Check-out 11:30am. Doubles 15,000dr.

## FOOD AND NIGHTLIFE

Waterfront places mostly have average food, lots of tourists, and prices that reflect the rent. Hidden treasures compensate for location with superb food and significantly lower prices.

**Taverna Xeri Elia** (☎52 886), in a trellised courtyard a 5min. walk inland on Tombazi. Classy, top-quality food and service at a range of prices. Entrees 1200-4000dr. Try the delicious *moussaka* (1000dr).

**Christina's Taverna** (☎53 615), on Spilios Charamis just to the right of Taverna Xeri Elia. Far off the beaten path, this is the place for brilliant home-cooking, so don't bother with the menu—just order whatever Christina has in the kitchen. Entrees 1200-1700dr. Open 11am-11pm.

**Taverna Psaropoula** (☎52 630). The best value of the waterfront restaurants. Entrees are on display, cafeteria-style, just inside the door; food is unremarkable but clean and fast. Full meals start at 3500dr.

**Captain George** (☎53 660). Rowdy by Hydra's standards, but still warm and thoroughly lovable, serving up hearty and classic Greek fare (entrees 1400-3500dr). The walls boast "Captain George" artwork by loyal local patrons.

**Anemoni** (☎53 156). Bear left up from the OTE. Greek pastries (100-500dr) in generous portions; stop by after dinner for fresh ice cream (300dr) and almond confections. Open 7am-11pm. For more savory goods, the **bakery** on Tombazi next to Vassilis Tours is the island's best. Pies and breads 100-500dr, ice cream 200dr. Open 7am-10pm.

If the urge to shake your groove thing overtakes you in Hydra, try **Disco Heaven,** up the white trimmed stairs just before the Sunset Restaurant on the west side of town. There's an indoor, A/C dance floor as well as an outdoor bar overlooking the sea. (☎52 716. Drinks 2000dr. Cover 1000dr. Open 11pm-late, summer only.) As the large contingent of artists might suggest, the Hydrian scene is much more about strolling the moonlit harbor, getting invited onto yachts for drinks, and wandering in and out of the waterfront bars. The perfect Hydrian night begins around 12:30am in the lounge seats of the **Pirate Bar,** tucked into the southwest corner of the harbor (☎52 711; cocktails 1200-2000dr; open 10am-late), then wanders slowly through the bar crowds down to **Salonicos,** stopping for drinks and munchies with everyone along the way, and ends with an early-morning swim in the deep, cool waters off the landing past Sunset Restaurant, around the cape to the east. (☎52 589. Cocktails 2300dr. Open 10pm-late.)

## SIGHTS AND THE OUTDOORS

**HYDRA'S MERCHANT MARINERS.** Despite its watery name, Hydra's land has always been too arid for lucrative agriculture. With few natural resources and a significant population of refugees from the Peloponnese, the Balkans, and Turkey, Hydra's inhabitants turned to managing the exports of others. Dodging pirates and naval blockades during the late 18th and early 19th centuries, Hydriot merchants emerged in 1821 as the financial and naval leaders in the revolt against Ottoman

rule, contributing two-thirds of the revolution's 200-odd ships. The Venetian-built mansions of these merchants-turned-heroes dot the hills behind the harbor, and are definitely worth a look. George Koundouriotis was one of the many Hydriot leaders in the Greek War of Independence, and his grandson, Pavlos Koundouriotis, became the President of Greece in the 1920s.

The **Koundouriotis house** is currently being renovated by the Ministry of Defense; it will eventually become a public museum. The **Tombazis mansion** on the east side of the harbor now houses a famous art school—look for paint-smeared artists on the balcony. The **houses of Votsis** and **Economou,** two Hydriots who also contributed to the island's naval fame, are closer to the crest of the hill, right on Voulgari. East of the harbor, in the **Tsamados mansion,** is the first **Pilot School** of the Greek Merchant Marine. Set off by winding, anchor-flanked stairs, it features maritime paintings and models. Most houses are privately owned, so ask at the tourist office for directions and then just knock on the door. *(Houses open roughly 9am-10pm. Free.)*

**BYZANTINE SIGHTS.** Those in search of peace need only check beneath the large clock tower that dominates the port. Stepping from the busy port into the courtyard of the **Church of the Assumption of the Virgin Mary,** you are immediately struck by the stillness and angelic whiteness of this place. The small church is certainly worth a trip if just for a peek of its gilded ceiling and a few wonderful moments of quiet contemplation. Before serving as a monastery, the structure was a convent, housing 18 nuns from 1648 to 1770. It is now dedicated to the *kemesis*, or ascension of Mary. The courtyard surrounds the tomb of Koundouriotis, his statue, and a statue of Miaoulis. Modest dress is required. Hidden away up the stairs is the lovely **Byzantine Museum,** with an extensive and impressive collection of Byzantine icons, frescoes, gospels, and ecclesiastical liturgical vessels. Noteworthy are the holy vestments and the brightly colored, beautifully preserved scenes from the life of Christ produced in the 18th and 19th centuries. *(Open 10am-5pm. 500dr.)*

**HISTORICAL ARCHIVES MUSEUM.** To the left of the ferry landing, the Historical Archives Museum of Hydra houses old Hydriot costumes, census records, a library, naval treasures, and relics of the revolution. Don't miss the heart of Admiral Andreas Miaoulis, which is stunningly embalmed and preserved in a silver and gold urn. *(☎52 355 or 54 142. Open Tu-Su 9am-4:30pm. 1000dr, children 700dr.)*

**MONASTERY HIKE.** An arduous 90min. hike up A. Miaouli from the waterfront will take you to the **Monastery of Prophitis Ilias** and, on a lower peak overlooking the harbor, the **Convent of Efpraxia.** While the nuns at Efpraxia do beautiful embroidery work, the monastery is the prettier of the two, and the monks may show you around. A donkey ride up the rocks will cost about 8000dr and wear out the donkey—inquire at the harbor. Modest dress is required at both the monastery and the convent. *(Both open 9am-5pm.)*

**FESTIVALS.** If you're in Hydra town during the **Miaoulia** (the fourth weekend in June), celebrate the feats of Admiral Andreas Miaoulis while watching an explosive mock battle held in the harbor. Greek Orthodox **Easter Weekend** (one week after Roman Catholic Easter) marks the other big festival of the year, with outdoor candlelight services on Good Friday and Holy Saturday and a ceremonial immersion of the Epitaph on Good Friday in the sea off Kamini beach.

## BEACHES

Various beach options tempt that pasty-looking skin to the sun. Within walking distance, pick your favorite rock cove anywhere around the western coast past the Sunset Restaurant. Here the water is cool and immediately deep. A 15min. walk further west along the coast takes you past the high-walled, cobbled-street artists' colony of **Kamini** (surreal at night). Just beyond it is the tiny, pebbly **beach** where the drop to the sea is less severe. Walking another 20min. along the lovely coast leads you to slightly more populous **Vlihos Beach,** guarded by a regiment of Hawaiian-style beach umbrellas. A 30min. hike east of town (or 10min. water taxi) lies

**Mandraki Beach** (a.k.a. the Mira Mare Hotel, but free for all), a genuine if gritty sand beach. This isn't the secluded beach of your dreams, but there are plenty of fun water toys to keep you busy. (Paddle boats 2500dr per hr., canoes 1500dr per hr., tubes 2500dr per hr.) If you have time and money, hire a water taxi or boat and head to the far side of the island, where the jet set measures a beach's trendiness by its inaccessibility. There's also room for you to find a quiet beach of your own—just make sure you agree on a pickup time before you get out. (Thanks, Mom.)

# SPETSES ΣΠΕΤΣΕΣ

Ancient *Pitiusa* (Pinetree Island), Spetses is a floating pine forest dotted with white and blue houses and expansive old villas. Although the island's warm beaches and clear, sparkling water draw their fair share of tourism—lavish vacation developments are popping up and weekends find the docks clogged with yachts—Spetses maintains its welcoming, laid-back atmosphere. Visitors to the island will want to soak up quality rays while sipping a cool daiquiri. Serene Spetses demurely and happily provides sun and fun without the self-conscious, tacky trimmings of many resort towns.

## SPETSES TOWN ☎0298

The vast majority of Spetsiots live in Spetses Town, as close to the water as possible. Cafes and bars string the 4km of water, interspersed with little pebble beaches every 50m—turning the town into a round-the-clock beach club. Jet-setters dock in Spetses's Old Harbor to the left (facing inland) of the ferry quay. Although topless sunbathing is technically illegal, Spetsiots know how to bend the rules.

### GETTING THERE AND GETTING AROUND

**Ferries:** Depart once daily to: **Piraeus** (4½hr., 3200dr); **Poros** (2hr., 1600dr); **Methana** (2¼hr., 1900dr); and **Aegina** (3hr., 2400dr) via **Hydra** (1hr., 1200dr). **Alasia Travel** (☎74 098) sells tickets and posts schedules. Open 8am-10pm.

**Flying Dolphins: Ticket office** (☎73 141), inland from the dock. **Hydrofoils** and **catamarans** to: **Piraeus** (2hr., 5-7 per day, 6400dr); **Hydra** (30min., 7 per day, 2300dr); **Poros** (1hr., 1 per day, 3300dr); and **Monemvasia** (2½hr., 2 per day, 4600dr.

**Water Taxis:** (☎72 072), docked across from the Flying Dolphin ticket office. To: **Kosta** (2500dr); **Old Harbor** (3000dr); **Kostovla** (4000dr); **Agia Marina** (5000dr); **Hinitsa** (6000dr); **Emilianos** (7000dr); **Porto Heli** (7000dr); **Zogeria** (7000dr); **Anarghiri Beach** or **Paraskevi Beach** (10,000dr); and trips around the island (15,000dr).

**Caïques:** These small boats dock between the ferries and water taxis. Leave 10am-noon and return around 4pm. Daily trips to: **Ag. Anarghiri** and **Ag. Paraskevi Beaches** (2000dr round trip); **Zogari Beach** (1500dr round trip); and **Kosta** on the mainland (350dr one way).

**Buses:** To: **Ag. Anangiri Beach** (20min., 3 per day, 400dr), from the far left side of the waterfront by the kiosk; and to **Anargyrios College** and **Lioneri Beach** from the plateia to the right of the waterfront by the Hotel Poseidon. Schedule posted.

**Taxis:** In front of the travel agencies to the left of the ferry dock.

**Moped Rental: Pap Bikes** (☎72 261 or 83 720) at the far left end of the waterfront; take the right fork at the kiosk and watch for signs on the left. 50cc mopeds for 4000dr per day. **Rent-a-Bike** (☎74 143) on the street running parallel to the waterfront, behind the Hotel Soleil, rents **mountain bikes.** 1500dr per day.



### ORIENTATION AND PRACTICAL INFORMATION

Restaurants and shops form a 2km line on either side of the port. Facing inland, the old harbor is a 20min. walk left of the boat landing.

**Tourist Agencies:** Several around the corner on the left side of the boat landing. **Alasia Travel** (☎74 497, 74 498, or 74 098), sells ferry tickets.

**Banks: National Bank** (☎72 286), left of the OTE, on the waterfront to the right of the ferry docks. Open M-Th 8am-2pm, F 8am-1:30pm. 24hr. **ATM.**

**Laundry:** (☎73 304) On the way to the police station on the left. 4000-5000dr per load. Open 7am-10pm.

**Police:** (☎73 100). Follow signs to the Spetses Museum; 150m before the museum. Also houses **tourist police** (☎73 744) in basement. Open 24hr.

**Port Police:** (☎72 245), on waterfront 50m left of ferry quay on 2nd floor. Posts ferry and hydrofoil schedules. Open 24hr.

**First Aid Station:** (☎72 472). Open M-F 8:30am-1:30pm; 24hr. for emergencies. Call police for doctor.

**Pharmacy: Kapelaki** (☎72 256), in the plateia, behind the port police. Open M-Sa 8:30am-1:30pm and 5:30-9:30pm, Su 10am-1:30pm and 5:30-9:30pm.

**Telephone: OTE** (☎72 199), on the waterfront, right of the Star Hotel, National Bank, and ferry docks. Open M-F 7:30am-2pm.

**Internet Access: Delfinia Net-Cafe** (☎74 385), left of ferry docks, between a few tavernas. Minimum 750dr per 30min., 1500dr per hr.

**Post Office:** (☎72 228), left of the ferry dock on the road parallel to waterfront behind Stelios Restaurant. Open M-F 7:30am-2pm. **Postal Code:** 18050.

## ACCOMMODATIONS

Good rooms are extremely pricey on the weekends but cheap during the week. Prices vary wildly. Ask around and bargain by letting owners know if you've heard a better quote—they'll invariably beat it. If possible, shop in the evening. If you're short on drachmas, say so. Both **Alasia Travel** (☎75 170) and **Mimeza Travel** (☎75 270) own hotels in town; ask about their lower scale accommodations that run about 8000-10,000dr for a double.

**Hotel Faros** (☎72 613; fax 72 614), in the plateia behind the port police. Large, simple rooms with private baths, phones, and fridges in an airy building. Singles 8000; doubles 13,000dr; triples 16,000dr; quads 22,000dr.

**Hotel Klimis** (☎72 334), on the waterfront to the left of the ferry docks is well worth a splurge. Classy, shining rooms have A/C, TVs, and fridges; beautifully tiled bathrooms. Doubles 18,000dr.

**Pansion Brazos** (☎75 152), just inland of the ferry docks. Unimpressive but convenient, rooms have baths, fridges, fans, and balconies. Singles 6000dr; doubles 7000dr.

## FOOD AND NIGHTLIFE

Tavernas abound in this tiny town, but many are rather pricey. **Kritikos Supermarket,** on the waterfront, is inexpensive. (☎74 361. Open 8am-2pm and 5-9pm.)

**O Roussos,** on the left side of the waterfront, past Hotel Klimis. Specializes in octopus, which you'll see drying on the clothesline outside. Octopus dishes around 2000dr. Open 11am-late.

**Il Passante** (☎72 027), in the plateia behind the port police. Pizzas (1700-2700dr) cooked on a wood-fired stove offer a break from the usual; omelets and pastas are also available. Open 11am-midnight.

**George's Restaurant** (☎73 309), on Ag. Marina Beach, is hearty home cooking–perfect for after a long day at the beach. Entrees run about 2000dr, but ask about daily specials. Open 11am-late.

**Politis** (☎72 248), on the waterfront, just to the right of the ferry docks. Run by the same family for nearly 40 years, this cafe serves full English breakfasts, all manner of cocktails, and pastries (300-1400dr).

Sports fans gather for drinks at **Socrates** for happy hour. (Open 9:30pm-midnight; all cocktails 900dr.) Try the fresh fruit cocktails. A younger crowd heads to **Mama's,** on the way to the Old Harbour, for expensive, *chic* drinks. Trendy Athenians can be found in bars along the Old Harbor *(Paleo Limani)* like **Mouraio, Club Starentos,** or **Naos.** Most open by 10:30pm and close around 1 or 2am. **Figaro** night club (☎73 220), past the old harbor, spins pulsing international beats. Halfway between the old and new harbors, **Spetsa Bar and Cafe** plays a mix of 60s, 70s, 80s, and classic rock. (☎74 131. Open 8pm-late. Drinks 1000-2000.)

## SIGHTS AND BEACHES

**SPETSES MUSEUM.** Housed in the center of town in the crumbling, late-19th-century mansion owned by Hadjiyanni Mexi, Spetses's first governor, the museum has a great view of the island. The imposing building itself is worth seeing, with an old island fireplace, stained glass windows, and carved wooden doors. Its collection includes a casket of the remains of Laskarina Bouboulina (see below), coins, costumes, mastheads, folk art, and religious artifacts. *(Follow the signs. ☎72 994. Open Tu-Su 8:30am-2:30pm. 500dr, students 300dr, EU students free.)*

**HOUSE OF LASKARINA BOUBOULINA.** Mme. Bouboulina was a ship's captain in the Greek War of Independence. Her heroic exploits are celebrated on Spetses with a mock naval battle, in which a small boat is blown up on the first Saturday after September 8th. *(Next to the park near the Dapia. ☎72 416. Open for guided tour only; English tours run from 9:45am-8pm. 1000dr, children 300dr.)*

**MONASTERY OF AGIOS NIKOLAOS.** The monastery is opposite a square of traditional Spetsiot mosaics, above the old harbor. A memorial plaque commemorates Napoleon's nephew, who was pickled in a barrel of rum stored in a monastic cell at Agios Nikolaos from 1827-32. The nuns give free homemade yogurt samples. *(Dress modestly: long pants for men, long skirts for women, no bare shoulders.)*

**BEACHES.** Spetses's surprisingly warm beaches are invitingly shallow; they're a major draw to the island. Big sandy **Ag. Anargiri,** on the opposite side of the island from Spetses Town, is the leader of a pack of beaches boasting several tavernas and a host of watersports. (Paddleboats 3000dr per hr.; kayaks 2500dr per hr.; waterskiing 45,000dr per hr.; windsurfing 3500dr per hr.; parasailing 7000dr per person, 9000 per couple; tubing 2000dr per person.) Its companion, **Ag. Paraskevi,** about 1km to the right facing seaward, has the same blanket of pine trees and a sandy-pebbly surface without the accompanying hubbub of its mentor. On the Anargiri-Spetses Town bus route, midway between the two, is the utterly peaceful **Xylocheriza.** Pure white, smooth stones contrast with the still, brightly colored waters of the bay. Refresh yourself after a swim with a hunk of watermelon (700dr) big enough for two at the snack bar. Although most easily accessed by moped, the bus does pass by the dusty road to the beach (10-15min. on foot); check with the driver about return times before you hop off. Also accessible by bus (leaving from in front of the Poseidon Hotel) are the popular **Kakiri** or **College Beach,** and **Ligoneri** beach. College Beach, in front of Anargirios College, is home to a popular bar and tanned tourists. **Agia Marina** beach is about a 30min. walk over the island from the far left end of the waterfront in Spetses Town, taking a right at the kiosk. It offers a few watersports (waterskiing 5000dr per person; kayaks 2000dr per hr.; paddleboats 3000dr per hr.), a beach bar and a good taverna.

# THE SPORADES AND EVIA

Viewed from the chaos of modern Athens, the Sporades and Evia circle like a family of enchanted sea-maidens. The matriarch is Evia, Greece's largest island after Crete; the island stretches from hospitable Karystos through Athenian protégé Halkida and the Aedipsos thermal springs. The Northern Sporades are her three daughters: quietly sophisticated Skopelos is the eldest, home to moonlit, jazz-filled harbors and a population of artists. Skiathos is the middle child, in a hurry to grow up, with the best party scene for miles. Innocent Alonnisos, the youngest, is a pristine wilderness crossed by hiking trails; the headquarters of MOM (Greece's save-the-wildlife organization) is based there. Skyros, in the east, is the grandmother, the purple-hilled keeper of the old ways. Invading Cretans, 5th century BC Athenians, 2nd-century BC Romans, 13th-century AD Venetians, and present-day foreign package tourists have all basked in the Sporades' sun; Evia remains the territory of Greek party animals.

**HIGHLIGHTS OF THE SPORADES AND EVIA**

**BECOME ONE** with the white-sanded, pine-forested Biotrope on Skiathos (p. 304).

**SCRIBBLE A PICTURE** of a Mediterranean monk seal and help save the endangered species by hanging your drawing in the conservatory on Alonnisos (p. 310).

**PONDER POETRY** by former resident Rupert Brooke while you snooze among pirate spoils in Skyros Town (p. 313).

**IMAGINE ZEUS AND HERA** falling in love in the thin air of Evia's Mt. Ohi (p. 322).

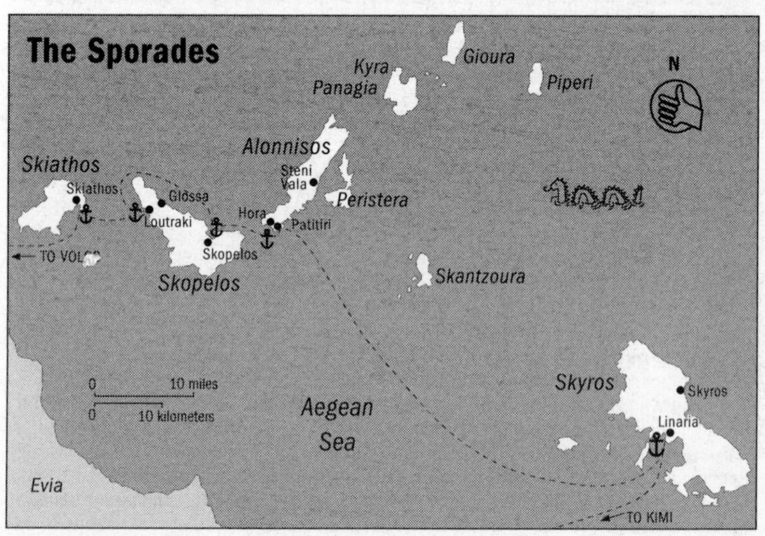

SPORADES

# SPORADES ΣΠΟΡΑΔΕΣ

## SKIATHOS ΣΚΙΑΘΟΣ

Welcome to the party hub of the Sporades. Tourism is a recent phenomenon here, as little Skiathos has grown up almost overnight into a glamorous dancing queen. If you're up for it, go with the flow, have fun, and hit the bars with the foreign tourists and their families. If you're looking to enjoy Skiathos's beauty on your own terms, sneak away to the otherworldly northern beaches between 6am and noon, while partiers sleep and the island's timeless beauty unfurls under the sun.

## SKIATHOS TOWN ☎0427

A touristy feeling pounces on you right away in Skiathos Town; if you survive the gauntlet of tacky tourist shops, dock hawks, and middle-aged visitors trying to blow big bucks, you'll be handsomely rewarded. Under its touristy exterior, Skiathos remains laid-back and lovely—a hidden trove of heavenly beaches, friendly natives, and delicious Dodoni ice cream (Δωδωνι, after the Oracle of Dodoni). The island remains one of the few places to purchase English translations of the works of 19th-century Skiathian monk and writer, Alexandros Papadiamantis (p. 27).

### GETTING THERE AND GETTING AROUND

**Ferries: Nomikos/Goutos Lines** (☎22 209 or 20 290), in the middle of the waterfront. Open 7am-9pm. Ferries run to: **Agios Konstantinos** (3½hr., 1-2 per day, 3300dr); **Alonnisos** (2hr., 2-3 per day, 1900dr); **Glossa** (½hr., 2-3 per day, 900dr); **Skopelos** (1½hr., 3-4 per day, 1400dr); and **Volos** (2½hr., 3 per day, 2700dr). To get to Skiathos from **Athens,** take the daily bus from the station at Liossion 260 to Ag. Konstantinos (2½hr., 16 per day, 2650dr), and then take the ferry.

**Flying Dolphins:** (☎22 018). To the left of the waterfront facing inland. Trips to: **Agios Konstantinos** (1¼hr., 3-4 per day, 6600dr); **Alonnisos** (1hr., 9 per day, 3800dr); **Glossa** (15min., 6 per day, 1800dr); **Skopelos** (35min., 6-9 per day, 2800dr); **Skyros** (2½hr., 1 per day, 8400dr); **Thessaloniki** (3¼hr., 6 per week, 8500dr); and **Volos** (1¼hr., 6 per week, 5500dr).

**Flights: Olympic Airways Office** (☎22 229 or 22 049), at the airport. Call 24hr. prior to takeoff to confirm flight. Open M-F 8am-4pm. Taxis from the harbor to the airport cost about 1000dr. Two flights per day (only one W) to **Athens** (50min., 16,800dr).

**Local buses:** The **bus stop** is at the far right end of the wharf, facing inland. The bus to **Koukounaries beach** (every 15min. 7am-1am, 320dr) makes stops along the main road. Heading out of Horio, sit on the driver's side for the best view. A schedule is posted at wharf bus stop and at Koukounaries.

**Taxis:** (☎24 461). Line up along the waterfront next to the Rooms to Let kiosk; prices are posted on the shack. Open 24hr.

**Moped Rental:** Rental shops litter the waterfront. Try **Alamo** (☎23 025), right along the harbor (3500-6000dr, including helmet and insurance).

### ORIENTATION AND PRACTICAL INFORMATION

The long waterfront, lined with travel agencies, tavernas, and bike and car rental dealers, is intersected by **Papadiamantis,** where the number of travel agencies is surpassed only by the vast number of high-class jewelry stores. Further inland, **Pandra** (at the National Bank) and **Evangelistra** (at the post office) intersect Papadiamantis. Parallel to Papadiamantis, beginning at Pandra, **Polytechniou** contains a string of bars. On the far right of the waterfront facing inland, a road winds from

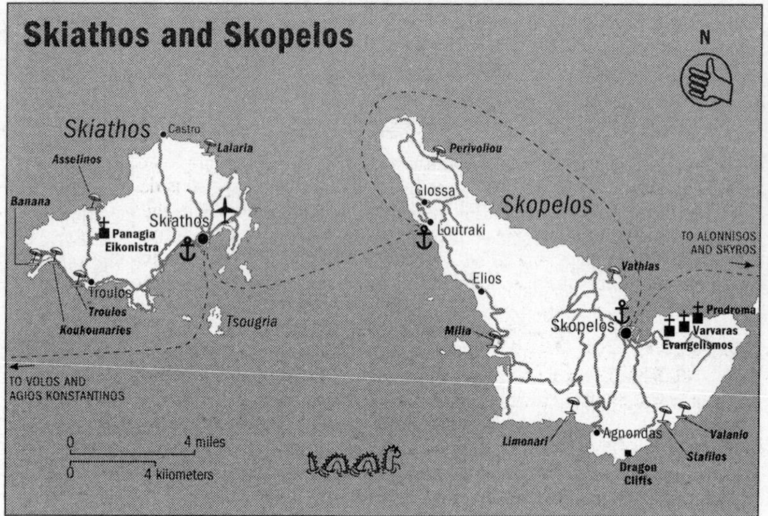


the bus stop up to the airport and several beaches. On the far left, along a harbor perpendicular to the main waterfront, is a row of fishing boats that charter daily excursions. The same mediocre **map** (500dr) is available everywhere. At the wooden kiosk in the harbor, tickets to a **boat** around the island cost 3000-5000dr.

**Tourist Police:** (☎23 392). A small white building on the right side of Papadiamantis, where the road forks around an electronic info kiosk. Not too helpful. Open 8am-9pm.

**Police:** (☎22 111), upstairs past the kiosk where Papadiamantis forks left. Open 24hr.

**Banks: National Bank** (☎22 400), midway up Papadiamantis on the left side. Offers **currency exchange** and an **ATM.** Open M-Th 8am-2pm, F 8am-1:30pm.

**American Express:** Papadiamantis 21 (☎21 463), on the left before the post office, in the Mare Nostrum Holidays agency. Tourist services. Open May-Oct. 9am-2pm, 5-9pm.

**Laundromat: Miele Laundry,** about 200m up Papadiamantis on a side street across from the National Bank. The owner is in the grocery store across the street, and sells tokens and detergent. 1800dr per load, 2000dr with their soap. Open 8am-11pm.

**Hospital:** (☎22 040), on the "Acropolis" hill behind Skiathos Town. Open 24hr., but **emergencies** only after 1pm (go figure).

**Internet Access: Skiathos Internet Center** is 1½ blocks down Miaouli (an alley cutting right off Papadiamantis opposite the Kodak camera shop). 1000dr per hr.

**Telephones: OTE** (☎22 399), on Papadiamantis, one block from the post office. Open M-F 7:30am-10pm; in winter M-F 7:30am-3pm.

**Post Office:** (☎22 011), at the intersection of Papadiamantis and Evangelistra. Open M-F 7:30am-2pm. **Postal code:** 37002.

## ACCOMMODATIONS

Most tourists make prior reservations for July and August, and tour groups often book most of the summer hotel rooms a year in advance. A burgeoning tourist industry means more and more local opportunists hawking their domatia at port-side. Be sure to **bargain.** Typical rooms run 6000-8000dr in winter, 8000-10,000dr in spring and fall, and 10,000-14,000dr in summer. Try **Evangelistra** and the streets parallel to it for domatia, or try the tourist police or **Rooms to Let** office in the port's wooden kiosk. (☎22 990 or 24 260. Open 8:30am-midnight.)

**Pension Danaos** (☎22 834), in an alley off Papadiamantis opposite the OTE. Attracts a crowd of young sunbathers/backpackers with amenities that cater to them: private baths, a communal rooftop terrace, tacky decorations, fridges and TVs in some rooms. Open May 1-Sept. 30. Singles 10,000dr; doubles 8000-15,000dr.

**Australia Hotel** (☎22 488), just left off Evangelistra, is not the brightest place around, but it's convenient, and the simple rooms with baths and small kitchens are cheap for 4 people. Doubles 8500-15,000dr; triples 12,000-18,000dr.

**Pension Nikolas** (☎23 062 May-Sept., ☎32 756 Oct.-Apr.), just off Polytechniou to the left past Kirki bar. A central location helps, as do the private baths and fridges. Some rooms with A/C. English spoken. Singles 6000-14,000dr; doubles 8000-16,000dr.

**Camping Koukounaries** (☎49 250), on the bus route to Koukouniares, ask the driver to let you off there. Has restaurant, mini-market, and campground 1km from the beach. 1800dr per person; 1000dr per tent; 750dr per car.

## FOOD

Meals in Skiathos fall conveniently into two categories: glamorous and functional. Foreign wads of cash pay for the ritzy food, which can be worth the splurge. Back-alley souvlaki stands and tiny tavernas off the main strip feed locals and broke backpackers. Cheap Greek food stands pack **Papadiamantis.**

**Chris, Jan & Deborah's Daskalio Pub** (☎(0941) 70 903), follow Papadiamantis to the kiosk and head right. Look for a brightly painted, triangular white building on the right. Come for the tasty curries (2500-4000dr) or "sponge of the day" (1500dr) and stay for the welcoming English pub crowd and funky decor. Pop music quizzes Tu, Th, and Sa at 11pm. Bar open 7pm-3am, food until 11pm. Open May-Sept.

**Tavern Alexandros,** on Kabadistrion, half-hidden in the alleys behind the Polytechniou bar strip; follow the signs. A loud, jovial crowd dances to live music between courses of Greek food on weekends. Entrees 1700-3000dr. Opens at 8 or 9pm.

**Mediterraneo** (☎23 860) along the waterfront is worth a splurge, if only to watch the moon from the elegant rooftop garden (entrees 1700-3000dr, veggie options available). Open 7pm-late.

## NIGHTLIFE

Indulge yourself at the innumerable bars in **Pl. Papadiamantis,** on **Polytechniou,** or on **Evangelistra.** Beware—island novelists have a tradition of writing from real life, and you may be immortalized as a minor character by a latter-day Papadiamantis. Expect to pay 600-1000dr for beer, 1500dr for cocktails, and 1000-2000dr cover on very popular Saturday nights. From Oct.-May, it's a ghost town; in July, it hops.

**Admiral Beubow,** on Polytechniou. A cozy place to begin (or end) the night, with plenty of comfy couches, a talkative crowd, a decor borrowed from *The Blues Brothers*, and a 600dr-per-pint Happy Hour (9pm-3am) most weekends.

**Kentavros** (☎22 980), off Pl. Papadiamantis, past the museum. Skiathos's oldest–and most popular–bar is decorated with a poster from *Casablanca.* 700dr beers, 1500dr cocktails, and everything from rock to jazz carry the night.

**Banana Bar** (☎21 232), on Polytechniou, a small street parallel to Papadiamantis; take Evangelista, then veer right. The largest TV in town entertains a rowdy tourist crowd. Beer 700-1200dr, cocktails 1500-2000. Open 9:30pm-4am.

**Blue Chips Bar** (☎21 935). Decor like the *Blue Lagoon* on ice. Chilly local crowd to match. Cover 1500dr, beer 1000dr, cocktails 1500-2000dr.

**Scorpion Club,** off Papadiamantis; follow the signs. Look for the building with thick, port-holed wooden doors. Bathed in an eerie green glow, this techno club's dance floor writhes with bodies. Drinks 1500-2000dr. Don't show until after 1am.

For more sedate entertainment, the open-air **Cinema Paradiso** screens recent Hollywood hits in English with Greek subtitles. Ask the American Express office (☎21 463) for July and August schedules. (☎23 975. 2000dr. Shows 9pm.) Concerts play at the **Bourtzi,** the small peninsula jutting out next to the Flying Dolphin dock.

### SIGHTS AND BEACHES

Author Alexandros Papadiamantis's 140-year-old house, set back off Pl. Papadiamantis about 1½ blocks inland, now serves as the **Papadiamantis Museum,** housing his few possessions. The museum honors the 19th-century realist who was one of Greece's best-loved prose writers. Info and short stories are available in English. (Open Tu-Su 9:30am-1pm and 5-8pm. 250dr.)

The island's main paved road runs along the south coast from Skiathos Town to the white-sanded, piney **Biotrope of Koukounaries.** Take the green buses from Skiathos Town's port to get there (3 per hr. 7:15am-1am, 320dr). The bus also stops at popular beaches along the route: **Megali Ammos** (stop 5), **Nostos** (stop 12), **Vromolimnos** (stop 13), **Kolios** (stop 14a), and **Troulos** (stop 18). Appropriately curved and yellow **Banana Beach** is a short walk from Koukounaries; follow the dirt road over the hill to the right, facing seaward. Once there, climb over the rocky jetty to the right to **Little Banana Beach**—drop your pants on the way. To reach quieter **Mandraki,** walk to the beach from stop 21. Magical **Lalaria,** a long stretch of white sand, blue water, and sea caves, is accessible only by boat; call the AmEx office (☎21 463) or any other waterfront tourist office about **boat excursions** (3000-6000dr per person).

Just east of Troulos, at bus stop 18, a road turns off for **Asselinos,** a beach on Skiathos's north edge. For a calmer afternoon, take the high road that forks after 2km—the right branch leads uphill to **Panagia Eikonistra** (The Blessed Icon Painter, or Panagia Kounistra), 8km from Skiathos Town. A small monastery with a grape arbor and taverna inside its walls, it's the most important surviving monastery on the island. A miracle-working icon is celebrated island-wide in the November 21 **festival** of the Presentation of the Virgin. Far on the northern coast stand the ruins of a medieval walled **castle** built in the 16th century as a refuge from marauding pirates. With independence in the 19th century, the castle's occupants moved to Skiathos Town. Only two of the town's original 30 churches remain—the **Church of the Nativity** has fine icons and frescoes, and a 17th-century *iconostasis.*

# SKOPELOS ΣΚΟΠΕΛΟΣ

Relaxed Skopelos sits between the whirlwind of Skiathos and the largely untouched wilderness of Alonnisos. It marks time from Ground Zero—the 1538 extermination of all the island's inhabitants by the pirate Barbaros. Still, the red-tiled roofs and tall white houses have grown back strong. By day, the pious head to the hills, where the island's monasteries and shrines hide in woods still heady with the fading sounds of *rembetika.* By night, the streets of Skopelos Town are filled with murmuring voices, and light drips down from cafes and onto the Aegean.

## SKOPELOS TOWN ☎0424

Past the *patisseries* of the waterfront, Skopelos Town becomes a 3-D chess match: you'll find castles and bishops peering sternly around whitewashed corners, while nights, dark and musical, sneak up on afternoons. On the left side of town (facing seaward), a seaside path ascends in whitewashed steps to the Castro.

### GETTING THERE AND GETTING AROUND

Boats dock at the concrete jetty on the left tip of the harbor, facing seaward. Buses and taxis leave from the right edge of town.

**Ferries: Nomicos/Goutos Lines** (☎22 363 or 22 055) runs to: **Agios Konstantinos** (4hr., 2 per day, 4100dr); **Alonnisos** (30min., 2 per day, 1100dr); **Skiathos** (1hr., 4-5 per day, 1400dr); and **Volos** (4hr., 3 per day, 3400dr).

**Flying Dolphins:** Tickets sold at the Flying Dolphin office right in front of the port (mobile (0222) 22 363 or (0424) 23 884). To: **Aedipsos** (45min., 2 per week, 6900dr); **Agios**

**Konstantinos** (2½hr., 3 per day, 8200dr); **Alonnisos** (15min., 9 per day, 2200dr); **Limni** (1hr., 2 per week, 8300dr); **Skiathos** (45min., 11 per day, 2800dr); **Thessaloniki** (4hr., 6 per week, 9300dr); **Trikeri** (1½hr., 1 per day, 4600dr); and **Volos** (2hr., 4 per day, 6800dr).

**Buses:** The stop is left of the waterfront facing inland. Bus lines run approximately 6 times per day to Stafilos and Agnondas; Panormos and Milia; and Elios, Glossa, and Loutraki. In summer, the Glossa-Skopelos Town bus stops at most beaches; ask the driver to let you off. Check the posted schedules at the stop or call **Thalpos Travel Agency** (☎22 907).

**Taxis:** (☎22 422 or mobile (094) 744 526). Available at the waterfront 7am-2am.

**Moped and Car Rental:** Shop around–most travel agencies arrange rentals. Mopeds 3500dr, cars 12,000dr. Prices vary by season, amenities, sound effects, and distance.

## ORIENTATION AND PRACTICAL INFORMATION

Tourist agencies, tavernas, and cafes line the waterfront. **Galatsaniou,** a fashionable street rich with trinkets and goodies, darts upward between restaurants, just before Cafe Armeon, at the center of the harbor. A chain of churches climbs the rocks to the left. **Platanos,** a shady plateia, is inland from the bus stop.

**Tourist Agencies:** Most **exchange currency,** rent mopeds and cars, sell ferry tickets, and run trips to nearby islands. **Thalpos Travel Agency** (☎22 947 or 23 466), on the 2nd floor behind Aktaion Cafe, can tip you off about everything from Dolphin tickets to catching octopi. English spoken. Open May-Oct. 10am-9pm; fax or telephone Oct.-May.

**Banks: National Bank** (☎22 691), on the right side of the waterfront, has a 24hr. **ATM.** Open M-Sa 8am-2pm.

**Emergency:** For police dial 100. For medical care, dial 22 222.

**Police:** (☎22 295), behind the National Bank.

**Medical Center:** (☎22 222). Follow the left-hand road inland from Pl. Platanos past Ag. Ioannis to the dead end, then go right at the signs. Open M-F 9am-2pm for free walk-ins; open M-F 24hr. for **emergencies.**

**Telephones: OTE** (☎22 399), 100m up from the water on Galatsaniou. Open M-Sa 7:30am-10pm, Su 9am-2pm and 5-10pm; in winter M-F 7:30am-3:10pm.

**Internet access: Cafe Armeon** (☎23 093). The first alley on the right off Galatsaniou. 1500dr per hour. Open 9am-1pm.

**Post Office:** (☎22 203). Follow the waterfront toward the bus stop, past the memorial, and look for the office in a plateia to your left. **Postal code:** 37003.

## ACCOMMODATIONS AND FOOD

In general, Skopelos's hotels shelter all-inclusive-resort tourists. Don't worry: the **Rooms and Apartments Association of Skopelos,** in the small stone building next to the town hall on the waterfront, can help you find a bed. (☎24 567. Open 10am-2pm, 6-10pm.) Prices vary by season, but are generally 5000-10,000dr for singles and 6000-12,000dr for doubles. **Pension Sotos,** 10m to the left of Thalpos Travel, is a gem, both for its setting and its diamond-in-the-rough price. A renovated Skopelian house, the pension provides baths and fans, and a common kitchen, fridge, quiet courtyard, and book exchange. (☎22 549; fax 23 668. Doubles 6500-12,000dr; triples 9000-16,000dr.) Dock hawks may also offer reasonable rooms.

Endless 350dr gyros and 600dr pizzas fill **Pl. Platanos.** If you want something less like a grease bomb, try **Greca's Creperie,** 20m right of the Folk Art Museum. A Parisian artist, Greca came to Skopelos decades ago on a UNESCO project to help children. Now she offers homemade crepes (600-2000dr) beside her internationally recognized prints. (Open 10am-3pm and 7pm-12:30am.) **Zorba's Taverna** may not have much style, but it does have healthy portions (entrees 1500-1800dr) and an uninterrupted view of the sea. From the Internet cafe, take the path left uphill to the paved road past the supermarket.

## ENTERTAINMENT AND NIGHTLIFE

A 10-minute stroll up the whitewashed steps at the far right of the harbor, facing inland, will bring you to **Anatoli,** the haunt of one of the world's last great *rembetika* singers, Giorgos Xintaris. Some nights (usually a little before midnight), you may be lucky enough to catch him with a group of friends singing the old songs. For new jazz and blues, **Platanos Jazz Club,** on the far right of the harbor facing inland, near the pier, lets you relax with a drink by candlelight under a gargantuan tree. (Beer 800-1000dr, cocktails 1600dr. Open 8am-3pm.) Skopelos's dance clubs cluster midway up a street off of Pl. Platanos: facing inland; it's the farthest ahead to the left. The talkative bartender at **Metro** will tell you about the island; you might also meet American painting students. Greek music plays. (☎24 446. Cover 1000dr. Beer 1000dr, cocktails 1800-2000dr. Open daily May-Oct., weekends Oct.-May.) **Kavnos** (☎24 300) is Skopelos's oldest bar—7 years and counting—and 1000dr beer and 1500-2000dr cocktails keep the crowd coming. Top-40, rock, and foreign music shakes the speakers (1000dr cover includes a drink).

## SIGHTS

Skopelos Town has an overabundance of churches. Ask for directions to **Panagia Papameletion,** a winding 10-minute walk inland; it dates from the 1660s. The four columns supporting the dome were "borrowed" from other Byzantine churches, which accounts for their differences in color and size. Just shoreward of the OTE, the meticulously maintained **Basilica of Agios Nikolaos** decorates its cielings with brightly colored icons and a marble statue of Mary. Up past Papameletion, Agios Spiridonas looks out over the whole bay; in 1821, locals and mainland revolutionaries debated Greece's fate here. The road up to **Castro** on the far right, facing inland, leads past seaside **Panagia Ston Pirgho** (the Virgin on the Rocks), built in the shape of a cross and dating from the Occupation. The road continues past the Armenian-influenced **Evangelismos** and the 11th-century **Agios Athanasias.**

Skopelos draws international students and recognition for its **Photographic Center of Skopelos** (☎24 121); call for more info. The **Folk Art Museum,** 200m left past the OTE, has a small and unexciting collection of island artifacts, but the meticulously researched first-floor exhibit on popular religion is worth a trip. (☎23 494. Open 11am-4pm and 6-10pm. 500dr, 18 and under free.)

## BEACHES

Traveling Skopelos's asphalt road by bus or car to Loutraki or Glossa gives you your pick of the lovely southern beaches. Archaeologists discovered the tomb of the ancient Cretan general **Stafylos** on a nearby hillside, along with a 15th-century BC gold-plated sword that's now in the Volos museum (XXX). Stafylos beach is crowded with families; nearby **Valanio,** over the hill to the left, is less full. Named for the trickling spring that was a gushing fountain in Roman times, today Valanio is advertised as the only nude beach on Skopelos. Past the small town of **Agnondas,** a dirt track cuts left to the bright blue beach of **Limonari;** if you'd rather not walk, take a water taxi. Further along the asphalt road is the wide, deep bay of **Panormos,** the ancient forest. From here, a 5min. walk leads to the isolated **Adrina** beaches, named for the female pirate who terrorized the islands, leaping to her death in this cove when cornered by angry islanders. **Milli,** accessible by paved road, has watersports and its own little islet called **Dassia.** Closer to Loutraki, dirt paths lead to the northern beaches of **Spilia, Marraki, Keramoto,** and **Chondroyiorghi.**

## HIKES FROM SKOPELOS TOWN

Due to Skopelos's predominantly dirt roads, the island is best explored by moped or on foot. The island's single, 35km-long asphalt road runs from the Skopelos bus station through Stafylos (4km), Agnondas (8km), Panormos (18km), Elios (24km), Loutraki (30km), and Glossa (32km).

**DRAGON CLIFFS.** According to local lore, a fierce dragon went on a flaming bender and ate almost everyone on Skopelos, until Ag. Rigine appeared on the scene and killed the dragon, thus becoming the island's protector. The Dragon Cliffs *(Drakondoschisma)*, where the creature was hurled to its death, are now a quiet picnicking spot with a sea view and an altar portraying the dragon's grisly demise. To find it, take the asphalt road from Skopelos Town, and turn left down a small dirt road disappearing into the woods about 1km before Agnodas beach.

**MONASTERIES OF MT. PALOUKI.** Two paved roads leave the town from the bus depot on the right end of the waterfront. To reach the monasteries, follow the left road, which circles the harbor and ascends Mt. Palouki. **Evangelismos** hails from the 18th century as part of the Monastery of Xiropotamos of Athos, but its enormous altar screen—the genuine article from Constantinople—is 400 years older. Take the left-hand fork up the hot, winding mountain road for 45min.; start early in the morning before the heat and bugs intensify, and in time to reach the monasteries before their 1-5pm daily closing. Up the right fork, another 45min. leads you to the **Monastery of the Transfiguration.** Its chapel, set in a flowered courtyard, dates from the 16th century. Another hour up the hill along the road takes you to two monasteries perched on precipitous ridges overlooking the sea. The first, the **Monastery of St. Barbara,** was built as a fortress in 1648. Nearby **Prodromou** contains icons dating back to the 14th and 15th centuries, and wall paintings. Once a monastery, Prodromou is now a cloister dedicated to St. John the Baptist; its astounding view surveys the entire coast. The small dirt path that begins behind the building snakes toward the smaller monasteries of **Agia Triada** and **Agia Taxianches.**

**MONASTERIES OF AGIOS IOANNIS.** At the end of the road, the quiet hilltop town of **Glossa** looks down on Skopelos's second port. For a four-hour round-trip hike from Glossa, walk the dirt track across the island to the **Monastery of Agios Ioannis,** clinging to a boulder above the ocean. Take the main road east from Glossa and turn left on the first dirt road to Steki Taverna; it's clear sailing after that. At the road's end, a path drops to the sea, and stone steps, cut in the escarpment, lead up to the monastery. The entire road is navigable by motorbike, up to the stairs. Another hike takes you to the eastern side of Skopelos, to the beautiful, secluded monastery of **Agia Anna.** Leave Skopelos Town and head toward Mt. Palouki on the road past Moni Vararas and Ag. Triada. The road ends soon after—watch for the old sign pointing the way to the church.

# ALONNISOS ΑΛΟΝΝΗΣΟΣ

Of the twenty-odd islands within Greece's new National Marine Park, only Alonnisos is inhabited. The fledgling tourist industry remains friendly to visitors who come to explore its sudden blues and wide open spaces. The untouched northern coast, with its cliffs awash in green pine and white-sanded boundary with the sea, draws hikers to its highland trails. Archaeological discoveries attest to the island's ancient prosperity, but it's hard to see past the influence of its tumultuous experience after the Second World War. In 1950, a crop disease annihilated its once-lucrative vineyards, forcing most of the island's men into construction work in Athens. A 1965 earthquake destroyed the Old Town; now, a government-directed housing project has turned Patitiri into the island's new center.

## PATITIRI Πατητηρι ☎0424

All boats dock at Patitiri, which is for all intents and purposes the only town on the island. Above, the whitewashed Old Town clings to the slopes of the hill. Sharp-angled and hastily built, it's not a postcard harbor, but it does serve as an easily accessible base to explore the rest of Alonnisos and the surrounding Marine Park.

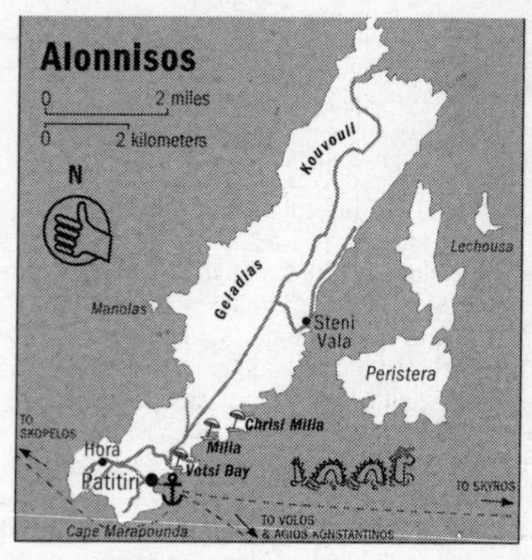


**ORIENTATION AND PRACTICAL INFORMATION.** From the docks, two main parallel streets run inland: **Pelasgon** on the left, and **Ikion Dolophon** on the right. **Ferries** run to: **Agios Konstantinos** (5½hr., 8-9 per week, 4400dr); **Skiathos** (2hr., 1-3 per day, 1800dr); **Skopelos** (30min., 1-2 per day, 1100dr); and **Volos** (5¼hr., 1-2 per day, 3750dr). **Flying Dolphins** go to: **Agios Konstantinos** (2¾hr., 2-3 per day, 8800dr); **Glossa** (35min., 4-5 per day, 3000dr); **Skyros** (1 per day, 8000dr); **Skopelos** (15min., 6-9 per day, 2200dr); **Skiathos** (1¼hr., 6-9 per day, 3600dr); **Thessaloniki** (4hr., 2 per week, 11,500dr); and **Volos** (2½hr., 5-6 per day, 7500dr). **Taxis,** right of the travel agencies, run until 2am; they respond to calls any time (taxi phone numbers are posted on phone booths). **Motorbikes** are available to rent at one of the numerous shops at the top of Ikion Dolophon. Expect to pay 3000-7000dr.

**Alonnisos Travel,** in the center of the waterfront, **exchanges currency,** finds rooms, books excursions, and sells ferry tickets. (☎/fax 65 511. Open 9am-10:30pm.) To the right, Pakis and friends at **Ikos Travel** offer similar services, plus ecological excursions, Flying Dolphin ticketing, and a book exchange. (☎65 320; fax 65 321. Open 6:15-7:15am, 9am-2:30pm, 3-10pm.) Up Ikion Dolophon, the **Port Police** are on the corner. (☎65 595. Open 24hr.) The **National Bank** with 24hr. **ATM** lies on the left. (☎65 777. Open M-Th 8am-2pm, F 8am-1:30pm.) The **police** (☎65 205) are on the top of the hill, near the **hospital.** (☎65 208. Open 9am-1pm, 24hr. for emergency.) **Internet access** is available at **Blue Point** on Ikion Dolophon, on the right just before the post office. (Open 9am-midnight. 1500dr per hr.) The **post office** is a 10-min. walk inland on the right. (☎65 560. Open M-F 7:30am-2pm.) **Postal code:** 37005.

**ACCOMMODATIONS.** The **Rooms to Let Office** next to Ikos Travel can lend a hand to travelers looking for a place to stay. (☎66 188. Open May-Oct. 9am-4pm.) **Panorama,** down the first alley on the left from Ikion Dolophon, rents bright rooms and studios with private baths, common fridges, and large, bougainvillea-covered common balconies with a port view. (☎65 240. Doubles 6000-10,000dr.) Inquire at Boutique Mary, on the right side of Pelasgon, for simple rooms with private baths at the **Dimakis Pension** next door. (☎65 294. Singles 5000-7000dr; doubles 6000-8000dr.) **Pension Dinas,** in a trellised courtyard set back from Pelasgon (across from The Sweet Devil), has spacious, airy rooms with full kitchen and big bath (☎65 266. Doubles 7000-10,000dr; triples 10-15,000dr.) Magdalini and Ilias Mpesinis rent immaculate **Rooms and Studios** with private baths, kitchens, and fridges. A gorgeous stone staircase and hand-painted decor adds to the atmosphere; it's worth the splurge. (☎/fax 65 451 or 65 972. Doubles 10,000-12,000dr; triples 12,000-15,000dr. Also has book exchange.)

**FOOD AND NIGHTLIFE.** Locals adore the little *ouzeri* **To Kamaki,** on the left side of Ikion Dolophon past the National Bank. Try the delectable warm octopus salad (1700dr). (Open noon-2:30pm, 7pm-late.) **Artolikoudies,** marked by the yellow sign inland on Pelasgon, serves delicious summer olive bread (400dr) and traditional pastries (250-400dr). **Pub Nefeli** (☎66 055), up at Cavos, the left end of the harbor facing the water, has a relaxed aura and full moon parties. Listen to Sting while you sip a cocktail (1800dr) under a gnarled tree and a grape-draped terrace at waterfront **Pub Dennis,** the island's oldest cafe-bar. **Club Enigma,** a bright blue building on Pelasgon, is *the* place to boogie (open June-Sept. W-Sa).

## HORA (OLD TOWN) Χωρα ☎0424

*The island's only bus runs from Patitiri to Hora (10min., every hr. 9am-3pm and 7-10pm, 300dr). Schedules are posted at the bus stop in both towns. Taxis are available (about 2000dr round-trip). A parching walk opens a glorious view—start uphill on Pelasgon and continue on the main road for 1½hr. Bring water. Lots of water.*

Set high on a hill to ward off pirates, Hora sprawls stony and proud, its crooked streets twisting into the dusty hills. The quiet old alleys open on incredible views of the island. From here, you can spy out your own private beach and head down toward it. Tiny 12th century **Christ Church** is run by Papa Gregorias, the village priest and local legend. Many great hikes in Alonnisos begin in Hora; you might want to stay in the Old Town instead of Patitiri proper. **Hiliadroma,** up behind the church, has brand-new rooms with private baths and unsurpassed views. Some rooms have kitchenettes. (☎65 814 or 65 469. Doubles 8000-10,000dr; triples 9000-12,000dr.) A typical bunch of cafes and tavernas sate your hiker's hunger.

**HIKES AND BEACHES AROUND HORA.** Only the south end of the island is inhabited, leaving stretches of mountain wilderness. Though a **moped** remains the quickest way to explore—Patitiri to Gerakas takes about two hours—it's worth **hiking.** Trails are marked at regular intervals, and are fairly well-established, but you may still want to pick up *Alonnisos on Foot*, a walking and swimming guide available at **Alonnisos Travel** (2800dr). A multitude of trails leads down the mountainside from the Old Town to pebbly, cliff-protected beaches. Among them, **Megalos Martias** is the largest and most established; nearby **Mikros Martias** is a contender for Ideal Greek Beach, with its rocks perfectly molded for semi-nude sunbathing sitting in the crystal water.

The road north from Patitiri, paved at first, cuts lengthwise across the island to the northern harbor of Fyrakos. A 90-minute walk on this road from Patitiri takes you to **Votsi,** the island's other significant settlement. Local boys cliff-dive at Votsi beach just outside the village (all their friends are doing it). Continuing north and downhill, pick from among the sandy, pine-girded beaches of **Platsouka, Vrissita, Milia,** and **Chrysi Milia,** where you can walk out 300m into the clear water. The beaches are also accessible by **rented boat** from Votsi; ask at the port. A 50-minute stroll from Patitiri brings you to the Byzantine monastery of **Agiri Anargyroi,** or you can head north to **Kokkinocastro,** where swimmers occasionally find ancient coins. The teeny fishing village of **Steni Vala,** 12km north of Palitini, with a population fluctuating between 25 and 60, is the only other bus stop (20min., 2 per day, 400dr)—the fantastic fish tavernas alone are worth the trip. Sandy **Glyla** beach is along the shore to the left of the village.

## NATIONAL MARINE PARK

*The park islands are accessible by specially licensed boat. Most trips, advertised and sold along the Patitiri harborfront, are all-inclusive single-day trips for 10,000-12,000dr. MOM's HQ is open May-Oct., 9am-3pm, 6pm-midnight.*

Surrounding Alonnisos are the 25 small, ecologically protected islets of Greece's National Marine Park. The largest and most important are Peristera, Skantzoura, Piperi, Kyra Panagia, Jura, and Psatnoura. They're strictly regulated and visited only by organized tour boats in summer. Psatnoura, Kyra Panagia, and Skantzoura are owned by nearby Mt. Athos (see p. 244) and are used in part for grazing goats. Visiting Jura and Piperi is forbidden in an effort to protect species once described by Homer, including the **Mediterranean monk seal.** The monk seals number only 800 total in the Mediterranean; a growing colony of 60-75 monk seals is now carefully monitored by MOM, an Alonnisos-based sea patrol unit named for the Latin name of the seals, *monachus monachus*. Unless you're a MOM official, forget about seeing the monk seals. Enthusiasts ***are*** free to draw a **"Save the Seals"** poster for the gallery in MOM's Alonnisos ferry dock headquarters. They provide the crayons, paper, and information in English about ecology and conservation efforts.

Besides their importance to living animals, the islands have a place in history. A shipwreck found off Peristera significantly changed archaeologists' understanding of ancient shipping, and **Polyphemus,** the Cyclops blinded by Odysseus's sizzling-hot pike, is said to have lived in a cave on Gioura. Though many islands claim this distinction, Gioura best fits Homer's description of Polyphemus's cavern and of the now-endangered brown goats with black crosses on their backs that inhabit it.

# SKYROS ΣΚΥΡΟΣ

From the sea, Skyros's cliffs and ripply hills spread out in greens and yellows under an infinitely blue sky. The hilly terrain once fortified the island against marauding pirates and is now trying to fight off modern culture. Skyros Town—its capital—and the island's northern and southern wilds remain traditional and separate, the last stand of ghosts, poets, and pirate kings.

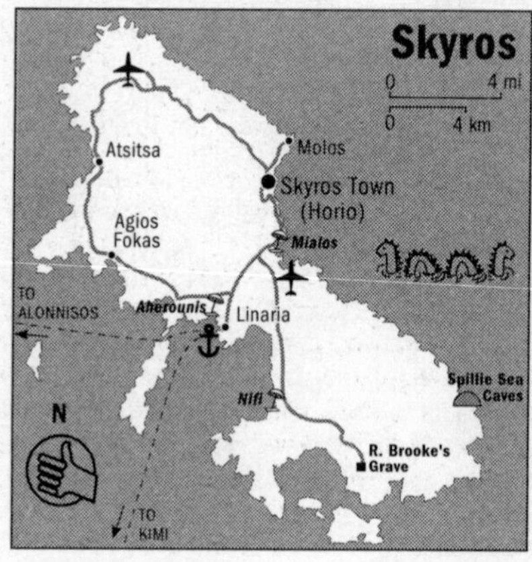


## SKYROS TOWN (HORIO) ☎0222

Stark-white, cubist Skyros Town huddles in the greening and fertile shadow of Ag. George. Within the last generation, the town's population has fallen from over 5000 to around 2000, as young people move away for better work or good schools for their children. In their place, outsiders are slowly discovering the town, to the surprise of longtime residents who follow traditional folkways: old men sew sandals by porchlight late into the evening, women embroider patterns learned from pirates, and a crazed goat-man spooks the streets at Carnival. Mazed and haunted, cobbled and china-plated, the town is a swiftly closing window to a strange dream.

### ORIENTATION AND PRACTICAL INFORMATION

The best way to get to Skyros is to take the **bus** from **Athens** to **Kimi** on Evia (3½hr., 2 per day, 2600dr), then the **ferry** to Skyros from Kimi (2 per day, 2300dr). No ferries run to the other Sporades. **Flying Dolphins** travel twice per day along two routes: **Alonnisos** (1¼hr., 8000dr), **Skopelos** (1¾hr., 8000dr), **Skiathos** (2¼hr., 8400dr), **Moudania,** and **Thessaloniki** (13,400dr); and **Alonnisos** (1¼hr., 8000dr), **Skopelos** (1¾hr., 8000dr), **Skiathos** (2¼hr., 8400dr), and **Volos** (4½hr., 14,100dr). Boats to Skyros arrive in **Linaria,** the tiny western port; a **local bus** to Skyros Town picks up when ferries and hydrofoils arrive (20min., 4 per day, 250dr); another bus runs from Skyros Town to **Molos** (10min., 4 per week, 270dr). Skyros Travel posts schedules. Tell the driver where you're going before you stash your bags below the bus, since each compartment corresponds to a certain location. Buses stop in Skyros Town (Horio—the Village—to locals) at the base of **Agoras,** the town's backbone road. The **military airport** (☎91 625), 20km from Skyros Town on the island's northern tip, flies to Athens (35min., 2 per week, 14,300dr); you'll have to take a cab there (2500dr). **Taxis** (☎91 666) wait by the central plateia or the bus stop; they aren't available late at night or during siesta hours. **Theseus Rent a Car** (☎93 099), 250m up from the bus stop, rents mopeds (3500dr) and cars (13,000-15,000dr).

Shops, pharmacies, bars, and restaurants ascend the hill along **Agoras.** Mazelike residential streets spider out in every direction along the hillsides. Buildings are

numbered counter-intuitively, and few streets are named; when venturing off Agoras, pick out landmarks on your way. At the far end of town, **Pl. Robert Brooke,** looking out across Molos and the sea, is dedicated to British poet Brooke and to "immortal poetry" (Αθανατι την ποησι). To reach Pl. Brooke, walk up Agoras through town until it forks at Calypso Bar and a kiosk. Head left along the wall, and walk up until you reach a sign pointing to "Brooke & museums" (right) and Γιαλος (beach, left). Veer right and follow the road to the plateia. The stairs to the right go past the **archaeological museum** on a 15-minute descent to the beach; stairs straight ahead and farther down lead to the **Faltaits Museum.**

**Skyros Travel,** past the central plateia on Agoras, sells **Flying Dolphins** and **Olympic Airways** tickets; it's also a de facto tourist office, organizing bus and boat excursions and helping visitors find lodging. (☎91 123 or 91 600. Open 9:15am-2pm, 7-10pm.) The port office in Linaria opens according to ferry and hydrofoil arrivals. **Skyros Nauftika Etairia** (☎91 790), midway up Agoras on the right just before Skyros Travel, arranges ferry tickets to and from Kimi. The **National Bank,** just past the central plateia, has a 24hr. **ATM** (open M-Th 8am-2pm and F 8am-1:30pm). The **hospital** (☎9222) is just out of town behind the Hotel Nefeli. Ask at the **police** station for doctors in town; turn right just past Skyros Travel, walk to the end of the road, and take another right. It's the white building with light blue gates. (☎91 274. Open 24hr., but small staff may be away on another call.) There are **pharmacies** on the right near the central plateia (☎91 617; open 8:30am-1pm and 6:30-10pm) and on the right past Skyros Travel (☎91 111 or 91 800; open 9am-2pm and 6pm-1am). **Internet access** is available at **Mepon Cafe** on Agoras across from Skyros Nauftika Etairia. (☎91 016. 3000 per hr., 1000dr for 20min.) The **OTE** is opposite the police. (☎91 399. Open M-F 7:30am-2pm.) For the **post office,** take the first right as you walk from the bus stop to the central plateia. There you can **exchange currency** and cash traveler's checks. (☎91 208. Open M-F 7:30am-2pm.) **Postal code:** 34007.

## ACCOMMODATIONS

Coming to Skyros and staying in a hotel is like coming to Greece to paddle in a pool—you've got to stay in a Skyrian house. You'll be met at the bus stop by old women offering domatia; you can also wander the narrow stairs with any sort of luggage, and you'll be asked the simple question, *"Domatia?"* The thick-walled houses are treasure troves, brimming with Delft ceramics, Italian linens, icons, embroidery, metalwork, and fine china bought from long-dead pirates who looted throughout the Mediterranean. Expect to pay between 5000-12,000dr for a room, depending on size and season. If you decide to stay in a Skyrian house, always **bargain** over the price and look carefully for landmarks and house numbers, as the streets may be extremely confusing, and it's easy to lose track of your domatia. The aid of a travel agency will cost you an arm, a leg, and the essence of the whole experience. If you arrive during siesta, the town is dead as a doornail, and your calls for a domatia may be answered only with snores from within.

**BOOTY CALL** During summer evenings in Skyros, mildly voyeuristic wanderers may catch a glimpse into its richly ornamented traditional homes, as the warm breezes nudge their lace curtains aside. Shelves laden with precious Delft and Italian china, copper dishes, linens, and lace line the walls. Much speculation surrounds the origin of these valuable wares in the houses' *aloni* (the area of the house set aside for decorations). The treasures may be pirate booty smuggled from shipwrecks and plundered vessels. Until the mid-nineteenth century, wealthy Skyrians had to defend their homes against the marauding buccaneers that provided their goodies. The delicate valuables that fill today's seaside abodes were then ferreted away in inland houses near the castle, the second homes of Skyrians who lived on the shore. These inland houses were used almost exclusively to hide the islanders' (originally pirate-stolen) stuff from more pirates—anything in houses too close to shore would be hauled off if the scurvy dogs came a-calling.

If you don't feel like searching for a room, you can ask at **Theseus Rent a Car** about the bright, airy rooms in the house downstairs. On the road from Pl. Rupert Brooke down to the beach, **Camping Skyros** offers the amenities of a restaurant and a mini-market, along with the opportunity to get back to nature with some horses and an old car in the same field. (☎92 458. 1500dr per person with tent).

## FOOD

After a long afternoon swim, you can't go wrong with Skyrian food. The incredible **O Pappas Kai Ego,** or "Grandpa and Me," toward the top of Agoras on the right—look for the light green chairs—serves a brilliant lamb *kleftiko* wrapped in parchment paper and dusted with cheese, as well as many Skyrian specialties. (☎93 200. Entrees 850-2200dr. Open 8am-2pm and 7pm-late.) **Sisyfos,** just before the central plateia, lets you ogle various vegetarian and traditional dishes before you try them. Ask the chatty owner about anything from the myth of Sisyphus to rooms to let. (Entrees 1100-1300dr. ☎91 505. Open 11am-2pm and 7pm-late.) Just before O Pappas, **Obelistirio** serves up a slow-cooked, just-shy-of-healthy, incredibly delicious 350dr gyro. (☎92 205. Open 6pm-2am.) Fill your dessert stomach at **Tapatsa** (☎92 071), next to the National Bank, for giant warm crepes (200-300dr) or waffles with ice cream (800dr) at their rooftop cafe. For a final nibble, walk to the unnamed **sweet shop** (☎91 005) on Agoras, where the Skyrian specialty *amigdolata* (sweet almond taffy covered with powdered sugar) costs 500dr per half kilo.

## SIGHTS AND FESTIVALS

**MONASTERY OF AGIOS GEORGE.** High above Skyros Town, the thousand-year-old **Monastery of Ag. George** and the **Castle of Licomidus** command magnificent views of Skyrian sunsets. Hoof it there, cutting up the hill behind the police station toward the asphalt road, then follow that—take either fork, but keep going up. What looks like a ruin from below is a beautiful, rose-gardened monastic complex. Wear good shoes, as the worn stones are slippery, and dress modestly: the official sign demands that you not be "half-naked" if you want to peek at the monastery's 11th-century fresco of Ag. George. Then climb to the *castro*, generally believed to be a stellar Venetian repair of an earlier Byzantine castle. If you need a miracle, light a candle in the church of Ag. George—his active presence often aids grateful locals, who have dedicated two-thirds of the island to him. *(Open Mar.-Aug. 7am-10pm, Sept.-Feb. 7:30am-6pm.)*

**FALTAITS MUSEUM.** The **Faltaits Museum,** just past Pl. Rupert Brooke, is the private collection of a Skyrian ethnologist, and shouldn't be missed. Tours available in English guide you through the frozen-in-time ancestral home of the Faltaits family. The extensive holdings include beautiful examples of embroidery, carved furniture, pottery, costumes, copperware, rare books, and relics from the island's annual carnival—it's an excellent introduction to the island's traditional culture. The wise, friendly staff speak perfect English, affectionately calling the museum "a place where the nine muses meet." Conferences and cultural activities are held here throughout the year, including a **theater and dance festival** in late July and August; ask the staff for dates and times. *(☎91 232 or 91 150; email falaits@otenet.gr. Open 10am-1pm and 5:30-8pm. 500dr.)* Down the stairs to the right of Pl. Rupert Brooke, the **Archaeological Museum** holds significant island artifacts, but may be a letdown after the rich Faltaits Museum. *(☎91 327. Open Tu-Su 8:30am-3pm. 500dr, EU students and children free.)* Both museums have rooms decorated as **traditional Skyrian homes.** Most Skyrians are very proud of their domiciles, too, so don't be afraid to knock on their doors in the evening and ask to look inside.

Skyros is best known among Hellenes for its **Skyrian Carnival,** running every weekend in February, culminating on the first day of Lent 40 days before Easter. On this *Kathari Deftera*, an old man dressed in a goat mask and costume covered with clanging sheep bells leads two young men, one dressed as a Skyrian bride and

**HAVING HIS DAY** Poet Rupert Brooke, known, among other things, for coining the expression "every dog has his day," was a British national hero long before his death. Golden-haired Brooke was the empire's articulate darling, lettered and muscled, bright and impetuous. He signed up with the Hood Battalion of the Royal Naval Division in September 1914: "Well, if Armageddon's *on,* I suppose one should be there." After the disastrous Antwerp expedition, he became more patriotic and more serious, continuing to fight for his country despite presentiments of death. Brooke sailed with the British Mediterranean Expeditionary Force in February 1915, during the ill-fated Dardanelles campaign. He made it to Limnos and Egypt before dying of blood poisoning aboard a French hospital ship at Skyros on April 23, Ag. George's Day. At night, by torchlight, he was buried about a mile inland. His grave, a simple wooden cross bearing his name and dates of birth and death, is accessible from Linaria on the southwestern part of the island by car or foot. In a prophetic poem, Brooke left instructions for those who might visit his final resting place: "If I should die, think only this of me: / There is some corner of a foreign field / That is forever England–."

the other as a 17th-century European (with a large bell hanging from his waist), on a wild dance through town to the monastery. The festival commemorates a land dispute between shepherds and farmers and draws upon many myths and religious customs. One hypothesis is that the transvestism refers to Achilles, who dodged the Trojan War draft on Skyros by dressing as a girl.

## BEACHES

The pleasant beach below town stretches along the coast through the villages of **Magazia** and **Molos** and continues around the point. Crowded and crawling with children in July and August, it's undeniably convenient. The local nude beach, ironically named *Tou papa to homa* (The Sands of the Priest), remains clean and uncrowded, just south of the local beach. To get there, follow the seaside road south past Club Skyropoula and some low-ceilinged concrete structures (10-12min.); a narrow, spiky-plant-lined, slippery dirt path leads downhill along a wire fence. Be especially careful on the last 10 ft. of the trail. From here, you'll have a beautiful view of the **Southern Mountain,** famous in local literature and poetry for its hourly color changes in the sloping island light. The nude beach is also accessible by a clumsy, slippery clamber southwards over the seaside rocks at the south end of the public beach (20min.), but it's more trouble than it's worth. Once home to nymphs, the now-deserted **natural spring** at **Nifi Beach,** south of Linaria, lets you frolic solo. Scenically barren beaches and **Rupert Brooke's grave** on the south portion of the island are accessible only by dusty paths or by boat. If you ask, buses from Linaria to Skyros Town will stop at the beaches of **Aherounis** on the west coast and **Mialos** on the east. Boats can explore the onetime pirate grottoes at **Spillies,** on the southeastern coast, and **Sarakino Island,** once Despot's Island and one of the largest pirate centers in the Aegean. During Ottoman rule, it was an important hiding-place for ships. Keep an eye out for the endangered **Skyrian horses.**

# EVIA EYBOIA

The second-largest island in Greece, Evia is propped up against the mainland like a sea horse tapping the eastern shore with its round belly. Halkida, the *omphalos* (belly button) and central port, is full of surplus Athenians and their attendant scooter-dust, and is a gateway to the Sporades, along with Kimi in the west. North and south, the coastal countryside flattens out into hundreds of roadside beach-villages before scrunching up again into the hilly, beautiful resort towns at island's end: Limni and therapeutic Aedipsos in the north and hospitable Karystos in the south. Though Evia is varied and lovely, it's also Ground Zero for Greek resort tourists—it may be harder than usual to find cheap, one-night accommodations.

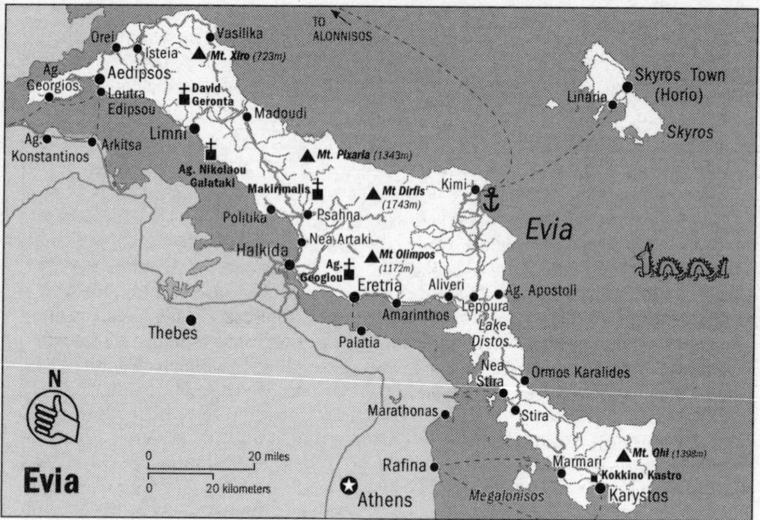


## HALKIDA Χαλκιδα ☎0221

Smoggy and loud, its car bumpers bumped by packs of passing tourists, Halkida (a.k.a. Chalkyda or Chalkis) requires guts. Just 20m from the mainland, it's a transit hub, with a major port and Evia's central bus station. Although the lively waterfront sparkles at night, it is a scene best viewed between pretty little villages.

### ORIENTATION AND PRACTICAL INFORMATION

Halkida's main thoroughfare is **El. Venizelou,** which runs inland perpendicular to **Voudouri** (the waterfront) for about 12 blocks before bending left into **Eikost Oktovriou.** The **Erippon Bridge** connects Halkida to the mainland, and points due west, with Halkida at your back.

If you arrive by **bus,** take a right from the ticket office and then your first left to intersect El. Venizelou. **Buses** travel to: **Athens** (2 per hr., 1400dr); **Karystos** (3½ hr., 2 per day, 2350dr); **Kimi** (1½ hr., 8 per day, 1700dr); and **Limni-Aedispos Springs** (3 hr., 3 per day, 2150dr). **Trains** go to **Athens** (17 per day, 900dr), and arrive on the mainland. Cross the bridge and take a left along the waterfront; Venizelou intersects the waterfront five blocks down from this bridge. **Flying Dolphins** leave from the dock to the right of the bridge. Purchase tickets to **Limni, Aedipsos,** and the **Sporades** at the shack on the waterfront just in line with the dock (☎21 521 or 21 621). **Taxis** (☎25 220) are available 24 hours.

If you have questions about Flying Dolphins, try your luck with the **port authority** across the bridge in the huge building (☎77 333 or 28 880). The **National Bank** is on El. Venizelou three blocks from the water, with a 24hr. **ATM** and **currency exchange.** (Open M-Th 8am-2pm, F 8am-1:30pm.) The English-speaking **tourist police** are only available in the mornings and are entirely inconvenient; their office is a 25-minute walk up Venizelou and onto Oktovriou, in the building with the regular **police.** Call instead. (☎77 777. Open 24hr. except when out on call.) To get to the **hospital** (☎21 901 or 21 908), take El. Venizelou toward the water and turn right on Arethousis, at the corner with the Citibank about 4 blocks inland. After 1½ blocks the street curves; jog one block left here onto Herakleos Giazeri and turn right; the huge hospital is four blocks down on the right. **Net Cafe** offers (of all things) **Internet access.** Take a right onto the waterfront and walk all the way down looking for the blue building on your right. (☎89 531. Open 10am-2pm. 1000dr per hr.) On the way you'll pass **Pl. Agios Nikolas,** spilling back from the waterfront, where the **public**

**library** and the **Church of Agios Nikolas** rest. The **OTE** (☎22 599) is one block further in at the intersection with Papanastasiou. The **post office** is on Karamourzouni, the second right after the National Bank, or the second left from the waterfront. (Open M-F 7:30am-2pm.) **Postal code:** 34100.

## ACCOMMODATIONS AND FOOD

Most hotels here are of the 25,000dr-a-night variety, catering to business travelers or Athenian families, so Halkida is not an ideal place to spend the night. That said, there are two good options. **Hotel Kentriko,** the pink building at Ageli Gobiou 5—the last left off El. Venizelou just before the water—has a Greek-Canadian proprietor happy to help you make sense of the city. The unexciting rooms have TVs, phones, and shared baths. (☎22 375 or 27 260. Singles 6000dr; doubles 8000dr; triples 9000-10,000dr. 24hr. reception.) On the mainland, **Hotel Hara** is a right turn on the street running uphill behind the Port Authority. The bright white rooms are a bargain for larger groups—look for the flags flying about a block down. (☎76 305, 306, 307, or 308; fax 76 309. Doubles 14,000-16,000dr; triples 16,000-18,000dr).

Like hotels, restaurants in Halkida are budget-busting. Several bakeries hide along side streets around Ag. Nikolas. Sample the mounds of sesame cookies at **Pinavoti Bakery** on the corner of Kerakleos Giazeri, toward the hospital, and snag some bread (150-800dr) for the road. (☎20 930. Open 7:30am-2pm.) The waterfront is trendy cafe central, with colorful umbrellas shading die-hard people-watchers at the outdoor tables. Order a *frappé* and join in the fun, but eat elsewhere—the prices will turn your stomach. Smirk as you munch a gyro (350dr) and look at the same waterfront view at **Thraki** (☎80 824), which peeks out of an alley to the left of the water. For a heartier sit-down meal, head to the right, past the port authority, to the cafes and smaller tavernas there.

## SIGHTS

The **Archaeological Museum,** on El. Venizelou across from the National Bank, is full of findings from the Classical and Roman eras. Stone horse heads accent the courtyard. There's a guard-to-visitor ratio of approximately 3 to 1. (☎76 131. Open Tu-Su 8:30am-3pm. 500dr, students 300dr, senior citizens 400dr, EU students and children free.) The white **Church of Ag. Nikolas,** facing the water and flying the Greek flag in the plateia of the same name, is big, rich, and full—a very alive place. (Open 9am-1pm usually.) You can trace the Halkidian life of **Nikos Skalkotas,** artist and composer, at his childhood and adult homes; he grew up at Kotsouparlou 35 in the maze behind Oktovriou street, and moved out to the pale yellow dock's-end cube past the internet cafe. Call the tourist police (☎77 777) for an appointment.

## DAYTRIPS FROM HALKIDA

### AEDIPSOS SPRINGS Λουτρα Αιδηψου

***Buses*** *run from* ***Halkida*** *(3hr., 3 per day, 2150dr). Ferries run to and from* ***Arkitsa*** *(45min., 9 per day, 550dr; buy tickets on the dock) on the mainland (30min. by bus from Ag. Konstantinos, 350dr). The* ***bus station*** *(☎22 250) is on Thermopotamou, which runs inland from 28 Oktovriou, the waterfront strip. The hot springs are in a large complex on a road heading inland from the left end of the waterfront facing the water, 200m past the post office. Open 7am-7:30pm. 400dr.*

The village of Aedipsos, northwest of Halkida on the coast of Evia, earned praise from Herodotus, Aristotle, and Aristophanes for its healing sulphurous waters. Aedipsos is worth a daytrip for anyone who wishes to enjoy the hot springs' relaxing vibes, but be aware that the spring's main patrons are those with "rheumatism, arthritis, and gynecological complaints." Locals advise not to swim longer than 30 minutes, as too much of the good bathing thing will leave you in a none-too-therapeutic stupor. Check out the various specialized pools and equipment. Uphill from the complex, the hot spring water cascades down a small waterfall and mixes with sea water, cooling the temperature a bit while maintaining a hot-tub feel.

## LIMNI Λημνη

*Limni is on the* ***Halkida-Aedipsos Springs*** *bus line (3 per day, 2150dr). Buses stop at the main intersection in town; ask before you get off when the next one comes.*

If there are tourists here, they're extremely well hidden. A 45min. bus ride south of Aedipsos takes you to the wooded cove of Limni (Lake). The fishing village remains friendly, curious about the rare outsider that stumbles upon it. The town takes a collective afternoon swim amid fishing boats and windsurfers. The splendid scenery and gorgeous setting—far from the phlegmy coughs of Aedipsos—will wow you, especially if you stay for the dazzling sunset and the star-filled night.

Limni is laid out in a "T", with the long waterfront intersecting the road upwards and outwards (to Aedipsos and Halkida). Facing inland, turn right on the waterfront for pastry shops and Pl. Eth. Antistassis, the main plateia. Turn left for most restaurants. After an afternoon dip, stop for *ouzo* and fresh cookies (50dr) at **Kafe-Ouzeri Andriola Ioanna** (☎56 830), the large pastry shop off Pl. Antistassis. If you're looking for an evening meal, get a char-grilled souvlaki stick (300dr) from the stand across from the bus stop and walk out on the fishing pier to watch the sunset bend hazy and fine across the northern mountains. After 10pm, you can pick from the waterfront restaurants' nightly specials. If you stay for the stars, you can stay in one of two hotels in town, both on the waterfront. **Hotel Limni** is to the far right, facing inland, past the small boat dock, and has unadorned rooms with bath. (☎/fax 31 316 or 31 748. Singles 4000-5000dr; doubles 7000-8000dr; triples 8000-10,000dr.) To the left, across from the bus stop, the **Plaza Hotel** has nicely furnished doubles in a renovated old house. (☎31 235. Doubles 9000dr.)

# ERETRIA Ερετρια ☎0229

Long, flat beaches meet the twinkling blue water in Eretria, where Athenian vacationers relax in languid sunsets. Though something of a bland resort now, the town rivaled ancient Chalkis (Halkida) as the island's most important city and as a trading power with the rest of Greece, Italy, and the Near East. In the 3rd century BC, Menedimos, the town's most famous son and a disciple of Plato, founded a school of philosophy here. The amazing archaeological finds, as well as access to Athens, make it a convenient base for exploration of the island.

**ORIENTATION AND PRACTICAL INFORMATION.** Eretria's beach curves into the joint formed by two perpendicular harborfront streets: the northwest waterfront and the southeast waterfront, which runs inland to become **Archaiou Theatrou. Ferries** to and from **Oropos** (20 min., 2 per hr., 300dr) dock in the middle of the northern waterfront. Eretria is also accessible by **bus** from **Halkida,** because every bus heading south to **Karystos, Kimi,** or **Amarinthos** swings through (2 per hr., 450dr). The **bus stop** is a sweet shop on the street running parallel to the ferry side of the waterfront. A complete bus schedule for the island is posted outside, but check inside the shop as some destinations require you to pre-purchase a ticket. **Taxis** (☎62 500) wait by the ferry dock. From the bus stop facing the street, turn right and walk 20m to find the **National Bank,** which **changes money** and has a 24 hr. **ATM.** (Open M-Th 8am-2pm, F 8am-1:30pm.) Call the **police** at 61 111. The **OTE** is another 20m to the left. (Open M-F 7:30am-1pm.) **Internet access** (yes, even here) is available at **Christos Cafe** on the southern waterfront. (☎61 604 or 62 337. 1500dr per hr. Open 10am-3am.) Turn right and then left two blocks before the waterfront to find the **post office.** (Open M-F 7:30am-2pm.) **Postal code:** 34008.

**ACCOMMODATIONS.** Eretria is mainly a resort town, so hotel owners may be confused to find that you only want a cheap room for the night. Athena runs a tight and wonderful ship at **Pension Diamado.** From the ferry dock facing inland, follow the waterfront around as it curves 90 degrees to the right; look for the blue and yellow Diamado's sign just before the Fat Indian Cafe. Spotless, charming rooms have baths, TVs, and fridges. (☎62 214. Doubles 10,000-11,000dr; triples 13,000dr.) Along this same stretch of waterfront, turn left at the sign and walk 200m to the

would-be jungle resort of the **Eretria Sunrise Hotel.** Don't let the overwatered garden phase you. The apartments are large, gorgeous, and fully equipped with kitchens, fridges, A/C, and baths. (☎60 004. Singles 12,000-15,000dr; doubles 17,000dr.)

**FOOD AND ENTERTAINMENT.** Warm crusty bread (150dr) makes a comforting start to a morning—stop into the **bakery** with the red and white awning between the post office and OTE. (Open 8am-2pm.) For lunch, try **Valkanos** at the potted plant intersection for the classiest gyro (350dr) around. (Open 10pm-late.) Tavernas along the southern waterfront serve the usual fare; expect to shell out 1200-2200dr for entrees. Eretria is no swinging disco town, but you can certainly relax with a drink at any of the waterfront **cafe-bars.** (Beers 600-1500dr, cocktails 1500dr and up.) **Cafe Antiques,** across from the ferry dock, is a bit pricey but bursting with carved knick-knacks and character. Catch an earful of blues, jazz, and eccentric mellow music nightly. (Cocktails 1800dr. Open 9am-3am.)

**SIGHTS.** The **Archaeological Museum** is at the inland end of Archaiou Theatrou, in a statued courtyard. The small collection displays some quality pieces, like three large *pithoi* south of the House of the Mosaics—the remaining six are in the museum at Athens—and the mysteriously six-fingered (and zero-headed) **Centaur of Lefkandi,** which dates from 750-900 BC. Exhibits are in Greek and French, but you can buy a red English guidebook for 2000dr. Museum admission lets you into the **House of the Mosaics** 10min. away; just trade your passport for the keys at the front desk of the museum. Coming out of the museum, walk to the right along the main road for three blocks, turning left at the marked road. The three 4th-century BC mosaics are incredibly well preserved and are among the oldest in existence. Walk all the way around the house for an easier view of the tiled sphinx and serpent. The Swiss School of Archaeology in Greece publishes a brochure on the house's history, available from the museum for 1000dr. (☎62 206. Open Tu-Su 8am-3pm. 500dr, students and senior citizens 300dr, children free.) Beyond the museum is a large excavated area of the Old City for you to explore.

## KARYSTOS Καρυστος ☎0224

Cut off from the rest of Evia by a mountain chain, Karystos blooms in summer: there are lush trees, pink flowers, sand that squishes between toes, glimmering bars, and teeming tide pools. The long bus ride from Halkida passes some unexciting strip towns, but the view of Marmari's bay and other windy landscapes more than compensates. Wind-generators stand guard over the sea, while sunlight flashes from wave to wave.

**ORIENTATION AND PRACTICAL INFORMATION.** Karystos is one of the few Greek cities organized into an easily navigable grid. The central plateia along the waterfront is, unsurprisingly, the center of practical life, while tavernas and bars stretch in both directions along the shore. The **bus** stops one block above the main plateia; look for the KTEL sign above a restaurant on the west (right, facing inland) side of the street. Buses from Karystos travel to: **Halkida** (4hr., 2 per day, 2350dr); **Marmari** (30min., 3 per day, 350dr); and **Stira** (45min., 1per day, 700dr). **Ferries** travel to **Rafina** (2hr., 2 per day, 1800dr); buy tickets across from where the boat docks at **Praktorio Millis Lines** (☎24 070) or at **South Evia Tours** (☎25 700 or 26 200, fax 29 011; open 9am-3pm and 5:30-11pm), on the right side of the main plateia, facing the water. South Evia Tours also sells tickets for **Flying Dolphins** to: **Tinos** (2 per week, 5300dr); **Mykonos** (2 per week, 6600dr); and to **Naxos** and **Santorini** (4 per week, 8400). **Taxis** (☎26 500) collect in the plateia.

The **tourist kiosk** (☎25 650) at the center of the waterfront has a few pamphlets. The English-speaking staff helps with bus schedules; for more help, including car rentals, head to South Evia Tours. **National Bank** is just inland of the bus stop. (Open M-Th 8am-2pm, F 8am-1:30pm.) To find the **police** (☎22 252), turn into the small alley inland of the bank and climb the stairs. Find a **pharmacy** (☎23 505) on the corner on the left past the bus stop. The **OTE** is on Amerikis, the next cross-

street inland of the bus. (☎22 399. Open 7:45am-1pm.) To reach the **post office** from the OTE, turn left on Amerikis and take the first right past the playground; you'll see the round yellow sign. (Open M-F 7:30am-2pm.) **Postal code:** 34001.

**ACCOMMODATIONS.** On the far right of the waterfront, **Hotel Galaxy,** run by a hospitable English-speaking couple, has some of the best rates; don't let the ostentatious lobby scare you. All rooms have baths, TVs, and A/C. (☎22 600; fax 22 463. Singles 6500-9200dr; doubles 9000-13,700dr; triples 13,500-17,500dr.) **Hotel Als** across from the tourist kiosk, has private baths, TVs, fridges, phones, and A/C. Some rooms have balconies. (☎22 202; fax 25 002. Doubles 10,000-13,000dr.)

**FOOD AND NIGHTLIFE.** The octopi *(oktopodia)* lined up to dry in the sun may clue you in to what this town likes to eat. At the very end of the strip (on the far right facing the water), you'll come to the all-Greek crowd at **Kalamia,** serving up hearty Greek fare. (☎22 223. Entrees 1000-5000dr.) For a cheap souvlaki fix, head to **Kotsika,** perpendicular to the waterfront, to the right of the central plateia (facing the sea). Four different gyros stands await your arrival. Miss McDonalds? Your inner hipster teen won't want to miss **Tastyland** (☎25 700) on the waterfront—don your disco gear and grab a burger to go (450dr).

By night, the *ouzeria* and restaurants along the shore gradually fade into bars and pubs. **Archipelagos,** on the beach at the right edge of town, packs a crowd with good music and an engaging view. (☎25 040. Beer 600-800dr, cocktails 1300-1500dr. Opens at 8am.) The discos and clubs are seasonal, open 2-3 nights a week, and at least 10min. away by car; check the posters plastered around the main plateia for hotspots and deals. The scene gets going around midnight. Taxi drivers may know what's up by virtue of where they've been taking people all night—don't be afraid to ask. You may want to take a cab there (500-2000dr) and especially back—navigating Karystos's mountain roads is treacherous, especially after a night with Dionysus. Serious dancing moves the **Barbados Disco,** 3km from town toward the mountains. (☎24 119. 1300dr cover includes a drink.) The bewitching blue glow of **Ostria Pub,** a bit further down the beach, will bathe you in color and sound. (☎25 678. Beer 700-1200dr, cocktails 1200-1500. June-Sept. Opens at 9am.)

For more immediate entertainment, the local **carnival** is off to the right of the waterfront; 150dr tokens will buy you a chance at all your favorite kiddie games. There's also a movie theater, **Ciné Agra,** on the right side of Sachtouri, the first street inland running parallel to the waterfront. Mostly American movies play nightly at 9 and 11pm for 1600dr a head; check posters out front for billing.

**SIGHTS.** Peek into one of the holes at the back of the **Fort of Bourtzi,** the impossible-to-miss structure on the waterfront. In the 11th century, your peephole was used to pour boiling oil on attackers. Today, the fort is regularly invaded by theater-goers swarming in to watch student productions; ask at South Evia Tours *(☎25 700 or 26 200)* about schedules. The **Archaeological Museum,** on the waterfront past the fort, shares a building with the public library and houses a few artifacts that attest to past military might. *(☎25 661. Open Tu-Su 8:30am-3pm. 500dr, seniors and students 300dr, EU students and children free.)*

**UNTITLED** According to Orthodox tradition, children must have a saint's name to be baptized. Some priests will reluctantly baptize an unorthodoxically named infant, but not without a certain amount of fuss and pointed questioning. Typically, children are named after a grandparent, and though there are a range of names to pick from, certain favorites pop up: Christos, Georgios, Maria, Anna, etc. Instead of celebrating birthdays, Greeks instead party on their **name-days,** held on the feast day of their namesake saint. For instance, on St. Eleni's feast day, women named Eleni get phone calls and cards, and hold parties. Sometimes people who share a name will team up—for instance, several Dimitrises might band together on their name day for a massive Dimitris bash. Otherwise, Greeks party-hop from one Pavlos or Athanasios or Katerina to the next, depending on whose name day it happens to be.

**DAYTRIPS FROM KARYSTOS.** With a free morning, you can explore the villages north of Karystos: Nikasi, Kalivia, Ag. Triada, Lala, Palea Hora, Mekounida, Arabia, and Myli. Palea Hora in the east and Nikasi in the west are good bases. Grab the **free,** painstaking "Paths in the Karystos Countryside" from the port tourist kiosk, then follow Aiolou, a block east of the plateia, out of Karystos toward Myli. Go straight at the crossroads toward **Palio Hora,** hugged by lemon and olive groves, or turn right for a sunnier, more difficult walk to **Myli.** The road rises sharply, following a stream to the village. The water flows from the three lions' mouths at a small roadside fountain. From Myli, a 20min. hike up the hill on the left and across the stone bridge leads to the 13th-century Venetian **Kokkino Castro** (Red Castle), named for the blood spilled there in a Greek-Ottoman battle. From Myli, it's a 2½hr. hike to **Arabia;** take the road toward Kokkino Castro, past the castle and across a stream, under the **aqueduct** *(kamares)*, left on the path toward the church of **Agia Katerina** (St. Catherine), and then down the stone path *(kalderini)* from the church to the village. To explore the western villages, take the **bus** from Karystos to **Nikasi** (220dr). From here, **Agia Triada** is 2hr. north and **Kalivia** is 1½hr. west. **Lala** is 1½ hr. north of Kalivia. Hikers looking for romance can climb **Mt. Ohi** (1398m), where Zeus and Hera fell in love. The refuge hut on the mountain is a 3-4hr. hike from Karystos. The refuge, made of unmortared stone blocks during the Pelasgian Period, may have been a temple to Hera or a signal tower. The ruin, now known as the **Dragon's House,** is reputedly haunted.

# NORTHEAST AEGEAN ISLANDS



For centuries, the northeast Aegean islands have had to protect themselves, a fate not unusual in Greece. Recent Turkish occupations have left a bad taste in the islanders' collective mouth; they may be wary of visitors as a result. Many islands continue to isolate themselves from the influx of tourism, hoping to preserve their traditions. Intricate, rocky coastlines and unassuming port towns enclose thickly wooded mountains, which give way to unspoiled villages and beaches. Despite proximity to the Turkish coast and a noticeable military presence (which may lead women traveling alone to feel uncomfortable), the northeast Aegean islands dispense a taste of undiluted Greek culture.

**HIGHLIGHTS OF THE NORTHEAST AEGEAN**

**LET SAPPHO INSPIRE YOU** under the volcanoes of Lesvos (p. 336), Greece's premier lesbian destination, and inspiration to poetic minds–from the ancient sensual lyricist Sappho to the Modernist Nobel Laureate Odysseus Elytis–for millennia.

**SEE GREEN** on the lush birthplace of Pythagoras and Epicurus, Samos Island (p. 328).

**BOW** before the Sanctuary of Great Gods of Anatolia on Samothraki (p. 349), where Alexander the Great's parents met, wooed, loved–and worshiped.

## IKARIA ΙΚΑΡΙΑ ☎0275

Ikaria takes its name from reckless young Icarus, who plunged to his death off the island's coast when his wax wings—made by his father Daedalus so they could escape the Cretan labyrinth—melted when he gleefully flew too close to the sun. Today, Ikaria's villages adhere to a daily schedule in which stores and restaurants are closed by day and open much of the night, keeping up the bad-boy lifestyle of their namesake. The island pays little attention to tourism, which is a mixed blessing: travelers don't face overwhelming attention, but they run into logistical problems. Bus service is minimal and utterly unreliable, banks are rare outside Agios Kirykos, which is separated by over 40 treacherous kilometers from Evdilos (the island's other main port) and the more populated villages of the north coast. Today's mostly Greek visitors generally arrive hoping to be healed by Ikaria's radioactive medicinal springs. Split by a rocky mountain chain, the odd landscape gives root to around 2500 species of plant, mostly herbs, which subtly color and scent the island. Large patches of Ikarian forest, devastated by fires in 1993 and 1997, are slowly growing back.

### AGIOS KIRYKOS Αγιος Κηρυκος

As Ikaria's main port, Agios Kirykos is the most convenient base for a visit to the nearby thermal springs; summer rooms are sparse due to the springs' popularity.

**ORIENTATION AND PRACTICAL INFORMATION.** The town's pier is marked by a large sculpture of Icarus plummeting to the ground, but getting here has become considerably easier and safer since Icarus's time; coming off the ferry, walk up the pier onto the main waterfront road, then turn right to reach the town plateia, which shelters all the tourist services.

Ikaria's new **airport** serves **Athens** (1 per day, 18,900dr) through the **Olympic Airways** office (☎22 214; open M-F 8am-2:30pm), and is on the island's northeast tip, near Fanari Beach. **Ferry tickets** are available at the plateia's **G.A. office** (☎22 426). Ferries run to: **Fourni** (1hr., 4 per week, 1300dr); **Paros** (4hr., 3 per week, 3300dr); **Patmos** (1½hr., 4 per week, 2800dr); **Piraeus** (10hr., 1-2 per day, 5300dr); and **Samos Town** (3hr., 5 per week, 2200dr). Boats alternate stops at **Evdilos** in the north and **Agios Kirykos,** where taxis await to shuttle passengers to the other port (2000-2500dr). **Flying Dolphins** cost twice as much and leave for **Fourni** (30min., 5 per week, 2510dr); **Patmos** (1hr., 6 per week); and **Samos** (1½hr., 6 per week, 3523dr). Three **caïques** leave for Fourni every week (1100dr). **Buses** cannot be relied upon, but, in theory, run twice daily between **Agios Kirykos** and **Armenistis** via **Evdilos** (1000dr.); and every 30min. to **Therma** (200dr). On the way to the town plateia from the ferry dock you will pass **Ikariada Travel,** which offers the friendliest and best English-speaking service. They can arrange rooms, vehicle rentals, excursion trips, or Flying Dolphin services. (☎23 322; fax 23 708. Open 8am-10pm.)

The **port police** (☎22 207), **police** (☎22 222), and **tourist police** (☎22 207) share a building; climb the steps left of Dolihi Tours and continue up the road (all open 8am-2pm). The **pharmacy** is next to the G.A. Ferry ticket office. (☎22 989 or 22 220. Open M-F 8:30am-2pm, 6-8:30pm; Sa 9:30am-2pm, 8:30-10:30pm; Su 11:30am-2pm.) For emergency after-hours care, try the pharmacist (☎(0932) 199 089). The local **hospital** (☎22 330 or 22 336) is two streets up from the pier. The island's banks, including the **National Bank,** are in Agios Kirykos, in the plateia near the ferry offices. (☎22 894. Open M-Th 8am-2pm, F 8am-1:30pm.) A 24hr. **ATM** is next door to Dolihi Travel. After hours, tourist offices and big hotels offer **currency exchange. Internet access** is available at the **Internet Club** to the left of Dolihi Travel. (☎22 864. 500dr per 20min.) About 100m up the street are the **post office** (☎22 413; open M-F 8am-2pm), and the **OTE** (☎22 399; open M-F 7:30am-3pm). **Postal code:** 83300.

**ACCOMMODATIONS AND FOOD.** Finding lodging can be rough on your first night, so check your port of arrival beforehand and call ahead for reservations. To reach **Hotel Akti,** climb the stairs on the right-hand side of Dolihi Travel and take your first right. A pleasant courtyard enhances basic rooms built around a lovely seaside patio. Owner Marsha knows tons about the island and is very accommodating. (☎22 694 or 23 905. Singles 6500dr; doubles with private bath 11,000dr.) The modern rooms of the **Hotel Castro** have TVs, baths, balconies, phones, and fridges, and are on the road leading left from the police station. (☎23 480. Singles 12,650dr; doubles 17,950dr.) Next to Hotel Akti is the **Hotel O'Karras,** offering simple sky blue rooms and spacious baths. (☎22 494. Singles 4000dr, with bath 5000dr; doubles 6000/7000dr.) Taverna **A Klimataria** is a block inland from the plateia; freshly prepared dishes, like fish in the shape of a grape arbor, enact the restaurant's name. (*Briam*, an eggplant dish, 1300dr; entrees up to 1500dr. ☎22 686. Open 11am-4pm, 7pm-midnight daily.) **Dedalos,** in on the right of the plateia, stirs up a wonderful omelette breakfast (up to 1000dr) and traditional Greek cuisine with ocean-side seating. (Entrees from 1200-1700dr. ☎22 473.)

**NIGHTLIFE AND BEACHES.** At **Flik-Flak,** 1km out of town, get down to popular radio tunes on Ag. Kirykos's hottest dance-floor. (☎41 587. Cocktails 1800dr. Open 11pm-4am.) *Barakia*, or little curb-side bars, line the stoned pathways leading inland from the plateia, where nightlife is just as easily overpowered by families. Standard prices of an 1800dr cocktail and 1000dr beer are offset by Top 40 hits and late-night Greek tunes. **Therino Cinema/Bar,** on the road to Therma, combines the outdoor showings of the latest films with a convenient spot to sip your *karpouzaki* (1700dr). Shows are nightly at 9:30pm; look for the posters next to Ikariada Travel. There are some rocky **beaches** west of the ferry dock. To the east of town, you can clamber down to the sandy beaches and crystal water of the coves past the tourist police office. **Agios Georgios,** between Fanari and the airport, is this part of the island's best beach.

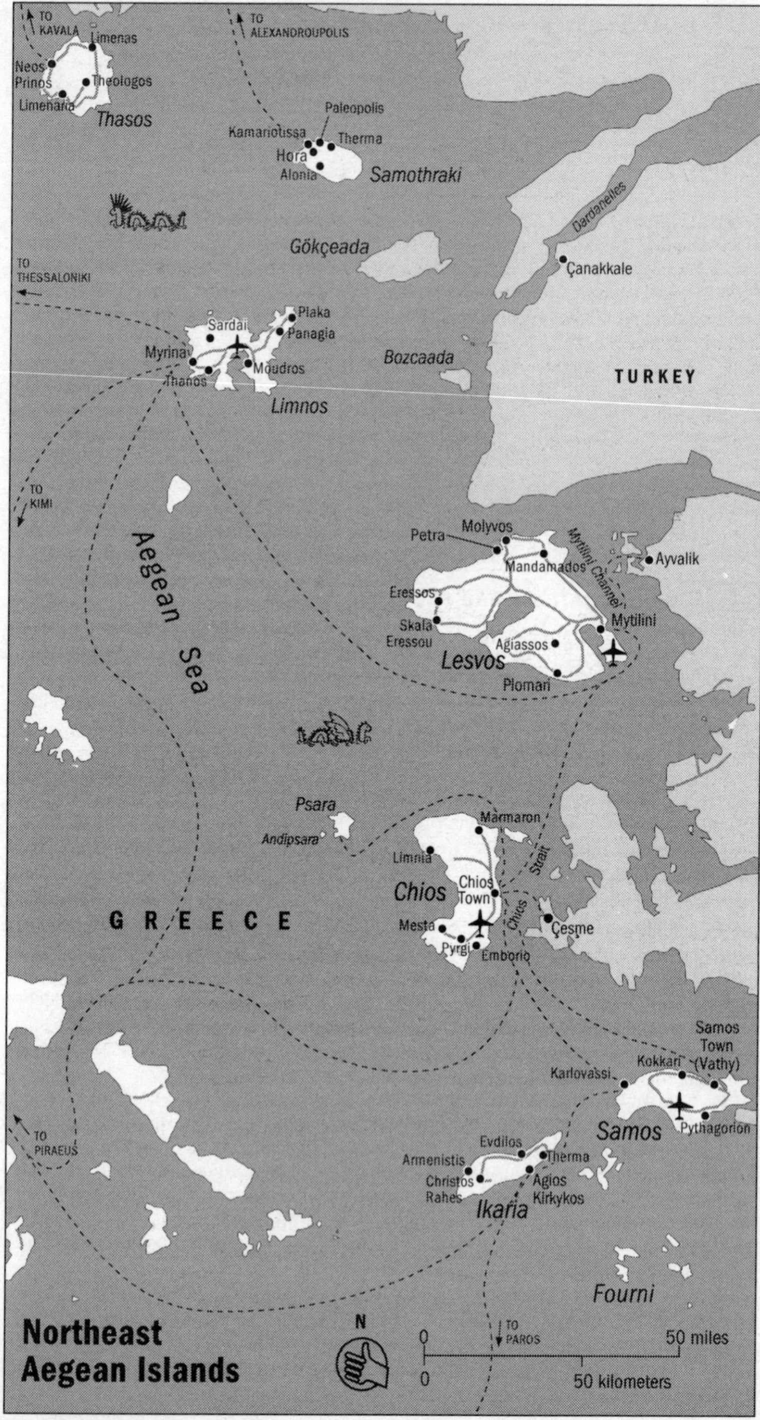

Northeast Aegean Islands

# EVDILOS Ευδηλος

Heading north from Agios Kirykos, the tiny road to Evdilos snakes along sheer cliffs through florid hill country, opening wide coastal vistas—and a safety risk to moped drivers. From the island's eastern heights you can see Samos, Patmos, and the Fourni Archipelago. On the way to Evdilos, the road passes a few tiny villages and beaches, many of which have limited tourist accommodations. The island's competing port town, Evdilos sports red-tiled roofs against its steeply sloping hill.

**ORIENTATION AND PRACTICAL INFORMATION.** **Buses** are supposed to run twice daily between **Agios Kirykos** and **Armenistis** via **Evdilos,** but service is unreliable at best (1000dr one way). The schedule reported by the tourist police is often inaccurate. **Taxis** may be your best bet; sharing a cab will cut costs. (☎31 275. Agios Kirykos to Evdilos 8000dr; Agios Kirykos to Armenistis 9000dr; Armenistis to Evdilos 3000dr.) The **post office** sits at the top of a set of white stairs that lead to the right of the plateia. (☎31 225. Open M-F 7:30am-2pm.) The **OTE** (☎31 559) is past the post office, across from the church. The **pharmacy** (☎31 394) is between the town and ferries arrival dock. In case of emergency call for **first aid** (☎31 228). The **port police** (☎31 007) is directly inland from the plateia, next to the pharmacy. **Blue Nice Holidays** handles ferries, Flying Dolphins, excursions, flights, and car rentals, **exchanges currency,** and posts a weekly schedule for ferries to Evdilos and Agios Kirykos, as well as Flying Dolphins serving Agios Kirykos. (☎31 990/991 or 31 428; fax 31 572. Open 9am-2:30pm and 7-10pm.) There is **no bank** in town.

**ACCOMMODATIONS AND FOOD.** Quality of lodging in Evdilos is a direct reflection of the price. For the best view of crashing waves and a gorgeous sunset, try **Apostolos Stenos' Rooms to Rent.** Ask for directions on the way. (☎31 365. Singles 8000dr; doubles 9000dr; prices are flexible.) The cheapest place in town requires a serious compromise in glitz, but not in cleanliness. **Hambas' Rooms** are very gentle on the budget; they're directly inland from the kiosk in the main square. (☎31 523. Singles 3000dr; doubles 5000dr.) **Ioannis Spanos** offers basic rooms with shared bath near the plateia at the base of the hill along the Agios Kirykos-Armenistis road. (☎31 220. Doubles 8000dr.)

Restaurant tables fill the plateia offering generally similar fare in a shared setting. Revered as the island's best taverna, and the town's first, **Kafestiatorio** uses only local Ikarian ingredients and meats to create inexpensive and delicious meals. (Entrees 1600dr, Greek salad 600dr. ☎31 273. Open 12:30pm-midnight daily.) **Cuckoo,** with tables strategically surrounding the square's central monument, focuses on *mezedes* and afternoon ouzo. Try the spicy squid in wine (1500dr) or 1300dr three-cheese *saginaki.* (☎31 540. Open M-Sa 10am-2pm, 4pm-midnight.) Catering to the late-night ferry arrivals with an array of sweets, coffees, and baked goods, **Ta Kimata** (☎31 952), next to Blue Nice Travel, is open 24hr.

## CHRISTOS RAHES

Stone idle fountains hidden under the canopy of shady green leaves mark the entrance to the shopping area of **Christos Rahes** (Χριστος της Ραχης), the apotheosis of a traditional Ikarian village. The best time to visit is after 11pm, when the locals have finished their daily livestock care and produce gathering, and are ready to run their daily errands, shopping until 3 or 4am. Visit the local **baker** on the main road below the plateia, where the brick oven-baked loaves (100dr), made daily, are left out for consumers to grab; deposit the money in a little basket on the honor system. Ikaria's best-organized **hiking** trails originate from here and are marked by little orange footprints. Pick up the very handy *Guide Map and Information* on the *Round of Rahes on Foot* (1000dr) at any bookstore or tourist shop. Among the highlights are the **Monastery of Evangelistria; Nas** is also within an hour's hike from here. Although difficult to reach—try a taxi—this little village is a must-see for any visitor to the island.

**YOU'VE GOT MAIL** Two things you need to know about Greek post offices: when to go, and what to wear. Anyone who has ever tried to send mail from Greece during the first week of the month may find that hundreds of Greeks seem to have had the same idea. This is because Greek post offices are not just for sending or receiving mail, but also for paying electric, gas, and light bills. It is thus fundamentally impossible to do any of the above in less than two hours. If you can't wait a week, at least go prepared. Women, this means tight (preferably short) clothing, and enough makeup to form a comfortable cushion between you and the person ahead of you in line. Men, break out the swim trunks and flip-flops, and please remember that shirts may inhibit your arm gestures when explaining how someone cut you off in line. Introverts, grumble quietly and constantly to yourselves; extroverts, push hard. At no time should you doubt the Greek gift for creating challenge where there was none before—after all, this is the country that gave us democracy.



### THERMA θερμα

A short distance from Agios Kyrikos on the way to the airport, Therma is one of the main reasons to visit Ikaria. It's very accessible; **boats** run here for 100dr from Agios Kyrikos based on demand, **buses** run every 30min., and the **walk** is only 2km on the path beside the police station. The village is built in a little valley with houses on the steep cliffs surrounding it. Elderly people crowd the main plateia while children clamber around the beach; people with ailments ranging from rheumatism to gynecological ailments venture to the three springs of Therma. Each of the springs is naturally radioactive and used for different treatments. 20min. in a warm bath costs a mere 450dr, so take your time.

### NAS Νας

West of Armenistis, the asphalt runs out, leaving a dirt road running to Nas, one of the Aegean's undiscovered gems. The inspiring beach, flanked by huge rock walls, separates an aggressive sea from a seductively serene river. Bordered by the beach, a freshwater pool forms the river's final destination, while a 25-minute hike south takes you to the small waterfall that forms its beginning. To reach the falls, head inland toward the wood past the pool. With no set path, the hike is best accomplished by staying close to the river, which may mean getting your feet wet. Approaching the final leg of the hike, notice the remarkable cavernous rock enclosure perched atop the eastern ledge. However, think twice about trying to claim it for a nap; this is a favorite haunt for local goats. The smallish waterfall lies a few minutes beyond this point.

**Camping** along the river is a regular event, despite being technically illegal. Inhabitants are a mix of short-term visitors in search of free lodging and an attractive setting in which to pitch a tent, and long-term Ikarians keen on perpetuating the summer of love with a commune-esque atmosphere and propensity for nudity. More conventional lodgings sit above the beach and river. **Artemis Pension** offers small but tasteful rooms with balconies. (☎71 485. Doubles with shared bath 6000dr, with private bath 9000dr.) The owner also runs mind/body exercise classes, has a relaxing taverna, and plays tunes from her great classic rock collection. A path to the river descends from the steps next to the taverna.

## FOURNI ☎0275

Although few visitors stay overnight, Fourni island presents rewards for both day-trippers and those willing to stay longer. Most come for the fresh seafood served at waterfront restaurants, but pleasant beaches and easy hiking are also easily accessible. The island consists of three little villages: Kampos, Chrysomilia, and Thymeria on the neighboring island of the same name.

The main port has more tourist facilities than one would imagine. Almost everything is either located on the waterfront or the main street that runs perpendicular to it. Weather-permitting, Fourni is easily accessible by daily **caïque** from **Ikaria** (4000dr round-trip). There is also limited **ferry** service three times per week from **Ikaria** (2500dr) and **Patmos** (3500dr). The **port police** (☎51 207) and **police** (☎51 222) share a white building at the end of the dock. The friendly, English-speaking staff answer questions about the island. Walking away from the water heading inland, there is a **doctor** (☎51 115; open M-F 7am-2pm), **pharmacy,** and **post office** (☎51 286; open 7am-1pm). To the right (facing inland) **Hotel Nectaria** provides spacious rooms with baths, fridges, and fans. (☎51 365. Doubles 8000dr; triples 1000dr.) Next door, **Toula Rooms** has immaculate studios with baths, kitchens, and fans (☎51 332. Doubles and triples 11-12,000dr.) The island's two best beaches, **Kambe** and **Psili Ammos,** are accessible from here.



# SAMOS ΣΑΜΟΣ

Although it is perhaps the most beautiful and definitely the most touristed island in the northeast Aegean, Samos manages to remain less frenetic than some of its Cycladic and Dodecanesian siblings by accommodating a more scholarly, mature crowd. While short-sighted tourists see Samos as little more than a necessary stepping-stone on the way to Kuşadası and the ruins of Ephesus on the Turkish coast (p. 553), this green island has been a destination in its own right for centuries. A procession of architects, sculptors, poets, philosophers, and scientists (among them Pythagoras, Epicurus, Aesop, and Aristarchus, who called the sun the center of the universe 1800 years before Copernicus) grew up playing on Samos's sandy beaches. Samos's residents cherish their sumptuous local red wine, *kokkino krasi*, more than anything else.

In summer 2000, wildfires devoured much of the lush greenery on the east side of the island. Touristed areas escaped significant damage, and visitors during 2001 will likely not see any damage around Samos Town. Ancient sites around Pythagorion remain intact, showing the fires' path only in the charred brush nearby.

## VATHY (SAMOS TOWN) Βαθυ ☎0273

Palm trees shade quiet inland streets, an engaging archaeological museum stands across from a garden, and red roofs speckle the neighboring hillside of Vathy, also called Samos Town, one of the northeast Aegean's most appealing port cities.

### GETTING THERE AND GETTING AROUND

**Ferries:** Service to: **Chios** (5hr., 4 per week, 2690dr); **Fourni** (2hr., 5 per week, 1800dr); **Lesvos** (8hr., 1 per week, 4090dr); **Mykonos** (6hr., 4 per week, 5100dr); **Naxos** (6hr., 4-7 per week, 4900dr) via **Paros** (4370dr); and **Piraeus** (12hr., 2-3 per day, 6700dr) via **Ikaria** (2100dr). Ferries to **Kuşadası, Turkey,** leave from Samos Town daily (1¼hr.; 8:30am and 5pm; 10,000dr for a one-way morning departure, 9000dr for a one-way afternoon departure, 11,000dr return for a daytrip; 3000dr Greek port tax). Turkish entrance **visas** must be purchased at the Turkish border by Americans ($45), British (UK£10), and Irish (IR£5), *if* they are planning to stay for more than one day.

**Flying Dolphins:** Zip from Samos Town to **Fourni, Ikaria, Kos,** and **Patmos,** in half the time and at twice the price.

**Flights: Olympic Airways** (☎27 237). Pass the municipal gardens and make a right after the church; the office is 20m up the street on your left. Flights to **Athens** (1hr., 5 per day, 15,500dr) and **Thessaloniki** (2 per week, 25,500dr). Open M-F 8:30am-3:30pm. Samos' **airport** (☎61 219) is 20min. drive past Pythagorion and is only reachable by taxi (3500dr).

**Buses:** Follow the waterfront past Pl. Pythagoras, turn left onto Lekati, and continue one block to the **station.** To: **Pythagorion** (12 per day), **Heraion** (3 per day), **Tsainadon** via **Kokkari** and **Lemonakia** (9 per day), **Avlakia** via **Agios Konstantinos** (7 per day), **Marathokambs** (1-2 per day), **Chrissi Ammos** (3 per week), **Vourliotes** (3 per week).

**Taxis:** (☎28 404). Available 24hr. in Pl. Pythagoras.

**Rentals: Pegasus** (☎61 831 or 62 047), near the dock. Mopeds around 5000dr. Cars around 12,000dr. Open 8:30am-10pm.

## ORIENTATION AND PRACTICAL INFORMATION

Samos Town unfurls around a crescent-shaped waterfront. **Pl. Pythagoras,** identifiable by its four large palm trees, consists of cafes, taxis, and a giant lion statue. Turn onto the side streets between the port and Pl. Pythagoras to hit the most densely packed pension neighborhood on the island. Heading along the waterfront away from the port, past Pl. Pythagoras, will take you to the **Municipal Gardens,** circled by the town's public amenities and the archaeological museum.

**Tourist Office:** (☎28 530 or 28 582), on a side street one block before Pl. Pythagoras. Open July-Aug. M-Sa 8:30am-2pm.

**Tourist Agencies: ITSA Travel** (☎23 605; fax 27 955; email itsa@otenet.gr), on the waterfront at the dock. Helps with travel and accommodations. Free luggage storage. Open 6am-midnight. **Samos Tours** (☎27 715), next door, provides similar services and further info. Free luggage storage. Open 6am-midnight and when boats arrive.

**Banks: National Bank,** on the waterfront just beyond Pl. Pythagoras, has a 24hr. **ATM.** Open M-Th 8am-2pm, F 8am-1:30pm.

**Laundromat:** (☎28 833), near Georgiou's Taverna, one block to the left side of the waterfront. Wash 1000dr, dry 800dr, soap 200dr. Open 8am-11pm.

**Police:** (☎22 100), after Pl. Pythagoras on the far right of the waterfront (facing inland). Doubles as the **tourist police.** Some English spoken.

**Hospital:** (☎27 426), a 10min. walk to the left as you leave the ferry dock. Open 24hr.

**Telephones: OTE,** across from Olympic Airways, behind the church. Open 7am-10pm.

**Internet Access: Net Cafe** (☎22 535) is on the waterfront past Pl. Pythagoras. 500dr per 30min. Open 9am-midnight.

**Post Office:** (☎27 304). Walk past the municipal gardens, turn right after the church and left after the Olympic Airways office. Open M-F 7:30am-2pm. **Postal code:** 83100.

## ACCOMMODATIONS

Samos has just few enough rooms to make it advisable to call head during the high season. If you arrive and all the beds listed below are filled, try the pensions around the Ionia or get help from a travel agent.

**Pension Trova,** Kalomiris 26 (☎27 759). Turn right at the end of the ferry dock and walk 100m along the waterfront to take a left onto E. Stamatiadou before the Hotel Aiolis. Take the second left onto Manoli Kalomiri and wrap uphill around the bend to hit Kalomiris. Cool, traditionally furnished rooms, some with bath and balcony, all with full hospitality. Singles 4000-6000dr; doubles with bath 5500-8000dr.

**Pension Avli,** Areos 2 (☎22 939). Turn right at the end of the ferry dock and walk 100m along the waterfront to take a left onto E. Stamatiadou before the Hotel Aiolis. Take the second right onto Manoli Kalomiri and then your second left onto Areos. Simple 70s-ish rooms around an elegant courtyard. Doubles 6000-7000dr. Open summer only.

**Pension Dreams,** Areos 9 (☎24 350), just up from Pension Avli. Compulsively neat rooms with fridge and bath. The balconies of some rooms rival your backyard in size. Singles 5000-6000dr, doubles 5000-7000dr; triples 6000-7500dr.

## FOOD AND NIGHTLIFE

Gourmands will find their time well-spent in savoring sweet Samian wine, served at all of the island's nearly indistinguishable restaurants, which otherwise offer a standard spate of traditional meals. **Gregory's,** just past the post office heading inland, is a worthy local favorite. The menu is the same as everywhere else in town, but it just tastes better here. (Entrees 1500dr. Open noon-2:30pm and 7pm-midnight.) Similarly priced and more conveniently located is **Christos** (☎24 792), in Pl. Nicolaos behind Pl. Pythagoras, with outdoor seating for optimal people-watching in the main square. The most popular bar at night is **Escape,** a five-minute walk on the way to the Pythagoras Hotel. A patio stretches out over the bay below. Come 3am, all taxis are heading out of town to the discotheque **Totem.** Its mountainside location outside of town means that no noise complaints quiet the music.

##  SIGHTS

The phenomenal **Archaeological Museum** sits behind the municipal gardens. Its broad collection looks at Samos' past glory as a commercial and religious center for worshiping Hera. Finds from ancient Heraion, the temple of Hera, and other local digs are enshrined in two recently renovated buildings full of informative notes; you'll find more proof of Heraion's bygone splendor here than at the crumbled remains at the site. The first building houses intricate Laconian ivory carvings of mythological notables, and awesome statues like a colossal 5m **Kouros** from 560 BC. Pieces of this magnificent *kouros* were found at different times, some of them built into existing walls and cisterns. There's also the stunning Geneleas group. A nearly life-size votive offering depicting a family, it's named after its sculptor; it once graced ancient Heraion's Sacred Way. In the second building, an exhibit on Hera-worship shows off offerings made to the goddess, remarkable for their workmanship and expense. Objects from Ancient Egypt, Cyprus, and the Near East testify to the island's extensive early trade. In the last room, a case of gorgeously nightmarish **protomes** (cauldron handles) is not to be missed. (☎27 469. Open Tu-Su 8:30am-3pm. 800dr, seniors and students 400dr, EU students free.)

During the months of July and August, Samos hosts a number of fine classical and jazz concerts featuring Greek artists as part of the **Manolis Kalomiris Festival.** Contact the tourist office for a schedule of events.

## DAYTRIPS FROM VATHY

### ANCIENT PYTHAGORION Πυθαγορειο

*A bus from Samos Town arrives at Pythagorion every hour (20min., 280dr). The beach town of Pythagorion, 14km south of Samos Town, sits atop the ancient city of the same name. The wildfires of summer 2000 left the town and ruins unscathed.*

The ancient city of Pythagorion, once the island's capital, thrived during the second half of the 6th century BC under the reign of **Polykrates the Tyrant.** Herodotus reports that Polykrates undertook the three most daring engineering projects in the Hellenic world, among them the **Tunnel of Eupalinos,** 1500m up the hill to the north of town. The "tunnel" was in fact an underground aqueduct that diverted water from a natural spring to the city below; it may owe its misnomer to its size, which just fits a person. An impressive 1.3km long, it's in remarkably good condition, although only about 200m of damp cavern are open to visitors. To reach the tunnel, walk back inland from the bus stop in town and follow the signs. The 20min. walk to the tunnel's entrance leads past minor ancient ruins, like a Hellenistic villa and some wells; rolling hills and grazing goats fill the intervals. *(☎61 400. Open Tu-Su 8:45am-2:45pm, last entrance 2:15pm. 500dr, students 300dr, EU students free.)* You can also check out Polykrates' second feat, the 40m deep **harbor mole** (rock pier), which supports the modern pier.

Blocks, columns, walls fragments, and entablatures are strewn throughout Pythagorion like Lincoln Logs after a floorquake. The presentation in the small **Archaeological Museum** is no different. A little over half of the collection fits into the building; many of the ruins are haphazardly scattered on the sidewalk in front. *(☎61 400. Open Tu-Su 9am-2:30pm. Free.)* On the south side of town are the ruins of the **Castle of Lycurgus,** built during the beginning of the 19th century by Lycurgus, a native of Samos and a leader in the Greek War of Independence. The **Church of the Transfiguration** is a pale blue variation on classic Orthodox architecture.

### HERAION Ηπαιον

*The bus from Pythagorion (10 min., 3 per day, 250dr) leaves you in Heraion Town. ☎95 277. Open T-Su 8:30am-3pm. 800dr, students 400dr.*

Polykrates' magnum opus is in Heraion (EAR-ion). Seven centuries of pilgrims had worshiped Hera on Samos when Polykrates began enlarging her temple. Eventually, 134 columns supported the 118m-long, 58m-wide 530 BC version of the **Temple of Hera.** Since a fire damaged it in 525 BC, it has been only minimally reconstructed. On the site, you'll see the lone standing column of the once-

majestic colonnade, and casts of the Geneleas group (now in the Samos Museum). A walk along the beach brings you back to the temple at your own pace. If you can't enter through the beachside back gate, a path brings you inland to the main road and main entrance farther along the beach, past two houses. Follow custom and wrap yourself up in your best toga and carry along a jug of libations on this path, which runs close to the ancient **Iera Odos** (Sacred Way) from Pythagorion to the temple.



## NORTHERN AND WESTERN SAMOS

**BEACHES.** The northern coast of Samos has many crowded, sandy-piled beaches and a few sparsely visited pebble beaches tucked into little coves. Most of the coast is easily accessible from the road to **Karlovassi.** Built on a peninsula 10km west of Samos Town, you'll find the eminently visitable northern village of **Kokkari,** skirted by white pebble shores and clear waters. **Lemonakia Beach,** 1km west of Kokkari next to Tsamadou, and the wide white beach west of **Avlakia** are both alluring. Kokkari, Lemonakia, and Avlakia are reachable from Samos town though the irregular KTEL bus service (7-9 buses per day). Infrequent buses (1-2 per day) shouldn't deter you from the splendid beaches of southwest Samos. A couple kilometers west of the peaceful red-roofed hamlet of **Marathokampos** is the spacious beach at **Votsalakia.** A bit farther is an even better beach at **Psili Ammos.**

**HIKES.** From the village of **Agios Konstantinos,** on the northern coast of Samos, you can trek into the mountains through the Valley of the Nightingales, where songbirds regale the green-treed valley just after midnight. Buses to Agios Konstantinos leave three times a week from Samos Town. The village of **Vourliotes,** 5km south of Avlakia, got hyped up by actress Melina Mercury, who exalted the village for years after her visit there. The cheap, delicious tavernas on the plateia might woo you too. Several kilometers above the town, the 16th-century monastery **Moni Vrontianis** polices the behavior of the populace below. (Modest dress required. Open 8am-noon, 4-6pm.) Two kilometers west of **Paleo,** a path (through a pond and up a series of ropes) leads to three successive waterfalls in the island's northwest corner.

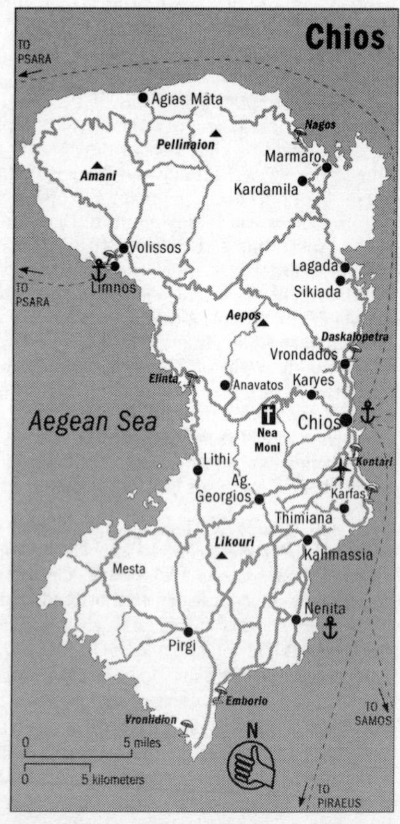


# CHIOS ΧΙΟΣ

Chios (KHEE-ohs) is where the wild things *were:* Orion hunted every last beast down, leaving the island's mountainsides to pine, cypress, and mastic trees, and to the native son Homer. Ever since, human occupants have cultivated and exported the trees' *masticha*—a bittersweet,

gummy resin used in varnish, cosmetic potions, chewing gum, floor wax, and (wonder of wonders) color TVs. Medieval Genovese and Venetian Crusaders (among them Christopher Columbus) made themselves at home here for a while, and in 1822 Chios hosted a failed Greek nationalist rebellion that resulted in 25,000 deaths. A military base and a center of Greek shipping for years, it only recently opened the gates to tourist infiltrators. As its striking volcanic beaches and medieval villages become more accessible, Chios flashes back to the pre-Orion days, as tourists on the way Çeşme do the Wild Thing all night long.

## CHIOS TOWN ☎0271

Many a merchant ship and the occasional tourist ferry dock at Chios Town. Shipping provides the lion's share of this affluent island's wealth, and tourists are the exception instead of the rule at the waterfront tavernas and trendy cafes. Aging Greeks and their hepcat grandkids alike spend their days lounging over *frappés* and backgammon boards. Inland, a crumbling medieval fortress keeps several centuries worth of island history intact within its decayed bulk—from the days of Byzantine occupation to the Nazi's razing of the town in the Second World War. Today, tourists and townspeople penetrate the fallen fortifications daily, partaking of the markets and tavernas that are the fortress's present-day occupants.

**ORIENTATION AND PRACTICAL INFORMATION.** Walking left from the ferry dock along the waterfront, you'll pass a bevy of cafes and restaurants. A right on **Kanari** takes you inland to **Pl. Vounakio,** the social center of town, where most services, buses, and taxis plant themselves on one side or another of the **Municipal Gardens.** Left of Vounakio lies the **market street,** where groceries and bakeries open for business weekday mornings and evenings. Between the ferry dock and the Municipal Gardens, fortress walls hug the Old Town, a residential area with a few small shops and tavernas.

**Ferries** go to: **Alexandroupolis** (1 per week, 7000dr); **Kos** (1 per week, 5000dr); **Leros** (1 per week, 4500dr); **Lesvos** (3hr., 1 per week, 3400dr); **Limnos** (1 per week, 4500dr); **Piraeus** (8 hr., 1-2 per day, 5800dr); **Rhodes** (1 per week, 7100dr); **Samos** (4hr., 3 per week, 3120dr); and **Çeşme,** Turkey (45min., 2 per day, 11,000-12,000dr, plus 3000dr port tax). American, European, and other non-Greek citizens will have to purchase a **visa** if staying more than one day (by date) in Turkey: Americans ($45), Australian (AUS$20), British (UK£10), Canadians (CAN$45), and Irish (IR£5). **Ferries** also go to the island of Psara (3 per week, 2200dr). Hatzelenis Tourist Agency (see below) sells tickets. There are 3 to 5 **flights** per day to Athens (17,400dr) on **Olympic Airways,** whose office is on the waterfront on Psychari. (☎23 998. Open M-F 8am-4pm.) **KTEL buses** (☎27 507 or 24 257) leave from both sides of Pl. Vounakio, right off the municipal gardens coming from the waterfront. **Blue buses** (☎23 086), in the plateia on Dimokratias, are for travel within the vicinity of Chios Town (9km), making 5-6 daily trips to Daskalopetra, Kontari, Karfas, Karies, and Vrondados. **Green buses,** on the left side of the municipal gardens, make trips to: **Emborios Beach** (4 per day, 720dr); **Pyrgi** (8 per day, 620dr); and **Volissos** (7 per week, 930dr). Red **taxis** (☎41 111) cluster in the plateia around the clock.

**THE SEXY SAINT** On July 22nd, every sinner on the island of Chios gathers by the beach at Volissos to celebrate the feast of Chios's own Saint Markella, one of the Orthodox faith's most beloved martyrs and the victim of a gruesome death. Her mother died when she was a child, and upon reaching adolescence, her blossoming beauty drew the lecherous gaze of her father. To resist his increasingly bold advances, she ran away to find refuge in the mountains. He pursued and found her; then began Markella's final escape. She ran as her father followed, shooting arrows at her. She prayed that the ground would swallow her, and it did—but only up to her waist. Markella's father attacked the trapped girl with his sword: he cut off her breasts and then her head, which he cast into the ocean. To this day, the girl's blood is believed to bless the waters around Volissos with its sacred healing powers.

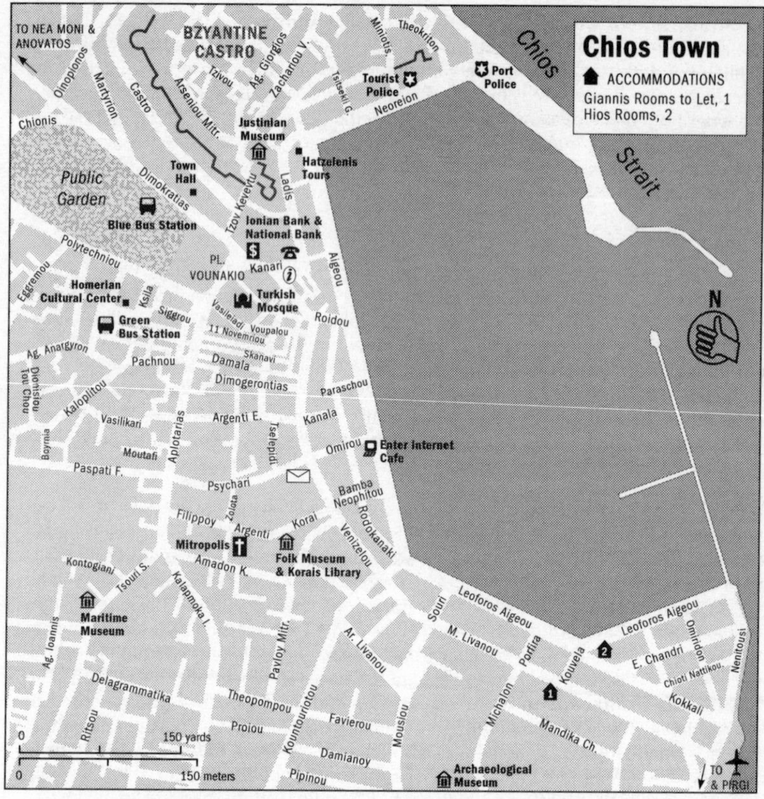


To reach the **tourist office,** Kanari 18, turn off the waterfront onto Kanari, walk toward the plateia and look for the "i" sign. They provide maps and help with transportation and accommodations. (☎44 344 or 44 389. Open Apr.-Oct. M-F 7am-2:30pm and 7-10pm, Sa 10am-1pm, Su 7pm-10pm; Nov.-Mar. M-F 7am-2:30pm.) **Hatzelenis Tourist Agency** (☎26 743 or 20 002; email mano2@otenet.gr) lies at the end of the ferry dock and the start of town; the extremely friendly staff sells **ferry tickets** for all lines except NEL. NEL has its own exclusive agency in the center of the waterfront. (☎23 971. Open M-Sa 7am-1:30pm and 6-9pm, Su 10am-1pm and 6-9pm, and often when boats arrive at night.) The **Ionian Bank,** Kanari 16, is next to the tourist office and offers a 24hr. **ATM** and **currency exchange.** (☎23 522 or 23 434. Open M-Th 8am-2pm, F 8am-1:30pm, Sa 9am-1pm.) A 24hr. **hospital** (☎44 303) is 2km north of Chios. The **OTE,** Kanari 1, is across from the Ionian bank, and phones are on the waterfront. (Open M-F 1am-10pm.) **Enter Internet Cafe,** Aigeou 98, on the second floor of a waterfront building, charges 500dr for 30min. (☎41 058. Open 9:30am-late.) The **post office** is one block inland on Omirou. (☎443 50. Open M-F 7:30am-2pm.) **Postal code:** 82100.

**ACCOMMODATIONS.** Most of Chios Town's accommodations are on the far end of the waterfront from the ferry dock, in high-ceilinged, turn-of-the-century mansions. In high season, seek help from a tourist agency to get a room. In a yellow building at the far right end of the waterfront, the uncommonly hospitable owners at **Chios Rooms,** Leofores 114, offer bright and breezy rooms with polished hard-wood floors, most with a sea view and some with bath. (☎20 198. Singles 4000-5000dr; doubles 5000-8000dr; triples 9000-10,000dr.) One block behind Aigeou on the waterfront, **Giannis Rooms to Let,** M. Livanou 48, has rooms with baths, a common kitchen, and a lovely backyard garden shaded by grapevines heavy with fruit. (☎27 433. Doubles from 7000-9000dr.)

**FOOD AND ENTERTAINMENT.** Myriad vendors set up shop near Pl. Vounakio. For lunch on the cheap, bite into the fresh *spanakopita* or *tyropita* available in **bakeries.** Though the waterfront establishments are well-patronized, they lack something. Love is in the ruins at elegant **Ouzeri Ikobou Plita,** Ag. Giorgios 20, where open-air tables nestle into the tumbledown walls of the Byzantine fortress. To get there, walk past Hatzelenis on Aigeou and make the fourth right. There's no menu; just eyeball the options and pick whatever looks good. (Entrees 1500-2000dr. ☎23 858. Open M-Sa 9pm-late.) Turning off the waterfront on the way to the Archaeology Museum brings you shortly to the **Two Brothers,** on Livanou, who serve good Greek grub in their garden restaurant. (Stuffed tomatoes 1200dr, lamb with potatoes 1500dr. ☎21 313. Open W-M noon-4pm and 8-midnight.)

Glitzy cafes and bars line the waterfront. Of these, locals drink at **Remezzo** and **Metropolis.** (Drinks around 1500dr. Open 9pm-3am.) Everyone stops by **La Loca,** above Mister Mac restaurant, to hop like a jumping bean in the Mexican aura. (500dr cover includes a 1500dr drink. Open 10pm-4am.) Late night in summer, the party moves south. Grab a taxi to a cluster of bars outside of **Karfas** (1500dr); **Stasi** is the hottest and has the cheapest cold beer. In **Kontari,** clubs like **Millennium** and **Fresh** (cover 2000dr) fill up Wednesday through Saturday. The municipal gardens in town host an **outdoor cinema** with shows nightly (1200dr).

**SIGHTS.** The recently renovated **Archaeology Museum,** Michalon 10, inland toward the left end of the waterfront, dissects Chios's role in the ancient Aegean world, with an extensive collection of artifacts and detailed explanatory placards. Don't miss the 3rd-century AD statue of Leda and the Swan, with just enough limbs left on both parties to suggest how the dirty deed was done. (☎82 100. Open Tu-Su 8:30am-3pm. 500dr, students 300dr, EU students free.) Relics of the town's past encircle Pl. Vounakio. To the right of the plateia, the walls of the **Byzantine Castro,** reconstructed by the Genovese, enclose the narrow streets of the **Old Town.** The castle houses a handful of well-restored 14th-century Byzantine wall paintings in the **Justinian Palace** as you enter from Vounakio. (☎26 866. Open Tu-Su 9am-3pm. 500dr, students 300dr.) The minaret of the nearby **Ottoman Mosque** is visible from far away, though almost every surface has a storefront built in front of it. The main room contains a Byzantine collection, but was unavailable for viewing at press time due to a much-needed restoration project in the summer of 2000. During the construction, only a short hallway of Byzantine paintings and a small courtyard of assorted Venetian, Genovese, and Ottoman sculptural pieces are open to visitors. (Open Tu-Sa 10am-1pm, Su 10am-3pm. 500dr, students 300dr.) The **Folklore Museum,** on the first floor of the **Korais Library,** is next to the **Mitropolis,** Chios Town's cathedral. The collection of textiles and tools is more extensive than most; there are no explanatory placards, just pretty designs. (Open M-Th 8am-2pm, F 8am-2pm and 5-7:30pm, Sa 8am-12:30pm.)

## NEA MONI Νεα Μονι AND ANAVATOS Αναβατος

*Check with the tourist office or the green bus terminal in Chios for information on excursions to both sites. (2-3 per week, 3500-4000dr). Taxi drivers may agree to drive you to the site, wait 30 minutes, and bring you back. From Chios, a taxi-tour of Nea Moni and Anavatos costs around 8000dr.*

On the eastern half of the island, several sites silently recall the invasion of the island by the Ottoman Turks in 1822, among them Nea Moni and Anavatos. Pine-covered mountains 16km west of Chios Town cradle Nea Moni (New Monastery). Built in the 11th century, the **monastery** was inspired by the miraculous appearance of an icon of the Virgin Mary to three hermits. Over the centuries, the monastery complex, always one of the world's most important Byzantine monuments, has been rebuilt and enlarged. An 1881 earthquake destroyed much of the complex itself, but most of its structures have been carefully restored. The main chapel was under restoration in the summer of 2000, and the work should

**A FORK AND A DREAM** Although it's built in the twisting alleyways of a medieval castle, little Pyrgi in southern Chios is most recognizable for its *ksista,* the unique geometric patterns that cover the walls of every house in the village. Instead of whitewashing their homes, as is common in the Cyclades, Pyrgian craftsmen first coat each house with a paint made from the gray stone at Emborio. The houses are then whitewashed, and, while the paint is still wet, the craftsmen press in geometric patterns with a fork, creating the village's trademark design. After both coats have dried, artists add splendidly colorful designs to the black-and-white geometry.



be complete by 2001. Before entering the main chapel, you'll pass through the inner narthex, where 11th-century gold **mosaics** are stunning despite their age; their artists are also responsible for the mosaics of Hagia Sophia in Istanbul. An adjoining chapel beside the entrance to the complex houses a **memorial**—gut-wrenchingly real, with its skulls and bones—to monks and villagers massacred by the Turks in 1822, when the island's population was reduced from 118,000 to 18,000. The skeletons were once 600 priests and 3500 women and children who vainly sought refuge in the chapel. Elsewhere on the island, 23,000 residents were killed and 47,000 sold into slavery. (Open 9am-1pm and 4-8pm. Free. Dress modestly.) An on-site **museum** displays church garments and religious items. Open 8:30am-1pm. 500dr. Free Su.)

Anavatos, 15km west of Nea Moni, is a beautiful, abandoned village built into the hillside. The village's women and children threw themselves from these cliffs in resistance to the 1822 invasion. A walk among the ruins of these fortifications provides amazing views of the hills. Stop into the church near to the right of the site's entrance to see a spectacular folk-art rendition of the massacre of 1822.

## PYRGI Πυργι

*Take the bus from Chios (8 per day, 620dr).*

The villages in the southern half of the island, called *Mastichochoria,* produce Chios's famous resin, secreted by squat mastic or lentisk trees. Pyrgi, high in the hills 25km from Chios, is tatooed with black and white geometric designs all over its buildings; they're gorgeous. If you'd like to stay, the **Women's Agricultural Tourist Collective** (☎(0271) 72 496) arranges rooms in private farmhouses in Armolia, Pyrgi, Olymbi, and Mesta. Unless you make reservations far in advance, you'll have to ask around at places with Rooms to Let signs. Pyrgi is also home to the 12th-century **Agioi Apostoloi** church, a replica of the Nea Moni. Thirteenth-century frescoes and paintings by a Cretan iconography school cover almost every inch of the interior. (Open M-F 9am-3pm. 100dr.) The caretaker can unlock the front gate for you; ask for Michalis Vassilis at Mix. Kolika 27, across from the OTE.

## SOUTHERN CHIOS

Only 6km south of Chios Town lies popular, sandy **Karfas,** victim of Chios' latest burst of development. Convenient to both the beach and the amenities of Chios Town, many tourists take up temporary residence here. Blue **buses** run from Pl. Vournakio in Chios (15 per day, 260dr). Hatzelenis Tours in Chios Town can set you up with a double with bath and kitchen by the beach at **Villa Anatoli** (☎20 002 or 32 235. 8000-12,000dr.). Farther south lies pristine **Emborio,** where beige volcanic cliffs contrast with black stones and deep-blue water below. The green **bus** from Chios Town (4 per week, 720dr) drops off at the harbor, from where the first beach is up the only road to the right (facing the water), and a smaller, less crowded shore is up the stairs to your right.

## NORTHERN CHIOS

Nine kilometers north of Chios Town, you'll find the pleasant, pebbly shores of **Vrondados** and **Daskalopetra.** Blue buses from Pl. Vournakio in Chios Town service both (5-6 per day). A two-minute walk from Daskolopetra beach takes you to the **Sanctuary of Cybele.** Here, sitting on the **Stone of Homer,** the bard is rumored to have taught to students gathered around. After Daskalopetra, the main roads wind northwest along the coast past Marmaron to **Nagos,** with its gray stone beach—perhaps a popular spot to cut Homer's classes. High in the hills toward the center of the island, the village of **Volissos,** Homer's legendary birthplace, is crowned by a Byzantine fort with a handful of modern-day habitations scattered around it. **Buses** run here from Chios (7 per week, 930dr).

# LESVOS ΛΕΣΒΟΣ

Unlike the tiny islands of the southern Aegean, Lesvos feels like its own country. Far closer to Turkey than to Athens, it's a strong Greek influence in the politically and culturally complex north Aegean. Lesvos's cosmopolitan, off-beat culture incorporates horse breeding, ouzo, and leftist politics with equal zeal. Huge, geographically diverse, and far from the mainland, the island attracts visitors who spend weeks exploring its therapeutic hot springs, monasteries, petrified forest, sandy beaches, mountain villages, seaside cliffs, and art colonies. Daytrippers may be overwhelmed; you'll need four or five days to get far beyond the main harbor.

Lesvos has one of the richest cultural and artistic legacies in the Aegean. Seventh century BC poet Sappho, fabulist Aesop, philosopher Aristotle, the original epicure, Epicurus, Nobel Prize-winning poet Odysseus Elytis, neoprimitive artist Theophilos, and art publisher and critic Tériade *all* made Lesvos home. This list of dignitaries isn't all; legend has it that Lesvos's population was once entirely female. The tale may date back to the Athenian assembly's 428 BC decision to punish the unruly residents of Mytilini by executing all adult males on Lesvos; the assembly actually repealed the sentence. Still, the idea of an Amazon isle appeals to grrl-power pilgrims paying homage to Sappho and the etymological roots of the word "lesbian." Poets retrace Elytis's footsteps and Sappho's fragments. Despite all the attention, Lesvosians resist tourist degradations.

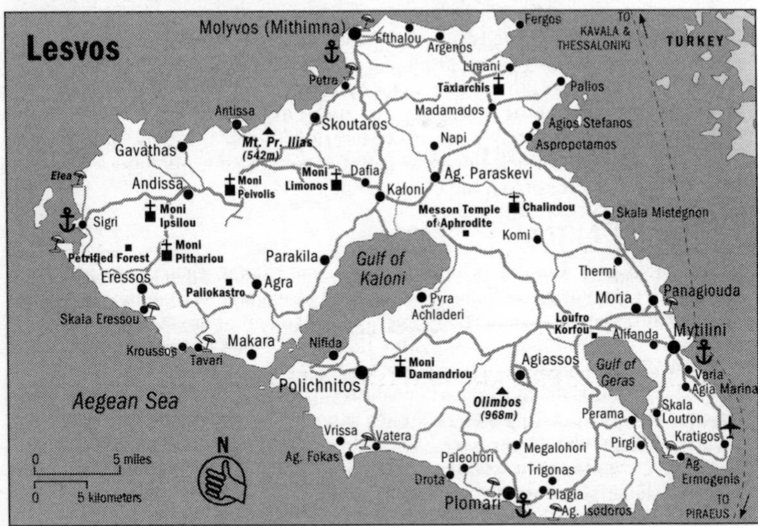

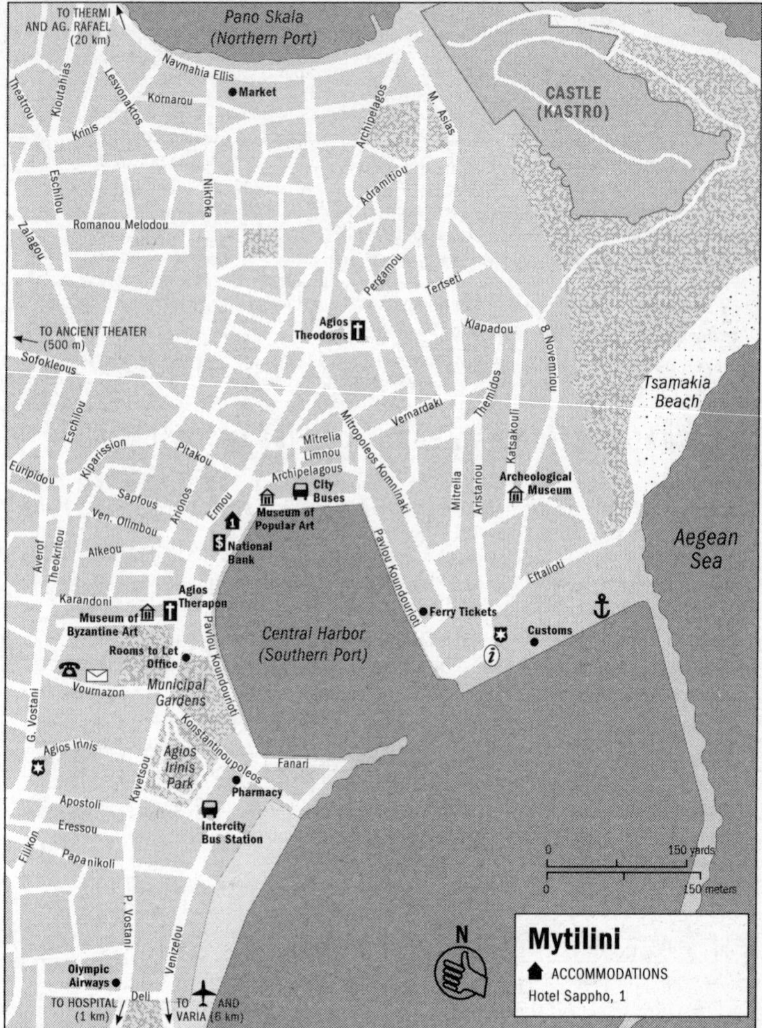


# MYTILINI Μυτιληνη ☎0251

Each morning, the wide harbor of the capital yawns into a modern, working city more reminiscent of Piraeus than of the tiny ports of nearby islands. Most come to Mytilini on business or en route to the rest of the island; aimless wandering in town will turn up decrepit buildings and quiet backgammon games alike.

## GETTING THERE AND GETTING AROUND

**Ferries: NEL Lines,** Pavlou Koundourioti 67 (☎22 220 or 28 480; fax 28 601), along the waterfront three blocks north along the pier. Open 7am-8pm. Service to: **Chios** (3hr., 1-2 per day, 3400dr); **Kavala** (12hr., 2 per week, 6500dr); **Limnos** (5hr., 4 per week, 4400dr); **Piraeus** (12hr., 1-3 per day, 7200dr); **Thessaloniki** (12hr., 2 per week, 8400dr); and **Aivali, Turkey** (16,000dr, includes 3000dr Greek port tax).

**Airplanes:** the **airport** (☎61 590 or 61 490) is 6km south of Mytilini in the direction of Varia; take a **green bus** from the intercity bus station. **Olympic Airways,** Kavetsou 44 (☎28 660), books flights to: **Athens** (5-6 per day, 16,900dr); **Thessaloniki** (7 per week, 22,400dr); **Limnos** (3 per week, 13,400dr); and **Chios** (2 per week, 7500dr).

**Buses:** Several round-trip buses per day go between Mytilini and every other major city on Lesvos; but routes are odd, and Mytilini's **intercity bus station** (☎28 873), 1½ blocks from the south edge of the harbor behind Ag. Irinis Park, is the only real bus station on the island. The first buses leave Mytilini at 9am and return in the afternoon. Service to: **Petra** and **Molyvos** (2hr., 5 per day, 1400dr); **Skala Eressou** (3hr., 2 per day, 2100dr); **Sigri** (2½hr., 2 per day, 2100dr); and **Plomari** (1½hr., 5 per day, 950dr); services reduced on Su. Local **blue buses** (☎28 725), based on the waterfront, run to: **Ag. Marina** and **Varia** (every hr. 6am-8pm, 250dr); **Ag. Rafael** and **Thermi** (every hr. 6am-9pm, 300dr); and **Loutra** and **Koundourtias** (9 per day, 170dr).

**Taxis:** Line up on the corner of Ermou and Vournazon.

**Moped Rentals: Golden Sun Rent-a-Moto** (☎22 722), in an alley off the waterfront past NEL lines agency, rents mopeds for 3700-7500dr.

NORTHEAST AEGEAN

## ORIENTATION AND PRACTICAL INFORMATION

A long, thin cement arm extends southward into the water from the main ferry landing, serving as both fishermen's haunt and makeshift beach (swim on the far side). Ferry and airplane tickets are sold at the offices on the southeast side of the inner harbor, while local buses leave from the station in the northwest bend. The inner harbor street is called **Pavlou Koundourioti,** but becomes **El. Venizelou** south of the Hotel Argo. The **old market** *(Palia Agora)* stretches north along Ermou one block west of the water.

**Banks:** The inner harbor has a **National Bank** with 24hr. **ATM** in its north center next to Hotel Sappho. Open M-Th 8am-2pm, F 8am-1:30pm.

**Public Toilets:** Pleasantly sanitary. 100dr, in the park.

**Emergency:** Dial **166** for an ambulance. Dial **199** for the fire brigade.

**Tourist Police:** (☎22 776), in the large passport control building at the ferry docks. Very helpful, with maps, brochures, and free advice. Open 7:15am-2:15pm and 5-8pm.

**Hospital:** (☎43 777, 46 334, or 40 501), southwest of town on E. Vostani. Open 24hr.

**Telephone: OTE** (☎28 199), 2 doors up from the post office.

**Post Office:** (☎28 836), on Vourhazon near the intercity bus station. Follow signs behind the park near the taxi stand. Open M-F 7:30am-3pm. **Postal Code:** 81100.

## ACCOMMODATIONS AND FOOD

For the cheapest rooms, head to the **Rooms to Let** office (Syllogos Enoikiazomentan Domation), just off the waterfront right after the Bank of Greece. (Open 9am-1pm. Singles 5000-6000dr; doubles 6000-8000dr.) Hotels along the waterfront have similar rates (doubles 11,000-13,000dr) but variable quality. **Hotel Sappho,** in the center of the western waterfront, is more than comfortable and one of the best deals. Rooms have A/C, TVs, phones, and sparkling white private baths. (☎22 888 or 28 415; fax 24 522. Singles 9000dr; doubles 12,500dr.)

It's often best to order from the waiter's list of specials. To get close to the taverna experience, head to the alley Thasou off Ermou, north of the port, to **To Katenilini** (meat 2000-2500dr, salads start at 700dr), where you'll find neither names nor menus—just superb food (2000-2500dr). Tiny **Oi Kolones,** behind the local bus station, offers big, meaty gyros (450dr). As you wait for your fries (300dr), chat about Lesvos with the owner, who hasn't left his storefront chair in years. Walk seaward on the southwestern quay to find fresh fish, hearty food, and an amusing split view of the harbor and a busy children's amusement park at **Taverna O Stratos.** (☎21 739. Entrees 800-3000dr; *saganaki* 800dr; *moussaka* 1400dr. Open 11am-late.) **Zacharoplasteio Valentino,** El. Venizelou 6, has the best almond confections in the city. (☎23 989. Almond cookies 50dr. Open at 9am.)

## SIGHTS

**ARCHAEOLOGICAL MUSEUMS.** Bright yellow signs cheerfully direct visitors to major monuments. The wonderful **old Archaeological Museum,** behind the ferry dock, has a collection of Lesvian artifacts organized to give a linear history of the island. The collection includes Mycenaean, Protogeometric, and Archaic pottery, Classical and Hellenistic vases and sculpture, and remnants from the excavations at Thermi, as well as masks, oil lamps, life-like figurines, and a gold-leafed crown, found and donated by fishermen. Don't miss the smaller building hiding behind the main museum, which contains rare Aeolian tablets. *(Argiri Eftalioti 7. ☎28 032. Open Tu-Su 8:30am-2pm. 500dr.)* Uphill, the **new Archaeological Museum** claims to be the largest and most modern in Greece, with exhibits that emphasize the island's Roman era. The mosaics are particularly interesting. *(On Pl. 8 Novembriou. Open Tu-Su 8:30am-3pm. 500dr.)*

**CASTLES AND THEATERS.** Nearby is the large **Gattelusi Castle.** Tucked away in a pine forest above town, the fortress stands resolute guard over photographers snapping scenic harbor shots. Originally constructed by Emperor Justinian on the site of a Byzantine castle, it bears the name of Francesco Gattelusi, who received Lesvos as dowry in 1355 after he married Justinian's daughter. Genoese, Ottomans, and Greeks have spent successive centuries maintaining the castle walls and underground tunnels. *(☎27 970. Open Tu-Su 8:30am-3pm. 500dr, students 300dr.)* The highest point on the north side of Mytilini is the 3rd-century BC **ancient theater,** built during the Hellenistic period, where 15,000 spectators attended performances and enjoyed near-perfect acoustics. The effect was so impressive that it inspired Pompeii to build Rome's first stone theater. *(Open Tu-Su 8:30am-3pm.)*

**OTHER MYTILINI SITES.** Art aficionados may want to stop at the **Museum of Popular Art,** immediately west of the local bus station on the waterfront. The museum houses authentic costumes and some beautiful period art from all over the island. *(☎41 388. Open M-Sa 9am-1pm and 6-8:30pm. 300dr, seniors and soldiers 200dr.)* If after all this you find you still have a spare hour in Mytilini, visit the enormous late 19th century **Church of Ag. Therapon,** west and one block inland on Ermou *(open 9am-7pm)*, and the neighboring **Byzantine Museum**. *(☎28 916. Open 7am-1pm and 5-8pm. 300dr.)* The church towers over a fish market full of sardines, octopi, and small sharks. Near the tall clock tower at the south end of the harbor is the impressive **Church of Ag. Theodoros,** housing the bones and skull of its patron saint.

**VARIA.** Only 4km south of Mytilini along El. Venizelou, the tiny, unassuming village of Varia (Βαρια) surprises wayfarers with the **Theophilos Museum,** featuring the work of the famous neo-primitivist Greek painter Theophilos Hadzimichali. *(☎41 644. Open May-Sept., Tu-Su 9am-2:30pm and 6-8pm. 500dr, EU students free.)* Next door, the **Musée Tériade** displays an excellent collection of Picasso, Miró, Léger, Chagall, and Matisse lithographs; explanatory blurbs are in Greek, English, and French. Tériade, a native of Lesvos born Stratis Eleftheriadis, was a leading 20th-century publisher of graphic art in Paris. *(☎23 372. Open Tu-Su 9am-2pm and 5-8pm. 500dr, EU students free.)* **Buses** to Varia leave the Mytilini waterfront depot every hour (20min., 250dr). Tell the driver you are going to the museum.

**AGIOS RAFAEL.** 20km into the hills above the capital is the monastery of Ag. Rafael in Thermi. The saint was particularly active in working modern-day miracles, making his chapel and grave a major place of pilgrimage. The door on the bottom level of the church, marked ΑΓΙΑΣΜΑ, leads to a source of holy water. Visitors can stay free for up to two nights, and nearby **Kafe-Estiatoriou O Fotis** offers "home cooking at fair prices." *(☎71 259. Bus from Mytilini runs every hr. for 300dr.)*

**META** Most of the large trucks causing traffic jams at the ferry docks have ΜΕΤΑΦΟΡΕΣ written on the sides. This is the Greek word for "shipping," but it transliterates directly to another English word: "metaphors." *Voila:* the etymological origin of the English rhetorical device which connects two different sets of ideas with one clever figurative leap, much like a large noisy truck connecting two destinations.

## MOLYVOS Μολυβος ☎0253

Hilly and cobbled, the artists' colony of Molyvos spills from the towering castle to the sea like a gingerbread village from a childrens' storybook. Its quaint charm and long stretches of sand make it one of the most visited spots on the island, yet the atmosphere remains serene and the prices reasonable.



**ORIENTATION AND PRACTICAL INFORMATION.** The bus stops at the base of town. **Buses** run from Molyvos to **Mytilini** (3-6 per day, 1400dr); in the summer, local buses run between Molyvos, **Petra,** and **Eftalou.** Check the tourist office for schedules and fares. Near the National Bank, **Kosmos Rentals** rents **mopeds** (5000-7000dr per day), **cars** (13,000dr per day), and **jeeps** (18,000dr per day), including full insurance, tax, and unlimited mileage. (☎71 997. Open 8am-1pm and 4:30-9pm.) Uphill on the left, just before a road that heads left to the public beach is the **tourist information office** where you'll find maps, schedules, and help finding rooms. (☎71 347; fax 72 277; email mithimna@aigaio.gr. Open April-October 7:30am-4pm.) Next door, the **National Bank** offers a **currency exchange** and a 24hr. **ATM** (open M-Th 8am-2pm and F 8am-1:30pm). Just beyond the bank, the road forks; head uphill and right at the next fork to the **post office** (open M-F 8am-2pm). If you head left at the fork instead, you'll find the local **laundry,** where 2500dr will get you clean clothes (☎71 622; open 9am-2pm and 6-10pm) and a **pharmacy** (☎71 427; open 9:30am-2pm and 6:30-11pm). Signs will direct you to the **police station** (☎71 222). **Internet access** is available at **Cafe Cinema** (open 8am-midnight, summer only) just up from the bus stop, and at **Cafe Pengola** (☎71 236) for 1600dr per hour, with an 800dr minimum. **Postal code:** 81108.

**ACCOMMODATIONS AND FOOD.** Signs for domatia dot the town and the helpful tourist office will be glad to find you a bed. Expect to pay 5000-8000dr for doubles in the low season and 8000-10,000dr in the high season. **Hotel Poseidon,** on the road to the public beach, has spacious and homey rooms with phones, TVs and fridges. The little balconies are a nice touch. (☎71 570 or 71 981. Singles 6000-8000dr; doubles 9000-11,000dr; triples 13,000-15,000dr.) **Camping Mithimna** is 1.5km out of town on the road to Eftalou. (☎71 079. 950dr per person, 650dr per tent.)

Tavernas are clustered in the harbor, at the far end of the leftmost seaside road, and they tend to be pricier than the tavernas hidden on the steep inland roads. **Taverna O Gatos,** midway up the hill before the post office, has served fresh traditional fare for 20 years. Ask the friendly staff if you can have a rooftop seat, the view is amazing. (☎71 661. Starters 500-1600, entrees 900-2000. Open 11am-late.) Herbivores rejoice, your prayers have been answered in the form of **Friends** gyros stand (☎71 567). Found on the seaside road, the friendly owner of Friends has created a hearty vegetarian gyro (350dr) stuffed with cucumbers, french fries, and green peppers instead of meat. A small **bakery** is nestled at the top of the uphill road just beyond the post office. (Sweet breads 250-350dr, cookies 50dr each. Open all day.)

**SIGHTS.** The dominating feature of the Molyvos skyline is the **Kastro,** the medieval castle. The view alone is worth a climb up, and the castle itself is superbly preserved and occasionally plays host to theatrical events; call the town hall for information (☎71 313 or 71 323) or keep an eye out for signs. The castle is open Tu-Su 7:30am-3pm. **Exhibitions** by local artists and a small **archaeological museum** may be found in the town hall. While you're there, you can ask about the **Museum of Popular Art.** Despite the culture that abounds, the town's biggest draw is the long, pebbly **public beach** that stretches southward toward Petra and is accessible from various points, one of which is the road to the left before the post office. Equally impressive are the black beaches of **Eftalou;** buses run in summer only.

## PETRA Πετρα ☎0253

This tiny artists' beach town suns itself on a fertile plain 5km south of Molyvos. Petra's thin strip of sandy beach earns the praise of repeat revelers and more: it won the EU's blue banner for cleanliness and environmental awareness in 2000.

Local buses run from **Molyvos** in the summer, but little Petra is certainly within walking distance from its big brother. See the tourist office for bus schedules if don't feel like making the hike. The **bus** stops in the central plateia on the waterfront. Facing inland, the road straight ahead holds the **post office** (open M-F 8am-2pm). The **National Bank** lies on a street to the right (open M-Th 8am-2pm, F 8am-1:30pm). Farther to the right on the water is **Nirvana Travel,** providing one-stop shopping for all of your tourist needs. Friendly owner Rebecca Michealides provides info, **currency exchange,** a book exchange, excursion bookings, and help with accommodations and car rentals. (☎41 991 or 41 977; fax 41 992; email nirvanat@compulink.gr. Open 9:30am-2pm and 6-10pm; available by fax, phone, and email in winter.) The **OTE,** to the left of the plateia on the road to Molyvos, provides telegram services (open M-F 7:30am-1:30pm). **Postal code:** 81109.



The **Women's Cooperative of Petra** can help you find a room and serves up home-cooked meals in the summer. (☎41 238; fax 41 309. Starts serving at 6pm, full meal 3000dr.) Otherwise you can hit the typical beachfront taverna strip, on the road to Molyvos. At night, head to **Magenta** bar and disco on Ermou (parallel to the waterfront). Open all year (7pm-late), the club spins a funky mix of R&B, latin, hip-hop, and soul (beers 500dr, cocktails 1300dr). If you can peel yourself off the sand, you can watch ouzo bottling at **Ouzo Petras,** Ermou 31, an ouzo store with its own old bottling equipment. (☎41 231. Open 10:30am-1:30pm, 6:30-10:30pm.) Before getting happy with your brand-new bottle of liquid licorice joy, climb up the rock in the center of town to the pretty **Church of the Holy Mary with the Sweet Smile** (open 8:30am-9pm, modest dress required).

## SKALA ERESSOU Σκαλα Ερεσου ☎0253

Skala Eressou's seemingly endless beach stretches across the opposite end of Lesvos from Mytilini, completely breaking from the concrete music of the capital. Laid-back and welcoming, Sappho's birthplace attracts an eclectic group of visitors—archaeologists, lesbian poets, and freckled families share the sand. Its western half remains one of the few legal nude beaches on the island.

**ORIENTATION AND PRACTICAL INFORMATION.** Two **buses** run from **Mytilini** each day (3hr., 2100dr). The bus stops in a large parking lot two blocks from the waterfront. Wonder woman Joanna at **Sappho Travel,** one block from the bus stop and before the waterfront, can help with accommodations, **currency exchange,** and other tasks in addition to booking tickets. (☎52 140; fax 52 000; www.lesvos.co.uk. Open 9am-11pm May-Oct., 9am-2pm and 5-9pm in winter.) There are **health clinics** in Eressou (☎52 132; open Tu-Th) and Skala Eressou (☎53 221; M and W 9am-1pm), behind the Hotel Sappho. The nearest **police** are in Eressou (☎53 222). In case of **emergency** call 52 122 or the **Health Center** in Antissa (☎54 440, 54 442, or 54 444). There is **no bank,** so bring either cash or traveler's checks. A few **card phones** are creatively hidden around town; there is one alongside Hotel Sappho. **Postal code:** 81105.

**ACCOMMODATIONS.** **Hotel Sappho,** on the waterfront to the right (facing the water), is a women's-only hotel with spacious rooms, original wall art, and a massage room. (☎53 495 or 53 233; fax 53 174. Singles 6000-8000dr; doubles 10,000-12,000dr; triples 12,000-14,000dr.) Further down the beach to the right, **Villa Manilena** has rooms with fridges and balconies right on the beach. (☎53 637 or 53 094. Doubles 6000-12,000dr; singles and triples available, prices vary.) There is unofficial camping at the far end of the beach, by the nude section farthest from town, with primitive women's facilities. This camping may be tolerated but is **illegal,** so camp at your own risk, and lather on repellent—the bugs are vicious.

**FOOD AND ENTERTAINMENT.** Outdoor cafes and the serene Aegean Sea surround the stone-layered **Square of Anthis and Evristhenous.** Across the bridge, **Yamas** is open all day for breakfast (800-900dr) or cocktails (1200-1500dr). Killer

milkshakes (800dr) are served at the cozy, brightly decorated tables, in addition to tasty North American food, like the veggie pizza (1000dr). Colorful restaurants with bamboo-covered wooden piers sit on the beach and exhibit flawless sunset views of **Sappho's Profile,** formed by the ridge of the western mountains. **Eressos Palace,** set back from the sun-chairs at the beach's west end, serves a hearty fresh *moussaka* (1300dr; entrees 1000-3400dr). To the far left of the walkway, past Yamas, is the **Bennetts' Restaurant,** run by Brit Max Bennett and featuring a refreshing variety of entrees (1200-2700dr). (☎53 624. Open 9:30am-3pm and 6-11pm.) **The Tenth Muse,** in the main plateia, is a popular lesbian bar. Revelers hang at the beachfront bars and cafes that spill onto the sand; after 1am it's hard to tell which bar mixed your cocktail (1000-1700dr).

**SIGHTS.** The 5th-century mosaics once housed in the early Christian basilica of **Ag. Andreas,** three blocks north of the beach, are now in Mytilini's Archaeological Museum. Near the church is the **Tomb of St. Andrew** *(open 9am-1pm).* Behind the church is a small, unimpressive **archaeological museum** featuring funerary *steles* and similar items. *(Open Tu-Su 8:30am-3pm. Free.)* Of greater interest is the large excavation of still-vivid **floor mosaics** that began in the summer of 2000. The uphill road traces the route of pilgrims to the remains of **Sappho's home** in Eressou—and to a transcendent hilltop view at dusk. The river, just west of Skala's center, is home to many rare and exotic birds; peak **bird watching** season is April to May. Farther inland at **Antissa** are the 700,000 year-old volcanically **petrified trees** of Lesvos, one of two such forests in the world (the other is on the Arizona-New Mexico border in the US). Although tourist raids have largely reduced the "forest" to a collection of stumps, it still holds roughly 200 plant and animal fossils and requires a good 90min. for proper appreciation. *(From Mytilini, take the bus to Sigri and walk or ride 8km to the forest. From Skala, you'll need to rent a moped or car.)*

## PLOMARI Πλωμαρι ☎0252

After arson destroyed Megalohori village in 1841, people resettled in the Turkish-inhabited region 12km south, now modern Plomari. From its earliest days, this southern coastal town has had a split personality—it's a resort town brimming with tavernas and trinket shops, and a crumbling fishing village full of octopi nailed to telephone poles to dry in the sun. The overall effect is aided and abetted by Plomari's large ouzo industry.

**ORIENTATION AND PRACTICAL INFORMATION.** Plomari is 40km by bus from Mytilini (1½hr., 950dr). The **bus** stops in the main plateia, where you'll spot a **National Bank** that has a 24hr. **ATM** and offers **currency exchange** (open M-Th 8am-2pm, F 8am-1:30pm). A road to the left wanders through shops and, to the left over a bridge, to a small plateia full of tavernas. On the right of town on the beachside road, facing inland, is the **OTE** and the **post office,** which also exchanges currency (open M-F 7:30am-1pm). **Saloon Cafe,** near the OTE, provides **Internet access** for 1500dr per hour (open 9am-evening). For the **police,** call 32 222. Call the 24hr. **Health Center of Plomari** (just outside town) at 32 151; in a **medical emergency,** dial 166. **Taxis** (☎33 331) wait in the main plateia, next to the bus stop. On the other side of the plateia, **Oceanis Rent-a Bike** (☎32 469 or 32 498) rents mopeds (3500-7000dr), cars (8000-14,000dr), and a few bicycles (800dr). **Postal code:** 81200.

**ACCOMMODATIONS.** While Plomari makes a wonderful daytrip, there are places to get a room should you want to relax a bit longer. The enormous **Hotel Oceanis** is owned by the same friendly proprietor of the rental shop. Rooms come with baths, phones, and balconies. (☎32 469 or 32 498. Singles 7000-8000dr; doubles 9000-10,000dr.) 500m along the road to Agios Isidoros is **Fnini Apartments.** Surprisingly well-priced rooms include kitchenettes, baths, and balconies over the water. (☎32 023 or 32 316. Doubles 4000-9000.)

**SIGHTS AND BEACHES.** The local ouzo is far better than the bottled industrial variety. Try a sample at the **Barbayanni Ouzo Factory,** roughly 2km east toward Agios Isodoros on the way to Plomari, which has its very own **Ouzo Museum.** (☎32 741. Open M-F 9am-7pm, Sa 9am-2pm.) An annual, week-long **Ouzo Festival** is held in late August and features song, dance, and, of course, free ouzo. Plomari also hosts several summertime religious celebrations and cultural events. The one-week **Festival of Benjamin** in late June commemorates the War of Independence leader with dancing and theatrical presentations. On Aug. 15, **Panegyri** is celebrated in time-honored Plomari style.

Beaches appear intermittently around Plomari. To reach small, rocky **Ammoudeli Beach,** turn onto Ag. Nikolaou and follow the signs; it's a 15min. walk south of town. If you continue straight on Ag. Nikolaou you will come to **Agios Nikolaos,** a church sparkling with icons spanning 400 years. 3km east of town, the sandy, golden expanse of **Ag. Isodoros** beach draws a large, bronze-colored following. The area is becoming a major resort, complete with a standard array of pricey hotels and restaurants, and makes a better daytrip than place to stay.

Just 15km north of Plomari on the slopes of Lesvos' Mt. Olympus, you'll find the ceramic crafts center of **Agiassos.** In town, an Orthodox church treasures an icon of the Virgin Mary made by St. Lucas, originally destined for Constantinople in AD 330. When the priest transporting it heard rumors of war, he hid the icon in Agiassos' church. On August 15, Agiassos hosts **Panagia,** a grand annual celebration in honor of the Virgin Mary. The village also boasts an **Ecclesiastical Museum** with Byzantine religious works (ask church officials and priests in town), a **Folk Museum** featuring traditional costumes.

# LIMNOS ΛΗΜΝΟΣ

Everyone who visits Limnos cries twice: once when they arrive and once when they leave, according to a saying. Tiny, remote, laced with dirt roads and spotted with sheep, the island's solitude sinks in slowly. Stubborn Limnos meets travelers on its own terms, somewhere between the two-storied capital, the flamingoes of the eastern salt lakes, and the silent military presence. In the direct, Hephaestan sunlight, bleating goats throng the roads, and from the mountain loneliness emerges a strangely fantastic island whose spaces and light are dreamlike.

Excitement on Limnos is largely seasonal. In the winter, the western salt plains of **Aliki** and **Hortaro Limni** host thousands of migrating flamingoes. On April 23, Ag. George's Day, the town of **Calliope** near Keros Beach holds a horse-racing festival. The hot springs of **Therma,** 4km outside of Myrina, can revive you after a night at Limnos' seaside discos; they usually open midsummer and advertise their locations by postering Myrina's harborfront.

The island's main archaeological sites are **Polichni,** excavated by the Italian Archaeological School in Athens on the east coast of the island; **Hephaestia,** a sanctuary dedicated to the Great Goddess Limnos, built in the 6th century BC 42km from Myrina on the northeast part of the island; and the flat, muddy, pillared **Sanctuary of the Caberoi,** north of Hephaestia, considered the most important excavation regarding the Caberian mysteries. Visit the **Archaeological Museum** in Myrina before trekking out to get a sense of what you'll find.

## MYRINA Μυρινα ☎0254

The island's capital and primary port is a well-proportioned fishing village. At night, the hilly skyline is dominated by an impressive, illuminated Venetian Castle. Each morning, Myrina is roused to the orange dawn by the harborside fishermen.

**ORIENTATION AND PRACTICAL INFORMATION.** The city has two main waterfronts on opposite sides of the **Kastro. Romeikos,** on the Greece-facing side, is longer, pebblier, and more popular; once-regal neoclassical mansions, cafes, and

pricey tavernas, line its sides, all the better for viewing spectacular sunsets behind Mt. Athos. **Turkikos,** facing Turkey, is the active port where ferries and hydrofoils dock; its beach is sandier, shallower, and bordered by the best fresh fish restaurants in town. To get to Romeikos from Turkikos, head inland up **Kyda** (the main artery) past most of the town, and take a left at the bridge to reach the waterfront.



**LIMNIAN 101** For instant status as an honorary islander, turn your sputtering tourist Greek into a convincing local dialect. First of all, you've got to lose those pesky ends of words. True Limnians drop most ending vowels: *andaxi* (ok) becomes "andax," *koritzi* (girl) becomes "koritz," and so on. Next, pick up the favorite local expression: "Qwa!" It's a general exclamation of surprise and disbelief, e.g. "*Qwa!* Brittany Spears is not coming to Greece because of a special effects accident?" Good, now *you* try. You can also earn yourself points for effort by mastering some local slang. One of the most commonly heard expressions on Limnos is "BRA-vo", with the accent on the first syllable for extra sass. It's used as an expression of approval ("You just got a cell phone that rings to the tune of 'Blue'? Bravo!") as well as assent ("You want to go to the nude beach today? Bravo, bravo."). If you're feeling saucy, you can just bust out whenever you feel like it and see what happens. Ready? BRA-vo!

**Ferries** depart from Turkikos and run to: **Agios Efstratios** (2hr., 6 per week, 1600dr); **Alexandropolis** (6hr., 2 per week, 3300dr); **Chios** (10hr., 2 per week, 5200dr); **Kavala** (6hr., 4 per week, 3700dr); **Lesvos** (6hr., 3 per week, 4200dr); **Piraeus** (22hr., 3 per week, 7000dr); **Rafina** (10hr., 4 per week, 5400dr); **Samothraki** (1½hr., 2 per week, 2500dr); and **Thessaloniki** (8hr., 2 per week, 5300dr). Visit **Nicos Vayakos' Tourist and Travel Agency** in Myrina's port plateia for ferry tickets and information. (☎22 900 or 22 460; fax 23 560. Open 8:30am-1:30pm, 7-10pm.) The **Olympic Airways** office (☎22 214; open M-Sa 8am-4pm) is on a street right off of Kyda, next to the post office. They book flights to: **Athens** (7 per week, 16,400dr); **Mytilini** (3 per week, 13,500dr); and **Thessaloniki** (6 per week, 16,200dr). You can also call the airport for reservations (☎31 204 or 31 598). The **bus station** (☎22 464) is in Pl. El. Venizelou, the second plateia along Kyda in the far left corner between a tourist agency and a coffee shop. Although buses serve all of the island's villages, you may get somewhere and find yourself unable to return. You'll be much better off renting a **bicycle** (1500-3000dr), **moped** (3500-9000dr), or **car** (9000-12,000dr); inquire at the harborfront at one of the many agencies. **Taxis** (☎23 820) are at your service in the main plateia, but they run without a meter, so agree on a price before starting your trip.

Kyda leads inland from Pl. 8 Octovriou, past a variety of shops, and into the town's central plateia where you'll find **taxis, card phones,** and the **National Bank** with 24hr. **ATM.** (☎22 414. Open M-Th 8am-2pm, F 8am-1:30pm.) The **dental clinic** is one floor up under the green cross. (☎25 401. Open M-F 8:30am-2pm, 5-9pm.) There's a **tourist information office** to the right along Pl. 8 Octovriou. (☎22 935. Open 8am-3pm, 7-11pm summer only.) One block farther on Kyda, Garofalidi runs to the right. Here you will find the **post office** (☎22 462; open M-F 7:30am-2pm) and a self-serve **laundromat.** (☎24 392. 1800dr for 1-2kg. Open M-F 9am-2pm and 5:30-10pm, Sa 8:30am-11:30pm, Su 11am-11:30pm.) Two doors down from the post office, **Joy Games** offers **Internet access** for 1200dr per hour. (Open 10:30am-11pm.) The **pharmacy** is also on Kyda. (☎22 500. Open M-Sa 6am-9pm.) The **pediatrician** is in a small alley off Kyda, 1 block before the bus station plateia—look for a sign hanging on the second-floor balcony. (☎23 773, home 23 477, mobile (095) 41 82 81. Open 8am-1pm, 6:30-9pm.) The **hospital** is in a large building all the way down Garofalidi on the left, a 10-15min. walk past the post office. (☎22 222 or 22 345. Open 24hr.) Call the **police** at 22 220. In case of **fire,** call 22 199. **Postal Code:** 84100.

**ACCOMMODATIONS AND FOOD.** Waterfront hotel rooms will cost at least 8000-10,000dr for doubles. The police station keeps a list of phone numbers of all available rooms to let, or you can follow one of the many signs off Kyda.

**Hotel Limnos,** at the ferry dock, offers hot showers and balconies with harbor views, as well as TVs, telephones, and fridges. The owners, Harry and Bill, know tons about Limnos. (☎22 153 or 24 023; fax 23 329. Doubles 10,000-12,000dr.)

The hands-down best fish in Myrina is at **To Limanaki,** in the far corner of Turkikos. Order from the glass tank near the kitchen, but remember quality doesn't come cheap: the day's catch will usually go for 2000-4000dr per (whole) fish. (☎23 744. Open 7am-late.) Souvlaki and gyros are on sale for 400-600dr up and down Kyda; **Demis Handmade Souvlaki** (☎22 438), in the same plateia as the OTE, is a local favorite. The restaurants along Romeikos have menus, prices, and specials posted along the waterfront; be sure to get a seaside table for the view of Mt. Athos. At night, cruise the cafe/bar strip at Romeikos.

**SIGHTS.** The **Kastro** that pierces the skyline and divides the waterfronts also houses several dozen deer; if you don't catch sight of them, you can at least enjoy the stunning view and the ruins of the 7th-century BC fortress, reworked by Venetians in the 13th century. Follow signs from Myrina harbor for the easiest ascent. The network of dungeons and tunnels underlying the kastro is only for daring explorers with flashlights. After you've worked up a gnawing hunger climbing, stop by any of the local pastry shops for *bougatsa*, an incredible Mediterranean cream pastry perfected in Limnian ovens and best before 9am. In the middle of Romeikos right next to Hotel Castro, the **Archaeological Museum** offers A/C and a fascinating collection from the sites on Limnos: Poliochini, Hephaestia, and the Sanctuary of the Caberoi. Don't miss the sacrificed bull-calf on the second floor. *(☎22 990. Open Tu-Su 8:30am-3pm. 500dr, students free.)*

**DAYTRIP FROM MYRINA: PLATI** Πλατη. Two winding kilometers up Garofalidi out of Myrina, tiny Plati—virtually unchanged since the Second World War—peeks around the Malliaris hills to face the water. Travel past sleepy-eyed donkeys and wheedling chickens, through milky foothills and down to the wide, trembling lip of the sea. The road ends in **Odos Anastasios Malliaris,** a street named for the illustrious founder and his grandson, the noted American economist. Follow the bend right to the town plateia to find two tavernas, a supermarket, and the ornate **Church of Ag. George.** From the plateia, a road sign reading "Beach" leads down to the shore. You can also ask for directions to the *langada*, a freshwater spring with a beautiful view of the sea.

**Plati Beach** attracts crowds of both loyal islanders and Brits—you'll find the latter at **Limnos Village. Villa Aphrodite,** the other waterfront resort, attracts a more continental set and has events almost every night (cover 1000-3000dr). The rowdy beachside taverna **O Tzimiz** (Jimmy's) is another local favorite (entrees 1200-3000dr). When Plati Beach gets crowded in high season, take a 15min. walk on the seaside road along the coast (with the water on your right) to a beach hamlet at the rocky road's end. Look for the ruins of old walls underwater, but don't wade near shore—there are seasonal jellyfish. The little island in the bay is a 30min. swim, but beware of motorboat cross-traffic.

# THASOS ΘΑΣΟΣ

Just off the coast of Kavala (p. 249) lies Thasos, the green jewel of the North Aegean. According to legend, Thasos was founded when the devoted brother of Europa gave up pursuing his abducted sister and settled on this remote island. "The Green Island" fully deserves its nickname, with its cool, forested mountains, thriving agriculture, and an isolated north coast that is a hiker's paradise.

As an ancient exporter of gold, silver, white marble, and its famous wine, Thasos attracted the unwelcome attention of Phoenician, Athenian, and Roman conquerors. This was just the beginning. A slew of invading forces used and abused the island. The Thassians who were not killed or sold into slavery were forced to hide, fleeing to mountain villages or caves. Along with most of northern Greece, Thasos

returned to Greek rule in 1912 at the conclusion of the First Balkan War. Since then, massive forest fires have threatened to obliterate the island's greenery, but the forests are slowly reviving. Today, Thasos thrives on trades like beekeeping, shepherding, farming, and jam-making. The quiet island is a nature lover's escape from the crazier party islands to the south.



## LIMENAS Λιμενας ☎0593

The island's capital and tourist center is built atop the foundations of the ancient city, and ruins pop up here and there in the streets. Also known as Thasos Town, Limenas sees the highest concentration of tourists, and is accordingly more crowded and expensive than the rest of the island.

### GETTING THERE AND GETTING AROUND

The village of **Prinos** (18km west) is the point of arrival and departure for ferries.

**Ferries:** The gray port police building and ticket booth post schedules. Ferries go to **Keramoti** (35min., 12 per day 7:15am-10:30pm, 400dr). From **Prinos,** ferries go to **Kavala** (1½hr., 8 per day 6am-8pm, 850dr) and **N. Peramus** (1½hr., 5 per day 8:30am-10pm, 850dr). Bus schedules between Prinos and Limenas are synchronized with the ferries. You must return to Kavala for ferry connections to other islands.

**Flying Dolphins:** Hydrofoils zip to **Kavala** from Limenas (45min., 6 per day 6am-5:30pm, 2000dr), and from Limenaria, on Thasos's south coast (45min., 8:20am and 3pm, 3000dr). Schedules are posted at the port police and ticket booth, and docked boats declare upcoming departure times with signs on board. Tickets can be bought on board.

**Buses:** The station (☎22 162) is across from the ferry landing, on the waterfront. Open 7:30am-8:15pm. To: **Limenaria** (1½hr., 11 per day 6:35am-8:45pm, 850dr), via **Prinos** (30min., 13 per day 6:35am-8:45pm, 360dr); **Panayia** (15min., 12 per day 6:45am-9:15pm, 230dr); **Skala Potamia** (30min., 12 per day 6:45am-7:15pm, 300dr); **Aliki Beach** (1hr., 4 per day 9:15am-4:15pm, 700dr); **Potos** and **Pefkari** (1¼hr., 11 per day 6:35am-8:45pm, 900dr); **Theologos** (1½hr., 5 per day 8:45am-4:15pm, 1150dr); and all the way around the island and back to **Limenas** (2½hr., 8 per day 6:35am-4:15pm, 2050dr). Ask at the tourist police or bus office for schedules.

**Rentals: Budget** (☎23 150), on street perpendicular to the waterfront. Cars 15,000dr, including 100km and damage waiver. Open 8am-1:30pm and 5-9pm. **Billy's Bikes** (☎22 410 or 22 490) is next door. Motorbikes 4000dr. Open 9am-2pm and 5-9pm.

**Taxi:** (☎23 841), near the ports.

**Water taxi:** Daily from Limenas to **Golden Beach** (leaves 10:30am, returns 5pm; 1000dr) and **Makryamos** (leaves 10:30am, returns 10:50am and 5:40pm; 500dr).

### ORIENTATION AND PRACTICAL INFORMATION

A small crossroads near the ferry landing connects the waterfront road and **28 Octovriou,** a jungle of souvenir shops and souvlaki joints running parallel to the water one block inland. With your back to the water, to the left is the **Old Port** and the ancient **Agora.** The small central plateia with its withering plane tree lies about two blocks farther inland.

**Tourist Agencies: Thassos Tours** (☎22 546), under the yellow sign, is right on the waterfront. Rents motorbikes (3000dr), suggests rooms, and has advice on tours of the island. Open 9:30am-10:30pm. **Thassos Tourist Services** (☎22 343), on 28 Octovriou behind the row of tavernas, has maps of the ancient agora, and **exchanges currency.** Open 9am-1:30pm, 6-9pm; closed Th.

**Bank:** There's a **National Bank** where 28 Octovriou meets the waterfront, with an automated 24hr. **currency exchange** and **ATM.**

**Police:** (☎22 500), on the waterfront by the port police. Open 24hr.

**Tourist Police:** (☎23 111 or 23 580), with the police. Open 8am-10pm.

**Port Police** (☎22 355), in the gray building with Greek flags at the waterfront's center. Open 6am-11pm.

**Health Center:** (☎71 100), in Prinos. Open 24hr. There is no hospital on Thasos; the nearest is in Kavala.

**Telephones:** The **OTE** is on 28 Octovriou, a block down from Thassos Tourist Services. Open M-F 7:30am-10pm.

**Internet Access: Niko's Games** (☎23 150), on the corner a few doors down from Thassos Tourist Services. 1000dr per hr. Open 10am-3am.

**Post Office:** Head inland from Thassos Tours and turn right at the fourth corner. Open M-F 7:30am-2pm. **Postal code:** 64004.

## ACCOMMODATIONS

There's no need to stay in a hotel on Thasos—the plentiful domatia are a much better deal. The streets behind 28 Octovriou are crammed with rooms to let signs; most cost 5000-6000dr per single; hunt around for a good price, and don't take anything over 6000dr. If you do want to stay in a hotel, check the large blue sign at the dock—it lists phone numbers for the pricey hotels, pensions, and campgrounds.

**Hotel Athanasios** (☎22 545). To find this wonderful exception to Thasos's hotels, walk down the waterfront with your back to the Old Port. Make a left after the Hotel Xenia. On the right, at the end of a narrow lane, the hotel is nearly swallowed up by grapevines and plane trees. Spacious, light rooms, some with baths, relax in an unhurried countryside calm. Singles 5000dr; doubles 6000dr; triples 7000dr.

**Hotel Lido** (☎22 929), just past the post office, toward the plateia. Basic rooms in the middle of town. Fridges, phones, and private baths. Singles 6000dr; doubles 7000dr.

## FOOD AND NIGHTLIFE

The waterfront is packed with cheap tavernas and *tsipouradika* (where fiery *tsipouro* replaces wine as an accompaniment to food; see **Moonshine,** p. 174). Nocturnal hot spots are scattered throughout Limenas. The **Island Cafe,** on the beach on Limenas's eastern edge, is popular early in the night, when MTV blares loudly and dancing moves to the sand (beer 800dr, cocktails 1500dr). Across the street is the more relaxed **Epekeina,** with tables and chairs on an open-air patio. Right on the plateia is the pounding **XXL Club,** which kicks out the jams to a different theme party (Mexican night, Absolut night, Pirate's Party) every night. (Cover 1000dr. Open until 3am.)

**Simi Restaurant** (☎22 517), in the old port on the waterfront. One of the best located and most popular spots in Limenas, with a laid-back atmosphere and lots of tasty fish and shellfish. Entrees 750-3400dr.

**Selinos Taverna,** some 800m in from the port; take the road past the post office, near the overgrown Temple of Hercules. Secluded and romantic, with Greek music playing softly in the background. Mixed meat, seafood, and rabbit-food options, like *kolikomezedes* (zucchini burgers; 700dr). Entrees 1000-2300dr. Open 6pm-1am.

**Restaurant Syrtaki** (☎23 353), past Simi and the old port at the very end of the waterfront road. An ocean-oriented view and menu. Entrees 950-3100dr.

## SIGHTS

Just past the Old Port are the ruins of the ancient **agora** and **acropolis,** built in the 5th and 6th centuries BC. The crumbled streets and toppled pillars invite you to scramble over them, and maps of the Old City are available at Thassos Tourist Services. Farther up the hill are the remains of a 4th-century BC Greek **theater.** As of summer 2000 it was being restored, with little visible beyond a tangle of stone, dirt, and uprooted trees. To find the theater, turn right behind the old port and continue to a fork in the road, just beyond the ruins of the **Temple of Dionysus.** The middle of

the three paths leads to the theater. Ringing the hills around Limenas are the well-preserved marble **city walls,** inscribed with Archaic reliefs.

The **Vagis Museum,** just outside of Potamia, displays sculptures by Thassian artist Polygnotos Vagis (1894-1965). Born in Potamia, Vagis emigrated to New York at age 14, where he studied art and began mixing Archaic forms and postures with modern movement and expression. A rival museum in Kavala (p. 252) holds more of his works. (☎61 182. Open Tu-Sa 10am-12pm and 6-7:30pm, Su 10am-1pm. Free.) Closed for renovation as of summer 2000, the **Archaeological Museum** near the old port displays mosaic floors and sculptures found on the site, including a colossal 6th-century BC statue of Apollo with a ram draped around his shoulders.



Beachgoers may have a hard time choosing among Thasos's beautiful sands. Between Panagia and Potamia, the golden, popular **Chrisi Ammoudia** stretches endlessly. To the south, **Aliki**'s twin coves, formed as sand shifted over a Roman marble quarry, shelter slabs of bleached white rock and crevices ideal for snorkeling. More isolated spots can be found along the water in both directions from Limenaria—just rent a bike or head out on foot, and pick a cove. For a guide to the superb **hiking** in the relatively untouched interior, pick up "Walking in Thasos" at any of the tourist agencies.

## LIMENARIA Λιμεναρια ☎0593

Limenaria, Thasos's thriving second town, is across the island from Limenas on a glorious curve of sandy beach on the island's southern tip. Much smaller and more relaxed than its bustling counterpart, Limenaria is a haven of unhurried calm, breeze-blown waves, and long, lazy sunsets.

**ORIENTATION AND PRACTICAL INFORMATION.** Limenaria's two main streets run parallel to the waterfront. One main crossroad, **Eth. Antistaxsis,** has **Speedy Rent-a-Car** (☎52 700; cars 10,000dr per day), and beyond that, the town's **OTE.** (☎513 599. Open M-F 7:30am-2pm.) The **post office** (☎51 296; open M-F 7:30am-2pm) and **National Bank,** with a 24hr. **ATM,** are both on the far right edge of the waterfront, facing inland. The **bus stop** is on the waterfront, a few blocks left from the post office. The **police** (☎51 111) are on the first street inland in the center of town. **Postal code:** 64002.

**ACCOMMODATIONS, FOOD, AND NIGHTLIFE.** Hotels and rented rooms abound throughout Limenaria, especially on the left part of the waterfront. Family-owned **Hotel Asterias,** on the waterfront to the left of Eth. Antistaxsis, offers rooms with baths and some ocean views. (☎52 497. Singles 5000dr; doubles 7000dr; triples 8000dr). Next door, **Hotel Molos** has pleasant, bright rooms, many with balconies that overlook the water. All have baths and shared fridges. (☎51 389. Singles 6000dr; doubles 8500dr; triples 9500dr.)

The entire waterfront in Limenaria fuses into one mega-restaurant, comprised of the town's numberless tavernas and snack bars. **Il Mare,** just opposite Eth. Antistasis, serves all kinds of seafood delicacies at the romantic tables right on the water. (Entrees 1500-3000dr.) Across from the bus stop, you'll spot popular **O Vasilis,** hung with fishing nets and specializing in fresher-than-fresh fish: you pick your still-swimming meal from the tank. (Entrees 1700-3200dr.) Right across is **Restaurant Maranos,** on the right edge of the waterfront, which offers a pleasant shady environment, classic *rembetika*, and many fish choices. (Entrees 1000-2800dr.)

Presto-change-o! Come nightfall, the wall of waterfront restaurants become a single long bar. **Istos Cafe-Bar** blares American music. (Beer 1000dr; cocktails 1500-2000dr.) Follow the signs two streets inland to the **Rock Cave Bar,** where the DJ spins underground rock and electronica. It's quiet enough to appreciate the music while holding a conversation. (Beer 500dr; cocktails 1000-1500dr.) The popular, massive disco **Bolero,** 1.5km east of town on the road to Pefkari, booms to a different liquor promotion every night. (Cover 1000dr. ☎52 180.)

# SAMOTHRAKI ΣΑΜΟΘΡΑΚΗ

One of the Aegean's northernmost islands, Samothraki (also called **Samothrace**) lies well outside the tawdry tour-group circuit, reserving its charms for the few who visit its pristine shores. When the first Thracian colonists arrived in the 10th century BC, they saw the same thing you'll see today when your ferry pulls into port: dry grassy fields spread outward from the base of the Aegean's tallest peak, the pine-blanketed 1670m Fengari "moon." An occasional lonesome tree flags the fields. Remote, scarcely developed, and full of beautiful wilderness, Samothraki attracts Greeks who would willfully choose swatting mosquitoes in a tent over clubbing until dawn. Though all kinds of people visit, there are, on the whole, more hiking boots than high heels, and guitars outnumber cell phones as handheld accessories. This laid-back crowd lends the place a grungy *joie de vivre*—a change from the run-of-the-mill island summer glitz of other islands.

Early on, Samothraki was a place of pilgrimage for Thracian settlers who worshipped the Anatolian Great Gods that preceded the Olympian pantheon. Philip II of Macedon and bride-to-be Olympia may have met here as candidates to join the religion; Sparta's Lysander and Julius Caesar's father-in-law, Piso, were initiates, too. Unlike other mystery cults, women, slaves, and all comers could gain membership. The religious center shut down after centuries of operation, when the Roman Empire banned all non-Christian practices in the 4th century AD.



## KAMARIOTISSA Καμαριοτισσα ☎0551

Even with tourist agencies along the waterfront road and the busy comings and goings of buses and ferries, Kamariotissa retains the untouched charm of the island. Don't come in search of crowds or nightlife; the town is so small that only the coastal road has streetlights.

**ORIENTATION AND PRACTICAL INFORMATION.** Everything in Kamariotissa is within a stone's throw of the waterfront. **Ferries** connect Samothraki with: **Alexandroupolis** (2½hr., 1-2 per day, 2300dr); **Kavala** (4hr., 3 per week, 2800dr); **Limnos** (3hr., Tu 11am, 2500dr); and **Piraeus** (19hr., Tu 11am, 8500dr). **Flying Dolphins** run to: **Alexandroupolis** (1hr., 21 per day, 4700dr); **Limnos** (1½hr., 4 per week, 4900dr); and **Maronia,** south of Komotini (1hr., Sa and Su 8:30am, 4700dr). For tickets and schedules, ask the port police or **Saos Tours** (☎41 505; open 7:30am-2pm and 6-10:30pm) and **Nikis Tours** (☎41 465; open 7:30am-2pm and 5-10:30pm). Saos Tours doubles as the island's main **bus station.** In summer, buses run to: **Alonia** (10 per day, 6:30am-7:30pm, 330dr) via **Hora** (230dr); the **campsites** (20min., every 10min. 8:30am-9pm, 680dr) via **Paleopolis** (250dr) and **Therma** (370dr); and **Profitis Ilias** (20min., 14 per day, 450dr) via **Psira Potomos** (350dr) and **Lacoma** (350dr). **Taxis** wait on the waterfront (8am-1am). Rent **mopeds** at **Niki Rent Motor Bikes** in the colorful, flag-adorned lot across from the pharmacy. (☎41 305. Mopeds 4000dr and up per day. Regular bikes 2000dr per day.)

Facing inland, past the waterfront docks on the left, a Greek flag marks the **port police.** (☎41 305. Open 24hr.) Nearby on the waterfront is the **National Bank,** which **exchanges currency.** (Open M-Th 8am-2pm, F 8am-1:30pm.) There is **no ATM** on the island, so bring plenty of cash. The bank in Hora, the island's capital 5km inland, processes **credit card** transactions. There's a **pharmacy** around the corner from the bank. (☎41 581. Open M-F 9am-2pm, 6-10pm; reduced Sa-Su.) The **Internet Cafe** is farther down the same block on the left. (1000dr per hr. Open 9am-2am.) The **post office, OTE,** and **police station** (☎41 203; open 24hr.) are in Hora. **Postal code:** 68002.

**ACCOMMODATIONS.** Although Samothraki has managed to escape the housing crunch that plagues the more heavily touristed islands, accommodations can still be hard to come by. Your best bet is to comb the streets off the port for homes offering domatia. Saos and Nikis Tours (see above) can brief you on the current room situation in town and will often help find accommodations. Doubles average 8000dr or 10,000dr with bath, although in July and August they can run higher. The rooms of **Evangelia Kordonia,** right uphill from the internet cafe, are bright and spacious, with electric fans and shared baths. (☎95 083 or 95 146. Doubles 8000dr and up.) Family-run **Vasiliki**

**Karoyiannis** has rooms with shared baths and ceiling fans on the street between Nikis and Saos Tours. (☎41 165. 6000dr.) For other cheap rooms with private baths, continue uphill and turn right at the road's end. **Xatzi Michaeli** has bright rooms with private baths, fans, and a shared fridge. Walk uphill on the road to the right of Saos Tours, go right at the market, and it's the first house on your left. (☎41 536. Doubles 10,000dr.)



**FOOD AND NIGHTLIFE.** The waterfront teems with tavernas specializing in fresh seafood. Most have no need for a menu—just go inside and point at your fish of choice. **I Sinatisi,** a few doors down from Nikis Tours, is the best in a row of fish tavernas. Excellent seafood appetizers pave the way for perfectly grilled fresh fish, with the setting sun as a natural, gorgeous backdrop. (Entrees 900-3200dr. ☎41 308. Open until 2am.) Another excellent spot is **I Klimataria,** on the left-hand side of the waterfront, which features old standbys and some more innovative dishes, such as *yiannotiko*, pork with vegetables and cheeses. (Entrees 1000-2500dr.) If fish just doesn't do it for you, check out **To Kehayiadiko,** a carnivore's paradise straight across from the port. Try any of the local goat dishes, or any of the variety of animals served on spits. (Entrees 1000-2100dr. ☎32 708.) While away the day at **Kafe Moka** with *loukoumades*, ice cream, and coffee. (Sweets 400-800dr. ☎31 332.) Nightlife in Kamariotissa is so laid-back, it's almost non-existent. Beyond a couple of chill *barakia* (little bars), the town mostly has a drink after dinner and dozes off. Both **Diva** (☎76 305), across from the ferry docks, and **Big Blue,** on the far right edge of the waterfront, are good spots for a relaxed drink by the dying light of the setting sun. Side-by-side across from the port are **Cafe Aktaion** and a nameless, popular vine-covered **bar,** which draw relaxed, easy-going crowds.

**DAYTRIP FROM KAMARIOTISSA: PALEOPOLIS.** Paleopolis and the **Sanctuary of the Great Gods,** Samothraki's premier attractions, lie 6km east of Kamariotissa. (Open Tu-Su 8:30am-8:30pm. 500dr, students free; free on Sunday.) Before the island's 8th-century BC Aeolian colonization, the chief goddess worshipped here was **Axieros,** or the Great Mother; three other gods completed the **Kabeiroi** group: Axiokersa, Axiokerson, and Kasmilos. These gods were assimilated into the Olympian Pantheon; Axieros was redubbed for the fertility goddess Demeter, while two of her consorts, believed to protect sailors, were associated with the twins Castor and Pollux. Disclosing initiation secrets was punishable by death, so the rituals remain shrouded in mystery. There were probably two levels of membership: first, the *myesis*, then the higher *epopteia*. The first purification took place in the **Anaktoron,** at the lowest part of the temple complex. The second rite took place in the **Hieron,** a courtyard whose five reconstructed columns now form the site's central attraction. In the **palace** at the southern end, aspiring initiates donned special vestments and were given a lamp. The palace abuts the Anaktoron, with its circular wooden platform upon which the newly inducted were presented.

The enormous cylindrical **Arsinoëin,** given to Samothraki by Queen Arsinoë of Egypt, demonstrates the importance of circles to the site. The walls (now preserved in the museum) are decorated with rosettes and heads of oxen. They once stood at the sacrificial site. The nearby **Sacred Rock** was the original center of the cult's practices. In the center, the Doric Hieron—containing pits for sacrifices, an altar for libations, and seats for the audience—saw the final stage of initiation. Confessing their worst deeds, the candidates were purified. A scrubby hillside is all that remains of an ancient **theater.** On top is the spot on which the **Winged Victory** (or **Nike**) **of Samothrace** once stood upon a marble base shaped like a ship's prow. Removed to Edirne, Turkey, it was then looted, by a French consul in 1683. It now presides over the Louvre in Paris, one of its greatest treasures. Above the sanctuary are the remains of the **ancient town** of Samothraki, where the apostle Paul lived for a year on his way to Kavala in AD 49-50.

Beside the ruins, the **Paleopolis Museum** is slightly underwhelming. It houses gargantuan entablatures from the **Arsinoein** and the **Hieron,** a weathered bust of the melancholy prophet **Tiresias,** and a galling cast of the Nike of Samothrace—a "gift" to Greece courtesy of the French. The relief of dancing girls symbolizes the marriage of Cadmus and Harmonia. The dance represented the onset of winter, a time of mourning to be followed by spring's renewal of life and bursting of seed. *(☎41 474. Open Tu-Su 8:30am-3pm. 500dr, students 300dr.)*

# CYCLADES ΚΥΚΛΑΔΕΣ

Happy is the man, I thought, who, before dying, has the good fortune to sail the Aegean Sea.
—Nikos Kazantzakis

When people speak longingly of the Greek islands, they are probably talking about the Cyclades. Whatever your idea of the Aegean—peaceful cobblestone streets and whitewashed houses, breathtaking sunsets, sunny hikes, Bacchic revelry—you can find it here. The islands' name derives from their spiral shape: the *kyklos* (cyclical) pattern around sacred Delos showed ancient worshipers that the island lay both at the center of the islands and at the center of their faith.



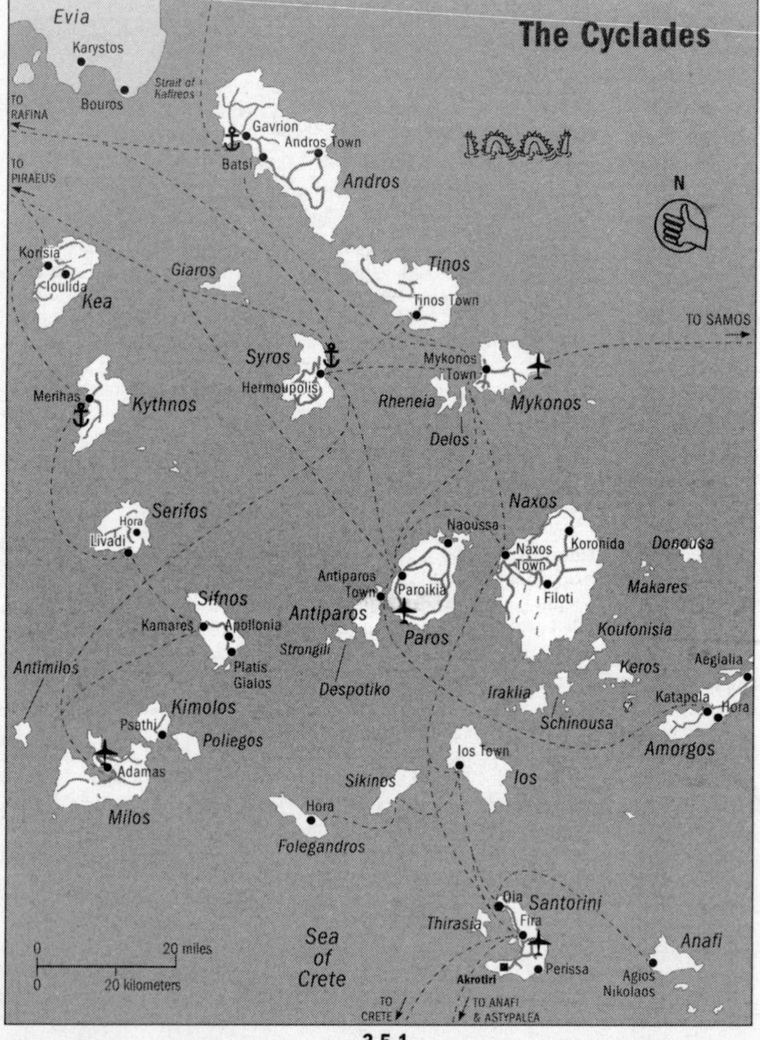

Today, the islands fall into a few broad groups. Although quiet villages and untouched spots still hide in their corners, Santorini, Mykonos, and Ios have become a partier's three-pronged mecca. Santorini is the most chic and expensive, with spectacular views along its black sand beaches. Mykonos ranks a close second in sophistication (and price); it uncorks some of the wildest nightlife on earth. Beer-goggled Ios can be summed up in three words: frat party run amok. All right, that was four words, but after a night on Ios you won't be able to count either. Paros, Naxos, and Amorgos also get their share of visitors, but they're less frantic, more pristine, and attract more families and hikers. Few non-Greek vacationers sprawl in the sand on Andros, Tinos, Syros, Folegandros, Sikinos, Milos, Kimolos, Serifos, Sifnos, Kythnos, and Kea (deep breath). The pint-sized Little Cyclades—Koufonisia, Donousa, Iraklia, and Schinousa—are isolated oases blissfully untouched by tourism.

Many tourist amenities on these islands are seasonal. Accommodations, especially, are only open April through October. During the summer high season, lodgings are scarce and expensive, so make reservations in advance.

**HIGHLIGHTS OF THE CYCLADES**

**LOSE YOUR MIND. LOSE YOUR PANTS.** Party naked on Ios (p. 394).

**A SYMPHONY'S STRAINS** accompany a sunset over lava-made cliffs and smoke-colored sand on Santorini's western coast (p. 399).

**GET COSMOPOLITAN** on the streets of Mykonos (p. 360), the Aegean's premier gay destination.

**POKE AROUND** the ruins of the Cyclades' ancient religious capital at Delos (p. 366).

**THE BIG BLUE** of film fame lives in the pristine hikes, dives, and the bleached Byzantine Hozoviotissa Monastery on a sheer cliff of Amorgos (p. 390).

**MODERN ART** coexists with Andros's whitewashed walls and Venetian ruins (p. 352).

**MILOS' SHIMMERING BEACH** casts back the sun from its pearly sand (p. 408).

# ANDROS ΑΝΔΡΟΣ

The magnificent hour-long drive from the ferry landing at Gavrio to Andros Town winds above Andros's famous, beloved beaches. This island is *the* weekend destination for Greece's wealthy ship captains, who, in their zeal to keep their hideaway unspoiled, restrict ferry access to the island. Streams and stone walls outline green and purple tiered fields; the island's 300 sandy beaches glow in solitude beneath the sun, each more breathtaking than the last. Athenian vacationers crowd in on the weekends, but Andros remains a quiet escape for those who delight in untrammeled ground and nights gazing out to sea.

## BATSI Μπατσι ☎0282

Centered around a long stretch of golden sand, Batsi is the tourist capital of Andros, with varied food and accommodations options and the liveliest nightlife. Visitors stroll the waterfront by night, pausing for a drink at a *kafeneion*.

**ORIENTATION AND PRACTICAL INFORMATION.** The main **bus stop** and the **taxi stand** are at the end of the beach in a small plateia. A single **bus** route passes **Andros Town** (5-7 per day, 650dr) and **Gavrio** (300dr), Andros's port. From Gavrio, **ferries** sail to: **Rafina,** Athens' minor port (2hr., 3 per day 11am-5pm, 2330dr); **Tinos** (2hr., 3 per day 9:45am-7:30pm, 1700dr); **Mykonos** (2½hr., 3 per day 9:45am-7:30pm, 2000dr); and **Syros** (2-3hr., Su 10pm, 1800dr). **Sea Jets** run once a week to **Rafina** (1hr., 4750dr); **Tinos** (50min., 3500dr); **Syros** (1½hr, 3595dr); **Mykonos** (15min., 5330dr); **Naxos** (2hr, 6000dr); and **Paros** (1¾hr, 5475dr). Check schedules and prices at ticketers in Gavrio before you depart—**Adamis Travel** (☎71 224, 71 591

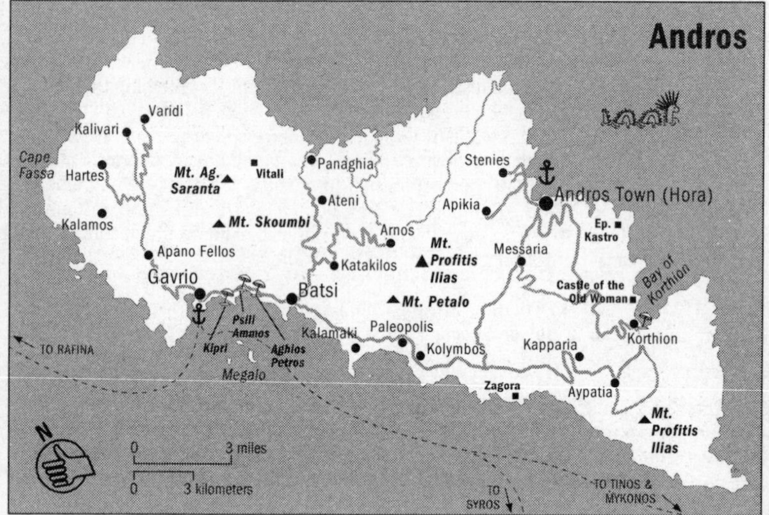




or 71 691) is one ticket service. Beach-bound **taxi boats** dock at the end of Batsi's beach. (Open 9:30am-1:30pm and 6-9pm. Round-trip 1500dr.) Renting a **moped** costs around 3500dr; try **Dino's Rent a Bike** (☎41 003) behind the post office.

Down the road to Andros Town and to the right, there's a branch of the **National Bank** with a 24hr. **ATM.** (☎22 400. Open M-F 8am-1:30pm.) The **post office** is down the road along the beach, inland from the "Hotel Karanassos" sign, across a dirt road from the hotel. (Open M-F 7:30am-2:30pm.) With your back to the water, the **pharmacy** is up the hill to the right of the waterfront, past the beach; another is on the waterfront next to Hotel Karnassos (both open 8am-2pm). Along the waterfront, a **kiosk** sells **international papers** and magazines. On a street parallel to the main road, before the National Bank, **Greek Sun Travel** offers **currency exchange,** info, and excursions. (☎41 198; fax 41 239. Open 9am-1:30pm, 6-9pm.)

**ACCOMMODATIONS AND FOOD.** It's easier but generally pricier to find accommodations in Batsi than in either Gavrio or Andros Town. Expect to pay 5000-7000dr per person per night for domatia (lower if you bargain). Many domatia studios have kitchens. It'll cost you 10,000-14,000dr for a double at a beachfront hotel. **Meltemi Studios** is worth the uphill walk; take the first set of stairs all the way up as you leave the beach with the water on your right (next to Batsi Gold jewelry store). The studios have an ocean view, kitchen, private bath, TV, fridge, and balcony. Larger suites have a full kitchen and private entrance. (☎41 016 or 41 702; fax 41 564. Doubles and triples 12,000-16,000dr; quads 18,000-24,000dr.) **Hotel Chrissi Akti** has a pool; indoors, there's A/C and a TV, fridge, and phone. (☎41 236 or 41 237; fax 41 628. Doubles 16,000dr; triples 19,000dr; quads 28,000dr.) **Hotel Karanassos,** one block from the beachfront, has breezy rooms with balcony and bath and a restaurant and bar. (☎41 480 or 41 481. Doubles 8000-14,000dr; triples 10,000-16,000dr; quads 12,000-18,000dr. Breakfast 1000dr.)

You'll find **Restaurant Sirocco** at the top of the first set of steps on your left as you leave the beach with the water on your right; head for the string of lights and the strains of jazz. Years ago, the owner Louie was born under the bar (literally); now he serves fab international food like homemade garlic bread (300dr), Shrimp Sirocco grilled in a spicy red sauce (3500dr), and a curry-lover's chicken *biryani* with yogurt (1800dr). (Open 6:30pm-midnight.) **Oti Kalo,** on the right side of the waterfront facing inland, ladles out nutmeg *moussaka* (1000dr), which complement its cheap wines. (Open noon to midnight.) There's a **supermarket** where the beach ends, on the right side of the waterfront.

**NIGHTLIFE.** To the left of the plateia, vine-covered, waterfront **Skala** plays trendy music and vends a vast variety of beers (600-3000dr) to a hepcat crowd. For a beat you can dance to, head to **Alpha Club,** halfway to Gavrio on the main road; the nightclub includes the first drink in its 1500dr cover, but you can skip the cover and go into the bar. (Beer 800dr; cocktails 1200-1500dr. Open till you go home.) **On the Rocks,** smack dab on the waterfront, is a good place to watch the sunset and drink cocktails (1500dr) while grooving to rock and dance music. **Capriccio Music Bar,** right next to the Ionian Bank, offers big, fun, fruity drinks like piña coladas and a gin fizz called the Bing Bamboo (1500-1700dr). Stick the drink decorations in your hair and dance to rock music in the ocean breeze. Clubbers can follow the party set to **Slammer** or **Nameless** behind the Ionian Bank.



**SIGHTS AND BEACHES.** For daytime partying, there's heaps of fun to be had around the bar at **Golden Beach,** accessible by taxi boat (beer 500dr). Or skip the lively, crowded central beach by walking or riding back toward Gavrio; stop at **Kipri, Psili Ammos,** or **Agios Petros** to swim in quiet beaches and in secluded coves. The ruins of the ancient capital **Paleopolis,** including the remains of a theater and a stadium, are *en route* to Andros Town; continue on 2km southeast to the **Bay of Korthion,** and Andros' finest swimming. Remnants of the **Castle of the Old Woman** are north of **Korthion,** 33km from Batsi; take a taxi, or rent a car or moped.

## ANDROS TOWN Ανδρος ☎0282

A sophisticated village with striking architecture, Andros Town (casually known as Hora) lies on a narrow peninsula jutting into the Aegean. Behind the town, the land rises in shelves of green, cut only by the road leading to Batsi. The wide, quiet cobbled streets lead past hotels, shops, and homes to the water, where blue waves pound the black rocks. Most tourists make Hora a daytrip from Batsi, leaving the town's 1500 residents an evening rest to themselves.

**ORIENTATION AND PRACTICAL INFORMATION.** The **bus** from Gavrio and Batsi drops you at a depot near a plateia where **taxis** wait (☎22 171). The **bus station** is coupled with a friendly restaurant, just to the right of the pedestrian section of **Agora,** the town's main street. A full schedule is posted in the outdoor waiting area. It's a good idea to arrive 15min. early. Walk down the stairs next to the high blue domes of the church to find the town center, all the way at the end of the main street toward the plateia with the **sculpture** of the unknown sailor and a view of Hora. The **Ionian Bank** is just off the plateia. (☎22 700. Open M-Th 9am-2pm, F 8am-1:30pm.) The **National Bank** is on the left farther down, on the way to the water (☎22 400. Open M-Th 8am-2pm, F 8am-1:30pm.) In an **emergency,** dial 23 991. The **police station** is at the far inland end of the main street. (☎22 300. Open 24hr.) There's a **pharmacy** at the corner of the plateia closest to the bus depot (open 8am-2pm); look for the green cross. Follow the signs to the **post office,** next to the plateia, which has **currency exchange.** (☎22 260. Open M-F 7:30am-2pm.) The **OTE** is across from the central plateia on the left. (☎22 199. Open M-F 7:30am-3pm.) **Postal code:** 84500.

**ACCOMMODATIONS AND FOOD.** Rooms are somewhat expensive and hard to find. In high season, doubles go for 5000 to 10,000dr; the numerous places on the beach get cheaper farther from the main strip. Keep an eye out for signs flagging the many domatia. **Hotel Egli,** next to the Ionian Bank, fills up quickly; rooms have a fridge, TV, and phone (some have bath), and there's a sofa lounge on each floor. Reception is next door at the hotel bar. (☎22 303 or 22 159. Singles 7500dr; doubles 11,000-15,000dr; triples 17,000dr; breakfast 2000dr.) Fruit markets and stands line the main agora, by the plateia. The tavernas and cafes are mediocre, but there are good *mezedes* to be had (and a local crowd to meet) at a taverna just before the steps down to the Museum of Modern Art.

**SIGHTS.** The **Museum of Modern Art** displays works by 20th-century Greek sculptor Michael Tombros. The weird noises from downstairs are *not* a mechanical failure—they're the clatter of electromagnetic art by Takis. Don't miss the enormous temporary exhibition space across the street a little farther downhill, with work by Henry Moore and others. (☎22 650. Open M, Th-Sa 10am-2pm and 6pm-8pm, Su 10am-2pm. 1000dr, students 500dr, EU students free.) The **Archaeological Museum,** 5min. down the main road from the bus station, has an excellent display on the Geometric village of Zagora and many post-Byzantine marble relics and *kouroi*, including a marvelous 2m statue of Hermes. The museum patio offers a lovely view of Andros Town. (☎23 664. Open Tu-Su 8am-2:30pm. 500dr, students and seniors 300dr, EU students free.) At the end of the main road, just above the water, the **Maritime Museum of Andros** trots out intricate ship models. The guard next door will give you the key. (Open M, W-Sa 10am-1pm and 6-8pm, Su 10am-1pm. Free.) Continue on the main road for a view of the offshore Venetian turret.

**BEACHES AND HIKES.** You'll find a sandy **beach** down the steps from the plateia by the museums. At the end of the peninsula, down the rocky face, the cove offers an excellent swimming hole beneath old Venetian arch ruins. Just be sure to watch out for sea urchins and a surprisingly strong undertow. Those yearning to see the island's more secluded spots—the many rivers, **waterfalls,** and mills in the island's interior—should search out **Cosmas,** who regularly leads **hikes** on weekends or by request. (2000-10,000dr, lunch included; email earthmessage@icgmail.com or ask for him around Andros Town.)

CYCLADES

# TINOS ΤΗΝΟΣ

From the summit of hulking Mt. Exobourgo, Tinos spreads below. In one direction, Hora's buildings, ferries, and beaches cluster together; away from the port, wildflowers, medieval dovecotes, and villages untouched by time contrast with the green mountains. The island's allure is perhaps most apparent to the thousands of pilgrims who have flocked to the Panagia Evangelistra Church in Tinos Town every year since the 1812 War of Independence. Its miracle-working Icon of the Annunciation—the *Megalochari* (Great Joy) or *Panagia Evangelistra*—was found by a nun in an underground church. Each year on the Feasts of the Annunciation (March 25) and Assumption (August 15), close to 30,000 pilgrims crawl on their knees up a red carpet from the port to the church; they then follow the icon in a 10km procession to the Kechrovouni convent.

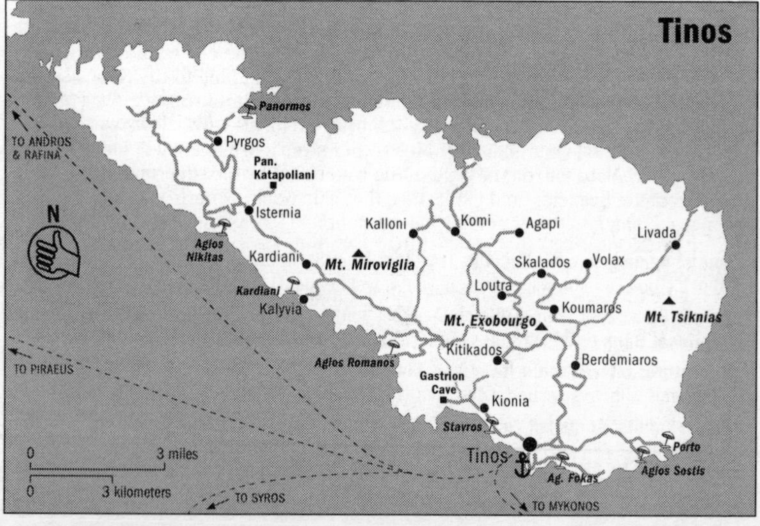

# TINOS TOWN Τηνος ☎0283

A stroll past the barrage of waterfront tourist shops reveals Tinos Town's two faces: peddlers sell both standard tourist wares and the jugs pilgrims use to carry Panagia's sacred waters home. The town is politically significant, too: on August 15, 1940, an Italian submarine torpedoed the Greek cruiser *Elli* as it docked in the harbor for the observance of a religious holiday. Mussolini declared war two months later. The cool sea breeze remembers the wind god Aeolus who once made Tinos his home.



## GETTING THERE AND GETTING AROUND

**Ferries:** Ferries arrive from Piraeus, Rafina, Mykonos, Syros, Andros, Thessaloniki, and Crete. From Tinos to: **Mykonos** (30min., 4-5 per day 11:15am-9pm, 1100dr); **Andros** (2hr., 2 per day 2:15pm-4pm, 1800dr); **Syros** (40min., 1-4 per day 10:15am-3:15pm, 1100dr); **Piraeus** (5½hr., 1-3 per day 10:15am-3:15pm, 4700dr); and **Rafina** (4hr., 2-3 per day 1:45pm-4:30pm, 3600dr). In high season, 2 per week to **Paros** (1700dr).

**Catamarans: Minoan Lines** sails a catamaran daily to: **Mykonos** (30min., 2275dr); **Paros** (1¼hr., 3385dr); **Naxos** (1¾hr., 3750dr); **Rafina** (3hr., 7225dr); and **Amorgos** (6¼hr., 6115dr). **Blue Star** runs a catamaran daily to Mykonos, Paros, and connects to Naxos and many other islands.

**Flying Dolphins:** (☎22 737), on the far left of the waterfront. Two per day to: **Mykonos** (2270dr); **Paros** (3460dr); **Naxos** (3850dr); **Santorini** (7970dr); and twice weekly to **Amorgos** (6200dr).

**Buses:** Leave across the street from the National Bank 3-5 times daily to: **Pyrgos** (750dr); **Panormos** (800dr); **Kalloni** (600dr); **Steni** (350dr); **Skalados** (420dr); **Kionia** (200dr); and **Porto** (230dr). A **schedule** is posted in the KTEL ticket agency (☎22 440) across from the bus depot. Open 8am-11pm.

**Taxis:** (☎22 470), next to Commercial Bank. Available 6am-2am.

**Cars and Mopeds:** It's worth getting your own wheels from a waterfront rental place. Try **Vidalis,** Zanaki Alavanou 16 (☎23 400; email vidalis@thn.forthnet.gr), on the main road leading out of town–ask for Christina. Mopeds 2500-8000dr; cars 6000-10,000dr. Open 8:30am-9pm. At **Jason's** (☎22 583 or 24 283), on the waterfront just before Alavanou, Jason himself can tell you anything you want to know about Tinos. Moped 2000-3000dr; car 6000-15,000dr. Open 8am-10pm.

## ORIENTATION AND PRACTICAL INFORMATION

Ferries land either on the central dock next to the bus depot or at the outside port near the children's park; walk along the waterfront to the center of town where sprawling **Megalochares** begins. This wide avenue leads uphill to the Neoclassical facade of the **Panagia Evangelistria Church.** Parallel to and to the right (facing inland) of Megalochares, **Evangelistrias**—"Bazaar" to locals—overflows with knick-knacks and religious paraphenalia. Most other streets are unnamed. Many of the hostels are off **Alabanou,** on the right of the waterfront by the supermarket. Hotels, tavernas, ticket agencies, and banks face the main dock. Waterfront tourist shops sell maps (500dr). In the directions below, right and left assume you face inland.

**Tourist Agencies:** At **Windmills Travel** (☎23 398), opposite the children's park by the outside port, Sharon will handle all your travel needs. Open 9am-3pm and 6-9pm.

**Banks:** Banks with 24hr. **ATMs** on the waterfront across from the bus depot include the **National Bank** (☎22 328 or 23 590). Open M-Th 8am-2pm, F 8am-1:30pm.

**Bookstore: International News and Magazines** (☎22 581), on the left of the waterfront, has a large selection. Open 8am-11pm.

**Public Toilets:** At the left end of the waterfront in Pl. Dolphin behind Hotel Lito.

**Police:** (☎22 100 or 22 255), in the same building as the **tourist police,** 5min. out of town on the road to Kionia (leave from the far left side of the waterfront).

**Telephones:** (☎22 499), up Megalochares on the right. Open M-F 7:30am-3:10pm.

**Post Office:** (☎22 247), on the far right end of the waterfront, behind the small plateia. Sells phone cards. Open M-F 8am-2pm. **Postal Code:** 84200.

## ACCOMMODATIONS

Tinos has plenty of accommodations, except during the Easter festival, Apr. 8-22 in 2001, and during July and August weekends when vacationing Athenians descend. Most waterfront hotels are expensive, so try your bargaining skills with the crowd of smiling faces holding **Rooms to Let** signs when you disembark.

**Yannis** (☎25 089), at the far right end of the waterfront, to the right of the Oceanis Hotel. Offers peaceful, airy rooms in a 75-year-old blue-shuttered home. Giannis himself will give you Greek lessons over a cup of Greek coffee in the garden sitting area. Common baths and refrigerators, kitchen and laundry facilities. Singles 5000dr; doubles 8000dr; triples with private bath and kitchen 12,000-16,000dr.

**Boussetil Rooms,** Ioannou Voulgari 7 (☎22 675). Walk up Alvanou, and turn right before the Mazda dealership. Come for the immaculate, new rooms with TV, private bath, and a shaded garden. Stay for the delicious homemade lemonade. Singles 5000dr; doubles 10,000dr; triples 15,000dr. 20% discount for *Let's Go* users.

**Vincenzo Rooms to Let,** 25 Martiou 10 (mobile 094 52 8888; fax 23 612); go up Alavanou, turn right onto 25 Martiou (across the street from the little boy fountain), and follow the signs. Simple rooms, private baths. Doubles 10,000dr; triples 15,000dr. Expect a price hike on the weekends.

**Tinos Camping** (☎22 344 or 22 548), a 10min. walk from the waterfront to the right—signs point the way. Well kept, with kitchen and laundry, showers, bungalows, and restaurant and bar. 1500dr per person; 900-1000dr per tent. Bungalows 5000-7000dr.

## FOOD

Tons of tavernas wait to usher you in for a bite. There's a **supermarket** two doors to the left of the post office. (Open M-Sa 8am-9:30pm, Su 9am-1:30pm.)

**Caffe Italia,** Akti Nazou 10 (☎25 756), behind the children's park near Windmill Travel. A secret of Tinos's gourmands, this small restaurant serves a range of authentic pastas (1800-2000dr) made to the exacting standards of its expatriate Italian chef Dora. Open 10am-3pm and 6pm-midnight.

**Mesklies** (☎22 151), on the left side of the waterfront; look for the sign. Mesklies is both a fine pastry shop, featuring ornately designed cakes (around 2000dr), and a tasty pizza restaurant (1200-2800dr). Wrap up your meal with *tyropitakia,* the dense, cheesecakey local specialty. Open 7am-3am.

**Pallada,** on the left side of the waterfront and inland by the bar street. Authentic Greek cuisine and local specialities so good you might want to bring bread from the bakery (see below) to wipe your plate. Try fava beans and spinach (900dr), or local sausage and potatoes (1000dr). Open 9am-4pm and 6pm-1am.

**Old-fashioned Wood-Burning Bakery,** across the pedestrian walkway from Pallada—follow your nose to their amazing fresh bread (180-360dr). Open 7am-3pm.

## NIGHTLIFE

Most of the town's bars are on "bar street" (parallel to Palada street), on the water to the left of the central port, behind Hotel Lito; the clubs are open from 9pm-3am. Swing a left onto Palada to find **Pyrsos,** with a large dance floor and huge pillow-padded benches draped with drink-sippin' patrons. (Beer 1000dr; cocktails 1500-1800dr.) **Monopolio Café** is a hip joint just down the street on the left from Pallada Taverna, on the waterfront; coffees from Greek to Irish run 400-1800dr. (Open

10am-3am.) **The Kaktos Club,** inside a windmill behind the Panagia Evangelistria Church, opens its incredible hilltop view to American music lovers; it also hosts special live music nights. **Kouros Bar,** on Bazaar across from Vinaki Pizzeria, is a snazzy coffee bar by day and people-watching heaven at night; balconies overlook the open market. (Bottled wine 4500dr, cocktails 1600dr. Open 11am-3am.) **Metropolis Club** plays the latest Greek tunes for a wall-to-wall, table-dancing crowd, while **Corsaire,** next to Mesklies, broadcasts good tunes under colorful lights. For those just raring up when the bars shut down, head for the bright orange doors of **Paradise,** a 15min. walk toward Stavros beach.

## SIGHTS



**PANAGIA EVANGELISTRIA.** In 1822, the Tiniote nun Sister Pelagia had a vision of the Virgin Mary telling her about an icon buried in an uncultivated field (once a church destroyed by 10th-century pirates). A year later, amid great rejoicing, the prophesied icon was unearthed and Panagia Evangelistria was built to house it. The church continues to draw daily visits from believers who consider it evidence of the Virgin's power and presence. The relic is said to have healing powers, and is credited with ridding Tinos of cholera, saving a sinking ship, and giving a blind man sight. Gifts of gold, diamonds, and jewels, and countless *tamata*—plaques praising Mary's healing powers—cover the chapel, the "Lourdes of the Aegean."

The **Well of Sanctification** is a natural spring that appeared when the icon was unearthed. Today it flows (from one of many faucets) below the marble entrance stairs to the chapel; visitors scoop up a bottle of it to drink or to carry as a talisman. To the right of the well is the mausoleum of the Greek warship *Elli*, sunk by an Italian torpedo in 1940. *(Open 7am-8pm. Free. Modest dress required.)*

Don't miss the **sculpture gallery** with its depiction of the exhausted Phidippides announcing victory after the Battle of Marathon. Other rooms feature works by hometown artists. *(Open 8:30am-3pm. Free.)*

**ARCHAEOLOGICAL MUSEUM.** Tinos' small Archaeological Museum, clearly marked on Megalochares uphill from the OTE, has artifacts from Poseidon's sanctuary at Kionia, a first-century BC sundial, some vases from Xombourgo, and wonderful 7th-century BC *pitnoi* (relief pottery) showing Athena bursting from Zeus's head. *(Open Tu-Su 8:30am-3pm. 500dr, students 300dr, EU students free.)*

**PYRGOS.** Take a **bus** 33km northwest of Tinos Town (1hr., 3-5 times per day, 750dr) to the artsy, picturesque town of **Pyrgos,** home to a School for Fine Arts and inhabited by Tinos' renowned marble sculptors. Several museums and exhibitions are dedicated to past residents, such as Giannouli Chalepas, whose *Sleeping Daughter* graces Athens' central graveyard. For classy souvenirs, head to **The Blue Trunk** (☎31 870), where marble and (cheaper) terra cotta statues are for sale; it's on Sardela street in Pyrgos, near three tavernas frequented by the locals.

## BEACHES

Rural Tinos rewards adventurers with secluded beaches and broad views of the countryside, a short drive away from Tinos Town. At **Kionia Beach,** lucky swimmers may glimpse a baby parrot fish or a school of tiger-striped wrasse. On the way back to Tinos Town from Kionia, there's touristy **Stavros Beach;** if you stay late, you can experience the nightlife at the locally acclaimed **Chroma Bar/Homa Club.** A short walk east on the opposite side of Tinos Town is the equally crowded **Agios Fokas Beach.** Swimmers should head south, since the north coast's waters are rough. To get to spectacular **Kardianis** beach, take the Pyrgos bus to Kardiani and travel down the winding street from the main road to the bay.

To the north, you'll find windswept **Kolimbithra Beach** and the small shore of lovely **Panormos Bay** (2km northeast of Pyrgos). Be careful not to get stranded there: Panormos has three tavernas and not much else, no night buses run on

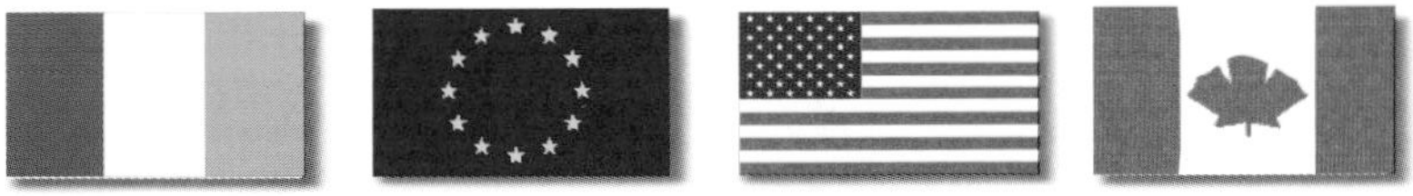

Tinos, and taxis are hard to find. If you rent a moped or car, the cliffs and landscapes along the road from Tinos Town to Panormos Bay form inspiring views.

For the best of the best, head east to **Agios Sostis** and **Porto.** Take the KTEL **bus** or drive all the way to the end of the road that arrives in Porto at the water's edge. From there, either climb left to the nudity-strewn rock beaches or head right toward the sand. The medieval-era **dovecotes,** 2000 in total, are built of intricate white lattices and are full of nesting birds; they've become the island's symbol.

Take the KTEL **bus** from Tinos Town (3-5 per day, 200dr) or drive left along the waterfront road out of town to explore the ruins of the 4th-century BC **temple** of Poseidon and Amphitrite and enjoy the clear-watered, fine sand beach.

## HIKING: MOUNT EXOBOURGO

If you have a car or moped, the villages that ring Mt. Exobourgo (Εξοβουργο Ορος; 14km north of Tinos Town) and the site of the Venetian Fortress **Xombourgo** are yours to explore. After withstanding 11 assaults, the 13th-century island capital fell to the Ottomans in 1715, the Ottoman Empire's last territorial gain. For a resplendent panoramic view of all Tinos, drive up to the foot of the fortress itself, or if you're feeling energetic, climb the mountain from the east foothill (near the village of Xinara or Loutra) on a trail lined with wildflowers and brilliant orange moss. At the gated entrance to Xombourgo, head left into the plateia to the little gate where the rocky trail to the top starts. The road detours to a church at a fork; go straight to get to the fort. Strong winds buffet Exobourgo, and the fort is occasionally closed as a result; stay low to avoid getting blown off the mountain.

The delightful hike from Tinos Town to Mt. Exobourgo takes 6-7 hours, but you can turn around and double back at any time. Alternatively, the trip from Tinos Town to Loutra and back takes 3-4 hours and takes you over much of the central island. Other direct routes up Mt. Exobourgo don't cut through all the villages; wooden signposts mark these trails. Whatever your route, bring water, provisions, comfortable shoes, and a buddy. Stick to the trail and be prepared for extremely high winds at all times.

**ASCENT TO KITIKADOS.** Begin by heading left behind the Panagia Evangelistria Church to unmarked **Agios Nikolau** (ask if you can't find it). Follow this road straight up and to the left, where the asphalt gives way to a broad cobblestone path that takes you past two white chapels within 45min. Along the ascent, look behind you to see the ferries coming in to port. Past the second white chapel is a small stone bridge with an arch; either go over the bridge for a 15min. visit to the unremarkable village of **Kitikados,** or continue on the main trail up to the island's main asphalt road and turn left. Continue across the road until you see a small trail marked with a wooden sign bearing a hiker and the word "Ksinara." Follow this path up to the right of the windmill. Once you pass the windmill, there is another trail marker on your right. Written in Greek, it indicates a direct ascent up to Mt. Exobourgo, looming in the distance, topped by a cross revealing the **fortress** Xombourgo. **Ksinara** is straight ahead, and **Tripotamos** is behind you. You can ascend Exobourgo from this point, or you can continue about 1½hr. through the quiet town of Ksinara.

**LOUTRA TO XOMBOURGO.** Follow the road through town until the church plateia and then head left to the narrow dirt-and-stone trail. This pathway begins your descent to the village of **Loutra,** where a convent school teaches young girls to weave carpets; to get there, turn right when you hit the asphalt road. At this point you should be about 2hr. into the hike. Continue on the asphalt past Loutra to Skalados; if you're hungry, turn right to enter the nice hillside taverna. From the taverna, head up and right on a street with steps to another asphalt road. Walk to the right about 15min. until you see the blue sign pointing toward **Volax.** It's worth stopping here to meander through the narrow, low-arched streets; peek into one of the many basket-weaving workshops in town. Then retrace your steps to the blue Volax sign and turn left onto the road. When you reach **Koumaros,** look for the **Asso-**

**ciation lounge** offering hospitality and dirt-cheap drinks and snacks. Once through Koumaros, the road turns into a stone stair trail that will take you up the northeast side of Mt. Exobourgo. At the foot of **Sacred Heart,** an impressive Catholic monastery, go diagonally through the plateia to the little gate on the left side. Ascend 20min. to the fort of Xombourgo, where your reward is a view of the entire island.

# MYKONOS ΜΥΚΟΝΟΣ ☎0289



Mykonos has long been the object of envy and desire. In ancient times, merchants vied with each other to supply pilgrims en route to the holy island of Delos. By the Byzantine and Ottoman eras, the pilgrim trade had given way to marauding pirates eager for the rich plunder to be found in the waters around the island. In the 70s, Mykonos' gay scene and wild nightlife secured the island's place among the premiere resorts of the Mediterranean. Today, the island is the playground of the sleek and chic—sophisticates the Greeks call *kosmopolitikos.* Though Mykonos' gay scene has lost its former preeminence, it's anything but dead, and it still helps the Mykonosian nightlife command international Bacchic awe. *Kosmopolitikos* flock here to lounge on the island's long, blond beaches and club until dawn in the frenzied alleys of the capital. As you might guess, the honor of joining this jetset levies a hefty tax, but Mykonos may just compensate for the crowds and the expense with some of the Cyclades' finest beaches and a wonderfully picturesque capital. While you won't experience unadulterated Greek culture on Mykonos, you'll still escape from the ordinary.

## MYKONOS TOWN Μυκονος

Mykonos Town owes its labyrinthine streets (closed to motor traffic in the afternoon and evening) to Mediterranean pirates. The maze-city was planned expressly to disconcert and disorient marauders; the plan has a similar effect on tourists. Despite the influx of visitors, the town has resisted large hotel complexes, and the drag queens and high fashion models seem to complement, not corrupt, the charm of the fishing boats in the harbor, basket-laden donkeys, and Petros the Pelican.

### GETTING THERE AND GETTING AROUND

**Ferries:** To: **Andros** (3hr., 1 per day, 2700dr); **Ikaria** (2 per week, 3200dr); **Naxos** (3hr., 1-2 per day, 1900dr); **Piraeus** (6hr., 2-3 per day, 5100dr); **Rafina** (1-2 per day, 4200dr); **Samos** (2 per week, 5100dr); **Santorini** (6hr., 3 per week, 3500dr); **Syros** (2½hr., 1-3 per day, 1600dr); and **Tinos** (45min., 3 per day, 1200dr).

**Flying Dolphins:** Boats to: **Andros** (2 per day, 5300dr); **Ios** (1 per day, 6350dr); **Naxos** (1 per day, 3600dr); **Paros** (1 per day, 3400dr); **Piraeus** (1 per day, 10,000dr); **Santorini** (1 per day, 6900dr); **Syros** (2 per day, 3100dr); and **Tinos** (2 per day, 2400dr); **Amorgos** (5 per week, 6200dr) and **Sikinos** (1 per week, 6600dr).

**Flights: Olympic Airways** (☎22 490 or 22 495; airport ☎22 327). Flights to: **Athens** (40min., 6-7 per day, 21,400dr); **Rhodes** (1hr., 4 per week, 24,400dr); **Santorini** (30min., 4 per week, 16,400dr); and **Thessaloniki** (3 per week, 28,400dr). There are no buses to the airport; a taxi from Mykonos Town costs 2000dr.

**Buses: KTEL** (☎23 360) has two stations in town. **North Station,** uphill from the ferry dock, serves: **Agios Stefanos** beach (every 30min., 230dr); **Ano Mera** and **Kalafatis** (10 per day, 250-340dr); and **Elia Beach** (8 per day, 330dr). **South Station,** uphill from the windmills at the opposite edge of town, serves: **Agios Ioannis** (every hr., 250dr); **Paradise Beach** (every 30min., 250dr); **Plati Yalos Beach** (every 30min., 250dr); and **Ornos Beach** (every 30min., 250dr). Schedules are posted at the stations.

**Taxis:** (☎22 400 or 22 700). Available at "Taxi Square," along the waterfront.

**Rentals:** Agencies surround both bus stops. Get ready to bargain. **Mopeds** 5000-7000dr per day. **Jeeps** 12,000-16,000dr per day.

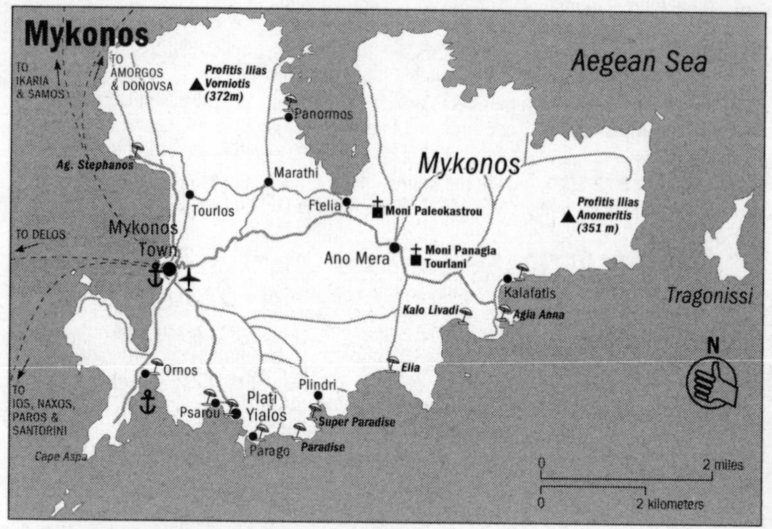




## ORIENTATION AND PRACTICAL INFORMATION

If you're facing inland, incoming boats dock at a pier on the far left of the waterfront. One road leads to the right along the water, past the town beach, to the center of town. Another road, parallel and above the first, heads uphill to the **North Station** bus depot, then wraps around Mykonos Town to the **South Station.** A turn-off on the road to South Station leads to the **airport.** Everything you could need or want is near the **waterfront**—banks, travel agencies, shops, cafes, tavernas, bars, and discos—but much of the real shopping, fine dining, and partying goes on in the narrow, winding **back streets** (especially Matogianni, Kalogera, Mitropoleas, and Enoplon Dinameon). On the right side of the waterfront is a pier for excursion boats headed primarily to nearby Delos. Past the pier is a series of churches, a lovely part of town called **Little Venice** (home to the islands' classiest bars and cafes), and a small hill with a line of windmills. The town's practicalities—post office, police, markets, and so forth—mostly lie in the **inland** vicinity of Lakka and South Station, and can be reached by following **Mitropoleas.**

**Tourist Police:** (☎22 482), in an office at the ferry landing. Very helpful English-speaking staff. Open 8am-11pm.

**Banks: National Bank of Greece** (☎22 932), in the center of the waterfront, offers **currency exchange** and **ATM.** Open M-Th 8am-1:30pm, F 8am-1pm.

**American Express:** (☎22 322), left of the bank (facing inland) inside **Delia Travel Ltd.** Limited travel services for cardholders. Commission-free check exchange. Open M-F 9am-9pm, Sa-Su 9am-3pm and 6-9pm.

**International Bookstore: International Press** (☎23 316), in a small plateia opposite Pierro's; follow signs from the waterfront. Eclectic books, magazines, and newspapers in English. Open 8am-midnight.

**Laundry:** (☎27 600), on Psarou, heading toward the windmills from the bus terminal. Full load 3000dr. Open 8:30am-10pm.

**Medical Center:** (☎23 994, 995, 996, or 997; fax 27 407), on the higher road leading from the port to South Station, just beyond the turn-off for the hospital. Doctors include a general practitioner, microbiologist, cardiologist, X-ray guru, and gynecologist. Open May-Oct. 8:30am-midnight; Nov.-Mar. 8:30am-9pm. In an emergency (24hr.), call an ambulance at 166, or the medical center mobile (094) 433 8292 or (097) 765 4737.

**Police:** (☎22 716 or 22 215), in Lakka past the South Station. Open 24hr.

**Telephones: OTE** (☎22 699), at the left end of waterfront in a big white building, uphill and to the right of the dock. Open M-F 8am-3pm.

**Internet Access: E@rth Internet Club** (☎22 791), Zani Pitaraki, gets connected close to little Venice. Open 9am-11pm. **Angelo's Internet Cafe** (☎24 106), on the street running between South Station and the windmills. Both charge 1000dr for 20min.

**Post Office:** (☎22 238), around the corner from the police in Laka, behind South Station. **Exchanges currency.** Open M-F 7:30am-2pm. **Postal code:** 84600.

## ACCOMMODATIONS



While Mykonos is certainly the most expensive of the Greek islands, contrary to popular belief, affordable accommodations aren't just a pipe dream—especially if you're willing to stay outside the immediate town. Most budget travelers find their niche in Mykonos's several festive campsites, which offer a myriad of sleeping options beyond the standard plot of grass. The information offices on the dock are numbered according to accommodation type: one for **hotels** (☎24 540; open 9am-midnight), two for **rooms to let** (☎24 860; open 9am-11pm), and three for **camping** (☎23 567; open 9am-midnight).

**Hotel Apollon** (☎22 223), on the waterfront. The oldest hotel in town is an antique-laden house with rooms overlooking the harbor. The owner's motto, "Smile and the world's your friend," shows in her friendliness and in her comfortable home. Common baths. Singles 9,000-14,000dr; doubles 11,500-16,000dr; triples 15,000-19,000dr.

**Zoris Hotel,** N. Kalogera 30 (☎22 167 or 24 168; fax 24 169). The nicest hotel around Kalogera. Feather pillows, handmade quilts, real showers, and a roof-top deck for sunbathers. Doubles 18,000-25,000dr. Singles 10% less.

**Hotel Philippi,** N. Kalogera 25 (☎22 294; fax 24 680; email chriko@otenet.gr), next to Zoris Hotel. Cheerful rooms around a bountiful garden provide an escape from the narrow, busy town streets. Private baths don't cost extra. Singles 7500-10,000; doubles 11,000-17,000dr; triples 15,000-22,000dr. Internet 30dr per min. Open Apr.-Oct.

**Hotel Terra Maria,** Kalogera 33 (☎24 212; fax 27 112). Don't confuse it with Chez Maria or the nearby Marios Hotel. A/C, private baths, fridges, TVs, and minibars. Central, but on a quiet side street with trees out back. Run by Petros, a former soccer star. Breakfast 2500dr. Doubles 15,000-24,000dr; triples 18,000-30,000dr.

**Hotel Karboni/Matogianni** (☎22 217; fax 23 264), on Matogianni, inland from the waterfront. This hotel-complex has lots of rooms; ask about the cheaper ones in the rear. Doubles 12,000-25,000dr; triples 18,000-27,000dr.

**Paradise Beach Camping** (☎22 852 or 22 129; www.paradise-greece.com), 6km from the port on the beach; the round-trip bus costs 250dr but there's a free pick-up and drop-off for port and airport. The liveliest place to stay in town, this enormous complex includes every imaginable type of accommodation, eatery, and entertainment venue. Located directly on crowded Paradise Beach, where nude bathers freely shed their inhibitions. Private rooms come with bath, fridge, and breakfast. 700-900dr per car. 400-700dr per motorbike. Luggage storage 350dr. Safety deposit box 250dr. Internet access 1000dr for 15min. 1300-2000dr per person; 900-1100dr per small tent, 1300-1500dr per large tent; 2-person beach cabin 6000-12,000dr, 4-person beach cabin 12,000-24,000dr; doubles 10,000-22,000dr; triples 12,000-26,500dr.

**Mykonos Camping** (☎25 915 or 25 916; fax 24 578; www.mycamp.gr; email mycamp@hotmail.com), on Paraga Beach, near Paradise Beach. On the bus route to Paradise Beach, there's also a free pick-up and drop-off at the port and airport. Smaller and quieter than Paradise Beach. Very clean. 1300-2000dr per person; 900-1100dr per tent; 1800-2500dr per tent rental; 2-person bungalow 8000-10,000dr.

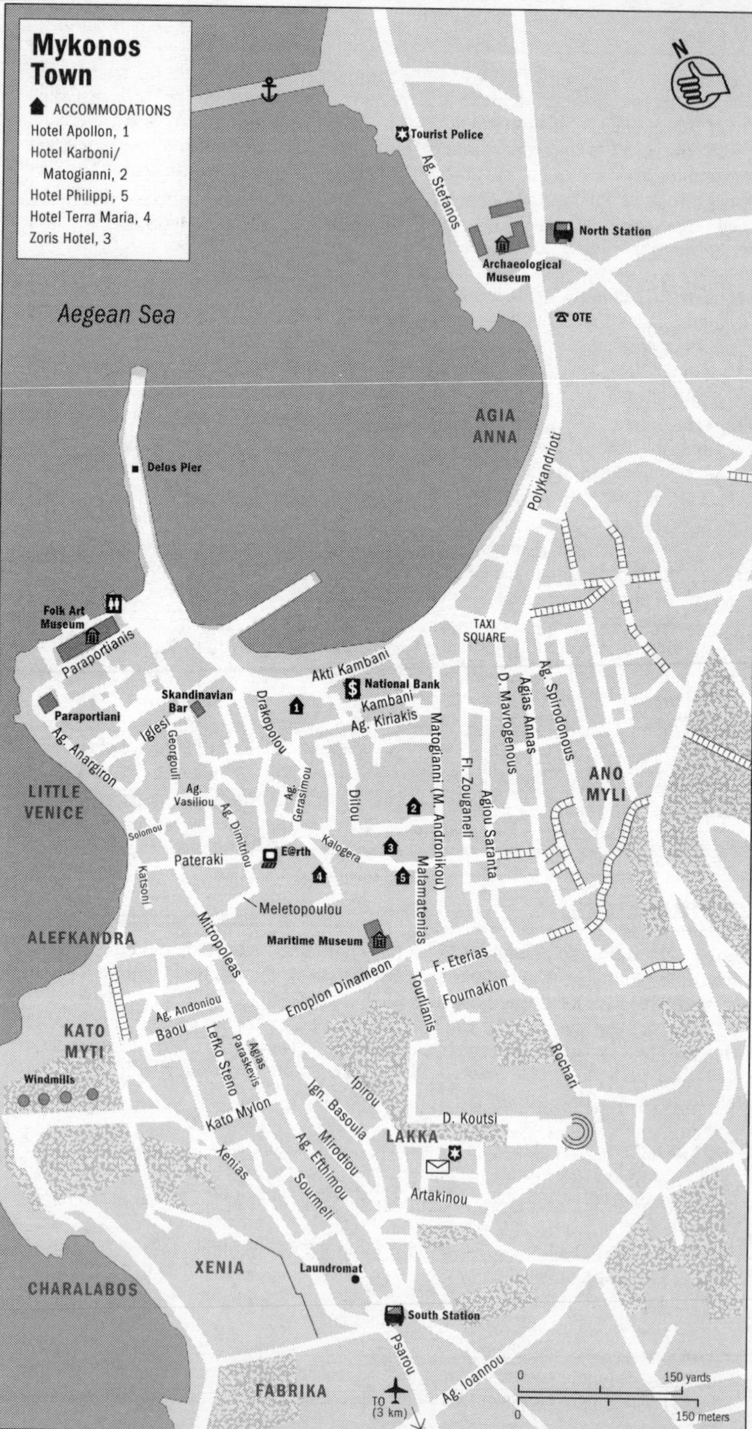
Mykonos Town
ACCOMMODATIONS
Hotel Apollon, 1
Hotel Karboni/ Matogianni, 2
Hotel Philippi, 5
Hotel Terra Maria, 4
Zoris Hotel, 3
Aegean Sea
Tourist Police
Ag. Stefanos
North Station
Archaeological Museum
OTE
AGIA ANNA
Polykandrioti
Delos Pier
Folk Art Museum
Paraportianis
Paraportiani
Skandinavian Bar
Akti Kambani
National Bank
Kambani
Ag. Kiriakis
TAXI SQUARE
Drakopolou
Iglesi
Georgouli
Ag. Anargiron
LITTLE VENICE
Ag. Vasiliou
Ag. Gerasimou
Ditou
Matogianni (M. Andronikou)
Fl. Zouganeli
D. Mavrogenous
Agias Annas
Ag. Spirodonous
ANO MYLI
Agiou Saranta
Solomou
Ag. Dimitriou
Kalogera
Pateraki
E@rth
Katsoni
Meletopoulou
Malamatenias
Mitropoleas
Maritime Museum
ALEFKANDRA
Enoplon Dinameon
F. Eterias
Fournakion
Tourlianis
Ag. Andoniou
Baou
Lefko Steno
Agias Paraskevis
KATO MYLI
Windmills
Rochari
Ipirou
Ign. Basoula
Kato Mylon
D. Koutsi
LAKKA
Mirodiou
Ag. Efthimou
Xenias
Sourmeli
Artakinou
XENIA
Laundromat
CHARALABOS
South Station
Psarou
Ag. Ioannou
FABRIKA
TO (3 km)
0 150 yards
0 150 meters

CYCLADES

## FOOD

Most choose to eat out on Mykonos, but budget travelers would do well to put together a picnic from the fruit stands that surround South Station. **Mykonos Mini-Market** offers carbs and more, at a short distance from the post office. (☎24 897. Open 7am-late.) Cheap creperies and souvlaki joints make guest appearances on nearly all of Mykonos's chi-chi streets. Otherwise, it's possible to lounge the day away (off the beach) at the cafes that line the waterfront, all of which serve the usual Greek food suspects. You'll pay dearly for the view, not for the cooking (*frappés* around 900dr, greek salads around 1200dr).

**Dynasty Thai Chinese Restaurant** (☎24 194), in Pl. Lymni, by the cinema on Meletopoulou. It ain't Greek, but if you endure the wait for an outside table and spicy, authentic Asian cooking, you'll be rewarded. Veggie dishes 1650-2000dr, beef and chicken dishes 2300-2500dr, Thai salads 2100dr. The owner recommends Peking duck (half for 5000dr, whole for 9950dr). Open 6:30pm-12:45am.

**Klimataria** (☎24 051), on Florou Zouganeli, the first street to your right as you face inland with Taxi Square in front of you—look for blue tables. Good prices for faithful Greek cuisine, and the menu speaks five languages. Stuffed vegetables 1400dr, lamb in a variety of seasonings 1900dr, fish soup 2000dr. Open 9am-1am.

**Nikos Taverna** (☎24 320), in Porto, in a cluster of restaurants inland from the excursion boat docks. A hoppin' place for fine Greek cuisine. Personable local pelicans often frequent the spot. Taste the baked calamari and cheese (2800dr) and the lamb *kleftiko*, which is baked with cheese in aluminum foil (2500dr). Open noon-2am.

**La Mexicana,** at the end of Kalogeri. Chicken enchiladas 2550dr, chicken, beef, or shrimp fajitas 3400-3850dr, vegetarian dishes around 2300dr. Happy Hour 6:30-8:00pm, with discounts on sangria (500dr), frozen margaritas (1300dr), and tequila shots. Open 6:30pm-12:30am.

**Alexi's,** in the back of Taxi Square. The oldest greasy spoon in Mykonos. Alexi puts on a show as he cooks up your gyro (400dr), hamburger (600-800dr), or belly-bursting souvlaki plate (2000dr). Breakfast (including a fried tomato) 1350dr. Open 10am-7am.

**Euthymios Euthymiou,** off Taxi Square; follow the divine smells. *Amigdalota* (almond cookies) 2000dr per box, *kalathakia* (walnut-tarts) 1800dr per box, and more commonplace goodies (croissants 500dr, sandwiches just 200dr). Open 8am-11pm.

## NIGHTLIFE

There's a good time to be had on Mykonos—perhaps the best in Greece (some say the world). Come nightfall, the young, the beautiful, the fabulous, and mere mortals enjoy the warm embrace of chic cafes, buzzing nightclubs, and a handful of pubs. After eleven the bars get packed; the most popular watering holes are in the vicinity of the waterfront, around Little Venice and Taxi Square. If you tire of dancing until dawn, head to **Cine Mant,** in Pl. Lymni off Meletopoulou, which shows two English-language films per day (☎27 109; 1800dr).

**Caprice Bar,** on the water in Little Venice. Popular but unpackaged, mod yet cheery. A perfect post-beach hangout, complete with breathtaking sunsets, feel-good music, and friendly, good-time company. Cocktails 1500-2000dr. Open Su-Th 6:30pm-3:30am, F-Sa until 4:30am.

**Montparnasse Piano Bar,** Ag. Anargyron 24. Savor the good life (literally and philosophically) with a cocktail by the bay window overlooking the water, while being serenaded by cabaret tunes from a live piano. Groovy, sophisticated, and mostly gay. Wine around 1000dr, cocktails around 2000. Open 7pm-3am.

**Pierro's,** on Matogianni. Pierro's gained its fame as the first gay bar in Greece and it maintains its reputation with its irresistible hedonism and the most fantastic dancing on the island. The crowd spills out into the plateia. Beer 1500dr, cocktails 2500dr.

**Icaros,** next-door and upstairs from Pierro's. Shares clientele, atmosphere, and a nightly drag show with its downstairs neighbor. Beer upwards of 1000dr, cocktails upwards of 1500dr. Open 11:30pm-4am.

**Skandinavian Bar,** near Niko's Taverna and the waterfront (follow the pumping bass). There's something for everyone in this two-building party complex, and though the evening starts slow, after midnight *everyone* passes through this place. Beers and shots around 1000dr, cocktails upwards of 1500dr. Open 8:30pm-3am, Sa until 4am.

**Mykonos Bar,** in Little Venice, next to inland side of the Caprice Bar. Watch Greek dancers perform the *zebekiko* and *zorba,* then join them until sunrise. Goofy, popular, and fun. Beer 1200dr, cocktails around 2000dr. Cover 1000dr and up. Open 10pm-4am.

**Veranda,** up the stairs off Venetias, in Little Venice. Aims for effortless grace, with a big veranda and slow movin' fans. This is the place for highbrow drink sipping. Cocktails 2200-2500dr. Open 6:30pm-3:30am.

**Mad Club,** on the waterfront beside Taxi Square, up a flight of stairs. Serves up pounding techno in an intimate bar-meets-jungle-gym setting. Take a break on the balcony overlooking the sea. Cocktails around 2000dr. Cover 2000-3000dr. Opens at midnight.

CYCLADES

## SIGHTS

The prime daytime activities on Mykonos are shopping and tanning, but you don't need to blow all your money. Losing yourself in the colorful alleyways of Mykonos Town at dawn or dusk is one of the easiest, cheapest, and most exhilarating experiences the island has to offer. At every corner, you're bound to stumble upon a miniature church or quiet corner glowing in ethereal Cycladic light.

A stroll to the **Castro** area—behind the Delos ferry pier, at the far left of the port if you're facing the sea—will take you to the **Paraportiani.** You'll recognize this cluster of white churches, probably the most famous of Mykonos' sights, from endless picture postcards. From there, walk through **Little Venice,** where the turquoise waters of the eager Aegean lap at the legs of cafe tables and chairs. Grab a seat at one of the waterfront bars in Little Venice to watch the sun set and the tide roll in. The line of stalwart **windmills** farther south along the waterfront also offers prime sunset seating. If you're up all night, see the sun rise over the Aegean by taking a walk along the winding road that leads from the North Bus Station up the hill overlooking the port.

Although cultural enrichment may not be Mykonos' primary draw, several museums fill the void. The **Archaeological Museum,** on the paved road between the ferry dock and the center of town, mysteriously lacks Cycladic art, but has an impressive 7th-century BC *pithos* (large terra-cotta storage jar) with relief scenes from the Trojan War. (☎22 325. Open Tu-Su 8:30am-2:30pm. 500dr, students and seniors 300dr, EU students free.) The **Aegean Maritime Museum,** around the corner from the inland end of Matogiannis, contains ship models, rare ancient coins with nautical subjects, and navigational instruments. The beautifully manicured back garden includes larger-than-life nautical instruments that the three-room interior can't contain, including ancient grave *steles* and a lighthouse. (☎22 700. Open Apr.-Oct. 10:30am-1pm and 6:30-9pm. 500dr, students 200dr.) The **Folklore Museum,** in the 300-year-old house of a former sea captain, is inland from the excursion boat docks near the Paraportiani. **Lena's House,** part of the Folklore Museum, is a 300-year-old home with 19th-century furniture; it remains exactly as its owner left it. The two provide background knowledge on the hand-crafted souvenirs of Mykonos. (☎22 591. Both open Apr.-Oct. M-Su 4:30-8:30pm. Free.)

## BEACHES

Although all the beaches on Mykonos are **nude,** the degree of nudity depends on where you go. To avoid finding yourself on the unspectacular Mykonos Town beach, get on the bus and head out of the city. Small **Ag. Stefanos Beach** is an easy bus ride (10min., every hr., 230dr) from the North Station, but it's close to the busy

**PETROS THE PELICAN** When it comes to glamour and beauty, even the most gawk-worthy visitors to Mykonos must compete with the island's prize pink pelicans. The first arrived in 1955, plucked out of the air by one of Mykonos' fishermen. Exhausted and mourning the death of its mate (found nearby), it had become separated from its migrating flock. The pelican was given to another fisherman, who named it Petros, for a soldier friend executed by Nazis during the Second World War. Nursing Petros back to health, the fisherman created a superstar. It wasn't long before Mykonian functions began to depend on the presence of their most famous fowl. Upon taking a trip to Tinos, the beloved bird sparked a **Pelican War**–it took an official task force comprised of the mayor, police chief, and important priests to retrieve him from the recalcitrant Tinians. Numerous official efforts were made to set Petros up with a "nice Greek girl," and distinguished people, including Jackie Onassis, have had cute girl pelicans flown to Mykonos to catch his eye. Unlike most visitors to Mykonos, however, pink pelicans practice strict monogamy, mating once and for life, and principled Petros refused to be corrupted by the charms of stardom. Meeting his end in 1985, unseen beneath a farmer's vehicle, Petros has been preserved in song (hits like "Dirge for a Pelican" and "Whitewash and Pink Feathers") and in the folklore museum, where his earthly portion is stuffed. The pelicans you see preening themselves in the streets of Mykonos today are merely trying to live up to Petros' distinguished legacy.



roadway leading to the airport, and its sands are often littered. The clear, shallow water of little **Ornos Beach** is a short hop away from South Station (10min., every 30min., 250dr), as is crowded **Psarou Beach** (15min., every 30min. 8:15am-2am, 210dr). Buses run from South Station to **Plati Yialos** (every 30min., 250dr), from where you can catch a **caïque** (around 400dr) to three other great beaches, Paradise Beach, Super Paradise Beach, and Elia. Or, you can take the bus directly to **Elia** from North Station (30 min., 8 per day, 330dr) or to **Paradise** from South Station (every 30min., 250dr). While **Super Paradise Beach** has the craziest reputation among Mykonos' bare-butt beaches, contemplative naked people while away the daylight hours at the far reaches of Elia's quiet shores, where broad sand beaches are divided by sections of craggy rock. Majestic and remote **Kalo Livadi Beach** is about a 5km walk back along the road to Mykonos from Elia; the bus to Elia stops at the turn-off, so ask the driver to let you off at Kalo Livadi to shorten your trek.

If you've got the time, head to **Panormos Beach** and take a walk to the nearby town of **Ano Mera** to see the icons in the convent of **Panagia Tourlianis.** Just north of Ano Mera is the 13th-century monastery of **Paleokastrou.** Nearby, atop the arid moon-like slope, the medieval fortification of **Durga** stares out at the island's wind-swept hills with a sweeping view.

# DELOS ΔΗΛΟΣ

Apollo wher'er thou strayest, far or near,
Delos is still of all thy haunts most dear
—Homeric Hymn to Apollo

An excursion to Delos—the sacred navel around which the Cyclades whirl—is a must-see, even for those who take little interest in mythology or history. The most famous sanctuary in the Cycladic islands, Delos claims *the* Temple of Apollo, built to commemorate the birthplace of the god and his twin sister, Artemis. A site of religious pilgrimage in the ancient world, Delos is today something of a giant, island-wide museum.

## A DRIFTING ISLAND GROWS ROOTS

After getting **Leto** pregnant with Artemis and Apollo, sleazy **Zeus** kicked her out, afraid of his wife Hera's (understandable) wrath. Desperately searching for a place

to give birth, Leto wandered the Aegean, but island after island refused Leto shelter (to avoid Hera's vengeance). At last she came upon a rocky, unknown floating island shrouded in mist. Frightened, the little island bobbed about furtively until Leto swore by the river Styx that it would come to no harm, and that her unborn child would live there forever, casting light upon its birthplace. The reassured island stopped drifting, but Leto's trials were far from over: Hera conned the goddess of childbirth, Eilythia, into prolonging Leto's labor for nine days, at which point the other gods bribed Eilythia into having mercy. Leto collapsed and gave birth beside the island's Sacred Lake. Upon the children's birth, the mist disappeared and the island was bathed in radiance; because it could now be clearly seen, its name was changed from Adelos ("invisible") to Delos ("visible"). Grateful Leto promised to make the island the seat of her son's worship, and the ensuing sanctuary—plus a good central location—transformed little Delos into a major religious and commercial center.



### HISTORY OF DELOS

With a central position among the Aegean islands, Delos's role as a a maritime and political powerhouse is hardly surprising. The five-kilometer long island is paired with larger **Rheneia,** whose inhabitants are also called Delians. Although first settled in the 3rd millennium BC, it was during the Mycenaean Period (1580-1200 BC) that Delos began to flourish. Mycenaean rule ended around 1100 BC, and a century later the Ionians dedicated the island to worshipping Leto. By the 7th century BC, Delos had become the political and mercantile center of the Aegean League of Islands, starting off three centuries of struggle for power between the Delians and the Athenians. The Delians put up a good fight, but slowly bled power to the mainlanders. During these years, the Athenians ordered at least two "purifications" of the island, in honor of Apollo. The second, in 426 BC, decreed that no one should give birth or die on its sacred grounds, meaning that all graves had to be exhumed, and the bodies within moved to a "purification pit" on nearby Rheneia. Living Delians who violated the birth edict were banished. The Athenians later instituted the quadrennial **Delian Games,** where they always (unsurprisingly) came home with all the medals.

After Sparta defeated Athens in the **Peloponnesian War** (403 BC; see p. 11), Delos enjoyed independence and wealth. Sweet prosperity soured during the Roman occupation in the second century BC, when prestigious Delos was reduced to the slave-trading center of Greece, where as many as 10,000 slaves changed hands every day. By the end of the second century AD, after successive sackings, the island was left virtually deserted. Today, its only residents are legions of leaping lizards, huge spider webs, and members of the French School of Archaeology, who have been excavating here since 1873.

## DELOS ARCHAEOLOGICAL SITE

*Most accessible as a daytrip from Mykonos Town.* ***Excursion boats*** *leave from the dock near Mykonos Town (35min.; Tu-Su every 30-45min. 9:30am-11:30am, returns 12:20-3pm; 1900dr round-trip). Most trips only let you explore the site for 3hr., but each boat line has several return trips in the afternoon, so you have some exploring time flexibility. Expensive* ***guided tours*** *in several languages by each excursion boat company (8000dr, including admission to the ruins). A more affordable and worthwhile option is to buy the* ***guidebook*** *by Photini Zaphiropoulou (in town or at the entrance to the site), which includes info, color pictures, and a map of the site (1700dr). Tinos, Naxos, and Paros, and other islands offer joint trips to Mykonos and Delos, but allow less time to explore.* ***Open*** *Tu-Su 8:30am-3pm. 1200dr, students and EU seniors 600dr, EU students free.*

Occupying almost an entire plateia mile of the small island, the archaeological site includes, in the center of the ancient city, the Temple of Apollo and the *agora*, the outlying parts of the city, Mt. Kythnos, and the theater quarter. While it takes several days to explore the ruins completely, you can see the highlights in approximately three hours. Most of your fellow ferry passengers will follow a similar

route when they disembark; reverse the route if you want some privacy. As always, bring a hat, good shoes, sunblock, and a water bottle. There is an exorbitantly priced cafeteria beside the museum, so it's wiser to pack snacks.

**SACRED ROAD.** The path beyond the admission booth points you toward the **Agora of the Competaliasts,** where Roman guilds built their shop-shrines. Continue on in the same direction and turn left onto the wide Sacred Road. Lining your walk are two parallel **stoas,** the more impressive of which (on the left) was built by Philip of Macedon in 210 BC and dedicated to Apollo. Follow this road to the **Sanctuary of Apollo,** a collection of temples built in the god's honor that date from Mycenaean times to the 4th century BC. The biggest and most important of the temples is on the right. The famous **Great Temple of Apollo,** or **Temple of the Delians,** was completed at the end of the 4th century BC. Its immense, partially hollow hexagonal pedestal once supported an 8m-high marble statue of the god of light. The plundered remains of the statue can now be viewed in the **Artemision,** down by the water on your left.



Following the direction of the Sacred Road north, 50m past its end, places you in the beautiful **Terrace of the Lions.** In the 7th century BC, at least nine marble lions looked onto the sacred lake from the terrace; only five remain on Delos, and the body of a sixth, pirated by the Venetians, guards the entrance to Venice's arsenal. The original lions were removed from their seats to the site's archaeological museum in fall 1999; replicas are expected to assume their posts in 2001.

**SACRED LAKE AND ENVIRONS.** Proceed up the small crest left of the terrace to the **House of the Hill.** Because the building was dug deep into the earth, this archetypal Roman house is still substantially intact. Downhill lies the **House of the Lake,** with a well-preserved mosaic decorating its atrium, and the desecrated **Sacred Lake,** drained in 1925 to protect against malaria. The most mythologically potent of the island's sites, the round form of the former lake today appears as a leafy oasis with a lone palm tree at its center (honoring Apollo's birth). On the lake's south side is the expansive Roman **agora.**

**AROUND MOUNT KYTHNOS.** From the museum you can hike up the path to the summit of **Mt. Kythnos** (112m); its peak offers a such a good view of the ruins that Zeus chose it to spy on the birth of Apollo and Artemis. Although the climb is not difficult, wear sturdy, comfortable shoes—some of the rocks in the stairs dislodge easily. Ascending the mountain coming from the direction of Temple of Apollo, you will pass several temples dedicated to Egyptian gods. Arguably the most spectacular antiquity on the island, the elegant bust in the **Temple of Isis** depicts the sun. The immense building blocks of the nearby **Grotto of Herakles** suggest that it's from Mycenaean times, but some experts suggest that it's a Hellenic knock-off of Mycenaean architecture.

At the base of Mt. Kythnos, head west along the edge of the ruins to reach the **House of the Dolphins** and **House of the Masks,** which contain their intricate, well-preserved, eye-popping mosaics of dolphins and *Dionysus Riding a Panther.* Continue on to the **ancient theater,** which has a rather sophisticated cistern (as cisterns go) called **Dexamene,** with nine arched compartments. Also, try to explore the maze of rooms toward the port from the theater: the **House of the Trident,** graced a mosaic of a dolphin twisted around a trident; the **House of Dionysus,** containing another mosaic of Dionysus and a panther; and the **House of Cleopatra.** The famous statue of Cleopatra and Dioscourides is sheltered in the museum; a plaster copy is on the site.

**ARCHAEOLOGICAL MUSEUM.** Behind the Terrace of the Lions is the museum, the best place to round off your exploration of the ruins. It contains an assortment of archaeological finds from the island, including the originals of many of the statues that you thought you were admiring on site. Many of Delos' best sculptural finds are far away at the National Archaeology Museum in Athens (see p. 104).

# SYROS ΣΥΡΟΣ

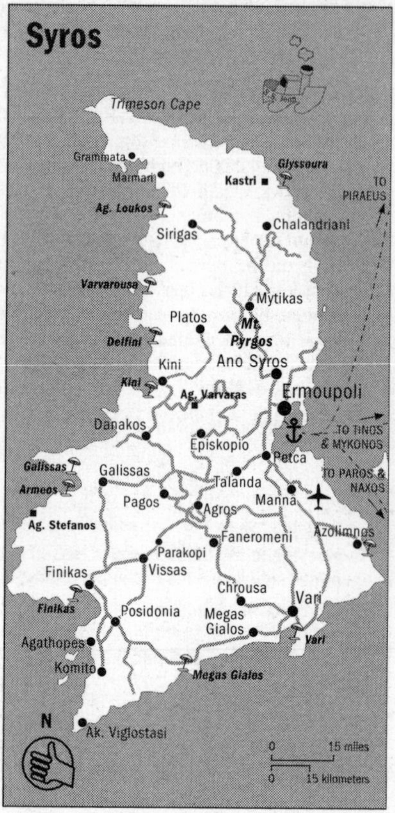

Although Syros first rose to commercial power as a Phoenician seaport, it was the 13th-century Venetians who turned it into the trading capital of the Cyclades. Steam-powered ships and the rise of Piraeus as the national port finally ended Syros's glory days. In the last 20 years, the island has regained its footing, largely due to the shipbuilding that now keeps the island afloat. International sailors ship in and out of town, and windsurfing has become *de rigeur*. You can always escape the madness of the port town Hermoupolis by following legions of Greek families to a seaside village or beach, or by heading to the medieval settlement of Ano Syros high above Hermoupolis on one of Syros's two peaks. Bold hikers will find uncharted terrain; everyone else can rely on the excellent public bus system.

Syros

Trimeson Cape
Grammata
Marmari
Glyssoura
Kastri
TO PIRAEUS
Ag. Loukos
Sirigas
Chalandriani
Varvarousa
Mytikas
Platos
Mt. Pyrgos
Delfini
Kini
Ano Syros
Kini
Ag. Varvaras
Ermoupoli
Danakos
Episkopio
TO TINOS & MYKONOS
Galissas
Galissas
Petca
Armeos
Talanda
TO PAROS & NAXOS
Pagos
Manna
Ag. Stefanos
Agros
Azolimnos
Faneromeni
Parakopi
Vissas
Finikas
Chrousa
Vari
Finikas
Posidonia
Megas Gialos
Vari
Agathopes
Komito
Megas Gialos
N
Ak. Viglostasi
0 15 miles
0 15 kilometers

## HERMOUPOLIS

## Ερμουπολις ☎0281

Bustling Hermoupolis is not only the Cyclades's largest city and capital, but (as the waterfront statue announces) it belongs to the winged messenger Hermes, god of commerce. Elegant Neoclassical buildings of Greek, Italian, and Bavarian design in Pl. Miaouli and Dellagrazia give the island an international appearance and offer a peek at the city's opulent past; they also explain its former nicknames—the "Manchester of Greece" and "little Milan." Though the city's roles in government and shipping make tourism a secondary concern, its vitality makes Syros an exciting, fully alive island. Athenian vacationers clog Hermoupolis's hotels from mid-July to September; you'll probably want to head for the island's countryside.

### GETTING THERE AND GETTING AROUND

**Ferries:** To: **Piraeus** (4½hr., 3-5 per day, 4450dr); **Rafina** (1 per day, 3000dr); **Tinos** (40min., 2-3 per day, 1100dr); **Mykonos** (1½hr., 2-3 per day, 1550dr); **Paros** (1½hr., 1-2 per day, 1550dr); **Naxos** (2½hr., 3 per week, 2150dr); **Ios** (4hr., 4 per week, 3750dr); **Santorini** (5hr., 1 per day, 4150dr); **Crete** (1 per week, 5450dr); and a few smaller Cyclades. Most boats depart from the right side of the harbor; be sure to ask.

**Flying Dolphins:** Depart daily from across the ferry docks on the left to: **Tinos** (2150dr); **Mykonos** (3000dr); **Paros** (3150dr); **Naxos** (4150dr); **Santorini** (8200dr); and **Ios** (7150dr). **Sea Jets** run once per day to: **Rafina** (1½hr., 6950dr); **Tinos** (15min., 2150dr); **Mykonos** (35min., 3000dr); and once per week to **Andros** (3715dr). **Minoan Lines** carries cars and passengers once per day to **Piraeus** (2hr., 8650dr).

**Flights:** There are 2-3 flights per day to Athens (15,000dr). You must take a bus or a taxi to the airport, southeast of Hermoupolis (☎87 025).

**Buses:** (☎82 575). Green **KTEL** buses leave from the depot near the ferry dock and travel regularly to: **Galissas** (18 per day, 270dr); **Kini** (6 per day, 250dr); and **Ano Syros** (3 per day, 220dr); less frequently on Su. A schedule is posted next to the buses.

**Taxis:** (☎86 222). The ferry landing and town hall in Pl. Miaouli have taxi stands.

**Rental Cars and Bikes:** On the waterfront. Try **Enjoy Your Holidays Rent a Car** (☎87 070 or 81 336; fax 82 739), Akti Papeidou 4. Small cars (Fiat Panda) 10,000dr per day; jeeps 14,000dr; bikes and scooters 4000dr. You can also buy ferry tickets here. Knowledgeable staff. Renting is popular, so call ahead. Open 9am-10pm.

## ORIENTATION AND PRACTICAL INFORMATION



When you get off the ferry, head right and walk down the waterfront for 3min. to **El. Venizelou,** beginning at the winged **statue of Hermes.** Activity in Hermoupolis centers around **Pl. Miaouli,** 2 blocks up El. Venizelou, where the town hall—a restored Neoclassical building—and its large marble plaza rest. Hotels and domatia are found all along the waterfront and the surrounding streets.

**Tourist Information:** Look for the "i" as you head right off the ferry–the booth is behind a statue wearing the helmet of Hermes. Free, helpful info on accommodations, good maps (400dr), and books on the island (500dr). Open 10am-6pm. The **Greek National Tourist Organization**'s Office of the Cyclades, Dodecanisou 10, offers free information and maps. Follow the sign 1 block to the right of Hotel Diogenes. Open 7am-2pm.

**Tourist Agencies: Gaviotis Tours** (☎86 606; fax 83 445), across from the bus depot. Provides schedules and prices. Sells ferry, hydrofoil, and flight tickets. Open 7am-1am.

**Banks: National Bank** (☎82 451), at the end of the first street on the right off El. Venizelou (going away from the waterfront), **exchanges currency.** Open M-Th 8am-2pm, F 8am-1:30pm. **Ionian Bank,** on Venizelou by Pl. Miaouli, has a 24hr. **ATM.**

**Police:** (☎82 610), behind the theater off the upper right corner of Pl. Miaouli. A **tourist police officer** is on duty all day.

**Port Authority:** (☎88 888 or 82 690). The office is at the end of the dock all the way to the right of the waterfront, with a Greek flag in front.

**Public Toilet:** On the right side of the first alley off the street with the National Bank and the post office on it. Look for the "WC" sign.

**Hospital:** (☎86 666), at the left end of the waterfront (facing inland) at Pl. Iroon, a 20min. walk from Miaouli.

**Pharmacy:** (☎82 220), at the center of the waterfront. Open 8am-2pm, 6pm-9pm.

**Telephones: OTE** (☎82 799), in the plateia. Open 7am-2:40pm.

**Internet Access: Net Café,** (☎85 330; http://users.otenet.gr/~dragon), in Pl. Miaouli, to the left, facing the town hall. A popular hangout. 1600dr for 1hr., 1000dr per additional hr. (600dr minimum). Ice cream, coffee, and drinks 350-1000dr. Open 8am-late.

**Post Office:** (☎82 596), 40m down the street from the National Bank. Open M-F 7:30am-2pm. **Postal Code:** 84100.

## ACCOMMODATIONS

Cheap domatia rooms abound (look around for "Rooms to Let" signs), and off-season prices are generally 20-40% cheaper. There's a large map with names and phone numbers of hotels at the ferry dock.

**Villa Nefeli,** Parou 21 (☎87 076). From the waterfront, head right and make a left on Hiou, just before Venizelou. Parou is the first left off Hiou–just follow the signs. Have a drink with Markos, the extra-friendly owner of this cozy traditional-house-turned-hotel, on the sunny roof garden bar, which has a full view of the harbor. Fridges. Doubles 12,000dr; triples 13,000dr.

**Ariadni Rooms to Let** (☎81 307 or 80 245), on Nik. Fylini near the ferry dock (look for signs). A dose of luxury, the hotel prides itself on its well-deserved class "A" rating. Spotless, radiant rooms, often with kitchen for no extra charge (try calling ahead). Doubles 17,000dr.

**Hotel Esperance** Akti Papguo and Folegandros 1 (☎81 671 or 81 434; fax 85 707), to the left of the ferry dock by the EKO gas station. Gleaming rooms with bath, TV, A/C, fridge, phone. The owner's wonderful, giggling mother will win you over. Breakfast 1500dr. Doubles and triples 19,000dr.

## FOOD AND NIGHTLIFE

For your grocery needs, there's a **mini-market** halfway up from the plateia on Hiou. (☎81 008. Open 8am-9pm.) Fresh produce stalls line the same street.

**Amvix Italian Restaurant,** (☎83 989), almost directly across from the ferry dock. Huge portions of amazing Italian food, including *tagliatelli carbonara* (1900dr) and all kinds of gourmet pizza (1600-2900dr).

**Restaurant Bakhos** (Βακχος). From the waterfront, make a left on Hiou; the restaurant is down at the end of Peloponnisou. Built in 1843, the building was a functioning pottery factory until 1922. Today, it spins out seafood specialties like haddock (1300dr) and grilled squid (1700dr). Salads 700-1200dr. Open 10am-2am.

**Kechayia Sweet Shop,** on the waterfront corner of El. Venizelou. Fabulous renditions of traditional local specialties like *chalvathopita*, a sweet concoction of almond paste, nuts, and chocolate (350dr) and *loukoumi* (450dr).

At night, the waterfront and Pl. Miaouli buzz with cafes, restaurants, dance clubs, and bars. On the right-hand strip of the waterfront, the **Cotton Club** is a hopping cafe/bar; just next to it, **Kimbara** is packed with wall-to-wall bodies and Madonna tunes. For the latest Greek music, hit the center of the waterfront, where **Odyssea** plays the Greek top 40 and serves beer and cocktails until the wee hours. For dancing, try **Arxaion**—it opens at 9am as a cafe and closes at 4am as a dance club. If you want some high rollin', **Kazino Eyeou**—Aegean Casino—is the only sin palace around. Men must wear pants and foreign visitors must leave their passport and 5000dr at the door. (☎84 400. Gambling starts 12:30pm.)

## SIGHTS

At the **Church of the Assumption** *(Kimisis Theotokou)*, on Ag. Proiou to the right of the plateia facing the town hall, you can contemplate a 1562 painting by a 20-year-old Domenikos Theotokopoulos before he was known as **El Greco** (see **It's El Greco to Me,** p. 470). The small **open market** on Hiou, between the lower left of Pl. Miaouli and the waterfront, hawks fresh produce, groceries, seafood, and snazzy souvenirs. From there, ascend to **Ano Syros,** a medieval Venetian settlement which Syros's Catholics still call home, by climbing the steps behind Pl. Miaouli (20min.) or taking the bus from the waterfront. You can wander its labyrinthine streets to the lofty Church of Ag. George above, and look over Hermoupolis and the coast below. The town hall's **Archaeological Museum** has a small collection of Cycladic art. (☎88 487. Open Tu-Su 8:30am-3pm. Free.)

## BEACHES

The closest beach is un-touristy **Agios Nikolau.** To get there, walk up El. Venizelou through Pl. Miaouli to the right of the Archaeological Museum. Head right and pass through Pl. Vardakas up to the right of the church of Agios Nikolau. Continue on the street until you see an archway and a stone stairway leading down to the beach. There is a roped-off area for swimming, but you can swim anywhere. The main beach at **Galissas,** a village to the west of Hermoupolis, is beyond crowded; every inch of sand is full of sun-lovin' life. It's *the* place to go. From Hermoupolis,

**buses** travel to Galissas (18 per day, 300dr), alternating between a direct 15min. route and a 45min. route that stops in other villages first (take the longer bus for a glimpse of the island). Climb past the chapel of Agia Pakou on the left side (facing the water) to discover nudist paradise: tiny, beautiful **Armeos Beach.**

Taking the scenic route to Galissas allows you to see the rest of Syros's southern beaches: **Poseidonia** (a ritzy resort area), **Finikas** (for watersports), **Angathopes,** and **Komito,** all developed for tourists. The beach resort of **Vari** is popular with families and package tour groups because of its shallow waters and relaxed atmosphere. North of Galissas is the tiny, quiet fishing village of **Kini,** ideal for the quintessential romantic sunset. If you happen to be in this picturesque hamlet on June 29th, the **Church of Ag. Peter** invites you and every other living thing within earshot to an all-night festival. *Bouzouki* strains accompany the plentiful *kakavia* (fish soup).



# NAXOS ΝΑΞΟΣ

"To Naxos steer," quoth Bacchus, "for it is indeed
My home, and there the mariner finds good cheer."
—Ovid, *Metamorphoses*

Naxos Town's gleaming marble Portara, the lone remaining arch of the grandest Greek temple to Apollo, serves as the portal into diverse and splendid Naxos. The island is the largest of the Cyclades; olive groves, wineries, teeny villages, and chalky white ruins fill its interior, and sandy beaches line the shore. Dionysus lived here back in the day, but even without mythology Naxos has had a colorful history. Prosperous since ancient times, the island's marble rivals that of neighboring Paros. When the Venetians under Marco Sanudi conquered the Cyclades in 1207, they made Naxos the capital of their Aegean empire. Spending a day navigating the wide mountain roads peels back these layers and reveals how they combine to make the island a self-sufficient paradise.

To properly experience Naxos, it's essential to escape the clutter of Naxos Town and get to the interior. Mopeds can be invaluable for combining trips to the beaches south of town and the inland sights and villages. Be careful, as even mostly paved roads have stretches of dirt with loose rocks. With patience, you can also use a combination of bus and foot to get almost anywhere you'd like to go. The most exhilarating aspects of Naxos' interior are the villages and hikes of the **Tragea** highland valley (a vastly green olive grove). Would-be hikers should pick up a copy of *Walking Tours on Naxos* by Christian Ucke, available from the tourist office in both English and German (4000dr).

## NAXOS TOWN Ναξος ☎0285

Naxos' capital reaches out to you before you've stepped from the ferry: as you float into the harbor, the Portara juts out into the sea on a peninsula, and the Chapel of Myrditiotissa floats on an island. Once inside Naxos Town, both the twisty historic quarter and the hard-nosed modern half step forward. Tightly-packed Old Naxos snoozes behind the waterfront shops, on the hill leading up to the Venetian castle. Low stone archways and trellises of flowers engulf the homes around the castle, while nearby, colorful markets bustle with activity. The new quarter opens on the far side of town near Agios Georgios beach and the waterfront. Hip bars and clubs there call you to shimmy after a day exploring the island.

### GETTING THERE AND GETTING AROUND

All **ferries** to Naxos dock in Naxos Town. The dock is at the left end of town. Mopeds are the best way to get around the island.

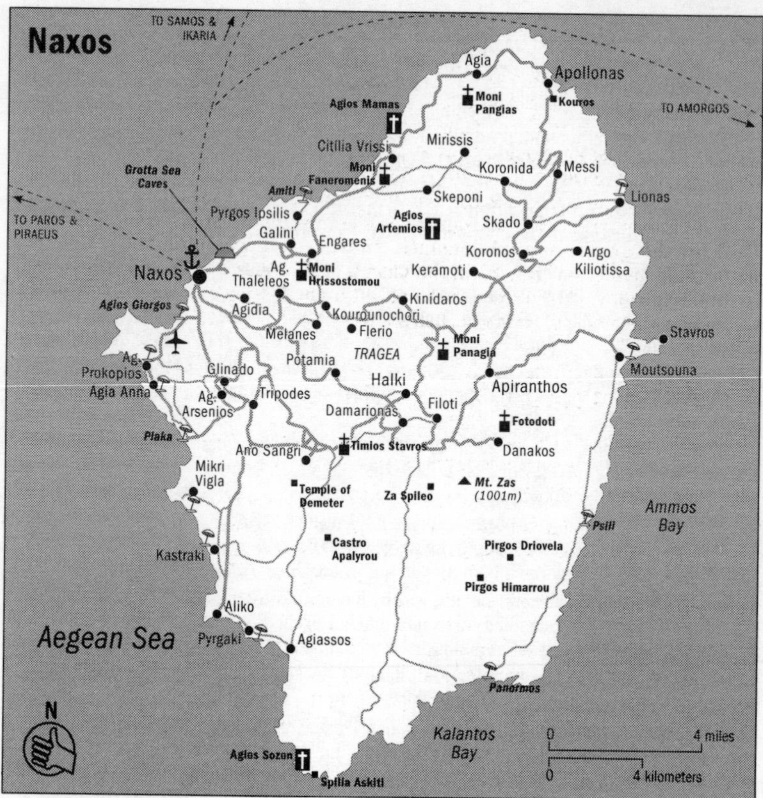




**Ferries:** To: **Amorgos** (3hr., 1 per day, 2300dr); **Crete** (7hr., 2-3 per week, 4960dr); **Ios** (1½hr., 6 per day, 2200dr); **Iraklia, Schinousa, Koufonisia,** and **Donousa** (1½hr., 3pm, 1430dr); **Mykonos** (2hr., 5 per week, 1740dr); **Piraeus** (7hr., 6-8 per day 9am-midnight, 5000dr); **Paros** (1hr., 6-8 per day 9am-midnight, 1400dr); **Santorini** (3hr., 6 per day, 2900dr); and **Syros** (2½hr., 1 per day, 2100dr). Ferries sail to **Kos** and **Rhodes** about twice per week.

**Flying Dolphins:** To: **Amorgos** (7600dr); **Andros** (6000dr); **Mykonos** (3500dr); **Ios** (4200dr); **Paros** (2700dr); **Santorini** (5600dr); **Syros** (4100dr); and **Tinos** (3900dr). Minoan Lines runs a route to **Piraeus** (3hr., 1 per day, 9600dr) and the **little Cyclades.**

**Buses:** (☎22 291), in front of the ferry dock. Check the **schedules** at the tourist office and the bus station across the street and to the left (facing inland). Buses to **Apollonas** (2hr., 3 per day 10am-1:15pm, 1050dr) and **Filoti** (5 per day 10am-3pm, 380dr) are often packed. Buses also run to: **Agia Anna beach** (15min., every 30min. 8am-midnight, 300dr), via **Agios Prokopios beach; Apiranthos** (1hr., 4 per day 10am-3pm, 550dr); **Halki** (30min., 6 per day, 320dr); **Engari** (1 per day, 220dr); **Pyrgaki Beach** (1hr., 3 per day 11am-2pm, 400dr); and **Tripodes** (3 per day 11am-2pm, 220dr).

**Flights:** An **Olympic Airways** desk is housed in **Naxos Tours** (☎22 095 or 24 000), at the right end of the waterfront. Two flights per day to **Athens** (20,100dr).

**Taxis:** (☎22 444), on the waterfront, next to the bus depot.

**Rentals: Ciao** (☎26 612), one block inland on the paved road to the right of the bus depot. Mopeds 3000dr per day. Open 8am-midnight. **Mike's Bikes** (☎24 975) rents tandem 64 cycles (2500dr per day). Also see **Rental Center** under **Internet Access.**

## ORIENTATION AND PRACTICAL INFORMATION

Avoid the dock hawks and pseudo tourist agencies on the dock (representing Naxos's disreputable accommodations) and make your way to the waterfront tourist information office (look for the "i"). Here you'll find stores and agencies galore. At the right end of the waterfront is the main road out of town, which runs along the waterfront and up to the right through **Pl. Protodikiou.** The Old Town is between this road and the shop-lined waterfront. You can enter the old market from many points along the waterfront; it's easiest to start from the entrance across the street from **Ciao's Motor Bike Rental,** by the friendly "Welcome to the Old Market" sign. Beware the lack of street signs.



**Tourist Office:** (☎24 358 or 25 201; fax 25 200; email chateau-zeugoli@forthnet.gr), 300m from the dock, by the bus depot. Bus, ferry, and hydrofoil schedules; car rental; **currency exchange;** international telephone; **luggage storage** 500dr; safety deposit 500dr; **laundry service** 2500dr. As for English-speaking Despina—she's a miracle-worker. Open 8am-midnight.

**Tourist Agency: Zas Travel** (☎23 330; fax 23 419), two offices along the waterfront and one in Ag. Anna (☎24 601). Telephone, **currency exchange, car rental,** and ferry/hydrofoil tickets. Open 8am-11pm.

**Bank:** The **National Bank** (☎23 053) is one of many on the waterfront offering **currency exchange** and an **ATM.** Open M-Th 8am-2pm, F 8am-1:30pm.

**English Bookstore: Vrakas** (☎23 039 or 22 226), behind a jewelry shop. Look for signs reading "gold-silver used books." Vrakas buys at half the original price, sells for 200-2500dr. Open 9:30am-11:30pm. **Zoom** (☎23 675), to the right of the National Bank, offers dozens of magazines from around the globe. Open 7:30am-midnight.

**Public Toilets and Showers:** Behind Toast Time on the street parallel to the waterfront. Turn left by the dock after Zas Travel and turn left again. Separate facilities for men and women. Toilets 100dr; showers 800dr. Open 6am-midnight.

**Police:** (☎23 100). On the main road heading toward Agios Georgios Beach from Pl. Protodikiou, 1km out of town. Open 24hr.

**Port Police:** (☎22 300), on Nikodemos, near Posto Travel, directly above the town hall. Near the bus depot on the waterfront. Open 24hr.

**Health Center:** (☎23 333 or 25 741). Turn right past Hotel Hermes and continue along that road for about 500m; it's on your left. Helicopter to Athens available for emergencies. Open 9am-9pm.

**Telephones: OTE:** by Hotel Hermes at the harbor's right end. Open M-F 7:30am-3:10pm.

**Internet Access: Rental Center** (☎23 395 or 25 584; email rentalcenter@nax.forthnet.gr), in Pl. Protodikiou. 2500dr per hr., 1000dr minimum. Friendly staff and good **car rental** rates, plus load of info on Naxos. Open 8:30am-11pm. **Veporia Play Room** (☎22 003), one block toward Ag. George Beach from Pl. Protodikou. Satellite TV, video games. Internet access 2000dr per hr., 1000dr minimum. Open 10am-5am.

**Post Office:** Walk down the waterfront (water on your right), and continue just beyond the main street that turns left. Pass a long playground on the right, and the post office will be on your left, up one floor. Open M-F 7:30am-2pm. **Postal code:** 84300.

## ACCOMMODATIONS

Most hotels on Naxos fill to capacity in late summer. Accommodations of all types can be arranged through the tourist office. For domatia, you'll pay around 3000-4500dr for singles, 4000-8000dr for doubles, 7000-10,000dr for triples, and 5000-10,000dr for studios (doubles with kitchenette and bath). Naxos has four roughly equivalent **beach camping** options, and their representatives wait eagerly at the dock. **Maragas Camping** runs a shuttle bus from the dock and frequent buses to Agios Anna beach (every 30min.; 300dr); it's the furthest campground, but virtually on the beach. (☎42 552 or 42 599. 900-1200dr per person; 300dr tent rental. Studios 8000-12,000dr; doubles with bath 6000-8000dr.) **Naxos Camping,** 1500m along Ag. Georgios beach, has a swimming pool. (☎23 500 or 23 501. 1000dr per person; 500dr tent rental. 10% discount for *Let's Go* readers.) **Apollon Camping** (☎24 417) and **Plaka Camping** (☎42 700) share similar rates and conditions.

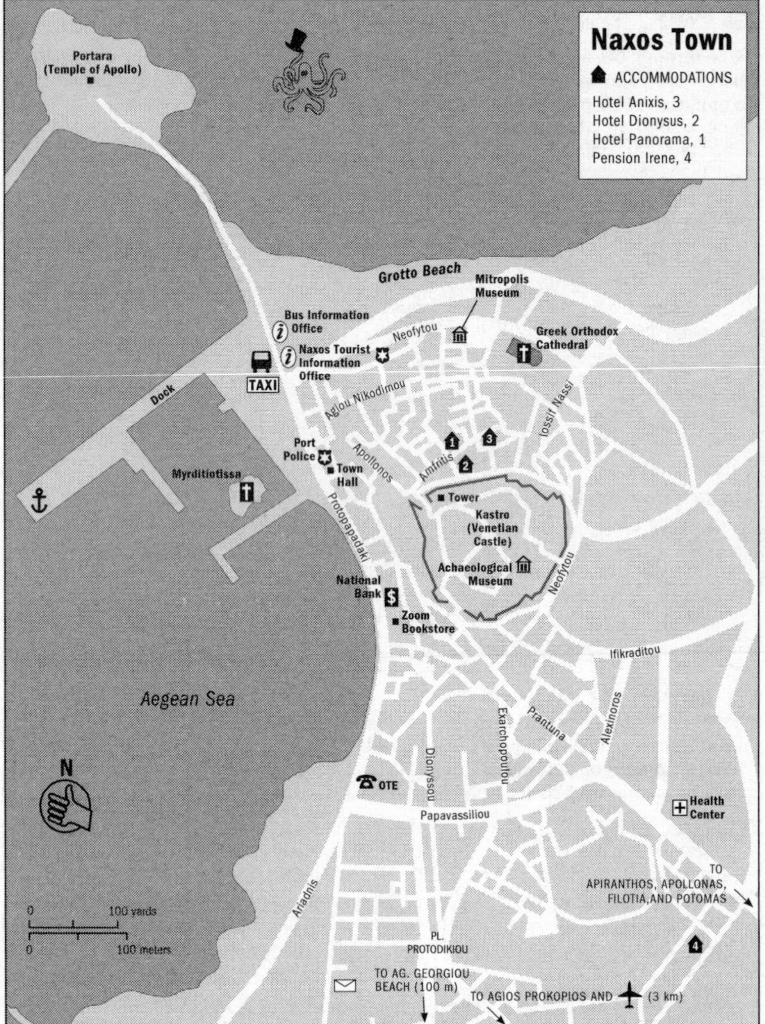


**Pension Irene** (☎23 169), in newer Naxos, up the hill from Galini Restaurant, 300m from Ag. Georgios beach. Inquire at the information office. A/C, TV, and a shuttle from the dock. Rooms have cooking facilities, fridges, and baths. Doubles 10,000dr; triples 12,000dr; quads 15,000dr.

**Dionysus** (☎25 201), just behind Panorama. Spartan, but utterly cheap. Reception open 10am-6pm and 10pm-midnight. Dorm 2000dr; singles 4000-5000dr; doubles and triples 5000-6000dr.

**Hotel Anixis** (☎22 112), also near Hotel Dionysos. Rooms with baths, TVs, and access to a lounge and laundry. Glass-enclosed roof garden lets you enjoy breakfast (900dr) while gazing at the Temple of Apollo. Doubles 12,000-14,000dr; triples 17,000dr.

**Hotel Panorama** (☎24 404), in Old Naxos, near Hotel Dionysos (follow signs pointing the way). Great for families. Quiet, airy rooms with fans and fridges; the owners are very proud of their panoramic views of the harbor and town. Breakfast 900dr. Singles 8000dr; doubles with bath 14,000dr; triples 17,000dr.

## FOOD

Wade through the sea of waterfront tables or park it at one of the many new cafes that decant cappuccinos. In Old Naxos, you'll stumble upon tucked-away *moussaka* havens. **Supermarkets** and fruit and grocery stands are everywhere.

**Galini** (☎25 206), 500m inland from Hotel Hermes; it's on your right just before the medical center. The best-kept secret in Naxos is worth the 10min. walk. Galini serves succulent fresh fish (1500-2500dr) without tourist crowds. Open noon-2am.

**Dolfini,** (☎24 320), up the steps from Ergo Bank. A slice of India (via Britain), in a lush garden washed by romantic tunes. They'll carry a variety of tasty curries to the marble tables. Entrees 1700-2000dr. Open 9am-2am.

**The Old Inn Garden,** (☎26 093), across the street from Ciao's Motor Bike Rental. This outpost of Deutschland serves healthy food in a scenic garden. Starters 900-1600dr, chicken souvlaki with mushrooms 1700dr. Peek into their flea market and have a romp in their playground. Open 6pm-3am.

**Giakoumis Taverna and Snack Bar Grill.** From Petros Travel, walk inland one block behind the waterfront, across from port authority. Fast, cheap, good food, traditional island music, and homemade wine keep the place packed. Souvlaki 400dr, Greek salad 800dr. Open 9am-2am.

**Cafe Picasso Mexican Bistro** (☎25 408). One block toward Ag. Georgios Beach from Pl. Kapodistrou. Some of the only Mexican food you'll find in Greece, from quesadillas (1300-1600dr) to burritos (2500-2900dr). Ease the salsa with a glass of sangria (600dr) or a frozen margarita (1200dr). Open 7pm-2am; kitchen closes at midnight.

**Rendez-Vous** (☎23 858). This bright pink waterfront palace concocts pastry: especially delicious *loukamades* (honey doughnuts, 750dr); ice cream and fruit bowls are served with sparklers. Takeout 20% cheaper. Breakfast served. Open 6am-2am.

## NIGHTLIFE

After-hours Naxos serenades evening wanderers with music from cafes and clubs. Take advantage of half-price Happy Hour, then relax all night, or get ready to gyrate at the hip waterfront clubs, which open at 11.

**The Jam,** behind OTE. Plays every style of rock plus a little reggae, all accompanied by owner Nikos on air guitar. Try the giant special cocktails—the Fiji is divine. If you get too hot, step out into the garden for a while. Happy Hour 5-10pm. Open 7pm-3:30am.

**Prime Cafe Bar** (☎23 747), on the waterfront. A comfy place to pass days and nights. If owner Yiannis doesn't know your face or your language yet, he will soon. Food and drink 500-1300dr. Happy Hour 7-11pm (cocktails 1600dr). Open 7:30am-3:30am.

**Super Island Bar and Club,** on the water along the paved road next to the bus depot. All Naxos goes to see and be seen here, kicking some serious moves. Step onto the terrace for fresh air and splendid views of the sea. 1500dr cover includes a drink. Open 11pm-3:30am, later F and Sa.

**On The Road** (☎22 262). A few blocks up the road from the OTE on the right. Packed during the off season when others turn off the taps, it's a refuge from the waterfront scene. Drinks 700-1500dr. Open after 5:30pm in summer, all day in winter.

**Lakridi Jazz Bar,** in Old Naxos on Old Market, close to the Captain's Cafe. Chill to Billie Holliday in the hot Naxian night. Delectable drinks 700-1800dr. Open 8pm-4am.

**Cine Astra** (☎25 381), on the road to Agia Anna from Pl. Protodikliou; a 15min. walk from the waterfront. Spend a low-key evening with the stars and Greek-subtitled English-language flicks. Shows 9 and 11pm. 1800dr, children 1500dr, students 1200dr.

## SIGHTS

The new **Mitropolis Museum** shouldn't be missed. An architectural achievement itself, it is built around an excavated site of a 13th century BC civilization. An ele-

vated walkway leads you through the reconstructed buildings; clear floors give the feeling of being inside them. (☎24 151. Open Tu-Su 8am-2:30pm. Free.)

The **Castro,** an old Venetian castle, looms over town, and merits the trek uphill. On the way, check out the coats of arms above the doorways of mansions inhabited by descendants of Frankish and Venetian nobility. At the top of the hill sits the **Archaeological Museum,** in the former Collège Français where Nikos Kazantzakis (p. 33), author of *The Last Temptation of Christ* and *Zorba the Greek*, studied. There's a significant collection of Cycladic figurines, an exhibit on Archaic and Classical sculpture, and pottery from Geometric through Roman times. (Open Tu-Su 8am-2:30pm. 500dr, students 300dr; free on Sundays and holidays.)

From the waterfront, you can see the white chapel of **Myrditiotissa** floating in the harbor on a man-made islet and the marble **Portara** archway, on its own peninsula. Climb up to it and view the unfinished beginnings of an ambitious temple dedicated to Apollo, begun on the orders of the tyrant Lydamis in the 6th century BC. This is one of the few archaeological sites in Greece where you can actually climb all over the ruins—with no admission, and no guards, open 24 hours, it's recommended for romantic sunsets or midnight star-watching.



## BEACHES

North of Naxos Town, you can snorkel among caves and reputed submerged Cycladic buildings looking for rocks and sea urchins. You'll have to head south, however, for Naxos's finest beach life, replete with hotels, rooms to let, bars, tavernas, discos, and creperies. The most remote, uncrowded beaches with the clearest waters are the farthest from town. There younger, beautiful, and less clothed bathers frolic among the windsurfers who come to Naxos from everywhere.

Near town, **Agios Georgios, Agios Prokopios, Agia Anna,** and long and sandy **Plaka** border crystal-blue water. A **bus** goes from the port to the beaches every half-hour (300dr). Unfortunately, unsightly modern buildings border them, and they're often crammed with sunbathers. On Plaka, stunning nude sunbathers stud the shore. At Ag. Georgios beach, **Flisvos Sportclub** runs windsurfing and catamaran rentals and lessons, and organizes weekly mountain bike excursions. The complex is complete with bar and restaurant. (☎24 308. Open 10am-6:30pm.)

The more secluded beaches at **Mikri Vigla, Kastraki, Aliko,** and **Pyrgaki** are accessible by **bus** from Naxos Town (4 per day, 400dr). Here desert meets sea; scrub pines, prickly pear, and century plants grow on the dunes. There is a small nudist beach on the southern protuberance of **Kastraki Beach.**

## DAYTRIPS FROM NAXOS TOWN

### APOLLONAS AND NORTHERN NAXOS

*From Naxos Town, catch the **bus** to Apollonas for a ride on an thrillingly beautiful coastal road (2hr., 1100dr). This bus service can be used easily to make a round trip (in either direction) of the central Naxian villages and the islands' northern coast; the bus goes on an interior and an alternate coastal route. The coast is lined with secluded, sandy beaches; those on moped can pick their spot and hike down along the goat trails.*

On the road to Apollonas you'll pass on your left the secluded beach at **Amiti,** down the road from Galini, and, farther on, the monastery of **Faneromenis** (the Virgin Revealer). The main attraction of Apollonas, one of the more famous *kouroi* of Naxos, is just a short walk from the harbor. While this **kouros** is nearly 11m tall, it's a bit less completely sculpted than the one in Flerio (see below). From the Apollonas bus stop, walk back along the main road uphill until you come to the fork in the road. Take a sharp right and walk up until you see the stairs at the Pros Kouro (Προς Κουρο) sign.

## CENTRAL NAXOS AND THE TRAGEA

The bus ride from Naxos Town to Halki takes you through cultivated mountainsides rich in olive trees, churches, and wildflowers. Look for the turn-off to **Ano Sangri,** an isolated town of winding flagstone streets 1km west of the road. You can get off the bus at the turn-off and walk the entire way (roughly 1½hr.). If you're up for the 30-minute amble south of Ano Sangri, you can see the 6th-century BC **Temple of Demeter** being reconstructed with original fragments and new Naxian marble. If you have a motorbike or car, an alternate route takes you from Naxos Town through Melanes to **Flerio,** where another magnificent Naxian **kouros** sleeps in a garden. This one was probably abandoned in its marble quarry because it broke before completion. Its owner runs a small *kafeneion* in the garden. From Flerio, backtrack and follow a road through three charming villages in a river valley—**Kato Potamia, Mesi Potamia,** and, farthest upstream, **Ano Potamia**—before reaching Halki. A map is essential—grab one at the tourist office in Naxos Town (500dr).

**Halki,** a placid village surrounded by Venetian towers, marks the beginning of the magnificent **Tragea,** an enormous, peaceful Arcadian olive grove. Restoration work in the **Panagia Protothonis,** across from the bus stop, has uncovered frescoes from the 11th through 13th centuries. The priest can let you in if it is closed.

Soon after leaving Halki you will reach Filoti, a village at the far end of the Tragea valley. Walking through the sylvan bliss is highly recommended. Footpaths off the main road will lead you into the dense **olive grove.** It is easy to get delightfully lost wandering among the scattered churches and tranquil scenery of the Tragea. If you do, take note of the sun and head west to return to the main road. If you're in Filoti from August 14 to 16, you'll see Naxos's largest celebration, the three-day-long **Feast of Assumption of Panagia** (the Virgin Mary).

## MT. ZAS

The slopes of Mt. Zas near Filoti offers superb views extending to Poros and the sea beyond. Serious hikers may want to check out the **Cave of Zeus,** the spot where an eagle gave the king of gods the power of hurling thunderbolts. This 150m deep cave is a good 1½-hour trek uphill from Filoti. Determined mythologists, or those simply looking for a good hike with excellent views, should bring a flashlight to appreciate the cave fully. Head up the road to Apiranthos for 20-30min. until a sign points to the right for Mt. Zas. Follow this road to its end, passing through a gate, just before a clearing with a potable **spring water fountain.** From there, keep going, staying on the left (uphill) whenever possible. Look for red arrows on stones, and be prepared to share the path with goats; don't expect any signs. After 45min. you'll reach cave's mouth, marked with a simple sign saying "cave." The grotto itself is large, cool, and rather slimy, and fun to explore.

## APIRANTHOS

A 15min. bus ride from Filoti brings you to the small town of Apiranthos, which houses an **Archaeological Museum** with many Cycladic artifacts, in a white building on the right side of the main street. Also in Apiranthos are a modest **folk art museum,** a **natural history museum,** and a **geological museum.** All four are "officially" open from 10am to 1:30pm, but it all depends on tourist traffic; many of the owners moonlight as goat herders. (Single ticket to all four.) Many Apiranthos homes are 300 to 400 years old, and lie in the shadow of the two castles that dominate the town. The mountain views from the edges of the town are stunning, and locals are cordial to the few tourists who come this way. More information is available at the unofficial **info center** inside the pricey Yasou Snack Bar, on the right past the Geological Museum. There are several cafes and tavernas on the main road to satisfy your hunger. From Apiranthos through **Koronos** and **Koronida,** a one hour drive away, the road snakes through interior mountain ranges. The terraced landscape, laden with fruit and olive trees, plunges into the valleys below.

# LITTLE CYCLADES

Goats overpoweringly outnumber human inhabitants in this tiny island group. Jumping off the beaten island-hopping track into the Little Cyclades lets you pursue perfect isolation and meditation. Peaceful walks, refreshing solitude, and a breathtaking nighttime sky await the adventurous traveler.

## KOUFONISIA Κουφονησια ☎0285

The littlest of the inhabited Little Cyclades (and the most popular), Koufonisia surrounds itself with a sparkling selection of beaches on the southeast side of the Koufonisia mainland, **Ano Koufonisia.** The charming small town of **Hora** serves as its capital. The endless views of the sea and of neighboring islands from **Kato Koufonisia** and rocky **Keros** lure visitors off of Ano Koufonisia. There may be few alternatives to the well-worn path from beach to taverna, but Koufonisia's total simplicity makes it totally relaxing.

**ORIENTATION AND PRACTICAL INFORMATION.** The **ferry ticket office,** up the main road in Hora, a few buildings past the blue-domed church, posts a ferry schedule on its door. (☎71 438. Open 9am-2pm and 6-10pm.) There are two **ferry** lines; one runs daily to Naxos (1550dr) via Schinousa (1100dr) and Iraklia (1100dr), and continues to Paros and Mykonos 3 times per week; the other runs daily to Donousa (1350dr) and 4 times per week continues to Amorgos (1600dr). Head straight off the ferry dock toward the tiny white village and the winding lanes of Hora. The heart of Hora can be reached by turning left at the second road, just past the card phone. Be sure to bring enough drachmas, as there is **no bank** on the island. **Currency exchange** is available at the **post office,** one block left at the first road away from the port. (Open 8:30-10am and 6:30-9:30pm.) The **OTE** is on the main road. (☎22 392. Open 8am-2pm and 5-10pm.) The **medical center** (☎71 370) is next to the ferry. A few **minimarkets** are on the main road. Just off the waterfront on the road up to Hora are the **police. Postal code:** 84300.

**ACCOMMODATIONS.** The small pensions around town fill up fast, so it's best to call ahead for accommodations. Walking along the main road reveals many homes with rooms to let, with prices around 10,000dr for doubles. **Hotel Koufonisia,** up the main road to the right, offers pickup service at the dock, not to mention large, furnished rooms with beds, desks, telephones, refrigerators, baths, and breakfast (300-500dr) in the pleasant cafe garden outside of the reception. (☎71 745. Doubles 10,000dr; triples 14,000dr.) **Hotel Keros,** just up the main road from the dock, is bigger and more expensive than the rest, but it's worth it. Hotel Keros has splendid waterfront views, a bright and airy cafe bar and TV lounge, and a lovely outdoor garden; it has ferry pickup and drop off, in-room phones, breakfast (500-1000dr), and a super-friendly staff. (☎/fax 71 600 or 71 601. Doubles 16,000-18,000dr; triples 18,000dr; quads 20,000-22,000dr.) **Pension Melissa** (☎71 454) is just up to the left from Katerina in the center of town (doubles 9000; triples 12,000dr).

**FOOD AND ENTERTAINMENT.** Throughout town you'll find good tavernas: seafood and standard Greek fare are the unanimous favorites (entrees 1400-2700dr). Their quality is uniform, and they're cheap. **Skoleio,** near the end of Hora's central road, bucks the trend by offering tasty crepes (dinner crepes 1400-1700dr); jazz and board games accompany your meal. Beyond star-gazing with your *meli* (honey), at night you can check out the rotating exhibits of the **Koufonisia Art Studio** (next to the post office; open 6pm-midnight) or **Eikazein,** a new gallery featuring the paintings and photographs of its owners (open 8pm-midnight). **Kalamia Music Cafe,** just across the beach next to the island's public telephone, is a pleasant place to cool your heels while waiting to use the phone.

**BEACHES.** Koufonisia's beaches spool out in a continuous ribbon along the southern coast. **Amos Beach** is closest to Hora, just to the right of the ferry dock (facing inland); it's mainly a spot to look at the nearby fishing boats and at spirited kids' soccer games. Continuing 10min. down the road behind the sand leads you to family-packed **Finikas,** with a convenient taverna beside it. Just on the other side of the ridge from Finikas waits much quieter **Fanos.** A 45min. walk from Hora, **Pori beach** is the best on the island, with water and sand magnificent even by Greek Island standards. If the sand gets too busy or broiling, head for the shaded rocks behind the beach, with its bay perfect for snorkeling. Regular boats also make trips to Pori there from the dock at Hora (500dr). Check the posted schedule for boat times. If these beaches get too hectic, peace costs just 500dr—the price of the daily ferry to Kato Koufonisia.

## DONOUSA Δονουσα ☎0285

A trip to Donousa takes you back in time to a Greek island as it would have been before tourism began. Lacking modern conveniences (banks, public transportation, a reliable tourist office), Donousa beckons those eager to abandon English.

The **tourist office** is on the left as you walk off the ferry dock; it sells ferry tickets and exchanges currency during its erratic opening hours. If it's closed during your visit, you can buy your ticket on the boat. Continue and bear to the right to find the **mini-market** (☎51 582). There are several tavernas, all visible from the dock, all serving similar Greek food (entrees 800-1800dr). **To Kima** (☎51 566), the island's main hangout, also sells phone cards and some groceries; it's right beside the dock. Up the hill behind it is the island's sole **public phone.** You can call the **doctor** at 51 506. Accommodations are mediocre, scarce, and expensive—singles cost around 10,000dr, doubles 15,000dr. Try the domatia, or seek out **Nikolas Sisalas** (☎51 570) or **Minalopolou** (☎51 603), both a short walk from the port. Some of the island's tastiest food comes from the **bakery** just above the tourist office (☎51 567).

The town **beach** allows children to splash under the watchful eyes of parents sipping Mythos. **Kedros beach,** a much nicer piece of shore, stretches out just over the ridge. Follow the road to the right of the white sign on the town beach to get to the tent-lined sand. Farther down the same road lies even more pristine **Livadi beach.**

## IRAKLIA Ιρακλια ☎0285

The few travelers who have stumbled upon Iraklia go to great lengths to conceal their whereabouts, lest their hideaway be discovered. The island's solitude is precious, along with the close ties between the local community and its rare visitors. Whether exploring its caves, basking on its beaches, or drinking a coffee under the starlight in a cafe, Iraklia's tangible and intangible charms will envelop you.

**ORIENTATION AND PRACTICAL INFORMATION.** **Express Skopelitis** runs **ferries** (1100-1700dr) to: **Naxos** (daily); **Paros** (4 per week); **Mykonos** (4 per week); **Schinousa, Koufonisia,** and **Amorgos** (daily); and **Donousa** (4 per week). In winter, ferries run to all destinations 4 times per week. **Hellas** runs ferries to **Naxos** (3 per week) and **Schinousa, Koufonisia, Amorgos, Naxos,** and **Donousa** (1-2 per week). **Flying Dolphins** run once per week to Schinousa, Koufonisia, Amorgos, Naxos, Paros, Mykonos, Syros, Tinos, Andros, and Rafina (1700-7500dr). Rent **mopeds** from **Iraklia Rent a Scooter;** they'll drive one to you. (☎71 564. 5000dr per day.) From the **port** of Agios Giorgios, head right along the road toward the town beach and Hora. This main road splits at **Perigali,** where you can pick up a useful island map (350dr). It comes back together on the far side of a ravine; on the right is all-purpose **Melissa,** a general store, ferry ticketer, telephone operator, post office, and domatia. (☎71 539; fax 71 561. Doubles with bath and fridge 5000-7000dr.) The island's only card phone is just outside. Call a **doctor** at 71 388. **Postal code:** 84300.

**ACCOMMODATIONS AND FOOD.** In July and August, call ahead to reserve accommodations—in most cases, your hosts will pick you up at the port. Stay at **Marietta's,** where the friendly service adds to the awesome location on Livadi Beach. (☎71 252. Doubles 8000dr.) **Alexandra,** at the top of Hora on the way to Livadi Beach, has four breezy rooms with baths and fridges, and a shared kitchen and veranda. (☎71 482. 8500dr; extra bed 2200dr.) **Maistrali,** up the hill just before Alexandra, rents studio apartments for 6000-10,000dr and sells postcards, foreign papers, and books; an attached restaurant serves good Greek food. It's also the late-summer disco hot spot for Athenians who flee the city to hear Nikos spin tunes all night long. (☎71 807. Opens at 7am for breakfast; dinner entrees 800-1600dr.) Domatia are generally quite adequate, but if you don't want to wrangle at the dock, call ahead to **Maria** (☎71 485) or **Anna's Place** (☎71 145).

Ten minutes down the road to Livadi, you'll find a delicious variety of grilled fish and Greek specialties at **Giorgios Gavalas' Place.** Dance late into the night with his sons, or ask Giorgios if you can participate in the next all-male Miss Iraklia contest. **O Pevkos** serves fresh fish across from **Maistrali.** At **Perigali,** locals hunch over backgammon games all night across from the town beach. Most eateries don't have set menus, and begin running out of choice dishes by 9pm. For a more energized hangout, especially in July and August, try **Bar Aki Music-Dance** in Hora, a new club that has the whole island grooving to its beat.

CYCLADES

**SIGHTS, BEACHES, AND THE OUTDOORS.** The shallow, clear waters of **Livadi Beach** echo the serenity of everything else on the island. Wade out and look at the ruins of the **Venetian Castle** overhead. To step into the Greece of 40 years ago, continue along the main road past Livadi to the town of **Panagia** (45min. from Hora), where you'll find a small taverna, a church, some cows, and not much else. The taverna, **To Steki** (☎71 579) also serves as a general store, bakery, and the only "gas station" on the island—fill up from a canister.

For the more adventurous, stalactite and stalagmite-scattered **Agios Ioannis Cave** will fascinate you with its tiny waterways you can crawl around in. There is a rough but helpful map of the path on the back of the Iraklia map available in Perigali. Bring a flashlight, candles, and matches, and get ready to get filthy. The steep, 1½ hour **hike** begins in Panagia, where a red arrow and the word "cave" are scrawled on a barn—if you don't see it, ask in To Steki. After 20 minutes along the stone wall-lined dirt path, you'll reach a wooden fence and another painted arrow pointing you through it. Follow the stone wall on your right until it meets another stone wall. The beaten path of the ascent becomes difficult to follow; just stay near this wall. After your climb, another wooden door stands at the intersection of two fences. Through this door, you'll begin a steep but more clearly defined 30min. descent along the back side of **Mt. Pappas** toward the two cave entrances. Crawling through the small entrance (with a hanging bell) brings you into the caves. You'll need the flashlight right away; leaving lighted candles along the way will help mark your path. To the left as you enter is an icon of St. John, who is celebrated in an August **festival** at the cave. There are said to be 15 rooms inside the cave. Be careful: the rocks are slippery, and daylight vanishes fast.

# SCHINOUSA Σχινουσα ☎0285

A multitude of isolated yet accessible beaches line the coast of the undiscovered island of Schinousa, all but guaranteeing an isolated communion with nature for the persistent traveler. The island is best enjoyed by exploring the landscape on foot and getting to know the friendly population—about 100 at last count.

**ORIENTATION AND PRACTICAL INFORMATION.** All boats dock at the tiny port of **Mersini,** with **Hora** a 10-15min. walk uphill. Call ahead for accommodations and you'll be picked up from the ferry, or grab a ride with a pension owner at the dock. **Ferries** go daily to: **Koufonisia** (1100dr); **Iraklia** (1100dr); **Naxos** (1400dr); **Koufonisia** and **Amorgos,** continuing to **Donousa** 4 times per week (1100-2000dr); and

**Iraklia** and **Naxos,** continuing to **Paros** and **Mykonos** 3 times per week (1400-2500dr). Nearly everything you'll need in Hora can be found on the main road, a 5min. walk from end to end. As you enter town, the **tourist info shop** and **supermarket** (☎71 930) is on the left, selling maps, postcards, fruit, and other provisions. Owner Giorgios Grispos, the island's tourist guru, **exchanges currency** at cruddy rates and sells **boat tickets.** He also runs **Central Travel Agency** (☎71 950; fax 71 176) on the path to Tsigouri Beach. Ask him for a free brochure with a map of the island. Two public **card phones** are down at the port and in the main plateia of Hora. The island doctor can be reached at 71 174. Follow signs to the **post office,** run out of a house off the main road. **Postal code:** 84300.



**ACCOMMODATIONS AND FOOD.** Nearly every restaurant or general store in town offers several rooms to rent in addition to their *moussaka* and Fanta. At **Meltemi,** friendly service by Elias and his family complements the large balconies (doubles 10,000-17,000dr); they also serve the best souvlaki in town (350dr). **Anesis** offers snappy new rooms with balcony's-eye views, fridges, and baths (☎71 180; doubles 10,000dr, triples 17,000dr); have a drink downstairs with the owner. **Pothiti Restaurant** has rooms with bath and balcony (☎71 184; triples 6000-8000dr) above one of Schinousa's two central tavernas—the other is **Panorama Restaurant.** Both prepare delicious daily specials; just go into the kitchen and choose your meal from what you see.

**NIGHTLIFE AND BEACHES.** At night there are two choices. In town, the **Margarita Cafe Bar** is complete with a DJ and a terraced cafe area overlooking the water (coffee 400dr, cocktails 1600dr; opens at 6pm), but the real fun is down by Tsigouri Beach. Walk down a rocky path at the beginning of Hora, off the main road, for 10 minutes to reach **Ostria Cafe,** an outdoor beach bar and restaurant, where you can spin music with the five fab brothers (Manolis, Agilos, Dimitris, Christos, and Antonis) who own the joint.

Schinousa's dirt roads love pedestrians as much as they hate cars. Grab some water, glance at a map, and walk until a particularly alluring cove catches your eye. **Tsigouri Beach** invites you to splash in the waves, play a round of beach volleyball, and rent kayaks or waterskis. Other beaches include **Livadi** (farther along the main road through Hora to the dirt tracks that lead down to the water) and **Psili Ammos** on the other side of the island, about a 20min. walk past the bakery.

# PAROS ΠΑΡΟΣ

Paros was famous in the ancient world for its slabs of pure white marble, which were shaped into Venus de Milo, the Nike of Samothrace, and parts of Napoleon's mausoleum in Paris. The unclouded marble contrasts with the blotched mythological and oral history of the island. When Hercules stopped in Paros on his quest for Hippolyte's belt, two of his sailors were murdered by the sons of the local big shot, Minos of Crete. Enraged Heracles slew Minos's sons and took off. In the 7th century BC, Greeks feared Paros as the home of sharp-tongued Archilochus, one of the earliest lyric poets and inventor of iambic verse, whose biting satire actually drove one allegedly unvirtuous Parian woman and her shamed father to suicide. Nowadays, the quarries have closed and the locals have warmed up considerably, as Paros has become a tourist favorite among the islands, ranking third after Santorini and Mykonos. Paros's allure comes in part from its large size, rolling agricultural fields, golden beaches, and tangled whitewashed villages.

## PAROIKIA Παροικια ☎0284

Behind Paroikia's (PAR-ah-kia) commercial facade, flower-filled streets wind through archways, and past whitewashed houses and one of the most treasured basilicas of the Orthodox faith. Wander through the *agora* (marketplace) to find

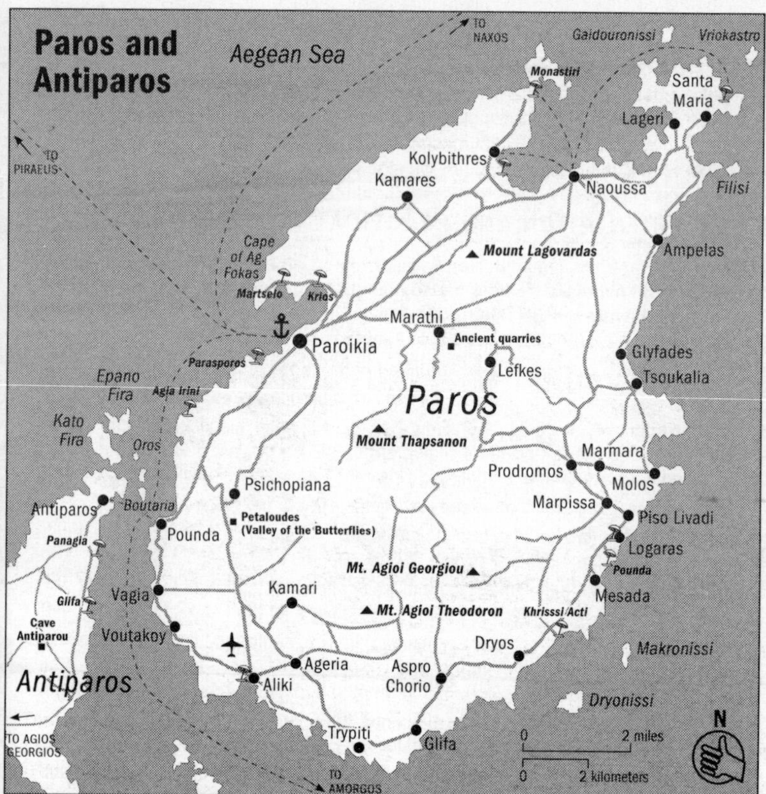


trendy clothing, snappy jewelry, local art, homemade goods, and the outdoor terraces of coffeehouses. While the beaches aren't much to write home about, this transportation hub is a convenient base for reaching almost any spot on the island.

## GETTING THERE AND GETTING AROUND

**Ferries:** To: **Amorgos** (3hr., 1-2 per day, 2740dr); **Crete** (8hr., 5 per week, 4950dr); **Ikaria** (4hr., 5 per week, 3350dr); **Ios** (2½hr., 7-9 per day, 2450dr); **Kos** (1 per week, 4350dr); **Piraeus** (5-6hr., 5-8 per day, 4950dr); **Naxos** (1hr., 5-10 per day, 1350dr); **Rafina** (3-5 per day, 4150dr); **Rhodes** (16hr., 1 per week, 6950dr); **Samos** (6hr., 6 per week, 4050dr); **Santorini** (3½hr., 7-9 per day, 3080dr); **Sikinos** (7 per week, 1750dr); **Syros** (1hr., 3-6 per day, 2450dr).

**Flying Dolphins:** Catamarans and hydrofoils speed to: **Amorgos** (1-2 per day, 5500dr); **Anafi** (6950dr); **Andros** (2 per week, 5500dr); **Crete** (9900dr); **Folegandros** (3 per week, 3800dr); **Koufonisia** (2 per week, 5423dr); **Ios** (2-3 per day, 4900dr); **Milos** (5730dr); **Mykonos** (1 hr., 2-4 per day, 3300dr); **Naxos** (4-7 per day, 2700dr); **Rafina** (9 per week, 8200dr); **Santorini** (3-4 per day, 6150dr); **Sifnos** (2 per week, 1920dr); **Sikinos** (3500dr); **Syros** (3-4 per day, 3100dr); and **Tinos** (4-5 per day, 3500dr). **Minoan Lines** go to **Piraeus** (3hr., 9700dr).

**Flights: Olympic Airways** (local ☎21 900; general information ☎0801 44 444), in the plateia by National Bank. Open M-F 8am-3pm. To **Athens** (around 2 flights per day, 20,400dr). Taxi to airport 2200dr; bus to Aliki 290dr. **Hellenic Star Airlines** (local ☎21 738; fax 22 146. Athens general information ☎(01) 961 1881; fax (01) 965 0373) has recently begun running inexpensive flights to Paros.

**Buses:** (☎21 395 or 21 133). Schedule posted in the shack a few blocks to the left of the windmill (facing inland). Prices range from 250-550dr. Buses run to: **Aliki** and the **airport** via the **Valley of the Butterflies** (30min., 10 per day, 250dr); **Chrisi Akti (Golden Beach)** (50min., 2 per day); **Marpissa** (35min., 15 per day); **Drios** (1hr., 12 per day); **Kamares** (20min., 2 per day); **Lefkes** (25min., 8 per day); **Naoussa** (15min., 33 per day); **Piso Livadi** (40min., 15 per day); **Pounda** (15min., 15 per day).

**Taxis:** (☎22 620), inland and to the right of the windmill.

## ORIENTATION AND PRACTICAL INFORMATION



Stepping off the ferry, cheap hotels, tourist-related offices, and the town beach lie to the left. The plateia is straight ahead, past the windmill and the tourist offices. To the right, a whitewashed labyrinth brims with shops, restaurants, and cafes. To the far right around the bend, the island's party district awaits.

**Tourist Agency: Polos Tours** (☎22 092 or 22 093; fax 21 983), next to the OTE. Has up-to-the-minute transportation schedules and rental services. Open 8am-1am.

**Banks: National Bank** (☎21 298). From the windmill, head inland to the plateia and to the right. It's in the fortress-like building at the far corner, past the playground. 24hr. **ATM** and **currency exchange** machine. Open M-Th 8am-2pm, F 8am-1:30pm.

**Luggage Storage:** Places around the port charge 1000dr per piece per day.

**Laundromat: Top** (☎23 424). Pass the bus station and turn right just after ancient ruins. Wash, dry, soap, and optional folding 2200dr. Open 9am-2pm and 5:30-9pm.

**Public Toilets:** Beside the small blue and white church to the left of the windmill. More toilets are to the right of the windmill beside the signs for the Frankish Castle.

**Police:** (☎23 333), across the plateia behind the OTE, on the 2nd floor above the photo shops. Open 24hr. **Tourist police** (☎21 673), in the same building. Open 9am-3:30pm. **Port Police** (☎21 240), off the waterfront, past the bus station. Open 24hr.

**Medical Clinic:** (☎22 500). Across the street from the toilets and the small blue and white church to the left of the windmill. Open M-F 7am-2:30pm. **Emergency** care 24hr.

**Telephones:** The **OTE** (☎21 399) is one block to the right of the windmill (facing inland). Open M-F 7:30am-2:30pm.

**Internet Access:** Internet cafes are multiplying like rabbits in Paroikia. **Cybercookies** (☎/fax 21 610), on Market street, charges 1200dr for an hour-long card. Special offers include 20min. free with one order of food, 45min. with two orders. Open 9am-2am. **Memphis Cafe** (mobile ☎(0030) 2842 3768) is left of the windmills on the waterfront. 500dr for 20min. Open 9am-1am.

**Post Office:** (☎21 236), on the left side of the waterfront, 2 blocks past the bus stop. Open M-F 7:30am-2pm. **Postal code:** 84400.

## ACCOMMODATIONS

There are many hotels and rooms to let along the waterfront and in the Old Town; a slew of new, inexpensive pensions have opened behind the town beach to the left of the plateia (when you're coming from the dock). Dock hawks are known to offer good deals in Naoussa, Piso Livadi, and Antiparos, among other places; remember to insist on seeing the rooms before you hand over any money or your passport. The **Room Association** (☎24 528) can help you in your hunt.

**Rena Rooms** (☎/fax 22 220 or 21 427). Turn left from the dock and take a right after the ancient cemetery ruins, or call ahead for pick-up from the port. Bright, spic-'n'-span rooms with fridges, ceiling fans, baths, balconies (some with sea view), and helpful owners. Free luggage storage. Doubles 6000-13,000dr; triples 9000-14,000dr. 20% *Let's Go* discount. Open Mar.-Nov.

**Pelagos Studios** (☎22 725 or 22 726; fax 22 708). Find Vassilis in the port or call and get picked up. Fully furnished rooms with kitchen, bath, TV, and even radio. Convenient

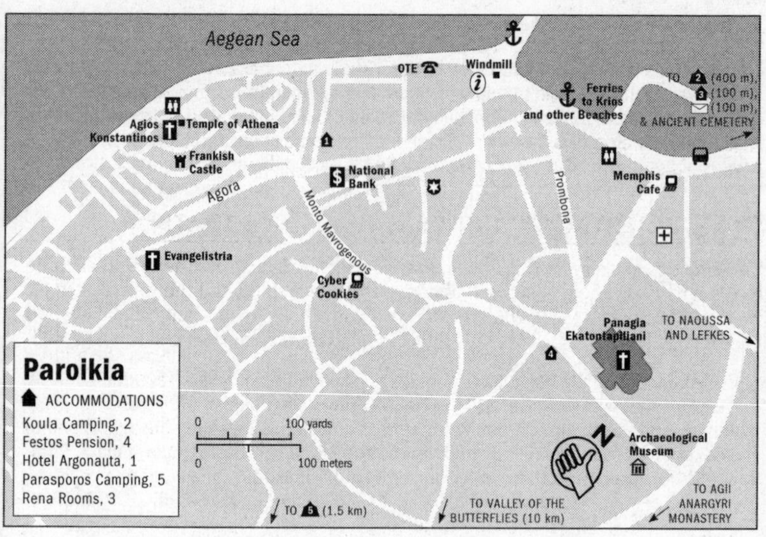




to Pariokia's nightlife, despite its peaceful, picturesque setting. Guest congregate on the flower-roofed outdoor patio where the owner serves complimentary *ouzo.* Doubles 8000-18,000dr; triples 10,000-20,000dr.

**Festos Pension** (☎21 635; fax 24 193). From the dock, walk to the left of the windmill, and take a right to head toward the Church of 100 Gates; take another right at the end of the road, and Festos will be on your left. Central location and private baths. Laundry 1000-1700dr. Luggage storage 300-500dr. Check-out 10:30am. 4-bedded dorm 3000-5000dr. Doubles 5000-12,000dr.

**Hotel Argonouta** (☎21 440, 22 278, or 22 090; fax 23 442), a large hotel next to the National Bank in the old part of town. Well-kept, A/C rooms with bath and balcony. Doubles 9000-18,000dr; triples 12-22,000dr.

**Parasporos Camping** (☎22 268 or 21 100), 1.5km south of the port; shuttle service available. Away from the hubbub, beside Delphini Beach. Showers, laundry, and kitchen. 1300dr per person; 600dr per tent; 1000dr tent rental.

**Koula Camping** (☎22 081 or 22 082; fax 22 740), 400m north of the dock across the street from the pebbly town beach. Market, laundry, and kitchen. 1500dr per person; 600dr per tent, 1000dr tent rental; 1000dr per car, 500dr per motorcycle.

## FOOD

**Happy Green Cow** (☎24 691), a block inland off the plateia in the narrow walkway behind the National Bank. Relish vegetarian food in a psychedelic setting. Mushrooms gratin with cheese and bechamel sauce 1900dr; burritos 1600dr. Open 7pm-midnight.

**Apollon Garden Restaurant** (☎21 875). Go down the winding side street off Market street, turn left approximately 100m past the Church of 100 Gates; keep an eye out for the signs. It's not cheap, but the enthralling garden and food are worth it. Octopus macaroni 1400dr; catch-of-the-day 1900dr for one, 3500dr for two. Open 5pm-1am.

**Nik's Hamburgers** (☎21 434). Walk right from the port; it's tucked away in one of the plateias. Paros's first hamburger joint, established in 1977. Nikburger 450dr, Nikfeast (2 burgers, chips, and salad) 890dr, fish and chips 950dr. Open 5-10pm.

**Bountaraki** (☎22 297). At the far right end of the harbor, with your back to the water. Prime waterside seating, with a menu that includes traditional dishes and vegetarian and seafood specialties (most entrees 1500-2400dr). Open 1pm-midnight.

## NIGHTLIFE AND ENTERTAINMENT

**Pirate Blues and Jazz,** tucked away in the Old Town, anchors several mellow cafes where you'll find eclectic music offerings. (Beers around 800dr, cocktails 2000dr, coffee 800dr, wine 800dr. Open 7pm-3am.) The cafes are found by heading away from the dock along the street that starts with the National Bank on the plateia. If a night of boozing doesn't thrill you, **Cine Rex,** 400m to the left of the dock along the waterfront, shows American movies in its outdoor theater; check signs in the plateia (2 showings per day, 1700dr).

The waterfront is the true home of pulsing Parian nightlife. Throngs sit on the sidewalk or the beach, sharing booze and singing songs; toward midnight, the tourist traffic forms a stream flowing eastward toward the thicket of clubs that sit at the edge of town. There are hangouts for English-speakers to the far-right end of the waterfront past the ferry dock, just before the small white bridge. **Saloon D'Or,** a popular cafe playing the greatest hits of the seventies and eighties, fills nightly with travelers. **The Slammer Bar** specializes in tequila slammers (500dr); friendly bartenders train the uninitiated. The **Parian Experience** consists of a mind-boggling party complex that rounds out any night on Paros. Follow the spotlight and the crowds to the far end of the harbor to reach **The Dubliner, Down Under, Cactus Shots Bar,** and the **Paros Rock Cafe,** all under one roof. Sit around or dance to any of the four simultaneously playing tunes. (Beer 700-800dr, cocktails 1400dr. 1000dr cover goes toward a drink.) If these four don't suit you, there are several other discos next door.



## SIGHTS AND MUSEUMS

**PANAGIA EKATONTAPILIANI.** The **Church of Our Lady of 100 Gates** looms over Paroikia's plateia in the shape of an imperfect Greek cross. It houses three separate churches, cloisters, and a large peaceful courtyard. Tradition holds that only 99 of the church's 100 doors can be counted—when the 100th appears, Constantinople will once again belong to the Greeks.

The Ekatontapiliani was supposedly conceived in the 4th century AD when **St. Helen,** the mother of Constantine, stopped here on her way to the Holy Land. While praying, Helen saw the True Cross and vowed to build a church befitting the site of her vision. She died before she could fulfill her promise, but in the 6th century, the Emperor Justinian commissioned young Ignatius, student of Isidorus of Miletus, to build her church. According to legend, the church's beauty drove Isidorus to a fit of jealousy in which he lunged violently at his pupil, Ignatius. In the ensuing scuffle, both fell to their deaths. The repentant architects can be seen bemoaning their fate on the sculpted bases of the columns across the courtyard. The main structure of the complex is the mammoth **Church of the Assumption.** The **Church of Agios Nikolaos** (the oldest of the three) and the **baptistry** flank this centerpiece to the north and south, respectively. The churches' architecture exhibits several centuries worth of masterful stonemasonry, containing much Byzantine iconography along with more recently created liturgical objects. Dress modestly: long pants for men, long skirts for women, and no bare shoulders. *(Open 8am-8:30pm.)*

In the courtyard are the tiny **Church Museum,** on the right, and the tiny **Byzantine Museum,** next to the entrance. *(Church Museum open W and F-M 9am-1pm and 5:30-9pm. 500dr. Byzantine Museum open daily 9am-1pm and 5-9pm. 500dr.)*

**OTHER SIGHTS.** The collection at the **Paroikia Archaeological Museum** contains more prized pieces than your average antiquities museum, including a 5th-century BC statue of wingless Nike, a large gryphon sculpture, and a piece of the marble **Parian Chronicle,** a history of Greece up to 264 BC. *(Behind the church next to the schoolyard. ☎21 231. Open Tu-Su 8:30am-3pm. 500dr, students 300dr, EU students free.)* A ramble through the Old Town will inevitably lead you past the lone remaining wall of the Venetian **Frankish Castle,** where you can see sections of marble and columns removed from the ancient Temple of Athena. The actual temple was a short dis-

tance away, on the site of the present day, gleaming white **Church of Agios Konstantinos.** Peep your head into this tiny church for a glimpse of candle-lit Byzantine iconography. To reach the church, walk left along the waterfront from the dock, and walk up the stairs at the Frankish castle sign.

Walking right along the waterfront will lead you past the **ancient cemetery,** where a series of huge, mostly Roman-era tombs lie scattered in the midst of a strip of mini-markets. The unpaved road behind the Archaeological Museum leads up to the **Agia Anargyri Monastery,** where you can admire the view and wander through dramatically sighing cypress groves.

## DAYTRIPS FROM PAROIKIA

**Marathi,** 5km from Paroikia in center of the island, is home to Paros's now idle marble quarries. Still considered to be among the finest in the world, Parian marble is translucent up to 3mm thick, with one-third the opacity of most other marble. A visit to the quarries is a serious undertaking: bring a flashlight, strong shoes, and don't go alone. Nearby **Lefkes,** 5km from Marathi, was the largest village on the island through the 19th century, when Parians moved inland to escape plundering coastal pirates. Today, it's a quiet village of 400 inhabitants with classic Cycladic architecture—the most attractive and unspoiled town in Paros' interior.

Boats run from Paroikia to the **beaches** of Krios, Martselo, and Kaminia (15min., 4 per hr. 9:30am-7pm, 400dr), north along the coast. The calm, secluded beaches to the south, **Parasporos** and **Agia Irini,** are an hour away by bus.



## VALLEY OF THE BUTTERFLIES

*Take the bus from Paroikia to Aliki (10min., 8 per day, 250dr) and ask to be let off at Petaloudes. Then follow the signs up the steep winding road 2km to the entrance. Open M-Sa 9am-8pm. 400dr.*

Just 10km south of town is the cool, spring-fed Valley of the Butterflies, or **Petaloudes,** where the rare (and tongue-twisting) *Panaxiaquadripunctaria* moth congregates in massive numbers during its mating season, from June to late September. The butterflies cloak the foliage, their zebra-striped wings blending into their surroundings until they expose their bright red underwings in flight. Every summer they return to this lepidopterous metropolis to mate, sleeping on the bushes during the day and getting busy at night. Because the sleeping patterns of the butterflies are vital to their mating patterns, it is important to cause as little distraction as possible: don't clap or talk loudly, and don't shake the bushes.

# NAOUSSA Ναουσσα ☎0284

Naoussa is Paros's second port after Paroikia, a natural harbor cradled by long, sandy beaches in the shape of crab claws. Persian, Greek, Roman, Venetian, Ottoman, and Russian fleets have anchored here; the tradition continues today as visitors from all over the world converge on Naoussa's beaches. Unfortunately, although you may see glimpses of an unspoiled Greek fishing village, much of the town's charm has been sucked out by the influx of package tours.

**ORIENTATION AND PRACTICAL INFORMATION.** Naoussa is easy to navigate. From the bus stop facing the water, the road heading left past the little bridge leads to the beaches of **Kolibithres** and **Monastiri.** For a nude beach, take the bus to **Laggeri.** To your right, one wide commercial street runs behind you; the Old Town lies to the right of this street.

**Buses** run continuously between **Paroikia** and Naoussa (15min., every 30min., 250dr). There are also buses (230-550dr) from Naoussa to: **Ampelas** (4 per day, 250dr); **Drios** (15 per day, 500dr); and **Santa Maria** (4 per day, 250dr). Check the schedule at the bus stop booth. **Taxi boats** leave Naoussa for nearby beaches. The blue booth across from the first stretch of cafes on the waterfront sells round-trip

tickets to: **Kolimbithies** (12min., every 30min. 10am-8pm, 700dr); **Laggeri** (20min., every 40min., 1000dr); **Monastiri** (15min., every 30min., 800dr); and **Santa Maria** (40min., 1 per day, 2000dr).

Naoussa's **tourist office** is across from the bus stop by the bridge, and offers general information on the town and its accommodations. (☎52 158. Open May-Sept. 15 10:30am-6:30pm.) For more specific advice about where to stay and how to move around in Naoussa and Paros, pop into **Free Spirit Travel Agency** (☎52 251 or 53 391; fax 52294; http://users.hellasnet.gr/frspirit). To find the 24hr. **police** station (☎51 202), walk left (facing the water) up the hill and turn left on the curving road before Mike's Moto Rent; at the top of the hill, turn left again, and shortly it'll be on your left. A **medical center** can be found by the bus stop on the main road (☎52 304); the doctor is available 9am-10pm. For 24hr. **emergencies,** call mobile (0944) 340 0940. Farther down on the right is the **General Bookstore,** selling international magazines and some books in English. (☎51 532. Open 9:30am-11:30pm.) You will find the **post office** 400m down the same road, just past the Santa Maria turn-off. (☎21 236. Open M-F 7:30am-2pm.) The multilingual **pharmacy** is on the main street inland. (☎51 550; **emergencies** 51 004. Open M-Sa 8:30am-2:30pm and 5:30-11pm, Su 10am-2:30pm and 5:30-11pm.) The **National Bank** is along the marina. (☎51 438. Open M-Th 8:30am-1:30pm, F 8:30am-1pm.) **Postal code:** 84401.

CYCLADES

**ACCOMMODATIONS.** For a small town, Naoussa has lot of places to sleep, but package-tour groups book most hotels months in advance. Rooms to let cost roughly 7000-13,000dr for doubles and 8000-15,000dr for triples; ask at the tourist office for help. **Villa Galini** is reached by heading inland past the bus stop, and turning right 700m ahead; signs mark the way. Traditionally decorated, airy rooms and a gregarious owner make for a pleasant stay; private baths, phones, and fridges make it comfortable. Call several days in advance for free pick-up from the port at Paroikia. (☎53 335; fax 53 336. Doubles 6000-16,000dr; triples 7200-19,200dr. Open Apr.-Sept.) To right of the waterfront with you back to the water lie a number of upscale pensions with spectacular views of the harbor. To reach **Pension Hara,** walk along the waterfront 300m past the port and climb the stairs that lead to the police station. You'll find impeccably clean rooms with balconies, TVs, and refrigerators. (☎51 011. Doubles 8000-17,000dr.) Just across the street, **Isabella** rents fully furnished apartments with kitchens, baths, and sea views. (☎51 090. Doubles 15,000-19,000dr.) Around the corner and up the hill a short distance is **Sakis Rooms,** with luxurious lodgings with bath, balcony, and fridge. Call for pick-up from the port at Paroikia. (☎52 171; fax 24 365; www.paros-online.com. Doubles 8000-20,000dr.) **Camping Naoussa** is on the road to Kolimbithies. Call for pick-up from the port. (☎51 595. 1300dr per person; 800dr per tent.) **Camping Surfing Beach,** 4km toward Santa Maria, offers waterskiing, windsurfing, diving, and other summer fun. (☎51 013 or 51 491; fax 51 937. 1500dr per person; 500dr per tent, 1000dr tent rental; 900dr per car, 400dr per bike.)

**FOOD AND ENTERTAINMENT.** Naoussan kitchens cook up famously fabulous seafood; their local specialty is the fish plate called *gouna*. If you follow the waterfront as it bends to the right, you will come to a crowded cluster of tavernas. **Diamantis,** behind the church, is an excellent choice for Greek fare; feast on the restaurant's specialty, lamb Diamantis, stuffed with feta cheese, tomatoes, peppers, and onions, and grilled slowly (1900dr). **Pervolaria** is a garden restaurant offering peaceful seduction just inland off the main road. Request the Greek specialties that don't appear on the menu. (☎52 490. Stuffed squid 1800dr, yogurt with fruit 1200dr. Open 7pm till late.) For unbeatable *loukamades* (600dr) and such, turn left off the commercial street at the Naoussa pastry shop and continue past the white church to **To Paradosiako** (open 5:30pm-1am).

There are several low-key cafes and bars mixed in with the tavernas—look for dimmed lights and listen for the groove. **Varelathiko** is a huge wooden disco that boasts Athenian style on an outdoor deck. Reminiscent of an old-fashioned barn,

the place is decorated with wine barrels and lanterns hanging from the ceiling. Head here for the latest in Greek music, a full bar, and all-night dancing; if the main road through the plateia doesn't take you here, the current of revelers surely will. (Cocktails 1500dr. Cover 100dr.) If you can't stay up that late, try your luck swatting mosquitoes at the **outdoor movie theater** next to Diamantis. (Shows nightly at 10pm.) Free Spirit Travel can set you up with beachside **horseback riding.** (7000dr for 1 hr., 10,000 for 2hr., 12,000dr for 3 hr.) On the first or second Sunday in July, eat, drink, and be merry as you cruise around Naoussa's harbor and watch traditional dancing in the **Wine and Fish Festival;** call the tourist office for details.

## EASTERN COAST OF PAROS

Road meets sea at **Piso Livadi,** 11km from Lefkes. If Paroikia's nightlife is not your bag, Piso Livadi is close to Paros' nicest beaches (from **Logara** to **Khrissi Acti**), will warm your heart and roast your skin. On the other hand, culture vultures will cringe to find that tourism spawned the town's development. **Perantinos Travel & Tourism,** across from the bus stop, provides information on accommodations, as well as an international phone. (☎/fax 41 135. Open 9am-10pm.) In general, doubles range from 12,000-16,000dr, depending on the season and quality—the resort-style locale will cost you a pretty penny. Up the street from the bus stop toward Paroikia are two straightforward hotels. **Hotel Piso Livadi** (☎41 387) offers doubles with bath (11,000-15,000dr) and triples with bath (15,000-18,000dr). The **Londos Hotel** (☎41 218) has doubles (9000-12,000dr) and triples (10,000-13,000dr).

CYCLADES

# ANTIPAROS ΑΝΤΙΠΑΡΟΣ

Literally "opposite Paros," Antiparos is so close to its neighbor that, according to local lore, travelers once signaled the ferryman on Paros by opening the door of a chapel on Antiparos. The small island is mostly undeveloped, with a teensy population to match Antiparos's size. Most travelers encounter Antiparos as a daytrip to see the caves, but it's easy to find a place to stay in the charming capital or near the beaches of this tiny island, which makes even peaceful Paros look frenetic.

## ANTIPAROS TOWN Αντιπαρος ☎0284

Virtually all of the island's 900 inhabitants live in town, where the ferry docks and most accommodations are.

**ORIENTATION AND PRACTICAL INFORMATION.** You'll arrive in Antiparos Town by ferry; a few waterfront restaurants and several hotels and pensions are at the harbor. Tourist shops, tavernas, and bakeries line the street leading from the dock to the tree-shaded central plateia, where a cluster of bars and cafes have opened. Go through the stone archway to the right of the plateia to reach the **Castle of Antiparos,** a village built in the 1440s. Take a direct **ferry** from **Paroikia** (30min., 15 per day, 460dr) or a bus to **Pounta** (15min., 15 per day, 250dr), followed by a boat to Antiparos (10min., 30 per day, 170dr). The only **bus** service on the island goes to the stalactite caves.

Waterfront **Oliaros Tours** assists with finding rooms, and has boat and bus schedules, an **international telephone,** and **currency exchange.** (☎61 231, in winter 61 189. Open 8:30am-10:30pm. Doubles with bath and fridge 5000-15,000dr.) The **National Bank** is open only in high season (M-F 9am-1pm). The **post office** is on the left side of the street leading from the waterfront to the plateia. (Open M-F 7:30am-12:30pm.) The road bends left past the post office and passes the diminutive **OTE,** on the right just before the road opens into the main plateia. (Open M-F 9am-noon and 6-10pm.) The self-service **laundry** is closer to the water on the same street as the post office. (Open 10am-2pm and 5-8pm. Wash, dry, and soap 2000dr.) Call the **police** at 61 202, or a **doctor** at 61 219. The **postal code** is 84007.

**ACCOMMODATIONS.** The **Mantalena Hotel,** to the right of the dock (when you're facing inland), has recently renovated rooms with private baths, fridges, and balconies, some of which afford a fantastic sea view. A family-owned establishment for 37 years, the hotel welcomes guests with *kourabiethes* (almond cookies). (☎61 206; fax 61 550. Doubles 10-15,000dr; 20% extra for another bed.) At the waterfront beach, the welcoming family at the **Antiparos Hotel** rents rooms with good views of the sea. (☎61 358; fax 61 340. Doubles 10,000dr; triples 12,000dr.) To the right of the harbor facing inland, around the bend on the road to Camping Antiparos, **Theologos Rooms to Let** offers sunny rooms with gleaming bathrooms and balconies. (☎61 244; fax 61 045. Doubles 7000-12,000dr; studios with kitchen 10-15,000dr; breakfast 400-900dr.) **Camping Antiparos** is 800m northwest of town on the well signposted way to Ag. Yiannis Theologos Beach. The beachside site has its own mini-market and restaurant, and is adjacent to the town nightclub. (☎61 221. Open May-Sept. 1100-1200dr per person; 300-400dr per tent.)



**FOOD AND ENTERTAINMENT.** The restaurants of Antiparos Town mostly serve excellent fish pulled from the same sea that you'll gaze at while eating. Inside town, **Taverna Klimataria** trades in the view for an idyllic garden setting roofed by blazing pink azaleas. Find it by heading down the main street and turning left down the alley next to the bookstore. (Calamari 1200dr, Greek salad 1000dr. Open June-Sept.) Open for all-day service on the waterfront, **O Spyros** and **Zorbas** turn the catch of the day into traditional dishes. (Entrees around 1500dr.) Following the lead of neighboring islands, Antiparos' plateia is packed with rock and roll watering holes. Late night, choose your favorite from among **Time Pub, Clown Pub, The Doors,** and many more (beer 500-700dr). **Cafe Yam** is a trendy spot to sip a cocktail out of doors. The whitewashed bar serves every drink imaginable. (Beer around 700dr, cocktails around 1500dr. Open 10am-2am.)

**SIGHTS AND BEACHES.** The cool, wet stalactite **caves** at the south end of the island are Antiparos' main attraction. (Open 10am-3:30pm. 600dr.) Names of famous visitors are written on the walls with their years of entry (alongside some slightly less famous 20th-century visitors who took it upon themselves to leave a mark). Some of the stalactites were broken off by Russian naval officers in the 18th century and "donated" to a St. Petersburg museum, while still more were destroyed by Italians during World War II. Despite all this amateurish defilement, the caves, which plunge 100m into the earth, are simply beautiful. The site doesn't offer any postings about its peculiar history, so see if the ticket-seller is in the mood to tell stories—how Queen Amalia lost her earrings here in 1840, or how the motley crüe of Marquis de Nointel, Louis XIV's representative in Constantinople, spent Christmas of 1673 inside. Excursion **buses** (20min., round-trip 1000dr) run from Antiparos Town's port every hour from the morning through early afternoon.

**Psaraliki Beach,** just to the south of town, is a pleasant place to take a dip, as is **Glifa,** a few miles down the east coast. On the west coast, **Agios Georgios** and the sandy stretch at **Livadi** make for enjoyable daytrips.

# AMORGOS ΑΜΟΡΓΟΣ

Much of Amorgos resembles its most enduring symbol, the Hozoviatissas Monastery, which burrows into the cliffs near Hora. Though hard to reach, unparalleled views and indulgent hospitality await you once there. The steep cliffs and clear waters were captured 20 years ago in the film *The Big Blue (Le Grand Bleu);* they remain just as startlingly big and blue now. King Minos of Crete was said to rule a second kingdom on Amorgos in ancient times; a 1985 discovery of Minoan artifacts atop Mt. Moudoulia affirmed the legend.

Despite the recent growth of tourism, Amorgos's relative inaccessability and a local community unwilling to commercialize have preserved the pervasive peace. Infrequent ferry connections generally stop at Amorgos's two ports in succession—**Aegiali** in the northeast and the larger **Katapola** in the southwest. Be sure to disembark at the right port, as transportation between the two is sporadic.

## KATAPOLA Καταπολα ☎0285

The island's central port waves to visitors with its windmill arms. Whitewashed houses, narrow streets, and the overhanging Venetian castle make up little Katapola; it's free of the bustle of many other Cycladic port towns, and retains its serene, communal atmosphere in which the whole town might spend the night huddled in front of *The Big Blue* or a football game.

**ORIENTATION AND PRACTICAL INFORMATION.** **Ferries** from both ports of Amorgos go to: **Astypalea** (3hr., 2 per week, 2800dr); **Mykonos** (2 per week, 3175dr); **Naxos** (4hr., 1-3 per day, 2300dr); **Paros** (1-2 per day, 2700dr); **Piraeus** (8-13hr., 1-3per day, 5000dr); **Syros** (5 per week, 3510dr); and **Tinos** (2 per week, 3140dr). Once a week, there are ferries to **Kalymnos** and **Kos,** and to **Santorini. Hydrofoils** zoom to: **Andros** (3 per week, 6745dr); **Ios** (1 per day, 4375dr); **Mykonos** (1 per day, 6420dr); **Naxos** (1 per day, 4600dr); **Paros** (2½hr., 1 per day, 5450dr); **Rafina** (3 per week, 9500dr); **Santorini** (1 per day, 4500dr); **Syros** (4 per week, 6830dr); and **Tinos** (1 per day, 5980dr). Frequent **buses** connect the villages of Amorgos in summer, running from Katapola to: **Aegiali** (45min., 6 per day, 450dr); **Agia Anna** (25min., 250dr); **Hora** (15min., 1 per hr., 250dr); and **Hozoviatissas Monastery** (20min., 250dr).

The town surrounds the ferry dock in a horseshoe shape, with restaurants, bars, and accommodations on either side. The large port rests at the center; most tourist services are between the ferry dock and the road to Hora. Across from the ferry dock is **Synodinos Tours,** which **exchanges currency** and has an international telephone and tickets to ferries and hydrofoils. (☎71 201; fax 71 278. Open 9am-2pm and 6-10pm.) Since there is a limited **post office** (open M, W, and F 10am-1pm) and **no OTE** in Katapola, Synodinos Tours sells stamps and phone cards, and handles registered mail. **Agricultural Bank,** across from the ferries, has a 24hr. **ATM.** The **police** (☎71 210) and **port police** (☎71 259; open 24hr.) are on the right on a side street heading inland from the main plateia. The **pharmacy** is next door to Synodinos Tours. (☎71 400. Open 9am-2:30pm and 6-10pm.) The **medical center** (☎71 257 or 71 208) is along the waterfront as it bends around the harbor, in the white building behind the two statues. For **medical emergencies** dial 71 805. **Public toilets** are at the start of the town beach across from **Amorgos Motor Center.** (☎71 007 or 71 777. Mopeds 2500-5000dr.) For **taxis** call 71 255. **Postal code:** 84008.

**ACCOMMODATIONS.** Katapola is small and well kept; the rooms echo the town. Pensions are a better bet than dock hawks. **Pension Amorgos** is close to the water and has a rooftop veranda with a view, stacked above its blue-trimmed rooms. (☎71 013 or 71 814. Doubles and triples 8000dr and up.) **Katapola Inn,** on the waterfront, has simple but cheap rooms. (☎71 007. Doubles or triples with bath 8000-10,000dr.) To reach **Big Blue Pension** from the ferry dock, walk toward town, turn right after the plateia with Pension Amorgos, and follow signs. The pension, one of many establishments cashing in on the popularity of the French film *The Big Blue*, is indeed big, with blue windows and doors, and the rooms are large. (☎/fax 71 094. Doubles 7000dr.) **Gavalas Taverna,** along the waterfront, has basic rooms with shared baths. (☎71 275. Singles 6000dr; doubles 8000dr.) **Community Campsite** is in town, by the road to Hora. Cross the small bridge on the quay, and follow the signs. Peaceful and clean, the campsite offers 24hr. hot water and meals for guests at a small cantina. (☎71 802. 820-1000dr per person; 650-800dr per tent.)

**FOOD.** Katapola's dining options tend toward simple, high-quality tavernas that are easy on the wallet. **Mourayio,** one of the first buildings left of the ferry dock, crowds early and empties late. The restaurant stuffs smiling diners with local specialties like octopus (1800dr) and *fava* (1000dr) and gritty live Greek folk music. (Open 10am-2am.) As always, the further you get from the dock, the less touristy your meal. **The Corner,** left on the waterfront past most of the tavernas, serves *pastitsio*, *moussaka*, *dolmades*, and *papoutsakia* for 1300dr each. (Open noon-1am; live music 8pm-midnight.) **Erato Cafe Bar,** on the right as you

disembark the ferry, spends its Clark Kent days as an authentic Italian joint (spaghetti *napolitana* 1000dr, *pizza al tonno* 1850dr); at night, it morphs into a Superbar. Beer and cocktails (700-1400dr) are served all day. (Open 2pm-3am.) **Gavalas,** on the opposite side of the waterfront, caters to vegetarian tastes. (☎71 275. Open noon-4pm, 6pm-2am.)

**NIGHTLIFE.** Like the island itself, nightlife is calm and soothing. Cafes and bars are open all day, dispensing ouzo and beer amidst cool sea breezes—drink to relax, not to pass out. **Katerina's Moon Bar,** opposite the ferry dock on the waterfront, serves excellent local liqueurs like Cretan *raki* (600dr) and delicious appetizers. Sample *dakos*, the island specialty of *paximathi* (dry bread) covered with tomato, onion, cheese and oregano (1200dr). Although not on the menu, salty sea urchin accompanies your ouzo. **Le Grand Bleu,** a waterfront bar one block away with a glowing blue interior, sells sodas and beers for 600dr, and the looped screenings of *The Big Blue* itself (in English with Norwegian subtitles) are free. Cool off with **Aegon**'s underwater decor and its ice cream-garnished cakes. (Cake 800-1000dr. ☎21 549. Open 8am-3am.)



**SIGHTS AND BEACHES.** In front of Katapola's main church, a sign points to a 40min. hike to the ancient town of **Minoa,** inhabited between the 10th and 4th centuries BC. Look for the base of the temple among the ruins with the bust of a statue still rising from within—the barely distinguishable acropolis once stood on the plateau above the temple. Various **beaches** provide sand and nudity outside of town, opposite the dock. Smooth-stoned, bare-skinned **Plakes** and **Agios Panteleimonas** are quiet, yet easily accessible.

## HORA Χωρα ☎0285

Katapola means "below the town"—the town is Hora. Also known as **Amorgos Town,** the island's capital lies 6km from the harbor along the island's only significant paved road. A fine example of Byzantine village planning, its winding streets were constructed to deter and confuse raiding pirates, and now allow visitors to meander along the cafe-lined walk to **Pl. Loza,** at the far end of town. Sights include a 14th-century Venetian **fortress,** a row of retired windmills perched on the mountain ledge above town, 45 Byzantine churches, and the first high school in Greece, built in 1829 (on your left as you head up to OTE).

Hora is home to Amorgos' main **post office,** tucked in a corner up from Pl. Loza (☎71 250; open M-F 7:30am-2pm), and its main **OTE,** on the right at the top of town (☎71 339; open M-F 7:30am-3pm). The **police** are in the main plateia with the big church, next to Cafe Loza. (☎71 210. Open 8am-midnight.) The **medical center** is on the main road into Hora from Katapola. (☎71 207. Open 24hr.) If you decide to spend the night, you can contract with the domatia owners that meet your boat, or look for "Rooms to Let" signs in town. **Pension Ilias Kastanis,** on the road to Monastiri, toward the lower end of Hora, has quality rooms and can provide pickup and drop-off at the port. (☎71 277. Doubles 5000-9000dr.) **Liotrivi,** below the bus station, prepares delicious twists on Greek standards—*kalogiros* (eggplant with veal, cheese, and tomato; 1500dr) and *exohiko* (lamb and vegetables in pastry shell; 1500dr) are the house specialities. Uplifting gormandizers will delight in the *karharia* (shark; 1200dr), prepared with garlic paste, mustard, and lemon sauce. (☎71 700. Open noon-1am.) Head to the chill **Vegara** for an omelette (700-1200dr), every type of coffee imaginable, sweet desserts, and eclectic art and music. (☎74 017. Open 9am-3am.) **Zygos** (☎71 350) serves peerless apple pie (600dr) and often has live music and dancing till 5am.

**HIKE FROM HORA.** Rugged mountains and a placid coast run alongside the road from Hora to Aegiali. A four-hour hike begins behind Hora and stretches up the mountains to the village of Potamos. Forty minutes into the hike, the crumbling, abandoned Byzantine church Christosomas (The Body of Christ) is hewn out of

small cave, a onetime hermit dwelling. The trail ascends past a series of monasteries, before descending to views of miniature Nikouria Island, which swimmers can reach from the beach by the main road. Lonely and deserted Agios Mammas Church is the last significant marker before Potamos appears. Aegiali lies directly below.

## HOZOVIATISSAS MONASTERY

*Catch a bus from Katapola to the monastery. ☎71 274. Open 8am-1pm and 5-7pm. Dress modestly.*

A trip to Amorgos is incomplete without a visit to otherworldly Hozoviatissas Monastery—one of the most exhilarating spectacles in all of Greece, and an inspiration to Le Corbusier among others. Built into the sheer face of the cliff, the whitewashed, 11th-century Byzantine edifice seems to be a living creature growing from the rock. Legend has it that attempts to build the monastery on the shore were twice thwarted; when the workers discovered their tools inexplicably hanging from the cliff, they figured it was an omen and recommenced construction there. If you complete the hike (up 350 stairs), the monks may reward you with cold water, *raki*, and *loukoumi* (Greek sweets). Before leaving, visit the downstairs exhibit, which includes writings, relics, and church items dating to the founding of the monastery. To soak up the hamlet's serenity and solitude, wander the chambers farther below. If solitude's not your thing, come in November when the entire island celebrates the **feast** of Panagia Hozoviatissa at the monastery.

The road from the monastery takes you to the crystal waters of **Agia Anna** and its two enchanting beaches; from the bus stop, one is at the end of the path through the clearing, the other at the bottom of the central steps. *The Big Blue* was filmed along these rocky shores. The villages in southern Amorgos are less memorable, but several beaches grace the coast. **Paradisia,** at Amorgos's southern tip, may be the island' best. It neighbors a Byzantine church's remains, and is accessible by a **bus** from Katapola that makes one round trip per day. Ask locals to direct you to the 60-year old remains of the **Olympia shipwreck.**

CYCLADES

# AEGIALI Αιγιαλη ☎0285

Aegiali, the island's other port, is as close as Amorgos comes to feeling touristy. As a result, the locals seem a little more road-weary of travelers than on other parts of the island. With a town beach and numerous rooming and camping opportunities, leisurely Aegiali serves as a base for exploring the island's northern parts.

**ORIENTATION AND PRACTICAL INFORMATION.** **Nautilus Travel** handles all ferries, **currency exchange,** and other travel services. (☎73 032; fax 72 231. Open 10am-1pm and 6-10pm.) **Aegialis Tours** (☎73 394; fax 73 395) handles car rental and bus and boat excursions. Both agencies are just inland from the waterfront. For **ferry** and **Flying Dolphin** schedules, see the listings for Katapola (p. 391). **Buses** run from the waterfront bus stop to **Katapola** via **Hora** (3 per day, 450dr). The **port police** are up the steps from the waterfront (open 9:30am-2pm and 6-9:30pm). The **post office** also has **currency exchange;** follow signs from the waterfront up the steps from the port. (☎73 037. Open M-F 7:30am-2pm.) A **first aid station** is above the town, by the road to Potamos. (☎73 222. Open 9am-1:30pm; available 24hr. for emergencies.) **Amorgos Motor Center,** on the waterfront, rents bikes. (☎73 444. 2500-4500dr per day.) Aspiring Jacques Cousteaus should ask **Amorgos Dive Ventures** (☎/fax 73 611) about beginner and PADI certified courses in scuba diving.

**ACCOMMODATIONS.** Look for "Rooms for Rent" signs going up the stairpaths in the middle of town. **Popi Chalari Rooms for Rent,** by the post office, has rooms with balconies overlooking Nikouria Island. (☎73 207. Doubles 6000dr.) To reach **Adonis Similidas Rooms to Let,** follow the middle stairpath and the signs for the bakery, which forms the first floor of this simple rooming establishment. (☎73 225. Doubles 6000dr.) **Amorgos Camping,** just outside town, by the road to Tholaria,

is a 10min. walk from the port and beach but provides free port pickup and drop-off. The site boasts laundry and cooking facilities, safety deposits, showers, a restaurant, and a bar. (☎73 500; fax 73 388. 1000dr per person; tent rental 500dr.)

**FOOD AND NIGHTLIFE. To Limani** (☎73 207), adorned by paintings of island life, is just inland from the waterfront, near the travel agencies. They improvise on standard taverna fare like Amorgian fish soup (1600dr) and octopus salad (1500dr). **Celini Cafe Bar,** across from the beach, satiates beachside patrons day and night with breakfasts, dinners, and a bar. (Calamari 1200dr; pasta with pesto 1000dr. Open 9am-3:30am.) **Skari,** a bar named for an attractive female figure and Celini's beachside neighbor, revolves around an outside patio and pool tables inside. **Paspartou,** next to the post office, mixes 50s Americana, Greek nautica, and serene views of Nikouria Island. (Drinks 500-1600dr. ☎73 016. Open 9am-3:30am.)



# IOS ΙΟΣ

If you're not drunk when you arrive, you will be when you leave. On Ios, beers go down and clothes come off faster than you can say *"Opa!"* Even before they arrive, revelers prepare for the madness with plentiful booze on the ferry ride over. There is everything your mother warned you about—people swimming less than 30 minutes after they've eaten, wine being swilled from the bottle at 3pm, drinking games all day along the beach, condoms scattered on dirt roads, men and women dancing madly in the streets, and so much more. Drinks are cheap and plentiful; Ios imports 1½ mega-truckloads of beer a day, and exports the same number of empty bottles each morning. The island has settled down a bit in the past few years, making a sincere and successful effort to bring families and the older set to enjoy the other, more peaceful side of Ios. Of its 35 beaches, only three have been fully developed for tourism, so there's plenty of unexplored territory. Those seeking quieter enjoyment of Ios's pleasures stay in Yialos Port, while the party animals cavort in Hora. Pilgrims to this mecca should prepare for loud music, hangovers, and the lustful stares of the inebriated.

## IOS TOWN Ιος ☎0286

### GETTING THERE AND GETTING AROUND

**Ferries:** Ferries set sail for: **Crete** (5hr., 1 per week, 4300dr); **Folegandros** (2hr., 3 per week, 1700dr); **Mykonos** (4-5hr., 1 per day, 3300dr); **Naxos** (1½hr., 6-8 per day, 2100dr); **Paros** (2½hr., 5-6 per day, 2600dr); **Piraeus** (8hr., 4-6 per day, 5500dr); **Santorini** (1¼hr., 4-6 per day, 1700dr); **Sikinos** (1hr., 3 per week, 1500dr); and **Syros** (5hr., 2-4 per week, 3800dr). Once a week, ferries go to: Anathi, Kifnos, Milos, Serifos, and Sifnos.

**Flying Dolphins:** Service to: **Amorgos** (2hr., 3-4 per week, 4500dr); **Mykonos** (2hr., 3-4 per day, 6280dr); **Naxos** (45min., 2 per day, 4200dr); **Paros** (1¼hr., 4 per day, 5200dr); **Rafina** (4-5hr., 1 per day, 8240dr); **Santorini** (35min., 3 per day, 3300dr); **Syros** (2½hr., 2-4 per day, 7500dr); **Andros** (3½hr., 1 per day, 8640dr); and **Tinos** (2½hr., 2-3 per day, 7050dr). There are also four round-trip excursions per week to **Sikinos** (2500dr) and **Folegandros** (3400dr).

**Rentals: Trohokinisi** (☎91 166), past the lot between the church and main road. Cars 16,000dr per day. **Free Riders** (☎91 330), on the main road. Mopeds 5000dr.

### ORIENTATION AND PRACTICAL INFORMATION

The good life centers around three locations, each 20min. apart along the island's paved road. The **port,** or **Yialos** (Γιαλοσ) is at one end; the **village,** or **Hora** (Χορα) sits above it on a hill, and frenzied **Mylopotas Beach** is 3km further. During the day, the winding streets behind the church are filled with charming wares and postcard

pushers. As the sun sets, they become the focus of nocturnal activity. You can do most of your "serious" business within five minutes of the village bus stop along the paved road. Frequent buses shuttle from port to village to beach and back (every 10-20min. 7am-midnight, 230dr).

**Travel Agencies: Tourist Information Center** (☎91 135) is a private travel agency immediately adjacent to the bus stop. Helps with transportation and accommodations. Open 8am-midnight. **Acteon Travel** (☎91 343 or 91 002) has offices all over the island. Open 7:30am-midnight.

**Banks:** In the village, **National Bank** (☎91 354), next to the main church, has an **ATM** and handles all your MasterCard needs. Open M-Th 7:45am-2pm, F 7:45am-1:30pm. The **Commercial Bank,** by the main plateia next to the Lemon Club, has 24hr. **ATM.** At the port, there is an **ATM** on the waterfront, to your left as you disembark from the ferry.

**Police:** (☎92 222), on the road to Kolitsani Beach, just past the OTE. Open 24hr.

**Port Authority:** (☎91 264), at the far end of the harbor by Camping Ios. Open 24hr.

**Medical Center:** (☎91 227), in new facilities at the port, 100m from the dock. Specializes in drunken mishaps. Open 10am-1pm and 6-7pm.

**Internet Access:** At the port, **Acteon Travel** charges 1000dr for the first 30min., 2000dr per hr. thereafter. Open 7:30am-midnight. In the village, travel agencies (Acteon, the Tourist Information Center), hostels (Francesco's, Markos), and bars (Fun Pub) all offer access for around 40dr per minute. **Postal code:** 84001.

CYCLADES

## ACCOMMODATIONS

The majority of affordable rooms are conveniently located in the village. A few options exist for those who would rather stay at the port (and avoid the late-night chaos). Alternatively, a tent, bungalow, or room on Mylopotas Beach lets you roll hazily from your mattress to the beach, foregoing coffee for a tequila sunrise.

**Francesco's** (☎/fax 91 223). With your back to the bank, take the uphill steps in the left corner of the plateia, then take the first left. Rooms with spectacular harbor views sit atop the terrace bar, where you'll **get drunk.** Big with young internationals. Dorms 3000dr; doubles 6000dr, with bath 8000dr; triples 9000dr/12,000dr.

**Pension Markos** (☎91 059; fax 91 060). From the bus stop, take the right just before the supermarket (uphill). It's on a side street to the left, with a sign visible from the street. Friendly and popular, with a happening pool where you can **get drunk** cheaply. Enjoy the view of the village and weekly barbecue. Doubles 10,000dr; triples 13,000dr.

**Kolitsani View** (☎91 061; fax 92 261). Follow the path past the OTE and look for the white archway. Five minutes from the village action, its quiet rooms have a family atmosphere close to Kolitsani Beach. The expansive view includes several beaches and even Santorini; you'll see the ferries arrive. **Get drunk** at the poolside bar. Free portside pickup. Breakfast and snacks served all day. Doubles 15,000dr; triples 18,000dr.

**Petros Place Hotel** (☎91 421; fax 91 866). Head left down the waterfront, turn right before the beach, and it's on the left. Baths in every room and a large outdoor swimming pool with bar where you can **get drunk.** Popular with package tours, it's fairly peaceful. Breakfast 800dr. Doubles 12,000-18,000dr; triples 15,000-18,000dr.

**Hotel Petradi** (☎/fax 91 510), equidistant from the village and the beach on the main road. Every room has a balcony with a romantic ocean view. Large patio. Quiet at night. Bar downstairs where you can **get drunk.** Doubles 10,000dr; triples 12,000dr.

**Camping Ios** (☎91 329). For those who want something affordable without the nonstop action of Far Out Camping. Open June-Sept. 2000dr per person; 500dr per tent.

**Far Out Camping** (☎92 301 or 92 302; fax 92 303), at the far end of the beach. The most luxurious campsite around. Club Med at rock-bottom prices, with a restaurant, a bar where you can **get drunk,** a minimarket, basketball, volleyball, a swimming pool, nightly movie, scuba-diving lessons, showers, laundry, internet access, live music, and parties where you can **get drunk.** Open Apr.-Sept. 1200dr per person; 300dr tent rental; small cabins 1500-2000dr; bungalows 2000-3000dr.

## FOOD

Most eating on Ios coincides with boozing, peaking in the middle of the night at cheap gyro joints open all night. More discerning palates will find several inexpensive restaurants interspersed among the ubiquitous bars and discos in Ios village, in the port, and on the beach. There's also **Ios Market** (☎91 035), across from the bus stop in Hora, and the **supermarket** in the main plateia.

**Waves Indian Restaurant and International Cuisine** (☎92 145), to the left of the waterfront road as you disembark from the ferries. This increasingly popular slice of heaven is run by a lovely Welsh windsurfer couple. *Divine* curries: veggie for 2000dr, shrimp *biryani* 3500dr. Takeout available. Opens at 10am for breakfast.

**Polydoros** (☎91 132), 2km north of the port on Koubara Beach, is where Ios's residents and true gourmands can be found delighting in snails (1400dr) and shrimp with tomato sauce and mouth-watering feta (2800dr), from a supremely laid back owner.

**Pithari,** near the National Bank. Hard-to-top Greek specialties in hearty portions will help keep you on your feet later, when you head out to **get drunk.** *Exohiko* (lamb wrapped in pastry) 2000dr; chicken *methismeno* (**drunk** chicken) 1400dr.

**Filippos Café Restaurant** (☎91 895 or 91 291), in Koubara, a 15min. walk down the main road from the port. The freshest fish on the island. Take your pick from the display in the kitchen. Enjoy the glittering harbor views as you savor fried squid (1600dr per kg) or fabulously grilled flat white stonefish.

**Lordos Byron,** uphill from the National Bank on the tiny street below the main drag. Exquisite Greek cuisine and forgotten recipes. *Strapatsada* (a special Greek omelette) 1200dr, *fava* dip 1000dr. Choose freely—it's all *katapliktiko*. Open 7pm-midnight.

CYCLADES

## NIGHTLIFE AND ENTERTAINMENT

Most of Ios's extraordinary number of bars are packed into the old village area. The discos, which are larger and louder, line the main road. Smaller bars hug the main village's main pedestrian street. Bacchantes warm up at daytime beachside bars, swill liquor from the bottle in the main plateia at sunset, hit the bars before 1am, and migrate to the discos and to other, more private, liaisons before sunrise.

**The Slammer Bar,** just uphill from the main plateia in the Village. Have the bartender whack your helmeted head with a hammer before you **get drunk** by downing the tequila slammer (tequila, Tia Maria, and Sprite; 900dr).

**Blue Note.** Follow the main pedestrian path as it curves to the left through the main plateia. Get some breathing room away from the plateia, and enjoy the company of the world's highest concentration of Swedes outside Sweden. **Get drunk** by downing 7 shots—you'll get a free t-shirt. Beer 700-1000dr, cocktails 1000-1500dr.

**Fun Pub,** on the main road just beyond the supermarket. Restaurant and bar playing the latest movies to entertain or rescue you from unwanted conversation while you **get drunk.** Beer 600dr, cocktails 800dr.

**Red Bull,** in the main village plateia. Another good place to fire up your mojo (shots 800dr) before you head out to tackle the rest of the scene. **Get drunk** on the Red Bull and Vodka energy special (1500dr).

**Lemon Club,** by the plateia. Sports a small stage with mirrors, poles, and industrial-strength A/C. Cheap beer (500dr), White Russians (1000dr), and whipped cream hands-free "blowjobs" (1500dr).

**Amadeus,** just through the main plateia. A small jazz and blues escape from the wildness outside the door; get names straight, then head back out. Drinks 500-1500dr.

**Scorpion Disco,** on the edge of town, en route to the beach. This crazy techno emporium is strategically located for those heading back to Mylopotas. 1000dr cover after 1am.

**Sweet Irish Dream,** in a large building near the "donkey steps." Most end up here, but many save it as the night's last stop. Come here after you **get drunk** (or after 2am) to dance on tables. No cover before 1am. Beer 700-800dr, cocktails 1200dr.

**Dubliner,** next to the bus stop. Proximity to the clubs makes it a great warmup–and the only place to **get drunk** on Guiness on tap. The large outdoor terrace attracts live bands. Beer 600dr, cocktails 1000dr.

## SIGHTS AND BEACHES

Pay a visit to the new Ios **Archaeological Museum,** in the town hall across from the bus stop, and bring a smile to the lonely faces of those at the door. (Open T-Su 8am-2pm. Free.) Other passably highbrow diversions include some castle ruins, a pile of rubble reputed to be **Homer's tomb,** and the ancient town near Hora. If you want to repent the night's excess at the solitary monastery, go to the windmills above the village and find the path near the top of the hill. There's an **Open Theatre Festival Program** every summer, held above the windmills on the island.

Beyond that, the **beaches** are the place to be. Most spend their days at **Mylopotas Beach,** a 20min. walk downhill from Ios town, or a bus ride from the port or village (runs 8am-midnight; 230dr). **Mylopotas Water Sports Center** has three different shack locations along the beach—look for the piles of red kayaks along the water's edge near the rental huts. Pick your poison: **windsurf** (3000dr per hr.); **water-ski, knee board,** and **wakeboard** (5000dr for 10 attempts); **canoe** (2000dr per hr.); **inner tube** (3000dr per hr.); **catamaran** (5000dr per hr.); **laser sail** (5000dr per hr.); or **snorkel** (1500dr per hr.). Ask about group package deals and rental options. (☎91 662; fax 91 451. Open Apr.-Oct.) The beach of Mylopotas, like the town, has music blasting everywhere. The outer reaches offer a modicum of privacy. The farther you go, the fewer clothes you will see (or wear).

Of course, there are prettier and less crowded beaches on Ios. If you continue uphill from the OTE, look for the path that leads down to the secluded beach and crystal pool of water at the little **Kolitsani** bay (a 15min. walk from Hora). Excursions leave daily by bus and boat for the nude beach at beautiful **Manganari Bay,** stopping, oddly enough, at the monastery (11am, return 6pm; 2000dr). Nudist, secluded **Psathi** on the eastern coast, is a 7km walk along donkey trails. An excursion goes to Psathi a few times per week, stopping at the ruins of **Paleocastro** (11am, return 6pm; 2000dr).

# FOLEGANDROS ΦΟΛΕΓΑΝΔΡΟΣ

Although its name is more than a mouthful, the island of Folegandros is a simple alternative to the more hectic Cyclades. Named after the son of King Minos—who made the first footprints on the island's shores—the island was secluded from outside influence for many centuries due to its high rocky cliffs and inaccessible port. The dry, rocky, steep hills are terraced with low, snaking stone walls worn by centuries of fierce wind. A sense of calm blankets this nearly treeless island in the silence of the jagged cliffs at sunset and the warmth of its inhabitants.

## HORA Χωρα ☎0286

The narrow streets and bright-white walls of Hora, also called **Folegandros Town,** will begin the island's convincing effort to win you over.

**ORIENTATION AND PRACTICAL INFORMATION.** After disembarking from the ferry, you can board the **bus** from the port **Kararostassi** to the main town of Folegandros, Hora (every 2hr. 8am-midnight, 220dr). On your way up, the **post office** will be on your left as you enter the village. (Open M-F 8:30am-2pm.) If you get off the bus with your back to the road you just came up, most of the village, including the **Medical Center** (☎41 222), will be down to your left. To your right lie a few hotels and the path up to the **Church of Panagia.** If you leave Pl. Pounta and head into town, on your left is **Maraki Travel,** which **exchanges money,** sells ferry tickets, and has **Internet access** for 1000dr per 30min. (☎41 273 or 41 221. Open

CYCLADES

10am-1pm and 5:30pm-10pm.) **Ferries** go to: Ios (5 per week, 1500dr); Kimolos (3 per week); Milos (3 per week); Naxos (2 per week, 2300dr); Paros (2 per week, 1900dr); Santorini (5 per week, 1700dr); Sifnos (3 per week); and Sikinos (5 per week, 1200dr). The **port office** (☎41 198) is open an hour before each boat.

Head straight past the next two plateias filled with trees, cut across right, and then down left again. A sharp right before the **market** leads to the **police** (☎41 249). If you continue on to the left you will come to a widening in the road where **buses** leave for **Ano Meria** (6km, 250dr). Check the posted listings for the bus, or call the one **taxi** (☎41 048) on the island, or rent a moped from **Moto Rent** (☎41 316) for 4000dr per day. **Sottovento Tourist Office** (☎41 444; fax 41 430) is by the bus stop too. As there is no bank, American Express office, or OTE office, they are your best for bet help of all kinds, including **currency change.** There are six **card phones** in Hora. Maps are available for 700dr, but the best guidance comes in the pamphlet from **Folegandros Snack Bar** (see below), with directions and tips. **Postal code:** 84011.

CYCLADES

**ACCOMMODATIONS.** Folegandros's increasing popularity has outpaced the (visibly in-progress) construction of lodgings. Most housing is consequently pricey: locals tell tales of legions of travelers arriving on the morning ferry only to leave in the afternoon when they can't find a room. But have no fear: welcome relief comes at **Pavlo's Rooms.** Down toward the port about 300m from the post office, Pavlo's has roof-sleeping with common baths charmingly housed in a converted stable. (☎41 232. Laundry 1200dr per load; breakfast 500-1000dr. 4000dr per person; doubles 12,000dr, with bath 15,000dr). **Camping Livadi** is another option. (☎41 204. 2300dr per person.) Up in Hora, there are many places with **Room to Let** signs. Most run about 12,000-14,000dr per night for a double in high season. **Maria's Rooms** have a lovely view of the island and sea. (☎41 265. Double 12,000dr; triple with kitchen 18,000dr.)

**FOOD AND NIGHTLIFE.** Several fresh fruit and bread **markets** line the road from Kararostassi. At **Folegandros Snack Bar,** across from Maraki Travel, Nikolas, the bionic serenading proprietor, provides vegetarian options, milkshakes, games, books, maps, and information on the island. Top off your meal with a special shot of Metaxa, *raki*, or ouzo, which Nikolas pours down patrons' throats as crowds cheer. (Open 24hr.) **Sik** specializes in vegetarian vittles like chick pea curry (1300dr). In Hora, taste the *fava* (600dr) or the roast chicken (1200dr) at **Nikos Cafe Restaurant** (opens at 5pm).

In summer, when the island's permanent population of 650 triples, Hora starts to rock. **Anoixto** caters to a lively crowd with funk and Latin. During the day, it's also a hip place to chill and grab some cool drinks (500-1200dr) or breakfast within the colorfully artsy decor. (Open 9:30am-late.) A calm place to chat, **Kellari Wine Bar,** in Pl. Pounta next to the medical center, sells an amazing selection of Greek wines in a small stone-walled room reminiscent of a castle winecellar. Try dry and fruity Limnos white (800dr a glass) or rely on hostess Isabel's expertise. (Open 7:30am-late.) **Astarti** plays the best selection of Greek music into the night—come try the *rakomelo* (*raki* with honey) and *pasteli* (a sesame and honey sweet).

## ANO MERIA

Get ready to work those calves; beyond Hora, Folegandros is best explored on foot. The **Church of Panagia,** above the town on Paleocastro hill, is an excellent place to watch the sunset or photograph whitewashed domes against the mountains and sea. (Open 6-8pm in summer; in winter only for religious festivals.) For a superb glance into Ottoman life, check out the **Folklore Museum** in Ano Meria. On an island whose history is empty of epoch-defining events, the olive presses, looms, and fishing nets detail the perpetual struggle against infertile soil and stormy harbors. Take the bus to Ano Meria and ask the driver to let you off there. (Open June-Aug. 5-8pm. Guidebook 2000dr.)

**Ano Meria** has many footpaths leading to secluded beaches, including **Livadaki,** the island's best. The steep, winding trails—the only access to these beaches—take at least an hour each; there are no tavernas at the end. A better option for families may be **Agali Beach** (see below), accessible by motor, by foot, or by boat from the port (check the schedule at any tourist office). The Sottovento tourist office heads day-long boat tours around the island that stop at several beaches; inquire upon arrival. A demanding hike across Paleocastro Hill leads to **Chryssospilia** (Golden Cave), a onetime refuge from pirate invasions. Local lore insists that a secret tunnel connects the cave to Panagia, though it's uncharted.

Those planning an extended stay in Folegandros or who want a more intimate acquaintance with island culture should look into **The Cycladic School** (☎41 137; fax 41 472), run by Anne and Fotis Papadopoulous. The school leads six- to twelve-day courses that focus on drawing and painting, as well as theater, music, sailing, diving, history, and philosophy. A day at the school includes a lecture, practice time, and excursions around the island. For more information, contact Anne and Fotis Papadopoulous, GR-840-11, Folegandros, Cyclades, Greece.

## AGALI AND AGIOS NIKOLAOS

The **hike** from Hora to Agali and Agios Nikolaos takes about an hour down to Agali and an additional 30min. to Ag. Nikolaos beach. Start from Hora and take the road toward Ano Meria. There's about 20-30min. of asphalt until you hit one of two dirt paths leading left off the road and down to the **beaches** and the terraced countryside. If the black tar burns your toes, distract yourself with the gorgeous views of both sides of the island. Across from one of several small white churches, you'll see the trail snaking down toward Agali. From here, you'll traverse rocky terraces and pass olive trees down the main dirt track (hang left) that heads straight to Agali. In Agali, you'll find a few tavernas, domatia, and a bunch of tents (if you climb up past the first tavernas on the right to the rocky trail that leads to Ag. Nikolaos beach). Between the two beaches are small rocky coves and beaches perfect for a cool, quiet swim.

# SANTORINI ΣΑΝΤΟΡΙΝΗ

Whitewashed towns balanced on plunging cliffs, burning black-sand beaches, and deeply scarred hills make Santorini's landscape nearly as dramatic as the volcanic cataclysm that created it. This eruptive past—and startling beauty—has led some to believe that Santorini is Plato's lost continent of Atlantis. The volcanoes have also enriched the soil, making Santorini a green oasis among the mostly barren Cyclades. The island vineyards allow a passion for wine making among residents (second only to their zest for drachma-dropping tourists).

According to Greek mythology, Santorini arose from a clod of earth given by the sea god Triton to the Argonauts. First inhabited by the Phoenicians, the island, then called Thira, was an outpost of Minoan society by 2000 BC. Around the turn of the 17th century BC, an earthquake destroyed the wealthy maritime settlement that was centered around Akrotiri, and all hope of recovery vanished when a massive volcanic eruption spread lava and pumice across the island around 1625 BC. The destruction of Santorini heralded the fall of Minoan prominence; it is believed that the volcanic eruption lead to a series of

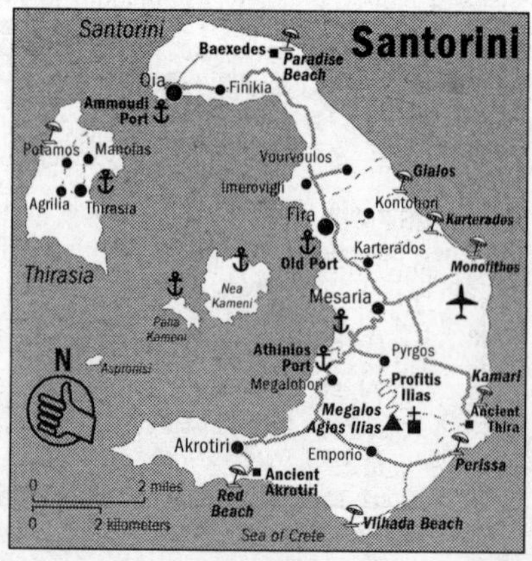

tidal waves that wreaked havoc on Crete, too. Natural disaster continues to threaten the safety of Santorini's residents: as recently as 1956, an earthquake caused serious damage to much of the island. Skeletons of many destroyed buildings are still visible today.

Modern Santorini is only the eastern crescent of what was once a circular island, originally called Strongili (round). The ancient eruption left a crust of volcanic ash stretching over the hollow center of the island, which later caved in to create the *caldera* (basin) that now forms Santorini's harbors and western rim. Thirasia and Aspronisi, the two small islands to the west of Santorini, are in fact a continuation of the original island's rim.

Santorini is easily accessible and incredibly crowded. The coastline, neighboring islands, and volcano make it a popular site for weddings and honeymoons. It's tempting to explore via moped, but inexperienced riders, poor bikes, and carefree drivers are a dangerous combination; traveling by foot or by Santorini's excellent bus service may be a better option. The island is on the expensive side, mostly due to the cost of importing water needed to combat the fresh water shortage.



## FIRA Φηρα ☎0286

The island's activity centers around the capital, Fira (FEE-rah). Aloft on a hill and far from the black sand beaches, the congested mess of glitzy shops, whizzing mopeds, and scads of hyperactive tourists can be shocking to newly arrived visitors stepping off the bus or ferry. Fortunately, the noisy roadside strip is only one part of this multifaceted town. Tourist traffic has made it almost too easy to find a hamburger or wiener schnitzel, but Fira's simple, pristine beauty and old-school Greek food still prevail. The city is perched on a cliff, and the short walk to the *caldera* at the town's western edge reveals a stunning view of the harbor. For all the kitsch and overcrowding, nothing can destroy the pleasure of wandering among the narrow cobbled streets, poking into craft shops, and arriving at the western edge of town in time to watch the sunset.

### GETTING THERE AND GETTING AROUND

**Boats** dock at one of three ports: Athinios, Fira, and Oia. Athinios is the most important and has frequent buses to Fira and Perissa Beach (30min., at least 20 per day, 380dr). The **port** of Fira is down a 587-step footpath from the town; you can take a **cable car** down (every 20min. 6:40am-10pm; 1000dr, children 500dr; luggage 500dr) or hire a **mule** (1000dr). Santorini's **buses** run frequently and can take you anywhere you want to go, but be warned that their convenience leads to overcrowding. To be sure that you make it onto your bus, arrive at the station ten minutes early, and rush ahead to the arriving bus. The estimated journey lengths below are based on ideal circumstances; busy buses often move much slower.

**Ferries:** To: **Ios** (1½hr., 3-5 per day, 1700dr); **Mykonos** (7hr., 2 per week, 3600dr); **Naxos** (4hr., 4-8 per day, 3000dr); **Paros** (4½hr., 3-5 per day, 3200dr); **Piraeus** (9hr., 4-8 per day, 6100dr); **Syros** (8hr., 3 per week, 4100dr); **Anafi** (2hr., 2 per week, 1900dr); **Folegandros** (1½hr., 3 per week, 1100dr); **Sikinos** (2 per week, 1700dr); **Thessaloniki** (15hr., 5 per week, 10,100dr); **Iraklion** (4hr., 1 per day, 3700dr); and **Skiathos** (12hr., 1 per week, 8000dr). **Flying Dolphins** go to similar destinations at half the time and twice the price.

**Flights: Olympic Airways** (☎22 493) has daily flights to: **Athens** (22,500dr); **Mykonos** (15,400dr); **Iraklion** (15,400dr); **Rhodes** (22,900dr); and **Thessaloniki** (30,400dr). From the bus depot, go straight across the main road, make your first right and then your first left. Open M-Sa 8am-4pm, M-Tu and Th-F 4-9pm.

**Buses:** To: **Akrotiri** (30min., 16 per day 9am-10pm, 400dr); **Athinios** (25min., 11 per day, 380dr); **Kamari** (20min., 62 per day, 270dr); **Oia** (30min., 30 per day, 280dr); **Perissa** (15min., 30 per day, 400dr); and **Monolithos** via the **airport** (30min., 25 per day, 260dr).

**Taxis:** (☎22 555) in Pl. Theotokopoulou beside the bus station.

**Moped Rental: Marcos Rental** (☎23 877), 50m north of the plateia. 4000dr per day, discounts for extended rentals. Helmets included. Open 8am-7pm.

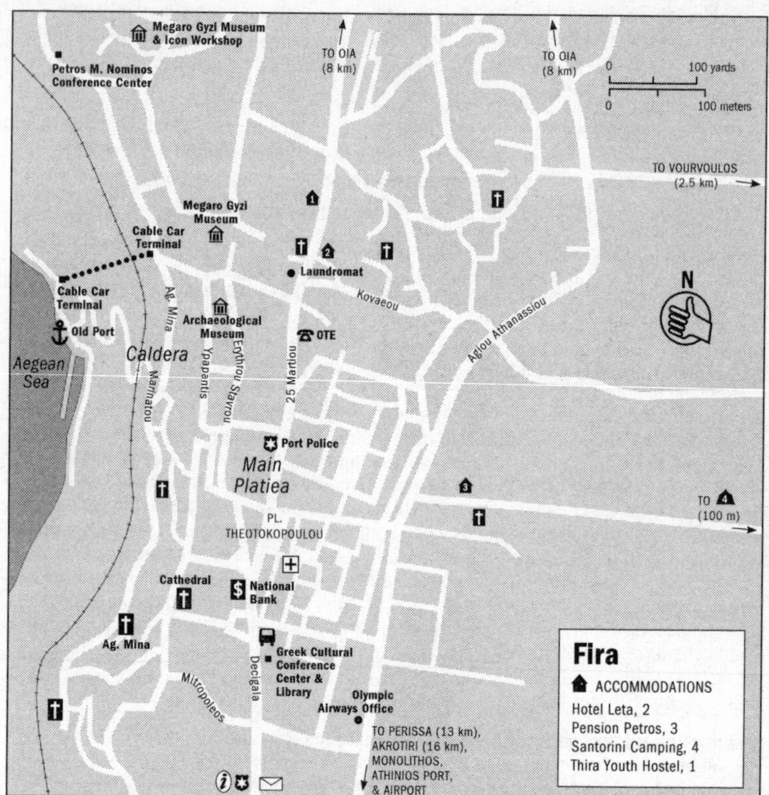


CYCLADES

## ORIENTATION AND PRACTICAL INFORMATION

Facing the street with the bus station behind you, walk right and uphill (north) to **Pl. Theotokopoulou,** full of travel agencies, banks, and cafes. At the fork in the road, the street on the right is **25 Martiou,** the main paved road. It leads from the plateia north toward Oia, and hosts accommodations, including the youth hostel. Head onto the left branch of the fork and turn onto any westbound street to find back streets with many of the best bars, stores, and discos. Farther west is the *caldera,* bordered by **Ypapantis** street, where expensive restaurants and art galleries are overshadowed by the spectacular view.

**Tourist Police:** (☎22 649), on the main road south of the bus depot. They share a building with the **police.** Open 24hr.

**Banks: National Bank** (☎22 906), on the road branching off 25 Martiou south of the plateia. Currency exchange. **24hr. ATM.** Open M-Th 8am-2pm, F 8am-1:30pm.

**American Express:** In the office of **X-Ray Kilo Travel and Shipping Agency** (☎22 624), on the *caldera.* All AmEx services. Open 8am-10pm.

**Laundromats: Penguine** (☎22 168), on 25 Martiou, north of the plateia on the left. 2hr. and 2700dr result in 7kg of clean clothes. Open 9am-10pm.

**International Bookstore: International Press** (☎25 301), in the plateia. Many magazines in many languages, with a small selection of popular reading books. Open 8:30am-midnight.

**Library: The Greek Cultural/Conference Center and Library** (☎24 960), off 25 Martiou, on the side street before the post office. The island's only library, with info about island events. Open 9am-2pm and 6-9pm; in winter 9am-2pm and 5-8pm.

**Public Toilets:** On 25 Martiou, beside the bus depot.

**Medical Center:** (☎22 237). Go downhill (south) from the bus station, make the first left, then make another left. Routine problems 9am-2:30pm. **Emergency** care 24hr.

**Telephone: OTE** (☎22 135), north of the plateia on 25 Martiou. Open 8am-2pm.

**Internet Access: PC Work** (☎25 551), in the upper right-hand corner of the platiea, coming from the bus stop, on the 2nd story. 700dr for 30min., 1000dr for 1hr. Open 9am-1am. **Lara Internet Cafe** (☎25 291). 700dr for 20min. Open 9am-2:30am.

**Post Office:** (☎22 238), 50m downhill (south) from the bus stop. Open M-F 8am-2pm. **Postal code:** 84700.



## ACCOMMODATIONS

In summer, the pensions and hotels fill up quickly and prices skyrocket out of budget range. The cheapest options (and the best bet if you arrive late) are the good quality **youth hostels** in Fira, Perissa Beach, and Oia. There are also accommodations in private homes all over the island. You can find substantially cheaper places in **Karterados,** 2km south of Fira, or any of the small inland towns along the main bus routes (try Messaria, Pyrgos, or Emborio). The hostels and many pensions will pick you up at the port.

**Pension Petros** (☎22 573; fax 22 615). From the bus station, go one block up 25 Martiou and make a right. Make a left at the bottom of the hill, then your first right. One in a line of new, and nearly identical, pensions. The owner Petros shares stories and bottles of his homemade wine with travelers. All rooms have baths and fridges. Free transportation to and from the port. Doubles 7000-16,000dr; triples 9000-19,000dr.

**Thira Youth Hostel** (☎22 387 or 23 864), on the left roughly 300m north of the plateia, set back 25m from the road to Oia. Lonely travelers join the happy throng in the courtyard of this old aristocratic mansion neighboring Fira's *caldera*. Quiet dorm rooms and pension-quality private rooms with baths. Quiet after 11pm. No smoking in dorms. Open Apr.-Oct. Large dorms 1800-3000dr; 3-4 person dorms 2000-4000dr; doubles 5000-10,000dr (bring your own toilet paper). Sheets 300dr, pillowcase 150dr.

**Hotel Leta** (☎22 540; fax 23 903). Just 100m from the plateia: walking up the main road, follow signs to the right after the laundromat. Downstairs rooms with bath 4000dr per person. Upstairs rooms with A/C, TVs, baths, and fridges: doubles 6000-15,000dr; triples 8000-18,000dr.

**Santorini Camping** (☎22 944 or 25 062; fax 25 065). Follow the blue signs leading east of the plateia. This shady campsite is the most festive spot in town, with a swimming pool (and poolside party), cafe, bar, and mini-market on the premises. 24hr. hot showers. Washing machine 1300dr (soap included). Internet access 700dr for 20min., 1200dr for 21-60min. Quiet hours midnight-8am. 450dr per motorbike. Open Apr.-Oct. 1500dr per person; 800dr per tent; 1200-2000dr per tent rental; 700dr per car.

## FOOD

Inexpensive restaurants are nearing extinction in Fira, but the few that are to be found are nestled within the tiny streets sandwiched between the plateia and the *caldera*. The *caldera* is lined with fine dining options that impose a hefty fee on their priceless views. Generic but convenient snack shops dot the plateia.

**Mama's Cyclades Cafe** (☎24 211). Head north on the road to Oia; it's on the left side. Advertised as the best American breakfast in Greece, and they're not kidding. Mama is a fabulous, affectionate character you must see to believe, and her breakfast special is

equally praiseworthy: 2 pancakes, 2 eggs, bacon, and toast or coffee for 1350dr. Greek specialties complement the menu. Open 7am-midnight.

**Nikolas Taverna.** Head uphill on the side street in the northwestern corner of the plateia (next to Pelican Travel), then take the first right at the Hotel Tataki. The menu's in Greek, but you can't go wrong: beef stew with noodles 2000dr, stuffed tomatoes 1500dr, eggplant with feta 1400dr, *raki* 300dr. Open M-Sa 12-4pm and 6-11pm, Su 6-11pm.

**Restaurant Poseidon.** A traditional restaurant in a garden down the stairs next to the plateia taxi stand, it's close to the buzz but worlds away. Rumored to have the best *tzatziki* (700dr) on the island, Poseidon serves enormous entrees with 2 side dishes each. Try *soutsoukakia*—Greek meatballs served with tomato sauce (1400dr)—or their specialty *potmapauia*—beef with lemon sauce. Open 7am-1am.

**Poldo,** up the street from the National Bank. Take-out includes vegetarian entrees like falafel (900dr), tabouli (700dr), and hummus (800dr). The long line is for the gyros: large (1000dr) and small (500dr). Open 24hr.

**Popou,** overlooking the *caldera* across the path from the Tropical Club. This candy store is full of sugary concoctions, so grab a plastic bag and start scooping (420dr per 100g). 14 varieties of licorice. Open 11am-midnight.

**Kastro's Cafeteria & Bar.** While you wait for the cable car next door, enjoy the view at this bargain basement sister of the Kastro Restaurant. Have an omelette (1500dr), a sandwich (800dr), or simply a cocktail (1900dr and up). The pricier version is upstairs, so make sure you're in the right place. Open noon-3pm and 6pm-1am.

CYCLADES

## NIGHTLIFE

Fira is host to one of the hippest disco scenes in Greece. The clubs, on the north end, gear up around 2am. Unfortunately, exorbitant covers make a club-crawl an unwise financial venture. Clubs generally share drink prices and covers, which vary according to the season: beers are around 800-1000dr, cocktails around 1000-2000dr, and covers start at 1000dr (soaring to upwards of 3000dr in the high season). The hippest are **Koo Club** and **Enigma** (facing each other on 25 Martiou), both of which crank into the wee hours. Chill on the outdoor decks and watch the steam rise on the dance floors inside. **Trip into the Music,** next door to Kira Thira Jazz Club, keep its dance floor crowded with a variety of tunes, including new British rock. At **Lava Club,** next to Enigma, there's techno-dancing and little talk. **Town Club,** next to Lava Club, pumps techno through a small room with a castle motif. Try one of the following bars for some pre-booty-shaking booze:

**Kira Thira Jazz Club,** across from Nikolas Taverna, on a side street parallel to the main road out of town. Mellow out to jazz (or, when there's no band, pop music) while sipping a gin fizz or piña colada (2000dr each). The brass hangs from the ceiling and the regulars kiss the DJ good night. Live jazz nightly in August. Open 9pm-late.

**Tropical Club.** High up on the *caldera,* a native Californian mixes signature cocktails as tasty as they are creative (around 1500dr). "Sunset coffees" like the Bob Marley *frappé* (dark rum, Kahlua, iced coffee, and cream) go well with sunset views over the *caldera.* Arrive by 8pm for prime balcony seating. Open noon-4am.

**Two Brothers Bar,** next to Poldo up the street from the banks. Hiding behind the exterior guise of a medieval prison, a relaxed crowd of regulars and wanderers congregates at the brothers' bar. Try a watermelon shot with your complimentary one-free-shot card. 500dr cover goes toward the cost of a drink. Beer around 700dr. Open 9pm-late.

## SIGHTS AND BEACHES

The **Petros M. Nomikos Conference Center,** above the cable car station, houses an exhibition center that currently displays life-size, 3-D reproductions of the magnificent **wall paintings of Ancient Thira;** the originals are some of the most prized pieces at the National Archeological Museum in Athens (see p. 104). Brightly col-

ored and intricately detailed murals provide hints of the factual existence and imaginative life of Santorini's wealthy ancient Minoan culture. (☎23 016, 017, 018, or 019. Open May-Oct. 10am-9pm. 1000dr, seniors and students 500dr, children under 18 free; audio tour 1000dr.) Just steps away from the cable cars you'll find Fira's **Archaeological Museum,** which holds an impressive array of vases, figurines, and statues, representative mostly of the Geometric period and from the site of Ancient Thira. (☎22 217. Open T-Su 8:30am-3pm. 800dr, students and EU seniors 400dr, EU students free.) The private **Megaro Gyzi Museum,** just northwest of Thira Youth Hostel, has an engrossing collection of old maps, engravings, and Greek island photographs covering the 15th through the 19th centuries. A few steps away is the **icon workshop,** where Catherine and George Ioannidou recreate the religious imagery of Byzantine Greece on wood-backed canvases. The museum hosts several classical music concerts and temporary art exhibitions in July and August. (☎23 077. Open May-Sept. M-Sa 10:30am-1:30pm and 5-8pm, Su 10:30am-4:30pm. 500dr, students 200dr.)



Reigning over the island from its lofty height, Fira lacks proximity to beaches. But it's the most convenient base for exploring them. The black sand sizzles in the sun—a straw mat and sandals are welcome accessories. Use your own two feet to reach one of Santorini's most secluded (though pebbly) black sand beaches: **Vourvoulou** (Βουρβουλου). To get there, head north of town and follow the signs; it's a one hour walk past fields and some of the least built-up enclaves of Santorini. Beside the beach is the cheap seafood taverna **To Limanakitou Vourvoulou.** (☎25 479. Appetizers 600dr, fish 8000dr per kg. Open noon-midnight.)

## THE OUTDOORS

When the hum of mopeds becomes a grating roar, hop on a boat and flee to the little islands along Santorini's *caldera* rim. The most popular boat excursion goes to the still active volcano, with a 30-minute hike up the black lava rocks to see the crater. Most boats make a swim-stop afterwards in nearby waters that are warmed in patches by hot sulphur springs. You'll have to swim through cold, cold water to get to the hot springs, so be prepared. A longer excursion goes to the inhabited island of Thirasia (Θηπασια); on the standard daytrip, you'll only have two hours to wander the island. Built along Thirasia's upper ridge, the villages of **Manolas** and **Potamos** have spine-tingling views of Santorini's western coast. Tour groups dock at **Korfos** or **Reeva.** From Korfos, you'll have to pant up 300 steep steps or catch a donkey ride (1000dr) to get to the villages; Reeva provides a paved road. **Boat tours** can be arranged through agencies all over Santorini. (Volcano and springs 2500dr, with Thirisia 4500-5500dr.)

# PERISSA Περισσα

Perissa isn't overly flashy, and its beaches are smooth and spacious. A youth hostel, nearby camping, and a casual nightlife scene make it more popular with student travelers. To get there, take the bus from Fira (15min., 30 per day, 400dr). If black sand seems passé, take the ferry to **Red Beach** at Akrotiri (☎82 093; leave at 11am and 12:30pm, return 4pm; 1500dr).

**ACCOMMODATIONS. Youth Hostel Perissa-Anna** is between the first and second bus stops heading into Perissa town; alternatively, if you get off at the final stop at the main plateia by the beach, walk inland along the main street for 500m; The hostel will be on your right. This friendly spot provides women's and mixed dorms, private rooms, cooking facilities, discounts at the market next door, and at other services around Perissa, use of a nearby pool, and free safety deposit boxes. (☎82 182. Hot showers 9am-9pm. Luggage storage 600dr. Linen 300dr for 3 days. Internet access 500dr for 15min., 900dr for 30min., 1500dr for 1 hr. 34-bed dorm 1200dr; 10-12 bed dorm 1600dr; private rooms 2000-4000dr.) Youthful **Stelio's Place** is a 7min. walk from the plateia: from the road leading out of town, turn left before

two side-by-side travel agencies; it's 50m down on your left. Stelio's has 21 spic-and-span rooms with private baths, fridges, a pool, and an adjacent bar (beer 500dr), as well as transportation to and from the airport or port. (☎81 860. Reservations recommended. Breakfast 1300dr. 3000-6000dr per person.) **Perissa Camping** is right off the main hub, adjacent to the beach in one of the few tree-covered spots on the island, though it's no forest. Enjoy their beach bar, mini-market, kitchen facilities, super-clean restrooms, discounts on nearby scuba package deals, and restaurant. (☎81 343 or 81 686. Internet access 500dr for 15min. 1500dr per person, children 750dr; 800dr per tent rental.) **Domatia** in private homes offer more privacy; proprietors hang around the dock at Athinios, but don't pay or hand over your passport without first seeing the room. (Doubles 6000-10,000dr.)

**FOOD.** Hitting where the main road meets the plateia at the beach, **Santo Food** crams french fries, *tzatziki*, and onions into its souvlaki; belly-bursting combos of Greek fast food specialities hover around 2000dr, and might easily fill two stomachs. Breakfast and vegetarian sandwiches are also served. (Open 24hr.) Across the street, delicious calzones, 10 varieties of pizza, and pasta await at **Bella Italiana.** (Calzones 1500-1700dr. Open 11am-1am.) Head back across the street for a beer at the **Full Moon Bar,** where the Canadian owner lovingly taps Guinness (1500dr) and other great drafts. DJs mastermind the music nightly, honing their craft for frequent theme nights. Listen to the Stones and the Doors and bask in MTV, Eurosport, or CNN. (Mixed drinks 1000-1500dr, beer 500dr. Open 8am-4am.)



## KAMARI Καμαρι

Although known as a black sand beach, Kamari Beach is actually covered in black pebbles, and the slippery seaweed-covered rock bottom makes wading especially difficult. But none of that really matters for most Kamari enthusiasts, who come to stare and be stared at from their beach chairs. The long, narrow beach area is covered in umbrellas, and edged into the ocean by pricey hotels, upscale shops, cafes, and nightclubs. Buses come from **Fira** (20min., 62 per day, 270dr), and a rocky shuttle boat scoots between Kamari and **Perissa** (every 30min. 9am-5pm or whenever a boatload has gathered, 1000dr). The boat leaves from in front of the Hook Bar at the right end of the waterfront, facing the sea.

**ACCOMMODATIONS.** Throughout town, doubles range from 10,000-24,000dr. **Kamari Tours** (☎31 390) has outlets all over, but the one on the right end of the harbor offers the most service. **Hotel Preka Maria** (☎31 266) rents rooms (12,000-15,000dr) and furnished 3-person apartments (12,000-18,000dr), with refrigerator, bath, a cooking sink, and access to a common swimming pool. It's close to the waterfront, on the northern end of town: heading away from the mountain, take a left before the Kali Bar and the hotel is 70m father on your right. **Kamari Camping** is 1km inland along the main road out of town. (☎31 453. Open June-Sept. 1200dr per person; 1000dr per tent.)

**FOOD AND ENTERTAINMENT.** To pick up an inexpensive snack along the waterfront, head to **Ariston** at the northern end of the waterfront, a bakery and small grocery selling fresh loaves (around 180dr, olive bread 300dr). (Open 6:30am-11pm.) At the northern end of the waterfront, **Mango** and **Dom** serve up a sexy combination: Mango is an upscale outdoor cafe, Dom is a futuristic indoor club. (2000dr cover buys 1 drink; cocktails 1700-2000dr. Open Su-Th morning-3:30am, much later on weekends.) For quieter entertainment, check out **Open Air Cinema Kamari** (☎31 974), on the way out of town, which shows new films and has a **Jazz Festival** every July. The **Canava Roussos** winery, 1km from Kamari Camping, will wine and dine you with its red, white, and rose *bouganvilla.* Try the house favorite, *mavrathiko* (100dr per glass), a sweet wine made with red grapes instead of the traditional white. (Open 10am-8pm.)

## OIA Οια ☎0286

Dazzling sunsets made the posh cliffside town of Oia (EE-ah) famous; its little stucco buildings piled together in postcard perfect disorder make it charming. In the aftermath of the 1956 earthquake that leveled the town (and much of the northwest tip of the island), inhabitants carved new dwellings into the cliffside among the shattered ruins of the old. The narrow cobblestone streets are pedestrianized for peaceful window-shopping at the town's many upscale boutiques. Although the budget traveler will not thrive long in Oia, it's possible to survive a pleasant day or two without too much fiscal damage, browsing the exquisite jewelry, craft, and embroidery shops, glancing at the menus of elegant restaurants, and exploring the many stunning clifftop views before choosing a spot to marvel at the sunset. Buses run from **Fira** to Oia (25min., 30 per day, 280dr), and a few ferries dock at Oia before continuing to Fira or Athinios.

**ACCOMMODATIONS.** The Karvounis family can help meet all your tourist needs. **Karvounis Tours** (☎71 290, 291, or 292; fax 71 291; email mkarvounis@ote.net.gr), on the main street beside the biggest church in town, answers questions about Oia and Santorini, in addition to selling ferry and airline tickets and arranging marriages—perhaps beyond the bounds of typical tourist needs. Email them with questions about accommodations. The Karvounis family's classy **Youth Hotel Oia** has spacious, impeccably clean rooms with baths and large mirrors, a courtyard, and a bar open for breakfast and evening drinks. The affordable, luxurious hostel makes painfully expensive Oia affordable. Happy hour lasts from 7:30-8:30pm, with cheaper-than-already-cheap drinks and the opportunity to watch the sunset from the roof patio. (☎71 465; fax 71 291. Rooms single-sex or mixed. Free safety deposit boxes. Wheelchair accessible. Open May-Oct. Dorms 3500dr, breakfast included.) Short-term domatia are difficult to come by; most proprietors expect a five-day stay.

**FOOD.** Dining will cost you a bit more than in Fira, but some restaurants serve exceptional food. **Petros,** Oia's oldest restaurant, at the end of Oia's main road (when you're heading toward Fira from the main church), overlooks the *caldera*. Try the fresh fish soup, or any of the outstanding, fresh seafood dishes (including octopus). Old Greek recipes provide a pleasant alternative to the common *moussaka*, and Petros Jr. continues the family tradition of making homemade wines. (Entrees 1000-2000dr. Open 6pm-late.) The family of Petros extends up the street to **Thalami Taverna,** where they cook up less exotic fare, but offer a better view of the *caldera*, all enhanced on Tuesdays by live music. (☎71 009. Chicken with blue cheese and mushrooms 2500dr, *fara* 1000dr, fried tomato balls 1000dr, Santorini salad 1700dr.) **Restaurant Lotza** serves well-seasoned dishes like curried chicken (2500dr), *gioourtlou* (minced meat, pita bread, and yogurt; 2400dr), and spaghetti

**(ONE IS) THE LONELIEST NUMBER** If you're traveling alone in Greece, be prepared for the inevitable question: *"mono sou?"* ("just yourself?"). Answer yes and you may be asked to clarify that you really did, for some incomprehensible reason, choose this kind of life. The solitary lifestyle is not exactly taboo in Greece, but it's certainly not customary or desirable, either. There is no Greek word for "privacy"—the closest word translates as "loneliness" or "solitude"—and there is no English word for *parea,* which means something like "company" (without the financial associations) or "gang" (without the criminal implications). Your *parea* can be the bunch of buddies with whom you do everything, or whoever you happen to be with at a given time ("I saw Nikos and his *parea* at the club..."). So don't be offended if Greeks commend you on your bravery, or console you for your apparent friendlessness. They are simply concerned: they come from a country of people-persons.

with seafood (2500dr), in a bohemian atmosphere (open 9am-late). There is a small **grocery/bakery,** close to the plateia where the buses stop; follow the signs to fresh loaves (around 300dr), croissants, and pies. (200-400dr. Open M-Sa 7am-9pm, Su 7am-2pm.) On your way back to Fira, stop by **Santorini Mou I Love You,** where the owner strums his guitar along with the featured music acts.

**BEACHES.** A 20-minute climb down the 252 stone stairs at the end of the main road leads to rocky **Ammoudi Beach,** where a few boats are moored in a startlingly deep swimming lagoon. It's worth climbing down and up the cliff to relax on the rocks and swim in the beautiful blue water. Re-energize with a meal of fresh fish at one of the three **tavernas** at the bottom of the stairs, where the fish is hauled straight from the net to the table. If you're not up to the climb back up, hire a **donkey** (1000dr per person) for a ride to the top.



## AKROTIRI Ακρωτηρι ☎0286

*Take the bus (16 per day, 400dr) from Fira. ☎81 366. Open Tu-Su 8am-7pm. 1200dr, students 600dr.*

The volcanic eruption that wrecked Santorini in the 17th century BC blanketed Akrotiri with lava and ash that, as they destroyed the island, ironically preserved the maritime city of Akrotiri in a more complete state than almost any other Minoan site. A highly sophisticated Bronze age society lived in Akrotiri, as its two and three story buildings show. In 1967, Professor Marinatos uncovered the paved streets of Akrotiri, lined with houses connected by a sophisticated central drainage system. Each house had at least one room decorated with wall paintings, some of which are unsurpassed in Greece. The originals are at the National Archaeological Museum in Athens; an initial visit to the replicas at Fira (see p. 403) helps to imagine the original architectural setting. Since no skeletons were found in the city, the theory is that everyone escaped before the effects of the 1625 eruption devastated the area. Less adventurous visitors tag along with the guided tours, but this once-bustling town hits hardest when seen at a slower pace; frequent signposts inform your roving.

Near ancient Akrotiri is the small modern village of Akrotiri. For sustenance and a fabulous sea view, head down the road to the right of the archeological site to reach the **Dolphin Fish Restaurant;** don't worry, the name is based on the popular icon in Minoan wall paintings, while the food consists of species of fish caught daily by the owner in local waters. For a swim, continue heading away from the ancient site and past the Dolphin Fish Restaurant to the **Red Beach,** a 20-minute walk from the Akrotiri bus stop. Though Santorini is famed for its black beaches, this ruddy beach is prized for its remote location and smooth sand.

## PYRGOS Πυργος AND ANCIENT THIRA Αρχαια Θηρα

*To reach Pyrgos, take the bus from Fira to Perissa (15min., 30 per day, 400dr), and ask the driver to let you off at Pyrgos. Ancient Thira can be reached as a hike from Pyrgos; alternatively, take a bus from Fira to Kamari (20min., 62 per day, 270dr) and climb the mountain beside the waterfront for 30min. to reach the ancient ruins.*

Once a Venetian fortress, the lofty town of Pyrgos is surrounded by medieval walls. Ottoman occupation through 1828 left a legacy of 25 blue- and green-domed churches dotting the horizon, one of which (near the top) houses the **Museum of Icons and Liturgical Objects.** (Open Tu-Su 10am-2pm. Free.) The fortress and museum are near one another; to find them through the maze of alleyways leading up the hill, follow the signs for adjacent Kafe Kasteli. A 40-minute hike from Pyrgos takes you to the **Profitis Ilias Monastery.** Built in 1711, it graciously shares its site with a radar station installed by military personnel who thought the monastery's proximity would make the station impervious to attack. (Open 5-9am and 5-6pm.) On July 20, the monastery hosts the **Festival of Profitis Ilias.**

From Profitis Ilias, it's a 90min. hike to the ruins of **Ancient Thira** *(open Tu-Su 8am-2pm)*. This trek takes you along the mountain that separates Kamari and Perissa and affords fantastic views of all Santorini. The way is poorly marked, with narrow dry-gravel paths on the steep mountainside, so strong shoes with good traction are a must. The ancient theater, church, and forum of the island's old capital are still visible, though less spectacular than the Akrotiri excavations.

### MONOLITHOS BEACH

Those who like their beaches sandy might want to check out Monolithos Beach. More popular with locals than with tourists, this small beach is easily accessible due to its proximity to the airport (15 buses per day, 250dr). If you want a bite to eat, the fish taverna **Skaramagas** is the least expensive on the strip. The owners catch the fresh seafood, keep what they need for the restaurant, and sell the rest to other establishments. Many locals come here for lunch several times a week to enjoy calamari (1500dr), Greek salads (800dr), and the famed *kakavia*, or fish soup (2000dr). (Open May-Oct. 11am-midnight.)



# MILOS ΜΗΛΟΣ

Though the ghost of past achievements continues to loom large—plastic replicas of the Venus de Milo pop up everywhere from the archaeological museum to taverna bathrooms—there's much to enjoy in Milos that France hasn't stolen. Mineral deposits and volcanoes have collaborated to create a wealth of breathtaking beaches. Thucydides' *Melian Dialogue* may have stirred up your hunger for history, which you can feed in the winding streets of Plaka, which conceal an ancient theater and spooky catacombs.

## ADAMAS Αδαμας ☎0287

This port town stuffs most of Milos's accommodations, food, and nightlife into the space of several blocks, causing congestion both vibrant and stifling. Most sights are elsewhere, but the centralized bus system makes it a base for exploring the rest of the island; a rented moped or car helps, too. Follow the waterfront to the right as you disembark from your ferry to reach the center of Adamas.

### GETTING THERE AND GETTING AROUND

**Ferries:** From Milos, ferries follow a twisted, complex, but well-posted schedule. Destinations are: **Folegandros** (2 per week, 1700dr); **Ios** (5hr., 2 per week, 2600dr); **Karpathos** (10hr., 1 per week, 7200dr); **Kassos** (9hr., 2 per week, 5900dr); **Kimolos** (2 per week, 1200dr, from Pollonia 550dr); **Kithnos** (1-2 per day, 2500dr); **Piraeus** (8hr., 1-2 per day, 5000dr); **Rhodes** (14hr., 1 per week, 1850dr); **Santorini** (3 per week, 3600dr); **Serifos** (3hr., 1-2 per day, 1600dr); **Sifnos** (1½hr., 3 per day, 1500dr); and **Sikinos** (4 per week, 2800dr). Ferries also head to the Cretan ports of **Agios Nikolaos** (6hr., 5 per week, 4900dr) and **Sitia** (6½hr., 5 per week, 5100dr).

**Buses:** (☎22 219). Buses stop in the busy area on the waterfront. They go to: **Pollonia** (6 per day, 260dr); **Trypiti** (every hr. 7:30am-11pm, 260dr); and other destinations. Check the schedule posted in the bus station or in travel offices.

**Flights: Olympic Airways** (☎22 380, at the airport 22 381), on 25 Martiou. Planes go once daily to **Athens** (14,700dr). Open M-F 8am-3pm.

**Taxis:** (☎22 219), stand along the waterfront. Available 24hr. Fixed fares are posted.

**Moped Rental: Moto Express** (☎23 227), just before the post office. Rentals limited to motorbike license-holders over 23. Bikes 2500-5000dr per day. Open 8am-10pm.

## ORIENTATION AND PRACTICAL INFORMATION

**Tourist Office:** (☎22 445), across from the dock. Multilingual staff. Ask for brochures, maps, ferry and bus timetables, and a complete list of the island's rooms and hotels. Open 10am-2pm and 6pm-midnight.

**Tourist Agencies: Milos Travel** (☎22 000 or 22 200; fax 22 688), on the waterfront, sells most ferry tickets. Open 7am-2am. John at **Vichos Tours** (☎/fax 22 120), next to the National bank, speaks English and knows all about the island.

**Banks: National Bank** (☎22 077), near the post office along the waterfront with 24hr. **ATM.** Open M-Th 8am-2pm, F 8am-1:30pm. There's another branch by Milos Travel.

**Police:** (☎21 378 or 21 204).

**Port Authority:** (☎22 100). Open 24hr.

**Medical Center:** (☎22 700, 22 701 or 22 702), in Plaka.

**Post Office:** (☎22 288). Take the waterfront road past the bus station, turn right before Agricultural Bank; it's 100m up, on the left. Open M-F 7:30am-2pm. **Post code:** 84801.

CYCLADES

## ACCOMMODATIONS

High season prices may wound your budget, but persistence is your friend. Domatia in Adamas's and Plaka's side streets will turn up affordable private rooms, since few tourists look beyond the port. To stay in Adamas, book far in advance.

**Semiramis Hotel** (☎22 117; fax 22 118). Follow the main road past the bus station, and bear left after the supermarket; it's straight ahead. Nikos and Petros tend excellent rooms with a shaded garden outside. Breakfast 1200dr. Doubles 13,000-20,000dr; triples 18,000dr; cheaper downstairs rooms with common bath 10,000dr.

**Paliohori Rooms to Let** (☎22 480 or 22 777), just up the road from Semiramis. Maria offers rooms with baths, ceiling fans, and fridges, starting at 9000dr.

**Manovsos Rooms to Let** (☎21 985 or 23 425), just before Semiramis. Gorgeous rooms; if you're lucky, you might score an honest-to-god bathtub. All doubles have fridges and TVs. A/C available. Reception 8:30am-9:30pm. Doubles 16,000dr; triples 18,000dr.

**Rooms Katris** (☎22 046). Walk along the water 500m past the bus station; turn left at the minimarket. Simple rooms with TV. Doubles 15,000dr.

**Camping Milos** (☎31 410; fax 31 412), at Achivadolimni Beach, 7km from port; before 6:30pm, buses pick up at the dock. New and sharp, with kitchen, laundry, car/bike rental, minimarket and restaurant. Bungalows with fridge and bath 12,000-17,000dr. Camping 1500dr per person; 1000dr tent rental; mopeds 300dr, cars 400dr.

## FOOD AND NIGHTLIFE

Large waterfront restaurants gather tourists around their beautiful views every night. There are also several cafes peppering the waterfront, where you can watch the flood of tourists drown the island every few hours.

**Flisvos** (☎22 275), before the bend in the waterfront, next to Kinigos. Superb, cheap food; the seafood packs them in (1800-2500dr). Vegetarian options available.

**Kinigos** (☎22 349), around the first bend on the waterfront. Straight-up grilled Greek fare like ever-popular gyro plate (1800dr) or seafood risotto (1950dr).

**Trapatseli's Restaurant,** a 5min. walk on the road to Achivadolimni Beach. It's worth the wait to score one of these elegant waterside tables. Octopus with pasta 2000dr.

There isn't a huge bar or disco scene in Adamas, but there are a few places to bebop the night away. **Notos Club,** to the left of the ferry dock facing inland, spins folk, Greek, and disco for your dancing pleasure. (cocktails 2000dr, beer 1500dr.) If a dark, wood-paneled, verging-on-seedy, fun bar strikes your fancy, head to **Vipera Lebetina** for slightly cheaper cocktails (1500dr) and the DJs spinning discs until the wee hours of the night.

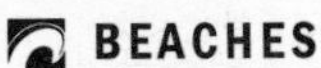

## BEACHES

Milos has emerged from centuries of volcanic eruptions with stunning **beaches** covered with exceptional rock formations and unique sand. Distinctive beaches line both the northern and southern coasts. In the north, **Sankiniko**'s gleaming white rocks give the impression you're swimming next to snow-covered mountains; you'll need a moped or car to get there. The pools of **Papafrankas,** regally enclosed by a stone arch, are right on the route to **Apollonia;** just ask the bus driver to let you off, or continue all the way to Apollonia for a stroll along the beach that edges this cute fishing village. On the south side of the island, happy **Provatas** and **Paleohori** beaches sport bars, music, comfy beach chairs, and bus access (bus from Adamas; 25min., 6 buses per day, 350dr). The real gem sits between them at **Tsigrados beach,** where natural stores of pearlite make for deep, soft sand that glimmers magnificently in the afternoon sun. Get there by moped, or trek from Provatas (1½hr.). Seven buses per day from Adamas journey to densely populated **Achivadolimni Beach** (15min., 350dr).

## DAYTRIPS FROM ADAMAS

### PLAKA Πλακα AND TRYPITI Τρυπητη

*Buses from Adamas run to Plaka (15min., every 30min., 260dr) and Trypiti (15min., every 30min., 260dr).*

Six winding kilometers from Adamas, Plaka rests on mountaintops. From the police station, follow the signs downhill through several twisty streets to the terrace of the **Church of Panagia Korfiatissa,** which leans into a view of lush countryside and blue sea only an arm's length away. Next door, the town's **Folk Museum** displays eerie mannequins in household settings. (☎21 292. Open Tu-Sa 10am-2pm and 6-9pm, Su 10am-2pm. 400dr, students and children 200dr.) Near the bus stop on the road to Trypiti, the **Archaeological Museum** houses artifacts unearthed at Fylakopi, including the mesmerizing *Lady of Fylakopi.* (☎21 620. Open Tu-Su 8:30am-2:30pm. 500dr, students 300dr, seniors 300dr, EU students free.) For a truly spectacular view, climb upward for 15min. from the bus station to the **Panagia Thalassitra Monastery** at the top of the old castle.

Outside teeny Trypiti, the **catacombs** hewn into the cliff face are the oldest site of Christian worship in Greece. The open-air ruins are small and without on-site plaques, but peering into the unlit corridors of the cool catacombs sparks the imagination. (☎21 625. Open Tu-Su 8:30am-1pm. Free.) You can still see part of a Dorian stone wall built between 1100 and 800 BC. A sign marks the spot where the **Venus de Milo** was buried around 320 BC; in the 19th century AD, she moved to the Louvre in Paris. A well-preserved theater dating from the Roman occupation provides a riveting ocean view; ask at the tourist office about performances there. A 20min. walk downhill from Plaka on the road through Trypiti will get you to the seaside fishing village of **Klima,** where whitewashed houses loom over the waves.

Archaeology buffs will want to scramble among the ruins of **Filakopi,** 3km from the fishing village of **Pollonia** (Πολλονια) toward Adamas, where British excavations unearthed 3500-year-old **frescoes** now displayed in the National Museum in Athens (see p. 104). There is a bus from Pollonia to **Papafragas** (15min., every 45min., 350dr), where dangling rock formations surround a pool of clear blue water. Buses run from Adamas to Pollonia (20min., every 45min., 260dr).

### KIMOLOS Κιμωλος

*Ferries run from Milos to Kimolos (2 per week, 1200dr).*

Pedestrian-friendly Kimolos is lovely at sunset, when the colors are most vivid over the sea and islands, and the ribbon of white rock around Kimolos' edges shines. Disembark at the small port of Psathi, and head left for Aliki Beach or continue up to Hora. The **Castro ruins,** in the center of town, are studded with lovely

little churches to be explored. From the Castro, an hour's hike will take you through mountains to the beaches of the eastern shore. Walk past the Castro with it on your left and continue past the Byzantine church, the minimalist town, and a public well (good to refill your bottle). Keep walking to a chapel; there, bear right and take the bright-red downhill path toward the valley, then over a stone bridge.

# SIFNOS ΣΙΦΝΟΣ

Sifniots are a festive bunch, dropping everything a whopping 13 times a year to celebrate religious festivals with food, drinking, dancing, and merriment that lasts for days. Even when they sober up and return to work, their zest persists in their happening nightlife, their distinctive cuisine, and their beaches, where people are as likely to be snorkeling or leaping from cliffs as bathing in the sun.



## KAMARES Καμαρες ☎0284

Kamares is a magnificent harbor filled with sailboats and yachts and surrounded by formidable brown cliffs in fierce contrast to the emerald sea. The excellent town beach sweeps the harbor rim, and a few tavernas line its shallow perimeters. Kamares is a gentle town pleasing to the senses, where days easily drift away. Here you can secure a room, swim, dine, and peruse shops featuring ornate local pottery; look for *keramiko* (ceramic) signs throughout the village.

### ORIENTATION AND PRACTICAL INFORMATION.

From Sifnos, **ferries** head to: **Folegandros** (45min., 1-3 per week, 1700dr); **Kimolos** (1½hr., 1 per day M-Sa, 1500dr); **Kithnos** (2½hr., 1-2 per day Sa-Th, 2000dr); **Ios** (3hr., 1-3 per week, 2610dr); **Milos** (1½hr., 1-2 per day, 1600dr); **Piraeus** (6hr., 1-2 per day, 4400dr); **Santorini** (4hr., 1-3 per week, 3000dr); **Serifos** (1hr., 1-2 per day Sa-Th, 1500dr); **Sikinos** (2½hr., 1-3 per week, 1930dr); and **Syros** (4½hr., 2 per week, 2100dr). For ferry tickets, head two doors down to **Katsoulakis Travel** (☎31 004, 31 700, or 31 213); they also have an office behind the museum in Apollonia. Weekly **hydrofoils** go to: **Milos** (3000dr); **Mykonos** (1½hr., 6100dr); **Paros** (1hr., 2000dr); and **Piraeus** (9000dr). From Kamares, **buses** go to **Vathi** (ever hr. 7:30am-11:30pm, 420dr) via **Apollonia** (220dr). **Sifnos Moto Car,** on the main road, rents cars and bikes. (☎31 793. Cars 18,000-22,300dr per day; mopeds 3000-8000dr per day. Open 8:30am-10pm.)

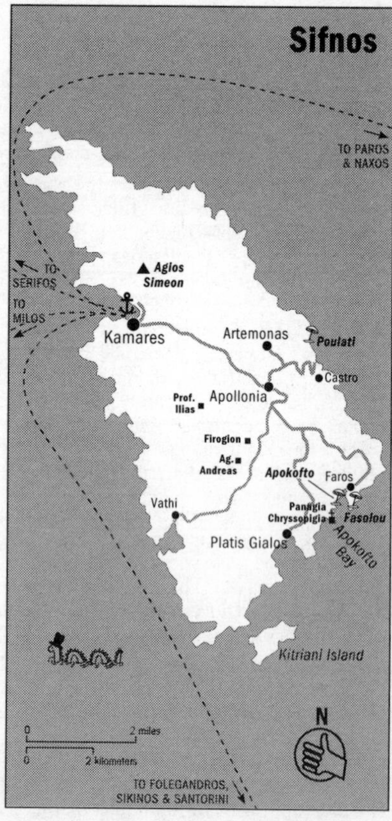


Just opposite the ferry dock, the **Community Information Office** helps find rooms, deciphers boat and bus schedules, exchanges currency, and stores luggage. (☎31 977. Hours depend on ferry schedule.) The **port authority** next door has sea travel

information. (☎33 617. Open 24hr.) The **Aegean Thesaurus Travel Agency,** along the waterfront as you walk from the dock to town, has an English-speaking staff that exchanges currency, finds accommodations, stores luggage, sells Flying Dolphin tickets, and organizes excursions around the island. (☎33 151; fax 32 190. Open 9:30am-10pm.) **Public toilets** are right next to the information office. There's an **International Press** on the main strip. (☎33 521. Open 9am-midnight.) In an **emergency,** call the **police** (☎31 210). A **doctor** can be reached at the clinic at 31 315, and a **pharmacy** can be reached at 33 033 or 33 541. **Postal code:** 84003.

**ACCOMMODATIONS.** During high season, you are unlikely to find a budget hotel room; inquire at **Room to Let** signs or by asking at one of the many waterfront tavernas. Doubles usually run 8000-12,000dr and triples 12,000-18,000dr. **Hotel Stavros** has clean, pleasant rooms with baths, many with panoramic views of the harbor's beach. Stavros and his English wife also offer travel services, car rental, maps (400dr), and a book exchange next door. (☎33 383 or 31 641; fax 31 709. Doubles 5000-10,000dr, with bath 8000-13,000dr; triples with bath 9500-15,000dr.) **Hotel Kiki,** farther along the waterfront road toward Apollonia, offers spotless rooms with baths, TVs, and balconies overlooking the harbor. (☎32 329; fax 31 453. Doubles 14,000dr; triples 16,500dr; breakfast 1500dr.) **Maki's Camping** lies across the road behind the beach in Kamares. (☎/fax 32 366. 1300dr per person, with tent 1700dr; breakfast 800dr). Another, more secluded campsite is calm, clean **Platis Yialos Camping,** amid trees and stone walls, a 10min. walk inland from the bus stop. (☎31 786. 1100dr per person; 700-810dr tent rental.)



**FOOD.** A local Sifniot specialty is chickpea soup, called *revithada* (700dr; served only Su). It gets polished off early, so try it for lunch. There are also several **groceries** and **bakeries** selling the local almond cookie delicacy, *amigdalota*. The tavernas serve food of roughly the same quality and price, but many have seaside seating. For Greek food with a charming twist, try the waterfront **Kamares Ouzeri.** Among the specialties prepared by the English-speaking chef and staff are the grilled stuffed calamari (1700dr), grilled chicken (1300dr), and *tzatziki* (600dr). **Ristorante Italiano de Claudio,** on the waterfront up the main street toward Apollonia, serves up a mighty fine grilled swordfish (3000dr), lasagna (1500dr), and *rigatoni delicati* (pasta with chicken, asparagus, and cream sauce; 1800dr). Sate your sweet tooth at **Pipi's Pastisseries,** which will lure you with heaven-sent apple pastry (450dr) and other delectables (open 7am-midnight).

**NIGHTLIFE.** A choice sunset-watching spot is **Cafe Folie,** at the far end of the beach. It's a bit pricey (beer 1000-2000dr, cocktails 2500dr), but the colorful, funky decor, Caribbean flavor, and proximity to the water justify the hefty price tag. **Collage** is closer to the dock, above a supermarket. Enjoy freshly squeezed fruit juices (800dr), juice cocktails (800-1000dr), and their alcoholic counterparts (1500dr); look for the sign hanging over an outdoor terrace. (Open 11am-3am.) The **Old Captain Bar,** just across the street, has beer and drinks (1000-1500dr), plays string music at sunset, then swings to country (courtesy of Tony) and calypso. (Open until 3am.) Farther along the road, **Mobilize** attracts a later crowd; the strobes pulse and the DJ takes requests until sunrise (open 10pm-6am).

## APOLLONIA Απολλωνια ☎0284

Apollonia, the island's capital, meanders about the hill haphazardly—pick a landmark to get your bearings by the main road, where all of Sifnos's roads converge. A few steps from the main road will submerge you in narrow streets, a rabbit warren of shops, bars, and charming houses.

**ORIENTATION AND PRACTICAL INFORMATION.** Everything you need to conduct your business is on the main plateia, where the **bus** from Kamares makes its first stop. Buses to Kamares (10min., 240dr) stop in the plateia in front of the

post office, while those to villages and beaches like Kastro (240dr) and Plati Yialos (440dr) stop around the corner near the Hotel Anthousa. Buses run to all three at least once every hour. An **International Press** is located off the plateia next to the meat market. **Aegean Thesaurus,** near the post office, is your source for **currency exchange,** accommodation assistance, bus and ferry schedules, and their 600dr island information packs. (☎33 526 or 33 151. Open 10am-10pm.) The **National Bank,** on the left before the medical center, has a 24hr. **ATM.** (☎31 237. Open M-Th 8am-2pm, F 8am-1:30pm.) There's an **OTE** on the road back to Kamares. (☎31 215 or 33 499. Open 7:30am-2:30pm.) From the other bus stop near Hotel Anthousa, head up the road to Artemonas to find the **medical center** (☎31 315) on your left and the **police station** (☎31 210) in a small white building on your right. The **Billiard Cafe,** on the road out of Apollonia to the right, plugs you into the **internet.** (1600dr per hr. Open 2pm until 1am.) Beside the main plateia is the **post office.** (☎31 329. Open M-F 7:30am-2pm.) **Postal code:** 84003.

CYCLADES

**ACCOMMODATIONS, FOOD, AND NIGHTLIFE.** Summer vacancies are rare in Apollonia; call a month in advance for reservations. **Hotel Sofia** is just off the plateia; head up the wide paved road from the main plateia until you see it on your left above the supermarket. (☎31 238. Doubles 12,000dr; triples 14,000dr.) **Hotel Anthoussa,** framed by trees and located above the pastry shop around the corner from Hotel Sofia, has luxurious accommodations with A/C, TVs, telephones, daily cleaning service, and 4000dr self-service laundry. (☎31 431; fax 32 207. Singles 7500-12,000dr; doubles 8500-15,000dr; triples 10,000-16,500dr.)

Restaurants are excellent and not as expensive as their beautiful exteriors suggest. The better tavernas are along the path across from the police. The restaurant at the **Sifnos Hotel** (☎31 624) serves the island specialty on Sundays—chick-peas with olive oil and lemon, cooked all night in special ovens in another town. Let Apostolos ladle it up along with years of wisdom about the island. The fricassee is a classic—goat and rice covered with greens and baked in a ceramic pot (1800dr). **Vegera,** on the road to Artemonas (just before the National Bank), brews yummy coffees and makes crepes (400-1600dr) on an open-air veranda under the island's spellbinding sunsets. Try the Sifniot specialty sweet, almond *amigdalota* (300dr).

Stroll along the street behind the museum to tap into the Sifniot nightlife. **Bodgi,** a bar and coffee house, is likely to catch your eye and ear: candles light up both levels and the outside terrace, and trip-hop tickles your tympanum (open until 4am). Down the street, **Argo** is packed until daylight, playing American and British rock early on and Greek dance hits late. Live Greek music comes alive every night until sunrise at **Aloni,** where the Greeks are. Take the road toward Artemonas to get there; the sunrise is divine.

**DAYTRIPS.** Travel in Sifnos is easy with the assistance of the map available at kiosks (400dr). Pack a picnic to nibble as you explore Apollonia's adjacent hillside villages. The quiet but expansive village of **Artemonas,** a 10min. walk from Apollonia, has a magnificent view and several fine mansions built by refugees from Alexandria. Enchanting **Castro** village is 3km east of Apollonia and can be reached by bus (15min., 240dr). This cluster of whitewashed houses and narrow streets rests on an ocean-facing mountaintop. You may find the tiny **Archaeological Museum** while walking through the former capital's streets. (Open Tu-Su 11am-2:30pm. Free.) There are no hotels, but ask around for domatia. Behind the Castro and next to **Epta Martires** (poke your head in) is the island's best spot for **diving.** Rocks form natural platforms for jumping into the deep water below. From Castro, the footpath leads to the sparkling cove at **Poulati,** popular for snorkeling.

Hourly buses run to **Platis Gialos,** 12km from Apollonia, where you can rent equipment for watersports. To the south, **Faros** has several popular beaches, connected by footpath. **Fasolou** and **Apokof** beaches have tavernas and tend to be busy. Farther along the path, you'll reach striking **Panagia Chrysopigi Monastery,** also accessible by the Platis Gialos bus followed by a 10min. walk. A bridge connects this 17th-century monastery's rocky islet to the mainland. The monastery lets

rooms; make reservations about two months in advance. (☎31 482. Doubles 4000dr.) If the walk to Chrysopigi works up an appetite, the restaurant on the beach to the left of the monastery serves authentic Sifniot cuisine like *mastelo*, lamb cooked in wine and spices, for 1270dr, and *kaparosalata*, a caper greens salad, for 750dr. (☎71 295. Open noon-11pm.) Forty days after Easter, the two day **festival of Analipsos** is celebrated at Chrysopigi. Other renowned Sifniot festivals fall during the summer, with one each in July, August, and September. Inquire at the tourist office to find out when you can join in the fun.

# SERIFOS ΣΕΡΙΦΟΣ



Sitting atop the crumbling Castro, you can take in the full panorama of Serifos's charms, from the fertile arc of the port to the mining-ravaged surrounding hills and the untouched distant beaches. Poor roads restrict the plague of Athenian vacationers in the port, leaving the rest of the island blissfully undiscovered. "Stony" Serifos got its name from Medusa. Perseus hunted her down and turned her shocking ugliness against her with a mirror. When he took her head back to Polydictes, king of Serifos, he found that Polydictes was putting the moves on Perseus's mom, Danae. Pissed-off Perseus flashed the Medusa's severed head at Polydictes and his royal court, freezing them (and their island) in stone.

## LIVADI Λιβαδι ☎0281

Livadi, Serifos's port, keeps visitors rested and full for daytime trips throughout the island. The white tower that is Hora (the island's other main town) hangs above the port, and can be reached by hike (40min.) or by frequent bus (250dr).

### ORIENTATION AND PRACTICAL INFORMATION

A walk along the waterfront will take you past the services. An island map that lists useful phone numbers is available at kiosks (300dr). Regular **ferries** from Piraeus and other Western Cyclades and occasional boats from Paros, Syros, Ios, and Santorini arrive in Serifos. From Serifos, ferries travel to: **Kimolos** (2hr., 6 per week, 1850dr); **Kithnos** (1½hr., 1 per day, 1800dr); **Milos** (3hr., 1-2 per day, 1700dr); **Mykonos** (1 per week); **Paros** (2 per week); **Piraeus** (4½hr., 1-3 per day, 3900dr); **Santorini** (6½hr., 1 per week, 3450dr); **Sifnos** (45min., 1-2 per day, 1450dr); and **Syros** (2 per week). **Flying dolphins** go once a day to Kithnos (3500dr), Milos, Piraeus (7500dr), and Sifnos, once per week to Kimolos (3550dr). Krinas rents **cars** (10,000-16,000dr per day) and **mopeds** (3000-7000dr). For **taxis,** call 51 245 or 51 435.

**Krinas Travel,** 50m from the dock, upstairs from Captain Hook (☎51 488; fax 51 164; open 8:30am-8:30pm), and **Apiliotis Travel,** on the waterfront to the left of a supermarket (☎51 155; open 9am-2pm and 6-8:30pm), vend hydrofoil and ferry tickets and have English schedules. The **Ionian Bank,** with 24hr. **ATM,** is along the waterfront. (☎51 780. Open M-Th 8am-2pm, F 8am-1:30pm.) The **port police** (☎51 470) are up the narrow steps, marked with a large Greek flag. For **police,** dial 51 300. The **pharmacy** is two doors to the left of Apiliotis. (☎(0932) 605 859. Open 9am-2pm and 6:30-9:30pm.) **Postal code:** 84005.

### ACCOMMODATIONS

Look for pensions on the waterfront, on the street parallel to the waterfront road, and on the road that bears left from the Milos Express office toward the excellent **Coralli Campgrounds.** (☎51 488. Bungalows 5000-10,000dr, depending on season and amenities). **Hotel Serifos Beach** is a block back from the beach, with a large blue sign on the main waterfront road. Away from the main strip, rooms are comfortable and quiet. (☎51 209 or 51 468. Singles 9000-13,000dr; doubles 11,000-15,500dr. Breakfast 1500dr.) **Hotel Areti,** up the hill on the first left as you exit the ferry, bears

blue shutters and a coat of whitewash. The hotel has a harbor view, with a backyard terrace and private balconies for each room. (☎51 479 or 51 107; fax 51 547. Open Apr.-Oct. Singles 11,000-12,000dr; doubles 14,000dr; triples 16,000-17,000dr. Breakfast 1200dr.) Waterfront **Hotel Albatross** has rooms with fridges, baths, and fans, plus a large garden. (☎51 148. Doubles 12,000dr; triples and quads 16,000dr.)

## FOOD AND NIGHTLIFE

Everything on the menu satisfies at local favorite **Mokkas,** one of the first tavernas along the waterfront. Come here for locally grown ingredients and simple, flavorful fresh seafood. Try the *fasolakia* (green beans with tomato sauce and olive oil; 1000dr), or the chicken Antonio (tender meat wrapped in bacon with divine cream sauce; 2000dr). For an inexpensive, stick-to-your-ribs meal, head to **Stamadis,** at the right end of the waterfront on the beach. The stuffed vine leaves (1000dr) and rabbit casserole with onions (1500dr) are delightful beside the open-air sea view. The **Marinos** market, far along the waterfront, sells fresh fruit. (Open 7:30am-2pm, 4:30pm-midnight.)

Unwind after a hard day at the beach at **Astra,** a bar and dance club in the middle of the waterfront (cover 1000dr), and at **Metalio,** 5min. down the road to Hora (beer 1000dr). **Roman,** in a small shop complex bursting with knick-knacks near Praxis, has a pool table, games, and a mellow scene (beer 600dr). Next door, **Alter Ego Music Club** bumps and grinds. (Cover 1500dr. Open after 11pm.)



## DAYTRIPS FROM LIVADI

### HORA Χωρα ☎0281

The dense white roofs of Hora (or Serifos Town) look postcard-perfect, with whitewashed houses tumbling down the hill like a handful of white dice. The 40min. **walk** there from Livadi begins at a stone staircase next to the Marinos market—follow the way. The footsore can catch the hourly **bus** from Livadi. The first stop on this route deposits you at Hora's **post office** (☎51 239; open M-F 8am-noon), while the second drops you in front of a well-stocked **supermarket** and a few tavernas. From here you can climb up a series of steps to the small **chapel** that crowns the town. The crumbling remains of the old **Castro** invite you to poke around them; follow the signs painted along the steps up. Rich yellow earth terraces, the green oasis of the port, and the blue Aegean spread out below. Getting lost in Hora's maze of stony, twisty streets is even better than knowing your way around—you'll discover quiet tavernas and markets along the circuitous alleyways. Domatia are available for around 12,000dr for a double; other tourist commodities are mercifully absent.

### NORTHERN SERIFOS

*Serifos's interior isn't very accessible without a car or moped, a map, and excellent driving skills. To rent wheels, call* ***Blue Bird,*** *just past Metalio Club. (☎51 511. Mopeds 4000-7000dr per day, cars 12,000-25,000dr.)*

Traditional villages, scattered churches and monasteries, and traces of ruins mark the northern part of the island. With transportation, you can visit the **Monastery of the Taxiarchs,** 10km beyond Hora toward the village of Galani. Built in AD 1400 on a site where a Cypriot icon mysteriously appeared (and to which it returns whenever removed), the monastery also houses an Egyptian lantern and several Russian relics. If you arrive close to sunset, you may meet the lone monk who has lived there for 20 years, and who might treat you to coffee and cherries. Arrange a visit in advance by calling ahead (☎51 027). By foot, the trip takes two hours. Since the monastery and town around the port have no facilities, bring all you need if you choose to hike.

# KYTHNOS ΚΥΘΝΟΣ

Everyone—from ritzy hot springs bathers to families with kids in tow—can find a niche in Kythnos. While the now crumbling Hotel Posidonon probably contained more rooms than there are tourists on the island, those who do choose to visit can delight in quiet beaches and simple small-town life.

## MERIHAS Μεριχας ☎0281

The main port, Merihas harbors most of the island's tourists in addition to its ferries. Making it your base of operations will help you explore the rest of Kythnos.

CYCLADES

### ORIENTATION AND PRACTICAL INFORMATION

The port town is littered with rooms to let, a few tavernas and businesses, and several waterfront **supermarkets. Ferries** sail to: Kimolos (1-2 per day, 2400dr); Milos (1 per day, 2600dr); Piraeus (1-2 per day, 3150dr); Serifos (1-2 per day, 1800dr); and Sifnos (1 per day, 2000dr). They run once per week to Santorini (3800dr) and Sikinos (3200dr) and twice per week to Folegandros (2900dr). **Hydrofoils** jet to Piraeus (1 per day, 6050dr). **Express Giorgios** goes to Kea (3 per week, 1500dr). Flying Dolphins go twice a week to Milos, Mykonos, Naxos, Paros, Serifos, Sifnos, Syros, and Tinos. **Buses** stop at the waterfront and go to Loutra, Driopis, and Kythnos Town (a.k.a. Hora), for 250-400dr. There are no posted bus schedules, so ask the driver about stops and fares. If you need a **taxi** or **bus,** search the streets to find one parked, or call 31 272 or 31 280.

The **tourist office** (☎32 250) by the dock dispenses general information, maps, and boat schedules, but is open erratically. Past the dock heading into town, up a flight of stairs on the left, is the helpful **Milos Express** travel agency, with room information and ferry tickets. (☎32 104; fax 32 291. Open 9am-2pm, 5pm-10pm.) Call the **tourist police** at 31 201; the **port police** (☎32 290) can help with ferry info. Farther along the waterfront, you'll find a representative of the **National Bank** who will **exchange currency.** The **pharmacy** is two doors left of Milos Express. There is no **OTE** or **post office** in Merihas. **Postal code:** 84006.

**ACCOMMODATIONS AND FOOD.** The abandoned hulk of **Hotel Posidonon** leers over the small and pebbly town beach; the few living accommodations populate the surrounding area. Walking with the sea on your right, turn left just before the children's playground to find a series of domatia including **Panayota Rooms To Let.** The roomy, clean rooms are equipped with 2-3 beds, kitchen, bath, fridge. (☎32 268. 8000-12,000dr.)

Multiple **supermarkets** line the waterfront with huge displays of fresh fruit. **Sailors Restaurant,** on the waterfront, hails you with flags a-waving; take your pick of its amazing selection of fresh fish—they're still flopping. Lobster spaghetti (3500dr), mixed fish (3000dr), and yummy fried Kythnos goat cheese (1000dr) are specials. After dinner, bring the crew to the **Byzantio Club** for a dish of ice cream with homemade fudge and whipped cream that will make you salivate for years afterwards (1600dr). (☎32 259. Open 9am-late.) Alternatively, trek uphill to **Akrotiri,** the only disco in town, which overlooks the tip of the island.

# KEA ΚΕΑ

The closest Cycladic island to mainland Greece, Kea (or **Tzia**) is colonized by an influx of Athenians, motoring through its dry, rocky landscape. Several underground water sources feed the island interior's sporadic cheery green olive trees, almond groves, and clumps of oaks. Visitors tend to go their own way,

and natives of this quiet island are more private and less ebulliently friendly than the Greek islander stereotype. Kea's gems are far-flung, the terrain is impressively forbidding, and bus service is notoriously unreliable; you'll need your own wheels.

## KORISIA Κορησια ☎0288

The traffic-clogged port town of Korisia resembles the gridlock of Piraeus more than a peaceful island port. **Myrina** travel office (☎21 313) sells ferry tickets, including those to **Lavrio** (5 per day, 1400dr), where you can catch a bus to **Athens** (2hr., 950dr). Across from the dock is the Flying Dolphin office, where Stefanos **exchanges currency,** provides info about the island (maps 1000dr), and sells tickets for speedy catamarans to **Piraeus** (5 per week, 4800dr). There are two banks on the harbor, the cream-colored **Piraeus Bank** (☎22 712), behind the beach with a 24hr. **ATM,** and **Alpha Bank** (☎22 702), just up the road to Hora. The **tourist police** can be reached at 22 100. You can rent a motorbike (4500-5000dr per day) at **Moto Center,** past Alpha Bank. (☎21 884. Open M-F 8:30am-2:30pm and 5:15-8:30pm, and Sa-Su 8:30am-9pm.) **Postal code:** 84002.

To stay at the port, try **Hotel Tzia Mas,** which has doubles with baths, terraces, and common fridges, on the beach. (☎21 305. 15,000dr. Breakfast 2000dr.) **Hotel Korisia,** right off the road running along the beach, rents nice new doubles. (☎21 484 or 21 355. 10,000-18,000dr.) Nearby rooms to let at **Athina** are large and clean. (☎21 467. 12.000dr.) Stuff your gullet at friendly **Tis Popis** (☎21 244), next to Piraeus Bank, where world traveler Popi will charm you with her delicious sweet and savory crepes. (1200-1400dr).

## IOULIDA Ιουλιδα ☎0288

Kea's capital will ease your nerves after the madness of Korisia. Its hillside mix of whitewashed buildings, meandering walkways, and Neoclassical architecture bathe you in tranquility. The **bus** from Korisia stops on a plateau just above the main road where there is a **National Bank** (open M-Th 8am-2pm, F 8:30am-1:30pm). Signs point to the **post office** through the archway and to the right. (☎22 325. Open M-F 8am-2pm.)

Head directly under the archway to find **Clue,** a bright lemon-drop of a cafe-sweetshop with a panorama of refreshments to cool you in the heat of day (milkshakes 1000dr; fresh juices 800dr; yogurt, honey, and nuts 600dr). Athenian kids cut loose in the after-midnight **nightlife** on the weekends, which centers around a few bars up the walkway, past the post office. **Léon** (☎(0932) 104 051) is the first and best of them, with outdoor tables an indoor dance floor. The crowds bounce to danceable technopop. **Mylos,** just next door, is a two-level indoor bar and restaurant with s a vine-covered terrace, live Greek music downstairs, and a more mellow, jazzy bar scene upstairs. At the end of the main street, heading out of town and overlooking the cemetery, is **Bar Kamini,** which blasts the latest Greek hits.

Ioulida's sights include the **Archaeological Museum** on the main walkway (open Tu-Su 8:30am-3pm; free), and the half-smiling **Lion of Kea,** a 6th century BC granite sculpture 15min. along the main path.

## AROUND KEA ☎0288

The beach road north of Korisia leads to the smaller, ritzier port of **Vourkari,** where the yachting set tie up their boats. A few pricey tavernas and shops line the waterfront. If you continue along the road, it leads to a dirt path to the 18th century monastery of **Panagias Kastrianis,** with its fantastic vistas of the north side of the island. If **beaches** float your boat, continue past Ioulida into the small, green, olive grove valley of **Pisses.** The island's campground, **Camping Kea,** is right there, with its shop, bar, and restaurant just behind a long stretch of sandy beach. You can get there by taxi or bus, as there is no port pickup. (☎31 302.

1400dr per person; 400dr per tent rental.) There are also several tavernas and mini-markets on the beach and up the main road back to Ioulida; 15min. up from the beach, you'll find **Galini Apartments,** which offers furnished doubles with beds, kitchens, baths, and terraces. (☎31 316. 15,000dr.) Continue past Pisses to reach the long dirt road behind the myriad small **coves of Koudouras,** dotted by the rare bright beach umbrella.

# DODECANESE
# ΔΩΔΕΚΑΝΗΣΑ

The Dodecanese are lean wolves and hunt in packs; waterless, eroded by the sun. They branch off every side as you coast along the shores of Anatolia. Then toward afternoon the shaggy green of Cos comes up; and then slithering out of the wintry blue the moist green flanks of Rhodes.

—Lawrence Durrell

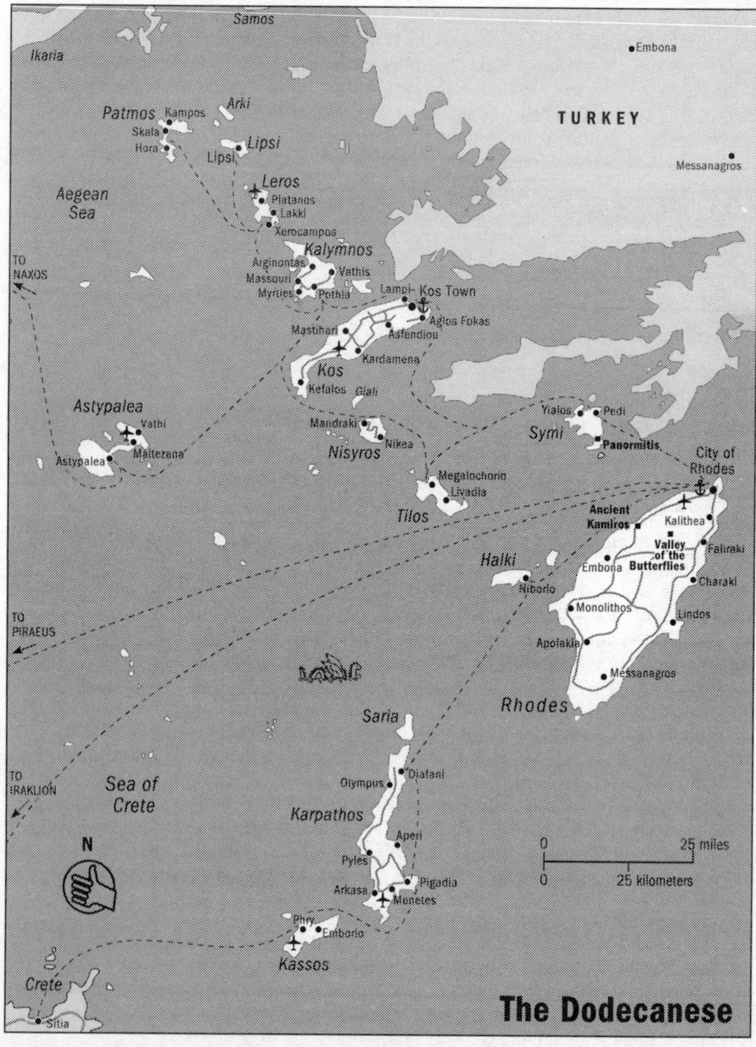

Thrown against the coast of Turkey, the Dodecanese, or Twelve Islands, are the farthest Greek island group from the mainland. Closer to Asia Minor than to Athens, these islands have experienced both more independence and more invasions than more central parts of Greece. In ancient times, the Dodecanese flourished before falling to Alexander the Great's Hellenistic empire. A favorite target of evangelizing biblical luminaries like St. Paul and St. John, inhabitants numbered among the first Greek Christians. Though they prospered in the early Byzantine years, the islands suffered from raids that later hurt the entire empire. Crusaders crashed in during the 14th century, building heavily fortified castles as bases for their religious wars. The Ottomans ousted them in 1522, and the lucky Dodecanese received special concessions for their proximity to Turkey. An Italian occupation rolled over the islands from 1912-1943. During the Second World War, Dodecanesian soldiers fought fiercely; they joined the Greek nation as citizens in 1948.

Eclectic architecture is the legacy of all these comings and goings: Classical ruins, Crusader castles, Ottoman mosques, and Mussolini-style public buildings all coexist. Ferry routes cut the Dodecanese off from the Cyclades, hurting tourism and making the islands less accessible; travelers who deal with the hassle and venture here will find landscapes that range from Rhodes's fertility to the pumice-crusted volcanic landscape of Nisyros. Kos's hopping nightlife, Rhodes's medieval city, the apocalyptic beauty of Patmos, the secluded beaches of northern Karpathos, and the hidden glory of Kalymnos leave picky visitors a slew of options. Nudging the Turkish coast, the Dodecanese also make an ideal transition point from Greece to Turkey (see **Turkish Daytrips,** p. 549).



**HIGHLIGHTS OF THE DODECANESE**

**THINK REVELATION** when visiting Patmos (p. 458), former home to vision-endowed gospel writer St. John, who inhabited this holy isle.

**SNIFF THE SULFUR** of the smoking, inactive Mandraki volcano on Nisyros (p. 441).

**REGENERATE** with a bathtime scrubdown on sponge capital Kalymnos (p. 452).

**STRAIN YOUR EARS** at the sublime whisper of millions of bright beating wings at the Rhodes's Valley of Butterflies (p. 438).

**SQUEEZE** into your tightest pants, then try to get into somebody else's on Kos (p. 443).

# KARPATHOS ΚΑΡΠΑΘΟΣ

Midway between Rhodes and Crete, windy Karpathos often receives no more than a passing glance from the deck of an overnight ferry. Those who disembark, however, enjoy a Karpathian hospitality that personifies Greece's famed welcoming spirit. Karpathos wasn't always so inviting—fighting first alongside the Spartans in the Peloponnesian War, then later falling to Rhodes in 400 BC. In 42 BC, Romans began a series of occupations, involving all the usual suspects: the Arabs, the Genovese pirate Moresco, the Venetians, and the Ottomans. Ottoman rule ended when Italians conquered the island during the First World War, later passing into German hands for a few years following the end of the Second World War. Despite its rowdy past, Karpathos has changed most markedly in the last fifty years. After a war-ravaged economy sent many a Karpathian to the eastern seaboard of the US, their prodigal Greek-American sons and daughters have returned to the island and invested heavily. As a result, Pigadia and the south, have suddenly modernized. The mountainous north remains a world unto itself, steadfastly preserving its traditions. Gorgeous beaches stretch to the southeast part of the island.

## PIGADIA Πηγαδια ☎0245

Pigadia, literally "the wells," was formerly called Possi, for "Poseidon Polis," but drew objections because the name also meant "drinking about." While this port town (also known as **Karpathos Town**) lacks the natural beauty offered by much of the island, it is the best base for accessing those resources.

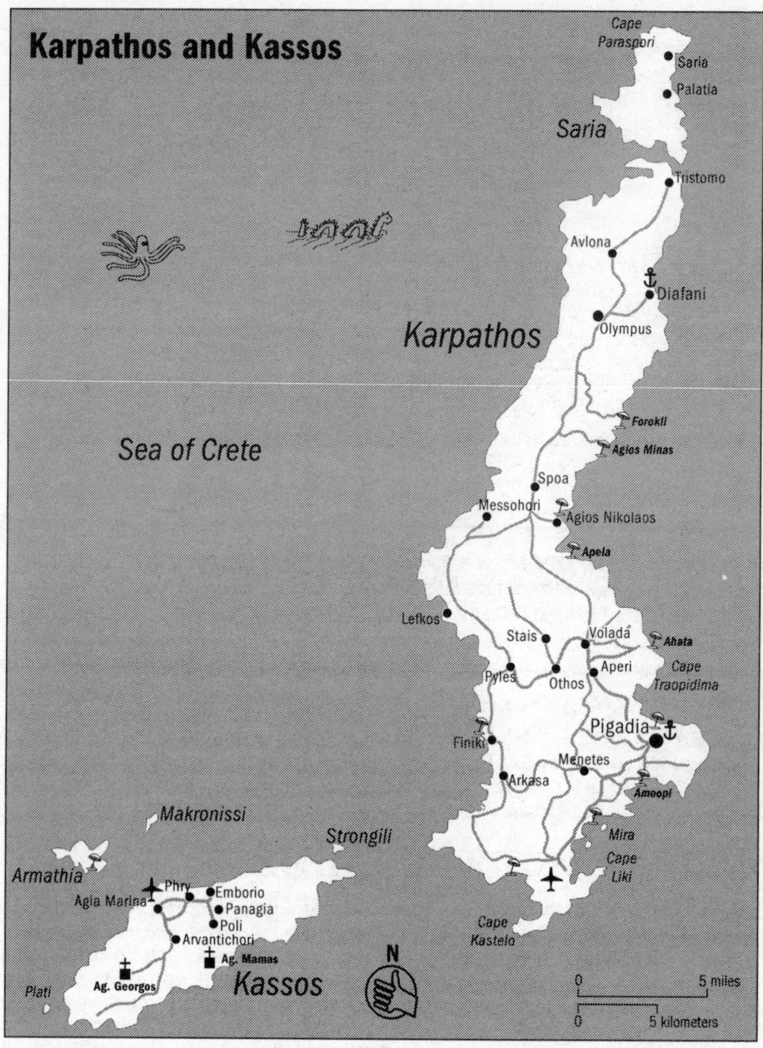




## GETTING THERE AND GETTING AROUND

Schedules for ferries can be obtained from Kassos Travel or Possi Holidays. Bus tickets are sold on board and no buses run on Sundays or local holidays.

**Ferries:** Ferries go to: **Iraklion** (6hr., 2 per week, 3500dr); **Kassos** (1½hr., 3 per week, 1480dr); **Paros** (17hr., 2 per week, 5025dr); **Piraeus** (21hr., 3 per week, 7800dr); **Rhodes** (5hr., 2 per week, 4175dr); and **Santorini** (12hr., 2 per week, 4860dr). For other Dodecanese islands, Rhodes is the connection hub. **Chrisovalandu Lines** and **Karpathos 1** run daily excursions to **Olympus** (leaves 8:30am, returns 6pm; 5000dr). Find them near the ferry docks or book reservations at **Karpathos** or **Possi Travel.**

**Buses:** One block up Dimokratias from the town center. Serving most southern villages (300-1000dr); check the schedule at the bus stop, Karpathos Travel, or with Manolis (☎22 192). Buses run from Karpathos town to **Aperi, Volada, Othos** and **Piles** (3 per

day). To **Menetes, Arkasa,** and **Finiki** (2 times per day). To **Amoopi** (2 per day) and to **Spoa Village** (once per day).

**Taxis:** (☎22 705). Taxis run 24hr. (2000dr to nearby villages). Government regulated taxi prices are posted at the station on Dimokratias.

**Rentals:** Facing inland from the bus station, walk right 2 blocks to find **Moto Carpathos** (☎22 382). Friendly and fair service. Mopeds from 3500-6500dr per day. Insurance is extra. Open 8am-3pm and 5-9:30pm. **Circle Rent A Car** (☎22 690), one block past Moto Carpathos. Cars 10,000dr per day.

## ORIENTATION AND PRACTICAL INFORMATION

Karpathos Town has three main ways running parallel to one another. The first runs along the water and is lined with tavernas. The second extends one block up and inland from the dock. The third contains the police and guest houses. The bus station is on Dimokratias, which connects the second and third main streets. If you need a map, you'll find the best ones at **Karpathos Travel** or **Possi Travel.**



**Tourist Agencies: Karpathos Travel,** Dimokratias 9 (☎22 148, 22 386; fax 22 754) between the bus station and waterfront, offers bus and boat schedules, arranges rooms, **rents cars** (43,400dr for 3 days), **exchanges currency,** and sells tickets for excursions to Lefkos, Diafani, and Olympus. Open M-Sa 8:30am-1pm and 5:30-9pm, Su 9-11am and 6-8pm. **Possi Travel** (☎22 235, 22 627; fax 22 252), nearby on Karpathion, sells **maps** (350dr) and books daily **excursions** (from 4000dr.). Open M-Sa 8:30am-1pm and 5:30-8:30pm, Su 10am-noon and 6pm-8pm. Branches also exist in **Amoopi** (☎81 150) and **Lefkos** (☎71 442).

**Banks: National Bank** (☎22 409), opposite Possi Travel, has **currency exchange** and an **ATM** that accepts Visa and MC. Open M-Th 8am-2pm, F 8am-1:30pm.

**Police:** (☎22 222). At the corner of Eth. Antistassis, next to the post office. Open 24hr.

**Port Police:** (☎22 227), next to the ferry dock. Open 24hr.

**Medical Assistance:** The **Health Center** (☎22 239) is a large white building 100m past Pl. 5 Octovriou on N.K. Matheou. In an **emergency** after 2pm, go directly there and ring the bell. No English spoken. Open 8am-1:30pm and 5-9:30pm.

**Hospital:** (☎22 228).

**Telephones: OTE,** uphill past the post office. Open M-F 7:30am-3pm.

**Post Office:** (☎22 219). Take the uphill road right of the bus station and follow the signs leading directly across from the police station. Open M-F 7:30am-2pm, Sa 7:30am-1pm. **Postal code:** 85700.

## ACCOMMODATIONS

Illegal freelance camping is usually tolerated on the town beach to the north.

**Elias Rooms for Rent** (☎22 446). From the bus station, walk up the stairs past the supermarket. Rooms are quiet but centrally located, and the high-hearted Elias knows lots about the island, especially ways to save money. Ask about the traditional room with a lofted bed. Singles 4000dr, with bath 5000dr; doubles 5000dr/6000dr.

**Hotel Avra** (☎22 388; fax 23 486). Facing inland at the bus station, turn right: Avra is a few doors down on the right-hand side. Don't be shy to ask the friendly owners for anything you might need (like breakfast). Kitchen and laundry facilities available. Singles 3000dr, with bath 4000dr; doubles 6000dr/8000dr.

**Harry's Rooms to Rent** (☎22 188). Facing inland at the bus station, turn right and take the first left. Very clean, astoundingly cheap, modern rooms with balcony and shared bath. Singles 2500dr; doubles 5000dr; triples 5500dr.

### FOOD AND ENTERTAINMENT

While you can always snack on savory pies (300-500dr) and pastries (400-600dr) from the ubiquitous sweet shops, the best dinner options lie inland along the paved **waterfront** road toward the beach. The fairly touristy cafes are popular in the evening. More club-like nightlife may be out of walking distance.

**Kali Karthia,** just past the school on the water at the north end of town. Fresh, cheap fish 7500dr per kg. Try *swpia* (1500dr), the chef's favorite. Open 7am-2pm and 7pm-1am.

**Ideal,** between National Bank and the church. One of the few waterfront tavernas with tasty, cheaper options. Plate of dips 500dr, pita gyros 300-400dr.

**Edem Music Cafe-Bar** (☎23 681), uphill from the post office. Completely packed by 10:30pm, Edem is the latest hotspot where your favorite hits provide the background for matchmaking potential. 1500dr cover includes first drink.

**Fillagri** (☎23 373). Follow the carefully painted and placed concrete blocks straight out of town. With four bars–three indoors and one outdoors–in an abandoned olive oil mill, the club handles over 1600 thirsty customers each weekend. Doors open at 11pm and don't close until the sun rises. Try the second floor **Gamma-3** for a more relaxed atmosphere fed by Greek and foreign tunes.

## OLYMPUS ☎0245

Words cannot convey the isolation and insularity of Olympus, where the living, centuries-old customs keep ethnologists and linguists in a tizzy. Eighty families seeking to escape attacking pirates founded the village 1750m above the sea, atop Mt. Profitis Ilias, in the 11th century; each family built one windmill, one house, and one church. Olympus supported itself by shipping its men off to do migrant work; because women took control of the household while their husbands were away, property is inherited matrilineally. Plaster-sculpted nymphs, angels, eagles, and Venetian lions adorn house exteriors, while the interiors are filled with hand-embroidered linens and ceramic plates. Tourist interest has led Olympians to preserve and, in some cases, rekindle craft traditions: cobbler Nikolaos Kanakis still hand-crafts the leather boots that were once Olympus's standard footwear, but at 65,000dr per pair, these boots aren't made for walking.

**ORIENTATION AND PRACTICAL INFORMATION.** To travel between Olympus and **Diafani,** take a **taxi** or the small **bus** that leaves Diafani (when the boat from Karpathos Town arrives; bus fare is included in the excursion ticket) and Olympus daily. A dusty **hike** along the valley floor is another alternative if you have the time, energy, and drinking water—it's a long, hot, uphill trip. **Minas,** at the village Mayor's office, is a great resource on what the area has to offer. His perfect English and fascination with the Internet and his hometown will yield much information for those desiring to know more about Olympus or Karpathos in general.

**ACCOMMODATIONS AND FOOD.** The best accommodations in Olympus are near the windmills at **Hotel Aphrodite,** where big rooms offer breathtaking views. (☎51 307 or 51 454. Doubles 7000dr.) Call ahead for reservations. Ask Nikos at the related **Parthenonos Taverna** to play the town's best lyre renditions. The best food in town is served at the **Milos Tavern,** in the windmill above the museum. Wait for the tour groups to leave, then enjoy watching the stuffed pitas bake in a wood-burning oven (350dr), or gaze dreamily from the balcony. The pasta-like *makarounes,* a village specialty, are served with cheese and sprinkled with onion (900dr). **Pension Olymbos,** around to the left of the bus stop near the start of the village, rents rooms with beautiful hand-carved beds, private baths, and placid balconies. (☎51 252. Singles 3000dr; doubles 3500dr, with bath 5000dr.) They also serve home-cooked food in the adjacent **taverna;** *pastitsio* and *moussaka* go for 1200dr a piece and are worth every *drachma.* Farther uphill, **Hotel Astro** has rooms and shared baths. (☎51 378. Singles 3000dr; doubles 5000dr; triples 7500dr.)

**SIGHTS.** Olympus itself constitutes the main sight of the region. If you just want more, check out the two working **windmills** overlooking the western cliffs; there, Olympian women grind the flour which they later bake in huge stone ovens, smoldering under the hillside. While you're there, brave the tiny ladder inside the windmill and watch it whirl from behind the scenes. If you're willing to bound over stone walls, visit the small collection of the three oldest chapels on Karpathos, **Agia Triada,** easily visible from the town above—look down to the right of the bus stop for earthy red arched roofs. Inside, 13th- or 14th-century **frescoes** geometrically represent birds and fish. Just past Parthenos Taverna, near the windmill, is the lavishly decorated **Kimisi tis Theotokou,** the largest church in the village. Gold foil blankets its altar, and breathtaking, handpainted biblical scenes adorn the walls. If the priest isn't around, ask at the restaurant for a key. Nightly *glendis* in the plateia by Kimisi lure villagers and foreigners with lyres and a *tsamiko*.

# SOUTHERN KARPATHOS

West of Pigadia, winding roads climb toward charming villages and cloud-covered mountains before descending into the beach-laden west coast.



## APERI

The southern city of Aperi was the island's capital in medieval times, when Arab raids forced Karpathians to abandon their coastal homes in 1892. Although it has surrendered this official status, it remains at the heart of Karpathos. The church here holds a **Panagia** (Virgin Mary) icon revered throughout Karpathos. Legend has it that the icon was discovered when a monk was chopping wood; blood began spurting from one of the logs, tipping the monk off to the fact that this was no ordinary bit of tree. Each time the icon was moved, it would disappear—only to reappear in an old church in Aperi. Building a bishop's church on the spot in 1886, the monk gave it a permanent home. (Open 8-11am.) West of Aperi, a walk through the last of Kato Horia's villages in **Pyles,** with its enchanting narrow alleyways, leads to olive groves and charming tavernas where you can find the town's famous honey.

Two kilometers west of Pyles, the road hits Karpathos's stunning west coast. From Pigadia, a number of coastal towns are accessible by bus. The windswept remains of five parallel Cyclopean walls mark the town of **Arkasa,** whose acropolis is perched on the hill of Paleokastro. The notable mosaic floors of **Agia Sophia** give quite a reason to visit this part of the island. **Alpha Hotel,** at the north end, is one of the few hotels to accommodate independent travelers. (☎61 352. Singles 4000dr; doubles 5000dr.) South of Arkasa, campers find shelter in a small beach cove near the sandy shore of **Agios Nikolaos.**

North of Arkasa, the miniature fishing port of **Finiki** today consists mostly of tourist amusements. **Dimitrios Fisherman's Taverna** (☎61 294 or 61 365) has earned local renown for its excellent preparation of Dimitrios' daily catch. The taverna also offers some of the town's very few rooms (doubles 6000dr). Continuing north along the coast, you'll come to the small beach town of **Lefkos,** where those willing to trade sandy beaches for a rocky cove will have a gorgeous stretch of coast to call their own. Inland, forested hiking terrain is shared only with the goats.

For the island's best beaches, take the unmarked dirt roads off the Pigadia-Airport mainway (use good walking shoes or private transportation). Those seeking a full body tan will adore the little stretch of sand named the **River of Birds.** Take the first dirt road headed to beautiful but sometimes crowded **Amoopi** beach and take a left as the road begins to hug the coast. Deep green-blue waves reaching for the shores across from Mira Isle can be reached by taking the first left before the built-up area preceding the airport. Long coves of sandy shores line the bay between Cape Kastelo and **Cape Akrotiri.** Follow the dirt road from the airport toward Arkasa and stops along the way will not disappoint.

# KASSOS ΚΑΣΣΟΣ

The spare, rocky landscape of Kassos is billed as "tranquil," but outside the small August influx, "comatose" may be a better word. Kassos is a world apart from its crazier Dodecanese siblings. Peace and quiet are its main attractions, along with a few remote beaches, intriguing caves, and humble archaeological sites. The best way to orient yourself is to note the island's layout as you approach it from the sea. One kilometer east of the port town of Phry, the even smaller town of Emporio has a very small, uninviting beach and three small tavernas. Clusters of homes dot the arid hillside above Phry and Emporio: moving clockwise, these are the villages of Poli, Panagia, Arvantichori, and Agia Marina. On the other side of the hill (not visible from the ferry), the villages of Kathistres and Chroussoulas lead the way to the island's caves. You can walk the entire loop in an hour.

## PHRY Φρυ

☎0245

Although the small port town of Phry isn't much to look at, it's the biggest and best that Karpathos has to offer.



**ORIENTATION AND PRACTICAL INFORMATION.** Transportation on and off the island is difficult; if you aren't flexible now, you'll learn how the hard way. **Ferries** run to: **Agios Nikolaos,** Crete (5hr., 3 per week, 4500dr); **Karpathos** (1½hr., 3 per week, 1800dr); **Piraeus** (17hr., 2 per week, 7829dr); **Rhodes** (6½hr., 3 per week, 5300dr); and **Sitia,** Crete (2½hr., 2511dr). **Flights** run to and from **Karpathos** (3 per week, 3500dr) and **Rhodes** (5 per week, 13,400dr). With island bus service cancelled, **taxis** are the most common way to get around. (☎41 183 or 41 278. 1000dr between villages.) **Moto Kasso,** on the main street in Phry, rents motorbikes. (☎41 746. Mopeds 3500dr per day.) All of Kassos' tourist services are in Phry. **Kassos Maritime and Tourist Agency,** right behind the church in Pl. Iroön Kasou, provides maps, friendly advice, and timetables. **Internet access** is available for those who really need it. (☎41 323 or 41 495. Open M-Sa 8am-2pm and 5-9:30pm, Su 7:30am-3pm.) The **Olympic Airways** office is right next door. (☎41 555. Open M-F 8am-4pm.) The **police station** is on the airport road. (☎41 422. Open 24hr.) The **port police** is on the road to Emporio. (☎41 288. Open 24hr.) A **National Bank** branch offers **currency exchange** in the supermarket next to the Anesis Hotel. (☎41 234. Open M-F 9am-noon.) The **hospital** is on Kriti, past the bus stop (☎41 333. Open M-F 8am-3pm.) The **OTE** is a few blocks inland (open M-F 8am-2pm). The **post office** is off Pl. Iroön Kasou (open M-F 7:30am-2pm). **Postal code:** 85800.

**ACCOMMODATIONS AND FOOD.** Kassos' two C-class hotels generally have plenty of rooms, except in August, when you should call ahead. **Anagenesis,** in Pl. Iroön Kasou next to the travel agency, has rooms with sea-view balconies and kind management; inquire at the travel agency. (☎41 495 or 41 323. Singles 5000dr, with bath 7000dr; doubles 7000dr/9500dr.) **Anesis,** on the main street, offers simple rooms with balconies and a taciturn owner; inquire at the supermarket below. (☎41 201. Singles 4000dr; doubles 5000dr.) **Rooms to let,** advertised by signs along the main road toward Emporio and the villages, charge 3500-6000dr for basic rooms. **Milos Taverna** in the plateia is another option. Smaller *kafeneia* fill the walk-paths right inside town. Both restaurants set up front-row seats for the island's big daily event: the arrival of boats at the port.

**SIGHTS AND THE OUTDOORS.** Leisurely excursions to the residential villages above Phry give a taste of island agricultural life. Maneuver through roadside sheep herds to reach **Panagia** and the showy homes left behind by Kassiot sea-captains. Athenians and former Kassiots who summer here are gradually refurbishing these once-impressive edifices. Panagia's annual August 15 **festival** is celebrated here. Ten minutes past the village of Kathistres, the entrance to the very

small cave of **Ellinokamara** is partially sealed by a Hellenic wall. Inside, inveterate spelunkers can clamber over slimy stones. Trek down the 1½km footpath beyond Ellinokamara where the cave of **Selai** bristles with stalactites and stalagmites.

From **Poli,** the 40-minute **hike** to **Agios Mamas Monastery** (6km from Phry) brings you to scenic overlooks of the southeast coast. The boulders you see from the monastery are reputed to be the hulls of three ships, turned to stone by vengeful monks. The one-time monastery of **Agios Georgios at Hadies** also merits a visit, not only for the magnificent views, but also for the gorgeous **Helatros beach** below.

# RHODES ΡΟΔΟΣ

**RHODES CODES**

**0241** for the northern half of the island;
**0244** for all locations south of Kolymbia on the east;
**0246** for all locations south of Kalavarda on the west.



Though Rhodes is the undisputed tourist capital of the Dodecanese, its sheer size shelters the centuries-old customs, natural resources, and serene escapes of the interior and smaller coastal towns. Sandy beaches stretch along the east coast, jagged cliffs skirt the west, and green mountains freckled with villages fill the interior; resort towns dominate the north. Kamiros, Ialyssos, and Lindos show the clearest evidence of the island's classical past, while medieval fortresses slumber in the City of Rhodes and in Monolithos.

## CITY OF RHODES ☎0241

The winding streets of the City of Rhodes blend medieval and Hellenistic architecture in stone and pebbles. The City of Rhodes was born in 408 BC when three city-states combined. It's been the island's capital for 20 centuries. Rhodes's twisty layout and charming harbor have made it one of the most beautiful cities of the ancient world, and it remains regal today. Remnants of the 14th-century occupation by the Knights of St. John—a surreal palace and the grand fortress surrounding the Old Town—still lend the city a note of strangeness.

### GETTING THERE AND GETTING AWAY

Schedules for ferries, Dolphins, and buses are at the EOT. Summer moped rental places are common throughout town. The bumpy cobblestone Old Town roads are dangerous on a moped, especially since locals drive superfast. Be careful.

**Ferries:** Service to: **Alexandroupolis** (1 per week, 11,600dr) via **Hios** (7000dr), **Lesvos** (7600dr), and **Limnos** (9400dr); **Agios Nikolaos,** Crete (1 per week, 6200dr); **Amorgos** (1 per week, 4600dr); **Astypalea** (2 per week, 5000dr); **Haifa,** Israel (36hr., 1 per week, 33,500dr); **Halki** (1 per week, 1900dr); **Iraklion,** Crete (1 per week, 6200dr); **Kalymnos** (1-2 per day, 4300dr); **Karpathos** (3 per week, 4400dr); **Kassos** (2 per week, 5300dr); **Kastellorizo** (3 per week, 2000dr); **Kos** (2-3 per day, 4000dr); **Leros** (1 per day, 4700dr); **Limassol,** Cyprus (17hr., 1 per week, 20,500dr); **Milos** (1 per week, 8450dr); **Mykonos** (1 per week, 6800dr); **Paros** (1 per week, 6900dr); **Patmos** (1-2 per day, 5400dr); **Piraeus** (1-4 per day, 9000dr); **Samos** (2 per week, 6500dr); **Santorini** (1 per week, 5100dr); **Sitia,** Crete (1 per week, 5950dr); **Symi** (4 per week, 2000dr); **Thessaloniki** (1 per week, 14,600dr); and **Tilos** (4 per week, 2800dr). Most ferries have student discounts. Daily excursions from Mandraki Port go to: **Kos** (round-trip 14,000dr); **Lindos** (2hr., 1 per day, round-trip 5000dr); and **Symi** and **Panormitis Monastery** (round-trip 4000dr).

**Flying Dolphins:** Hydrofoils head to the northeast Aegean islands, Turkey, and the rest of the Dodecanese. To: **Fourni** (12,400dr); **Halki** (W 2 per day, 3230dr); **Kos** (2 per day,

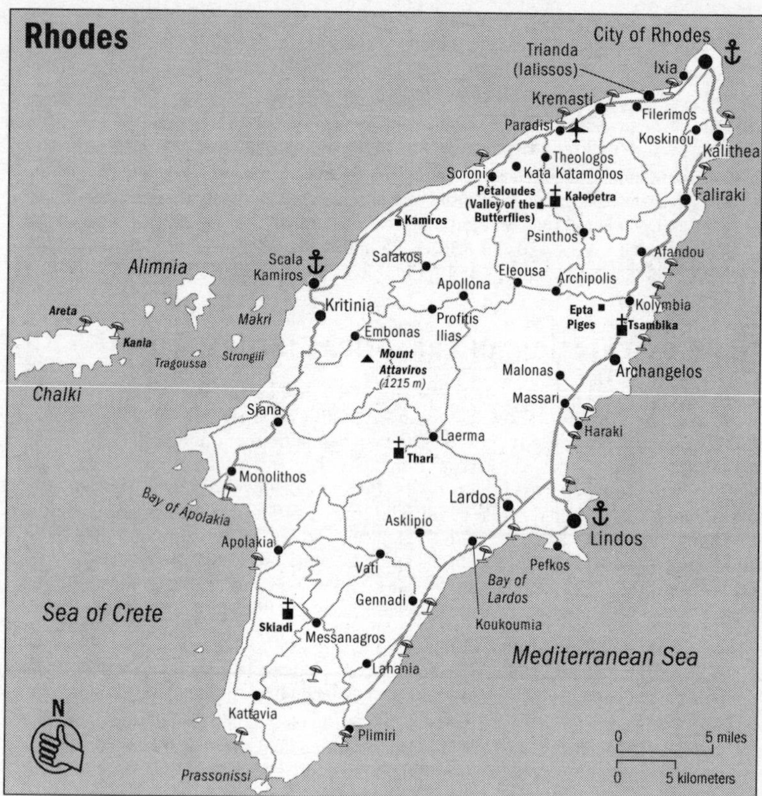




6500dr); **Kalymnos** (W and Sa 2 per day, 8532dr); **Leros** (W 2 per day, 9823dr); **Marmaris** (2 per day, 6750dr plus US$10 in Turkey); **Nisyros** (Su 2 per day, 5400dr); **Patmos** (M-F 2 per day, 10,700dr); **Symi** (F 2 per day, Sa 4 per day; 2900dr); and **Tilos** (Su 2 per day, 5300dr). Call **Nearhos** agency for more further hydrofoil information (☎78 052, 78 053; fax 20 272). The **Katamaran Dodekanissos Express** (☎22 461, 75 655) travels between **Kalymnos, Leros, Kos, Halki, Nisyros, Tilos,** and **Symi** twice daily during the summer from Kolona harbor.

**Buses:** Stations lie on opposite sides of Papagou at Pl. Rimini.

**East** station is served by **KTEL** (☎27 706, 75 134; fax 24 268). Service east to: **Afandou** (16 per day 6:50am-11pm, 450dr); **Archangelos** (14 per day 6:50am-11pm, 600dr); **Faliraki** (20 per day 6:50am-9pm, 450dr); **Gennadi** (6 per day 8:30am-6pm, 1250dr); **Haraki** (10am and 3pm, 750dr); **Kolymbia Beach** (8 per day 8:15am-7:30pm, 600dr); **Laerma** (1pm, 1200dr); **Lardos** (6 per day 8:15am-6pm, 1050dr); **Lindos** (13 per day 8:30am-6pm, 1000dr); **Malona** and **Massari** (5 per day 6:50am-2:30pm, 750dr); **Pefkos** (6 per day 8:15am-6pm, 1100dr); **Pilona** (1 per day, 950dr); **Tsambika Beach** (9am, 650dr); and **Vliha** (9am and 3pm, 1000dr).

**West** station is served by **RODA** (☎26 300). Service west to: **Embana** (3 per day, 1150dr); **Kalavarda** (9 per day 5am-9:20pm, 600dr); **Kalithea** and **Calypso** (34 per day 6:45am-11pm, 450dr); **Kamiros** (1 per day 1:30pm, 1000dr); **Koskinou** (16 per day 6am-9:10pm, 400dr); **Kritinia** (1 per day, 1000dr); **Monolithos** (1 per day, 1400dr); **Paradisi Airport** (27 per day 5am-11:30pm, 450dr); **Petaloudes** (9:30 and 11:10am, 1000dr); **Salakos** (5 per day 6:15am-9:20pm, 800dr); **Soroni** and **Fanes** (9 per day 5am-9:20pm, 500dr); and **Theologos** (13 per day 5am-9:20pm, 420dr).

**Flights: Olympic Airways,** Ierou Lohou 9 (☎24 571, reservations 24 555, airport 83 400 or 83 403), near the central OTE. Open M-F 7:30am-9pm. The **airport** (☎91 771) is on the west coast, 16km from town, near Paradisi, accessible by public bus (5:55am-

11:45pm, 400dr). Flights to: **Athens** (5 per day, 21,500dr); **Iraklion,** Crete (4 per week, 18,500dr); **Karpathos** (4 per day, 9400dr); **Kassos** (1 per day, 10,000dr); **Kastellorizo** (1 per day, 7500dr); **Kos** (3 per week, 11,000dr); **Mykonos** (3 per week, 19,500dr); **Santorini** (3 per week, 19,500dr); and **Thessaloniki** (2 per week, 28,500dr).

**Taxis:** (☎27 666), in Pl. Rimini. Radio taxis also available (☎64 712, 64 734, 64 756, 64 778, or 64 790). Check price list for out-of-town destinations. Open 24hr.

**Rentals: Mandar Moto,** Zephiros 3 (☎34 576, 30 665), in the Old Town. Take Sokratous to Pl. Hippokratous and continue on Aristotelous until Pl. Evraion Martiron. Mopeds 4000-7000dr per day. Open 8am-11pm. **Margartis Motors,** I. Kazouli 23 in the New Town near Agia Maria church. (☎37 420, 39 485) Wide and numerous selection. Scooters 3000-5000dr. Mountain bikes start at 1000dr. Motor bikes 5000-10,000dr per day. Open 8am-8pm daily.

## ORIENTATION AND PRACTICAL INFORMATION

The city is divided into two districts: the **New Town,** stretching to the north and west, and the **Old Town** below it, within the medieval fortress walls. All international and most domestic ferries use the **Commercial Harbor** outside the Old Town. **Mandraki,** the New Town's more traditional Greek island waterfront, docks private yachts, hydrofoils, and excursion boats. Beaches are to the north, beyond Mandraki, and along the city's west coast. The tourist office, both bus stations, and a taxi stand are in **Pl. Rimini,** beneath the fortress's turrets at the junction of the Old and New Towns. To get there from the small fishing and excursion boat-lined Mandraki, head a block inland keeping the park on the New Town side to your left. The New Town is a mecca for nightlife; **Orfanidou** has been popularly dubbed **Bar Street.**



**Greek National Tourist Office (EOT):** (☎23 255/655), up Papagou a few blocks from Pl. Rimini at the intersection of Makariou. Incredibly helpful advice on the essentials for your visit. Free maps, brochures, and accommodation advice. Open M-F 7:30am-3pm.

**Tourist Office:** (☎35 945), in the small yellow building in Pl. Rimini. Bus, ferry, and excursion schedules, some accommodations advice, and **currency exchange.** Far less helpful than the EOT. Open M-Sa 8am-9pm, Su 8am-3pm.

**Budget Travel: Castellania Travel Service** (☎75 860/862; fax 75 861), in Pl. Hippokratous at the intersection of Sokratous and Aristotelous in the Old Town. Low-priced **ISIC** and **GO25 cards** issued (2600dr), international telephones, free **luggage storage.** Open 8:30am-11:30pm; in winter 8am-1pm and 4-8pm.

**Consulates: The Voice of America** (☎24 731), southeast of the city, just past Sigourou street. Handles emergencies. Open M-F 8am-4:30pm. A **British Vice-Consul** is available M-Sa 8am-2pm through **Lloyd's Travel Bureau,** 25 Martiou 23 (☎27 306 or 27 247).

**Banks:** Many banks are in the New Town, few in the Old Town; **ATMs** are widespread throughout both. **Ionian Bank,** Pl. Symi 4 (☎27 434), offers currency exchange. Open M-Th 8am-2pm, F 8am-1:30pm, Sa 8:30am-1pm. The **National Bank** has an office in Pl. Museum with an ATM. Open M-Th 8am-2pm, F 8am-1:30pm. In the New Town, the **National Bank** (☎27 031) in Pl. Kyprou has currency exchange. Open M-Th 8am-2pm, F 8am-1:30pm, Sa 9am-1pm.

**American Express: Rhodos Tours Ltd.,** Ammohostou 23, P.O. Box 252 (☎24 022). Open M-F 9am-1:30pm and 5-8:30pm, Sa 7:30am-3pm.

**Laundry: Happy Wash Express Service Laundry,** has two locations both in the New Town. 38 Alex. Diakou (☎35 693) and Dilberaki 97 (☎21 546). Open 9am-11:30pm daily. 1000dr for wash and dry. **Express Laundry,** 5 Kosti Palama (☎22 514), directly across from the Pl. Rimini bus station, offers full wash and dry for 1000dr. Open daily 8am-11:30pm. The only **Old Town laundromat** is on Platonos 33, near Yiannis taverna (☎76 047). Open 8am-10pm. Wash and dry 1500dr.

**Police:** (☎23 294), on Eth. Dodekanission, 1 block behind the post office. Open 24hr. **Lost and found** open M-F 8am-2pm.

**Tourist Police:** (☎27 423 or 23 329), in the GNTO building, speak English.

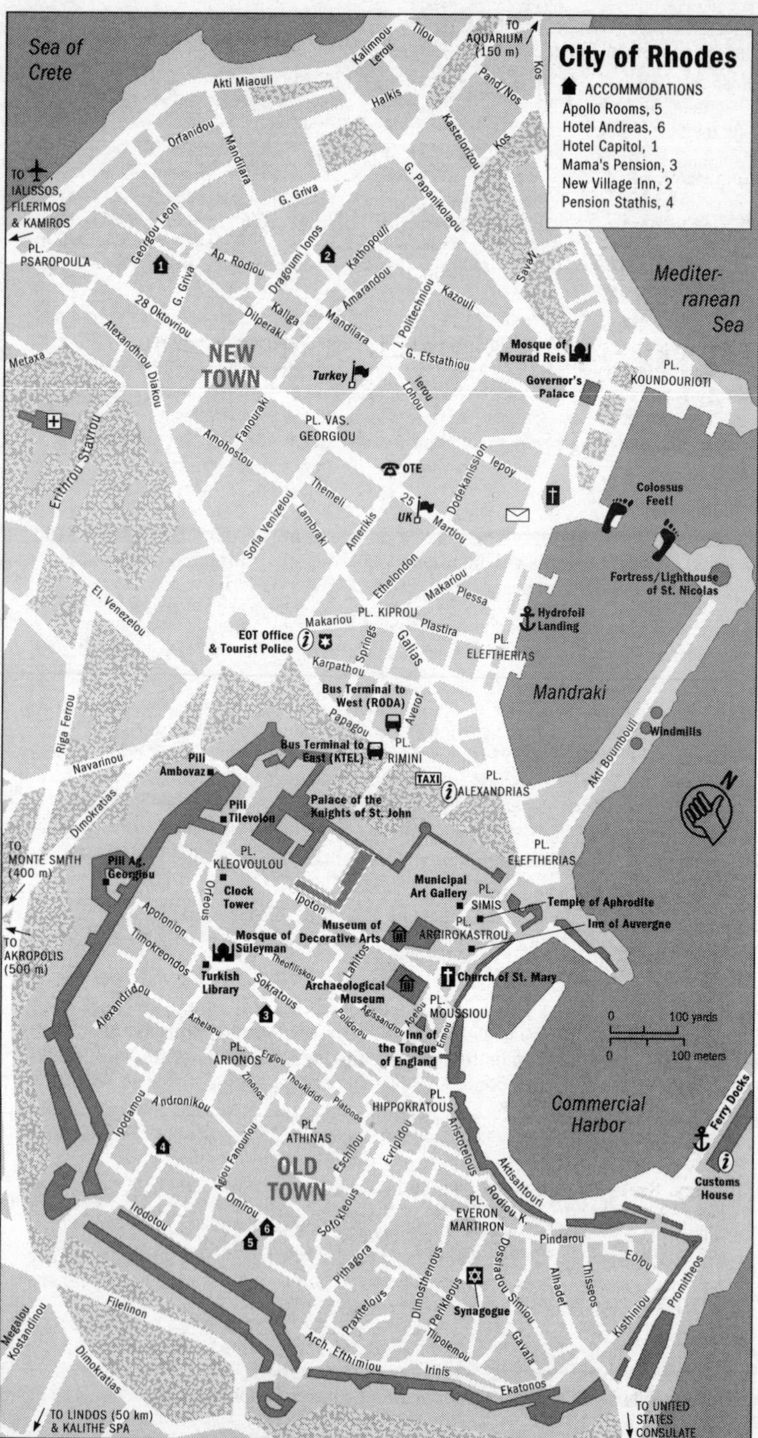
City of Rhodes
ACCOMMODATIONS
Apollo Rooms, 5
Hotel Andreas, 6
Hotel Capitol, 1
Mama's Pension, 3
New Village Inn, 2
Pension Stathis, 4
Sea of Crete
Mediterranean Sea
NEW TOWN
OLD TOWN
Mandraki
Commercial Harbor
TO AQUARIUM (150 m)
TO IALISSOS, FILERIMOS & KAMIROS
TO MONTE SMITH (400 m)
TO AKROPOLIS (500 m)
TO LINDOS (50 km) & KALITHE SPA
TO UNITED STATES CONSULATE
Mosque of Mourad Reis
Governor's Palace
PL. KOUNDOURIOTI
Turkey
PL. VAS. GEORGIOU
OTE
UK
Colossus Feet!
Fortress/Lighthouse of St. Nicolas
Hydrofoil Landing
PL. ELEFTHERIAS
EOT Office & Tourist Police
PL. KIPROU
Bus Terminal to West (RODA)
Bus Terminal to East (KTEL)
PL. RIMINI
TAXI
PL. ALEXANDRIAS
Windmills
Pili Ambovaz
Pili Tilevolon
Palace of the Knights of St. John
PL. KLEOVOULOU
Pili Ag. Georgiou
Clock Tower
Municipal Art Gallery
PL. SIMIS
Temple of Aphrodite
Inn of Auvergne
Museum of Decorative Arts
PL. ARGIROKASTROU
Mosque of Süleyman
Turkish Library
Church of St. Mary
Archaeological Museum
PL. MOUSSIOU
Inn of the Tongue of England
PL. ARIONOS
PL. HIPPOKRATOUS
PL. ATHINAS
PL. EVERON MARTIRON
Synagogue
Ferry Docks
Customs House
0 100 yards
0 100 meters

DODECANESE

**Port Authority:** or Central Harbor Master (☎22 220 or 28 888), is on Mandraki just left of the post office. Complete boat schedules. Open 24hr.

**Hospital:** (☎22 222 or 25 555; general first aid 80 000), on Erithrou Stavrou, off El. Venizelou. Open for emergencies 24hr. **Visitor's clinic** open 5-9pm. Be prepared to wait for medical attention.

**Telephones: OTE,** Amerikis 91 (☎24 599), at the corner of 25 Martiou in the New Town. Open 6am-11pm.

**Internet Access: Minoan Palace,** Ir. Polytechniou 13 (☎20 210), at corner of G. Efstathiou in the New Town. 1000dr per hr., minimum 30min. Open 9:30am-2am. In the Old Town, **Mango Bar,** Pl. Dorisos 3 (☎24 877, 28 324 or 32824) 1200dr per hr. Open 10am-2am.

**Post Office: Main branch** (☎22 212 or 34 873), on Mandraki, along the waterfront and next to the Bank of Greece. Open M-F 7:30am-8pm. **Parcel service** 7:30am-2pm. Also a **mobile branch** in the Old Town on Orfeos, near the Palace of the Grand Masters. From Pl. Museum, head down Ipoton. Open M-F 7:30am-2pm. **Postal code:** 85100.

DODECANESE

## ACCOMMODATIONS

### OLD TOWN

Pensions are scattered about the narrow pebbled paths around Omirou Street in the quiet, charming Old Town, the preferred resting place for most travelers.

**Mama's Pension** Menekleous 28 (☎25 359), off Sokratous, directly above Mike's Taverna. Mike himself will treat you to a cheap room, Greek hospitality, and live musical renditions of familiar songs with a twist late into the night. Dorms 2500dr per bed; doubles 6000dr.

**Pension Stathis,** Omirou 60 (☎24 357). Animated Stathis welcomes all–travelers, tourists, families–to quiet, spacious rooms surrounding a vine-covered courtyard. French, Italian, and English spoken. Nightly folk music from nearby theater. Check-out noon. Laundry 1200dr. Dorms 2500dr; singles 6000dr; doubles 6000-8000dr.

**Apollo Rooms,** Omirou 28C (☎32 003 or 63 398). Great budget accommodation with a courtyard ideal for meeting fellow travelers. Just grab any room if the owners are absent. Simple rooms with shared baths 2500dr. per night.

**Hotel Andreas,** Omirou 28D (☎34 156; fax 74 285). Rooms with bunk beds are ideal for families or groups. Roof terrace offers one of best panoramic views. Laundry, international telephone, Internet access in rooms. Doubles 7000dr, with bath 9000dr; triples with bath 12,000dr; quads with bath 14,000dr.

### NEW TOWN

The New Town is rather charmless—maybe ugly. Expensive hotels line the coast, but affordable pensions can be found along the narrow streets of Rodiou, Dilberaki, Kathopouli, and Amarandou.

**New Village Inn,** Konstantopedos 10 (☎34 937). Owned and well run by a nice couple. Open-air corridors lead to exceptional rooms surrounding tile-covered courtyard. Singles 5000dr; doubles 8000dr.

**Hotel Capitol,** Dilberaki 65-67 (☎62 016 or 74 154). Has quiet, spacious rooms with private baths in an old home with distinct character, once inhabited by Rhodes's mayor. Singles 7000dr; doubles 8000dr; triples 12,000dr; quads 14,000dr.

## FOOD

In the Old Town, the food tends to be mediocre, the waiters aggressive, and the prices high. The New Town cafes are similarly overpriced, but a burgeoning expat community has brought with it a sophisticated international palate.

**Yiannis,** Sokratous-Platonos 41 (☎36 535), just off Sokratous away from the New Town. Exquisite traditional Greek food in huge portions at good prices, not to mention a complementary refreshing post-meal watermelon offering. Try the *stifado, keftedes,* or special *mousaka* for 1100-1800dr. Elliniko plate feeds 3 (2800dr). Open 10am-12am.

**L'Auberge Bistrot,** Praxileous 21 (☎34 292). From the synagogue, walk south on Perikleous; take your 1st right, then 2nd left. The covert location makes this gastronomic gem even more worthwhile. A friendly French couple has created an unforgettable bistro where jazz vibrates through arty decor. Two starters 600-1200dr; entrees 1800-2500dr.

**Niohorio,** I. Kazouli 29 (☎35 116). Local grill house serving the basics (gyros 250dr, souvlaki 1200dr). Carnivores are well advised to stop in (sausages 600dr, meatballs 600dr). Open noon-midnight.

**Da Capo,** G. Leontos 12 (☎76 790, 37 806). Traditional Greek food (1700-2000dr) and an extensive list of pizzas (1600-1800dr) on its inviting patio and balcony. Stands out among the New Town's invariable restaurant options. Open 2pm-midnight.

**Chalki,** Kathopouli 30 (☎33 196). Sensuous aromas of Hellenic delights draw locals and foreigners. Food is fresh but pre-made daily. Entrees 1800dr, salad 900dr. Open noon-3pm, 6pm-midnight daily.

## NIGHTLIFE AND ENTERTAINMENT

### OLD TOWN

Nightlife focuses around Militadou street, off Apellou. The street becomes so crowded that walking is nearly impossible, and trying to get into one of the bars is no easier. The atmosphere is friendly, as all the locals seem to know one another.

**Cafe Havana/Theater Bar,** 9 Militadou (☎0944 314 724, 0932 278 587). One block south of Sokratous—two brilliant answers to the ostensibly difficult question of where to grab a drink in the Old Town are the focus of bar life. Try the *Scorpio* to really tickle your insides (1500dr).

**Club Caprice** (☎35 995), on Militadou, is a medieval looking bar (turned club after midnight), where alcohol-happy locals and tourists groove to the latest hits. 1500dr cover includes one drink; use it to try the *Olympic 2004* specialty (1500dr).

**Mango Bar,** Pl. Dorieos 3 (☎24 877, 28 324 or 36 957). Walk up Ag. Fanouriou from Sokratous street. A pre-game bar with the cheapest draft beer in town (100dr). Surf the web and throw back a few before heading out.

**Hamam,** in Pl. Arionos, provides a unique cleansing; visit the single-sex Turkish bath. (☎27 739. 500dr. Open Tu 1-6pm, W-F 11am-6pm, Sa 8am-6pm.) The **sound and light show,** with entrance from Pl. Rimi, is one of the Old Town's numerous attempts at a cultural offering. (☎36 795. Shows in English start at 8:15pm. 1500dr, students 1000dr.) **St. Francis Church** (☎23 605), at Dimokratias and Filellinon, echoes with sublime organ recitals Wednesday nights at 9pm. Check with the tourist office for performances in the **ancient theater** near Monte Smith. In the winter, the **National Theater** (☎29 678), off the Mandraki next to the town hall, stages occasional productions, and nearby **Rodon** shows new flicks and subtitled classics (1200dr). **Folk Dance Theater,** Andronikou street, stages hokey Greek dances and songs. (☎29 085 or 20 157. M, W, F 9:20pm. 3000dr, students 1500dr.)

### NEW TOWN

The only thing skeezier than New Town cafes are the Romeos of **Bar Street,** their hands slithering indiscriminately around unsuspecting women. Nightlife here is neither shy nor tame. Although popular bars and clubs are scattered throughout the New Town, crowds flock to Orfanidou, unanimously referred to as Bar Street. Popular places have expensive drinks, while empty bars will cut deals. The five-minute walk from end to end will give you a feel for each place's atmosphere.

**Down Under,** Orfanidou 37 (☎32 982). Join loud rock table-top dancers at one of the most popular bars on the strip. Drinks from 1500dr.

**Colorado Pub,** Orfanidou 57 (☎75 120). Three rooms attract crowds by covering all necessary bases and moods. Live bands, a smashing club atmosphere, and an escape to a mellow pub, all in one. Cover 1500dr.

**Scorpio,** Orfanidou 28 (☎22 109). Despite the bar-like appearance, Scorpio's dance floor is the liveliest until the wee hours of morning. Take advantage of their specials like 4 shots of tequila for 1000dr.

**La Scala,** a sprawling complex southwest of town by the beachside Rodos Palace Hotel in Ixia, is the king of Rhodes's nightclubs, accompanied by covers fit for royalty. Strap on your heels and shorten your skirts if you hope to fit in. Watch for special party nights.

**The Blue Lagoon,** 25 Martiou 2 (☎76 072, 32 632). Walk the plank to enter this bizarre, Disneyesque pirate-scape. The extensive investment in design draws chuckles while you sip high-quality drinks. It opens at 8:30am, just in time for your morning poolside beer. Missing the Blue Lagoon Special (1800dr) is a crime.

**Dracula's Palace,** adjacent to the Blue Lagoon, is the island's only haunted-house-like experience. Entrance 1500dr.



### OUTSIDE THE CITY

**Excursion boats** trace the beach-filled coast from the City of Rhodes to Lindos, leaving the city in the morning and returning in the afternoon; it's a great way to escape the crowded beaches of the western coast. The boats make several stops, including Faliraki. Schedules and prices are posted at the dock along the lower end of the Mandraki (starting at 3500dr). **Waterhoppers** (☎38 146) and **Dive Med Centres** (☎61 115) offer **scuba diving** lessons and trips to Kalithea (lessons 12,000dr; non-diving passengers 6000dr), as well as trips for certified divers.

**Rodini Park** is a forested area with streams, trails, a restaurant, and some small, harmless animals left over from the park's days as a zoo. Bus #3 runs to the park regularly. The snorkeler's heaven of **Kalithea,** 10km south of Rhodes Town, features a deserted spa at the beach cove's meager snack bar (not-so-great cheese pie 350dr; soda 250dr).

## SIGHTS

Few islands are known for a sight you'll have to imagine; Rhodes is one of them. The wonder of the ancient world, called the **Colossus of Rhodes,** a 35m bronze statue of Helios astride the harbor entrance at Mandraki, leaves no earthly trace today. Legend has it that the Colossus toppled in a 237 BC earthquake. Two bronze deer are now frozen right where a colossal foot would have crushed them. A new Colossus is in the works, in an effort to make Rhodes a worldwide wonder again.

**PLAY IT AGAIN, DIMITRI** Tired of dancing your heart out to the same American movie soundtracks you've heard all summer? Shake your booty over to a more Greek version of a disco (an *ellinika tragoudia*) for line-dancing like you've never seen before. The key to line-dancing is to pick up on the syncopated beat–one, three, four–and to move your legs in some variant of the grapevine, kicking where appropriate (the tricky part). Arms hug each others' shoulders or hands are clasped and held high, depending on the dance's rules or the drunken whimsy of your newfound countrymen. Tip: dance lines always move from left to right. When the moves get more complicated and an inspired couple takes the floor, it's polite to get down on one knee and clap out the beat. If it's a good night, somebody will set out ouzo shots on the floor, which local acrobats pick up and drink without using their hands (Greek break-dancing, if you will). What's a little broken glass in the name of tradition?

## OLD TOWN

Scattered throughout the pebbled inclines of the Old Medieval Town (constructed by the **Knights of St. John**) are small bronze plaques that label historical sites and museums. The plaques balance the material tourism of **Sokratous** street, the main shopping strip, formerly an Ottoman bazaar. The street is now lined with a poor imitation of the bazaar, with rip-off jewelry stores, restaurants, and junkshops. Upon conquering the island, the Knights redecorated the capital city, giving it a homier feel and replacing Hellenistic ruins with medieval forts and castles.

**PALACE OF THE GRAND MASTER.** At the top of the hill, the tall square tower, said to be the work of Grand Master Pierre d'Aubusson, marks the entrance to the Palace of the Grand Master. With 300 rooms, moats, drawbridges, huge watchtowers, and colossal battlements, the palace survived the long Ottoman siege of 1522, only to be devastated in 1856 by the explosion of 300-year-old ammunition in a depot across the street. At the beginning of this century, after years of use as a prison by the Turks and Italians, the citadel was restored and embellished by Italians determined to outdo even the industrious Knights. Many of the floors now bear **mosaics** taken from Kos. The interior decoration was completed only a few months before the start of the Second World War; the Italians had little chance to savor the fruits of their labor. The two outstanding exhibits on the north and southwest sides of the ground floor use archaeological findings and visual aids to tell a detailed version of Rhodes's extensive history. *(☎23 359, 75 674, 34 719. Open Tu-Su 8am-7pm, M noon-7pm. 1200dr, students 600dr.)* For an unparalleled bird's-eye view of the entire fortified city, wait for a Tuesday or Saturday and take a **walk** along the **city walls.** *(Open Tu and Sa 2:45-8pm. 1200dr, students 600dr.)*

DODECANESE

**PLATEIA ARGYKASTROU.** Dominating one side of the plateia with its beautiful halls and courtyards, the former **Hospital of the Knights** has been reborn as an **Archaeological Museum.** Its treasures include the small but exquisite first century BC *Aphrodite Bathing* and the 4th-century *Apollo.* *(☎27 674. Open Tu-Su 8:30am-2:30pm. 800dr, students and seniors 400dr.)* The **Avenue of the Knights,** or Ipoton, sloping uphill near the museum, was the main boulevard of the city 500 years ago.

A Byzantine fountain burbles at the center of Pl. Argykastrou. The 14th-century **Palace of Armeria,** now the **Archaeological Institute,** is on the right side of the plateia. Connected to the palace is the **Museum of Decorative Arts,** with Dodecanese costumes, carved sea chests, and ceramic plates. *(Open Tu-Su 8:30am-2:40pm, 6:45pm in the summer. 500dr.)* **Pl. Museum** is after the low archway; to its left is the **Church of St. Mary,** an 11th-century Byzantine building that was a Gothic cathedral by the time the Knights of St. John were through with it. Most of its interior frescoes were obliterated when the Ottomans transformed the building into the Enderoum Mosque. The Italians then re-converted the mosque to a church, which has since become an **icon museum.** *(Open Tu-Su 8:30am-3pm. 500dr, students 300dr.)* The **Inn of the Tongue of England** is a 1919 copy of its 1483 predecessor, destroyed in one of many defensive battles. The Order of the Knights of St. John of Jerusalem consisted of seven different religious orders, called "tongues" because each spoke a different language. Their inns, now government offices lining both sides of Ipoton, are closed to tourists. Because each tongue guarded one segment of the city wall, parts of the wall are labeled "England" or "France" on the map.

**PLATEIA SYMI.** To the right inside Eleftherias Gate, at the base of the Mandraki with your back to the arch, are the **Municipal Art Gallery**'s contemporary paintings by local and national artists. *(Open M-Sa 8am-2pm. 500dr.)* Behind the ruined 3rd-century BC **Temple of Aphrodite** in the middle of the plateia stands the 16th-century **Inn of the Tongue of Auvergne,** with an Aegean-style staircase on the facade.

**PLANE TREE WALK.** Evidence of the city's Ottoman era is most clear in Pl. Kleovoulou. A walk down **Orfeos,** better known as the Plane Tree Walk, will take you past a large **clock tower** that marked the edges of the wall separating the knights' quarters from the rest of the city. The walk opens the highest viewpoint in the Old Town. The setup was identical during the Ottoman Era, but the boundaries

changed; the Old Town housed Muslims and Jews, while Christians lived outside its walls. Climbing the tower leads you to a small cafe. *(Open 9am-11pm. 1000dr includes a drink at the bar.)* The **Mosque of Süleyman,** below the clock tower, dates from the early 19th century. Its red plaster walls, garden, and stone minaret distinguish it. The original mosque on this site was built after Sultan Süleyman the Magnificent captured Rhodes in 1522. You can view the mosque from its exterior or from the clock tower.

**TURKISH HORA.** The **Turkish library,** built in 1793 opposite the mosque, houses 15th- and 16th-century Persian and Arabic manuscripts. *(Open 10am-1pm and 4-7pm. Donation expected.)* Other Old Town Ottoman-era buildings and monuments are in various states of decay, but the 250-year-old baths and the **hamam** (Turkish bath) in Pl. Arionos are worth a peek. Note the way sunlight streams through one dome's small carved stars. *(☎27 739. Open Tu 1-6pm, W-F 11am-6pm, Sa 8am-6pm. 500dr.)*

**JEWISH QUARTER. Pl. Martyron Evreon** (Square of the Jewish Martyrs) lies in the heart of the old Jewish Quarter. The Jewish community was an integral part of Rhodes's history from its inception; for example, Sephardic Jews fled the Spanish Inquisition and added a Spanish flair to some Old Town medieval architecture. In 1943, 2000 Jews were taken from this square to Nazi concentration camps. A little way down Dossiadou is the **Shalom Synagogue,** restored by the 50 Jewish men and women who survived the war. Services are Friday at 5pm; dress modestly. Oriental rugs cover the stone mosaic floor and "eternal lamps" hang overhead. To see the interior, ask Lucia (who lives above it) to contact the caretaker, Mr. Soviano.



### NEW TOWN AND MANDRAKI

If you're not blinded by the flashing display of consumer culture, you'll find stately Italian architecture throughout the modern business district. The bank, town hall, post office, and National Theater are among the Mussolini-inspired stone buildings presiding over wide Eleftherias. Opposite them is the majestic **Governor's Palace** and a cathedral built by the Italians in 1925. The cathedral replicates St. John's Church, leveled in an 1856 explosion. Three defunct **windmills** stand halfway along the harbor's pier. The **Fortress of St. Nicholas,** at the end of the pier, guarded the harbor from 1464 to the end of the Second World War. Opposite the cemetery is **Villa Kleovoulos,** which housed author **Lawrence Durrell** during his appointment with the Foreign Office from 1945-47. A number of Durrell's books are set in Greece, including his most celebrated *Reflections on a Marine Venus*, which takes place on Rhodes. Look for the small plaque. Named after Süleyman's admiral, who died trying to capture Rhodes from the Knights of St. John in 1522, the **Mosque of Mourad Reis** is an important remnant of the Ottoman presence. The small, domed building inside is his mausoleum. Turbans indicate male graves, flowers indicate female ones. Greece's only **aquarium,** also a marine research center for the Dodecanese, exhibits creatures of the Aegean depths at the northern tip of the island. *(☎27 308 or 78 320. Open 9am-9pm. 600dr, students 400dr.)*

## FALIRAKI Φαλιρακη ☎0241

Faliraki ain't for the faint of heart. Here, beach bunnies hop between the sand and the bars all day long. The bars—named for alcohol-induced impotence (e.g. The Brewer's Droop) and advertising wall-to-wall foam parties—attract a wild crowd and pack the city's rooms—another reason to make Faliraki a day-into-night trip.

**ORIENTATION AND PRACTICAL INFORMATION.** Faraliki is located 15km south of the City of Rhodes. There are two main bus stops in Faliraki, one on the City of Rhodes-Lindos road and one on the waterfront. **Buses** run to the **City of Rhodes** (14 per day, 450dr) and from the waterfront bus stop, to **Lindos** (14 per day, 800dr). Faliraki is also a base for boat trips to **Kos** (11,000dr), **Lindos** (4000dr), and **Symi** (5000dr). Grab a **taxi** at the stand next to the waterfront bus stop, or call 85 444 (2200dr to the City of Rhodes). Ermou is the main thoroughfare connecting

the beach with the City of Rhodes-Lindos highway. Directly opposite the waterfront bus stop, to the right of Ermou, is the **first-aid station** (☎85 555; open 8am-6pm). Dr. Zanettullis (mobile ☎(094) 582 747) can be reached 24 hours a day. For an **ambulance,** call 22 222. The **pharmacy** is on the main road up to the highway; look for the green cross. (☎85 998. Open 9am-10:30pm.) The **Janus Travel Agency,** on Ermou, offers **currency exchange, phones,** and **safe-deposit.** (☎86 179 or 86 169. Open 8:30am-10pm.) The **Agricultural Bank,** on Ermou (open M-Th 8am-2pm, F 8am-1:30pm), has a 24-hour **ATM.**

**ACCOMMODATIONS AND FOOD.** Lodgings in Faliraki are hard to find, as most places rent their rooms to British package tour companies. **Hotel Faliro** is inland on Ermou, past Hotel Edelweiss. Rooms have full baths. Free pool and snack bar are perks. (☎85 483/399. Doubles 7000-9000dr.) Close to the water directly on Ermou, **Savitas Studios** offer sizeable rooms with fridge and full bath. (☎85 293, 86 448, 86 449 or 85 369. Doubles 8,500dr.) **Hotel Edelweiss,** on Ermou, is an older hotel offering currency exchange and great beach-and-bar access. (☎85 305. Doubles 9500-12,000dr.) A great budget option is Rhodes's only **campsite** (☎85 516 or 85 358), off the main road 1500m north of Faliraki. It has a market, well-pressured hot showers, and an impressive pool; ask the bus driver to let you off.

Dining in Faliraki way too often means inhaling a burger, greasy fries, and a soda at any of the fast-food joints. Ermou hosts most of these indiscreetly un-glamorous establishments, while the Rhodos-Lindos road has more restaurant options, generally equally poor in quality or class. A meal will run you a standard 1000-1500dr. **Cookies Bakery,** halfway between the main road and the beach, between a tourist shop and a side street, serves the gooey kind of baklava (400dr) that leaves honey dripping down your face. (☎86 276. Open 8am-1am.) **Sarantis,** on the City of Rhodes-Lindos road where Ermou ends, is a family-run restaurant with a seafood focus. (Dover sole 1950dr, cod 1750dr. Open 6pm-midnight.)

**ENTERTAINMENT AND NIGHTLIFE.** With each sunset, the sunburned masses migrate inland from the beach toward uniformly priced beer (600-700dr) at jubilant bars on Ermou; later there is a second exodus to a handful of popular dance clubs. **Chaplin's,** on Ermou by the beach, is a popular daytime party spot, especially during Friday afternoon karaoke competitions (shots 500dr). **Jimmy's Pub** (☎85 643) inland on Ermou, is a British bar with Guinness on tap; additional stimuli include soul music and TVs throughout the bar. Head on up to the free-of-cover club above the Pub, popular after midnight. **The Brewer's Droop,** a few doors down from Jimmy's Pub, serves up daily movies, frozen margaritas (choose from banana, pineapple, melon, or strawberry; all 1500dr), and the occasional frozen orgasm ("screaming" or "multiple"). The bass starts bumping after midnight when pub crowds migrate to clubs. The most convenient option for Ermou indulgers is **Sinners,** a popular stop-over for house and techno music's biggest names. (Cover 2000dr, includes one drink.) Friendly big, new, and posh **Millennium,** is set back in a shopping center on the City of Rhodes-Faliraki road, and quickly becoming Faliraki's most popular dance club. (☎86 603. Cover 1800dr with first drink.)

## LINDOS Λινδος ☎0244

With whitewashed houses clustered beneath a castle-capped acropolis, Lindos is perhaps the most picturesque town on Rhodes. World-famous writers, poets, painters, and professors congregate here. Vines and flowers line narrow streets, and pebble mosaics carpet courtyards. Charm like this hasn't remained a secret, however, and in summer, the streets of Lindos make the City of Rhodes look like a desert island. The crowds, astronomical prices, room shortage, and notorious heat make lovely Lindos a better destination outside of July and August.

**ORIENTATION AND PRACTICAL INFORMATION.** Lindos is a pedestrian-only city: all traffic stops at **Pl. Eleftherias,** where you'll find the **bus** and **taxi** sta-

tions. Buses to and from Lindos fill quickly, so its best to arrive early. Buses connect Lindos to: **Esperides** (3 per day, 800dr); **Faliraki** (16 per day 7am to 7pm, 9500dr); **Kolymbia Beach** (3 per day, 700dr); **Pefkos** (9 per day, 300dr); **City of Rhodes** (16 per day, 1000dr); and **Calypso** (3 per day, 750dr). **Excursion boats** from Rhodes depart at 9am and return at 5pm, hitting the **City of Rhodes** and **Turkey,** among other pit stops, as they travel along the coast.

Past the **Telebank** 24-hour **ATM, Acropolis** street leads through the eastern part of town and up to the acropolis. **Apostolou Pavlou,** another main street, runs perpendicular to Acropolis just past the **Church of the Assumption of Madonna,** whose stone belfry rises above the middle of town. Houses are distinguished only by their numbers. **Pallas Travel,** on Acropolis, has a **free map, exchanges currency,** and arranges excursions. (☎31 494; fax 31 595. Open M-Sa 8am-11pm, Su 9am-1pm and 5-10pm, in summer. Minimal hours in the winter.)

Critical and not-so-critical services huddle at the intersection of Apostolou Pavlou and Acropolis. The **pharmacy** is just past Yianni's Bar. (☎31 294. Open M-Sa 9am-11pm, Su 9am-3pm.) Sheila Markiou, an American expat, runs the superb **Lindos Lending Library** with more than 7000 English, Italian, German, French, and Greek books. To get there, walk to Pallas Travel and bear right where the road forks; the library is up and to the left. (☎31 443. Open M-Sa 9am-8pm, Su 9am-4pm.) Sheila also runs a **laundry** service out of the store (2500dr wash, dry, and soap). The **medical clinic** is to the left before the church. (☎31 224. Open M-Sa 9am-1:30pm and 6-8pm; open 24hr. for emergencies.) **Lindanet Cafe** provides the cheapest year-round **Internet** services. (☎32 142. 1500dr per hr. Open 10am-11pm daily.) There are **public toilets** across from the information office near the taxi/bus station (100dr). The **police** are at Ap. Pavlou 521. (☎31 223. Open M-F 8am-3pm; open 24hr. for emergencies.) The **post office** is just uphill and to the right of the donkey stand. (☎31 214. Open M-F 7:30am-2pm.) **Postal code:** 85107.

DODECANESE

**ACCOMMODATIONS.** Package tours hog even the tiniest pensions, making Lindos a difficult place to spend the night. One option is to arrive in the morning before the tour buses rumble in and ask the tour companies' offices if they have any empty rooms. To reach **Pension Electra** 85107 Lindos, from the main plateia, take the first left downhill after the donkey stand and follow signs for the acropolis. Rooms with A/C, fridge and bath. (☎31 266. Double 14,000dr.) Cheapest and simplest rooms with shared bath (6000-8000dr). At the end, follow the turn-off with stairs for the acropolis and continue downhill toward the beach. The **pension on Acropolis** offers a garden, terrace, baths, air-conditioning, and fridges (doubles 12,000dr; triples 14,000dr). **Pension Katholiki,** around the corner from Electra, has more rooms, all with baths, kitchens, and access to a rooftop view; inquire at Acropolis 57. (☎31 445. Doubles 16,000dr, off-season 10,000dr. A/C 2000dr extra.) **Pension Lindos** offers beautiful studios near the Omega Supermarket. (☎31 369. Doubles 10,000dr.)

**FOOD AND ENTERTAINMENT.** Eating poses yet another challenge to the budget traveler in Lindos: restaurant prices range from expensive to exorbitant, leaving souvlaki-pita bars, creperies (crepes start at 800dr), and grocery stores on the two main streets as virtually the only cheap alternatives. "Snack bar" shops serve the healthiest option in Lindos (yogurt with honey and fresh fruit 700dr).

To prepare for the climb to the acropolis, or to refuel upon your descent, have some *foccaccia* (600-900dr) or *panzerotti* (700dr) at **Il Forno Bakery,** around the corner from the bookstore. All ingredients are imported from Italy and handmade by the Italian owner. (open M-Sa 8am-9pm, Su 8am-1pm). In an inviting courtyard near the National Bank of Greece, **Gelo Blu** serves over 18 flavors of delicious *gelato* made from natural ingredients (from 800dr). Good, potent espresso, cappuccino, and iced drinks accompany the chocolate fudge cake. (☎31 761. Open 9am-12am.) Those who find a way to reach family-run **Ta Mezedakia,** a 10-minute drive south of Lindos in Gennadi, will find the seafood fresh and the prices right. (☎43 627. Open noon-1am.)

Lindos' nightlife is relatively tame; municipal law requires music to stop at midnight. If you are not ready to call it a day, head to **Amphitheatre,** an open-air nightclub not far from town. Free cabs shuttle you from Lindos plateia to the dance floor, where you can groove with a view of the acropolis and the sea. (1500dr cover includes first drink. Open midnight-4am.) Less energetic types might try **Antika,** on Apostolou Pavlou in the center of town, a beautiful bar with a pebble mosaic floor, a lush indoor garden, board games, monthly foreign magazines, and daily papers (pint of beer 500dr; open 2pm-1am). The **Museum Bar** is another subdued, perhaps vegetative, option. Watch CNN, MTV, ESPN, or the Discovery Channel on one of their three televisions, or in the afternoon, select an American movie from their (limited) collection. The sangria is fruity and refreshing (1000dr) and the coffee freshly brewed (400-600dr).

**SIGHTS.** Lindos's ancient **acropolis** stands on sheer cliffs 125m above town, caged by scaffolding and the walls of a Crusader fortress; from the highest point on the acropolis, the lowest point in the city can be seen. Excavations by the Danish Archaeological School between 1902 and 1912 yielded everything from 5000-year-old Neolithic tools to a plaque inscribed by a priest of Athena in 99 BC that lists the dignitaries who visited Athena's Temple—Hercules, Helen of Troy, Menelaus, Alexander the Great, and the King of Persia. The winding path up to the acropolis is veiled in lace tablecloths sold by local women, making for a surreal, frilly ascent. Right before the final incline, don't miss the ancient Greek *trireme*, which the artist Pythokreitos carved into the cliffside as a symbol of Lindos's inextricable ties with the sea. Lined with staircases, the daunting 13th-century **Crusader castle** looms over the entrance to the site. The arcade, built around 200 BC at the height of Rhodes's glory, originally consisted of 42 columns laid out in the shape of the Greek letter "Π." The large stone blocks arranged against the back wall served as bases for bronze statues that have been long since melted down. The remains of the **Temple of the Lindian Athena,** built by the tyrant Kleoboulos in the 6th century BC, come into view at the top of the steps. Legend has it that this area, once a tremendously important religious site, held a temple as early as 1510 BC. The one that remains is one of the few ancient temples with inner walls still fairly intact; colonnades flank both sides. Kleoboulos's tomb, inscribed with his timeless maxim, "Nothing in excess," is across the way. At the southwest foot of the acropolis are the remains of the **ancient theater.**

As you leave the castle, make a U-turn to your left to reach the imposing **Doric Stoa** (arcade), whose 13 restored columns dominate the entire level. Donkey rides to the acropolis aren't worth the fare (1000dr one way), as the 10min. walk isn't strenuous. A cave called the **Voukopion,** on the north side of the rock face (visible from the donkey path), may have been used for special sacrifices that could not be performed in the acropolis. The cave probably dates from the 9th century BC, and was later transformed into a sanctuary for Athena by the Dorians. *(☎31 258. Open M 12:30pm-6:40pm, Tu-Sa 8am-6:40pm. 1200dr, students 600dr. Ask for the free pamphlet on the brief history and explanation of the layout.)*

## RURAL RHODES

**EPTA PIGES.** Eleven kilometers south of Faliraki, just before Kolymbia, a road to the right leads down 3km to Epta Piges. Constructed by Italians seeking potable water for nearby Kolymbia, the aqueduct now quenches thrill-seekers, who slide through 150m of pitch-black tunnel. Laughers and shriekers alike end up in a large, picturesque freshwater pool; if the destination sounds nicer than the journey, take the path next to the tunnel that is used to return from the pool. A decent streamside taverna (with peacocks) sits at the entrance before the tunnel. To get there, ask a Lindos/Archangelos bus driver to let you off at the tunnel. Continue inland past Epta Piges to visit the 13th- and 15th-century frescoes of the Byzantine **Church of Agios Nikolaos Fountoucli,** 3km past Eleousa. Three **buses** per day stop at Eleousa on the way to the City of Rhodes. Villagers in **Arthipoli,** 4km away, rent rooms.

**TSAMBIKAS MONASTERY.** From the coast road, Tsambikas Monastery is easily marked by the restaurant that sits below it. A 1km road leads up to the restaurant; the Byzantine cloister and its panoramic views are 1km farther up a steep trail. The monastery takes its name from the sparks *(tsambas)* that were reportedly seen atop the hill. Upon climbing up to investigate, locals discovered a Cypriot icon of the Virgin Mary that had mysteriously appeared here, miles and miles from home. Angry Cypriots ordered that the icon be returned, and the locals obliged, but the icon kept returning. By the third time, everyone agreed that Rhodes must be the icon's proper home. To this day, some women ascend the mountain to pray to the Virgin Mary for fertility. Should the prayer work its magic, Junior will be named Tsambikos if it's a boy or Tsambika if it's a girl. Maybe it's not what your first choice, but a deal's a deal. One bus runs to the long and flat sandy **Tsambika Beach,** 1km south of the turn-off for the monastery (650dr); any bus that passes the turn-off should let you off here for a worthwhile day in the sun.

**KAMIROS.** Though the smallest of the three ancient cities of the Rhodian State, Kamiros far surpasses Ialyssos and the City of Rhodes in intricacy and preservation. The history of this ancient city has been pieced together from the evidence found in its cemeteries. People have lived here since Mycenaean times, but after the devastating earthquake of 226 BC, the city was reconstructed with a typical Hellenistic layout and design. The cistern on the north side of the temple dates to the 5th or 6th century BC, and the stone stoa (shaped like the Greek letter Π) is from at least the 2nd century. Visit the precinct of Athena Kamiros on the acropolis to get a clear sense of the city's impressive chessboard layout. *(Take a bus from Kamiros to the City of Rhodes (2 times per day 10am, 1:30pm; 1100dr). ☎ 40 037, 75 674. Open Tu-Su 8am-6:40pm. 800dr. Non-EU students 400dr. EU students Free.)*

DODECANESE

You can hike to picturesque **Profitis Ilias,** where 3 old Italian hotels long for restoration beside gorgeous orchards. Follow dirt roads to Salakos, where a path leads straight to the peak. *(Buses (5 per day, 850dr) from the City of Rhodes run to Salakos.)*

**VALLEY OF BUTTERFLIES.** Seven kilometers inland from the village of **Theologos, Petaloudes,** or the **Valley of Butterflies,** is a popular visiting spot with or without the company of the little fluttering guys. During the summer, Jersey tiger moths flock to the valley's Styrax trees, attracted to its resin (also used in making incense) and the area's unique shadiness. While resting to live out their final days in the trees, the moths fast, living only on water and body fat to conserve energy for rigorous mating sessions. After the deed is done, they die of starvation. The valley and its many trees are worth a walk throughout the year, but are a particularly welcoming reprieve from summer's sun-beaten coasts. The valley is accessible from an entrance next to an old mill, or from the main entrance farther uphill. The trail winds around a blue-green stream that collects in lily-covered pools and glides under cute little bridges. Avoid clapping and stomping to incite the moths to flight, like other foolio visitors do: noise interrupts the moths' action. *(☎ 81 801. 750dr, students half price.)* Hike up 300m from the end of the 1km trail to the **Monastery of Kalopetra,** home to a restored mosaic, where fresh yogurt and honey from the caretakers will accompany a panoramic view of the island.

# SYMI ΣΥΜΗ

Rumor has it, at least according to Symians, that visitors who daytrip here from Rhodes often end up staying for months. Indeed, both residents and foreigners seem to cherish and want to preserve this paradisiacal island—a refreshing change of mindset after the consumer ethic of many heavily touristed islands. The island's **Panormitis Monastery** (p. 441) rests in a remote spot at Symi's southern end, separated from the northern port of Yialos by an uninhabited, hiker-friendly mountain range. Indeed, until the 19th century, monasteries were the only dwellings on the island's steep, barren shores. Shipbuilding, sponge-diving, and fishing moved in later, as Symi received special treatment from the Ottoman sultans, eventually

becoming the capital of the Dodecanese. While Symi-made ships still have a reputation for their speed, sponge-diving is long-gone. Spice-growing has taken over, giving the island a measure of financial stability, along with recent tourism. A growing population of foreign residents gives the island a slightly cosmopolitan flair to match the colorful mosaic of houses that brighten its port.

## SYMI TOWN ☎0241

Symi Town, the only real town on the island, is divided into two sections. From the east end of the waterfront (left facing inland), several sets of several hundred stairs lead to **Horio,** perched above the port, yield views of orchard-covered mountains and the sea. Constructed in the middle ages as a fortification against pirate raids, the village's winding pathways are populated by sympathetic village folk peering from white-washed clefts. The port, **Yialos,** has most of the island's visitor services to boot. A string of islets leads boats into the harbor, where a rainbow of houses welcomes visitors. Though many of its 19th-century houses were abandoned when the sponging industry collapsed, the Greek government declared the port a historic site in 1971.



### ORIENTATION AND PRACTICAL INFORMATION

**Ferries:** Daily to **Rhodes** (2500dr). Two per week to: **Kalymnos** (3500dr); **Kos** (2700dr); **Nisyros** (2500dr): **Piraeus** (8400dr); **Tilos** (1800dr); and **Kastellorizo** (2300dr). There are ferry ticket offices where they dock and one is just after the footbridge, one the next block, turn right for yet another block inland.

**Flying Dolphins:** Four per week to **Rhodes** (2850dr). One per week to: **Astypalea** (8470dr); **Kalymnos** (6890dr); and **Kos** (5000dr).

**Bus:** A green van stops on the east waterfront past Pl. Ikonomou. On-the-hour transportation to: **Horio** (5min., 200dr) and **Pedhi** (10min., 200dr).

**Taxis:** Most congregate near the bus stop on the east waterfront, but the island's four taxis can be reached at their mobile phones (get the numbers from the travel agency).

**Symi Motobike Center** (☎71 926) is the only harbor rental shop, with another branch in Pedhi (☎71 954). Prices range from 5000-8000dr. Open 8am-9pm daily.

**Travel Agency: Symi Tours** (☎71 307/689), a block inland from the waterfront gold shop. Sells ferry, hydrofoil, and plane tickets, handles **currency exchange,** and helps find accommodations. Open 9am-1pm and 6:30-9:30pm.

**Banks: Ionian Bank** (☎71 122), on the waterfront left of the ferry landing, has a 24hr. **ATM.** Both banks open M-F 8am-2pm.

**Police:** (☎71 111), next to the Yialos clock tower, in a big white building on the waterfront. English spoken. Open 24hr.

**Medical Center:** (☎71 290), next to the church, directly opposite Hotel Kokona. Open M-F 8am-1pm; after hours, call the police.

**Telephones: OTE,** inland along the left side of the park in the middle of the harbor; follow signs from Neraida restaurant. Open M-F 7:30am-3:10pm.

**Internet: Vapori Bar,** over the footbridge, set back about 50m from the 90° turn to the east side of the harbor. Open 5pm-late. 2000dr per hour.

**Post Office:** (☎71 315), in the same building as the police, up the flight of stairs on the left. Offers **currency exchange.** Open M-F 7:30am-2pm. **Postal Code:** 85600.

### ACCOMMODATIONS

Most travelers don't spend the night; that still doesn't seem to phase the small flock of dock hawks at the port. Luckily, expensive list prices drop fast with perseverance. Prices listed are high season; expect a 2000dr decrease in the low season.

**Hotel Kokona** (☎72 620 or 71 451), over the footbridge and to the left of the old church tower. Light breezes blow the lemon-fresh scent through light balcony curtains. All rooms with baths and balconies. Doubles 9000-10,000dr; triples 12,000dr; quads 12,000-15,000dr. Breakfast 1000dr.

**Dallaras Snack Bar** (☎72 030), in the Horio, ask around; directions in the Horio are difficult. Small, attractive rooms in a nearby house. Doubles with shared bath 7500dr.

**Hotel Maria** (☎71 311), next to Hotel Kokona. Large rooms with kitchen facilities and baths on a cute courtyard. Doubles 7000-9000dr.

## FOOD AND ENTERTAINMENT

Waterfront tavernas pale in comparison with the eclectic menus and often more reasonable prices in **Horio.**

**Georgios' Restaurant** (☎71 984), at the top of the 200 stairs to the Horio. Authentic, family-owned restaurant goes beyond the basic Greek menu. Try the peppers *florini* (red peppers stuffed with feta 1200dr), and lamb *exohiko* (lamb baked in aluminum foil with potatoes, cheese, and oregano; 1800dr). Open 7pm-2am.

**Manos Fish Restaurant** (☎72 429) cooks up fresh fish right from the tank/sea. Mix and match to your personal taste and be sure to try the house wine (1200dr). Open from 10am-midnight.

**Jean and Tonic Pub** (☎71 819), in Horio, up the hill from George's. Happy Hour 8-9pm, friendly conversation all night long. Open 8pm-late!

**To Vapori** (☎72 540) Surrounded by a little square of bars, classy Vapori stands out with **Internet access** and Happy Hour (6:30-8:30pm). Open 5pm-late.



## SIGHTS

At the top of the road to Horio, signs point toward the small **Archaeological Museum,** with well-labeled Classical and Byzantine pieces, island costumes, and utensils. *(☎71 114. Open Tu-Su 8:30am-2:30pm. 500dr, seniors 400dr, under 18 200dr.)* The museum ticket also covers entrance to the nearby **Chatziagapitos Mansion,** which displays everyday objects owned by Symiots of yesteryear, in an old naval family's exquisite village home. *(Open Tu-Su 8:30am-2:30pm.)* The curators of both museums are happy to explain it all to you.

In Yialos, a yellow neoclassical building at the back of the main waterfront strip floats the **Naval Museum.** It recounts the history of sponge-diving on the island with equipment, photographs, and maps. *(☎72 363. Open Tu-Su 10am-2pm. 300dr.)* Signs also lead through a maze of streets to the ruins of the old **castle,** where little remains within the Cyclopean walls aside from the **Church of Megali Panagia.**

**CUCKOO FOR KOUKKOUMAS** Think singles bars stink? Visit Symi during the festival of Koukkoumas for a taste of matchmaking, Symiot-style. Traditionally, Koukkoumas begins on the evening of May 1. Unmarried girls with living parents silently gather water from seven homes in which the housewife is named Irene. Later that evening, the girls toss their rings into the water and place the water on a roof for the night. The next morning, the would-be brides use the gathered water to bake salty pies. All baking must be done with their hands behind their backs. A long day's baking gives way to singing, dancing, and salty pie eating. During the festivities, a young girl with living parents takes each ring and utters a male name. Before sleeping that night, the would-be brides, dehydrated from extensive dancing and copious salt consumption, go to another house to drink water. If an unmarried male who shares the name spoken by the young girl resides in that house, she's found her husband.

## DAYTRIPS AROUND SYMI: PANORMITIS MONASTERY

*Four weekly **tour buses** and one **tour boat** run from **Yialos;** tour boats from **Rhodes** stop here as well. Mopeds aren't fit for the gravelly terrain around the site. By foot it's a rigorous full-day **hike.** Open 10am-1pm. Dress modestly. Free toilets are to the left of the complex. Museums 400dr.*

In the southern part of the island, the grand Monastery of the Archangel Michael—the friend of travelers—chimes out a welcome to visitors from its elegant belltower. The monastery was built in the 15th century at the spot where a local woman happened upon an icon of Michael. As is often the way with icons, it was brought to Yialos but kept returning to Panormitis. The palatial buildings of the monastery, dominated by an elegant central belltower, contain two small **museums,** one with ecclesiastical relics and worshipers' gifts and one with folkloric exhibits. The small on-site church focuses around an exceptional wooden altar screen, famous for its power to grant wishes. Tokens in the museum represent supplicants' requests. Allow the crowds to leave first to really enjoy the museum.

If you want to **hike** but think the day-long trek to Panormitis is too ambitious for you, take the red paths that mark hiking trails off the main road. They lead through a forest dedicated to **James Brown** to a remote **monastery** and isolated **beaches.**

DODECANESE

## BEACHES

Symi's tiny coves shelter a few excellent beaches at Agios Marina, Nanou, and Marathounda on the east side of the island. They are the most impressive and are accessible only by boat. Boats also go to tranquil, sandy Sesklia Island, south of Symi (3000dr round-trip). Excursion boats line up with destinations and prices posted in the morning (round-trip 1500-2000dr). Twenty minutes below Horio is Pedhi, the island's only other town easily accessible by bus from Yialos. The small fishing port lacks Yialos' stateliness and Horio's architecture, but stretches out a humble patch of sand sheltered in the natural harbor. Find a better sandy, serene beach—enclosed on each side by amicable cliffs—at Agios Nikolaos, an easy 30-minute hike farther east. Tiny Nos Beach is very close to the port if you need a quick dip; it's a 10-minute walk north along the waterfront from Yialos, past the shipyard. Nimborio, 45-minute on foot past Nos, has a mediocre, pebbly beach, but the views make the walk worth it. You can also take a taxi boat (800dr round-trip).

# NISYROSΝΙΣΥΡΟΣ

Greece's *other* volcanic island, Nisyros isn't as dramatic or as popular as Santorini, but retains its virgin landscape, its hospitality, and its islander community. An idle volcano pulls your eyes skyward to the clifftop monastery and picturesque hikes through the enduring greenery on this hidden treasure of the Aegean.

## MANDRAKI Μανδρακι ☎0242

Nisyros's tiny, whitewashed port town, Mandraki meets you with its dingy ferry dock. Beyond it, you'll be relieved to see the winding stone-paved streets and handsome views that make the city a pleasant and comfortable stopover.

## ORIENTATION AND PRACTICAL INFORMATION

Virtually all of Mandraki lies to the right of the port. Walking along the waterfront, small alleys lead inland to residential areas and the orchards above them. Most travelers' hunger can be satiated on the waterfront and the parallel inland road.

**Ferries:** 4 per week to: **Kalymnos** (1500dr); **Kos** (1600dr); **Piraeus** (7500dr); **Rhodes** (2800dr); **Symi** (2400dr); and **Tilos** (1300dr).

**Flying Dolphins:** 2 per week to: **Rhodes** (5600dr); **Tilos** (3000dr); **Halki** (6000dr); and **Kos** (3200dr).The **Catamaran** runs a similar schedule with the same prices.

**Buses:** Buses (7am-8pm, 230-350dr) go to: **Emporio** (20min., 5 per day); **Nikea** (45min., 5 per day); **Pali** (10min., 6 per day); **Volcano** (30min., 2 per day); **Loutra** (5min., 6 per day) and **White Beach** (5min., 6 per day). Daily excursion buses to the **Volcano** run once per day when the boats from Kos arrive. 2000dr includes entrance.

**Taxis:** From Mandraki, **Babis'** (☎31 460) and from Nikea, **Irini's** (☎31 474).

**Moped Rentals: Alfa Rent** (☎31 580). Bicycles 1000dr per day, mopeds 3000dr-6000dr per day. Open 8:30am-9pm.

**Tourist Office:** Next to the ferry dock. Provides maps and advice on transportation and accommodations. Open 9:30am-2pm and 4-6pm.

**Travel Agency:** Dimitris at **Nisyrian Travel** (☎31 411, fax 31 610), to the left of the ferry dock, is very knowledgeable about the island. They arrange excursions, walks, accommodations, Greek Evenings, and special boat trips. Open 8am-9pm daily. **Enetikon Travel** (☎31 180; fax 31 168), on the right side of the road leading into town, on the rocks. Multilingual staff. Open 9am-1:30pm and 6-9pm.

**Banks:** A representative of the **National Bank** works in **Diakomitalis Tours** (☎31 459). Open M-F 8am-1:30pm. Diakomitalis also handles all transportation **ticket** sales, car rentals and exchange.

**Port Authority:** (☎31 222), in a white building near the dock. Open 24hr.

**Police:** (☎31 201), in the same white building as the Port Authority.

**Post Office:** (☎31 249), in the *same* white building. Offers **currency exchange** and houses the savings bank. Open M-F 7:30am-2pm. **Postal code:** 85303.



## ACCOMMODATIONS AND FOOD

Doubles cost around 6000-7000dr. Reserve ahead, especially during the August festival for the Virgin Mary. On the road leading left from the dock, **Three Brothers Hotel** offers well-maintained seaside rooms overlooking the ocean, with baths, fridges, and friendly service from the brothers three. English is spoken very well. (☎31 344. Average prices for singles 6000dr; doubles 8000dr.) Across the street, **Hotel Romantzo** has rooms with baths, fridges, and a charming roof garden with an ocean vista. (☎31 340. Doubles 6000dr; triples 8000dr.) In Mandraki, on the road parallel to the waterfront, **Taverna Nisyros** has studios with bath and kitchenette. (☎31 460. Rooms 6000dr.)

The taverna is also where Polyxeni cooks up a storm of Nisyrian specialties that will satisfy all for under 2000dr (*moussaka* 900dr, fresh *boukounies* or lamb chops 1500dr). Wandering away from the waterfront, a small sign points to **Y Fabrika,** on one of the side streets leading from the town hall plateia to the water. Go down the steps for books, music, and superb Greek *mezedes* at this cozy and friendly *ouzeri* (octopus 1000dr, *raki* 200dr, beer 400-500dr). **Captain's** (☎31 225), at the water's edge, sells cheap fish (swordfish 1800dr) and the island's specialty, *soumada* (almond juice; 500dr per serving) and a tuna pasta (1500dr).

## DAYTRIPS AROUND NISYROS

**MANDRAKI VOLCANO.** The volcano, dormant since 1888, is the island's main attraction, for good reason. Inside the crater, the smell of sulphur overpowers the nose, and scalding steam jets up eerily against the island's pumice landscape. There are audible rumblings in parts of the crater. A 20-minute walk uphill from its famous and popular neighbor, the **Alexhandros Crater** leads a quieter life. Virtually unvisited but no less spectacular, the crater is accessible via a small walking trail

that begins behind the toilets and leads over the mountain. *(20min. bus from Mandraki (2 per day, 350dr) gives you 45min. to wander around in the crater. Renting a moped lets you spend more time exploring; drive carefully, as the roads are narrow. 200dr.)*

**NEARBY VILLAGES.** The quiet hillside village of **Nikea** looks across to the island of Tilos to the southeast, and has a bird's-eye view of the volcano. Life in Nikea centers around its sweetly picturesque plateia, where the village church and a few cafes set up shop. Halfway between Mandraki and the volcano, a sign marks the turn-off to **Emporio,** 1km away. The once-abandoned village is gradually being refurbished by summering Athenians and foreigners. Both towns are accessible by bus from Mandraki Port.

**MONASTERY OF OUR LADY SPILLANI.** This tiny monastery nests within a deceptively inflated outer shell on the cliff at the end of the Mandraki. The monastery's sacred icon used to reside in a small cave just above Mandraki's port, but it had a habit (like most icons) of mysteriously disappearing from the sanctuary and turning up on the site of today's monastery. Monks took a hint and built a new home for the icon, making a large replica of it in 1798 to display in the new church. The tender gazes of Christ and the Virgin Mary kill pain and are faithfully pleaded with by many to cure disease and injury. The church also has relics of **Ag. Haralambos** in its antechamber. Recently, on the rear face of the icon of the Virgin Mary, an altar boy discovered the iconographer's hidden portrait of **Ag. Nikolaos,** which had been covered with an old cloth for over two centuries. Pictures of the back of the icon are now on display as well. To get up to the monastery, follow signs and climb the narrow uphill steps across from the church with the pink bell tower. *(Open 10:30am-3:30pm. Donations welcome.)*



**BEACHES.** Steaming black volcanic rocks can torment the toes; still, there's a small, secluded beach behind the monastery's cliff; its soothing sand and green-blue waters pamper swimmers. Past the **hot springs of Loutra,** on the road to Pali, **White Beach;** go there from Mandraki (6 buses per day, 250dr). The island's best beach is larger, cleaner, and 4km east of Pali (past the **Oasis** taverna; ask the bus driver to let you off). Depending on demand, Enetikon and Nisyrian Travel organize trips to the nearby island of **Giali** for its better beaches (2000dr round-trip). To experience the gorgeous sands of Giali and the island's source of *kakavia* (Greek bouillabaisse), you can leave with the worker boat, departing each day at 7:30am and returning at 3:30pm. Bring your own lunch.

# KOS ΚΩΣ

> Cos is the spoiled child of the group. You know it at once without even going ashore. It is green, luxuriant, and a little disheveled.
>
> —Lawrence Durrell

The booming nightclubs and packed bars of modern Kos gloss over the past and live in the now. Famous figures in literature and medicine have lounged on these beaches. Kos is the sacred land of **Asclepius,** god of healing, the birthplace of **Hippocrates,** father of modern medicine and the Hippocratic oath, and the home of the poet **Theocritus** and his teacher **Philetas.** In ancient times, Kos was a major trading power with a population of 160,000—eight times that of today. An episcopal seat of the Byzantine Empire, the island became a target for predatory naval forces. The Knights of St. John prevailed in 1315, seizing control and turning Kos into one of their outposts. Since then, its history has mirrored that of the other Dodecanese in passing under Italian, German, and British governments.

Rivaling Rhodes in terms of sheer numbers, Kos tends to draw a younger, louder, more intoxicated crowd. Don't be dismayed by the raucous bars and mammoth hotels along the lengthy stretches of golden beach.

## KOS TOWN ☎0242

In Kos Town, the minarets of Ottoman mosques spike above grand Italian mansions, the massive walls of a Crusader fortress, and scattered ruins from the Archaic, Classical, Hellenistic, and Roman eras. The combination of ancient, medieval, and modern makes Kos a historian's paradise by day, while its bars make it a dissipated hotspot by night. A panoply of architectural styles attests to Kos's constant changes in ownership. On the downside, the town is one of the most expensive in the Dodecanese, and package tour agents who contract with pension owners have left very few rooms for independent travelers.



### GETTING THERE AND GETTING AROUND

**Ferries:** Service to: **Kalymnos** (1¼hr., 1-3 per day, 1400dr); **Leros** (2½hr., 1 per day, 2100dr); **Patmos** (4hr., 1-2 per day, 2800dr); **Piraeus** (11-15hr., 2-3 per day, 7500dr); and **Rhodes** (4hr., 2 per day, 3400dr). One per week goes to: **Kastellorizo** (4300dr); two per week go to: **Nisyros** (1700dr) and **Symi** (2500dr). Ferries also go to: **Tilos** (2 per week, 1900dr). Greek (and Turkish) boats run to **Bodrum,** Turkey every morning (10,000-13,000dr round-trip). Turkish boats leave in the afternoon and return the next morning (8000-13,000dr round-trip). Since travel is international, prices are not regulated by the Greek government. **Port Authority** (☎26 594) is at the corner of Megalou Alexandrou and Akti Kountouriotou. Visitors leaving with Turkish boats requiring an overnight stay also need a visa (3000dr).

**Flying Dolphins:** Two per day to **Kalymnos** (2800dr) and **Samos** (6500dr). One per day to: **Leros** (4100dr) and **Patmos** (5500dr). Two per week to: **Agathonisi** (5980dr); **Astypalea** (6000dr); and **Tilos** (3850dr). Also to: **Fourni** (3 per week, 7200dr); **Lipsi** (6 per week, 3900dr); **Nisyros** (3 per week, 3640dr); **Symi** (1 per week, 5000dr); and **Rhodes** (2 per day, 6800dr).

**Flights: Olympic Airways,** Vas. Pavlou 22 (☎28 331/332), runs to **Athens** (2-3 per day, from 17,300dr). Open M-F 8am-3:30pm. On Sa-Su, call ☎51 567. Olympic runs a **bus** (1000dr) from Kos Town to the **airport** 2-4 times per day. Schedule posted. Taxis from Kos Town to the airport cost 5000-5500dr.

**Buses:** (☎22 292, fax 20 263). Leave from Kleopatras street near the inland end of Pavlou behind the Olympic Airways office. M-Sa to: **Asfendiou-Zia** (40min., 3 per day, 350dr); **Antimachia** (40min., 6 per day, 450dr); **Kardamena** (45min., 6 per day, 600dr); **Kefalos** and **Paradise** (1hr., 6 per day, 800dr); **Marmari** (35min., 11 per day, 300dr); **Mastihari** (35min., 5 per day, 550dr); **Pyli** (30min., 5 per day, 350dr); and **Tigaki** (30min., 12 per day, 350dr). Sunday schedules are reduced. Schedule posted by the stop. Buy tickets on the bus.

**City Buses:** Akti Koundouriotou 7 (☎26 276), on the water. To: **Asclepion** (15min., 16 per day); **Agios Fokas** (57 per day); **Messaria** (8 per day); **Lampi** (25 per day); and **Thermae** (20min., 9 per day). Fares 150-250dr.

**Taxis:** (☎22 777 or 22 333), near the inland end of the Avenue of Palms.

**Rentals:** Laws restricting rentals to those with proper motorbike licenses are more strictly enforced here than on other islands. However, driving behavior does not reflect this stringency, and drivers should exert caution. For **Sernikos,** Herodotou 19 (☎23 670), take your first right off Megalou Alexandrou and go 2 blocks. **Mike's** (☎21 729) is at the corner of Amerikis and Psaron. Mopeds 2500dr per day. Bikes 500-1000dr per day. **George,** P. Tsaldari 3 (☎28 480), near the port authority, rents quality bikes. Mopeds from 2500-5000dr per day. Bikes 500-1000dr. Open 8:10am-8pm.

### ORIENTATION AND PRACTICAL INFORMATION

The dignified walls of the Castle of the Knights of St. John overwhelm the vista as ferries pull into the harbor of Kos Town. Walk left (facing inland) from the harbor to reach the **Avenue of Palms,** also known as **Finikon,** framed by the stately trees. Continuing along the waterfront past the Palms leads to **Vassileos Georgios** and the

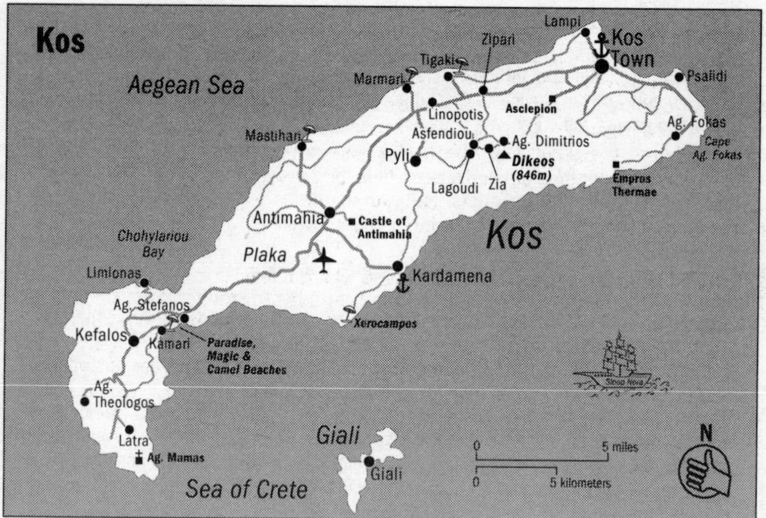




rocky beach alongside it. Turn right onto the Palms, follow it to the next corner of the fortress, and you'll come upon **Akti Koundouriotou,** another waterfront street that wraps around the harbor. Here you'll find the city bus station, boats to Turkey, travel agencies, restaurants, and Kos's thriving nightlife. Branching inland off Akti Koundouriotou are the town's main arteries: **El. Venizelou** leads through a row of travel agencies directly into the shopping district, and **Megalou Alexandrou,** a few blocks down, heads to **Pl. Palaiologou,** the ruins of ancient Kos Town, and eventually the inland villages. The town's other sandy beach begins near the end of Akti Koundouriotou.

**Tourist Office:** Vas. Georgiou 1 (☎24 460 or 28 724; fax 21 111; email dotkos@hol.gr). Free maps and info on transportation, events, and accommodations. **Greek National Tourist Office,** on Akti Miaouli in the same building as the tourist police, provides maps, brochures, and schedules. Open M-F 8am-8:30pm, Sat 8am-3pm.

**Tourist Agencies:** No single agency in Kos has comprehensive boat information. Two large ferry companies, **DANE** and **GA,** and two hydrofoil lines, **Ilio** and **Dodecanese Express,** serve Kos and its neighbors. **Pulia Tours,** Vas. Pavlou 3 (☎26 388, 24 194, or 21 130; fax 26 388), near the waterfront end of this main road, sells DANE and hydrofoil tickets, organizes day excursions, offers rental assistance and **currency exchange,** and helps in finding rooms. Open 7am-11pm.

**GA Office** (☎28 545; fax 24 864), on Vas. Pavlou across from the National Bank, serves the other lines and offers similar tourist services. Open 7:30am-10pm.

**Banks: National Bank** (☎28 167), in back of the Archaeological Museum, one block inland from the water on A.P. Ioannidi. 24hr. **ATM.** Open M-Th 8am-2pm, F 8am-1:30pm. After hours, **exchange currency** at any travel agency along the waterfront.

**American Express:** (☎28 429). Full AmEx services at the **Credit Bank** (*Trapeza Pisteos*), Akti Kountouriotou 5, near the city bus stop. Open M-Sa 9am-2pm and 5-9pm.

**Emergency:** (☎22 100). **Ambulance,** ☎22 300.

**General Information:** ☎132.

**Police:** (☎22 100), on Akti Miaouli in the big yellow building beside the castle. Some English spoken. Open 24hr. **Tourist police** (☎22 444) in the same building. Open 7:30am-2pm.

**Hospital:** (☎28 050). On Mitropoleos, between El. Venizelou and Hippocrates. For **information,** call 28 013. Open 24hr.

**Telephones: OTE** (☎22 499), at L. Virona and Xanthou, around the corner from the post office. Open M-Sa 7:30am-10pm, Su 8am-10pm.

**Internet Access: Del Mar Internet Cafe,** Megalou Alexandrou 4A (☎24 244), is small and crowded. Limited service at 1500dr per hr. **Multitech,** El. Venizelou 55 (☎23 584) has video games, Play Station and email.

**Post Office:** El. Venizelou 14 (☎22 250). Follow signs from Vas. Pavlou, which lead past Pl. Eleftherias and the fruit market, and turn left onto Venizelou. Open M-F 7:30am-2pm. **Postal Code:** 85300.

## ACCOMMODATIONS

Hotel vacancies are rare in summer, so start searching for rooms early. Most inexpensive places are on the right side of town if you're facing inland. It is best to seek out your own room, since Kos's dock hawks are notorious; if your boat docks in the middle of the night, you may have no choice. Camping on public land is illegal.

**Pension Alexis,** Herodotou 9 (☎28 798 or 25 594). Take the first right off Megalou Alexandrou, on the back left corner of the first intersection. The aromas of fresh jasmine from the garden won't smother you nearly as much as Sonia and Alex's hospitality will. If rooms are full, the proprietor will set you up with a mattress and sheets on the patio or cut you a deal at his elegant **Hotel Afendoulis.** View-friendly verandas, and common baths. Prices are flexible, especially if you're carrying *Let's Go.* Doubles 5500-7000dr; triples 7500dr. Try Sonia's famous feta omelette for breakfast (1000dr).

**Hotel Afendoulis,** Evrilpilou 1 (☎/fax 25 321 or 25 797), right down Vas. Georgiou practically on the beach. Traditional wood-paneled rooms around a central sitting courtyard. All have private baths. Doubles 7500-9000dr. Breakfast 1000dr. Ask about the cheaper cellar rooms.

**Meropis Hotel,** Meropidos 5 (☎22 789), near the post office. Old, basic rooms with shared or private bath. Good proximity to the center while maintaining enough distance for a good night's sleep. Singles 6000dr; doubles 8000dr.

**Anna Sofou Rooms,** Artemisias 1 (☎26 158), where Venizelou becomes Artemisias. High-ceilinged rooms and baths could use refurbishment, but it adds character. Cheap for Kos. Doubles 5000dr.

**Kos Camping** (☎23 910 or 23 275); 3km southeast from the center and accessible by public transport. Shady, well-maintained setting right across from the beach. Mini-market, bar, laundry facilities, cooking room, rental assistance, and security boxes. 1750dr per person. You can bring your own tent (800dr) or rent one (1000dr). Buses run to and from the center every 30min.

## FOOD

The fruit and vegetable **market** in Pl. Eleftherias, on Vas. Pavlou, inside a large yellow building with a picture of grapes over the doors, caters to tourists and is not as inexpensive as it looks; mini-markets have cheaper fruit (open M-F 7am-9pm, Sa 7am-6pm, Su 10am-2pm).

**Ampavris,** (☎25 696) on E. Georgiou. Take the road past the Casa Romana; it's about a 15min. walk from town. A true diamond in the rough, and one of the few places on Kos to find authentic cuisine. Stuffed flower buds 900dr, entrees 1000-1800dr.

**Hellas,** Psaron 7, at corner of Amerikis. Huge portions of tasty Greek dishes in a service-friendly atmosphere. Lamb *kleftiko* 1500dr, *moussaka* 1200dr. Good vegetarian options available. Open noon-1am.

**Andonis' Taverna** (☎25 645), on the corner of Amerikis and Paleo Polemiston. If you're looking for that hidden taverna only locals eat at, this is the place. Excellent traditional dishes in large portions. Hospitality reigns. Try the *mekri meze* (1700dr, serves two).Main dishes from 1500-2000dr.

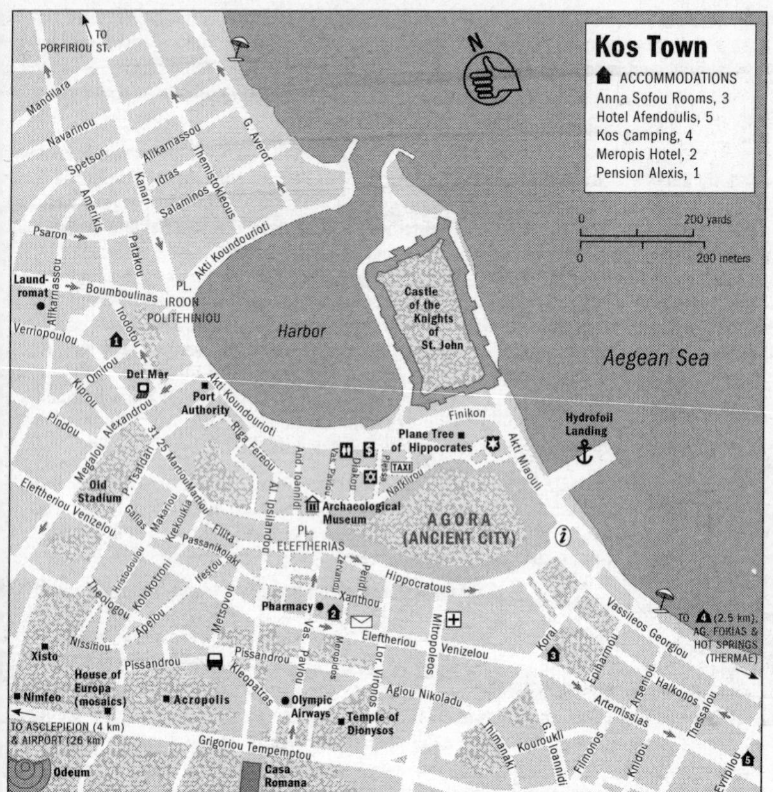




**Nick the Fisherman,** Averof 21, at corner of Alikarnasou. Daily catches straight to your plate at the best *psarotaverna* in town. Ask for Larry's friendly service. Mussels 1600dr, sea-urchins 1600dr; entrees from 1500-2000dr. Open 8am-12am.

## NIGHTLIFE

Prepare for masses of young people wearing skin-tight clothes and looking for a good time. Most bars are in two districts. The first is around **Exarhia** (a.k.a. **bar street,** between Akti Koundouriotou and the ancient agora), the area around **Vas. Pavlou.** Beers go for 800-1000dr, cocktails for 2000dr. Most places open at 9pm, fill by 11pm, and keep on keepin' on until dawn. The second district, **Porfiriou,** is cheaper and more subdued bus has equally thirsty patrons. Its waterfront dance clubs in the north near the beach mark the endpoint of a night's pilgrimage. **Orfeas** (☎25 713), on the corner of Fenaretis and Vas. Georgiou, shows American movies (adults 2000dr).

**Fashion Club,** Kanari 2 (☎22 592), by the dolphin statue rotary. Kitsch (peanut-vending machines) meets de rigueur (elegant candles) at Kos's most ostentatious club, but the friendly dance floor isn't nearly as pretentious as the bouncers would have you think. 2500dr cover includes first drink. No cover for the large fashion TV-filled cafe in front.

**Hamam Club** (☎28 323) near the agora, next to the taxi station in Pl. Diagoras. The exotic former bathhouse now refreshes and soothes you with aural massage: live, outdoor acoustic sets play until midnight over a hopping dance club floor. Enjoy crazy drinks made by a crazy barman in one of the one-time private bathing rooms.

**Heaven** (☎23 874), on Zouroudi, along the waterfront. Opposite the beach, with the appropriate cabana theme. A big, loud, popular outdoor disco. 2000dr cover includes first drink and is sometimes waived early in the evening. W night foam parties.

## SIGHTS

**ROMAN RUINS.** The run-down field of ruins bounded by Nafklirou, Hippocrates, and the waterfront was the agora; it's now dominated by a population of sunbathing cats. The remains of a **Temple of Aphrodite** and the more impressive 2nd-century AD **Temple of Hercules** lie beside two Roman roads: the **Cardo** (axis), perpendicular to Grigoriou, and the **Decumana** (broadest), parallel to Grigoriou and intersecting Cardo. Nearby, you'll find an ancient gymnasium, a swimming pool from the Roman era, and an early Christian basilica built over a Roman bath. At the end of the Decumana, the wood-sheltered 3rd-century AD **House of Europa** has a mosaic floor depicting Europa's abduction by that bully, Zeus. The **odeum,** a well-preserved Roman theater, lies across the street. The 3rd-century AD **Casa Romana,** uncovered by an Italian archaeologist in 1933, is down Grigoriou. The meager ruins of a **Temple of Dionysus** stand opposite the Casa Romana. *(Open 24hr. Free.)*

DODECANESE

**ARCHAEOLOGICAL MUSEUM.** Hellenistic and late Roman sculptures dominate findings from the island's many archaeological sights. A celebrated statue, found at the Kos Odeon and presumably of Hippocrates, stands in the northwest room. A 2nd-century AD Roman mosaic in the central courtyard depicts Hippocrates and a colleague entertaining the god Asclepius. Statues of Dionysos, Artemis, and Aphrodite occupy the North room and Atrium. *(In Pl. Eleftherias. ☎28 326. Open Tu-Su 8:30am-3pm. 800dr, students 400dr.)*

**CASTLE.** Ironically, the invading Knights of St. John, who built the massive 15th-century castle, came to Kos to heal the sick. The once-removable bridge that marks the connecting entrance from the Square of Hippocrates linked the island castle to the mainland. Destroyed by an earthquake in 1495, the fortress was rebuilt by Grand Master Pierre d'Aubusson. In the 16th century, elaborate double walls and inner moats reinforced the castle to resist Ottoman raids; now, it's one of the best-preserved examples of medieval architecture in Greece. *(Take the bridge from Pl. Platanou across Finikis. ☎28 326. Ask for the helpful pamphlet available at the door. Open Tu-Su 8am-2pm. 800dr, students 400dr.)*

**OTHER SITES.** The gigantic **Plane Tree of Hippocrates,** allegedly planted by the great physician 2400 years ago, has grown to an enormous 12m diameter in Pl. Platanou. It's alluring to envision Hippocrates teaching and writing beneath its noble foliage; it's deflating to realize that the tree is only 500 years old. A spring beside the tree leads toward an ancient sarcophagus used by the Ottomans as a cistern for the **Hadji Hassan Mosque.** Behind the tree, the monumental former **Town Hall,** originally the Italian Governor's Palace, now houses police, justice, and governmental offices. The most impressive Ottoman structure is the **Defterdar Mosque** in Pl. Eleftherias. Nearby, on Diakou, is the abandoned art deco **Synagogue of Kos,** in use until the Second World War. The city's Byzantine **Greek Orthodox Cathedral** looms large on the corner of Korai and Ag. Nikolaou. Near the Casa Romana are the ruins of an even older (5th century BC) and more striking Hellenic mansion. *(Open Tu-Su 8:30am-2:30pm. 600dr, students and seniors 300dr.)*

## ASCLEPION Ασκληπιειον

*4km west of Kos Town. Take the **bus** in summer (15min., 16 per day), or a bike or moped. Follow the sign west off the main road, and go as straight as you can. Taxis are 500dr. ☎28 763. Open June-Sept. Tu-Su 8am-7pm. 800dr, students 400dr.*

The ancient sanctuary of **Asclepion** devotes itself to the healer god. In the 5th century BC, **Hippocrates** opened the world's first medical school here to encourage the development of a precise medical science. Combining early priests' techniques

with his own, Hippocrates made Kos the foremost medical center in ancient Greece. Many present-day doctors travel here to take their Hippocratic oaths.

Most of the ruins at the Asclepion date from the 2nd and 3rd centuries BC. Carved into a hill overlooking Kos Town, the Aegean, and Asia Minor, the complex contained three levels. A sacred forest of cypress and pine trees still adjoins the site. If you ignore the swarming tourists, it's easy to envision the structures as they once stood. Inside, you'll find 2nd-century AD Roman baths, complete with *natatio* (pool), *tepidarium* (tepid-temp), and *caldarium* (sauna). The three stacked levels, called *andirons*, remain fascinating. The lowest *andiron* holds a complex of 3rd-century AD Roman baths and a preserved cistern. Climb the 3rd-century BC steps to the remarkable second *andiron* and the elegant 2nd century AD columns. **Temple of Apollo** and the 4th-century BC **Minor Temple of Asclepius**. The 60-step climb to the third *andiron* leads to the forested remnants of the **Main Temple of Asclepius** and an overview of the site, Kos Town, and the Turkish coast opposite.

## CENTRAL KOS

Claustrophobes will be pleased at how quickly Kos Town's urban fracas gives way to pastoral landscapes north of town. The island's northern reaches stretch out flat, with bike-laned roads. So slap on that sunscreen, strap on your helmet, grab your map, and head for the beach. Take the main road east of town to pedal past a sandy, crowded stretch on the way to the stinky hot springs of **Empros Thermae,** near the road's end and marked by several parked bikes and a Kantina. **Lampi Beach** is at the northernmost tip of the island. West of there, you'll find the tourist strip mall of **Tigaki** (10km west of Kos), where umbrellas and beachside tavernas reign. A nude beach lies between Tigaki and Marmari for the liberated. If cycling or motorbiking doesn't interest you, buses run to **Empros Thermae** (9 per day), **Lampi** (34 per day), **Marmari** (10 per day), and **Mastihari** (4 per day).



The main road out of Kos Town heads 9km southwest to the modern village of **Zipari,** with the ruins of the early **Christian Basilica of St. Paul.** From there, a twisting road slowly winds through the green foothills of the Dikeos Mountains to **Asfendiou,** five small settlements that you can hike without encountering a soul. Buses from Kos go to Asfendiou (40min., 3 per day, 350dr). Continue up this road to **Zia,** a delightful and refreshing small village set in the forests of Mt. Dikeos, host to spectacular island views and worth some quality wandering time. **Ag. Georgios,** in the center of town, also accommodates incredible 13th and 14th-century frescos. South of **Lagoudi,** one of the prettiest of the five villages, the road becomes narrower (a mule path) and the hills become wilder. Uphill 8km farther, you'll come to the compact ruins of old **Pyli,** which include 14th-century frescoes in a Byzantine church built within a castle. Buses from Kos (30min., 5 per day, 350dr).

## SOUTHERN KOS ☎0932

Hills, ravines, and the occasional pasture roll across Southern Kos, which is edged by the best **beaches** on the island. Get a moped to explore more freely; a private taxi will also do the trick. Head to **Ag. Theologos** for the best beach or to the fascinating village of **Zia.** The tiny island of **Kastri** is a short swim from the shore, tempting those who want to frolic on its rock formations. Amongst the beaches stretching up to Kardamena: **Camel** is mildly busy and beautiful; **Paradise** is popular and has its own bus stop; and further north, Hawaiian-flavored **Magic** is empty and enticingly blue. The bus will let you off at any of the beaches.

A few oceanside ancient columns distinguish **Kefalos,** Kos' ancient capital. Get outside this crowded, blah town to the surrounding beaches. North of Kefalos, picturesque **Limionas** spreads a delicious harborside meal beside a sunset view at **Limionas** restaurant. The cheap fish comes fresh from the owner's nets. (*Barbounia* 9000dr per kg, octopus 1200dr, Greek salad 800dr. ☎422 002. Open 10am-11pm.) A gorgeous, deserted beach stretches along the coast to **Mastihari.** **Agios Theologos,** 4km west of Kefalos, is one of the island's quietest and most drop-dead-gorgeous beaches. To get there, walk for an hour on the dirt path that branches to the right from the bus stop; you'll likely have the beach to yourself.

# ASTYPALEA ΑΣΤΥΠΑΛΙΑ

Few travelers venture to butterfly-shaped Astypalea, the westernmost of the Dodecanese islands. Jagged hills and secluded orange and lemon groves make it an excellent place to unwind, but infrequent ferries and almost total lack of Flying Dolphin service repulses intruders almost as effectively as its mountaintop fort once did. For those in dire need of tranquility, it might be worth the effort, planning, and patience required to reach the undiscovered coves of Astypalea.

## ASTYPALEA TOWN ☎0243

Surrounded by tawny hills, Astypalea Town is composed of Skala (or Pera Yialos) by the port, and Hora, at the top of the hill. It's the only major city on the island, and all of the services and amenities you'll need can be found here.



**ORIENTATION AND PRACTICAL INFORMATION.** **Ferries** run to: **Amorgos** (2½hr., 3 per week, 2800dr); **Kalymnos** (3hr., 4 per week, 2600dr); **Kos** (3½hr., 1 per week, 3000dr); **Naxos** (5½hr., 2 per week, 4600dr); **Paros** (7hr., 2 per week, 3800dr); **Patmos** (2 per week, 2450dr); **Piraeus** (10-13hr., 4 per week, 6800dr); **Rhodes** (5hr., 2 per week, 5000dr); and **Santorini** (4hr., 1 per week, 3200dr). **Flying Dolphins** serve **Kos, Kalymnos, Symi,** and **Rhodes** (1 per week, twice as fast and twice as expensive). Daily excursions go to the neighboring islands of **Ag. Kyriakis, Kounoupi,** and **Syrna** (1500dr). The ever-changing **bus schedule** is chalked up where the waterfront meets the main road to Hora. **Buses** run as far as **Livadia** and **Analipsi** (400dr); frequency varies by season. Renting a **moped** is one of the best ways to see he island from Astypalea Town. **Moto Center Astypalea** (☎61 263 or 61 541), on the waterfront near the ferry dock, and **Moto Rent Vergouli** (☎61 351), on the main road to Hora, rent motorbikes from 2500dr (open 8am-2pm and 4:30-9pm). Just before the town's small beach, the **police** are in a small building (☎61 207; open 8am-7pm). The **port police** are in a white building with a Greek flag, on the waterfront between the town and the port (☎61 208; open 8am-10pm). In case of **emergency,** call 61 544.

The **National Bank** is under the Aegean hotel (☎61 224; open M-Th 8am-2pm, F 8am-1:30pm); the waterfront has a **24hr ATM.** A **tourist information** center (☎61 412, 61 114, or 61 206) runs from the Town Hall in **Hora,** directly across from the gift shop. **Astypalea Tours** (☎61 571 or 61 572; fax 61 328), on the main road to Hora, can handle transportation, accommodation and information questions; they're also the **Olympic Airways** local agent, whose planes depart from Analypsis **airport** (☎61 410; open 10am-1pm and 6-10pm). The **OTE** is above the Maistrali Restaurant. (☎61 212/5. Open M-F 7:30am-2pm.) The **post office** (open 7:30am-2pm), **currency exchange** (☎61 223), and several **supermarkets** (open 9am-1pm and 5-9pm) are all in this section of town. **Postal code:** 85900.

**ACCOMMODATIONS.** Rooms on the island fill with an annual influx of summering Athenians in July and August, but vacancy is the norm the rest of the year. Bargain in the off season. **Akti Studios and Rooms** are ideally set at the edge of town across from the ferry dock—look for the large "Rooms To Let" inscription on the side of the building. Doubles with water-scraping balconies overlook the entire town. Ask about cheaper back-side rooms. (☎61 114 or 61 281. Fridge and private bath. Around 10,000dr.) Along the central waterfront, **Hotel Astynea** rents simple rooms with phone, fridge, balcony, and private bath. (☎61 040 or 61 209; fax 61 041. Singles 5000-7500dr; doubles 7000-10,000dr.) Rooms are similar to those at **Camping Astypalea,** 2.5km east of town, near Marmari; a hip bar, self-service restaurant, mini-market, post, and exchange services are a bonus. Follow signs or take a bus toward Maltezana. (☎61 338. 1100dr per person; 800dr per tent.)

**FOOD AND ENTERTAINMENT.** Restaurants roll out near the waterfront in Astypalea Town and on the square in Hora. At waterside **Albatross,** tapestries and a straw roof create a cozy atmosphere to try a tasty but random assortment of Chinese, German, and Italian foods. (Excellent *souzoukakia* 1300dr, *Armenkio souvlaki* 1000dr, barbecued chicken 1400dr. ☎61 546.) With tables stunningly set on the beach below Albatross, **To Akrogiali** serves a local Astypalean concoction, *astakomakaronada* (12,500dr per kg) and other daily catches from 6000dr per kg. (☎61 863. Open 8am-3am daily.) Finish your meal with a slice of pie (800-1300dr) at **To Magazi,** looking out on the Castro. Follow the road across from the fifth windmill to get there. (☎61 889. Open 10am-2pm, 8pm-2am.) In Hora, **To Aigaion** (☎61 730), a snack bar/*mezedopolon*, is the only one of its kind on the island. It's across from the windmills, and ideal for breakfast (400-1000dr), an afternoon *frappé* (500dr), or a late-night drink to lively Greek and English hits until 5am.

**SIGHTS.** The **Archaeological Museum** in Astypalea Town houses a small, well-presented collection of artifacts unearthed from around the island, including stone inscriptions, early Christian sculptures, and Mycenaean grave findings. Before heading up to the castle, stop to see some of the better-preserved objects once held within the fortification. The museum is on the main road to Hora, just inland from the waterfront. (Open M-F 8am-2:30pm, 6pm-12:30am. Free.) In **Hora,** a striking row of windmills leads to a path up to the 1413 **Castro,** originally a line of defense built by the Knights of St. John; later, the Turks moved in, leaving the most significant architectural presence. Much of the structure remains intact. Exploring the chamber lets you gaze out across the island and nearby islets with a clear view. Occasional concerts are held there; ask at the tourist office for details. **Portaitissa Monastery** is to the right of the entrance and is the island's most sacred church.



# NEAR ASTYPALEA

Head out from Hora to find good beaches. A 20min. hike southwest along the coast takes you to **Tzamaki Beach,** an uncrowded refuge for nude bathers that's much better than **Livadia,** a beach closer to town. Four kilometers farther along a dirt path, the sand and palm trees at **Agios Konstantinidos** make it the western island's best beach. Great beaches surround the southwest part of the island past Tzamaki, like **Ormos Kaminakia** and **Ormos Vatses.** From there, the hidden cave of **Spilia Negrou** is accessible by boat, and worth the venture if you can convince a local fisherman to take you. A right turn after the sixth windmill in Hora circuitously leads past a military base to the monastery of **Agios Ioannis,** which looks out over a small waterfall—perhaps the most charming sight on the island.

Northeast of Astypalea Town, the main road leads toward the other "wing" of the butterfly-shaped island, passing the campsite and several sandy beaches. Signs prohibiting nudity are a red flag for a good beach below. The road is a bus route, and in addition to designated stops, sympathetic drivers make informal stops.

Lackluster buildings and ominous construction mar the colorful gardens and gentle landscapes of the fishing village of **Maltezana** (officially known as **Analipsi**), 10km northeast of Astypalea Town. Home to miraculously intact **Roman mosaics and baths** next to the small port, Maltezana is accessible by **bus** (4 per day, 250dr). **Psili Amo** beach near the airport is one of the island's best, with sands that invite everyone, but no one comes. Vathi's natural harbor divides into **Exo Vathi** and **Mesa Vathi** 2km farther; there's a decent beach nearby at **Agios Andreas.**

# KALYMNOS ΚΑΛΥΜΝΟΣ

In Kalymnos the infant's paint-box has been at work again on the milky slopes of the mountain.
—Lawrence Durrell

Although the first inhabitants of Kalymnos have yet to be identified, the ruins at Embrio and Vathis suggest that Phoenicians successfully colonized the island around 2000 BC. However, Kalymnos is better-known for its sponge-diving industry than its ancient history. In years past, Kalymnian men would spend five or six months of the year diving in the Libyan Sea, south of Muammar Al-Quaddafi's Line of Death. Sponges still lurk in warehouses, tourist kiosks and factories, and restaurant display-cases, harkening back to the island's glory days as the sponge capital of the world. But the sponges are dying off, as is Kalymnos's economy. West-coast tourism has resuscitated the economy somewhat, keeping the interior rather barren. The rugged central mountains cascade into wide beaches and blue-green water, luring the occasional intrepid mountaineer.



## POTHIA Ποθια ☎0243

During the turn-of-the-century Italian occupation, locals antagonized the Italians by painting their houses blue, Greece's national color. Pink and green buildings have since infiltrated Pothia's blued streets and, although slightly grayed, this relatively large town (pop. 11,500) remains more colorful than its whitewashed Aegean counterparts. Behind the bustle of the busy port, narrow back streets are lined with stellar classical leftovers. Pothia isn't made for tourists—there are few rooms, few agencies, and few attractions—but that's part of the appeal.

### GETTING THERE AND GETTING AROUND

**Ferries:** To: **Astypalea** (3hr., 2 per week, 2500dr); **Kos** (1hr., 1 per week, 1400dr); **Leros** (1hr., 1-2 per day, 1400dr); **Lipsi** (2hr., 3 per week, 2000dr); **Nisyros** (3 per week, 1600dr); **Patmos** (3hr., 1-2 per day, 2500dr); **Piraeus** (10hr., 1-2 per day, 7000dr); **Rhodes** (6hr., 1 per day, 4300dr); **Samos** (2 per week, 3100dr); **Symi** (3 per week, 3300dr); **Thessaloniki** (1 per week, 13,500dr); and **Tilos** (3 per week, 2300dr). Daily **excursions** head to the splendid island beaches on **Pserimos** (2000dr round-trip) or **Mastihari** (3 per day; 900dr one way).

**Flying Dolphins:** Daily to: **Agathonisi** (4980dr); **Fourni** (6800dr); **Ikaria** (6180dr); **Kos** (3-4 per day; 2800dr); **Leros** (3 per day; 3600dr); **Lipsos** (3600dr); **Nisyros** (1 per week, 3400dr); **Patmos** (4900dr); **Rhodes** (8750dr); **Samos** (6145dr); **Symi** (6785dr) and **Tilos** (4075dr). Also to **Astypalea** (1 per week, 5000dr). A hydrofoil to **Turkey** departs once a week (10,000dr).

**Buses:** Buses leave every hour on the hour 8am-10pm to: **Kastelli** (50min., 250dr) via **Hora** (10min.); **Myrties** (20min.); **Massouri** (25min.); and **Panormos** (15min.). Fares 100-250dr. Also to: **Argos** (2 per day 7am-1:50pm, 200dr); **Emporio** (8am and 4pm, 300dr); **Plati Gialos** (3 per day 9:15am-3pm, 250dr); and **Vilhadia** (7 per day 8am-7:30pm, 200dr). Buses to western towns leave from the town hall in harbor center. Buses to **Vathis** (4 per day 6:30am-6pm, 300dr) depart from the northeast corner of the waterfront. Buy tickets before boarding at Themis mini-market, next to the town hall, and insert them into the automated validating box on the bus.

**Flights: Olympic Airways** (☎29 265; fax 28 903). Take the first left past the National Bank; it's 50m down on the left. Open M-Tu and Th-F 8am-1:30pm and 5-8:30pm, W and Sa 8am-1:30pm.

**Taxis:** (☎50 300 or 50 303). Congregate in Pl. Kyprou up Eleftherias 7am-9pm. Taxis also operate as taxi buses for people going in one direction.

**Moped Rental: Kastas Katrivesis,** behind the port police at the end of the dock. Mopeds 2500-4000dr per day, with partial insurance. Open 8:30am-9pm. **Scooteromania** (☎51 780; home 50 193) is down a little alley off the waterfront between the cafes. Mopeds from 2000-5500dr. Open 9am-9pm. Both places only rent to those with and International Driver's License unless they have an EU license.

## ORIENTATION AND PRACTICAL INFORMATION

Ferries arrive at the far left end of the port (facing inland). The road leading from the dock bends around the waterfront until it runs into the large, cream-colored municipal building, a church, and the town hall. Narrow, shop-lined **Eleftherias** heads one-way inland at this point, leading to **Pl. Kyprou,** home to the **post office, telephone, police,** and **taxis.** The waterfront road continues past town hall to a strip of fish tavernas and one unparalleled sweet shop. The second most important avenue, **Venizelou,** intersects Eleftherias at the end of the harbor near **Agios Christos Church.** Continue on this road to reach the western part of the island. Follow the harbor promenade past the police station to access the road to Vathis. Most streets in Pothia are unnamed, but following the landmarks is relatively easy.

**Tourist Office:** At the time of press, the new tourist office had not opened. Contact the town hall (☎59 142) for updated information.

**Tourist Agencies:** No one agency will satisfy all your tourist needs, especially if you're looking at boat schedules. **Magos Travel** (☎28 777, 50 777, or 28 652; fax 22 608), on the waterfront near the port police, sells hydrofoil tickets and **GA** ferry tickets. Open 8:30am-9pm. **DANE Sea Lines** (☎23 043 or 24 083), next to the tourist office and marked by a yellow flag, represents the other ferry line serving Kalymnos to Leros, Patmos, Kos, Rhodes, Piraeus, and others. They also have hydrofoil services (from 1400dr-7000dr). Open 9am-2pm and 5-10pm.

**Banks:** A few banks on the waterfront have full services, including **National Bank** (☎29 794), with an **ATM** and **currency exchange.** Open M-Th 8am-2pm, F 8am-1:30pm.

**Police:** (☎29 301). Go up Eleftherias and take the left inland road from the taxi plateia. English-speaking help can be found in a blue and yellow Neoclassical building on the right. Open 24hr.

**Port Authority:** (☎29 304), in the yellow building across from customs at the end of the dock. Provides ferry information. Open 24hr.

**Hospital:** (☎23 025), on the main road to Hora, 1.5km from Pothia. Open 24hr.

**OTE:** (☎29 599). From the taxi plateia up Eleftherias, take the inland road on the right. Open M-F 7:30am-3:10pm.

**Internet: Neon Internet C@fe** (☎50 980) is off a side street from the waterfront behind the town hall. Six computers and other video games. 1000dr per hour.

**Post Office:** (☎28 340), just past the police station on the right. Has **currency exchange.** Open M-F 7:30am-2pm. **Postal code:** 85200.

## ACCOMMODATIONS

Pickings are slim in Pothia when it comes to lodgings. There are better options in Myrties or neighboring Plati Gialos, though transportation is tricky; the tourist office may help. Camping is legal on all the island's beaches, but uncommon.

**Pension Greek House** (☎29 559), one block in front of the sponge factory. A sparkling flower-covered home; rooms have baths and fridges. Doubles 8000dr; triples 10,000dr.

**Faros** (☎28 077 or 47 790), above the Adelfia Cafe directly across from the port police, offers very simple doubles with nice balconies overlooking the entire port. Doubles 6000dr with shared baths. Ask about the roof-top room; although smaller, it has its own bath and a huge terrace.

**Pension Niki** (☎48 135 or 28 528). If there are any vacancies, Niki will be waiting at the dock when you arrive. A little tough to find. Take a left of the waterfront road on the first main street; the bank will be on your left. Look for a little sign or ask around. Rooms are of decent size in a quieter part of town and all have their own baths and **fans.** Doubles 5000 per night, 4000 if you stay more than one night.

## FOOD AND ENTERTAINMENT

Nightlife in Pothia is pretty tame. Most folks enjoy a few drinks in the harbor bars and tavernas before heading to the clubs in Massouri.

**Xefteris.** From the town hall, head up Eleftherias and take the first right, then the first left directly into the taverna's outdoor garden. Out of the way and not at all touristy, even though it's the island's oldest restaurant. *Dolmades* (stuffed vine leaves) 1200dr, stuffed zucchini 1200dr. Open noon-1am.

**Navtikos Omilos Restaurant.** Isolated at the far left end of the harbor (facing inland). Depending on the season, you have front row seats to either an amusement park (June-July) or the ocean. You and the excursion groups from Kos will dine cheaply and well. Spaghetti *neapolitana* 650dr. Open 8am-3pm and 6:30-11pm.

**Alachouzou** (☎29 446) past the church and along the waterfront. This pastry-lover's paradise has been making only 5 of the classic honey-drenched Greek desserts for over 35 years, and it has perfected all of them. Try the house specialty, *galaktobouriko* (custard sandwiched between *phyllo* dough and drenched in sweet syrup; 350dr, 500dr if you sit down), with homemade vanilla and chocolate ice cream (cone 200dr). Open 9am-2:30pm, 6pm-1am.

**Apothiki** (☎51 890), past the town hall on the waterfront road. Pothia's trendiest night-time haunt. Stylin' young locals sip *frappés* and cocktails. Open 10am-3pm, 5pm-2am.

**Cine Oasis,** off the waterfront, at the end of a short alleyway plastered with movie posters. Nightly shows at 8:45 and 10:45pm. Adults 1400dr, children 1000dr.

DODECANESE

## SIGHTS

**POTHIA.** Learn first-hand about the island's historic industry at the sponge shop of **Nikolas Gourlas,** on the waterfront near the port police. Mr. Gourlas speaks English and will be happy to show you around the factory, where sponges are cleaned and chemically treated. (Sponges from 500dr.) The **Nautical Museum,** on the second floor a few doors down from the town hall, houses traditional island wares and clothing in the one-room **Folk Museum**, and explores the life and work of the island's sponge divers. Read plaques all about the island's famous industry, or ask the curator, a former diver, about the experience. *(☎51 361. Open Tu-Sa 8am-1:30pm, Su 10am-12:30pm. 500dr, students 300dr.)* Follow the blue signs from Venizelou to the **Archeological Museum of Kalymnos,** in the former mansion of turn-of-the-century Kalymniot sponge barons Catherine and Nikolaos Vouvalis *(☎23 113. Open Tu-Su 9am-2pm. Free.)*

From the port police, take the roads to the left to reach the beach at **Therma,** 2km away. Arthritic patients once came to the sanitarium to wade in its painkilling **sulphur mineral baths.** Now, a pleasant, crowded beach has replaced the baths (out of operation for 3 years) as the main draw. A short walk around the bend leads to a quiet swimming spot. Tranquil **Vlichadia beach** (6km from Pothia), the island's only **scuba diving** site, lies west of Therma. Inconvenient buses keep it peaceful.

**VATHIS VALLEY.** Although most of Kalymnos sprouts grass and wildflowers, thriving mandarins, limes, and grapevines cover the valley at Vathis (6km north-east of Pothia), which begins at **Rina** village. There's no beach here, but you can swim from the pier. The exquisite scenery and quietude compensate make sand unnecessary. Within swimming range on the north side of the inlet is **Daskaleios,** a stalagmite cave. In Rina, the **Hotel Galini** has decent rooms with baths and balconies. (☎31 241. Doubles 7500dr.) The three tavernas on the tiny waterfront rent rooms at similar prices.

# Hmm, call home or eat lunch?

Nathan Lane for YOU[SM].

No doubt, traveling on a budget is tough. So tear out this wallet guide and keep it with you during your travels. With YOU, calling home from overseas is affordable and easy.

If the wallet guide is missing, call collect 913-624-5336 or visit www.youcallhome.com for YOU country numbers.

**Dialing instructions:**
*Need help with access numbers while overseas? Call collect, 913-624-5336.*

**Dial the access number for the country you're in.**
**Dial 04 or follow the English prompts.**
**Enter your credit card information to place your call.**

| Country | Access Number | Country | Access Number | Country | Access Number |
|---|---|---|---|---|---|
| Australia **v** | 1-800-551-110 | Israel **v** | 1-800-949-4102 | Spain **v** | 900-99-0013 |
| Bahamas **+** | 1-800-389-2111 | Italy **+ v** | 172-1877 | Switzerland **v** | 0800-899-777 |
| Brazil **v** | 000-8016 | Japan **+ v** | 00539-131 | Taiwan **v** | 0080-14-0877 |
| China **+ ▲ v** | 108-13 | Mexico **u v** | 001-800-877-8000 | United Kingdom **v** | 0800-890-877 |
| France **v** | 0800-99-0087 | Netherlands **+ v** | 0800-022-9119 | | |
| Germany **+ v** | 0800-888-0013 | New Zealand **▲ v** | 000-999 | | |
| Hong Kong **v** | 800-96-1877 | Philippines **T v** | 105-16 | | |
| India **v** | 000-137 | Singapore **v** | 8000-177-177 | | |
| Ireland **v** | 1-800-552-001 | South Korea **+ v** | 00729-16 | | |

**YOU**[SM]
*Service provided by Sprint*

**v** Call answered by automated Voice Response Unit. **+** Public phones may require coin or card.
**▲** May not be available from all payphones. **u** Use phones marked with "LADATEL" and no coin or card is required.
**T** If talk button is available, push it before talking.

# WEST COAST OF KALYMNOS

## HORA

Pera Castro and Argos overlook the town of Hora, once Kalymnos's capital but now little more than another of Pothia's tentacles. One kilometer or so beyond Hora, just after the road begins to descend into Panormos, a few white steps and a sign by the side of the road lead to the shell of the **Church of Christ of Jerusalem.** Byzantine Emperor Arcadius built this church to thank God for sparing him in a storm while at sea. The half-domed stone blocks with carved inscriptions are from a 4th-century BC temple to Apollo that stood on the same site. By incorporating these pre-Christian buildings, the church served as a symbolic victory of Christianity over the Olympians. The beachside footpath leads to a quiet **cove** with strange rock formations. Bring your waterproof shoes to avoid sea urchins, if you dive in.

Many **hikes** originate off the road to Panormos from Pothia. There is no map or official guide; ask a road-side kiosk owner or tourist office for information. The main road branches at Panormos. One offshoot goes to **Kantouni,** a village with a crowded, less-than-spectacular beach and an excellent dining-and-dancing establishment—**Domus Restaurant** (☎47 959)—on the waterfront; don't miss the rooftop sunset, and dance the night away at one of the most celebrated spots for quality nightlife. Encounter concealed natural platforms ideal for dives of all heights by venturing left (facing the sea) along the rocks of Kantouni beach. Another road from Panormos leads 2km to the sandy, flat and less crowded beach of **Plati Gialos,** one of the island's best. A stay at **Pension Plati Gialos** (☎22 014) is sure to captivate you. The pension is perched on a cliff with a memorable view of the coastline and fresh, quiet, sun-filled rooms to wake up in; follow the paved road to the top of the hill, where you will find the reception desk (doubles 6000dr).

DODECANESE

## MYRTIES

Besides its own crowded, grey-sand beaches, Myrties is named for the abundance of wild blueberries that once covered it's rolling hills above the beach. Short boat trips to tiny, rocky islet of **Telendos** (15min., every 30min., 200dr) originate here. A city occupied the fault line where an AD 554 earthquake separated Telendos from Kalymnos, and traces of it have been found on the ocean floor, but the rift is invisible from the surface. The Roman ruins on Telendos are modest at best, but a few small, secluded beaches fringe the island; turn right from the ferry dock for the best of them, including the bare-all variety. The Byzantine Monastery of **St. Constantine**, open only for liturgy, is past the beaches to the right. Its dome is visible from the Pothia-Emporios road near Myrties. Accommodations in Telendos are generally only full in August. Most pensions charge 5000-7000dr for a double. **Uncle George's Pension,** near the docks, has an excellent restaurant and rooms with baths. (☎47 502. Doubles 6000dr; studios with kitchenette 7000dr.) **Restaurant Noufaro** (☎47 822, 48 110), on the main road in **Armeos,** just outside Myrties, makes the best *bifteki* around (1700-1900dr per main entree). A great view of Telendos and candle-lit tables from the veranda centered around a cute fountain makes it worth the slight transportation inconvenience. (Open 11am-12am daily.) Before leaving Myrties, take a last look back at Telendos. Many claim that the profile of a woman mourning her husband is visible in the rock along the left side of the mountain.

## MASSOURI

The pebbly beaches and the nightclubs at Massouri are always crowded. Establishments open late, and the clientele arrive even later—always after midnight. With only one paved road running through Massouri, all the bars and clubs are within 5min. of one another on foot and crowds in each vary from night to night. **Neon Internet C@fe** (☎48 318) has a branch here where an hour goes for 500dr. The **Pink Elephant** boasts Guinness (600dr), hard cider (600dr), and an assortment of cocktails (1000dr). **Nadir** bar hosts Happy Hours from 8-9pm, making that 1700dr double its worth. The real hot spots are the dance clubs **Club Dorian Tropical** and

Kalymnos's only outdoor club, **Kastro,** a little farther north on the main road. Each charges a 2000dr cover that includes a free drink. Follow the road for another 500m to get to the *bouzoukia*, where a Greek *glendi* continues late into the night.

# LEROS ΛΕΡΟΣ

Mental hospitals and military *junta* prisons don't fit into the paradisical picture of the idyllic Greek island, but Leros has a lot of history, both recent and ancient. The goddess Artemis, a fleet-footed hunter and generally independent woman, was the island's first occupant; she chose Leros, as did the Persians, the Knights of St. John, and the influential Italians, who saw in Lakki's natural harbor the potential for an ideal naval base during the Second World War. The prettiest sights on the island are the old Italian mansions of faded reds, oranges, and blues that line the harbor of Agia Marina. After the war, the Greek government chose Leros as a site for mental hospitals. Because these institutions garnered negative responses for their poor treatment of patients, the island was held back from leaping onto the tourist bandwagon. In many respects, this has proved its saving grace, allowing for a degree of tourism that hasn't yet threatened the island's serenity.



## LAKKI Λακκι ☎0247

Lakki, an uninviting port town and the ferry-goer's introduction to Leros, has borne the brunt of the island's problematic recent past. Passing through this transportation hub is necessary for most trips to Leros. The waterfront hails from the Italian occupation, and resembles an abandoned movie set populated with a cast and crew on an eternal coffee break. A grand rotary-dotted boulevard fronts large art deco buildings quietly deteriorating. Public sentiment seems to be shifting in favor of preserving these edifices as a historical reminder rather than letting them crumble as a political symbol. Lakki has done little to cultivate tourism from which neighboring towns have prospered, yet the town contains the island's largest stores and banks. Few people choose to tour or stay in Lakki.

**ORIENTATION AND PRACTICAL INFORMATION.** **Ferries** float away to: **Kos** (1 per day, 2100dr) and **Kalymnos** (1-2 per day, 1800dr) and from **Xirocampos** to **Myrties** (1-2 per day) and **Patmos** (1 per day, 1500dr). Kos and Patmos connect with more comprehensive ferry service. **Flying Dolphins** leave from Ag. Marina. A **taxi station** (☎22 550 or 23 070) is next to the police station. **Kastis Travel and Shipping,** King George 9 (☎22 500; fax 22 872), along the waterfront directly across from the taxi stand, offers comprehensive travel assistance and if Mr. Kastis is there, he'll share his grand knowledge of the island. Virtually all tourist services are on or just inland from the waterfront. The road to the rest of the island runs perpendicular from the rotary. The closest beach is 1km west in **Koulouki,** which makes for a scenic walk along the coast and one of the island's better swims. The old mental hospital is 2km to the west. For **tourist information** (☎22 937), look for the sign on the waterfront. A **National Bank** (☎23 583) is along the waterfront, and an **Agricultural Bank** (☎23 234) sits inland from the police station, at the left where the road separates (both open M-Th 8am-2pm, F 8am-1:30pm, with **24hr. ATM**). The **police** are at the far end of the waterfront from where ferries dock (☎22 222; theoretically open 24hr.). To find the **port police,** head inland by the waterfront school near the ferry dock and take the first left into a seemingly abandoned building. (☎22 224. Open 24hr.; you may have to ring the doorbell.) A **hospital** (☎23 251 or 23 554) is two blocks inland of the waterfront school and open 24hr. For a **pharmacy,** head inland at the cinema and take the second right. (☎23 367. Open daily 8am-1pm and 5-9pm.) The **post office** is a block inland from Leros Palace Hotel. (☎22 929. Open M-F 7:30am-2pm.) **Postal code:** 85400.

**ACCOMMODATIONS AND FOOD.** Most wisely avoid using Lakki as a base to explore the island, but ferry schedules may necessitate overnight stays here. Rooms can be pricey, but the town's unpopularity gives bargaining travelers the upper hand. **Hotel Katerina** is by far the best bet in town with clean, if slightly institutional, rooms. Their van may be waiting at the ferry for pickup, but if not, walk along the main street from the port, head inland at the cinema, and take the second right. (☎22 460; fax 23 038. Singles 8000dr; doubles 10,000dr.) **Hotel Artemis,** a few blocks inland before Leros Palace Hotel, is the next best option. (☎22 416. Singles 8000dr; doubles 10,000dr.) The large and well-maintained **campground,** 3km southeast, between the mental hospital and Xero Kampos, has standard facilities. (☎23 372 or 097 7633 146. 1200dr per person; 1000dr per tent; 650dr per tent rental.) The owner also runs **Leros Diving Center.** (Excursions from 15,000dr with proper qualification.)

There are a couple of notable exceptions to the boring string of restaurants along and just inland of the waterfront. The island's largest and cheapest **Spanos supermarket** lies two blocks inland from the police station. Next to the post office, inland from Leros Palace Hotel, **To Petrino** (☎24 807) serves carefully prepared meals in the sort of setting that keeps you lingering all night. The menu changes but consists of starters (around 700dr) and large meat-heavy portions (around 1700dr). **Kali Parea**, the best and cheapest along the waterfront, grills a superior souvlaki (400dr). Beachside **Koulouki,** 1km west of town on the coast road and an island favorite, serves lamb with pasta (1400dr), prawns (1400dr), and other goodies under a canopy of trees (☎24 935; open 9am-midnight). The few Lakkians who venture out after dinner head to the waterfront for the seldom-crowded **Puerto Club** (☎24 347, open 10pm-3am daily), or the island's outdoor waterfront **cinema.** (Films 9:15pm, in English with Greek subtitles. 1500dr, children 1300dr).

DODECANESE

## AGIA MARINA Αγια Μαρινα ☎0247

Seeming like the island's true capital, Agia Marina is probably the most charming town in Leros. This harbor town has lured in loads of tourists, and now supplies most island administrative and commercial services. Though the town is noted for its nightlife and has the island's only Flying Dolphin service, there aren't as many rooms in Agia Marina as you'd expect, and more visitors stay in **Alinda.** With no beach in town, Agia Marina lends itself to eating, drinking, and promenading.

Waterfront **Kastis Antonis Travel,** right near the dock, is extremely useful for exchange, excursions, and all other travel arrangements. (☎22 140. Fax 23 500. Open M-Su 8:30am-1:30pm, 5:30-8:30pm.) An **Agricultural Bank** (open M-Th 8am-2pm, F 8am-1:30pm, **no ATM**) is next to the **National Bank** with a 24hr. **ATM.** A 24hr. **police station** (☎22 226) and a number of moped rentals sit along the waterfront, alongside a burgeoning collection of boutiques and tourist shops. The **post office** (☎85 400) and **OTE** (☎23 199; fax 25 549) are in the same building along the road to Platanos' plateia, leading left from the National Bank. Ag. Marina's self-serve **laundry** (☎(093) 462 349) is located on the parallel street from the main Platanos road.

Directly next to Kastis Travel, **Ta Koupia** (☎24 204) makes some of the best chicken souvlaki in existence for a mere 350dr. When the moon rises, Agia Marina becomes naughtier and livelier than its daytime calm hints. Evenings begin at the waterside cafes or at the locals' preferred watering hotel, **To Meltemi;** they end at trendy **Apothiki** (☎22 968) for Greek music, or **Apocalypse** for funk and soul. **Enallatiko** plays the latest English hits all day and night and is Ag. Marina's flourishing center of nightlife with an elegant harbor view. **Internet** services are also available (☎25 746. 1500dr per hour; open 8am-1am daily). Bars hug the waterfront and are distinguishable only by the colors of their chairs; some charge covers (around 1300-1800dr), depending on the evening and almost solely in August.

# PATMOS ΠΑΤΜΟΣ

Declared the "Holy Island" by ministerial decree, Patmos makes its historical and religious significance as plain as day—portside signs warn that nudity and other indecent behaviors will not be tolerated here. Still, modern Patmos is lively and sophisticated, balancing its long religious history and its role as a place of spiritual pilgrimage. Artisans find secular inspiration here, too: galleries and craft stores proliferate in larger towns. Though more tame than its neighbors, visitors won't have to spend the night in self-flagellation—Patmos is only part monastic.

In ancient times, Patmians worshipped **Artemis,** the huntress said to have raised the island from the sea. **Orestes** built a grand temple to her after seeking refuge on Patmos from the Furies, who were pursuing him for murdering his mother Clytemnestra (she, in her turn, had murdered her husband and Orestes' father). With the arrival of **St. John,** exiled from Ephesus, Patmos became a center of fledgling Christianity. John purportedly wrote the **Book of Revelations** here, in a grotto overlooking the main town. His words "I…was on the isle that is called Patmos, for the word of God, and for the testimony of Jesus Christ" are the island's unofficial motto. In the 4th century AD, when Christianity spread with the Byzantine Empire, a basilica replaced the razed Temple of Artemis. In the 11th century, the fortified Monastery of St. John was built on a hill overlooking the entire island.



## SKALA Σκαλα ☎0247

Built along a graceful arc of coastline, the colorful port town of Skala gives only a hint of the island's diverse terrain. The town didn't develop until the 19th century, when the pirate threat subsided and living by the water became safe. The main administrative buildings, housing the post office and customs house, were constructed during Italian occupation (1912-1943). Today, whitewashed churches blend in with village buildings, cafes, bars, tavernas, shops, and galleries. Skala is the most convenient place to stay on Patmos, particularly if you'll rely on the bus.

### GETTING THERE AND GETTING AROUND

**Ferries:** Most are run by **DANE** (☎31 314; fax 31 685) or **G.A. Ferries** (☎33 133, 31 205, or 32 575; fax 32 180), both near the plateia. Ask about student discounts. Daily to: **Kalymnos** (2½hr., 1700dr); **Kos** (4hr., 2700dr); **Leros** (1½hr., 5000dr); **Piraeus** (10hr., 6500dr); and **Rhodes** (10hr., 5600dr). Also to: **Lipsi** (3 per week, 1100dr); **Samos** (4 per week, 1700dr); **Agathonisi** (4 per week, 1550dr). Ferries run once per week to: **Nisyros** (3200dr); **Tilos** (3200dr); and in summer **Thessaloniki** (21hr., 11,500dr). Private **excursion boats** go daily to **Lipsi** (1500dr one-way, 2500dr round-trip) and to **beaches** around the island (1000dr round-trip); deals are posted on the waterfront.

**Flying Dolphins:** Service to: **Agathonisi** (40min., 2 per week, 3980dr); **Fourni** (1hr., 3 per week, 3500dr); **Ikaria** (50min., 1 per day, 3780dr); **Kalymnos** (1hr., 2 per day, 4900dr); **Leros** (30min., 2 per day, 3360dr); **Lipsi** (20min., 2 per week, 2620dr); and **Samos** (50min., 2-3 per day, 3645dr).

**Buses:** Across the little park, left of the police station. 11 per day (every hour, on the hour) to **Hora** (10min.); 7 per day to **Grikou** (15-20min.); 6 per day from **Hora to Grikou;** and 4 per day to **Kampos** (20min.; 8:15am-6:30pm). All fares 250dr. Buy tickets on the bus from the ticket boy. An ever-changing schedule is posted at the bus stop.

**Taxis:** (☎31 225). Congregate in the main plateia 24hr. in summer, but are difficult to catch, especially in the post-disco flurry (3-6:30am). Taxis to Hora 1000dr.

**Car Rental: Patmos Rent-a-Car** (☎32 203 or 32 923). Turn left after the post office and look for it on your right, next to the Art Cafe (2nd floor). Cars 11,000dr and up. Open 8:30am-2pm, 4pm-9:30pm.

**Moped Rental:** Available all over Skala. For the friendliest and most straightforward service around, **Express Moto** (☎32 088) is a left after the tourist office; take the first

right. New models 2000-5000dr per day. Open 8am-8pm. At **Theo Girogio** (☎32 066), new models are 3000-6000dr per day. Open 8:30am-9pm. Both are service-oriented, and they also rent mountain bikes (from 600-1200dr. per day).

## ORIENTATION AND PRACTICAL INFORMATION

Skala's amenities are all within a block or two of the waterfront. Excursion boats dock opposite the line of cafes and restaurants, while larger vessels park in front of the Italian building that houses the police and post office and borders the main plateia. Moving straight inland from the Post office, a street lined with shops and souvlaki stands leads to the OTE. Across from the welcome cafe, a parallel road leads to Hora and is lined with a few pensions. Skala is on a narrow part of the island; you can walk from the water to the opposite coast in about 10 minutes.

**Tourist Office:** (☎31 666), in the big Italian building across the dock. Maps, brochures, bus schedules, information on all ferries, and help with accommodations. Ask for the free Patmos Summertime guide, which includes maps of Skala and the island. Open M-F 9am-3:30pm and 4-10:30pm, Sa 11am-1:30pm and 6:30-8pm. **City Hall** in Hora can also provide information (☎31 235 or 31 058). The **Welcome Cafe,** next to the dock, is open 24hr. and has space for baggage storage.

**Port Authority:** (☎31 231 or 34 131), to the left of the ferry dock, next to the snack bar. Information on ferries. Open 24hr.–just knock long and loud if it's late.

**Tourist Agencies:** All over the waterfront, but each offers info on only the ferry lines for which they sell tickets. Consult the tourist office or the port police for complete schedules and then ask where to buy your ticket. **Apollon Tourist and Shipping Agency** (☎31 724, 31 324, 34 105, or 31 105; fax 31 819) is the local agent for **Olympic Airways** and can assist with rentals. Open 7am-10pm.

**Banks: National Bank** (☎34 050), in the far end of the plateia. Cash advances on MasterCard, **currency exchange,** and **24hr ATM.** Open M-Th 8am-2pm, F 8am-1:30pm. Exchange at the post office and **Apollon Agency** as well.

**Police:** (☎31 303), upstairs from the tourist office. Open 24hr.

**Tourist Police:** (☎31 303), housed with the police above the tourist office.

**Hospital:** (☎31 211), on the main road to Hora, across from the monastery Apokalipsi (2km out of Skala). Open 8am-2pm. In an **emergency,** call the police at ☎31 087 or 31 571; they know doctors' schedules and will contact them.

**Telephones: OTE** (☎31 399); follow the signs in the main plateia. Open M-F 7:30am-3:10pm. The cafe-bar at the dock also has an international phone.

**Internet Access: Millennium Internet Cafe** (☎29 300) past the OTE, has 4 computers and video games. 2000dr per hr. Open M-Sa 9am-11pm.

**Post Office:** (☎31 316), on the main plateia, next to the police. Open M-F 7:30am-2pm. **Postal code:** 85500.

## ACCOMMODATIONS

Even the plethora of early morning boats are greeted by a battalion of locals offering **domatia** (singles 5000-7000dr; doubles 7000-10,000dr). There are many rooms on Vas. Georgiou, on the street leading to the OTE and up the hill before the junction to Kambos and Lampi—signs are easy to spot.

**Flower Stefanos Camping at Meloi** (☎31 821, 31 754), 2km northeast of Skala, and a 2min. walk from Meloi Beach. Follow the waterfront road all the way to the right (facing inland) and look for signs. Mini-market, laundry, spotless showers, grill facilities, motorbike rentals (from 2500dr per day), and a tasty budget cafe all between the bamboo stalks. For free shuttle service, watch for the rainbow van at the port. 1500dr per person; 750dr per tent rental. Open May 15-Oct. 15.

**Pension Sydney** (☎31 689, 32 118). Follow the road along the waterfront, a sign on your left is right before the road to Lambi and Kambos. Boasting all-you-can-drink **free water and home-made wine** straight from the owners' private well and vineyard, this quiet and cozy pension is centered around a courtyard containing these invaluable commodities. A 2 min. walk to the sea on either side of the island. Doubles with balconies and private baths 7000-12,000dr.

**Jason's Rooms** (☎31 832 or 31 838), near the OTE on the opposite side of the street. Cheerful and very large rooms, a friendly manager, book exchange, and convenient lobby card phone makes Jason's popular with backpackers. Singles with shared bath 5000dr; doubles 7000dr, with bath 10,000dr.

**Maria Paschalidis** (☎32 152 or 31 347). Walk left from the ferry dock and right onto Vas. Georgiou. Maria's "Rooms to Let" sign is roughly 50m on the left, after Pizza Zacharo, across from the basketball court. A peppy pension with jasmine-scented rooms. Doubles 7000dr, with bath 8000dr; triples 9000dr, with bath 10,000dr.

## FOOD

Several seafood restaurants featuring expensive fish entrees line the waterfront, and standard touristy tavernas abound. **Grocery stores** and **sweet shops** cluster around the main plateia. Patmos is known more for its desserts than tavernas; try the *pouggia*, a ball of honey and nuts smothered in dough and sometimes powdered sugar (220-300dr), or cheese pie, a pastry shell filled with local cheese, eggs, milk, and cinnamon (350-450dr).



**Pantelis** (☎31 230 or 31 920), behind the central strip of cafes on the street parallel to the waterfront. Cheaper than Old Harbor (below) but equally delicious, serving over 50 Greek dishes each day, many vegetarian. *Gigantes* 800dr. Open 11am-11pm.

**The Old Harbor Restaurant** (☎31 170), on the waterfront road to Meloi; look for the woodwork balcony. Reputed to be the island's best seafood, but the best doesn't come cheap: mid-sized serving of *barbounia* 3000dr (800dr per kg). Open 6pm-midnight.

**Grigoris** (☎31 515), across from the bus stop at the corner of the road to Hora. Central location and quick service. Great swordfish souvlaki for 1400dr or home-made *spanakopita* 400dr. Open noon-3pm and 6pm-1am.

## ENTERTAINMENT

Perhaps in deference to the island's holy element, the nightlife tends to be free of the rowdy excesses found most anywhere else. The increasing number of tourists, however, ensures a standard palette of cafes and discotheques easily balanced with pleasing night-time strolls along the ever-busy waterfront.

**Koncolato** (☎32 323), a bright club and bar popular with both regulars and tourists under Cafe Aman's ownership. Open 11pm-late.

**Cafe Aman** (☎32 323), a chic cafe resting below the magnificently lit church of Agia Paraskevi. Draws a pre-bar crowd early in the evening, but many stay all night. Open 9am-4am.

**Kahlua Club** (☎32 405), by the gas station, 5min. down the road to Melloi. Liveliest of the few dance floors on Patmos, getting much livelier as the night wears on. 2000dr cover includes the first drink. Open 10:30pm until late.

**Art Cafe** (☎33 092). Vibrant paintings by Katerina's progenitor liven the inviting cafe-bar where an older clientele is known to listen to owners Nikos and Katerina play DJ all the leisurely night long. A lush roof garden affords great views of the harbor. Frappes are 500dr, fresh fruit juices from 700dr, and cocktails 1500dr. Open 9am-4am.

# HORA Χωρα

The white houses of Hora and the majestic walls of the Monastery of St. John the Theologian above form a landmark visible for all of Patmos. Hora's streets are a

**APOCALYPSE NOW?** In the Book of Revelation, the Bible says that in the years before the Second Coming, people will bear the Sign of the Beast (the number 666). This doesn't ordinarily bother the rest of the world, but in Greece, all hell broke loose over it (figuratively, at least at press time). The furor began when the European Union passed the Schengen Treaty, an agreement which, among other things, called for each person in the EU to be issued an electronic ID card. Pretty harmless, right? Not according to many Greeks, who swear that the bar codes on the IDs are designed around the infamous three sixes. Each bar code, it seems, possesses three bars corresponding to the number six: one at the beginning, one in the exact middle, and one at the end. Are these bar codes really the mark of the Antichrist as prophesied by the Book of Revelations? The powerful Greek Orthodox Church has called on all believers to shun the new IDs as evil; only time will tell.

maze, hiding sprawling gardens behind grand doors in the shelter of the monastery, and making it impossible to give precise directions. The map of Patmos at kiosks and tourist shops comes with a questionable illustration of the town; you'll need to pick **landmarks** to find your way back to where you started.

Take care of business before arriving, as a few card phones and a mailbox at the bottom of the hill are the only links between Hora and the outside world. From the bus and taxi station, both the monastery and main plateia can be reached by walking left and following signs. Hora is 4km from Skala, a trip that you can tackle by **bus** (10min., 10 per day, 200dr), by **taxi** (1000dr), or by **foot,** although it's a steep hike. The bus stops at the top of the hill outside the town, which is also the point of departure for buses from Hora to Grikou. Hora's restaurants and cafes share the spectacular view over the surrounding countryside and of the whitewashed town. Post-sightseeing hunger can be sated at **Vangelis' restaurant.** To reach it, head toward the monastery and follow signs to the central plateia. Peek into the pots and pans to pick your portion, and grab a seat on the rooftop garden to enjoy the spectacular view as you eat. (☎31 967. *Moussaka* 1200dr. Open noon-2pm and 6pm-1am.) **Cafe Stoa,** in the main plateia across from Vangelis, is the center of Hora's nightlife and the home of that rare find, the 1200dr cocktail. Be prepared to take a cab home if you're staying in Skala—the last bus from Hora leaves at 10:30pm, long before you'll be ready to say good night. (☎32 226. Open 5pm-2am.)



## MONASTERY OF ST. JOHN THE THEOLOGIAN

*☎31 398. Monastery and treasure museum open M, Th, F, Sa, Su, 8am-1:30pm; Tu, W 8am-1:30pm, 4-6pm. Treasury 1000dr; monastery free. Try not to visit the monastery at midday in summer–it's a tourist zoo and you'll have to tag along with a guided group. Off-season visitors may be offered an informal private tour by one of the monastery's 20 monks (down from 1700). Visitors to the monastery should dress modestly–no shorts.*

The turreted walls and imposing gateway of the Monastery of St. John the Theologian make it look more like a fortress than a place of worship. At the time of its founding by St. Christodoulos in 1088, the monastery was a constant target of pirate raids; pragmatic considerations took precedence over aesthetic ones. A memorial to St. John, who visited the island in the first century AD, was transformed into a citadel with battlements and watchtowers. As you enter the courtyard centered around the well of Holy Water, notice the 17th-century **frescoes** on the left that portray stories from *The Miracles and Travels of St. John the Evangelist*, written by John's disciple Prochoros. To the upper right, a fresco portrays St. John's duel of faith with a local priest of Apollo named Kynops; the Saint threw the heathen into the water at Skala, where he froze into stone. The rock is still in the harbor—ask any local to point it out. The monastery holds ten chapels within its walls, which allows maximum prayer while respecting the Orthodox dictum limiting masses to one per day per altar. The **Chapel of the Virgin Mary** is covered with 12th-century frescoes, hidden behind the wall faces until 1956 tremors shook things up and exposed them. The **treasury** guards icons, ornamented stoles

(some donated by Catherine the Great of Russia), a copy of St. Mark's Gospel, and an 8th-century Book of Job. Look for Helkomenos, an icon painted by **El Greco,** near the end of the exhibit. The **Chapel of the Holy Christodoulos** holds the remains of the monastery's illustrious founder, and the skull of St. Thomas. Shortly after Christodoulos's death, some visitors attempted to steal his saintly remains, so the monks defended his body with a marble sarcophagus and a silver reliquary.

**APOCALYPSIS MONASTERY.** Between Skala and the Monastery of St. John in Hora, the Apocalypsis monastery is built on the site where St. John stayed while on Patmos. Two kilometers from both Skala and Hora, on the winding road that connects them, you'll find the large white complex of interconnected buildings. Most people come here to see the **Sacred Grotto of the Revelation,** adjacent to the Church of St. Anne. In this natural cave, St. John dictated the *Book of Revelation*, the last book of the New Testament, after hearing the voice of God proclaim "Now write what you see, what is to take place hereafter" (Rev. 1:19). When God spoke to St. John, he cleft the ceiling of the cave with a three-pronged crack representing the Holy Trinity. Silver plating marks the spot upon which St. John is presumed to have slept. *(☎31 234. Dress modestly. Open M, W, and F 8am-1:30pm, Tu, Th and Su 8am-1:30pm and 4-6pm. Free.)*



## RURAL PATMOS

Arriving in Skala, visitors are welcomed by a sign that reads *Patmos: Beautiful Beaches Nestled in Tradition.* As the sign attests, the island has no shortage of great, varied beaches. For an undisputedly amazing unrestricted view of Hora and Skala, visit **Aspris Bay**—at sunset, if you can. The closest shore to Skala is **Meloi,** a quick 2km walk north. Large trees flank the back of the sandy beach, so grilling in the sun is optional. A bit farther north, **Agriolivado** has yet another sandy beach, an alternative to more-crowded **Kambos** nearby, which is a pleasant yet discovered option for beachgoers, with frequent bus service (15min., 4 per day, 250dr). Its numerous hotels help pump in the tourists; the town itself has an inviting plateia and a few waterfront restaurants.

Just over the hill from Kambos, **Vagia Beach** is a world apart—rocky, secluded, and serene. Go east along the road to Livadia, and follow the path down to an appealing, unmarked beach set against a small cliff. A bit farther east, cliff-lined **Livadia beach** and **Livadia Restaurant** share spectacular views of the string of islets just offshore. While bus service extends only as far as Kambos, the hikes or bikes required to get to farther beaches provide you with solitude and peace. North of Kambos, the beach at **Lambi** is famed for its multicolored pebbles—rare and growing rarer, as tourists pocket them for souvenirs. The strong winds that attack this part of the island make swimming difficult.

# CRETE ΚΡΗΤΗ

In middle of the sable sea there lies
An isle called Crete, a ravisher of eyes,
Fruitful, and manned with many an infinite store;
Where ninety cities crown the famous shore,
Mixed with all-languaged men.
—Homer, *Odyssey*

According to a Greek saying, a Cretan's first loyalty is to his island, his second to his country. The insular Cretan mindset—shaped by centuries of bitter resistance to relentless invasion—causes them to view even their fellow Greeks as foreigners. Cretans are nonetheless friendly to the outsiders that continue to invade, or vacation in, their beloved island, and visitors will enjoy a heaping dose of that old Greek hospitality. Like the long-mustached men in black who sit by the harbor polishing their high boots, the island welcomes you, but prefers to keep its distance.

Records of Cretan life reach back to 6000 BC, when neolithic inhabitants dwelled in open settlements and placed terra-cotta statuettes on mountaintops to honor their deities. When settlers arrived from Asia Minor around 3000 BC, Cretans began to forge a civilization that would mark Greece, the Mediterranean, and all of Europe. Through the next two millennia, Crete's Minoans developed unprecedented technological and artistic abilities, constructing enormous palaces which still astound archaeologists and casual observers alike. Excavations of these palaces in this century have turned up shards of decorated pottery, colorful frescoes, intricate jewelry, ceremonial horns, stone libation vessels, small sculptures, and tablets written in Linear A and Linear B (see p. 24).

Three catastrophes—an earthquake, a tidal wave from an eruption in ancient Santorini, and a probable Mycenaean invasion—leveled Minoan society; three times, the Minoans rebuilt from the ground up. Three distinct artistic styles—creatively titled the Early, Middle, and Late Minoan Periods—accompanied each period. The Early Period's iconography makes it famous: women on thrones appear repeatedly, suggesting that early Minoan society may have been the primeval utopian matriarchy of social scientists' speculation. The Middle Period brought a political and artistic high point, as the Palace at Knossos (see p. 472) dominated a prosperous Aegean marine empire. Later Greeks dated their own origins to the Middle Period, when Zeus was born on Mt. Ida, the mythical Minotaur munched men in the Knossos labyrinth, and the Athenian king Theseus wrested power from Crete's Minoans and handed it to the Achaeans of mainland Greece.



## HIGHLIGHTS OF CRETE

**CLAMBER** amidst remnants of Minoan palaces at Knossos (p. 472), Phaistos (p. 478), and Malia (p. 481).

**HIKE** the Samaria Gorge, the longest gorge in Europe (p. 492).

**ARAB, VENETIAN, AND OTTOMAN ARCHITECTURE** strut their stuff in the harbors of Rethymno (p. 482) and Hania (p. 487).

**HANG ABOVE THE LIBYAN SEA** from cave-riddled cliffs at Matala (p. 476).

**EXPLORE THE GHOST TOWN** that was Europe's last leper colony, at Spinalonga (p. 500), off the coast of Agios Nikolaos (p. 496), Crete's most sophisticated resort town.

In the 8th century BC, the Dorians (see p. 10) occupied the island, carpetbagging with their own ideas about jewelry-making, sculpture, pottery, and language. Conquering Romans set up camp, only to find the island an increasingly unstable aristocratic hangout because of frequent intercity fighting. Next, Crete fell under rickety Byzantine rule, resulting in the construction of lovely Byzantine churches (if not much else), until the Arabs conquered Crete in 827. The Byzantines eventually regained the island, but lost it again to Frankish crusaders who conquered Constantinople in 1204. After being sold to Venice, Crete became a commercial hub, with fortified ports ringing the island. Crete's populace split into haves and have-nots under the Venetian nobles and Cretan aristocrats.

Despite Byzantine control, Cretans look back on this period far more fondly than on the Ottoman occupation that followed. From the late 17th century until Prince George's liberation of the island in 1898, Crete was Ottoman (see p. 15) turf. After the Balkan Wars of 1913, Crete joined the Greek state. During the Second World War, the island met German occupation with passionate guerrilla resistance; the period is now regarded with great pride in Crete. From the end of the war on, Crete escaped conquerors and attacks as a part of the Greek nation.

Today Crete is divided into four main prefectures: **Hania, Rethymno, Iraklion,** and **Lasithi.** The island's inhabitants have this division firmly etched in their minds, and transportation networks are based on the prefectures. It's easy to get around within a prefecture, but transportation from prefecture to prefecture can be slightly more complicated, so make your plans with the divisions in mind.

**GETTING THERE** **Olympic Airways** and **Air Greece** run cheap, fast, domestic flights from Athens to **Sitia** on the east, **Iraklion** in the center, and **Hania** on the west. You might also try **Cronus Airlines** (☎(821) 51 100) and **Aegean Airlines** (☎(821) 63 336). Consult the **Practical Information** of your destination for more information on flights. Most travelers take the **ferry** from Athens (**p. 81**) to Crete, landing in Iraklion, Hania, Sitia, or occasionally Rethymno or Agios Nikolaos. Boats run frequently during the summer, but they're always prone to irregularity. Larger boats run more frequently and dependably. All prices listed are for deck-class accommodations; bring a sleeping bag to snooze on the deck.



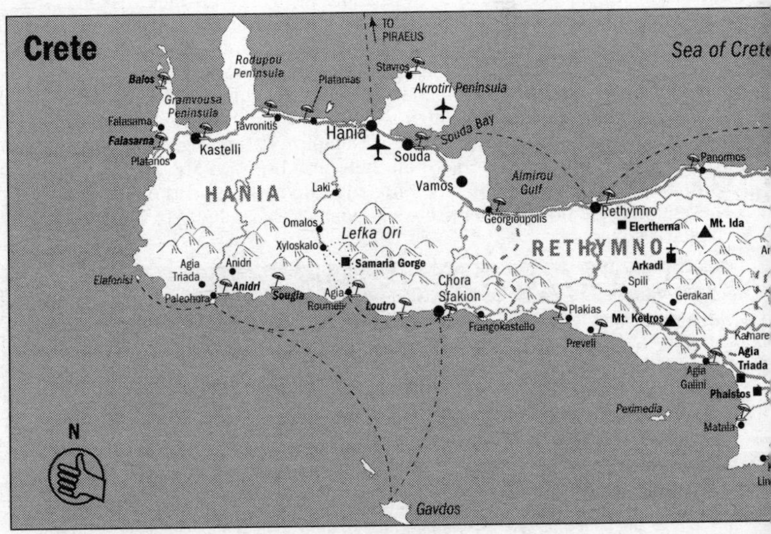

# IRAKLION PREFECTURE

Iraklion Prefecture revolves around its cosmopolitan capital, which shares its name. As with most of Crete, the touristed areas are pressed along the beaches in the north, while the southern half of the province and the mountains that sandwich each side host fewer visitors and stick more closely to traditional life.

## IRAKLION Ηρακλειο ☎081

The fifth-largest city in Greece, Iraklion is Crete's capital and primary port. The chic native population lives life in the fast lane, which translates into an urban brusqueness unique among the cities of Crete, and the most diverse nightlife on the island. While architectural aesthetes find Iraklion's unplanned jumble—Venetian monuments sandwiched between Turkish houses and two-story concrete flats—utterly offensive, others find in the mosaic of buildings a valuable reminder of the city's impressive history. Iraklion's museums and the nearby palace of Knossos are reminders of this past, with the most significant artifacts from the far reaches of Crete. The biggest bus station and port on the island are here, making this central, capital city a convenient base to explore the rest of the island.

### GETTING THERE AND GETTING AROUND

#### BY PLANE

Inexpensive, popular flights on **Olympic Airways, Air Greece,** and **Aegean Airlines** zip between Iraklion and the other large cities of Greece. Planes fly to: Athens (45min., 13-15 per day, 19,300-21,300dr); Rhodes (45min., 6-7 per week, 21,800-22,300dr); Thessaloniki (2hr., 1-2 per day, 29,800-30,300dr); and Santorini (40min., 2 per week, 15,300dr). Discounts available for those under 24 or 26, or over 60. To get to and from the Iraklion airport, take bus #1 to the **airport** from **Pl. Eleftherias** every 10min. (170dr). Cabs to the airport cost 2000-2500dr. Inquire about flights at **Travel Hall Travel Agency,** Hatzimihali Yiannari 13, one block southwest of Pl. Eleftherias. ☎341 862 or 282 112; fax 283 309. Open M-Tu and Th-F 9am-4pm and 5:30-9pm, W 9am-5pm, Sa 9am-2pm.



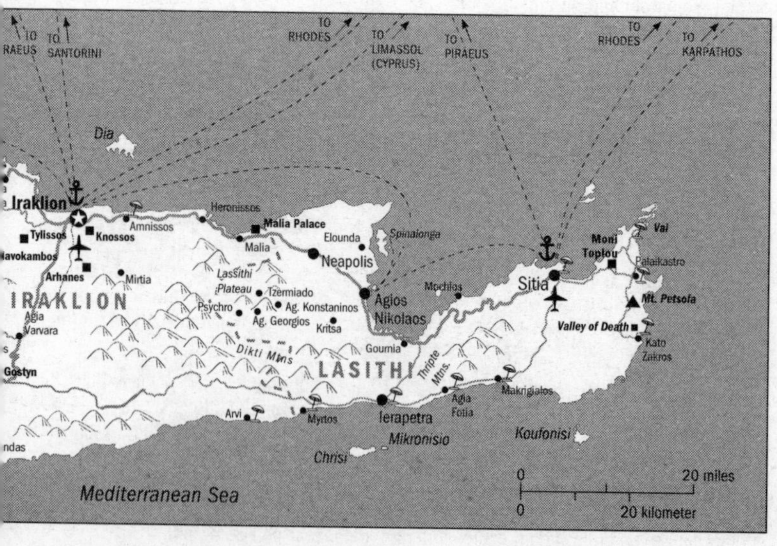

## BY BOAT

Both **ferries** and **speed boats** dock at Iraklion. Boat **offices** line 25 Augustou, most are open 9am-9pm. Boats run to: Athens (14hr., 3 per day, 7000dr); Santorini (4hr., 2 per day, 3700dr); Paros (9hr., 7 per week, 5200dr); Naxos (7hr., 3 per week, 5200dr); Mykonos (8½hr., 5 per week, 6000dr). **Speed boats** service these destinations in about half the time, for twice the price. Do you really think time is money?

## BY BUS

If you'll be arriving in Iraklion from elsewhere in Crete, you'll have a fairly easy time. But if you're planning to bust out from the city, some planning is necessary, since there are several **KTEL** bus terminals. Check to make sure you match the station to your destination.

**Terminal A** (☎245 017 or 245 020), between the old city walls and the harbor near the waterfront, serves: **Agios Nikolaos** (1½hr., 20 per day, 1450dr); **Lasithi** (2hr., 2 per day, 1450dr); **Hersonissos** (45min., every 30min., 650dr); **Malia** (1hr., every 30min., 800dr); **Sitia** (3¼hr., 4 per day, 2950dr); **Ierapetra** (2½hr., 7 per day, 2200dr); and **Arhanes** (30min., 15 per day, 360dr).

**Hania/Rethymno Terminal** (☎221 765) is opposite Terminal A, beside the ferry landing. Buy tickets in the cafe building. Service to **Hania** (17 per day, 2900dr) and **Rethymno** (1½hr., 18 per day, 1550dr). From Hania and Rethymno, connections may be made to Plakias, Samaria, Hora Sfakion, and Akrotiri.

**Terminal B** (☎255 965). To reach Terminal B, which is outside the Hania Gate of the old city walls, take local bus #135 from Terminal A (340dr). Buses run from Terminal B to: **Phaistos** (1½hr., 8 per day, 1300dr) via **Gortys** (950dr); **Agia Galini** (2¼hr., 7 per day, 1600dr); and **Matala** (2hr., 5 per day, 1600dr).

CRETE

## BY CAR AND MOPED

**Taxis: Tariff Taxi of Iraklion** (☎210 102 or 210 168). Open 24hr. When taking a taxi from the airport or port, beware of drivers who claim that a hotel you name is closed or full; they may be drawing commission from a rival hotel.

**Car Rental:** Rental car companies are scattered along 25 Augustou. Make the owners compete for your business by quoting prices from their neighbors. **Cosmos,** 25 Augustou 15 (☎241 357 or 346 173, fax 220 379), charges 10,000dr for a one-day rental. Renting for more days reduces the price up to 30%. Open April-Oct. 7:30am-9pm, Nov.-Mar. 8am-1pm and 5-9pm.

**Moped Rental:** Cheap rentals line Handakos, El Greco Park, and 25 Augustou. Check if the quoted price includes the 20% tax and insurance (50cc bikes cost around 5000dr per day when you rent for several days, tax and third-party liability insurance included).

## ORIENTATION AND PRACTICAL INFORMATION

Although Iraklion spreads telescopically, the area bordered by the waterfront and **Dikeosinis, Doukos Bofor,** and **Handakos** streets contains most necessities. The city has two centers. **Pl. Venizelou** (also known to tourists as **Lion Fountain** or **Four Lion Square**), home to Morosini Fountain, is where Handakos meets Dikeosinis and 25 Augustou in the center of town. **Pl. Eleftherias** is at the intersection of Doukos Bofor and Dikeosinis on the east side of the old city. Be warned that many of the street names are given as **numbers,** so that 1866 and 25 Augustou are street names; this guide lists the address number *after* the street name.

**Tourist Office:** Xanthoudidou 1 (☎228 203, 244 462), opposite the Archaeological Museum in Pl. Eleftherias. Free city maps, lists of hotels, message board for travelers, bus schedules, and some boat schedules. Staff is friendly and helpful but busy. Info on cultural events and museums. Open M-F 8am-2:30pm; hours Sa and in the evening in July and August.

**Travel Agencies:** Several agencies line 25 Augustou. **Arabatzoglou Bros. Shipping Agents Travel Bureau,** 25 Augustou 54 (☎226 697 or 226 698; fax 222 184), has a knowledgeable staff when it comes to ferry schedules. Open 8am-9pm.

**Banks:** The banks on 25 Augustou have 24hr. **ATMs** and **currency exchange. National Bank,** 25 Augustou 35 (☎304 850). Open M-Th 8am-2pm, F 8am-1:30pm.

**Luggage Storage: Washsalon,** Handakos 18 (☎280 858). 500dr per day. Open 8:30am-9pm.

**Bookstores: Planet International Bookstore,** Kidonias 23 (☎281 558; fax 287 142), on the corner of Hortatson and Kidonias. The 4-floor megastore sells books in a number of languages, with a broad selection of classics and travel literature. Open M-F 8:30am-2pm and 5:30-8:30pm, Sa 8:30am-noon.

**Library: Vikelaia Municipal Library** (☎399 237 or 399 249), across from Morosini fountain. Limited selection in English, French, Italian, Russian, and Chinese. Most international books are philosophy, literature, classics, and history—peruse them in the luxurious reading room (full A/C!) on the second floor. Open M-F 8am-3pm, M and W 5-8pm. Public **Internet access** expected in 2001.

**Laundromat: Washsalon,** Handakos 18 (☎280 858). 2000dr for wash and dry, soap included. Be very clear with care instructions. Open 8:30am-9pm.

**Public Toilets:** In El Greco Park, look for the underground, blue, cage-like entrance by the swings. Also in the public gardens near Pl. Eleftherias. 150dr. Open 6am-9pm.

**Emergency:** ☎ 166.

**Tourist Police:** Dikeosinis 10 (☎283 190 or 289 614), one block from intersection of 25 Augustou and Dikeosinis. Open 7am-11pm.

**Police:** Pl. Venizelou 29, in a blue building hidden among the cafes. Open 24hr. One station for the east side of town (☎284 589 or 282 677); another station in the same building serves the west (☎ 282 243).

**Port Police** (☎244 956 or 244 912), in the harbor.

**Hospital: Venizelou Hospital** (☎237 502 or 237 524), on Knossou; take bus #2 from Pl. Venizelou (20min.). **Panepistimiako Hospital** (☎392 111); take a bus from Astoria Hotel in Pl. Eleftherias. The **medical center,** Iatrikos Kritis (☎342 500), is on the southern side of Pl. Eleftherias. Open 7:30am-9pm.

**Telephone: OTE,** Minotavrou 10 (☎395 276 or 395 275), on the left side of El Greco Park as you enter from 25 Augustou. Open 7:30am-1pm.

**Internet Access: Gallery Games Net,** Korai 14 (☎282 804), is on the next street past Dedalou in the direction heading away from Pl. Eleftherias. 500dr for 30min. Open 10am-midnight. **Netc@fe,** on 1878, gets you connected for a similar fee. To reach it, walk toward the waterfront on Handakos, turn left on Vistaki, and then right onto 1878.

**Post Office: Main office** (☎289 995), in Pl. Daskalogianni off Giannari. Open M-F 7:30am-8pm. **Branch** in El Greco Park. Open M-F 8:30am-3pm. **Postal code:** 71001.

## ACCOMMODATIONS

**TOOTING THEIR OWN HORN** When taking a **taxi** from the airport or port, beware of drivers who claim that the hotel you name is closed or full. It's a common scam for taxi drivers to get payoffs from hotels for bringing customers there. Insist on your own destination, and if the cabbie won't comply, threaten to get out of the taxi.



Iraklion has a bunch of cheap hotels and hostels, most near **Handakos** at the center of town. Others are on **Evans** and **1866** near the market.

**Rent a Room Hellas,** Handakos 24 (☎288 851), 2 blocks from El Greco Park. Formerly the HI Youth Hostel. Institutional large dorm rooms, with a garden bar on the fifth floor. 24hr. hot water. Breakfast 700-1300dr. Dorms 2200dr; doubles 4500-6000dr; triples 6000-8000dr. Extra bed 1000-1100dr.

**Hotel Rea** (☎223 638; fax 242 189), on Kalimeraki. From Pl. Venizelou, walk down Handakos and turn right after Rent a Room Hellas. Airy, cool rooms and jasmine-scented reception. Hot showers. Free luggage storage. Breakfast downstairs or in your room 950dr. Rents cars (12,000dr per day, 30% off for hotel guests). Singles 6000-7500dr; doubles 7500-8500dr; triples 9000-1050dr.

**Youth Hostel,** Vyronos 5 (☎286 281; fax 222 947). From the bus station, with the water on your right, take a left on 25 Augustou and a right on Vyronos. Midnight curfew. 24hr. hot water. Sheets 200dr. Luggage storage 500dr. Check-out 10am. Private rooms available. Breakfast 700dr, beer 400dr. Dorms 2000dr; singles 3000-4000dr; doubles 5500-6000dr; triples 7000-8000dr.

**Hotel Paladion,** Handakos 16 (☎282 563). Functional private rooms in a convenient location. Singles 4000dr; doubles 6000dr; triples 8000dr; quads 9600dr.

## FOOD

The ritzy cafes around the **Morosini Fountain,** near El Greco Park and in Pl. Venizelou, are perfect for lounging. Budgeteers should take a left off 1866, one block from the plateia, to reach tiny **Theodosaki** street, where 10 colorful tavernas serving big, cheap dishes (around 1000dr) are jammed side by side. If there's no menu, fix the price before you sit. Souvlaki joints abound on **25 Augustou.**

The best show in town is the **open-air market** on 1866, starting near Pl. Venizelou. Stalls piled high with sweets, spices, fruits, vegetables, cheeses, meat, and Cretan muscle shirts line both sides of the narrow street. (Open M-Sa 8am-2pm, Tu and Th-F 5-9pm.) **Amalthia,** named after the goat that nursed Zeus, has cauldrons of yogurt that far eclipse the filtered, pasteurized brands found elsewhere. The store serves traditional sheep's milk yogurt (800dr per kg), as well as local cheeses like

the Cretan version of *gruyère*. Amalthia's cheeses fill the pastries made at **Kirkor,** Pl. Venizelou 29. (Open 5:30am-midnight.)

**Thraka,** Platokallergon 14. The wood paneled joint around the corner from the Morosini Fountain in Pl. Venizelou. Tons of fun, thanks to a 30-year tradition of serving only grilled ham gyros and souvlaki cooked over charcoal. Try the souvlaki with *thraka* bread crust (550dr). Open M-Sa 10am-5am.

**Tou Terzaki,** Loch. Marineli 17 (☎221 444), behind Agios Dimitrios chapel, off Vyronos, one block from 25 Augustou. Cosmopolitan Iraklion types grab an outdoor table and order the best of Cretan cuisine. The quiet patio seems far away from the busy city center just around the corner. Fried squid 1400dr, stuffed tomatoes 1300dr. Open M-Sa for lunch and dinner.

**Lychnostatis,** Ioannou Chronaki 8 (☎242 117), 30m past El Greco Park on the same street as the OTE. Local devotees of all age groups make for a relaxed, intimate meal at this quiet taverna. Goat with tomatoes 1100dr. Open noon-1am.

**Antonios Nerantzoulis,** Agios Titou 16 (☎346 236), behind the Agios Titus Church. Run by the same family since 1900, this bakery is famous for *oktasporo* and *kalitsounia* (2000dr per kg), plus common baked goods. Open M-Sa 7am-3pm, Tu and Th-F 5-8pm.

**Tierra del Fuego,** Theotokopoulou 26 (☎341 515), down the street behind Xalkiadaki market off El Greco Park. A Cretan take on Mexican food, this ideal date spot hides in a lush garden behind a deceptively dull entryway on a business street. Salads 700-950dr, mixed plates 1600dr, vegetarian tacos 1200dr. Open 8:30pm-2am.

## NIGHTLIFE AND ENTERTAINMENT

Trading tourist kitsch for genuine urban energy, Iraklion outdoes the resort towns with its pulsing nightlife. Day or night, the huge atrium-like **Aktarika Cafe,** across from Pl. Venizelou, brims with hip, black-clad twenty- and thirty-something Iraklionites and the people who watch them. (*Frappés* 700dr, cocktails 1700dr. Open 9am-2:30am; DJ on duty 11am-4pm and 8pm-2:30am.) Around 11pm, the young and the restless of all nationalities overflow the small streets off **Pl. Venizelou.** To cross Androgeou street you must ford a river of chic young Cretans drinking, smoking, and chatting. As the night proceeds, these activities merge with the rhythms of techno, pop, and Greek music along the waterfront. A walk down D. Beaufort takes you to **Privilege Club** and **Yacht** next door. Continuing along the water, **Limenico** has a dance floor for bumping and a terrace for talking. The doors of Iraklion's clubs generally demand a sharp and tidy appearance, and ask for a 2000dr cover, which includes one drink.

Schedules for Iraklion's **movie theaters** are posted in front of the tourist police office. Join Greeks and tourists at sites throughout the city during the months of July, August, and September for Iraklion's annual **summer festival,** a cultural combination of plays, concerts, theater, ballet, and folk dancing. (Shows begin at 9:30pm. Schedules at the tourist information office. Tickets around 2000dr; reduced student prices.)

## SIGHTS

### IRAKLION ARCHAEOLOGICAL MUSEUM

*Off Pl. Eleftherias. ☎226 092. Open M 12:30-7pm and Tu-Su 8am-7pm. 1500dr; students and EU seniors 800dr; classicists, fine arts students, under 18, and EU students free. Illustrated guide 1500dr.*

Iraklion's main attraction, after Knossos (p. 472), is the superb Archaeological Museum. While most Cretan museums offer a hodgepodge of local finds strung across millennia, the Iraklion Museum—by appropriating major finds from all regions of the island—presents a comprehensive and chronologically organized

CRETE

**IT'S EL GRECO TO ME** Although he made his name at the Spanish court, **Domenikos Theotokopoulos** (1541-1614) clung to his Greek heritage throughout his artistic career. Born in Venetian-ruled Iraklion, the Cretan artist melded his early Byzantine training with the teachings of the Venetian and Roman schools, where he trained with masters like Titian, Raphael, and Michelangelo. **El Greco,** as he came to be known, was a master of **Mannerism,** a style of painting that places internal emotion above nature. His reputation was built on portraits and religious imagery that featured strangely elongated figures–perhaps influenced by his own fingers, which were made long and sinewy by years of disease. His best-known work, *The Burial of the Count Orgaz,* staged a historical event in the contemporary world, a strong tradition in Western art. Although El Greco moved to Toledo, Spain, in 1576, the Spanish subjects and contexts of his work never eclipsed his feeling that he was a stranger in there. Throughout his career, El Greco would continue to sign his paintings in Greek.

record of the Neolithic and Minoan stages of the island's history, with a nod to the Hellenistic and Roman periods in its final rooms. A visit to Knossos, and most any of the other Minoan palaces around the island, is incomplete without seeing the museum's inventory of the royal and everyday artifacts that once decorated the throne room and the woodshop. Of particular interest are the original **wall paintings of Knossos** on display here.

**ROOM 3.** In room 3 you'll find the most lauded discovery from the palace of Phaistos (p. 478), the cryptic **Phaistos disc.** Scholars have been unable to decipher the 214 pictographs that adorn the solid clay disc, as they wind from the circumference to the center. The intricate impressions suggest they were made by means of metal stamps, an ancient form of printing. The disk might convey a religious or magical hymn or astrological chart. Or absolutely nothing. The plot thickens further: some archaeologists speculate that the disc didn't originate on Crete.

CRETE

**ROOM 4.** Three displays vie for your attention in room 4. Two topless **snake goddesses** wear layered skirts, cats on their heads, and flailing serpents in each outstretched arm. It's not actually known whether they're supposed to be goddesses or priestesses. The clothes are revealing in more ways than one: from the figure, you can see the cut and fashion of Minoan costume, the use of snakes symbols for eternity, the high status of women in the Minoan religious hierarchy, and the way the female form was idealized in Minoan society. Nearby, the **bull head libation vase** dazzles with white mustache, tight curls of hair, and red eyes made of painted rock crystal. The vase is pierced by two holes, one for filling and one for spilling. The sacred liquid used may have been blood from a sacrificial bull. While the original wood horns have not survived, one of the eyes is still preserved in its socket. Adjacent is another stately drinking vessel, an alabaster libation vase shaped like a lioness's head. Room 4's grand finale is an **ivory acrobat,** probably leaping a bull in a Minoan ritual (p. 478).

**OTHER ROOMS.** If you take a close look at the gold jewelry in room 7, you will discover an intricate **bee pendant** from Chryssolakkos at Malia. The pendant is composed of two bees joined delicately at their stingers, forming a cage with their antennae that encloses a golden ball and a honeycomb lying at the center—a cherished image on Crete. Room 6 stores the **Palaikastro vase,** covered with a complex pattern of spiraling tentacles that move toward geometric abstraction. The virtuoso, marine-style Minoan painter's amazing technical abilities and remarkable aesthetic sensibilities shine out in the vase. The jumble of tentacles, suction cups, seaweed, shells, and ink complement the shape of the two-headed amphora perfectly, in a mix of chaos and order. In rooms 10 and 11, the **Goddess of the Poppies** stands with raised arms and ritually significant opium flowers sprouting from her head. The austere power of this and other **household goddesses** shows a significant change in the Minoan concept of women than represented in the statues in room 4.

**MINOAN HALL OF FRESCOES.** Upstairs is the **Minoan Hall of Frescoes,** the museum's most controversial exhibit. These are the original wall paintings found at Knossos—replicas adorn the reconstructed palace. Sir Arthur Evans didn't spare these priceless finds his revisionist hand; in restoring the frescoes, he added his own ideas about the original compositions. Depicting ancient Minoan life, these frescoes capture ladies offering libations, blue monkeys frolicking in palatial gardens, and Minoans in procession. They're breathtaking. But before you get too excited, check out the restoration work up close: minimal traces of the original pieces left room for some major extrapolation. In fact, subsequent study of the **Prince of Lilies** revealed that the fragments actually depicted three figures: a priestess in a lily crown, and two boxers flanking her.

## OTHER SITES

**KAZANTZAKIS REMEMBERED.** With views of Iraklion, the sea, and Mt. Ida to the west, the austere **Tomb of Kazantzakis** offers a peaceful and charming respite from crowded Iraklion. Because of his unorthodox beliefs, Nikos Kazantzakis, the author of *The Last Temptation of Christ,* was denied a place in a Christian cemetery, and was buried alone in this tomb. The tomb is a wonderful place to watch the sun set, or to contemplate the city. To reach the tomb from the city center, head down Evans until you reach the Venetian walls and the Martinengo Bastion, then turn left and walk about 100m further; the tomb is atop the city walls beside the football stadium. Alternatively, you can follow the crumbling outline of the city walls to the tomb. The village of **Varvari** outside of Iraklion is home to the **Kazantzakis Museum,** where true devotees can see many of the author's original manuscripts, as well as photos of his theatrical productions. A slide show (in English) provides historical background. *(Take a bus from Terminal A to Mirtia (570dr) and follow the signs; make sure to check return schedules. ☎741 689. Open Mar. 1-Oct. 31 M, W, and Sa-Su 9am-1pm and 4-8pm, Tu and F 9am-1pm. 1000dr, students and children 300dr.)*

**CHURCHES.** Several interesting churches hide in the modern maze of Iraklion's streets. Magnificent **Ag. Titus Church,** on 25 Augustou, is a converted mosque. Its architecture combines Muslim geometric designs and Christian regalia. The stained glass windows are all shapes instead of figures. Every night, it is lit up; note the *tamata* (charm-like votives) that represent the churchgoers' prayers. In Pl. Venizelou, **San Marco Church,** built in 1239, houses a changing exhibition space that features things like monastery frescos from the 14th-17th centuries. *(☎399 399, ext. 228. Open 9am-10pm. 1500dr.)* Built in 1735, the **Cathedral of Agios Minas** graces Pl. Agia Ekaternis. *(☎282 402. Open 7am-11pm.)* **Ag. Catherine's Church of Sinai,** also in the plateia, served as the first Greek university after the fall of Constantinople in 1453. The church has six icons by the Cretan master Damaskinos as well as other icons from around Crete. *(☎288 825. Open M-Sa 9am-1:30pm, Tu and Th-F 5-7pm. 600dr.)* San Marco and Agios Minas churches share their plaza with a small church building that contains the **Icons Museum,** a collection of extant Byzantine altarpieces and other ceremonial objects. *(☎288 825. Open M-Sa 8am-1:30pm, Tu, Th, and F 5-7pm. 500dr.)* A priest gives tours of the **Armenian Church.** Head away from the town center on Kalokerianou and take a right on Lasthenous after Yianni's store—the church is left of the bend. *(☎244 337.)*

**HISTORICAL MUSEUM.** The collection of the undervisited Historical Museum includes a scale model of the city with historical background, Byzantine and medieval works, a folk collection, finely woven tapestries, photos from the Second World War Nazi invasion, displays on Kazantzakis, and perhaps the only **El Greco** painting on Crete—the 1578 work View of Mt. Sinai and the Monastery of St. Catherine. *(On the corner of Grevenon and Kalokerianou, across from the Xenia Hotel. ☎283 219. Open M-Th 9am-5pm, F 9am-2pm, Sa 9am-2pm. 1000dr, students 750dr, under 12 free.)*

**VENETIAN IRAKLION.** As you rove the city, take in the various Venetian monuments: **Morosini Fountain,** centerpiece of Pl. Venizelou, and the nearby reconstructed **Venetian Loggia,** now a town hall. The 17th-century **Venetian Arsenal,** off Pl.

Koundouriotou near the waterfront and the Koules Fortress, guards the old harbor. *(☎246 211. Open M-F 8am-6pm, Sa-Su 10am-5pm. 500dr, students 300dr.)* For an unexpected dose of peace and beauty, walk along the olive tree lined southeast section of the **Venetian walls.** Also accessible from Iraklion is **El Greco**'s home village of **Fodele,** full of orange trees and history (see **It's El Greco to Me,** p. 470).

## DAYTRIPS FROM IRAKLION

### KNOSSOS Κνωσσος

*From Iraklion, take bus #2 (every 20min., 260dr), which stops along 25 Augustou and in Pl. Eleftherias. Buy your bus tickets at a nearby kiosk in advance. ☎231 940. Open 8am-7pm, in winter 8am-5pm.* ***Admission*** *1500dr; students and seniors 800dr; classicists, fine arts students, and EU students free; in winter, free on Su.* ***Guides*** *1500-2200dr. Helpful and enlightening* ***tour*** *in English, Italian, German, French, or Dutch (1hr.; 3000dr, 2000dr for students). Make sure your guide is official and has the required papers.*

Legend and fact are close cousins at the palace of Knossos, famous throughout the world and history as the site of King Minos's machinations, the labyrinth and its Minotaur, and the imprisonment (and winged escape) of Daedalus and Icarus. Cretans were once ridiculed for claiming Minoan roots, but Sir Arthur Evans won them the last laugh when his excavations confirmed their legacy.

At about $150m^2$, Knossos is the largest and most complicated of Crete's **Minoan palaces.** (The others are at Phaistos (p. 478), Malia (p. 481), and Zakros (p. 508)). Arthur Evans, one of Heinrich "Troy 'n' Mycenae" Schliemann's British cronies (see p. 119), purchased the hill that concealed Knossos in 1900. Evans spent 43 years and a fortune excavating it. Armed with the evidence he unearthed, he set out to restore the palace he found, with creativity and woeful inaccuracy. Walls, window casements, stairways, and columns were reconstructed in reinforced concrete, and copies of the magnificent frescoes replaced the originals, which are now a must-see in **Iraklion's Archaeological Museum** (p. 469). Indeed, a visit to Knossos is not really complete without seeing the Archaeological Museum's collection of decorations and everyday objects that cluttered the palace. Restorations saved some walls from collapse, but Evans' reconstruction crossed from preservation to destruction. Visiting throngs and the brightly painted walls make the complex look something like a Disney-esque "Minoanland." Nonetheless, the present-day reconstruction is well marked and provides visitors with a more satisfying explanation of the site than you'll find at other, less visitor-friendly Minoan palaces.



#### THE SITE

**ENTRANCE.** Visitors enter through the western court, following the path used for ceremonial processions in ancient times. The path wraps around to the Corridor of Procession. The entrance in the western court is bordered by three large circular pits that resemble giant wells. These pits held remnants of early religious houses called *kouloures.* The *kouloures* didn't jive with Evans's vision for the palace, so his reconstruction skips over them entirely. Continuing through the entrance, you'll see a series of **magazines** (storage rooms with large clay jars) on the left. Look closely for the darker sections of wall, which were blackened by the burning of oil in storage jars during a long-ago earthquake. The hall past the magazines served as the ceremonial entrance, called the **Corridor of the Procession** after the wall fresco that once adorned it. A copy of the fresco, which depicts youths holding instruments and libation vessels while visiting a goddess, now resides in the **South Propylon** on your left. The **Grand Staircase** lies ahead. Turn around and enter the central court near the south entrance to visit the inaccurately reconstructed **Priest-King fresco.**

**CENTER STAGE.** The large open space in the middle of the site, the **Central Court,** was the heart of the palace and the arena for **bull-leaping** (see p. 478). To its left is the **Throne Room,** where the original, preserved limestone throne still sits in its

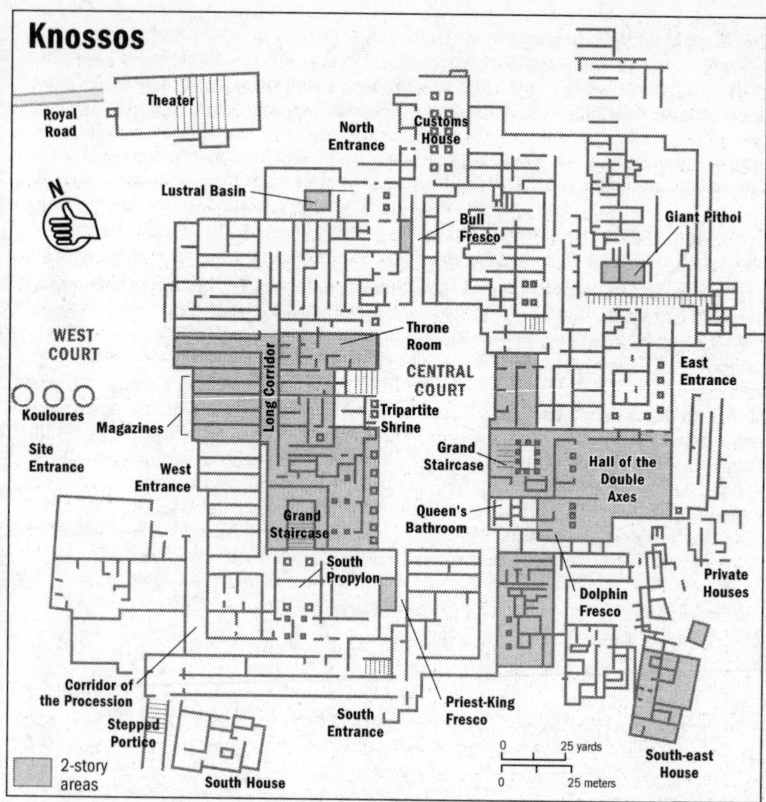




majesty, surrounded by paintings of gryphons. A priestess—not King Minos—probably occupied this seat. A wooden replica of the throne sits outside, erected where a pile of charred remains were found.

**BLUEPRINTS** All of Crete's palaces share a basic layout, with a vast network of rooms–sometimes rising to three stories–grouped asymmetrically around a central court. Devastating natural disasters have reduced most to ruins: first erected around 1900 BC, the palaces were destroyed by earthquakes around 1700 BC, rebuilt a century later on the same site, and promptly re-destroyed around 1650 BC. Each palace held royal apartments, artisans' workshops, extensive storehouses for oil, wine, and grain, and offices for scribes, who frantically tried to keep tabs on all the hoopla. The palaces were important religious centers. The **west wing** was always devoted to a mother goddess, but sacred elements could be found everywhere. Built from a central court outward, Minoan palaces had haphazard-looking exteriors. Near Eastern architecture from trading partners in ancient Egypt and Mesopotamia influenced their design; carefully chiseled stone in large square slabs, decorative stucco, massive pillars and ceremonial stairways, and sophisticated drainage systems made the palaces snappy looking and functional. Shunning exterior windows, Minoan architecture disseminated light from the inside by means of light wells and wooden colonnades. Cool, light, and airy, the interiors of Minoan palaces were bedecked with bright **frescoes** depicting bull-leaping ceremonies, magical gardens, wild goats, and nubile dolphins.

**ROYAL QUARTERS.** Leading down to the royal quarters is the grand staircase, an elegant structure that is the most architecturally sound part of the palace, as it was built into living rock. Because of its solid foundation, two stories below the main court survived through otherwise devastating earthquakes. Don't miss the **Queen's Bathroom,** where over 3000 years ago, she flushed her own toilet and took milk baths while gazing up at marvelous dolphin frescoes. The king had his quarters in the **Hall of the Double Axes.** The double axe, a sacred Minoan symbol, is carved all over the palace and in the Iraklion Museum. The word for double axe, *labrys*, and the tangled maze of the palace's layout (like Daedalus' maze to imprison the Minotaur) both contributed to the present-day word "labyrinth."

**OTHER SIGHTS.** Pause a moment to catch the cool breeze at the **Queen's Megaron;** planners intentionally placed the queen's sitting room at that naturally air-conditioned spot. Climb above the throne room to see replicas of frescoes and the grand **pothoi**—jars so big that Minos's son was said to have drowned in one filled with honey. Throughout the palace, note the drainage system, the occasional mason's marks on the shiny, cut-stone architecture, and the I-shaped cement bumps on the ground that mark where doors slid into the walls to let in or keep out the sunlight. The areas painted red around each window and door were originally made of wood; they cushioned the walls from frequent seismic shock, but ultimately facilitated the palace's destruction by fires after the earthquake and tidal wave of Thira (modern Santorini, p. 397) in 1450 BC.

## ARHANES Αρχανες

*Buses run from Iraklion (30min., 15 per day, 360dr).*



A safe, comfortable, pretty suburb of Iraklion, Arhanes still retains much of its past as an ancient and medieval village in its interior old quarter, and in its museum collection and Minoan cemetery. Once used as a burial ground by Minoans and Mycenaeans, who wanted to raise their dead above the earth so the living would continue in their shadow, modern Arhanes is composed of winding tree-lined streets, neat pastel houses with clay tile roofs, and a thriving grape export industry. Arhanes' **wine factory,** behind the clock tower, is open seasonally for visiting.Only a daytrip for most visitors, Arhanes remains startlingly bereft of tourist menu billboards and harassing hosteliers.

Pleasant street-ramblings aside, Arhanes' official attractions are its **Archaeology Museum** and the sites where the collection originated. To reach the museum, head from the bus stop toward the center of town, keeping an eye out for the signs. Though the collection is small, the museum provides a good understanding of the area's sites. Its one room holds relics from Phourni, Anemospilia, and the Minoan Palace at Arhanes, as well as photos of finds now in Iraklion's Archaeological Museum (see p. 469). The most sensational of the Arhanes Museum's objects is the **bronze dagger** used for human sacrifice, found at the **Shrine of Anemospillia,** a 17th-century BC shrine on Mt. Iouktas outside of town. The sacrifices were most likely an attempt to appease the gods, perhaps to prevent the kind of earthquake that eventually destroyed the shrine. (Open M and W-Su 8am-2:30pm. Free.)

The museum's artifacts come primarily from the *tholos* graves at the nearby **Minoan Cemetery,** used throughout the Palace Period (2400-1200 BC). *Tholos* A in the burial ground was the first unlooted royal burial site found on Crete. Most of its objects have been moved to Iraklion, but some remain in the Arhanes Museum: terra-cotta *pithoi*, child and adult sarcophagi, baby burial jars (eek!), and skeletons from Phourni are among the finds. *Tholos* D yielded up a wealthy woman sporting flashy clothes and jewelry. Phourni Building 4 housed a wine press and a vat for treading grapes, and an *amphora* for the wine itself. To see the cemetery after checking out its contents, follow Kapetanaki street out of town and look for signs to the site; it's northwest of Arhanes. (Open Tu-Su 8am-2:30pm. Free.)

## GORTYS Γορτυνα

*From Iraklion, take one of the buses that go to Matala or Phaistos, and ask the bus driver to stop at Gortyna (950dr). You can also take the bus from Mires (270dr). ☎(0892) 31 144. Open 8am-6pm; in winter 8am-5pm. 800dr; students and EU seniors 400dr; under 18, classicists, fine arts students, and EU students free.*

Gortyna, site of the Greco-Roman city Gortys, is a fun stop for the historically minded, 45km south of Iraklion. In 67 BC, when Crete fell to the Romans, Minoan Gortys was made its capital. Coming from Iraklion on the paved road to Matala, the first stop is the 7th-century **Basilica of Saint Titus,** Crete's first Christian church. Built on the site where ten saints were executed in AD 250, the Basilica's *berma* (half dome with windows) grandly overlooks a courtyard full of fallen columns. Behind the church is the **Roman odeon,** where the famous **Law Code of Gortys** is lodged in the walls. Called the "Queen of Inscriptions," it is the most important extant source of pre-Hellenistic Greek law. Written in a Dorian dialect, it dates from 450 BC and is one of the first European attempts to codify legislation. Across a small wooden bridge from the odeon is the perpetually green **Platanos tree,** under which distinguished brothers Minos (an early Cretan ruler), Sarpidon (a Trojan warrior), and Rodaman (the family under-achiever) were born.

After you exit this part of the site, re-enter on the other side of the entrance booth to find a small, fenced-off **museum** with 13 sculpted figures. Left of the museum is a larger-than-life **statue** of Roman emperor Antonious Pius. If he seems sort of nondescript, you're on to something—resourceful Romans changed the statue's head every time a new emperor came to power.

Outside the site, you have two options. The first is an expanse of ruined structures: head 50m toward Iraklion and turn right at the sign. You'll first hit the **Sanctuary and Sacrificial Altar of Pythian Apollo.** Nearby is the **Nymphaion,** which was the end of an aqueduct that brought spring water from Zaros. A few steps further are arguably the most impressive ruins at Gortys: the **Praetorium,** which was the seat of the Roman administrator. Built in the 4th century BC, the Praetorium was ahead of its time: it had a full-scale water-heating system. If you take the other path, you'll find the 7th-century BC **acropolis** on the hill west of the odeon. To get there, continue 50m down the main road toward Matala, take a right after the river, and walk 200m; when you reach the corner of the fence, hike up the road for 30 minutes. Temple ruins and pottery dedicated to Athena Poliouchos are at the road's end.



# ZAROS Ζαρος ☎0894

Zaros's name has spread far and wide for its water, and little else, but this wee mountain town is a fully-stocked base for a day spent hiking in the mountains of Iraklion prefecture. Zaros is the capital and political center of a union of villages that includes neighboring Vorisia, Kamares, and Moroni. Upon arrival, you may be alarmed to discover that the ultra-pure "Zaros" spring water originates in this slightly gritty mountain town, but the surrounding landscape and warm Cretan hospitality are as refreshing as its bottled export.

**ORIENTATION AND PRACTICAL INFORMATION.** Zaros' one main road has everything but a **bank,** which you'll find in nearby Mires. The bus stops at the downhill start of the road, where the **police station** sits (☎31 210). You can also call the **Mires police** (☎22 222). Two **buses** run from Zaros to Mires (40min., 370dr) and Iraklion (70min., 1000dr) every day. Walk uphill to reach Zaros's downtown center, which includes the **pharmacy** (☎31 386; open M-F 8:30am-2pm and 5-8pm) and the **post office.** From the bus stop, walking to the right and away from main road leads to an immediate left turn where you'll find the **medical center** (☎31 206) and the flag-marked town hall (open M-F 9am-1:30pm); for **emergencies** at any hour call the hospital in Mires (☎(0892) 23 312). The **postal code** is 70002.

**ACCOMMODATIONS AND FOOD.** **Keramos Rent Studios** is the better of your two housing options. Walking uphill, turn left before the post office; it'll be on your left. The father makes all the traditional wood furniture by hand in this family-run operation, and the wife and daughter tend to guests with breakfasts of Cretan delights like *pitaraki* (Christmas pastry). Most studios have kitchenettes; all have baths and central heating in winter. (☎31 352. Singles 6000dr; doubles 8000dr; triples 11,000dr; breakfast included.) **Charikleia Rent Rooms,** in a cottage across from the police station, offers shared baths and a common, leafy courtyard. (☎31 787. Singles 4000dr; doubles 6,000dr; 1000dr per person for breakfast.)

Beyond the end of the village, the main street becomes **Votomos Lane,** where a number of tavernas take shelter in the greenery. About 200m beyond the Idi Hotel (a 20min. walk from town), a restaurant run by **Petrogiannakis and Ieronimakis** is known across Crete for outstanding fish raised from eggs on the premises. After touring the fish farm, savor trout (1500dr per kg) and salmon (8000dr per kg) cooked by the owner's mother. If the sound of the babbling brook is too near to think of seafood, try the pork chops (1400dr). (☎31 071 or 31 454. Open 9am-midnight.) **Papadaki Rena,** behind Keramos Studios, sells sweets and gifts; try the *tulta* cream cake or *baklava,* for around 250dr. (☎31 055. Open 8am-10pm.)

**SIGHTS AND HIKES.** Zaros has been Crete's source of health-giving **water** since the days of ancient Gortyna. At the water-bottling plant just above town, you can see the trucks loading bottles to take to the far reaches of the island. Every July and August, the village celebrates its aquatic bounty in an annual **water festival.** Zaros also holds an annual **summer festival** every August (2000dr).

Hikes and walks through gorges and up to surrounding monasteries can be quite breathtaking; check the map in front of the police station for ideas. At the end of the road beyond the Idi Hotel and Votomos tavernas is the **lake** of Votomos, which draws visiting Greeks from surrounding areas. Take the path behind the lake to reach the hike through the gorge up beyond the Agios Nikolaos Church. This climb makes a satisfying daytrip through the fast-changing scenery of the mountainside, but be warned that the way is oftentimes poorly marked and the path slippery with much loose gravel. Another path up the mountains leads to the **Monastery of Vrondisi,** where you will find impressive frescoes said to be painted by El Greco himself. Every May, the annual **Paniel festival and bazaar** takes place here to commemorate the ascent of Thomas. Trails and streams up through the hills around the monastery lead to a cliffside sanctuary dedicated to Cretan saint **Agios Euthymios.** Shepherds keep large bottles of olive oil in the sanctuary, and bring hikers into the shrines' three cave chambers to meditate before frescoes of the saint. Yet another mountain road leads to the **Kamares Cave,** where Rhea hid her infant son Zeus from his father's voracious appetite. Archaeologists made some important finds here, including ceramics and skeletons now in the Iraklion museum.

CRETE

## MATALA Ματαλα ☎0892

Anyone who visited Matala 20 years ago probably only has blurry memories of a hallucinogenic trip—the caves along Matala's seaside cliffs were supposedly once full of LSD-dosed psychedelia-lovers listening to groovy music. Today's Matala is a far cry from that old hippy city: there's an admission fee and fence barring access to the caves that counter-cultural hedonists once called home. But the party isn't entirely over: a short hike beyond the main drag, magnificent nude beaches are gorgeous reminders of those bygone days.

**ORIENTATION AND PRACTICAL INFORMATION.** Matala's single main street holds most necessities; when it hits the waterfront, the road bends to become a covered market, with steps leading down to a taverna-lined waterfront. Before the covered market, a pension-filled road branches off, heading eventually to Red Beach, up and over the hill. **Buses** go to: Iraklion (1¾hr., 3-6 per day, 1600dr); Phaistos (20min., 3-5 per day, 300dr); and Agia Galini

(45min., 3-6 per day, 700dr). **Monza Travel,** in the plateia, rents **mopeds** (3500dr) and helps with accommodations. (☎45 732 or 45 359; fax 45 763. Open 9am-11pm.) Several motorbike rental shops **exchange currency.** The **laundromat,** on the left side of town as you enter, charges 2500-2800dr per wash and dry. (Open M-Sa 9am-5pm.) The **post office** across the street opens sporadically. The **police, hospital,** and **pharmacy** are in Mires, 17km northeast. In an **emergency,** call 22 222 for police; dial 22 225 or 23 312 for a doctor. **Public toilets** are east of the post office, on the way to the beach. **Internet access** is available at the **Kafeneio Coffee Shop,** on the right side of the road about 100m past the bus stop (1200dr per hr.). **Postal code:** 70200.

**ACCOMMODATIONS.** Though hotels in the center of town tend to be pricey, don't try sleeping on the main beach or in the caves; it's illegal, and police raid them. Instead, look outside of town for reasonable prices in a quieter setting. Walk 200m toward Phaistos and follow the blue signs to the energetic hacker (butcher *and* internet fanatic in one) at **Dimitri's Villa.** His gleaming rooms have baths, balconies, fridges, safes, and phones. *Let's Go* users get a 25% discount on bike rentals and a free lift from Mires. (☎/fax 45 002 or 45 003; fax 45 740; mobile (093) 248 3939; www.c-v.net/crete/hotels/matala/dimitris_villa. Singles 3500dr; doubles 4700dr; triples 5300dr). If Dimitri's 13 rooms are full, continue on to the neighboring **Georgia Hotel** (☎45 761), which offers comparable rooms in price and quality. If you're set on staying in town, **Pension Matala View,** on the road to Red Beach, offers cool rooms with bathrooms, balconies, and fridges, and a common kitchen facility. (☎45 114. Singles 4000dr; doubles 5000dr; triples 6000dr.) **Matala Camping,** just off the main road east of the post office, lets you snooze in a slightly wooded grove beside the beach. (☎42 720. Showers available. 1100dr per person; 750dr per small tent; 750dr per car; 1350dr per RV.)

**FOOD AND ENTERTAINMENT.** Only a few restaurants in town cater to the budget palate. For good souvlaki (300dr) and gyros (500dr), head to **Notos,** between the waterfront and the covered market (open 9am-1am). On the west end of the beach, **Nikos at Plaka** specializes in fresh fish, in case your imagination wandered to the bottom of the ocean while you lounged on the beach (calamari 1600dr); they serve traditional Greek foods for around 900dr as well. (☎45 335. Open April-Oct. daily 11am-midnight.) **Kantari,** on the main plateia, is a popular place to catch Latin and other world music. (☎45 404. Opens at 9am. Beers 500dr; drinks 100-1300dr.) In tiny **Kahlua** (☎45 253), near the end of the main road, you can gulp flaming shots of sambuca with the owner, Effie. **Yorgos** is owned and bartended by energetic Yorgos himself, who will win you over with his spunky dancing, chit-chat, and ice-cold beers. (☎45 722. Opens at 6pm.) The partying goes on until around 6am.

**SIGHTS AND BEACHES.** Matala attracts visitors with its three tiers of spectacular **caves** beside the beach. As you sit in their cool, dim interior, reflect on the caves' previous occupants—Nazis searching for British submarines, singer-songwriter Joni Mitchell, and even Roman corpses. (Open 8am-4pm. 500dr.)

Matala is blessed with some of Crete's best **beaches,** many of which are spawning grounds for endangered **sea turtles.** Environmentalists run a kiosk providing info on the turtles and their habitat; if you want to support their cause, pick up a purple **Save the Turtles t-shirt** (3500dr). A 45min. hike past the pension-lined street and up and over the steep, roughly-marked hill will bring you to a magnificent strip of sand called **Red Beach.** Cliffs surround this taverna-free nudist beach. Bring drinking water and an umbrella: the beach has no shade, leading to speculation that it may take its name from the lobster skin tone of unprepared visitors and not from its clay-colored sand. Five kilometers from Matala, the long, pebbly **Kommos Beach** stretches out, with one taverna and an enclave of nude bathers. Archaeologists are currently excavating a Minoan site that overlooks the beach. To get there, take the bus to Matala-Iraklion (260dr) and walk a dusty 500m down to the beach.

**BULL LEAPING, PART I** Jump. Jump. Jump. You see them everywhere in museums, the mysteriously smiling youths jumping over bull horns. Minoans made a game of frolicking with bulls in an arena, though in a very different way than today's Spanish bullfighters. Minoan bull games took place in the large central court in palaces like Knossos and Phaistos, as the main event after a boxing match. The court's ground-level exits were blocked, and fans crowded the upper windows and balconies. Scantily clad boys and girls then danced around the court, inviting the bulls to chase them. As things heated up, a kid would lead a running bull up a platform, then leap over the pursuing animal. More treacherous stunts went down at mid-court, where an athlete would grab the bull's horns and launch a spectacular flip off its rearing head.

## PHAISTOS Φαιστος ☎0892

***Buses** from Phaistos go to Iraklion (1½hr., 8 per day, 1300dr); Matala (20min., 5 per day, 300dr); and Agia Galini (25min., 6 per day, 390dr). ☎42 315. Open year-round 8am-variable times. 1200dr; students and all EU seniors 600dr; classics students, under 18, and EU students free.*

Seated imperiously on a plateau with magnificent views of the mountains, the Minoan palace complex of Phaistos (also spelled **Festos**) is second in importance only to Knossos (p. 472). Unlike Knossos, Phaistos attracts fewer tourists and has undergone less interpretive renovation. Four palaces have been discovered on the site: the first, built around 1900 BC, was destroyed by the earthquake that decimated Crete around 1700 BC. The second structure was leveled by a Mysterious Cataclysm in 1450 BC; traces of two even older palaces were detected by an excavation in 1952. Since the excavations, minor reconstruction work has been done on the walls, chambers, and cisterns. Built according to the standard Minoan blueprint, the complex included a great central court surrounded by private royal quarters, servants' quarters, storerooms, and chambers for state occasions.

CRETE

Today visitors enter Phaistos and immediately see the **West Courtyard** and **theater area** on their right. On the left, you'll see the intact grand staircase. At its top is the **propylaea,** consisting of a landing, portico, central column, and light well. Cut through the **main hall** to reach the **central court,** which has a magnificent view of the Messara Plain. The main hall encloses a central and fenced-off **storeroom,** where you can view *pithoi* similar to those at Knossos, and other goodies.

Outside of the main court, columns and boxes mark the place where sentries used to stand guard. Beyond this area, plastic-roof-covered **royal apartments** with a queen's **megaron** are similar to the famous queen's bathroom at Knossos, and a lustral basin (covered purifying pool) recalls that of the Knossos throne room. In the nearby **peristyle hall,** the remains of columns can be seen lining the walls. Northeast of the central court are the narrow halls of the palace **workshops** as well as the seven-compartmented room where the renowned **Phaistos disc,** now in the Archaeological Museum in Iraklion (see p. 469), was discovered.

## AGIA GALINI Αγια Γαληνη ☎0832

A rather unremarkable riff on the typical Cretan beach melody, Agia Galini's popular beach and hilly streets are hard to make out through the fog of package tourists that fill them. The pebbly-sandy beaches pull in the tourists en masse. The town's main street runs down a steep hill from the bus station to the harbor, and contains all the practical necessities. Off the main drag, more frivolous streets run, well stocked with restaurants and some accommodations. Turn left from the harbor to reach the long beach, where more tavernas await your thirst. The **bus station** offers service to: **Iraklion** (1½hr., 6-7 per day, 1600dr); **Rethymno** (1hr., 3-4 per day, 1300dr); **Matala** (1hr., 2-5 per day, 650dr); and **Phaistos** (30min., 5-6 per day, 650dr). **Ferries** run to **Paveli** and back once a day; they leave at 10am and return at 5pm

(round-trip 5000dr). Next to the bus station is a **taxi service** (☎91 486, mobile 094 952 172). Across the street, **Monza Travel** provides info and rents mopeds and cars. (☎91 278. Open 9am-11pm. Mopeds 4000-5000dr; cars 10,000-12,000dr.) The street is full of **exchange** places. Heading downhill from the bus stop, you'll pass a **doctor** (☎91 056, emergency 932 688 564 ), and a **pharmacy** (☎91 168. Open M-Sa 9am-2pm and 5-9pm, Su 10am-2pm.). Across the street is the **police station.** (☎91 210. Open 24hr.) The **post office** is just up the street from the doctor. **Postal code:** 74056.

Pensions are occasionally affordable and close to the beach. On the main road, **Phaistos** (Φαιστος) offers rooms with bathrooms. (☎94 352. Doubles 8000dr.) Next door, **Manos** has rooms with shared and private baths. (☎91 394. Doubles 7000-8000dr; triples 7000-12,000dr.) **Camping Agia Galini No Problem** has a pool, mini-market, and taverna serving food fresh from the family farm (salad and two entrees 3500dr). Call for the free minibus service; alternatively, walk along the beach until the path starts climbing the hill and make a left, and then turn right twenty meters down the path. (☎91 386 or 91 141; fax 91 239. Laundry 1000-1200dr for wash. 10% discount for *Let's Go* users. 1000-1400dr per person; 500-700dr for children 6-12; tents 500-800dr; cars 300-500dr.) At night, you can chill at a mellow waterfront bar or, if you're feeling saucy, trot your booty over to the **Juxebox,** where the bartender is known to toss napkins in the air to keep the party hoppin.' (☎91 154. Open 10pm-7am, Happy Hour until midnight. Beers 500-1200dr; drinks 1500-200dr.)

## HERSONISSOS Χερσονησος ☎0897

Hersonissos's (kher-SON-i-suss) 150 bars, discos, nightclubs, and mountain villages to the south are a playground for English and German youngsters. Bungee-jumping, bumper cars, and waterslides clutter the beachfront, and Cretan culture is preserved only in a well-polished open-air museum. You don't need to know the Greek word for vodka here—your bartender won't know it either.

CRETE

### ORIENTATION AND PRACTICAL INFORMATION

Hersonissos is just 26km east of Iraklion. The lone main road, **Eleftheriou Venizelou,** has offices, markets, and discos. Perpendicular streets lead either to the beach or to the hills. Turning left beyond the Hard Rock Cafe on your way to Iraklion puts you on **Dimokratias,** a less congested stretch of supermarkets and travel agents.

**Buses:** There is no station, just a kiosk near the Hard Rock Cafe. Bus service to: **Iraklion** (45min., 4 per hour, 700dr); **Malia** (20min., 4 per hour, 250dr); **Agios Nikolaos** (55min., 17-20 per day, 850dr); **Sitia** (2½hr., 2400dr); and **Ierapetra** (2hr., 1650dr).

**Taxi:** 24hr. station (☎23 723 or 22 098) on El. Venizelou beside the medical center.

**Car and Motorbike Rental:** Several agencies on El. Venizelou. **Eurorent,** El. Venizelou 31 (☎24 958; fax 24 371), rents cars (7500dr per day with full insurance and tax included) and motorbikes (5,000 per day).

**Tourist Agencies: Mareland Travel** has 5 branches; the main one is on Dimokratias (☎24 424; fax 24 150). Open 8:30am-11:30pm. **Zakros Tours,** Dimokratias 12 (☎22 626; fax 22 137). Open 8am-10pm. Both rent cars, sell boat and plane tickets, exchange currency, find rooms, and have maps.

**Banks:** Several on El. Venizelou **exchange currency** and have 24hr. **ATMs,** including the **National Bank,** El. Venizelou 106 (☎22 377). Open M-Th 8am-2pm, F 8am-1:30pm.

**Public Toilets:** Across from the Zakros Tours office on El. Venizelou. Free.

**Tourist Police:** Minoos 8 (☎21 000). Turn toward the beach before Club 99 as you walk into town from Iraklion. Offers **currency exchange.** Open 8am-11pm.

**Police:** Minoos 8 (☎22 100 or 22 222).

**Medical Services: Medical Emergency of Kriti** (☎22 063 or 22 600 or 22 111; fax 21 987; mobile (0944) 517 170), at the corner of El. Venizelou and Kassaveti, near the

Hard Rock Cafe. Open 24hr. **Cretan Medicare,** El. Venizelou 19 (☎25 141 or 25 142 or 25 143; fax 24 064), in the western outskirts of town. Open 24hr.

**OTE:** Eleftherias 11 (☎22 299). Heading into town from Iraklion, turn left after Pelekis Jewelry. Open 7:30am-9:30pm.

**Internet Access:** Internet Cafe, Papadogi 10 (☎25 292); coming from the Hard Rock Cafe, go left after the toilets. Email 750dr per 30 min.

**Post Office:** (☎22 022). Open M-Sa 7:30am-2pm. **Postal Code:** 70014.

## ACCOMMODATIONS

Tour companies book up a majority of the rooms in town for the entire season.

**Selena Pension,** Em. Maragaki 13 (☎25 180). Walking from the bus kiosk on the main road away from Iraklion, take a left just past Enjoy Bar. Small rooms have private bath and balcony in a convenient, relatively quiet location. Singles 3000-5000dr; doubles 7000-10,000dr.

**Camping Hersonissos** (☎22 902), in Anisara. Take a bus or walk 3km toward Iraklion; it's on the right. Restaurant, supermarket, bar, and 24hr. hot water. 1150dr per person, 700dr per tent, 650dr per car. Open April-Sept.

**Camping Caravan** (☎22 025; fax 24 718), in Limenas; walk or bus 2km east toward Agios Nikolaos until the Lychnostatis Museum. English spoken. Restaurant and bar. 24hr. free hot water. 1100-1300dr per person, age 6-10 600-750dr; 850-1050dr per tent; 670 per car.

CRETE

## FOOD AND ENTERTAINMENT

The Hersonissos waterfront sports the usual assortment of restaurants serving "traditional Greek food"—often code for inferior pre-packaged facsimiles. A number of sandwich and fast food places line the main road.

Hersonissos' mediocre beach confirms it: you've come for the **nightlife.** Most clubs open at dusk and close at dawn. You can't stray two storefronts without encountering another bar or disco; they generally charge no cover, with beers costing between 800dr and 1300dr, and drinks around 1500dr. The **Black Cactus,** El. Venizelou 72, is a good place to start, with Happy Hour from 8:30-11:30pm (disco ball spinning throughout). Afterwards, head to the endless line of clubs along the waterfront. On the western end of the beach, **Status** can't contain its crowd. Skedaddle around the corner to the **Camelot Dancing Club,** where locals and tourists alike crowd in for international rave and house music. On El. Venizelou, **Disco 99** provides more room to do the shuffle. Please remember, *real* tourists do not leave town without a t-shirt from the **Hard Rock Cafe** (1500dr). The open-air museum **Lynchostasis,** roughly 1km toward Agios Nikolaos, exhibits Cretan houses and a windmill, and hosts ceramics and weaving workshops. During the harvest season, you're invited to tread grapes or bake pumpkin pie. (☎23 660. Open Tu-Su 9:30am-2pm. Tours at 10:30am, 11:30am, and 12:30pm. 1250dr, students 800dr, kids 12 and under 600dr; tour included.)

**Elli Taverna,** Sanoudaki 2 (☎24 758). Heading toward Iraklion, take a right after Cretan Medicare, and this modest taverna will be on your left. There's no menu, so peek inside the pots to choose from dishes like broccoli (800dr), lamb fricassee (1500dr), or beans (600dr), all cooked fresh in olive oil produced by the owner. Open 7am-2am.

**Taverna Kavouri,** Archeou Theatrou 9 (☎21 161). Walk toward Iraklion, turn right before the Hard Rock Cafe onto Peace and Friendship street, and walk left around the bend. Kavouri's fifteen tables under grapevines are an enjoyable, authentically Greek escape from the waterfront. Lamb 2800dr, *moussaka* 1100dr, chicken with lemon 1300dr. For dessert, try fried *tiganites* with ice cream (900dr). Open 5pm-midnight.

**Selena Restaurant** (☎25 180), beneath Selena Pension. Slip into this side street to escape the commotion of town. Selena serves house wine from their own vineyard and fresh rabbit (2500dr) from their farm (ask for it grilled or stewed in wine). Greek salad 800dr, *tzatziki* 550dr. Open 10am-9pm.

## MALIA Μαλια ☎0897

Mediterranean climate and nearby Minoan palace aside, Malia, with its pubs and Guinness taps, comes closer to evoking the pages of *Hello!* magazine than those of Homer or Kazantzakis. Young British tourists, booked months in advance on pre-packaged holidays, leap to Malia's beach like salmon in a mating frenzy. Locals refer to these hordes as *barbares* (what the ancient Romans used to call the ancient Greeks) and insist that there is more to Malia than simply partying like a rock star. Many visitors only come for a daytrip to see the palatial Minoan site. If you're ready for the mayhem of an overnight stay, however, bring condoms, a jersey from your favorite football (soccer) team, and lots of drachmas.

**ORIENTATION AND PRACTICAL INFORMATION.** **Buses,** which drop off on the main road, leave from a number of stops throughout the city for: **Iraklion** (1hr., 2-4 per hr., 800dr) via **Hersonissos** (20min., 250dr); **Agios Nikolaos** (1½hr., 2 per hr., 800dr); and **Lasithi** (1½hr.; leaves 8:30am, returns 2pm; 1300dr). **Taxis** (☎31 777 or 33 900) idle at the intersection of El. Venizelou and the National Bank road. **Altino Travel Service** (☎33 658; fax 29 620), across from the old church on the way to the beach, has maps, travel advice, and a rental service for **cars** (13,000-15,000dr) and **motorbikes** (5000-6000dr per day).

The main road from Iraklion, **Eleftheriou Venizelou,** should satisfy your practical needs, while the two converging paths to the beach, full of discos and watering holes, pander to the primal. The old village (between the main road and the inland hills) has lots of bars and cheaper rooms; to reach its center, turn left onto 25 Martiou at the Hertz car rental agency. A number of banks on El. Venizelou have 24hr. **ATMs,** including the **National Bank** across from the taxi station. (☎31 833 or 31 152. Open M-Th 8am-2pm, F 8am-1:30pm.)

There are **no police** in Malia; in **emergencies,** dial 22 222. There are two **24hr. medical centers: Medical Emergency of Kriti** (☎32 227 or 33 100), across from the old church, and **Cretan Medicare** (☎31 661, 662, 663). The **Internet Cafe,** Dimokratious 78, is on your right-hand side, about a ten minute walk past Altino Travel Service on the way to the beach. (☎29 563. 750dr per 30min.) The **OTE** is in the old village; follow signs from 25 Martiou at the Bimbo Cafe. (☎31 299. Open M-F 7:30am-2:30pm.) The **post office** is off El. Venizelou behind the old church. (☎31 688. Open M-F 7:30am-2pm.) **Postal code:** 70007.

**ACCOMMODATIONS AND FOOD.** Finding reasonably priced rooms in Malia can be a challenge, with beachside spots both booked and pricey. Affordable housing is in the old village, where some Greek speakers are found; wander around the sidestreets of **25 Martiou** and look around for a place that suits you. Walking away from the bus drop-off toward Agios Nikolaos, make a right onto 25 Martiou and then a left on Konstantinou to reach **Pension Aspasia,** home to large, balconied rooms, common baths, and a roof for sunbathing. Keep an eye out for the smallish sign and potted plants in front. (☎31 290. Singles 3000dr; doubles and triples 6000dr.) More Spartan rooms are found at **Pension Menios,** one door down from Aspasia. (☎31 361. Singles 4000dr; doubles 5000dr; triples 7000-7500dr.)

The most popular dishes in Malia are the "English" breakfast (600dr), the "steak" dinner (1900dr), and pizza (1500dr). Far into the old village, on the road leading to the OTE, sunny Greek youths take the limelight in traditional **Cafe Mylos;** hip modern Greek music plays as you order *mezedes* (500-700dr) or a big Greek salad (700dr)

from the leatherbound wooden menu. (Open 9am-3pm and 5pm-3am.) Ironically (and perhaps appropriately), the most faithful Greek food in Malia—Greek salad (1200dr) and *stifado* (2400dr)—is prepared by a Dutch chef, at **Petros** in the old village. (Open 5pm-1am.) On the main road, omnipresent **banana vendors** sell bunches for 400-500dr.

**ENTERTAINMENT.** The Beach road is home to many of Malia's more popular dance clubs, blaring with pop, house, international, rave, and dance music. Clubs open around 9pm, get really packed by 1am, and stay that way until 4am (weekdays) or 6am (weekends, including Thursday). With two halves on either side of the road, the crowd at **Malibu** blocks traffic, so you'll likely find yourself joining the party. (400dr cover to enter, redeemable at the bar after 1am, beers and drinks 1000-1500dr.) **Zoo** has no cover, but it does have sturdy cages for those craving a little cage-dancing. The smoke screens and strobe lights of **Apollo** enhance the hardest beats. (500dr cover, redeemable at the bar; beers and drinks 1000-1500dr.)

At the bars toward the end of the Beach road, there's less dance and more chatter, with recent Hollywood movies and old British comedies playing all day and almost all night for free; the **Charlie Chaplin** and **Oscars** have large screen TVs (open 11am-1am). For a quieter night of Dionysian delight, head for the cobbled Old Town, where a hybrid Greek-British libation is poured down willing throats every night in open-air pubs, complete with darts and grapevines.

**SIGHTS.** Though few natives take much interest in the place these days, Malia was one of three great cities of Minoan Crete. Malia's **Minoan Palace** lacks the labyrinthine plan of Knossos and Phaistos, but it's complicated enough to rank third among Minoan architectural puzzles. First built around 1900 BC, the palace was destroyed in 1650 BC, rebuilt on a larger scale, and then destroyed again (by that Mysterious Cataclysm) around 1450 BC. Notice the **Hall of Columns** on the north side of the large central courtyard, with its six columns supporting the roof. The **loggia,** a raised chamber on the west side, was used for state ceremonies; west of it are the palace's living quarters and archives. Northwest of the loggia and main site is the **Hypostyle Crypt,** possibly a social center for Malia's intelligentsia. The plot is well marked enough to notice these structures, and the admission fee includes an entrance to a small gallery with a three-dimensional reconstruction of the site and extensive photographs of its excavation. Follow the road to Agios Nikolaos 3km to the east and turn left toward the sea, or walk along the length of the beach and then 1km through the rocky fields. (☎31 597. Open Tu-Su 8am-3pm. 800dr, students and seniors 400dr, EU students free.)

CRETE

# RETHYMNO PREFECTURE

While many of the resort towns of eastern Crete seem to have sprung from the brains of British booking agents, the vacation spots of western Crete have grown naturally around towns rich in history and character. This end of the island is far less built up, with modest seaside towns filling only short sections of the shore with tavernas, leaving the long stretches to the birds, waves, and satisfied hikers. The meld of Ottoman, Venetian, and Greek architecture here complements the blue waters of the southwest coast and the sheer cliffs of the Samaria Gorge.

## RETHYMNO Ρεθυμνο ☎0831

The capital of the Rethymno prefecture, the city of Rethymno (or Rethymnon) is steeped in ancient folklore and spicy with urban panache. According to Greek myth, Zeus was born of Rhea to the god Cronus in the cave of Idaion Andron outside Rethymno. Cronus was on the verge of eating the baby to prevent Zeus's predicted future one-upmanship, but Cretan *kourites* (spirits) danced up a storm to distract the jealous king. Once safely away from Cronus, baby Zeus nursed from the goat Amaltheia and ate honey from golden bees.

CRETE

According to archaeologists, Rethymno has been occupied since the late Minoan period. Overrun by Mycenaeans in the 14th century BC, the city survived the Hellenistic, Roman, and Byzantine periods, until the Franks sold the island to the Venetians for 520lb. of silver. Rethymno—especially the Arkadi Monastery—played a major role in the fight for Greek independence in the 1860s.

Crete's many conquerors—Venetians, Ottomans, even Nazis—have had a profound effect in Rethymno's old city. Arabic inscriptions on the walls, a skyline full of minarets, and the Venetian fortress guarding the harbor unite in a distinctive, single cultural atmosphere that overflows the city like the Greek folk music spilling out of its cafes and garden restaurants. Even the most restless travelers may find their wanderlust inexplicably sated as they lounge beside contented locals, sipping *raki* into the wee hours of the morning.

## ORIENTATION AND PRACTICAL INFORMATION

**Pl. Martiron,** between Rethymno's **Old City** to the north and **New City** to the south, is about a 15min. walk from anywhere you'd want to go. To get to the plateia from the bus station, climb the stairs at the back of the station's parking lot onto **Igoumenou Gavriil** and go left; Pl. Martiron is just after the **public gardens.** The **waterfront** lies at the northern edge of the old city, with a maze of ancient streets filling the space between the main thoroughfare of Igoumenou Gavriil, which turns into **Koundouriotou** as it runs east toward Iraklion. The formidable Venetian **Fortezza** sits at the western edge of the waterfront, while the western end turns into a fine beach at the city's edge.

**CRETAN HOMEBREW** Intrigued, nervous, or delighted about what's in that **raki** Greeks are so willing to share with tourists? Here's the scoop: *raki* is a powerful form of hard liquor made from the bits of the grape left over after the wine-making process (much like mainland *tsipouro*). The remnants of pulp, pits, and skin are distilled five times to make good *raki,* which should slip down your throat accompanied by a pleasant burning sensation. Beware of poorly distilled *raki*—it can be as lethal as moonshine or Irish *poitin.* (Local word has it that *raki* that's only been distilled once can blind you.) *Raki* hospitality is enshrined in the earliest Cretan laws, and there's still no tax on the substance. Ouzo is better known amongst the tourist crowd, but *raki* devotees will diss ouzo as a watered-down, sugary version of *raki.*

**Buses: Rethymno-Hania station** (☎22 212), south of the fortress on the water on Igoumenou Gavriil. Service to: **Iraklion** (1½hr., 18 per day, 1550dr); **Hania** (1hr., 17 per day, 1600dr); **Agia Galini** (1½hr., 3-4 per day, 1300dr); **Plakias** (1hr., 4 per day, 950dr); and **Arkadi Monastery** (45min., 3-4 per day, 550dr).

**Flights: Olympic Airways,** Koumoundorou 5 (☎24 333 or 22 257), opposite the Public Gardens. Open M-F 8am-8pm, Sa 8am-4pm.

**Ferries:** Buy tickets to Athens (7:30am, 7000dr) at any travel office.

**Taxis:** (☎25 000, 22 316, 24 316, or 28 316). Available 24hr. at Pl. Matiron 4.

**Tourist Office:** (☎29 148), by the waterfront on El. Venizelou, east of the old city. Free maps of town, bus, and ferry schedules, info on rooms and restaurants. Open M-F 8am-2:30pm. M-Sa 8am-2pm.

CRETE

**Banks:** The several blocks of Koudouriotou west of the public gardens sprout over five banks, several with 24hr. **ATM.** The **International Bank** is at the intersection of Koudouriotou and Dimokratias.

**Bookstore: International Press,** I. Petichaki 15 (☎24 111). Sells books, newspapers, and magazines. Open 9am-11pm. **Spontidaki Toula,** Souliou 43 (☎54 307), buys and sells new and used books. Open 9am-11pm.

**Laundromat:** Tombasi 45 (☎56 196), next to the hostel. Wash 1500dr, wash and dry 2500dr. Open M-F 8am-2pm and 5-8pm. 20% discount for hostel guests.

**Tourist Police:** Venizelou 5 (☎28 156; fax 53 450). Open M-F 7am-2:30pm.

**Police:** (☎25 247) in Pl. Iroon. Open 24hr. In an **emergency,** dial 100.

**Port Police:** (☎25 276), at the Venetian Port.

**Hospital:** Trandalidou 18 (☎27 814), in the southwest corner of town. From Igoumenou Gavriil at the bus station, take Kriari and turn left onto G. Trandalidou. Open 24hr.

**OTE:** Koundouriotou 23 (☎22 699). Open M-Sa 7am-3pm.

**Internet Access: Cafe Galero** (☎25 750), at Rimondi Fountain. 800dr per 30min., 1400dr per hr. Open 7am-3am. The **Youth Hostel** also has a terminal open to guests.

**Post Office: Main branch,** Moatsou 19 (☎22 303), west of the public gardens in the New City. Open M-F 7:30am-8pm, Sa 7:30am-2pm. **Caravan office,** on the beach by the second dock. Open 7:30am-2pm. **Postal code:** 74100.

## ACCOMMODATIONS

The adorable streets near the fortress and the Venetian port are lined with ideally located but expensive hotels and rooms to let.

**Youth Hostel,** Tombazi 41-45 (☎22 848; www.yhrethymno.com). From the bus station, walk down Igoumenou Gavriil, take a left at the park traffic light, and walk through the Guora Megali gate; Tombazi is the first right. Fun, bustling outdoor gardens and bar (beer and wine 400dr). Outdoor beds available. Hot showers 8-10am and 5-8pm in winter, more in summer. Reception open 8am-noon and 5-9pm. Breakfast 400-500dr. Internet access 350dr per 15min. Beds 1800dr per person, sheets 150dr. 20% discount at neighboring laundry.

**Olga's Pension,** Souliou 57 (☎53 206, 28 665, or 54 896; fax 29 851), off Antistassios. The rooms are oddly shaped to match their fantastic, homespun decoration. Enjoy fare from **Stella's Kitchen** downstairs in the rooftop garden, with its view of all Rethymno and beyond (open 7am-midnight). Check out the Greek coins that decorate the stairwell, and bask in the owner's friendliness. All rooms with ceiling fans, some with bath. Singles 5000-7000dr; doubles 7000-9000dr; triples 10,000-11,000dr.

**Hotel Paradisos,** Igoumenou Gavriil 37 (☎22 419). From the bus station, walk down Igoumenou Gavriil; the hotel is on the left, across from the entrance to the public gardens. Clean, very quiet rooms. Singles 3000dr; doubles 4000dr; triples 5000dr.

**Elizabeth Camping** (☎28 694), 3km east of town at the beginning of the old road to Iraklion. Take the hotel bus from Rethymno station (every 15 minutes until 9pm, 170dr). Pitch your tent on shaded grass. Free parking next to reception; otherwise, pay 600dr to park next to your tent. The staff lends supplies, guitars, and books to occupy you at the nearby beach. Self-service **taverna** open 8:30am-1am. Seafood grilled Tu, Th, Sa (1200-1700dr). Laundry 1200dr. Open mid-Apr. through Oct. 1650dr per person, 1100-1500dr per tent depending on size; single person and tent 2200dr. 10% discount with a Minoan Lines ticket.

## FOOD AND ENTERTAINMENT

An **open-air market** next to the park, between Moatsou and Koundouriotou, opens at 6 or 7am and closes around 1 or 2pm on Thursdays; selection diminishes by 9 or 10am. For affordable nighttime eats, tourists and locals head to **Pl. Petichaki.**

**Taverna Kyria Maria,** Moskovitou 20 (☎29 078), behind the Rimondi fountain. Kyria Maria serves up generous breakfasts (1200-2300dr), rabbit with onion, lettuce, or tomato (1800-2000dr), and octopus in wine sauce (2000dr). Exquisite, free cheese pies accompany the after-dinner shot of *raki*. Open mid-Mar. to Oct. 10am-11pm.

**Dimitris,** Ag. Varvaras 35 (☎28 933). If you order the owner's homebrewed *raki* (200dr), you'll get a plate of snacks, usually olives, cheese, and meat. Oven-roasted potatoes (500dr) are the specialty. Adored by locals. Open 8am-2pm and 5-11pm.

**Katerina's,** Melissinou 34 (☎57 024). Seating beneath the Fortezza, and *raki* from the lovely Katerina herself. Lamb with Greek herbs, greek salad, ouzo, and *tahiki* for two costs 4000dr. Open 8am-midnight.

The bar scene in Rethymno centers around Petichaki and Nearchou streets near the west end of the harbor. The happening **Rock Café Club,** Petichaki 8, and the **Fortezza Disco Bar,** Nearchou 14 (☎21 493), serve pricey beers (1000dr). They also bookend several Greek *bouzouki* places, including **Odysseas** (☎29 233), beside the Rock Cafe. **Baja-Opera Club,** at the intersection of Salaminos and Messologiou, packs in the crowds with its A/C dance floor and techno and house tunes. (☎51 593. Beers 1500dr, drinks 2000dr.) For a slow and steady drink with a chatty Greek crowd, head to the bar at **Kafeneio Sta Vrysakia,** Moschovitou, behind Rimnodi Fountain. (☎(09) 777 50 431. Beer 500dr, wine 1000dr per kilo.)

## SIGHTS

The **Venetian Fortezza,** built in 1580, is certainly Rethymno's most impressive sight. Although most of the buildings inside were either destroyed by Ottomans or bit the dust three centuries later during the Second World War, the walls of the citadel are in excellent condition. (☎28 101. Open Tu-Su 8am-7pm. 900dr, children 700dr.) Rethymno's **Archaeological Museum** occupies a former Ottoman prison adjacent to the fortress. The museum has enough Minoan artifacts and information about their sites to keep an archeology enthusiast occupied for 90min. or so. (☎54 668. Open Tu-Su 8:30-3pm. 500dr, students and seniors 300dr, EU students free.) The **L. Kanakakis Center of Contemporary Art,** Himaras 5, at the corner of Salaminus, displays lots of 19th and 20th century modern Greek paintings, and hosts

temporary exhibits. (☎52 530. Open April-Oct Tu-F 9am-1pm and 7-10pm, Sa-Su 11am-3pm; Nov.-Mar. Tu and Th-F 9am-2pm, W 9am-2pm and 5-9pm, Sa 9am-3pm. 500dr.) The **Historical and Folklore Museum,** Vernardou 28-30, showcases traditional arts, farming tools, and a varied collection that shows the physical remains of Cretan society from the past several centuries. (☎23 398. Open M-Sa 10am-2pm. 500dr, students 200dr.)

Tattooed with graffiti and untamed by museum keepers, Rethymno's Ottoman monuments blend quietly into the scenery: the **Neratzes Minaret** on Antistassios; the former Franciscan church **Nerdjes Mosque,** a block away on Fragkiskou 1 (called St. Francis on many maps); the **Kara Pasha Mosque** on Arkadiou near Pl. Iroon; and the **Valides Minaret,** which presides over the gate called **Porta Megali** at Pl. 3 Martiou. The **public gardens** lie at the inland end of Igoumenou, beside the southwest corner of Pl. Matiron. Their leafy environs are a cool retreat from the Greek sun, but beware the ostriches that gawk on the premises in the small **zoo.**

Rethymno's **Wine Festival** (usually in July) is a crowded all-you-can-drink celebration, with a local dance troupe performing each evening. The city's **Renaissance Festival,** featuring theater, concerts, and exhibitions, is held in the fortress in July and August. Call the tourist office for schedules and other information.

## DAYTRIP FROM RETHYMNO: ARKADI MONASTERY

*Take the bus the 23km from Rethymno (40 min, 3-4 per day, 550dr; return trips an hour later). ☎83 076. Site open 8am-8pm, Museum 8am-1:30pm and 2:15-8pm. 500dr.*

CRETE

The site of one of the most famous battles in the Greek struggle for independence from the Ottomans, Arkadi Monastery (Μονη Αρκαδη) became a symbol to accompany the motto *Ελευθερια η θανατος*—"Freedom or Death." Modern Greeks refer to the event as the Holocaust of 1866. In November of that year, Greeks and Turks fought in a two-day standoff at the monastery. When Greek defenses finally gave way, the monks and *kleftes* holding out in the monastery set off their own ammunitions supplies, sacrificing themselves to kill hundreds of Turks. The story of Arkadi inspired support for Cretan independence in Western Europe, and the original structure has since been permanently memorialized on the 100-drachma note. Today a few monks maintain what is left of the monastery: the frame of the church and the outer complex, the roofless chamber where the ammunition was detonated, and a small museum containing a portion of the church's original decoration, including Byzantine paintings and orthodox vestments. Despite its devastation, the church is still a stunning example of 15th century Cretan Renaissance architecture.

# PLAKIAS Πλακιας ☎0832

Sunny and secluded, Plakias has remained wonderfully underdeveloped and inexpensive compared to most Cretan beach towns. The crystal-clear waters of the south coast, as well as mountain villages and a remote monastery within hiking distance, make Plakias an ideal escape from the surrounding tourist mainline.

**ORIENTATION AND PRACTICAL INFORMATION.** You'll be able to find anything you need either on the beach road or on the paths that scatter inland from it. **Buses** drop off and pick up at the beach, and run to: Rethymno (4 per day, 1000dr) and Preveli (1 per day, 400dr). **Monza Travel** (☎31 433; fax 31 883), on the beach road, rents cars (12,000dr) and mopeds (5000dr). Behind Monza Travel are a **doctor** (☎31 770, mobile 094 859 983; open M-Sa 9:30am-1:15pm and 5:15- 8:30pm, Su 5:30-8:30pm) and **pharmacy** (☎31 666; open M-Sa 9:30am-1:15pm and 5:15-8:30pm, Su 5:30-8:30pm). **Police** are 20km away in Spilli (☎22 027); in an **emergency,** dial 100. The **hospital** (☎(0831) 27 814) is in Rethymno. The yellow **post office** trailer sits on the beach in summer (open M-F 8:30am-2pm); an office with permanent foundations is 1km north in Mirthios. **Postal code:** 74060.

**ACCOMMODATIONS.** From the bus stop, with your back to the water, go left and follow the signs pointing inland about 250m to reach the **Plakias Youth Hostel.** Set in an olive grove, this heavenly hostel goes all-out with hot showers, good music, and cheap alcohol, making it a much raved-about backpacker oasis. Reception is open 9am-noon and 5-9pm, but if you arrive after 9pm, grab an open bed and settle up in the morning. (☎32 118; www.yhplakias.com. Internet access 250dr for 10min. Open March-Nov. Beds 1700dr, sheets 200dr.) At **Pension Kyriakos,** at the end of the road with the doctor and pharmacy, rooms are decked out with kitchenettes and private bathrooms, and Kyriakos insists on treating all his guests to *raki*. (☎31 307. Singles 5000-6000dr; doubles 7000-8000dr; apartments for 3-4 11,000dr.) To reach **Camping Apollonia,** walk eastward from the bus stop and take a left at the Old Alianthos Taverna. Follow this road for about 100m until you reach a complex that includes a pool and snack bar—it's not a country-club, it's the campsite. (☎31 318. Free showers for campers. Laundry 1000dr. Bike rental 1500dr per day, motorbikes 4000dr per day. Open May-Oct.; reception open 8:30am-9:30pm. 1200-1350dr per person, 750dr per child ages 4-10; 600-750dr per tent; 750dr per car; 400dr per bike; 1400dr per caravan.)

**FOOD AND ENTERTAINMENT.** To avoid the crowds, walk 40min. west along the beach to **Alyykes,** a family restaurant that only serves food fresh from its own farm. Work off your meal with a post-dinner romp on the beach 100m down the road. (☎32 116. Calamari 1200dr, octopus 1450dr. Open May-Oct. 10am-11pm.) Locals highly recommend the special *stifado* (1300dr) and butter beans (900dr) at the **Old Alianthos Taverna,** at the eastern end of the beach road. (☎31 851. Open daily 11:30am-10:30pm.) Quiet Plakias starts to hum come nightfall when its bars light up on the outskirts of town. **Meltemi,** 100m past the end of town grinds nightly from 11pm to 6am. (☎31 305. Beers 1000dr.)

**HIKES AND BEACHES.** Pass a pretty day **hiking** through the villages that dot the hills around Plakias and escaping into the gorges that punctuate the trek. You can take a **bus** to **Preveli Monastery,** or ask in town for directions on how to complete the fantastic (but complicated) two-hour **hike.** (Open 8am-1:30pm and 3:30-8pm. Modest dress required. 700dr, students 350dr, under 14 free.) From there you can reach **Preveli Beach** by walking 1km along the road to a dirt parking area; make the one-hour climb down. Scramble up again to catch the Preveli-Plakias bus back, or take the ferry to **Plakias** (1000dr) or **Agia Galini** (2500dr).

CRETE

# HANIA PREFECTURE

The westernmost tip of Crete is ringed with gorgeous beaches and cleft by the much-beloved Samaria Gorge; tourists flock to these natural wonders in droves. But it's also Zorba country, with small villages and beaches off the beaten track and awaiting exploration. If you want to party in a beachside club, look no further. If you want to flee pounding techno and foam-filled orgiastic scenes, seek out patience and a moped, and escape is yours.

## HANIA Χανια ☎0821

Crete's second largest city, Hania (KHAHN-ee-ah) responds to its yearly avalanche of summer tourism with Cretan hospitality, despite the port town's urban sophistication. Down by the Old Venetian Harbor, the revelry starts. Visitors meander through winding streets, listening to folk music from streetside cafes or waiting for the setting sun to silhouette the lighthouse and nearby Ottoman domes.

## ORIENTATION AND PRACTICAL INFORMATION

To get to the city center from the bus station, turn right onto Kydonias and walk for two short blocks, then turn left onto **Zymvrakakidon,** which runs along one side of a large public plaza called **Pl. 1866.** At the far end of Pl. 1866, the road becomes **Halidon** and leads to the **Old Venetian Harbor,** full of outdoor restaurants, narrow alleyways, and high-ceilinged interiors. Intersecting with Zymvrakakidon and Halidon at their meeting point is another major road, **Skalidi,** to the left (facing Halidon); to the right it becomes Chatzimichali, and then Giannari. A short distance later, Giannari forks into Tzanakaki and El. Venizelou. If you're arriving by ferry, you'll dock in the nearby port of **Souda.** Take the bus from the dock, which stops at the supermarket on Zymvrakakidon by Pl. 1866 (15min., 260dr). Hania's business district stakes out the area across from the **Municipal Market** around the intersection of **Gianari** and **Tzanakaki.** Its shops and restaurants cluster around the splendid Venetian Harbor. Beach bathers should head west of the harbor along the waterfront to find a long, thin stretch of well-populated sand at **Nea Hora.**

**Buses:** The **central bus station** (☎93 306) fills a block between Kydonias, Zymvrakakidon, Smyrnis, and Kelaidi. To: **Platanias** (every 30min., 350dr); **Paleohora** (3 per day, 1600dr); **Hora Sfakion** (3 per day, 1500dr); **Kastelli** (13 per day, 1000dr); **Samaria Gorge** (4 per day, round-trip 2800dr); **Elafonissi** (1 per day, 2500dr); **Sougia** (1 per day, 1550dr); **Rethymno** (17 per day, 1600dr); and **Iraklion** (17 per day, 2900dr).

**Ferries: ANEK Office,** Pl. Market 2 (☎27 500). *Lato* and *Lissos* go to **Piraeus** (9½hr., 1 per night at 8:30pm, 5900dr). Call ahead in July-Aug. about an additional morning departure between 8 and 9am, with a 30% discount fare. Open 7:30am-8:30pm.

**Flights: Olympic Airways,** Tzanakaki 88 (☎57 701, 702, 703), near the public gardens. Tickets sold M-F 8am-3pm. Phone reservations M-F 7am-9pm, Sa 8am-3pm. Flights to **Athens** (4 per day, 18,000dr plus 3300dr tax).

**Moped and Car Rental:** Several agencies are on Halidon. Mopeds 4000-7000dr per day. Cars go for around 8000-10,000dr per day.

**Tourist Office:** Kriari 40 (☎/fax 92 624), just off Pl. 1866. Free maps of Hania and Crete. Open M-F 7:30am-2pm. Private tourist agencies near Pl. 1866 also offer travel advice in English. The **Tourist Information Center,** Kanevaro 10, on the east side of the harbor, has info on rooms to let. Open M-F 9am-2pm and 6-9pm, Sa 9:30am-2pm.

**Banks: National Bank** (☎28 810), on the corner of Nikiforou, Foka, and Tzanakaki streets. **ATM.** Open M-Th 8am-2pm, F 8am-1:30pm.

**Luggage storage:** You can leave your bags at the bus station while looking for a room. 400dr per bag. Open 6am-9pm, closed 6:30-7:30pm.

**Police:** Irakliou 23 (tourist ☎53 333, general ☎28 730). Open 7:30am-8pm.

**Emergency:** dial 100. For a 24hr. **ambulance,** call 166.

**Hospital:** (☎27 000). On the corner of Dragoumi and Kapodistriou; plans to move in September 2000 to Mournies, 6km south of Hania. Consult the tourist office. Outpatient clinic open M-Sa 12:30-2pm and 6-9pm, Su 8am-9pm.

**OTE:** Tzanakaki 5 (☎35 519). Open 7am-10pm. Telex and telegram M-F only.

**Internet Access: Sante** (☎94 737), a cafe toward the west end of the harbor on the waterfront, offers Internet access upstairs. 30min for 500dr, 500dr deposit. Open 8am-2am. **Vranas Internet Cafe,** on the corner of Kalinikou Sarpaki and Agion Deka, beside Mitropoleos Square (☎58 618). 1 hr for 1000dr, 200dr deposit. Open 8am-late.

**Post Office:** Tzanakaki 3 (☎28 445). Open M-F 7:30am-8pm, Sa 7:30am-2pm. **Postal Code:** 73100.

## ACCOMMODATIONS

There are many inexpensive pensions in the Old Town. New Town overlooks the harbor, with its convenient location with access to fabulous views and noisy night

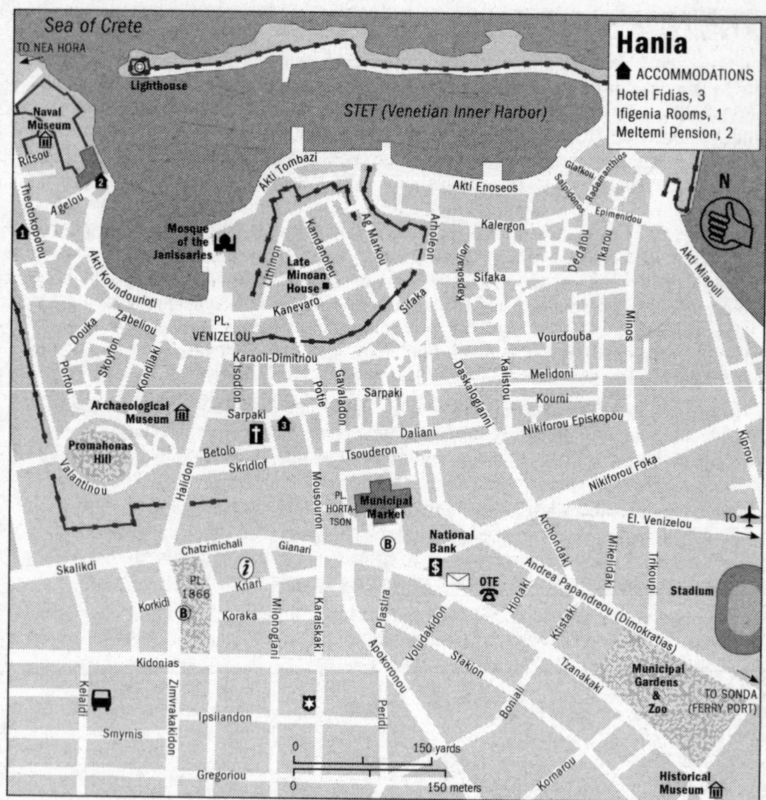


spots. Small hotels sprout from the beaches to the west, but expect to pay dearly for the brown sands of **Nea Kydonia** and **Agia Marina.** The **Association of Rooms to Let: Unikreta Travel Agency,** Dor. Episkopou 20, one block left of harbor center, can help you find a room. (☎43 601; fax 46 277. Open M-F 9am-2pm.) Also worth trying is the Tourist Information Center (see listing above). Beware of people at the station trying to entice visitors to stay in their rooms: hawking at the bus station is illegal.

**Hotel Fidias,** Sarpaki 6 (☎52 494). Walking toward the harbor on Halidon, turn right onto Athinagora; half a block past the cathedral on the right, Athinagora becomes Sarpaki. Charming, communal atmosphere. Exceptionally friendly staff, comfortable rooms; kitchen facilities; free luggage deposit; hard-to-find singles. Reception open 7am-10pm. Singles 2000-4000dr; doubles 3000-4500dr; triples/dorms 4500-6000dr, depending on season. 15% senior discount in winter.

**Meltemi Pension,** Agelou 2 (☎92 802), at the west side of the harbor, next to the Naval Museum. Rooms are as tall and expansive as you could ask of a Venetian Harbor residence, with the added luxuries of showers, wooden floors, marble-topped desks, and fabulous harbor views. The **Meltemi Cafe** downstairs serves *frappés* (600dr), breakfast (1300-1600dr), and cocktails (1300dr) come nightfall. Singles 5000dr; doubles 7000-12,000dr; triples 10,000-14,000dr.

**Ifigenia Rooms,** at Ant. Gampazi and Parados Angelou. Michalis Boulakas (mobile ☎944 501 319) owns a number of snappy rooms around the west end of the harbor. Prices range substantially in terms of season, luxury, and jacuzzi possession. Doubles 7000-18,000dr; triples 16,000-17,000dr.

## FOOD AND ENTERTAINMENT

You could construct a fantasy meal from the selection of exotic foodstuffs available at the open-air **Municipal Market** in (surprise!) Pl. Market. In a stately warehouse built at the intersection of Giannari and Tzanakaki in the center of town, vendors hock their wares to hordes of locals and tourists. (Open M-Sa 8am-2pm, Tu and F 6-9pm.) For other cheap options, try the **supermarket** (☎90 558) in Pl. 1866, on the right as you walk from Halidon. (Open Sa-Th 8am-9pm, F 8am-6pm.)

**Anaplous** (☎41 320), on your right as you walk from the harbor on Sifaka. This romantic open-air bistro is set in pink stone ruins. Nikos, the innovative chef, boasts of offering the only *pilino*—pork and lamb cooked 6-7hr. in ceramics—in Greece. Breaking the clay costs 7000dr and serves 3. Other dishes average 1900dr, including the excellent lamb *foukaki* (1980dr). Stellar vegetarian options abound, like *boureki* (seasoned zucchini, 1680dr). Anaplous moves to a Venetian house across the street during winter. Open 7pm-midnight.

**Tamam,** Zabeliou 49 (☎96 080). Tamam is notable among the many beautiful open-air restaurants on and around Zabeliou. Intimate dinners of superb calamari (1500dr), *hounkiar beyiendi* (chicken in eggplant puree, 2100dr), and vegetarian alternatives. Extensive wine list. Open M-Th 6pm-12:30am, F-Su noon-12:30am.

**Akrogiali,** Akti Papanikoli 19 (☎73 110), on the waterfront in **Nea Hora,** a 12min. walk westward along the water past the Maritime Museum. Gaze across the road at Nea Hora's white beaches as you scarf down fresh seafood gathered from the deep blue Mediterranean beyond. Open M-Sa 7pm-1am, Su 11am-1am.

Hip rock clubs like **Mythos,** Akti Koundourioti 52, and **Street,** right next door, offer a club/bar scene for a 2000dr cover that includes one free beer or drink (ensuing beers and drinks 1000-2000dr). The clubs are open until 3:30am on weekdays, and until people go home on weekends. **Mylos,** a must-see dance club for red-blooded beach-party devotees, is only a 2000dr taxi ride away in Platanias (see **Near Hania,** p. 491). For nightly traditional music and dancing in a relaxed setting, sit down and sip a slow drink in the narrow confines of **Kafe Kriti,** an outpost of Cretan culture on Kalergon on the east side of the harbor.



## SIGHTS

**VENETIAN INNER HARBOR.** The **Venetian lighthouse,** an oddly rickety tower of stone, guards the entrance to Hania's stunning architectural relic, the Venetian Inner Harbor. The inlet has retained its original breakwater and Venetian arsenal, and the Egyptians restored the lighthouse during their occupation of Crete in the late 1830s. On the west side of the main harbor, the **Maritime Museum** describes the tumultuous (often ferocious) 6000 years of Crete's naval and merchant history in maps and models. The second floor houses a large exhibition on Crete's remarkable expulsion of the Nazis in 1941. *(☎91 875. Open daily Apr.-Oct. 10am-4pm, Nov.-Mar. 10am-2pm. 600dr, students 350dr.)* In the **Venetian Shiphouse,** at the east end of the harbor where Arhdeon meets Anti Bnoseos, a temporary museum is set up with a new theme each summer—consult the tourist office. *(☎28 435.)* The melange of Ottoman and Venetian architecture in the **waterfront alleys** reflects the city's past. At the corner of Kandanoleu and Kanevaro, just north of Kanevaro on **Kastelli Hill,** visitors can look upon much earlier reminders of Hania's ancient Kydonian Bronze Age prosperity, including the **Late Minoan House** (c. 1450 BC) and other fenced-off and unmarked monuments. A small collection of gondolas and more modern vessels dock in the harbor at night, offering moonlit cruises to tourists.

**MUNICIPAL GARDENS.** Inland, past the public market off Tzanakaki, Greeks of all ages mellow out in the shade of flora of all varieties in the **Municipal Gardens,** *Dimotikos Kypos*, once the property of a *muezzin* (Islamic prayer caller). The garden also boasts an **open-air movie theater** that shows international films *(☎41*

*427; 1800dr)*, in addition to a small zoo of several goats, many birds, and a flock of free-range pigeons for petting. UNICEF sets up an annual **International Fair** in the gardens—consult the tourist office for details.

**SFAKIANAKI.** This 19th-century neighborhood with tree-lined streets is beyond the gardens to the east. The **Historical Museum and Archives,** Sfakianaki 20, might interest Greek speakers and costume specialists with its small display of Cretan weaponry, photos of 19th-century generals, and a tattered Cretan flag. *(☎52 606. Open M-F 9am-1pm. Free.)*

**ARCHAEOLOGICAL MUSEUM.** The **Archaeological Museum,** on Halidon about 40m past the cathedral toward the water, features a broad collection of Cretan artifacts, ranging from early Minoan to Hellenistic times. Once a Venetian monastery, then the mosque of Yusuf Pasha, these high-ceilinged halls are lined with mosaics, grave *steles*, clay shards of Linear B, and even some scraps of Linear A: get your gold, glass, stone, or clay! *(☎52 606. Open T-Su 8:30am-3pm. 1000dr, students 300dr.)*

**TRADITIONAL CRETAN MUSEUM.** Directly across from Hania's cathedral is the Traditional Cretan Museum, where models of all sizes recreate in several rooms the handicrafts and agricultural lifestyle of Crete's people in recent history. *(☎90 816. Open M-F 9am-3pm, 6-9pm. Free.)* Chess lovers should visit the masterful Athenase Diamantopouioi, who has run the Chess Center, Potie 51, for over 50 years. Take home a handmade chess or backgammon set for 3000dr and up. *(☎42 217. Open 9am-2pm and 5-8:30pm.*

# NEAR HANIA

## PLATANIAS Πλατανιας

Half an hour to the west by bus (every 30min., 350dr), Platanias (plat-AHN-yaas) shelters long, pretty beaches and ten tourists for every local. Platanias's fame sprang from a large rock island just offshore, better known as a petrified sea monster called the Kracken. Perseus turned the Kracken to stone with the aid of Medusa's severed head. (For a cinematic retelling, check out the special effects wizardry of *Clash of the Titans*.) Present-day Platanias's most famous phenomenon, swanky rock club **Mylos,** whoops any MTV beach party for sheer numbers of

**BULL LEAPING, PART II** While many Minoans enjoyed jumping over bulls (see **Bull Leaping, Part I,** p. 478), one Minoan queen jumped a bull. Poseidon, the sea god, had given **King Minos** a white bull specifically to slaughter in the god's honor, but Minos neglected to axe the bull as promised. Aphrodite then set out for twisted retribution: she filled his wife **Pasiphaë** with a burning lust for the fine bull. Pasiphaë hired master engineer **Daedalus** to build a sexy cow costume to catch the bull's eye. After a (literal) roll in the hay, Pasiphaë gave birth to the hideous **Minotaur,** a fearsome, beast with a bull's head (and a bullheaded attitude to match), a man's body, and a taste for human flesh. Minos shut the bully bastard into an inescapable **labyrinth** designed by Daedalus; to feed the monster, he taxed mainland Greece seven maidens and seven youths every year. The Minotaur gobbled the younguns year after year until dashing Athenian prince **Theseus** volunteered to be sacrificed. Theseus met, wooed, proposed to, and conspired to escape with **Ariadne,** Minos and Pasiphaë's all-human daughter. Ariadne gave Theseus a ball of string to find his way around the labyrinth; within the maze, he killed the monster, retraced his path, and escaped by ship with Ariadne. Theseus then ditched Ariadne on the beach of Naxos (p. 372), Bacchus' favorite hangout. Men. Soon, Bacchus himself quieted Ariadne's grief and married her. Back in Crete, Minos imprisoned Daedalus and his son **Icarus** for their role in the whole mess. Resourceful Daedalus manufactured wax wings for them, going for the ultimate jailbreak. With freedom in sight, Icarus ignored dad's warning not to fly so close to the sun; his wings melted, and he plummeted to his death.

gyrating hotbodies. The converted, well-polished bread mill draws nightly crowds of sharply dressed young Euros from midnight until morning. (Take the last bus from Hania, get off at the bus stop at Platanias Center, and continue walking away from Hania. After about 450m, a huge sign will alert you to the right-hand turnoff that leads past an enormous parking lot to Mylos, the **beach,** and copious booty. Beers 1500dr. Cover 2000dr, includes one drink. To get home, either take a cab (2000dr), or party until the 6:30am bus arrives the next morning.)

## AKROTIRI PENINSULA

Just northeast of Hania is the sparsely populated peninsula of Akrotiri, home to Zorba's hill at Stavros, several monasteries, and beaches that will make you say "this is why I came to Greece." At the small, white sand beach of **Kalatnos,** 16km from Hania, sunbeds with umbrellas go for 1000dr per day. Kalatnos lies on the route of the bus to **Stavros,** another glorious beach with a handful of demure resort hotels, all looking up at a mining hill you may recognize from the movie *Zorba the Greek*. Take the bus (1hr., 4 per day, 400dr) and get off at the end of the line in front of **Christiana's Restaurant** (☎39 152; call ahead to ask about occasional music offerings at night), and the smooth sands of Stavros will be at your toetips. Rent an umbrella and a deckchair for 1000dr per day, or take a walk down to the rockier, though no less lovely, end of the beach. Get your refreshments 30m inland at **Zorba's Original Tavern.** Both Stavros and Kalatnos make excellent daytrips for travelers staying in Hania and hankering for secluded, unpolluted beaches.

At the midpoint of the southern coast of the peninsula and accessible by car is **Loutraki.** This stunning beach is near a vast military complex but free from the sight of such an ominous entity. An offshore island is home to a Venetian castle that the government has recently restored and plans to open to the public in 2001. Ask at the tourist office at Hania (p. 488) for the most current details.

About 6km from Kalatnos on the way to Stavros (16.5km from Hania) is the monastery of **Agia Triada** (☎63 310), which was built in 1606 near ruins of a Minoan temple (c. 1700 BC) and has produced traditional olive oil since 1632. Tour the grounds and small museum, with its collection of mostly 19th-century pieces and three Byzantine paintings (1635-45). Take the experience home in the form of some Agia Triada olive oil, bottled or canned with an English label (600dr for 250ml) or *raki* (1200dr for a pretty bottle). Modest dress is requested: long skirts for women, long pants for men, and no bare shoulders. (Open 8am-2pm and 5-7pm. 300dr.) Monastery buffs who just can't get enough may want to trek the 4km up a stubby Cretan hill (complete with wild goats and narcissus flowers) to **Gouverneto,** a similar monastery. (☎63 319. Open 8am-12:30pm and 4:30-7:30pm.)

## BALOS Βαλος

The beautiful and secluded lagoon of Balos rests on the northwestern tip of Crete. Chartered boats reach this shore; some brave the slight hassle of driving, but are richly rewarded for it. To drive from Hania, take the main road past Platanias and through Kissamos for about 90min. until you reach a dirt road. There you'll find a small white **chapel** with a spring of healing water; watch out for wasps, or you may find yourself in need of those healing powers. Driving for another 30min. until this road ends leaves you at the top of a 45min. hike downhill to the lagoon. The view of Balos' brilliant blues, greens, and whites, and the surrounding islands is worth an extra moment before heading down to the lagoon.

# SAMARIA GORGE Φαραγγι της Σαμαριας

***Open** May 1 to Oct. 15 6am-4pm. For gorge information, call the **Hania Forest Service** (☎ (0821) 92 287), or pick up info at the tourist offices in Hania, Rethymno, or Iraklion. **Buses** for Omalos and Xyloskalo leave Hania (2 per day, 1400dr each way). Early buses (6:15-8:30am) will place you in Xyloskalo for a day's hike, while the 1:45pm bus will put you in Omalos, ready to go the next day. If you spend the night in the mountain setting of Omalos, nod off at Gigilos Hotel on the main road. (☎ 0821 67 181. Singles 4000dr;*

*doubles 6000dr.) From **Rethymno,** take the 6:15 or 7am buses through Hania to Omalos (2550dr). Early risers can take the 5:30am bus from **Iraklion** through Rethymno and Hania to Omalos (3850dr). **Admission** 1200dr, children under 15 and organized student groups free. Hang on to your ticket; you have to give it back at the gorge's exit.*

The most popular excursion on Crete is the five- to six-hour hike down the largest gorge in Europe, the Samaria Gorge, a formidable 16km pass through the **White Mountains National Park.** Sculpted by rainwater over the course of 14 million years, the gorge retains its allure despite mobs of international visitors. Those who remember to take their eyes off their feet will enjoy towering beauty: rare, native plants peek out from sheer rock walls, wild *agrimi* goats clamber around one of their last natural homes, and endangered gryphon vultures and golden eagles soar overhead. Humans have settled here for centuries, as the 1379 church of **Saint Maria of Egypt,** the source of the gorge's name, attests. While under Ottoman rule, Cretan rebels hid out in the gorge's caves.

Though it's possible to reach the gorge from any number of major tourist towns, **Hania** is the closest and allows the most flexibility over the hour you start the trek. The 44km, 1½-hour bus ride from Hania to **Xyloskalo** places you at the start of the trail and offers spectacular scenery, though the town boasts little more than toilets, a cafeteria, a shop, and the ticket booth— the last of their kind that you'll see for several hours. From Xyloskalo, you begin your descent, following a noisy but nearly dry river, passing between cliff walls as high as 600m and as narrow as 3½m. Much of the hike is shaded by clumps of pines and by the walls of the gorge itself. The hike ends in **Agia Roumeli** on the south coast (see below)—from there, experienced hikers can try the 10-hour hike to **Hora Sfakion** (see below) along one of the more outstanding coastlines in the country, or a path from Xyloskalo that ascends **Mt. Gingilos** to the west. If you're only interested in the dramatic tail of the gorge, you can start at Agia Roumeli; the path to the trail begins behind Hotel Livikon at the rear of the village. Known as "Samaria the Lazy Way," the two-hour climb to the north takes you to the gorge's narrow pass, known as the **Iron Gates.**



Whichever route you choose, bring water, trail snacks, and good walking shoes. The gorge is dry and dusty in summer, and well-worn stones on the path are slippery. Often, the altitude makes the top of the gorge cold and rainy. If you get tired on the hike, keep an eye out for the **donkey taxis** that patrol the trail, although they are sometimes few and far between. Be sure to bring enough **cash** to get to the gorge and home again, as there are no banks on either end. Please observe the Hania Forest Protection Service's rules concerning litter.

**AGIA ROUMELI.** At the end of the hike is the small town of **Agia Roumeli,** where the inhabitants make a living selling food, souvenirs, and lodgings to tired hikers. If you stay, you can sleep directly at the point where the path meets the town, at **Hotel Livikon,** in a room with a balcony and bathroom. (☎91 363. Doubles 6000dr; triples 7000dr.) **Ferries** run from Agia Roumeli quite frequently from April to October: to **Hora Sfakion** (2 per day, 1500dr) and to **Sougia** and **Paleohora** (1 per day, 1000-2100dr). From November to March, there are three ferries per week; call in advance for their times. The last **bus** from **Hora Sfakion** waits for the last ferry (bus and ferry are scheduled at 7:30pm and 6pm respectively, so you can make the complete round-trip from Hania, Rethymno, or Iraklion in one day if you leave on a morning bus. (One-way bus from Hora Sfakion to Hania 1600dr, to Rethymno 1600dr, to Iraklion 3100dr.)

## HORA SFAKION Χωρα Σφακιων ☎0825

The scenic town of Hora Sfakion, often called simply Sfakion, lacks the intimacy of Plakias to the east or Paleohora to the west, but serves as the transportation hub of the south coast. The pebbly cove and fishing fleet look tempting from afar, but up close they turn out to be polluted—thankfully uncharacteristic of other southern ports. Nonetheless, Hora Sfakion is an adequate, and most likely a necessary resting spot after the Samaria Gorge hike, as well as a good base for daytrips to the area's smaller gorges and lovely beaches.

**ORIENTATION AND PRACTICAL INFORMATION.** The town consists of one main harborfront road opening off a plateia 50m uphill from the ferry dock. Four **buses** per day go to Hania (2hr., 1600dr; last at 7pm), Rethymno (1½hr., 1600dr; change at Vrises) and Iraklion (3100dr; last at 7pm; change at Vrises). Buses also run to Agia Galini (2hr., 1 per day, 2200dr). If your ferry is late, don't worry—the buses wait for the boats to arrive. Boats from Hora Sfakion travel to **Agia Roumeli** (1¼hr., 4 per day, 1500dr). From April to October, most routes stop in **Loutro.** In winter, travelers go by foot or fishing boat. As always, it is a good idea to check schedules with the ticket office (☎91 221). Boats also run to **Gavdos,** a sparsely populated island that is the southernmost point in Europe (Sa-Su 9am). **Caïques** to Sweetwater Beach leave at 10:30am and return at 5:30pm every day (500dr each way). Uphill from the plateia, you'll encounter the **OTE** (☎91 299; open M-F 7:30am-3:15pm) and, eventually, the flag-bedecked 24hr. **police station** (☎91 205) and **port police** (☎91 292). Walking from the plateia toward the street, you'll see the **post office** (☎91 244; open M-F 7:30am-2pm) and the travel agency **Sfakia Tours** (☎/fax 91 130; open 8am-9:30pm), which sells bus tickets and rents cars (9000dr per day). **Postal code:** 73011.

**ACCOMMODATIONS AND FOOD.** A bed in Hora Sfakion is often a necessary expense that hoteliers know to charge dearly for. The cool, grotto-like **Hotel Xenia,** at the far end of the street, has spacious rooms with refrigerators and phones. (☎91 490; fax 91 491. Singles and doubles 7500-12,000dr; triples 8500-12000dr.) **Lefka Ori,** on the waterfront, rents rooms with views of the harbor. (☎91 209. Singles 4000dr; doubles with bath 5000-6000dr; triples 8000dr.) **Hotel Alkyon,** also on the waterfront, offers neat and tidy rooms. Late risers beware: checking out after noon will cost you 50% more. (☎91 180. Doubles 6000-8500dr; triples 7000-9500dr. Laundry service 1500dr per load. Open 8am-1pm.) No-frills **Starris** modestly awaits at the end of the back street. (☎91 220 or 91 201; fax 91 152. Singles 4500-5000dr; doubles 5000-6000dr; triples 6000-7000dr.) The town's restaurants are limited to those downstairs from the hotels (entrees 1500-4000dr); the **markets** are a good place to stock up on food. There's a market on the main street, and one on the back street, too. The only disco, **Underground,** rocks nightly, in case you're not too exhausted from your hike. (Open 10pm-morning. No cover.)



## PALEOHORA Παλαιοχωρα ☎0823

Once a refuge for the embattled rear guard of the 1960s counterculture, Paleohora (pahl-eo-KHOR-ah) has since calmed down to a state of contented middle-aged charm. The town, 77km south of Hania, is a peninsular retreat with a rocky harbor on its east side and smooth beaches lying on its west, all set against the splendor of the Cretan mountains.

**ORIENTATION AND PRACTICAL INFORMATION.** The amenities, lodgings, and restaurants of Paleohora town cluster around the main thoroughfare, **Venizelou,** which runs the center of the peninsula from north to south. Heading north on Venizelou takes you to Hania, and south to the ruins of an **old castle.** Venizelou crosses **Kentekaki,** which leads west to the beach and east to the harbor.

One to two **ferries** per day leave this modest port for: **Sougia** (45min., 1000dr); **Agia Roumeli** (1½hr., 1 per day at 9:30am, 2100dr); **Loutro** (2¼hr., 2700dr); and **Hora Skafion** (2½hr., 2800dr). One boat per day departs Paleohora for **Elafonisi** at 10am and returns at 4pm (1hr., 1300dr each way). A boat goes to **Gavdos** three times a week (3½hr.; post boat leaves M and Th 8:30am, returns 2:30pm, tourist boat goes at the same time Tu; tourists may ride either boat; 3100dr each way.) More tourist boats run in summer. **Syria Travel** (☎41 198; fax 41 535) is a general tourist office that is helpful for ferry information and tickets, as well as basic information about the region. For information about boats, tickets, and much more, visit the travel agent across from the tourist office on the main street, at **Notos Rentals** (☎42 110 or 41 140). The **bus station,** with buses to **Hania** (2hr., 3 per day, 1600dr), is on

Venizelou on the northern edge of town. A bus departs for **Samaria** at 6am (1400dr); a boat returns you to Paleohora from Agia Roumeli at 4:45pm (round-trip 3150dr). For a taxi, call **Paleohora Taxi Office** (☎41 128 or 41 061). Walking toward the center of town from the bus station, you'll find the **National Bank,** with 24hr. **ATM** three blocks up on your right. (☎41 430. Open M-Th 8am-2pm, F 8am-1:30pm.) Half a block farther and also on your right is the helpful **tourist office** (☎41 507. Open W-M 10am-1pm and 6-9pm); a block and a half farther, on your right again, is the **OTE.** (☎41 299. Open June-Sept. M-Sa 7:30am-10pm; Oct.-May M-F 7:30am-3pm.) The **port police** (☎41 214) are farther down the main street. Turning left toward the harbor at the OTE leads to the **police station** (☎41 111), one block down on your left. The port lies past the police station toward the harbor. Notos Rentals also runs a **laundry** (open 8am-2pm and 5-11pm). There is a **doctor** on Venizelou (☎41 380), one street past the bus station heading away from town; the **public health center** (☎41 211) is behind the OTE, heading away from the beach. There is a **pharmacy** on Venizelou across from the OTE. (☎41 498. Open 8am-2:30pm and 4:50-11:50pm.) **Internet access** can be found across from OTE at **PC Corner,** on Venizelou. Get connected and pay 400dr for your first 10min., then 25dr for each additional minute. Alternatively, pay 3000dr for three hours. (☎42 422. Open M-Sa 9:30am-2pm, 6-11pm, Su 6-11pm.) To find the **post office,** head to the beach from the OTE and make a right. (☎41 206. Open M-F 7:30am-2pm.) **Postal code:** 73001.

**ACCOMMODATIONS.** Some small hotels line the road closest to the harbor. In the middle of the harbor stands a tall white building marked **Dream Rooms,** run by Nikos Bubalis and his extremely friendly wife; rooms with balconies look out onto the picturesque harbor and the surrounding mountains. (☎41 112. Singles 4000-5000dr; doubles 5000-7000dr; triples 6000-8000dr.) A bit farther along the waterfront heading away from the ferry dock is **Christos Restaurant and Hotel,** which has comfortable doubles with private bathrooms. (☎41 359. 7000-9000dr; A/C 2000dr extra per night.) Away from the harbor, **Savas Rooms** offers quiet, shady rooms with private bathrooms. To get there, walk from the bus station north toward Hania for about 50m; Savas is on your left at the edge of town. (☎41 075. Singles 4000-5000dr; doubles 6000-7000dr.) **Camping Paleohora** is a 10min., well-signposted walk east of town. With its own on-site restaurant, the campsite is close to Club Paleohora, the town's popular disco, and a **beach.** To reach it, walk north on Venizelou (away from the town), turn right just after the bus station, take the second left on the last paved road before the beach, and walk 1km to the site. (☎41 120. Open April-October. 1000dr per person; 500dr per tent; 500dr per car; 500dr per child; children under 4 free.)



**FOOD AND ENTERTAINMENT.** **Markets** and **tavernas** stand along Venizelou and its surrounding streets; a row of restaurants serve traditional Greek food along the waterfront from standard tourist menus at the usual mid-range prices (*tzatziki* 400-600dr, *moussaka* 1000-1200dr, *baklava* 500-700dr). Notable among these is **Christos Restaurant.** Vegetarians and carnivores alike will appreciate the homemade Greek, Asian, and European dishes at the **Third Eye Vegetarian Restaurant;** to get there, turn right after the pharmacy, walk three blocks, turn left, take an immediate right, and the Third Eye will be on your left. All things veggie are delicious and under 950dr, while meat lovers are penalized in price but fortunately not flavor. (☎41 234. Entrees are around 1400dr. Open Apr.-Oct. 8am-3pm and 6pm-midnight.) **Club Paleohora,** across from Camping Paleohora, is the town's popular open-air disco. Follow the directions to the campsite, or utilize the minibus that transports clients from **Skala** bar in front of the port to the disco every 30min. from midnight to 4am. (☎42 230. Open M-Sa 11pm-5am, Su 11pm-6am. Cover F-Sa 1000dr includes one beer; drinks 800-1500dr.)

**DAYTRIP FROM PALEOHORA: ELAFONISI (Ελαφονισι).** Elafonisi is a beach across from a small uninhabited island at the southwestern corner of Crete. Although the beach on the mainland side is lovely, you may want to escape the

tourists there by wading 100m through crystal-clear water to the beach on the island. On its mainland side are sunchairs (1000dr), restrooms (150dr), and a taverna that serves reasonably cheap meals. (Open 8am-8pm. Souvlaki 600dr, burgers 700dr, water 300dr, beer 500dr.) If you miss your boat and want to stay overnight in Elafonisi, **Elafonisi Restaurant Bar** has private bungalows or rooms for reasonable prices. (☎(0822) 61 274. Singles and doubles 6000-8000dr.)

The cliffside monastery of **Chrisso Kalitissas** is kept up by nuns today. Built from and supported by the cliffs, it's blessed with a magnificent ocean view. Reach it by walking 5km up the road from Elafonisi. The monastery will be in view on your left when you come to an unmarked but well-paved road; turn left, then make another left at the end of this road. *(Take the ferry from Paleohora along the south coast (leaves 10am, returns 4pm; 1300dr each way), or take the bus from Hania (leaves 8am, returns 4pm; 2500dr each way). Admission to monastery free.)*

### ANIDRI Ανιδρι

Escape the crowds at Paleohora's beach at nearby Anidri Beach, which may be reached by car or foot. A fantastic day-hike from Paleohora takes you to the small village of Anidri and then on to the beach itself. The hike begins five minutes' walk past **Camping Paleohora,** where the road forks; the higher road to the left will take you through the mountains to the village of Anidri in about an hour. Continue on from the village cafe, heading beyond its patio, which opens onto a road with a sign pointing to a church. Follow this road to its end and make a right; when this next road ends, make another right. You'll reach a stone road with a sign pointing back to the cafe; turn left and go down it to the dry riverbed. Follow the signs and stone markers to the beach (about 40min. from town). The beautiful path is poorly marked and fairly difficult—your only company will be roaming **goats.** Make sure to wear good walking shoes, and bring water and trail snacks.

The beaches at the bottom, especially the beach farthest left, are magnificent, with sheer cliffs running right into the water at their edge. To head back, walk eastward along the dirt road that traces the waterfront, which will take you back to the right branch of the fork near Camping Paleohora. This path can be gentle alternative for reaching the beach without risking the snares of the mountain path (30min.).



# LASITHI PREFECTURE

Lasithi Prefecture starts wrong: the road east from Iraklion along the north coast passes through overcrowded, overpriced resort towns with mediocre beaches edged into the ocean by tavernas with an imported northern ambiance. As the road continues east along the coast, though, it becomes gradually quieter and more scenic; inland, it hits smaller villages sustained not by tourism but by thriving local agriculture. The spectacular, endlessly winding main highway joining Agios Nikolaos, Ierapetra, and Sitia grips the side of mountains, ascending and descending through deep valleys. The locally favored destinations east of Agios Nikolaos are entirely worthwhile. Heed the advice of locals who nudge you toward the island's eastern edge, where stretches of pristine coastline fill the gaps between white villages and olive plains.

## AGIOS NIKOLAOS Αγιος Νικολαος ☎0841

Occupying a small peninsula on the northeast edge of Crete, Agios Nikolaos is a nouveau chic resort town where posh vacationers huff and puff their way up steep, boutiqued streets, then stop in at a harborside cafe to catch their breath at great leisure. Meander through its sparkling, hilly streets and you'll find beach-obsessed patrons, one-stop holiday-makers, and hikers on their way to more obscure destinations. There are few bargains in Agios Nikolaos or in its satellite beach towns, but the intense nightlife, diverse array of intriguingly glamorous tourists, and remnants of indigenous Cretan culture make for a lively concoction.

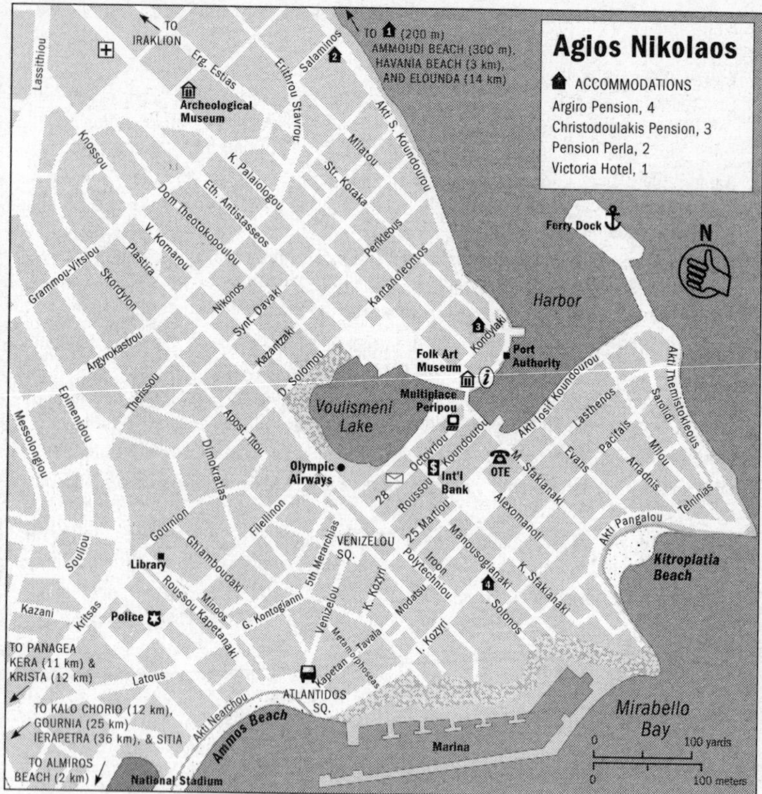


## ORIENTATION AND PRACTICAL INFORMATION

Agios Nikolaos is easy to navigate—it's set on a small peninsula, with beaches on three sides and most services, hotels, restaurants, and discos in the center. Facing the water from the bus station, turn right and you'll be on **Eleftheriou Venizelou.** Turning right on this road again will lead to a rotary with a monument, after which the road turns into **Roussou Koundourou,** which leads to the harbor. Don't confuse the nepotistic street names: R. Koundourou, I. Koundourou, S. Koundourou...

**Flights: Olympic Airways Office,** Plastira 20 (☎22 033), overlooking the lake. Open M-F 8am-3:30pm. The closest **airport** is in Iraklion.

**Buses:** (☎22 234), in Pl. Atlantidos, across town from the harbor. To: **Iraklion** (1½hr., 20 per day, 1450dr) via **Malia** and **Hersonissos; Lasithi** (1½hr., 2 per week, 1150dr); **Ierapetra** (1hr., 7-9 per day, 750dr); **Sitia** (1½hr., 3-5 per day, 1550dr); and **Kritsa** (15min., 8-11 per day, 250dr). Buses to **Elounda** (20min., 14-20 per day, 250dr) and **Plaka** (40min., 6-8 per day, 360dr) leave from the tourist office.

**Ferries: Nostos Tours,** R. Koundourou 30 (☎22 819), sells tickets for departures all over Crete. Open 8am-1:30pm and 5-9pm. To: **Piraeus** (12hr., 5 per week, 7500dr) via **Milos** (7hr., 4 per week, 5000dr); **Rhodes** (12hr., 3 per week, 6300dr); **Sitia** (1hr., 5 per week, 1600dr); **Kasos** (6hr., 3 per week, 3300dr); **Karpathos** (7hr., 3 per week, 4100dr); and **Spinalonga** (2 per day, 5000dr). Ferries to **Cyprus** and **Israel** available.

**Taxis: 24hr.** station (☎24 000 or 24 001), at the bridge beside the tourist office. Taxis abound around the monument on El. Venizelou.

**Car and Moped Rental:** Shop around on A. Koundourou. Car rentals average around 10-12,000dr per day, and motorbikes around 4000-6000dr per day.

**Tourist Office:** S. Koundourou 21A (☎22 357 or 24 165; fax 82 534). Cross the bridge at the harbor and take a right to reach the tourist office. Assists with accommodations, **exchanges currency,** sells phone cards and stamps, and gives transportation schedules and a **map.** Open Apr.-June and Sept.-Nov. 8am-9:30pm, July-Aug. 8am-10pm.

**Banks:** Several on 28 Octovriou have 24hr. **ATMs,** including the **National Bank** (☎28 735). Open for **currency exchange** M-Th 8am-2pm, F 8am-1:30pm; the bank's ATM is on R. Koundourou.

**Emergencies:** For **24hr. emergencies,** go to **Cretan Medicare,** Palaiologou 20 (☎27 551, 552, 553; fax 25 423).

**Police:** Stavrou 25 (☎22 751); walk up Paleologon; right after the hospital. 24hr.

**Tourist Police:** Stavrou 25 (☎26 900), in the same building as the police. Regulates hotels, registers complaints, and gives general info. Open 8am-2pm.

**Medical Care:** There is a hospital (☎25 221) on Paleologou, at the north end of town. From the lake, walk up Paleologou, one block past the archaeological museum.

**Pharmacies: Dr. Theodore Furakis** (☎24 011), in Pl. Venizelou. Open M-F 8am-2pm.

**OTE:** (☎95 333), on the corner of 25 Martiou and K. Sfakianaki. Open M-Sa 7am-midnight, Su 7am-2:30pm.

**Internet Access:** **Multiplace Peripou,** 28 Octovriou 25 (☎24 876). Internet 1500dr per hour. Sells CDs and books. See below for more information. Open 9:30am-2am.

**Post Office:** 28 Octovriou 9 (☎22 062). Open M-Sa 7:30am-8pm. Branch at Metamorphosis 8 (☎22 276) for packages only. Open M-F 7:30am-2pm. **Postal code:** 72100.

CRETE

## ACCOMMODATIONS

Many larger hotels in Agios Nikolaos fill up months in advance. There are lots of **pensions** offering clean, cheap rooms, but their rooms are also in great demand, so make a reservation. Look for cheaper accommodations inland on the east side of the harbor, although some pensions on the western waterfront are also affordable. The **tourist office** has a bulletin board with many of Agios Nikolaos' pensions and their prices. Prices listed are 20-40% less in the off-season.

**Christodoulakis Pension,** Stratigou Koraka 7 (☎22 525). With your back to the tourist office, turn right and climb the street next to the taxi station, then make the second left onto Stratigou Koraka. Common kitchen facilities, large common balconies for sunbathing. Singles 4000-5000dr; doubles 5000-6000dr; triples 7500-8500dr.

**Argiro Pension,** Solonos 1 (☎28 707). Make the fourth right, walking away from the bus station (off Kapetan Tavila onto Polytechiou) and then the first left. Quiet, cool rooms (with common or private baths) in a stately old house with a serene, jasmine-scented garden. Doubles 4800-5500dr; triples 7000dr.

**Pension Perla,** Salaminos 4 (☎23 379). Walk away from the harbor on S. Koundorou. Big rooms, some with balconies and harbor views. Comfortable TV lounge and fridge space. All but 2 rooms have private bath. Singles 4000dr, doubles 5000-8000dr, triples 6000-9000dr.

**Victoria Hotel** (☎22 731; fax 22 266), about 1km from the harbor on S. Koundourou, near Amoudi Beach. A clean, white stucco hotel. Rooms with baths, phones, and balconies. Singles 5800dr; doubles 8300dr; triples 7000-11,000dr. Breakfast included.

## FOOD

While Agios Nikolaos's waterfront is infected with a super-chic strain of the mediocre-tourist-restaurant virus, there are tasty and semi-cheap eats to be found. There's a **Spar Supermarket** near the archeological museum on

Paleologou, large enough to satisfy even an American. (Spar-brand ouzo 1150dr for 700ml.)

**Sarri's,** Kuprou 15 (☎28 059), one block from Pl. Venizelou. Sarri's cooks up freshly harvested food from the family farm. Vine-covered retreat transplants you from the nearby city center. Post-feast, enjoy the free *raki* and cherries in a quiet arbor. *Tzatziki*, chicken, potatoes, and a glass of wine 1600dr. Open 8:30am-4pm and 6pm-midnight.

**Loukakis Taverna,** S. Koundourou 24 (☎28 022), a ten-minute walk past the tourist office. The business from locals hasn't slowed since this family-run taverna opened in 1952, and the tourists are fairly innocuous. Veal *stifado* 1200dr, chicken *okra* 1200dr, and plenty of vegetarian dishes 400-800dr. Open 9am-11pm.

**Cafe-Creperie Central,** R. Koundourou 6 (☎22 011). This sunny cafe folds up sweet and savory crepes (750-950dr, additional toppings 100dr), along with a spread of baked goods (sandwiches 450-550dr).

## NIGHTLIFE AND ENTERTAINMENT

Join the happy throng at the upscale clubs around the harbor on I. Koundourou or S. Koundourou. Alternatively, you might take in a movie at the **open-air theater** on Kazantzaki; from October to April, flicks are also available indoors at the **Rex** theater on M. Sfakianaki (1500dr).

**Multiplace Peripou,** 28 Octovriou 25 (☎24 876). After dinner, Greek youths stream in to sip *frappés* (500dr) and play or watch a game of *tavli*. View of the lake and seashells preserved under glass tabletops. One-stop entertainment spot with a cafe, Internet access (1500dr per hr.), and book and record store. From Oct.-May, the club cafe hosts live music twice a week, from Greek traditional to jazz acts. Occasional cover 2000-3000dr. Open 9am-2am.

**Rififi** (☎23 140). A harborside rendezvous for backpackers and other tourists to sip coffee (600dr) and alcohol (cocktails 1500dr, beers around 1000dr). Open 11am-3am.

**Sorrento Bar,** on the waterfront. A good place to begin a night of debauchery, with dancing bartenders and free shots of "fluffy" at the door. Cocktails 1500dr, beer 900dr.

**Lipstick Night Club** (☎22 377), on the waterfront. Join modern Bacchic frenzy with local kids. Free tequila at the door and shooters with drinks on Friday. Open 10:30pm-late.

CRETE

## SIGHTS AND BEACHES

Around hilly Agios Nikolaos, you'll find a bathtub for goddesses, goat-inhabited archaeological sites, and cheap shopping.

The last week of June or the first of July brings **Nautical Week,** when Greek seamen race in the waters around Agios Nikolaos. For landlubbers, there's nightly music and dancing around town. Call the tourist office for details. Facing the harbor are two islands. On the near one, endangered mountain goats, nicknamed **Kri-Kri,** have unconsciously booted off human inhabitants. The Greek government has barred people from the Kri-Kri's island because of its archeological value; the people of Agios Nikolaos have ordained it the island of all saints. On the last weekend of June, the fisherman dock their boats in the harbor and gather passengers to ferry over to the island for the **Feast of All Saints.** The rest of the year, only the tender of the goats may set foot on Kri-Kri Island. The more distant island is also unihabited; the municipality limits its use to the Boy Scouts.

**MARKET.** You can shop for inexpensive clothes at the weekly **market,** where sundry items like paintings, knock-off Prada bags, swimming trunks (300dr), and underwear (4 for 1000dr) can be purchased. Goodies like watermelon (100dr per

kg), tomatoes (50dr per kg), and Cretan honey (1000dr per 500g) are sold at the top of the hill. (On Eth. Antistassios, next to the lake. Open W 7am-1pm.)

**MUSEUMS AND ARCHAEOLOGICAL SITES.** The **Archaeological Museum,** on Paleologou, houses an extensive collection of artifacts, like Minoan sarcophagi with bones still inside, a well documented coin collection from Greek and Roman times, and art from the under-represented 7th-century Daedalic period. Don't miss the stunning Goddess of Myrtos in the second room. (☎24 943. Open Tu-Su 8:30am-3pm. 500dr, students 300dr, EU students, classicists, fine arts students, and under 18 free.) Train your eye before you buy crafts at the weekly market by visiting the **Folk Art Museum,** next to the tourist office. Tapestries, embroidered clothes, furniture, and icons, are lovingly displayed. (☎25 093. Open Su-F 10am-4pm. 300dr, under 12 free.)

One kilometer before Kritsa on the road from Agios Nikolaos, Crete's Byzantine treasure, the **Panagia Kera,** honors the Dormition of the Virgin in several narrative cycles. A patchwork of smoky 14th-century paintings adorns the central nave, while the wings bear 15th-century Byzantine frescoes. (Open 8:30am-3pm. 800dr, students and seniors 400dr.)

**BEACHES.** All of Agios Nikolaos's beaches are rated blue flag beaches by the EU, which means they're the cleanest of the clean. The constant sunshine and lack of rain makes these beaches perfect for sunning. Three of the more mediocre beaches are a quick walk from the main harbor, but the farther you venture, the better it gets. Lazy folks sunbathe on the concrete piers that jut out from S. Koundourou, while others head to **Ammos Beach** by the National Stadium, **Kitroplatia Beach** between Akti Panagou and the marina, or **Ammoudi Beach** farther up S. Koundourou away from town. Those with greater aspirations catch the hourly bus to Ierapetra or Sitia and get off at **Almiros Beach** (1.5km east of Agios Nikolaos), the area's best beach. Almiros is Agios Nikolaos's only natural beach, and nature unsurprisingly abounds just up the hill, where an EU-protected **wildlife reserve** merits exploration. A river runs through the reserve and gushes cold water into the sea at Almiros; the hot springs hidden under the ocean surface mix with the cold jet for a titillating hot-cold swim. Sandy **Kalo Horio,** 10km further, is less crowded; take either bus and tell the driver to let you off at the **Kavos Taverna.** Another beautiful, somewhat touristy spot is **Havania Beach,** at the Havania stop on the Elounda bus.



## DAYTRIPS FROM AGIOS NIKOLAOS: SPINALONGA

*Private boats and travel agencies in Agios Nikolaos offer guided daytrips to this island (5000dr). Bring your bathing suit; most boats make 20min. swim stops.*

The most touted—and most disconcerting—excursion in eastern Crete is the trip to Spinalonga Island (Σπιναλογκα). A short distance across the clear sea from the town of Plaka, the island has a dichromatic scheme: robust green brush softens the harsh lines of the orange stone fortifications. This island-wide museum's simple coloring doesn't even hint at the island's long and bizarre history.

**MERCHANTS OF VENICE** Venetian merchants lived in Crete centuries ago, but their buildings still dominate the island's appearance. Impenetrable, gargantuan fortresses and city walls, certain to last for centuries more, confine Rethymno, Hania, Iraklion, Agios Nikolaus, Sitia, Ireapetra, and Spinalonga in the same heavy, restrictive fort-and-wall uniform. Both fortifications showed why Venice was interested in Crete: its lucrative and much-envied role as a merchant island. The symbol of Venice, a seated **griffon** holding a **book,** adorns these walls even today. The Venetians applied the symbol to new cities in their empire, with two variations: open book and closed book. Across Crete, the book is always open, indicating that the island surrendered peaceably and by contract, without raising arms.

In 1204, after their purchase of the entire island of Crete, the Venetians destroyed fortresses in Barba Rossa and Agios Nikolaos before investing 75 years building a third, almost impregnable fortress on Spinalonga. When Crete gained independence in 1898, the Greeks were determined to rid the island of all non-Greeks, including the Turks who had taken over Spinalonga. In a kill-two-birds-with-one-island scheme, they established a leper colony there, simultaneously frightening away the Turks and sequestering the infected who previously inhabited mountain caves. On October 22, 1904, the first lepers arrived at their new home. In 1954, the government determined that a combination of the medicines Dopsin and Promil was effective in treating leprosy; three years later, the colony was closed and the surviving residents were taken to Athens and cured. Spinalonga had been the last leper colony in Europe. During those 53 years, 1100 lepers lived on the island and sixty children were born to leper families. The children, born free of the disease, were rushed away to the mainland, where relatives or rich, infertile couples adopted them. The island was reopened in 1970, leaving a good thirteen years to ensure the absence of bacteria for visitors' safety.

When you arrive at the island, you will enter as the lepers did, through **Dante's Gate,** a grim, dark procession through an iron-barred tunnel. Emerge to walk down **Market** Street past reconstructed Venetian and Turkish houses. For the first nine years of the colony's existence, the lepers were not only poor, but also exploited by their corrupt governor, who sold them food at exorbitant prices. It was only in 1913 that inhabitants began receiving social security payments of one drachma per day—a large allowance at the time. Opportunistic Cretans were quick to capitalize on the lepers' new wealth, setting up of shops and tavernas along Market Street.

At the end of the street is the **Church of Agios Pandelemonis,** founded by the Venetians in 1709 and dedicated to the Roman doctor Pandelemon, the saint of the sick in the Greek Orthodox faith. The lepers later used this church to pray for miraculous cures and maintained an ardent faith in the power of Pandelemon to protect the ill. Stairs lead from the church to the **laundry,** where water collected into tubs was heated over fires used to rinse bandages. The **hospital,** halfway up the hill, is identifiable by its eight-window facade. Although patients went to Santa Barbara Hospital in Athens for major operations, this hospital oversaw non-invasive surgery and general care for the lepers. It's lofty location theoretically allowed the wind to carry away the unpleasant odor of rotting flesh.

Beyond the laundry are steps to the sea. To the left of the steps are the modern concrete **apartment buildings** that housed the lepers. At the bottom of the steps is the original arched entrance to the **fortress.** In front is the **disinfecting room,** where everything from bedsheets to clothing to coins was sterilized (a hole in the ceiling released the steam). It now houses a minimalist photographic history of the area. From the fortress, you can see across the water to Plaka. In 1941, German troops withheld provisions from the island to starve the inhabitants, and several lepers attempted to escape across the channel. Some survived the swim, only to meet with the German gunfire awaiting them in Plaka. When the president of the leper community threatened a mass suicide if they were not treated as prisoners of war, the Germans provided enough food for the lepers' survival through the war.

Continuing on the path around the rest of the island, you will find the small orange-roofed **Church of Ag. George.** Built in 1661 by the Venetians, this is where lepers took communion. Past this church, at the top of the ramp leading back to Dante's Gate, is the cemetery and its 44 unmarked graves.

## LASITHI PLATEAU
## Οροπεδιου Λασιθου

☎0844

The inland route to Agios Nikolaos bypasses the jagged northern coastline and traverses the Lasithi Plateau, ringed by steep, crumbling mountains. This rural plain is home to twelve small, white-washed villages full of exhausted donkeys and yeomen husbanding their fields. The residents of the region once harnessed

CRETE

the plains' persistent breezes with thousands of wind-powered water pumps; black-and-white pictures of their windmill-strewn fields adorn the walls of travel agents across the northern coast. The mills have lost their sails as electric pumps have taken over in recent decades, but modern life has otherwise taken the coastal road and bypassed Lasithi. Only a daytrip for most travelers, the tranquil plain possesses sufficient natural wonders and Old World hospitality to make a longer stay worthwhile. The fabulous Dikteon Cave may pull you to the area, but its traditional Cretan charm will convince you to explore more thoroughly.

**ORIENTATION AND PRACTICAL INFORMATION.** It's best to visit Lasithi on wheels (with a rental **car** or **moped**). Those who use the infrequent bus service may find themselves stranded for hours in a town, or limited to the few towns within walking distance. All the basics can be found in Tzermiado, the capital of Lasithi and the first and only large village you pass through upon entering the plain. The bus stops at the center of the town's main plateia in front of the Kronio Restaurant. If you're coming from **Iraklion,** take the coastal road 8km past Gournes, and then turn right on the road to **Kastelli** (not the one on the west coast). After about 6km the road forks right to Kastelli; stay left, heading toward **Potamies,** pausing to ogle the giant plane tree in the center of Potamies: it takes 12 men to wrap their arms around the trunk. Continuing on through Krassi, the main road winds around mountain ridges, cuts through the ruins of the stone windmills of the Seli Ambelou pass, and finally descends into the Lasithi Plateau. If you're heading from **Malia,** you have two options. The more manageable road is reached by heading west along the coastal road and turning left about 3km outside of town at the turn-off for **Mochos;** this road takes you onto the road that passes through Krasi, described in the directions from Iraklion. Your second option from Malia is to follow **25 Martiou** out of town, and follow the signs. This road is faster than the Mochos route, but it is largely unpopulated and involves even more hairpin turns. **Buses** run between Lasithi Plateau and **Agios Nikolaos** (1½hr., 2 per week, 1150dr), **Malia** (1 per day; leaves Malia 8:30am, leaves Lasithi 2pm; 1250dr), and **Iraklion** (2hr., 2 per day, 1450dr). The **tourist police** for Lasithi Plateau are in Agios Nikolaos, but the regular police station is a few doors down from Kronio. (☎22 208. Open 24hr.) The **OTE** is further down the same road. (☎22 299. Open M-F 7:30am-3:10pm.) The **Agricultural Bank** is across the street from the Kronio and exchanges currency. (☎22 390. Open M-F 8am-1:30pm.) The **pharmacy** is 100m from the bus stop along the road to Agios Nikolaos. (☎22 310. Open 10am-1pm and 6-9pm; hours extended M-F.) A **medical center** (☎22 602) is open 24hr. for emergencies and basic primary care; walk away from the police station on the road with the Agricultural Bank, make your first left, and follow this road for 1km. The **post office** is next door to Kronio. (☎22 248. Open M-F 7:30am-2pm.) **Postal code:** 72052.

CRETE

**ACCOMMODATIONS AND FOOD.** In **Tzermiado,** you'll find **Hotel Kourites** by following the road with the pharmacy and the hotel, beyond the Texaco. If no one is at reception, check in at the hotel's other building and taverna. The big bedrooms come with baths, balconies, and breakfast. (☎22 194. Singles 6000dr; doubles 8000-10,000dr.) In **Agios Konstantinos,** your only option is **Maria Vlassi Rent Rooms,** behind Maria's embroidery shop on the road from Tzermiado. (☎31 048. Singles 3000dr; doubles 4000dr.) In **Agios Georgios,** there are several good choices: **Dias Hotel,** on the main road, has sunny rooms with sinks and 24hr. hot water. The rooms are decorated with the owner's handmade crafts; you may find her sewing as you arrive. (☎31 207. Singles 2500dr; doubles 4000dr; breakfast 600dr; 500dr student discount.) **Hotel Maria,** on the opposite side of town, sports the latest in today's traditional style; go to Rea Taverna on main street to request a room. (Singles 5000dr, doubles 6000-7000dr.)

Most restaurants in Lasithi Plateau are linked to hotels. An exception to the rule is **Kronio Restaurant,** the oldest taverna in Lasithi, at the center of **Tzermiado.**

People don't just come for the food (*moussaka* 1200dr, *stifado* 1600dr, Greek salad 800dr): the corner at Kronio is a meeting place for the incredibly friendly villagers to settle utilities bills, and a favorite coffee shop of the village priests. The **Kri Kri Taverna,** in the center of town, lavishes tender affection on its food. Ivy-covered walls and a homey fireplace make a strange but splendid combination (*moussaka* 1200dr, omelette 700dr). On the main road in **Agios Konstantinos,** the **Dikti Taverna** has excellent *moussaka* (1000dr) and Greek coffee (150dr). In **Agios Georgios,** the only restaurants are attached to hotels.

**SIGHTS.** **Agios Georgios** is home to a **folklore museum,** whose models of humans and stuffed fowl are more amusing than edifying. Next door is the **El. Venizelou Museum,** a hall completely dedicated to honoring the former prime minister of Crete and president of Greece, who was born in Hania. (Open Apr.-Oct. 10am-5pm. Combined admission to both museums 800dr, students 500dr, under 12 free.)

The village of **Psychro** serves as a starting point for exploring **Dikteon Cave,** 1km away. At the turn of the century, archaeologists found hundreds of Minoan artifacts crammed into the cave's ribbed stalactites; many are now at Iraklion's **Archaeological Museum** (p. 469). Arthur Evans, who also dug up Knossos (p. 472), excavated this spot and, in a blast of misguided enthusiasm, blew apart the entrance. To get there, follow signs from Ag. Georgios. Local members of the Association of Ass Drivers will probably offer to taxi you (4000dr round-trip); the uphill walk is grueling, but it should take less than an hour. (Open 8:30am-3pm. 800dr, students and EU seniors 400dr, EU students free.) The **Kronion Cave** can't compete with the spelunker behemoth of Dikteon, but it's free from Dikteon's crowds and merits a quick side trip. Clear signs in Tzermiado will direct you the 2km to the grotto, the mythical home of Zeus' parents, Cronus and Rhea. The last kilometer is badly marked and manageable only by foot. Stay on the people path (there are lots of goat paths), and don't forget a flashlight.

CRETE

## IERAPETRA Ιεραπετρα ☎0842

Although German tourists have made inroads, Ierapetra (ear-YEP-eh-tra) still welcomes more Greeks than foreigners. Touted as Europe's southernmost city, the title is dubious: the most urban aspect of Ierapetra is its tangled, unplanned streets, and it's otherwise quite small. After centuries of foreign rule, the city's architecture shows its cosmopolitan past. In day-to-day life, on the other hand, the old rural ethic shines through in the hospitality of the town's denizens.

**ORIENTATION AND PRACTICAL INFORMATION.** Although small, Ierapetra can be difficult to navigate. It has three main plateias, connected by three roads running north-south. With your back to the **bus station,** Lasthenous 41 (☎28 237), **Pl. Plastira** will be on your right. Walking straight for a block on **Lasthenous,** which then turns into **Koundouriotou,** brings you to **Pl. Eleftherias,** the central square where most businesses are located. Keep walking in the same direction for about 100m to reach another plateia: **Pl. Kanoupaki.** South of it is the Old Town district. The **police station,** in Pl. Eleftherias (☎22 560), is in the big yellow building on the waterfront. Ierapetra is under the jurisdiction of the Agios Nikolaos **tourist police** (☎(0841) 26 900). The **National Bank,** in Pl. Eleftherias, has a 24hr **ATM.** (Open M-Th 8am-2pm, F 8am-1:30pm.) **Tourist agencies** on the street parallel to the water distribute free city **maps.** The **Ierapetra Express office,** Pl. El. Venizelou 25, is helpful. (☎28 673 or 22 411. Open 8am-1:30pm and 4-9pm.) **Radio Taxi** (☎26 600 or 27 350) lines up cars in Pl. Kanoupaki. The **hospital** is north of the bus station, left off Lasthenous at Kalimerake 6. (☎22 488 or 22 766. Open 8:30am-1:30pm, **emergency** care 24hr.) The **OTE** is at Koraka 25. (Open M-F 7:30am-1pm.) Chic **Polycafe Orpheas,** Koundoutitou 25, just past Pl. Eleftherias, offers **Internet access** at 1000dr for 30min. (☎80 462. Open M-Sa 9am-11pm.) The **post office,** Stilianou Houta 3, is in Pl. Kanoupaki. (☎22 271. Open M-F 7:30am-2pm.) **Postal code:** 72200.

**DIONYSUS'S DESCENDANTS** Though the Greek Orthodox faithful would never take part in the lusty, booze-soaked orgies of old-time Bacchic revelry, remnants of Dionysian rituals still influence the **Pre-Lenten festivals** throughout Greece. Echoes of ancient celebrations of nature and spring (and, of course, their king, Dionysus) run through present-day festivals: dressing up in costumes and disguises, drinking to excess, and even dancing around a fire (as Galaxidi's residents do) conjure up pre-Christian rites. Like in Britain and America, where Halloween precedes All Saints Day, the Pre-Lenten festivals begin the season of fasting and prayer that is Lent. As with Roman Catholic parties during Mardi Gras (also just before Lent), the Orthodox faithful cut loose with old-school Dionysian holdovers as part of their modern-day lives.

**ACCOMMODATIONS.** For the most part, Ierapetra makes its beds for upscale tourists, who want only the best after a day snoozing on Chrissi Island. When bargain-hunters land in town, they avoid the mainland and knock on doors in the streets surrounding the bus station, or just head back to Agios Nikolaos for the night. Make a sharp right out of the bus station and you'll see signs leading to the sparkling **Cretan Villa,** Lakerda 16. The 205-year-old building's white stucco-walled, brick-floored, high-ceilinged rooms hide a central garden. The owner, a University of Missouri alum, speaks fluent English. All rooms have private baths. (☎28 522. Singles 6000-8000dr; doubles 9000-11,000dr; triples 10,000-13,000dr.) Find **Hotel Coral,** Ioanidou 18, in the Old Town, by following Kyrva from Pl. Kanoupaki and taking a right after passing the port police. You'll find large, remarkably private rooms with private baths (bathtubs!), fridges, and free luggage storage. (☎22 846 or 28 743. Doubles 5000-7000dr; triples 8000dr; A/C 1500dr extra per night.) For your camping pleasure, **Koutsounari,** 7km from Ierapetra on the coastal road to Sitia, supplies ground, restaurant, bar, and beach. Take the bus to **Sitia** via **Makri Gialo** (20min., 1 per hr., 220dr) and ask to be let off at the campgrounds. (☎61 213. 1300dr per person; 900dr per tent.)

CRETE

**FOOD AND ENTERTAINMENT.** Nearly all of Ierapetra's waterfront restaurants are identically priced. The most enjoyable eatery in Ierapetra is **Veterano,** in Pl. Eleftherias, with an ideal view of the palm-edged main plateia. Sip your cappuccino, spy on the bustling populace, and contemplate a second piece of *baklava* (500dr), or perhaps *kalitsounia* (150dr), an Ierapetrian sweet cheese tart. (Open 7:30am-midnight.) It's a safe bet to head to **Napoleon,** Stratigou Samovil 26, on the waterfront near the old village. Everyday, the Mrs. cooks up the seasonally priced fish, meats (1500dr), and vegetables (800dr) that the Mr. bought fresh that morning. (Open M-Sa 8am-midnight.) **Gorgona Taverna,** Stratigou Samovil 12, also serves fish and large portions of traditional meals like *giovetsi* (1600dr). On Saturdays there's a **street market** with fruits, veggies, and textiles on the corner of Papagou and Kalimerake. (Open 7am-1:30pm or 2pm. Tight, tight Levis 50,000-60,000dr.)

Nightlife in Ierapetra is low-key, but several bars on Kyrva fill up with tightly dressed Greeks who groove all night long. **Priority Club,** Kyrva 18, is the hippest of the bunch (cocktails 1500dr), but you can also mellow to the oldies, jazz, classic rock, and Greek music mixed by the DJ at **Acropolis,** Markapolou 51. From Pl. Kanoupaki, head to the waterfront and make a left. (Open summer 9pm-4am.)

**SIGHTS.** Few of Ierapetra's historical sights are open for visiting. In the Old Town are a 19th-century **mosque** and a decaying **Ottoman fountain** *(Krini)* covered with Greek graffiti. The 13th-century restored **Venetian fortress** *(Kales)* at the extreme south end of the old harbor indicates that the Venetians didn't think Ierapetra deserved first-rate defense measures. Still, the fortress is a pleasant lookout, though there's not much room to stretch your legs. (Open Tu-Su 8:30am-3pm.) The **Kervea festival,** held each summer in July and August, features music, dance, and theater performances at the fortress; call the town hall for information (☎24 115).

Ierapetra's **Archaeological Museum,** at Pl. Kanoupaki on the waterfront, has a few Minoan artifacts from the south coast and a worthwhile collection of Greco-Roman statues. One unique sarcophagus in the second room, adorned by hunting scenes, embodies the simple elegance of Minoan painting. (Open Tu-Sa 8:30am-3pm. 500dr, EU students free.)

**DAYTRIP FROM IERAPETRA: CHRISSI.** Ierapetra's star attraction is Chrissi, an island eight nautical miles away from the mainland. Free from stores and crowds, Chrissi is completely flat, adorned by green pines and surrounded by transparent green sea. Pack a lunch and bring water; there's nothing but two tavernas near the dock (open all day). **Ferries** depart May through October daily at 10:30am and 12:30pm, returning at 5pm and 6pm, respectively (6000dr, including return; 1500dr beach chair charge).

## SITIA Σητεια

☎0843

A winding drive on coastal and mountain roads from Agios Nikolaos leads to the fishing and port town of Sitia. Despite strong efforts on the part of the municipality to promote tourism, Sitia has maintained a teflon resistance to each summer's increasingly heavier batch of holiday-makers, staying devoted to its residents. Tourists nearly blend with locals at the harborside tavernas, and pelicans walk the streets at dawn. Sitia makes a great base for your exploration of Crete's east coast, and it's the most convenient port for departures to Rhodes.

### ORIENTATION AND PRACTICAL INFORMATION

**Pl. Iroon Polytechniou** sits at the center of town on the waterfront; most practical necessities can be found here. With your back to the bus station, exit to the right. Make another right, then a left, and **Venizelou** will take you there.

**Buses:** The station (☎22 272) is outside of town off Venizelou. To: Agios Nikolaos (1½hr., 4-6 per day, 1550dr); Iraklion (3¼hr., 3-5 per day, 2950dr); Ierapetra (1½hr., 3-5 per day, 1300dr); Vai (1hr., 3-5 per day, 600dr); and Kato Zakros (1hr., 1-2 per day, 1050dr).

**Ferries: Port Office** (☎25 555). Three ferries per week go to: **Rhodes** (12hr., 6000dr); **Kassos** (4hr., 2600dr); and **Karpathos** (5hr., 3400dr). Five per week go to: **Piraeus** (16-17hr., 7600dr) via **Agios Nikolaos** (1½hr., 1600dr) and **Milos** (9hr., 5200dr).

**Flights: Airport** (☎24 666) connects to Athens (3 per week, 2 per week in winter; 23,200dr). No buses to airport. Taxis cost 1000dr for the ride 1km uphill.

**Taxis:** (☎22 700) in Pl. Venizelou. Cabs are usually available 24hr. on weekends.

**Rentals: Porto-Belis Travel,** Karamanli 34 (☎22 370; fax 23 830) rents **cars** (7300-9300dr) and **mopeds** (7500dr and up).

**Tourist Office:** (☎28 300), on waterfront. From Pl. Polytechniou, head along the water. **Maps, currency exchange,** accommodations. Open M-F 9am-9pm; Sa-Su 10am-9pm.

**Banks: National Bank** (☎22 250 or 22 218), in Pl. Venizelou. 24hr. **ATM.** Open M-Th 8am-2pm, F 8am-1:30pm.

**Tourist Police:** Therissou 31 (☎24 200). From the plateia, follow Kapetan Sifi 2 blocks to Mysonos; go left and continue until it becomes Therissou. Open 7:30am-9pm.

**Police:** (☎22 266 or 22 259), in the same building as the tourist police. Open 24hr.

**Hospital:** (☎24 311), off Therissou past the youth hostel, away from town. Open 24hr.

**OTE:** Kapetan Sifis 22 (☎28 099). From the main plateia, head inland past the National Bank for 2 blocks. Open M-F 7:30am-10pm.

**Post Office:** Main branch, Dimokritou 8 (☎22 283; fax 25 350); from the plateia on the waterfront, walk inland on Venizelou and go left on Dimokritou; it will be on your right. Open M-F 7:30am-2pm. **Postal Code:** 72300.

## ACCOMMODATIONS

It's wise to call ahead and book a room if you'll be coming in August. The youth hostel is friendly, but for more privacy, look behind the west end of the waterfront on Kornarou and Kondilaki.

**Youth Hostel,** Therissou 4 (☎22 693). Leave the bus station to the right, walk inland and follow the signs for the major road to Iraklion and Agios Nikolaos. As you bear left, the street becomes Therissou; the hostel is 150m up. Reception 9am-noon and 6-9pm; if no one is around, find a bed and register later. Call ahead to get a free ride from the bus station. Common kitchen. 24hr. hot water. Dorms 1600dr per person; singles 2500dr; doubles 3500-4000dr; triples 4500-5000dr; sheets 100dr. Camping on the small lawn 1200dr per person, tents free.

**Venus Rooms to Let,** Kondilaki 60 (☎24 307). Walk uphill on Kapetan Sifi from the main plateia and make your first right after the OTE. All rooms have balconies and access to common kitchen facilities; some have private bath. The luxurious top-floor offers a couch and flower-wreathed balcony. Doubles 4000-8000dr depending on the season; prices 20% higher for a triple.

**Rooms to Let Apostolis,** Kazantzakis 27 (☎22 993 or 28 172). From the main plateia, head inland on Kapetan Sifi and turn left onto Foudalidi, then right one block further onto Kazantzakis. Bright granite stairs lead to spacious rooms with private baths, wash basin and linens. A basic common kitchen area opens onto a balconied dining area. Doubles 7000dr; triples 9000dr.

## FOOD

The waterfront offers typical tourist fare to light *bouzouki* strumming. There's less of a view of the water but more local life at the tavernas on the inland streets.

**Cretan House,** K. Karamanli 10 (☎25 133), right of the main plateia as you face the water. Most diners take outdoor tables on the waterfront, but the interior is more colorful, with Cretan artifacts like a threshing plow and a brick oven. Friendly staff serves a huge variety, including Cretan recipes like *mezethra, kouloukopsomo* (crunchy bread topped with tomatoes, cheese, and spices), and Stana ("Cretan Viagra"). Specialty appetizers 700-900dr, entrees around 1400dr. Open 9am-1:30am.

**Taverna Michos,** V. Kornarou 117 (☎22 416), one block up from the main plateia. Sitia's best restaurant, according to the locals. Serves swordfish-prawn souvlaki with rice and delicious Cretan vegetables (1600dr), and lamb stew in wine sauce (1600dr). Whet your appetite with their *dolmades* (800dr). In winter, live music on Fridays and Saturdays. 15% discount for seniors. Open all day in summer; shorter hours in winter.

**Mike's Creperie,** El. Venizelou 162 (☎25 207), left of the main plateia. Sweet and salty crepes make for a different type of taverna on the waterfront. Crepes around 800dr. Open M-Sa 10am-4pm.

## NIGHTLIFE AND ENTERTAINMENT

People-watching is a mainstay of Sitian nightlife, especially along the row of restaurants and cafes near the main plateia, where moonlight softens the rugged boats and colors the evening with romantic brush strokes. A night out begins here at places like **Scala,** El. Venizelou 193, a bar with late-night DJs that draws a younger crowd. (Cocktails 1500dr. Open 5pm-3am.) After midnight, everyone heads to **Hot Summer,** about one kilometer down the road to Palaikastro by the beach, where a swimming pool replaces the staid dance floor. The über-chic, the young, and the talkative self-segregate at three fully-stocked bars, and half the fun is figuring out which crowd is where. (Cover around 1000dr, redeemable at the bar; cocktails 1800dr.) Around 3am, head westward several kilometers out of town to **Planetarium Disco,** where you can stand on the sweeping balcony or shuffle your feet on the dance floor of one of Crete's largest clubs. (1500dr cover, includes one drink. Open in summer 1am-dawn.)

## SIGHTS

Away from the waterfront on the hill high above town, the **fortress** provides scarce protection for most of Sitia's inhabitants, but a good view of their environs. (Open Tu-Su 8:30am-3pm. Free.) It hosts Sitia's **Kornareia Festival,** running from June to August, with free open-air theater and concerts. In mid-August, just before the grape harvest, Sitia hosts the **Sultanina Festival,** a four-day celebration of Sultanina golden raisins. The festival features unlimited wine, dancing, and music (2000dr).

The prison-like **Archaeological Museum,** directly behind the bus station across the street, represents the particularly rich excavation sites around Sitia, where many peak sanctuaries and villas were located in Minoan times. As a result, the collection offers clues to both average and upper-class Minoans' daily lives. Be sure to note the Late Minoan **Palaikastro Kouros** statuette, a small ivory and gold masterpiece with strong Egyptian influences that reflect eastern Crete's connection with the kingdom of Pharaoh. (☎23 917. Open Tu-Su 8:30am-3pm. 500dr, students and seniors 300dr, EU students and under 18 free.) Sitia's **Folk Art Museum** houses traditional 19th-century Cretan items; walk up Kapetan Siphi from the main plateia and the museum is on the right. (☎22 861. Open Tu-Sa 9:30am-2:30pm, Tu 5-8pm. 500dr.) Stop by **Sitian Arts,** Vitsentzou Kornarou 145, to witness the local arts of blue pottery and watercolors. The knowledgeable owner can arrange a visit to his pottery workshop in nearby Agia Fotia. (☎/fax 22 600. Open 9am-1pm and 4:30-8pm.) The town's **beach** extends 3km east toward Petra. Close to town, the beach is narrow and squeezed out by a busy roadway, but the road turns inland some at the distant end, leaving an empty expanse of beach.

## DAYTRIP FROM SITIA: VAI Βαι

*Buses from Sitia (1hr., 4-6 per day, 600dr) via Palaikastro (250dr) stop in the parking lot in front of the beach. (Parking: cars 600dr; motorbikes 250dr.) A tourist information booth offers currency exchange. First aid is near the toilet, at the back of the parking lot. For emergencies call the police (☎61 222).*

Not long ago, tourists headed east to Vai to escape the beaten path. Today, several buses roll into this outpost every day, depositing tourists eager to swim at a smooth, blue-flag (super-clean), sandy **beach,** and, afterwards, to rest under the shady fronds of Europe's only indigenous **palm tree forest.** Legend has it that the forest sprouted from dropped date seeds that 2nd-century BC Egyptian soldiers littered on their way to war. In the 60s and 70s, Vai became a haven for British bands like Cream and Led Zeppelin, who would camp out, rock out, and smoke out under the palms. Nowadays, camping, fires, and drugs are all prohibited to keep the forest (and the visitors) healthy. (Umbrella and deck chair 1000dr.)

For more secluded bathing and a better beach, face the water and head left, up, and over the craggy hill. Although camping is forbidden in the park itself, many unfurl sleeping bags in this cove to the south of the palm beach. If sandy pajamas and the possibility of arrest don't appeal to you, rent a room in quiet **Palaikastro,** 8km back toward Sitia (see p. 507). Although there is one **restaurant** and a **snack bar** (small sandwiches 500-600dr) in Vai, you're better off packing a **picnic** or eating in Palaikastro or Sitia. A **watersports center** offers jet-skis (6000dr for 10min.), pedal boats (3000dr per hr.), and scuba diving (15,000dr per session), among other activities. (Open 10am-6pm; reduced prices for larger parties.)

# PALAIKASTRO Παλαικαστρο ☎0843

The slow pace of life in town and the excellent beaches that dot the periphery of the village of Palaikastro create an ideal balance of tranquility and diversion.

**ORIENTATION AND PRACTICAL INFORMATION.** Palaikastro is a stop on two bus routes, running from Sitia to Vai and Kato Zakros; exploring the beaches with a car makes the trip even better. **Buses** leave from the main plateia for: Sitia

(45min., 3-4 per day, 450dr); Vai (15min., 3-4 per day, 250dr); and Kato Zakros (30min., 1-2 per day, 650dr). You may buy tickets at the kiosk in the plateia or on the bus. For **taxis** call 61 380 or 61 271. The village has the bare necessities in its main plateia. **Lion Car Rental,** in the plateia across from the church, rents **cars** (around 9000dr per day) and **exchanges currency.** (☎61 482 or 61 511, mobile (0944) 58 1665; fax 61 482. Open 9am-1pm and 6-9pm.) The **tourist information office,** 100m down the road to Sitia on your right, **exchanges currency,** has room and restaurant info, and gives out **maps** that point the way to the beaches. (☎61 456. Open M-Sa 9am-10pm.) A few doors away, the **police station** (☎61 222), one flight upstairs in the building marked by Greek flags, provides general info and help with emergencies. A **doctor** (☎61 204) calls on the village once per week, seeing patients in the mayor's building, down the road immediately left of the tourist office. The **OTE** (☎61 225) is in the same building as the tourist office and shares the same hours. **Internet access** is available at **Kazamias Rent-a-Car,** just past the tourist office. (☎61 093. Open 9:30am-1:30pm, 5:30-9:30pm. 500dr for 20min.)

**ACCOMMODATIONS AND FOOD.** You can find rooms and hospitality in the home of **Yiannis Perakis.** Once off the bus, look for a gravel path that starts about 200m past the center of Palaikastro; follow it as it forks to the right. Look for Pegasos Taverna on your left; the pension is up the gravel path on the left. Lemon trees and bougainvillea flowers invite you to bright rooms. (☎61 310. Singles 3000dr; doubles 5000dr; triples 6500dr.) On the same path as Yiannis, **Pegasos Rooms,** above Pegasos Taverna, offers balconies, fridges, and private baths. (☎61 479. Singles 6000dr; doubles 8000dr; triples 9000dr; 5-person apartments 12,000dr.)

For the basics, visit the village's **mini-market** (and **bakery**) opposite the church entrance, 20m down the road to Vai. **Restaurant Mythos,** in the plateia, is a local favorite with good prices. (Traditional entrees 1000-1400dr, vegetables 600dr. Open 6am-1am.) **Hotel Hellas** serves all the standards and has the best view of the plateia. (Greek salad 750dr, stuffed eggplant 950dr. Open 8:15am-1am.) The family restaurant **Vasios Nasiakos,** 300m past Pegasos in the next village, serves tasty Cretan food to a local crowd. (Entrees 1000-1300dr. Open summer 7pm-1am.)

**BEACHES.** If you're looking for activities outside of Palaikastro, take the bus headed for Kato Zakros and ask the driver to let you off at **Chochlakes.** From this village, you can walk through the valley to the secluded beach and bay of **Karoumes.** Take the road east from Palaikastro on its way to the tiny village of **Agathias,** beyond which lie many of Crete's most scenic and least visited beaches. Past Agathias, the road forks; its right branch leads to the **Minoan Palace** at **Roussolakos,** while the left branch leads to **Chiona Beach.**

## VALLEY OF DEATH AND ZAKROS ☎0843

*Buses travel from Sitia to Kato Zakros, stopping in Palaikastro and Zakros (1hr., 2 per day, 1050dr). Ask the bus driver to drop you at the gorge's entrance, approximately 2km down the road from Zakros's main plateia. The 11am bus from Sitia allows enough time to hike the gorge, visit the ruins, and take a quick swim. Zakros's bus stop is in the main plateia, along with three taxis, an OTE (☎93 220), and the police station (☎93 323).*

A four kilometer natural gorge, confoundingly titled the Valley of Death, connects the quiet village of Zakros or Apo Zakros (upper Zakros) to the beach enclave of Kato Zakros (lower Zakros). The wildlife showcases the area's natural diversity: goats graze by the mountain road, snakes and scorpions make themselves visible in the valley, and elegant geese strut the streets of Kato Zakros.

Those seeking a physical challenge should hike (4km, about 70min.) through the **Valley of Death** (or **Death's Gorge**), leading from Zakros to Kato Zakros. Although Samaria (p. 492) is larger, Death's Gorge equals it in beauty and far surpasses it in tranquility. Although it's impossible to wander too far astray in a gorge, the path is poorly and sporadically marked with crude red arrows. Bring along plenty of water and trail snacks, and long pants to avoid many a stray bramble. Keep an eye

out for **phaskomilo,** a tea plant with small, fuzzy, green leaves. Its scent is naturally refreshing, a marked change from the odor of the onion plants (identified by their small purple flowers) that also inhabit the valley.

At the end of the gorge, turn left on the dirt path—bear right when you see the sign for the palace that leads you to the coast and the **Minoan Palace** (☎93 105) of Kato Zakros. Destroyed in 1450 BC, the royal rubble extends up a hill. Check out the labyrinthine turns of the palace up close. Minoan kings once bathed in pools near the bottom of the hill, now home to innumerable turtles. (☎93 105. Open 8am-3pm, last entrance 2:30pm. 500dr, students and seniors 300dr, EU students free.)

Keep walking along the path away from the palace and you'll arrive at Kato Zakros and its wheelchair-accessible beach. The waterfront is largely free from clutter and deck chairs, and the beach is quiet and pleasant, if pebbly. **Restaurant Nikos Platanias** cooks up fish from the Mediterranean and veggies from the owner's farm. (☎93 375. Entrees around 1300dr.) To stay overnight, ask at the restaurant or follow the signs to **George's Villa.** George treats his guests to his own good humor in rooms that overlook the brilliant blue Mediterranean and unspoiled beach. Call for a ride from the bus stop. (☎26 883 Doubles 8000-12000dr, triples 9000-13,000dr.)

# CYPRUS ΚΥΠΡΟΣ

Would that I go to Cyprus, the island of Aphrodite,
Where the Loves who soothe mortal hearts dwell.
—Euripides

From the ancient temples and Roman mosaics scattered on its shores to the Green Line that runs through its capital city, Cyprus is an island of ancient harmonies and modern tensions. After enduring a succession of conquerors including the Phoenicians, Greeks, Persians, Ptolemies, Romans, Arabs, Crusaders, Ottomans, and Britons, the island now exists independently, although uneasily. Contrasting landscapes—sandy beaches, the cool Troodos mountain air, the developing industrial cities—mean that a change of pace is just a short bus ride away. While visiting Cyprus can be expensive, more and more tourists are making the trip. The Cypriots are generally welcoming and English-speaking, making life that much easier for travelers.

**HIGHLIGHTS OF CYPRUS**

**STAY OVERNIGHT AT A MOSQUE-TURNED-HOSTEL,** sup with poets at an art cafe, and stare into the foundations of one of the world's oldest cities at Larnaka (p. 517).

**FROLIC** on the fabulous beaches of frenetic Agia Napa (p. 524).

**CROSS THE GREEN LINE** to Turkish-occupied territory in Lefkosia, the world's last divided city (p. 542).

**DIP YOUR TOES** in Aphrodite's Divine Tub of Love and Beauty (p. 536).

**HIKE** the shady, piney Troodos Mountains, where French poet Arthur Rimbaud once hid out (p. 538).



# HISTORY AND POLITICS

## ANCIENT AND MEDIEVAL CYPRUS

**REALLY OLD.** The remains of round stone and mud dwellings date settlement on Cyprus back to roughly 7000 BC. Millennia later, Cyprus's wealth of copper and ore made it the most popular island around, leading to an increase in Cypriot trade and cultural exchange with their neighbors during the **Bronze Age** (2500-1050 BC). Linguists are unsure whether *Kypros*, from which the word "copper" is derived, first referred to the island or the metal itself.

| **3000 BC: POPULARITY CONTEST** | The discovery of copper in the foothills of the Troodos mountains makes centrally located Cyprus the place where the cool kids go. Copper is used to make shiny, pretty things. |
|---|---|

In the midst of all the copper-working, **Mycenaean** (see p. 7) traders from the Peloponnese swung by, initiating a long-lasting Hellenic influence in Cyprus. The 12th century BC saw the rise of city-kingdoms Paphos, Salamis, Kition, and Kourion, the spread of Greek language, and the use of basic written notation. The arrival of **Phoenician** traders and bullies in the first millennium BC forced the Greeks to share political control until the **Assyrians** arrived in the 7th century BC; the Assyrians dominated the island for a century, until the **Egyptians** seized control for a brief spell. They were soon overthrown by the **Persian** king. Pro-Hellenic **Evagoras I,** who forced the Persians out of Salamis and spread the Greek language throughout his kingdom, initiated the most significant resistance to Persian rule by Cypriots.

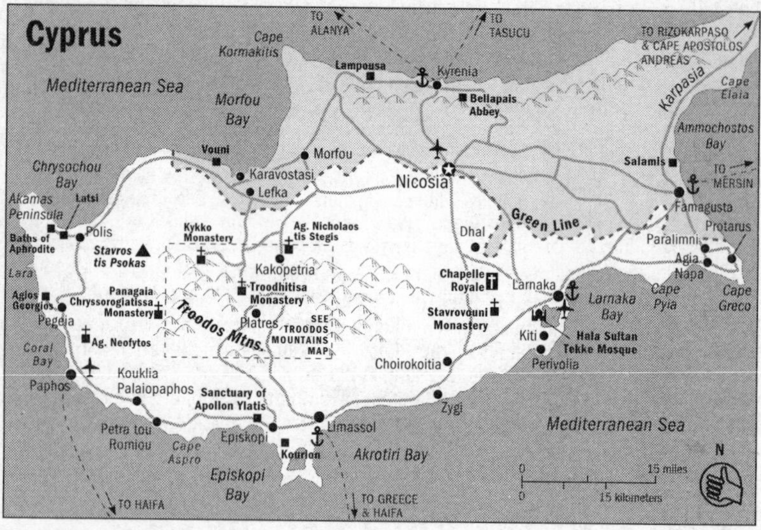


**GETTING IT TOGETHER.** As Persian expansion stagnated, **Alexander the Great** (see p. 12) absorbed Cyprus into his growing empire. In 295 BC, following Alexander's death, the rather strict **Ptolemies of Egypt** claimed Cyprus, abolished the city-kingdoms, and unified the island. While cultural and religious institutions remained unchanged, the Greek alphabet came to replace the local syllabic script. Two centuries later, in 58 BC, Rome annexed the island, and in AD 45 the apostle **Paul** and the Cypriot apostle **Barnabas** introduced Christianity to the island. The new faith spread, and when the Roman governor converted in 46, Cyprus won the prize for becoming the world's first Christian territory.

# BYZANTINE TO OTTOMAN RULE

**ISLAND FOR SALE.** After Constantinople was proclaimed capital of the eastern half of the divided Roman empire (see p. 14), Roman civic thought, Greek philosophy, and Greek Orthodoxy were synthesized on Cyprus. These centuries were bad times for the Cypriots: devastating earthquakes rocked their world in AD 332 and 342, a 40-year drought left everyone thirsty, and fierce Arab raids in the 7th century made the islanders feel like fish in a barrel. In 1191, **Richard the Lionheart,** en route to the Crusades in Jerusalem, overran the island; he took provisions for the Christian armies and robbed the island of its treasures. Unable to carry the island around, he sold it to the **Knights Templar.** In turn, they passed responsibility on to **Guy de Lusignan,** a minor French noble who had been involved in the Crusades.

| AD 1191: SHIPWRECKED! | Richard the Lionheart's fiancée and sister claim mistreatment at the hands of Cypriots following an emergency docking in Limassol. Rich captures island; mother warns, "You are *not* bringing that *thing* into my house!" |
|---|---|

**NOT A NICE GUY.** The feudal system of the **Lusignan Dynasty** (1192-1489) oppressed the lower classes and suppressed Cypriot traditions and religion, but compensated with Gothic churches, cathedrals, and castles. The Crusaders were forced to retreat after getting beaten up in Palestine, so the Lusignans invited Crusader families to hang out in Cyprus. As a result, in the late 13th century Cyprus became the wealthiest island in the eastern Mediterranean. Profiting from the Lusignans' dynastic intrigues, the **Venetians** annexed the island in 1489. Even with

strengthened Cypriot military defenses, however, the island was no match for the encroaching Ottomans. In 1570, following a two-month siege, Lefkosia surrendered to the Turks under Lala Mustafa. The fall of Famagusta one year later marked the beginning of the **Ottoman period** in Cyprus, as well as the introduction of a brand new ethnic element to the island.

| 1821: GREEK WAR OF LIBERATION | The sultan smells a conspiracy on Cyprus. Four hundred and eighty-six Christians are convicted of sympathizing with the mainland freedom-fighters; heads roll. See **Greek Nationalist Revolt,** p. 16. |
|---|---|

Cypriot peasants welcomed the Ottoman abolition of feudalism, probably because they acquired land in the process. The Orthodox Church also flourished, serving as a powerful administrative machine for the sultan. In the 19th century, Great Britain defended the Ottoman territories against Russian expansion, in an effort to defend its own colonies. Landing at Larnaka in July of 1878, British forces assumed control of Cyprus as a **military base.** Although Cypriots received no political freedom under the British, as a consolation prize they benefited from the construction of many public works: roads, bridges, improved water supplies, a railway, schools, and hospitals.

## CYPRUS IN THE 20TH CENTURY

In 1955, **General George Grivas,** in conjunction with **Archbishop Makarios,** founded the **EOKA** (National Organization of Cypriot Fighters), an underground *enosist* (pro-union) movement demanding union with Greece. When the United Nations vetoed the Greek request to grant Cyprus self-government, an enraged Grivas and the EOKA initiated guerrilla warfare aimed at the British government. In response to increased EOKA activity, the underground Volkan (Volcano), under the leadership of **Rauf Denktaş,** founded the **TMT** (Turkish Resistance Organization). TMT was a paramilitary organization designed to fight the *enosists* and to push for **taksim,** or partition of the island between Greece and Turkey. Weary of the perpetual violence (especially the violence aimed at itself), Britain, along with the foreign ministers of Greece and Turkey, agreed in 1959 to establish an **independent Cypriot republic.** On August 16, 1960, Cyprus was granted independence and became a member of the U.N.; in March 1961, it was admitted to the British Commonwealth.



| 1963: KEEP YOUR HANDS TO YOURSELF | Fighting breaks out in Cyprus when Prez and Veep disagree. The British government posts soldiers across the center of Lefkosia, telling both groups to stay on their own side, or they will turn this island around and go straight home. |
|---|---|

**LET'S BE FRIENDS.** The new **constitution** stipulated that a Greek Cypriot president and a Turkish Cypriot vice-president were to be appointed through popular election, and that the Greek to Turkish ratio in the House of Representatives would be 70 to 30. In 1959, Archbishop Makarios became the mixed republic's first president, and **Fazıl Küçük,** leader of the Turkish Cypriot community, was elected to the vice presidency unopposed. In 1963, Makarios proposed 13 amendments to the constitution, intending to make bicommunal life easier, including the abolition of the president's and vice-president's veto power and the introduction of majority rule (in a country where the Greek Cypriots are the huge majority). When the unenthusiastic Turkish government threatened to use military force if these amendments were implemented, renewed violence broke out between the EOKA and the TMT, resulting in the division of Nicosia along the **Green Line** (p. 542). In February 1964, the U.N. dispatched a "temporary" peacekeeping force that has been renewed indefinitely and remains in place today.

**BREAKING UP IS HARD TO DO.** In 1968, Makarios and Küçük were both re-elected by an overwhelming majority, although in the years following they were subjected to several coup attempts. In 1971, General Grivas snuck back in to Cyprus to found the militant **EOKA-B** and to revitalize the call for *enosis.* The violence exploded into an international affair in 1974, when the Greek Cypriot National Guard (*sans* General Grivas, who died in Limassol the same year), assisted by the military **junta** in Greece, overthrew Archbishop Makarios and replaced him with **Nikos Sampson,** an EOKA member who favored immediate *enosis.* This new government lasted all of five days, after which the Turkish army invaded Cyprus from the north to protect Turkish Cypriots from the National Guard. Early in 1975, the North declared itself the **Turkish Federated State of Cyprus (TFSC),** officially partitioning the island.

# RECENT YEARS

In November 1983, Turkish-occupied Cyprus proclaimed itself independent as the **Turkish Republic of North Cyprus (TRNC).** Although only Turkey has recognized the new state, the TRNC has established trade relations in Europe and with several Arab states. In 1992, the U.N. significantly pared down its peacekeeping mission, leaving Cypriots to resolve their situation without much international intervention. **Glafkos Clerides,** former head of the conservative **Democratic Rally (DISY),** became head of the Republic of Cyprus in 1993. Led by Rauf Denktaş, North Cyprus still lags behind the Republic of Cyprus economically, but retains the support of Turkish-Cypriots and, in recent years, thousands of settlers from mainland Turkey. The two men still lead their respective island halves today, and hope for cooperation is growing.

**EU OR NOT EU?** Greek officials are hopeful for the Republic of Cyprus's acceptance into the European Union, a prospect with uncertain implications for the political status of North Cyprus. Turkey is not a candidate for admission to the EU in either the first or second round, and has warned that it would seek to annex North Cyprus if the Republic of Cyprus were to join the EU. In early August 1997, Turkey and North Cyprus agreed to work toward partial defense and economic integration. The agreement came just five days before U.N.-sponsored talks between Greece and Turkey, and incensed the Greek government.

**WE CAN WORK IT OUT.** The peace talks' hope for cooperation faded further in late 1997, when the Republic of Cyprus placed an order for a shipment of **S-300 missiles** from Russia. Both the Turkish government and the Turkish Cypriot government threatened that the delivery of these weapons would prompt an immediate increase in the Turkish military presence on the island. The missiles were deployed to Crete instead. In the past few years, negotiations to resolve the missile situation have progressed in fits and starts with periodic US involvement, including the mediation efforts of the current US Ambassador to the U.N., **Richard Holbrooke.** While missiles are still a sore subject for both sides, talks about the political status of the island began in 2000 and have been somewhat successful. Though Clerides and Denktaş don't meet face to face, they have been discussing the formation of a federation or a loose confederation of the Greek and Turkish Cypriot governments. As of July 2000, the talks remained inconclusive; tensions rose in June after a massive **fire** of mysterious origins devastated the agricultural plains of Cyprus. Fortunately, the fires were contained before they reached the coast and will not greatly affect Cyprus's tourist industry.

# CYPRIOT SPECIAL EVENTS

Cypriots observe not only Greece's holidays (see p. 35), but also hold their own regional and local festivities; following are a few of the most significant:

**Dec. 26: Boxing Day.** The day after Christmas. Cypriots still celebrate this throwback to the days of British colonization.

**Feb. 18-March 13: Carnival.** The most notable celebrations are in Limassol (p. 525).

**March 13: Green Monday,** the beginning of Lent. In areas of more strict observation this initiates seven meatless weeks of Lenten fasting.

**Apr. 1: Greek Cypriot National Day,** commemorating the creation of the Republic.

**June 19: Kataklismos,** or Flood Festivals. Across Cyprus, **Pentecost** marks the beginning of days of feasting and celebration, remembering Noah's deliverance from the Flood, and paying homage to Aphrodite.

**Oct. 1: Cyprus Independence Day.**

# ESSENTIALS

**ENTRANCE REQUIREMENTS.** Tourists with valid passports from Australia, Canada, Great Britain, Ireland, New Zealand, and the US do not need a **visa** to enter Cyprus for stays of up to 90 days; South Africans and Turks do need visas (£5). Tourists wishing to stay longer should probably first leave Cyprus and then reenter.

## GETTING THERE

**YOU CAN'T GET THERE FROM HERE.** Southern Cyprus is not accessible from northern Cyprus, nor is northern Cyprus accessible from southern Cyprus. If your travels originate in North Cyprus and you have a Turkish stamp in your passport, you can *never* enter the south. The quickest way to get to the south from the north is to fly somewhere else first, then hop a plane to southern Cyprus. To get to there without flying you must take a detour: catch a ferry to **Taşucu,** Turkey, a bus to **Marmaris,** a ferry to **Rhodes,** and on to southern Cyprus (2 days). Ask the Turkish authorities not to stamp your passport: a **Taşucu** stamp reveals that you've been to North Cyprus.

CYPRUS

Cyprus lies 64km from Turkey, 160km from Israel and Lebanon, and 480km from the nearest Greek island. **The Republic of Cyprus** (southern Cyprus) is accessible from Greece and other European and Middle Eastern countries by airplane or ferry. Both **Limassol** and **Larnaka** are accessible by ferry from a number of points, including Rhodes, Crete, and Hafia. There are two international airports, in **Larnaka** (p. 517) and **Paphos** (p. 530); see the **Transportation** section for each city for more information on fares and routes. Cyprus is accessible by plane on **Olympic Airlines** (US ☎(800) 223-1226; Cyprus ☎(02) 46 21 01; www.olympic-airways.gr), **Cyprus Airways** (US ☎(212) 714-2190; Cyprus ☎(02) 44 30 54; www.cyprusair.com.cy), and many major airlines. Roundtrip fares from Athens to Larnaka cost about US$135 (for more information on finding flights, see **Essentials,** p. 61).

## CONSULATES AND EMBASSIES

### IN YOUR COUNTRY

**Australia:** 30 Beale Cr., Deakin, Canberra, ACT 2600 (☎6281 0832; fax 6281 0860).

**Canada:** 365 Bloor St. E., Suite 1010, Box #43, **Toronto,** ON M4W 3L4 (☎(416) 944-0998; fax 944-9149); 2930 rue Edouard Mont Petit, Suite PH2, **Montréal,** QC H3T 1J7 (☎(514) 735-7233).

**Greece:** Odos Irodotou 16, Athens (☎723 27 27; fax 723 19 27).

**UK:** 93 Park St., London W1Y 4ET (☎(0171) 499 82 72; fax 491 06 91).

**US:** 2211 R St. NW, Washington, D.C. 20008 (☎(202) 462-5772; fax 483-6710).

## IN CYPRUS (LEFKOSIA)

**Australia:** High Commission, Annis Comninis 4 (☎473 001; fax 366 486), 500m east of Pl. Eleftherias off Stasinou. Open M-F 7:30am-2:50pm.

**Canada:** Odos Them. Dervi 15 (☎45 16 30; fax 45 90 96).

**Egypt:** Egypt 3 (☎465 144; fax 462 287). Open M-F 8am-2pm.

**Greece:** Lordou Vyronos 8 (☎441 880; fax 473 990). Open M-F 9am-noon.

**Israel:** I. Grypari 4 (☎445 195). Open M-F 8am-4pm.

**Lebanon:** Vas. Olgas 1 (☎442 216; fax 467 662). Open M-F 8:30am-1:30pm.

**Syria:** Androkleous 1 (☎474 481; fax 446 963). Open M-F 8am-2pm, Sa 8am-1pm.

**UK:** High Commission, Alexanderou Pavlou (☎473 131; fax 367 198), west of the old city. Open M and W-F 7:30am-2pm, Tu 7:30am-1pm and 2-5:30pm.

**US:** Metochiou and Ploutarchou (☎476 100; fax 465 944). Open M-F 8am-5pm.

# MONEY

The main unit of currency in the Republic of Cyprus is the **pound (£),** which is divided into 100 cents. Coins come in 1, 2, 5, 10, 20, and 50 cent sizes; bank notes in denominations of £1, 5, 10, and 20. Cyprus imposes no limit on the amount of foreign currency that may be imported, but amounts in excess of US$1000 should be declared on Customs form D (NR). No more than £50 in Cypriot currency may be brought into or taken out of the country. Banks are generally open M-F 8:15am-12:30pm; see the **Practical Information** section of each city for more detailed info.

The prices quoted below were effective in the summer of 2000. As inflation and exchange rates fluctuate, present prices may differ by as much as 30%. (For information on traveler's checks, ATMs, credit cards, and other financial matters, see the **Money** section of **Essentials,** p. 41).

| CYPRIOT POUND (£) | |
|---|---|
| **US$1 = £0.60** | **£1 = US$1.68** |
| **CDN$1 = £0.41** | **£1 = CDN$2.45** |
| **UK£1 = £0.91** | **£1 = UK£1.10** |
| **IR£1 = £0.73** | **£1 = IR£1.37** |
| **AUS$1 = £0.36** | **£1 = AUS$2.78** |
| **NZ$1 = £0.28** | **£1 = NZ$3.52** |
| **SAR1 = £0.09** | **£1 = SAR11.68** |
| **EUR€1 = £0.58** | **£1 = EUR€1.74** |
| **100DR = £0.17** | **£1 = 583.38DR** |
| **TL10,000 = £2.98** | **£1 = TL3,376** |

# GETTING AROUND

A reliable highway system serves much of Cyprus, but take caution on the winding mountain roads. **Cars** drive on the left side of the road; be prepared for British rotaries. Almost all Cypriot rental cars have manual transmission and standardized rates: the cheapest compact cars should cost £13 per day, small **motorbikes** £5, and larger motorcycles £7-8. Cypriot law requires that seatbelts be worn in front seats of cars, and an **international driver's license** or a **national driver's license** from your home country is required. A temporary Cypriot driver's license, good for six months, can be obtained from district police stations with a photo ID and £3.

There is one island-wide **bus schedule** available at tourist offices. This schedule provides all necessary information, including prices for buses and private taxi service. Bus service is less frequent in winter and is less dependable in rural areas of Cyprus. Buses run between all major cities except **Paphos,** which requires a connection in Limassol in order to reach Larnaka or Lefkosia. **Service taxis** are the most reliable form of transportation on Cyprus and are quite affordable. Each taxi seats 4-7 passengers; in the winter they stop running an hour earlier (every 30min. M-Sa 5:45am-7:30pm, Su 7am-6:30pm; £2.10-5.50). After 7pm, transportation is limited to expensive **private taxis.** Hitchhiking is uncommon, and neither locals nor tourists are likely to offer rides. Limited bus service is available to the **Troodos Mountains.** See the **Getting There, Getting Around,** and **Practical Information** for each town or city for more information.

# PRACTICAL INFORMATION

**199** for ambulance, fire, or police. **192** for night pharmacies in Cyprus.

**BY MAIL.** **Post offices** are open Monday through Friday from 7:30am to 1:30pm. Some have afternoon hours (4-6pm) and Saturday hours (8:30-10:30am). Poste Restante (see **Keeping in Touch,** p. 58) is available in Lefkosia, Larnaka, Paphos, and Limassol. **Airmail** is available and takes 3-4 days to travel to Europe. Faster, more expensive courier services are also available. The cost of sending a 20g letter varies by destination: to **Europe** and **Middle East,** 31¢; **US, Africa,** and **Asia,** 36¢; **Australia** and **New Zealand,** 41¢. Sending a **postcard** costs 26¢ to everywhere but Australia and New Zealand, which costs 31¢.

**BY PHONE.** Southern Cyprus has fairly reliable telephone service (administered by **CYTA**). Direct overseas calls can be made from all public phones, but you need a **phone card** to activate them even if you plan to use your own service provider. Cards are available in denominations of £3, £5, and £10 and are sold at banks and kiosks. Private phones in hotels may have a 10% surcharge. For instructions on how to call in and out of Cyprus, see **Keeping in Touch,** p. 58.

**PHONE HOME** The country code for Cyprus is **357.** The international access code for Cyprus is **080.**

**ACCOMMODATIONS.** In general, off-season prices (Oct.-May) are about 20% lower than the rates quoted in this book. Lefkosia, Troodos, Paphos, and Larnaka all have **HI youth hostels;** expect hostels to be clean, if a bit run down, with free showers, kitchens, and common rooms. Although Cyprus has few formal campgrounds, some travelers sleep on beaches and in forests. This has obvious risks, but should you choose to do so, choose a discreet campsite. Women should not camp alone. It is generally a good idea to make reservations in advance; the **Cyprus Tourist Office** (p. 517) is available to help travelers find accommodations. For more information on **Accommodations,** see p. 55.

**TIPS FOR TRAVELERS.** Getting around in Cyprus is like traveling in Greece: most Cypriots speak English, and the country's main industry is tourism. There are a few additional things to be aware of when visiting this divided island. Picture taking is forbidden at the top of Mt. Olympus and at the Green Line in Lefkosia (p. 542). **Women** (or anyone) traveling alone should feel safe, as the police take the harassment of women very seriously in Cyprus. It was only two years ago that homosexuality was legalized in Cyprus, but **gay and lesbian travelers** shouldn't have any trouble getting around the country. A few stares and comments may be thrown your way, but as with any form of hassling, ignore it and keep moving. In general, Cypriots are known for their hospitality and truly enjoy showing travelers around their country. For more information on **Specific Concerns,** see p. 71.

**CTO OFFICES.** Tourist offices in Cyprus are extremely helpful and efficient. There are offices in Limassol, Lefkosia, Larnaka, Paphos, Polis, Agia Napa, and Platres. The main office is the **Cyprus Tourism Organization (CTO),** P.O. Box 4535, Limassol 19, Lefkosia 1390 (☎(02) 337 715; fax 331 644; email cto@cyta.com.cy). The CTO offices provide free maps and info on buses, museums, and events. A particularly helpful publication available at tourist offices is *The Cyprus Traveler's Handbook* (free). Officials generally speak English, Greek, German, and French.

**Greece:** 36 Voukourestiou, Athens (☎361 01 78; fax 364 47 98).

**US:** 13 E. 40th St., New York, NY 10016 (☎(212) 683-5280; fax 683-5282; email gocyprus@aol.com; www.cyprustourism.org).

**UK:** 213 Regent St., London W1R 8DA (☎(0171) 569 8800; fax 287 6534; email ctolon@ctolon.demon.co.uk).

# COASTAL CYPRUS

Nothing on Cyprus draws visitors like its magnetically lovely beaches. The volume of coastal tourism in the area confirms it has not shaken its colonial feel—in the summer it seems as if Brits outnumber Cypriots. Still, if you stray even a block inland from the beach there is Cypriot culture to be found, particularly in Paphos, where nearby monuments make for a quick transition between marble and sand.

## LARNAKA Λαρνακα ☎04

Larnaka gets its name from the ancient Greek word for coffin *(larnax)*, an allusion to the final resting place of **St. Lazarus** in the city's central church. Fortunately, tropical Larnaka (pop. 70,000) isn't as grim as its moniker implies. Larnaka is one of the oldest continually inhabited cities in the world. Segments of the ancient city walls and aqueducts, Bronze Age temples, and the Hala Sultan Tekke Mosque—which dates back to the first Arab invasion of Cyprus in AD 647—poke through into the present. Elsewhere, graffiti reading *"Hellas, Enosis, EOKA"* elicits memories of the violent movement for union with Greece a few decades ago. Sunny Larnaka has lately become a leisure hotspot, quieter and cleaner than Limassol and a convenient base for travelers.

CYPRUS

### GETTING THERE AND GETTING AROUND

**Flights:** (☎692 700). Most flights into and out of Cyprus land at the **Larnaka Airport** located 6km west of town. **Taxis** to the center of town cost £3-5 and are the main mode of transport into town. **Bus #19** (Kiti bus) runs from Pl. Ag. Lazarus to the airport by request to the driver. (14 per day 6:20am-7pm, off-season M-F 6:20am-5:45pm, with reduced service on Sa; £0.50.)

**Buses:** Intercity buses leave from Leforos Athinon by the marina on the waterfront opposite Four Lanterns hotel. Look for a sandwich board with the schedule or ask at the CTO for current schedules, as they change constantly. **Kallenos Buses** (☎654 850 or 644 666) go to **Lefkosia** (M-F 6 per day 7am-4pm, Sa 4 per day until 1pm; £2 through Agia Napa) and **Limassol** (M-F 4 per day 8am-4pm, Sa 3 per day until 1pm, £1.70). **EMAN** (☎03 721 321) buses go to **Agia Napa** (M-Sa 9 per day 8:30am-5:30pm, Su 4 per day until 4:30pm, £1). **A.L.** (☎650 477) bus #19 leaves Pl. Lazarus and stops at **Ag. Helenis, Artemidos, Meneou, Kiti,** and **Tersefanou** (13-14 per day 6:20am-7pm, £0.50).

**Service Taxis: Travel & Express** (☎661 010), in Pl. Vasileos Pavlou, adjacent to the Sun Hall Hotel; and **Kyriakos,** Ermou 2C (☎655 100). All run to **Lefkosia** (M-F every 30 min. 6am-6pm, £2.40); **Travel & Express** runs to **Limassol** (M-F every 30min. 6am-6pm, £3). Service taxis will pick up and drop off anywhere in the city if you call ahead; they are much cheaper than private taxis. On Sundays taxis run until early afternoon; prices may be roughly £0.50 or higher.

**Private Taxis: Makris'** private taxi service (☎652 929), based in Pl. Vasileos Pavlou across from the CTO, is shamelessly expensive, but it's 24hr. (£0.65 per km in the day, £0.88 per km at night).

**Car Rental: Phoenix Rent-A-Car,** Makariou III 65 (☎623 407 or 622 314; fax 650 460; www.phoenix.com.cy). Prices from £10 per day. Unlimited mileage. Minimum age 25.

## ORIENTATION AND PRACTICAL INFORMATION

**Leoforos Athinon** (a.k.a. the **Finikoudhes,** "Palm Tree Promenade," or simply **Athinon**) runs along the waterfront at the heart of the tourist district and hops with various eateries and night spots. **Pl. Vasileos Pavlou,** one block west of the north end of Athinon across from the **Marina,** marks the city center, where most practical facilities (including the post office, police station, and tourist office) can be found. One block west of Pl. Vasileos Pavlou's south end is **Pl. Ag. Lazarus,** home to the municipal market and the youth hostel. **Larnaka Fort** presides over the southern end of Athinon; just past it is the old **Turkish Quarter.**

**Tourist Office: CTO** (☎654 322), in Pl. Vasileos Pavlou, provides information and maps for all of Cyprus. Open M-Tu, Th-F 8:15am-2:15pm and 4-6:15pm; W, Sa 8:15am-2:15pm; off-season hours vary. There's also a **24hr. airport branch** (☎643 000).

**Banks:** The main branches of three major banks are in or near Pl. Vasileos Pavlou. **Bank of Cyprus,** next to the AmEx office, has a 24hr. **ATM,** traveler's checks, and **currency exchange.** (☎653 181. Open M-F 8:15am-12:30pm, in summer also M 3:15-4:45pm.) **Popular Bank** (☎652 222, Open M-F 8:15-12:30pm and Wed. 3:30-6:30pm), and the **Hellenic Bank** have 24hr. **ATM** services throughout the city.

**American Express:** (☎652 024), in the office of **Mantovani Plotin Travel,** across from the CTO. No traveler's checks or currency exchange. Money check forms available for those drawing funds from AmEx cards. Guarantees personal checks for use at local banks. Open M-F 8am-1pm and 3:30-7pm, Sa 9am-noon; winter afternoons 2-5:30pm.

**Police:** (☎804 040), on the corner of Makariou III, one block north of the tourist office at the intersection of Leoforos Gkiani Timagia and Leoforos Georgiou Griva Digeni. English spoken. Open 24hr.

**Hospital:** (☎630 300 or 630 312), off Grigori Afxentiou street, at the intersection of Ag. Elenis and Konst. Zachariada.

**Telephones: CYTA,** Z. Pierides 7-9 (☎640 257). Follow Lordou Vyronos toward the waterfront; the office is on the right, before Zinonos Kitieos. Open M-F 7:30am-6pm, Sa 7:30am-1pm (noon in winter). **Phone cards** in £3, £5, or £10 amounts available at most kiosks. **Telecard phones** throughout the city.

**Internet Access: Web Internet Cafe,** Lordou Vyronou 54 (☎654 954; www.web-cafe.com.cy), with computer use £2 per hr.; printing £0.20 per page. **Theathine Internet Cafe/Bar** (☎623 133), 95B Athinon, on the 2nd floor of the Tuck Inn. Movies play at the bar, which morphs into a dance club after dark. £2 for the 1st hr., £0.25 per 15 min. thereafter. Drinks from £1-3.50. Open M-F 11-1am, Sa-Su 11am-2am.

**Post Office: Main branch,** in Pl. Vas. Pavlou (☎802 600). Open Sept.-June M-Tu, Th-F 7:30am-1:30pm and 3-6pm, Sa 9-11am; July-Aug. M-F 7:30am-1:30pm and 4-7pm, Sa 9-11am. **Postal code:** 6900. **Pl. Ag. Lazarus branch** (☎630 182) open Sept.-June M-F 7:30am-1:30pm, Th 3-6pm; July-Aug. M, F 7:30am-1:30pm. **Postal code:** 6902.

## ACCOMMODATIONS

While Larnaka is less expensive than neighboring Agia Napa, rooms are just as scarce in summer. Pricey resort hotels line the waterfront, but cheaper options can be found a few blocks inland. Prices tend to be £5-7 less in winter. For those staying in the area for more than 5 days, Larnaka is a good base. Flats can cost £5 less per person for longer stays.

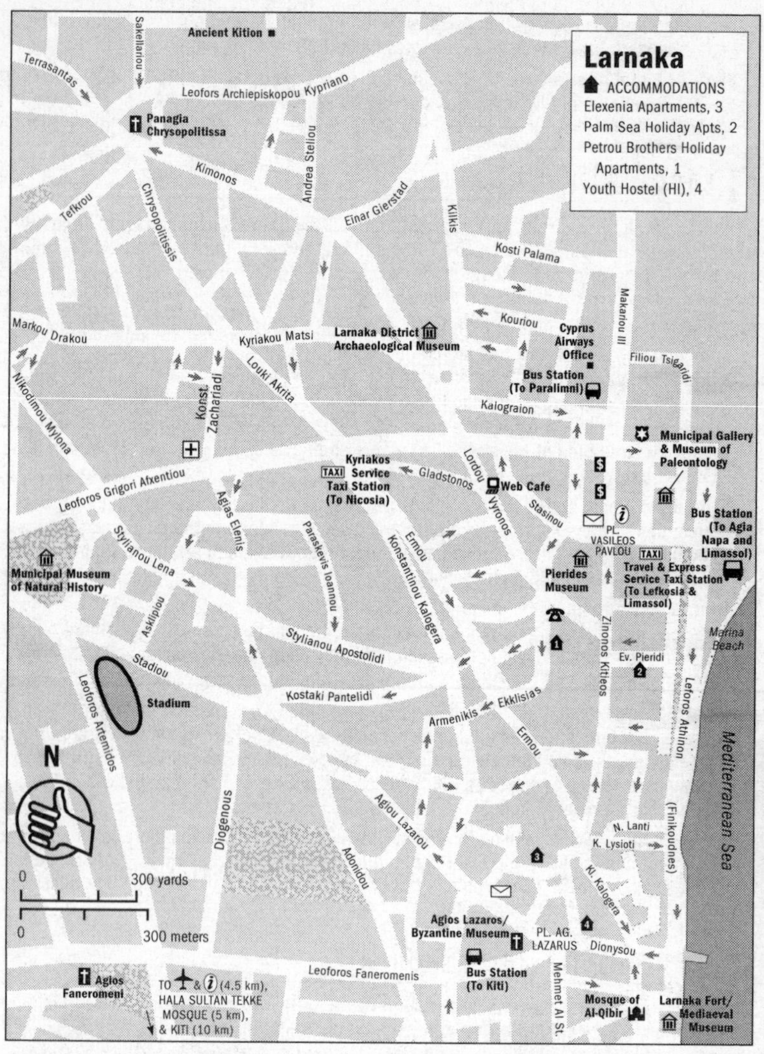


CYPRUS

**Petrou Bros. Holiday Apartments,** Armenikis Ekklisias 1 (☎650 600/601; fax 655 122; www.petrou.com.cy), 2 blocks from the waterfront. Immaculate and spacious modern flats with bathrooms, showers, telephones, kitchens, balconies, A/C, sun roof, and 24hr. reception. Laundry, travel services, parking, breakfast, and sun roof available (£2-3 each). Doubles £22; quads £30; 6-person suite £40; off-season £5-8 less.

**Youth Hostel (HI),** Nikolaou Rossou 27 (☎621 188), in Pl. Ag. Lazarus near Ag. Lazarus church. Housed in a former mosque, friendly management maintains harmony over 3 large rooms (female, male, coed) with 10 beds each, and 1 room for a family. The hostel, but not the front desk, is open 24hr; guests can sign in anytime. No luggage storage. Relatively empty, so private space may be available. Some kitchen facilities. Bring sheets or rent them for £1. £4 per person.

**Palm Sea Beach Holiday Apts,** Evanthias Pieridou (☎659 232; fax 625 726), 3 blocks from Pl. Vasileos Pavlou between Athinon and Zinonos Kitios. Great views of the ocean

and Marina from in-room balconies, all with kitchen, TV, fold-out couch, full baths. Attentive staff. Peak summer season rates begin £18, A/C £2 extra.

**Elexenia Hotel Apartments,** D. Demetriade 1 (☎653 478; fax 651 466), at the corner of D. Demetriade and Nicholas Rossou, just off Pl. Ag. Lazarus. Bright, cheerful rooms at bargain rates. A/C, TV, and kitchen facilities. Singles £11; doubles £12; triples £13.

## FOOD

Most of Larnaka's tavernas and bars are on the waterfront. Larnaka offers an array of international cuisines, including Chinese, Armenian, Lebanese, Italian, French, and Indian. Prices include 10% service charge and 8% VAT (see p. 41).

**1900 Art Cafe,** Stasinou 6 (☎653 027), across the street from the tourist office. Run by a painter and a poet, the cafe brims with artistic and intellectual exchange, as well as carafes of local wine (£2.50) and coffee (£1). With swanky taverna/bar seating upstairs, the downstairs operates as a traditional *kafeneion*, and contains the first movie projector in Cyprus. Quiet during summer, its cozy fireplace draws in locals all winter. Serves some of the only vegetarian dishes available in the city. Most entrees £3.50. Open W-M 9am-2pm, 6pm-midnight.

**Kali Kardia,** Zehra 8. Go south on Pialepasa from Larnaka Fort and turn right on Barbaros; this tiny joint is at the end of road. Kali Kardia serves authentic Cypriot cuisine for those pining for a home-cooked meal. Kebabs, souvlaki, and salads £1 for take-out, £2 for dining in. Open 6pm-midnight.

**Militzis Restaurant,** Piale Pasha 42 (☎655 867), 1 block south of Larnaka Fort. This spacious seaside spot glories in carnivorous delights and a charming view; 3 large clay ovens create *psita,* cooking up an assortment of fresh meat (£4) and lamb dishes (only £2.25). Great wines £3-6. Open 12:30pm-midnight, closed M in winter.

**Mavri Helona,** Mehmet Ali 11 (☎650 661), on a small side street by the church of Ag. Lazarus. Toy turtles lead to the upstairs dining room. A welcoming and lively crowd of singers, musicians and large groups of local buddies gather until midnight Tu-Sa nights to munch a variety of *mezedes* (£6.50), kebabs (£3-4), and fish (£4-5). Wines £3-4, beers £1.25. Opens at 6pm Tu-Sa, closed Aug.

**Cuckoo's Nest,** 10 Piale Pasha (☎628 133). Walk about a block south of Larnaka's Fort and don't blink or you'll miss it. Huge portions and great prices. Try the popular *kotoletes, mezedes* for 2 (£8), fresh cod (£2.65) or steak (£2.50). The hospitality, seaside seating, and indoor A/C are pluses.



## NIGHTLIFE AND BEACHES

The area around the **Hard Rock Cafe** shimmies with fun, teen-centered nightlife. Most of the clubs rage on until dawn. If daylight fun is more your thing, check out the Marina area for watersports and lots of sunshine, although you'll do better to explore beaches out of town. Pretty, less-crowded white sand **beaches** are situated to the northeast, on the way to Agia Napa. (EMAN buses 8:30am-5:30pm, £1.) You can also try a **Larnaka-Napa Sea Cruise** day trip organized by a private company; see **Mr. Karotsakis,** who oversees watersports and sea cruises. (☎656 949/954; larnaka.napa.sea.cruises@cytanet.com.cy) Otherwise, you're left with the **Marina** at the north end of town, which borders the bustling beach—a dismal mixture of packed dirt and cigarette butts crammed with baking vacationers.

**Stone Age Pub,** Watkins 9 (☎624 526). Feel especially hip after schmoozing in this joint. Drinks from £1.50-2. No food.

**Hard Rock Cafe,** next to Stone Age (☎664 292), is a hangout for Larnaka's youth, who congregate along Athinon. Not necessarily the real thing, but definitely cool.

**Club Memphis,** on Athinon next to Snack Boy. Its foam parties are infamous. A dubious entrance leads to an underground craze of the intense dancers enduring the wee hours

of the morning. On Athinon next to Snack Boy. Cover £5, one drink included. Athinon also provides quieter late-night snack and dessert locations perfect for people watching or overlooking the calm night sea.

**Nitro Cafe,** 15 Leoforos Gregori Afxentiou (☎664 909). A zenith of popular inland cafeterias, drawing mostly local crowds with a DJ spinning a soulful mix of house, American R&B, and Greek pop. Open M-Sun 10am-whenever.

## SIGHTS

Within walking distance of each other, Larnaka's major historical sights draw the many tourists passing through the city. The CTO offers **free walking tours** for travelers or daytrippers in a hurry. (☎654 322, W 10am beginning at the CTO; ☎630 576, F 10am beginning at Larnaka Fort.)

**CHURCH OF AGIOS LAZARUS.** Most recently rebuilt after a devastating fire in 1970, this beautifully adorned 9th-century church rests on the rather creepy sepulcher of Lazarus, whom Jesus personally raised from the dead. The church is one of the most important Orthodox sites of pilgrimage, especially on the Saturday of Lazarus during Lent. Legend holds that Lazarus journeyed to Cyprus and became the island's first bishop, living in Kition for 30 years before dying again. Lazarus's tomb is down the steps near the *iconostasis*. The church's belfry was added in 1857 and lends a Byzantine ambience. The courtyard holds a small **Byzantine museum** with ecclesiastical art, and the **Epitafio,** worth a peek. *(Take the first left north of the Larnaka Fort. Dress modestly: long skirts for women, pants for men, no bare shoulders. Museum ☎652 498. Open 8am-12:30pm and 3:30-6:30pm. £0.50. Services Su 6-9:30am.)*

**HALA SULTAN TEKKE MOSQUE & SALT LAKE.** This must-see mosque's setting is exotic and picturesque: it hangs over the edge of the Salt Lake, which dries up completely in summer. Palm trees surround one of the most sacred pilgrimage sights for Muslims, after Mecca and Medina. Also called the **Tekke of Umm Haram,** it was constructed in AD 649 during the Arab invasion of Cyprus and rebuilt in 1816 over the site where Umm Haram (Muhammed's maternal aunt) fell from a mule and broke her neck around AD 449. The mosque also houses the tomb of Jordanian King Abdullah's great-great-great-grandmother, who died in exile in Cyprus in 1929. *(Take bus #19, bound for Kiti, from Pl. Ag. Lazarus (15min., 14 per day, £0.50). Tell the driver "Tekke." After you're dropped off, walk along the paved road for 1km. Open summer 7:30am-7:30pm. Free.)*

CYPRUS

**LARNAKA FORT.** Built to protect Larnaka harbor by Venetians in the 15th century and rebuilt by Ottomans in 1625, the small fort served as a prison during the British occupation (1878-1959). The small upper-level museum contains artifacts and photographs from local excavations and churches, as well as early Byzantine artifacts and a medieval armory and pottery. Climb the sea wall for a panoramic view of the surrounding town. *(At the southern end of Athinou and a block east of Pl. Agiou Lazarou. ☎630 576. Open M-F 7:30am-7pm; Sa, Su 7:30am-5pm. £0.75.)*

**PIERIDES FOUNDATION MUSEUM.** This private museum was the home of Demetrios Pierides (1811-1895), a collector of Cypriot artifacts; his descendants still occupy the top floor of the house. Bronze Age ceramics, Cypriot folk wood carvings and silverware, as well as some of the earliest cartography of the island are all in four large rooms. Modern sculptures, chiefly from the past decade, are displayed in the adjacent yard. *(Zinonos Kitieos 4, diagonal from CTO entrance. ☎651 345 or 652 495. Open M-F 9am-1pm and 3-6pm, Sa 9am-1pm, Su 10am-1pm. £1, under 18 free.)*

**TORNARITIS-PIERIDES MUSEUM OF PALEONTOLOGY AND MUNICIPAL CULTURAL CENTER.** Five colonial-style warehouses are home to the Paleontology Museum and Municipal Gallery. The **Paleontology Museum** is two rooms filled with wood, fossilized fish, and the bones of dwarf pygmy elephants and hippopotami who once mysteriously migrated to Cyprus. Pieces date back over 490 million years to the Cambrian period. The **Municipal Gallery**'s small but impressive set of

modern abstract works and rotated featured collections inspect Cypriot politics and culture. The curator is eager to expound on the art and to refer aesthetes to private galleries throughout the island. *(Pl. Evropis, in the old customs warehouse at the end of Athinon. Call a day in advance to arrange a tour. Gallery ☎628 587, Paleontology ☎658 848. Open Tu-F 10am-1pm and 5-7pm, Sa-Su 10am-1pm; winter 4-6pm. Free.)*

**KITION.** Now mostly underground, the temple complex of the ancient city forms the substratum of Larnaka. Settled in the early 13th century BC and abandoned soon after, Kition was rebuilt in 1200 BC by refugees from the Peloponnese. The site's four main small temples were damaged in 4th-century BC wars with the Phoenicians and Egyptians, and were later leveled by earthquake and fire in 280 BC. Part of the ancient Cyclopean wall and the **Temple of Astarte** (the Phoenician goddess of fertility) now poke up. The site requires an active imagination—only barely discernible foundations remain; many parts are covered by vegetation. *(The site's entrance is hard to find. Walk north from the archaeological museum on Kilkis with the museum on your left. Turn left on Leontiou Machaira, and left again onto Ioanni Paskirati; the entrance is at the end of the road. Signs lead the way. Open M-F 7:30am-5pm. £0.75.)*

**OTHER SIGHTS.** The **Larnaka District Archaeological Museum** has 2 main rooms, one dedicated to ceramic artifacts from the prehistoric period to the middle Bronze Age, and the other full of findings from ancient Kition. *(Follow the signs and head west on Leoforos Grigori Afxentiou; turn right on Klimonos. It's at the intersection of Kilkis and Klimonos. ☎630 169. Open M-Sa 9am-2:30pm, Th 3-5pm, Su 10am-1pm. £0.75, Cypriot citizens free.)* In the center of the **Municipal Gardens,** listen to the shouts of children playing in the adjacent playground mix with squawks from turkeys, buzzards, canaries, flamingos, and peacocks at the **Municipal Museum of Natural History.** Over 5000 individually labeled Cypriot insects will set your skin crawling. Stuffed local animals—from street cats to extinct moufflons—fill 6 small rooms. (*On Stadiou across from the stadium, in the Municipal Gardens. Open Tu-Su 10am-1pm and 4-6pm. £0.20.)* Muslims anxious to teach travelers about their religion still use the medieval **Mosque of Al-Qibir** as a place of worship. *(Across the street from the Larnaka Fort, ☎665 752. Open sunrise-sunset, about 3:30am-10:30pm in summer. Free.)*

CYPRUS

## DAYTRIPS FROM LARNAKA

### PANAGIA ANGELOKTISI

*Take bus #19 (25min., 14 per day, £0.40), from Pl. Ag. Lazarus in Larnaka, to Kiti; tell the driver "Panagia Angeloktisi." Open M-F 8am-4pm, Sa 10am-4pm, Su 9am-noon and 2-4pm. Modest dress required. Donations welcome.*

The church "built by the angels," Panagia Angeloktisti, lies in **Kiti,** a little residential village. Much of the church was built in the 11th century, atop (and incorporating) a 5th-century ruin of a prior sanctuary. A spectacular 6th-century **mosaic** in the central apse depicting the Virgin Mary with Christ, surrounded by the Archangels Michael and Gabriel, is the oldest Cypriot mosaic still in its original setting. The church's narthex was built in the 14th century by the Gibelet family, a prominent Latin noble family in medieval Cyprus.

### STAVROVOUNI MONASTERY

*Open to men 8am-noon and 3-6pm, 2-5pm in the winter. No photography or video. Free. Note: Women are not allowed to enter the monastery, only the church at the foot of the entrance, and only with proper attire.*

Panoramic views of Cyprus's countryside, from Larnaka to Lefkosia and beyond, spread out below "Cross Mountain" monastery's 700m peak, which is just 40km outside Larnaka. This 4th-century monastery was founded by Constantine the Great's mom (and the one who converted him), **Saint Helen.** Stavrovouni was erected atop the ruins of an ancient temple to Aphrodite. On the way home from Jerusalem, Helen is said to have left a fragment of the True Cross there, following

a dream's instructions. The isolation and internal harmony of the peak are reminders of the importance of religious history in Cyprus. The devout monks are eminent icon painters and produce some of the island's best honey and cheese, even as they follow a strict regimen. At the foot of the rocky cliff lies the small 18th-century monastery of **Agia Varvara (Barbara),** also noted for its monks' icon painting.

## CAPE GRECO

East of Agia Napa, on **Kyrou Nerou,** resort hotels give way to an empty coast preserved as a national forest. Several rough surface roads connect mainland Cyprus to the sea; the mostly unmarked hiking trail, 8km from town, leads to **Cape Greco.** For a solitary—and breathtaking—communion with Cyprus's southeast coast, trek around Cape Greco and the Red Villages on a rented moped or bicycle: look for rentals in nearby Agia Napa.

Maps of hiking trails can be obtained from the **CTO** and are quite helpful. The cape has remained undeveloped because of a military radar installation, giving aspiring secret agents the chance to swim beneath two space-age radar dishes. On Kyrou Nerou, the main road, signs point to **Agiou Anargyroi,** a small church that stands in splendid isolation over the sea. Next to the church, stairs descend to sea caves large enough to wander inside: a flashlight would help explorers. There are no hotels, no tavernas, and no sand—just craggy coves cascading into the magnificent blue sea. Fishermen and adventurous tourists can discover the unruffled isolation of this bit of the Mediterranean.

### PROTARAS AND PARALIMNI

Named for the crimson soil that feeds the agriculture of the Red Villages, seven "built-up areas" make up the district. Signs lead in a ring from village to village, with less than 5km between each. Navigation by primary roads is straightforward.

North on the main road from Agia Napa, at the resort town of Protaras, pure white sand spreads over the villages' best beaches. Since it's so expensive to stay in Protaras, it's better to daytrip to its beaches. Northeast of Protaras, the road turns toward the drab modern village of Paralimni, which pulls visitors to the 18th-century church of **Agia Panagia** in the center of town, and makes a good base when accommodations in Agia Napa or Protaras are hard to come by.

**Buses** to and from Paralimni and Protaras originate at the **Paralimni-Dherynia Bus Co. headquarters** (☎821 318) in Pl. Ag. Georgios, with service to **Larnaka** (5 per day M-F 8am-4:30pm, 4 per day Sa 8am-1:30pm, in winter 3 per day; £1) via Dherynia and Frenaros. Buses to Lefkosia (South Nicosia) run from Ag. Georgios Sq. in **Paralimi** (7:30am, £2.50) and from the hotel area in **Protaras** (7am, £2.50). The Paralimni **taxi** office is at Eolias 9, and has 24hr. service. (☎096 37 020. Service to/from Agia Napa £3-5.) The **San Antonio Hotel,** Gregoriou Afxentiou 123, about 500m outside Pl. Ag. Georgiou in Paralimni, is a somewhat pricey but very welcoming option. Motherly owner Maria gladly aids travelers and answers questions. Private baths, spacious rooms, balconies, swimming pool, and continental breakfast included. (☎821 561. £15 per person.) Enjoy traditional fresh fish *meze* harborside in Paralimni's **Loukiana.** Prices are steep, but the peaceful nautical ambience makes it a worthwhile splurge. (☎828 580. Open M-Sa 5pm-midnight.)

CYPRUS

### DHERYNIA

Two kilometers north of Paralimni and a stone's throw from the Green Line is the small village of Dherynia, home to many refugees from Famagusta. The **#2 bus** (☎821 318 or 825 607) runs through Agia Napa, Paralimni, Protaras, and Dherynia. The bus departs from **Dherynia** (4 per day M-Sa 10am-5:30pm, £0.50) and reverses its route in **Agia Napa** (4 per day M-Sa 8:30am-3:15pm, £0.50). **Police** are at Ammochostou 47, near the traffic light on the road for Paralimni. Several tourist lookouts nearby allow views of the "ghost town" of Turkish-occupied **Famagusta.** The closest viewpoint can be found by following signs from the main road to the **Famagusta Beach View.** (☎730 433. £1, drink and leaflets included.) The viewpoints look out over what was once Cyprus's second-largest city; now, Farmagusta lies hauntingly frozen in time, its construction cranes unmoved for twenty-five years.

## AGIA NAPA Αγια Ναπα ☎03

Agia Napa thrives on the heavy tourist traffic of sunbaked visitors. Mopeds zip past sparkling beaches and a vast array of English-language multicolored signs. This once-quiet farming and fishing village has become a haven for young tourists ready to get freaky all night long. Thirty years ago, most tourists flocked to **Famagusta,** 16km to the north, allowing Agia Napa's ruined monastery and white sandy beaches to lie peacefully vacant. When Turkish forces occupied Famagusta in 1974, Agia Napa was transformed almost overnight into a glitzy, brassy tourist resort, even as it absorbed a large refugee community from North Cyprus.

**ORIENTATION AND PRACTICAL INFORMATION.** **AirTour-Cyprus,** Makarios 17, books flights out of Larnaka airport. (☎721 265. Open M-Tu and Th-Sa 8am-1pm and 4-6:30pm, W and Su 8am-1pm; afternoon hours reduced in winter.) The **bus station** is across from the Hellenic Bank; service is provided by **EMAN** (☎721 321) to: **Larnaka** (M-Sa every hour, 10 per day 8am-5pm, Su 4 per day 9am-4pm; in winter 5 per day, every 2 hours 8am-4pm; £1); **Lefkosia** (M-Sa 8am, £2); and **Paralimni** and **Protaras** (M-Sa 10 per day 9am-7pm, Su 5 per day 9am-6pm; in winter M-Sa 8 per day every hour until 5pm, no Su service; £0.50). Expensive but effective and conveniently located, **Agia Napa Taxi** (☎721 111/888), just uphill from the monastery off Makarios, offers 24hr. service and negotiable rates. **Bikes and mopeds** are ideal transportation in Agia Napa. To reach **Ham-Yam's Car, Motorcycle & Bicycle Rentals,** take a right on Nissi from Makarios; it's about 3 blocks on your left. Ham-Yam's is the only place to offer full insurance coverage, and is worth the slightly higher prices. Daily scooter rentals start at £7.50. (☎723 045 or 721 825. Open 8am-8pm daily, off-season closing at 1pm.)

Trying to navigate Agia Napa by addresses and street signs is an exercise in futility; instead, establish landmarks using a map. The town centers around the **Agia Napa Monastery** and the bar and taverna-laden streets that wind up the hill from it. **Makarios,** in front of the monastery, is the main road, with banks, shops, and most tourist services along it. Uphill, Makarios becomes Dinokratias, which leads north to Paralimni. Toward the sea, **Leoforos Nissi** heads west of Makarios to Larnaka and Nissi beach. A free **map** will help; get one from the **CTO,** Kyrou Nyrou 12, just off Makarios. (☎721 796. Open M-Sa 8:30am-2:20pm, M-Tu and Th-F 3:15-6pm, until 5pm in winter.) The **Hellenic Bank,** on Makarios, has a 24hr. **ATM.** (☎721 488. Open M-F 8:15am-12:30pm.) For **Internet access, Virtuality,** Eleftherias 2, uphill from the monastery, is the only choice. (☎723 290. Open 4:30pm-2am. £2 per hour.) The **police** (☎721 553) are north of town on the road to Paralimni. The closest **hospital** (☎821 211) is 10km north in Paralimni. The **post office** is at D. Liperti 1A. (☎701 550. Open M-F 7:30am-1:30pm, Th 3-6pm, Sa 8:30-10:30am.) **Postal code:** 5330.

CYPRUS

**ACCOMMODATIONS AND FOOD.** Inexpensive rooms are always elusive in Agia Napa, and in August they're nearly nonexistent—**call ahead** for reservations. Consider spending your nights in **Paralimni** if you can't find somewhere to stay. Be prepared for 24hr. noise at some less glam establishments, most easily encountered through word of mouth or following signs. To get to **Xenis Rooms,** Democratias 34, go up the road to Paralimni until you have to turn. A left, a right, and a walk to the top of the hill will get you to Xenis's four single rooms, each with bath and kitchen. (☎721 086, £7.) Just before Xenis Rooms, across from Mary's Supermarket, are the **Paul Marie Hotel Apartments,** which offer a quiet retreat, currency exchange, a pool table, two bars, a rooftop pool, and 24hr. service. (☎722 480. Studio £20; 1 bedroom £26; £3 for an extra bed.)

Good, cheap food is also hard to find in Agia Napa: try the supermarkets and 24hr. takeout shops, which serve the same food as restaurants, at cheaper prices. Cypriot *mezedes* and fresh fish prepared over real charcoal grills make **Lime Light,** on Liperti, on the left as you pass the post office on your right, is a local favorite; its owners see food as the center of the universe. (☎721 650. Open M-Sa 10am-2pm. Specials from £5, starters £1-3.) **Jasmin's Inn,** D. Solomou 1, is known

for an extensive menu and large portions. Table-top dancing and karaoke, partly influenced by the fearsome "Viagra cocktail," takes over part of the restaurant after 11pm. (☎721 731. Open 8am-2am daily, closed in winter. Entrees £3-5.) **Jasmin Kebab House,** D. Solomou, across from Jasmin's Inn, offers the cheapest and tastiest takeout in town. (☎721 436. Vegetarian dish £1.60, gyros plate £1.80.)

**NIGHTLIFE.** After dark, the bass thumps in Agia Napa's watering holes and discos and continues until morning, accompanied by flashing neon lights and the grinding bodies of Agia Napa's revelers (many of them foreigners in search of a summer beach party). After sundown, people gather in the streets around **the Square** to sample drink specials outside such pubs as the **Volcano Pub** (☎721 049), **Minos Pub,** and **Mariella Pub.**

The crowds dwindle after 1am as people migrate to the dance clubs. **Gas,** on Makariou, can cram 2500 people into its cavernous, bubble-filled, retro interior; two rooms of 70s and 80s hits and garage music blast from the latest electronic equipment. **The Kool Club,** near the intersection of Makariou and Nissi, booms the latest house and garage and throws a giant load of foam on top. The retro and house music at **Starsky & Hutch** and **Carwash** contrasts with the techno, house, and garage at **The Castle,** Tefkrou Anthia 37 (☎723 978. 18+. Open 12:30-4am.) Chat up your honey in the outdoor "Chill-Out" space as a break from speaker-top dancing to the newest house beats. While the pubs have no cover, the clubs often charge £5 (or £3 with the flyer handed out in the Square); women may get a break on cover.

**SIGHTS.** Inside the walls of the 16th-century Venetian **Monastery of Agia Napa,** an octagonal, dome-covered, marble fountain lies within a beautiful courtyard full of flowers, plants, and trees, including a famous, gargantuan 600-year-old sycamore outside the west entrance. In the monastery's small chapel, only a few icons hang. Off the main courtyard, you might hear the well that supplies water to the inner chapel, which is built into a cave. The well is said to have appeared when a group of Christians, hiding from pirate attacks, were saved from dehydration by the appearance of the Virgin Mary pointing to the corner spring. Since this **Miracle of Panagia,** the well has never run dry. (Open 7:30am-5pm. Services every Saturday 6pm. Free.) Every summer Sunday at 8pm, locals perform Cypriot **folk dances** in the plateia near the monastery.

The **Tornaritis-Pierides Municipal Museum of Marine Life,** Agias Mavris 1825, in the basement of the town hall, catalogues Cyprus's coral-reefed beaches through a collection of giant shells, fossilized fish, and stuffed migratory birds and marine animals from around the Mediterranean. An explanation of local efforts to save sea turtles, common victims of beachside development, appears too. (☎723 409. Open M-Sa 9am-2pm, Th 3-6pm. £1, students and soldiers free.)



# LIMASSOL Λεμεσος ☎05

A perpetual barrage of cultural festivities entertains foreigners and natives in this bustling industrial metropolis. Limassol is an unrepresentative but cordial introduction to Cyprus as port of entry for most passenger ferries. A maximum of 1½ hours from almost anywhere on Cyprus, many use it as a base for further exploration. While the city's elegant restaurants, designer stores, and embassies contribute a of sophistication lacking in other Cypriot cities, rapid growth and a lack of urban planning have taken their toll on the city proper, nurturing an endless row of hotels. The region's jewels—the ruins of Kourion and the gorgeous beach that dwells below—lie 10km to the west on the Akrotiri Peninsula (p. 529).

## GETTING THERE AND GETTING AROUND

**Bus #1** runs to the port from the station near the Anexartisias market, and **bus #30** runs from the **new port** to downtown Limassol (every 30min., Sa every hr.; £0.35); most pick it up in front of the CTO. After ships arrive, buses wait near the customs building; otherwise, the stop is outside the port gates. A taxi to town costs £2.50.

**Buses:** Check times with the CTO. **KEMEK** (☎747 532), 400m north of the castle at the corner of Irinis and Enosis, serves **Lefkosia** (M-F 5 per day, Sa 3 per day; £1.50) and **Paphos** (M-Sa 6-10 per week, £1.50). **Kallenos** (☎(04) 654 850) picks up by the old port on the sea front road, and heads for **Larnaka** (M-Sa 3-4 per day, £1.70). To reach the **Troodos Mountains,** contact **Kyriakos,** Thessalonkis 21 (☎362 061), which serves **Platres** (6 per week; M-Sa 11:30, return 7am; £2). Buses to Polis are via Paphos, as buses to Agia Napa, Paralimni, and Protaras are via Larnaka. The **Episkopi Village** and the **Kourion archaeological site** bus stops in front of Limassol Castle (every hr. 9am-1pm; returns 11:50am, 2:50, and 4:50pm June-Sept.; £0.60).

**Ferries: Poseidon Lines** (☎745 666; fax 745 577). Open M-F 8am-12pm and 3-5pm, Sat. 10am-2pm. **Salamis Tours** (☎355 555; fax 364 410) run to: **Haifa,** Israel (11hr., 2 per week, £50); **Rhodes** (18hr., 2 per week, £44); and **Piraeus** via **Rhodes** (45hr., 2 per week, £47).

**Cruises: Salamis Tours** (☎355 555; fax 364 410), **Louis Tourist Agency** (☎363 161; fax 363 174), and **Paradise Island Tours** (☎357 604; fax 370 298) stop at Haifa, Israel, and Port Said, Egypt.

**Service Taxis:** Taxis run 6am-6:30pm to **Lefkosia** (£3.45), **Larnaka** (£3), and **Paphos** (£2.50). Contact **Makris** (☎365 550) or **Kyriakos** (☎362 061). Free port pickup.

**Private Taxis: New Faithful Taxis** (☎354 444, 365 527, or 377 633).

**Bike and Moped Rentals:** Agencies cluster on the shore road, near the luxury hotels. Try **Allipsos** rentals along the Promenade (☎376 1650), with 24hr. service. Motorbikes £6.50 per day. For longer rentals, you'll find lower rates in Polis.

## ORIENTATION AND PRACTICAL INFORMATION

Centrally located on the south coast, 50-70km from most other major cities in South Cyprus, Limassol is the island's transportation hub. Passenger boats arrive at the **New Port,** 5km southwest of the town center at the **Old Port.** The Old Port area contains the one and only significant structure in Limassol, the **medieval castle.** Shops kindled by package tourists from the new center crowd the Castle in the day, while candle-lit local tavernas offering fresh fish dishes emerge after 10pm. The blocks neighboring the town hall contain all the necessary tourist services. A number of exquisite dining and entertainment venues are east on **Ag. Andreou,** parallel to the waterfront two blocks inland. Approximately 6km east of the town center, a row of resort hotels and apartments lines the waterfront.

**Tourist Office: CTO,** Spiro Araouzos 15 (☎362 756), on the waterfront one block east of the castle. Open M-Tu and Th-F 8:15am-2:30pm and 4-6:30pm, W 8:15am-2:30pm, Sa 8:15am-1:15pm. Office at the **New Port** (☎343 868) open immediately following arrivals. Another office in **Dassoudi Beach,** George I. Potamos Yermassoyias 35 (☎323 211), opposite the Park Beach Hotel (open same hours as Limassol office).

**Tourist Agencies: Salamis** (☎355 555), on 28 Octovriou, offers package tours and cruises. Open M-Sa 8am-1pm and 3-5pm.

**American Express:** Archiepiskopou Kyprianou 1 (☎362 045), is in the offices of **A. L. Mantovani and Sons.** Open M-F 8am-12:45pm and 2:30-5:30pm.

**Banks:** All three major banks are in the town center around Agia Napa church. Open M-F 8:15am-12:30pm with 24hr. **ATM** service. **Popular Bank,** one block from the Old Port CTO, has a convenient ATM for travelers waiting for the bus.

**Bookstores: Marilyn's Book Swap,** Kitou Kyprianou 51 (☎353 564). Open M-F 9am-1pm, Sa 9am-2pm. Wide selection of second-hand books; trade one in for store credit. **Kyriakos Bookshop,** Panayides Building 3, Grivas Dighenis (☎747 555), at the roundabout near the Museum of Archaeology. The largest selection of paperbacks, dictionaries, educational books, and magazines in the city.

**Laundromat:** (☎368 293), on Kaningos, near the Archaeological Museum. Same-day service or do it yourself. Wash £2, dry £1. Open M-Tu and Th-F 7:30am-1pm and 2-5pm.

**Police:** (☎330 411), on Gladstone and Leondios next to the hospital. Open 24hr.

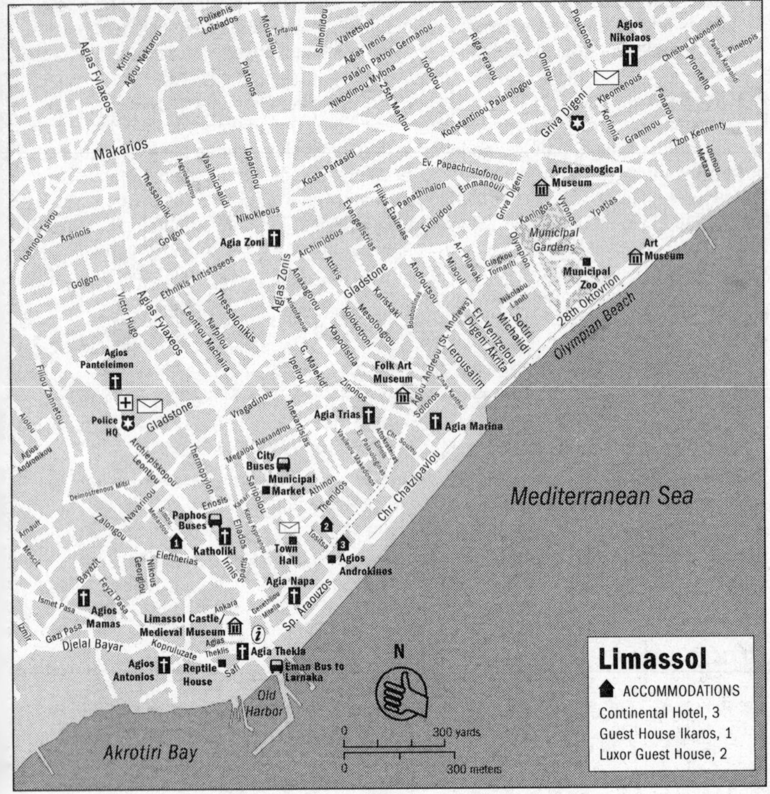


Hospital: **Government General Hospital,** outside Limassol near the village Polemidia; take the #15 bus. There are many private doctors and clinics which can be recommended through the CTO.

**Telephones: CYTA** on the corner of Markos Botsaris and Athinon.

**Internet Access: Cybernet Café,** Eleftherias 79 (☎745 093). £1.50 for 1hr., £1 per additional hr. Open 1pm-2am. **Netwave Internet Club,** Makarios 153 (☎730 239). £2.50 for 1 hr., £1 per additional hr. Open M-F 3:30pm-midnight, Sa-Su 1pm-midnight.

**Post Office:** The main office (☎330 190) is next to the central police station on Gladstone. Open May-Sept. M-Tu and Th-F 7:30am-1:30pm and 4-6pm, W 7:30am-1:30pm, Sa 9-11am. Oct.-June daily 3-5pm except W. **Postal Code:** 3900.

## ACCOMMODATIONS

Quirky guest houses around the town center are Limassol's budget best. Solo travelers, especially women, may prefer the more upscale hotels on the waterfront.

**Guest House Ikaros,** Eleftherias 61 (☎354 348). Tapestries, fish tanks, animal skins, lawn ornaments, and chandeliers. Cheap, big rooms with shared bath. First daily shower free, second £0.50. Call for reservations. Singles £5; doubles £10.

**Luxor Guest House,** Ag. Andreou 101 (☎362 265). Understated decor lends a simple elegance to this guest house. Shared baths, some balconies. Singles £5; doubles £10.

**Continental Hotel,** Spiro Araouzos 137 (☎362 530). Well priced for a seaside hotel; affords privacy and convenience. Private baths, phones. Breakfast included. Singles £15; doubles £25; triples £35; A/C £2 extra. Ask about a student discount.

## FOOD

There are tavernas, small kebab houses, and cafes throughout the city. The best option for the health- and wealth-conscious traveler is the **Municipal Market,** in a huge warehouse on the corner of Saripolou and Kanari. A lunch of fruits, veggies, bread, and cheese costs less than £1. (Open M-F 6am-1pm, M-Tu and Th-F 4-6pm.) Piddling alleyways around the castle in the Old Port area are home to some of the most intimate and fresh tavernas, while the center of the tourist district, 5km southwest, is home to more fast-food options.

**Cuckoo's Nest,** Ag. Andreou 228 (☎362 768). You'd be crazy to pass up a meal in this pleasantly nautical joint. Cheap village wine (£2.25 per bottle) flows freely under the fishing nets strewn across the ceiling. *Meze* £4, entrees £1.25-3.

**Mikri Maria,** Ankara 3 (☎357 676). Endearingly unpretentious, serving exquisite food cooked over hot coals. Try the delicious grilled *lountza* and *halloumi* or the refreshing *tzatziki.* Live guitar music in winter. Entrees £3-5.50. Open M-Sa until 10:30pm.

**Sidon,** Saripolou 71-73 (☎342 065), next to Municipal Market. Upscale restaurant with a Lebanese twist in a stunning stone room. Vegetarian *meze* £5.50, entrees £4-12.

**Ta Kokkalakia,** Ag. Andreou 239 (☎340 015). The zebra hide isn't likely to win points with animal rights activists, but the exotic garden and bar will please all. Eclectic African menu including ostrich steak and South African sausage, and an impressive South African wine selection. Entrees £5-11. Open M-Th 6pm-11pm, F and Sa 6pm-midnight.

## NIGHTLIFE

Local bars and cafes are on Ag. Andreou and near the castle, while dance clubs are at the edge of town in the tourist district. For disco dance clubs, **The Hippodrome,** on Georgiou, is the place to get down as the neighboring bars dwindle after 1am. Cover can be free for the ladies by obtaining a flyer from PR representatives. Popular dance hits and house music get even the uniformed bartenders/bouncers to leave all worries behind.

**Graffiti,** Ag. Andreou 244. Well-dressed twentysomethings congregate at this tree-laden open-air bar for good music and trendy atmosphere. Try the blue orgasm (£3.50) or the barman's special (£3-4), guaranteed to get the night in gear.

**Paradozo,** Irinis 140. Largely open-air bar with plenty of nooks for conversation. Cologne for males and black for all are prerequisites. Open 8pm-2am, weekends until 3-4am.

**The Green Movement,** Ag. Andreou 259 (☎369 595). The 200-year-old building is testament to Limassol's fine architectural past with sand-white columns prevailing from a marble patio. It serves as a bar, a stage for spontaneous jam sessions, and a meeting room for political and environmental discussions. Open M-F 10am-midnight.



## SIGHTS

**CASTLES.** The **Limassol castle,** where Richard married Queen Berengaria in 1191 (crowned the Queen of England), is the lone building of historical significance in Limassol. Richard gained possession of Cyprus after defeating Cypriot Isaac Comnenus, who had reportedly mistreated some survivors of a shipwrecked fleet on the way to the Third Crusade (see p. 15). The castle has not only interesting architecture but also a working olive press in the side yard. Destroyed by earthquakes and Genoese assaults, the only traces of the old Byzantine fort are in the western wall of the building. In the early 14th century, the Knights Templar fortified the castle's walls and covered the Gothic windows. Later, the Knights of St. John con-

verted the great Western Hall into a Gothic church and the chapel into a series of prison cells. The Ottomans claimed the castle in 1570, and the spacious West Hall was used as a prison under the British regime until 1940. Today, it is the **Cyprus Medieval Museum,** home to a scattered collection of medieval armor and religious objects, kept in what were prison cells only decades ago. *(☎305 419. Open M-F 9am-5pm, Sa-Su 10am-1pm. £1.)*

The **Kolossi castle** played a crucial role during the Crusades, when both the Knights Templar and the Knights of the Order of St. John briefly made it their headquarters. When the latter moved to Rhodes in 1310, Kolossi's wealth of vineyards made it their richest overseas possession. *(9km west of Limassol; take bus #16 (every 20min., £0.40). Open June-Sept. 7:30am-7:30pm. £0.75.)*

**SITES.** The **Archaeological Museum,** on the corner of Kaningos and Vyronos, contains an assortment of funerary *steles*, jewelry, statues, and terra-cotta figurines. *(☎330 132. Open M-F 7:30am-5pm, Sa 9am-5pm, Su 10am-1pm. £0.75.)* The **Folk Art Museum,** Agiou Andrew 253, houses 19th- and 20th-century embroidery and costumes. *(☎362 303. Open M-F 8:30am-6:30pm. £0.30.)* Kids and snakophiles may enjoy the **Reptile House,** at the Old Port, showcasing poisonous scaly critters from around the world, with eight species local to Cyprus. The friendly owner is more than happy to answer questions about anything from reptilian mating patterns to the rarities of Cyprus's finest scales. *(☎372 779. Open 9am-6pm. Adults £1, children £0.50).* The attractive **Municipal Gardens,** on the waterfront, between Olympion and Vyronos, are home to Cyprus's largest zoo and the **Municipal Open Air Theatre** that hosts an array of concerts and local Cypriot theatrical performances. *(Reserved for performances from 6-11pm, pending. The CTO has schedules.)*

**BEACHES.** The city's long stone beach might be a little too rocky and too near the busy port for the discerning beach-goer, but a new breakwater has made the area more pleasant for swimming. **Dassoudi Beach,** 3km east of Limassol, is far better. *(Take bus #6 from the Kanaris market; every 15min.; £0.50.)* The crazy **Ladies Mile Beach,** just west of the new port, is popular with locals and tourists alike. Clear blue seas preside over light grainy sand. *(Take bus #1.)* When making the excursion to Kourion, be sure to spend some time at luckily undiscovered **Kourion beach.** Lined with tourist tavernas serving fresh fish and other Cypriot delights, this relatively small beauty of a beach is worth the 15-minute walk from Kourion's reception area. *(The bus to Kourion continues to the beach area; just ask the driver.)*



## FESTIVALS

Limassol is host to an array of special events throughout the year; details are available at the CTO and in *This Month's Principal Events.* At summer's end, Limassol's gardens are transformed into a tribute to Dionysus for the Limassol **wine festival,** where participants are given a bottle to fill with as much of the local wine as they can handle. The general intoxication is compounded by music, dance, and theater. A bottle of your favorite vintage makes a great souvenir at the evening's close. (Admission £1.50.) From May to August, Limassol's abounding cultural selection of activities is centered at **Kourion.** People flock from around the world for **Shakespeare Nights** at the theater of ancient Kourion. Hand-picked performers from all of Cyprus and abroad work year-round to produce weekend shows. **Carnival,** 50 days before Orthodox Easter (usually in February), is celebrated with more vim and vigor in Limassol than anywhere else in Cyprus.

## DAYTRIP FROM LIMASSOL: KOURION

*12km west of Limassol.* ***Buses*** *leave Limassol Castle bound for ancient Kourion every hour on the hour (9am-1pm), returning at 11:50am, 2:50, and 4:50pm (£0.70). Mopeders to Kourion usually go via Episkopi village. There are no signs for Kourion until you're within about 2km of the site, so a map is essential. Open June-Sept. 8am-7:15pm; Oct.-May 8am-5pm. £1. Guidebook (£3) available at reception area.*

Vivid images of mythology and ancient life are recalled through the remarkably well-preserved ruins of Kourion—well worth a visit. First settled during the Neolithic period, Achaeans from Argos colonized Kourion during the 14th and 13th centuries BC; it would become famous for its **Sanctuary of Apollo Hylates,** fittingly meaning "of the forest" (8th century BC, 3km west from main road), and its **Stadium** (2nd century AD, 1km west of the main settlement and the basilica). In the 4th century AD, an earthquake destroyed several Cypriot coastal cities, leveling Kourion. The city was rebuilt in the 5th century, only to be burned in the 7th during an Arab raid. As a result, the **Temple of Apollo** and other parts of the Sanctuary of Apollo are largely reconstructed. A photo of the pre-reconstruction sanctuary hangs in the front office.

The majestic 2nd-century Roman **amphitheater** is open to a splendid view of the sea. It is used for **Shakespeare Nights** in June (see **Festivals,** p. 529), occasional summer concerts and theatrical productions, and weekend theater in September. The earliest structure on the site, the theater was used for dramas during Greek and Roman times, but by 300 AD, civilization-on-display had degenerated to animal fights and professional wrestling. Practically adjacent lie the **Baths and Annex of Eustolos,** built in 360 AD with mosaic floors only dating to the 5th century.

Across the road from the basilica lie a group of ruins under excavation. In the northwest corner are the remains of the **House of Gladiators** and its mosaic gladiator pin-ups, for which the house is named. The **House of Achilles,** next to the ancient theatre, has beautiful mosaic floors depicting the Rape of Ganymede and Achilles' revelation to Odysseus of his identity. A guidebook will assist in further explanation of the plentiful houses and small palaces surrounding these major sites. The nearby **Museum of Kourion** provides clear explanations of the artifacts. *(In Episkopi village. Open M and W-F 7:30am-2:30pm, Th 3-6pm. £1.)*

## PAPHOS Παφος ☎06

Paphos, the favorite city of Aphrodite, became the capital city of Cyprus under the Ptolemies of Egypt. Under their rule, the city grew fabulously wealthy, developing into a cosmopolitan commercial center and remaining thus under later Roman conquerors. When a 4th century BC earthquake ended its supremacy, the capital—and the political and social prestige—moved to Salamis (near modern Famagusta), and Paphos dwindled. In recent years, however, Paphos has reemerged as the most worthwhile destination of the Republic. Crystal waters brush the shores once occupied by ancient civilizations, while beautiful sites clutter the streets.

CYPRUS

### ORIENTATION AND PRACTICAL INFORMATION

Paphos is divided into two sections. **Ktima Paphos** (the upper section, referred to simply as "Paphos") is centered around **Pl. Kennedy,** where you'll find the shops, budget hotels, and services. **Kato Paphos** (the lower section) lies roughly 1km south, hosting luxury hotels, holiday villas, and most of the city's nightlife. **Leoforos Apostolos Pavlou** runs south from Ktima to Kato Paphos. **Vasileon** runs up the west coast to Coral Bay and is lined with costly resorts, rental places, and cafeterias. Unless noted, everything listed below is in Ktima Paphos.

**Flights: CTO** (☎422 833). Most flights arrive in Larnaka, but **Paphos International Airport** receives various European airlines and many chartered flights. Get there by private taxi from the city center or Kato Paphos (£5). **ALEPA** (☎234 410) runs to the airport (5 per day 9am-5pm; £0.50, plus £0.50 per piece of luggage); call for reservations.

**Buses: Nea Amoroza Co.,** Pallikaridi 79 (☎236 822 or 236 740), in Pl. Kennedy. Minibuses go to **Polis** (10 per day M-F 6:20am-6pm, £1); some continue on to **Pomos Village** (3 per day M-F 11-4pm, 3 per day Sa; £1.10). Service to **Limassol** (M, Tu, Th, F 8:30am and 2:30pm, W and Sa 8:30am and 1pm; £2).

**City Buses: ALEPA Bus** (☎234 410) runs the municipal bus #11 between Ktima Paphos and Kato Paphos (every 15min., £0.50). Catch one in Ktima Paphos, up the road from the post

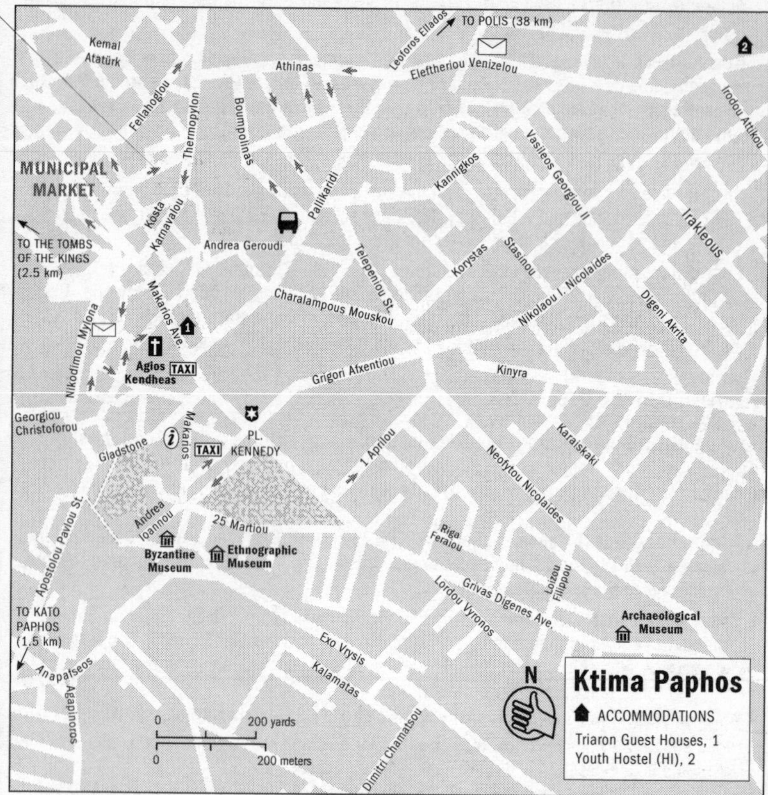


office at the market, or in Kato Paphos at any of the yellow benches on the road to town. ALEPA bus #10 goes to **Coral Bay** (20 per day, £0.50) along the coastal road. Bus #15 starts at Geroskipou Beach with stops along the coastal road (every 15-20min. 8am-7pm). Check the schedules available in the tourist office, as they are often subject to change.

**Service Taxis:** To **Limassol** (every 30min. M-Sa 5:45am-6:30pm, Su 7am-5:30pm; £2.50). Contact **Travel & Express** on Eagorou (☎233 181).

**Moped Rental:** There are several shops in Kato and Ktima Paphos and along Apostolos Pavlou, the coastal road. Cheaper options lie along Ap. Pavlou, while convenience is concentrated in Kato Paphos. Rent early in the day; rentals often run out during peak seasons. £2.50-6.50 per day. **4U Car & Bike rentals** is on Tomb of the Kings avenue (☎252 656 or 251 112). **Pentaras Rentals,** Ag. Antoniou 5 (☎241 965 or (09) 603 838), in Kato Paphos, has a few cheap cars and bikes (£5-15 per day). Call ahead. Open M-F 8am-1pm, 3-7pm, Sa-Su 8-1pm.

**Tourist Office: CTO,** Gladstone 3, just outside of Pl. Kennedy (☎232 841; fax 232 841). Open M-Tu and Th-F 8:15am-2:30pm and 3-5:15pm, W and Sa 8:15am-1:30pm.

**Travel Agency: Iris Travel,** Gladstone 10A (☎248 933 or 237 585; fax 233 960), opposite CTO. Ferry tickets to Rhodes, Crete, and Israel (from £44, student discounts up to 20%). Airline tickets to London and Greece (about £40. Student discounts up to 40%). Open M-F 8am-1pm and 4-7pm, Sa 8am-1pm. Helpful **VK Developers,** El. Venizelou 56, is right near the hostel (☎910 400; fax 910 195).

**Banks:** Concentrated around Pl. Kennedy on Makariou. All have 24hr. **ATMs.** Open M-F 8:30am-12:30pm. ATMs can be found on any major road.

**Police:** (☎806 060) on Grivas Digenes, in Pl. Kennedy, opposite the Coop Bank. English spoken; like a second tourist office. Open 24hr.

**Hospital: Paphos General** (☎240 111), on Neophytos Nicolaides, offers free first aid. English spoken. A long walk; you'll probably want to take a taxi. **St. George's Private Hospital,** El. Venizelou 29 (☎247 000), on the way to the youth hostel, has casualty and ambulance services. English spoken. Open 24hr.

**Telephone: CYTA** (☎230 228), on Grivas Digenes. Open 7:30am-7:30pm.

**Internet Access:** Scattered throughout the city. **Maroushia Fashion Cafe** (☎247 240 or 247 241) is directly on Pl. Kennedy, No. 6. Check email (£2 per hr.) while young locals play games or pool, or converse over an afternoon *frappé.*

**Post Office: Main branch,** on El. Venizelou. Open M-F 7:30am-1:30pm and (except W) 3-6pm, Sa 8:30-10:30am. Smaller office (☎240 223) on Nikodhimou Mylona. Open M-F 7:30am-1:30pm, Sa 8:30-10:30am. The post office in **Kato Paphos** (☎240 226) is on Ag. Antoniou. **Postal Code:** Ktima Paphos 8900; Kato Paphos 8903.

## ACCOMMODATIONS

Finding affordable accommodations in Paphos is a chore. Solo travelers should stick to the youth hostel or the guest house; groups might try renting a flat. Prices are higher in Kato Paphos, where the nightlife is better and the beaches are closer.

**Triaron Hotel Guest House,** Makarios 99 (☎232 193). Fairly large rooms, common living room with TV, and kitchen access make this ideally located budget option a brilliant choice. Singles £5; doubles £7.

**Youth Hostel (HI),** El. Venizelou 45 (☎232 588); walk 15min. from the plateia on Pallikaridi to Venizelou, then turn right. Out of the way, but clean and cheap. Two single-sex rooms with eight beds each; family room available. Kitchen and laundry facilities. £5 per bed for the first night, £4 per night thereafter.

**Violetta Flats,** Dionissiou 7 (☎234 109; fax 220 734), in Kato Paphos. Seven flats with kitchen, TV, and private bath. Well situated for enjoying the nightlife, poorly situated for avoiding it. Singles £14; doubles £16. A/C £2 extra.

**Zenon Gardens Geroskipou Camping** (☎242 277), east of the tourist beach, 3km from Paphos Harbor. Your best bet if you don't need to be in town. Mini-market, restaurant, and kitchen. £2 per site; £2 per 3 people; £1 per small tent. Open Mar.-Oct.

## FOOD AND NIGHTLIFE

Restaurants in Kato Paphos are geared to pound-laden foreigners, while those in Ktima Paphos can be affordable and even elegant, with local tavernas hidden among the winding streets.

**Vasano Kebab House,** Agapinoros 25 (☎242 635), Kato Paphos, for those craving the ultimate souvlaki and *sheftalia* in Paphos. Take-out is available, but a conversation with friendly locals is worth some sedentary leisure. Souvlaki £1.

**Athens,** Pallikaridi 47 (☎232 613). The place for anyone who remotely likes sugar. Scrumptious traditional pastries, cookies, and *tiropites*. Pastries £0.40 and under!

**Peggy's Miranda Cafe,** in Pl. Kennedy. Run by and for British expats, it has a colonial flavor, plus continental breakfast (£2) and a book swap. Open M-Sa 8am-4pm.

**Euro Surf Cafe,** Gladstone 1 (☎239 239), has reasonably priced quality light meals (sandwiches £1-1.50, beer £0.80). **Internet access** (£2 per hr.), and the best ham-and-cheese sandwich in Cyprus. Open until 9pm.

Virtually all of the area's nightlife centers around Ag. Napas and Ag. Antoniou, a couple of blocks inland from the waterfront in Kato Paphos; just look for bright lights and listen for loud noise. **Club 12,** on Ag. Andreou, draws all the crowds after 1am with heavy bass and the latest techno tunes. (☎(0191) 230 4848. Cover £5.) **Summer Cinema** (☎247 747 or (09) 632 229) on the waterfront, is a trendy open-air club

CYPRUS

just far enough from package hotels for the locals to call it their own. **Boogies,** on Ag. Antoniou across from the post office, is Paphos's favorite karaoke bar: after 2am, slurred but earnest Backstreet Boys renditions give way to equally enthusiastic dancing. The animated Australian hosts could persuade dead aristocrats from the neighboring tombs to karaoke. (☎244 810. Open 9pm-4am.) **Limanaki,** on the waterfront by Paphos Fort, is the place in town to watch the sunset. (Open 10am-2am.)

## SIGHTS

**MOSAICS OF KATO PAPHOS.** Over $2000m^2$ of mosaic floors from the **House of Dionysus,** the **House of Theseus,** and the **House of Aion** lie under weather protection tents adjacent to the ruins of the houses they were originally kept in. The city's, and the Eastern Mediterranean's, most dazzling ancient relics were discovered accidentally—by a farmer plowing his fields. In 1962, they were excavated by a Polish expedition that found largely intact mosaics covering 14 rooms of the expansive Roman **House of Dionysus,** named for the jug of wine depicted in many well labeled scenes. The mosaics are not unique for their time period, but are amazingly well preserved (and thus rare) examples of the norm for aristocratic decor during the Roman Period. The floors depict vibrant scenes from Greek mythology and daily life using the naturally occurring hues of the stones. Toward the water rests the **House of Theseus,** dating from the 2nd to 6th centuries AD. These ruins reveal what had once been a decadent building with marble statues, columns, and mosaic floors. Two mosaics of Theseus and Achilles are accessible by walkways. *(Enter through the gate at the start of the pedestrian way past the parking lot on the Paphos Fort road. Walk up the dirt path about 200m to the reception booth. ☎240 217. Open 7:30am-7:30pm daily. £1. Guidebook £3.)*

**TOMBS OF THE KINGS.** Apostolou Pavlou street, connecting Ktima and Kato Paphos, is lined with monuments to the Roman, early Christian, Byzantine, and Venetian periods of Cypriot history. About 2km before of Kato Paphos, a sign directs you to Paleokastra's **Tombs of the Kings.** Although those interred in the stone tombs were local aristocracy, not kings, the 2nd century remnants bear a strong resemblance to Egyptian peristyle court tombs. The larger tombs consist of an open court encircled by burial chambers, with Doric columns carved out of the underground rock and stairways leading down to the interiors. These Hellenistic and Roman tombs were later used as hideouts by Christians fleeing persecution. The most impressive are tombs 3, 4, 5, and 8, which have wonderfully musky, barely touched, extensive underground passages to wander through. *(☎240 295. Open 8am-7:30pm. £0.75.)*



**MUSEUMS OF KTIMA PAPHOS.** The **Archaeological Museum,** on Grivas Digenes, 1km from Pl. Kennedy, has an array of Bronze Age pottery, tools, sculpture, statues, and artifacts from the Houses of Dionysus and Theseus. Better to visit after having seen the Houses of Kato Paphos (above). *(☎240 215. Open M-F 7:30am-2:30pm and 3-5pm, Sa-Su 10am-1pm. £0.75.)* The private collection at the **Ethnographic Museum,** displayed in the owner's home at Exo Vrysi 1, just outside of Pl. Kennedy, takes you through different historical phases of Cypriot vocational and domestic life in a very realistic and worthwhile demonstration, complete with traditional costumes and daily tools. The garden is the highlight of the museum, with a 3rd century BC Hellenistic tomb, Christian catacombs, and *kleftiko* ovens. *(☎232 010. Open M-Sa 9am-6pm, Su 10am-1pm. £1. Guidebooks £3.)* Across the way, the **Byzantine Museum,** Andreou Ioannou 5, has icons and religious relics from local monasteries and churches, including frescoes, wood carvings, metal art works, vestments, manuscripts, and printed books. The main attraction is the oldest preserved icon in Cyprus, of Agia Marina, dating to the 7th or 8th century. *(☎231 393. Open M-F 9am-5pm, Sa 9:10am-1pm. £1.)*

**CATACOMBS OF AGIA SOLOMONI.** Descend into the dark catacombs that include a chapel with deteriorating Byzantine frescoes. Dedicated to Ag. Solomoni (Hannah), the chapel sits on the site of an old synagogue. Part of the deepest chamber is filled with lucent water, which you may not notice until you're

drenched in it. A marked tree—said to cure the illnesses of those who tie a cloth to it—marks the entrance to the catacombs. St. Paul was whipped for preaching Christianity at nearby **St. Paul's Pillar,** on the site of the Catholic church where current excavations continue. *(Tombs opposite Apollo Hotel on Ap. Pavlou. Open 24hr. Free.)*

**OTHER SIGHTS.** The remnants of an *agora* are north of the mosaics enclosed in Kato Paphos's archaeological park. The limestone Roman **odeon,** a small, roofed, semi-circular theater, is still used for dance and song performances. Pick up a schedule at the CTO. *(Open 7:30am-7pm. £0.50. You can get in free by taking a left off Ap. Pavlou onto a little side street between Ploutarchou and Ag. Lamprianou, but the park is difficult to navigate without the map available at the entrance.)* Built in the late 7th century on a hill overlooking the harbor, the **Byzantine Castle** *(Saranda Kolones)*, named as such for its many granite columns, was intended to protect inhabitants from Arab pirates. When an earthquake destroyed the castle in 1222, the Lusignans built the **Paphos Fort** at the end of the pier, which was later rebuilt by Venetians and Ottomans. Though empty, the fort is fun to walk through and the view is expansive. *(Open 10am-5:45pm. £0.75.)*

## BEACHES

The two most popular beaches stretch along **Geroskipou** to the east (more touristy) and **Coral Bay** to the north (bigger and sandier). For Geroskipou, take bus #11 from Ktima Paphos (3 per hr., £0.50); to reach Coral Bay, take bus #15 from Geroskipou (every 20min., £0.50). **Cape Lara** is host to lovely, empty sandy beaches and is a nesting site for Green and Loggerhead Turtles from June until September. The **Lara Sea Turtle Project** was conceived in 1971 to protect the turtles by ensuring that nesting continues. Turtle nests can be viewed in the Project's hatchery enclosure. Alas, there's no public transportation to Cape Lara; your best bet is a jeep excursion or motorbike. Follow signs for **Agios Georgios** from Coral Bay to find a tiny sandy beach that sits below the uninteresting church. On the road to Ag. Georgios, there are sea caves with limestone rocks peering over clear deep waters. Bask uninterrupted or explore the nearby caves. **Sundy Beach,** about 2km down the dirt road to Cape Lara, is a long stretch of practically untouched golden sand, and arguably the most secluded beach in the area.



## DAYTRIPS FROM PAPHOS: KOUKLIA

Adjacent to the modern village of Kouklia are the ruins of the great **Temple of Aphrodite** and **Paleopaphos** (Old Paphos), once the capital of a kingdom encompassing nearly half of Cyprus. The temple itself was the kingdom's religious center and a destination for pilgrims from every corner of the Roman world. Built in the 12th century BC, it thrived until the 4th century AD, when the edicts of Emperor Theodosius and a series of earthquakes reduced it to rubble. The scant remains—merely piles of rocks—make little sense without a guide. *A Brief History and Description of Old Paphos*, published by the Department of Antiquities, is available in the adjoining **Paleopaphos Museum.** *(☎432 180. Open M-F 7:30am-5pm, Sa-Su 9am-4pm. Admission to ruins, city, and museum £0.75.)* The sites are most easily seen from the excursion buses. Renting a moped is **not advisable**—the road is very dangerous; service taxis are a much safer bet.

# POLIS Πολις ☎06

Aphrodite herself took a bath in this coastal resort; for better or for worse, she no longer bathes alone. Tourism has gained a foothold in Polis, which is much smaller, cheaper, and more relaxed than Paphos, 37km to the south. Accessible by minibus and taxi, and blessed with plentiful hikes, lovely beaches, cheap accommodations, and good dining, Polis is becoming a popular base for budget travel.

**ORIENTATION AND PRACTICAL INFORMATION.** Limited street signs can make Polis difficult to navigate, although most traveler destinations are clearly

marked and consolidated in the plateia. The plateia, about 1½km from the irenic shores, is home to several locally flavored cafes and all of the town's tourist services. **Minibuses** (☎236 740 or 236 822) pass through Polis from Paphos (10 per day M-F 6:30am-7pm, 5 per day Sa 9am-4pm; £1). **Spirides Taxi Service** (☎516 161) is in the plateia. **Pegasus** (☎321 374 or 322 156), also in the plateia, rents cars, mopeds (£4 per day), mountain bikes (£3 per day), and apartments. **A&H Petrides Motors Ltd.** (☎321 541, 322 227, and 321 578, after-hours service 321 971), lies to the right of the main pedestrian way on a side street and rents motorbikes (£4-11), cars, and apartments. The **CTO** office is the island's newest, offering enthusiastic advice for day-trips and accommodations. (☎322 468. Open M-Sa 9am-1pm, 2:30-5:45pm in the summer.) The **police** are one block from the plateia in the direction of the beach and speak some English. (☎321 451. Open 24hr.) Around the plateia you'll find three **banks** with 24hr. **ATM**. (Open M-F 8:15am-noon.) The **Lemon Garden** (☎321 443), away from the plateia past the Hellenic Bank, rents and sells **sports equipment** such as jet skis, mountain bikes (£1.50-4 per day), and diving equipment (£5-15). Two **pharmacies** (☎321 253 or 321 167) are down the street from the post office. High speed **Internet access** can be found above **The Piazetta** at Pavlou Georgiou 3. (☎321 518. £2.50 for 1hr., £2 for each additional hr.) The **hospital** (☎321 431) is about a short walk from the plateia toward the campground. The **post office** is also in the plateia. (☎321 539; open M-F 7:30am-1:30pm, Th 3-5pm.) **Postal Code:** 8905.

**ACCOMMODATIONS.** **Elena's Rooms to Let** are a five-minute walk from the beach along the main road from the plateia. Rooms have TVs and refrigerators. (☎321 244 or (09) 675 474. £10-15 per night.) The **Lemon Garden** has a unique combination of quality rooms, food, and atmosphere. All rooms come with kitchenette, private bath, A/C, a view, and swimming pool access. (☎321 443. Doubles £14-16; larger rooms £16-20.) **Akamas Hotel** is the cheapest hotel in the area, on the corner when first entering the plateia on the road from Paphos. There is 24hr. reception, though the owner is sometimes found at La Piazetta on the pedestrian way. (☎321 521 or (09) 603 293. £6 per night.) Other inexpensive **rooms to let** (£5-6 per person) on the road to Latsi and to the beach and are clearly marked; inquire at a cafe if you get tired of looking. Campers are in luck: the **Campground** (☎321 526), 1½km from the town center in a fragrant, seaside eucalyptus grove, is open from Mar.-Oct.; to get there just follow the signs. It has shower facilities, a playground, and a bar that hosts beach parties every Thursday and Sunday. (£1 per person; £1.50 per tent; tent rental £2.) Call ahead in peak season as space is limited. Near the Baths of Aphrodite, 10km from Polis, a large field often holds several tents. Camping here is **illegal** but many choose to ignore the rules as long as the field remains clean; some campers seem to have taken up semi-permanent residence. The field also leads to the two main hiking trails of the Akamas peninsula.

**FOOD.** The plateia cafes and restaurants serve pretty uniform fare (Cypriot with an Italian flare) at pretty uniform prices. At **Mario's Garden Café,** located down a set of stairs beyond the Akamas Hotel, a formerly dilapidated Turkish house has become a whimsical garden cafe and bar, with statues, quirky furniture, and a central bonfire. Mario's daily specials may be the best meal in town. In town, **Arsinoe,** across from the church, serves the catch of the day. (Swordfish £3.50, fish *meze* £4.50. Open 8am-1pm and 7pm-1am.) The area's best souvlaki can be found at the main junction before reaching the road to the plateia. **Altholis' Kebab House** offers large pita souvlaki, one of which will satisfy even the largest of appetites. (☎321 270 or 321 955. Souvlaki £1, £1.50 with fries.)

**SIGHTS.** The churches of **Agios Andronikos** and **Agia Kyriaki** in Polis were built in the 15th century. In the latter half of the 16th century, invading Ottomans converted Agios Andronikos into a mosque and plastered over its frescoes. Now the plaster is being removed and the church restored. Ask for a key from the CTO to see the church yourself.

The uniquely beautiful and magically alluring pools of the Baths of Aphrodite, carved out of limestone by natural springs, are the mythical site of Aphrodite's first encounter with, and later marriage to, Akamas, the son of Theseus. The baths are where the goddess would come to cleanse herself after nocturnal exploits. According to legend, all who bathe in the pool stay forever young—unfortunately for aging tourists, the baths are strictly look-but-don't-swim. *(Take a bus from Polis: M-F 9:30, 10:30am, 2:30pm; £0.50.)*

**HIKING THE AKAMAS PENINSULA.** The easternmost home of European vegetation, the peninsula contains a remarkable array of about 600 plant species and over 160 bird species, some of which (especially the stationary varieties) are marked along the trails. Stretching to the Cape of Arnaouti, this area is a must for travelers. The two primary hiking trails, the **Aphrodite** and the **Adonis,** begin at the Baths. Both take 2-3hr., although with a side trip to **Fontana Amaroza,** the Aphrodite can take closer to half a day. The trails take the same path for the first 2km, leaving coastal scrub behind in favor of fragrant forest. They split at the ruins of **Pyrgos tis Rigainas,** believed to be a medieval monastery, where picnic tables and a potable well sit among huge oak trees. From here, the Adonis continues left, running along a series of placid streams and returning to the main road just east of the tourist pavilion. The Aphrodite continues to the right, ascending **Mt. Sotiras** before descending toward the coast into a field cleared by forest fire. It then hugs the coast all the way back to the Baths. Near the coast, the turnoff for Fontana Amaroza (the Fountain of Love) leads to a shipwreck and sea caves as well as the fountain itself. While it may have worked wonders in the past, today the *fontana* is an unimpressive stagnant pool; a hike would aim more at the scenery than the fountain itself. The CTO has free maps of the Akamas Peninsula and a helpful booklet on the vegetation and animal life.

**VILLAGES EAST OF POLIS.** Along the road to **Kato Pirgos** (65km), placid farming villages preside over lovely, deserted stretches of **beach** that are slightly rockier than those to the west. By the turnoff for Makounta and Kinousa, shaded picnic tables line a stretch of beach. Trekking east of **Pomos** demands a 45min. detour around the village of **Kokkina,** currently occupied by the Turkish military. Minibuses from Paphos continue to Pomos (£1.15), as do buses from Kato Pirgos.

About 10km south of Polis, the village of **Androlikou** has been abandoned since the Turkish military forced the Turkish-Cypriots who inhabited the village to evacuate; today goats wander among crumbling buildings. The dirt road veering off from Prodromi is the only way there. Ten kilometers further south, the happier village of **Dhrousha** has narrow winding streets, beautiful houses, and panoramic views. Both villages are best visited by following signs from route E709, which runs south from the road between Polis and Latsi.



# TROODOS MOUNTAINS ΤΡΟΟΔΟΣ

Comprised of some of the world's most geologically unique terrain, winding and underdeveloped roads, crisp mountain air, authentic village life, and Byzantine churches tucked amongst its pine-covered mountains, the Troodos are the perfect escape for hikers who wish to avoid Cyprus's summer heat. A peaceful and rejuvenating natural experience in June and early July can turn frustrating and costly in August, when the urban crowds descend, especially on weekends. In winter, **Mt. Olympus,** the highest point in Cyprus (1951m), is host to hundreds of skiers.

Public transportation to and around the area and between the villages is infrequent; scheduled stops are unreliable at best, nonexistent at worst. The best way to get around is to get a hold of your own wheels. Some hitch, but *Let's Go* does not recommend it and locals and tourists are unlikely to be friendly to hitchhikers. In the mountains, those over 17 with a valid license can easily rent mopeds (standard transmission, more than 100cc). Cars are available in Limassol, Paphos,

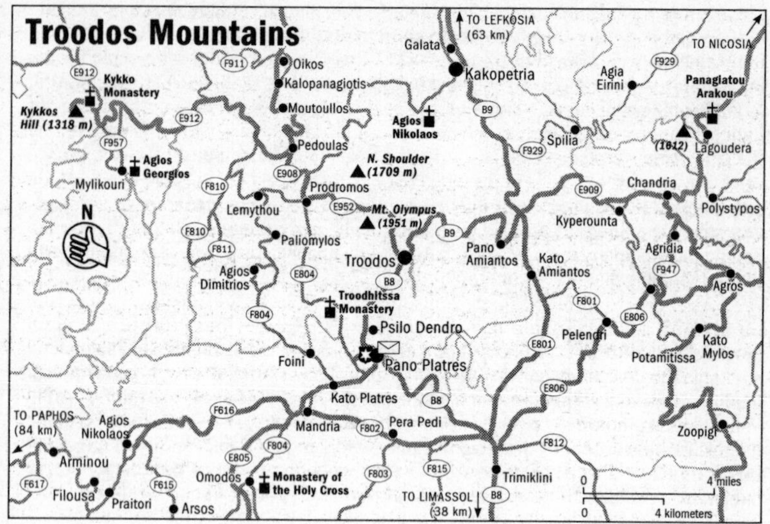


Polis, or Lefkosia for those over 23. Be careful: mountain roads are tortuous, winding, bumpy, and steep.

## PLATRES Πλατρες ☎05

Platres offers beautiful fresh mountain air and the sound of rushing streams; high branches veil the town's fountain, dainty parking area, and departing roads. Devoted to eateries and accommodations, relatively cheap and accessible by public transportation, the town offers no sites of its own, but evokes a relaxing communion with your surroundings.

**ORIENTATION AND PRACTICAL INFORMATION.** Platres is divided into the **pano** (upper) and **kato** (lower) sections. Pano Platres contains most tourist facilities, while Kato Platres is largely residential. Hiking trails are the area's main form of entertainment. **Zingas Bus,** in Lefkosia, runs to Platres on a reservation basis, so call ahead. (☎(02) 463 989. M-Sa 12:15pm, £2.) Buses from Platres for Lefkosia are also by reservation only (M-Sa 6am). From Limassol, a **Kyriakos service taxi** leaves at 11:30am, returning at 7am. (☎421 346. M-Sa, £2.) Kyriakos has an office in Platres (☎364 114) for transit in the area. **Pantelis private taxis** run within the mountain villages (☎423 333 or (09) 429 453; £5 to Troodos Square, £7 to Omodos). **Top Hill Souvenirs,** on the main street, down the hill from the post office, rents **mountain bikes.** There are some great bike routes in the Troodos—ask the staff for guidance. (☎422 022. 21-gear bikes £4 per day. Open 10am-6pm.) The **tourist office** is left of the parking lot in the plateia. (☎421 316. Open M-F 9am-3:30pm, Sa 9am-2:30pm.) The **Bank of Cyprus** is opposite the tourist office, and **Popular Bank** is just up the hill. Both have a 24hr. **ATM.** (Open M-F 8:15am-12:30pm.) The **hospital** is below Pano Platres. (☎421 324. Open 24hr.) The **police** are opposite the tourist office in a converted military chapel. (☎421 351. Open 24hr. English spoken.) The **CYTA,** next to the post office, sells phone cards. (Open M-F 7:30am-1:30pm.) The **post office** is to the left of the tourist office. (☎422 629. Open M-F 7:30am-noon and 3-5pm.) **Postal Code:** Kato 4815, Pano 4820.

**ACCOMMODATIONS, FOOD, AND ENTERTAINMENT.** From the post office, go down the hill and bear left to find **Kallithea Hotel,** where the friendly owner offers simple rooms, some with a balcony or patio. (☎421 746. Doubles £11;

breakfast included.) Ask about the rooms across the street, which are practically in the trees and offer large serene balconies (doubles £9; breakfast included). To find **Lanterns,** walk downhill from the post office and bear right; the simple rooms have private bath. (☎422 661. £10 per person; breakfast included.) **To Psilo Dentro,** a fish farm 2km north of Platres on the road to Troodos, serves sumptuous trout under a canopy of tall trees. (Whole trout £4.20. Open 8am-5pm.) Directly below the hill from the post office is the **Petit Palais Hotel Restaurant,** offering a large selection of entrees (£3-5) and crepes (£1-2). Cafes serving standard snack foods line the plateia and are constantly inhabited by tourists. For picnics, two large **grocery stores** are downhill from the post office; bear right one block past Lanterns. **Soforla Supermarket** (open 7:30am-9pm) and **Cherryland** (open 7am-10pm) stock all the necessities, plus ice cream bars.

**SIGHTS.** Five kilometers from Platres on the road from Prodromos, eight monks and countless animals make their home in the **Troodhitissa Monastery.** Although the monastery has decided not to allow visitors, those with genuine interest in unconventional architecture and history might try to visit. Dedicated to the Virgin Mary, the intimidatingly devout monastery was built to house a miracle-working icon. During the chaos of the iconoclastic movement in the 8th century, a monk hid the icon in Troodos, where it was protected by a pillar of fire. More than a century later, a sign revealed the site of the icon; the monastery now stands on the site.

**PLATRES TRAILS.** **Psilo Dentro restaurant,** 2km north of Platres on the road to Troodos, marks the starting point for three main hiking trails. A helpful map of Platres area hikes and bicycle routes is available at the Platres tourist office. Most hikes lead toward various vantages of **Kaledonia Falls,** the Troodos region's most celebrated and picturesque spot. Although not impressively high, the delicate trickles of water are lovely. Left of the restaurant, a path accessible by car and mountain bike reaches the falls early, affording postcard views before continuing through a forested path for 3km (about 1-2hr. uphill). The trail ends by the Troodos's presidential palace, built by the famous French poet **Arthur Rimbaud.** At the end of the trail, veer left to reach the Platres-Troodos road. To the right of the restaurant, the path joins with an easterly trail before reaching a junction. From here, yellow signs lead to either the top of Kaledonia falls or the south shoulders of Mt. Olympus. Also to the right of the restaurant, the least impressive but most ambitious trail leads to the unremarkable **Mesopotamos Monastery;** the 9km (a generous 4hr.) dirt track is accessible to mountain bikes.

CYPRUS

## OMODOS ☎05

Ten kilometers southwest of Platres, Omodos is a place where old village folk smile kindly as you walk past local wineries. The handmade cordial lace, gorgeous sunsets, and lack of exhaust fumes are an added bonus. Your introduction to the town will be the lively, cobbled plateia, where you can buy a bottle of dry local wine (£2-3) or fiery *tsipouro*, a Cypriot-made whiskey, from any one of the elderly, congenial vendors.

**PRACTICAL INFORMATION.** No buses run to Omodos, but a **taxi** from Platres will run £6-7. There is **no CTO,** but this largely residential village is very easy to navigate. The **hospital** (☎421 254) is directly outside the plateia and holds unreliable hours, but the **doctor** is always on call (☎(097) 26965). The closest **police** station is in Pano Platres. The **post office** is on the street to your left when facing the monastery's entrance (open M-F 8am-noon). **Postal Code:** 4820.

**ACCOMMODATIONS AND FOOD.** Rooms to let do exist at what seems like a village-wide fixed price (doubles £15), although a lengthy stay in Omodos would only be convenient for those with private transport. **Konstantina's Rooms to Rent** (☎421 376) come furnished with sizable balconies, refrigerators, and private

baths. **Taverna Makrinar** is planted in the heart of Omodos (follow signs from the plateia). *Bouzoukia* strum into the night in this traditionally decorated taverna. Try the *moussaka* (£3) and local wine (£3.50-4). (☎421 151. Open M-F 8:30-10am, 2:30pm-3am.) Be sure to take advantage of **free wine** tasting at the cafe on the corner outside the monastery's side entrance.

**SIGHTS.** The labyrinthine streets of gentrified Omodos lead past souvenir shops, an arts center, traditional whitewashed homes, and a restored wine press (*linos*, officially declared an "Ancient Monument" when restored in 1980-84). Elderly women sit in their doorways along the main paths embroidering beautiful pieces of lace; purchase some for a gift or souvenir. The plateia is also home to the famous 14th century **Monastery of the Holy Cross.** The upper level of the monastery is closed to visitors due to the reconstruction following a 1996 earthquake, but the church and a number of other structures are still open (M-Sa 8am-6pm, Su noon-6pm). To the left of the main entrance in the monastery is the door of the room that St. Helen stayed in when visiting. Alive with biblical history, the church contains the bloodstained piece of rope used to tie Christ that St. Helen brought with her; it lies hidden from the public. The skull of Apostle Philipos, the bones of 26 saints, and a unique icon of Christ whose eyes seem to follow you wherever you stand are some of the amazing relics contained within the monastery.

## TROODOS Τροοδος ☎05

Penetrating Cyprus's clear skies in the mountains that bear its name, the Troodos district hoards magnificent views of the entire island. However, Troodos itself is merely an aggregate of tourist and camping facilities that provides another launch point for exploration. Just 10km north of Platres, the area can be reached by **Clarios Bus Co.** in Lefkosia if you make reservations. (☎453 234. Leaves M-F 11:30am, returns 6:30am; £1.10.) A **private taxi** costs £17 from Lefkosia and £5 from Platres. You can also **hike** uphill (at least 2hr.) from Platres. The **Troodos campground,** 2km north of the plateia in a pine forest, provides laundry facilities, a mini-market, a bar/restaurant, and a first aid station. The exceptionally accommodating owner will be happy to answer your questions and offer assistance should you need it. (☎422 249. £1.50 per person.)

**TROODOS TRAILS.** Four spectacular hikes originate in the Troodos area. Detailed maps are available at all Cyprus tourist offices. From Troodos, **Artemis** begins 200m up the road to Prodromos. The circular trail wraps around **Mt. Olympus** for 7km, or roughly 3½hr. Although relatively flat and mostly covered in black pines, the hike provides majestic views of Cyprus in its entirety. From the Troodos post office, the **Atalante** trail essentially mimics the Artemis trail at a lower altitude. The trail runs 12km (about 5hr.), ending at the Prodromos-Troodos road, near the chromium mine camp. A fresh mountain water spring 3km into the hike will sustain hikers, allowing ceaseless photography of the striking views from Limassol to the Northern occupied territory, and everything between. The 3km **Persephone** trail leaves from the coffee shop in Pl. Troodos and gradually descends to a divine lookout point among huge slabs of limestone rock. The **Kaledonia** trail, the shortest, begins 2km from Troodos on the road to Platres, passes the Kaledonia Falls, and ends at Psilo Dentro restaurant near Platres.

## KAKOPETRIA Κακοπετρια ☎02

Kakopetria is popular with urban Cypriots and foreign tourists alike. Wood and stone traditional village houses perch beside the fresh mountain stream that flows through the center of town. According to local legend, the large rock perched on the hillside rolled over and crushed a couple as they walked past the church, initiating a tradition in which newlyweds sit on the rock to ensure marital stability. Lately, Kakopetria has become a model of the nation's trend toward "agrotour-

ism," ideally a seamless blend of tourism and tradition. While a bit contrived, the result is an aesthetic success, ensuring tasteful tourism within its lively plateia.

**ORIENTATION AND PRACTICAL INFORMATION.** **Clarios** (☎453 23 34) runs buses to **Kakopetria** from **Lefkosia** (10 per day M-F 6:10am-5:30pm, July-Aug. 13 per day M-F 6:10am-7pm, Su 2 per day; £1.10) and back to Lefkosia from **Kakopetria** (9 per day M-F 4:30am-2:30pm, July-Aug. Su 6am and 4:30pm; £1.10). Some buses continue to **Troodos** by reservation. **Private Taxis** from Lefkosia cost £15.

Kakopetria consists of the main drag, **Makarios,** which leads into the village, passes through the plateia, and continues to the adjoining village of Galata. The "Old Road" lies across the stream and can be accessed with a turn off Makarios at the Village Pub. All three major banks (**Hellenic Bank, Popular Bank,** and **Bank of Cyprus**) are in the plateia and have 24hr. **ATM** service. (Open M-F 8:15am-12:30pm.) The **police station** is right up the hill from the Bank of Cyprus (☎922 420/255. Open 24hr.). A **pharmacy,** on Makarios, is toward the Lefkosia-Troodos road. (☎922 020. Open M-F 9:30am-9pm.) The **post office** is up the hill from the Bank of Cyprus. (☎922 422. Open M-F 7:30am-1:30pm.) **Postal Code:** 2810.

**ACCOMMODATIONS AND FOOD.** Kakopetria has a number of budget domatia above or behind restaurants, many along the stream with clearly visible signs pointing you in their direction. For those looking for a longer, more expensive getaway, try staying in one of the agrotourism inns, gorgeous restored homes rented out for several days.

**TUTTI FRUITY** Citrus fruits, apples, and watermelons are succulent treats found only seasonally in most of the world. But Cyprus's booming **agrotourism** industry brings people to traditional homes, country life, and oh-so-ripe fruit. The old dwellings have been beautifully restored and allow city-folk to get a glimpse of old village farming life, work, and table—for a fee. Saturday morning *laiki agora* brings together farmers from nearby villages, facilitating the trade of their produce to visitors staying in the hotels and inns, combining tourism and the farmstand. Try bargaining with the wrinkled men selling fresh tomatoes or fruit, and take part in a tradition older than most of the *archaia* you visit.



To reach the best deal in the mountains, follow signs for the police station from the plateia, then turn right: the modern rooms of **Hekali Hotel,** Gr. Digenis 22, are an improvement on the area's rooms to let. All have TV, phone, and balcony with peaceful views of the village. (☎992 501; fax 922 503. Handicapped accessible. Singles £14; doubles £22.) Three rooms below **Serenity Coffeeshop** are on Old Kakopetria street, between the bridge and Linos Inn. The quiet, intimate location beside a forest and stream explain the name. (☎922 602. Singles £15; doubles £20.)

Kakopetria has more dining options than neighboring towns. Restaurants on the plateia cater to tourists serving Cypriot and more mainstream dishes, while cheaper kebab houses are a bit off to the side. Follow the signs over a log bridge to arrive at **Maryland at the Mill,** looking out over a neighboring former mill along the stream. This slightly upscale eatery serves up a fresh trout specialty (£5.50) among other sumptuous entrees (£1.50-5; open M-F noon-11pm, Sa-Su noon-3:30pm and 7:30-11pm). **Plateia Pizza** dishes up sizable orders of what the chef calls Australian pizza (try vegetarian or "South of the Border," £3.40 and up) on a large outdoor patio. (Open 8am-midnight, delivery until 10pm.)

**SIGHTS AND ENTERTAINMENT.** Nightlife in Kakopetria centers around its single nightclub. **Clarion Brand Disco,** Makarios 21, across the stream from the plateia, lights up the night; shuffle in your hiking boots alongside teenagers from neighboring villages, who gather to hear their favorite Greek dance hits. (Cover £3-

5. Open F, Sa 7pm-2am.) For a less raucous night, stroll the byways of Old Kakopetria and savor the view.

Well-preserved village houses line the cobbled streets. Kakopetria and its smaller neighbor, **Galata,** have five Byzantine churches between them dating to the 13th century. The most notable, 11th-century **Agios Nikolaos tis Stegis,** shines 3km southwest of Kakopetria on the road to Troodos. Local buses fetch the elderly from surrounding villages for Sunday morning services. Frescoes dating back to 1320 ornament the walls. The caretaker provides a tour detailing the history of the church and its frescoes upon request. (Open Tu-Sa 9am-4pm, Su 11am-4pm.) For ambitious hikers looking for a long daytrip, an 8km uphill hike from Ag. Nikolaos tis Stegis to Troodos Square is an option. The trail is well maintained and buses departing from Troodos for Kakopetria and Lefkosia at 6:30am are by reservation only; call **Clarios Bus Co.** (☎453 234).

The monastery of **Panagiatou Arakou,** 16km southeast of Kakopetria in the village of Lagoudhera, displays elaborate 12th-century frescoes, including the dome depiction of Christ Pantokrator restored in 1968. (Open 8am-7pm daily.)

## KYKKO MONASTERY Movη Kυkkο

*From the Leonidou station in Lefkosia, Kambos (☎(09) 623 604 or 02 94 253; open 9am-6pm) sends buses to Kykko Monastery (leaves Lefkosia at noon and returns at 6am the next day; £3.50, £1.75 each way). Most access Kykko by car. For rental opportunities, see Lefkosia (p. 542) or Limassol practical information (p. 525). Rooms are available, but are meant for those who've come for religious purposes.*

Kykko Monastery, 20km from Pedhoulas in the northwest part of the mountains, prides itself on being the wealthiest and most prestigious monastery on Cyprus. Standing strong and solitary in the depths of the Troodos mountains, this architecturally daunting building is the result of centuries of renovation after each of four accidental fires in AD 1365, 1541, 1751, and 1813. The monastery was founded in the early 11th century by the hermit Isaiah. He was rewarded with the Apostle Luke's **icon of the Virgin Mary** after curing the Byzantine Emperor's daughter; it's one of three icons in the world blessed by the saint herself. The celebrated icon has survived intact, but is too holy to be viewed directly and is consequently completely ensconced in mother of pearl and silver casing; not even the monks have seen it, per the Virgin Mary's request. The gaudiness of the casing is in keeping with the rest of the monastery; the palatial courtyard seems more suitable for revelry than religion.

During the Cypriot struggle for independence (p. 512), Kykko was a communication and supply center and the home of **Archbishop Makarios III.** Only 1.5km away was the secret headquarters of the first military leader of the struggle, General George Grivas. Today, the surprisingly friendly monks seem very aware of their monastery's historical importance and are willing to give extensive explanations upon request. The sanctity of the space prohibits photography, but they sell a video of the interior in their giftshop.

The **tomb of Makarios,** first president of the Cypriot Republic (p. 512), is in the hills 2km west of Kykko. By Makarios's request, the site, guarded by two Greek Cypriot soldiers, is partially open to the east so that on the day of Cypriot reunification, sunlight will enter his tomb, and he can celebrate with his people. Just above the tomb, the path leads up to an icon of the Virgin, called the *throni* (small throne). Scarves covering the path are the gifts of sick children hoping to be cured.

# NICOSIA ΛΕΥΚΩΣΙΑ ☎02

Landlocked Lefkosia, sliced in two by the barbed-wire Green Line, has the sad distinction of being the last divided city in the world. The more modern New City is separated from the Old by Venetian walls, built on top of the ancient Roman town of Ledra in a failed attempt to fend off Ottoman cannons. In 1570, the Ottomans took only seven weeks to conquer Lefkosia (p. 511), proving the uselessness of the

walls. They ruled the city for several hundred years before British imperialists arrived in 1878; the British crown governed Cyprus until independence in 1960, when Lefkosia became the capital of the island nation. In the aftermath of 1974, Lefkosia was split into Turkish and Greek sections (p. 513), and today it remains the under the watchful eye of the UN. Passage across the Green Line is sanctioned from the Ledra checkpoint on the southern side.

**CROSSING THE GREEN LINE** The infamous Green Line is Nicosia's main attraction. The only spot on the border where photography is permitted is Ledra, where the military has erected a makeshift shrine to the north. Crossing the Green Line from the south is fairly easy—just follow the strict regulations, and don't bother trying to get information about North Nicosia on the southern side: Greek Cypriots have not crossed the line for over 20 years. You will not be permitted to cross if you are a Greek citizen or if you are of Greek descent. Head for the **Ledra Palace Checkpoint** between the Greek Cypriot and Turkish walls. This former hotel, its interior gutted and its exterior marred by bullet holes, stands on neutral territory and houses U.N. troops. You will need to show your passport on the Greek Cypriot side and again on the Turkish side, where you'll fill out a general information form in order to receive a special visitor's visa (£3-4, fluctuating based on currency rates). **Do not let them stamp your passport.** If they stamp your passport, you will not be readmitted to Greek Cyprus. They will, however, give you a form to be stamped by someone at another window. Hold on to this form—you will need it to cross back after your visit.

1. You may enter North Cyprus 8am-1pm, but must return by 5pm. No exceptions. You cannot start a trip through North Cyprus and Turkey by crossing the Green Line; guards will not allow you to cross with a large backpack or bag.
2. Cars are not allowed—you must cross by foot.
3. As in other areas of Lefkosia and Cyprus, do *not* take pictures of anything that has to do with the military or police.
4. You are officially not allowed to buy anything on the Turkish side. If you wish to buy food, you must exchange your much desired Cypriot pounds for Turkish lira. Also, any items purchased in the north will be confiscated upon your return to the south.
5. If you have a problem, ask the U.N. soldiers (in blue berets) for help.



# LEFKOSIA (SOUTH NICOSIA)

The Old City of Lefkosia, as it is commonly called by Greek Cypriots, caters to history-hungry and politically inclined tourists. Outside the Venetian walls that embrace the Old City, the New City sprawls, an expanding metropolis. At the moment, the city is restoring the old Laiki Yitonia (the pedestrian shopping district) and constructing new museums and monuments, catering to tourists as it preserves its history. Lefkosia is geared toward bureaucrats rather than backpackers, and its only attraction is the grim Green Line. The city offers the true Cyprophile a chance to interact with the island without the frills of coastal tourism, and gives an intimate view of the political strife that has shaped modern Cyprus.

## GETTING THERE AND GETTING AROUND

**Buses: Kallenos** (☎654 850), in Pl. Solomos, runs to **Larnaka** (7 per day M-F 9am-6:30pm, Sa 9, 11am, 1pm; £1.50). **Kemek,** Leonidou 34 (☎463 989), runs to **Limassol** (5 per day M-F 6:30am-4pm, £1.50) and **Paphos** (M-Sa 6:30am, £3). **ALEPA** (☎625 027), near Pl. Solomos, runs to **Limassol** (M-Tu and Th-F 12:30pm and 3:45pm, £1.50) and **Paphos** (M-Tu and Th-F 3:45pm, W and Sa 12:45pm; £3). **EMAN,** Pl. Eleftherias 2 (☎473 414), picks up at the bus stop 100m east of the post office for

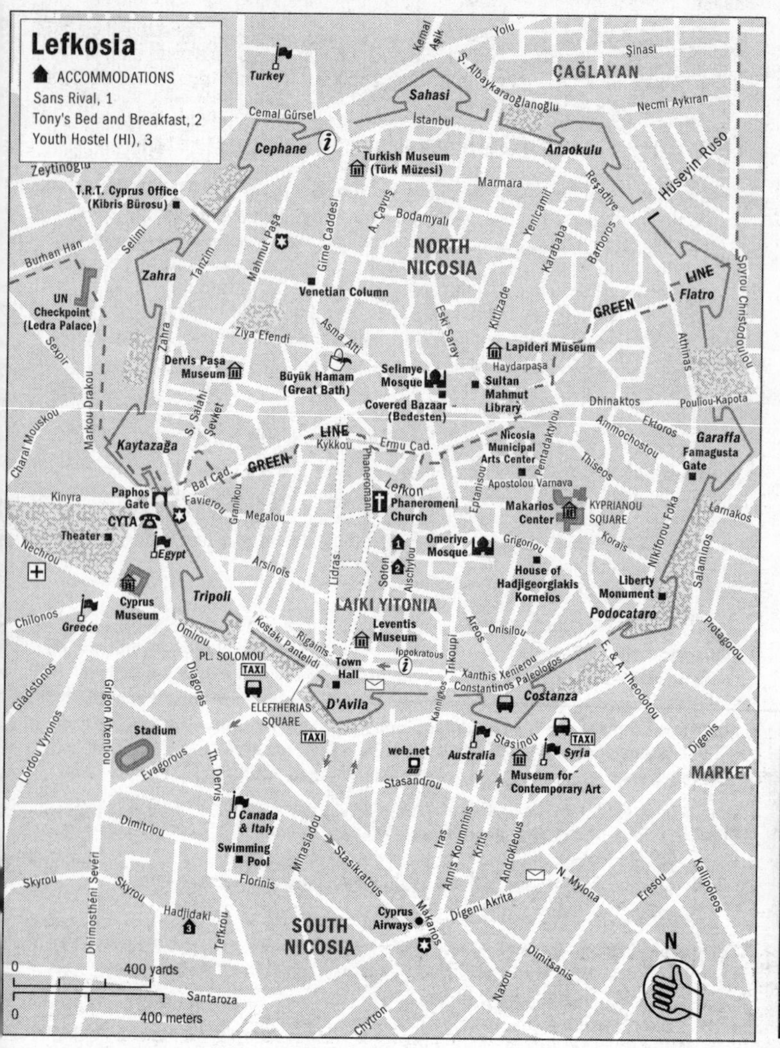


Agia Napa (M-F 3pm, £2). **Paralimni-Dherynia,** Stasinou 27 (☎444 141), at Kyriakas Taxi, runs to **Parlimni, Protaras,** and **Agia Napa** (M-F 1:30pm, £2.50). **Zingas** (☎463 989), at the Kemek office, runs to **Prodromos, Pedoulas,** and, if you make a reservation, **Platres** (M-Sa 12:15pm, £2). **Clarios** (☎453 234), 200m east of Pl. Eleftherias on Costanze Bastioon, runs to **Kakopetria** (13 per day M-Sa 6:10am-7pm, £1.10; Su 2 per day, £1.90) and **Troodos** (by reservation). **Kambos,** on Leonidou, runs to **Kykko Monastery** (M-Sa leaves at noon and returns 6am the next day, £2). A free route map of all the urban **Lefkosia buses** is available at the CTO (☎473 414 or 778 841).

**Service Taxis: Makris** and **Kyriakos** merged into **Travel & Express** (☎661 010), and they run taxis every 30min. (M-Sa 5:45am-6:30pm, Su 7am-5:40pm) to: **Limassol** (£3.45), **Larnaka** (£2.40), and **Paphos** (£6). Call ahead. **Solis** (☎46 63 88), on Tripolis Bastion, runs taxis (M and W-Sa 1:30pm, £5) and a minibus (M-Tu and Th-Sa 11:30am, £4) to **Polis.**

**Private Taxis:** Are easily summoned from street sides and corners. Taxi stations are in Pl. Eleftherias, or call **National Taxi** (☎666 300) on Platialpirou for service as well. Open 24hr. Private taxis are expensive, running about £0.65 initial charge and £0.22 for every subsequent km in the day or £0.88 initial charge at night.

## ORIENTATION AND PRACTICAL INFORMATION

The easiest way to orient yourself in Lefkosia is to use the Venetian walls. The Green Line, running east to west at the north end of the city, divides the **Old City** into Greek and Turkish sectors. Within the walls, travelers can find most budget lodgings, museums, tavernas, and sights. From **Pl. Eleftherias,** Evagoras heads southwest into the New City, while **Lidras** street, the primary pedestrian and tourist core, runs north intersecting the Green Line. Intersecting Evagoras are Makarios Ave., Diagoras, and Th. Dervis, which leads to the youth hostel. **Laiki Yitonia,** southeast of Lidras street, is the prominent pedestrian and tourist district. The New City is more spread out, making transportation on foot difficult; visitors to the New City are dependent on a rental car, motorbike, or the bus. Sheet metal barriers or white and blue dividers confront you when you walk down the streets. **Do not ignore the signs forbidding photography.**

**Tourist Office: CTO,** Aristokypros 11 (☎674 264), in the Laiki Yitonia; entering Pl. Eleftherias from the New City, turn right and follow signs from the post office. Free maps, a list of buses, and a guide to events in the city will prove helpful. Open M-F 8:30am-4pm, Sa 8:30am-2pm. A free English-language walking tour through the old village of Kaimakli leaves from here (2hr., M and Th 10am).

**Embassies and Consulates:** See p. 514.

**Banks: Bank of Cyprus:** main branch, Phaneromeni 86 (☎477 774), offers **ATM** and **currency exchange.** Open M-F 8:15am-12:30pm. A convenient branch (☎365 959) in Laiki Yitonia on Drakos with 24hr. **ATM.** Open M-F 8:30am-12:30pm. Additional ATMs are located throughout the city.

**American Express: A.L. Mantovani and Sons,** Agapinoras 2D (☎443 777), 1km south of Pl. Solomos down Makarios. Open M-F 8am-12:45pm and 3:30-6pm. Deals mostly with travelers checks and currency exchange.

**Public Toilets:** In the parking lots along the Venetian walls (follow the W/C signs). Surprisingly sanitary and toilet paper is blessedly abundant.

**Police and Fire Station:** (☎303 090). The 2 buildings are next door to one another, 150m east of Paphos Gate on Digenis, inside the wall. Open 24hr.

**Hospital:** (☎451 111), at Omirou and Nechrou streets. Open 24hr.

**Telephone: CYTA,** Egypt 14 (☎470 200). Customer service open M-F 7:15am-1:30pm; cashier open M-F 7:15am-6pm, Sa 7:15am-1pm. 24hr. telecard machine outside.

**Internet Access: Web.net cafe** at Stasandrou 10C (☎753 345), at the beginning of the New City. Enjoy the virtual garnish and consistent availability of over 20 computers while soaking in the latest beats (£2.20 per hour). The snack bar offers drinks from £0.60-1.30. Open M-Sa 10:30am until late and Su 5:30pm until late.

**Post Office: Main office** (☎303 231) on Constantinos Paleologos, east of Pl. Eleftherias. Open M-Tu and Th-F 7:30am-1pm and 4-7pm, W 7:30am-1pm. Branch offices on Digenis, Palace, and Loukis Akitas (☎302 531). **Postal Code:** 1903.

## ACCOMMODATIONS

Lefkosia's few budget accommodations lie within the city walls.

**Sans Rival,** Solon 7 (☎474 383), in the Laiki Yitonia. Generally booked. Elevators take you to red-carpeted hallways leading to fairly spacious rooms with spartan decor and A/C. Singles £13; doubles £16.

**Tony's Bed and Breakfast,** Solon 13 (☎666 752 or 667 794; fax 454 225), in the Laiki Yitonia. Traditional decorations and a Victorian staircase lead to rooms of various sizes, all with radio, phone, hot water pots, fridge, and TVs. A large rooftop patio looks over the old city. Singles £11, with bath £14; doubles £20-22; triples £32; quads £40. A/C £1 extra per night; full English breakfast included.

**Youth Hostel (HI),** Hadjidaki 1 (☎674 808). Overgrown plants drape the entrance to this house turned hostel. Little supervision and few guests. Kitchen, yard, and front veranda provide meeting spots for travelers (if you can find any). Separate sex rooms have 6 beds, and a family room has 5 beds. Showers included. Sheets £1. Dorms £4.

## FOOD

Dining choices in Lefkosia include tavernas with live music, pubs, pizzerias for the *neolaia*, and full restaurants. Touristy joints around Laiki Yitonia serve Cypriot *mezedes*, while in the depths of the backroads in the Old City, smaller restaurants cater to locals. For the cheapest option in Lefkosia, head to the **municipal market** on the corner of Digenis Akritas and Kallipolis, a huge warehouse filled with food stands. Hanging pigs will make you either ravenous or vegetarian. (Open 6am-1pm and 4-6pm.) A colorful streetside **produce market** near Pl. Eleftherias along Constantinos Paleologos beckons veggie lovers (open W 9am-1pm and 4-6pm).

**Mattheos** (☎475 846), behind Phaneromeni Church, near a small mosque. Older couples crowd the tables pouring onto the street. Taverna-style food at low prices. *Koupepia* (stuffed grape leaves) and *mousaka* £3 each. Open 5am-7pm.

**Berlin #2 Cafe** (☎474 935), on the corner of Lefkon and Phaneromni. This popular takeout joint serves up *kebab*, salad, and pita (£2.50) in the shadow of a UN guard station. Open M-Tu and Th-F 7:30am-6:30pm; closes early W and Sa.

**Natural Choice,** Chytron 11 (☎362 674), in the New City, convenient to the youth hostel. Wash down your fresh, seasonal stuffed veggies or chicken curry (£2-4) with a huge slab of sugarless apple pie (£0.75). If you don't feel healthy enough after the meal, stock up on vitamins or self-help books in the adjacent health food store.

## NIGHTLIFE AND ENTERTAINMENT

For late night entertainment, scattered coffeeshops, pubs, and dance clubs are voyeur-beckoning cabarets that keep Lefkosia nights busy. **Dance clubs** appear mostly in the outskirts of the New City. For the latest tunes, try the Strovolos area along Ag. Prokopiou and Leoforos Georgiou Griva Digeni or **Zoo,** Stasinou 15. Also a restaurant, this slightly upscale joint draws large crowds and is *the* most popular dance spot in Lefkosia. (☎758 262. Open daily 10am-1am and weekends until 4am.)

**Ta Kala Kathoumena,** Nikokleous 21 (☎464 654), tucked into an alley behind Paneromni Church. Lefkosia's young intellectuals gather at night for debate, backgammon, coffee and drinks (£0.40-£1.20). Open 11am-midnight or when the crowd abates.

**Zanettos Taverna,** Trikoupi 65 (☎765 501), near Omeriyeh Mosque. Open since 1938, this taverna is lined with paintings of local landscapes. Stairs lead to lofted seating where you can relish meat and fish *meze* (£6), kebabs, and fantastic *Halloumi* specials (£2). Open daily from noon-4pm and 5pm-midnight.

**Odyssea Pub,** Pl. Eleftherias (☎451 174). Unbelievably crowded watering hole, popular with twentysomething Cypriots; people watch with a good beer from 11pm on. Beer £1.25-2. Open 8am-4am.

## SIGHTS

**FAMAGUSTA GATE.** Along the Venetian Walls at the end of Theseus street is the recently restored Famagusta Gate. The main entrance to old Lefkosia, built in 1567, it now hosts plays, concerts, exhibitions, and lectures; check the schedule at the CTO. *(Open M-F 10am-1pm, 4-7pm. Free.)* A short ways down Korais street, a marble monument, the **Freedom Statue** or *Agalma Eleftherias*, depicts fourteen Cypriots, each representing a period of the island's history, being released from the iron bars that have restrained them.

**LEVENTIS MUNICIPAL MUSEUM.** This museum, which won the European Museum of the Year award in 1991, chronicles the history and social development of Lefkosia from 3000 BC to recent years. Peer through the glass at your feet as you walk over an authentic ancient tomb. The second floor consists mainly of traditional costumes, household items, and weaponry. Don't overlook the photographic chronology or the courtyard garden with its authentic Turkish baths. *(Hippocratis 17. ☎451 475. Open Tu-Su 10am-4:30pm. Free. Handicapped accessible.)*

**PHANEROMENI CHURCH.** A point of nationalist pride to Greek Cypriots, the Phaneromeni Church survived a Turkish attempt to transform it into a mosque. Dating to the 14th century, the ornate *iconostasis* is engraved with Old Testament images. *(In the center of the Old City off Ledgras street. Open 6am-8pm daily. Free, but donations are welcome.)*

**PLATEIA ARCHBISHOPRIC KYPRIANOS.** Pl. Archbishopric Kyprianos consists of a 15th-century Gothic monastery that houses the **Makarios Cultural Center.** Also in the plateia, the **Byzantine Art Gallery** has the island's largest collection of icons, with over 150 pieces from the 8th to the 18th centuries. Icons from occupied northern Cyprus hold special significance to local refugees. *(☎430 008. Open M-F 9am-4:30pm, Sa 9am-1pm. £1, groups of 6 or more £0.50 per person.)* The **Folk Art Museum** presents Cypriot woodcarving, embroidery, pottery, basketry, and metalwork from the 18th to 20th centuries. *(☎463 205. Open M-F 9am-5pm, Sa 10am-1pm. Admission £1. Guidebook 50¢.)* The neighboring **Greek Independence War Gallery,** founded in 1961, contains photographs and items from the struggle for *enosis*, the union of Cyprus with Greece. *(☎302 465. Open M-F 9am-4:30pm, Sa 9am-1pm. £0.50.)* Also in the area is the **St. John Cathedral,** built in 1662 by Archbishop Nikiforos with a single nave and five pointed arches. The tablets adorning the entrance were transferred from Venetian and Frankish buildings. *(Open M-F 8am-noon and 2-4pm, Sa 9am-noon. Free.)*



**OTHER SIGHTS.** Near Pl. Kyprianos is the luxurious, 18th-century **House of Hadjigeorgiakis Kornesios,** known also as the **Konak Mansion** and home of the famous *dragoman*, or Ottoman interpreter. With an enchanting courtyard and a floor plan in the shape of the letter $\pi$, the monument is a significant example of the urban architecture of the last century of Ottoman Rule. *(Patriach Gregory 18. ☎305 316. Open M-F 8am-2pm, Sa 9am-1pm. £0.75.)*

The **Ledra Museum and Observatory** allows tourists to investigate the Northern part of the city from the 11th floor windows atop the Woolworth building. Free binocular usage and guiding plaques aid viewing. *(☎679 369. Corner of Arsinois and Ledra. £0.40.)* The **Lefkosia Municipal Gallery of Contemporary Art** has three floors of works from established and up-and-coming abstract, expressionist, and sculptural Cypriot artists. *(Crete 1. On the edge of the New City across from the Ömeriye Mosque. Open Tu-Sa 10am-5pm and Sa 10am-1pm. Free.)*

The **Ömeriye Mosque**'s easy-to-spot huge minaret makes it a landmark. It is one of the only mosques still in operation in southern Cyprus and dates back to the 14th century. The prophet Ömer may have rested at the mosque's locale when passing through Lefkosia. *(Tillirias 8. At Trikoupi and Tillirias Sq.)* The **Turkish Baths** are across from the mosque. *(☎477 588. Baths open to women W and F 8am-3pm; for men Tu, Th, and Sa-Su 8am-7pm, W and F 3-7pm. £4.)*

**CYPRUS MUSEUM.** Here you'll find the most extensive collection of ancient art and artifacts on the island, from pre-Hellenic periods through the Byzantine era. Amateur archaeologists can compare local jewelry across eras, while everyone will feel dwarfed by ancient, larger-than-life terra-cotta figures. *(Mouseiou 1, near the Paphos Gate. ☎303 112. Open M-Sa 9am-5pm, Su 10am-1pm. £1.50.)*

**BOTANICAL GARDENS.** Next to the archaeological museum sprawls the colorful botanical gardens, a spot popular with locals for picnics. The gardens' aviaries showcase most of the island's indigenous species. *(Open 8am-10pm. Free.)*

# NORTH NICOSIA

North Nicosia is overrun with green-clad troops, who have been instructed to be kind to tourists. Unlike the conservationism affecting its southern counterpart, modernization has seized the Old City of North Nicosia. The glitzy highrises of Girne Caddeşi contrast with the barbed wire and oil barrels of the Green Line and the crumbling walls of the Old City.

## ORIENTATION AND PRACTICAL INFORMATION

From the south at the **Ledra Palace** crossing, a roundabout with a Turkish **victory monolith** in the middle is 500m up the street. Follow the city walls to **Girne Gate** (Kyrenia Gate). From there, **Girne Caddeşi,** the main street, runs to the main square, **Atatürk Meydanı,** and continues to the Green Line.

Because of the fluctuating value of the Turkish lira, prices for goods and services in North Nicosia are listed in US dollars. For **police,** dial 155; **emergency ambulance,** dial 112; **fire,** dial 199. The helpful **tourist office,** at the extreme northwest of the city on Bedrettin Demirel Cad., 2km from Girne Gate, is a good place to begin your tour of the city. (☎228 96 29. Open M 9am-6pm, Tu-F 9am-5pm; in winter M-F 8am-5pm.) Only **Turkey** has a full embassy in North Cyprus, at Bedrettin Demirel Cad. (☎227 23 14. Open M-F 9am-noon.) The following countries have "representative offices," offering some consular services: **Australia,** 20 Güner Türkmen Sok. (☎227 73 32; open Tu, Th 8:30am-12:30pm); **Germany,** #15 28 Kasım Sok. (☎227 51 61); **UK,** 29 Mehmet Aleif Cad. (☎228 70 51 or 228 38 61; open M, W, F 9am-1:30pm; Tu, Th 9am-1:30pm, 2:30-5pm); and **US,** 6 Saran Sok. (☎225 24 40; open M-F 8am-1pm, 2-3:30pm) Several offices along Girne Cad. offer **currency exchange** (open M-F 8am-1pm, 2-4pm). **ATMs** are near Atatürk Meydanı; the one outside **Türkiye İş Bankası** takes foreign cards. The **police** (☎228 33 11) are on Girne Cad. close to Atatürk Meydanı. A **hospital** (☎228 54 41 or 223 24 41) is 3km from the town center on the road to Girne, roughly 700m from the Victory Monument. Look for the *Hastane* sign. **Pembe Telefon,** 30m right of the post office, has metered booths and sells phone cards. (Open M-F 7:30am-2pm, 3:30-5:30pm.) Inexpensive **restaurants** crowd the area near the Girne Gate; typical Turkish fare goes for around $3.50.

CYPRUS

## SIGHTS

The **Selimiye Camii** mosque, formerly **Agia Sophia Cathedral,** is a bizarre sight: a seemingly ancient cathedral looming in the shadow of its two soaring minarets. Despite the *seccade* (prayer rugs) and Islamic calligraphy, the saints carved in the arches above the door and the flying buttresses testify to the edifice's original purpose. Refurbished by the Ottomans in 1570, the Roman Catholic cathedral was originally built in the Gothic style in 1326 by French architects at the behest of Queen Alix of Champagne. From Atatürk Meydanı, with Girne Gate at your back, continue down Girne Cad., looking left for the twin minarets. Beside it is the **Bedesten,** the 14th-century Orthodox **Cathedral of St. Nicholas.** Ottomans first converted it into a covered market and then a barn.

With your back to the mosque, head straight for a block and take a left to get to the 700-year-old **Büyük Hamamı,** once part of a 14th-century church. Since the time

of the building's construction, the city has risen about 2m, leaving the *hamam* slightly subterranean. (Open daily 8am-10pm. Bath, exfoliation, and massage by professional male masseur. $15.) Just a dice throw away is the **Kumarcılar Hanı** (Gamblers' Inn). Formerly for 17th-century traveling merchants, it now houses Northern Cyprus's Antiquities Department (open M-F 8am-2pm). A block or two to the east and beyond the Selimiye Mosque is the Gothic-era **Haydarpaşa Camii,** once a Lusignan church, and today a gallery. Face the Green Line and follow it to the right to the **Derviş Paşa Museum.** The former mansion of a notable 20th-century Cypriot newspaper owner, it has been converted into an unimpressive ethnographic museum displaying clothing and household goods. (Open M 9am-2pm, 3:30-7pm; Tu-Su 9am-7pm. $1.80, students $0.40.)

# DAYTRIPS TO TURKEY

The Turkish Aegean coast is full of ancient Greek ruins, funky beach towns, beautiful mosques, and moving war memorials. Daytrips to Turkey are cheap and easy from several Greek islands, including Samos (p. 328), Kos (p. 444), and Chios (p. 332). To go for the day, just catch a ferry to the Aegean coast. Not every Turkish daytrip is accessible by direct ferry. If your destination is Çanakkale, Eceabat, İzmir, Efes, or Selçuk, you'll need to head to Bodrum or Kuşadsı and catch a bus to your destination. Bus connections are listed below, with prices in US$ (as Turkish lire fluctuate widely). For a more on the rest of Turkey's sites and sounds, check out *Let's Go: Turkey 2001.*

**GETTING TO TURKEY** Non-Greek citizens need to purchase an **entrance visa** at the Turkish border if they're staying more than one day (by date) in Turkey: Americans ($45), Australian ($20), British (£10), Canadians ($45), and Irish (£5). Ferry schedules are variable, so check with a tourist office when making plans. For info on purchasing tickets, see the Practical Information section for each town. Ferries run from the following Greek islands to towns on the Aegean coast (3000dr Greek **port tax** not included here):

**Samos:** Ferries leave Samos Town daily for **Kuşadası** (1¼hr., 8:30am and 5pm, 10,000dr for a one-way morning departure, 9000dr for a one-way afternoon departure, 11,000dr return for a daytrip).

**Chios:** Boats from Chios Town to **Çeşme** (45min., 2 per day, 11,000-12,000dr).

**Kos:** Greek and Turkish boats leave from Kos Town for **Bodrum** every morning (10,000-13,000dr round-trip). Additional Turkish boats leave in the afternoon and return the next morning (8,000-13,000dr round-trip).

## BODRUM ☎252

"The Bedroom of the Mediterranean," Bodrum comes to life at night. Streaks of colored light from pounding dance clubs play over the yacht-filled harbor. While Bodrum's nightlife is notorious, the surrounding Acadian Peninsula is famous for its silica beaches, lush forests, secluded coves, and ancient ruins. As a multitude of visitors agree, it's easy to get sucked into Bodrum's rhythm of sun, shopping, sightseeing, and watersports—an innocent prelude to nightfall's bacchanalian delights.

### ORIENTATION AND PRACTICAL INFORMATION

Small blue signs label the streets of Bodrum; main streets radiate from the **Castle of St. Peter. Cumhuriyet Cad.,** the main commercial drag, runs along the beach. Ferries and yacht cruises leave from the breakwater, and **Kale Cad.** runs from the left of the castle to a mosque. **Belediye Meyd Cad.,** the street to the left of the mosque facing inland, becomes **Neyzen Tevfik Cad.,** along the west harbor coast.

See **Getting to Turkey** (p. 549) for Kos-Bodrum **ferries.** Travel agents sell tickets back to Greece. **Bodrum Express Lines** (☎316 40 67 or 316 10 87; fax 313 00 77) has offices in the *otogar* (station) and near the castle. Walk past the castle toward the sea; the office is on the left. **Ferries** run to **Kos** (1½hr.; daily 9am, return 4:30pm; arrive 30min. early for passport check). **Bodrum Express** also runs **hydrofoils** to **Kos** (15min.; daily 9am, return 4:30pm; $21, round-trip $24) and **Rhodes**

TURKEY

(2¼hr.; Sa 8:30am, return 4pm; $43, round-trip $48, open return $63). **Buses** run daily to **İzmir** (4hr., 2am-6pm, $7) and **Selçuk** (3hr., 2am-6pm, $8); contact **Pamukkale Lines** (☎316 13 69). The **tourist office,** 48 Barış Meydanı, gives away free brochures and **maps** at the foot of the castle. (☎316 10 91; fax 316 76 94. Open Apr.-Oct. 8:30am-5:30pm; Nov.-Mar. M-F 8am-noon, 1-5pm.) **ATMs** pepper shopping areas. In an **emergency,** dial 316 12 15. The **police,** 50 Barış Meydanı, are at the foot of the castle, next to the tourist office. (☎316 10 04. Open 24hr.) If you need a place to sleep it off, try **Emiko Pansiyon,** Atatürk Cad., 11 Uslu Sok.; from the *otogar*, follow Cevat Şakir Cad. towards the water, turning left onto Atatürk Cad. After 50m, turn right down the alley marked with the *pansiyon*'s sign. It's the second building on your left. Run by Emiko, a Japanese woman fluent in English, this *pansiyon* offers 8 simple rooms with hardwood floors and bath. (☎/fax 316 55 60; email emiko@turk.net. Guest kitchen. Breakfast $2. Laundry $3. Singles $15; doubles $20.)

**HALICARNASSUS.** The ancient city of Halicarnassus was the home of **Herodotus,** writer of The Histories, and is famous for the 4th-century BC funerary monument to King Mausolus that was magnificent enough to be declared one of the seven wonders of the ancient world. To reach the site, turn on to Kirkateyn Sok. from Neyzen Tevfik Cad. (Open summer Tu-Su 8am-noon and 1-5:30pm; off-season closes 5pm. $1.60, students $1.)

## NIGHTLIFE AND ENTERTAINMENT

All of the following except for Halikarnas Disco are on Cumhuriyet Cad. For a wild taste of England in Turkey, hop over the western ridge of Bodrum to Gümbet, where more discos and bars glitter in the night (30min. walk or 10min. *dolmuş* ride; *dolmuş* leave the *otogar* every 10min.; $0.40).

**Halikarnas Disco,** Z. Müren Cad. At the end of Cumhuriyet Cad., 1km from the center of town. This famed open-air disco juts out into the ocean, where its strobe lights reflect off the sails of nearby yachts. Daily shows featuring 25 performers, great music, and a celebrity-style entrance tunnel make this club the definitive Bodrum experience. $18 cover charge includes one local drink. Beer $3; cocktails $6.

**Hadi Gari** (☎313 80 97). Next to the luminous castle, the oldest disco in Bodrum fuses elegance and funkiness. Stylish customers groove on the outdoor dance floor. Others recline on cushions in the softly lit interior. Beer $3; *rakı* (a potent Turkish liquor) $3.60; cocktails $4-8. Restaurant by "day" (6pm-midnight), dance club by night (midnight-4am).

**Greenhouse** (☎313 09 11). A much-favored dance bar that extends onto the beach, with a laid-back atmosphere. Enthusiastic international and Turkish DJs. Everyone ends up here. Beer $1.80; *rakı* $3; cocktails $5. Open daily midnight-5am.

**Karşı** (☎(532) 256 44 17). Sexy bartenders and an enticing and diverse crowd make for a sultry evening of intrigue and alluring glances. The bar loudly dispenses underground, jazz, blues, and pop. Beer $3; *rakı* $3; cocktails $4-8. Open daily 10am-5am.

**Sensi** (☎316 68 45). For a riotous ride in bar craziness, join the mostly British crowd at Sensi, where table dancing, karaoke, and wig-wearing 70s nights keep this joint quaking. Beer $1.80; *rakı* $2; cocktails $3.60-5. Open daily 5pm-5am.



# İZMİR ☎232

İzmir, formerly ancient Smyrna, has risen from a tumultuous past to become Turkey's third-largest city and second-largest port. Reputedly the birthplace of Homer, Smyrna gained prominence in the 9th century BC and thrived until Lydians destroyed it 300 years later. After the Ottoman Empire's defeat in the First World War, the Greek army occupied İzmir, hoping to annex it. Turkish nationalist leader Mustafa Kemal—Atatürk—defeated overextended Greek forces, who left in 1922.

**ORIENTATION AND PRACTICAL INFORMATION.** İzmir's principal boulevards radiate from roundabouts, called *meydan*. **Cumhuriyet Meydanı,** on the waterfront, is the city's financial center. Budget hotels, inexpensive restaurants, several bus company offices, and the **Basmane train station** circle **9 Eylül Meydanı.** To get to the city center and to Basmane from İzmir's new intercity bus station, Yeni Garaj, walk two flights down from the upper level, where buses arrive, to the ground level, where city buses and *dolmuş* depart. Take city bus #601, 605, 50, 51, 53, 54, or 60. All of these buses pass through 9 Eylül Meydanı; the best way to make sure you get off in this square is to sit near the bus driver and tell him you want "Basmane Meydanı." Buy bus tickets from the kiosk before boarding ($0.50).

Getting to İzmir from Greece requires both a **ferry** (to **Bodrum, Kuşadası,** or **Çeşme,** see **p. 549**) and a **bus.** Buses run daily to İzmir from **Bodrum** (4hr., 2am-6pm, $7); **Kuşadası** (1½hr., every 20min. 6am-10pm, $4); and **Çeşme** (1¼hr.; every 30min. 6:30am-6pm, 9pm, midnight; $3.25). One ferry per week runs to **İstanbul** (20hr.; Su 2pm; from $18.75, students $15). **Local buses** head just about everywhere, including: **Bodrum** (4hr., every hr. 7am-1am, $10); **İstanbul** (9hr., every hr. 9am-1am, $18); and **Kuşadası** (1hr., every 90min. 8:30am-5:30pm, $3.25). The broken-English-speaking **Tourism Information Office,** 1/1D Gazi Osman Paşa Bul., has free **maps.** (☎445 73 90 or 489 92 78; fax 489 92 78. Open June-Sept. M-F 8:30am-6:30pm, Sa-Su 9am-5pm; Oct.-May M-F 8:30am-5:30pm, Sa 9am-5pm.)

**SIGHTS.** İzmir's **Archaeological Museum,** near Konak Sq., offers perhaps the finest collection of statuary outside of İstanbul. Finds from Ephesus and local sites stand beside elaborate sarcophagi and a few extraordinary statues. (Open Tu-Su 9am-5pm. $2.50.) In the center of the Konak district lies the **Hisar Camii,** İzmir's 400-year-old treasure of a mosque. Decorated with beguiling floral tiling and fantastic Turkish carpets, this mosque is the most famous site in İzmir, within the **konak** itself. İzmir's **agora,** the marketplace and town center, was built in the 4th century BC, destroyed by an earthquake in AD 178, and rebuilt by Roman emperor Marcus Aurelius. Find the leftovers of ancient columns and more interesting tombstones by walking south on Gazi Osman Paşa Bul. and turning left on Anafartalar Cad. (Open daily 8:30am-5pm. $1.25.) Above the city at Mt. Pagus, the **Kadifekale** surrounds an unsavory, intriguing park. Alexander originally built the walls in the 4th century BC, but various conquerors frequently altered and restored it. The area may be unsafe after dark, but the view from it is fabulous. *Dolmuş* marked "Mezarlık" leave from the agora entrance on Anafartalar Cad. and ascend Mt. Pagus on the way, offering a thrilling panorama of the bay ($0.40).

## ÇANAKKALE ☎286

Çanakkale, though not terribly scenic, is an easy base for exploring Gallipoli and Troy. The easiest way to get to Çanakkale is by bus from **İzmir** (5hr., $7.50). **Dolmuş** ($0.50-1) run from under the small bridge over the Sarı Çay inlet to **Troy** (25min., leaving throughout day when the *dolmuş* fills ($0.80). **Ferries** to **Eceabat** (30min., 5am and every hr. 7am-1am) require a token ($1) from the token window next to the small PTT booth. Practically everything relating to the mechanics of budget travel (food, accommodations, and travel agencies) lies within the one-block area around the **ferry dock** and the clock tower. The English-speaking staff at the **Tourist Office,** 67 İskele Meydanı, distributes maps. (☎/fax 217 11 87. Open M-F 8am-7pm, Sa-Su 10am-6pm.) The **police** (☎212 14 66) are off İnönü Cad. **Tours** of the Gallipoli battlefields and the city of Troy are available and include lunch, an English-speaking guide, transportation, and admission to the sights. **TJ's Tours** (☎814 29 40; fax 814 29 41; email TJs_TOURS@excite.com), provides daily tours to Gallipoli (12:30pm, $19) and Troy (8:45am, $14) when there's sufficient demand. Call ahead to reserve a space. **The Hassle Free Travel Agency,** 61 Cumhuriyet Meydanı (☎213 59 69; email hasslefree@anzachouse.com), provides daily Gallipoli tours (Apr.-Nov. 11:45am, Dec.-Mar. 10:45am; $19), and almost-daily Troy tours that depart from Anzac House (Apr.-Nov. 8:45am, Dec.-Mar. 7:45am; $14).

TURKEY

## TROY

*Take a* dolmuş *from Çanakkale; they run from under the small bridge over the Sarı Çay inlet (25min., $0.80). Open daily June-Sept. 8:30am-7:30pm; Oct.-May 8am-5pm. $2.50.*

For the casual visitor with no romantic attachment to **Homer,** Troy's jumbled, partially excavated ruins might seem disappointing—the site is confusing and doesn't immediately strike the romantic imagination. But for lovers of Greek myth or of Homer's poems, it's magic. A tour (see p. 551) is a good idea, since a guide's explanations of Troy's history and the excavation process liven it up. For those interested in archaeology as a discipline, in particular, Troy is a rare gold mine among ancient sites, and for everyone, a must-see for any trip to the Aegean Coast.

Troy's lifetime spans a huge continuum of civilization, from the early Bronze Age to the late Roman Empire. During 110 years of sporadic excavation, archaeologists have split these into numbered periods. Troy began as a fishing settlement in 3000-2500 BC, evolved into an affluent city-state from 2500-2200 BC, and eventually became the city of Homer's **King Priam** from 1275 to 1240 BC (though the date is disputed), before its fall to ruin for four centuries. Reborn as a fishing village around the 3rd century BC, Troy rose to importance as V.I.P.s from Alexander the Great to Julius Caesar took an interest. The fall of Rome wrecked Troy again; after being inhabited for 35 centuries, the city lay buried for 13 more until **Heinrich Schliemann** (p. 119) arrived to dig it all up. Playing finders-keepers, Schliemann helped himself to some ancient treasure; his keepsakes can be seen today in the Pushkin Museum of Fine Art in Moscow.

## ECEABAT ☎286

Eceabat is a short ferry ride across the straits from Çanakkale (every hour on the hour, $0.75), and is the closest major town to the Gallipoli battlefields. The town's excellent tour company and hostel, combined with its location, make it the best base for exploring the battlefields. The sea and ferry docks edge one side of Eceabat's main square. The road parallel to the sea is **Cumhuriyet Cad.** Facing away from the sea, the road off to the left one block beyond Cumhuriyet Cad. is **Zübeide Hanım Cad.** İlhami Gezici, nicknamed TJ for his eerie resemblance to Las Vegas darling Tom Jones, owns and runs **TJ's Tours** (☎814 29 40; fax 814 29 41; email TJs_TOURS@excite.com). TJ himself gives the tours of the battlefields ($19) and general advice for tourists. **ATMs** are at İş Bankaşı in the main square and at Ziraat Bankaşı, past the Gul Restaurant.

## BATTLEFIELDS OF GALLIPOLI

*Gallipoli is spread out, so it's a good idea to take an* ***organized tour,*** *many of which provide lunch, excellent English-speaking guides, and transportation to the memorials. Tours are available from Çanakkale (p. 551) and Eceabat. Bring your bathing suit, since tours often make a short swim stop. Museum open 8:30am-noon, 1-5:30pm. $1.20.*

About 10km northwest of Eceabat lie the battlefields of Gallipoli, the backdrop of a major First World War offensive that attempted to take Constantinople and create a Balkan front. Eighty thousand Turkish soldiers and more than 200,000 Allied troops died in the bloody stalemate. Australian and New Zealander forces suffered especially severe losses. The battle launched its hero, **Atatürk,** on a rapid rise toward his status as Turkey's founding father. Each year, thousands of Australians and New Zealanders make pilgrimages to Gallipoli's war cemeteries, and April 25, the date of the Allied landing, remains a day of remembrance and grief.

A **museum** displays battle photographs, uniforms, weapons, skeletal remains, and—to demonstrate the intensity of the fighting—two bullets that collided in midair. Four kilometers from the museum is **ANZAC Cove,** where the Australia-New Zealand Army Corps first landed on April 25th. A stone monument is inscribed with a moving tribute by Atatürk to the young men of all nationalities who died fighting. Seven kilometers uphill from the museum, the **Lone Pine Memorial** marks the site of an unsuccessful Australian attempt to break the stalemate; a short walk north from the Lone Pine brings you to **Johnston's Jolly,** where the still-visible trenches of the Australians and Turks lie so close together that they actually line both sides of the road. More memorials and battle sites follow the road uphill to **Conkbayırı,** the highest point of the battlefield.

## SELÇUK ☎232

Selçuk serves as a base for exploring nearby Ephesus, besides its own notable archaeological sites. The Selçuk castle dominates the city's skyline, with the Basilica of Saint John, where the apostle John is buried, the İsa Bay Camii, and the ruins of the Temple of Artemis. The House of the Virgin Mary *(Meryemana)* can also be reached from Selçuk.

**ORIENTATION AND PRACTICAL INFORMATION.** The İzmir-Aydın road, **Atatürk Cad.,** is one of Selçuk's main thoroughfares. **Dr. Sabri Yayla Bul.,** also called **Kuşadası Cad.,** meets Atatürk Cad. from the west, and **Şahabettin Dede Cad.** meets Atatürk Cad. from the east to form the town's main crossroads. Selçuk is reachable by **bus** from **Bodrum** (3hr., 2am-6pm, $8) or **İzmir** (take a Bodrum- or Kuşadası-bound bus and ask to be let off at Selçuk; 1hr.; $4). Buses head to: **Bodrum** (3hr.; every hour 7:30am-8:30pm, 10:30pm, 12:30am; $9); **İstanbul** (10hr.; May-Sept. 7 per day 9:45am-midnight, Oct.-Apr. 3 per day; $19.50); and **İzmir** (1hr., every 20min. 6:30am-8:30pm, $3.25). **Minibuses** run to **Kuşadası** (20min.; every 20min. May-Sept. 6:30am-12am, Oct.-Apr. 6:30am-8:30pm; $1.20). The **tourist office,** 35 Agora Çarşısı, Atatürk Mah., at the intersection of Kuşadası Cad. and Atatürk Cad., has free city **maps.** English is spoken. (☎892 63 28; fax 892 69 45. Open M-F 8:30am-noon and 1-5:30pm; Apr.-Dec. also Sa-Su 9am-5pm.) A **bank,** 17 Namık Kemal Cad., **exchanges currency** and **traveler's checks** and has an **ATM.** (☎892 61 09 or 892 65 14. Open M-F 8:30am-5:30pm.) The **police** (☎892 60 16) have an office beside Türkiye İş Bankası, and a booth at the corner of the *otogar* on Atatürk Cad.

**SIGHTS.** The stunning Selçuk mosque **İsa Bey Camii** was built in 1375 on the order of Aydınoğlu İsa Bey. It features columns taken from Ephesus, which the Ephesians had pilfered from Aswan, Egypt. Restored in 1975, the mosque has regained much of the simplicity that 600 years of wear and tear had eroded. Scattered inside the courtyard is a collection of Ottoman and Selçuk tombstones and inscriptions. The mosque's facade features Persian-influenced geometric black and white stone inlay. *(Open 10 min. before and 10 min. after times of prayer.)* A few hundred meters down Dr. Sabri Yayla Bul., walking away from town with the tourist office on your right, are the sad remains of the **Temple of Artemis.** Once the largest temple in the ancient world, and considered one of the seven wonders of the ancient world, it now is a lone reconstructed column twisting upward from a bog that approximates the area of the temple's foundation. *(8:30am-5:30pm. Free.)*

**EFES MÜZESI.** Directly across from the town's tourist office, Selçuk's Efes Müzesi (Ephesus Museum) houses a world-class collection of Hellenistic and Roman recent finds from Ephesus; most earlier pieces are in Vienna. The collection includes an infamously erect Priapus statue, **Beş,** that graces postcards throughout Turkey. While this particular piece was found in the vicinity of Ephesian brothels, the image of the generously endowed demi-god wasn't a smutty novelty, but a fairly common image in the ancient world. The museum houses an excellent collection of statuary, including a multi-breasted statue of **Artemis,** exquisite busts of Eros, Athena, Socrates, and emperors Tiberius, Marcus Aurelius, and Hadrian. *(Open daily 8:30am-noon, 1-5:30pm. $5.)*



## EPHESUS ☎232

*From Kuşadası or Selçuk, take a free* ***shuttle service*** *from any hotel and pansiyon. Otherwise, from the Kuşadası* otogar, *take a* ***dolmuş*** *toward Selçuk and tell the driver to stop at Efes (30min., $1). From the Selçuk* otogar, *take a Pamukkale-bound* dolmuş *toward Kuşadası (5min.; May-Oct. every 30min., Nov.-Apr. every hr.; $0.50).* ***Taxis*** *run from Selçuk to Ephesus ($4) and to the House of the Virgin Mary (9km, $21 round-trip including 45min. to visit the site). The site is an easy* ***walk*** *(3km, 25min.) from Selçuk along a fig-shaded path, beside Dr. Sabri Yayla Bul. Bring water and sunscreen. A good guidebook to Ephesus costs about $2.50 in Kuşadası's souvenir shops or at the entrance to the site; it provides history for the ruins and a more lengthy explanation of the many sights. ☎892 64 02. Open 8am-6pm. $6.50. The best time to visit is early in the morning.*

From early archaic times to the 6th century AD, Ephesus's glorious prosperity just lasts and lasts. To this day, its concentration of Classical art and architecture is surpassed only by Rome and Athens (p. 97). The ruins rank first among Turkey's ancient sites in sheer size and state of preservation; extensive marble roadways and columned avenues give an authentic impression of this ancient metropolitan gateway to the eastern world.

Once you reach the site, you'll see the **Vedius Gymnasium** on the left down the road from Dr. Sabri Yayla Bul. toward the lower entrance. It was built in AD 150 to honor then-emperor Antonius Pius and **Artemis,** the city's patron goddess. Beyond the roadside vegetation, the remains of the **stadium** open up in a horseshoe. The original Greek semi-circular theater followed the land's contours to add natural emphasis to the staged dramas. Romans plunked their own stadium right on top of the Greek theater, interpreting "drama" in another way, staging martial spectacles, bloody gladiator games, wild beast hunts, and public executions. Just inside the lower entrance, a dirt path leads off to the right; on the right side of the fork, you'll find the ruins of the **Church of the Seven Councils,** where the Third Ecumenical Council met in AD 431. Beside the Church of the Seven Councils, the **Archbishop's Place,** destroyed by Arabs in the 6th century AD, remains in ruins.

At the main entrance gate, a tree-lined path points to the **Arcadiane,** Ephesus's main drag. Buried under a dense swarm of tourists, the 30m by 145m **Grand Theater** is a stunning, heavily restored beast; its *cavea* (seating area), carved into the side of Mt. Pion, seats 25,000. The **Street of Curetes** begins at a slight incline. Ruts in the road are evidence of the enormous concentration of traffic between the temple and the city, and gaps between the slabs reveal glimpses of the city's **sewer system.** At the very bottom of the Street of Curetes is the **Library of Celsus,** restored by Austrian archaeologists. The large building behind the library was probably the **Temple of Serapis,** an Egyptian god of grain. Farther up the Street of Curetes, the imposing ruins of the AD 118 **Temple of Hadrian** are on your left marked by a double-layered column construction. Several friezes depict the creation of Ephesus, and a bust of the goddess Cybele adorns the keystone. A little farther up the hill on the left are the ruins of the exquisite **Fountain of Trajan.**

Two pillars in the middle of the road mark the **Gate of Hercules;** farther uphill and to the left is the **Prytaneion.** Dedicated to the worship of **Vesta** (Hestia to the Greeks, and goddess of hearth and home), the Prytaneion contained an eternal flame tended by Vesta's priestesses, the **Vestal Virgins.** Vesta was vital to the Romans, and the Vestal Virgins thus gained a social standing *almost* as high as men. Thanks, guys. Immediately adjacent, the **odeon,** or *bouleterion*, remains in fine repair. The small, once-covered theater seated around 1500, and served as a performance space and meeting hall. The **state agora** on the right was the heart of political activity from the 1st century BC until the city's final demise. On the left after the odeon lie the upper **baths.**

# APPENDIX

## CLIMATE

The climate is fairly uniform throughout Greece; the islands are a bit milder, and higher altitude areas (especially in the north) are cooler—expect it to be much colder on mountainous hikes. **Summer** is sunny, hot, and sticky with humidity. **Winter** temperatures hover around 50°F. October to March is the rainy season.

| Avg. Temp. (lo/hi), | JANUARY | | APRIL | | JULY | | OCTOBER | |
|---|---|---|---|---|---|---|---|---|
| Precipitation | °F | in. | °F | in. | °F | in | °F | in. |
| **Athens** | 55/43 | 2.5 | 68/52 | 0.9 | 91/73 | 0.2 | 75/59 | 2.0 |
| **Thessaloniki** | 48/36 | 1.8 | 68/50 | 1.6 | 90/70 | .9 | 72/55 | 2.3 |
| **Trikkala** | 48/32 | 3.4 | 70/46 | 3.2 | 95/66 | 0.8 | 77/54 | 3.2 |
| **Naxos** | 59/50 | 3.6 | 68/55 | 0.8 | 81/72 | 0.1 | 75/64 | 1.8 |

To convert from degrees Fahrenheit to degrees Celsius, subtract 32 and multiply by 5/9. To convert from Celsius to Fahrenheit, multiply by 9/5 and add 32.

| °CELSIUS | -5 | 0 | 5 | 10 | 15 | 20 | 25 | 30 | 35 | 40 |
|---|---|---|---|---|---|---|---|---|---|---|
| °FARENHEIT | 23 | 32 | 41 | 50 | 59 | 68 | 77 | 86 | 95 | 104 |

## METRIC CONVERSIONS

| | |
|---|---|
| 1 inch (in.) = 25.4 millimeters (mm) | 1 millimeter (mm) = 0.039 in. |
| 1 foot (ft.) = 0.30 m | 1 meter (m) = 3.28 ft. |
| 1 mile = 1.61km | 1 kilometer (km) = 0.62 mi. |
| 1 ounce (oz.) = 28.35g | 1 gram (g) = 0.035 oz. |
| 1 pound (lb.) = 0.454kg | 1 kilogram (kg) = 2.202 lb. |
| 1 fluid ounce (fl. oz.) = 29.57ml | 1 milliliter (ml) = 0.034 fl. oz. |
| 1 gallon (gal.) = 3.785L | 1 liter (L) = 0.264 gal. |
| 1 square mile (sq. mi.) = 2.59km$^2$ | 1 square kilometer (km$^2$) = 0.386 sq. mi. |

## TELEPHONE CODES

See **Keeping in Touch** (p. 58) for full information and advice about telephone calls in Greece and Cyprus, including international access.

| | | COUNTRY | CODES | | |
|---|---|---|---|---|---|
| Australia | 61 | Greece | 30 | South Africa | 27 |
| Canada | 1 | Ireland | 353 | Spain | 34 |
| Cyprus | 357 | Italy | 39 | Turkey | 90 |
| France | 33 | Japan | 81 | UK | 44 |
| Germany | 49 | New Zealand | 64 | US | 1 |
| | | **GREECE CODE** | **30** | | |
| Aegina | 0297 | Itilo | 0733 | Olympia | 0624 |
| Agia Galini | 0832 | Kalamata | 0721 | Osios Loukas | 0267 |
| Agios Nikolaos | 0841 | Kalambaka | 0432 | Paleohora | 0823 |
| Agria | 0423 | Kalavrita | 0692 | Parga | 0684 |
| Alexandroupolis | 0551 | Kalymnos | 0243 | Paros | 0284 |
| Amorgos | 0285 | Kardamyli | 0721 | Patmos | 0247 |
| Andritsena | 0626 | Karpathos | 0245 | Patras | 061 |
| Andros | 0282 | Karpenisi | 0237 | Petalidio | 0722 |
| Arahova | 0267 | Karystos | 0224 | Piraeus | 01 |
| Astypalea | 0243 | Kassos | 0245 | Poros | 0298 |

| GREECE CODE 30 | | | | | |
|---|---|---|---|---|---|
| Athens | 01 | Kastoria | 0467 | Pouri | 0422 |
| Cape Sounion | 0292 | Kavala | 051 | Pylos | 0723 |
| Kephalonia | 0671 | Kea | 0288 | Rafina | 0294 |
| Chios | 0271 | Killini | 0623 | Rethymnon | 0831 |
| Corfu | 0661 | Kimi | 0222 | Rhodes | 0241 |
| Corinth | 0741 | Kithnos | 0281 | Samos | 0273 |
| Delphi | 0265 | Kos | 0242 | Samothraki | 0551 |
| Dimitsana | 0795 | Kyparissia | 0761 | Serifos | 0281 |
| Edessa | 0381 | Kythera | 0735 | Sifnos | 0284 |
| Epidavros | 0753 | Lefkada | 0645 | Sithonia | 0375 |
| Eritrea | 0221 | Lesvos | 0251 | Sitia | 0843 |
| Folegandros | 0286 | Lia | 0664 | Skiathos | 0427 |
| Galaxidi | 0265 | Limni | 0227 | Skopelos | 0424 |
| Gythion | 0733 | Limnos | 0254 | Skyros | 0222 |
| Halkida | 0221 | Litohoro | 0352 | Sparta | 0731 |
| Hania | 0821 | Matala | 0892 | Symi | 0241 |
| Hersonissos | 0897 | Methoni | 0723 | Syros | 0281 |
| Hora Sfakion | 0825 | Metsovo | 0656 | Thasos | 0593 |
| Ierapetra | 0842 | Milos | 0287 | Thebes | 0262 |
| Igoumenitsa | 0665 | Monemvasia | 0732 | Thessaloniki | 031 |
| Ikaria | 0275 | Mt. Athos | 0377 | Tinos | 0283 |
| Ioannina | 0651 | Mycenae | 0751 | Tripoli | 071 |
| Ios | 0286 | Mykonos | 0289 | Volos | 0421 |
| Iraklion | 081 | Nafplion | 0752 | Xilokastro | 0743 |
| Isthmia | 0746 | Naxos | 0285 | Zagorohoria | 0426 |
| Limni | 0674 | Neapolis | 0734 | Zakynthos | 0695 |

| CYPRUS CODE 357 | | | | | |
|---|---|---|---|---|---|
| Agia Napa | 03 | Nicosia | 02 | Platres | 05 |
| Larnaka | 04 | Pano Platres | 05 | Podromos | 0295 |
| Limassol | 05 | Paphos | 06 | Polis | 06 |

# GLOSSARY OF GREEK TERMS

**acropolis** a fortified, sacred high place atop a city
**adelfos** brother
**adelfi** sister
**afto** this
**aftokinito** car
**agape** love (see *erotas*)
**agora** the ancient city square and marketplace
**alati** salt
**alithea** truth
**ammos** sand
**amphora** a two-handled vase for oil or wine storage
**angouri** cucumber
**apse** nook beyond the altar of a church
**architrave** lintel resting on columns and supporting the entablature, below a frieze
**arhontiko** mansion
**arni** lamb
**astinomio** police; pigs
**astra** stars
**Archaic Period** 700-480 BC
**arnaki** lamb
**Asia Minor** Turkey, especially its once-Greek Aegean coast
**aspro** white
**astakos** lobster
**atrium** house's open interior courtyard; typically Roman
**avga** eggs
**avgolemono** egg-lemon soup
**avrio** tomorrow
**basilica** church with a saint's relic; especially holy
**bouleterion** meeting place of an ancient city's legislative council
**bouzouki** stringed instrument
**Byzantine Period** AD 324-1453
**caïque** fishing or passenger boat, usually wooden
**capital** decorated top of a column
**castro** castle or fortifications (often built by Italians)
**cella** inner sanctum of a classical temple
**chora** see **hora**
**chrono** year (or time, in a grandiose sense)
**chryso** gold
**cigara (tsigara)** cigarettes
**Classical Period** 480-323BC
**Corinthian column** ornate, leaf- or flower-engraved top (or capital) of a column
**cornice** top of the entablature of a temple
**Cyclopian walls** massive irregular-cut Minoan and Mycenaean stone walls, so called because only a Cyclops could lift such stones
**demos** people, citizens
**dimarchio** town hall

APPENDIX

**dolmades** warm stuffed grape leaves with sauce of egg and lemon
**dolmadakia** cold stuffed grape leaves
**domatia** rooms to rent in private homes; rooms to let
**Dorians** the invaders of 1100 BC and their descendants
**Doric column** cigar-shaped columns with wide fluted shafts, cushion tops (or capitals), and no bases
**efimerevon** 24hr. pharmacy
**eleftheria** freedom
**eleftheri/os** single, free
**entablature** upper parts of a temple facade, atop columns
**epicremeni/os** upset, sad, disappointed
**erotas** erotic love or sex; "let's do it"="na kanome erotas" (see *agape*)
**erotevmeni/os** madly in love
**esoteriko** domestic
**etos** year
**exoteriko** international
**exedra** curved recess in classical/Byzantine architecture
**exonarthex** outer vestibule in a Byzantine church
**Faneromeni** Virgin Revealer
**fevgato** flighty
**feta** soft, white, omnipresent goat-milk cheese
**filaki** (accent on la) kiss
**filaki** (accent on ki) jail
**forum** Roman marketplace
**frappé** Greek iced coffee
**frieze** illustrated middle part of a temple exterior (in particular, the entablature); see *metopes* and *triglyph*
**frourio** medieval castle; often called a Kastro or Castro
**gaiduri** donkey (masculine)
**gaidara** donkey (feminine)
**galaktopoleio** dairy shop
**galaktobouriko** cream pastry
**Geometric Period** 1100-700 BC
**ghala** milk
**glika** sweets
**gyro** greasy, pita-wrapped lamb sandwich (mmm)
**haroumeni/os** happy
**Hellenistic Period** 323-46 BC
**heroon** shrine to a demigod
**hora (chora)** island capital or main town in an area
**iconostatis** screen that displays Byzantine icons
**Ionic column** slender column topped with twin scrolling spirals and with a fluted base
**iperastiko** long distance (phone calls, transportation)
**kafeneio** cafe and social hub
**kaimaiki** specialty ice-cream with *mastika (*gum)
**kalamarakia** baby squid
**kasseri** hard yellow cheese
**kastro** castle or fortifications
**Katharevoussa** uppity "pure" Greek literary language, taken from ancient Greek
**kathemera** every day
**kathemerino** daily
**katholikon** monastery's main church or chapel
**kato hora** the lower part of a village
**kefalos** head
**kefi** The Mood for fun
**KKE** Greek communist party
**koine** "common" Greek used before the Byzantine era
**kore** female statue
**kotopoulo** chicken
**kouros** male nude statue
**ktapodhi** octopus
**KTEL** local bus service
**ladhi** oil
**leoforos** avenue
**leoforeo** bus
**libation** gift of food or liquor to a god
**limani** port
**logariasmo** check
**magiritsa** tripe soup with rice
**malaka** nasty obscenity that connotes masturbation
**mastika** chewing-gum or gum
**mavro** black
**megalo** big (opposite of *mikro*)
**megaron** large hall in a house or palace
**melizanes** eggplants
**meltemi** an unusually strong north wind in the Cyclades and Dodecanese
**metopes** painted or sculped square block in a Doric frieze that contains scenes with figures; *metopes* are separated by *triglyphs*
**meze, mezedes, mezedakia** appetizers to go with ouzo
**mikro** small (opposite of *megalo*)
**Minoan Period** 3000-1250 BC
**mitera** mother
**moni** monastery or convent
**moro/moraki** baby
**moschari** veal
**moussaka** a layered, lasagna-like dish made with layered eggplants and cheese
**moustarda** mustard
**Mycenean Period** 1600-1100 BC
**naos** holy innermost part of a temple or church
**narthex** vestibule on the west side of a Byzantine church
**nave** church aisle
**ne** yes
**Neolithic Period** 3000-2000 BC
**nomos** Greek province
**nosokomeio** hospital
**odeion** semi-circular theater
**odos** road
**ohi** no
**oikos** house
**omphalos** belly-button
**opa!** much-used expression; hey!; oops!; look out!
**ouzeri** *ouzo* tavern serving *mezedes* and other yummy treats
**ouzo** Greek national liquor
**omorfia** beauty
**ora** time (hour)
**OTE** the Greek national telephone company
**paleohora** old town
**palaestra** classical gymnasium
**Panagia** the Virgin Mary
**pano** high or upper
**panigiri** local festival, often religious
**Pantokrator** a mosaic or fresco of Christ in a Byzantine church dome
**papaki** duckling (slang for moped)
**pareia** a group of friends
**patera** father
**pedi** child; "ela, pedia" means "come on, kids"; used to call the *pareia* at any age
**pediment** triangualar, sculpture decorated space in an ancient temple's facade
**peplos** mantle worn by ancient Greek women; Athena's nightgown
**periptero** street kiosk
**peristyle** colonnade around a building
**philos** buddy, friend
**pima** poem
**piesi** high blood pressure, nerves
**piperi** pepper
**pithos** ceramic storage jar
**plateia** town square
**pleio** ferry
**polis** city-state
**portico** colonnade or *stoa*
**pronaos** outer column-lined temple porch
**propylaion** sanctuary entrance flanked by columns
**prytaneion** administrative building
**psaras** fisherman
**psaria** fish
**psomi** bread
**raki** Cretan local liquor
**retsina** sharp white wine
**rhyton** cup shaped like an animal's head
**Roman period** 46 BC-AD 324
**satyr** lusty follower of Dionysus
**simera** today
**skala** port for an inland town
**souvlaki** oh-so-tender meat on a skewer (usually lamb)
**spili, spilia** cave, caves
**stele** a stone slab that marks a tomb

**stoa** in ancient marketplaces, an open portico lined with rows of columns
**taverna** restaurant or tavern
**techni** art, craft, skill
**tholos** Mycenean earth-covered, beehive-shaped tomb
**tiri** cheese
**triglyph** part of a Doric frieze comprised of 3 vertical grooves that alternate with *metopes*
**trireme** ancient ship with 3 sets of oars
**tsipouro** mainland bathtub liquor
**tsoutsoukakia** meat balls in tomato sauce
**varka** boat
**volta** evening walk
**vouno** mountain
**voutiro** butter
**xechasmeni/os** forgotten
**xeri** dry
**xeri carpi** nuts, dry snacks
**yiayia** grandmother
**yialos** waterside (port, beach)
**zaccharoplasteio** sweetshop
**zakhari** sugar

# GREEK ALPHABET

The Greek alphabet has 24 letters; the chart below can help decipher signs. The left column gives the name of each letters in Greek, the middle column shows lower case and capital letters, and the right column shows the pronunciation.

| LETTER | SYMBOL | PRONUNCIATION | LETTER | SYMBOL | PRONUNCIATION |
|---|---|---|---|---|---|
| alpha | α Α | *a* as in father | nu | ν Ν | *n* as in net |
| beta | β Β | *v* as in velvet | ksi | ξ Ξ | *x* as in mix |
| gamma | γ Γ | *y* as in yo or *g* as in go | omicron | ο Ο | *o* as in row |
| delta | δ Δ | *th* as in there | pi | π Π | *p* as in peace |
| epsilon | ϵ Ε | *e* as in jet | rho | ρ Ρ | *r* as in roll |
| zeta | ζ Ζ | *z* as in zebra | sigma | σ (ς) Σ | *s* as in sense |
| eta | η Η | *ee* as in queen | tau | τ Τ | *t* as in tent |
| theta | θ Θ | *th* as in health | upsilon | υ Υ | *ee* as in green |
| iota | ι Ι | *ee* as in tree | phi | φ (φ) Φ | *f* as in fog |
| kappa | κ Κ | *k* as in cat | xi | χ Χ | *ch (h)* as in horse |
| lambda | λ Λ | *l* as in land | psi | ψ Ψ | *ps* as in oops |
| mu | μ Μ | *m* as in moose | omega | ω Ω | *o* as in glow |

# COMMON WORDS AND PHRASES

| PEOPLE | | |
|---|---|---|
| Woman or wife | γινεκα | yee-NECK-ah |
| Man or husband | ανδρος | AHN-dras |
| Mother/Father | μιτερα/πατερα | mee-TER-ah/pa-TER-ah |
| Sister/Brother | αδελφη/αδελφος | ah-del-FEE/ad-del-FOS |
| Aunt/Uncle | θεα/θεος | THEE-ah/THEE-os |
| Mother-in-law/Father-in-law | πεθερα/πεθερος | peh-the-RA/peh-the-ROS |
| Godmother/Godfather | νονα/νονος | no-NA/no-NOS |
| Cousin (f/m) | ξαδελφη/ξαδελφος | ksa-del-FEE/ksa-del-FOS |
| Grandmother/Grandfather | γιαγια/παπους | yah-YAH/pah-POUS |
| Group of friends | παρεια | pah-RAY-ah |
| Friend (f/m) | φιλη/φιλος | FEE-lee/FEE-los |
| Lover (f/m) | αγαπιτη/αγαπιτος | a-ga-pi-TEE/a-ga-pi-TOS |
| Neighbors/neighborhood | γιτονια | yee-ton-YAH |
| Neighbor | γιτονισα | yee-TON-ee-sah |
| Crazy guy | ο τρελος | oh treh-LOS |
| God | θεος | thay-OS |
| **DESCRIPTIONS** | | |
| beautiful (f/m) | ομορφη/ομορφος | OH-mor-fee/OH-mor-fos |
| ugly | ασκιμο | AS-kee-mo |
| big | μεγαλο | me-GAL-oh |
| medium | μεσεο | me-SAY-oh |

| | | |
|---|---|---|
| small | μικρο | mee-KRO |
| happy (f/m) | χαρουμενη/χαρουμενοσ | har-OU-men-ee/os |
| sad | λιπετερο | lee-pe-ter-OH |
| funny | αστειο | ohs-TEE-oh |
| simple | απλα | ap-LAH |
| old (thing) | παλεο | pah-LYO |
| old (person; f/m) | γερη/γερος | YEH-ree/YEH-ros |
| sturdy (f/m) | γερη/γερος | yeh-REE/yeh-ROS |
| summertime | καλοκαιριανο | kah-lo-kar-ee-an-OH |
| wet | βραιμενο | vreh-MEN-oh |
| dry, brittle | ξερι | kser-EE |
| fried | πιγανιτο | tee-gan-ee-TOH |
| virgin | παρθενος | par-then-OS |
| wordsmith | λογοτεχνης | lo-go-TECH-nis |
| **USEFUL WORDS** | | |
| stop | σταματα | sta-MA-tah |
| shit | σκατα | ska-TA |
| asshole | γαμοτο | gah-MO-to |
| darling | λατρεια | lah-TREE-ah |
| maybe; I'm thinking about it | το σκεπτομε | toh SKEP-to-meh |
| it does (not) matter | (θεν) πειραζι | (then) peer-ADZ-ee |
| I love you | Σαγαπαω | SAH-gap-AH-o |
| I miss you | Μου λιπις | mou LEE-pis |
| I want you | Σε θελο | seh THEL-oh |
| **GREETINGS** | | |
| good morning | καλημερα | kah-lee-MEH-rah |
| good evening | καλησπερα | kah-lee-SPE-rah |
| good night | καληνυχτα | kah-lee-NEE-khtah |
| yes | ναι | NEH |
| no | οχι | OH-hee |
| please/you're welcome | παρακαλω | pah-rah-kah-LO |
| thank you (very much) | ευχαριστω πολυ | ef-hah-ree-STO (po-LEE) |
| excuse me | συγνομη | seeg-NO-mee |
| hello/goodbye (polite, plural) | γεια σας | YAH-sas |
| hello/goodbye (familiar) | γεια σου | YAH-soo |
| OK | ενταξι | en-DAHK-see |
| Mr./Sir | κυριος | kee-REE-os |
| Ms./Madam | κυρια | kee-REE-ah |
| What is your name? | Πως σε λενε; | pos-se-LEH-neh? |
| My name is ... | Με λενε | me-LEH-neh ... |
| **QUESTIONS AND WAYS TO GET HELP** | | |
| Do you speak English? | Μιλας αγγλικα; | mee-LAHS ahn-glee-KAH? |
| I don't speak Greek | Δεν μιλαω ελληνικα | dhen mee-LAHO el-leen-ee-KAH |
| I don't understand | Δεν καταλαβαινω | dhen kah-tah-lah-VEH-no |
| I need a ticket | Χπειαζομαι ισιτεριο | chree-AH-soh-meh eeseeTERio |
| Can I see a room? | Μπορω να δω ενα δωματιο; | bo-RO nah-DHO E-nah dho-MAH-tee-o? |
| why? | Για τι; | yah-TEE? |
| where? who? when? | πoυ; πιος; ποτε; | POO? pYOS? POH-teh? |

APPENDIX

| | | |
|---|---|---|
| Seriously!? | σοβαρα; | so-vah-RAH?! |
| I am lost | χαθηκα | HA-thee-ka |
| I am ill | Ειμαι αρροστος | EE-meh AH-ross-toss |
| Help! | Βοητηεια! | vo-EE-thee-ah! |
| Go away! | Φυγε! | FEEG-he! |
| **TIME** | | |
| What time is it? | Τι ωρα εναι; | tee-O-rah EE-neh? |
| yesterday | χθες | KTHES |
| today | σημερα | SEE-mer-a |
| tomorrow | αυριο | AV-ree-o |
| first | πρωτο | PRO-to |
| morning | πρωι | pro-EE |
| evening | βραδι | VRAH-dhee |
| later tonight | αποψε | ah-PO-pseh |
| last | τελευταιο | teh-lef-TEH-o |
| **DIRECTIONS** | | |
| Where is ... ? | Που εναι; | pou-EE-neh ... ? |
| I'm going to ... | Πηγαινω για | pee-YEH-no yah ... |
| When do we leave? | Τι ωρα φευγουμε; | tee O-rah FEV-goo-meh? |
| restaurant | εστιατοριο | es-tee-ah-TO-ree-o |
| post office | ταχυδρομειο | ta-khee-dhro-MEE-o |
| market | αγορα | ah-go-RAH |
| museum | μουσειο | mou-SEE-o |
| pharmacy | φαρμακειο | fahr-mah-KEE-o |
| bank | τραπεζα | TRAH-peh-zah |
| church | εκκλησια | eh-klee-SEE-ah |
| hotel | ξενοδοχειο | kse-no-dho-HEE-o |
| room | δοματιο | dho-MAH-teeo |
| suitcase | βαλιτσα | vah-LEE-tsah |
| airport | αεροδρομειο | ah-e-ro-DHRO-mee-o |
| airplane | αεροπλανο | ah-e-ro-PLAH-no |
| train | τραινο | TREH-no |
| bus | λεωφορειο | leh-o-fo-REE-o |
| ferry | πλοιο | PLEE-o |
| ticket | εισιτηριο | ee-see-TEE-ree-o |
| hospital | νοσοκομειο | no-so-ko-ME-o |
| port | λιμανι | lee-MA-nee |
| toilet | τουαλετα | twa-LE–ta |
| police | αστυνομεια | as-tee-no-ME-a |
| archaeology | αρχαιολογια | ark-ha-o-lo-GEE-a |
| bar | μπαρ | BAR |
| doctor | γιατρος | yah-TROS |
| right | δεξια | dhek-see-AH |
| left | αριστερα | ah-rees-teh-RAH |
| here, there | εδω, εκει | eh-DHO, eh-KEE |
| open, closed | ανοιχτο, κλειστο | ah-nee-KTO, klee-STO |

| PRICES | | |
|---|---|---|
| How much? | Ποσο κανει; | PO-so KAH-nee? |
| I need | Χρειαζομαι | khree-AH-zo-meh |
| I want | Θελω | THEH-lo |
| I would like ... | Θα ηθελα | thah EE-the-lah ... |
| I will buy this one | Θα Αγορασω αυτο | thah ah-go-RAH-so ahf-TO |
| Do you have? | Εχετε; | Eh-khe-teh? |
| bill | λογαριασμο | lo-gahr-yah-SMO |
| newspaper | εφημεριδα | eh-fee-meh-REE-dha |
| water | νερο | ne-RO |
| good | καλο | kah-LO |
| cheap | φτηνο | ftee-NO |
| expensive | ακριβο | ah-kree-VO |

| NUMBERS | | |
|---|---|---|
| zero | μηδεν | mee-DHEN |
| one | ενα | Eh-nah |
| two | δυο | DHEE-o |
| three | τρια | TREE-ah |
| four | τεσσερα | TES-ser-ah |
| five | πεντε | PEN-dheh |
| six | εξι | E-ksee |
| seven | επτα | ep-TAH |
| eight | οκτω | okh-TO |
| nine | εννια | en-YAH |
| ten | δεκα | DHEH-kah |
| eleven | ενδεκα | EN-dheh-kah |
| twelve | δωδεκα | DHO-dheh-kah |
| thirteen | δεκατρια | DHEH-kah TREE-ah |
| fourteen | δεκατεσσερα | DHEH-kah TES-ser-ah |
| fifteen | δεκαπεντε | DHEH-kah PEN-dheh |
| sixteen | δεκαεξι | DHEH-kah E-ksee |
| seventeen | δεκαεπτα | DHEH-kah ep-TAH |
| eighteen | δεκαοκτω | DHEH-kah okh-TO |
| nineteen | δεκαεννια | DHEH-kah en-YAH |
| twenty | εικοσι | EE-ko-see |
| thirty | τριαντα | tree-AN-dah |
| forty | σαραντα | sa-RAN-dah |
| fifty | πενηντα | pen-EEN-dah |
| sixty | εξηντα | ex-EEN-dah |
| seventy | εβδομηντα | ev-dho-MEEN-dah |
| eighty | ογδοντα | og-DHON-dah |
| ninety | ενενηντα | en-EEN-dah |
| hundred | εκατο | ek-ah-TO |
| thousands | χιλιαδες | hil-ee-AH(dhes) |
| million | εκατομμυριο | eka-to-MEE-rio |

# INDEX



## A

# D



# E

## H



## I

# J



# K



# L

# M

INDEX

## R



## S

# T

## U



## V

INDEX

www.lowealpine.com

Lowe
alpine

Will you have enough stories to tell your grandchildren?